LINCOLN'S LIEUTENANTS

BOOKS BY STEPHEN W. SEARS

The Century Collection of Civil War Art

Hometown U.S.A.

The Automobile in America

Landscape Turned Red: The Battle of Antietam

George B. McClellan: The Young Napoleon

The Civil War Papers of George B. McClellan:
Selected Correspondence, 1860–1865

To the Gates of Richmond: The Peninsula Campaign

For Country, Cause & Leader:
The Civil War Journal of Charles B. Haydon

Chancellorsville

Mr. Dunn Browne's Experiences in the Army:
The Civil War Letters of Samuel W. Fiske

Controversies & Commanders:
Dispatches from the Army of the Potomac

On Campaign with the Army of the Potomac:
The Civil War Journal of Theodore Ayrault Dodge

Gettysburg

The Civil War: The Second Year Told by Those Who Lived It

Lincoln's Lieutenants:
The High Command of the Army of the Potomac

LINCOLN'S LIEUTENANTS

The High Command of the Army of the Potomac

STEPHEN W. SEARS

Mariner Books
Houghton Mifflin Harcourt
BOSTON   NEW YORK

First Mariner Books edition 2018
Copyright © 2017 by Stephen W. Sears
Maps copyright © 2017 by Earl McElfresh, McElfresh Map Company LLC

For information about permission to reproduce selections from this book, write to trade.permissions@hmhco.com or to Permissions, Houghton Mifflin Harcourt Publishing Company, 3 Park Avenue, 19th Floor, New York, New York 10016.

hmhco.com

Library of Congress Cataloging-in-Publication Data is available.
ISBN 978-0-618-42825-0 (hardcover) | ISBN 978-1-328-91579-5 (pbk.) |
ISBN 978-0-544-82625-0 (ebook)

Book design by Chloe Foster

Printed in the United States of America
DOC 10 9 8 7 6 5 4 3 2 1

For Bruce Catton (1899–1978)
for his many kindnesses, and
for showing how it's done

Maps

Contents

Introduction

IN HIS MEMOIR, General Régis de Trobriand cast a look back at his four years in the Army of the Potomac and remarked on that army's unique wartime role. This one particular army, he wrote, simply by being based at Washington, became "the army of the President, the army of the Senate, the army of the House of Representatives, the army of the press and of the tribune, somewhat the army of every one. Everybody meddled in its affairs, blamed this one, praised that one, exalted such a one, abused such a one. . . .".

This meddling — pervasive and never-ending — led the Army of the Potomac's officer corps, all too often, to worry about the enemy in the rear as well as the enemy in front. On that account, these particular lieutenants of Mr. Lincoln's were challenged as no other generals, North or South, in the Civil War. That challenge came atop the already stark perception that in this contest "between armies of the same nation & blood" (as Major Henry L. Abbott put the matter), it was command that made the difference.

In spring 1861 General-in-Chief Winfield Scott collected those at-hand regular-army officers who had not joined the secessionists and put them under Irvin McDowell in defense of the capital. Soon enough routed at First Bull Run, McDowell's Army of Northeastern Virginia gave way to a name change and a new commander, George Brinton McClellan. McClellan played a major role picking generals for his newly christened Army of the Potomac, and many of his choices were in their turn "McClellanized," a contagious disease diagnosed by critics as "bad blood and paralysis."

The era of McClellan, lasting until November 1862, witnessed the largest campaign of the war, on the Virginia Peninsula, the bloodiest single day in the nation's history, at Antietam, and in between the brief reign of General John Pope, who blundered his way to the Potomac army's second defeat at Bull Run. It was an era when generals, from army headquarters down through corps, division, and brigade, indulged themselves in the politics of war. Historian Bruce Catton called it the Era of Suspicion.

The press was cosseted and leaked to. The Radical Republican congressional Committee on the Conduct of the War grilled allegedly Democratic generals for supposedly disloyal acts. Among the McClellanized there was talk around the campfires and in headquarters tents of intrigues and betrayals and coups.

To be sure, in the fighting on the Peninsula and at Second Bull Run and at Antietam, many of McClellan's and Pope's subordinate generals fought capably and some brilliantly. The defeats and doubtful outcomes were due to the generals commanding (and due as well to the best general on all these fields, Robert E. Lee).

Lincoln's decision to replace McClellan with Ambrose Burnside marked the apex of the Era of Suspicion. Burnside was not appointed for his command skills (which he himself loudly disclaimed) but because he was thought to be apolitical and would cushion the effects of McClellan's dismissal. Burnside's subsequent dismal fall at Fredericksburg was not in the least cushioned by his officer corps — which officer corps then, in spring 1863, openly rebelled against Joe Hooker in the aftermath of the defeat at Chancellorsville.

In tracing the saga of the high command of the Army of the Potomac, the darkling doldrums of McDowell, McClellan, Pope, Burnside, and Hooker give way at last to comparatively sunny uplands when George Meade and then U. S. Grant take command. The road from Gettysburg to Appomattox would prove to be marked by brutal casualties and its share of command lapses and blunders in the officer corps, yet talk of disloyalty and conspiracies and coups to undercut the army and its generals was largely absent. Politicking would reemerge in securing Lincoln's reelection in 1864, but by this time the Potomac army had become Mr. Lincoln's army; the politics were tolerated for a vital cause.

The high command that closed the war in April 1865 was a world apart from the high command that opened the war. This had become a largely self-taught army led by volunteer officers from civilian life. Four years of fighting cost twenty-one of its generals their lives, but somehow, through trial and tribulation unimagined, the Army of the Potomac kept its identity and its purpose and its resolution steadfast until final victory.

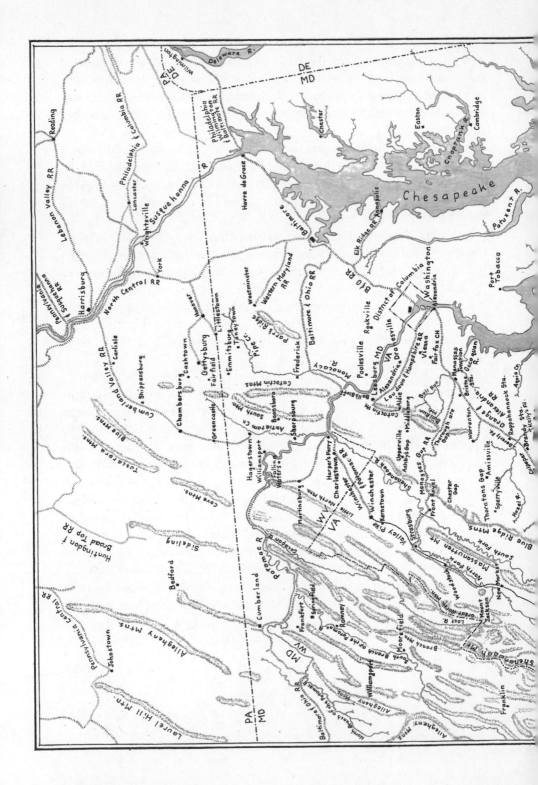

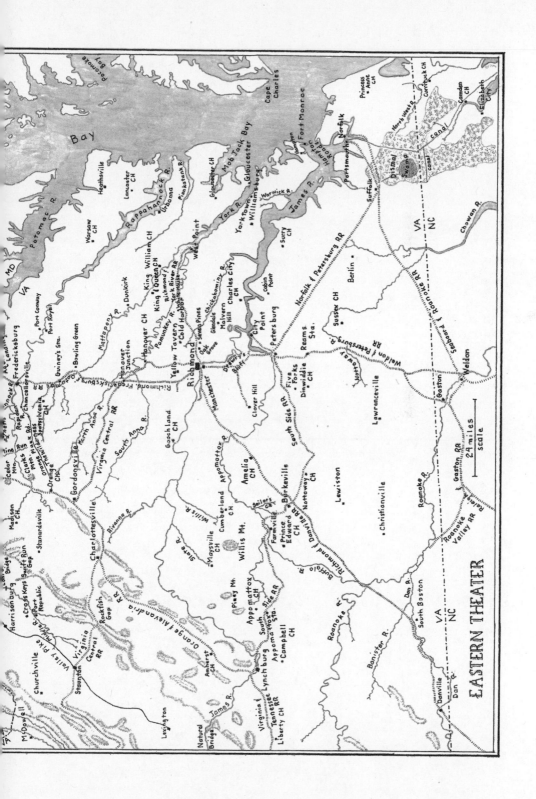

EASTERN THEATER

1. *"Civil War Seems Inevitable..."*

"GENERAL SCOTT SEEMS to have *carte blanche*. He is, in fact, the Government, and if his health continues, vigorous measures are anticipated." So wrote Edwin M. Stanton, late attorney general in James Buchanan's cabinet (and future secretary of war in Abraham Lincoln's cabinet), in a letter to the former president dated May 16, 1861. The subject of this observation was Lieutenant General Winfield Scott, whose arching self-esteem would surely have brought forth an imperial nod of agreement at Stanton's characterization.[1]

The notion that General Scott was "the Government" was Stanton's insight that the army appeared to be the power in the land—or at least in the Northern half of the land—and therefore to one and all Scott, as general-in-chief, *was* the army.

In fact Scott's role during the secession crisis and now the war crisis had traced an erratic course. But then Winfield Scott was by nature erratic. His heroics in uniform went back to the battles of Chippewa and Lundy's Lane in the War of 1812, and the regular army he afterward nourished showed its mettle under his brilliant command in the War with Mexico. He was appointed army general-in-chief in 1841 and brevetted lieutenant general in 1855. In the meanwhile "Old Fuss and Feathers" squabbled publicly with one fellow general or another, ventured disastrously into presidential politics as the Whig party's candidate in 1852, and in a fit of pique moved army headquarters from Washington to New York so he would not have to associate with President Franklin Pierce, who had defeated him so handily. Scott remained implanted in New York during the tenure of Secretary of War Jefferson Davis, with whom he carried on a vitriolic feud.[2]

As the election of 1860 approached, the South was swept with blazing pledges of secession and disunion should Abraham Lincoln and the Black Republicans gain the presidency. Because the fatal split of the Democratic party made that outcome a virtual certainty, General Scott concluded it was time and past time for statesmanship to prevail. He regarded himself,

Lieutenant General Winfield
Scott, hero of the Mexican
War, had been general-in-
chief for two decades when
civil war threatened.

in his seventy-fifth year, as a senior statesman. He would offer his thoughts
on the impending national crisis.

Election Day was November 6, and on October 29 Scott presented to
President Buchanan his "Views suggested by the imminent danger of a
disruption of the Union by the secession of one or more of the Southern
States." He opened with the startling assertion that to "save time" in making his arguments, he conceded the right of secession, but "instantly bal-
anced by the correlative right" of the national government to regain its
violated territory by force if necessary. This lawyerly stipulation — Scott
had briefly been an attorney in the early years of the century — would delight Southern secessionists and dismay Northern Unionists. He warned
should the Union be broken up by whatever "political madness may contrive," its fragments could never be reunited "except by the laceration
and despotism of the sword." Scott's acceptance of the legality of secession revealed political naiveté, but his warning of secession's poisonous
fruit reflected the reality of war as experienced by the nation's premier
warrior.

After an excursion into a fantastical alternative to civil war — the peaceful partition of the nation into four confederacies, each dictated by "natural boundaries and commercial affinities" — Scott returned to earth with
specific military advice to forestall the "danger of an early act of rashness
preliminary to secession." By an act of rashness he meant the seizure of
one (or more) of the forts guarding ports and harbors on the southern Atlantic and Gulf coasts. Most had skeleton garrisons or no garrisons at all.

He named them — Forts Jackson and St. Philip, on the Mississippi below New Orleans; Fort Morgan at Mobile Bay; Forts Pickens and McRee at Pensacola in Florida; Fort Pulaski at Savannah; Forts Moultrie and Sumter in Charleston Harbor; Fort Monroe guarding Hampton Roads in Virginia. "In my opinion, all these works should be immediately so garrisoned as to make any attempt to take any one of them, by surprise or *coup de main*, ridiculous."

In addition to Buchanan, Scott directed a copy of his "Views" to the secession-minded secretary of war, John B. Floyd of Virginia, who saw to its private circulation in the South. Wider circulation came with its publication in Washington's *National Intelligencer* on January 18, 1861. Buchanan would remark that the general's paper "was sufficient to set the South on fire. . . . Never was a prediction better calculated to produce its own fulfillment. . . ." Indeed, Scott's offhand stipulation of the right of secession earned him widespread suspicion among Northerners. The general was, after all, well known to be a Virginian born and bred.[3]

As ill written and ridiculously fanciful as much of Scott's paper was, his more reasoned and timely military advice concerning the all-but-empty coastal forts deserved a more thoughtful hearing than it got. This was due to Scott's florid rhetoric, to James Buchanan's indecisiveness, and to the bitter sectional division within Buchanan's cabinet. But garrisoning the forts ran up against another difficulty — a severe manpower shortage. Scott explained to Secretary of War Floyd that there were just five companies of regulars "within reach." For the nine forts that he urged be adequately manned, he could furnish at short notice perhaps 400 or so additional troops. Buchanan took this as a conundrum. Such paltry reinforcements, however parceled out, might be interpreted by Southern hotspurs as an admission of weakness, even as an incitement to that "early act of rashness." Better, he thought, to do nothing provocative.[4]

The fact of the matter was that in 1860 the United States army was exceedingly small, exceedingly scattered, and exceedingly unprepared to meet a sectional crisis. Army appropriations for that year were the smallest they had been in any year since 1855. The end-of-year returns showed only 16,367 officers and men on the rolls — 14,663 of them present for duty. Of the number present, 372 were line officers, just five of them (including Scott) general officers. The line strength of the 1860 army comprised 197 companies, of which 179 were posted west of the Mississippi River, in the Departments of the West, Oregon, California, Texas, New Mexico, and Utah. The Department of the East — east, that is, of the Mississippi — contained but 18 companies.[5]

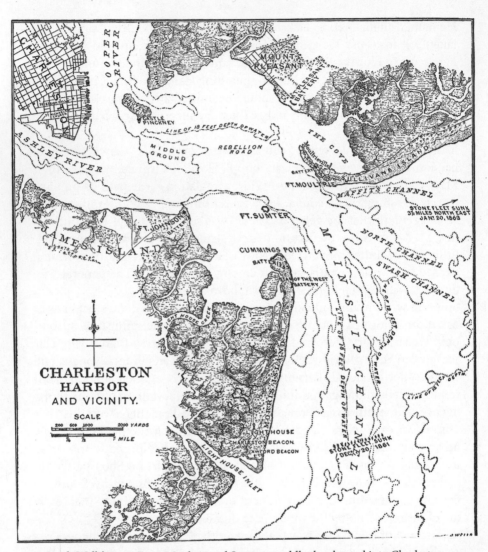

In Jacob Wells's map, Forts Moultrie and Sumter straddle the channel into Charleston Harbor. Batteries at Forts Johnson and Moultrie and Cummings Point ring Sumter.

Scott reported to Secretary Floyd the installations most at risk. He recommended instructions go immediately to commanders at the Florida and Charleston Harbor forts and Fort Monroe on Hampton Roads "to be on their guard against surprise and *coups de main.*" So far as Scott could learn, however, his advice was falling on deaf ears. He wrote Kentucky senator John J. Crittenden on November 12, "My suggestions seem to have no good effect at Washington; in other words, I have had no acknowledgment from either President or Secretary; nor has a single step been taken."[6]

In fact one small step had been taken. On the day of the presidential election, Secretary Floyd called for an inspection of the forts at Charleston Harbor, where the potential for trouble seemed greatest. He chose Major Fitz John Porter, assistant adjutant general, for the task. Major Porter was marked as one of the army's bright young men. West Point class of 1845, he had won two brevets for gallantry and suffered a wound in the War with Mexico. He returned to West Point as an artillery instructor, and had been in the adjutant general's office since 1856.

Porter reported on November 11 — five days after Lincoln's election — that he found an "inflammable and impulsive state of the public mind in Charleston — to a great extent characteristic of the feeling manifested throughout the State." The principal post, Fort Moultrie, was manned by two companies of the 1st Artillery, ten officers and sixty-four enlisted men, only thirty-six of whom were present for duty. Moultrie was in a dilapidated condition, and its unguarded state "invites attack, if such design exists." Fort Sumter, in splendid isolation out in the harbor entrance, was more defensible, but at the moment it was unmanned and unfinished, with just a portion of its ordnance mounted. Major Porter recommended reinforcing the Moultrie garrison and a general upgrading, but due to the high temper of the times, "much delicacy must be practiced."[7]

In command at Fort Moultrie was an old-timer named John L. Gardner, a Massachusetts Yankee not thought to be the sort to practice much delicacy. Colonel Gardner wanted drilled recruits to fill out his two companies, and a reinforcement of two companies to occupy Fort Sumter out in the harbor, "the only proper precaution." Gardner's proposals appeared to Washington more provocative than delicate, and he was relieved. His replacement was Major Robert Anderson, 1st Artillery. The major was a gentlemanly Kentuckian whose wife hailed from Georgia. It was hoped he might be more agreeable to those inflammable and impulsive Charlestonians.

On November 13 Anderson reported to General Scott at army headquarters in New York for instructions. He was informed by the testy general-in-chief that there were no instructions to give. Scott explained that all military matters relating to the Charleston forts were closely held by Secretary of War Floyd. Unofficially, however, Scott talked over the situation with the major, including the advisability of shifting the garrison to the one defensible spot in the harbor — Fort Sumter.[8]

Events were moving fast now, generating upheaval in the Buchanan administration. On November 10, in promised response to Lincoln's election, the South Carolina legislature had called for a convention to consider an ordinance of secession. December 17 was the date announced for the convention, and there seemed little doubt that South Carolina was set to leave the Union. At Charleston, Major Anderson had been in command of Fort Moultrie hardly a week before he stated flatly to Washington that Fort Sumter "*must* be garrisoned immediately if the Government determines to keep command of this harbor." That was what his indelicate predecessor, Colonel Gardner, had said, and it reflected as well what General Scott had whispered in Anderson's ear.[9]

In the capital President Buchanan was tugged to and fro by conflicting advice from his divided counselors. He himself denied the legitimacy of secession, and sought consensus on South Carolina's threat to secede. He found none. On December 4 he was to deliver his annual message to Congress on the state of the Union — which was clearly perilous — and then he must say *something* on the subject.

In the cabinet, Secretary of the Treasury Howell Cobb of Georgia regarded secession as both legal and proper. Jacob Thompson of Mississippi, Interior secretary, warned that coercion against South Carolina would drive his state into the secessionists' camp — and likely drive there as well the other cotton states of the Deep South. Secretary of War Floyd of Virginia, not an announced secessionist, was widely believed to face in that direction behind the scenes. In contrast, Lewis Cass of Michigan, secretary of state, wanted action taken against any secessionists, anywhere, and was seconded by Attorney General Jeremiah Black of Pennsylvania and Postmaster General Joseph Holt of Kentucky. So far as President Buchanan was concerned, General-in-Chief Scott's unfortunate admission, in his "Views," that there was nothing illegal about a state seceding, drowned out the military advice he offered about securing the federal forts in disaffected states.

James Buchanan was lacking in strong convictions, and his annual message to Congress on December 4, 1860, reflected the cacophony of advice he had received over the past weeks. He pleased no one and irritated nearly everyone. His one initiative was a suggestion that Congress compose "an explanatory amendment" to the Constitution to clarify key issues relating to slavery. Buchanan denied the right of secession, but implied that when all was said and done, the government was powerless. "Our Union rests upon public opinion and can never be cemented by the blood of its citizens shed in a civil war. If it cannot live in the affections of its people it must one day perish." William H. Seward, the senator from New York who had opposed Lincoln for the Republican nomination and was now preparing to enter the president-elect's cabinet, rendered a sardonic verdict on Buchanan's address: "I think the President has conclusively proved two things, 1st, That no State has the right to secede, unless it wishes to; and 2d, That it is the President's duty to enforce the laws, unless somebody opposes him."[10]

During December, however, the temper of the cabinet underwent major change. Howell Cobb resigned to return to Georgia to foster secession there, and Unionist Lewis Cass resigned in disgust at Buchanan's lack of backbone. Secretary Floyd, caught up in a War Department corruption scandal, was forced to resign at year's end. As reconstituted, and with the addition of Edwin Stanton as attorney general, the Buchanan cabinet took on a definite Unionist cast. At the same time, as South Carolina's march toward disunion gathered speed, attention focused more sharply than ever on the Charleston forts. In this matter even Buchanan had to admit that military expertise was required, and so early in December General-in-Chief Winfield Scott was finally called to Washington for consultation.

The general soon recognized this was to be no mere visit, so he reestablished army headquarters in the capital, on 17th Street across from the War Department. For himself he took up quarters at Wormley's, a celebrated free mulatto restaurateur and caterer on I Street. The choice of Wormley's was perfectly characteristic of Winfield Scott. He was seventy-five, and in the dozen years since his last major active service, in Mexico, he had not aged gracefully. This was due in part to his old war wounds but in greater measure to his gormandizing. Always an imposing figure at six feet four and a quarter inches (he never neglected to mention that last quarter inch), Scott now weighed 300 pounds and was afflicted with gout and serious edema. Even so, dining extravagantly remained his singular pleasure. His military secretary, Lieutenant Colonel Erasmus Keyes, recorded Scott's invariable response when served his favorite dish, Maryland terrapin: "He would, while leaning his left elbow on the table, having some of the terrapin on his fork, held raised about six inches above his plate, exclaim: 'This is the best food vouchsafed by Providence to man!'"

Scott's days as field commander were obviously past, for he walked with difficulty and could no longer mount a horse, and only got about by carriage. Anecdotes about his pomposity and his vanity fill the pages of Colonel Keyes's memoir (Keyes quoted Scott, "At my time of life, a man requires compliments"), yet during that secession winter the old soldier buckled down to business and spent long hours at work at his headquarters. The folderol so long associated with Old Fuss and Feathers was set aside in these crisis times.[11]

Scott only now became aware of the full record of the administration's vacillation on the matter of the Southern forts. He urged Buchanan to reinforce Fort Moultrie at Charleston, but his effort was futile. So the general gave thought to how he himself might influence the man who, in some two and a half months, would be in the White House — President-elect Abraham Lincoln of Illinois.

On December 17 a mutual friend of the two men, Illinois congressman Elihu B. Washburne, called on Scott in Washington to learn what was happening at Forts Moultrie and Sumter. He described Scott to Lincoln as outraged that Buchanan would not act on the forts. Not one of his recommendations had been accepted, said Scott, and he felt powerless and frustrated. Washburne quoted the general, "I wish to God that Mr. Lincoln was in office. I do not know him, but I believe him a true, honest and *conservative* man." He wanted to know if the president-elect was "a *firm* man." He was indeed firm, Washburne told him. The old general seemed cheered at that, and said, "All is not lost." Lincoln asked Washburne to present his respects to Scott and to tell him confidentially, "I shall be obliged to him to be as well prepared as he can to either *hold,* or *retake,* the forts, as the case may require, at, and after the inauguration."[12]

On December 20, 1860, in a unanimous vote, after no debate, the delegates to the convention meeting in Charleston passed an ordinance of secession. Edmund Ruffin, that most tireless of workers for Southern independence, reported in his diary, "... when all the signatures had been affixed, & the President holding up the parchment proclaimed South Carolina to be a free and independent country, the cheers of the whole assembly continued for some minutes, while every man waved or threw up his hat, & every lady waved her handkerchief." The convention's next act was to send three commissioners to Washington to negotiate the transfer of the Charleston forts and various other properties from the United States to the sovereign republic of South Carolina.[13]

Six days later Major Anderson took matters into his own hands. He had been told, early in December, that it was Secretary Floyd's order that he might defend himself if attacked, but only with such troops as he already had. Beyond permitting him to fight back, which he had intended to do anyway, this was of little help to Major Anderson. But more guidance was on the way. On December 9 Major Don Carlos Buell of the adjutant general's office arrived at Fort Moultrie to deliver fresh verbal instructions from Floyd. Anderson's predicament was quickly apparent to Buell, and contrary to his orders he determined to give his fellow officer a written directive, and to add to it a twist of his own. Buell explained that if need be Anderson might defend whichever of the forts was most defensible, "whenever you have tangible evidence of a design to proceed to a hostile act." This last was Major Buell's own interpretation . . . or invention. In handing the memorandum to Anderson, he said, "This is all I am authorized to say to you, but my personal advice is, that you do not allow the opportunity to escape you."

Major Anderson could discern hostile designs just about anywhere he looked, especially after South Carolina officially seceded. Now he had, in writing, the authority he needed to act. At dark on the day after Christmas he gave the Charleston militiamen standing watch on Fort Moultrie the slip and he and his little garrison, with most of their supplies, rowed across to Fort Sumter. That night Anderson wrote his wife, "Thanks be to God . . . for His having given me the will and shewn the way to bring my command to this Fort. I can now breathe freely."

Effectively, and even with a certain subtlety, the army had now seized a starring role in the drama being played out at Charleston. To those officers on the scene, Colonel Gardner and Majors Anderson, Porter, and Buell, it had become obvious that the men of the 1st Artillery were going to be gobbled up, and the forts with them, while Washington dithered. "I would rather not be kept here to '*Surrender*' when a demand is made for the Fort," Anderson had written a friend. "I don't like the name of '*having surrendered.*'" And General Scott, at their meeting in November in New York, had unofficially but unmistakably steered Anderson toward the direction he finally took.[14]

The response in Washington was shock and concern. In cabinet Secretary of War Floyd denounced Anderson for disobeying his orders and demanded Fort Sumter be abandoned and the garrison returned to Moultrie, or that Anderson give up Charleston entirely. But Floyd's influence was about gone now — he would resign on December 29 — and other voices spoke out in Anderson's defense. The new attorney general, Edwin Stanton, was one of them. Stanton said that turning over Fort Sumter now would be a crime equal to Benedict Arnold's, and any president giving such an order would be guilty of treason. The case was discussed up one side and down the other, with the commissioners from South Carolina entering the debate. But Fort Sumter remained in the government's hands.[15]

When he learned of the efforts to recall or to surrender Anderson and his garrison, General Scott angrily pitched into the fray. In a December

28 memorandum to Floyd, employing the third person for imperial emphasis, he wrote, "Lieut General Scott . . . begs to express the hopes to the Secretary of War — 1. That orders may not be given for the evacuation of Fort Sumter; 2. That 150 recruits may instantly be sent from Governor's Island to re-inforce that garrison with ample supplies." Getting no reply, two days later Scott took the case to the president: "It is Sunday; the weather is bad and General S. is not well enough to go to church. But matters of the highest national importance seem to forbid a moment's delay. . . . Will the President permit Genl. S. without reference to the War Department, & otherwise as secretly as possible, to send two hundred and fifty recruits, from New York Harbor, to reinforce Fort Sumter, together with some extra muskets or rifles, ammunition & subsistence?" There was no response from Buchanan.

The calendar turned to 1861, and the president continued to vacillate between the pleadings of his Unionist cabinet members and the arguments of the South Carolina commissioners. Buchanan, whatever else might be said of him, was stubbornly indecisive. The commissioners finally recognized their mission as fruitless and quit Washington for Charleston, tossing insults at the administration in their wake. "It is all over," Buchanan was heard to say, "and reinforcements must be sent."[16]

The task of reinforcement was already occupying General Scott. His first thought was to send regulars from Fort Monroe aboard the steam sloop *Brooklyn,* but then changed his mind. The *Brooklyn* was too noticeable and the plan too obvious to stay secret, and seemed likely to endanger the fragile peace at Charleston. Scott thought perhaps a civilian craft might slip into the harbor there with less notice. So the merchant steamer *Star of the West* was quietly chartered in New York, loaded with troops and supplies, and on January 5, 1861, set out ostensibly on her usual New Orleans run.

The matter was not managed quietly enough. The secret was leaked by the press, and warnings soon reached Charleston. Batteries were manned at Fort Moultrie and on Morris Island, flanking Fort Sumter. When the *Star of the West* entered the harbor at first light on January 9 the only one who did not know of her mission was Major Anderson, for the War Department's alert had failed to reach him. The South Carolina batteries opened fire on the steamer, scoring one minor hit, and when the puzzled Anderson did not order counterbattery fire from Fort Sumter, the *Star of the West*'s civilian captain put about and steamed out to sea and safety.

The brief encounter might have escalated into a casus belli, except that Fort Sumter, at the heart of the issue, took no part in it. Both Charleston and Washington backed off. South Carolina might declare itself a sovereign nation, but at the moment that was not much more than talk — it was too soon to start a solo war with the United States. As for the United States, it was presided over by a lame duck president desperately anxious to avoid any confrontation anywhere over anything during the seven or so weeks left in his term. An uneasy truce settled over Charleston Harbor.[17]

As the uproar over the *Star of the West* episode wound down, South Carolina found itself no longer alone in disunion. By February 1, 1861, six more Deep South states passed ordinances of secession — Mississippi, Florida, Alabama, Georgia, Louisiana, and Texas. In their first flush of independence they seized various United States military installations, arsenals, and coastal forts within their borders. A call was issued for a convention of the seceded states to meet in Montgomery, Alabama, on February 4 to form a new government under the sun.

General Scott continued pressing his active role in events. As he surveyed the various federal forts and installations in the disaffected states, he recognized that beyond Fort Sumter the one other site still practical for the government to try and hold was Fort Pickens, guarding Pensacola

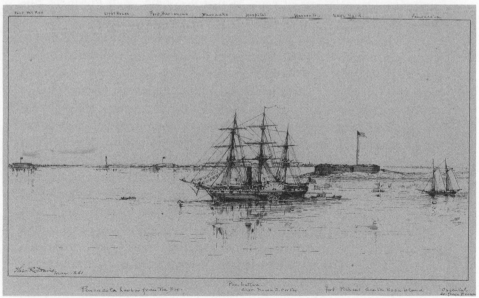

Theodore R. Davis, an artist for *Harper's Weekly*, did this study of Fort Pickens and the side-wheeler USS *Powhatan*, jointly keeping the flag flying over Pensacola Harbor in Florida, in May 1861. *Powhatan* had brought fresh reinforcements to Pickens.

Harbor in Florida. On January 3 Scott dispatched orders to the commanding officer there to prevent the seizure of the fort "by surprise or assault." On January 10 — the day Florida seceded — Lieutenant Adam J. Slemmer pulled his little garrison out of its barracks and into Fort Pickens at the harbor entrance. The *Brooklyn* sailed from Fort Monroe with a company of regulars, anchoring off Fort Pickens to await events. Because Lieutenant Slemmer could be reinforced and resupplied from the seaward side (and because Floridians were less inflammable and impulsive than South Carolinians), Fort Pickens never became a tinderbox issue like Fort Sumter. Yet like Sumter it was a symbol of the government's resistance to the breaking up of the Union.[18]

Frustrated by the *Star of the West* fiasco, Scott resolved on a second effort to reinforce Sumter. For this he called in Gustavus V. Fox, an Annapolis graduate with a distinguished naval career behind him. Fox was a strong Unionist and a fresh thinker. He submitted a scheme to reach the fort by slipping into the harbor past the batteries at night with light-draft tugboats. "My plan will be adopted if it becomes certain that reinforcements will be sent," Fox wrote his wife on February 7. He had the approval of both Scott and Joseph Holt, Floyd's successor as secretary of war, but Major Anderson was reluctant — he feared the attempt would be seen by South Carolina as an act of war — and that doomed it in President Buchanan's eyes.[19]

With that disappointment, General Scott turned his concerns from distant Forts Sumter and Pickens to Washington and the scheduled consequences of the November election — the counting of the Electoral College ballots on February 13, and the inauguration of Lincoln on March 4. The capital was virtually undefended, and there were frequent rumors that bands of conspirators would overturn the electoral count or prevent the inauguration of the Black Republican president. Mutterings of coup d'état were in the air. Senator Seward: "Treason is all around and amongst us, and plots to seize the capital and usurp the government." Senator Charles Sumner: "It is feared that the Departments will be seized & occupied as forts."

The general-in-chief would have none of that. "I have said that any man who attempted by force or unparliamentary disorder to obstruct or interfere with the lawful count of the electoral vote . . . should be lashed to the muzzle of a twelve-pounder and fired out of a window of the Capitol." Let the word go out, said the general: "While I command the army there will be no revolution in the city of Washington!"[20]

That sounded well and good, yet in truth General Scott's brave words

General Charles Stone and daughter. In early 1861 Stone raised militia companies to defend Washington.

rang hollow. As 1860 ended, there were no regular troops stationed in the capital beyond the 300 or so marines at the Navy Yard barracks and some 50 ordnance men at the Washington arsenal. The officer who would make good Scott's boast and turn matters around in Washington was named Charles Pomeroy Stone.

Stone had been posted to the artillery after graduating from West Point in 1845, and in the War with Mexico he was brevetted for Molino del Rey and Chapultepec, catching the eye of Winfield Scott. He left the army in 1856, and in 1860 was working in Washington as a topographical engineer. On the last day of the year he called on his old commander to pay his respects and to ask if there was anything he might do for him. Indeed there was, said Scott.

In the District of Columbia just then were four old-time militia companies of varying sizes and varying capability — and perhaps of varying loyalty. If properly organized and led, Scott said, they might form the core of a security force for the capital and defend the government if called upon. "These people have no rallying-point," he told Stone. "Make yourself that rallying-point!"

So on the 1st of January 1861 Charles Stone was appointed colonel and inspector general for the District of Columbia, and the next day mustered into United States service. This made him the first man to demonstrate literally his loyalty to his country in its crisis, and (in his own words) "the first man mustered into the service for the defense of the Capital. . . ." Therefore by extension Charles Stone was the first officer in what came to be called the Army of the Potomac. Stone would be quite unable to encompass the irony of it all when, thirteen months later, he was arrested and imprisoned for disloyalty to his country. "Why, if he is a traitor," Winfield Scott would rage, "I am a traitor, and we are all traitors!"[21]

That was in the unimaginable future when Colonel Stone set to work. By appealing to "well-known and esteemed gentlemen of the District," Stone set about raising volunteer militia companies. He recruited from fire companies and such skilled trades as masons and stonecutters and carpenters. By mid-February he had on the rolls thirty-three new companies of infantry and two troops of cavalry. By then, too, half a dozen companies of regulars had been brought to Washington. Duty officers in the capital were made responsible for the defense of key buildings — Major Irvin McDowell guarded the Capitol, Captain William B. Franklin, the Treasury, Captain Andrew A. Humphreys, the Smithsonian. Colonel Stone took responsibility for the White House. Ohio governor Salmon P. Chase told a friend, "Gen. Scott writes me that he thinks Washington will be sufficiently protected from attack."

Loyalty was everywhere being tested in these unsettled times. Perhaps inevitably questions were raised about the loyalty of Virginia-born Winfield Scott. Governor Chase, soon to be in Lincoln's cabinet, wrote the general of reports "that, in a certain contingency, you mean to throw up your commission." Chase insisted that "imbecility, or treason, or both, mark all the action of the existing administration. . . . General, you must not resign. Reflect, rather that you and not this condemned and expiring administration, now impersonate the American people." Chase proposed that Scott ignore any order of Buchanan's that involved "the surrender of posts or stores to rebels or traitors."

Various of Lincoln's advisers assured the president-elect of Scott's devotion to the Union. Simon Cameron, another prospective cabinet member, wrote Lincoln that Scott "bids me say he will be glad to act under your orders in all ways to preserve the Union. . . . The old warrior is roused, and he will be equal to the occasion." Scott himself wrote Lincoln, "The President-elect may rely with confidence on General S.'s utmost exertions in the service of his country. . . ." Still, the suspicious Republican governor of Illinois, Richard Yates, sent his own emissary, Thomas S. Mather, to Washington to interview Scott and appraise his motives and where he stood.[22]

All the while the general was abused by Southerners for disloyalty to the state of his birth. There was even a personal encounter arising from the overheated secession rhetoric in the capital. At a dinner party Scott was stirred to a boil by the outspoken senator from Georgia, Robert Toombs.

By Scott's account, Toombs and his fellows damned the president and Major Anderson and the Union, "and behaved in their discourse like madmen." At that, Scott "seasoned every dish and every glass of wine" with the refrain "The Union must be preserved!" Then, reported Elizabeth Blair Lee, "Mr. Tombs & Genl Scott had a *bout.* . . . The first called the Old Hero a liar — whereupon the Genl rushed into him — but they were promptly parted." Mrs. Lee concluded that "Civil War seems inevitable — even at friendly dinner parties."[23]

On February 4 the seceded states met in convention in Montgomery to form their new nation, the Confederate States of America. In short order the delegates organized a government, wrote a constitution, and on the 9th proclaimed Jefferson Davis of Mississippi provisional president. On February 13, in Washington, as scheduled, the Electoral College met to officially confirm Abraham Lincoln's election as president of the United States — or now, of the disunited States. Scott's promise held good, and the electoral counting in the Capitol was not interrupted. The army was in charge. As the general put it, there would be no revolution in Washington so long as he commanded the army.[24]

The greater test of the capital's security came on March 4, the day of Lincoln's inauguration. General Scott and Colonel Stone put on a flawless performance. They now had a solid core of regulars plus militiamen and volunteers of various stripes under command. When Lincoln and Buchanan rode in the procession from Willard's Hotel to the Capitol, their carriage was closely flanked by cavalry. Sharpshooters were stationed atop buildings along the route, and cavalry details blocked off each intersection as they passed.

Close by on Capitol Hill stood a battery of light artillery commanding the scene. Nearby were General-in-Chief Scott and the head of the Department of the East, Brigadier General John E. Wool, prepared to assume control should anything untoward take place. At seventy-seven Wool was older even than Scott, their joint service (and their wounds) dating back to the War of 1812. They made a picture of contrasts: Scott, hugely ponderous and adorned in gold braid and epaulettes, and Wool, slim and spare and brittle-looking, seeming relics of another time, monuments to old battles and past glories. Artillerymen stood ready at their pieces, canister stacked close at hand. From time to time aides arrived with the latest intelligence for General Scott. "He was evidently very anxious — everyone was anxious," recalled one of the gunners. The procession made its slow way to the Capitol, and after a time Lincoln could be seen on the platform, delivering his inaugural address. Scott watched intently. Finally Thurlow Weed, the Albany editor and Republican power broker, hurried up to the general, calling out, "It is finished! He is President! He is safe!"

"Thank God," said Scott. "Thank God."[25]

In his inaugural address Lincoln referred only indirectly to the beleaguered forts: "The power confided to me will be used to hold, occupy, and possess the property and places belonging to the Government, and to collect the duties and imposts. . . ." In so doing, he said, there need be "no bloodshed or violence; and there shall be none, unless it be forced upon the national authority. . . . In *your* hands, my dissatisfied fellow-countrymen, and not in *mine,* is the momentous issue of civil war. The Government will not assail *you.*" His unspoken reference was to Fort Pickens at Pensacola as well as Fort Sumter at Charleston, but all attention at the moment focused on Sumter. Lincoln spoke to his hope that the potentially explosive confrontation there might in some way be defused, and for that he envisioned an atmosphere of patient deliberation. "My countrymen, one and all, think calmly and *well* upon this whole subject. Nothing valuable can be lost by taking time."

On the matter of Fort Sumter there was a considerable distance between president-elect and president. Back in December, in Springfield, Lincoln wanted General Scott to understand that the Charleston forts should be held, or if taken by the secessionists, should be retaken after the inauguration. To Francis Preston Blair — Old Man Blair, elder statesman whose influence went back to the days of Andrew Jackson's Kitchen Cabinet — Lincoln wrote the same thing: "According to my present view, if the forts shall be given up before the inauguration, the General must retake them afterwards." Since then, however, this taking (and retaking) of forts had become a wholly new issue. Now, according to the latest advices from Major Anderson, simply holding on to Fort Sumter suddenly seemed almost impossibly difficult.[26]

During the more than two months since he occupied Sumter, Anderson had kept Washington fully up to date about the growing array of heavy guns ranging in on him. What was less clear from his reports was his own situation. Then, in a packet of dispatches sent on February 28 and received in Washington on the day of the inauguration, Anderson finally recited the exact circumstances he and his eighty-five officers and men (plus forty-three civilians) were facing. His rendition, in the words of Secretary of War Holt, "takes the Department by surprise. . . ."

What Major Anderson had neglected to mention was the limited quantity of his supplies. How long they could hold out, General Scott observed, "cannot be answered with absolute accuracy," but if not resupplied by about April 15 they faced starvation. As Anderson put it, their relief, "rendered necessary by the limited supply of our provisions," would require a force of 20,000 men. This startling news arrived on President Lincoln's desk on his first day at work, bearing Scott's equally startling endorsement. Scott saw "no alternative but a surrender . . . we cannot send the third of the men (regulars) in several months. . . ."[27]

As if this were not surprise enough, in circulation at the same time was what Scott termed a supplement to his "Views," that earlier effort at statecraft he had prepared just previous to the election. Dated March 3, before Major Anderson's revelations were known, Scott's new paper was addressed to William H. Seward, Lincoln's secretary of state. The general presented the new administration with four options.

First, he said, adopt one of the "conciliatory measures" — he mentioned the compromise on slavery proposed by his friend Kentucky senator John J. Crittenden — then making the rounds in Washington, "&, my life upon it, we shall have no new case of secession" and the early return of most if not all the seceded states. Without such a "benign measure," he warned, the slave states of the Upper South "will, probably, join the Montgomery confederacy in less than sixty days. . . ."

The second possible course would be to adapt to present circumstances and collect the duties on foreign goods outside the ports from South Carolina southward around to the Gulf, or close and blockade those ports. Then, presumably, wait for the cotton-states Confederacy to wither away.

The general's third option was coercion and civil war, which he presented in an apocalyptic vision. To conquer the seceded states, he said, would require an army of 300,000 and take two or three years. That army would require a general with the genius of a Wolfe, conqueror of French Canada, or a Desaix or a Hoche, famed commanders in Revolutionary France. And after all the blood and treasure was expended, the consequences would be "fifteen devastated *provinces* — not to be brought into harmony with their conquerors; but to be held, for generations, by heavy garrisons. . . ."

Scott's fourth alternative was starkly simple: "Say to the seceded States — *wayward sisters, depart in peace!*"

Secretary Seward, who shared these views and who strongly influenced Scott in their writing, had the paper circulated among the like-minded, and leaked at least the gist of it to the newspapers. Lincoln made no recorded response to the general's latest attempt at statecraft. There was nothing particularly new here and the options posed were not unrealistic, and the general did not declare a preference for one nonwar option over another. And certainly what America's first soldier had to say about the dreadful prospects of a civil war merited sober attention. Little good to Scott's reputation came of it, however. His melodramatically stated fourth option, about the wayward sisters departing in peace, attracted the most attention, mostly negative.[28]

The immediate, pressing problem was what to do about Fort Sumter and Major Anderson and his garrison. Lincoln called on Scott for advice, and on March 6 Scott convened a meeting at the War Department that included the army's chief engineer, Joseph G. Totten; the old and new secretaries of war, Joseph Holt and Simon Cameron; and the new secretary of the navy, Gideon Welles. Scott had organized the *Star of the West* expedition to relieve Sumter, and afterward supported Gustavus Fox's plan for that purpose, but now he insisted that such opportunities were gone. What changed his mind were the latest advices from Sumter. As one of Anderson's officers put it, to strengthen or provision the garrison "openly by vessels alone, unless they are shot-proof, is virtually impossible, so numerous and powerful are the opposing batteries." That those batteries were positioned by one of Scott's Mexican War favorites, P.G.T. Beauregard of Louisiana, added to the old soldier's dismay.

By Welles's account, Scott expressed his "apprehensions, perhaps convictions that hostilities were in his opinion imminent and inevitable." He described the formidable difficulties of resupply by sea, and said the subject was "one for naval authorities to decide." The next day the participants reconvened at the White House, without Holt but with the addition of Secretary of State Seward. Scott, supported by engineer Totten, doubted that as a military operation it was practical to attempt to reinforce Sumter. Secretary Welles, however, said his officers "were confident that the navy could reinforce the garrison with men and provisions." Seward opposed any attempt for fear it would drive the slave-holding border states into the arms of the nascent Confederacy. In that regard, everyone's concern was Virginia, where a state convention was then sitting, waiting on events. "No conclusion was arrived at," Welles reported.[29]

On March 9 Lincoln sent General Scott an interrogatory. How long, the president asked, could Major Anderson hold Fort Sumter with his present force and supplies? Could the general, "with all the means now in your control," supply or reinforce Anderson within that time? If not, what additional means would be required to do so? Scott's response was dispiriting. Anderson might hold out unsupported for another month or so. He, Scott,

Major Robert Anderson and his officers posed for Charleston photographer George S. Cook at Fort Sumter on February 8, 1861, the source for a woodcut engraving in *Harper's Weekly* on March 23. Seated from left, Abner Doubleday, Anderson, Samuel W. Crawford, and John G. Foster. Standing from left, Truman Seymour, G. W. Snyder, Jefferson C. Davis, R. K. Meade, and Theodore Talbot.

could do nothing effective to relieve him within that time. To reinforce and resupply the garrison with any hope of success, he said, would require a force of 25,000 men, with "a fleet of war vessels & transports." To assemble and train such an expedition would require six to eight months. "It is, therefore, my opinion and advice, that Major Anderson be instructed to evacuate the fort so long gallantly held by him and his companions, immediately upon procuring suitable water transportation." Scott drafted a proposed evacuation order.

Over the next few days Lincoln and his cabinet continued arguing the tangled Sumter question. Scott's professional military judgment to give up the fort carried considerable weight with the secretaries of war and navy, Cameron and Welles. The one strong voice for supporting Anderson was Postmaster General Montgomery Blair, himself a West Pointer and an advocate of the reinforcement scheme proposed earlier by his brother-in-law, Gustavus Fox. Fox was still on the scene, and the president welcomed his knowledge, experience, and assurances. Fox told his wife, "Our Uncle Abe Lincoln has taken a high esteem for me and wishes me to take dispatches to Major Anderson at Fort Sumpter . . . and to obtain a clear statement of his condition. . . ."[30]

In consideration of the increasingly doubtful prospects for holding Fort Sumter, Florida's Fort Pickens came again into sharp focus. That fort *could* be reinforced and resupplied. If Sumter should be given up to the secessionists, Pickens would remain the symbol of the North's stand against disunion. The president duly ordered that Pickens be reinforced. On March 12 Scott sent a dispatch aboard the *Mohawk* bound for Pensacola, addressed to Captain Israel Vogdes of the company of regulars aboard the *Brooklyn* still riding at anchor off Fort Pickens. "At the first favorable moment," the dispatch read, "you will land your company, re-enforce Fort Pickens, and hold the same till further orders." In due course the regulars went ashore and Fort Pickens was secured then and thereafter for the Union.[31]

The Fort Pickens drama would play out offstage, as it were, but Fort Sumter remained glaringly at center stage. On March 15 the president polled the cabinet: "Assuming it to be possible to now provision Fort Sumter, under all the circumstances is it wise to attempt it?" Five of his counselors, including the secretaries of war and navy, were opposed to any such effort. Treasury Secretary Chase was on the fence, only in favor if war did not result. Postmaster General Blair was the sole unequivocal supporter of reprovisioning the fort. The evacuation of Sumter, Blair wrote, "will convince the rebels that the administration lacks firmness and will therefore . . . so far from tending to prevent collision, will ensure it. . . ."

In preparing his demur, Secretary of War Cameron called on General Scott for his own response to the president. Scott read Lincoln's question as a political one. Having already spelled out his professional military judgment on the matter, he would now issue a political judgment. He had earlier lectured the White House on national policy in his October 29 "Views" and in his supplemental March 3 "Views," and had no reservations about doing so again. His focus now was on the border states of the Upper South.

Beyond the military arguments against reprovisioning Sumter, Scott wrote, it was doubtful "whether the voluntary evacuation of Fort Sumter alone would have a decisive effect upon the States now wavering between adherence to the Union and secession." The general-in-chief would give up Fort Pickens as well. "Our Southern friends . . . are clear that the evacuation of both the forts would instantly soothe and give confidence to the eight remaining slaveholding States, and render their cordial adherence to this Union perpetual."

Scott's memorandum was a shocker, and canny Simon Cameron pigeonholed it until he found a use for it. Cameron had allied himself with Secretary Seward in a scheme a later generation would call appeasement. Seward was seeking to buy peace with the South at any price, and was going behind the president's back to do it. He was privately in touch with Confederate officials to assure them that Sumter would be given up, and he leaked similar stories to the Northern press, all designed to lighten the reaction on both sides when, inevitably (as he saw it), the Fort Sumter garrison was evacuated. In this regard he and Cameron recognized the general's memorandum as ammunition for their campaign. But they needed to time its release for maximum impact.[32]

Mr. Lincoln was moving slowly and cautiously through the dangerous, entangling thicket of decision making. His counsel from the army was unanimous — General-in-Chief Scott, chief engineer Totten, and Major Anderson and his Fort Sumter officers were all agreed that to reinforce and resupply Sumter could not be done peacefully, and there was nowhere near enough available force to attempt it anyway. Gustavus Fox promised he could slip a few men and some supplies into the fort in the dark of night, but even so Fox would have to repeat the operation with some frequency and ever-growing risk. Still, the president had pledged, as his constitutional duty, to "hold, occupy, and possess the property and places belonging to the Government. . . ." Furthermore, he had promised the secessionists, "The Government will not assail *you*." Now, time and options were running out.

Public pressure built inexorably. "We trust this period of indecision, of inaction, of fatal indifference, will have a speedy end," editorialized the *New York Times*. "The people want *something* to be decided on — some standard raised — some policy put forward. . . ." The diarist George Templeton Strong grumbled, "The bird of our country is a debilitated chicken, disguised in eagle feathers. . . . The country of George Washington and Andrew Jackson (!!!) is decomposing." In consequence of Seward's leaks about the impending surrender of Fort Sumter, General Scott came in for his share of the blame. "Growls about Scott's 'imbecility' are growing frequent," Edwin Stanton observed.[33]

Gus Fox returned from his fact-finding trip to Charleston and Sumter on March 24. He remained convinced his plan for resupplying the fort was feasible so long as he had proper naval support. In these unsettled times the president was always glad to hear from anyone with a positive plan, and Fox told his wife, "I have seen Abe often. . . ." These White House discussions reviving the idea of aiding Sumter persuaded Simon Cameron to spring General Scott's bombshell on the administration. On March 28 Cameron sent to the president Scott's memorandum urging the surrender not only of Fort Sumter but of Fort Pickens as well, as a way of appeasing the secessionists.

To Lincoln, Scott's memorandum came as "a cold shock," quickly graduating into anger. He immediately sent for the general-in-chief. Scott's giving up Fort Sumter as a matter of military necessity was not new, but he had never before mentioned any military necessity for surrendering Fort Pickens. Colonel Keyes, after hearing the general's accounting of his meeting with Lincoln, entered in his journal that the president "seemed to indicate a want of consistency in General Scott's own views concerning Fort Pickens." Lincoln issued the general a thinly veiled warning that "his administration would be broken up unless a more decided policy was adopted, and if General Scott could not carry out his views, some other person might. . . ." That prospect, Keyes noted, "seems to have disturbed General Scott greatly."[34]

That evening of March 28 there was a state dinner at the White House, and at a late hour, as the other guests departed, the president asked the cabinet members to remain. In an "agitated manner" he read them Scott's memorandum. Seward and Cameron were of course not surprised, but the reaction of the others was stunned amazement. It was loudly remarked that the general had never suggested any military need to surrender Fort Pickens. Quite the opposite — orders had already gone out to reinforce it. Montgomery Blair was the most outspoken. "Mr. President," he said, "you can now see that General Scott . . . is playing the part of a politician, not of a general. . . ." Before he sent them home, Lincoln called a cabinet meeting for noon the next day.[35]

. . .

March 29, 1861, became for Abraham Lincoln a day of decision, with General Scott's memorandum acting as catalyst. When the cabinet met that day in the president's office, the conversation ranged widely but without resolution. Above the fireplace mantel an engraving of Andrew Jackson looked down, perhaps accusingly, on the wavering statesmen. Finally Attorney General Edward Bates suggested that each of the counselors summarize his views on the Sumter and Pickens questions in a written brief. The lawyer president found this to his liking.

Secretary of War Cameron did not attend the meeting, and no brief of his is on record. The rest of the cabinet, most notably the nimble Seward, insisted Fort Pickens must remain in Union hands. Thus the appeasers, pulling back to the safety of the majority, left their proxy Scott alone on the limb. Now, too, only Seward and Interior Secretary Caleb Smith advocated giving up Fort Sumter unconditionally.

Montgomery Blair had harsh words for the general-in-chief: "I have no confidence in his judgment on the questions of the day. His political views control his judgment, and his course as remarked on by the President shows that, whilst no one will question his patriotism, the results are the same as if he was in fact traitorous." Blair went on to say that if Fort Sumter was voluntarily surrendered to South Carolina, "it will strike a blow against our authority from which it will take us years of bloody strife to recover from." For his part, said Blair, "I am unwilling to share in the responsibility of such a policy." Indeed, he had his resignation already prepared.

Montgomery Blair's resolution on Fort Sumter was strongly endorsed by his influential father, Francis Preston Blair. After the cabinet meeting, Old Man Blair buttonholed the president and told him, not mincing words, "It would be treason to surrender Sumter." He must not listen to old Scott, who was timid and supine and under Seward's thumb. In the eyes of the nation, of the world, of history, "submission to secession would be a recognition of its constitutionality." Lincoln put him off by refusing to say if Sumter would be given up. In fact he had already reached a determination on that subject.[36]

Gus Fox had discussed with the president the particulars of mounting an expedition of some sort to Fort Sumter, and Fox drew up a memorandum of the ships, men, and supplies required. Now, although the head of the army opposed him, Lincoln had a cabinet majority with him in favoring aid to Sumter. On March 29 he sent Fox's memorandum to Secretaries Cameron and Welles, along with a directive: "I desire that an expedition, to move by sea, be got ready to sail as early as the 6th. of April next, the whole according to memorandum attached. . . ."

What set this apart from earlier schemes for Sumter's reinforcement and resupply was its purpose — and by newly defining that purpose, Lincoln cut the knot that had tied up the Sumter question for so long. The expedition he ordered would be for the sole purpose of provisioning. Moreover, the governor of South Carolina, Francis W. Pickens, would be notified beforehand of that purpose. Lincoln instructed his messenger what to say to Governor Pickens: "I am directed by the President of the United States to notify you to expect an attempt will be made to supply Fort-Sumpter with provisions only; and that, if such attempt be not resisted, no effort to throw in men, arms, or ammunition will be made."

To be sure, in case of need, men, arms, and ammunition would be onboard the expedition, but the intent was announced in advance to be peaceful — provisions only for a garrison manning a United States military installation in peacetime. No coercion and no aggression were intended or would be initiated. Mr. Lincoln, in short, was fulfilling the pledges made in his inaugural. Of equal significance, with deliberation he was placing the decision to make war or to continue a peaceful standoff in Charleston Harbor entirely in the hands of the secessionists.[37]

In something over two weeks Fort Sumter's larder would be empty, and that set off a frenzy of activity in Washington and New York. Little of it involved the general-in-chief of the army. Thanks to his inept lectures on policy, Winfield Scott found himself bypassed, sometimes inadvertently, sometimes deliberately, in these busy days.

The president put the Sumter expedition in the charge of Gus Fox, who shuttled between Washington and New York, chartering vessels, collecting supplies, gathering manpower. At the same time, Secretary of State Seward, scrambling to regain the ground he had lost, put together virtually on his own hook a parallel expedition to powerfully reinforce Fort Pickens. He might have lost out on Sumter, but he would declare himself the ultimate savior of Pickens. Seward sought an army equivalent of Gus Fox, and found him in the person of Captain Montgomery C. Meigs. A West Pointer, an energetic and experienced engineer, Meigs was just then supervising construction of the Capitol building extensions and the Washington Aqueduct. Seward hustled Meigs to the White House to help him sell the Pickens project. Lincoln asked if Fort Pickens could be held. "I told him certainly, if the Navy had done its duty and not lost it already," Meigs wrote. That sort of jaunty confidence was music to the president's ears.

On Easter Sunday, March 31, Seward put Meigs together with Scott's military secretary Erasmus Keyes and told them they had until 3 o'clock that afternoon to prepare a plan for reinforcing Fort Pickens and to bring their plan to the White House. When the two presented themselves to the president at the appointed hour, Colonel Keyes held back, saying he had not had time to clear the plan with General Scott. Meigs had no such reluctance. "I'm not General Scott's military secretary," he said, "and I am ready to report." Their plan was approved on the spot, and Lincoln sent them to see the general-in-chief with the admonition, "Tell him that I wish this thing done. . . ."

When Meigs and Keyes reported to Scott, they brought Seward with them. This proved a wise precaution, for the general's already dark mood grew blacker when he learned why they were there. He was being asked to approve a reinforcing expedition that was new to him, that he had no part in planning, to a fort he had recommended be evacuated. And his erstwhile ally Seward was smugly telling him that the commander-in-chief had rejected the general-in-chief's advice and was ordering him instead to reinforce Pickens and "hold it to the last extremity." However humiliated he felt, the old soldier drew himself up to his full six feet four and a quarter inches and exclaimed, as only Winfield Scott could, "Sir, the great Frederick used to say, 'When the King commands, all things are possible!' It shall be done!" The necessary orders went out over General Scott's signature.

Within a week the Pickens expedition was on its way, and by April 16 men and arms and supplies were coming ashore at the fort without event. Despite some dark, devious, and secret machinations by Seward, the expedition demonstrated finally that the end justified the means. Fort Pickens was safer than ever for the Union. By that time, however, the tinderbox at Charleston had ignited.[38]

The Sumter expedition had gotten the go-ahead on April 4, but only after a last-minute effort to avoid confrontation. Lincoln met with a representative of the secession convention then sitting in Richmond, and by report discussed a tradeoff: If the convention would disband and Virginia disavow secession, the president would withdraw Major Anderson's garrison. "He promised to evacuate Sumter if they would break up their Convention, without any row or nonsense . . . ," presidential secretary John Hay later wrote. "The President was most anxious to prevent bloodshed." But by now peacemaking was riven with mistrust and, wrote Hay, "they demurred."[39]

On April 4 Lincoln himself wrote out instructions for Major Anderson. The major was told "an expedition will go forward; and, finding your flag flying, will attempt to provision you. . . . You will therefore hold out, if possible, till the arrival of the expedition." Gus Fox, given quasi-official rank as Captain Fox in recognition of his seafaring days, was ordered to direct "the transports in New York having the troops and supplies on board to the entrance of Charleston Harbor, and endeavor, in the first instance, to deliver the subsistence." Should this effort be opposed, the navy had leave to force a passage into the harbor, whereby Captain Fox had leave to land men as well as supplies at Fort Sumter. Fox was assured that South Carolina's Governor Pickens would have the president's avowal of its passive intent beforehand.[40]

In New York Fox chartered the merchant steamer *Baltic* and several auxiliary vessels to carry men and provisions, and the navy promised him three of its prime warships, *Powhatan, Pocahontas,* and *Pawnee,* plus the revenue cutter *Harriet Lane,* for support. General Scott had no role in the planning, nor was he asked to play one. Captain Fox wrote his wife, on the eve of setting off for Charleston, "I cannot shrink from a solemn duty, which, if successful is pregnant with great results for our beloved country."

The Sumter expedition promptly went completely awry. A villain of the piece was Secretary Seward, who with means too clever by half had managed to snatch away the powerful steamer *Powhatan,* intended flagship of the Sumter squadron, and use her in his Fort Pickens adventure. No one in the fledgling Lincoln administration seems to have been able to follow or understand what Seward was up to, and when they did, it was too late. Then, to make matters a great deal worse, the weather blew up a gale, scattering and delaying the rest of Fox's little fleet. When he finally arrived in the *Baltic* off Charleston Harbor at first light on April 12, Fox expected to find the navy squadron waiting for him. Instead he found only the cutter *Harriet Lane.* Soon enough, Fox wrote, "as we drew in saw that the forts had all opened fire upon Sumpter and that Major Anderson was replying gallantly."[41]

Four days earlier, a State Department clerk had reached Charleston and delivered to Governor Pickens Lincoln's message about provisioning Fort Sumter. The governor promptly telegraphed President Jefferson Davis in Montgomery for instructions. Davis and his cabinet cast a cold and suspicious eye on this tactic of Lincoln's, for thanks to a bit of espionage they were privy to Major Anderson's reaction to it. In his reply to Washington — seized and read by the authorities in Charleston — Anderson confused this newly devised relief expedition with Gus Fox's earlier plan for landing reinforcements as well as provisions at Sumter. That plan he had opposed, and therefore he expected the worst of this one: "I fear that its result cannot fail to be disastrous to all concerned. . . . I frankly say that my heart is not in the war which I see is to be thus commenced."

Anderson's dispatch with its calamitous misreading of his instructions, appearing to contradict Lincoln's promise to Governor Pickens, cast the issue in stark relief. Robert Toombs, the Georgia firebrand who nearly came to blows with General Scott at that Washington dinner party back in January, crystallized the dilemma facing the Davis government. As avid as he was for the South's independence, Toombs warned his colleagues that initiating an attack on Fort Sumter now would set off a civil war beyond imagining. "You will wantonly strike a hornet's nest which extends from mountains to ocean," he declared, "and legions, now quiet, will swarm out and sting us to death. It is unnecessary; it puts us in the wrong; it is fatal."

Yet to stand by and allow Sumter to be provisioned (and apparently reinforced) would only prolong the standoff, depriving the newborn Confederacy of the initiative in the dangerous game playing out at Charleston. In that event, perhaps with time secession would even be talked to death, or compromised to impotence. Very likely the border states of the Upper South, especially Virginia, would see no cause to join the new nation. Of the two potential flashpoints, Fort Pickens was a considerably more dubious proposition than Fort Sumter. At Sumter the military issue would not be in doubt. Lincoln had given Davis and his colleagues a choice, but as they saw it, it was no choice at all.

On April 10 Confederate Secretary of War L. P. Walker wired General Beauregard, in command at Charleston, that if he had no doubt of the authenticity of the message of "the Washington Government to supply Fort Sumter by force you will at once demand its evacuation, and if this is refused proceed, in such manner as you may determine, to reduce it." In a fateful misreading of intentions, Lincoln's professed resolve to provision Sumter peacefully was not credited in Montgomery.[42]

The next day, April 11, Beauregard sent aides out to the island fortress in a small craft with a politely worded demand that Major Anderson and his men evacuate; the honors of war would be accorded them. Anderson's reply was a politely worded refusal. He remarked, in an aside, "I will await the first shot, and if you do not batter us to pieces we will be starved out in a few days." This last initiated another round of exchanges, "to avoid the effusion of blood." In the end there appeared to be no way to guarantee an evacuation date due to starvation. So Major Anderson was handed a final note saying that General Beauregard "will open the fire of his batteries on Fort Sumter in one hour from this time." The note was marked 3:20 on the morning of April 12.

And so at 4:30 a.m., April 12, 1861, ten minutes late, the Civil War began. The first shot was fired from a signal gun at Fort Johnson, on James Island.

Theodore Davis's watercolor shows the war's first shot bursting over Fort Sumter, fired from Fort Johnson (far left). In the foreground is the Rebels' battery at Cummings Point.

Captain Abner Doubleday — future major general in the Army of the Potomac — fired the first of Sumter's guns in reply. Beauregard had promised to ring Fort Sumter in a circle of fire, and it was an apt metaphor. His batteries were sited at the points of a triangle, bearing on Sumter in the center at an average distance of just 1,800 yards. Among his forty-three guns were sixteen heavy mortars, ideal for dropping shot and shell, and hot shot, into the fort's interior. Sumter actually mounted more guns, but only those in protected casemates could be used, and in any event ammunition was very limited. This first battle of the war was no contest.

The bombardment continued all day on the 12th, paused during the night, and resumed in greater intensity on the 13th. The fort was rapidly being knocked to pieces; the wooden barracks were afire, the spreading flames threatening the magazine. Major Anderson had continued to resist in hopes of rescue by the squadron he imagined would storm into the harbor, but finally by afternoon he could hold out no longer. He ran up a white flag. The official surrender ceremony took place the next day, April 14. As Anderson fired a salute to his flag, an errant spark exploded a stack of ready ammunition, and two privates of the U.S. 1st Artillery died. There were no other deaths on either side in the thirty-four-hour bombardment.[43]

Aboard the *Baltic* off the harbor entrance, Gus Fox watched all this in mounting frustration. "As we drew near," he wrote, "I saw, with horror, black volumes of smoke issuing from Sumpter." One of his late-arriving vessels brought him news of the *Powhatan*'s defection, and his frustration turned to fury. As he told his wife, he could hardly wait "to place the blow on the head of that timid traitor W. H. Seward. He who paralyzes every movement from abject fear." The sole accomplishment of the Fox expedition was to transport the surrendered Major Anderson and his garrison back to New York.

Even with his entire squadron at hand and not delayed by weather, it is doubtful Fox could have done much more than prolong Fort Sumter's agony. And had he attempted to provision the fort by force (as the Confederates anticipated) rather than peacefully, the question of who fired the first shot might have been muddled. On that score at least Fox could take some satisfaction. He explained matters to Anderson on the voyage to New York. "I told the Major how anxious the Prest was that they (S.C.) should stand before the civilized world as having fired upon bread. . . ."[44]

2. *An Army for Battle*

ON SATURDAY, APRIL 13, like everyone else, Mr. Lincoln read in the papers of the firing on Fort Sumter. Evening brought news of Major Anderson's surrender. Earlier the president had learned from General Scott the technicalities of his military options, so he was prepared. On Sunday morning the 14th, he met with the cabinet and explained that he had drafted a proclamation calling out the militia.

The proclamation — dated April 15, 1861 — announced that because the laws of the United States were opposed "by combinations too powerful to be suppressed by the ordinary course of judicial proceedings," the president was calling out the militia to the "number of seventy-five thousand, in order to suppress said combinations. . . ." Lincoln acted in accordance with the Militia Act of 1795. It limited call-ups to three months' service in any one year, so unless this proved to be a ninety-day war, other arrangements for an army, or armies, to suppress these too-powerful combinations would have to be made.

The proclamation, reported the *New York Times*, "will thrill like an electric shock throughout the land, and establish the fact that we have a Government at last." The attack on Sumter and the call for militia did indeed electrify the North. Mass meetings and rallies in city and town overflowed with flag-waving and patriotic oratory. Volunteers rushed to answer the president's call, fulfilling quotas many times over. "The heather is on fire," wrote Harvard professor George Ticknor. "I never before knew what a popular excitement can be. . . ." In New York, where the Stars and Stripes even flew from the steeple of Trinity Church, diarist George Templeton Strong watched the 6th Massachusetts militia regiment march past on its way to Washington: "Immense crowd; immense cheering. My eyes filled with tears, and I was half choked in sympathy with the contagious excitement. God be praised for the unity of feeling here!"

To be sure, Lincoln's proclamation generated equal unity of feeling in the South. On April 17 the Virginia convention adopted an ordinance

George Hayward's watercolor depicts New York City's 7th Regiment of militia receiving cheers at the corner of Broadway and Courtland Street, April 19, 1861, on its way to the seat of war at Washington. Hayward's work was widely distributed as a lithograph.

of secession and scheduled a popular-vote referendum, the outcome of which was hardly in doubt. In North Carolina, Governor John W. Ellis wired Secretary Cameron, "I can be no party to this wicked violation of the laws of the country and to this war upon the liberties of a free people. You can get no troops from North Carolina." Ellis's state would leave the Union on May 20. In Tennessee, Governor Isham G. Harris pledged not a single man "for purpose of coercion, but 50,000, if necessary, for the defense of our rights. . . ." Tennessee was welcomed into the Confederacy on May 16. Two days later Arkansas joined. Lincoln's calling out the militia raised the count of Confederate states from seven to eleven.[1]

The militia companies answering the president's call in the North, or responding in defiance of it in the South, were a variegated lot. Some were smartly outfitted and drilled, many others were ramshackle in appearance, equipment, and training. Yet by their very existence these state-sponsored militias allowed North and South to be at war after Fort Sumter without a pause for mobilization. Their mutual rush to the colors left no time in the two sections for any sober second thoughts about the consequences of the nation going to war with itself.

Consequently, the immediate issue for Winfield Scott was the safety of Washington and the government. Virginia was certainly leaving the Union (the May 23 referendum made it official), and should slave state Maryland follow, Washington would be encircled, severed from the rest of the North. To build an army to defend the capital, it was absolutely necessary to keep Maryland in the Union.

As of April 15, seven companies of regulars had arrived in Washington, supported by nine companies of District of Columbia militia mustered into Federal service. Editor Alexander K. McClure asked General Scott the size of his force to defend the capital. "Fifteen hundred, sir; fifteen hundred men and two batteries," said the general. McClure asked about Beauregard's force at Charleston. "General Beauregard commands more men at Charleston than I command on the continent east of the frontier," said Scott, and noted that it might take Beauregard three or four days to march on Washington. "General," said McClure in alarm, "is not Washington in great danger?" That roused the old generalissimo. "No, sir, the capital can't be taken," he declared; "the capital can't be taken, sir!"[2]

In January it had been Charles Stone who saved Washington from any possibility of a coup d'état. Now, in April, to the rescue came the unlikely, unmilitary figure of Benjamin Franklin Butler, lawyer-politician and brigadier general of Massachusetts militia. Ben Butler would often enough make himself a thorn in the Potomac army's side. Just now, however, his bluff and brass were exactly what was needed.

On April 18 the first troops reached Washington in response to Lincoln's call-up — five companies of Pennsylvania militia (mustered at Harrisburg by the industrious Major Fitz John Porter, who in November had gauged the situation at Charleston for the War Department). Their passage through Baltimore was met by a jeering, rock-throwing mob of would-be secessionists. Secretary of War Cameron warned Maryland's Governor Thomas H. Hicks of "unlawful combinations of misguided citizens" seeking to prevent the transit of Federal troops across his state. Baltimore posed great potential for trouble because there was no unbroken rail passage through the city. The two lines from the north terminated at the President Street Station. The cars were then hauled by horse teams along a light-rail track on Pratt Street a mile or so to the Baltimore & Ohio's Camden Station for passage over the Washington branch of the B. & O. The Baltimore mob vowed it would do better next time.

Next time was the next day, April 19. The 6th Massachusetts militia — the regiment George Templeton Strong had so admired when it passed

THE LEXINGTON OF 1861.

The 6th Massachusetts militia, on its journey to Washington, battles its way through a secessionist mob in Baltimore on April 19, 1861. In rendering the scene, printmaker Currier & Ives evoked the patriots on Lexington Green on April 19, 1775.

through New York — arrived at the President Street Station at midday. The regiment's slow passage along Pratt Street grew uglier by the minute, and finally the growing mob blocked the track, forcing four companies of the 6th to leave the cars, shoulder their muskets, and proceed on foot. That triggered a full-scale riot, with bricks and paving stones raining down on the troops and much scuffling. Inevitably a shot was fired, then many shots, and before police restored order, four soldiers were dead and thirty-six wounded. The mob counted a dozen killed and an undetermined number hurt. The 6th Massachusetts reached Washington that evening blood-stained and grim-faced. Here was a mark of true civil war. Patriots North and South were reminded of the events on Lexington Green on this same date eighty-six years earlier.[3]

Ben Butler now strode upon the stage. The Baltimore authorities, cowed by the mob, shut the city to further passage of Federal troops. Butler led the Massachusetts regiments answering the president's call, and on General Scott's advice, detrained his men at the head of Chesapeake Bay, embarked them on a ferryboat, and bypassing Baltimore landed at Annapolis. There he was met by Governor Hicks, who said his state would go up in flames if any more Yankee soldiers tried to cross it. Ben Butler — rotund, balding, cockeyed, and cunning, more politician than soldier — easily bluffed his way past the governor.

The branch railroad at Annapolis connecting with the B. & O.'s Washington line at Annapolis Junction had been disabled by the secessionists, but Butler's men were up to the challenge. Track was repaired and a damaged locomotive put to rights by Private Charles Homans, 8th Massachusetts, who said he ought to be able to fix it, for it had been built in the shop back home where he worked. The 7th New York militia followed Butler to Annapolis, with regiments from Massachusetts and Rhode Island not far behind. The 7th New York was marched to Annapolis Junction to entrain for Washington.

These were days of isolation and apprehension in the capital. General Scott said Washington was "now partially besieged, threatened, and in danger of being attacked on all sides in a day or two or three." There was concern about the loyalty of the District militia companies. "We were not certain but that . . . we would have to look down the muzzles of our own guns," Lincoln's secretary John Nicolay wrote his fiancée. "We were not only surrounded by the enemy, but in the midst of traitors." The president told the convalescing Massachusetts militiamen, "I don't believe there is any North. The Seventh Regiment is a myth. Rhode Island is not known in our geography any longer. *You* are the only Northern realities."

At last, on the seventh day, the suspense ended. At noon on April 25 the 7th New York arrived at the Washington depot to the cheers of a welcoming crowd. In their natty gray uniforms, behind their brass band, the New Yorkers were a spectacle as they marched up Pennsylvania Avenue to the White House to salute the president. They returned along the avenue to the Capitol, where they were quartered in the House Chamber. Washington was declared safe.

The next step was to permanently safeguard the capital's railroad lifeline through Maryland, and Ben Butler saw to that. Concluding that laws federal and state were being flouted, Butler gathered 950 troops and a battery, marched into Baltimore, and put the city under martial law. Troops patrolled the streets, arms were seized, arrests made. Soon enough, rail service through Baltimore was back to normal. Strutting about in his gaudy militia uniform, Butler played the proconsul's role to the hilt. General Scott sent him starchy notes ordering him to stop issuing proclamations and generally to cease and desist. Yet there was no taking back results. Butler was sent off to Fort Monroe on the Virginia Peninsula, but in the name of self-preservation the Federals' iron grip on Baltimore and on Maryland did not relax.[4]

Secretary of War Cameron, looking back on these first weeks of war, explained that upon taking office, "I found the nation without an army; and I found scarcely a man throughout the War Department in whom I could put my trust. The Adjutant General deserted. The Quartermaster ran off. The Commissary General was upon his death bed. More than half the clerks were disloyal." It was a scant foundation on which to build an army to defend the Union.

Adjutant General Samuel Cooper resigned to take the same post in Richmond. Quartermaster Joseph E. Johnston followed Virginia out of the Union. (Commissary General George Gibson lingered until September before he expired.) There were departures right and left. "I hardly knew who to trust any more," said Lincoln.[5]

For Winfield Scott, the most painful defection was that of Robert E. Lee. Scott once said that if a president should ask him about a commander for some great battle "to be fought for the liberty or slavery of the country . . . I would say with my dying breath, let it be Robert E. Lee." His hope was that in time Lee would succeed him as head of the army. Scott called Lee to Washington from his posting in Texas, and he reported the day after the inauguration. Lee said he could not turn his hand against the South, especially his native Virginia, but Scott persuaded him for the moment to think there would be no fighting. But on April 18 Lee met with Francis Preston Blair. War was at hand, said Blair. At Lincoln's instruction he offered Lee command of the field army being raised in the capital. Lee replied that he "could take no part in any invasion of the Southern States." He went to Scott's office with his decision. "Lee," the old warrior said sadly, "you have made the greatest mistake of your life; but I feared it would be so." On April 20 Lee resigned his commission, and accepted command of Virginia's forces.

Virginia's secession generated rumors that General Scott himself would follow his native state into the Confederacy, and indeed he was invited to do so. Scott's friend Senator Crittenden sought assurances from the general. "I have not changed," said Scott. "I have not thought of changing. Always a Union man." Virginia's newspapers redoubled their invective against the "arch-traitor."[6]

With Washington's lifeline to the North secured, the task now was to organize the militiamen and volunteers arriving in the capital in growing numbers. The proclamation calling out the militia also called Congress into special session — on the 4th of July. Until then, the Lincoln administration on its own would take the Union to war. "We are gathering a great army," Secretary of State Seward observed to Scott. "What I do not yet foresee is how it is to be led. What are we to do for generals?" That was indeed the burning question, Scott replied. "Unfortunately for us, the South has taken most of those holding the higher grades."

So it seemed. After Lee's defection, Scott considered Albert Sidney Johnston, Department of the Pacific, but Johnston also elected to go south. At the Department of Texas, David E. Twiggs not only went south with unseemly haste but surrendered nine companies of regulars to the Texas secessionists. Of other major department heads, the Southern background of William S. Harney, Department of the West, made him suspect. John E. Wool, Department of the East, was older than Scott and equally incapable of serving in the field. Thus the general officers of the regular army had all either gone over to the Confederacy or were unsuited for field command. "We have captains and lieutenants, that, with time and experience, will develop, and will do good service," Scott said hopefully. Just then there was precious little time . . . and precious little experience. Except for Scott and Wool, not a single Union officer had led as much as a brigade, in war or in peace.

(Excepting Twiggs, these noteworthy defectors were all West Pointers. They formed the tip of an iceberg of defectors. Nearly a quarter of the West Pointers on active duty in 1861 joined the Confederacy. Among West Pointers in the classes 1830 to 1861 who served in the Civil War, nearly 30 percent went south. Of the 239 cadets at the Academy at the time of the secession crisis, 88, nearly 37 percent, took up the cause of the Confederacy. As these statistics became known, numerous critics rose up to condemn the Military Academy as the "nursery of treason.")[7]

The War Department was in no sense prepared to manage this rush to war. A third of the department clerks quit or went south. Secretary Cameron was besieged by contractors "patiently waiting for hours to catch a part of the drippings from the War Department." The various bureaus — woefully understaffed, lacking any retirement policy, overstocked with overage officers — had long been directed in the fashion of sinecures, slow moving and swathed in red tape.

The place of Adjutant General Cooper was taken by the pedestrian, tippling Lorenzo Thomas, Scott's chief of staff at the army's New York headquarters. Highly capable Montgomery C. Meigs replaced Quartermaster Joe Johnston. Meigs did not immediately take his post due to cabinet squabbling. Meigs had been Seward's protégé on the Fort Pickens expedition, which Cameron resented being undertaken behind his back. The war secretary may also have worried that Meigs's watchdog reputation with supplier contracts might conflict with his own less rigorous ways of doing business. Meigs tartly remarked in his journal that the administration "had better make me Q.M. Gen'l than to keep up the present already rotten system. . . ." Lincoln agreed. Captain Meigs became Colonel Meigs and then Brigadier General Meigs and finally, on June 13, the army's quartermaster general.

These first militia arrivals were quartered in any available space. There were Massachusetts men in the Senate Chamber and the Capitol Rotunda, New Yorkers in the House Chamber, Rhode Islanders in the Patent Office. Troops sheltered in the Treasury Building and the Navy Yard and the "Palace of Aladdin," where the inaugural ball had been held. Proper encampments and drill grounds would in time be established, but meanwhile sheltering and feeding and arming the thousands of would-be soldiers stretched the petty army bureaucracies to and beyond their limits. Yet the soldierly raw material and the patriotic spirits were there. Presidential secretary John Hay visited the 1st Rhode Island and was impressed. "When men like these leave their horses, their women and their wine, harden their hands, eat crackers for dinner, wear a shirt for a week and never black their shoes — all for a principle, it is hard to set any bounds to the possibilities of such an army."[8]

Such an army would not be built of ninety-day militia, however, and clearly the regular army was too small for the task ahead. Volunteers signed for years rather than months were needed. Secretary of War Cameron was overwhelmed with the militia call-up, so it fell to other hands, particularly those of Secretary of the Treasury Salmon P. Chase, to plan an army "for the war." The self-important Chase was more than willing to insert himself into military matters (especially the appointing of generals), and he was quick to propose a call for nonmilitia volunteers. Lincoln asked him to develop the idea, and Chase convened a three-man board of officers — the new adjutant general, Lorenzo Thomas, Major Irvin McDowell, and Captain William B. Franklin — to advise him on forging a new army. McDowell had administrative experience in the adjutant general's office. Franklin, first ranked in the West Point class of 1843, was supervising an extension of the Treasury Building and conveniently at hand. Because of Thomas's existing workload, most of the planning fell to McDowell and Franklin.

They proposed simply expanding the regular army, with its "national" structure of numbered regiments, through volunteers "for the war." Chase called this politically naive and would have none of it. The states were providing the men; state pride and state rights had to be accommodated. Chase, former Ohio senator and governor, said he would "rather have no regiments raised in Ohio than that they should not be known as Ohio regiments." The regular army would be expanded, but parallel to it would be raised an all-volunteer army of state-named regiments whose men were enlisted for three years. This decision was tacit acknowledgment that the United States of 1860–61 was but a loosely woven compact of states, so loosely woven that in the South secession rent the fabric; while in the North a one-dimensional "national" army would not be tolerated.

A May 3 presidential proclamation authorized enlarging the regular army by 22,714 officers and men, and called initially for 42,034 three-year enlistees for the volunteer army. Chase was right — the politics of the case ruled. The regulars would never achieve their enlistment quotas, while the framework for the North's future armies was built of state-sponsored three-year volunteers. On May 16 Chase pondered his handiwork. The call for three-year volunteers was oversubscribed, he noted, and the governors were pleading with the War Department to take them all. Chase calculated that soon there would be a force of 30,000 to 35,000 troops in Washington. "Of course under these circumstances, there is a good deal of talk of forward movement, and plans for a campaign are much discussed. Nothing, however, is decided."[9]

It was none too soon for such thoughts. The Confederacy did not wait for Virginians to vote themselves out of the Union before seizing strategic sites across the state. Within five days of Lincoln's proclamation, Southern militia occupied the naval base at Norfolk and Harper's Ferry on the Potomac, key to the lower Shenandoah Valley. Of most immediate concern was the Confederate force at Manassas Junction, where the Manassas Gap Railroad joined the Orange & Alexandria, just 25 miles southwest of the capital. Jefferson Davis signaled the site's importance by putting General Beauregard, "hero of Fort Sumter," in command there.

Before any decisions on campaigning, it was necessary to fully secure Washington by seizing Alexandria and Arlington Heights, just across the Potomac in Virginia. Within hours of Virginia's May 23 secession referendum, Federal troops took up a bridgehead on the sacred soil. They met no resistance and suffered but one casualty.

Before the war, Elmer Ellsworth had sought to revitalize the militia system by leading the French army–inspired Chicago Zouave Cadets in dazzling displays of drilling and marching. Abraham Lincoln took a liking to the boyish Ellsworth, and invited him to be one of the president-elect's

Colonel Elmer
Ellsworth, carrying the
Confederate flag he has
just torn down, falls
mortally wounded as
one of his men kills the
assassin, hotelkeeper
James Jackson. By
Arthur Lumley.

escorts on the trip east to Washington in February. On May 24, as Colonel Ellsworth led his New York Fire Zouaves into Alexandria, he spied a
Confederate flag flying from the roof of the Marshall House hotel. Impul-
sively, Ellsworth rushed up the stairs to the roof and cut down the offend-
ing banner. As he came down the stairs, flag tucked under his arm, he encountered the hotelkeeper, James T. Jackson. Taking offense at this act of
trespass, Jackson shot the colonel dead. Jackson in his turn was killed by
one of Ellsworth's men.

The deadly exchange filled many newspaper columns, and the body of
the North's first slain hero lay in state in the East Room of the White House.
President and First Lady led the mourners. Washington was dressed in
crepe. "The entire country seemed up in arms," wrote a soldier who escorted Ellsworth to his grave, ". . . and the resolve to crush the rebellion
was sealed in Ellsworth's blood."[10]

· · ·

With half a dozen brigades gathered at Washington, there was, as Treasury Secretary Chase noted, much talk of forward movements. This was men enough to start an army, and so the War Department organized one. On May 27 a new department was carved out of the Department of the East and called the Department of Northeastern Virginia, and an army was assigned to the new department and called . . . the Army of Northeastern Virginia. Which army in due course, rising from the fire like the phoenix, became the Army of the Potomac.

General Scott wanted Joseph K. F. Mansfield for the army command. Colonel Mansfield was a white-bearded old-timer, West Point 1822, once wounded, thrice brevetted for gallantry in Mexico, now heading the Department of Washington. But Scott's choice was overridden in a charge led by Secretary Chase. The April 15 call for 75,000 militia had included provision for five major generals and seventeen brigadier generals of volunteers, to be parceled out among the states answering the call. Ohioan Chase "recommended" (as he modestly put it) Ohioan Irvin McDowell for the post. Chase exerted far more political leverage than anyone speaking for Joseph Mansfield of Connecticut, and McDowell assumed command of the Army of Northeastern Virginia on May 28.[11]

Scott had no quarrel with McDowell's qualifications—he had served on Scott's own staff as well as in the adjutant general's office—but he objected to seeing Mansfield, a full colonel, oversloughed by a major, a major by brevet at that. The general-in-chief, said McDowell, "was cool for a great while." Diplomatically, McDowell rejected a major generalship and settled into the army command as a brigadier general.

Matters of promotion agitated not a few regular officers in these frantic early weeks of war. When he learned that Captains William Franklin and Montgomery Meigs were jumped to colonel, Major Samuel P. Heintzelman grumbled to his diary, "It is a great outrage on a great many officers of the Army." (Heintzelman was mollified when his own colonelcy was backdated to match Franklin's and Meigs's.) For career soldiers, stuck in grade decade after decade in the stultifying antebellum army, wartime expansion meant promotion and accelerated seniority. It was also evident, from McDowell's abrupt elevation, that who one knew in the national and state capitals (and how one made oneself known) would have much to do with rank and position in this war.[12]

Irvin McDowell was forty-two, a tall, overstuffed figure lacking any grace of movement or presence. William Howard Russell, correspondent for the *Times* of London, described him in his diary: "Grey & iron tuft, broad jowl and smooth face, keen blue eye, good brow, block head, square

Irvin McDowell was promoted to head of the Army of Northeastern Virginia after some two decades of staff rather than command duty.

stout clumsy figure & limbs," McDowell neither smoked nor chewed tobacco and did not touch alcohol or even coffee or tea. Secretary Chase analyzed him as "a loyal, brave, truthful, capable officer. . . . He resorts to no acts of popularity. He is attended by no claquers & puffers." Yet, Chase admitted, his protégé was marked by a "rough indifference" that alienated fellow officers, and he lacked any warmth toward the troops. "Having none of the vices of ordinary mortals and but few of their weaknesses," wrote artillerist John C. Tidball, who knew McDowell from the old army, "he imagined himself on a higher plane than they. . . ."

McDowell graduated midway in the Academy class of 1838 and was commissioned in the artillery, then returned to West Point to teach tactics. In Mexico he served on the staff of General Wool, and was brevetted for Buena Vista. The rest of his antebellum service was in the adjutant general's office and on General Scott's staff. He took a leave in 1858–59 to study military institutions in France, a career plus, for at the time France was regarded as the font of the military art. His lack of command experience made him no different from nearly all his fellow serving officers. It was his work for Secretary Chase on the plan for a volunteer army that helped him up that last rung to army command.[13]

While McDowell and the War Department went about organizing and finding officers for the Army of Northeastern Virginia, plans were afoot for taking it to war. On May 2 General Scott handed the president a strategic war plan prepared by a newly minted major general of volunteers named George Brinton McClellan. Thirty-four-year-old McClellan was a longtime favorite of Scott's and had caught the eye of Secretary Chase. McClellan headed Ohio's volunteer forces. He had ranked second in West Point's class of 1846, and when he resigned his commission eleven years later for a career as a railroad executive, he was regarded as one of the army's brightest, most promising officers. After Fort Sumter, New York, Pennsylvania, and Ohio had all sought him to lead their troops. Ohio won the bidding, and McClellan was in Cincinnati organizing a projected 30,000-man force.

On April 27 McClellan had sent to Scott a grandiose "plan of operations intended to . . . bring the war to a speedy close." With sufficient arms, said McClellan, the Northwest would furnish an 80,000-man army he would lead across the Alleghenies to fall on Richmond. With Scott's Eastern army advancing in conjunction with McClellan's Western one, this would relieve Washington and "secure the destruction of the Southern Army." Should he not be needed to relieve Washington, McClellan sketched war on an even larger canvas. With his 80,000 men he would march south from Ohio through Kentucky and Tennessee to Nashville, where he anticipated a battle. Victorious there, he would push on to Montgomery, Alabama, at the time he was writing, the capital of the Confederacy. The Eastern army would meanwhile advance through the Carolinas and Georgia, and the combined armies would then sweep up the Gulf ports of Pensacola, Mobile, and New Orleans. This "second line of operations would be the most decisive."

In annotating McClellan's plan for the president, Scott pointed out its impracticabilities, such as manpower limitations imposed by the three-months' militia call-up, and its grave logistical shortcomings, relying on "long, tedious and break down (of men, horses, and wagons) marches." Scott sketched a plan of his own. Rather than McClellan's piecemeal approach, he would envelop the seceded states "by a cordon of posts on the Mississippi to its mouth from its junction with the Ohio, and by blockading ships of war on the sea board."

Scott filled in details in his reply to McClellan. He would rely heavily on a constrictive blockade of the South Atlantic and Gulf ports. A 60,000-man army, "in which it is not improbable you may be invited to take an important part," would advance aboard transports, supported by gunboats, down the Mississippi, taking New Orleans and Forts Jackson and St. Philip near the river's mouth. A cordon of posts would keep the river open. (In a second letter, Scott raised the count of troops to 80,000, one column waterborne on the Mississippi, a second column "to proceed as nearly abreast as practicable by land.") He projected a starting date of November 10, six months hence. His scheme would "envelop the insurgent States and bring them to terms with less bloodshed than by any other plan." Scott added a cautionary note. "A word now as to the greatest obstacle in the way of this plan — the great danger now pressing upon us — the impatience of our patriotic and loyal Union friends." Pressure was building from every quarter for "instant and vigorous action, regardless, I fear, of consequences. . . ."[14]

While not submitting his design as a formal plan of operations, Scott advanced it widely, inside and outside the administration, as a grand strategic plan for suppressing the rebellion. In his memoir, E. D. Townsend of Scott's staff recalled the general frequently explaining "to the President, and other influential men" that by maintaining a strict blockade of the Southern coastline and sending a strong force to open the Mississippi, "the Union spirit will assert itself; those who are on the fence will descend on the Union side, and I will guarantee that in one year from this time all difficulties will be settled." But, he warned, should the South be invaded at any point, "I will guarantee that at the end of a year you will be further from a settlement than you are now."

As it had during the Sumter crisis, the cabinet divided over Scott's plan. Secretary of State Seward, self-appointed peacemaker, favored it as the least confrontational. He commissioned Quartermaster Montgomery Meigs to formulate a strategy. There must be no rush to battle, said Meigs, but "a policy defensive in the main, offensive only so far as to occupy important positions in the border states. . . ." Postmaster Montgomery Blair objected. To Blair, Meigs was repeating Scott's staid policy of compromise and accommodation, of overestimating the secessionists' hold on the Southern people. "This is a fundamental and fatal error and if . . . we fail to go to the relief of the people of the South they will be subjugated. . . ." An immediate advance would "be hailed with joy by the people of the South everywhere."[15]

Scott's strategic plan was debated in the newspapers, and his scheme to enfold the insurgent states in the coils of economic pressure inspired someone to christen it the "Anaconda plan." A Cincinnati printmaker issued a sketch map of the Confederate states encircled by a huge black anaconda, titling it "Scott's Great Snake." Conservatives were generally supportive. To New York diarist George Templeton Strong "the programme

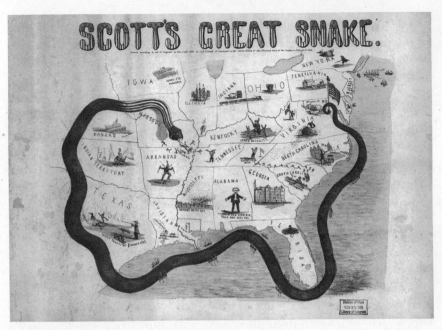

Printmaker J. B. Elliott interpreted General Scott's so-called Anaconda plan literally, as a threat to economically strangle the eleven largely uncivilized states of the newborn Confederacy. A Kentuckian straddles a fence labeled "armed neutrality."

looks sensible and promising." On the other hand, the *Chicago Tribune* was among those more Radical papers demanding immediate action. Unionists in the South "will be crushed out . . . long before the anaconda has got the whole country enveloped in its coils." Horace Greeley's *New-York Tribune* had no tolerance for further delay, blaring out "the Nation's War Cry: Forward to Richmond! Forward to Richmond!"

General Scott, content to have his grand strategy under review, was in no hurry to be more specific. He revealed his dilemma to William T. Sherman, an old regular newly returned to the service in command of the U.S. 13th regiment. "Genl. Scott knows what he is about," Sherman told his wife; "— he never designed for the 1st 3 mos. to do any thing more than to Secure his key points — open the Roads & prepare materials, but there are so many pushing him that he says he may be beaten, by Genl. Impatience." On June 17, in conversation with the historian John Lothrop Motley, Lincoln remarked, "Scott will not let us outsiders know anything of his plans." While this was said lightly, it spoke of frustration. Once again, as with Fort Sumter, the president was being pressed inevitably toward a major military decision.[16]

Two major concerns marked Lincoln's thinking. First, as of mid-June the ninety-day militia enlistments were two-thirds used up. The June 26 return showed seventeen of the twenty regiments as three-months' troops. After the drama of his proclamation, after the public outpouring of support, to send men who had rushed to the colors home in late July with nothing to show for their patriotism would be a political disaster. As Senator John Sherman put it, their enlistments "will melt away, and they go home having done nothing, and little likely to enlist again."

The other concern was Beauregard's army at Manassas Junction, just 25 miles from the Capitol. Its strength was said to be 25,000. The Northern public would hardly tolerate McDowell's Yankee army sitting and staring at this arrogant enemy display for six months until the Anaconda plan could start. (Or, as the satirist Robert Henry Newell put it, until the "great anaconda has gathered itself in a circle around the doomed rabbit of the rebellion, and if the rabbit swells he's a goner.") Greeley's *Tribune* grew overheated at the very thought: "Again, we repeat, On to Richmond!"[17]

A pair of skirmishes further stirred press and public impatience. On June 10, from Fort Monroe, Ben Butler mounted a surprise assault on an enemy camp at a church known as Big Bethel. It was a disaster. Regiments fired into each other, maneuvers were disjointed, and finally the troops beat a humiliating retreat. A week later, in northern Virginia, an Ohio regiment was ambushed at Vienna and routed. The Ohioans scattered into the woods, leaving eight dead and bearing tales of enemy "masked batteries" that resonated through the raw, impressionable army.

News from the West was better. General McClellan had been put in command of the Department of the Ohio, and with the patronage of Scott and Secretary Chase named major general in the regular army, ranking him second only to Scott himself. McClellan sent a column into western Virginia to drive out a Confederate incursion, and on June 3 the Yankees surprised and routed the Rebels at the village of Philippi. The papers christened it the "Philippi Races" and pointed to it as a model for McDowell's army.[18]

Finally General-in-Chief Scott bowed to the stark reality of a Confederate army at Manassas Junction, a day or two's march from Washington. He had McDowell prepare a plan for an offensive. Beauregard was posted behind a small stream called Bull Run, covering the junction of the two railroads, the Orange & Alexandria and the Manassas Gap. McDowell called for a 30,000-man army, with a reserve of 10,000. "I propose to attack the main position by turning it, if possible, so as to cut off communications by rail with the South. . . ." He expected militia general Robert Patterson, heading the Department of Pennsylvania, to prevent a Rebel force in the Shenandoah Valley—commanded by former U.S. quartermaster Joe Johnston—from reinforcing Beauregard. The battle should establish "the prestige in this contest on the one side or the other."

McDowell testified that in discussing the plan with Scott, "I mentioned to the general that I felt tender on the subject of General Patterson and General Johnston." He was reassured by Scott's promise: "If Johnston joins Beauregard he shall have Patterson on his heels."

The president concluded he could delay no longer regarding the Army of Northeastern Virginia. On June 29 he convened a meeting at the White House to hear McDowell's Manassas plan. The room was crowded: General Scott, Quartermaster Meigs, New York militia general Charles Sandford, the Department of Washington's Joseph Mansfield, and McDowell and his senior officer, Daniel Tyler. McDowell spread his maps and presented his plan. Scott objected to this rush to battle, calling again for an advance down the Mississippi in the fall. But by now the old warrior sensed the pro forma quality to his presentation. Meigs argued for a quicker end to the contest—making war now in Virginia promised to be less expensive and more efficient. McDowell's plan carried the day. Lincoln approved it without substantive objection, although General Sandford did observe that Patterson should be firmly posted to hold Joe Johnston in the Valley. Scott set a date—July 8, just over a week hence.

Nothing about this meeting and this decision implied rejection of the basic wisdom of General Scott's Anaconda plan. Indeed his scheme would become (although not under that discredited name) an important element in the Union's war strategy. What was rejected that 29th of June was any notion of patiently seeking some military strategy that might resolve or limit this small-bore beginners' war before it became a no-holds-barred, all-out war.

It was confidently predicted that when General McDowell's offensive succeeded there would be no need for Anaconda plans and their like. When he expressed concern about the rawness of his troops, McDowell was told not to worry: "The answer was, 'You are green, it is true; but they are green, also; you are all green alike.'" That defined the risk. The possible destruction or at least crippling of the secessionist movement defined the reward. As Meigs put it, "One good battle & the back of the rebellion is broken."[19]

The June 26 return gave McDowell just six brigades. But companies and regiments were coming into the capital in a growing rush now, and by July

Newspaper artist Alfred R. Waud sketched General Scott preparing orders for
the advance against the Rebels at Bull Run. From left, staff aides George W.
Cullum, Schuyler Hamilton, and Henry Van Rensselaer.

8, the date Scott had set for the advance, McDowell would count eleven
brigades plus a miscellany of regiments as a reserve. From Scott and Mc-
Dowell emerged an army command structure of brigades formed into divisions.

Five divisions were marked out for the Army of Northeastern Virginia.
The First Division was led by Daniel Tyler, brigadier general of Connecticut militia. Under Tyler were the brigades of Colonel Erasmus D. Keyes,
former military secretary to General Scott; Robert C. Schenck, former
Ohio congressman, now brigadier general of Ohio militia; Colonel William T. Sherman, the reenlisted regular who would win his fame on more
distant battlefields; and Colonel Israel B. Richardson, a fourteen-year regular who left his Michigan farm to return to the wars.

The Second Division was under Colonel David Hunter, a rare regular
of abolitionist bent. His two brigades were led by Andrew Porter, colonel
of the new U.S. 16th regiment; and Colonel Ambrose E. Burnside, a Rhode
Islander fated for a checkered career in the Army of the Potomac.

The Third Division was led by Samuel P. Heintzelman, whose colonelcy
only came after thirty-five years' service. His three brigades were under
Colonel William B. Franklin, Topographical Engineers; Colonel Orlando
B. Willcox, West Point 1847; and Colonel Oliver Otis Howard, the youngest West Pointer (1854 class) in this gathering army.

Brigadier General Theodore Runyon, New Jersey militia, had the Fourth Division, a general reserve. Under him were four regiments of New Jersey militia and four of New Jersey three-year volunteers.

The Fifth Division was commanded by Colonel Dixon S. Miles, the longest serving (thirty-seven years) among the regular officers. Colonel Louis Blenker, late of the Bavarian Legion, led one of Miles's brigades, and Colonel Thomas A. Davies, a West Pointer who had last seen army service in 1831, the other.

It was General Scott's intent to place West Point regulars, or ex-regulars, in all the command postings, and he came close to his goal. Of McDowell and his sixteen chief lieutenants, thirteen were Academy graduates. Andrew Porter had attended the Academy for six months in 1836–37, afterward joining up for the War with Mexico. Schenck and Runyon gained command as brigadiers of militia; the third militia brigadier, Tyler, was a West Pointer, class of 1819.

The German Blenker won a brigade after leading the 8th New York Volunteers to Washington. A similar route to command was taken by Willcox (1st Michigan), Richardson (2nd Michigan), Burnside (1st Rhode Island), and Davies (16th New York), all of whom had resigned from the antebellum army. Howard, a serving officer, resigned to command the 3rd Maine Volunteers. The other serving officers were McDowell, Heintzelman, Hunter, Keyes, Porter, Franklin, and Miles. Nine of the army's eleven artillery batteries were commanded and manned by regulars. While some commanders had experienced Indian fighting on the frontier, only five — Richardson, Porter, Heintzelman, Franklin, and Miles — had experienced actual war combat, in Mexico.

Scott's determination to fill the upper command slots with regulars and ex-regulars did not extend to regimental and company postings. Indeed, he was adamant about not doing so. Whatever the fate of this opening campaign being pressed on him, he believed the war's decisive battles would be won by an invigorated regular army, with only assistance from the volunteers. He opposed seeding volunteer units with experienced junior officers from the regulars, and the War Department made it difficult for regulars to resign to take rank with the volunteers. Nor could regular noncoms and enlisted men be transferred to leadership roles in volunteer companies. In his past wars the old general had found volunteers (and their officers) a trial, and he could not bring himself to forecast a major role for them in this potentially far greater conflict.[20]

Scott's July 8 campaign start came and went and nothing and no one was ready. In his diary for July 10 Heintzelman reported, "Gen. McDowell

& staff were here. . . . Much talk & but little done." Orlando Willcox wrote his wife, "One thing is certain, there is a great lack of competent colonels & generals, and all the regiments require drilling badly." Yet when hardbitten regulars like Israel Richardson took to the drill field, they got results. Sergeant Charles Haydon, 2nd Michigan, watched him in action: "When they saw Richardson tramping up & down the field on foot, his great iron sword sheath hung to his side with chains, rattling like a log chain on a pole bridge, giving orders loud enough to be heard a mile . . . & keeping them on the jump by the hour, they thought the Devil had surely come." After a busy two weeks, Colonel Willcox believed there was progress: "We are all alive for the grand move which cannot be put off long. . . . I have no fear of the result." General McDowell did not share such optimism. "This is not an army," he told a visitor. "It will take a long time to make it an army."

As that army girded for battle, cheering news arrived from General Mc-Clellan in western Virginia. Two small but significant victories, at Rich Mountain and Corrick's Ford, allowed McClellan to claim that "secession is killed in this country." His extravagant proclamation to the troops was widely applauded: "You have annihilated two armies, commanded by educated and experienced soldiers, and entrenched in mountain fastnesses fortified at their leisure. . . . You have proved that Union men, fighting for the preservation of our Government, are more than a match for our misguided and erring brethren . . ." The press was ecstatic. "We like the works and ways of Gen. McClellan," said the *New-York Tribune*. The *New York Herald* headlined, GEN. MCCLELLAN, THE NAPOLEON OF THE PRESENT WAR. The *Louisville Journal* suggested eastern Virginia "will next be *McClellanized* in the same finished style."[21]

William Howard Russell of the *Times* of London had met General Scott back in April and was engaged and entertained. Affectionately christening him "old Vanity," he added, "but he really is a fine old lump of martial glory." Now in July Russell revisited army headquarters and found Scott sadly worn down from his labors: "The General has become visibly weaker since I first saw him. He walks down to his office, close at hand, with difficulty . . ." Nevertheless, Scott pledged to Russell that when fighting commenced he would take the field in his carriage, "which is always ready for the purpose . . . ; nor is he unprepared with precedents of great military commanders who have successfully conducted engagements under similar circumstances."

Russell had famously covered the war in the Crimea and the Sepoy Mutiny, and while he found Washington infused with martial spirit, he was unimpressed with this army's state of readiness. He found the artillery badly equipped, with "the worst set of gunners and drivers which I, who have seen the Turkish field-guns, ever beheld." The cavalry "would go over like ninepins at a charge from Punjaubee irregulars." Russell's countryman, newspaper artist Frank Vizetelly, remarked on the pretensions of these amateur warriors. "Verily, a cosmopolitan army is assembled here. As one walks he is jostled by soldiers dressed in the uniforms of the Zouaves de la Garde, the Chasseurs à Pied, Infanterie de la Ligne, and other French regiments — so great, apparently, is the admiration of our cousins for everything Gallic."

General McDowell, while he spoke confidently to Russell of his hopes for the campaign, did not seem in very high spirits. He knew little certain about Beauregard's forces and positions, and complained of a lack of cavalry for scouting. Russell thought him "not so much disposed to undervalue the Confederates" as before. "I said as I parted I wished him success," Russell entered in his diary that evening. Then, recalling his earlier stay in Charleston, he mused, "Cd. I help doing so, & yet I wished the same to Beauregard."[22]

Meanwhile, along the upper Potomac, Robert Patterson, major general of militia, was trying to organize his own ninety-day army and doing General Scott's bidding at the same time. Long-ago credentials had earned Patterson command of the Department of Pennsylvania. In the War of 1812 he enlisted in the militia and ended the war as captain of regulars. He left the army in 1815 but returned in 1846 as major general of volunteers in Mexico, where he led a division under Scott. Now, age sixty-nine, he had charge of Pennsylvania's militia units.

Harper's Ferry was seen as vital to holding the lower Shenandoah Valley, and when the secessionists seized the place a week into the war, Scott put a premium on regaining it. Patterson was assigned the task. He proposed crossing the Potomac upstream at Williamsport to outflank the Rebels at Harper's Ferry. Scott's approval was hedged about with cautions: ". . . we must sustain no reverse; but this is not enough, a check or a drawn battle would be a victory to the enemy, filling his heart with joy, his ranks with men, and his magazines with voluntary contributions." This proved exactly the wrong thing to tell a man of Robert Patterson's mild military temperament.

Patterson's Army of the Shenandoah reached Williamsport and on June 16 edged across the river. Harper's Ferry was found abandoned and the

In an 1861 cartoon, Lincoln defends flag and eagle by fending off a secessionist planter. General Scott directs his troops to the rescue, led by a noose-bearing soldier to deal with "all traitors." At left, Buchanan says, "I am glad, I am out of the scrape!"

Confederates withdrawn to Winchester up the Valley. "Harper's Ferry has been retaken without firing a gun," Patterson reported. Scott's response was deflating: Patterson should send to Washington all the regulars in his army. Patterson counted on his few regulars to stiffen the spines of his many militia, and without them he recrossed the Potomac to safety in Maryland.[23]

So began a lasting confusion in Robert Patterson's mind as to his mission and how to carry it out. Joe Johnston stoked his confusion. Finding Harper's Ferry a military cul-de-sac, Johnston had abandoned it for Winchester. Should he take the offensive, he had a choice of Potomac crossings at Harper's Ferry or Williamsport, forcing Patterson to cover both. Should he be called to Beauregard's army, he could march south to the Manassas Gap Railroad and put his army aboard the cars to Manassas Junction, outdistancing any pursuit by Patterson. In operational terms, the two Confederate forces were acting on the inside track (literally, the Manassas Gap's track), leaving the Federals on the longer outside track.

Scott worried that should Patterson act too aggressively against Winchester, Johnston might fall back to Manassas, hardly what was wanted. "Remain in front of the enemy" was the general-in-chief's injunction. But

Patterson must not advance, or offer battle, "without a well-grounded confidence in your continued superiority." Patterson proceeded to demonstrate a complete lack of confidence in his continued superiority.

Patterson counted his army at 18,200, the largest share ninety-day militiamen shortly to be mustered out, but among the officers were a number who would make their marks in the Army of the Potomac. These included Alpheus S. Williams, David B. Birney, Abner Doubleday, George H. Gordon, Charles P. Stone, Daniel Butterfield, John Newton, and Patterson's chief of staff, Fitz John Porter. None advanced their careers by serving in Patterson's Army of the Shenandoah, an army utterly barren of accomplishment.[24]

On July 1 Scott notified Patterson that McDowell would advance within a week or so on Manassas Junction "for aggressive purposes." Dutifully, Patterson once again crossed the Potomac at Williamsport and pushed ahead to Martinsburg. The Army of the Shenandoah remained at Martinsburg, 20 miles from Winchester and the Rebel army, for one day shy of two weeks. Patterson told Washington he dared not advance farther . . . for fear of being lured into a trap by a greatly superior enemy. On July 4 he counted Johnston's army as 15,000 to 18,000 men. By July 6 he had Johnston reinforced from Manassas to 26,000 men. On July 13 he telegraphed, "Johnston is in position . . . to be re-enforced, and his strength doubled just as I would reach him." (During this period, Johnston's returns showed him with 10,600 men.)

Patterson relied on deserters and other informants for his picture of the enemy. David Hunter Strother of Patterson's staff gave Johnston 12,000 to 15,000 men at most, based on direct observation. Chief of Staff Fitz John Porter refused to credit Strother's figures. Instead he endorsed increases in the enemy's force to as much as 44,000 men and sixty-three guns — reinforcements miraculously dispatched from Manassas even as Beauregard prepared to receive battle from McDowell. Strother wrote of Patterson and his officers, "These men of war seemed to be entirely satisfied with information obtained from other quarters, and I was equally well satisfied that this information had been furnished them by persons in the employ of the enemy."[25]

On July 9 Patterson convened a council of war to try and resolve his dilemma. What should they do in regard to aiding General McDowell? Should they advance, and how far? Would they be falling into a trap? Could anything be accomplished before the ninety-day enlistments were up? One staff man spoke knowingly of the ease with which the enemy transferred troops by rail back and forth between Manassas Junction and

Winchester at the rate of 12,000 men a day. Captain John Newton insisted, "Our present position is a very exposed one. . . . Our whole line is a false one." The field officers agreed they were at risk where they were and that they should retire to Charlestown, close by Harper's Ferry. Indecision paralyzed Patterson's resolve, and he stayed at Martinsburg for another week.

General Scott was dissatisfied with Patterson's "tardy movements, he not having got down to within anything like striking distance of Johnston's camp." By now Scott and his old Mexican War comrade-in-arms were talking past each other. Scott had accepted Patterson as a trained soldier and awarded him considerable leeway to find a way to defeat or at least neutralize Johnston. Patterson felt cast adrift in a vast sea of troubles. He lacked the self-assurance for independent command, desiring instead a dependent command, with step-by-step directions from the general-in-chief. In time Scott grew more incisive in his orders. On July 13 he wired Patterson, "If not strong enough to beat the enemy early next week" — when McDowell expected to go to battle against Beauregard — "make demonstrations so as to detain him in the valley of Winchester. . . ."[26]

Such clarity came too late. On the same date, Patterson insisted that if he advanced, Johnston's strength would be doubled "just as I would reach him." Making a demonstration risked being crushed by overwhelming force. Fitz John Porter abetted his delusion. Porter would be asked by a congressional committee if it was the feeling in Patterson's staff "that it was absolutely beyond your power to hold Johnston?" Porter replied that it was. The enemy would "gradually draw us forward until the time came when they would suddenly strike us, and make a dash at Manassas."

Reinforcements from Washington briefly ignited in Patterson what one of his men called the "old martial fire." On July 15 he marched from Martinsburg to within a dozen miles of Winchester and ordered a reconnaissance. On the morning of July 16 his scouting party advanced along the Valley Pike until it encountered a Rebel outpost. After a scattering of shots the party hastened back. By Patterson's reckoning, that was the demonstration Scott demanded of him, accomplished by the date expected of him. He ordered the Army of the Shenandoah back to Charlestown. By day's end on July 17 Patterson was bivouacked 23 miles from Winchester.

That night Scott telegraphed Patterson, "Do not let the enemy amuse and delay you with a small force in front whilst he re-enforces the Junction with his main body." In a second telegram Scott sharpened his tone. He expected "to hear that you had felt him strongly, or, at least, had occupied him by threats and demonstrations. . . . Has he not stolen a march and sent re-enforcements toward Manassas Junction?"

Patterson took this as a display of bad temper on the general-in-chief's part. He was indignant: "The enemy has stolen no march upon me. I have kept him actively employed, and by threats and reconnaissances in force caused him to be re-enforced. I have accomplished in this respect more than the General-in-Chief asked or could well be expected, in face of an enemy far superior in numbers. . . ."

Even as Patterson was writing that dispatch at midday on July 18, Joe Johnston, freed from any threat, started his army toward the Manassas Gap Railroad and the Manassas battlefield. General Patterson would not credit, or acknowledge, the enemy's departure from his front for two days.[27]

It would have brought aged, ailing Winfield Scott immense satisfaction, when his army reached the field of battle that July day in 1861, to summon his carriage to carry him to the scene so that he might personally supervise victory over the secessionists. He had said as much to Russell of the *Times,* surely holding up the example of Marshal Saxe directing from a litter the triumph at Fontenoy in 1745. Instead he played the role of generalissimo back in Washington, coordinating by telegraph the efforts of his field generals, Irvin McDowell and Robert Patterson.

McDowell set his army in motion on July 16, even as Patterson started his timid reconnaissance toward Winchester. General Scott, dining with editor Henry Raymond of the *New York Times,* played down the movement as simply a preliminary to the grander vision of his Anaconda plan. That evening the general-in-chief made an appearance at a White House levee. When he left early — it was whispered he must be preparing to take the field at the head of the army — he was applauded by numerous well-wishers.[28]

McDowell expected to find Beauregard entrenched behind Bull Run, shielding his railroad supply link at Manassas Junction. The Rebels were also said to have an outpost at Fairfax Court House. Handling intelligence with far more skill than Patterson, McDowell estimated Beauregard's force at 25,000 (only 3,000 too high), with the potential of 10,000 reinforcements. He was led to believe that if Patterson did his duty, Joe Johnston would not furnish those reinforcements. McDowell reported his own army at about 35,000. Twenty of the fifty infantry regiments were ninety-day militia whose time was nearly up, some in days. He had no illusions about the battle readiness of his force, nor about achieving surprise; he expected Washington's papers to fully report the start of his march.

His was to be a two-phase offensive, with the outpost at Fairfax Court

House the first target and the Bull Run line the second. The short opening march on the 16th was designed not to tax the green troops. It took Daniel Tyler's First Division northwest to Vienna. David Hunter's Second Division made a very public departure — Ambrose Burnside's lead brigade assembled on Pennsylvania Avenue and Burnside, his horse garlanded with flowers from admiring spectators, led the way across the Long Bridge to Annandale. Also camping at Annandale was Dixon Miles's Fifth Division. Sam Heintzelman's Third Division angled slightly southward toward Fairfax Station on the Orange & Alexandria. Theodore Runyon's Fourth Division, its regiments unbrigaded, acted as reserve.

It was McDowell's plan to position Tyler, Hunter, and Miles to envelop Fairfax Court House on the 17th. To the south, Heintzelman would take position to outflank Beauregard's Bull Run fortifications and sever his railroad lifeline. McDowell intended no assaults on entrenched positions. As Colonel Sherman explained, General Scott "will allow no risks to be run — He thinks there should be no game of hazard here. All the Risks should be made from the flanks."[29]

The first day's march was more adventure than war, with cheering crowds and bands playing "John Brown's Body" and "Dixie." Day Two began more soberly with 3:00 a.m. reveille. McDowell intended to fall on Fairfax Court House from three directions by 8:00 a.m. In this war, with all the imponderables of communications and topography and the mischances of the battlefield, nothing proved more frustrating than trying to coordinate two, or three, or four separate columns so they reached their appointed places at their appointed times. Poor McDowell started from scratch — no command experience, a vestigial staff, green field officers leading green troops. Inevitably July 17 disappointed. McDowell summed it up ruefully: "None of us got forward in time."

He laid blame on the indolence of the troops. They "stopped every moment to pick blackberries or to get water. They would not keep in the ranks, order as much as you pleased." But McDowell was guilty of a heavy dose of official caution. Three things, he insisted, "will not be pardonable in any commander: 1st. To come upon a battery or breastwork without a knowledge of its position. 2d. To be surprised. 3d. To fall back." As a consequence, scores of skirmishers preceded and flanked the columns, scrambling through woodland thickets and briar patches, slowing the march to a crawl. "Hardly a musket shot was fired," a man wrote, "but our commanders were fearful of masked batteries, and proceeded as timidly as old maids eating shad in the dark."[30]

Ambrose Burnside's brigade, in Hunter's Second Division, had the lead on July 17. Just short of noon the entrenchments at Fairfax Court House came in sight, and Colonel Burnside rode to the front, ordered muskets loaded, and delivered a little speech reminding the men of their duty to the Union and to their families and friends back home. He could have saved his eloquence. When skirmishers warily advanced, they found the town empty. The quarry had flown.

On the flank, Tyler's First Division encountered the same delays as the other columns. Two miles north of Fairfax the road forked — left fork to Fairfax, right fork to Germantown and the Rebel rear. McDowell had designated Germantown as Tyler's target, but granted him discretion to move on Fairfax "should he deem it best." Tyler pondered the matter for some time. When he finally chose the right fork to Germantown, he was only in time to see the Fairfax garrison escaping to the west and safety.

In Fairfax, after tearing down the Confederate flag flying over the courthouse, the troops began breaking into houses and looting. "No goths or vandals ever had less respect for the lives & property of friends and foes," Sherman wrote his wife; ". . . for us to say we commanded that army is no such thing — they did as they pleased." Furious at these displays of indiscipline, McDowell ordered each regimental commander to appoint a provost marshal with a ten-man squad "to preserve the property and arrest all wrong-doers. . . ."[31]

July 18 was to see the army closing on the Rebels' main line, turning their right, and threatening their railroad supply line, but like July 17, the 18th did not go as planned. For one thing, provisions ran short. Subsistence trains were slow to march and misdirected. The troops set out carrying three days' rations, but their eating habits proved as undisciplined as the rest of their soldiering. Some wolfed down all their rations the first day; by the end of Day Two most of the rest were hungry and marching on empty stomachs.

Daniel Tyler's First Division had the lead now, and McDowell's orders for the day were explicit. Tyler was to move west on the Warrenton Turnpike to Centreville, some three and a half miles from Bull Run. No resistance was expected at Centreville. "Do not bring on an engagement," Tyler was told, "but keep up the impression that we are moving on Manassas." The First Division's mission, in short, was a reconnaissance.

McDowell turned to Heintzelman's Third Division, the intended key to his campaign. He meant Heintzelman to swing south and cut the railroad near Bristoe Station while the rest of the army confronted the Rebels behind Bull Run. It was thought the need to regain his supply line should pry Beauregard out of his entrenchments. But to the south was rough country, the roads little more than pathways, narrow and crooked, and the flanking distance greater than expected. "We would become entangled," McDowell explained to Washington, "and our [gun] carriages would block up the way. I was therefore forced to abandon the plan of turning the enemy's right. . . ." He would now have to come up with an entirely new campaign plan on the fly.[32]

McDowell had hardly absorbed this blow when word came that Tyler's advance was engaged along Bull Run. Musketry and cannon fire could be heard. McDowell rode hard for headquarters to find out what had happened in his absence. What happened, he found, was General Tyler ignoring orders and taking matters into his own hands.

Daniel Tyler, West Point 1819, had last served in 1834. He did not interrupt a successful business career to volunteer for the Mexican War, but in this new war he accepted command of Connecticut's militia. He was a vigorous sixty-two, bearing a certain hauteur of command. Tyler seems to have resented McDowell — twenty years his junior — as army commander and grudgingly accepted his own secondary role. On July 18 he seized on his brief moment of independent command.

Tyler learned that the Rebels from Fairfax and Centreville had marched off south by west to the Bull Run crossings leading to Manassas Junction. A skirmish party from Israel Richardson's brigade took the advance, Tyler and Richardson leading. Within sight of Bull Run the road forked, right fork to Mitchell's Ford, left fork to Blackburn's Ford. An enemy force was visible beyond Mitchell's Ford, but Blackburn's appeared undefended except for a two-gun section of artillery. Might this be, Tyler wondered, a nearly open road to Manassas Junction?

Major John G. Barnard, the army's chief engineer, joined the advance. He cautioned Tyler and Richardson that McDowell wanted no fight with the Rebels that day . . . but a reconnoiter of Blackburn's Ford might be in order; not "that this point would be *attacked*. But a reconnaissance would be but the carrying out of a demonstration." There was a fine line to be trod here, and neither Tyler nor Richardson had the experience or temperament to follow it. Tyler brought up a pair of 20-pounder Parrott rifles, which soon drove off the enemy guns. With a nod from Tyler, Richardson sent in a battle line. This triggered a blast of musketry from across the run, and Richardson's blood was up.

Israel Richardson, West Point 1841, was a large, rough-hewn man of forty-six who saw considerable service in Mexico, earning the nickname "Fighting Dick." He was awarded brevet promotions for Contreras, Chur-

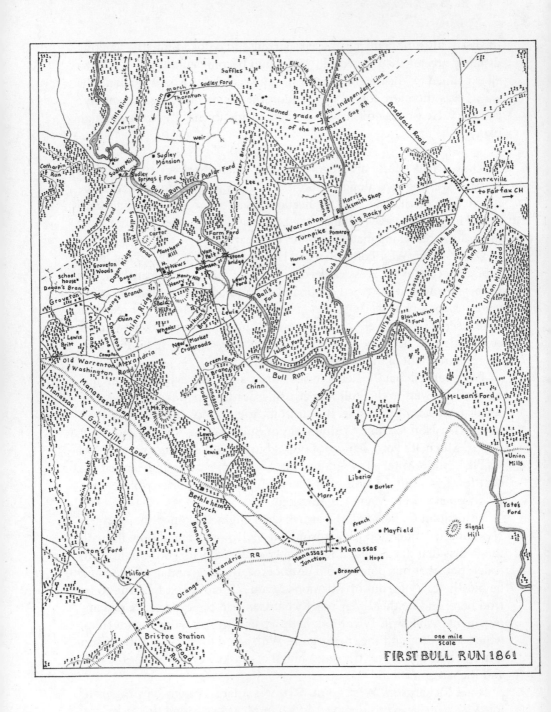

FIRST BULL RUN 1861

ubusco, and Chapultepec. He left the army in 1855 but rejoined shortly after Sumter to command the 2nd Michigan Volunteers. Richardson's training regimen was by regulars' standards, causing his company captains to petition the governor with grievances. But on May 29, to everyone's relief, widower Richardson took a wife. "Col. Richardson was married yesterday morning," Sergeant Haydon noted in his journal. "The effect was excellent. He was never so pleasant before as at battalion drill yesterday." The new bride insisted on going off to war with him and on this day was waiting back at Centreville.[33]

Richardson's brigade tangled with a Virginia brigade under James Longstreet, who here first revealed a deadly talent for defensive warfare. "It appeared to me that there were 5,000 muskets fired at once," said Tyler. This fire so demoralized the militiamen of the 12th New York that they fled in wild disorder. Richardson rode into their midst, shouting, "What are you running for? There is no enemy here! I cannot see anybody at all!" It was unavailing.

Major Barnard protested to Tyler that surely they knew all they needed to know about the defenses of Blackburn's Ford, and should defer to McDowell's standing orders. Tyler had boasted the enemy "would run whenever menaced by serious attack," but now saw the fallacy in that argument. Richardson wanted to step up the assault; he would "clear out those fellows" in two hours. But Tyler had seen enough and ordered Sherman's brigade to cover the withdrawal. By this time, too, the general commanding was on the scene. "Gen. McDowell arrived during the cannonading," Sherman wrote, "and I think did not like it."

Federal casualties in the affair at Blackburn's Ford came to 83, including 19 dead. (Confederate casualties were 68.) McDowell was displeased with Tyler for exceeding his orders, but one thing was clarified: Any frontal attack on the Bull Run line promised to be costly. Sam Heintzelman declared Blackburn's Ford "a disgraceful affair & Gen. Tyler is not excusable." As to Israel Richardson, his straight-ahead style of battle-leading lived up to his Fighting Dick reputation. This could prove a valuable asset in an army of volunteers, but it also put him right in the front line, not the safest place for a valued commander. Richardson left the field grudgingly, but at Centreville his mood was lightened when, as Sergeant Haydon reported, "His pretty young wife embraced him in a most distracting manner when he returned."[34]

General Beauregard accepted the encounter at Blackburn's Ford as proof that the Yankee army under his West Point classmate Irvin McDowell might actually be held at bay by his Bull Run defenses. He took heart.

He had telegraphed Richmond that he needed reinforcements "at the earliest possible instant and by every possible means." Even as the clash at Blackburn's drew blood, in the Valley Joe Johnston had his army marching for Piedmont Station on the Manassas Gap Railroad . . . and Robert Patterson knew nothing of it. With reinforcements promised, the tactician in Beauregard was aroused. He would attack the Yankee army at Centreville —a flank attack, a grand wheel from the right of his line against the left of McDowell's. He massed his forces on his right, and set the date for the offensive as Sunday, July 21.[35]

As for General McDowell, if he could not turn the Confederates' right flank, and if he rejected any thought of a frontal assault against the defended Bull Run crossings, he had no choice but to explore turning their left flank. On the evening of July 18 he called in chief engineer Barnard and his assistant, Daniel P. Woodbury, and set them the task of finding a hidden path to an undefended upstream crossing of Bull Run. Friday the 19th had to be devoted to reprovisioning the troops, so Barnard had the day to reconnoiter. Battle might be set for the next day, Saturday, July 20.

The obvious Bull Run crossing on Beauregard's left was the Warrenton Turnpike bridge, known to history as the Stone Bridge. If obvious to the Federals, it would be obvious to the Confederates, and the Stone Bridge appeared well defended. Consulting his map with a local Unionist named Mathias Mitchell, Barnard pointed to a ford at Sudley Springs, said to be two or three miles upstream from the Stone Bridge. The map showed no public road from the Warrenton Turnpike to Sudley Springs, but Mitchell said there was a farm road "by which, opening gates and passing through private grounds," they might reach the ford.

On the morning of July 19 Barnard and Woodbury with a troop of cavalry set out to trace the prospective route. After a time they struck a farm road they assumed must lead to Sudley Springs. But soon they came on a Confederate cavalry vedette, and fearful of giving the scheme away, they turned back. The reconnoiter satisfied neither Barnard nor McDowell, leaving the flanking plan mired in uncertainty.

Having no word from General Scott, McDowell assumed Patterson was holding Johnston in the Shenandoah, so there was no overriding urgency for him to attack. He gave thought to a reconnaissance in force to confirm the flank-march route, whatever the cost to secrecy, but ruled it out. Achieving surprise was his priority. It was decided to attempt a covert reconnaissance after dark. Whatever the result, there was now no prospect of opening the contest on July 20. That night, under a full moon, Woodbury and engineer Horatio G. Wright again tried to trace the flanking route. But again enemy cavalry was encountered and they gave up the attempt. Major Barnard satisfied himself, by further inquiries, that the still-unseen flanking route was feasible, and he so reported. With that, McDowell designated Sunday, July 21, as the day of battle.[36]

The army was massed around Centreville, its camps overrun by civilians who had come out from Washington to perhaps witness the battle that would extinguish the rebellion. There were a dozen or so members of Congress and leaders of Washington society and even the secretary of war, Simon Cameron. The troops, under the eyes of the visitors, displayed their best behavior. Colonel Oliver Otis Howard, the most Christian of Christian soldiers, assembled his brigade for prayer. As he described the moment, "The God of battles was entreated for guidance, for shielding in the battle, and for care of those so precious in our far-away homes."

That morning of July 20 McDowell telegraphed Washington that unofficial word had just reached him from Patterson's headquarters "that he has fallen back." McDowell added, without comment, "There are rumors that Johnston has joined Beauregard." These rumors were enough to send Cameron hurrying back to the capital to order up reinforcements, but the secretary was also acting to fill gaps appearing in the army's ranks. Despite a personal appeal by McDowell, the 4th Pennsylvania militia insisted on discharge on the 20th when their ninety days were up. Brigade commander Franklin said of the 4th, "When the remainder of the brigade marched forward, it marched to the rear." A New York militia battery also insisted on its discharge. But other militiamen were made of sterner stuff. The 1st Connecticut, for example, its time up on July 21, voted to see the campaign through before going home — a decision that would cost it seventeen casualties.

The rumors McDowell reported were enhanced by the sounds of trains coming and going at Manassas Junction. "I heard the cars running Friday and Saturday, both up from Richmond and down the other way," said Israel Richardson. "We heard them running all night." When later reminded of such reports, McDowell was exasperated. "But, great God! I heard every rumor in the world. . . . 'We heard the cars coming in last night.' Well, I expected that. I expected they would bring into Manassas every available man they could find." What he did not expect was those men being from Johnston's army. That had not been part of the bargain, he said.

Whatever truth lay behind these rumors, General McDowell could hardly change his plans or delay them either. Already he had lost a day provisioning the troops, and a second day confirming the feasibility of his new flanking plan. Time was expiring for his three-months' militia, who made up 40 percent of his infantry. To pull back and rethink the campaign would demoralize the troops, end any hope for retaining the militia, and certainly set sparks flying in Washington. A march to battle often creates a momentum all its own, and Irvin McDowell was being swept along by its force.[37]

McDowell called a conference of his division and brigade commanders for Saturday evening to present his battle plan. It was not a council of war, open for debate. As Heintzelman put it, "The plans were detailed, but no opinions asked." The battle orders were carefully drawn. Tyler's First Division "will move at 2.30 a.m. precisely" on the Warrenton Turnpike to threaten the Stone Bridge crossing, and shield the flanking column immediately following. At a blacksmith's shop just west of Cub Run, Hunter's Second Division was to turn off to the right on the farm road reported to lead to Sudley Springs. Heintzelman's Third Division, closed up behind Hunter, formed the other half of the flanking column. At midpoint on the flank march, Heintzelman was to turn off to the left to Poplar Ford on Bull Run, halfway between the Stone Bridge and Sudley Springs. Richardson's brigade would mount a diversion at Blackburn's Ford. Miles's Fifth Division at Centreville would act as a battlefield reserve and guard the army's base. In general reserve farther to the rear was Runyon's Fourth Division, holding the routes to Washington.

Tyler was to demonstrate at the Stone Bridge with artillery at "full daybreak." At that signal, Hunter would cross the Sudley Ford "and then, turning down to the left, descend the stream." This would uncover Poplar Ford, allowing Heintzelman to cross. The flanking column, attacking the enemy's left in two-division strength, should then uncover the Stone Bridge for Tyler to cross.

(Beauregard's battle order of the same date, also to be executed on July 21, was a striking contrast to McDowell's. Where McDowell was precise in planning, timing, and purpose, Beauregard was vague, convoluted, and incomplete. It would seem that cadet McDowell, ranked twenty-third in the Military Academy class of 1838, had paid more attention to his lessons than cadet Beauregard, ranked second in class.)[38]

Until Saturday, July 20, the mood at army headquarters in Washington was cautiously optimistic. McClellan's victories in western Virginia had buoyed spirits earlier in the week. By first reports, McDowell's advance appeared promising. General Scott would say, "We had all become animated and sanguine of success." Nevertheless, Scott's unease with Robert Patterson was borne out that Saturday. Patterson's aide Major William W. Rus-

sell arrived to explain his chief's actions — or inactions. A "very much annoyed" Scott demanded to know why Patterson had not advanced. Russell
repeated what Patterson had directed him to say: His orders were to make
demonstrations, not "to drive" Johnston. At that, "the general turned in his
chair very fiercely on me, and said very excitedly, 'I will sacrifice my commission if my dispatches will bear any such interpretation.'" Major Russell
withdrew in dismay.

That night came a confirming telegram from Patterson: "With a portion of his force Johnston left Winchester by the road to Millwood on the
afternoon of the 18th." In the firm grip of his delusions, he added that
Johnston's "whole force" came to some 35,200. On Sunday, July 21, on the
raging battlefield, McDowell would be handed a dispatch from General
Scott: "It is known that a strong reinforcement left Winchester on the afternoon of the 18th, which you will have to beat."[39]

In Washington on Saturday, July 20, William Howard Russell, the *Times*
of London, roused himself to take the field to inspect the Federal army in
action, engaging a horse and gig for passage to the prospective battlefield.
At 11 o'clock Sunday morning, with "a flask of light Bordeaux, a bottle of
water, a paper of sandwiches, and having replenished my small flask with
brandy," Russell set out to report on the first major battle of this American
war. As it happened, he arrived many hours too late for any actual battle
reporting.[40]

When General McDowell went off to war that morning (a good deal
earlier than Mr. Russell), he was unaware of an important advantage in his
favor. His new plan to turn the enemy's left flank was, by chance, the ideal
tactic to use against a general who had massed his army on his own right
flank. Of his eleven brigades, Beauregard posted nine of them to launch
or to support his wheel to the right to strike the Yankees at Centreville. To
guard his left at the Stone Bridge he assigned a single brigade — actually a
demi-brigade — of 1,100 men under Nathan Evans. Major Evans's closest
support was a mile and a half downstream.

Bull Run formed a deceptive military barrier. Meandering southeasterly from the Bull Run Mountains to empty into the Occoquan, it was neither very wide nor very deep, but its banks were steep and wooded, and in
the vicinity of Manassas Junction the only passages for artillery and wagons were the fords or the Stone Bridge. Beauregard's line guarded these
fords downstream from the Stone Bridge some eight miles to where the
Orange & Alexandria crossed the stream. South of Bull Run, where Mc-

English correspondent William Howard Russell, caricatured viewing the Bull Run battle from a safe distance while imbibing London stout.

Dowell intended to do his fighting, the ground was gently rolling with alternating farm fields and patches of woodland but open enough for maneuvering both infantry and artillery.

When his failed reconnaissances revealed enemy cavalry vedettes north of Bull Run, McDowell grew concerned that his turning movement might be prematurely discovered. Thus Tyler's division, pushing straight for the Stone Bridge, served as a screen for the flanking column—Hunter's Second Division and Heintzelman's Third, 11,500 men and twenty-two guns. They faced the longest march but should begin it in secrecy.

McDowell's timetable was designed to mesh everything seamlessly, but did not account for the independent-minded Daniel Tyler. Tyler exerted little effort getting his men early on the road, then put his most unsoldierly commander, political general Robert Schenck, in the lead. Proceeding slowly, flanked by five companies of skirmishers stumbling through the dark woods in search of ambushes and masked batteries, the column crept ahead. It was 5:30 a.m. before Schenck's brigade and those of William Sherman and Erasmus Keyes traversed the mile and a half from their camps to the blacksmith's shop and cleared the entrance to the farm road for the flanking column. "Started at 2½ a.m. & stopped at Centreville till 5½ a.m.," recorded an impatient Sam Heintzelman.[41]

With McDowell's battle plan already running some three hours late, the flanking column encountered a fresh delay. The civilian guide Mathias Mitchell, only let into the scheme on Sunday, explained that in fact there were two farm roads leading to the Sudley Springs crossing. The more direct one he had described to Major Barnard passed at one point close by

Bull Run and within sight of any Rebels on the far bank. If they needed a secret march, said Mitchell, they should take the other farm road, which looped well to the north and out of sight of the enemy. This produced, wrote Orlando Willcox, "a very hot march & incessant delays & halts. . . ."

McDowell was so alarmed by the delays that he altered his plan. At the turnoff by the blacksmith shop, "in doubt whether there would be an attack above at all," he halted Heintzelman's third brigade, under Otis Howard, and held it there in reserve should it be the enemy who seized the moment. The flanking column, already hours late, was reduced from five brigades to four.

(Beauregard did try to seize the moment. He attempted to put his own flank attack into motion that morning . . . without the least success. His orders were either not received or too badly drawn to be understood. In the end he was saved from folly by the Yankee guns signaling the start of their assault, and history was spared the spectacle of the two armies circling about each other, each lunging for the other's left flank.)[42]

Shortly after 6:00 a.m. Tyler positioned a 30-pounder Parrott rifle overlooking the Stone Bridge and as ordered fired the first of three thunderous rounds to open the battle. Nothing very much happened. From Israel Richardson's position in front of Blackburn's Ford on the left, three batteries began a measured bombardment, attracting no response from the enemy. From the right there was only silence.

In the flanking column Sam Heintzelman heard the signal gun clearly, but it only signified that his and Hunter's divisions, assigned the lead roles, were going to be quite late to the battle. The farm road they were following was hard going, especially where it narrowed through forest. Without access to the Poplar Ford shortcut, Heintzelman's division trailed behind, eating Hunter's dust and suffering the rising heat of what promised to be a scorching day.

It was 9:30 a.m. when Ambrose Burnside's lead brigade reached Sudley Springs, and the hot, tired men and animals paused to refresh themselves while splashing across Bull Run. They had marched 10 miles already, and were still 2 miles from the prospective battlefield. Hunter soon brought his other brigade, under Andrew Porter, across the ford, but the flanking column was so elongated that it was 11 o'clock before William Franklin's lead brigade of Heintzelman's division reached Sudley Springs, and well after that by the time Orlando Willcox's trailing brigade was across.

With no reaction from the enemy, McDowell felt it safe to give up his vigil at the blacksmith's shop, and rode off to join the flanking column. He had gained one of his major goals — he was across Bull Run in force, without a fight, and positioned to turn the enemy's left flank. The Rebels must meet his advance not from behind their defenses but out in the open. Yet he was three hours or more behind schedule, with likely consequences. Certainly his fortuitous (if unknown) advantage of catching his opponent off balance and out of position would dissipate.

Had his column reached Sudley's at daylight as planned, McDowell anticipated Tyler keeping the Rebels at the Stone Bridge "amused" (in the military parlance of the day) long enough for Hunter and Heintzelman to storm their flank. But Rebel Major Nathan Evans did not stay amused for long. When at 9 o'clock his cavalry vedette reported Hunter's division approaching Sudley Springs, Evans left a token force at the Stone Bridge — to amuse Tyler — and marched off to meet the Yankees. At the same time, Confederate signal officer Porter Alexander spotted the flanking column and warned Beauregard, "I see a body of troops crossing Bull Run about two miles above the Stone Bridge. . . . I can see both infantry and artillery." Battle was about to be joined.[43]

At midmorning, as the two armies squared off for battle, a curious phenomenon caught many eyes. Confederate signal officer Alexander left the best description. It was very hot and very still, he wrote, and off to the west "I began to notice clouds of dust begin to form. . . . And as the sun got higher the dust clouds in the west also grew denser & taller, until they became veritable pillars in the air hundreds of feet high & covering many degrees of the horizon & evidently slowly approaching." Both sides took alarm. The Confederates feared it was Patterson's Yankee army marching down from the Shenandoah on Joe Johnston's heels. The Federals feared it was heavy Rebel reinforcements from Manassas or the Valley about to turn their flank. Although it proved to be only Johnston's lumbering artillery and supply trains, the phenomenon impelled action. Beauregard and Johnston took serious notice of the threat to their left. McDowell hurried the troops at Sudley's, and sent off couriers to bring up Howard's brigade and to tell Tyler to find a way to push across Bull Run. McDowell's concern now was stranding half his army on one side of Bull Run and half on the other.[44]

By the same happenstance that put Daniel Tyler's division first in line that morning, the first fighting of the day saw David Hunter in command . . . with equally unfortunate results. Hunter was fifty-nine (that very day), an 1822 Academy graduate who left the army in 1836 but returned five years later to the mundane role of paymaster. In the two decades since he had seen neither line duty nor action. He owed his present divisional command to his staunch Republicanism. He showed no acquaintance with the art of command.

A scouting party reported that a mile ahead was a Rebel battle line posted on a modest elevation called Matthews Hill. With his demi-brigade Major Evans threw down the gauntlet. In accepting Evans's challenge, Hunter ignored the chain of command and reached into Burnside's brigade to call out the 2nd Rhode Island and personally march it into action. It was about 10:30 a.m. Burnside dutifully brought forward his other three regiments to strengthen the blow, but for a reason of his own, Hunter ignored him and instead ordered up from the rear his other brigade, under Andrew Porter. All the while the 2nd Rhode Island made the fight for Matthews Hill alone, colonel and major mortally wounded, stalled and stretched thin. Hunter seemed to think only in terms of single regiments and of leading them himself, and soon enough his reward for misjudgment was a nasty neck wound. Andrew Porter succeeded him.

Under Porter and Burnside the pace picked up, yet they could not make up for this newest delay — following a long morning of delays — resulting from Hunter's misadventure. By the time support reached the beleaguered 2nd Rhode Island, two Confederate brigades rushed up from Beauregard's reserve. Both were from Joe Johnston's army. (When later asked when he first learned that Johnston had evaded Patterson and was facing him, McDowell dryly remarked it was that morning, on the battlefield, when "I made some prisoners.")[45]

Ambrose Burnside graduated from West Point in 1847 and reached Mexico too late for the fighting, so except for some skirmishing with Apaches in New Mexico Territory, July 21, 1861, was his baptism of fire. His commanding presence served him well. The problem for volunteers and militia alike was inexperience — simply maneuvering from column to line of battle. As they stumbled about, Burnside took hold of the 1st Rhode Island militia, the regiment he had led to war, and set it into position as an example.

Burnside's brigade held the left of the line and Andrew Porter's the right. Although Porter left the Academy after six months, he earned his stripes with the Mounted Rifles, winning two brevet promotions in Mexico. He shifted his brigade to outflank Matthews Hill, taking with him Captain Charles Griffin's battery. There was a pause when Burnside sent to Porter for his battalion of regulars. His far flank needed shoring up, said Burnside. Major George Sykes halted his regulars and had them load. "He then made a short speech," wrote one of the men, "cautioning them to keep from getting excited, and to fire low." The battalion moved at the double-quick to brace the endangered flank. "Major Sykes, you regulars are just what we want," Burnside cried. "Form on my left. . . ."[46]

By now Heintzelman's Third Division was across Sudley Ford, and Mc-Dowell called for it. William Franklin's brigade had the lead, but McDowell fed it into the battle piecemeal rather than as a unit. Like David Hunter, the inexperienced McDowell envisioned the battle tactically as a matter of individual regiments and individual batteries. One regiment went off to the far left to support Sykes's regulars, and Captain James Ricketts's battery unlimbered on Dogan Ridge on the far right. The effect, belated as it might be, was to overlap both flanks of the Matthews Hill defenders.

The Confederates' critical position was made more critical by the abrupt appearance of a new Yankee force that had crossed Bull Run from the east rather than from the north. Leading it onto the battlefield was Colonel William T. Sherman. Like most Union commanders that day, Sherman had never been under fire before, yet already he had displayed initiative. Early that morning when Tyler's division pulled up in front of the Stone Bridge, Sherman searched out a way to get across Bull Run upstream when the call came to do so. It was about 11:00 a.m. when McDowell's courier reached Tyler with the order to "press forward his attack." Sherman promptly started his brigade toward the fording place he had found (called Farm Ford), with Erasmus Keyes's brigade following. A half mile beyond Bull Run they came on the fighting. With his column well closed up, flags flying, Sherman joined the battle. "They had had a pretty severe fight . . . ," he noted, "and the unexpected arrival of my brigade seemed a great relief to all."

It was past noon now, and the Rebels saw it was time and past time to give up Matthews Hill and get away while they could. Because they were as green as the Yankees, a good many simply ran for it — across the Warrenton Turnpike, up the broad slopes of Henry Hill where Beauregard was cobbling together a second line. "Victory! Victory!" McDowell's adjutant James Fry shouted; "We have done it! We have done it!" One of Sherman's men recorded McDowell's reaction: "General McDowell, our Commander-in-Chief, now came jingling on the field, waving, first his glove and then his hat, calling us 'Brave boys' and telling us, with the grand air of Caesar, that we had won the day. He passed away like a splendid dream."[47]

Irvin McDowell had reason to feel relieved as well as triumphant. His flanking column had fought its way far enough back downstream to reach the Warrenton Pike and a linkup with the rest of the army — Tyler's First

Division on the far bank of Bull Run, Miles's Fifth Division at Centreville. His task now was to pull his forces together to finish the job.

Of Tyler's command only Sherman's and Keyes's brigades crossed to join the fighting; Schenck's brigade and the divisional artillery remained behind holding the Stone Bridge crossing. Otis Howard's brigade of Heintzelman's division, held back at the start of the march, was still tramping through the woods toward Sudley Ford. Burnside's brigade, fought out, its ammunition exhausted, had gone to the rear for reorganization. McDowell therefore had at hand five brigades to renew the fighting—Porter's, from Hunter's division; Franklin's and Willcox's, from Heintzelman's division; and Sherman's and Keyes's, from Tyler's division—some 12,200 men. In support were the regular batteries of Ricketts and Griffin, and the volunteer Rhode Island battery of Captain William Reynolds.

All this had taken a great deal longer than anticipated. Evans's bold stand at Matthews Hill gained another two hours or so for Beauregard and Johnston to build up a defense. Now, as the Rebels stopped running and took position on Henry Hill, it began to appear that the Yankee cries of victory were somewhat premature.

It was a moment demanding decisive action on McDowell's part, yet he remained curiously indecisive. Direction of his lieutenants seemed to elude him. He established no headquarters but roamed about, and in his absences officers all too often had to act without orders. When Heintzelman reached the field, for example, he searched in vain for a plan, for guidance: "I did not find any one to give orders. . . . We found the enemy had been driven back & I stopped a few men to see what was going on & to make inquiries."[48]

Andrew Porter's brigade also lacked direction. Porter took command of the Second Division after Hunter's wounding, and Lieutenant William W. Averell, West Point 1855, took the brigade. Averell began on his own to feed regiments serially into the battle on the right. The 27th New York was repulsed, with Colonel Henry W. Slocum, future Army of the Potomac general, falling wounded. Major Joseph J. Bartlett, another future Potomac army general, rallied the regiment. Averell sent in two militia regiments, the 8th New York and the 14th Brooklyn. Without support, without firm leadership, they too were driven back by the strengthening Rebel line on Henry Hill. "The 8th New York broke and never afterwards formed to any extent," Averell complained.

The same undisciplined leadership afflicted the Union left. Fixed in his independent ways, Tyler launched an offensive against Henry Hill without orders. At the far left of the Federal line Keyes had the best angle to attack Henry Hill. Had Tyler brought Sherman into the assault, the combined 5,300 men could surely have swept the defenders off the hill. But Tyler utilized just two regiments of Keyes's brigade, the 2nd Maine and the 3rd Connecticut. Attacking bravely but without artillery support, they were beaten off. Tyler gave no thought to a reinvigorated assault. Daniel Tyler's command efforts on July 21 were of less use than even David Hunter's.[49]

Now General McDowell did take a decision, and it proved a disastrous one. His first thought, after gaining Matthews Hill, was to chase the seemingly disorganized Rebels off Henry Hill with his artillery alone — Ricketts's and Griffin's batteries firing from Dogan Ridge on the right, Reynolds's Rhode Island battery from the center. Most of these guns were rifled, outranging the defenders' smoothbores. The Confederate line, however, did not appear to waver under this bombardment, and so McDowell elected to assault Henry Hill head-on — not with his infantry, but with his artillery.

This was a tactic from the Napoleonic Wars, and even in his inexperience it is surprising that McDowell chose it. In France he had studied the latest in the military arts, and surely knew of the tactical debates about coping with the new weaponry of the day, rifled artillery and rifled muskets. It may be that at the critical moment he could think of nothing better to do. Still, ordering batteries to unlimber within 300 yards of enemy artillery and infantry was an exceedingly high-risk tactic.

Certainly Charles Griffin and James Ricketts thought so. Their six-gun batteries were chosen for the task. Both were West Pointers who had made the artillery their careers. Both fought in Mexico and knew their business thoroughly; neither had any illusions nor any tolerance for fools. Ricketts put the matter bluntly: "I saw at a glance, as I thought, that I was going into great peril for my horses and men."

Henry Hill is more an elevated plateau than a defined hill, and McDowell ordered Ricketts and Griffin to advance their guns onto the edge of the plateau. Artillery chief William Barry, seeming without a mind of his own, expressed no qualms about the scheme. But when Barry delivered the order to Griffin, sparks flew. ("I will say that before this battle we were never on good terms," Griffin said of Barry. "We never have been on good terms.") Where were the infantry supports? Griffin demanded. Major Barry said the 11th New York Fire Zouaves, the late Elmer Ellsworth's command, were coming up. Then let the infantry seize the ground, said Griffin, and he would advance his guns to that line. Those were not General McDowell's orders, said Barry. Far better ground for the guns, said Griffin, was a ridgeline off to the right (Chinn Ridge, it was called) from which they could enfilade Henry Hill. Not the general's orders either, said Barry. Griffin knew the undisciplined Fire Zouaves and insisted they would be poor support, but Barry was adamant. So was Griffin. "I will go; but mark my words, they will not support us."

James Ricketts sent back an officer to appeal the order directly to Mc-Dowell. McDowell was coldly polite; he "would comply" with Major Barry's orders — which orders, of course, carried out *his* orders. Andrew Porter, to whose brigade Griffin's battery was attached, was left speechless by the move. "I cannot tell you my feelings," he later said to Griffin; he feared the order to advance the guns to Henry Hill might have been thought as originating with him.

Not only were McDowell's artillery tactics reckless in the extreme, but infantry support for the guns became a catch-as-catch-can operation: Any officer who came on any unoccupied troops might (or might not) send them forward. Barry collected a battalion of marines from Porter's brigade and directed them to the batteries. Heintzelman took charge of ordering in the Fire Zouaves, of Willcox's brigade: "They rushed forward & in a few steps both parties came in sight of each other & fired & the Zouaves ran & I believe the enemy also. I tried to rally the Zouaves but failed." Nothing daunted, he led another of Willcox's regiments and one from Franklin's brigade toward Henry Hill.[30]

Meanwhile on the plateau, the two batteries were engulfed in a maelstrom of fire and smoke and noise. Their eleven guns (one of Griffin's was out with a jammed round) dueled with thirteen Confederate pieces, posted as close as 300 yards. Most of the defenders here were under the determined Thomas J. Jackson, who gained his famous nickname that afternoon. At this range the Rebel smoothbores were more effective than the Federals' rifled Parrotts, whose gunners were unused to cutting fuzes for such short ranges. Sharpshooters took a mounting toll of the batteries' gunners and horses. "We presented a better mark for them than they did for us," said Lieutenant Charles E. Hazlett. Now came what Griffin termed the critical moment of the battle.

A column of troops without distinctive uniforms or flags emerged from the woods to the right of the Federal guns. Convinced they were Confederates, Griffin trained on them a two-gun section loaded with canister. Before he could give the order to fire, Major Barry rushed up to stay the order; those men were support troops, he said. "They are Confederates; as certain as the world, they are Confederates!" Griffin insisted. "I know they are your battery support," Barry assured him. Dutifully Griffin retrained his guns—and in a matter of minutes the alleged support troops rushed them, firing a murderous volley from 40 yards away, and, in Griffin's grim summary, "that was the last of us." The two batteries were soon overrun. Ricketts was shot down and captured, and except for three pieces Griffin managed to get away, everything was lost.

(Later a seething Griffin came on Barry watering his horse in a brook. "Said I, 'Major, do you think the Zouaves will support us?' Said he, 'I was mistaken.' Said I, 'Do you think that was our support?' 'I was mistaken,' he said. 'Yes,' said I, 'you were mistaken all around.'")[51]

This abrupt turnabout was not the end of the fighting on Henry Hill, but it marked the beginning of the end. Brave and desperate—and entirely disjointed—efforts were made to retake the guns, and three times they were retaken, and three times lost. Orlando Willcox remembered the din as earsplitting: "I shouted 'charge bayonet!' but although among the file closers, my voice could not reach the files in front of me, & the whole regiment was swept back as by a tornado." It was every officer for himself. Heintzelman came upon the regrouping 14th Brooklyn. "I joined it, but at the first fire they broke & ran." For his trouble Heintzelman was hit by a musket ball that broke his right arm.

William Franklin pushed two regiments of his brigade into the battle for the batteries, but inexperience left the attempt in ruins. "The 5 & 11 Mass regts. . . . behaved very badly," Franklin confided in a letter to a friend. "Both fired when they were in column, and the 11th killed one Capt. and two Sergts. & three privates of their own by the fire. They had no commands to fire and only fired from excitement." The 2nd Wisconsin, clad in gray, attacked up the slope of Henry Hill amidst the smoke and was fired on by comrades who saw only their gray uniforms. After a stiff fight on the plateau they fell back, only to be mistaken this time for charging enemy troops and again peppered by friendly fire. The 2nd Wisconsin suffered 88 men killed and wounded this day, with no knowing how many were hit by fellow Yankees.

The disjointed effort to retake the batteries cost the officer corps. In addition to Heintzelman's wounding, brigade commander Willcox was wounded and captured while directing a charge. Colonel James Cameron, brother of Secretary of War Simon Cameron, was killed leading the 79th New York. Colonel Cameron's command lost 198 men to all causes, the most of any Union regiment that day.[52]

More Rebel reinforcements—the last of Joe Johnston's brigades from the Valley, just off a train at Manassas Junction—rushed onto the field. McDowell's only fresh force, Otis Howard's brigade, was caught in their path and crumpled. "Up to 3 o'clock in the afternoon I had done all and more than all that I had promised or agreed to do," McDowell would testify; "it was this last straw that broke the camel's back—if you can call 4,000 men a straw, who came upon me from behind fresh from the cars." He worded his decision prosaically: "Gentlemen, it seems evident that we must fall back to Centreville." In fact, his army had already taken that decision.

To a man this was an army exhausted from the day's long marches, exhausted from blazing heat and raging thirst, and most of all exhausted from the stress and terror of a first experience of combat. "The Volunteers up to that time had done well," Sherman wrote, "but they were repulsed regiment by regiment, and I do think it was impossible to stand long in that fire." Captain James Fry, McDowell's adjutant, described this latest enemy countercharge of fresh troops as indeed the last straw: "The men seemed to be seized simultaneously by the conviction that it was no use to do anything more and they might as well start home." And so they did.[53]

There was at first no cause for panic. George Sykes's regulars, discipline intact, formed a rear guard. The men plodded along, heedless of order and organization. The shortest route across Bull Run to Centreville was the Stone Bridge, but the troops knew nothing of that, and nothing any officer might command could sway them. They knew only the way they had come and they would return the same way—the brigades of Burnside, Porter, Franklin, Willcox, and Howard by way of Sudley Springs, the brigades of Sherman and Keyes by Farm Ford.

The Confederates were initially as disorganized by victory as the Federals by defeat. Their most determined pursuit was launched along the Warrenton Turnpike from the Stone Bridge crossing, where Robert Schenck's brigade was posted. In his report political general Schenck transmuted his failure to initiate any defense into a masterful withdrawal, "rallying together and arriving at Centreville with closed ranks. . . ." In consequence (as General McDowell put it), "the retreat soon became a rout, and this soon degenerated still further into a panic."

On the Warrenton Turnpike the better part of three Federal divisions with their guns and wagons and ambulances had to crowd across the narrow wooden suspension bridge over Cub Run. With them went several score carriages and buggies bearing the frightened civilians who had come out from Washington to watch the battle. The brigades of Sherman, Keyes, and the irresolute Schenck, following the turnpike straight from

Colonel Ambrose Burnside, foreground, waves forward his Rhode Island brigade to hold their Bull Run lines. By Alfred R. Waud.

the battlefield, had mostly cleared the Cub Run bottleneck by the time Hunter's and Heintzelman's divisions, marching roundabout from Sudley Springs, reached the turnpike just west of the bridge. The pursuing Rebels were free of any opposition until within a quarter mile of Cub Run. They posted a two-gun section of artillery on a rise overlooking the crowded Cub Run bridge. Its first shot was perfectly aimed, exploding directly over the bridge and causing a supply wagon to upset in the middle of the span.

This shot, and a dozen or so that followed, induced utter, unreasoning panic among the throng still west of Cub Run. Infantrymen splashed across the stream, some throwing aside their rifles in their haste to escape. Teamsters and ambulance drivers and cannoneers cut the traces and fled, leaving the vehicles and guns to the enemy. As Keyes recorded it, "A scene of confusion ensued which beggars description. Cavalry horses without riders, artillery horses disengaged from the guns with traces flying, wrecked baggage-wagons, and pieces of artillery drawn by six horses without drivers, flying at their utmost speed and whacking against other vehicles, soldiers scattered everywhere, running, some without arms or caps."

Correspondent Russell reached the scene too late to witness any of the Union fighting, but in time to record the Union retreat. "A more disgraceful rout was never witnessed," was his verdict. And having not made the effort to cover the actual battle, "disgraceful rout" became the theme of his letter to the *Times:* "The retreat on their lines at Centreville seems to have ended in a cowardly rout — a miserable, causeless panic." When copies of the *Times* reached America a month later, Russell, by labeling soldiers cowards who (unseen by him) had fought bravely enough earlier that long day, inflicted a lasting injustice on the Army of Northeastern Virginia.[54]

The panic subsided soon enough but disorder persisted as the army gained Centreville. "When I got across Bull Run," Heintzelman entered in his diary, "I found that not a Regt. could be rallied, nor even a company." He found a doctor to dress his wounded arm, and "I got a good drink of whiskey & took a nap of half an hour. . . . We soon got orders for the Army to retreat to Washington."

At first McDowell hoped to build a defense at Centreville, behind which he might gird for another try at the Rebels. But he found that Dixon Miles, heavily primed with brandy, had so muddled orders to his reserve division that roads were unguarded, inviting a Confederate flank attack. McDowell's lieutenants urged him to fall back to Washington. Indeed, a sizable part of the army had already chosen that course and set off for their old camps on the Potomac and in and about the District.[55]

In Washington the Sunday quiet was tempered by the faint but persistent rumble of cannon fire, sounding like a distant summer thunderstorm. In midafternoon Mr. Lincoln was made uneasy by a series of garbled telegrams from the field. He called on General Scott, who assured him that such reports proved nothing. Finally came a telegram from McDowell, marked 4:00 p.m., saying he was advancing his reserves across Bull Run, "having driven the enemy before him." On that encouraging note the president left for a carriage drive. But at 6 o'clock Secretary Seward burst into Lincoln's White House office "with a terribly frightened and excited look," as presidential secretary John Nicolay described him. "The battle is lost," Seward cried. "The telegraph says that McDowell is in full retreat, and calls on General Scott to save the capital."

That evening Lincoln and cabinet members and army staff crowded into Scott's headquarters to hear a tide of worsening news. Adjutant General Thomas read the dispatches aloud as they were delivered from the telegraph office. (At one point Thomas faltered and caught Secretary of War Cameron's eye to inform him his brother was dead on the field.) General Scott calmly took charge, sending out alerts to the city's defenses and arranging reinforcements for the army. "We know that you and your experienced officers will do all that is proper and possible," he wired McDowell. "We are not discouraged."

For twenty-four hours and more, wild rumors had Washington besieged, the enemy at the gates. At a White House gathering Scott burst out in frustration, "I have fought this battle, sir, against my judgment. . . . I deserve removal because I did not stand up, when my army was not in condition for fighting, and resist it to the last." That roused the president. "Your conversation seems to imply that I forced you to fight this battle," he said. Seeing slippery ground here, Scott backed off. "I have never served a President," he said, "who has been kinder to me than you have been."[56]

Starting at daybreak on Monday, July 22, in a steady rain, the beaten army returned. Those who did not see action on Sunday and avoided the panic — Runyon's Fourth Division, Miles's Fifth, Richardson's and Schenck's brigades — returned in good order. Those encamped west of the Potomac generally escaped notice. But into the District came several thousand tired and disheveled men, remnants of a lost battle, to crowd the capital's streets and byways and barrooms. Each had a story to tell. "One of them sat in the rain on the stone foundation of brother's front fence," Elizabeth Blair Lee wrote. "I asked if he was hungry? No! Thirsty? no, sick? no, — wounded no no only mad — we are beat & badly because we have no generals — no competent officers. He was almost heart broken from his tone & manner. . . ."

When the Federal Bull Run losses were tallied, they came to 460 dead, 1,124 wounded, and 1,312 missing or captured, total 2,896. Twenty-seven guns were lost on the battlefield or on the retreat. Confederate losses were a thousand less, 1,897, but their count of killed and wounded exceeded that of the Federals by 18 percent, confirming the closeness of most of the fighting.[57]

No generals, no competent officers, the disheartened soldier told Mrs. Lee, and there was justice in his complaint. Certainly McDowell justly censured Patterson's failure to detain Johnston. Further, when Johnston evaded Patterson's feeble grasp on July 18 and started for Manassas, McDowell was not told of it for three days. Forewarned, he might have launched his attack a day earlier. General Scott recognized all this. One of his first acts was to relieve Patterson, sending him home with his ninety-day militia. Patterson's best intentions were crippled by his wildly exaggerated count of Confederate numbers, rendering him (so he believed) helpless to hold Johnston in the Valley. On July 27 Robert Patterson was mustered out of the militia, and out of the war.

Of McDowell's four active division commanders, only Sam Heintzelman stood out. Combat experience in Mexico and on the Texas border hardened him to battle, and he displayed initiative and aggressiveness in putting in attacks, and was persistently courageous under fire, costing him a battlefield wound. His wounding ended the possibility of a more coherent attempt to capture Henry Hill. David Hunter, before *his* wounding, displayed little tactical aptitude, and his stay with the Army of the Potomac was brief. The Fifth Division's Dixon Miles was plainly drunk on July 21, before witnesses. He was found so by a court of inquiry, but "for the good of the service" was not court-martialed and instead confined to lesser duties. Daniel Tyler's unmerited sense of entitlement made him a less-than-loyal subordinate. Three times he ignored McDowell to follow his own independent course — at Blackburn's Ford on July 18, in his snail-like march to the Stone Bridge on July 21, and in his feeble assault on Henry Hill that afternoon. Tyler was mustered out with his Connecticut militia in August, and never called to the Army of the Potomac.[58]

The brigade commanders had limited opportunity to shine in this campaign, and their individual performances were promising at best ... or less than that. Israel Richardson showed aggressiveness in troop leading at Blackburn's Ford, profiting by his Mexican War experience. In Sunday's battle Erasmus Keyes was hardly noticeable in his brief test under Tyler's erratic generalship. Political general Schenck's primary skill proved to be papering over a striking lack of initiative during the retreat; he suffered fifty-two men and a battery captured.

William Sherman stood up well to his first combat — knee and coat collar nicked by bullets, his horse hit — and aggressively pushed his men into action. Afterward he displayed the strong opinion of an old regular about the lesson to be learned from Bull Run — the need for discipline in the ranks. After the battle, Lincoln was reviewing Sherman's brigade when an officer came up to him with a grievance. In a dispute over terms of service, he said, Colonel Sherman threatened to shoot him as a mutineer. In a stage whisper, for all to hear, the president said, "Well, if I were you, and he threatened to shoot, I would not trust him, for I believe he would do it."

Ambrose Burnside proved a determined troop leader, respected by his men. He would muster out with his Rhode Island militia, but within a year, his career on the rise, he would rejoin the Potomac army. Andrew Porter, a hard-nosed regular, utilized his Mexican War experience to perform as well as any of his fellows, but his lack of a West Point commission limited his prospects. William Franklin and Orlando Willcox did as best they could with their limited opportunities. Franklin complained that "brigade commanders had to act as field officers of all the regiments in their brigades . . ." Willcox, wounded on Henry Hill, was captured and not exchanged for more than a year. Otis Howard's brigade, the last to reach the battlefield, was just in time to take a pounding and join the retreat. Howard's regiments were all three-year enlistees, yet Howard appeared to exercise limited control over them; they fled as readily as the militia.[59]

Irvin McDowell, handcuffed by incompetents and victimized by misfortune, felt he deserved a different fate. Testifying to a congressional committee, he was blunt about Patterson's failures. "I hold that I more than fulfilled my part of the compact. . . ." McDowell did almost everything right until trapped in the white-hot glare of battle. He operated his campaign on clear directions, and brought his army to the battlefield with consideration for the rawness of the troops. He recognized the impracticality of his first plan and changed it on the fly to a soundly conceived second plan. His flank movement, although delayed by chance and mischance, was a success: The enemy was forced out from behind his defenses and brought to battle on an uncluttered field.

Then the shooting started. Lacking experience of command, McDowell's decisions began to miscarry. The tactical handling of his forces was flawed. The failure to immediately follow up the victory at Matthews Hill was serious. Spearheading the assault on Henry Hill with the two artillery batteries was fatal. His army, lacking the discipline to overcome adversity, stumbled back in defeat and fell into rout. The panic at the Cub Run bridge was the least of it, but what everyone remembered afterward. Scott's adjutant E. D. Townsend stated it simply: "Want of competent officers was the reason for the general panic. . . ."[60]

Early on Monday, July 22, a telegram went out from the army's adjutant general in Washington addressed to Major General George B. McClellan at Beverly, in western Virginia. "Circumstances make your presence here necessary," it read; ". . . come hither without delay."

"The fat is all in the fire now and we shall have to crow small until we can retrieve the disgrace somehow," presidential secretary John Nicolay told his fiancée. "The preparations for the war will be continued with increased vigor by the Government." On July 22 President Lincoln signed an act authorizing the enlistment of 500,000 three-year volunteers. On the 25th he signed a second bill, rushed through the Congress in response to the Bull Run defeat, authorizing 500,000 additional enlistments. The ninety-day war was over and done with. The Union was now at war for the long run, and the president saw this with perfect clarity. Amidst the handwringing over Bull Run, Lincoln spoke of the grim arithmetic of the moment. "There is nothing in this except the lives lost," he said, "and the lives which must be lost to make it good."[61]

3. *A New Army, a New Era*

CALLING MCCLELLAN TO WASHINGTON was a decision easily reached. As Treasury Secretary Salmon Chase put it, to erase the ugly stain of Bull Run required a general with "the prestige of victory." No one else met that standard. Beyond his small but well-publicized victories in western Virginia, Major General George Brinton McClellan was outranked by no one in the United States army but Scott himself, certainly a factor in deciding on a new general for the Union's principal army.

Winfield Scott's role in the matter was ambiguous. He was later heard to say that McClellan was "called here by my advice," but he qualified that in writing that "if I did not call for him, I heartily approved of the suggestion. . . ." Whatever the advice, Lincoln acted quickly and decisively to put the beaten army back on its feet by giving it a new commander. No doubt the president recalled McClellan from his time at the Illinois Central, for which he did legal work when McClellan was the railroad's vice president. Certainly he remembered him as a war planner from the strategy papers McClellan exchanged with Scott back in the spring. And Lincoln was aware how well McClellan's campaign had played in the press, resulting in gains in Northern support for the war.[1]

There was surprise at the erstwhile captain of cavalry's rapid climb, at age thirty-four, to the army command. Yet in his fifteen years between West Point and Fort Sumter, George McClellan did not languish in obscurity. In the Mexican War he ably served Scott as a subaltern in the engineers, gaining two brevet promotions. He afterward commanded the Company of Engineer Soldiers at the Academy, then embarked on a wide range of assignments. These included engineering projects, outpost duty on the frontier, explorations in Texas and for the Pacific Railroad Survey, a secret mission to Santo Domingo to chart sites for a naval base, and selection by Secretary of War Jefferson Davis to observe the Crimean War and to study the organization of the armies of the Great Powers. McClellan was marked as one of the army's rising stars. But for the young captain

George Brinton McClellan strikes a Napoleonic pose at Mathew Brady's photographic
studio in Washington upon taking command of the Army of the Potomac.

the prospect of joining the 1st Cavalry for frontier-policing duty was decidedly anticlimactic. McClellan left the army in 1857 for the railroad business, first with the Illinois Central, then as president of the eastern division
of the Ohio & Mississippi.

After Sumter, Ohio, Pennsylvania, and New York vied for his services.
Good fortune eased McClellan's path. He intended to serve his home state
of Pennsylvania as head of its Pennsylvania Reserves, but the offer of that
post was misdirected and he accepted Ohio's offer instead. That cast him
under the eye of Ohioan Chase — "General" Chase, he was coming to be
called. In a letter to McClellan, Chase explained that "the country was indebted to me — may I say it without too much vanity? — in some considerable degree, for the change of your commission from Ohio into a commission of major-general of the army of the Union, and your assignment
to the command of the Department of the Ohio." The elevation of his protégé McClellan helped salve Chase's hurt over the unhappy fate of his protégé McDowell.[2]

The journey east to his new command would have turned the head of someone far more modest than George McClellan. At every stop of his special train crowds gathered, alerted by telegraph. "My progress was one continued & universal ovation," he remembered. In the capital his welcome reached to the highest circles of government. "I find myself in a new & strange position here," he wrote his wife. "Presdt, Cabinet, Genl Scott & all deferring to me — by some strange operation of magic I seem to have become *the* power of the land."

McClellan assumed command of the new Division of the Potomac on July 27. It comprised the Department of Northeastern Virginia, under Irvin McDowell, and the Department of Washington, under Joseph K. F. Mansfield. "Neither of them like it much — especially Mansfield," McClellan confided to his wife. Poor Mansfield was twice a bridesmaid. In May Scott had nominated him for the army command, only to have Secretary Chase thrust McDowell past him. Now Mansfield was pushed aside in favor of a general twenty-three years his junior. Mansfield would wait more than a year to gain a posting in the Potomac army.[3]

Ahead of McClellan loomed an enormous task, no less than building a new army upon the ruins of the old one. He recognized his priority as restoring the defeated army's confidence in itself. "Everybody is sick in body or in heart," Otis Howard wrote his wife. "Applications for leave, resignations & discharges have been the order of the day. . . ." Irvin McDowell displayed no talent for morale building; George McClellan displayed that talent in abundance. He regularly rode out to the camps to see the troops — and to be seen by them. On his favorite mount, a big bay called Dan Webster, he looked every bit the general commanding. The young volunteers, first-time soldiers all, took to cheering him to the echo. In response he raised his cap high and gave it a jaunty twirl, and the cheering only grew louder. To symbolize the new era, McClellan awarded the army a new name. The Division of the Potomac became the Department of the Potomac, and the Army of Northeastern Virginia became the Army of the Potomac.

Correspondent Russell of London's *Times* gained an audience with the new army commander. "A short stout young man," he entered in his diary, "dark haired, clear blue eyes, rather a Napoleonic head . . . dark moustache, close hair, dark complexion — very kind, our talk was of all sorts of things in war." Especially welcome to Russell was the general's parting assurance: "Promised me all kind of facility." Another of George McClellan's talents was cultivating the press.[4]

Lincoln asked his thoughts for carrying on the war. On August 2 Mc-

Clellan wrote his wife, "I handed to the Presdt tonight a carefully considered plan for conducting the war on a large scale." His plan was all of that. The "first great struggle" would take place in Virginia, for which he required an army of 273,000 men, with 600 guns. First he would capture Richmond, then occupy Charleston, Savannah, and the Gulf ports, as he had earlier proposed to General Scott. Now he reduced Scott's Mississippi River expedition to a supporting role. Other movements — into Unionist East Tennessee, into Missouri, into Texas, against South Atlantic enclaves — were also secondary or diversionary, supportive of the Napoleonic grand army he would command personally.

McClellan spelled out his ideology for conducting a civil war. An ordinary war, he wrote, sought to "conquer a peace and make a treaty on advantageous terms." Here, however, he would not only defeat the Confederates in the field, but "display such overwhelming strength, as will convince all our antagonists, especially those of the governing aristocratic class, of the utter impossibility of resistance." Defeat their armies, seize their strongholds, but sheathe the iron fist in a velvet glove. By "pursuing a rigidly protective policy as to private property" — slave property — "and unarmed persons . . . we may well hope for a permanent restoration of peaceful Union." The blow when it fell must be a mighty one. "Rebellion to be crushed in one campaign," he noted.

McClellan read his paper to the cabinet on August 3. It was grand strategy in general terms, incorporating (but shrinking) Scott's Anaconda plan, lacking both a timetable and operational detail. No one in the administration, in this fourth month of war, was going to object to McClellan's recipe for putting down the rebellion firmly but humanely, for reunion without revolution.

There was no recorded reaction from General Scott; possibly he was not shown a copy. Already there was rising discord between the old general and the ambitious young one. McClellan mentioned to his wife a squabble with the general-in-chief, which "perhaps disgusted the old man, who by the way, is fast becoming very slow & very old. He cannot long retain command I think — when he retires I am sure to succeed him, unless in the mean time I lose a battle — which I do not expect to do."[5]

McClellan's confident mood in this August 2 letter lasted just two days. On August 4 he issued an alert to his commanders: "Information has been received which goes to show that the enemy may attack us within the next forty-eight hours." On August 6 he repeated the warning, with greater urgency. On August 8, to General Scott and the president, he laid out an apocalyptic vision. The Confederate army at Manassas, at least 100,000 strong, "intend attacking our positions on the other side of the river, as well as to cross the Potomac north of us." The Potomac army, outnumbered two to one, "is entirely insufficient for the emergency." He must have, without a moment's delay, men and arms from all nearby garrisons. All nearby military departments should be merged into one central department, under his direct command.

McClellan was in a state. That evening he wrote his wife, Ellen, "I have hardly slept one moment for the last three nights, knowing well that the enemy intend some movement & fully recognizing our own weakness." As to General Scott, "I do not know whether he is a *dotard* or a *traitor!* . . . He *cannot* or *will* not comprehend the condition in which we are placed & is entirely unequal to the emergency. . . . He understands nothing, appreciates nothing & is ever in my way." A week only grew his panic: "I am here in a terrible place — the enemy have from 3 to 4 times my force — the Presdt is an idiot, the old General in his dotage — they cannot or will not see the true state of affairs."[6]

General Scott saw the true state of affairs perfectly well, and recognized the utter improbability of McClellan's emergency. "Relying on our numbers, our forts, and the Potomac River, I am confident in the opposite opinion . . . ," he told Secretary Cameron. "I have not the slightest apprehension for the safety of the Government here." He and McDowell had no reason to doubt their original intelligence on the enemy at Manassas. Winfield Scott knew enough of war, and of war's logistics, to be confident that the Rebels could not have nearly tripled the size of their army in the eighteen days since the Battle of Bull Run.

Scott threatened to resign over the incident, and the president had to step in. McClellan withdrew his August 8 letter, but Scott was not appeased. It seemed, he wrote, that "all the greater war questions are to be settled, without resort to or consultation with me. . . ." He saw little hope the situation would change. What he did hope was that his successor would be Henry W. Halleck, a learned and well-thought-of officer he was calling east from California.[7]

The picture of the enemy McClellan sketched in his alarming August 8 dispatch to Scott and Lincoln set a precedent that haunted him for the rest of his service. He drew that picture, he said, from "spies, letters and telegrams." Nothing is on record for any of these sources except for one Edward B. McMurdy, a Confederate deserter. As McMurdy told it, his "opinion as to the strength, plans etc. of the Rebels" earned him an interrogation by General McClellan himself. The general, said McMurdy, "told me that I had saved Washington City and in all probability the very existence of the Government. . . ."

Awarding the Rebel army 100,000 men — three times its actual strength — ended talk of crushing the rebellion at one blow with a display of "overwhelming strength," of marching at the head of a 273,000-man grand army across the length and breadth of the Confederacy. Once George McClellan accepted the underdog's role, he never surrendered it. His own army would grow substantially, yet the enemy's army grew ever faster. On August 19 he raised the Rebels' count to 150,000, against his own 55,000; on September 8 he reported a Rebel column of 100,000 just to target Baltimore; on September 13 he gave the Army of the Potomac's strength as 81,749, and added, "The enemy probably have 170,000!" (Confederate returns for October 1861 reported just over 44,100 effectives.)[8]

This delusion of being hugely outnumbered lasted from McClellan's second week of command to his last week of command. It dominated his decisions strategically, operationally, tactically, administratively. The inflated numbers in letters to Ellen, where he held nothing back of his beliefs and opinions, confirm the sincerity of his self-deception. Once started on this path, he would not — could not — change his doomsday perspective on the Confederate threat.

The initial delusional counting was entirely McClellan's own doing, but soon enough he acquired a collaborator in Allan Pinkerton. Founder of a Chicago detective agency, Pinkerton had done investigative work for McClellan during his railroad days, and McClellan called on him to direct intelligence gathering for the Army of the Potomac. Pinkerton took the nom de guerre E. J. Allen and worked out of the provost marshal's office, but he remained a civilian in McClellan's employ. Pinkerton drew on spies and interrogations of those from "the other side" — prisoners, deserters, refugees, contrabands. He displayed the same credulousness that infected Robert Patterson and Fitz John Porter counting Joe Johnston's Valley army (and McClellan listening to deserter McMurdy), with the same consequences. Worse, Pinkerton and McClellan agreed to "make large" in counting Confederate regiments, to allow for those not yet found. Exaggerated troop counts multiplied by exaggerated regiment counts produced monumental overcounts. Finally, Allan Pinkerton was a sycophant, anxious to tell McClellan what he expected to hear. In time the detective's intelligence gathering degenerated into wholly unsupported "general estimates" as he tried to keep pace with McClellan's ballooning assumptions.[9]

• • •

Driven by this self-generated crisis, McClellan accelerated a wholesale revamping of the army's officer corps. Like General Scott, he was determined to fight this war with only professional officers (particularly those he personally favored and promoted), and in these early weeks of welcome he generally had his way. Of the Army of Northeastern Virginia's sixteen division and brigade commanders, nine would not have a place that fall in the Army of the Potomac.

The first to go, with their ninety-day charges, were the three brigadiers of state militias. Theodore Runyon went out of the war, Daniel Tyler would serve in the West, and Robert Schenck took various posts in other departments. Two division commanders soon followed. Dixon Miles was deposed (but not cashiered) for being drunk on July 21, and David Hunter went to the Western theater. Then brigade commander Thomas A. Davies followed him.

The case was different for three of the former army's brigade commanders. Orlando Willcox, wounded and captured on Henry Hill, would languish in Southern prisons until exchanged in August 1862. Ambrose Burnside, an especial friend of McClellan's, would take command of an expeditionary force against the North Carolina coast. William T. Sherman professed disgust at the indiscipline of the volunteer army and the administration's lack of backbone to correct it. As he explained, "Our adversaries have the weakness of slavery in their midst to offset our Democracy, and tis beyond human wisdom to say which is the greater evil." When Robert Anderson, of Fort Sumter fame, now commanding in Kentucky, offered Sherman a posting as his deputy, he jumped at it. As for erstwhile army commander McDowell, McClellan granted him the opportunity to retrieve his military fortunes. "I then thought him an honest, well meaning man of generous impulses," he later wrote . . . and added, "I was sadly deceived." McDowell took a division in the new army.

Of the remaining Bull Run commanders, Sam Heintzelman, William Franklin, Erasmus Keyes, Israel Richardson, and Otis Howard — all West Pointers, all in due course brigadier generals — all retained infantry commands in the Army of the Potomac. So did Louis Blenker, the onetime Bavarian Legion lieutenant, with his German brigade. Old regular Andrew Porter, with fighting experience but without a West Point diploma, was sidetracked into provost marshal duty.

Of these seven, McClellan was only well acquainted with Porter and Franklin. He had no immediate cause to complain of the others. Still, such as Heintzelman, Keyes, Richardson represented a class of officers from the antebellum army that he inherited unbidden, an older generation (militarily speaking) that in time he came to regard with reservations. In faint praise of Richardson, for example, he wrote, "An officer of the old army; 'bull headed', brave, a good disciplinarian & of moderate ability." They might (or might not) demonstrate leadership; certainly they bore his careful watching.

Another unbidden commander in the new army was George A. McCall, an old regular who had fought the Seminoles in Florida and won brevets in Mexico. When Pennsylvania's Governor Andrew G. Curtin lost McClellan, his first choice to lead the Pennsylvania Reserves, due to a misdirected telegram, the post went to McCall. As their ranks filled, the Reserves formed a three-brigade division. By McClellan's evaluation, McCall had been an "admirable officer, but advancing age & other causes had weakened his powers."

Patterson's Army of the Shenandoah might be gone, but its pool of officers remained. McClellan quickly tapped it. One pick was Charles P. Stone, who that winter and spring had swiftly assembled a force to protect Washington. McClellan had Stone promoted to brigadier general, gave him a Corps of Observation, and sent him to the upper Potomac. McClellan remained convinced the Rebels were poised to storm across the Potomac in Stone's sector. Stone reported everything quiet. So far as he could tell, the enemy demonstrated "a feeling of alarm lest we should attempt a crossing in force. . . ."[10]

McClellan knew Fitz John Porter from their mutual postings at West Point in the early 1850s. At the outbreak of war Major Porter, in the adjutant general's office, urged McClellan to join up: "Such men as you and Cump Sherman and Burnside are required to counterbalance the influence of Davis, Bragg & Beauregard." Porter felt stranded in the War Department, and when McClellan gained the Department of the Ohio Porter sought him out. "Dear Mac," he wrote. "Can you help me up a peg or two — I have done much for Cameron but a politician is not to be relied upon." But Porter was ordered to Patterson, where his cautious counsel did nothing to stiffen that general's spine. The press pilloried Porter for abetting Patterson's failure. Porter could scarcely bear that burden, he told McClellan, "and see my companions, my juniors, rising to distinction and position while I must plow along in a beaten and lonely track." The order to report to the Potomac army was a godsend.

Fitz John Porter at thirty-eight was tall and handsome, with a commanding bearing. He became George McClellan's constant counselor and most loyal army supporter, a position that in the end led to his undoing.

Fitz John Porter was
McClellan's most trusted
confidant as well as his
unofficial second in
command.

Yet never would he waver in his admiration for the Young Napoleon, as
the press had dubbed the new army commander. The two thought alike,
with firmly conservative military and political beliefs. In coming campaigns Porter acted as McClellan's chief adviser and unofficial second in
command, and as such he showed no reluctance to fight McClellan's battles for him when it came to that.[11]

McClellan also had his way getting two other serving officers he had
befriended in the antebellum army. In Texas he made the acquaintance of
Don Carlos Buell, whom he described as "one of the best men in the army."
After his sub rosa advice to Major Anderson in December to occupy Fort
Sumter, Buell found himself in the military doldrums. Appealing to Lincoln and Secretary Cameron, McClellan obtained Buell for a divisional
command. William F. "Baldy" Smith was known to McClellan from West
Point days. In April 1861, from his posting in the capital, Smith had alerted
McClellan to offers of command coming his way. Smith himself entered
the war as colonel of the 3rd Vermont, and McClellan soon saw to his appointment as brigadier general and gave him a brigade and then a division. He was generous in his praise of Baldy Smith: "He possessed great
personal courage, & a wonderfully quick eye for ground & for handling
troops."[12]

Other prospective generals found their own routes to the Army of the

Potomac. Former Lieutenant Colonel Joseph Hooker had arrived from California in June to offer his sword to the Union. Hooker graduated from West Point in 1837 and compiled an outstanding record in the War with Mexico, where at various times he was chief of staff to five generals and won three brevets for gallantry. He left the army in 1853 to seek his fortune on the West Coast, with poor results, and the war struck him as the only likely way to restore his prospects. He enlisted in his cause Oregon's Senator Edward Baker, a friend of Lincoln's, and he lobbied the congressional delegation of Massachusetts, his home state. Lincoln endorsed the application, but when it reached General Scott's desk it was pigeonholed; Hooker had run afoul of Scott at a court of inquiry in Mexico and the old general had a long memory.

Undaunted, Hooker persuaded one of the generals he had served in Mexico to present him to the president. Never at a loss for words, Hooker highlighted his resumé and brashly concluded, "And while I am about it, Mr. President, I want to say one thing more, and that is, that I was at the battle of Bull Run the other day, and it is neither vanity or boasting in me to declare that I am a damned sight better general than you, Sir, had on that field." His candor caught Lincoln's attention. By McClellan's account,

Generals Joseph Hooker (far left),
Philip Kearny, and Daniel Sickles
(right) wrangled command postings
with the Potomac army despite their
unrepentant private lives.

the president asked him about Hooker. "I told him that in the Mexican War Hooker was looked upon as a good soldier but an unreliable man, and that his course in California had been such as to forfeit the respect of his comrades — that he was then a common drunkard and gambler." Despite McClellan's talebearing, Hooker's lobbying got him on a list of nominees for brigadier general. The Senate confirmed, and command of a Potomac army brigade followed.[13]

Like Joe Hooker, Phil Kearny made his own way to the Army of the Potomac. Philip Kearny decided he was born to be a soldier. No more dashing figure ever served in the Potomac army. Winfield Scott called him "the bravest man I ever knew and a perfect soldier." Kearny was born in New York City to privilege, took a degree from Columbia College, and inherited a million dollars upon his grandfather's death, leaving him free to indulge his dream of a military life. In 1837 he gained a commission in the 1st Dragoons commanded by his uncle, Stephen Watts Kearny. After two years' frontier duty, Lieutenant Kearny was sent to France to study cavalry tactics at the Royal School of Cavalry at Saumur. From there, on leave, he campaigned in Algeria with the famed Chasseurs d'Afrique. Back in America, he married and fathered four children, coauthored a cavalry-tactics manual, and grew so bored with army duty that he resigned his commission. War with Mexico sent him back to the service. He recruited a company of dragoons for Scott's campaign against Mexico City. In leading a cavalry charge at Churubusco his left arm was shattered, requiring amputation.

The peacetime army failed to satisfy Kearny's itch for action, or to reconcile him to domestic life either. His wife left him, taking their children, and he for the second time resigned his commission and in 1851 went off to see the world. In Paris, in his dragoon uniform with the pinned-up sleeve, he cut a dashing figure, and won the heart of a young visiting American named Agnes Maxwell. Back at his New Jersey estate he and Agnes lived together openly while he sought a divorce, roiling the sensibilities of Victorian high society. Diarist George Templeton Strong recalled that Kearny lived "under a very dark cloud . . . and was cut by many of his friends." Finally a divorce was granted, the liaison sanctified by marriage, and the unrepentant Kearny returned to Paris. In 1859 he was once again off to war, this time with Napoleon III's Imperial Guard. He was awarded the Legion of Honor for Magenta and Solferino.

Fort Sumter sent Kearny rushing back to America, where he sought a command from New York. General Scott supplied a glowing testimonial — "He is among the bravest of the brave and of the highest spirit and bearing" — but Governor Edwin D. Morgan, eyeing Kearny's scandalous private life, turned him away. New Jersey's Governor Charles S. Olden was happy to turn a blind eye, for Theodore Runyon's departure left the New Jersey brigade leaderless. Its command, and rank, went to Phil Kearny. In hindsight, said McClellan, he should have put this cavalryman par excellence in command of the cavalry arm.[14]

New York's Governor Morgan, however prudish his view of Phil Kearny, turned a blind eye of his own when the subject was Dan Sickles, owner of a truly scandalous reputation. Governor Morgan needed to raise regiments for the Union cause, and politician Sickles was good at that task. The Army of the Potomac would become the most politicized of all the Union's armies, yet from first to last it contained surprisingly few pure exemplars of the species *political general*. Its most notable specimen was Daniel Edgar Sickles.

New Yorker Sickles was a lawyer of faint ethics, nurtured on rough-and-tumble Tammany Hall politics. He served in the late 1850s as Democratic congressman from New York's Third District, and thrived on the political game in Washington . . . until February 27, 1859. On that date, a block from the White House, in broad daylight, he shot and killed his wife's lover, Philip Barton Key, Washington's district attorney and son of Francis Scott Key of "Star-Spangled Banner" fame. In a lurid trial Sickles won acquittal thanks to a legal team that included Edwin M. Stanton, future secretary of war in Lincoln's cabinet. (Innocent by reason of temporary insanity, a legal first, was the defense's ploy.) Shocked society was shocked anew when Sickles took his adulterous wife back to his bed and board. Sickles, himself a well-practiced adulterer, was troubled mostly by the affair's affront to his personal honor. Dan Sickles would prove just as sensitive to any affront to his military honor.

His political career in limbo, Sickles turned his energies to recruiting troops to put down the rebellion. He raised regiments enough for a brigade, christening it the Excelsior Brigade after New York's state seal. When Republican Governor Morgan tried to steal away the Excelsiors, Sickles went straight to the White House, stressing this shining example of Democratic support for the war. He came away with the provisional rank of brigadier general, and the Excelsiors were brigaded with the Potomac army. Sickles made no apologies for his limited military experience — a long-ago interlude with the New York militia — and his glad-handing bonhomie was popular with the troops. But for the well-bred in the officer corps, Sickles's reputation proceeded him. Gentlemanly Charles Wainwright, Joe Hooker's artillery chief, recorded in his journal that one day at headquarters he was introduced to Sickles, "but fortunately he did not offer to shake hands."[15]

As the Bull Run regiments were refitted and as new regiments of three-year (and some two-year) volunteers poured in from the North, they were arranged in brigades and the brigades in divisions. Silas Casey, a crusty old regular talented as a drillmaster, saw to the infantry's instruction. Helping drill the recruits were threescore newly minted second lieutenants from West Point. These youthful drillmasters were from the 1861 class and, graduated a year early to meet the crisis, the 1862 class. From this combined class of '61 would come such Potomac army officers as Adelbert Ames, Emory Upton, Judson Kilpatrick, and class "Immortal" (last in ranking) George Armstrong Custer.

By mid-October McClellan had ten divisions organized. Nine of their ten commanders were West Pointers, either serving officers or regulars returned to service for the war. The sole irregular was Republican political general Nathaniel P. Banks. Banks, former Massachusetts governor, ten-term congressman, and Republican party founder, replaced Robert Patterson at Harper's Ferry. Banks never actually led any fighting during his eight months with the Army of the Potomac. Still, politician Banks (like politician Ben Butler) would in time inflict many headaches on the Potomac army.[16]

The nine other divisions in this initial formation of the Army of the Potomac were led by what McClellan called "instructed officers." From the old Army of Northeastern Virginia he selected Irvin McDowell, Sam Heintzelman, and William Franklin. From the old Army of the Shenandoah came Charles Stone and Fitz John Porter. McClellan won the bidding for Don Carlos Buell and Baldy Smith. Joe Hooker's presence owed much to President Lincoln, and George McCall's to Pennsylvania's Governor Curtin. McCall as well as Banks would not have been McClellan's choices, but he regarded the other eight as the best available at the moment.

On the new army's October roster of brigade commanders were seven who had been at Bull Run — Erasmus Keyes, Israel Richardson, Louis Blenker, Otis Howard, Henry Slocum (wounded colonel of the 27th New York), James S. Wadsworth (a wealthy New York grandee and volunteer aide to McDowell), and Charles D. Jameson (who led his 2nd Maine in the attack on Henry Hill). From Patterson's old command came John Newton, a Virginian who had stayed true to his West Point oath, and Daniel Butterfield, former officer in the New York militia. Dan Sickles was there through political connections, and Phil Kearny owed thanks to New Jersey's Governor Olden. From New York's militia staff came George W. Morell, a West Pointer first in the class of 1835. John H. Martindale, a classmate of Morell's at the Academy (graduating third), had like Morell resigned from the army to take up the law.

Other of these October brigade commanders would make significant marks in the Army of the Potomac, including several whose services McClellan went to some lengths to obtain. When Winfield Scott Hancock, whom McClellan had known in Mexico, arrived in Washington from his California posting, he was directed to stay quietly at Willard's rather than report for orders at the War Department. McClellan interviewed him, and Captain Hancock, who feared being stuck in the Quartermaster's Department, welcomed the offer of an infantry brigade and the brigadier's rank to go with it.

In the case of John F. Reynolds, McClellan acted directly against the intentions of General Scott. Reynolds was commandant of cadets at West Point when war broke out, and was assigned a regiment of regulars. McClellan bid for him, but Scott ordered him to General Wool, at Fort Monroe. Hardly had Wool acknowledged the assignment of "such an able and experienced officer" when fresh orders sent Reynolds to the Army of the

Potomac. McClellan went over Scott's head to Secretary of War Cameron: "I respectfully insist that Brig. Gens. Don Carlos Buell and J. F. Reynolds, both appointed upon my recommendation and for the purpose of serving with me, be at once so assigned." Cameron had pledged "to aid you with all the powers of my Department," and McClellan held him to it. Reynolds of Pennsylvania was given a brigade in the Pennsylvania Reserves.

A second Reserves brigade went to Pennsylvanian George G. Meade — rather to Meade's surprise. Captain Meade paced impatiently in Detroit, from where he was conducting a Great Lakes survey. "If I had been in Washington for the last year," he complained to his wife, "ready at the right time to maneuver & push matters I might now be a Col. or Brig. Genl. . . . I mean that these things are obtained not on merit, but on influence." His appeal to fellow Pennsylvanian Simon Cameron went for naught, but his wife knew the strings to pull. Margaret Meade had a family friend, the state's attorney general, write Pennsylvania's Senator David Wilmot in praise of Captain Meade, and six weeks later Meade was a brigadier general of volunteers and shortly he had his brigade.[17]

Avuncular John Sedgwick — "Uncle John" to all and sundry — was called east in June after twenty-five years of varied army duty in Florida, Mexico, and across the Great Plains. He was serving as inspector general in the Department of Washington when McClellan found him and gave him a brigade. "He was one of the best and most modest soldiers we had," McClellan wrote, ". . . thoroughly unselfish, honest, and true as steel." McClellan also sought out his West Point classmate Darius Couch, who had served in Mexico and then left the moribund 1850s army. After Sumter, Couch raised the 7th Massachusetts and led it to Washington, where McClellan assembled a brigade for him.

Major Abner Doubleday, who fired the first shot in defense of Fort Sumter, had abolitionist leanings and did not approve of the Potomac army's officer corps as McClellan shaped it. Doubleday's brother reported the major's views to Radical Republican senator Zachariah Chandler: "It is a great misfortune that our most important military officers are strong proslavery men." He listed McClellan, Andrew Porter, Fitz John Porter, George Morell, John Newton, "and fifty others whose nominations will come before the Senate, nominations not fit to be made. . . . The policy of McClellan is to put down the rebellion & leave us politically (as far as the institution peculiar is concerned) where we began." Such allegations were designed to feed Zach Chandler's Radical appetite . . . and did. To complaints he appointed too few Republican generals, Mr. Lincoln replied, "It so happened that very few of our friends had a military education or were of the profession of arms. It would have been a question whether the war should be conducted on military knowledge, or on political affinity. . . ."[18]

Secretary of State Seward gave thought to solving command problems by attracting to the Union cause the celebrated revolutionary soldier Giuseppe Garibaldi, of the movement to unify Italy. In Seward's approach to the Italian hero, Garibaldi got it in his head he would replace Winfield Scott as general-in-chief. As to that, he said, if the administration would confer upon him powers "to effect some good," the first power he would exercise would be to abolish slavery. He was disappointed when it was explained that such a grant of powers was not possible. He could effect no good without full powers, said Garibaldi, and negotiations broke off.

In his memoir McClellan recorded with relish the proposal he received from another famous revolutionary hero, György Klapka of Hungary, whom Seward's agent approached. General Klapka's terms were a $100,000 advance plus a salary of $25,000; he would act as McClellan's chief of staff while he learned the language, then take over the army command. "He failed to state what provision he would make for me," McClellan wrote, "tho' it is not improbable that I would have fared better with him than with my own government."[19]

In these first months of war, naming general officers to divisions and brigades in the Army of the Potomac was more easily accomplished than finding qualified regimental and company officers. In the July bills authorizing enlistments, Congress had provided for companies to elect their own officers, and for those to then elect the regimental officers. This was long-standing practice in the state militias. But on August 6 Congress reversed itself. Rather than the troops electing them, company and regimental officers would be appointed by the state governors. This simply bowed to reality, for in practice governors had frequently done the appointing from the first. If the states had to provide the men, the reasoning went, the governors reserved the right to appoint their officers. This could — and did — become very much a matter of political patronage. It was only self-interest, an observer noted, to appoint colonels and lieutenant colonels, majors and captains, who "would produce the more agreeable consequences at the next election-time. . . ."[20]

To be sure, most governors conscientiously sought out professionals to lead their troops. First choices were West Pointers who had left the service. Next came serving officers, especially native sons. Initially the dilemma for serving officers was an uncertain future professionally in the

General-in-Chief Scott and his commanders. From left: George McClellan, Silas String-
ham, Irvin McDowell, Franz Sigel, John Wool, John Dix, Nathaniel Banks, Samuel
Heintzelman, Scott, Robert Anderson, John Charles Frémont, Benjamin Butler.

volunteers. In the event, General Scott's insistence on keeping the regular
army intact, as the solid core for this new army of volunteers, led the War
Department to make it difficult for regulars to resign their commissions
to seek more rank in the volunteers. But after Bull Run extinguished all
thoughts of a ninety-day war, staying on in the regulars became unpalat-
able for many. As George Meade put it, "It is rather hard for me after 25
years faithful service to have to go as a Capt. outranked by *hundreds,* many
of whom were hardly born when I entered service." Pennsylvania's Senator
Wilmot was Meade's salvation.

Others took different paths. Fort Sumter found Otis Howard, West
Point 1854, teaching mathematics at the Academy. He offered his services
to the governor of Maine, his home state. But regiments were then being officered by election, not by appointment. James G. Blaine, Speaker
of Maine's House of Representatives, arranged for Lieutenant Howard to
stand for election in absentia as colonel of the new 3rd Maine. He was duly
elected, resigned his commission, and led his regiment to Washington.
Times were changing, however. Six weeks later Baldy Smith, also a serving
officer, went to war as colonel (by appointment) of a Vermont regiment
of volunteers while retaining his rank in the regular army. The coming of
McClellan further relaxed restrictions on regulars transferring to the vol-

unteers, at least in the infantry — "I do not think it possible to employ our Army officers to more advantage than in commanding divisions, brigades, and regiments of new troops," he said.

In addition to former regulars, serving regulars, and militia officers, there came candidates from the armies of Europe. They descended on Washington in a steady stream, wrote Russell of the *Times*: "Garibaldians, Hungarians, Poles, officers of Turkish and other contingents, . . . remainders of European revolutions and wars, surround the State department and infest unsuspecting politicians with illegible testimonials in unknown tongues."

When all these sources were exhausted, governors were left with only civilians to appoint. Most often those who raised the regiments and the companies, and those who assisted, were appointed to the command posts. Not infrequently these volunteer entrepreneurs demonstrated capabilities that translated into training leadership and, it was hoped, battle-field leadership as well.

Not all so demonstrated. Régis de Trobriand, colonel, 55th New York, described a certain retired merchant who spent $20,000 raising a regiment of cavalry "of which he was, of course, commissioned colonel. His camp was near us; he was never there. On the other hand, he displayed his uniform continually on the sidewalks of Pennsylvania Avenue and in the bar-rooms of the great hotels. He was present at all the receptions at the White House, at all the evening parties of the ministers. . . ." Sustained by "the double power of money and of political influence, he was nominated brigadier-general . . . and, without ever having drawn his sabre from the scabbard, he returned home, to enjoy in peace the delight of being able to write the title of 'General' upon his visiting-cards."

Such pasteboard colonels and brigadiers, de Trobriand went on, flourished in the Army of the Potomac due simply to that army's natal attachment to Washington. Political influence — "one of the most flagrant vices of the system applied to military affairs" — showed not only in appointments but in promotions, and operated in direct proportion to one's proximity to the capital.[21]

At the other end of the spectrum were those civilians of unwarlike background who in uniform grew very warlike indeed, carving out noteworthy high-command accomplishments in the Army of the Potomac. Among them were Francis Barlow, Alpheus Williams, David Birney, James Wadsworth, Hiram Berry, Joseph Bartlett, Joshua Chamberlain, and de Trobriand himself.

The first step in this process was to separate the wheat from the chaff.

On July 4, 1861, on Pennsylvania Avenue in front of the White House, President Lincoln (standing) and General Scott (seated) reviewed New York's Garibaldi Guard regiment. Engraved after Frank Vizetelly.

The War Department called for military boards to examine the "capacity, qualifications, propriety of conduct, and efficiency of any officer of volunteers." The results of these examinations, or the threat of them, were soon evident. McClellan appointed two boards on September 20, and a week later twenty-seven commissioned officers had resigned from just one division. On November 1 thirty-eight officers were discharged; on November 16 over a hundred.

Major Charles S. Wainwright, 1st New York Artillery, served on one such board and recorded in his journal the examination of three captains and four lieutenants of artillery, all volunteers. Of the captains, the first passed; he was thought weak on tactics but appeared to have sufficient intelligence. The second was nearly illiterate and unable to grasp anything of tactics, even though Wainwright coached him beforehand. The third was simply "too old a dog to learn new tricks." Of the lieutenants, two resigned rather than face examination, another was "totally lacking in every respect," and only one was "evidently capable and intelligent, and was passed." Admittedly, officers of artillery were required to gain far more specialized knowledge than those of infantry, yet Wainwright's experience suggests the leadership problems inherent in building an army out of volunteers.

In addition to supporting the examining boards, McClellan widened the use of courts-martial, where proceedings were exempt from political pressures. In some cases the men took it upon themselves to force out incompetent officers. "Our regiment has taken a purge this week," Captain Edward S. Bragg of the 6th Wisconsin told his wife. "We have *forced ten resignations* from officers, and put better men in their place. . . . The men who resigned, did not have our confidence, and we placed the dose to their lips, and made them swallow it."

Conscientious fledgling officers studied the manuals to school themselves in drilling, tactics, and administration. Charles Haydon, 2nd Michigan, described the trials of a volunteer-company captain of his acquaintance, a lawyer in civilian life: "He knew nothing abt the drill & was compelled to trot up & down through the mud for 2 hours in great heat, vexation & confusion. . . . I have seldom seen a man more blowed & he swore most prodigiously, which I never heard him do before." Future general Francis Barlow wrote in July 1861, "I confess I understand but little of the practical duties of an officer in battle & no one else here does. We ought to be instructed in it." Barlow set as his course that "in battle I should obey orders when they were given & use my discretion when they were not."[22]

Equipping the artillery arm not only required more matériel than the infantry, but officers of artillery were marked as something of a breed apart. The science and tactics of gunnery were not easily or quickly acquired. At the same time, the notion of flexibility of command in the artillery ran counter to long-standing tradition. Cannon were considered adjuncts of the infantry force, commanded and directed for infantry's benefit. In this initial building of the Army of the Potomac no provision was made for independence of command in the artillery. As it happened, a veteran battery captain might well have a far better grasp of the use of guns on a battlefield than the infantry brigadier of volunteers giving him orders.

As chief of artillery, McClellan kept on Major William F. Barry, a tall, austere-looking West Pointer and Mexican War veteran. Barry had held the same post under McDowell — and by no means distinguished himself at Bull Run. But Barry's talents were organizational and administrative, and at this time he was well suited for the post. He established an artillery rendezvous called Camp Barry at Bladensburg, Maryland, and there the organization, fitting out, and training for the army's batteries proceeded apace.

Major Henry J. Hunt commanded the artillery reserve and its adjunct, the siege train. Nineteenth of thirty-one in West Point's class of 1839, Hunt was assigned to the artillery and found a home there. He displayed an instinct for the battlefield, performing brilliantly in Scott's march on Mexico City, where he won brevets for Contreras and Churubusco and was wounded at Molino del Rey. A hard-faced, intimidating man of forty-two,

Hunt was known for his candid speech and his short temper — and for his dedication to his craft. McClellan knew Hunt's fighting record in Mexico, and giving him charge of the reserve batteries came as close to an artillerist's independent command as was then available in the Potomac army.[23]

The plan for the artillery arm called for attaching four batteries of field artillery to each division — not to brigades, as in McDowell's army — with one of the four a regular-army battery. This regular battery would serve as the core of the divisional artillery, spreading a leavening of discipline and organization to the volunteers. The regulars' captain was divisional chief of artillery. In the October organization, eleven regular batteries were attached to divisions, with eight others in Hunt's artillery reserve. Expecting to be fighting in heavily wooded Virginia, limiting the need for long-range guns, McClellan set as a goal equipping one-third of the field artillery with rifled guns and two-thirds with the shorter-range 12-pounder smoothbore Napoleon. Still to come was the siege train — the heavy guns and mortars of position — that McClellan wanted should he have to besiege Richmond.[24]

Rank and command in the artillery would long remain corrosive issues. Early on, McClellan bent the rules somewhat to at least advance Barry and Hunt from major to colonel. Barry made brigadier general as a staff administrator, but line commander Hunt's promotion to that rank was a year away. As to battlefield command of the guns, McClellan showed no pioneering spirit. A board of officers studied the matter, but it merely confirmed that practices differed in different armies and made no recommendations. McClellan stayed with tradition. The Army of the Potomac's chief of artillery would be restricted to administrative duties. He was to inspect batteries and "be responsible that they are properly equipped and supplied." He could not exercise command in the field "unless specially ordered by the commanding general." Divisional artillery would be directed tactically by infantry commanders.

General Scott's embargo on regular officers transferring to higher rank in the volunteers stayed in force longer for the artillery than for the infantry. Trained artillerymen were as scarce as they were essential; just then a battery captain was far more valuable than an infantry colonel. Captain John C. Tidball, 2nd U.S. Artillery, cast a rueful eye on what this meant to him and his fellow regulars. "This prohibition, although advantageous to the formation of a good artillery, proved of great personal disadvantage to this class of officers. Their comrades in other branches of the service pushed ahead of them in rank, and gained a start that was not made up even after the embargo was raised."

If McClellan's views on artillery command were uninspired, he at least had high expectations for that arm. He envisioned the big guns as the equalizer for his perceived inferiority in infantry. His campaign strategy evolving that first winter of the war would be shaped by his need to get his big guns to the battlefront to counter the enemy host.[25]

When it came to the cavalry arm, McClellan was not only uninspired, he displayed neither expectations nor vision. "The difficulties attending the organization of a suitable cavalry force were very great," he wrote in his memoir, "and it cannot be said that they were ever satisfactorily overcome." For his time of command, that understated the case. This might seem a strange turn of affairs for a onetime captain of cavalry, author of a cavalry manual, and originator of the famous McClellan saddle. In truth, when it came to cavalry George McClellan was one of those generals, wrote Captain Moses Harris, 1st U.S. Cavalry, "who, destitute of experience, was dominated and controlled by theory."

Captain McClellan, 1st U.S. Cavalry, resigned his commission in 1857 without serving a day with his regiment. His manual, *Regulations and Instructions for the Field Service of the United States Cavalry in Time of War*, was largely translated from Austrian and Russian cavalry regulations, and it bore little relationship to American conditions and experience. The McClellan saddle, too, was drawn from European models.[26]

By circumstance, the Potomac army got a slow start forming a cavalry arm. In the rush to the colors after Fort Sumter, the War Department made a point of not accepting volunteer cavalry regiments. The expense of equipping and maintaining cavalry was considerable, and in any case the ninety-day enlistment was deemed far too short a period to train horse soldiers. For the Bull Run campaign McDowell had but seven companies of cavalry, all regulars, and used them primarily to help cover the army's retreat. The defeat roused the War Department to finally accept the cavalry regiments the governors had been pressing on it, and to catch up ordering the necessary cavalry mounts, arms, and equipment.

There was no shortage of cavalry recruits. As veteran trooper Benjamin W. Crowninshield put it, in 1861 cavalry was seen as an elite corps, "and men preferred to enlist in that branch . . . because the would-be trooper preferred riding to walking, with perhaps an idea that at the end of a march his horse would be put up at some peripatetic livery-stable." None of the cavalry volunteers, including their officers, "had any definite idea of the duties," he concluded.

Still, by October 15 the Potomac army had one full or partial regiment of volunteer cavalry attached to nine of its ten divisions, plus three and a half regiments yet to be assigned. From the initial cavalry officers' pool, three West Pointers would rise to become general officers of cavalry in the Army of the Potomac — William W. Averell, David McMurtrie Gregg, and George D. Bayard. At the time, however, they were hamstrung by a lack of any system for cavalry to act in a unified and independent fashion, under independent command. Instead, explained Moses Harris, cavalry was distributed broadcast "at the disposal of generals without experience, who still further divided it so that each brigade, almost, was provided with its troop or squadron whose duty it was to add to the importance of the general by following him about, to provide orderlies for dashing young staff officers and strikers for headquarters." McClellan offers a prime example of this dilution of strength. Attached to his headquarters was one regiment of regular cavalry, part of another, and three regiments of volunteer cavalry.

For the Potomac army's chief of cavalry McClellan chose his West Point classmate George Stoneman. After a posting with the 1st Dragoons during the Mexican War, Stoneman saw duty in the Mormon Battalion on its overland march to California in 1846–47, and afterward served with the 2nd Cavalry. In the spring of 1861 he attracted notice by defying General Twiggs's surrender to the Texas secessionists and leading his command to Union ground. When General Scott attempted to transfer Stoneman to the Western theater, McClellan again went over the general-in-chief's head, this time directly to the president. Stoneman, he wrote, "is invaluable in the duty to which I have assigned him."

That duty, it turned out, was to organize and train the cavalry and nothing more. As with Barry in the artillery, Stoneman's role was administrative. The chief of cavalry was denied a tactical role unless granted by the general commanding. The divisional infantry general would manage the cavalry as well as the artillery attached to his command. McClellan's knowledge of cavalry operations was, as Captain Harris remarked, purely theoretical. In his manual, direction of the horse soldiers lay in the hands of infantry commanders, and his discussion of cavalry reconnaissance made no provision for independent operations. In these hectic fall days filled with hurried measures to forestall a phantom Confederate army, McClellan treated his cavalry as an afterthought.[27]

To manage all the details of this assembling and organizing, McClellan relied primarily on himself, impelled by his conviction that he would be attacked at any moment by superior forces. For the paperwork and the fol-

On a reconnoiter from a Virginia hilltop outside Washington in the fall of 1861, General McClellan strikes a pose dictating an order. With him is his chief of staff, Randolph Marcy (center), and Fitz John Porter. Watercolor by the Prince de Joinville.

low-up, however, he had to rely on his staff. The two key staff members for this purpose were Randolph B. Marcy and Seth Williams, both of whom he brought with him from the Department of the Ohio.

Marcy was a seasoned regular with nearly three decades of frontier service. McClellan first met him in 1851, when he was assigned to Captain Marcy's expedition to trace the source of the Red River of Texas. Although George McClellan displayed a chronic problem dealing with his superiors, on this posting he got on well enough that he gained an introduction to Marcy's daughter. In the 1850s pretty Mary Ellen Marcy was courted (so it seemed) by every love-struck subaltern in the U.S. army, notably by future Confederate general Ambrose Powell Hill. But McClellan proved the most persistent and eventually won her hand. War promoted Randolph Marcy to be his son-in-law's chief of staff.

Seth Williams, a clean-shaven, balding, amiable Yankee from Maine, was a career adjutant of expertise and efficiency. "I never met with a better bureau officer, perhaps never with so good a one," McClellan wrote of Williams. "He thoroughly understood the working of the adjutant-general's department . . . and thus exerted a great influence in bringing about the excellent organization of the Army of the Potomac." By way of affirmation, every Potomac army commander, from first to last, would depend on "Father Seth."

Two other staff posts were critical to operating the army in the field. Albert J. Myer, expert in flag and torch signaling and military telegraphy, was named signal officer. Myer had been called to the Bull Run battle too late to bring his signaling equipment, so he set out on July 21 with an observation balloon, inflated at a gas main in Washington, only to see it become wedged between two trees. For the next campaign, the Army of the Potomac would be well equipped for telegraphic and flag and torch signaling, and would have a balloon train as well.

The staff position of chief engineer went to John G. Barnard, a carryover from McDowell's army. Barnard, graduating second in the West Point class of 1833, was well regarded in the antebellum army for his skill at coastal fortifications. Barnard had not shown well as a battlefield scout at Bull Run, but defensive fortification was his primary skill. He began, and would carry out under McClellan's watchful eye, the extensive ring of forts around Washington.

The post of chief topographical engineer went to Andrew A. Humphreys, a twenty-three-year veteran of "topo" service in the old army. Talented and ambitious, Humphreys demonstrated how a vigorous personal campaign could lead to a brigadier's star. A Pennsylvanian, he courted his state's Congressman James H. Campbell and Senator Edgar Cowan. The head of the U.S. Coast Survey, A. D. Bache, was brought into his corner. Humphreys's wife called on Vermont's Senator Solomon Foot, with whom Humphreys had served on a West Point curriculum board. "I really believe Campbell has an affection for me of no ordinary kind," Humphreys explained to his wife, "and that Bache too is attached to me. And Mr. Foote the fine old fellow. . . ." Brigadier General Humphreys dutifully sent thank-you letters to all concerned.[28]

A royal adornment to the staff was a contingent from the House of Orléans, the Prince de Joinville and his two nephews, Robert d'Orléans, Duc de Chartres, and Philippe d'Orléans, Comte de Paris and pretender to the French throne. McClellan found useful staff work for the young aides-de-camp Robert and Philippe, and the two became known to the troops as Captain Chatters and Captain Perry. Joinville served the commanding general as adviser and confidant.

In his 1855–56 assignment to observe the Crimean War and the command structures of European armies, Captain McClellan duly noted the composition of the various army staffs. Yet he drew no lessons from the role of staff in directing on the battlefield operations and maneuvers in the name of the commanding general. Appointing Randolph Marcy as chief of staff was an innovation on McClellan's part, yet he entrusted Marcy with no operational responsibilities. Allan Pinkerton, the "off-the-books" intelligence chief, was another innovation, yet Pinkerton provided no finished intelligence estimates for decision, only raw data, and only to McClellan. It was clearly George McClellan's intention not only to command an army of some 100,000 men on campaign, but to do so in every respect entirely at his own direction.[29]

4. *Quiet Along the Potomac*

IN THE WEEKS FOLLOWING BULL RUN, General Beauregard grew eager to stir up matters by harassing the Federal army at Washington. Although second in command to Joe Johnston, Beauregard was the more aggressive-minded of the two. Johnston appeared content to await a further assault behind the line of Bull Run. Beauregard argued for pushing up close to the capital's defenses. "From these advanced positions, we could at any time concentrate for offensive or defensive purposes." He finally pressed the reluctant Johnston into agreement . . . and thereby made General McClellan very nervous.

The Rebels had followed the retreating Yankees as far as Centreville and established themselves there. Now they advanced to Fairfax Court House, and from that foothold set up outposts at Falls Church and on Upton's, Munson's and Mason's hills overlooking Washington. Beauregard visited these outposts and delighted in the view they afforded on a clear day of the Capitol's unfinished dome.

Leesburg, Virginia, some 35 miles up the Potomac from Washington, was yet another Confederate outpost, one that McClellan regarded as particularly worrisome. He fully expected the Rebels to cross the Potomac from Leesburg in great force to strike at Baltimore or at Washington's exposed northern flank. He had posted General Stone on the opposite shore in Maryland to try and stem the Rebel tide until help arrived. In that event, McClellan promised "to move up with my large reinforcements & assume command myself."[1]

It was against this backdrop of supposedly ever-widening Confederate menace that rumors spoke of a plot to take Maryland out of the Union. The picture was hazy and undocumented, but suggested that the Maryland legislature, scheduled to meet at Frederick on September 17, would secretly pass an ordinance of secession and signal its action to Johnston, who would then (as McClellan phrased it) "at once move into Maryland & raise a general disturbance." Secretary of State Seward, a Grand Inquisitor regarding matters of loyalty and disloyalty, was ready to act on this intelligence. McClellan took part in a "full consultation" with Lincoln, Seward, and Secretary of War Cameron. It was decided, wrote McClellan, "to nip the whole affair in the bud" by arresting all the Maryland legislators thought to be secession-minded.

The key figure here was McClellan. He made military necessity the decisive factor in this highly irregular, extralegal proceeding. In his delusion of being hugely outnumbered, he claimed "the danger was great — in a military point of view we were not prepared to resist an invasion of Maryland." The arrests were carried out by General Banks in Frederick and by Pinkerton detectives in Baltimore. All those arrested were Democrats. No evidence was found (then or later) that otherwise secession would have been proclaimed, with Joe Johnston storming into Maryland to secure it for the Confederacy, and in due course the legislators were released. McClellan was unrepentant; the threat "seemed at the time to be thoroughly reliable . . . & have no apology to make."[2]

Not content with flaunting their banners in sight of the Capitol, the Rebels imposed a blockade by closing navigation on the lower Potomac with a string of batteries on the Virginia shore 20 to 25 miles south of Alexandria. "The importance of keeping open the navigation of the Potomac is so obvious that no argument is necessary on the subject," said Navy Secretary Gideon Welles. McClellan did argue the case, and in any event he said it was the navy's problem. The navy said it was a joint problem, requiring the army's help to destroy the batteries.

As Gustavus Fox discovered, gaining cooperation from General McClellan on this subject was most elusive. Fox, who led the naval expedition to Fort Sumter, was now assistant secretary of the navy. At his urging, the Potomac flotilla initiated a joint army-navy operation to seize Mathias Point, a key site commanding the river. The navy would provide warships, transports, and landing barges; the army would provide 4,000 soldiers. On the appointed night no soldiers appeared. Fox went to the president, and together they went to McClellan. McClellan said his engineers told him troops could not be put ashore in such numbers. Fox said the navy would handle the landing in all its details, and the operation was rescheduled for the next night. "But the next night they did not go," Fox testified. "They never went, and we never knew what the reason was." Lincoln "manifested more feeling and disappointment than I have ever seen him exhibit before." The press reported "general alarm is felt throughout the North at the 'Closing of the Potomac.'"

The presence of the Rebel batteries did impel McClellan to at least take

General McClellan and members of his headquarters staff visit Brigadier George W. Morell at Miner's Hill, Virginia. From left, Morell (at stump), Alexander V. Colburn, Mc-Clellan, Nathan B. Sweitzer, Prince de Joinville, Comte de Paris.

measures to guard the Potomac army's left flank, and so Joe Hooker got his first taste of field command. He was posted in lower Maryland with two brigades of infantry and a battery. McClellan's concern was a Confederate crossing into Maryland in force from their battery positions, but Hooker (like Stone on the upper Potomac) found no evidence of imminent threat. Their focus, he thought, was defending against an assault, not delivering one.

Hooker was contemptuous of the batteries, remarking that passing ships "are as likely to be struck by lightning as by the rebel shot." With the navy's cooperation, he proposed landing a strike force of infantry and light guns "very quietly any night" on ground overlooking the batteries. This, he said, "would compel them to abandon their guns the first day we opened fire on them." But McClellan's attention was not engaged. He believed his own grand plan would, in the fullness of time, render the batteries harmless.[3]

The navy promoted a second joint operation, against Norfolk, where a menacing Confederate warship was taking shape. The outbreak of war found the steam frigate *Merrimack* laid up at Norfolk for repairs, and she was burned and scuttled when the navy yard there was given up. By report, the Rebels had raised the *Merrimack* and were converting her with armor into a new breed of war vessel, an ironclad ram. Montgomery Meigs warned Cameron, "She was to go down to Newport News some fine morning & sink all the fleet and I believe she could do it." The navy entertained schemes for destroying the *Virginia* (as she was renamed) in dry dock. Engineer Barnard pursued the idea, and Sam Heintzelman submitted a plan of attack. But weeks, then months, went by and McClellan found one reason or another to shelve the project. Like the Rebel batteries, he said, Norfolk's fall was an assured part of his grand plan. The navy, unpersuaded, rested its hopes on an ironclad of its own, then under construction in New York, called the *Monitor*.[4]

McClellan's reaction to these various schemes was exasperation with an administration that seemed bent on questioning him and interfering. "I can't tell you how disgusted I am becoming with these wretched politicians," he told Ellen. "There are some of the greatest geese in the Cabinet I have ever seen — enough to tax the patience of Job." Navy Secretary Welles was "weaker than the most garrulous old woman you were ever annoyed by." Secretary of State Seward was "the meanest of them all — a meddling, officious, incompetent little puppy." He found visits by President Lincoln, whom he termed "nothing more than a well meaning baboon," a particular trial, and he extended the insubordination he practiced on General Scott to the president. William Howard Russell recorded in his diary a call he made on McClellan at army headquarters, only to be turned away by an orderly. "General's gone to bed said he & can see no one. He sent that message to the President who came here to see him 10 minutes ago."[5]

At the seat of war (as the newspapers called it) in Washington, the public mood in these weeks, and the mood of Congress, was turning sour. The Army of the Potomac held grand reviews, widely reported, and appeared fit and ready for service, yet Confederate flags waved defiantly just across the Potomac, and nothing was done about the blockade of the lower river. Along the upper Potomac depredations against the Baltimore & Ohio Railroad and the Chesapeake & Ohio Canal added to Washington's sense of isolation. Correspondent Russell made note, "M'Clellan is still reviewing, and the North are still waiting for victories and paying money, and the orators are still wrangling over the best way of cooking the hares which they have not yet caught."

The special session of Congress ended August 6 and it would not meet again until December 2, but its members were restive. Two of the most fervent Radical Republican senators, Benjamin Wade and Zachariah Chandler, sniped at McClellan and his static army. "So there they stay in perfect contentment behind their entrenchments," Wade complained, "occasionally sending forth with great exultation a *bulletin* announcing that *the Capital is safe. . . .*" As for Zach Chandler, his disdain warped his spelling: "I am greatly dissatisfied with Genl McLelland. He seems to be devoting himself to parades & military shows instead of cleaning the country of rebels." These were not men McClellan wanted as enemies.

There was discontent in the administration as well. In his diary Attorney General Edward Bates demanded to know why the Potomac blockade was allowed to stand. It "makes the impression upon both parties to the contest, and especially to foreigners, that we are both weak and timid. . . . We absolutely need some dashing expeditions — some victories, great or small, to stimulate the zeal of the Country." General McClellan's first dashing expedition only made matters worse.[6]

Joe Johnston worried over his advanced outposts, and on September 28 he ordered Falls Church and Upton's, Munson's, and Mason's hills evacuated. Word reached Baldy Smith that night, and he ordered everyone forward pell-mell to seize the outposts. Smith's columns stumbled blindly into each other and opened fire. Worst hit was a Pennsylvania regiment uniformed in gray. One of the Pennsylvanians called it "midnight horror at Munson's Hill. . . . Who is responsible for sending upon such an expedition *men dressed in the garb of the enemy*?" McClellan said the positions had to be seized "at all hazards." He told his wife, "They can no longer say that they are flaunting their dirty little flag in my face, & I hope they have taken their last look at Washn."

The seizure of the nettlesome outposts ought to have gained him some reward for boldness, some praise from the impatient press. Instead a scent of the ludicrous lingered over the affair. The Rebels had only a single battery to defend the outposts, so they improvised artillery from logs and old stovepipes — "Quaker guns," the press christened them. "In the terrible batteries behind the hill there is but a derisive log, painted black, frowning upon the Federal army," mocked the *New-York Tribune*. "All the world laughing" about the wooden guns on Munson's Hill, noted correspondent Russell. "I wonder if McC. is all they think." Russell called him "'the little corporal' of unfought fields."[7]

There remained, in these weeks, the awkward presence of Lieutenant General Winfield Scott. Russell remarked on that too: "Poor old Scott is now a mere pageant & is scarcely heeded by any one here. . . . Two months ago, and his was the most honoured name in the States . . . holding an enormous boa constrictor of a Federal army in his hands, which he was

Rebel Gun at Munsons Hill — a regular Quaker.

On evacuating Munson's Hill, overlooking Washington, the Rebels left behind this piece of wooden ordnance that artist Alfred Waud termed "a regular Quaker."

preparing to let go as soon as he had coiled it completely round the frightened Secessionist rabbit." Now, like Shakespeare's Caesar, "none so poor to do him reverence."

But the general-in-chief had defenders. William H. Aspinwall, a prominent New York merchant and financier, urged the administration to retain Scott: "He is loved and revered by the people in the Eastern and Middle States, and from these come the sinews of war at present. His loss would tell fearfully in those quarters." Aspinwall had mentored McClellan in his railroad days, and now he wrote to urge him not to permit Scott to resign. Aspinwall cautioned that party politics was at work. "The idea has been put forth that the Republicans will try & crowd Frémont ahead of you. . . ." "Pathfinder" John Charles Frémont, Western explorer, the Republicans' first presidential candidate back in 1856, was presently major general in charge of the Western Department at St. Louis. Aspinwall feared that if Scott gave up his post before McClellan was firmly established as his probable successor, "political influences would be at work" to have Frémont appointed."[8]

McClellan did not heed Aspinwall's advice. Following their August blowup over the question of an imminent attack on Washington, McClellan simply paid no heed to the general-in-chief. "Genl Scott is the most dangerous antagonist I have," he wrote Ellen on August 14; "— either he or I must leave here — our ideas are so widely different that it is impossible for us to work together much longer." Scott wrote Cameron, "Are these new neglects & outrages, on the part of my junior, tho' virtually approved, in the highest quarter, to be borne with, by me?" In the face of all this, and because of failing health, he determined to resign his post. But he would "try to hold out till the arrival of Major Genl. Halleck, in the hope that I might be permitted to place the chief command of the army in wise & competent hands, & myself to retire."[9]

On September 27 the antagonism between Scott and his junior sparked an ugly scene in Scott's office. The gathering included the two generals, the president, and cabinet officers. In response to a question about the size of the forces at Washington, Scott said that no reports had been made to him, at which (by Gideon Welles's account) Secretary of State Seward read off a detailed recitation of the numbers, to which McClellan "replied that the statement approximated the truth." Scott's "countenance showed great displeasure," Welles wrote. General-in-chief of the armies of the United States, unable to obtain such reports, yet Secretary Seward "is possessed of facts which are withheld from me." Turning to Lincoln he asked, "Am I Mr President to apply to the Secretary of State for the necessary military information to discharge my duties?" Simon Cameron tried to calm the waters with the remark that everyone knew how meddlesome Seward was, always prying into the business of the other departments. "It was a pleasant way of breaking up an unpleasant interview," Welles wrote, "and we rose to leave." But Scott was not done. He drew himself up in front of McClellan and said, "When I proposed that you should come here to aid, not supersede me, you had my friendship and confidence. You still have my confidence."

Writing to Ellen that night, McClellan said that General Scott had "raised a row" with him. "I kept cool, looked him square in the face, & *rather* I think I got the advantage of him. In the course of the conversation he very strongly intimated that we were no longer friends. I said nothing. . . . I presume war is declared — so be it."[10]

Scott's hope of dictating his successor came to nothing. In San Francisco his candidate, the scholarly former captain Henry W. Halleck, now a prominent lawyer and businessman, had accepted a commission as major general readily enough, but it seemed the order calling him east was not precisely drawn; true to his fussy nature he stayed where he was until it was corrected. He would not reach Washington until November. As for Pathfinder Frémont, he dashed whatever hope the Radicals had of seeing him general-in-chief by misadministering the Department of the West so badly that Secretary Cameron had to travel to St. Louis to sort out the mess. At a cabinet meeting on October 18 it was decided that Scott must retire. The news soon reached McClellan, and he wrote Ellen, "It seems to be pretty well settled that I will be Comdr in Chf within a week." He noted with satisfaction that the president had honored Scott's request for retirement, "but *not* in favor of Halleck."

McClellan closed his letter by noting, "The enemy have fallen back on Manassas — probably to draw me into the old error. I hope to make them abandon Leesburg tomorrow." That objective produced his first offensive undertaking as head of the Army of the Potomac.[11]

On October 17 Charles Stone, posted on the upper Potomac across from Leesburg, telegraphed, "A large body of the enemy seems to have suddenly left the vicinity of Leesburg." The next day he reported enemy picket posts on his front abandoned. By reference to "the old error," McClellan meant he would not be drawn into another attack on the well-defended Manassas and Centreville positions. But if he could pick off Leesburg, the northern anchor of the Confederate line, preferably by clever maneuver, it might silence his critics.

He would employ bluff. On October 19 he ordered George McCall with the Pennsylvania Reserves to advance up the Virginia side of the Potomac to Dranesville, within a dozen miles of Leesburg. To General Stone, at Poolesville in Maryland, went instructions to enhance the bluff. When McCall sent out reconnaissances from Dranesville on the 20th, Stone was to "keep a good lookout upon Leesburg, to see if this movement has the effect to drive them away. Perhaps a slight demonstration on your part would have the effect to move them." Stone read this as setting him a clear objective: He was, in conjunction with McCall, to push the Rebels out of Leesburg.

On the afternoon of October 20 Stone advanced a brigade and a battery to Edwards Ferry, a Potomac crossing five miles from Leesburg. Confederate troops were sighted, and Stone made a show of preparing to cross the river while shelling the area vigorously. The enemy was seen to retire. At the same time, Stone sent a lesser force upstream three miles to Ball's Bluff to mount a second diversion. A crossing there was considerably more difficult than at Edwards Ferry due to Harrison's Island in the middle of the river — and, on the Virginia shore, the looming presence of Ball's Bluff, a hundred feet or so above the water. The bluff was seen to be unguarded. Makeshift flotillas of scows and skiffs served to deliver troops from the Maryland shore to Harrison's Island, and from there to the foot of Ball's

Bluff. By Stone's order, Colonel Charles Devens took half of his 15th Massachusetts across to Harrison's Island, and Devens sent a small detachment over to the Virginia shore. It was verging into night now, and by the light of the moon the scouting party scaled Ball's Bluff and in the distance saw what it took to be an enemy encampment. What the scouts saw, however, was simply an illusion, shadow tents created by moonlight filtering through the trees. A report of the supposed discovery was sent to General Stone.

Stone had reported to McClellan the success of his feint at Edwards Ferry and the crossing of the scouting party at Ball's Bluff. While awaiting further orders, Stone was handed the report of the phantom enemy encampment. To activate his intended diversion, he ordered Devens to attack the camp at dawn the next morning. He reinforced him with the 20th Massachusetts, and gave him the option of withdrawing after the assault or of taking a position atop Ball's Bluff, "which he can undoubtedly hold until re-enforced. . . ."

But already that October 20, a Sunday, General McClellan had written off the operation, and with it any prospect of winning a game of bluff against the Rebels. His second thoughts came after inspecting McCall's position at Dranesville. He saw risk there. He told McCall not to advance any farther for fear of triggering an enemy attack from Centreville, and ordered him back to Washington. On Monday morning McCall took his division back to its old camps.

Thus one day after initiating his Leesburg ploy, McClellan put it out of mind. He also put Charles Stone's "slight demonstration" out of mind. He made no reply to Stone's report of his day's work . . . nor did he inform Stone that McCall's division had been withdrawn. Stone proceeded with his plans for Monday quite unaware that the operation had ended and its other, much larger component had marched away.[12]

Colonel Nathan Evans commanded at Leesburg. At Bull Run back in July Evans had seen through McDowell's bluff at the Stone Bridge and challenged the Yankee advance. Now, three months later, he called McClellan's bluff. Evans had not evacuated his Leesburg posting as believed but simply rearranged his troops. Learning that McCall was gone from Dranesville, he was free to deal with the threats at Edwards Ferry and Ball's Bluff. He went in with guns blazing.

Early on Monday, October 21, Colonel Devens shuttled five companies of his 15th Massachusetts across to the Virginia shore and up the steep face of Ball's Bluff. He was joined by Colonel William R. Lee with two companies of his 20th Massachusetts. The little force set off to attack the enemy camp, as ordered. They found no camp, for there was none, nor did they find Rebel soldiers anywhere. Devens sent off a report of this to General Stone. Devens might then have ended the diversion, but he elected to wait where he was should Stone have further orders. Then Evans discovered the interlopers, and sharp skirmishes began to echo through the woods.

Back at Edwards Ferry, Stone decided it was impractical for him to be directing matters at Ball's Bluff, three miles distant. Devens had reported it quiet there. He turned over the Ball's Bluff force to Colonel Edward D. Baker. He briefed Baker on the situation as he knew it: McCall's division at Dranesville threatened Leesburg from the southeast; Baker was to discover whether it was practical to threaten Leesburg from the east. He left it to Baker's discretion "to retire the troops from the Virginia shore . . . or to pass over re-enforcements in case he found it practicable and the position on the other side strong and favorable. . . ."[13]

Edward Baker was literally a politician in uniform. An old friend of Abraham Lincoln's, he served as a congressman from Illinois, raised and led a regiment in Mexico, then went West, where in 1860 he was elected senator from Oregon. Sumter set him to recruiting again, especially seeking Western adventuring types, and Baker's so-called California brigade was assigned to Stone's division. During the special session just ended Baker had taken the Senate floor in full uniform to denounce secessionists root and branch. Today marked his first war service, and he galloped off to Ball's Bluff to take command there.

Baker arrived about 10:00 a.m. Instead of calling on Devens for an appraisal or crossing to investigate firsthand, he ignored the discretion granted him by Stone and said, "I am going over immediately, with my whole force, to take command." (On later visiting the site, General Alpheus Williams wrote, "One is filled with astonishment that any man of the least military pretentions should have crossed at such a place with such means.") Baker put all his energies into hastening the little flotilla shuttling between the Maryland shore and Harrison's Island, then between island and the Virginia shore. His reinforcements were agonizingly slow — William Lee's 20th Massachusetts, Isaac Wistar's 1st California, Milton Cogswell's 42nd New York.

When Baker finally reached the battlefield about 2:15 that afternoon, the firing was heavy and becoming heavier. Charles Devens, a lawyer in peacetime, felt great relief at Baker's arrival. The Federals were pushed steadily back into a clearing of some 10 acres at the edge of the bluff. The inexperienced Baker mismanaged their deployment, and the Confederates seized all the advantages of position. Henry L. Abbott, 20th Massachusetts, de-

Confederate colonel Nathan Evans (left) and Federal general Charles Stone play a deadly game of bluff at Ball's Bluff, as the routed Yankees attempt to escape across the Potomac.

scribed the Federals' position as barely wide enough for two regiments in line and "a short rifle shot" in depth, "one of the most complete slaughter pens ever devised."

As the Federal battle line collapsed in on itself, Colonel Baker rushed to the front to try and rally the faltering men and was shot dead. Colonel Lee told Devens, "The day is utterly lost; I do not see anything that can be done but to retreat." The 42nd New York's Colonel Cogswell attempted a breakout downstream to Edwards Ferry, where Stone might evacuate them safely. He was stopped in his tracks. Nothing was left now but to fall back down the bluff and try somehow to ferry the men across to Harrison's Island. This led only to further disaster. There were nowhere near enough scows for the task, and then the largest of them capsized and carried a score to their deaths. By Lieutenant Washington A. Roebling's account, "The boats were swamped of course & nearly 100 drowned; those who did not surrender were bayonetted & many drowned in trying to swim over — the river was full of floating dead bodies. . . ."[14]

Until midafternoon of this calamitous day General Stone had little understanding of what was going on at Ball's Bluff. He reported optimistically to McClellan, "I believe this command can occupy Leesburg to-day."

McClellan raised no cautions or objections with Stone. A jumbled head-quarters dispatch confirmed in Stone's mind that on his left McCall's division was threatening Leesburg.

One of Stone's staff, sent to investigate the rising sounds of battle, returned with news of Baker's death, and Stone began to grasp the truth. He relayed the grim report to Washington and hurried to the scene. "I am occupied in preventing further disaster," he wired McClellan; beyond the loss of Baker, he said, several commanders were captured or missing. He added, "Any advance from Dranesville must be made cautiously." Only from McClellan's reply did Stone learn McCall had long since left Dranesville, and the concerted move against Leesburg by their two divisions had been an empty promise.

Initially McClellan insisted that Stone retain a foothold on the Virginia shore at Edwards Ferry, but wiser heads prevailed. General Banks told him, "Opinion of many officers is strongly against any advance now." When the president was shown this dispatch, he endorsed it, "I think Banks & Stone better not *advance at any risk*." McClellan agreed, and went up the river to see to the case for himself. "McClellan was here raising the Devil about matters," Lieutenant Roebling wrote.

Federal casualties came to 82 killed, 158 wounded, and 681 taken prisoner, a total of 921. The officer corps suffered disproportionate losses. Baker was dead, Lieutenant Colonel Wistar (1st California) wounded, and Colonels Cogswell (42nd New York) and Lee (20th Massachusetts) were wounded and captured. Only Colonel Devens (15th Massachusetts) escaped unharmed.[15]

Lincoln followed the Ball's Bluff battle in the telegraph office at McClellan's Washington headquarters. With him were the general, Secretaries Seward and Cameron, and his secretary John Hay. Lincoln expressed concern that his old friend Edward Baker was said to be in the fighting. Then a telegram from General Stone was shown him. He looked stunned as he read it, Hay wrote, and after a moment's silence, with an "expression of awe and grief" he announced, "Colonel Baker is dead." There followed what Hay described as "simple and hearty eulogies" for the fallen senator.[16]

Reaction to Ball's Bluff was muted at first. "It is an obscure story as yet," wrote New York diarist George Templeton Strong on October 23. But soon Senator Baker's death and the severe casualties aroused a clamor. *Frank Leslie's Illustrated Newspaper,* echoing Tennyson on Balaklava, demanded to know who had sent Baker into the "jaws of death," and insisted that "the ignorance or incompetence which directed the attempt is without excuse."

Other papers were just as angry. The Ball's Bluff disaster, coming three months to the day after the Bull Run disaster, inspired much commentary on what that said about the newly proclaimed Army of the Potomac. Before long Ball's Bluff took on a significance far beyond its military outcome.

McClellan quickly declared who was responsible for the defeat. In a circular to his division commanders he wrote, "The disaster was caused by errors committed by the immediate Commander — *not* Genl Stone." He distanced himself from any responsibility, saying he withdrew the troops from "the other side, since they went there without my orders. . . ." He elaborated the point to his wife: "That affair of Leesburg on Monday last was a terrible butchery . . . ; it was entirely unauthorized by me & I am in no manner responsible for it. The man *directly* to blame for the affair was Col Baker who was killed — he was in command, disregarded entirely the instructions he had received from Stone, & violated all military rules & precautions."[17]

That was an accurate-enough appraisal of Edward Baker's command role. He made no initial effort to evaluate the situation, he ignored the option to withdraw granted him by Stone's orders, and having taken the decision to fight and to reinforce, he wasted some four hours supervising the crossing of the reinforcements, a quartermaster's job. When he finally took the command, any orderly withdrawal was next to impossible. In his inexperience, his deployments certainly "violated all military rules & precautions."

On the other hand, McClellan's denial of responsibility was specious. His initial orders to Stone implied that McCall would be close at hand to apply pressure on Leesburg, yet instructions for actual cooperation between the two divisions were lacking. The affair had an off-the-cuff quality about it, confirmed that Sunday when McClellan thought better of his bluff and ordered McCall's division back to its old camps — and then inexplicably neglected to inform Stone of that fact. Alpheus Williams, of Banks's division, nicely summed up the operation: "It was therefore plainly an unpremeditated and unprepared effort, and failed, as nine of ten such hasty affairs will." When Ball's Bluff became a cause célèbre, the dispatches between Stone and headquarters were sealed, and McClellan distanced himself from the distasteful affair.[18]

So it was that with no one else to blame, Charles Stone became the highly visible symbol of the Ball's Bluff debacle. The role and responsibility of army commander McClellan was successfully obscured. Senator Baker's transgressions swiftly transmuted into martyrdom — the hero slain in the front line rallying his troops — with any contrary judgments drowned out amidst the obsequies.

General Stone's primary command error (as it turned out) was to embrace McClellan's vague instructions too enthusiastically. Had he limited his "slight demonstration" to Edwards Ferry, it is likely that the whole affair would have ended harmlessly when he called for further instructions and roused McClellan to reveal he had canceled the mission. Stone believed that by adding a second threat to Leesburg from Ball's Bluff he would carry out McClellan's objective very nicely. False reports — the phantom Rebel camp on Sunday night, the reported quiet at Ball's Bluff on Monday morning — lulled Stone into a false sense of confidence; then events moved too swiftly for him to control.

Stone was appalled by the venomous newspaper reporting on the battle and his part in it. A Baker staff man sent a report of the battle to the *New-York Tribune* that Stone characterized as "the extraordinary production of a fertile imagination." Stone's own report on Ball's Bluff, with its measured criticisms of Baker, was pilfered from his headquarters by a *Tribune* reporter and published on October 30. "I was bound not to care for the barking of newspaper correspondents and editors," said Stone, and in response to the barking he wrote a supplementary report that was more specific in its criticisms of Baker. It was necessitated, he said, by the "persistent attacks made upon me by the friends (so called) of the lamented late Colonel Baker, through the newspaper press. . . ."[19]

Stone's protests and his attempts to set the record straight were confined to army channels and did not become public. He was warned by a McClellan staff man, "Don't write or say anything now. Keep quiet. Your military superiors are attacked." The press, without contradiction, fanned the issue into heat until Congress convened and took over the debate and widened it dramatically.

Charles Stone was old army, a martinet regarding duties and regulations. During his command in Maryland, numbers of runaway slaves would come into the army camps seeking refuge. The administration, intent on keeping slave-state Maryland in the Union, made it policy to order the fugitives returned to their officially loyal masters. Stone carried out the policy to the letter, then went a step beyond. He cautioned the troops against "advising and encouraging insubordination and rebellion among the negro servants in their neighborhood." Violators would face the civil courts, "dealt with as the laws of Maryland prescribe for such offenders."

There was abolitionist sentiment in Stone's command, and a Massachusetts soldier complained to his governor, John A. Andrew, of having to play the part of slave catcher. Governor Andrew wrote to Secretary of War Cameron about this "dirty and despotic work" ordered by General Stone. Massachusetts, he said, "does not send her citizens forth to become the hunters of men. . . ." This rebuke found its way to Stone, and he made bitter complaint. He termed it illegal usurpation of authority "to permit any governor to give orders affecting the discipline of any regiment which the government of the nation has intrusted to my command." This was forwarded to Governor Andrew, and from Andrew the exchange went to the press and to Massachusetts's Senator Charles Sumner . . . and with that the Stone case went spiraling out of control.[20]

Charles Sumner was a dominating figure in the antislavery movement, in the Republican party, and in the Senate of the United States, and from the Senate floor he took aim at Charles Stone. He introduced a resolution "that our national armies shall not be employed in the surrender of fugitive slaves," and announced, "I have a special interest at this moment because Brigadier General Stone has seen fit to impose this vile and unconstitutional duty upon Massachusetts troops." This goad further enraged Stone. He reissued to the troops his general order about not interfering with the return of slaves to their masters, and dashed off an incendiary letter to Senator Sumner. The senator's speech, he wrote, was evidence that while the soldier in the field "is receiving the shot of the public enemy in the front, he is at the same time receiving the vituperation of a well known coward from a safe distance in the rear."[21]

The Ball's Bluff debate was in full flower when Congress convened on December 2, 1861. In the Senate Zachariah Chandler proposed a congressional committee to investigate both Bull Run and Ball's Bluff, "with the power to send for persons and papers." The matter had advanced to a joint committee of the two houses to investigate *any* military defeat when Senator John Sherman — brother of the general — proposed expanding the committee's reach into every aspect of the war, not just battlefield disasters. Thus the Committee on the Conduct of the War, approved by the Senate 33 to 3 and concurred in without debate by the House. The joint committee had seven members, five Republicans and two Democrats, with "Bluff Ben" Wade of Ohio as chairman. The voices of such Radicals as Wade, Chandler, and George W. Julian promised to dominate the committee hearings, and the case of General Charles Stone would in time take on entirely new dimensions.[22]

McClellan evaded responsibility for Ball's Bluff so far as the public was concerned — "The people should be made to thoroughly acquit *him* of the affair," a *Chicago Tribune* correspondent advised his editors — but the Potomac army's singular lack of accomplishment in these months drew increasing criticism. Radical Republicans Wade, Chandler, and Lyman Trumbull joined forces even before Congress convened, to "worry the administration into a battle," as John Hay put it. Hay called them the Jacobin Club, for their whiff of French Revolution politics. Chandler was outraged that the army would go into winter quarters: "If we fail in getting a battle here now all is lost, and up to this time a fight is scarcely contemplated. . . . Washington is safe therefore let the country go to the devil."

On the evening of October 25 the Jacobins met with General McClellan at the home of Postmaster Montgomery Blair. For three hours they dinned their ideas for an ultra war policy into the general's ear. Wade demanded a battle in Virginia immediately, for the sake of Northern morale and to keep up the war effort. "We exhorted him for God's sake to at least push back the defiant traitors." McClellan parried their thrusts by blaming the army's inaction on General Scott. So long as Scott was general-in-chief, he said, his hands were tied.

The next evening the Jacobins took their turn at Lincoln. They reprised the arguments they had used with McClellan. Lyman Trumbull feared that if the generals put the army into winter quarters "with the capital besieged," it would lead to widespread demoralization and the possibility that the Confederacy would be recognized by foreign governments. Chandler told Lincoln that he "was in favor of sending for Jeff Davis *at once,* if *their* views were carried out." While the president defended what he called McClellan's deliberateness, he was concerned.

Afterward he went to McClellan's headquarters and they discussed the Jacobins' message. While the president deprecated the popular impatience for an advance, the "On to Richmond!" cries of the past summer, he warned McClellan that the impatience was real and must be taken into account. "At the same time, General," he said, "you must not fight till you are ready." That was a comfort to McClellan, for it perfectly reflected his own conviction.[23]

"I presume the Scott war will culminate this week," McClellan told Ellen on October 30, "& as it is now very clear that the people will not permit me to be passed over it seems easy to predict the result." In his conceit at having triumphed over the general-in-chief, McClellan made something of a Faustian bargain. Having shed the blame for the army's inaction from his shoulders to Scott's, he left himself without cover or excuse for the future. The Army of the Potomac's course would now be entirely his responsibility.

The next day he wrote Ellen, "I have been at work all day nearly on a letter to the Secy of War in regard to military operations." Lincoln had told
him that Scott's letter of resignation would be accepted on November 1,
and that he would succeed Scott as general-in-chief. As was the case when
he was named head of the Army of the Potomac, the president called on
him for a statement of his plans. In preparing this paper, McClellan remarked, "I have not been home for some 3 hrs, but am 'concealed' at Stanton's to dodge all enemies in shape of 'browsing' Presdt etc." He did not
celebrate this elevation to the nation's highest military posting. "I feel a
sense of relief at the prospect of having my own way untrammelled, but I
cannot discover in my own heart one symptom of gratified vanity or ambition." The way ahead was strewn with roadblocks. "I have a set of scamps
to deal with — unscrupulous & false. . . ." He hoped for God to light his
way. "But it is terrible to stand by & see the cowardice of the Presdt, the
vileness of Seward, & the rascality of Cameron — Welles is an old woman
— Bates an old fool. The only man of courage & sense in the Cabinet is
Blair, & I do not altogether fancy him!"

To help guide him past these unscrupulous scamps, he had sought out
Edwin M. Stanton, and not only for concealment from a browsing president. McClellan intended his paper to put on record "that I have left nothing undone to make this army what it ought to be & that the necessity for
delay has not been my fault." He would as well lay out his conditions for
taking offensive action. Stanton's formidable legal skills could help frame
his arguments. As attorney general, Stanton had tried to brace up Buchanan during the last months of his administration, and his professed
stance as a War Democrat and fervent Unionist attracted him to McClellan. He also professed to share McClellan's contempt for those in the administration attempting to manage the war, and he played a major role in
writing and editing this October 31 paper.[24]

For the Army of the Potomac McClellan laid out two unappealing options: "Either to go into winter quarters, or to assume the offensive with
forces greatly inferior in numbers. . . ." After accounting for those places
requiring garrisons — Washington, Baltimore, the upper and lower Potomac — he counted 76,285 men ready to take the field. Against this field
army he set a phantom enemy army — an army invented by him initially
and since enhanced by largely vacuous intelligence sources. McClellan
awarded the Rebels "a force on the Potomac not less than 150 000 strong
well drilled & equipped, ably commanded & strongly intrenched."

To redress the imbalance, McClellan called for straining every nerve
to direct new forces to the Army of the Potomac. He demanded a halt to

Louis Blenker's largely German division staged a parade by torchlight, with lighted transparencies, before General McClellan's Washington quarters to celebrate his promotion to general-in-chief. Drawing by Alfred Waud, November 3, 1861.

operations elsewhere and the resulting "superfluous strength" sent to him from every department, East and West; "a single will should direct & carry out these plans." He set November 25 as the deadline for his demands. To shut down the war elsewhere in order to double the size of the Army of the Potomac to achieve parity with the enemy host, and to do all this in just twenty-five days, was as deliberate as it was delusional. Clearly, McClellan's real motive was to avoid any offensive movement that winter — while demonstrating (as he told his wife) "that the necessity for delay has not been my fault."[25]

November 1 brought McClellan official notification that he now commanded the nation's armies. That evening Lincoln called on his new general-in-chief. "I should be perfectly satisfied if I thought that this vast increase of responsibility would not embarrass you," he said. Quite the contrary, McClellan replied, "I feel as if several tons were taken from my shoulders today." It was a relief, he said, to know that at last he could deal directly with the president and secretary of war. "Draw on me for all the sense I have, and all the information," Lincoln said. In addition to his present duties as head of the Army of the Potomac, "the supreme command of the army will entail a vast labor upon you." McClellan replied, "I can do it all."[26]

On his first day at work as general-in-chief, McClellan discovered things in a tangle. "I find the 'Army' just about as much disorganized as was the Army of the Potomac when I assumed command," he told Ellen; "— everything at sixes & sevens — no system, no order — perfect chaos." A prime example of perfect chaos was Pathfinder Frémont's Western Department at St. Louis, where incompetence and corruption flourished. Henry Halleck, belatedly arriving from San Francisco, was not at loose ends for long. John Hay wrote on November 7, "They are taking his measure, that they may cut out a piece of work for him to do." Two days later Halleck replaced Frémont in the newly named Department of the Missouri.[27]

Meanwhile a second major command in the Western theater became vacant. William T. Sherman had gone west after Bull Run to serve in Kentucky under Robert Anderson, and when Anderson's health failed Sherman replaced him. Kentucky presented a mare's nest of problems, however, and Sherman's temperament proved unsuited to solving them. He telegraphed McClellan asking to be relieved and returned to his old brigade. McClellan sent Thomas M. Key of his staff to investigate the case. Key believed Sherman suffered from nervous exhaustion, and so McClellan sent him to serve under Halleck where his responsibilities would be less and he might recover his mental balance.

The Kentucky post required a strong administrator, and McClellan recognized that sort was just then commanding a division in the Potomac army—Don Carlos Buell. He hesitated to part with Buell, for he had gone to some trouble to pull him out of General Scott's clutches. But this was a critical position to fill, and on November 9 Buell was ordered to the new Department of the Ohio.

To lead the division vacated by Buell, Erasmus Keyes was advanced from brigade. Keyes was fifty-one, a West Pointer whose original branch was the artillery. He saw antebellum service as Scott's aide and in 1860–61 as Scott's military secretary, and he led a brigade at Bull Run. Keyes, of an older military generation, was not one of McClellan's favorites, in part (Keyes believed) because of his Republican leanings. Seniority gained him his promotion.[28]

Another November addition to the Army of the Potomac's high command was Edwin Vose Sumner. Sumner was old army personified. He was sixty-four and in his forty-third year of active duty. He entered the regular army as a second lieutenant in 1819, led at various times infantry, dragoons, and cavalry, and at last, in 1855, made colonel. In Mexico he won two brevets for gallantry and was wounded at Cerro Gordo. In "Bloody Kansas" in the 1850s, commanding at Fort Leavenworth, he played a largely static role. He headed the Department of the Pacific after Albert Sidney Johnston resigned to go south. When David Twiggs defected, Sumner filled Twiggs's vacated regular-army brigadier general's slot, making him McClellan's senior lieutenant.

Sumner was given command of a new division comprising the brigades of Otis Howard and William H. French, and later of Thomas F. Meagher.

McClellan and his principal generals, taken by Mathew Brady on November 4, 1861. From left: William F. Smith, William B. Franklin, Samuel P. Heintzelman, Andrew Porter, Irvin McDowell, McClellan, George A. McCall, Don Carlos Buell, Louis Blenker, Silas Casey, Fitz John Porter.

White-haired, white-bearded, ramrod-straight, Sumner looked the part and played the part of old-army martinet and drillmaster. He believed in musketry and cold steel. He did not believe in fieldworks — "I think they have a tendency to make the men timid, and do more harm than good." His booming voice echoed across the drill grounds, and the men called him Old Bull, and Bull of the Woods. Otis Howard described his first meeting with Sumner: "As he stood there before me, a tall, spare, muscular frame, I beheld a firm, dignified man," but he found Sumner's kindly eye and courtesy to his juniors (which meant most everyone) disarming.[29]

For the Potomac army's high command, the shortage of trained staff officers, and the inadequacy of many of the regimental officers, was a constant trial. "I have been busy all day," Sam Heintzelman noted in his diary, "though nothing of much importance — details I would not have to attend to with a good staff." George Meade told his wife, "The men are good material and with good officers might readily be moulded into soldiers; but the officers, as a rule, with but very few exceptions, are ignorant, inefficient & worthless." Even after weeding out the worst, "those who take their places are no better." John Reynolds agreed. Volunteers, he wrote, "are un-

der no discipline and with the officers they have can never be disciplined or drilled. I almost despair...."

Phil Kearny was at his wits' end with the volunteer officers of his brigade. He cataloged their sins: "unmitigated indifference of the officers to their men ... the 'shilly-shally' manner in which the colonels promulgate the orders sent to them to execute ... their absolute non-comprehension of the simplest of military axioms." Kearny's method of educating his lieutenants was to intimidate them with his incandescent personality. "It is strange that he makes himself so obnoxious to those under his command," said Heintzelman. Discontent came naturally to Phil Kearny, and he glared at the general commanding. "I blame Gen. McClellan," he wrote. "Instead of maintaining our previous simplicity, he has initiated the forms of European despotism — unnecessary large Staffs & suites with high titles, mingled with foreign princes. The cry of affected exultation at his appearance, mammoth Reviews without meaning — this is the misfortune."[30]

McClellan's method of raising the morale in the Army of the Potomac, and through the press the morale of the home folks as well, was to stage frequent reviews — of brigades, of divisions, of virtually the whole army.

He even staged a review in honor of his wife. Ellen wrote her mother-in-law, "A review was given to *me*. . . . I had a Maj. Genl's salute of seventeen guns given me as we drove in to the ground & altogether we had a very exciting & merry day."

The largest of these army reviews took place at Bailey's Cross Roads, near reclaimed Munson's Hill, on November 20, 1861. Seven divisions, some 65,000 infantrymen, went through their paces, and there were blaring bands and parading cavalry and fifteen batteries firing salutes. The president, the cabinet, the diplomatic corps, and some 20,000 spectators took in the show. *Harper's Weekly* described the scene as "enlivening and brilliant beyond description." McClellan declared that he "never saw so large a Review in Europe so well done — I was completely satisfied & delighted beyond expression."[31]

In addition to drill, in addition to reviews, were special-duty assignments. The Rebels' closing of the Potomac forced the army to collect much of its own forage, and George McCall's division drew the assignment. In November and December McCall's three brigades, under John Reynolds, George Meade, and E.O.C. Ord, took turns venturing into Fairfax County on foraging expeditions. Reynolds's and Meade's efforts proceeded without event, but when Ord's turn came, on December 20, he collided at Dranesville with a Confederate party, under cavalryman J.E.B. Stuart, on the same mission.

Ord was a late addition to the Army of the Potomac. He was a West Pointer with long service in the artillery who found himself stranded at distant Fort Vancouver, Washington Territory, until a friend in a high place rescued him. The friend, Major Julius P. Garesché, was the capable assistant of Adjutant General Thomas — capable enough that people signed what he put in front of them. Major Garesché saw to Ord's promotion in one jump from captain to brigadier general, with orders to report for a Potomac army brigade. On this day at Dranesville Ord showed his fitness for the post.

The fighting lasted two hours, and ended with Stuart beating a hasty retreat. The difference was veteran gunner Ord's handling of his artillery. His battery dominated, blowing up a caisson and (as Stuart admitted) with "every shot of the enemy . . . dealing destruction on either man, limber, or horse." Confederate losses at Dranesville came to 194, including 43 killed. Ord counted 68 casualties. Afterward Meade asked Ord how his infantry had behaved. "He replied," Meade wrote, "*better* than he expected but not so well as they ought — that there was much shirking & running away on the part of both *officers & men.* Still he persuaded 2 regiments to maintain their ground & finally to charge."

General McCall hurried to the scene and reported "the rout of the enemy was complete." Meade thought this outcome might have saved McCall his command. Meade had heard concerning McCall "that McClellan was very anxious to *get rid of him* & only desisted from at once taking away his command by a sense of consideration for his feelings & former reputation." Blunt-talking George Meade considered this unfair to McCall — "With all his weaknesses he is nevertheless as good as most of the other Genls. of Division."

The *New York Herald* termed Dranesville "a splendid little affair." It was the Potomac army's first measurable victory, and while it could not make up for Bull Run or Ball's Bluff, it was a step in the right direction. It demonstrated that with leadership green troops would fight. In a first action "shirking & running" was to be expected, but Ord got them to stand their ground and to charge.[32]

The tangles in the Western commands that winter only confirmed McClellan's determination to hold his fire. It was clear from Halleck's and Buell's dispiriting reports that neither was ready to advance and certainly neither had any "superfluous strength" to send to McClellan to enable *him* to advance. In his strategy papers, McClellan emphasized Virginia as the paramount theater of war, and while describing the Confederate army on the Potomac as 150,000 strong, he gave no hint of his own strategy for how or where (or when) he would bring that army to battle.[33]

McClellan also remained firm in his belief that the war must be conducted in as humane a fashion as possible if the nation was ever to be truly reunited. Peter H. Watson of the War Department reported a conversation with McClellan soon after he became general-in-chief. Watson argued that no arranged peace was possible with the Rebels; that they were in earnest and the war would have to be prosecuted even to the point of subjugation. McClellan differed. "He thought we ought to avoid harshness and violence — that we should conduct the war so as to avoid offence as far as possible." If subjugation became the war's object, said McClellan, he would feel obliged to lay down his arms.

He expressed a like sentiment on limiting the war's objectives. E. D. Townsend of the adjutant general's office recorded McClellan's remark "that if the Government expected him to fight with the South *to free the slaves,* they would be mistaken, for he would not do it." Writing his confidant Samuel L. M. Barlow, McClellan explained, "*I* am fighting to preserve the integrity of the Union & the power of the Govt — on no other issue. To gain that end we cannot afford to raise up the negro question — it must be incidental & subsidiary." On this matter he said he was in step with Lincoln. "The Presdt is perfectly honest & is really sound on the nigger question — I will answer for it now that things go right with him."[34]

McClellan's seeming respect for Lincoln was a mercurial thing, however. Five days after the general-in-chief's favorable comment in writing to Barlow, Lincoln, his secretary John Hay, and Secretary of State Seward paid an evening call at McClellan's quarters. An orderly said the general was attending a wedding and they said they would wait. After an hour McClellan returned and, in Hay's words, "without paying any particular attention to the porter who told him the President was waiting to see him, went up stairs," passing the doorway of the room where the visitors waited. After half an hour the orderly was sent to remind the general of his guests, "and the answer came that the General had gone to bed."

"I merely record this unparallelled insolence of epaulettes without comment," Hay entered in his diary. Lincoln did not seem bothered by the snubbing (indeed, the second such snubbing in a little over a month), remarking that "it was better at this time not to be making points of etiquette & personal dignity." McClellan's arrogant temper was still on him a few days later when he wrote Ellen of a White House function "where I found 'the *original gorrilla*,' about as intelligent as ever. What a specimen to be at the head of our affairs now!"[35]

The president might not be overly concerned about etiquette, but he was decidedly concerned about getting answers from his new general-in-chief. When November passed with no discussion or plan or promise of an advance, he sent McClellan an interrogatory. What he had in mind was a particular strategy — a turning movement against the Confederate army entrenched at Manassas. This idea had been floating around army headquarters since July, when Sam Heintzelman proposed it as an alternative to McDowell's plan for fighting at Manassas. Possibly Lincoln had seen this memorandum; possibly he simply studied a map, for it was obvious that the weakness of Johnston's position was his railroad supply line.

Lincoln's idea was to cut the Orange & Alexandria south of Manassas Junction by assembling a force on the Occoquan River, 15 miles south of Alexandria, and marching west from there another 20 miles to seize the railroad. He would move part of the turning force by water up the Occoquan and the rest overland, leaving sufficient strength to mask the Manassas position. If either force was attacked, the other could take the attackers in the rear. "Both points will probably not be successfully resisted at the same time." He called on McClellan for the numbers available for such a movement, and asked, "How *long* would it require to actually get in motion?"

General McClellan's self-esteem would hardly allow him to embrace a plan of campaign from a civilian, even if (or especially if) the civilian was the commander-in-chief. In any case, he had long since looked at the Occoquan turning movement and rejected it as inadequate to his grander vision of one great war-ending campaign.

On December 10 he returned the president's interrogatory with the blanks filled in. He gave the total of the two Federal forces Lincoln proposed as 104,000 men, and said the movement might commence between December 15 and 25. Then to quash the idea he called up the phantom Rebel army. Recent information, he said, "leads me to believe that the enemy could meet us in front with equal forces *nearly*." That meant, in his awkward phrasing, taking the grave risk of dividing in half the 104,000-man Potomac army in the face of an equal force *nearly* (100,000, say) "in front" at Manassas, then finding the 52,000-man turning column facing an equal force *nearly* on the Occoquan — in short, violating conventional wisdom by dividing one's army when outnumbered three to two by one's opponent.

(The actual numbers, McClellan's 104,000 versus Johnston's 44,000, suggest the wisdom of the Occoquan plan as step one in a war-winning strategy. Of all McClellan's potential chances to crush or cripple his foe, none was missed by a greater margin than this.)

McClellan softened his rejection with an alternative. "I have now my mind actively turned towards another plan of campaign that I do not think at all anticipated by the enemy nor by many of our own people."

In the ten days between receiving Lincoln's interrogatory and responding to it, McClellan discussed this new "plan of campaign" with his chief engineer, John G. Barnard. McClellan's was a wider and more dramatic turning movement than Lincoln's Occoquan plan, and its target was not the Confederate army but the Confederate capital. The Army of the Potomac would advance by water to the little tobacco port of Urbanna, some 15 miles up the Rappahannock River. From there it was about 50 miles south by west to Richmond — one day's march to the York River, two days' march hence to the Rebel capital, said McClellan. If secrecy held, if cavalry destroyed the railroad bridges between Manassas Junction and Richmond,

"MASTERLY INACTIVITY," OR SIX MONTHS ON THE POTOMAC.

As the military stalemate in the East stretched from 1861 into 1862, an artist for *Frank Leslie's Illustrated Newspaper* labeled the period "Masterly Inactivity." McClellan (left) and Beauregard glare at each other and snowball fights rage across the Potomac.

he was confident his army could beat Joe Johnston's to Richmond. There he would fight the showdown battle, preferably defensively, on ground of his own choosing.

When sketched on a map the scheme looked attractive, for nowhere did it encounter a fortified enemy. But General Barnard was taken aback. He described the plan as "impractical, if not otherwise imprudent." There were any number of serious transportation problems to be overcome, with the Confederate batteries on the lower Potomac and the safety of Washington of paramount concern. He wondered how long a movement of 100,000 men could be kept secret. Between Urbanna and Richmond there was a swamp and three rivers to cross, making it highly unlikely that the Federals would win the race. Indeed he feared for both the practicality and the security of the landing ground at Urbanna. In retrospect, Barnard questioned "whether such a scheme could really have been soberly entertained."

Privately, Barnard was appalled that McClellan had meekly allowed things to come to such a pass, especially the blockade of the Potomac:

"Who was George B. McClellan — a young man unknown to fame — that this whole country should wait for ⅔'d of a year for some stupendous thing which he would *ultimately do,* while the enemy in numbers vastly inferior was shutting us up in our very Capital! Bah!"[36]

However that may be, it seems that after his response to Lincoln's interrogatory, McClellan further discussed his Urbanna plan at least in general outline with the president, for Lincoln wanted him to explain it to Secretary of the Treasury Chase. Chase complained of having trouble raising money for a war seemingly stuck on dead center, and would welcome assurance that an advance by the Potomac army was imminent. McClellan called on Chase on December 12 and outlined his Urbanna strategy. As Chase remembered the conversation, "Nothing but great energy and great secrecy could insure the success of such a movement, but with these its success seemed certain." Chase said existing financing should hold until mid-February 1862; McClellan assured him "that the whole movement would be accomplished before the 1st of that month." At a subsequent meeting "of leading capitalists" in New York, Chase pledged "my entire confidence in our young general, and my certain assurance that we were to have no going into winter quarters."[37]

General McClellan was bearing false witness, however. As early as December 2 George Meade was writing his wife, "We are not positively informed that we are in winter quarters, but the men are allowed to make themselves as comfortable as they can. I can not say I am pleased with this — to remain inactive for 4 months. . . ." Secretary Chase, two weeks after his meeting with McClellan, found nothing whatever being done to carry out the promised movement.

Nor would anything be done. On December 23 the general, scheduled to be the first witness before the Committee on the Conduct of the War, was too ill to testify. Doctors diagnosed his condition as typhoid fever. On the 27th the president told a visitor that General McClellan "is now quite sick," and under date of December 31 a *New-York Tribune* reporter wrote, "Gen. McClellan is worse today, much worse. The danger of typhoid fever is unconcealed." There was speculation about a successor, he added.

Mr. Lincoln dropped by Quartermaster General Meigs's office to pour out his troubles. "General, what shall I do?" he asked. "The people are impatient; Chase has no money and he tells me he can raise no more; the General of the Army has typhoid fever. The bottom is out of the tub. What shall I do?"[38]

5. *Grand Army, Grand Campaign*

GENERAL McCLELLAN'S TYPHOID FEVER did not prove to be life-threatening but it was debilitating, and for three weeks — the last week of December to mid-January 1862 — he was hors de combat. The uncertainty of the disease and the method used to treat it lent a sense of near-crisis to the period. "The Genl, it seems, is very reticent," Attorney General Bates noted on December 31. "Nobody knows his plans. The Sec of war and the President himself are kept in ignorance of the actual condition of the army and the intended movements of the General — if indeed they intend to move at all. . . ."

The press reported McClellan's chief of staff (and father-in-law) Randolph Marcy also had typhoid, and that both were being treated by homeopathic physicians. Homeopathy was widely regarded as quackery. General Meade thought McClellan's choice of doctors "has astonished all his friends, and very much shaken the opinion of many in his claimed extraordinary judgment." Meade blamed it on the foolish doings of the Marcys, disciples of homeopathy, and noted that McClellan's brother John, a prominent physician in Philadelphia, "is very indignant & says he will never enter his brother's house again."[1]

McClellan's inability to testify before the Committee on the Conduct of the War on December 23 inflicted a check to his fortunes. Had he invested his case with the authority of his position, and addressed concerns over the seeming lack of progress, he might have defused the committee's prospective hostility. Instead, Chairman Ben Wade called in McClellan's place his lieutenants. Their testimony revealed fissures in the Potomac army's high command and raised questions about McClellan as a military executive.

The first day's testimony, on December 24, by Sam Heintzelman and Israel Richardson, made it clear that the general commanding paid little heed to the army's old guard. After McClellan arrived in Washington, Heintzelman entered in his diary, "I have been several times to see Gen. McClellan, but he is hard to see & two weeks ago I thought he stood on his dignity, so I have not been to see him since." Heintzelman told the committee that little had changed since.

Samuel Heintzelman, fifty-six, bloodied at Bull Run, gnarled and feisty and talkative, was a general full of ideas who could not get anyone to listen. He was first to propose the turning movement against Manassas by way of the Occoquan. He proposed a strike at Norfolk, where the *Merrimack* was metamorphosing into the *Virginia*. He proposed taking Fort Monroe as a base for advancing up the James and York rivers to open the way to Richmond. All met the same fate: "McClellan had not noticed those I left for him with the Chief of his staff, Marcy." Heintzelman was asked if McClellan had ever called a meeting or council of his generals. He replied that he had not, and thought there would be no harm in his doing so — to listen to "the ideas of men of some experience." Asked about the size of the Rebel army, he displayed a streak of common sense rare in this army: "I think their force is very much overestimated, very much indeed. . . . Occasionally we get a man from their lines, but I have very little confidence in what they tell us."[2]

Israel Richardson, who had pitched into the Blackburn's Ford fight preliminary to Bull Run, testified he knew nothing of councils of war, had no idea of the force of the enemy, and had heard nothing from the general commanding. He had led infantry in Mexico and appeared content to lead infantry in this war, and said the men he trained were as good soldiers as any the Rebels had. Chairman Wade, pressing for a battle before winter set in, asked him the best way to boost morale — "By laying in camp" or "by smelling a little powder?" Richardson did not bite on that, but he had opinions when asked about volunteer cavalry. Regular cavalry, he insisted, was quite sufficient for cavalry's traditional duties as advanced guards and to carry reports and messages. Volunteer cavalry was "worse than nothing at all." He would auction off their horses and turn them into infantrymen, "whereas they are now good for nothing." "Fighting Dick" Richardson's heart was with the foot soldier.

A third old-guard general, George McCall, answered "No, sir," when asked if he "counselled with the general-in-chief in regard to an expedition of any kind against the enemy." McCall counted the Rebel army as 180,000, saying this was the thinking at headquarters "whence I learned it." He gave no opinions that might get him into trouble at headquarters, where he knew he was not admired.[3]

Other testimony revealed McClellan's favorites among his lieutenants. When William Franklin was asked how often McClellan "consulted the principal officers of his army upon the subject of the prosecution of the war," he replied, speaking only for himself, that he and the general consulted quite often. He acknowledged knowing something of McClellan's plans, and Chairman Wade pounced. Would he disclose what he knew to the committee? "We are all sworn to secrecy." Franklin said this was told him in confidence. He was asked for his own strategic views. In this disguise he hinted at what McClellan favored (and did not favor) about an advance. Were he in command he would reject any movement "to the left of Manassas" — the Occoquan plan — and instead move by water to the Rappahannock or the York — the Urbanna plan. Were this done rapidly and secretly, the enemy at Manassas "would be bound to evacuate their position there and go down to Richmond . . . and fight us there just where we pleased."

Per McClellan's staff, said Franklin, the enemy had 180,000 to 200,000 men between Richmond and Washington. He spoke of the shipping needed for a change of base, of the risk of a premature attack on the batteries blockading the Potomac ("It might turn out to be another Bull Run"), and Ben Wade grew agitated. The war's cost would soon reach $600 million, and he saw nothing accomplished "commensurate with the exertions the nation has made." If McClellan was a Bonaparte or a Wellington, "then we could repose upon him with confidence. But how can this nation abide the secret counsels that one man carries in his head, when we have no evidence that he is the wisest man in the world?" General Franklin had no answer for that.

McClellan's closest army confidant, Fitz John Porter, went before the committee with a chip on his shoulder. He showed little tolerance for these civilian interrogators. When Wade asked his opinion about whether the army should go into winter quarters or "attempt an enterprise to dislodge the enemy," Porter rejected the question. "I decline giving any information whatever in relation to future movements." His testimony was marked by "I decline to answer." So far as the committee could learn, of all his generals McClellan spoke only with William Franklin and Fitz John Porter. "It does seem to me that you military gentlemen would do well to compare opinions upon these matters," Wade advised.[4]

Irvin McDowell's testimony was everything Porter's was not. He was forthcoming with his answers and respectful of the committee's inquiry. While not privy to McClellan's plans, "I have had my own general views upon the subject, which I have expressed to him." He sprinkled his narrative with references to military history and the variables of the military art — his testimony ran to fifteen pages in the printed record — and it was obvious that the committee regarded him as a model witness.[5]

Augustus Tholey's lithograph eulogizes McClellan's high-command sway over the Union army. From left: Otis Howard, Phil Kearny, George Thomas, Ambrose Burnside, Winfield Scott Hancock, Winfield Scott, McClellan, William Rosecrans, Joe Hooker, Lew Wallace, Ben Butler, George Custer, and John Logan.

Wade might claim committee members were sworn to secrecy, but the seal of confidentiality was easily broken. It was leaked to the *New-York Tribune* that the committee was hamstrung by the generals' refusal to reveal anything of McClellan's plans. The committee was limited to summoning witnesses and making recommendations to the Congress and the executive . . . and (it seemed) to the press. Committeemen were not shy delivering recommendations. On December 31 they called on Lincoln. Wade was unsparing: "You are murdering your country by inches in consequence of the inactivity of the military." (Lincoln sent a note to McClellan in his sickroom, saying he found the committee "in a perfectly good mood" and he should not be uneasy about its investigations — intending, no doubt, to soothe the general's fevered brow.)

A week later the committee met again with the president, this time with the cabinet present. No words were minced. Wade and his colleagues called for McDowell's promotion to major general so he might supersede McClellan as head of the Army of the Potomac. Secretary Chase defended his protégé as "the best man for the place he held known to me," but admitted McClellan tasked himself too severely. He should delegate some of the burdens of command by consulting freely with his lieutenants, "communicating to them full intelligence of his own plans of action, so that, in the event of sickness or accident to himself" army movements would not be delayed. Lincoln said that he would call on McClellan for his views.[6]

In fact the president had already determined to take a direct hand in military affairs. He sought status reports from the two Western theater commanders, Don Carlos Buell and Henry Halleck, only to learn that neither was close to being ready to advance, in concert or separately. He endorsed Halleck's response, "It is exceedingly discouraging. As everywhere else, nothing can be done." It appeared, in the two months since becoming general-in-chief, that McClellan had done as little to get the war off dead center in the West as in the East. The president sent to the Library of Congress for a copy of Halleck's manual *Elements of Military Art and Science.*[7]

Quartermaster General Meigs, in response to Lincoln's plaint that the bottom was out of the tub, suggested the president consult with some of McClellan's lieutenants. If the enemy was as strong as McClellan insisted, there was danger of an attack, and the need to "select the responsible commander for such an event." On January 10, 1862, Lincoln convened an ad hoc evening war council at the White House.

Present were Secretaries Seward and Chase, Thomas A. Scott of the War Department, and Generals McDowell and Franklin. Lincoln recounted the trials of the moment — straitened conditions at the Treasury, loss of public credit, the Jacobinism of Congress, the delicate condition of foreign relations, bad news from the Western theater, and (according to McDowell's notes) "more than all, the sickness of General McClellan." He had been to McClellan's quarters but could not see him; "if General McClellan did not want to use the army, he would like to '*borrow it*,' provided he could see how it could be made to do something." For that, he pressed the two generals.

McDowell was ready with a plan. His was an elaborated version of Sam Heintzelman's (and Lincoln's) Occoquan plan. He would form the Potomac army's divisions into four corps. Three corps would confront the enemy at Centreville and Manassas. The fourth "would operate on his right flank, beyond the Occoquan . . ." So soon as the Confederates left their fortifications to defend their railroad lifeline, "we must succeed by repeated blows in crushing out the force in our front, even if it were equal in numbers and strength." (McDowell did not buy into McClellan's phantom Rebel army.)

The president asked Franklin what he would do with the command. He said he would take the army "to York River to operate on Richmond." Such a movement would require shipping, and Tom Scott said the War Department was fully taxed to furnish transports for just the 12,000 men of a recent coastal incursion at Port Royal, South Carolina. On that sobering statistic Lincoln adjourned the war council. He told McDowell and Franklin to consult with the army staffs on an advance and then to meet again the following evening.[8]

McDowell and Franklin spent January 11 at the staff departments — Quartermaster's, Commissary, Ordnance — documenting resources for the two plans. Franklin asked, Should they not clear all this with General McClellan? McDowell said they were assigned by the commander-in-chief, but to assuage Franklin's concerns he sought out Secretary Chase. Chase said it was a matter of direct orders from the president. He also revealed what McClellan had told him in December of his Urbanna plan, furnishing more data to the two generals.

Another caller on Secretary Chase that day was Edwin Stanton, and Chase described to him the ongoing war council at the White House. Stanton had earlier gained access to McClellan's sickroom to warn him that the Radicals were counting on his death and "already dividing among themselves your military goods and chattels." Ever the opportunist, Stanton scurried to the general's bedside to alert him that the process was fully underway.

That evening the council met again, with one addition, Postmaster Montgomery Blair. McDowell read a paper setting out the two plans — his, keeping the army's base at Washington and launching a turning movement against Manassas; and Franklin's (as proxy for McClellan), shifting to a new base on the lower Chesapeake and advancing on Richmond by way of the York River. McDowell argued that the York route was sure to be heavily defended and would require a siege train and a great deal of water transport. "I do not think a move by water of so large a force as I deem necessary could be counted upon under a month." Franklin admitted that if the Army of the Potomac "was to be moved *at once,* it would be better to march it into Virginia than to transport it by vessels."

Seward said that what was needed was a victory anywhere. Chase thought victory would be better achieved against the Rebel army just 25 miles away; beyond risking time and money, "we should have as many difficulties to overcome below as we now have above." Montgomery Blair spoke for the York River route. Blair was the one cabinet member with a military background—he graduated West Point in 1835 and served in the Seminole War before giving up his commission for the law—and he was listened to with respect. Blair wanted the Army of the Potomac based on the Virginia Peninsula, from which to strike at Norfolk and at Richmond. He thought the difficulties of changing the army's base overdrawn. He said the plan "of going to the front from this position was Bull Run over again." For a change of base, Lincoln wanted to hear from Quartermaster General Meigs, and asked the council to reconvene the next day, the 12th.[9]

To the council that Sunday Meigs explained that to change the army's base to the lower Chesapeake would require four to six weeks to collect the transports to move the first 30,000 men. The discussion seemed to favor a more immediate move on Manassas. Lincoln announced that General McClellan had come to see him that morning and would soon resume command, and that he would join them on Monday for a final council meeting. That evening, to Senator Orville H. Browning, the president remarked, perhaps not entirely in jest, that he was thinking of taking the field himself.

The January 13 gathering at the White House was tense and difficult. McClellan's attitude bordered on the childish. He visibly sulked through Lincoln's explanation that it was simply concern over his lingering illness that had produced the informal war council. McDowell outlined the results of his and Franklin's study of plans for an advance. McClellan responded curtly, "You are entitled to have any opinion you please!" and resumed his sulk. Meigs described the scene: "All looked to McClellan, who sat still with his head hanging down, and mute. The situation grew awkward."

Meigs pulled his chair close to McClellan's and whispered that he should say at least something about an advance; could he not promise some movement against Manassas? "I cannot move on them with as great a force as they have," McClellan said. How many have they? Meigs asked. "Not less than 175,000 according to my advices," McClellan said, and when Meigs repeated that Lincoln expected something from him, he said, "If I tell him my plans they will be in the New York Herald tomorrow morning. He can't keep a secret, he will tell them to Tad." Tad was Lincoln's eight-year-old son.

Finally Chase asked McClellan directly what he planned to do with the army, and when. McClellan replied that it was unclear what forces he could count on, that coordination with the Western armies was essential.

He said he was unwilling to discuss specific plans in such a gathering — the fewer who knew military secrets, the better — and would only do so if ordered by the president. At that, Franklin heard Chase mutter, "Well, if that is Mac's decision, he is a ruined man." Lincoln asked if he had at least matured in his own mind a plan and when it might commence. McClellan said he had. Then, said the president, "I will adjourn this meeting." By Meigs's account, Lincoln "yielded in despair to his wilful General."[10]

This series of meetings on January 10–13, 1862, importantly changed — or hardened — attitudes. Lincoln, while relinquishing the reins to the recovering McClellan, realized he must closely monitor his stubbornly uncooperative general and press him for information and for action. It marked a turning point. Thereafter nothing would come easy in the relationship of president and commanding general.

McClellan's performance was inexplicable. His audience was far from hostile. Indeed, Chase and Blair were his two influential advocates in the cabinet, Seward supported an advance of any sort, and Meigs and Thomas Scott were sympathetic to his logistical needs. No harm could come from outlining strategy in front of his lieutenants McDowell and Franklin. Commander-in-Chief Lincoln had every right and reason to know how and when McClellan intended to implement that strategy. Instead of seizing the moment to rally support, McClellan's response was yet another example of his especial "insolence of epaulettes" (as John Hay had put it). For McClellan it was opportunity lost . . . and never regained. As his hitherto ally Chase would write, "I had now so far lost confidence in him, that I was convinced a change ought to be made."

McClellan would now view Lincoln and the administration more contemptuously than ever. He found civilian control of the military all but intolerable. He assigned McDowell to his growing list of enemies, convinced he had originated these January meetings "hoping to succeed me in command." McClellan was even suspicious of William Franklin, who "might have insisted upon my being informed of what was going on."[11]

A second occurrence on January 13 produced a major impact on McClellan, and on the Potomac army's officer corps — Edwin M. Stanton succeeded Simon Cameron as secretary of war. Cameron was a graduate of rough-edged Pennsylvania politics whose skills had not translated into managing the War Department. Stanton was one of Cameron's sharpest critics, complaining that "arms, clothing, transportation, provisions, are each and all subjects of peculation and spoil." Lincoln termed Cameron

Arthur Lumley sketched the new secretary of war, Edwin Stanton, hosting a reception for generals and staff officers at the War Department on January 20, 1862. From left: Stewart Van Vliet, George Sykes, Stanton, McClellan, Daniel Sickles, Irvin McDowell, Lorenzo Thomas, Seth Williams, and George Stoneman.

"incapable either of organizing details or conceiving and advising general plans." Replacing him signaled another presidential effort to get the war off dead center.

Edwin Stanton was a chameleon-like figure, taking the coloration of whatever politics or faction or major figure best served his purposes. As Buchanan's attorney general he played a fiercely Unionist Democrat in a divided cabinet. For the Lincoln administration he advised such disparate Republicans as William Seward and Salmon Chase. When his nomination went before the Senate, he easily won over Republican lawmakers. "He is just the man we want," said the Radical William Pitt Fessenden. "We agree on every point: The duties of the Secretary of War, the conduct of the war, the negro question, and everything else."[12]

McClellan, in contrast, took Stanton as a fellow conservative Democrat who shared his scorn for the president, the cabinet, and ultras of every stripe. McClellan's appeal to Stanton was his posting. "I believe the life of the Republic depends on that man," Stanton predicted. McClellan wrote his confidant Samuel Barlow, "Stanton's appointment was a most unexpected piece of good fortune, & I hope it will produce a good effect in the North." He wrote Randolph Marcy, "Stanton's appointment has helped me

infinitely thus far, & will still more in the future." In expressing these sentiments McClellan had yet to experience Stanton's inconstancy and his bull-
dog inner nature. Sam Ward, a Washington lobbyist who bore scars from
the sharp edges of Stanton's temperament, labeled him "a dangerous foe —
a sleuthhound sort of man who never lost his scent or slackened his purpose." Stanton quickly took aim at the Potomac army. "This army has got
to fight or run away," he told an editor; "the champagne and oysters on the
Potomac must be stopped."[13]

Stanton had introduced McClellan to Malcolm Ives, correspondent for
James Gordon Bennett's *New York Herald,* in a plot to gain support from
the nation's largest newspaper. One day after complaining at the White
House war council that Lincoln was sure to leak army secrets to the *Herald*
(and to eight-year-old Tad), McClellan leaked those secrets to Malcolm
Ives . . . of the *Herald.* "What I declined communicating to them," he told
Ives, "I am now going to convey through you to Mr. Bennett. . . . I am going to give you *all* the knowledge I possess myself, with no reserve. . . ." He
instructed Randolph Marcy to see Bennett personally to assure him, "I am
anxious to keep Mr B. well posted & wish to do it fully."

Ives described McClellan as "guileless and innocent as a child," but this
guilelessness of McClellan's was actually guile, and he manipulated Ives for
his own purposes — to flatter Bennett into editorial backing and, in particular, to paper over his own difficulties with the Committee on the Conduct of the War.[14]

On January 15 McClellan sent a note to Lincoln saying he was going
before the committee and hoped to "escape alive." Interviewing McClellan afterward, Ives's reportage overflowed with bonhomie. He wrote that
Chairman Wade told the general he was "exceedingly anxious to sustain
him." To the committee's concerns, McClellan replied that he "thoroughly
appreciated the embarrassments referred to," promised action soon, "and
the interview ended in a manner satisfactory to all parties." Wade and
Zach Chandler recalled it rather differently. When asked why he had not
advanced against Manassas, the general explained there were too few Potomac bridges to ensure a line of retreat. Chandler retorted, "If I understand you correctly, before you strike at the rebels you want to be sure of
plenty of room so that you can run in case they strike back." Wade added,
"Or in case you get scared."[15]

Wade and his colleagues may have found General McClellan an elusive
target, but General Charles Stone was a different matter. Ball's Bluff had
inspired Congress to form the Committee on the Conduct of the War, and
its members felt duty-bound to uncover responsibility for the death there

of Senator-Colonel Baker, one of their own. The first Ball's Bluff witnesses added little to the newspapers' indictment of Stone. Stone himself, testifying on January 5, hewed to his battle reports. This testimony might have marked the end of it, with Stone slandered by the press and the committee but retaining his command. Then, starting on January 10, came a parade of witnesses bearing tales impugning not Stone's military conduct but his loyalty.

Leading the parade was Colonel George W. B. Tompkins, 2nd New York militia. His regiment had not been at Ball's Bluff, but Tompkins had a tale to tell anyway. He claimed General Stone trafficked with the enemy, exchanging sealed packages under flags of truce, communicating with Rebel officers. Maryland secessionists, he said, had a "good opinion generally" of Stone. Tompkins and his men no longer wanted to serve under him. "No confidence in his skill as a general, or in his loyalty?" coached Chairman Wade. "Both," said Tompkins. He was followed by other 2nd New York officers — ten of the thirty-six witnesses at the inquiry were from this regiment — who parroted his testimony. These statements had two characteristics in common: The supposed evidence was undocumented and entirely hearsay; and the presentations were well rehearsed. It was in fact a conspiracy to bring down Charles Stone.

At Bull Run the 2nd New York had balked, Colonel Tompkins being charged with "misbehavior before the enemy" in refusing to obey an attack order. When Stone inherited the regiment, he cracked down hard. To Tompkins's misbehavior charge Stone had since added a charge of filing a false muster, a fraud designed to gain the pay of nonexistent soldiers. Two of Tompkins's officers were also under charge by Stone, one for filing a false muster, the other for falsifying quartermaster records. Both had to be released from arrest to testify.

The committee ignored this perjury, even after McClellan informed it of the pending "disgraceful charges" against Tompkins and his fellows. Nor was it moved by testimony that Stone's dealings with the enemy were proper under truce flags. The "sealed packages," for example, were letters and provisions for the Ball's Bluff prisoners. The committee had ruled: Charles Stone was not only an apologist for slavery (as Governor Andrew and Senator Sumner portrayed him) but (now revealed) for secession as well. At Ball's Bluff the martyred Baker was a sacrifice to Stone's treason.[16]

At the first whiff of disloyalty the committee rushed its case against Stone to incoming Secretary of War Stanton. Stanton appeared to regard the Stone affair as a test of his fealty to Wade, Chandler, and company. On January 28 he sent an order to McClellan to have Charles Stone relieved of

Brigadier General Charles Stone was the victim of a witch-hunt carried out by the congressional Committee on the Conduct of the War.

his command and arrested. Stanton issued the order without a glance at the alleged evidence in the committee testimony.

Before acting on the arrest order, McClellan urged Chairman Wade to permit Stone to meet the charges against him. On January 31 Stone came before the committee a second time. The session was a farce. Wade refused to let Stone see the testimony impeaching him. He offered a general summation of the accusations, and Stone could only answer in generalities. On military matters he was handicapped by McClellan's ban on revealing any Ball's Bluff orders issued from headquarters. On the matter of his loyalty Stone was utterly disbelieving that it could be questioned — he who had almost single-handedly rendered Washington safe in those perilous early months of 1861. To question his loyalty, said Stone, "is one humiliation I had hoped I never should be subjected to." Wade was unmoved, and sent Stanton a further report of "conflict of testimony" in the Stone case.

In talking with one of Stone's officers, McClellan remarked of the committee, "They want a victim." The officer agreed: "Yes — and when they have once tasted blood, got one victim, no one can tell who will be the next victim!" McClellan was in a quandary. He had acquitted Stone of any military wrongdoing at Ball's Bluff, and he surely did not doubt his loyalty.

Yet just as surely, he suspected the Wade Committee was casting him as its next victim. McClellan might claim Stanton's appointment "has helped me infinitely thus far," yet he stood unwilling to spend any of that capital in argument with the new secretary of war. He threw Charles Stone to the dogs.

He did so using an Allan Pinkerton report of a refugee from Leesburg who claimed he had overheard Confederate officers praising Stone as "a fine man" and "a brave man and a gentleman." Saying the man's statement "tended to corroborate some of the charges made against General Stone," McClellan handed Pinkerton's report to Stanton. The arrest order was executed. On February 10 Charles Stone was lodged in solitary confinement in Fort Lafayette on New York Harbor.[17]

Stone was imprisoned for more than six months. His every attempt to learn the charges against him and to gain a hearing ran up against the malevolent secretary of war. In violation of the Articles of War, no charges of any kind were brought against him. Lawyer Stanton had no intention of bringing a hearsay case to court-martial. Instead, he offered up General Stone to public view as an example of what could happen in this war to a West Pointer, a Democrat, who (it was said) was soft on slavery and trafficked with secessionists. Only the dedicated efforts of Stone's civilian supporters finally persuaded Congress to pass legislation that led to his release, in August 1862.

When the Committee on the Conduct of the War's report and Ball's Bluff testimony was published in 1863, the New York Times editorialized, "The whole chapter, from beginning to end, has been as impenetrable as the veil of Isis. There was something behind, but that was all that could be made out. . . . As it is, Gen. Stone has sustained a most flagrant wrong — a wrong which will probably stand as the worst blot on the National side in the history of the war."[18]

That was one year later. In February 1862 the newspapers painted Charles Stone's alleged treachery and his imprisonment in the darkest of hues. The Times summed up a listing of Stone's transgressions, leaked by the Wade Committee, as "treasonable complicity with the rebels." Particularly telling, said the paper, was testimony against Stone by his own men. Washington's Elizabeth Blair Lee was appalled "that my country has produced another Arnold & worse." In New York, diarist George Templeton Strong reported widespread astonishment at the arrest. He recalled Stone's creditable work in Washington a year earlier, but wondered if all the censure and abuse by the press after Ball's Bluff might have left Stone "disgusted with the cause of the country. . . ." Attorney General Bates feared a precedent "for congressional interference with the command of the army, which might lead to the terrible results seen in France, in the days of the revolution."[19]

Stone's arrest cast a long and lasting shadow over the Potomac army's officer corps. The generals were shocked and outraged and alarmed. "I dont believe he is disloyal," Heintzelman told his diary, and as to General McClellan, "I dont think that he took a sufficiently decided stand under the circumstances. It is the greatest outrage. . . ." Phil Kearny also thought McClellan failed to stand by his lieutenant. "He has *sacrificed* Stone, either under undue political pressure, or to cover a threatened inquiry as to Balls Bluff." Captain Henry Abbott, who fought at Ball's Bluff, wrote that to question Stone's capability was one thing, but to doubt his loyalty "is simply ridiculous. I wouldn't send a private to the guard house on such absurd charges as have been trumped up to enable Charles Sumner to have a gentleman dragged away in the night . . ." Marsena Patrick of the inspector general's office agreed as to the source of Stone's ordeal: "There is no doubt that Stone has been sacrificed to the malevolence of Senator Sumner and his clique of abolitionists."

George Meade saw the Stone persecution as part of a larger pattern that winter. Horace Greeley's *New-York Tribune,* he wrote, "is becoming more violent & open in its attacks on McClellan & all regular officers." So far as these ultras in the press and in the Congress were concerned, "the more violent they become, the more open and bold, the sooner the question of putting them down or yielding to them will have to be settled." Brigadier William Burns congratulated Ohio's Samuel S. Cox for his speech in the House "against Greeley in his partisan, fanatical, ignorant onslaught against McClellan & the Army."[20]

As new commander of Stone's division McClellan picked John Sedgwick. Modest Uncle John declared himself pleased at McClellan's confidence in him, but added, "I enter upon the duties with a great deal of diffidence. It is a large command (thirteen thousand men), occupying an important position, and, I fear, above my capacity; however, I shall do my best." David Bell Birney took over Sedgwick's brigade. Birney was an atypical Potomac army general — a lawyer, a Republican, son of noted abolitionist James G. Birney. He entered the army by way of the Pennsylvania militia, and proved to be of that class of civilian-soldiers who rose through a cold, hard, acquired talent for command.[21]

The winter of 1861–62 was not the best of times for the Potomac army's high command. The residue of defeat at Bull Run and Ball's Bluff clung to the officer corps. The affair at Dranesville in December raised morale, but still it qualified as merely an affair. "We want a great victory . . . ," Sam Heintzelman grumbled. "Why don't we advance somewhere?" McClellan's increasingly public trials further sapped confidence throughout the chain of command. "I feel greatly troubled about our public affairs & think . . . the radicals are getting the control of both Congress & Executive," wrote Marsena Patrick. The implied menace of the Committee on the Conduct of the War was as chilling to the generals as the winter winds of Virginia.

Winter bred ill health as well as discontent. Typhoid fever felled Baldy Smith as it did General McClellan and Chief of Staff Marcy. Edwin Sumner was badly injured when his horse stepped in a posthole and threw him. At sixty-four Sumner required two months to recover. Phil Kearny's health was not robust, but he nevertheless managed to host an elaborate dinner party on New Year's Day to brighten the spirits of the officers of his New Jersey brigade and fellow generals Franklin, Heintzelman, French, and Howard. Kearny had taken for his headquarters an Alexandria mansion abandoned by its secessionist owners, and he put on a spread: six courses, from soup to nuts and including chicken, turkey, and venison. The wines were well chosen and there was much toasting. Of the eighteen guests, only Otis Howard and Robert McAllister, 1st New Jersey, saluted with glasses of water. "Gentlemen," Howard announced, "look at Colonel McAllister and see how healthy he is, showing clearly the value of temperance." The others lifted their wineglasses in toast.

Pleased with his New Year's Day party, Kearny repeated the performance on Saint Valentine's Day. There were twenty-five guests, from his own brigade plus a dozen division and brigade commanders. "They came from the extreme Right & the extreme Left" of the Potomac line, he noted. The party broke up at midnight in great good cheer. "It was really a sumptuous affair," Kearny wrote proudly.[22]

Winter storms ended talk of an immediate advance in Virginia. Brigadier W.T.H. Brooks wrote home, "We are mud fast, certainly not able to advance and could hardly retire if necessary. I never saw or heard of as much mud." With the Potomac army idled, McClellan promoted a scheme to send 70,000 of its infantry and 250 of its guns to Kentucky to initiate a drive into Tennessee. It spoke to an element of his grand design — cutting the Confederacy's main east–west railroad line, to prevent the Rebels from shifting troops from the West to oppose his prospective campaign in the East. He said he would take personal command in Kentucky.

Secretary Stanton dispatched Thomas Scott to Kentucky to work out the logistics of transporting this force by rail and steamboat. Scott reported,

A *Harper's Weekly* cartoon, published in January 1862, depicts a flock of geese, "The Small Politicians of Congress," cackling at General-in-Chief McClellan.

"It is an immense undertaking, *but can be done*." Yet like the schemes to take control of the upper Potomac, to break the blockade of the lower Potomac, to attack Norfolk and the ironclad *Virginia*, the Kentucky plan withered away. "I have not been able to impress the importance of this movement on General McClellan to the extent that I desire," Stanton complained. Some three weeks after activating the Kentucky project, McClellan dropped it. "At present no troops will move from East," he telegraphed Scott. "Ample occupation for them here."[23]

His response was due in part to the march of events. Quite apart from the Army of the Potomac, the Northern war machine lumbered into motion. In November an army-navy task force had seized Port Royal on the South Carolina coast. In January Ambrose Burnside led a second such expedition against the North Carolina coast at Roanoke Island and New Bern. On January 19 George H. Thomas (late of Patterson's Army of the Shenandoah) gained a victory at Mill Springs in Kentucky. On February 6, in Tennessee, a gunboat flotilla and an army under Brigadier General Ulysses S. Grant conquered Fort Henry, on the Tennessee River. On February 16 Grant won a sweeping victory at nearby Fort Donelson, on the Cumberland, capturing some 14,000 Rebel troops. On February 25 Nashville fell to Don Carlos Buell. The Army of the Potomac celebrated. "All these victories have created quite an excitement in camp, the men are hurrahing and the bands playing half the time," Charles Wainwright noted in his diary. Fitz John Porter had the "glorious news" read to his assembled brigades. "The men were delighted, and received in honor of the event a ration of whiskey."[24]

In the aftermath of the January war council, McClellan took a first step to advance his Urbanna scheme. On January 17 he engaged John Tucker, an assistant secretary of war, to work out the shipping required "to move at one time, for a short distance, from Annapolis to the mouth of the Rappahannock, about 50,000 troops, 10,000 horses, 1,000 wagons, 13 batteries and the usual equipments of such an army." Tucker reported the project feasible.[25]

Stanton managed to loosen McClellan's tongue, pressing him to develop his plan for the president. McClellan met with Lincoln on January 24 and explained in more detail his Urbanna plan, including the logistics worked up for him by John Tucker. The president continued speaking for the Occoquan plan — "You and I have distinct, and different plans for a movement of the Army of the Potomac," he told McClellan — and in view of their disagreement McClellan returned to his headquarters and began composing a detailed study to illuminate (as he wrote) "the differences between the two plans discussed this morning."[26]

Taking to his commander-in-chief role with determination, Lincoln seized the initiative to try and resolve the impasse himself. McClellan was taken aback to receive two executive orders. President's General War Order No. 1, dated January 27, designated February 22, Washington's birthday, for a general movement of the Union's land and naval forces against the insurgents. President's Special War Order No. 1, dated January 31, applied to the Army of the Potomac. Its immediate object was to seize "a point upon the Rail Road South Westward of what is known as Manassas Junction," the details to be left to McClellan but to start on or before February 22.[27]

Upon receiving the latter directive on Friday, January 31, McClellan secured Lincoln's permission "to submit in writing my objections to his plan, and my reasons for preferring my own." He spent the weekend completing and refining the paper he had begun the week before, and when he submitted it to Secretary Stanton on Monday, February 3, it ran to twenty-two pages. It was entirely his own composition; apparently he consulted no one in its writing.

The president, too, visited the subject that weekend, composing another of his interrogatories. If McClellan answered his questions satisfactorily, he wrote, "I will gladly yield my plan to yours." He asked:

1st. Does not your plan involve a greatly larger expenditure of *time,* and *money* than mine?

2nd. Wherein is a victory *more certain* by your plan than mine?

3rd. Wherein is a victory *more valuable* by your plan than mine?

4th. In fact, would it not be *less* valuable, in this, that it would break no great line of the enemie's communications, while mine would?

5th. In case of disaster, would not a safe retreat be more difficult by your plan than by mine?

Lincoln dated his interrogatory February 3 and it reached McClellan about the same time he submitted his own paper. Deciding he had covered the president's questions, he made no reply.

McClellan's paper opened with a self-serving account of assembling a well-drilled army "to which the destinies of the country may be confidently committed." Next came a lengthy discrediting of the president's Occoquan plan, invoking elaborate cautions and protections against "the masses of the enemy . . . elated by victory, and entrenched in a position long since selected, studied, & fortified." A victory (unlikely against these odds) would not be "decisive of the war, nor securing the destruction of the enemy's main Army."

McClellan proclaimed his Urbanna plan decisive of the war. Landing at Urbanna on the Rappahannock would position the army one long march to the York River, and two marches to Richmond. The enemy would abandon Manassas-Centreville to save Richmond and Norfolk. "He *must* do this, for should he permit us to occupy Richmond his destruction can be averted only by entirely defeating us in a battle in which he must be the assailant. . . ." The terrain was favorable, with roads "passable at all seasons of the year." Thirty days would be required to gather the transport for the change of base. "If at the expense of 30 days delay we can gain a decisive victory which will probably end the war, it is far cheaper than to gain a battle tomorrow that produces no final result." Victory at Richmond would make the North indomitable — Burnside in North Carolina, McClellan in Virginia, Buell in Tennessee, Halleck on the Mississippi. The Confederacy could not long survive.

McClellan's case for changing the army's base rested squarely on his fixed delusion about Confederate numbers. What he termed "the masses of the enemy" numbered, by countings then current, 170,000 or 175,000 or 180,000 or even 200,000. (Johnston's returns for February 1862 gave him 42,200 men on the Potomac line.) McClellan counted his own forces from 110,000 to 140,000 (the latter figure included 30,000 fresh troops garrisoning Washington). To counter this perceived imbalance, he would so surprise and outmaneuver Johnston that the battle for Richmond, when it came, would be fought defensively on ground of his own choosing. He ignored the serious flaws detected by engineer Barnard — doubt about Urbanna as a safe or suitable landing site, doubt about keeping the movement secret, doubt about being able to reach Richmond before Johnston. "Nothing is *certain* in war — but all the chances are in favor of this movement," said McClellan.[28]

The president noted that if McClellan answered his questions satisfactorily, he would "gladly yield my plan to yours." He did yield to McClellan's Urbanna plan, but not gladly. Lincoln was not (and never would be) persuaded of the wisdom of the Army of the Potomac changing its base to the lower Chesapeake. Yet he hardly felt qualified to overrule a general staking his military reputation on the matter. Naming McClellan commander of the Potomac army and general-in-chief of all the armies, he could hardly dismiss him over a battle plan, nor did he consider doing so. His two war orders achieved their purpose — finally pinning McClellan to a concrete plan of action. Now he would monitor every detail and every consequence of the plan as it evolved.

On February 14, 1862, Secretary of War Stanton authorized the collecting of shipping for the movement. The Army of the Potomac was going to change its base.[29]

As with all matters of military planning and strategizing that winter, the general officers of the Army of the Potomac — with the exception of Fitz John Porter, William Franklin, and John Barnard — were excluded from the Urbanna deliberations. Stanton was "quite surprised" that there had never been a council of war in McClellan's army. "I told him," wrote Sam Heintzelman, "that I never had a word about this Army than what I learned from the newspapers & the conversations with the officers around me. . . ." This exclusion, and the false starts and general inaction on the Potomac line, produced restiveness in the command.

Thanks to Heintzelman's creditable Bull Run record, there was a move from the civilian quarter to award him an independent command "to be sent South" in some vaguely defined attempt to get the war moving. His troops would be from Pennsylvania — his native state — raised by activist governor Andrew Curtin. Vice President Hannibal Hamlin supported Curtin's idea, as did the Jacobins Ben Wade and Zach Chandler. They were drawn to Heintzelman because he refused to return fugitive slaves to their owners. (The general was no abolitionist, yet he did not care to be a slave catcher either.) He was caught between his professional wish for independent command, and the major generalship that would go with it, and the possible perception of an intrigue against the general commanding. Like so many other fresh ideas, nothing came of this one. He concluded that McClellan learned of the matter and "had some feeling against me."[30]

Another source of high-command discontent was the matter of forming army corps — and the promotions thereby for their commanders. McDowell, presenting his plan to the ad hoc war council in January, called for combining the Potomac army's divisions into corps. Military wisdom of the time specified a corps structure for large armies so as to simplify directing maneuvers and engagements. McDowell's plan, for example, had three corps masking the enemy while a fourth corps moved independently against his communications.

Testifying before the Committee on the Conduct of the War, Generals McDowell, Heintzelman, and Meigs all spoke approvingly of corps for the army. But Fitz John Porter, well known to have McClellan's ear, qualified his answer to the corps question: "Just at this present moment I do not think it necessary. When the time comes, it will be so organized." That was McClellan's committee testimony. By Chairman Wade's account, the idea of forming corps was not regarded with much favor by McClellan: It was "a delicate matter" to appoint generals to corps command before being tried in battle. He would "himself manage this entire army in some battle or campaign," then promote those who tested best. The committee was unpersuaded, and added the forming of army corps to its badgering of Lincoln. Stanton adopted the corps idea and joined his voice to the chorus pressing the president on the issue.[31]

An issue demanding more attention was the continuing presence of Confederate forces virtually holding Washington hostage. Their batteries on the lower Potomac crippled commerce on the river. Along the upper Potomac there was no through rail traffic to the capital, and commerce on the Chesapeake & Ohio Canal was regularly interrupted. McClellan was pressed from every quarter to do something about this humiliating semiblockade. While he agreed on the importance of the Baltimore & Ohio, the primary rail link between East and Midwest, he would not be rushed into anything he considered high risk.

The capital's growing sense of isolation roused the Wade Committee. In a meeting at the War Department, McClellan assured the senators he planned action soon on the upper Potomac. He must prepare lines of retreat before risking his men. He had made that same argument in his earlier testimony, and once again it set off Chairman Wade. With "150,000 of the most effective troops in the world," said Wade, surely they could beat off any force brought against them, "and if any of them came back, let them come back in their coffins." The committee's journal reported, "To which General McClellan made no reply."[32]

With the Urbanna plan approved, McClellan felt free to act on the upper Potomac. On February 26 he was at Harper's Ferry with Nathaniel Banks's and John Sedgwick's (late Charles Stone's) divisions. McClellan telegraphed Stanton that a light pontoon bridge "was splendidly thrown" across the Potomac and 8,500 men, eighteen guns, and two squadrons of cavalry crossed and secured the far shore. He wrote Ellen, "I crossed the river as soon as the bridge was finished & watched the troops pass. It was a magnificent spectacle — one of the grandest I ever saw." Step two of the operation called for building a permanent bridge resting on canal boats anchored in the river. This span would supply outposts at Harper's Ferry and at Winchester, and allow the Baltimore & Ohio to rebuild its railroad bridge at the Ferry. The canal boats were floated to the site from Washington on the Chesapeake & Ohio Canal, which ran alongside the north bank of the Potomac, to be passed through a lock into the river for the bridge building. On the 27th McClellan sent Stanton a second, more sober telegram: "The lift lock is too small to permit the canal boats to enter the river so it is impossible to construct the permanent bridge as I intended." He was canceling the operation and returning the troops to their postings. Instead he would adopt a "safe and slow plan" for the railroad-bridge building.

After much fingerpointing, it was discovered that the lock in question was only used by the narrower (by 5 or 6 inches) canal boats plying the Shenandoah. The engineers had gone to the C. & O. for canal boats without revealing the purpose, and ended up with standard C. & O. freighters — and to an army engineer one canal boat looked pretty much like any other. Treasury Secretary Chase was inspired to a rare display of wit: "The expedition, it was said, and not untruly, died of lock-jaw."[33]

When Stanton brought McClellan's telegrams to the White House, sparks flew. Lincoln asked what it meant. Stanton said it meant "that it is a damned fizzle. It means that he doesn't intend to do anything." In a rare display of real anger, Lincoln pounded his fist on the table and exclaimed, "Why in hell didn't he measure first!" Secretary John Nicolay remembered the exchange as the only time in his White House years that he heard Lincoln curse.

Harper's Ferry, photographed by C.O. Bostwick from the foot of Maryland Heights. The railroad bridge was burned by the Confederates in June 1861. The Chesapeake & Ohio Canal lock that McClellan intended to use to lower canal boats into the Potomac for bridge building is at the left foreground, just out of the picture.

Chief of Staff Marcy was called in and subjected to the presidential wrath. "Why in the damnation, General Marcy," Lincoln asked, "couldn't the General have known whether a boat would go through that lock, before he spent a million of dollars getting them there? I am no engineer: but it seems to me that if I wished to know whether a boat would go through a hole, or a lock, common sense would teach me to go and measure it. I am almost despairing at these results. Everything seems to fail. The general impression is daily gaining ground that the General does not intend to do anything. . . ." Poor Marcy said he was sure it could all be explained, but Lincoln curtly dismissed him.

In due time, McClellan's "safe and slow plan" achieved the goals of the ill-fated Harper's Ferry expedition. The B. & O. bridge was rebuilt, and Banks occupied Winchester and the lower Valley. But in the short term, the fiasco widened the gulf between president and general. To be sure, Lincoln could hardly expect the general commanding to go about measuring canal boats and locks personally. Still, the episode revealed witless planning, incompetence, and a whiff of the ludicrous. Correspondent Horace White reported that "Lincoln swore like a Philistine when he learned the upshot of the affair, & there was wailing & gnashing of teeth among the imperial staff. . . . It was Ball's Bluff all over again, minus the slaughter."

What heightened the president's frustration with McClellan was the lack of a viable second choice. When Ben Wade demanded that he fire McClellan, Lincoln asked who should replace him. "Why, anybody!" Wade said. "Wade, *anybody* will do for you," Lincoln said, "but not for me. I must have *somebody*." Lincoln was still angry about the canal-boat debacle when he talked to Senator Charles Sumner two days later. By Sumner's account, "The Presdt. thought that Genl. M. should have ascertained this in advance, before he promised success. Since his return Genl. M. has not seen the Presdt, who has made up his mind to talk plainly to him."[34]

The basic premise of the Urbanna plan, as McClellan presented it, required getting the jump on Joe Johnston — landing at Urbanna and marching to Richmond before Johnston at Manassas realized what was happening. McClellan undertook the Harper's Ferry venture hoping it would not unduly alarm Johnston, that in fact it might distract him into tending to his threatened northern flank. But the Confederate batteries on the lower Potomac posed an altogether different problem.

McClellan intended to embark the army at Alexandria and sail it down the Potomac to Chesapeake Bay and up the Rappahannock to Urbanna. This could only succeed if the Rebel batteries commanding the river were disabled by the army beforehand or suppressed by the navy en route. The alternative was to avoid the Potomac entirely in favor of the more roundabout Chesapeake route, shifting the army over to Annapolis for embarking. McClellan worried the problem for more than two weeks.

He finally conceived a truly grandiose plan. He would lead virtually the entire Army of the Potomac — he estimated 118,000 men — against the Potomac batteries. Writing to General Halleck, he said he expected to open the Potomac within a week: "It will require the movement of the whole Army in order to keep 'Manassas' off my back." Once the Potomac was cleared, "I shall bring here the water transportation now ready . . . & then move by detachments of about 55,000 men for the region of sandy roads & short land transportation."

On the face of it, this appeared to compromise the critical surprise element in the Urbanna plan. He proposed to march the bulk of the army south from Washington 30 miles or so along the Virginia bank of the Potomac and fend off Johnston's supposed host long enough for the batteries to be destroyed. McClellan had claimed to want neither a premature battle nor a premature enemy withdrawal . . . and this movement promised one result or the other.

Perhaps he was simply pruning expectations. Rather than trying to beat Johnston to Richmond, he would settle for half a loaf—limiting the surprise to landing at undefended Urbanna and aim from there to establish a new base at West Point on the York River. This would cut off the defenders on the lower Peninsula, gain him the York as a supply route, and secure the terminus of the Richmond & York River Railroad to support (in good time) a march on the Confederate capital.

Besides pruning expectations, McClellan believed he must act simply to save his job. Chief of Staff Marcy had told him that Lincoln was "in a hell of a rage" over the Harper's Ferry fiasco. Furthermore (as McClellan explained to Halleck), "the abolitionists are doing their best to displace me & I shall be content if I can keep my head above water until I am ready to strike the final blow." Marsena Patrick heard stories of "a powerful cabal that will overthrow him if he does not move within a few days." Patrick passed the warning on to Marcy, and asked if McClellan knew of the plots against him. "He knows them all," Marcy told him. Putting the Potomac army into action, regardless of target, regardless of consequences, ought to keep the commanding general in his job.[35]

Rumors regarding McClellan's tenure suffused the officer corps. General Meade wrote his wife, "I hear it whispered that Genls. Sumner & McDowell, the one backed by his cousin the Mass. Senator, and the other by his great friend Sec. Chase, have united their forces with the Fremonters to affect McClellan's destruction." Should these ultras get their way, he added, "I shall give the country up. . . ." Pathfinder Frémont frequently cropped up in these rumors. McClellan's enemies "are the friends of Frémont," Washington lobbyist Sam Ward explained, "resolved to retaliate upon Mc the treatment which their limping demigod . . . recd at the hands of the proSlavery Democrats."

There was substance behind these rumors (except those involving Frémont), for Lincoln's patience was nearly at an end. He told a visitor that even if a Washington or a Napoleon or an Andrew Jackson led the Army of the Potomac, "they would be obliged to move or resign the position. . . . One thing I can say, that the army will move, either under General McClellan or some other man, and that very soon."[36]

On March 2 McClellan convened a gathering of his lieutenants—his first such as army commander or as general-in-chief. Generals Heintzelman, McDowell, Franklin, and Hooker spent the day going over details of the movement against the Potomac batteries with Chief of Staff Marcy. McClellan joined them in the evening and led further discussion. He did not extend instructions beyond the attack on the batteries.

The conference resumed the next day with the rest of the division commanders to produce a memorandum "in accordance with Gen. McClellan's plan." Sam Heintzelman welcomed this opportunity, at long last, to exchange ideas with the general commanding. "Gen. McDowell, myself & some others are in favour of doing this in a different manner & to produce the result he wishes, with others much greater," he entered in his diary; "will accomplish what he proposes & if successful cut the rebel communications." Heintzelman was proposing the movement against the Potomac batteries be adapted to carry out the Occoquan plan that he and McDowell — and Mr. Lincoln — had all earlier advanced. But no exchange of ideas took place that day. "As Gen. McClellan did not attend the conference we could not put forth our views."[37]

McClellan scheduled a final, dress-rehearsal gathering of his generals on the Potomac batteries operation for March 7. But at 7:30 that morning the president summoned him to the White House, apparently to make good on his pledge "to talk plainly." The sole account of the interview is McClellan's, written years later for his memoir. McClellan quoted Lincoln introducing "a very ugly matter." It had been represented to him, said the president, that the Urbanna plan was conceived "with the traitorous intent of removing its defenders from Washington, and thus giving over to the enemy the capital and the government. . . ."

By his account, McClellan jumped to his feet and, "in a manner perhaps not altogether decorous towards the chief magistrate, desired that he should retract the expression, telling him that I could permit no one to couple the word treason with my name." Lincoln said he was only repeating what others had said. He would put the issue to rest, said McClellan. His generals were to meet that morning concerning the Potomac batteries, and he would appoint them a council of war and submit his Urbanna plan to their vote. "I also said that in order to leave them perfectly untrammeled I would not attend the meeting." Thereupon, he reported, "I heard no more of treason in that connection."

McClellan's recollection is more fiction than fact. As of March 7, 1862, very few people in the army or in the administration — none of them Radicals or congressional ultras or abolitionists — even knew of the Urbanna plan. Certainly no one on the short list who did know considered George McClellan a traitor, whatever they thought of him. It is far more likely that Lincoln spoke bluntly about the risk of shifting the Potomac army's base

In a rare Alfred Waud cartoon, Uncle Sam introduces General McClellan to President Lincoln and Secretary of War Stanton and their failed general (perhaps intended to be Winfield Scott, perhaps Irvin McDowell). Their playbill features daily performances of "Onward to Richmond by a Select Company of Star Generals."

far from Washington while (by McClellan's own count) a much superior Rebel army lay just 25 miles away at Manassas. Perhaps he warned his general that when the Urbanna move became known there would be an outcry, perhaps a very ugly outcry, about his leaving the capital exposed to serious danger. For his part, McClellan saw a council of war as the means of securing both his plan and his job.[38]

Later that day, Lincoln offered a visitor an elliptical but telling comment on his dealings with General McClellan: "We won't mention names, and I'll tell you how things are. . . . Suppose a man whose profession it is to understand military matters is asked how long it will take him and what he requires to accomplish certain things, and when he has had all he asked and the time comes, he does *nothing*."[39]

The twelve brigadier generals called to army headquarters that morning were startled to find themselves a formal council of war. The twelve were division commanders Edwin Sumner, Irvin McDowell, Sam Heintzelman, Erasmus Keyes, William Franklin, Baldy Smith, George McCall, Andrew Porter, Fitz John Porter, Louis Blenker, Henry Naglee (sitting in for Joe Hooker, returned to his division in lower Maryland), and engineer John Barnard. Only Franklin, Fitz John Porter, and Smith knew of McClellan's plan of campaign, and their information was sketchy. Only Barnard had a working knowledge of the plan for changing the army's base.

Chief of Staff Marcy outlined the Urbanna plan for the generals. McClellan had now decided to avoid the Potomac batteries entirely and instead embark the army from Annapolis for transport down the Chesapeake. Shipping would be readied within a week. When he finished his presentation, Marcy buttonholed Heintzelman (among others) to explain the real significance of the war council. Marcy said there was a strong effort to have General McClellan superseded, "& that he would be unless we approved his plans." Pathfinder Frémont was rumored his successor, but more probably it would be Henry Halleck.

Discussion of the new strategy and the change of base went on until late afternoon. Heintzelman remarked on the lack of any actual deliberations. "There was a great deal of talk that I consider irrelevant." McClellan came in at one point to more fully explain his views. McClellan and Marcy left the room, and the president of the war council, Sumner, its senior member, called for a vote on the Urbanna proposition. "To my great surprise," wrote John Barnard, "eight of the twelve officers present voted, offhand, *for* the measure, *without* discussion. . . ."

Of the four dissenters, Barnard was on record as objecting to (among other things) the Urbanna landing site as inadequate and impractical and unsafe; Sam Heintzelman and Irvin McDowell favored instead the Occoquan plan; and old Sumner apparently felt the closer the enemy was, the easier it was to get at him. In summing up for the minority, Heintzelman said he "would not go off from an enemy in front, to try and find him somewhere else." The four represented the old guard of the old army, with none owing his place to General McClellan. On the other hand, of the eight-man majority, six (William Franklin, Fitz John Porter, Andrew Porter, Baldy Smith, Louis Blenker, and Henry Naglee) held their commands thanks to McClellan or were his known favorites, and the other two (George McCall and Erasmus Keyes) felt the need to curry favor to retain their commands. McDowell compared the voting to a political caucus, with the decision "determined on personal grounds." Barnard, "speaking pretty strongly," proposed a reconsideration of the vote, but was told that being in the minority at a war council meant he had no right to move a reconsideration. It was then proposed to make the vote unanimous, to express the officer corps' support for the beleaguered commanding general. The minority indignantly rejected the idea. "This excited considerable feeling," Heintzelman noted.[40]

The war council had been instructed to report to the White House when it reached a decision, and that evening Lincoln told the generals he welcomed the advance. "Napoleon himself could not stand still any longer with such an army," he said. By Heintzelman's account, "We soon got into a discussion, each party setting forth their views." Barnard said he heard neither a valid reason nor an intelligent answer to the main question of changing the army's base.

Lincoln's and Stanton's concern beyond any other was the safety of Washington, and the Navy Department's Gus Fox was called in to consult on the matter of the Rebel batteries. Could the navy open the Potomac for the army to return by the quickest route should the capital be threatened? Fox offered, on a week's notice, two big steam frigates from Hampton Roads as well as the new *Monitor* just then on her way from New York. Lincoln told the generals to return the next morning for his decision. Before adjourning, exercising his commander-in-chief prerogative, he called for a vote on the propriety of organizing the Army of the Potomac into corps. The vote in favor was unanimous.

At 10 o'clock the next morning, March 8, the twelve generals reassembled at the White House to meet with Lincoln and Stanton. McClellan was not present, nor was he consulted on the day's decisions. By means of two General War Orders, Lincoln announced his acceptance of the majority's vote on the Urbanna plan, but with certain qualifications. He would permit an advance guard of 50,000 men to sail from Annapolis for Urbanna, with another 50,000 to follow only on condition that the Potomac batteries were destroyed or the Rebels abandoned them and withdrew from Manassas. And the capital must be left securely defended. Sam Heintzelman, frustrated with the council's actions, handed the president a paper explaining the minority's preference for the Occoquan plan. "A defeat of the enemy here," he argued, "will give us the prestige our arms lost at Bull Run & which cannot be gained at any other point."[41]

The president, Heintzelman reported, "told us that he had decided to form Army Corps & that he knew no better plan than to take the five senior Generals of the Army of the Potomac: Banks, Sumner, McDowell, Heintzelman & Keyes. There were some blank faces, as I am confident some others expected a place." McDowell, Sumner, Heintzelman, and Keyes would command First through Fourth Corps of the field army. Banks's corps would remain behind as part of Washington's defenses.

In his memoir McClellan condemned the president's assignment of corps commanders as arbitrary, done without consulting him; "not one of them was well fitted for their duties." But in private McClellan had long since acknowledged the need for a corps organization, and in January he drew up a list of commanders for a projected six-corps army. He awarded the first three corps to Sumner, McDowell, and Heintzelman; the fourth was headed by Fitz John Porter rather than Erasmus Keyes. His other two corps went to William Franklin and Andrew Porter. Now McClellan could anticipate opening his campaign with three of his four corps commanders — Sumner, McDowell, and Heintzelman — on record as opposing the army's change of base. The fourth, Keyes, voted for the Urbanna plan yet he was not on McClellan's own corps list.[42]

Lincoln's final act set the starting date for the Potomac army's change of base as March 18, ten days hence, "and the General-in-chief shall be responsible that it so move as early as that day."

Heintzelman noted that Lincoln put on a good face in announcing his decision. "He urged us all to go in heartily for this plan." But privately the president confessed he acted with considerable reluctance. "We can do nothing else than accept their plan and discard all others," he told Stanton. "We can't reject it and adopt another without assuming all the responsibility in the case of the failure of the one we adopt." However disappointed, Lincoln was not (and would not be) prepared to dismiss McClellan solely over this issue of grand strategy.

However mixed its reception, General McClellan's plan to change the Army of the Potomac's base would proceed. But presently it would proceed in a much altered state, thanks to the Rebels.[43]

Joe Johnston spent an uneasy winter in his lines at Manassas and Centreville. In February his second in command, P.G.T. Beauregard, was posted to the Western theater, leaving Johnston to brood alone on his diminishing prospects. From October 1861 to February 1862 the count of his army actually fell by 1,900 men, to 42,200. He could barely subsist that force over his long and vulnerable railroad supply line. General McClellan, his old friend from the old army, was known to be amassing a force greatly superior to his. As he wrote Jefferson Davis on February 16, thus far they had "relied upon the season to prevent action by the enemy." That reliance could not last much longer.

Davis agreed, and summoned Johnston to Richmond to announce a major shift in military policy. Attorney General Thomas Bragg entered in his diary, "The Pres't said the time had come for diminishing the extent

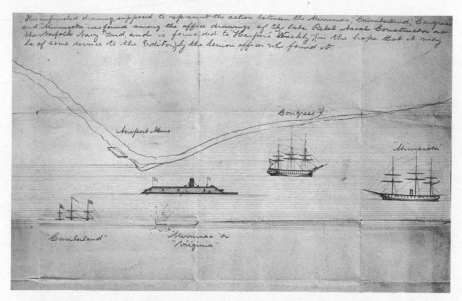

This unfinished drawing, supposed to represent the action between the "Merrimac," "Cumberland," "Congress" and "Minnesota" was found among the office drawings of the late Rebel Naval Constructor at the Norfolk Navy Yard, and is forwarded to "Harper's Weekly" (in the hope that it may be of some service to the Editor) by the Union officer who found it.

In a drawing by an unknown Confederate naval officer, USS *Merrimack* (reconstructed as the ironclad CSS *Virginia*) engages the *Cumberland* (at left, sunk), *Congress*, and *Minnesota* (right) off Newport News in Hampton Roads on March 8, 1862.

of our lines — that we had not men in the field to hold them and must fall back." For Johnston that meant falling back behind the Rappahannock. On March 5 unusual activity was seen among the Federals across the Potomac in lower Maryland (this was Joe Hooker preparing his part in McClellan's planned move against the Rebel batteries), and it triggered Johnston's worst fears. To forestall his southern flank being turned, he ordered troop withdrawals from Manassas and Centreville to begin on the morning of March 8.[44]

By happenstance, that same morning the ironclad ram CSS *Virginia* steamed out of her Norfolk berth and devastated the Federal blockading squadron in Hampton Roads. Frigates *Cumberland* and *Congress* were sunk, steam frigate *Minnesota* driven aground and helplessly facing the *Virginia*'s next sortie. The calamitous news reached Washington on Sunday morning, March 9, generating shock nearly as great as Bull Run the previous July.

Peter H. Watson of the War Department brought the first dispatches to the White House, then Secretary Stanton rushed in "very much excited, and walked up and down the room like a caged lion," as John Nicolay described him. The president's office soon filled — Secretary of State

Seward, Secretary of the Navy Welles, General McClellan, Quartermaster Meigs, chief engineer Joseph Totten — and "there was great flutter and excitement." By Welles's account, Stanton was "almost frantic" reckoning the disasters to come — the *Merrimack* (as everyone called her that day) would wipe out the blockading fleet, take Fort Monroe, capture Ambrose Burnside's army on the North Carolina coast, burn Washington, put every seaboard city under tribute.

During this diatribe Stanton glared accusingly at Welles, who amidst the hubbub was the calmest man in the room. Welles said the *Merrimack* was hardly seaworthy enough to go ranging up and down the Atlantic coast, and she drew too much water to ascend the Potomac as far as Washington. In any event, he expected the Union's own ironclad, the *Monitor,* to be at Hampton Roads by now, and was waiting to hear from Gus Fox, at Fort Monroe. Welles pointed out that after General McClellan refused to act against Norfolk in the fall, the navy had assumed the threat of the *Merrimack.* Had the *Monitor* been completed "within contract time," her first orders would have taken her to Norfolk to destroy the Rebel ironclad "before she came out of dry-dock."[45]

Finally, in late afternoon, came a dispatch from Gus Fox. He reported that the *Monitor* had reached Hampton Roads the previous night, after the *Virginia*'s depredations, and that morning, when the *Virginia* reappeared the *Monitor* challenged her. "These two ironclad vessels fought part of the time touching each other, from 8 a.m. to noon, when the Merrimac retired. . . . The Monitor is uninjured and ready at any moment to repel another attack."

Now came a rush of dispatches. Hooker reported the Rebels' Potomac batteries abandoned. Banks reported the enemy gone from the upper Potomac. Contrabands said that for the last two days Confederate troops were leaving Manassas and Centreville. McClellan hurried to his outposts to confirm the news. It was all true. "I am arranging to move forward to push the retreat of rebels as far as possible," he telegraphed.[46]

On March 10, with much fanfare, the Army of the Potomac marched off westward to seize the Rebel positions at Manassas and Centreville, and possibly catch up to Johnston's retreating army. "At two o'clock of that day," wrote an irreverent *New-York Tribune* correspondent, "Gen. McClellan parted with his wife, according to the approved Hector and Andromache fashion, and, amid the waving of handkerchiefs from the most highly-born ladies of Washington . . . took the field." McClellan went to war with seven divisions, some 75,000 men, under Generals McDowell, McCall, Frank-

Quaker guns in the evacuated Confederate lines at Centreville, March 1862. The platforms suggest real guns taking the place of the fake guns if attacked.

lin, Blenker, Sumner, Fitz John Porter, and Baldy Smith. The men went "prepared for desperate work," wrote Captain Rufus Dawes, 6th Wisconsin. "They had made their wills, written their farewell letters, and wanted to fight." Soon came word that the enemy was gone. "The boys were really greatly disappointed. . . ."

Johnston had a head start, and the Federals lacked the cavalry force for serious pursuit. McClellan recast the expedition as a practice march, to give the troops a few days of living in the field. He pronounced the works at Manassas and Centreville formidable; "it is evident that they had a very large force here," he told his wife. George Meade told *his* wife much the same: "It would have given us a good deal of trouble to have driven them out." McClellan made the case in his 1864 *Report*: "That an assault of the enemy's positions in front of Washington, with the new troops composing the army of the Potomac, during the winter of 1861-'62, would have resulted in defeat and demoralization, was too probable." This overlooked the fact that no one — not Generals Scott and McDowell in 1861, not proponents of the Occoquan turning movement in 1862 — had ever proposed frontal assaults on these positions.[47]

The *Philadelphia Press* warned, "If the rebel army, that since July has insolently menaced Washington, now escapes scot free, not all the newspaper panegyrics of the ingenious daring metropolitan editors can maintain that popular confidence in McClellan." Reporters inspecting the entrenchments were scornful: "From some of the embrasures projected *maple logs,* the ends painted black." These Quaker guns were reminiscent of the Munson's Hill "batteries." Said the *Tribune,* "The fortifications are a damnable humbug and McClellan has been completely fooled." Nathaniel Hawthorne spoke of "the tremendous shock with which we were brought suddenly up against nothing at all!" Elizabeth Blair Lee made note, "McClellan will have to achieve his Victories rapidly to hush up the sneering laugh of his enemies in the rear."[48]

McClellan's first impulse was to go ahead with his Urbanna plan. The Confederates' withdrawal relieved Washington from any immediate threat of attack, and the abandoned batteries left the Potomac open to passage by the army. He telegraphed Stanton on March 11 that he proposed occupying Manassas "& then at once throwing all the forces I can concentrate upon the line agreed upon last week."

But soon enough came sobering second thoughts. Johnston's army behind the Rappahannock was a good deal closer to Richmond than before . . . and a good deal closer to Urbanna as well. Any surprise achieved by an Urbanna landing would hardly last long enough to win a race to Richmond; indeed there was nothing certain even about defending Urbanna against the Rebel host. Perhaps Johnston had gotten wind of his plan, "and that was the main cause of their leaving." Already he might be lying in wait for the Yankees.

McClellan could either give up his change-of-base plan or find a different and secure base from which to launch it. He did not hesitate. He was too committed to his grand campaign, had worked too hard for its approval, to surrender it. The Potomac army would take Fort Monroe as its new base from which to strike at Richmond.

Fort Monroe had always been the backup option. As McClellan put it in his February 3 paper, "The worst coming to the worst — we can take Fort Monroe as a base, & operate with complete security, altho' with less celerity & brilliancy of results, up the Peninsula." To be sure, from there it was some 75 miles to Richmond rather than the three-day unopposed march from Urbanna he had prophesied. There would be no advantage of surprise, no prospects for celerity and brilliancy. The *Virginia*, from her base at Norfolk, promised to crimp prospects by blocking access to the James River. So long as the Rebel ironclad remained a threat, the Federals would have to rely solely on the York.[49]

At his field headquarters at Fairfax Court House McClellan was surprised to see in the *National Intelligencer* for March 12 Lincoln's War Order No. 3: "Major General McClellan having personally taken the field at the head of the Army of the Potomac, until otherwise ordered, he is relieved from the command of the other Military departments." This was, to McClellan, a demotion, insultingly announced by newspaper.

Lincoln had delegated to former Ohio governor William Dennison the task of informing the general of his new status, but the press reached Fairfax Court House before Dennison did. It was the president's judgment, Dennison explained to McClellan, that while commanding the Potomac army on campaign he could not at the same time meet the duties of general-in-chief. No new general-in-chief was appointed, implying that in due course the conqueror of Richmond might resume the post. "You command the Army of the Potomac wherever it may go," Dennison soothed him. "Everything is right — move quick as possible." Apparently mollified, McClellan set to work revamping his campaign.[50]

Fort Monroe was a secure base, but putting the army ashore there required also securing Hampton Roads. "Can I rely on the Monitor to keep the Merrimac in check?" McClellan telegraphed Gus Fox. As witness to the fight of the ironclads, Fox declared the *Monitor* the superior of the two, but warned of a disabling hit. "The Monitor may, and I think will, destroy the Merrimac in the next fight; but this is hope, not certainty." McClellan suggested blockading the channel into Norfolk. That, he was told, could only be done by first silencing the enemy shore batteries, and for that the *Monitor* would be needed. The navy's flag officer on the scene, Louis Goldsborough, was opposed. "The risk to the 'Monitor' would be too great at present — far too great I think." Standoff remained status quo in Hampton Roads.[51]

On March 12, at Fairfax Court House, McClellan convened his second war council in less than a week. His purpose was twofold: to demonstrate to a skeptical administration the support of his lieutenants for his (revised) campaign plan; and thereby to gain a vote of confidence as general commanding. This second council comprised only the four new corps commanders — Sumner, McDowell, Heintzelman, and Keyes — plus chief engineer Barnard.

"No objection appears to be made to my being one of the Commanders," Heintzelman was pleased to write of the corps postings, "but Sumner, McDowell & Keyes are objected to, McDowell particularly." The four had been selected by the president on the basis of seniority — Sumner was in his forty-third year of service, Heintzelman in his thirty-sixth, Keyes in his thirtieth, McDowell in his twenty-fourth. Even McClellan, in his private list of intended corps commanders, had bowed to seniority in regard to Sumner, Heintzelman, and McDowell.

Edwin Sumner, turning sixty-five that winter, was the oldest general officer in the Potomac army, and while respected for his stalwart soldierly qualities, "unfortunately nature had limited his capacity to a very narrow extent," as McClellan phrased it. Sumner's generalship was best expressed leading a brigade or at most a division. He was confused at the council. With the enemy withdrawn and out of immediate reach, he thought he was voting for McClellan's original Urbanna plan. By his own admission, "I was never more surprised in my life when I embarked at Alexandria to learn that the whole army was going down to Fort Monroe." The others paid closer attention.

While McClellan respected Heintzelman as "a very brave man & an excellent officer," he deferred judgment on him heading a corps. He did not defer judgment on Erasmus Keyes. McClellan strongly resented Keyes's appointment, labeling him "of very moderate ability; very prissy, & entirely unfit to command a corps." To complete his failings (as McClellan saw them), the man was a Republican with abolitionist sentiments. Keyes realized his handicap. "Jeff Davis has not a greater repugnance to, nor less confidence in, Republicans than has McClellan," Keyes wrote. "I was about to enter upon a campaign laden with disfavor at headquarters." McClellan resented Irvin McDowell, like Keyes, for personal and political reasons. The January ad hoc war council held while McClellan lay ill was plotted by McDowell (so McClellan believed) to recapture the Potomac army command. Moreover (by way of confirmation), it was Radical Republicans on the Committee on the Conduct of the War who pressed Lincoln to put their pet McDowell at the head of the army.

Baldy Smith spoke for the younger generation of officers around McClellan in expressing disgust with Lincoln's appointments. He termed McDowell "a vain, arrogant man" intriguing for independent command. "The three others had no claim to their positions except by seniority and senility." McClellan was uncomfortable dealing with these generals in council, and with having to put his modified plan to their vote.

In fact there was little room for deliberation. Only Keyes had favored the Urbanna plan, but now it was evident (except perhaps to Sumner) that the Urbanna site was too risky, leaving Fort Monroe "as the safer, surer way." Barnard posed the one stumbling block: The possibility of a *Virginia* sortie "paralyzes the movements of this army by whatever route is adopted." But the reports of Fox and Goldsborough on the *Monitor's* prowess were enough to gain the council's approval of Fort Monroe as the new base. Anticipating the vote, McClellan had already shifted the embarkation point from Annapolis on the Chesapeake back to Alexandria on the Potomac.[52]

The president's war orders included the strict injunction that no change of base would be permitted "without leaving in, and about Washington" force enough, in the joint opinion of McClellan and his corps commanders, to "leave said City entirely secure." The council agreed that every fort must have "a competent military garrison" and there should be "a movable column of 25,000 men." Sumner named a total of 40,000 men for the capital's defense. Lincoln's approval of the new plan carried a touch of impatience. Once Manassas and Washington were secure, he wrote, take "a new base at Fortress Monroe, or anywhere between here and there; or, at all events, move such remainder of the army at once in pursuit of the enemy by some route."[53]

To toast his triumph over adversity and enemies of every degree, McClellan called for his wife to join him at the Fairfax headquarters for a celebratory luncheon with the corps commanders. Then, reflecting on months of speculation and one final week of upheaval, he sat down to compose an address to his army. He sought to motivate and inspire, and for his closing he paraphrased Napoleon's 1796 address to the Army of Italy.

"I have held you back," he explained, "that you might give the death-blow to the rebellion that has distracted our once happy country." He termed the Army of the Potomac now "a real Army — magnificent in material, admirable in discipline and instruction, excellently equipped and armed; — your commanders are all that I could wish. The moment for action has arrived. . . ." He linked his fate with theirs, his duty to lead them to the decisive battlefield. "I am to watch over you as a parent over his children; and you know that your General loves you from the depths of his heart. . . . I shall demand of you great, heroic exertions, rapid and long marches, desperate combats, privations, perhaps. We will share all these together; and when this sad war is over we will all return to our homes, and feel that we can ask no higher honor than the proud consciousness that we belonged to the ARMY OF THE POTOMAC."[54]

The president's order to form army corps roused headquarters to a frenzy of paperwork. On March 14 McClellan roughed out the assignment of divisions to the four corps of the field army, and to Banks's Fifth Corps that would remain to defend Washington. Over the following days the organization was subjected to continual juggling. Heintzelman, for example, noted in his diary, "I got F. J. Porter's & Hooker's divis. in place of Franklin & Casey. I am sorry to lose the latter, but both I get are good." Commanders were shifted about. Baldy Smith negotiated himself out of serving under McDowell, but Franklin had no such luck; "I am afraid that that old rascal saw further through a millstone than I did," he wrote ruefully.

The initial command vacancies were the divisions of the four promoted corps commanders. Rufus King advanced from a brigade under McDowell to command of McDowell's division. Darius Couch, the senior of Keyes's brigade commanders, was awarded Keyes's division. Charles Hamilton came over from Banks's command to take Heintzelman's division.

Phil Kearny was ordered from Franklin's division to command Sumner's old division in the Second Corps, but Kearny balked. The issue, he said, was leaving behind the New Jersey brigade, which he had worked hard to tame. "Genl. McClellan," he told his wife, "behaved most unhandsomely to me, he did not dare to pass me over, but assigned me to command a Division, but not to take my Brigade with me. I flatly refused. It was a dirty trick." He labeled Franklin "ungenerous" in not releasing the Jersey brigade to go with him. He remained head of the Jerseymen under Franklin, and Israel Richardson took Sumner's old division. Ultra-Christian soldier Otis Howard was relieved to be serving under Richardson rather than Kearny, whom he feared was still "a very corrupt man, profane, a high liver, hard drinker, licentious."[55]

McDowell's First Corps, as constituted, comprised Franklin's First Division, its brigades under Kearny, Henry Slocum, and John Newton; George McCall's Second Division (Pennsylvania Reserves), with the brigades of John Reynolds, George Meade, and E.O.C. Ord; and Rufus King's Third Division, with brigade commanders Lysander Cutler, Christopher C. Augur, and Marsena R. Patrick.

Sumner's Second Corps contained Richardson's First Division, with the brigades of Otis Howard, Thomas F. Meagher, and William H. French; John Sedgwick's Second Division, with brigades under Willis A. Gorman, William W Burns, and N.J.T. Dana; and Louis Blenker's largely German

Third Division, its brigades under Julius Stahel, Adolph von Steinwehr, and Henry Bohlen.

Blenker's division would not set sail for the Peninsula, however. Lincoln was pressured by Radicals to rehabilitate their hero Pathfinder Frémont following his banishment from the Department of the West, and felt obliged to give Frémont command of a new Mountain Department, in far-western Virginia. Frémont needed troops, and was given Blenker's. "I write this to assure you that I did so with great pain, understanding that you would wish it otherwise," Lincoln told McClellan. "If you could know the full pressure of the case, I am confident you would justify it. . . ." McClellan did wish it otherwise, but professed understanding. Nevertheless, he marked the loss of Blenker's division as another entry in his accounting of Washington's meddling.

Heintzelman's Third Corps was made up of Fitz John Porter's First Division, with the brigades of John H. Martindale, George W. Morell, and Daniel Butterfield; Joe Hooker's Second Division, its brigades under Cuvier Grover, Nelson Taylor, and Samuel H. Starr; and Charles Hamilton's Third Division, with the brigades of Charles Jameson, David Birney, and Hiram Berry.

Keyes's Fourth Corps also consisted of three divisions: Couch's First Division, containing the brigades of John J. Peck, Lawrence P. Graham, and Henry S. Briggs; Baldy Smith's Second Division, with brigades under Winfield Scott Hancock, W.T.H. Brooks, and John W. Davidson; and Silas Casey's Third Division, with the brigades of Henry M. Naglee, William H. Keim, and Innis N. Palmer.

Henry Hunt commanded the artillery reserve and George Sykes, the infantry reserve. Philip St. George Cooke commanded the cavalry reserve, its regiments and companies scattered throughout the army.

Nathaniel Banks's Fifth Corps, the divisions of Alpheus Williams and James Shields, remained a part of the Army of the Potomac for barely three weeks. On April 4 it was transferred to the Department of the Shenandoah and thereafter served in northern Virginia.[56]

One name missing from the army's refurbished high command was political general Dan Sickles. On duty in lower Maryland Sickles had ingratiated himself with Joe Hooker, and he further feathered his nest when Edwin Stanton, who got him off in his 1859 murder trial, took the war office. Sickles christened his posting Camp Stanton. But the Senate refused to confirm him brigadier general. New York's Republican governor Edwin Morgan, feuding with Democrat Sickles, made his voice heard in the Republican-controlled Senate. Sickles hurried away to do battle for his rank.

He marshaled editorial support from New York's *Herald* and *Tribune*. After much string pulling and arm twisting, Sickles's name was resubmitted, and on May 13 the Senate confirmed him (in a 19–18 vote) as brigadier general. Meanwhile, the Excelsior Brigade went to war under command of Colonel Nelson Taylor.

The promotion process could be erratic. "I hear there is great opposition in the Senate to the confirmation of our friend 'Baldy,'" George Meade wrote his wife in reference to Baldy Smith. "In addition to the anti-McClellan party, he has managed to make himself unpopular with his troops, who have influenced the Senators from their states." W.T.H. Brooks, commanding the Vermont brigade of Smith's division, explained how that worked. Disgruntled Vermont soldiers aired their complaints about Vermonter Smith to their hometown papers — "The Vermont papers contain many queer letters," Brooks noted — which were in turn read by Vermont's senators. The general's supporters twice postponed the vote in order to firm up their case, and Baldy Smith finally gained his brigadier's star. Politics, domestic as well as army, had ever to be in the thoughts of the Potomac army's generals.[57]

On March 13 Secretary of War Stanton wrote McClellan, "Nothing you can ask of me or this Department will be spared to aid you in every particular." This profession of faith obscured the many and varied sins of Edwin Stanton.

With the post of general-in-chief now vacant, Stanton set up a War Board — the heads of the army bureaus, plus advisers — to assist him and the president in managing the war. The War Board spent a good deal of time second-guessing the generals, especially General McClellan. Its most prominent adviser was Major General Ethan Allen Hitchcock. The grandson of Revolutionary War hero Ethan Allen, Hitchcock graduated West Point in 1817 and served until 1855, notably as Winfield Scott's inspector general in the Mexican War. In 1861 the mild-mannered Hitchcock was enjoying retirement, investigating philosophy, spiritualism, and alchemy. In General Scott's eyes, Hitchcock (like Henry Halleck) was a military intellectual much needed to tame the rebellion, and Scott pressed him to return to the service. Although in poor health, Hitchcock agreed to serve on Stanton's War Board.

In his diary he recorded an eventful first day. "On reporting to the Secy — almost without a word of preface, he asked me — if I would take McClellan's place in command of the Army of the Potomac! I was amazed. I told him, at once, *I could not*. He spoke of the pressure on the President against McClellan, saying that the president and himself had had the greatest difficulty in standing out against it." Two days later Stanton "explained or stated the most astounding facts, all going to show the most astonishing incomprehency of McClellan. I cannot recite them; but one *after* another the Secy stated fact after fact until I felt positively *sick.*" Stanton, he added, "is dreadfully apprehensive of a great disaster."

Hitchcock found Edwin Stanton an intimidating taskmaster. He wrote his nephew, "My Chief is narrow-minded, full of prejudices, exceedingly violent, reckless of the rights and feelings of others, often acting like a wild man in the dark, throwing his arms around, willing to hit anybody, so he hits somebody, and makes a *big stir.*"

A "big stir" nicely described Stanton's intent on April 2 when he approached Lincoln's friend Illinois senator Orville Browning. As Browning recorded it, Stanton said that if Browning would propose to Lincoln that Illinois's Colonel Napoleon Bonaparte Buford be promoted major general and given command of the Army of the Potomac, "he would second my application." Buford was a regular of nondescript record serving in the Western theater whose singular military distinction was his name; perhaps that was what caught Stanton's attention. (U. S. Grant would remark of N. B. Buford's fitness for command, "He would scarcely make a respectable Hospital nurse if put in petticoats. . . .")

These flailing, irrational attempts to replace McClellan never reached Mr. Lincoln's desk. They demonstrated, however, the gulf between secretary of war and commanding general on the eve of the Peninsula campaign. By Browning's account, Stanton expressed "the opinion that McClellan ought to have been removed long ago, and a fear that he was not in earnest, and said that he did not think he could emancipate himself from the influence of Jeff Davis. . . ."

Stanton's irrationality took a fresh turn when on April 3 he closed all government recruiting offices. His intent (he later said) was to straighten out tangled recruiting practices, then reopen a reformed system. His folly by this act was anticipating victory by the Yankee armies as presently constituted — particularly by the Army of the Potomac. Being "dreadfully apprehensive" about McClellan's generalship, it required a leap of faith by Stanton to suppose the Potomac army would put down the rebellion in short order.[58]

For McClellan and his allies, his enemies were easily identified. "The fire in the rear is a terrific one; but I am still confident that the anti-McClellan party, the proper name of which is the Abolition Party, will be signally overthrown," wrote Democratic senator Benjamin Stark. On March 17 Senate Radicals, in secret session, narrowly failed to pass a motion of censure recommending McClellan's dismissal. Fitz John Porter, acting at McClellan's behest against this fire in the rear, sought editorial support from his friend Manton Marble, proprietor of the *New York World,* the city's leading Democratic journal. The country, Porter wrote Marble, could only be reunited by McClellan executing his plans. "But treason is at work and the abolition element is working with southern rebels to produce dissensions and break up our army." The *World's* Washington correspondent promised McClellan his paper "shall continue to counteract your detractors as best we may."

McClellan also looked for help in the conservative press through his home front confidant Samuel Barlow: "Do not mind the abolitionists — all I ask of the papers is that they should defend me from the most malicious attacks. . . ." He was confident about the forthcoming campaign, and hopeful about his support. "I shall soon leave here on the wing for Richmond — which you may be sure I will take. The Army is in magnificent spirits, & I think are half glad that I now belong to them alone. . . . *The President is all right* — he is my strongest friend."[59]

On March 17, one day before Lincoln's deadline, the first troops of the Potomac army embarked at Alexandria bound for Fort Monroe. McClellan's thought was to lead with McDowell's First Corps, landing it as a unit to flank the defenders on the lower Peninsula. But it proved impossible to mass the shipping for such an effort, and the embarkation proceeded instead by divisions "according to convenience." The First Corps was shifted to the end of the line, but its mission stayed the same — a decisive card to play to advance the campaign, said McClellan, "wherever the state of affairs promised the best results." McClellan might condemn Irvin McDowell's motives, yet he recognized him as his only lieutenant with the experience of having commanded a battle.

Heintzelman's Third Corps was best posted to meet the deadline, and Charles Hamilton's division was first to go. "All is confusion & the troops embarking slowly," Heintzelman complained at the Alexandria docks. Soon the kinks were worked out and the movement picked up speed — Heintzelman's Third Corps, Keyes's Fourth Corps, and Sumner's Second Corps to follow. The First Corps was scheduled to start arriving on the Peninsula in mid-April.

In charge was John Tucker, the assistant secretary at the War Department who had sketched out the logistics of the Urbanna move for McClellan back in January. Tucker managed a logistical tour de force. Infantry, artillery, cavalry, wagons, and gear of infinite variety were embarked at Al-

In this artist's composite, General McClellan, before his quarters at Camp Seminary at Alexandria, prepares to go to war. His mother-in-law, Mary Marcy, and his wife, Ellen, are in the doorway. The McClellans' daughter and nursemaid are at an upstairs window.

exandria, and some stores and forage from Annapolis on the Chesapeake. Tucker chartered steamers of every description — ferryboats, excursion craft, side-wheelers, packets — to the number of 113, plus 188 schooners and 88 canal boats and barges under tow. In some three weeks they delivered to Fort Monroe 121,500 men, 14,592 animals, 1,150 wagons, 44 batteries, 74 ambulances, "and the enormous quantity of equipage, &c., required for an army of such magnitude." Assembling, embarking, and disembarking this mass of men and matériel was in the hands of Quartermaster General Montgomery Meigs and Stewart Van Vliet, Potomac army quartermaster. Tucker pridefully summed up: "I respectfully but confidently submit that, for economy and celerity of movement, this expedition is without parallel on record."[60]

Taking headquarters at Alexandria, McClellan plunged into the complex staging of forces and their embarkation. Anticipating a rapid march up the Peninsula to West Point and the railroad from there to Richmond, he directed that sufficient locomotives and cars be standing by to supply an army of 130,000 in the final battle for Richmond. He also gave thought to a role for Ambrose Burnside's force in coastal North Carolina, placed under his command.[61]

He even found time to take under his wing London *Times* correspondent William Howard Russell, ostracized since his unsparing reporting on Bull Run. Gauging a friendlier tone now on the correspondent's part, McClellan granted him a pass to cover the campaign and welcomed him aboard. But the unforgiving Stanton unceremoniously ordered Russell off the ship. "I hear that he will not admit foreign correspondents because he cannot *punish* them if they give aid to the enemy," Russell wrote in disbelief. "Hideously outraged," he sailed for home on the next Atlantic packet.[62]

Another of McClellan's tasks was organizing a secure defense "in, and about Washington," as the president insisted he do. Initially this presented no problem. After the Harper's Ferry canal-boat fiasco, Nathaniel Banks had shepherded the slow rebuilding of the Baltimore & Ohio's bridge at Harper's Ferry and occupied the lower Shenandoah Valley. McClellan anticipated Banks's corps covering both the Valley and the Manassas-Centreville position, serving as the 25,000-man "movable column" the corps commanders had specified. Then Stonewall Jackson upset this best-laid plan.

Joe Johnston told Jackson not to let the Yankees take forces out of the Valley to aid McClellan. On March 23 Jackson struck at James Shields's division at Kernstown, just south of Winchester. Jackson miscalculated and was repulsed by Shields's second in command, Nathan Kimball. Yet the Federals took Kernstown for an omen. Surely it meant the Rebels were strengthening their Valley forces, and therefore Banks dared not reduce his. New arrangements would have to be made.[63]

McClellan took little care with these new arrangements, and his scheme did not at all match what the corps commanders had specified to guard

Washington. James Wadsworth commanded the capital's garrison. Reporting verbally to Stanton on March 30, McClellan said 50,000 men — 30,000 from Banks and Wadsworth's 20,000 — would be "left around Washington." Then, in a memorandum for Stanton dated April 1, McClellan spelled out the "approximate numbers and positions of the troops left near and in the rear on the Potomac."

John Hay made note that on the evening of March 31 McClellan called on the president. "He was much more pleasant and social in manner than formerly. He seems to be anxious for the good opinion of everyone." The next morning, April 1, Lincoln called on McClellan at Alexandria as he prepared to depart for the Peninsula. On neither occasion did McClellan raise anything substantive. Reporting these conversations to Senator Browning, Lincoln said he had taken McClellan's measure as best he could. He had no doubt of his loyalty or of his ability to prepare an army for battle, but "as the hour for action approached he became nervous and oppressed with the responsibility and hesitated to meet the crisis, but that he had given him peremptory orders to move now, and he must do it."

Like the ad hoc council of war on January 13, these meetings offered General McClellan an opportunity to make his case, in particular to explain his dispositions for the defense of Washington — in short, to share confidences with the president. He made no effort to do so. Instead he hurried aboard the steamer *Commodore* for the voyage downriver to Fort Monroe. "I feared that if I remained at Alexandria," he wrote Ellen, "I would be annoyed very much & perhaps be sent for from Washn."[64]

McClellan's April 1 memorandum called for posting 18,600 men in the Manassas-Warrenton area, 1,350 in lower Maryland, and 35,500 in the Shenandoah Valley — a total of 55,450 acting as a "covering force" for Washington. Allowing 18,000 for Wadsworth's garrison brought McClellan's grand total to 73,450. Nowhere was there a plan for the disposition of these forces (especially Banks's), nor any rationale for how all this demonstrated a secure defense of the capital. When Stanton realized that nearly half the impressive total was not "in, and about Washington" but well distant in the Shenandoah Valley, he took alarm.

Stanton passed McClellan's memorandum on to General Wadsworth. Wadsworth was a civilian in arms, a Republican grandee from New York State who had served as a volunteer aide to McDowell at Bull Run and who had little use for McClellan. He reported that of his 19,000-man Washington garrison, four of his best regiments were earmarked for the Potomac army and another 4,000 men were ordered off to Manassas. Further, of the troops left to him, nearly all were "new and imperfectly disciplined."

Further, three regiments of trained artillerymen from the forts had been appropriated by McClellan and replaced by raw infantry "entirely unacquainted with the duties of that arm. . . ." Further, whatever Banks's role in defending Washington, his corps was just then on the far side of the Blue Ridge.

Stanton bundled together Wadsworth's paper, the corps commanders' report on the capital's defenses, Lincoln's War Order No. 3, and McClellan's memorandum and sent them to Adjutant General Lorenzo Thomas and General Hitchcock of the War Board. He told them to report on whether McClellan had complied with the president's instructions, and if not, "wherein those instructions have been departed from." There were, it proved, quite a few departures.

First of all, almost a quarter of the total, some 18,600 men, did not exist —they were overcounted or counted twice or yet to be counted with the army. McClellan included Blenker's division among the Valley defenders, but Blenker had orders to report to Pathfinder Frémont. To this was added Wadsworth's documented woes. When it was all sorted out, it was found that rather than the 50,000 men McClellan promised Stanton on March 30, rather than the 73,450 promised in McClellan's April 1 memo, rather than the 40,000 the corps commanders had specified, the actual troop count "in, and about Washington" was 26,761.

Hitchcock and Thomas and their fellow War Board members, Stanton wrote, "agreed in opinion that the capital *was not safe*." Senator Charles Sumner reported Mr. Lincoln's reaction: "When the Presdt. became aware of this, he was justly indignant."

In fact, Washington was in no danger. With proper direction there were forces enough in this scheme to defend it. Had he put his mind to it, McClellan could have foreclosed debate by counting correctly, by allocating troops correctly, by explaining to Lincoln and Stanton exactly how this broad network of forces served to guard the capital. Instead he once again displayed the "insolence of epaulettes." To his wife, on departing Washington, he wrote, "Officially speaking, I feel very glad to get away from that sink of iniquity." A historian of the time, John C. Ropes, took note of the general's impatience to reach the Peninsula, "where the cheers of the troops should replace the cold and somewhat sceptical talk of the drawing-rooms and lobbies of the capital."[65]

6. *Toward the Gates of Richmond*

IN THE OLD ARMY, a posting to Fort Monroe was much sought after and warmly remembered. The largest of all the coastal fortresses, its cannon commanding Hampton Roads, Monroe was built on a spit of land called Old Point Comfort at the tip of the Virginia Peninsula. Old Point with its Hygeia Hotel was a celebrated watering place in the antebellum years. Now, under command of General John Wool, it was a seat of war.

Actual war was some days and some distance off. Sam Heintzelman led the parade of generals to the fort, bringing his wife along for dining and a stay at the Hygeia. "I dont think the campaign will be a long one . . . ," he confided to his diary. "We will soon have so overwhelming a force that it will carry all before it." The Confederates under John Magruder were said to be well fortified at Yorktown, on the York River some 20 miles from Fort Monroe, with an outpost midway between. Heintzelman had word that Magruder's force was about 7,500, "certainly not to exceed 10,000."[1]

The *Commodore* reached Fort Monroe on April 2 and McClellan went quickly to work. He intended an army-navy envelopment of Yorktown. He estimated the Confederates there at 15,000, well entrenched. While three divisions confronted Yorktown, two others would turn it on the left, or James River side. He anticipated the navy neutralizing the Rebel water batteries at Yorktown and across the York at Gloucester Point, opening the York for a sweep upriver to West Point by McDowell's First Corps.

McClellan labeled naval cooperation vital. At Yorktown the navy should concentrate its most powerful shipboard batteries. At the Navy Department Gus Fox concurred. He wrote Flag Officer Goldsborough, "I should like to see you knock down the town for them, they consider it as saving several months in the campaign."

Goldsborough read the situation very differently. The sortie of CSS *Virginia* on March 8 shocked him to his very marrow. All the wooden warships of his North Atlantic Blockading Squadron were seemingly helpless against the Rebel ironclad. The *Monitor* might be the *Virginia*'s equal, but with both vessels apparently invulnerable, on her next sortie the *Vir-*

The Army of the Potomac disembarks from steamers at Fort Monroe. A watercolor by the Prince de Joinville, the French nobleman serving on McClellan's staff.

ginia might simply ignore the *Monitor* and attack the rest of the blockading squadron and the army's transports. In that event Goldsborough would resort to ramming. Further, he needed his gunboats to counter the *Virginia*'s consorts, which might attempt to ram (or even board) the *Monitor*. Finally, he believed his wooden gunboats no match for shore batteries. "I dare not leave the *Merrimack* and consorts unguarded," he told McClellan. Taking Yorktown must be the army's task, not the navy's.

McClellan acknowledged this change of plan in writing the army's chief of engineers, Joseph Totten. Yorktown was the campaign's first objective, and "this *may* involve a siege (at least I go prepared for one) in case the Navy is not able to afford the means of destroying the rebel batteries. . . ." He wanted a full complement of engineering officers "to establish batteries & perhaps open some trenches." On April 3 he outlined his plan for Ellen. "I hope to get possession of Yorktown day after tomorrow. Shall then arrange to make the York River my line of supplies. . . . The great battle will be (I think) near Richmond as I have always hoped & thought."[2]

April 4, 1862, a Friday, marked the official start of the Peninsula campaign. Taking the road to Yorktown early that morning was Heintzelman's Third Corps, Fitz John Porter's division in the lead, Charles Hamilton's following. Heintzelman's Third Division, under Joe Hooker, had not yet arrived, and so John Sedgwick's Second Corps division served as general reserve. Uncle John wrote his sister, "We march at daylight, sixty thousand men and the finest artillery in the world. I do not think we can be whipped." McClellan's orders to Heintzelman were specific: "Do not attack unless you see that the rebels are actually evacuating the place. I wish to cut off their retreat with Keyes' column before pressing them on our right." Marching in parallel on the Hampton Road to the left was the flanking column — two of Erasmus Keyes's Fourth Corps divisions, Baldy Smith's in the lead, followed by Darius Couch's. The two columns, by design, were headed by trusted McClellan loyalists, Porter and Smith.

In all, the Federals mustered 55,000 men. They found the Rebels' advanced line abandoned, opening the way to Yorktown. "Everything has worked well today," McClellan wrote Ellen. "I have gained some strong positions without fighting & shall try some more maneuvering tomorrow."[3]

Tomorrow — April 5 — proved a defining moment in the Peninsula campaign. For General McClellan it was a day of unpleasant surprises. Morning saw a downpour of rain, and the roads he had described in his February 3 paper as "passable at all seasons of the year" were, when it rained, impassable. Charles Howard, Otis Howard's brother and staff aide, described them: "The entire surface for miles is under layed by 'quicksands' which give way as soon as teams begin to cross over the surface — such depth of mud & such frightful roads I never saw." Men could march, with difficulty, but guns and vehicles bogged down.

What was worse, the enemy front was not found where expected. Resistance was anticipated at Yorktown, and Fitz John Porter dutifully reported encountering Rebels "who as the mist rose were seen crowding the ramparts." But from the flanking column Keyes sent notice of strong breastworks blocking his way. "It is my opinion that we shall encounter very serious resistance." Later, "I am stopped by the enemy's works at Lee's Mill, which offer a severe resistance." He reported the Warwick River barred the way, dammed in several places and "nowhere fordable."

McClellan based his plan to outflank Yorktown on a map furnished him at Fort Monroe. It traced the course of the Warwick River closely paralleling the James before emptying into that river, showing a half dozen miles of dry ground between the James and Yorktown, easily room enough to turn the Rebel position. The map drew on a U.S. Coastal Survey chart of the James that showed only a narrow strip of coastline — and did not reveal that the Warwick originated close to Yorktown and flowed straight across the Peninsula toward the James. The only defenses marked were at Yorktown. McClellan, it seems, expected an obliging General Magruder to let himself be cooped up there, like Lord Cornwallis eighty-one years before.[4]

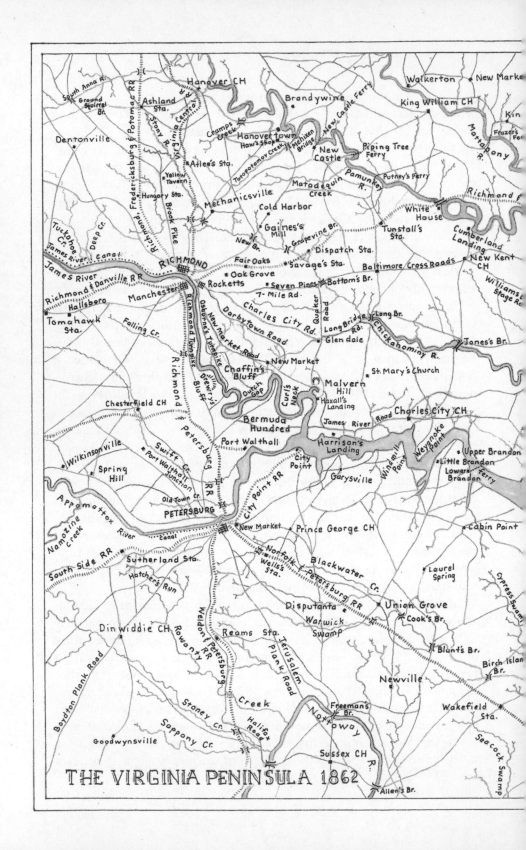

THE VIRGINIA PENINSULA 1862

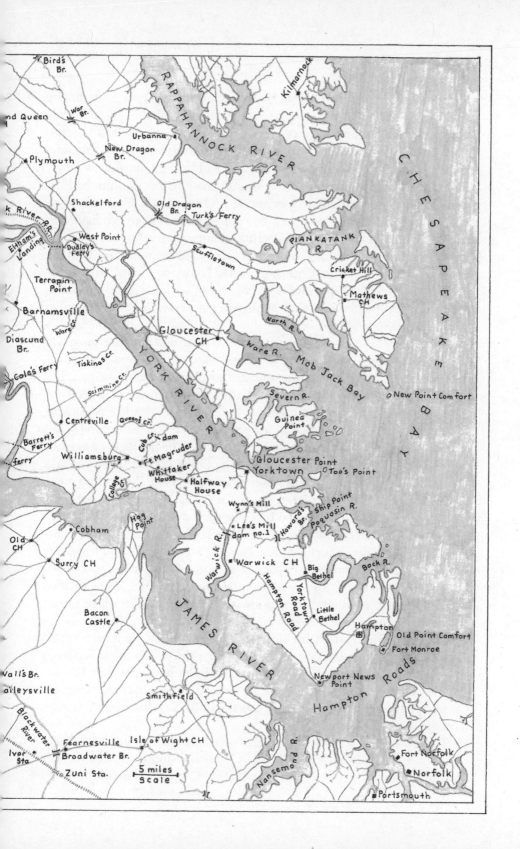

Instead, Magruder had turned the Warwick into a barrier by damming and earthworks. That was not the end of his creativity. In the old army Magruder was known as Prince John for the theatricals he liked to stage. Now he put on the performance of his life. Musketry and cannon fire met the Yankees. Drummers beat the long roll and buglers signaled assembly and officers shouted commands. It was all charade. Prince John had but 11,000 men, 6,000 of them in garrison at Yorktown and Gloucester Point, so he multiplied his few into many by ruse. Regiments marched in circles, appearing then reappearing from behind stands of trees. Or they marched in plain sight — one Louisiana regiment marched from Yorktown to the James and back six times. Cheering greeted "reinforcements" from Richmond. Magruder "did splendidly," wrote Mary Chesnut. "It was a wonderful thing, how he played his ten thousand before McClellan like fireflies and utterly deluded him."[5]

George McClellan, so highly organized in mind and purpose, proved to be unnerved by the unexpected. Boldness faded to caution. Nothing happening on April 5 had been foreseen; nothing was going as planned. The rains of spring promised to play havoc with movements by road. The real Warwick River bore no resemblance to the map's Warwick River, blocking his intended line of advance. The navy was no help. Keyes's reports of defenses extending to the James was the last straw. The intelligence must be wrong — surely Magruder would not attempt to man the citadels of Yorktown and Gloucester Point plus miles of fieldworks with just 15,000 men.

Earlier McClellan told chief engineer Totten that taking Yorktown "*may* involve a siege." He now decided his siege train was the surest solution to the knotty problem confronting him. That afternoon orders went to Quartermaster Van Vliet at Fort Monroe: General McClellan feels it necessary "to resort to some of the operations of a siege, and he wishes you to forward without delay ... the siege train and mortars." McClellan notified Goldsborough, "I cannot turn Yorktown without a *battle*, in which I must use heavy artillery & go through the preliminary operations of a siege."[6]

The final blow in this day of blows was a dispatch that night from Washington telling McClellan that McDowell's First Corps was "detached from the force under your immediate command." The president took this action because he deemed the force left in front of the capital insufficient for its safety; the numbers were "much less than had been fixed by your corps commanders as necessary. ..."

There was a choice in selecting the force held back to guard Washington, and Lincoln had left it to Stanton. Four divisions were not yet embarked for the Peninsula — Sumner's Second Corps division under Israel

Richardson, and McDowell's three First Corps divisions. A thought-out choice would be to hold back General Sumner, who with Richardson and a selection of troops culled from McClellan's scheme would be quite sufficient to protect the capital. Instead Stanton, overreacting to imagined danger — or simply acting from malice — withheld the entire First Corps. This blunder had consequences both imagined and real.

McClellan fired a telegram of protest to the president. "In my deliberate judgment the success of our cause will be imperilled by so greatly reducing my force when it is actually under the fire of the enemy," and he called for at least the division of his favorite, William Franklin. To his wife he called McDowell's retention "the most infamous thing that history has recorded. . . . The idea of depriving a General of 35,000 troops when actually under fire!"

The officer corps shared his anger. Sam Heintzelman: "At what a time to do such a thing. It is a great outrage." William Franklin: "The bad faith to McClellan was such an outrageous thing." Erasmus Keyes: "The plan to which we are reduced bears scarcely any resemblance to the one I voted for." Youthful, melodramatic Philippe d'Orléans of the staff described reactions among lesser officers: "Some are discouraged, others lose control of their language or sulk in silence, one even hears talk of calling upon the nation, upon the army, for a coup d'etat."[7]

At the front, Baldy Smith was not as taken in by Magruder's charade as corps commander Keyes, and early on April 6 he sent Winfield Hancock's brigade to see if the enemy line might be forced. "Knowing General Keyes to be irresolute . . . ," Smith wrote, "I took it upon myself to give Hancock orders," then told Keyes in a "conversational way" what he had done. As they talked, a dispatch arrived from headquarters. Keyes read it and without a word passed it to Smith. On General McClellan's orders, no offensive operations were to be undertaken until the engineers had examined the enemy lines. Hancock meanwhile reported the gap they were looking for, at a place called Dam No. 1. "I had only to reply to him to come back to camp," Smith wrote. He never doubted that had his initiative been rewarded there would have been no siege of Yorktown.

A second gap, at Wynn's Mill, was discovered by Heintzelman's division commander Charles Hamilton. The two of them reported the finding to McClellan and his confidant Fitz John Porter and made application to launch an assault with Hamilton's division. But, Heintzelman wrote, "the siege was determined upon without my being consulted." It was apparent General McClellan was not inviting battlefield initiatives by his lieutenants.

Winslow Homer, on assignment from *Harper's Weekly*, did this pencil and wash drawing of Willis Gorman's Second Corps brigade reconnoitering before Yorktown.

Baldy Smith would have been dismayed to learn that the aborted sortie at Dam No. 1 furnished McClellan with the rationale to go to ground at Yorktown. Hancock brought back four prisoners, who talked freely enough to a Pinkerton interrogator to suggest they were members of the Prince John Players. The interrogator's notes read, "Force of enemy 40,000. Johnston 8,000 exp'd. last night. Says they have 500 guns in position. . . . Says that the big fight will be here. . . . It is understood they have brought all the guns from above and in a few days 100,000 men." The report reached McClellan on April 7 and he swallowed it whole. He telegraphed Stanton, "All the prisoners state that Gen J. E. Johnston arrived in Yorktown yesterday with strong reinforcements. It seems clear that I shall have the whole force of the enemy on my hands, probably not less than one hundred thousand (100,000) men & possibly more. In consequence of the loss of Blenkers Division & the First Corps my force is possibly less than that of the enemy. . . ."

(On April 5 Prince John Magruder had telegraphed Richmond, "I have made my arrangements to fight with my small force, but without the slightest hope of success." Joe Johnston, when he later reached the Yorktown lines, remarked unkindly of his old friend, "No one but McClellan could have hesitated to attack.")

The phantom Confederate army, last credited at Manassas, was once again rooted in General McClellan's imagination, where it would haunt him for the rest of the Peninsula campaign.[8]

To Stanton McClellan laid out his dilemma. He faced a Rebel army larger than his own, manning a line too strong to be breached without heavy artillery of the siege train. His plan had been to land the First Corps to turn the Gloucester Point batteries. It would require several weeks (although he did not mention that) to position McDowell's divisions and build batteries for a coordinated assault. Now, lacking McDowell, he could not spare the troops to attack Gloucester Point "without materially impairing" his main column. It was the same argument he had used against the Occoquan plan — one dared not divide one's army in the face of a superior army. The siege train would even the odds. Unspoken was the fact that even should Washington relent and McDowell arrive as originally scheduled, the siege of Yorktown would still last as long as need be.

Siege warfare was the military art George McClellan knew well. As a young lieutenant of engineers he had taken part in the siege of Vera Cruz in 1847 during the War with Mexico. On his assignment abroad in 1855 to observe the Crimean War he had made a careful inspection of the siege of Sevastopol and studied its logistics. Now he sent to his wife for his books on the subject, and as his own siege progressed he wrote her, "I *do* believe that I am avoiding the faults of the Allies at Sebastopol & quietly preparing the way for a great success."

Great success would require much time to marshal many resources. Depots were established and the boggy roads corduroyed and bridges rebuilt. Chief engineer John Barnard laid out the siege lines and battery positions. Chief of artillery William Barry supervised arming the siege pieces. Fitz John Porter, director of the siege, was assigned "the guarding of the trenches, the assembling and distribution of the working parties, &c., &c." The general commanding oversaw every detail.[9]

While McClellan petitioned Lincoln and Stanton, his lieutenants were busy letter writing. Fitz John Porter wrote editor Marble of the Democratic *New York World* of the need for command questions to be decided by "an educated soldier not a politician who would sacrifice millions of lives for his own advancement. . . . Such an ass as Stanton would ruin any cause. . . ." Erasmus Keyes wrote *his* friend, Republican senator Ira Harris of New York, "The line in front of us is . . . one of the strongest ever opposed to an invading force in any country," and pleaded with Harris to use his influence to ensure "that the force originally intended for the capture of Richmond should be all sent forward." Another special pleader was Thomas M. Key of McClellan's staff, who appealed to Senator John Sherman and to Secretary of the Treasury Chase to have "the whole original force employed as contemplated when this great movement was commenced." Chase wryly observed, "McClellan, surrounded by a staff of letter-writers, gets possession of public opinion, and even those who know better, succumb."[10]

McClellan telegraphed Franklin that he was pressuring the administration for the release of at least his division. "Do all you can to accomplish it. Heaven knows I need you here." In reply, Franklin reported McDowell saying "he had nothing to do with having his corps taken from your command . . . it was intended as a blow at you. That Stanton had said that . . . all of the opponents of the policy of the administration centered around you — in other words that you had political aspirations." (By way of confirmation, Senator Charles Sumner, writing on April 22, heard Stanton admit he had very little confidence in McClellan "& that he was not disposed to send the re-inforcements which he desired.")

Franklin's dispatch, if further evidence was needed, clinched McClellan's disdain for the secretary of war. McDowell, his claim of innocence ignored, was adjudged disloyal and an intriguer. "After all that I have heard of things which have occurred since I left Washington & before," McClellan wrote the president, "I would prefer that Genl McDowell should not again be assigned to duty with me." His charge of intrigue was upheld (in his mind) when McDowell was assigned an independent command, the new Department of the Rappahannock. Four commands now defended Washington and its approaches — McDowell's Department of the Rappahannock, Banks's Department of the Shenandoah, Frémont's Mountain Department, and Wadsworth's District of Washington . . . and no general-in-chief to coordinate them.

On learning the army had gone to ground at Yorktown, Mr. Lincoln sent his general some considered advice. By the returns, McClellan would soon have 100,000 men. "I think you better break the enemies' line from York-town to Warwick River, at once. They will probably use *time,* as advantageously as you can." McClellan relayed this advisory to Ellen and added, "I was much tempted to reply that he had better come & do it himself." In his reply he poured out all his problems, all his needs, all the enemy's great strengths of position and manpower, and insisted the First Corps was key to his plans. "I feel fully impressed with the conviction that here is to be fought the great battle that is to decide the existing contest."[11]

In his response (April 9) the president set about explaining to his general the larger issues of the moment and thereby to reason with him. "Your dispatches complaining that you are not properly sustained, while they do not offend me, do pain me very much," he began. He observed that now "is the precise time for you to strike a blow. By delay the enemy will relatively gain upon you — that is, he will gain faster, by *fortification* and *re-inforcements,* than you can by re-inforcements alone . . . it is indispensable to *you* that you strike a blow. *I* am powerless to help this." He asked McClellan to do him the justice to recall that he had warned that "going down the Bay in search of a field," instead of doing battle at Manassas, "was only shifting, and not surmounting, a difficulty — that we would find the same enemy, and the same, or equal, intrenchments, at either place. The country will not fail to note — is now noting — that the present hesitation to move upon an intrenched enemy, is but the story of Manassas repeated.

"I beg to assure you that I have never written you, or spoken to you, in greater kindness of feeling than now, nor with a fuller purpose to sustain you. . . . *But you must act.*"

The president enunciated the divide between commander-in-chief and general commanding — his pragmatic strategy to move against the Rebel army in some fashion while it was within easy reach at Manassas, versus McClellan's perfectionist maneuvering to force the enemy host into one imagined Napoleonic war-ending battle before Richmond. The immediate issue concerned *time* and its consequences. McClellan would expend all the time necessary to refine and polish and perfect his plan. Lincoln sought action now, to deny the enemy the many uses of time to dig in and to reinforce.

McClellan offered no response to Lincoln's letter, but brightened when told that Franklin's division would join him, and, "if the safety of this city will permit," McCall's division would follow. He thanked the president for the release of Franklin, and said that siege preparations were progressing: "Siege guns & ammunition coming up very satisfactorily — shall have nearly all up tomorrow. The tranquility of Yorktown is nearly at an end." That was written on April 14. Yorktown would experience more or less tranquility for another three weeks.[12]

The withholding of the First Corps would became a cause célèbre . . . invented by General McClellan. In his 1864 *Report* he termed it a most discouraging blow. "It frustrated all my plans for impending operations. . . . It left me incapable of continuing operations which had been begun. It compelled the adoption of another, a different and a less effective plan of campaign. It made rapid and brilliant operations impossible. It was a fatal error."

Except for McClellan's discouragement, nothing in his catalog of complaint was true. He had already determined to lay siege to Yorktown before learning of the First Corps' retention. Impending operations were not disjointed; McDowell had never been scheduled to begin reaching the Peninsula before mid-April. Nor was the progress of the siege delayed; even after Franklin's division arrived (starting April 19), no use was made of it. It was McClellan's failure to heed his aggressive-minded lieutenants — Baldy Smith, Winfield Hancock, Sam Heintzelman, Charles Hamilton — that compelled "a different and less effective plan." It was Confederates in their phantom numbers who "made rapid and brilliant operations impossible."[13]

"The curiosity & anxiety about Yorktown is feverish," the *New-York Tribune*'s managing editor wrote in prodding his reporters for more Potomac army news. To quiet critics, the bloated Pinkerton report of Confederate strength that McClellan had found so persuasive was fed to the press. On April 9 an Associated Press reporter wrote, "By the time the roads are in condition for the Union Army to move the rebels may be able to meet them with one hundred thousand men." He counted 500 enemy guns.

The papers that April were full of successes elsewhere. At Shiloh on the Tennessee River U. S. Grant gained victory in a bloody battle, and on the Mississippi General John Pope captured Island No. 10. There were victories on the Atlantic coast, at Fort Pulaski in Georgia and at Fort Macon in North Carolina. Admiral David Farragut seized New Orleans, the Confederacy's largest city. "Glorious news come borne on every wind but the South Wind," White House secretary John Hay wrote; ". . . the little Napoleon sits trembling before the handful of men at Yorktown afraid either to fight or run. Stanton feels devilish about it. He would like to remove him if he thought it would do."

The stalemate of the North's largest army reinvigorated McClellan's critics. In his diary Attorney General Edward Bates delved into McClellan's mental makeup: "I do believe that the Genl. has such a morbid ambition of originality that he will adopt no plan of action suggested by another — He must himself *invent* as well as execute every scheme of operations. And yet it seems to me that he has but small inventive faculty — Hence his inevitable failure."

But McClellan did not lack for supporters. Samuel Barlow assured him that "the dastardly conduct of those in Washington, who seek to drive you from the Army, or into a defeat, to serve their own selfish ends, is beginning to be understood. . . ." Montgomery Blair, his advocate in the cabinet, pointed out (somewhat cynically) that dear-bought victories "will perhaps do more to raise you in the estimation of people generally than successes achieved by strategy merely. So come what will, you will be in no danger of losing reputation." Blair's influential father, Francis Preston Blair, also had advice for the general: "There is a prodigious cry of 'On to Richmond' among the carpet knights . . . who will not shed their blood to get there. . . . If you can accomplish your object of reaching Richmond by a slower process than storming redoubts & batteries in earth works, the country will applaud the achievement." In thanking Blair for his counsel, McClellan spoke of "the difficulties placed in my path by some who ought to be my friends," but he added, "I do not for a moment doubt the result of this operation. I will take Y. — take it too without an undue loss of life."[14]

Yorktown was not a full-fledged siege, designed to surround the enemy. Lord Cornwallis found no escape in 1781; in 1862 Joe Johnston could stand and fight or abandon his lines as he chose. McClellan's purpose was to mass his heavy ordnance to pulverize a section of the enemy line to allow an infantry assault. Fourteen batteries were constructed, to hold 109 pieces ranging from 20- and 30-pounder Parrott rifles up to 100- and 200-pounder Parrotts and massive 10- and 13-inch siege mortars. A steam sawmill provided lumber for the gun platforms and magazines. Working parties dug parallels and built redoubts. The labor and engineering required were enormous. Chief engineer Barnard estimated six hours of bombardment would finish the Rebels.

(On April 13, from his confinement in military prison on New York Harbor, Brigadier General Charles Stone wrote to Adjutant General Lorenzo Thomas asking that his arrest be suspended so that he might be "permitted to serve in some capacity before Yorktown." As with his requests to see the charges against him, Stone received no response.)[15]

On April 16 Baldy Smith made a demonstration at Dam No. 1 on the left, where earlier he and Winfield Hancock had briefly seized a gap in the Rebel lines. Smith acted on McClellan's order to stop the enemy from strengthening the spot; if a foothold was gained, assistance "will be promptly afforded." Then McClellan changed the mission: "Upon reflection I think it will, under present circumstances, be wiser to confine the operation to forcing the enemy to discontinue work." Here was an echo of his vague instructions to Charles Stone at Ball's Bluff. Smith sent in W.T.H. Brooks's Vermont brigade and it won a small lodgment on enemy ground. McClellan looked on for a time and returned to headquarters, apparently satisfied. What happened afterward, he said (in another echo of Ball's Bluff), "was in direct violation of my orders. . . ."

The Vermonters' calls for help went unanswered and they were counterattacked and driven out of their lodgment. A rescue attempt only added to the casualty list. Smith admitted "my own fault of not seeing the advantage I had gained." The cause of that, he said, was a balky horse which threw him and left him stunned. (It was said that "everybody behaved splendidly except the General's horse.") A different story got back to Vermont and to Washington, and to the newspapers. Smith's confirmation as brigadier general was then being contested, and on the House floor Vermont congressman Justin Morrill charged him with being drunk on the battlefield. McClellan condemned the accusation as a malicious slander. Smith demanded a court of inquiry and was cleared of the charge, after which he wrote a caustic letter to Morrill, demanding a "retraction as public as the libel." A Senate investigative committee cleared Smith, and his promotion was confirmed.

In fact there was never point or purpose to the fight of April 16. In General Brooks's words, "No great object and no great effect." It was settled that the bombardment and assault would be at the Yorktown end of the line. Artillery could have achieved McClellan's ambiguous wants. All Dam No. 1 demonstrated was the continued presence of cracks in the Potomac army's command structure.[16]

On April 29 Sam Heintzelman told his diary, "The conduct of Gen. McClellan is giving great dissatisfaction in this Army, particularly about Gen. Porter. No less than three Generals spoke to me about it & one of them this morning was afraid his name would have to be changed to Porter before he would be able to do anything." Heintzelman did not identify the three, but one was surely division commander Israel Richardson. "The favorites of Gen. McClellan," Richardson wrote his wife, "are put forward in this war, for instance Fitz John Porter, Franklin, and Smith. They may, however, be whipped as other favorites were at Bull Run, and others get the credit at last." Numerous of his lieutenants found McClellan hard to see and aloof to their concerns at any time.

Rhode Island's Governor William Sprague, who had served as an aide to Ambrose Burnside at Bull Run, was sent to the Peninsula by Secretary Stanton to investigate McClellan's running of the army. "I regret exceedingly to note the want of harmony," Sprague reported. The new corps organization was being "wholly nullified . . . Keyes, Sumner & Heintzelman are subordinate to Porter, Smith and to Franklin."

It did appear that the general commanding dealt only with these favorites. He made little effort to conceal his contempt for Erasmus Keyes. In the Dam No. 1 affair he issued orders directly to Baldy Smith, ignoring Keyes, Smith's superior. There was a move to get rid of Keyes entirely. In

David Hunter Strother, staff officer and artist under the name Porte Crayon, took as a subject for satire the siege-addicted McClellan.

a rare conciliatory mood, Stanton asked McClellan, "Would it assist you any to have Franklin made commander of a corps instead of Keyes, if it can be done?" McClellan was quick to approve. Then he grew concerned about the reaction in the officer corps to such a blunt move, and the idea was dropped.[17]

McClellan discovered how messy it was to get rid of a general. Charles Hamilton, who took Heintzelman's old Third Corps division, was an abrasive sort with a nose for intrigue. He resented McClellan's rejection of his scheme to attack at Wynn's Mill early in the siege, he resented Fitz John Porter assigning his division excessive siege digging, and he wrote highly disrespectful letters to Washington about all this. McClellan termed this misconduct and relieved Hamilton.

Charles Hamilton had Republican friends in Congress, and Mr. Lincoln found himself with a petition signed by twenty-three senators and eighty-four representatives demanding Hamilton's reinstatement. Among the signers were the Jacobins on the Committee on the Conduct of the War, always ready to discomfort McClellan. Lincoln wrote McClellan that he would like to accommodate Congress in this matter, "yet I do not wish to be understood as rebuking you." McClellan replied in high dudgeon — the discipline of the army would not permit Hamilton's restoration; he was removed for cause. "You cannot do anything better calculated to injure my army . . . than to restore Gen Hamilton to his Division." There the matter rested, prime evidence of the partisan politics swirling about the Army of the Potomac.

To replace Hamilton McClellan selected the mercurial Phil Kearny. Kearny confessed he would "not act to my own injury a second time." He had found his principled loyalty to his New Jersey brigade stifling, forcing him to serve with "unfitting, unpractised juniors." Ambitious to gain "my due military weight," he welcomed leading a division in the Third Corps along with Porter and Joe Hooker. Corps commander Heintzelman entered in his diary, "Gen. Kearny relieves Gen. Hamilton. I fear he will be troublesome."[18]

As April turned to May, McClellan put the final touches on his carefully calculated scheme for bombarding Yorktown. Batteries were completed, guns mounted, magazines filled, parallels dug. Heintzelman's Third Corps would spearhead the assault. Detective Pinkerton counted 100,000 to 120,000 as "under rather than over the mark of the real strength of rebel forces at Yorktown." McClellan expected a showdown battle, telling Baldy Smith, "I can not realize an evacuation possible." That was the last thing he wanted. "I do not want these rascals to get away from me without a sound drubbing," he told Ellen. The guns would open at first light on May 5.

Visitors crowded into headquarters in anticipation of the great battle. It was like those expectant days before Bull Run. There was Montgomery Blair from the cabinet, John Tucker from the War Department, Gus Fox from the Navy Department, former Ohio governor William Dennison, even the French minister, Henri Mercier. Uncle John Sedgwick expressed a widespread confidence: "It seems that this must be their last stand, and if beaten here they must leave Virginia."

McClellan told Ellen of impatience building in Washington. "I feel that the fate of a nation depends upon me & I feel that I have not one single friend at the seat of Govt — any day may bring an order relieving me from command — if such a thing should be done our cause is lost. If they will simply let me alone I feel sure of success. . . ."[19]

Joe Johnston, having hardly one soldier for every two Pinkerton credited him with, watched events closely. On April 29 he signaled Richmond, "The fight for Yorktown . . . must be one of artillery, in which we cannot win. The result is certain; the time only doubtful." During the night of

May 3 the Confederate guns unleashed a tremendous barrage, after which the lines fell silent. At first light on May 4, Sam Heintzelman ascended in an observation balloon. "We could not see a gun on the rebel works or a man," he would enter in his diary. "Their tents were standing & all quiet as the grave." He shouted to watchers on the ground that the Rebels were gone, and in due course a telegram went out from Potomac army headquarters to Washington: "Yorktown is in our possession."[20]

As first reports of the Confederate evacuation reached headquarters, the Comte de Paris hastened to wake the general commanding. McClellan judged the reports indefinite and went back to sleep. The young Frenchman diplomatically entered in his journal, "The American mind is slow to grasp an idea to which it is not accustomed beforehand." Heintzelman, scheduled to lead the assault on Yorktown, ordered Hooker and Kearny to have their men cook three days' rations and be ready to march. Then he waited for orders. Finally, impatiently, he rode to headquarters and found it only beginning to stir. Orders for a pursuit were issued four hours after Heintzelman found the Rebel works silent as the grave.[21]

The chief of cavalry, George Stoneman, led the pursuit. With the Potomac army lacking a unified cavalry command, Stoneman made do with a pickup force—two regiments from the cavalry reserve and one each from the Second and Third Corps. The infantry divisions of Joe Hooker (Third Corps) and Baldy Smith (Fourth Corps) would follow.

Snags and confusion marked the officer corps. Hooker only began his march at 1 o'clock, for Dan Butterfield, serving that day as "general of the trenches," would not immediately give up a thousand of Hooker's men detailed for digging. The delay left Hooker's division trailing Smith's on the roads leading to Williamsburg. Smith too had been delayed. Aeronaut Thaddeus Lowe had a balloon posted with the Fourth Corps, and Lieutenant George Armstrong Custer, West Point 1861, was aloft at first light to report the enemy trenches empty. Corps commander Keyes, however, urged caution. In forwarding Custer's sighting to headquarters, he wrote, "I have no idea the works are abandoned. I shall make no movement to cross without orders from higher authority." By then Custer was back on the ground and showing the way through the empty works.

Before long, all three of the corps commanders, Heintzelman, Keyes, and Sumner, were on their way to Williamsburg, where Stoneman was skirmishing with the Confederate rear guard. General McClellan, remaining at Yorktown to ponder his next move, failed to clarify command of the pursuing forces.[22]

McClellan quickly overcame any disappointment at not bringing the enemy to a climactic battle at Yorktown. "I am now fully satisfied of the correctness of the course I have pursued," he told Stanton. "Our success is brilliant. . . ." He repeated the claim to the retired Winfield Scott, making note that the Rebels' numbers "are stated to be from 100,000 to 120,000." To Ellen he boasted, "Results glorious. . . . The enemy's works of very great strength. He must have been badly scared to have abandoned them in such a hurry."

Celebration was widespread. The *New-York Tribune* headline read, REBELS RAN AWAY LAST NIGHT — THE "LAST DITCH" FILLED. In Albany the city fathers rang church bells and fired a 100-gun salute. But the army's artillerists grieved. For weeks, wrote the Comte de Paris, they "have counted down the hours that separated them from the bombardment which promised them no end of pleasure." Alexander Webb, artillery adjutant, was "tearing out his hair" at the prospect of breaking down the batteries and removing them.

Joe Johnston's evacuation could also be interpreted as Joe Johnston's escape — a repetition of his Manassas escape. "The retreat of the rebels I fear will play the devil with McClellan," Joe Hooker remarked. William Cullen Bryant's *New York Evening Post* recalled all those reports from Potomac army headquarters "of the immense numbers of men which the rebels had congregated on the peninsula, of the impregnable nature of their defences, of the necessity of our slow and careful approach . . . the universal expectation of some grand result when everything should have been prepared." Instead, it was "the mouse brought forth by the laboring mountain."[23]

The abandonment of Yorktown and Gloucester Point opened the York River, a key element in McClellan's design. By evening on May 4 the navy had reconnoitered some 25 miles upriver as far as West Point, where the Pamunkey and Mattapony rivers join to form the York, and where the Richmond & York River Railroad had its terminus. The navy reported no obstructions in the river and no batteries on the banks.

McClellan initially designated McDowell's First Corps his force of maneuver, to turn Gloucester Point while the rest of the army turned Yorktown. That scheme came undone when Yorktown could not be turned (so McClellan decided) and when the enemy was found to be 100,000 strong (so McClellan believed). Franklin's division was the remnant of the plan. For two weeks Franklin's men stayed aboard their transports in expectation of attacking Gloucester Point. But on May 3 McClellan decided he would be outnumbered attacking Yorktown, and ordered Franklin's division disembarked to reinforce Heintzelman. Now came a rush to get

Franklin's troops and artillery back aboard the transports to exploit the opening of the York. Only at first light on May 6 did Franklin set off up the York bound for West Point.[24]

George McClellan revealed something of his command philosophy by electing to remain behind at Yorktown on May 4–5. As the campaign shifted abruptly from the static of siege to the fluidity of pursuit, he assumed the role of military executive rather than warrior general. He explained in his memoir, "I therefore pushed with redoubled energy the arrangements to throw a force by water to the mouth of the Pamunkey, and had not the slightest reason to suppose that my presence was at all necessary at the front." Yet there was nothing to be done at Yorktown not already being done by Franklin and the engineers and the navy. What needed doing was far more likely to be at the front, at Williamsburg, where the first battle of the campaign was pending.

And in that event, McClellan did not hurry to the sound of the guns. On his one previous battlefield, at Rich Mountain in western Virginia in 1861, he made no move against the enemy's front when his flanking column under William Rosecrans ran into a noisy firefight in the enemy's rear. Rosecrans managed to prevail, yet General McClellan "was bound, as a military man, to have made the attack in his front, for the purpose of preventing the enemy from falling on me with too heavy a force." On the morning of May 5, 1862, at McClellan's headquarters, the sound of the guns was again heard. At 9:00 a.m. he reported, "Enemy still at Williamsburg — heavy firing now going on." His only response was to sit down at 9:30 and write to his wife proclaiming his triumph at Yorktown.[25]

Williamsburg was a dozen miles from Yorktown and a place well suited for defense. The Peninsula narrows here to just seven miles wide, and the space to be defended was reduced to half that by the winding courses of College Creek and Queen's Creek, emptying into the James and the York respectively. Magruder had marked Williamsburg as his fallback position should the Yorktown–Warwick River line not hold, and he put his men to digging. The lower Peninsula's two main roads — the York and Hampton roads — came together in front of Williamsburg, and there Magruder erected a large earthen redoubt he unblushingly named Fort Magruder. Left and right as far as the two creeks were thirteen small redoubts. Major Charles Wainwright, Joe Hooker's chief of artillery, described the approach as "ugly enough for some five hundred yards, the rebel redoubt, Fort Magruder, having a raging fire down it."

Johnston had not intended to defend Williamsburg. With the York now open to the Yankees, he was anxious to fall back on Richmond to avoid being cut off by a landing high up the York — the move Franklin was preparing. Then it began to rain, which Johnston knew would slow the retreat to a crawl. He told James Longstreet to occupy the Williamsburg defenses and block the enemy pursuit.

Command of the pursuit was jumbled from the start. That morning, McClellan sent to Heintzelman saying that when Kearny joined Hooker and Baldy Smith in the pursuit, "I would be glad to have you take control of the entire movement." That was clear enough — Kearny and Hooker were in Heintzelman's Third Corps and pursuing by way of the York Road. But then Smith's division, on the left on the Hampton Road, pushed into the lead. Smith belonged to Keyes's Fourth Corps, and suddenly that became an issue.

Although Edwin Sumner's Second Corps was held at Yorktown, at noon on May 4 Sumner received McClellan's order "to take command of the troops ordered in pursuit of the enemy." This was a McClellan second thought. If Baldy Smith's division led the pursuit, that meant a role for Smith's corps commander, Erasmus Keyes, and that was not to McClellan's liking. At Yorktown Sumner's left-wing command had included Keyes's Fourth Corps as well as his own Second, and now that directive was tacitly extended . . . absent the Second Corps. Keyes's only role at Williamsburg would be as supernumerary, shepherding his other two divisions to the front.[26]

It was intended to pursue on parallel roads, but a burned bridge on the Hampton Road turned Baldy Smith's troops into a crossroad leading to the York Road at a country tavern called Halfway House, some five miles from Fort Magruder. They reached there ahead of Hooker, blocking his path. From a contraband Hooker learned of a second crossroad just ahead that intersected the Hampton Road beyond the burned bridge, a route that ought to bring him in on the flank of the Rebels at Williamsburg. Impatient to break out of the traffic jam, Hooker proposed taking it — in effect completing an exchange of positions with Smith. Heintzelman, in command of the movement (as he thought), "heartily approved of it."

As Hooker set off on his flanking march, Heintzelman rode ahead to the front to (as he thought) take command. At headquarters at the Whittaker house he met Stoneman, Baldy Smith . . . and Edwin Sumner. Regardless of McClellan's earlier grant of command, Heintzelman now found himself under Sumner's orders as senior officer on the battlefield. "Seeing Gen. Sumner," Heintzelman wrote in annoyance, "I of course became a spectator. . . . I sat down and quietly waited developments."[27]

At sunset Sumner determined to storm Fort Magruder with Baldy Smith's infantry. He made no reconnoiter. The Comte de Paris described Sumner unflatteringly: "Packed into a tight jacket without insignia, his neck wrapped in a big red bandanna, wearing a huge pointed hat and holding in his hand a riding crop that he shakes fitfully, the grand old man, wizened, white-bearded, has an air of stupidity that perfectly expresses his mental state." McClellan's confidant the Prince de Joinville, traveling with the advance, urged Smith to protest the attack. "I told him General Sumner was not a man to reason with," Smith said, and suggested Joinville try to dissuade the old general. With a Gallic shrug, Joinville said that would be impertinent. "Officers came to me to try & induce Sumner to desist," Heintzelman said, "but he could nowhere be found." Sumner had led the way into the woods and in the growing darkness lost direction. Seeing only folly ahead, Smith ordered a halt. His column endured a wet night in the woods. A mile or so away on the left, Hooker's men also spent the night lying on their arms.[28]

Monday, May 5, dawned gloomy with a hard rain, but Joe Hooker would not be deterred. He was ordered to pursue a retreating enemy, he wrote, "& finding him I deemed it my duty to engage him without regard to numbers. . . ." He faced the Rebels' right flank. He knew Smith's division was also at the front, separated from him by a marshy woodland, and he supposed supporting forces must be on the way. Hooker sent no word of his intentions to his superiors, Sumner and Heintzelman; the sound of his guns would be sufficient notice of a battle — a battle he expected them to join.

At 7:30 a.m. Hooker opened with his divisional artillery. As Battery H, 1st U.S., unlimbered, it was met by a sharp fire. Men and horses were hit and panic seized the gun crews and they fled. Major Wainwright, divisional artillery chief, tried to drive them back to their pieces with shouts and sword but to no avail. "Never in my life was I so mortified, never so excited, never so mad," Wainwright told his diary that night. Finally he turned to his reserve, a New York battery that had been his first command, and called for volunteers. The New Yorkers soon had Battery H back in action.[29]

Hooker engaged his infantry and expected Smith's division at the center of the line to respond to his opening gambit. There was no response. Returned from his night in the woods, General Sumner appeared unable — or unwilling — to grasp the situation. Hooker's posting on the Hampton Road was Heintzelman's doing, the firing there was Hooker's own doing, so Sumner showed little interest in it. What alarmed him was a potential

Edwin V. Sumner badly
bungled his initial Civil War
independent command, at
Williamsburg, May 5.

attack on his center. Sumner had demonstrated such alarmist tenden-
cies at Yorktown, twice turning out entire commands to repel attacks that
never came. Bull Sumner shared McClellan's belief in an all-powerful
enemy.

The command situation was decidedly peculiar — three corps commanders, with Sumner by seniority in overall command despite having
no troops of his own on the scene, directing just two divisions, each from
a different corps. "Everyone hears this battle and yet the troops are not
given the order to move," wrote the Comte de Paris. Heintzelman, unable
to get Sumner's attention to Hooker's needs, was exasperated. "The firing
on General Hooker's front getting to be pretty heavy, I began to feel uneasy
about him, and left to join him."

For all his concern about fending off an attack, Sumner was very slow
to bring up support. Keyes claimed he issued marching orders to his two
divisions in reserve at Halfway House, Darius Couch's and Silas Casey's,
that should have brought them to the front by 9:00 a.m. Instead, they were
late by four and seven hours respectively. Keyes blamed conflicting orders
from Sumner.[30]

Before going to the scene of Hooker's fighting, Heintzelman did manage to persuade Sumner to order Phil Kearny's division over to the Hamp-

ton Road to reinforce Hooker. The order reached Kearny at 10:45 at Halfway House, and he pushed through "the masses of troops and trains that encumbered the deep, muddy single defile." Sumner rejected a plea from Hooker for immediate support from Smith's division or at the least to have Smith mount a diversion.

Joe Hooker was much in need of support. Finding no threat elsewhere, Longstreet shifted to the offense. The fighting quickly rose in pitch, much of it in dense, dripping woodland with the contestants half-blinded by mist and drifting battle smoke. The weight of the attack, some 10,350 Confederates against 9,000 Federals, fell against Hooker's left flank, and his line was steadily bent back toward the Hampton Road. The Rebels broke through to the road and captured two of Wainwright's batteries. Hooker rode into the battle line, directing fire, shifting troops into the fight, shouting encouragement. As Wainwright's remaining battery cleared the Rebels off the road with a blast of canister, Hooker's horse was spooked and pitched the general into a ditch. He leaped up, muddy but unbowed, calling out, "Don't fall back — the rebels are whipped! Reinforcements will be here in a few minutes."

Corps commander Heintzelman was there too, appraising the situation, sending to hurry up Kearny, sending to Sumner "to reinforce us & make a strong demonstration." ("He did neither, nor sent me any reply.") He told Hooker they must hold. This was the first battle since Bull Run and it would ruin the army — and ruin the both of them — if they fell back. To demonstrate his resolve, he lined the Hampton Road with cavalry with orders to shoot into the fugitives if need be. He collared a regimental band and ordered it to play. "Play, damn it! Play some marching tune! Play 'Yankee Doodle,' or any doodle you can think of, only play something." Faintly at first, then more strongly, "Yankee Doodle" and then "Three Cheers for the Red, White, and Blue" echoed through the drenched smoky forest.[31]

The first support for Hooker came indirectly. Back at Halfway House the word finally got through to Couch's Fourth Corps division and John J. Peck's brigade. Peck reported matter-of-factly, "About 11 a.m. I came up with Casey's command, which was halted, and, hearing heavy firing to the front, passed on by it to the headquarters of General Keyes." John Peck, West Point 1843, had won two brevet promotions in the Mexican War, and now he honored the soldierly instinct to march to the sound of the guns. By early afternoon he linked Smith's left with Hooker's right and was well engaged.

Still, Hooker's situation was sliding from serious to critical, with many of his men out of ammunition. It was 2:45 p.m. when Phil Kearny led his division onto the field at the double-quick. A staff officer met them and exclaimed, "General Hooker sends to General Kearny for God's sake to come on!" Kearny wrote his wife, "The time was critical, ten minutes later & the Division that had commenced the fight would have been panick stricken, as at Manassas." He did not exaggerate. Heintzelman wrote *his* wife, "A moment before our reinforcements arrived the men gave way being out of ammunition." Hiram Berry's brigade led the charge — "fired three volleys on the enemy and charged bayonets, recaptured all the artillery. . . ." Hooker's exhausted men fell back and Kearny's replaced them, pushing the Confederates back to their starting point. "I think I rank you," Kearny said to Hooker, who replied, "Certainly, general, you do," and Kearny took command of the field.[32]

Phil Kearny's way was to lead by example. He came on a bewildered New Jersey company that had lost its officers. "Well! I am a one-armed Jersey son-of-a-gun, follow me! Three cheers!" He told the 2nd Michigan, "Men, I want you to drive those blackguards to hell at once! . . . Will you do it?" Lieutenant Charles Haydon told his journal, "He was answered by a yell which reached the enemies' line above the roar of the battle. . . ." Kearny had commanded the division for only a week, so to show himself to the troops he rushed out to the skirmish line, drew the Rebels' fire (losing two of his staff killed), and rode back into his lines shouting, "You see, my boys, where to fire!" The fight turned in his favor, and he assured Heintzelman, "General, I can make men follow me to Hell!"

Sam Heintzelman was not to be outdone in matters of personal leadership. Lieutenant Haydon was astonished to see his corps commander by the roadside "more enthusiastic than I ever supposed he could be. He swung his hat, hurrahed for Michigan most lustily & swore as hard as ever saying 'give them hell God damn them, give the steel dont wait to shoot.'" Heintzelman would profess himself satisfied with the fighting on the Hampton Road, as antidote to Bull Run and giving "character and confidence to our army. . . . Kearny and Hooker have managed or others for them to carry off all the honors of this fight."[33]

All during the contest on Hooker's front Sumner remained in a fog of indecision. The Whittaker house was a mile or so from the fighting and screened from it by dense woods. "The sounds around us proved we were in the midst of a battle but we could not see what was going on," wrote the Comte de Paris. Cavalryman Stoneman made "a final try" at Sumner: "He wants him to bring up more troops, form a reserve and make an assault

Alfred Waud's wash drawing portrays Philip Kearny leading his Third Corps infantry division at the double-quick on the Hampton Road at Williamsburg on May 5.

aimed at disengaging Hooker and deciding the contest." Sumner would not be budged.

That morning an elderly black man came to Baldy Smith and told of a way around the Rebels' left flank. He said that a woods road led off to the right, crossed a dam over Cub Creek, and ran behind the enemy defenses. A redoubt guarded the dam crossing, he said, but it was empty. A staff man confirmed the man's story. Here was a way to flank the enemy on the right and thereby counter the threat to Hooker on the left.

Smith took his proposal for a flank march to Sumner, and in his mem-oir recorded Sumner's response: "Not taking in the situation at all, he, after much urging, finally told me that I could send one brigade to the first fort but no further. I left General Sumner with a feeling of admiration for the old plantation Negro who had shown more knowledge of strategy than the second officer in rank in the Army of the Potomac." Smith chose Winfield Hancock's brigade, quietly reinforced it with two additional regiments and a battery, and in confidence told Hancock to advance as far as he safely could and to call for any help he needed.

At the dam Hancock found the guarding redoubt empty. Ahead was a second redoubt, also empty. "I accordingly advanced . . . and took quiet possession." A mile ahead lay Fort Magruder. It was noon when he sent back to Smith detailing his progress and calling for a second brigade to secure his conquests and to continue the advance. Smith sent to Hancock that a brigade and a battery were on the way to him. The battery reached him; the infantry did not.

Twice W.T.H. Brooks's brigade set out for Hancock only to be summarily recalled by Sumner. At the Whittaker house Sumner had no sense of the battlefield. He acted on the fighting according to what he could hear of it. When John Peck reached the front and plunged his brigade into the woods, he set off an outburst of firing that alarmed Sumner into his first recall of Brooks. Then (as Sumner reported it), "at 3 o'clock p.m. the enemy made a furious attack upon my center. . . . I had not many troops to meet it, and for a little time I was exceedingly anxious." That triggered Brooks's second recall. No one else reported any such "furious attack" on the center. It was, in fact, the rising pitch of musketry as Kearny rushed to Hooker's aid over on the Hampton Road.

Hancock reported "three positive orders from General Sumner to retire." Twice he delayed obeying by sending back fresh reports and waiting for a response. Finally, shortly after 5 o'clock, with Sumner's third directive in hand, he ordered a withdrawal. Just then the Rebels obliged him by attacking. They had a third of Hancock's infantry force and no artillery, and the Yankees wrecked the attack before it was fairly begun. Hancock set up his battle line with precision, and to seal his victory he called for a counterattack. "The papers had it that he said, 'Charge, gentlemen, charge,'" explained Major Thomas W. Hyde, 7th Maine. "But he was more emphatic than that: the air was blue all around him." The Rebels fell back in rout. That day Phil Kearny claimed he could make men follow him to Hell. With his fighting blood up, Winfield Scott Hancock might have made the same claim.

Major Hyde analyzed his own response to the battle, his first, and discovered that his fighting blood was up as well. "In action I have never felt a fear yet simply because I have had too much to do and have been obliged to incite the men by example — for any soldiers will fight if their officers are brave men." It was, he saw, the starkest sort of challenge of successful battlefield leadership.[34]

At 5:30, as Hancock claimed his victory, there was a stir at the Whittaker house. "Everyone turns," the Comte de Paris wrote. "A group of riders are advancing rapidly along the road. We recognize the General. His arrival instantly creates a sensation." McClellan shared the moment with

Ellen: "As soon as I came upon the field the men cheered like fiends & I saw at once that I could save the day."

The general commanding was very late staking his claim. As early as 1:00 p.m. staff aide Major Herbert Hammerstein reached Yorktown with reports of serious trouble at Williamsburg. The Prince de Joinville was another early supplicant; he "finally decides to see what is delaying the General and make him come at all costs." Corps commander Keyes sent to McClellan for reinforcements, "but above all come yourself." Baldy Smith twice sent aides to Yorktown to tell the general "if he did not wish his army to be beaten by the enemy's rear guard, he had better come and take command."

General McClellan remained the reluctant warrior, even though this was manifestly the first battle of his grand campaign. To reach the battlefield that afternoon on a fast horse — and McClellan had a fast horse — took an hour to an hour and a half, yet it was 4 o'clock or later before he set out. Soldier-historian Francis W. Palfrey, in his account of the campaign, saw Williamsburg as setting a precedent. "Curiously enough, there was almost always something for McClellan to do more important than to fight his own battles."[35]

Indeed, there was no more battle to fight by the time McClellan reached the field. That night he telegraphed Stanton, "I find Joe Johnston in front of me in strong force, probably greater a good deal than my own & strongly entrenched"; they "intend disputing every step to Richmond." In closing he recited what was becoming the leitmotif of the Peninsula campaign: "My entire force is undoubtedly considerably inferior to that of the Rebels, . . . but I will do all I can with the force at my disposal."

But by morning on May 6 Johnston was gone. McClellan did not immediately attempt to follow. The men were out of provisions and supplying them over the atrocious roads challenged the quartermasters. In any event Johnston had a good lead and (as Williamsburg had demonstrated) a dangerous rear guard.

There was still the matter of William Franklin's amphibious operation. Early May 6 Franklin set off up the York toward a landing at West Point, some 18 miles beyond Williamsburg. The thought was to cut off the Confederates' retreat so the pursuing force could bring them to battle, but the long delay re-embarking Franklin's division made that increasingly unlikely. Now it became a question of whether Franklin himself was in danger of being cut off.

William B. Franklin, with his generals and staff, photographed by James Gibson in May 1862 at Cumberland Landing on the York River. Seated from left: Andrew A. Humphreys, Henry W. Slocum, Franklin, William F. Berry, and John Newton.

By morning on May 7 Franklin had his three brigades ashore at Eltham's Landing, near West Point. Johnston moved against the Yankees during the day, but only to hold them in check while his trains passed by safely on the Williamsburg Stage Road. The Rebels pinned Franklin in his bridgehead, inflicting 186 casualties. "I congratulate myself that we have maintained our position," said Franklin. He was fortunate Johnston was not more aggressive, for McClellan in his caution required four days to cover the 18 miles to Eltham's Landing. "We are now again united and Joe has lost his best chance of catching us in detail," he told Ellen. Franklin's move at least eased the army's logistical burden, and the divisions of Sedgwick, Richardson, and Porter followed upriver from Yorktown.[36]

McClellan termed Williamsburg (as he had termed Yorktown) "a brilliant victory," even though once again Johnston escaped his clutches. "The enemy were badly whipped, but will probably fight again," he told Stanton. The enemy, in fact, had inflicted substantially more casualties than they suffered — 2,283 to 1,682 — and justly claimed to have stopped the Yankee pursuit in its tracks.

Among the Federals there was full agreement on one matter. As McClellan put it, "Sumner had proved that he was even a greater fool than I had supposed & had come within an ace of having us defeated." Sam Heintzelman wrote, "I am more satisfied than ever about the bad management of Sumner & his inexcusable neglect to not support me." Darius Couch called Williamsburg "a miserably fought affair," Baldy Smith called it "a beastly exhibition of stupidity and ignorance," and both blamed Sumner. The press joined the chorus. "Genl. Sumner seems troubled by the newspaper attacks: some of them are virulent," wrote Otis Howard, and in consequence "he often profanes the name of God."

Bull Sumner had five infantry divisions and Stoneman's cavalry under command, and in that strength there was potential for an important victory at Williamsburg. But in Fitz John Porter's phrase, Sumner "put too few in action and too many at rest." Barely half the Federals joined the fighting. Two divisions in Heintzelman's Third Corps, Hooker's and Kearny's, were fully engaged. In Keyes's Fourth Corps, however, just two of the nine brigades — Peck's and Hancock's — saw action. Silas Casey's division contributed nothing.[37]

Given a direct order to march from point A to point B, Edwin Sumner was the soldier to carry it out. Given discretion, given command independence, as at Williamsburg, revealed him beyond his depth. McClellan's remark that Sumner "was even a greater fool than I had supposed" suggests he had long suspected the old general's failings. Nevertheless, at the last minute on May 4 he had replaced Heintzelman as commander of the pursuit with Sumner, for no better reason than to subordinate Erasmus Keyes.

In his journal the impressionable Comte de Paris often reported headquarters gossip as fact. That is evident in his accounting of General Keyes at Williamsburg. He had Keyes acting as éminence grise at the Whittaker house, whispering distorted advice in Sumner's ear out of concern for his own personal safety: "Keyes fears the slightest danger to his person and uses his keenest intelligence to foresee and avoid it. I am not afraid to write this since it is the unanimous opinion of the whole army." Philippe would hardly have written that unless he believed "the opinion of the whole army" was shared by the general commanding.

There is no knowing the origin of this canard. Keyes's previous battle record, at Bull Run, was middling but showed no trace of quailing under fire. Erasmus Keyes knew he was "laden with disfavor at headquarters," and so he determined to do nothing less (and nothing more) than to obey orders. The passive role he played at Williamsburg only fed the mendacious gossips.

Sam Heintzelman's command role was equally awkward, but there was nothing passive about *his* response. At Williamsburg, as at Bull Run, he was the only Union officer of senior rank to distinguish himself. So soon as he confirmed (personally) the Confederate evacuation of Yorktown, he alone had his troops prepared and provisioned to march. He authorized Hooker's flanking movement. When faced with Sumner's intransigence on May 5, he obtained Kearny's release to support Hooker, and then went himself to the battleground and devoted his considerable efforts to keeping Hooker in the fight and to bringing up Kearny in time to save the day. In looking back on Williamsburg, Heintzelman wrote, with pardonable pride, "If I had not been on the ground it would have been a disastrous defeat and ruinous to the Army of the Potomac." However that might be, he at least earned the right to make the claim.[38]

Joe Hooker's term for an officer's proper conduct was "soldiership," but in the fighting on the Hampton Road his own record of soldiership was mixed. He proved a bold and inspiring leader, important that day since only three of his twelve regiments had seen battle before, at Bull Run. Nor did he back down when the fighting became more than he had bargained for. His failing was his decision to open the battle without notice to his superiors. He assumed they would follow his lead, and when Sumner did not it was left to Heintzelman to plot a rescue. The heads of Hooker's brigades — Cuvier Grover, Francis E. Patterson (son of Robert Patterson of the ill-fated Army of the Shenandoah), and Nelson Taylor (filling in for absent Dan Sickles) — held their men to the defense with determination. Never lacking for brass, Hooker afterward wrote to a friend, "On the 5th inst I fought a great battle which will reflect character upon the Army of the Potomac and fame upon my Division."

At Williamsburg Phil Kearny displayed an abnormal relish for battle. He determined not just to lead his men to the field but to show them what to do when they got there — by personal example. In riding right into the skirmish line to draw the enemy's fire, he was reprising old battles at Churubusco in Mexico or Solferino in Italy. Such conduct would be daring for a company captain; for a general of division it was simply foolhardy. To be sure, Kearny's lust for action and his intolerance for fear made a winning formula that particular afternoon. "It is true, that I was fearfully exposed at times . . . ," he told his wife; "I was the only officer, mounted & quite in view, the only object aimed at by the enemy hardly fifty feet from me. But I could not do otherwise, we had very desperate work before us. . . ."

Kearny's brigade commanders — Hiram G. Berry, David B. Birney, and Charles D. Jameson — were put on their mettle by such bravado. At one point Kearny took Jameson with him to an exposed spot on the battle line to reconnoiter, and Jameson was very conscious of the bullets zipping past them. Afterward his aide asked him if he thought the reconnaissance an unjustifiable risk. "I certainly do," Jameson replied. Then why take the risk? Jameson explained that he had not dared flinch or show the slightest impatience at remaining exposed for so long. "Why, what would Kearny have thought of me!"

Winfield Hancock's decisive repulse of the Rebels at the opposite end of the battlefield became in the public mind the highlight of the Williamsburg fighting. McClellan telegraphed his wife news of the "brilliant victory," and added, "Hancock was superb yesterday." Ellen showed the telegram to a reporter, and the press added "Hancock the Superb" to its list of Northern heroes. Hancock had indeed done well in his first combat. He handled his forces skillfully, stretched his orders to make the most of his opportunity, and met the enemy's attack with well-controlled aggressiveness.[39]

McClellan's initial report on Williamsburg, telegraphed to Washington a few hours after he reached the field on May 5, was released to the press . . . and was greeted with outrage in the Third Corps. McClellan described Hancock's exploits, including "a real charge with the bayonet," and concluded, "His conduct was brilliant in the extreme." The sole mention of Joe Hooker said he "has lost considerably on our left." Phil Kearny was not mentioned at all. When the newspapers reached the Third Corps camps, it was said "to be dangerous to go near Kearny, and Hooker is terribly severe."

The two generals proved as aggressive with pen as with sword. Hooker sent copies of his Williamsburg report to New York's Senator Ira Harris, to Oregon's Senator James Nesmith, to New Jersey's Senator John C. Ten Eyck, urging Congress to call for its publication. Whether McClellan's failure to acknowledge the fighting record of Hooker's division "arises from his ignorance of soldiership, his determination to award merit only to favourites and kindred I do not know; . . . I am shocked, nay appalled by that man's ingratitude." Phil Kearny was in even higher dudgeon. "McClellan has painfully disappointed even those who expected very little from him — even me, who have *sifted* him from the first," he wrote a Washington lobbyist friend. "Still, I never expected to find him introducing a want of fair play to those who carry out his fighting, *whilst he stays in the rear.*" The general commanding, he complained, "forestalls the glory of the victors, by vamping up . . . a mere flurry of a skirmish, where Hancock (a charming officer and gentleman) with preponderating numbers, drives, for an instant, a paltry few of the enemy. . . ."

Heintzelman spoke to McClellan about doing justice to the Third Corps, amends were made, and a revised report went to the press. This did not silence Hooker and Kearny, but it took the edge off their charges.

Yet neither of these egotistical, ambitious men was ready then (or ever) to make up with the general commanding.[40]

Williamsburg might have served as a fair test of the corps system installed by Lincoln and accepted reluctantly by McClellan — Third Corps divisions and Fourth Corps divisions advancing against the enemy on parallel roads, to join before Williamsburg, with Heintzelman in overall command. But McClellan inserted Sumner into the mix and the high command structure became overpopulated, unwieldy, and unresponsive. Now, having created the mess, McClellan piously presented a plan for cleaning it up.

On May 8 he petitioned Stanton to revamp the corps arrangement, "experience having proved it to be very bad & it having very nearly resulted in a most disastrous defeat." Had he not reached the field when he did, "we would have been routed & would have lost everything." He wanted a return to organization by divisions, or the authority to relieve incompetent corps commanders. Stanton's reply (drafted by Lincoln) stated the president's unwillingness to see the corps organization voided, but also his unwillingness to see the general "trammelled and embarrassed . . . on the eve of an expected great battle." Therefore McClellan might temporarily suspend the present organization "and adopt any you see fit until further orders."

Mr. Lincoln once again composed a private letter to his general to try and reason with him. He said he had acted to form army corps based on the unanimous opinion of the army's twelve generals of division and "also on the unanimous opinion of every *military man* I could get an opinion from, and every modern military book. . . ." McClellan's opposition to this was seen "in quarters which we cannot entirely disregard . . . as merely an effort to pamper one or two pets, and to persecute and degrade their supposed rivals." He was told that McClellan had no consultation or communication with Generals Sumner, Heintzelman, and Keyes, "that you consult and communicate with nobody but General Fitz John Porter, and perhaps General Franklin."

"I do not say these complaints are true or just" — they did not come from the three corps commanders, he noted — "but at all events it is proper you should know of their existence. . . ." He was blunt: "Are you strong enough — are you strong enough, even with my help — to set your foot upon the necks of Sumner, Heintzelman, and Keyes all at once? This is a practical and very serious question for you."

McClellan again made no response to a presidential letter, but he was wise enough in the ways of army politics and protocol to know he could not rid himself of these senior corps commanders by force or fiat. Instead he would dilute their influence by carving out of existing forces two additional army corps, the commanders of which would be . . . Fitz John Porter and William Franklin. Porter's Fifth and Franklin's Sixth Corps were activated on May 18. (Franklin remarked on the special relationship he and Porter enjoyed with McClellan: "I knew that a jealous feeling had grown up about Gen Mc's friendship for Gen P & me, and I purposely kept away from HdQrs for days together in order to silence slanderous tongues.")

In the Army of the Potomac's new order of battle, Sumner's Second Corps retained its two divisions, under Richardson and Sedgwick. Heintzelman's Third Corps now comprised Hooker's and Kearny's divisions only, losing Porter's division. Keyes's Fourth Corps lost Baldy Smith's division, leaving it with Couch's and Casey's divisions. Porter's new Fifth Corps consisted of his own division (now under George W. Morell), George Sykes's division (two brigades of regulars and one of volunteers), and Henry Hunt's reserve artillery. The new Sixth Corps contained Franklin's division (originally in the First Corps and led now by Henry W. Slocum) and Baldy Smith's division.

Since McClellan seems to have had a decent respect for Heintzelman's abilities (or so Heintzelman thought: At Williamsburg McClellan "congratulated me warmly on our success"), the new scheme at least gave him three corps commanders he could rely on. Reducing the corps to two divisions each, however, significantly weakened their striking power, especially for independent operations. Furthermore, the two additional corps diluted command responsibility and authority within the larger army structure.[41]

These army corps negotiations took place while Lincoln and Stanton and Treasury Secretary Chase were at Fort Monroe taking a hand in advancing the campaign. For months the navy had vainly sought the army's help for an expedition to seize Norfolk, where CSS *Virginia* was based. On arriving at Fort Monroe on May 6, the president summoned Flag Officer Goldsborough and General Wool and set them to breaking the stalemate. A landing was made and on May 10, with General Wool and "General" Chase in the van, troops of the Monroe garrison marched into Norfolk. It was a bloodless capture — the last Confederates left the day before — and cause for celebration. In his delight, Stanton "fairly hugged" General Wool.

The more momentous accomplishment of the Norfolk expedition was to hasten the fate of CSS *Virginia*. The evacuation of Yorktown meant that Norfolk's days were numbered, and the Confederates planned to shift the *Virginia* to a new base well up the James where, acting as a floating battery, she would continue her control of the river. She drew too much water to cross the sandbars at the river's mouth, however, and before she could be sufficiently lightened the Yankees' abrupt capture of Norfolk trapped her. On May 11 the great ironclad was run aground and blown up. "So ended a brilliant week's campaign of the President," Chase wrote, "for I think it quite certain that, if he had not come down, Norfolk would still have been in possession of the enemy, and the 'Merrimac' as grim and defiant and as much a terror as ever."[42]

Yorktown's evacuation had inspired Lincoln to journey to Fort Monroe for a face-to-face consultation with his army commander. McClellan sent regrets; affairs at the front were critical; "I dare not leave for one hour." This was a valid excuse for those several days when the army was divided between Williamsburg and Eltham's Landing, but by May 9 the danger was over. McClellan even granted his army a day of rest. He could have boarded a gunboat on the York and reached Fort Monroe in a few hours. But he did not.

There was much he might profitably have discussed with Lincoln — the corps-command matter, strengthening the army with McDowell's corps, the latest intelligence on the Rebel army, utilizing the James now that the *Virginia* was destroyed, the probability and prospects of a next battle. His telegrams on these days were filled with these and other vital issues. Yet once again McClellan's contempt for Lincoln, and for Stanton and Chase too, led him deliberately to refuse to share confidences, to refuse to clear up misunderstandings, to refuse to clarify his intentions and spell out his needs. This missed opportunity would be McClellan's last-ever chance to meet personally with the president while in a position of relative strength, with the events of the day in his favor.[43]

The death of the *Virginia* caused McClellan's eyes to brighten. "I can change my line to the James River & dispense with the Railroad," he told Stanton. The James was navigable right to Richmond, and the Union navy wasted no time to try and exploit that fact. On May 15 a flotilla headed by the ironclads *Monitor, Galena,* and *Naugatuck* approached Drewry's Bluff, seven miles from Richmond and the last river outpost guarding the capital. Atop the high bluff was a battery of eight heavy guns. Commander John Rodgers anchored flagship *Galena* broadside to the Rebel battery and "resolved to give the matter a fair trial."

The *Galena* was a makeshift, with armor of iron plates and bars bolted in overlapping layers, like giant fish scales. Goldsborough termed her "a most miserable contrivance," and he was proven right. Rebel gunners put

The Union navy's attempt to open the James River to Richmond was repulsed at Drewry's Bluff on May 15. An unidentified artist, probably a Yankee crewman, represented from left, the *Aroostook, Monitor,* flagship *Galena, Port Royal,* and *Naugatuck.*

forty-three shells and solid shot into and through the *Galena,* leaving her armor shattered and her gun deck running with blood. Rodgers fell back out of range. The *Naugatuck* went out of action after her 100-pounder gun burst. The *Monitor* was unharmed, but the two guns in her turret would not elevate enough to reach the top of the bluff. The navy gave up immediate hopes for bombarding Richmond into surrender.[44]

With that McClellan's ambitions for the James languished. To renew the attack on Drewry's Bluff, the navy called on the army for help, which (said the general), "I will not be in position to afford for several days." Several days passed, then several weeks, and in the end no help was forthcoming. General McClellan was instead coming to terms with the new reality of his grand campaign.

He had prophesied fighting the war-ending battle for Richmond at a place of his own choosing, dictating the terms of the contest. Now the terms were different. He wrote Lincoln, "I must attack in position, probably entrenched, a much larger force, perhaps double my numbers." He pleaded for reinforcements. He reversed himself on employing the despised Irvin McDowell: "Any commander of the reinforcements your Excellency may designate will be acceptable to me, whatever expression I may have heretofore addressed to you. . . ." In contemplating the daunting odds, McClellan's thoughts turned again to his siege train. In this arm he was confident of his superiority. If unable to contrive a battle on advantageous terms, he would make Richmond hostage to a siege.

To transport the siege pieces and mortars to within range of the Confederate capital required either the James River or the Richmond & York River Railroad. By McClellan's accounting, opening the James at Drewry's Bluff called for greater risk—dividing his army in the face of a superior army—than he dared assume. On the other hand, as Johnston fell back toward Richmond, the Potomac army pushed after him astride the railroad, at hand to carry siege guns as well as supplies. A supply line combining the York and Pamunkey rivers and the West Point railroad was McClellan's bird in the hand, and he committed to it.[45]

May 1862 found McClellan dealing with Washington from a position of relative strength. However long it had taken, the siege of Yorktown ended in his favor. However badly managed, Williamsburg ended with the enemy in retreat. Whatever the opportunities missed, the Army of the Potomac, its flanks protected by the navy, its supply line secure, was steadily closing on Richmond. At McClellan's direction the war in the East was nearing some sort of resolution. Much the same—and at the same time—could be said of the war in the West. Following the great battle at Shiloh in Tennessee in April, Henry Halleck massed an army of 100,000 and began a slow, steady advance on the Rebels' main Western army entrenched at Corinth, in northern Mississippi. On May 18 McClellan offered Ellen a prediction: Soon he would "close up on the Chickahominy & find out what secesh is doing. I think he will fight us there, or in between that & Richmond—& if he is badly thrashed (as I trust he will be) incline to believe that he will begin to cry peccavi & say that he has enough of it—especially if Halleck beats him at Corinth."[46]

The president had conceived a similar vision, and he determined to greatly strengthen the blow aimed at Richmond. Only a major reinforcement, he believed, would pressure McClellan into an offensive.

Lincoln based his decision on highly assertive dispatches from the Shenandoah Valley. Following defeat at Kernstown on March 23, Stonewall Jackson had withdrawn up the Valley, with Nathaniel Banks trailing along behind to see him off. "Jackson is flying from this department," James Shields, one of Banks's generals, announced on April 20; "he gave the whole valley up for lost." On April 30 Banks assured Washington, "There is nothing more to be done by us in the valley." Irvin McDowell had advanced his First Corps to Fredericksburg, roughly halfway between

Washington and Richmond, so it appeared to the president that the Rebels' two primary corridors of invasion, via Fredericksburg-Manassas and via the Valley, were now secured or blocked. The capital should be safe.

Three military departments were parties to Lincoln's calculations. Banks's Department of the Shenandoah comprised two divisions, some 20,000 men, under Shields and Alpheus Williams. McDowell's First Corps (Department of the Rappahannock) — the divisions of George McCall, Rufus King, and a new division, replacing Franklin's, under E.O.C. Ord — was at Fredericksburg and numbered 30,000 men. Pathfinder Frémont had about 14,800 men in the Mountain Department, in the Alleghenies west of the Shenandoah. Relying on the optimistic reports from the Valley, Lincoln reasoned that Banks could spare one of his two divisions to reinforce McDowell's First Corps for the advance on Richmond while, with Frémont, still containing any threat from Jackson.

"The President has directed the transfer of General Shields, with his division, to your department," McDowell was told on May 1. As soon as might be, then, Irvin McDowell, at the head of an army of some 40,000 men, would join McClellan's campaign against Richmond. All this was initiated by the president with the best of intentions, to strengthen McClellan's hand to such a degree that he would have no excuse to further postpone his long-promised attack. By the returns, this reinforcement would give the Army of the Potomac something over 140,000 fighting men — perhaps matching, or nearly so, the enemy's numbers as variously imagined by the general commanding.[47]

The post of general-in-chief being vacant, Lincoln took this decision without benefit of hardheaded military advice. This proved a misfortune. In fact, the addition of Shields's division was quite unnecessary, McDowell's First Corps by itself being a more-than-generous reinforcement for the Peninsula. (Joe Johnston reported his strength on May 21 as 53,688. McClellan reported 102,670 men present for duty on May 20.) Setting out from Fredericksburg, said McDowell, would be "an easy four days' march" to link up with the Potomac army. He could start on short notice. But McClellan's repeated plaints of confronting "perhaps double my numbers" drowned out more reasoned calculations. So, fatefully, McDowell was forced to wait for Shields . . . and wait . . . and wait . . . and wait.[48]

Two black clouds combined to darken the sunny view of events in the Shenandoah Valley. The first was the bluster of James Shields. A onetime state senator from Illinois, Shields was a political general with actual military credentials, having led a brigade in Mexico. In the Valley his division had the advance, and he deduced (or invented) most of the intelligence on

Jackson's movements. Shields's bravado was not shared by fellow division commander Alpheus Williams. Williams was a self-taught citizen-soldier who came to command via the state-militia route. He had no illusions about Jackson's intentions. "We fear he has been largely reinforced," he wrote on April 29, "and intends to turn upon us here or wait for us in his present strong position." Williams was writing not to General Banks nor to Secretary Stanton nor to Mr. Lincoln but to his daughter, and his prescience went unrewarded.

The second black cloud was the lack of unified command in the field. Originally Washington's three-department scheme made sense. McDowell's Department of the Rappahannock was simply the Potomac army's First Corps in disguise, scheduled for the Peninsula. Frémont took his primary task in the Mountain Department as an offensive into East Tennessee. The Department of the Shenandoah under Banks guarded the Valley. Now, however, the lack of a coordinator produced lassitude among the various generals. Shields, on whose division everyone was now waiting, required twelve days just to collect himself and his men for the move, and then another eleven days to finally reach Fredericksburg. Only McDowell registered any sense of urgency, but Shields did not quicken his pace.

Banks was slow to recognize that his declaration of victory in the Shenandoah might be premature. He was told to fall back to Strasburg, there to secure his Manassas Gap Railroad supply line and to guard the lower Valley. Not until May 22, the day Shields reached Fredericksburg, did Banks notify Stanton that by all reports Jackson was back in the Valley. He estimated Jackson's forces at 16,000 and his own, under Alpheus Williams, at 6,800; "the probabilities of danger are so great, that it should be assumed as positive and preparation made to meet it."[49]

The danger was indeed great. From his desk in Richmond, Robert E. Lee urged Jackson to push back into the Valley with intent to tie up the Federals there and prevent reinforcements going to the Peninsula. "The blow wherever struck, must, to be successful, be sudden and heavy," Lee wrote, and Jackson prepared to carry out that instruction.

Banks found Frémont of no help to meet the threat. The Pathfinder never displayed any interest in cooperating with Banks to secure the Valley to begin with, for his sights were trained on East Tennessee. Intent on his own concerns, Frémont was taken aback when on May 8, at the village of McDowell on the southwestern rim of the Valley, one of his lieutenants was surprised and badly knocked about by Jackson. What this might portend was unclear. General Banks, to his unending regret, did not make enough of it.

Irreverent staff man David Strother took note of the effect Stonewall Jackson had on the Potomac and Shenandoah Valley armies. "Here I am," Jackson tells his puzzled foes.

The troops that ought to have been immediately at hand to reinforce Banks in this time of need — the all-German division of Louis Blenker — had instead embarked on a bleak odyssey. When Blenker was pulled out of the Potomac army for transfer to Frémont, he was supposed to linger in the Valley if needed by Banks before reporting to the Mountain Department. But en route the Germans fell through an administrative crack. Ill led, ill disciplined, and ill provisioned, they disappeared from military view. "Where is Blenker, and what are his orders?" Stanton telegraphed plaintively. Footsore and hungry, Blenker's men turned to foraging and plunder. "The Dutch brigades are composed of the most infernal robbers, plunderers, and thieves I have ever seen," one of Frémont's generals wrote. In due course Blenker's demoralized division reached the Mountain Department, but in the meantime Banks gained no use of it. Instead of the hunter, General Banks now became the hunted.[50]

Following the linkup with Franklin on May 9, the Army of the Potomac advanced slowly up the Peninsula, following after rather than pursuing the Rebels and closing on the Chickahominy River. McClellan privately felt rather positive about his prospects. He wrote his wife that he expected "to fight a very severe battle on the Chickahominy, but feel no doubt as to the result. . . . Secesh is gathering all he can in front of me — so much the better — I will finish the matter by one desperate blow. I have implicit confidence in my men & they in me!"

Much effort was expended on logistics. Supply bases were established on the Pamunkey first at Eltham's, then at Cumberland Landing, finally at White House Landing. From White House the Richmond & York River Railroad ran 23 miles to Richmond. The retreating Confederates did only minimal damage to the railroad, which was repaired apace with the advance. Five locomotives and eighty cars were delivered by barge from Baltimore.[51]

McClellan's mood soured on receipt of a telegram from Secretary Stanton on May 18. While announcing that McDowell's corps would, at last, join the campaign, conditions were attached. McDowell, so soon as Shields arrived, would march from Fredericksburg by the shortest route to join the Army of the Potomac. His would be a semi-independent command, its four divisions making it twice the size of any corps in the army. McDowell would come under McClellan's command, but with a proviso — McClellan must issue McDowell no order putting his corps out of position to cover Washington. The First Corps would be the army's fixed right wing, ready to march back to the capital in case of need. That was the price McClellan must pay for approaching Richmond roundabout by way of the Peninsula. If Lincoln expected McClellan's thanks for this generosity of reinforcement, he was disappointed.

McClellan sent the president a ten-page telegram that was a litany of complaint and fault-finding. He wanted McDowell explicitly placed under "my orders in the ordinary way, & holding me strictly responsible for the closest observance of your instructions" about covering the capital. McClellan's grievance was due in part to his suspicion of McDowell's motives and in part to concern about a divided command. Having made his point about safeguarding Washington, Lincoln assured McClellan he had full command over McDowell. McClellan also argued against sending the First Corps overland instead of by water. He claimed there was little hope that McDowell could join him overland in time for the imminent "desperate battle" against an enemy in numbers "greatly exceeding our own." Lincoln observed that McDowell's four- or five-day march overland would compare favorably to the ten days it had taken to deliver Franklin's division by the water route.[52]

Sam Heintzelman entered in his diary on May 20 a "considerable talk" with McClellan. Shown the telegrams from Washington regarding Mc-Dowell, Heintzelman said that with the First Corps "we will in 48 hours be in Richmond." He compared McDowell idle at Fredericksburg with Patterson idle in the Valley during the Bull Run campaign, and hoped history would not repeat. He suggested bringing up Ambrose Burnside's force from North Carolina to combine with John Wool's command at Fort Monroe for a march up the south bank of the James. "With McDowell on the right & Burnside on the left we soon would occupy Richmond." Because McClellan apparently could not think so boldly (or because he did not originate the idea), nothing came of it.

McClellan's lieutenants again got busy lobbying. Heintzelman wrote to Henry Wilson, chairman of the Senate's Committee on Military Affairs, to report that "we have now arrived at a crisis" and pressing him to urge all the reinforcements possible. Brigadier Hiram Berry of Maine wrote in a similar vein to a fellow Mainer, Vice President Hannibal Hamlin. Fitz John Porter wanted *New York World* editor Marble to know that McDowell's corps was useless posted at Fredericksburg. "Washington has been perfectly safe ever since this army landed at Old Point, yes, ever since it sailed from Alexandria." Porter read the Army of the Potomac as devotedly conservative, thereby causing "our enemies in the rear (the abolitionists) to be looked upon with contempt."[53]

By May 20 the Federal advance confronted the Chickahominy. The river takes its rise northwest of Richmond and meanders east by southeast, passing in front of the city and emptying into the James. At its normal stage, McClellan would write, it was some 40 feet wide, "fringed with a dense growth of heavy forest-trees, and bordered with low marshy lands. . . . It was subject to frequent, sudden, and great variations in the volume of water, and a single violent storm of brief duration sufficed to cause an overflow of the bottom-lands for many days, rendering the river absolutely impassable without long and strong bridges." His description, written from experience, was heartfelt.

To McClellan's surprise, Johnston had pulled back his right far enough that the Chickahominy crossings at Bottom's Bridge and the railroad were undefended. The bridges were destroyed, but the engineers went to work on new ones. "Unless he has some deep laid scheme that I do not fathom," McClellan wrote of Johnston, "he is giving up great advantage in not opposing me on the line of the Chickahominy." At headquarters Israel Richardson found as "many different opinions as there are persons are expressed about the enemy and their intentions." John Sedgwick had the same impression: Either the Rebels would hold them off only long enough to evacuate Richmond, or there would be a desperate battle for the city. "I cannot tell which rumour to favour."

With Bottom's Bridge and the railroad bridge rebuilt, Keyes's Fourth Corps pushed ahead along the railroad a half-dozen miles to a crossroad called Seven Pines. Heintzelman's Third Corps took a supporting position behind Keyes, anchoring the army's left. In his continuing distrust of Erasmus Keyes, McClellan on May 25 ordered Heintzelman to take command of Keyes's corps as well as his own.

There was assumed risk in this advance. The Third and Fourth Corps, now with only two divisions each, were isolated from the rest of the army on the south bank of the unpredictable Chickahominy. On the north bank, Porter's Fifth Corps advanced to Mechanicsville to anchor the army's right. In rear of Porter was Franklin's Sixth Corps and then Sumner's Second. Sumner was directly opposite Keyes, three straight-line miles from Seven Pines but more than a dozen miles roundabout by the road passing over Bottom's Bridge. Hurriedly the engineers set to work bridging the river between the army's left and right wings.[54]

On May 23, a Friday, Lincoln and Stanton visited McDowell at Fredericksburg to prod things along. Shields's division had finally arrived, and it was agreed to devote the weekend to "a good ready" for a Monday start. On Saturday, back in Washington, Lincoln telegraphed McClellan to confirm that McDowell's reinforced corps would start its march on Monday to join him. "We were all in high spirits," McDowell would write a friend. ". . . The wagons were all loaded, the orders given and we were to march. . . ."

But just hours later that Saturday there was a countermand. Word came from the Shenandoah that Stonewall Jackson had sprung at Banks's command and driven it into hasty retreat. "In consequence of Gen. Banks' critical position," Lincoln telegraphed McClellan, "I have been compelled to suspend Gen. McDowell's movement to join you." McDowell called it "a crushing blow to us." Said the president, "The change was as painful to me as it can possibly be to you or to any one."

General Banks, lacking the divisions of Shields (by Lincoln's order) and Blenker (by misadventure), and quite misreading the enemy, found himself in an untenable position. The Valley here is bisected by Massanutten Mountain, allowing the Confederates two separate lines of advance — and pinning Banks to two separate guarding outposts, at Strasburg and Front Royal. On May 23 Jackson swept up the Front Royal garrison and two days later smashed the retreating Banks at Winchester. To Senator Sumner, Lincoln said, "Banks's men were running & flinging away their arms." Another Bull Run, Sumner concluded. On May 27 Banks got his tattered command across the Potomac to safety in Maryland. Jackson pursued to Harper's Ferry.[55]

Whatever the misfortune to Banks, Lincoln recognized in Jackson's thrust north to the Potomac an opportunity to trap the Rebel column in the Valley. On the 24th orders went to McDowell to start 20,000 of his men westward toward Front Royal, and to Frémont to push eastward in the direction of Strasburg. "This movement must be made immediately," the president told Frémont. Everything depended "upon the celerity and vigor of your movement," he told McDowell.

McDowell protested that cooperation between himself and Frémont "is not to be counted upon. . . . I shall gain nothing for you there, and shall lose much for you here." The president overrode him. He used Jackson's offensive to goad McClellan to battle before Richmond — just as his war orders back in January dragged a campaign plan out of his reluctant general. Lincoln argued that every Confederate brigade in the Valley was one less brigade defending Richmond, signaling opportunity for McClellan. "I think the time is near when you must either attack Richmond or give up the job and come to the defence of Washington."

McClellan assured Lincoln that "the time is very near when I shall attack Richmond," and he deciphered Jackson's intentions: "The object of enemy's movement is probably to prevent reinforcements being sent to me." He wrote Ellen the president "is terribly scared about Washington — & talks about the necessity of my returning to save it! . . . A scare will do them good, & may bring them to their senses." But the goad seemed to take effect. On May 26 he wrote, "The net is quietly closing & some fish will soon be caught."[56]

It was McClellan's intent to press Keyes and Heintzelman ahead along the south bank of the Chickahominy, uncovering additional crossing sites for reinforcements. Then came reports of a large Rebel force to the north at Hanover Court House, seeming to menace his right. He had to "take every possible precaution against disaster & to secure my flanks against the probably superior force in front of me." On May 27 Fitz John Porter engaged what was in fact a quite small enemy force, a railroad guard, near the courthouse. Porter's superiority in numbers (about three to one) gained him the field. The Federal killed and wounded came to 285, about the same as the Confederates, although in their disjointed retreat they lost 731 prisoners.

McClellan elevated Hanover Court House into "a glorious victory over superior numbers . . . one of the handsomest things of the war. . . ." Porter did destroy bridges on the railroads connecting Richmond with Jackson in the Shenandoah, but overall the Hanover operation crucially delayed strengthening Heintzelman and Keyes across the Chickahominy. Bridges were completed and Sumner prepared to cross, but he was held back until Porter's return. This was a risk he had to run, said McClellan, and for the usual reason — "The enemy are even in greater force than I had supposed."[57]

Silas Casey was fifty-four, gray-haired and stern, an infantry officer all his military life. He graduated West Point in 1826, did his share of Indian fighting, and was twice brevetted and once wounded in Mexico. He was initially drillmaster to the Potomac army, introducing new regiments to the rudiments of drill before their postings; his manual *Infantry Tactics* was adopted by the Union army. Casey's own division was a pickup affair of poor reputation. Washingtonian Elizabeth Blair Lee made note that "Casey's troops were notorious here this whole past winter for bad discipline & bad conduct in every way." Responding to complaints about his division's readiness, Casey said that two-thirds of his regiments, and their officers, "were almost entirely new at the time of taking the field." Silas Casey's division, then — the smallest and rawest in the army — was hardly an ideal choice to be the sharp point of McClellan's advance on Richmond.

As May ended, the Potomac army was positioned astride the Chickahominy in the shape of a great fishhook. The shank, lying along the north bank of the river, was made up of (top to bottom) Porter's Fifth Corps at Mechanicsville, Franklin's Sixth, and Sumner's Second. The hook, curving across the river to the south bank at Bottom's Bridge, was formed by Heintzelman's Third Corps and Keyes's Fourth. Casey's division, of Keyes's corps, was the barb.

Casey's three brigades were posted across the Williamsburg Stage Road a thousand yards in advance of the Seven Pines crossroad. Engineers started to lay out defenses there, but the work had not progressed very far. Back at Seven Pines was the entrenched balance of Keyes's corps, the division of Darius Couch. Couch was uneasy. "I considered our position as very faulty," he would write. "Two small corps separated from the main army by an ugly river and only 9 miles from Richmond." General Keyes thought Casey's advanced position was pushing the enemy "as much as he will bear," and would "be glad when I learn that General Sumner is across so as to strengthen my right." Sam Heintzelman, in overall command, also thought that Seven Pines was far enough for the advance. For all his talk of an enemy with numbers twice his own, McClellan was strangely unconcerned about leaving Keyes's and Heintzelman's corps in isolation south of the Chickahominy. "Richmond papers urge Johnston to attack now he has us away from gun boats," McClellan told Washington. "I think he is too able for that."[58]

During the night of May 30 the Peninsula was wracked by a thunderstorm of monumental proportions. "Last night we had another of those rains in which the very sluice gates of heaven seem to be opened, and the water drops in masses for hours," wrote Charles Wainwright. The Chickahominy rose rapidly and became a thrashing torrent. Joe Johnston greeted the storm as a godsend. So soon as the Yankees reached and then crossed the Chickahominy, he had begun to plot an offensive against his divided enemy. He concluded that the most inviting target lay south of the river, and scheduled his attack for May 31. The storm's aftermath left the Federals inattentive, and at the same time the raging Chickahominy threatened the two bridges the engineers had completed to link Sumner's corps with Keyes's.[59]

The offensive the Confederates aimed at Seven Pines proved to be a high-command fiasco — of the twenty-two brigades Johnston intended to throw against the Yankees that day, only nine and part of a tenth actually got into action. Nothing, however, lessened the initial stunning blow struck at Casey's division. Casey and Keyes both later insisted they were not caught by surprise on May 31, but in fact the configuration of the battlefield made surprise almost inevitable. Hardly 200 yards in advance of Casey's lines was thick forest, and the only warning came from his picket line as it was overrun by the charging Rebels. Innis Palmer, commanding one of Casey's brigades, would admit that the suddenness of the attack routed him out of his tent, leaving behind his midday meal, all his gear, even a letter from his wife.

At the first alarm, Casey told Henry W. Wessells, commanding the center brigade of the three, to brace the picket line with the 103rd Pennsylvania. The 103rd had been in the army barely a month when it was shipped to the Peninsula, and at the first enemy fire it panicked and (in Casey's words) "broke to the rear and could not again be brought into the fight." This demoralized the rest of the battle line, which soon enough joined the rush back to the second line, at Seven Pines. Wessells was wounded and a second brigade commander, Henry M. Naglee, had his horse killed and was four times nicked by bullets. General Casey, one of his men wrote, "rode up and down his lines ... bare-headed, his long gray hair floating over his shoulders, encouraging his men by voice and example to a heroic resistance."[60]

Keyes's second line, Couch's division — the brigades of John J. Peck, Charles Devens, and John J. Abercrombie — did its best to halt the Rebels' momentum. Except for Peck's engagement at Williamsburg, these troops were untested in combat. Numbers of Casey's fleeing men burst through this second line and kept rushing toward the rear. "If found necessary you will fire upon them" was Heintzelman's blunt order. He corralled a company of the 2nd Michigan as a provost guard, which collected in an hour a thousand of Casey's stragglers. A thousand others did not stop until they crossed the Chickahominy at Bottom's Bridge.

General Keyes, trying to come to grips with the expanding battle, ordered Couch to take two regiments from Abercrombie's brigade on the right and threaten the flank of the attackers. This struck Couch as too little and probably too late, and he protested. Keyes was adamant, and Couch dutifully moved off to the north. He soon ran into far more Rebels than he could handle, and was driven away from the rest of his division to Fair Oaks Station on the railroad. In his isolation, Couch looked to the rear and the Third Corps, and also sent an aide to Sumner's corps across the river.[61]

In the fighting at Seven Pines the Federal high command was plagued by miscommunications. The attack began about 1:00 p.m., and thirty minutes later, hearing nothing from Keyes, Heintzelman sent two of his staff to investigate the sounds of musketry. At 2:30 Heintzelman telegraphed army headquarters that nothing had been received from Keyes, "therefore I presume there is nothing serious." Ten minutes later Heintzelman telegraphed that his aides had returned to say that Casey's division was being driven in and "Genl Keyes reports that the enemy are pressing him upon the railroad." Heintzelman said he had ordered up Kearny's division and was going to the front himself. "I rode rapidly to the front & met the road full of stragglers from Casey's Division," he noted in his diary. ". . . I tried to rally some of the Regts in the center as they fell back but only partially succeeded." Keyes claimed he sent to Heintzelman for support the moment he realized the weight of the attack, but his messenger was "unaccountably delayed."[62]

In the case of David B. Birney, leading a brigade in Kearny's division, it was a matter of too many orders rather than too few or too late. Heintzelman ordered Birney to advance along the railroad to brace the right at Fair Oaks. Phil Kearny, however, had his own ideas. He thought it better to establish a new line "& to let the enemy *butt* up against it than to

In the Seven Pines fighting, Samuel Heintzelman led the army's left wing, Third and Fourth Corps, posted south of the Chickahominy.

do this unsystematic haphazard thing; ... to send me *piece-meal* is like 'throwing good money after bad.'" Heintzelman rejected his argument, but Kearny was not deterred. General Heintzelman, he would write, was brave enough in battle but burdened with an "ossified small brain." Birney had started up the railroad when Kearny recalled him to his original posting and told him to obey no one's orders but his. One of Heintzelman's staff found Birney there and once again ordered him to the front. Birney concluded that Heintzelman's orders must supersede Kearny's, and directed his command up the railroad. His brigade tied in with Couch's isolated force at Fair Oaks, but once again Kearny ordered him back to his original position. Birney insisted the order be confirmed, Kearny repeated it, and Birney's brigade ended the day where it began.

An angry Heintzelman relieved Birney and charged him with disobedience of orders. Kearny assured Heintzelman that Birney had not disobeyed intentionally, but he failed to confess his own responsibility for the mix-up. A court-martial would acquit Birney, but his arrest had gotten into the papers and he was embittered. For his part, Heintzelman persuaded himself that David Birney would never "do any good service as I am satisfied that he is a coward, or at least will avoid close contact with the enemy whenever he can." This was unjust, the consequence of Kearny's overstepping — and concealing — his command role that day. (Later, seeing Birney's report and other evidence, Heintzelman would write, "I blame Kearny for all this trouble Birney got in.")[63]

While Birney endured his misadventures along the railroad, Phil Kearny pitched headlong into the fighting, as he had at Williamsburg. "I was again sent for to redeem the blunders & short comings of others," he told his wife. With Hiram Berry's brigade, he struggled up the Williamsburg Road against the tide of fugitives from the front. He ordered battery commander George E. Randolph to load canister and fire into the fleeing men. Randolph loaded but hesitated firing and Kearny did not repeat the order. Men were running like sheep, said Kearny. "I flew at them. Hurrahed at them, waved my cap, & turned them, & led them into the fight again."

Before he could stabilize the defenses at Seven Pines, a new wave of Confederate attackers collapsed the center of this second line, threatening to cut off Kearny as Couch had been cut off earlier. Veteran campaigner that he was, Kearny had reconnoitered the prospective battlefield, and now he traced a way to the rear ahead of the enemy and dug in his troops, and those he had corralled on the way, in a third line — "from which," he said, "I never should have been taken." Here he and Heintzelman blocked any further advance of the enemy. Heintzelman was pleased to receive a dispatch from McClellan that began, "You have done what I expected of you in relieving the disaster of Casey."[64]

The Rebels' offensive lost headway due to more than just this final battle line established by Kearny and Heintzelman. Edwin Sumner on this day went a good way toward redemption for his Williamsburg failings. This time he was asked to do what was entirely within his capabilities.

Over the last ten days General McClellan had been suffering from a malarial fever he first contracted during the Mexican War, and May 31 found him confined to his cot. At the first sounds of battle he roused himself enough to alert Sumner's Second Corps. Sumner's two divisions, under John Sedgwick and Israel Richardson, were posted three-quarters of a mile north of the Chickahominy and directly opposite Seven Pines. Two bridges had been completed on Sumner's front.

Rather than simply calling the troops to arms, ready for marching orders, Sumner formed up and marched them directly to the bridges — Sedgwick's to the Grapevine Bridge, Richardson's to the Lower Bridge a mile and a half downstream — and kept them waiting there in column. Before them the Chickahominy was in full flood, scouring across the bottomlands, smashing at the bridge causeways, twisting and tearing at the

Alfred Waud painted Edwin Sumner's Second Corps infantry crossing the Grapevine Bridge over the turbulent Chickahominy River to save the day at Seven Pines.

central spans over the main channel. On receiving Heintzelman's terse situation report from the front ("Genl Caseys first line broke and ran. I have ordered forward Kearnys Division and go forward myself. I need reinforcements from Sumner"), McClellan ordered the Second Corps to cross.

As Sumner gave the order to start Sedgwick's men forward, an engineer rushed up to him and said he would not be able to get across the bridge. "Can't cross this bridge!" Sumner roared. "I can, sir; I will, sir!" But, said the engineer, couldn't he see the bridge beginning to break up right before their eyes? "It is impossible!" That was not a word old Sumner tolerated. "Impossible! Sir, I tell you I *can* cross. I am ordered!"

To Edwin Sumner, it was indeed a matter of orders, of going from point A to point B, and he was just the man for that. So it proved. Sedgwick's marching column actually weighted down the bridge enough to keep it from washing away. The Lower Bridge did wash away, after only one brigade had crossed, and the rest of Richardson's men moved up to the Grapevine Bridge crossing. Just one artillery battery could be brought over, but that one proved enough for the work at hand.[65]

Once across the river, Sedgwick's division pushed ahead to Fair Oaks where, in the nick of time, it went into line alongside Darius Couch's beleaguered force. For more than three hours Couch had stood off repeated attacks with the two regiments he started with, two others he collected in the meantime, and a single battery, at the cost of more than 400 casualties. Upon seeing Sumner, Couch would write, "I felt that God was with us and victory ours."

The Rebel assaults here were pressed by Joe Johnston himself, trying to salvage something from his badly managed offensive. But Sedgwick's men were up to the task. Uncle John saw to that. One of his staff wrote, "The General rode into and through showers of bullets as imperturbably as if they were so many hail-stones." He tolerated no faint hearts. "He ran out into the field," wrote Lieutenant Henry Ropes, 20th Massachusetts, "and saw a Corporal running in with the usual story 'driven in.' Sedgwick caught the fellow by the neck, violently kicked his rear before all the soldiers, and ordered him back." Bull Sumner too was in his element, calling out to a New Hampshire colonel, in a voice loud enough for the men to hear, "If they come out here, give 'em the bayonet; give 'em the bayonet, they can't stand that." By Ropes's account, "Genl. Sumner ordered our whole line to advance. We rushed on with tremendous cheers, the whole together at a charge. The Rebels did not wait for the bayonets but broke and fled."

A deciding factor in this struggle at Fair Oaks was the Union artillery. The Confederates failed to bring up any guns for support, giving James Brady's battery, from Couch's division, and Edmund Kirby's battery, from Sedgwick's, unimpeded fire at the attacking infantry. Captain Brady ran out of canister, but he made do by firing shell and case shot without fuzes, "bursting the shell as it left the gun." For Lieutenant Kirby, May 31, 1862, was sweet revenge for July 21, 1861, when his Battery I, 1st United States Artillery, lost its guns on the Bull Run field and he was wounded. On this day Kirby fired 343 rounds and had the satisfaction of watching the enemy quit the field, seen off by final rounds from his guns.[66]

At midnight General McClellan met Heintzelman at Dispatch Station on the railroad for a report on the left wing. "The General is painful to see," the Comte de Paris wrote of McClellan, who was wan and weak from the malaria. Heintzelman "makes us a sad picture of Keyes's rout," adding that Casey's division should not be counted on in a renewed battle. But for June 1 Heintzelman was confident. He still had his own Third Corps intact — Kearny's division plus Hooker, who had not been engaged — and Couch was still game to fight.[67]

On the evening of the 31st Joe Johnston had been badly wounded in the fighting against Sedgwick, and his second, G. W. Smith, assumed the command. On Sunday morning, June 1, Smith renewed the battle but without much direction or conviction. McClellan, still ill, left the fighting to his lieutenants — in the Seven Pines area to Heintzelman, in the Fair Oaks area to Sumner — and on both fronts the Confederate attacks were repulsed before noon and they gave up the field.

On the left, Joe Hooker took over from Kearny, and the ground lost the day before was retaken. Hooker (wrote Heintzelman) "after a little firing told the men to fix bayonets & charge. They did so & drove the rebels a mile." As he had on Saturday, corps commander Heintzelman got right into the midst of the fighting and today was exultant at the outcome. Hooker's division, said one of its officers, "saved the left wing under Heintzelman and the old fellow hugged Genl. Hooker like a bear." His fighting blood up, Heintzelman turned to Kearny to support the advance. But to his surprise, "Gen. Kearny rode up to me & begged me to stop. He had no reliance on my reserves & thought if we were repulsed it would go hard on us." Reluctantly Heintzelman countermanded the order. Apparently the sight of so many fugitive troops the day before turned even Phil Kearny cautious.

On the Fair Oaks front Israel Richardson's division met the attack with what Richardson described as "the heaviest musketry firing that I had ever experienced." Once again the Rebels failed to bring up artillery to support their assaults, and the Federal batteries dominated. The brigades of William H. French and Otis Howard were the most heavily engaged and lost between them 800 men.

General French was a choleric-looking old regular with a facial tic that led his men to call him Old Blinky. Alcohol was a problem for French and in time it would sully his reputation, but on this day he managed his men capably enough in repelling repeated attacks. "Not for one moment in the entire fight during this contest for the mastery did our lines blench" was his high-flown but accurate summing-up.

Otis Howard's brigade was put into action piecemeal, its regiments filling gaps or extending lines. Going into battle here for the first time was Lieutenant Colonel Francis Channing Barlow, who led his 61st New York from in front. His men entered a wood where, he wrote, "a most violent firing began on both sides. The singing of the balls was awful. In about 3 minutes men were dying & groaning & running about with faces shot & arms shot & it was an awful sight." But the 61st persisted in its advance, and when recalled "came out in beautiful order." Civilian-soldier Barlow was well satisfied with his first battle-leading: "I was in the thick of it. . . . The men cheered me violently during the fight & when we came out."

Otis Howard, too, led from up front that morning. "In order to encourage the men in a forward movement I placed myself, mounted, in front of the Sixty-fourth New York," he wrote. They had hardly started their advance when Howard was hit in the right arm, and soon after he was hit again, in the right elbow. The surgeons found the arm hopelessly shattered and that night amputated above the elbow. The next day, as Howard waited at Fair Oaks Station to be evacuated, one-armed Phil Kearny arrived to commiserate. "General," he said, "I am sorry for you; but you must not mind it; the ladies will not think the less of you." (Kearny spoke from experience.) Howard laughed and remarked that at least they could buy their gloves together. "Sure enough!" said Kearny, and they shook on that with the hands left to them.[68]

At midday on June 1 the firing died out and the battlefield fell largely silent. McClellan telegraphed Washington, "We have had a desperate battle in which the Corps of Sumner, Heintzelman, & Keyes have been engaged against greatly superior numbers." He sketched in the two-day struggle, reciting one negative ("Casey's Division which was in first line gave way unaccountably & discreditably") but crediting the rest of the high command with checking and then everywhere repulsing the enemy. "Our loss is heavy, but that of the enemy must be enormous."

At 2 o'clock on the afternoon on June 1, at G. W. Smith's headquarters amidst the retreating Confederate army, Jefferson Davis dismissed Smith as commander of what was now to be known as the Army of Northern Virginia and appointed Robert E. Lee in his place.[69]

7. *The Seven Days*

NEAR THE END of the fighting on June 1 General McClellan appeared on the battlefield. His lieutenants had matters well in hand and little required his attention. "Sumner and his generals press themselves around the General, excited and triumphant," wrote the Comte de Paris, who went on to sketch the scene. Sumner "has an even more withered air than usual"; the Irish Brigade's Thomas Meagher "caracoles from right to left, always followed by a big green guidon, as if to say . . . 'I am the most Irish of the Irish'"; William French "twitches his nose and winks his left eye convulsively." An exception to the animated group was "the silent and contrite figure of Couch, wandering in vain in search of his division . . . cut off the previous day."

McClellan gave thought to striking at the retreating enemy with Porter's and Franklin's corps. But the river was reported running higher and more violent than ever, making bridging impossible. McClellan crumpled the dispatch in his fist, wrote the Comte de Paris, "but he limited himself to this gesture of impatience." The Battle of Seven Pines would not be followed up.

On June 2 the general commanding issued an address to his troops. As he had promised, "you are now face to face with the rebels, who are at bay in front of their Capital. The final and decisive battle is at hand." He asked of them one last crowning effort, and he renewed his pledge: "Soldiers! I will be with you in this battle and share its dangers with you." Read to the troops at dress parade, it "was greeted by many and loud cheers," wrote a staff man.

McClellan pledged to Washington as well. He claimed victory at Seven Pines and said he would move quickly to build on it. "I only wait for the river to fall to cross with the rest of the force & make a general attack." He telegraphed his wife, "One more & we will have Richmond & I shall be there with Gods blessing this week."

But that night, in his solitude, he turned introspective in a letter to Ellen. June 1 marked his first-ever look at the scene of a major battle. He found it deeply disturbing. The impression in his mind's eye of Seven Pines was crowded with the images of hundreds of gravely wounded men awaiting care and, scattered across the muddy, trampled field, scores of killed from the previous day's fighting. He had seen battle dead before, in Mexico, but this scene was different — different in scale, different because these killed and wounded men were *his* men. He was confident of ultimate success, he wrote. "But I am tired of the sickening sight of the battlefield, with its mangled corpses & poor suffering wounded! Victory has no charms for me when purchased at such cost."[1]

Seven Pines proved to be the only Peninsula combat George McClellan experienced this close up. His revulsion at the bloody arithmetic of battle pointed to something deep-rooted in his military character — a reluctance to accept the human toll necessarily expended by a commander to win a battle or a campaign. As he put it in another letter, "Every poor fellow that is killed or wounded almost haunts me!" In his address to the army he promised his men he would join them in the fighting to come and share its dangers. But critically at issue was whether in battle he would — or could — demonstrate the "moral courage," the ruthless acceptance of responsibility, to risk and to expend those lives, in whatever numbers required, to gain victory.

McClellan's incaution in pushing forward his left wing, and his misjudgment in thinking Johnston "too able" a general to risk countering that move, put the Army of the Potomac in jeopardy on May 31. Fortuitously, Johnston's planning was so bungled that the Federals rallied and finally halted the assault, and then on June 1 regained the lost ground. From his sickbed McClellan's direction was limited to ordering Sumner's Second Corps to support the embattled left. The Federals lost 5,000 men and the Confederates 6,100, and the two armies ended the battle about where they began it.[2]

In reporting to Washington on the fighting, McClellan drew on Heintzelman's dispatches to denounce Silas Casey's division for giving way "unaccountably & discreditably" on May 31. As at Williamsburg, McClellan's report was highly judgmental of events where he was absent; and it too was released to the press. The press expanded the story. Correspondent Samuel Wilkeson pictured Casey's troops as "sweeping in a great shameful flow down the Williamsburg road." Casey's men, wrote Wilkeson, "had been taught nothing save how to march and camp, and . . . deteriorated daily under the command of a General who had neither youth, enthusiasm, pride, or combativeness."

Casey tried to defend himself and his men. Just because his division was "the subject of a false and malicious telegram, it is certainly no reason that it should be deprived of that which is justly its due." He said his long casualty list earned his division credit, not discredit. The "unaccountably & discreditably" charge was withdrawn, but the damage was done. Beyond doubt Casey's division had been severely handled. On June 23 McClellan relieved Casey, replacing him with John Peck. Casey would not again serve in the field. While the matter was handled awkwardly, McClellan's summation was accurate enough. At Seven Pines "the division of Gen Casey was broken in such manner as to show that its commander had failed to infuse proper morale into his troops."[3]

Seven Pines was a battle suited to Bull Sumner's dedicated if limited generalship. "The old man seemed to be making up for Williamsburg," wrote Charles Wainwright. Scorched by the press after the earlier battle, Sumner sought vindication on May 31. When a McClellan dispatch crediting Sumner's role in the fighting was garbled in the *New York Herald*, Sumner insisted McClellan make it public as originally written. He did so, and Sumner sent a copy to his wife endorsed, "Show this dispatch to our friends." Alerted, he had assembled his men and marched them right to the Chickahominy bridges, thus wasting not a moment in crossing when the order came . . . saved moments that saved Keyes and Heintzelman. In the fighting Sumner grasped the measures needed, and competent lieutenants John Sedgwick and Israel Richardson carried them out.[4]

The Comte de Paris, so contemptuous of Erasmus Keyes at Williamsburg, conceded that "General Keyes . . . this time is not afraid to expose himself" to enemy fire. Keyes's horse and accouterments were hit three times by musketry during the chaotic fighting on May 31. A staff man wrote, "Keyes again rode up cheering and encouraging all around him, and his presence and words then as many other times during the day infused new vigor and determination into the men. . . ."

Still, Keyes found himself tarred by the same brush used on Casey, and belittled by the same rumors about his fortitude that Philippe earlier reported. Keyes wrote New York's Senator Ira Harris that "great injustice has been done to my corps & to me in giving currency to the idea that Casey's Division *ran at once*." Most of the Fourth Corps, he insisted, was much longer under fire than that; he himself "was under hot fire for six consecutive hours on the 31st & . . . I personally reformed my lines many times." But Erasmus Keyes had been caught in a situation not of his making, in a posting not of his choice, and could only try to stem what became (whether sooner or later) a stampede. To Chief of Staff Marcy, an old friend, Keyes wrote, "I *cannot of course believe* that Genl. McClellan is going to frown on me for my conduct on the 31st," but should he in any way disapprove, Keyes appealed "to our old associations" to allow him to resign quietly and not suffer the humiliation of being relieved.

McClellan lacked cause to relieve Keyes, but he distrusted him sufficiently to post him in the coming weeks far from the sound of the guns. For his part, Keyes sought intervention from Treasury Secretary Chase: "I am called a Republican and if you know the manner in which McClellan & his clique make war on republicans, you will understand what pressure I am obliged to sustain." He sought "the favor to have me ordered out of this army in some way which will not reflect on my capacity or devotion to the cause."[5]

Darius Couch, heading Keyes's other division, was cut off at Fair Oaks Station with hardly a third of his command. He defended the spot stubbornly until Sumner came to his relief, and was not forgiving of McClellan's failure to recognize his division's hard fight. Like Keyes, he wrote privately to Chief of Staff Marcy: "If I am obnoxious to Gen. McClellan, let him send me to another field. I am willing to do anything, in order that the men know that they saved the left wing of the army."

Sam Heintzelman initially reacted to the attack in slow motion, due to the ninety-minute delay in reporting from the front. But as he had at Williamsburg, he rushed to the scene, thrust himself into the fighting, pushed reinforcements forward and posted them, and his reporting brought Sumner's Second Corps into the battle. McClellan held out his hand, Heintzelman wrote in his diary, "& remarked calling me by name, 'You have done what I expected, you have whipped the enemy.'"

In answering the call on the 31st, Phil Kearny sought to reprise Williamsburg and play the part of rescuer. While he again demonstrated that as a battlefield leader of troops he had few peers, his command arrogance limited his performance. He overrode Heintzelman's orders to David Birney merely on the grounds (as he told his wife) that "weak old fool" Heintzelman "mismanaged me as usual." Kearny then did not admit it was he who was accountable for Birney's supposed inaction. In his memoir Baldy Smith termed Phil Kearny "ungovernable," a trait very much on display at Seven Pines.

In the second day's fight there were no surprises by the Rebels, and no lapses by the Federal command. June 1 proved an incisive reversal of May

The Young Napoleon sits stubbornly unmoving upon the bank of the Chicka-hominy. The telegraph trumpets victories, and the eagle praises his genius and tells him, "Take that City at your leisure." Lithograph by B. Duncan.

31. "I believe the report that the rebels are retreating," Heintzelman wrote. "They cast their last die & lost."[6]

On May 30, as Joe Johnston prepared his assault on Seven Pines, far to the west in Mississippi P.G.T. Beauregard evacuated Corinth, slipping away from the clutches of Henry Halleck's Federal army. This event triggered, on the part of General McClellan, an extended series of Beauregard sightings. Remarkably, the first came on May 30, McClellan reporting to Stanton, "Beauregard arrived in Richmond day before yesterday, with troops & amid great excitement." On June 10 he passed on further intelligence of Beauregard's arrival, and proposed "detaching largely" from Halleck's army to strengthen his own. Halleck bristled, reporting Beauregard and his army still a presence in Mississippi. McClellan continued to post Beauregard sightings regardless, thereby considerably inflating the host defending Richmond.[7]

As the Potomac army battled at Seven Pines, the campaign the president was managing in the Shenandoah Valley rushed toward its own climax. McDowell from the east and Frémont from the west sought to trap Stonewall Jackson. On May 30, having chased Banks into Maryland, Jackson started back up the Valley. By Jackson's calculation, McDowell and Frémont were aiming for Strasburg, "and are both nearer to it now than we are." In Washington, Quartermaster Meigs was writing, "Jackson's army is being gradually surrounded. I pray that the movement may be successfully carried out & that he may be caught in the web we have woven with care and labor in the last week."

McDowell's 20,000 men in the Valley saw James Shields's division in the van. Shields had just reached Fredericksburg to join the march to the Peninsula, but having campaigned in the Valley he seemed best suited to spring the trap. The Pathfinder, for all his experience in the mountains of the West, was finding the Alleghenies a terrible place to make war. Still, by May 31, despite their many trials, he and Shields were poised to head off Jackson at Strasburg. "It seems the game is before you," Lincoln telegraphed them.

Then both Federal generals blinked. On June 1 Shields halted and turned to defend against James Longstreet's command that rumor of the most improbable sort had brought from Richmond to threaten him. Frémont feebly skirmished with the Rebel rear guard while the last of Jackson's troops hurried through Strasburg. "The latest information from the Shenandoah Valley," wrote Lincoln's secretary John Nicolay on June 2, "indicates that Jackson's force has slipped through our fingers there, notwithstanding that he was almost surrounded by our armies."

"Do not let the enemy escape from you," the president demanded of McDowell and Frémont. They attempted pursuit, but on June 8, at Cross Keys, Jackson rounded on Frémont and drove him back. The next day, at Port Republic, Shields in his turn was driven back. A resigned Lincoln told Frémont to give up the chase and stand on the defensive. Shields was ordered to rejoin McDowell's command. The Valley campaign was over, and Stonewall Jackson had won it decisively.[8]

Lincoln's directions to his generals in the Shenandoah reflected sound military instincts. He discounted Jackson's threat to Washington, recognized Jackson's intent to tie up Federal forces in the Valley, and without hesitation seized on the moment to cut off Jackson's escape. Despite all the obstacles of terrain and weather, he managed to position Shields and Frémont in time to spring the trap. The failure was theirs. James Shields proved all bluster, Pathfinder Frémont, all excuses. Neither would redeem his lost military career.

The president's strategy for energizing McClellan's stagnant campaign went awry at the very start, when from the best of motives he pulled

Shields's division out of the Valley to join McDowell for transfer to the Peninsula. Had he not had to wait for Shields, McDowell and his three divisions at Fredericksburg ought to have joined McClellan by mid-May . . . at which Richmond, seeing the Yankees so strongly reinforced, would surely have recalled Jackson to defend the capital.

Lacking a general-in-chief, Lincoln's only source of professional military advice was Stanton's War Board and the ineffectual Ethan Allen Hitchcock. No one seems to have pointed out that without Shields's division the Valley's defenders were seriously "out of balance" and a tempting target for Jackson. "Messrs. Lincoln & Stanton are not as great Generals as they had supposed themselves to be," remarked W.T.H. Brooks. John Gibbon wanted the war left to the generals, "who ought to know what they are about, and if they don't I think it very certain nobody else does."

In fact it was still possible to achieve an exalted state of reinforcement even after Jackson's escape. George McCall's division that had remained at Fredericksburg was started to the Peninsula (by water) on June 6. The president determined that Frémont and a rejuvenated Nathaniel Banks ought to be enough to keep a grip on the Valley, so on June 8 McDowell was directed to the Peninsula "with the residue of your force as speedily as possible." That residue comprised the divisions of Shields, Rufus King, and James B. Ricketts (replacing E.O.C. Ord). But by now Shields's division, in Lincoln's homely phrasing, "has got so terribly out of shape, out at elbows, and out at toes" that it required refitting. Still, McDowell promised that he with King and Ricketts would join the Potomac army before June 20.

That order never came. Once again, affairs in the Valley turned perplexing. Lincoln told McClellan he had hoped to send him more force, "but as the case stands, we do not think we safely can." The continued bumbling of Frémont and Banks kept the Valley's defenses in disarray, and General Lee, with calculation, added to the perplexity. He dispatched three brigades to strengthen Jackson, greatly alarming the Yankees, then recalled Jackson and his entire command to the defense of Richmond. Frémont and Banks crowned their ineptitude by failing to discover that Jackson was gone.

Lincoln saw the reports of these Rebel reinforcements for the Valley as another McClellan opportunity. Every soldier sent away from Richmond was one less soldier the general would have to face — if he acted promptly. The logic of that quite escaped McClellan. Secure in his delusions about Confederate numbers, he replied that if 10,000 or 15,000 men "have left Richmond to reinforce Jackson it illustrates their strength and confidence." Detective Pinkerton fed the general's fantasy, reporting the Rebel army was "variously estimated" as 150,000 to 200,000 strong. McClellan took the 200,000 figure as his benchmark for the campaign.[9]

During the First Corps' checkered chronicle, Irvin McDowell met growing disdain from the Potomac army's officer corps. McClellan was convinced of McDowell's perfidy in angling for an independent command, and told Stanton if he could not have full control of McDowell's men, "I want none of them, but would prefer to fight the battle with what I have & let others be responsible for the results." Fitz John Porter tipped off *New York World* editor Manton Marble that McDowell was "a general whom the army holds in contempt and laughs at — and has no confidence in." Israel Richardson spoke of "the gay and accomplished Gen. McDowell . . . who puts one in mind very much of a second Jack Falstaff. . . . We should like much to have his troops to assist us, but don't want *him*." McDowell wrote a friend, "Yet I, who have been striving and struggling to get down to join McClellan's army . . . find myself thoroughly misunderstood both by the press and by the people . . . with a not worthy motive ascribed to me."

The net result of Jackson's Shenandoah Valley campaign was that his two divisions joined the Peninsula battles while just two divisions (of four) of McDowell's reached McClellan. The unsettling situation sent the president up to West Point to seek counsel from the retired Winfield Scott. The old general advised dispatching McDowell's corps to the Peninsula, and offered his thoughts on a general-in-chief and on a response to the Valley debacle. On June 26, the day after he returned to Washington, Lincoln combined the Union forces remaining in northern Virginia and in the Shenandoah Valley into a new Army of Virginia, to be commanded by one of Halleck's Western generals, John Pope.[10]

George McCall's Pennsylvania Reserves division was assigned on arrival to the Fifth Corps. It boasted three promising brigadiers, John F. Reynolds, George G. Meade, and Truman Seymour. The Fifth was now the largest corps in the Potomac army and, under Fitz John Porter, the particular favorite of General McClellan.

McClellan gained a second substantial reinforcement by working himself free of General Wool at Fort Monroe. John Wool, seventy-eight, wily veteran of army politics, ran his Department of Virginia as an independent fiefdom, holding fast to his troops and deflecting McClellan's pleas that he garrison the army's rear areas at Yorktown, Williamsburg, and White House. Lincoln resolved the impasse by an exchange of department heads — Wool taking the place of John A. Dix at the Middle Department in Baltimore, Dix taking over at Fort Monroe. The Department of Virginia was folded into McClellan's command, and two-thirds of Dix's troops — eleven regiments — attached to the Potomac army. Dix's regiments and the 20,000 men of McCall's division, said Sam Heintzelman, "ought to carry us into Richmond."[11]

Edwin Sumner was given charge of the three corps now posted south of the Chickahominy — his Second, Heintzelman's Third, Keyes's Fourth. Armed with semi-independent status, Sumner resumed his alarmist habits. On June 1, even as the Rebels' retreat ended the Seven Pines fighting, he announced, "I have good reasons to believe that I shall be attacked early in the morning by 50,000 men," and he called out the Third Corps for support. Heintzelman disagreed, detailing his reasoning to Sumner. It was wasted effort. On June 3 Heintzelman's diary read, "The promise of a pleasant day till Sumner created, or rather tried to create, a stampede." June 8: "Gen. Sumner has another stampede & paraded his troops & Kearny's. I could not see the slightest necessity." Sumner was only calmed when McClellan shifted headquarters south of the river and the three corps commanders resumed their normal roles.

Phil Kearny loudly complained about Sumner ("Bull in a china shop"), and raised objection when John C. Robinson replaced the injured Charles Jameson as head of one of Kearny's brigades. Robinson was a veteran officer with a good record, and Kearny was rebuffed. "Gen. McClellan has written a letter & sent it through me," Heintzelman wrote, "as severe & unexceptional as a letter well can be written. It will do Kearny good. He is always finding fault & making exceptions."

No objections met two other new brigade commanders. John C. Caldwell replaced wounded Otis Howard in the Second Corps. Caldwell was a school principal from Maine, a Republican whose party affiliation gained him the colonelcy of the 11th Maine and a promotion to brigadier general. Charles Griffin, the fiery artillery veteran who lost his battery at Bull Run, gave up the guns for an infantry brigade (and a brigadier's star) in the Fifth Corps, replacing the promoted George Morell.[12]

On June 2 headquarters set forth a reorganization of the Army of the Potomac's artillery arm. On taking command, McClellan had shifted the assignment of batteries from brigade to division, with a general army artillery reserve. In the new scheme, each corps took roughly half the batteries assigned to its divisions to form a corps artillery reserve. The Second, Third, and Fourth Corps carried out this reorganization in time for the next battle. Porter's Fifth Corps, to which Henry Hunt's artillery reserve was attached, had no separate corps reserve. The thought here was to give the corps commanders more flexibility for tactical purposes. The guns still remained under control of infantry generals, however; artillery flexibility directed by artillery officers was yet to come.[13]

So soon as the Chickahominy flooding subsided, McClellan put his engineers to bridge building. By mid-June there were ten bridges, and Franklin's Sixth Corps was brought across. Only Porter's reinforced Fifth Corps remained north of the Chickahominy, guarding the right flank and the railroad. The four corps south of the river entrenched themselves. Francis Barlow grumbled that the army lay crouched behind earthworks along the whole line. "I don't know whether we are to be the attacking or the attacked party." Phil Kearny grumbled too. "We always seem to take a nap after every Battle, which thus completely throws away all the good results." Still, confidence was building. "Richmond is sure to fall," Hiram Berry wrote. ". . . I trust when Richmond falls the war closes."

On June 15 McClellan outlined for his wife, but not for Washington, his plan for capturing Richmond. Lincoln was given only the vague assurance that "we shall fight the rebel army as soon as Providence will permit." The site of the next battle, McClellan told Ellen, would be Old Tavern, elevated ground a mile south of the Chickahominy and some five miles from Richmond. "If we gain that the game is up for Secesh — I will have them in the hollow of my hand." At Old Tavern he would mass 200 guns to "sweep everything before us," then advance the heavy guns and mortars and invest Richmond — "shell the city & carry it by assault."

Much to McClellan's embarrassment, on June 12–15 Jeb Stuart expanded a reconnaissance into a complete circuit of the Army of the Potomac. General Lee concluded that "McClellan will make this a battle of posts. He will take position from position, under cover of his heavy guns, & we cannot get at him without storming his works. . . ." Lee determined to seize the initiative. He took as his target Porter's Fifth Corps north of the Chickahominy, and assigned Stuart to reconnoiter. The Rebel troopers traced Porter's lines, and to conceal his purpose Stuart continued on around the Federals, returning to Richmond along the bank of the James.

Pursuit was a family affair, directed by Philip St. George Cooke, head of the cavalry reserve and Stuart's father-in-law. Cooke set off on Friday the 13th and his luck foundered. Lacking an independent cavalry force like Stuart's, Cooke had to paste together a command. Then he was hobbled by faulty intelligence that gave the Rebel column an infantry component. Cooke ordered up infantry of his own — Gouverneur Warren's brigade — thus limiting the pace of the pursuit to that of the foot soldiers. He never

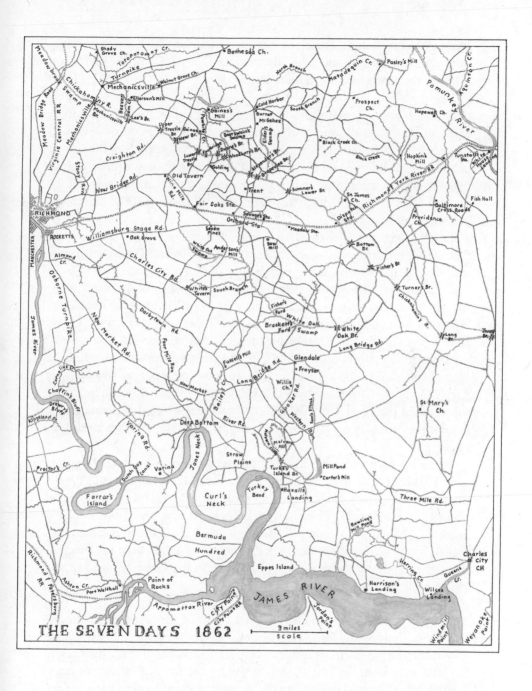

THE SEVEN DAYS 1862
3 miles scale

came close to catching Stuart. "I have just returned after a weary tramp (and an unsuccessful one foolishly managed) . . . ," Colonel Warren reported; "the rebels have been quite enterprising."[14]

Set against Union successes in other theaters that spring, the drumbeat of demands and complaints and excuses from the Peninsula increasingly wore on Washington. John Nicolay invoked an 1862 version of Murphy's Law: "McClellan's extreme caution, or tardiness, or something, is utterly exhaustive of all hope and patience, and leaves one in that feverish apprehension that as something *may* go wrong, something most likely *will* go wrong." Quartermaster Meigs was sure "McClellan never did & never will give an order for attack."

For his part, McClellan shared his alienation with his lieutenants. George Meade wrote his wife that he and Franklin and Baldy Smith visited McClellan, who "talked very freely of the way in which he had been treated, and said positively, that had not McDowell's corps been withdrawn, he would long before now have been in Richmond." McClellan passed on to Ellen the latest capital gossip: "I learn that Stanton & Chase have fallen out; that McDowell has deserted his friend C & taken to S!! . . . that Honest A has again fallen into the hands of my enemies & is no longer a cordial friend of mine! . . . Alas poor country that should have such rulers." He named caution his watchword: "When I see such insane folly behind me I feel that the final salvation of the country demands the utmost prudence on my part & that I must not run the slightest risk of disaster. . . ."

Fitz John Porter took up his commander's cause with virulent dedication. He urged *New York World* editor Marble to reveal to the country the nefarious conspiracy of the Lincoln administration. "The secy and Prest ignore all calls for aid. They have been pressed and urged but no reply comes. . . . I wish you would put the question, — Does the President (controlled by an incompetent Secy) design to cause defeat here for the purpose of prolonging the war, or to have a defeated General and favorite (McDowell) put in command . . . ?"[15]

On June 24 McClellan ordered the first move of his intended battle for Richmond. Taking the lesson of Casey at Seven Pines, for the advance on Old Tavern he put his most experienced lieutenant, Sam Heintzelman, and his best troops, on the firing line. "It will be chiefly an Artillery & Engineering affair," he told Heintzelman. "Keep your command as fresh as possible, ready for another battle — I cannot afford to be without Heintzelman, Kearny & Hooker in the next effort."[16]

William Waud, an artist for *Frank Leslie's Illustrated Newspaper,* drew an impromptu reconnoiter at Mechanicsville on the eve of the Seven Days. On the roof (from left), McClellan, Prince de Joinville, William Franklin. Fitz John Porter points at left.

In joining battle for Richmond, McClellan counted under his immediate command 105,800 men of all arms. While he based his strategic and tactical decisions on confronting a Confederate army 200,000 strong, in fact the two armies were a close match. General Lee, who culled reinforcements from every direction in addition to calling in Jackson from the Valley, counted just over 101,000 in the Army of Northern Virginia. Back in April Lincoln had warned his general that the Confederates "will probably use *time,* as advantageously as you can." That proved a major understatement.[17]

Wednesday, June 25, 1862 — Day One of the Seven Days — did not witness anything very auspicious militarily. The Third Corps' Heintzelman assigned Joe Hooker to advance his lines a mile or so to Oak Grove, a conspicuous stand of timber (like Seven Pines) in this heavily wooded landscape. Gaining that objective, said McClellan, would be a major step toward seizing Old Tavern, prospective jumping-off place for the siege and assault on Richmond.

Hooker posted Dan Sickles's Excelsior Brigade on the right, astride the Williamsburg Stage Road, and Cuvier Grover's brigade on the left, with Joseph B. Carr's in reserve. Grover, veteran of the hard fighting at Williamsburg, led with a skirmish line two regiments strong, pushing aggressively through the woods and driving the Rebel pickets. Today marked political general Sickles's first real test. It did not go well. He put out an undermanned skirmish line and the advance was too slow to keep pace with Grover. The Rebels punched back, striking the least experienced Excelsior regiment, the 71st New York, which (in Sickles's words) "broke to the rear in disgraceful confusion."

McClellan and entourage rode up to consult and to restart the advance. Generals and staffs, wrote the Comte de Paris, were "seated on the parapet ... hearing a few bullets whistle and quite a lot of cannon balls; one of them plants itself in the parapet, causing several people to scatter." That was as close as General McClellan came to sharing the dangers of the battlefield with his men during the Seven Days.[18]

This advance to Oak Grove on June 25 cost the Federals 626 casualties and came to nothing, for that evening Heintzelman was called back to the starting point. McClellan's abrupt turnabout was triggered by a dispatch from Fitz John Porter at Fifth Corps headquarters north of the Chickahominy. A contraband just in from Richmond, Porter wrote, "says a large portion of Beauregard's army arrived yesterday and that the army expected to fight today or tomorrow and fight all around. . . . He saw the troops arrive and heard the cheering welcome to them. They say we have one hundred thousand (100,000) men and they two hundred thousand (200,000) and that Jackson is to attack in the rear."

This singular piece of unsubstantiated intelligence brought all three of McClellan's deepest fears boiling to the surface — a supposedly eyewitness Beauregard sighting, a count of 200,000 for Richmond's defenders, and an imminent attack by the renowned Stonewall Jackson. At 6:15 that evening he sent a despairing telegram to Secretary Stanton: "I shall have to contend against vastly superior odds if these reports be true. . . . I regret my great inferiority in numbers but feel that I am in no way responsible for it as I have not failed to represent repeatedly the necessity of reinforcements. . . . I will do all that a General can do with the splendid army I have the honor to command & if it is destroyed by overwhelming numbers can at least die with it & share its fate. But if the result of the action . . . is a disaster the responsibility cannot be thrown on my shoulders — it must rest where it belongs."[19]

Having assumed the identity of martyr and shed accountability for whatever might happen, McClellan converted his energies from offense to defense, to saving his army. He directed Chief of Staff Marcy to order the four corps commanders south of the Chickahominy to look to their defenses: "You cannot too strongly impress upon the Generals the fact that I wish to fight behind the lines if attacked in force." Earlier McClellan had begun stockpiling stores afloat on the James with an eye to helping the navy force the Drewry's Bluff defenses. Now he redoubled that effort, his purpose to secure a haven on the James for the army if need be. He notified Flag Officer Goldsborough that the navy's cooperation was "of vital importance & may involve the existence of this Army." He sent to Ambrose Burnside in North Carolina to sever the railroad Beauregard was supposed to be using to transport his army from Mississippi. (Upon second thought, he ordered Burnside's men to Fort Monroe. They reached there after the fighting was over.)

As if to legitimize his fears, McClellan was handed Pinkerton's newest "summary of the general estimates" of the Confederate army — 180,000 men, endorsed with Pinkerton's caution that this number was probably "considerably short" of the enemy's actual strength.[20]

Fitz John Porter's Fifth Corps was well posted to meet an attack from Richmond. His main line was a half mile east of Mechanicsville behind Beaver Dam Creek, where it emptied into the Chickahominy. It was inherently a strong position, fortified originally by Joe Johnston. George McCall's recently arrived division manned the line, John Reynolds's brigade on the right, Truman Seymour's on the left, George Meade's in reserve. They were supported by six batteries. Except for Seymour's brigade at Dranesville (under E.O.C. Ord) back in December, these Pennsylvania Reserves were new to battle, but they were well led, well drilled, and well posted. The posting was mostly the work of Reynolds. A West Pointer, a twenty-year regular, Reynolds had won two brevets in Mexico and was highly regarded by McClellan, who had pulled strings to get him for the Army of the Potomac.

Lee's plan for June 26 called for an advance down the north bank of the Chickahominy, coordinated with Stonewall Jackson's Valley army striking Porter's right and rear. Lee anticipated this envelopment forcing the Yankees to abandon their position, perhaps without a fight. By plan, Porter would be heavily outnumbered, leaving only some 30,000 Confederate infantry in the Richmond lines to confront the more than 76,000 Federals south of the river. There seemed great risk here, but Lee had taken his opponent's measure — his cautious, deliberate pace — and read in the Northern press the wildly inflated estimates of Confederate numbers issued by Potomac army headquarters, and he recognized McClellan's commitment to siege warfare. "He sticks under his batteries & is working night & day," Lee wrote President Davis. "I will endeavour to make a diversion to bring McClellan out."[21]

But like Joe Johnston at Seven Pines, Lee's complex battle plan fell to pieces. Just five brigades, 13,000 men, got into action on June 26, hardly a fifth of the intended force. Jackson's army never reached the battlefield, never fired a shot. Instead of an overpowering envelopment, Beaver Dam Creek became a bloody, hopeless series of frontal assaults.

Much of John Reynolds's antebellum service was in the artillery, and he posted his batteries to cover every approach with direct fire and crossfire. The infantry was well protected in rifle pits. The fighting at Beaver Dam Creek lasted some six hours and was never in doubt; "night closed the action with the enemy defeated and discomfited," Reynolds wrote. The Rebels lost 1,475 men, the Federals, 361. Back in the fall Reynolds despaired of ever turning volunteers into disciplined soldiers. Now he had words of praise for his Pennsylvanians: "The conduct of the troops, most of them for the first time under fire, was all that could be desired and creditable to their State and Country." Reynolds himself was widely praised for his first battle, Truman Seymour declaring that "much of the credit of this day belongs justly to him; his study of the ground and ample preparations . . . justify his high reputation as a soldier. . . ."[22]

At noon that June 26, before the fighting began, McClellan telegraphed Stanton confirming that Jackson was closing in, threatening his communications. Stanton should "not be discouraged" by reports that the army's lifeline was cut, even that Yorktown was lost. "I shall resort to desperate measures & will do my best to out manoeuvre & outwit & outfight the enemy." He telegraphed his wife, "I think the enemy are making a great mistake, if so they will be terribly punished. . . . I believe we will surely win & that the enemy is falling into a trap. I shall allow the enemy to cut off our communications in order to ensure success."

These two telegrams implied some bold, aggressive intention. In fact they were advance cover for the reality that General McClellan, facing what he took as implacable odds, was giving up his campaign, retreating from the gates of Richmond. To fall back down the Peninsula would be to admit utter defeat. Instead (to his mind), the Rebels' "great mistake" was focusing on the Potomac army's railroad lifeline. He would "outwit the enemy" by giving up the railroad, slipping the army away southward, and starting over with the James River as his new line of communications. In due course, operating from the James — and greatly reinforced — he might still "ensure success."[23]

Victory at Beaver Dam Creek (or Mechanicsville, as the battle was named) left McClellan momentarily exultant. "Victory of today complete

& against great odds," he told Stanton. "I almost begin to think we are invincible." He crossed to Porter's, and to Marcy back at headquarters he sang the praises of McCall's division: "Tell our men on your side that they are put to their trumps & that with such men disaster is impossible." In the Sixth Corps, "cheer after cheer rang all along the line, the bands came out for the first time in a month."[24]

By Baldy Smith's account, McClellan, on his way to Porter's that evening, stopped at the Sixth Corps. Smith and Franklin urged him to seize the moment — bring the Fifth Corps south of the river, destroying the bridges behind it. Then, said Smith, "we who were fresh should attack in force . . . and capture Richmond before Lee could make the long detour by Mechanicsville" to defend it. This exactly defined the risk Lee was taking, but failed to move McClellan. He reckoned a Rebel army 200,000 strong would leave a force at least the size of the Potomac army to hold Richmond even as Lee maneuvered north of the river. Of his and Franklin's scheme Smith wrote ruefully, "This was not done."

McClellan remained at Porter's until after midnight, debating options. In his report, Porter laid out the daunting dilemma as he and McClellan imagined it. It was necessary "to select which side of the Chickahominy should be held in force, there being on each side an army of our enemies equivalent . . . to the whole of our own."

Porter wanted reinforcements to hold the Beaver Dam Creek line, but McClellan's concern was its open right flank. The alternative was to fall back four miles or so to a position near Gaines's Mill covering the Chickahominy bridges, the links to the rest of the army. McClellan said he would return to headquarters, evaluate the situation there, and telegraph Porter his decision. A staff man overhead their parting words. "Now, Fitz, you understand my views and the absolute necessity of holding the ground, until arrangements over the river can be completed. Whichever of the two positions you take, *hold* it." Porter replied, "Give yourself no uneasiness; I shall hold it to the last extremity."

McClellan was being less than forthcoming with his favorite general. He did not reveal his intention to retreat to the James — an intention developed sufficiently by that time to outline it to the Comte de Paris and other staff during their ride back to headquarters. Porter's understanding was quite different. As he explained to historian John C. Ropes, "McClellan left me after 12 o'clock that night to decide, after returning to his headquarters, whether I should remain at Beaver Dam & be reinforced or move as quick as possible to the selected position at Gaines' Mill where I would

be reinforced from the right bank, or he would attack Richmond and I resist Lee's attack even to my destruction, & thereby to prevent Lee going to
the defense of Richmond."

Apparently General McClellan was more comfortable asking his lieutenant to fight to the last ditch to secure a victory rather than to protect a
retreat.[25]

McClellan chose the Gaines's Mill option, and at first light on June 27
Porter skillfully broke contact with the enemy at Beaver Dam Creek and
steered his command to its new position. South of the river McClellan
surveyed his battle line for potential reinforcements for the Fifth Corps.
Anticipating that line as well as Porter's to be attacked by the enemy host,
he asked the four corps commanders there how many troops they could
spare for Porter and still hold their lines for twenty-four hours.

From the Sixth Corps on the Chickahominy opposite Porter, Franklin
marked Henry Slocum's division as the lead reinforcement. Next came the
Second Corps, and Bull Sumner volunteered half his corps to cross the
river if ordered. To Sumner's left was the Third Corps of Sam Heintzelman, who offered two of his six brigades. The Fourth Corps was on the
far left, and General Keyes, mindful of his ordeal at Seven Pines, was cautious to a fault. "As to how many men will be able to hold this position for
twenty-four hours, I must answer, all I have, if the enemy is as strong as
ever in front. . . ."

To prepare for the retreat, McClellan sent engineers to survey the roads
leading south to the James, and to bridge White Oak Swamp, the major
barrier the army would have to cross. Ammunition and rations were called
up from the White House depot. McClellan's posture was everywhere defensive. To prepare Stanton, he telegraphed he was contending "at several
points against superior numbers" and might be forced "to concentrate between the Chickahominy & the James. . . ."[26]

The Gaines's Mill position marked out by chief engineer John Barnard
was an elevated plateau about two miles wide by a mile deep overlooking the four military-bridge crossings of the Chickahominy. A sluggish
stream called Boatswain's Swamp curled around the northern and western
sides. Elder's Swamp bordered the plateau on the east. These streams were
thickly edged with timber and undergrowth. The plateau itself was largely
open, but the sloping sides were well wooded. The approaches offered little cover for attackers. If the Fifth Corps was to hold its position "to the last
extremity," this was good ground for it.

Posted on the left, facing west, was the division of George W. Morell, his brigades led by Dan Butterfield, John Martindale, and Charles Griffin. For most of these troops and their generals, this would be their first battle. Morell, head of the 1835 Academy class, served two years before leaving the army for railroading and then the law. He reentered the service on the staff of the New York militia. Dan Butterfield, businessman-in-arms, was also a former New York militia officer. Martindale, a classmate of Morell's, never served a day before resigning for a career in the law. Charles Griffin of the regulars was the only one of the four with battle experience, fighting his battery at Bull Run. Facing north (from where Stonewall Jackson was expected) was George Sykes's division — two brigades of regulars, under Robert C. Buchanan and Charles S. Lovell, and Gouverneur Warren's brigade of volunteers. Except for Sykes, these officers had not seen action previously. Sykes, who covered the army's retreat at Bull Run, was a twenty-year man. McCall's division that fought on the 26th was posted as corps reserve.

There were ninety-six guns on the plateau, supporting the lines or in reserve. Three of Henry Hunt's reserve batteries of heavy guns were posted on the right bank to fire on Rebels advancing along the left bank. The Fifth Corps counted some 27,000 men. When engineer Barnard left that morning for headquarters, Porter thought it was agreed that Barnard would explain to McClellan "the necessity for additional troops, and also to send me axes, that the proper defenses might to some degree be prepared."

Porter recalled bitterly that his request never registered at army headquarters. Barnard "found McClellan asleep, went to sleep himself & paid no attention to my request," conduct he termed criminal. (Barnard admitted that when he found "the commanding general was reposing, I went to my tent and remained there until afternoon.") In due course Porter renewed his call to headquarters for help, but reinforcements arrived very late and axes arrived, unhelved, even later. Whatever few fieldworks the defenders threw up were hasty makeshifts.

Porter expected reinforcement that morning after seeing the head of Slocum's division approach the bridges but then turn back without explanation, "and I supposed the attack would be made upon Richmond." In fact, in yet another of his second thoughts, McClellan countermanded Slocum's movement out of concern that the Sixth Corps, lacking Slocum's division, could not contain an attack *from* Richmond. Porter waited six hours with growing impatience for some response from Barnard's mission. Only at 2:00 p.m. did he signal headquarters, "If you can send Slocum over please do so."[27]

For George McClellan, Gaines's Mill was a battle not seen, not understood, not really sensed. He did not stir from headquarters at the Trent house, a half mile south of the Chickahominy crossings; his only links to the two fronts were the telegraph and couriers. He took no initiatives, waiting instead upon the enemy's initiatives. What was the strength of the attackers? Porter was asked: "The General wishes to be exactly informed before he gives you an order."

Throughout the day, as McClellan awaited intelligence from Porter's battlefront, alarms raised by the generals facing the Confederates' Richmond lines south of the river clamored for his attention. Joe Hooker reported "the passage of 2 or 4 thousand Rebel troops" toward Sumner's Second Corps. Baldy Smith reported "six or eight regiments have moved down to the piece of woods in front of General Sumner." Smith then warned, "The enemy are massing heavy columns" facing his own lines. Franklin confirmed: "Three regiments are reported to be moving from Sumner's to Smith's front." Sumner added an alarm: "Enemy threaten an attack on my right near Smith." Aeronaut Thaddeus Lowe made an ascension and announced, "By appearances I should judge that the enemy might make an attack on our left at any moment." A McClellan staff man summed up: "In fine the enemy appears to be intending to sweep down the Chickahominy on both sides."

The perpetrator of these impending attacks south of the river was Prince John Magruder, whose notion of a good defense was a pseudo-offense. As he had done in those first days at Yorktown, the vastly outnumbered Magruder emptied out his bag of tricks to hoodwink the Yankees. Columns of troops marched hither and yon in plain sight. In plain hearing came shouts of command and drummers beating the long roll. There were bursts of picket-line firing and sudden artillery barrages.

Not everyone was fooled by these antics. Colonel Samuel K. Zook, 57th New York, reported no enemy in his front. Zook had crept out in advance of the picket line "and saw a whole lot of niggers parading, beating drums, and making a great noise." Zook's report was overlooked amidst the general intelligence din. Prince John's efforts met the same credulous response on June 27 as they had at Yorktown in April—the phantom Confederate army of General McClellan's invention acting exactly as he anticipated it would.[28]

The day before, at Mechanicsville, Lee had hoped to drive the Federals into the waiting arms of Stonewall Jackson approaching from the flank and rear, but Jackson failed to appear. On the 27th Lee sought to repeat that tactic. He could commit some 54,000 men (twice Porter's strength before any reinforcement). But Gaines's Mill looked to be an even stronger position than yesterday's. There seemed little choice except to storm the Yankees. Again Jackson was very slow getting his Valley army to the field, and until late in the day the Richmond army's assaults, while fiercely made, were piecemeal and poorly supported. As late as 4:10 that afternoon Porter could report that he "found everything most satisfactory. . . . Our men have behaved nobly and driven back the enemy many times, cheering them as they retired." Slocum was arriving now, and Porter even considered counterattacks.

Initially Porter fought his battle with a certain passivity, believing McClellan understood his situation, accepting his role as decoy to occupy the enemy while the rest of the army advanced on Richmond. In that belief he had waited until 2 o'clock in the afternoon, when already under heavy attack, to even ask for Slocum's division. Caught up in the pseudo-attacks in front of him, McClellan was oblivious to the intensity of the real attacks across the river. Andrew Humphreys ascended in Lowe's balloon and reported the aerial view of Porter's battle "for the first time that afternoon showed me how serious it was; for although we were but a short distance from the field the strong wind prevented my hearing the musketry. . . ." The reality on the ground was captured by Richard Auchmuty of Morell's staff, who described the Fifth Corps caught in "a storm of shot, shell, and musketry, which made the trees wave like a hurricane."

Within an hour of Porter's confident 4:10 dispatch the battle turned against him. William F. Biddle of the headquarters staff, sent across the river to report on the fighting, found Porter sitting his horse at the rear of the battle line. "The bullets were coming thro the woods & dropping all around," Biddle recalled. "Genl. Porter pointed to the woods & said, 'You can see for yourself, Captain — we're holding them, but it's getting hotter & hotter.'" Shortly after 5 o'clock Porter telegraphed in desperation, "I am pressed hard, very hard. About every Regiment I have has been in action. I have asked several times for assistance, and unless I receive, I am afraid I shall be driven from my position."

McClellan adjured Porter to "hold your own" and pledged, "You must beat them if I move the whole Army to do it & transfer all on this side." It was an empty pledge. In asking — not ordering — his generals on the Richmond front to furnish what they could to Porter, McClellan met firm resistance. "I do not think it prudent to send more troops from here at present," said Franklin. "Everything is so uncertain that I think it would be hazardous to do it," said Sumner. Just two brigades — French's and Meagh-

The Federal left at Gaines's Mill, a lithograph after Prince de Joinville. Fitz John Porter gives orders to Comte de Paris and Duc de Chartres.

er's — crossed the river after Slocum, and they arrived only in time to pick up the pieces.[29]

For Porter and his lieutenants to maintain a command grip on the battlefield became all but impossible as the fighting rushed toward a decision. Morell's and Sykes's line was stretched too thin to maintain reserves. When the line wavered or regiments exhausted their ammunition under the relentless assaults, Porter reached into McCall's division for support. Truman Seymour described the resulting turmoil: "Regiment after regiment advanced, relieved regiments in front, in turn withstood, checked, repelled, or drove the enemy, and retired, their ammunition being exhausted, to breathe a few moments, to fill their cartridge boxes, again to return to the contested woods." The regiments of Seymour, Meade, and Reynolds were scattered beyond control.

The Comte de Paris, directing reserves to the front, rushed up to George W. Taylor's New Jersey brigade, Slocum's division, and braced Taylor in rapid-fire French. The startled Taylor turned to his aide and asked, "Who the devil is this, and what is he talking about?" His bilingual aide explained it was the Comte de Paris of General McClellan's staff, in his ex-

citement lapsing into his native tongue. Despite his doubts, Taylor said, "Very well then, give him the Fourth Regiment and go see where he puts it." (Shortly the 4th New Jersey was surrounded and captured; the young Frenchman escaped.)

On the northern front, facing Jackson, George Sykes posted his veteran regulars as a steadying second line, but soon they too were fully committed. Sykes's left, Gouverneur Warren's volunteer brigade, was subject to repeated assaults. "Oh I wish you could have seen that fight," Colonel Warren wrote his fiancée-to-be, "when our regiment rushed against a South Carolina one that charged us. . . . Nothing you ever saw in the pictures of battles excelled it. . . . In less than five minutes 140 of my men were killed or wounded and the other regiment was completely destroyed." Warren, who was nicked by a spent bullet, handled not only his own brigade but directed any other regiments that came under his eye in the confusion.[30]

Dispersing Slocum's reinforcing division far and wide by regiments, even by companies, was deemed essential by Porter, but it offended Henry Slocum's military sensibilities. He would send a bill of particulars to Secretary Stanton "which preclude the idea of any credit being due Genl. Porter for his services on that occasion." He spoke of Porter's abundant artillery, "yet he made but little use of it," of Porter's "absurd disposition of his infantry force," of his scattering of reinforcements. By Slocum's accounting, "nine thousand brave men, two thousand of whom were of my division, were unnecessarily — I had almost said wantonly — sacrificed. . . ."

Porter responded with harsh words of his own. General Slocum, said Porter, had failed to report to him, "with whom his presence and advice might perhaps have averted some of the disasters he claims to have arisen." Slocum needed to explain "his absence from his command and the battle field," and why he left "without authority the north side of the Chickahominy." This contretemps went unresolved, and marked the first of Slocum's poisonous dealings with the Potomac army's high command.[31]

The sun was low in the sky, blood-red in the haze of battle smoke, when in one final convulsive charge the Confederates overwhelmed Porter's line right and left and surged onto the plateau. Sykes's regulars fell back in fair order, but where unit organization was fragmented, command collapsed and retreat became disordered. Former artillerist Charles Griffin attempted to rally his brigade, and any other infantry he could collect, to defend the divisional artillery. "Men, this battery must not be taken," he pleaded. "I cannot cover your retreat; you must cover mine." His effort was unavailing and most of the guns were lost. "Gen. Griffin wept hot tears and was unable to give any order," reported the Comte de Paris. George McCall, at sixty old before his time and ailing, "exhausted by fatigue and opium, could no longer hold his horse and his speech had lost all coherence," wrote the count. He also witnessed Dan Butterfield, on foot, his horse killed, separated from his scattered brigade, put his hat on the point of his sword and "advancing entirely alone, encouraged his men and sought to reform the disorganized regiments." George Morell also rushed forward alone, seized a flag, and planted it as a rallying point for the fugitives.

One general the Frenchman did not see was John Martindale, of Morell's division. Apparently Fitz John Porter did not see Martindale either. From the moment he arrived on the field, Martindale had voiced objections, remonstrating against Porter's positioning of his brigade, against Porter's posting of the artillery. When it came to Martindale leading his brigade in battle, Porter found him wanting. Porter made the case bluntly: "He abandoned the field at Gaines Mill in the day time or just before dark."

The singular high command casualty that day was John Reynolds, who lost his way in the confusion and was captured. He was taken to Confederate general D. H. Hill, a onetime messmate of his in the old army. "Reynolds, do not feel so bad about your capture. It is the fate of wars," said Hill. Some six weeks later Reynolds would return to the Potomac army in a prisoner exchange.[32]

The closing moments of the fighting witnessed an astonishing, hell-for-leather charge by five companies of the 5th U.S. Cavalry. Philip St. George Cooke's reserve cavalry was posted behind Boatswain's Swamp at Porter's direction to guard the flank. Looking for redemption after failing to catch son-in-law Jeb Stuart in the recent brazen circumnavigation of the Federal army, Cooke chose not to sit by idly in the crisis. Acting "without orders, of course," Cooke sent in the 5th Cavalry to rescue the threatened artillery line on the plateau.

It was a disaster. The Rebels stood their ground and shot the charging troopers to pieces. The survivors sheered off and galloped back through the artillery line, creating the impression of a Rebel cavalry charge, and in the chaos batteries were lost. But the charge did give the attackers pause, and other batteries limbered up and escaped. About as many guns were saved as lost. Porter insisted Cooke's ill-chosen tactic was the turning point of the battle. In fact the battle was already well lost.

Darkness saved the Federals from being driven into the river, and the arrival of French's and Meagher's brigades restored enough order to prevent a rout. "I was obliged to charge bayonets by the heads of regiments to force a passage through the flying masses," French reported. Irishman Thomas Meagher, inspirited with Irish whiskey, galloped about in a drunken show of rallying fugitives.

"On the other side of the Chickahominy the day is lost," McClellan wired Sam Heintzelman. "You must hold your position at all cost."[33]

As the survivors of Porter's beaten command trailed back across the Chickahominy in the darkness, their way marked by pitch pine torches, McClellan called in his generals for orders. The gathering was lit by a fire of pine logs that cast flickering shadows across the clearing. A reporter thought the scene worthy of commemorating in a "grand national painting. The crisis, the hour, the adjuncts, the renowned participants. . . ." Present were corps commanders Porter, Franklin, Sumner, and Heintzelman. The outcast Keyes was not summoned; his corps, the army's reserve, would lead the march to the James. By Heintzelman's account, McClellan sketched out two possible courses of action — to give up the present campaign and withdraw the army to a new base on the James, or "to abandon this side &

our wagons & with all the troops fight a battle on the other side. . . . Gen. McClellan professed a desire on his part personally to concentrate the Army & risk it on one general Battle." This was a bravura gesture. As the Comte de Paris tactfully put it, "Heintzelman fought it and did not have trouble dissuading him from it." Without debate, the retreat, already decided upon, was official. The last to cross the river destroyed the bridges.

In the midnight hour General McClellan, his grand campaign in ruins, anguished captive to his delusions, telegraphed Secretary Stanton his unique summary of the Gaines's Mill battle. South of the Chickahominy "we repulsed several very strong attacks," while north of the river the troops "were overwhelmed by vastly superior numbers even after I brought my last reserves into action. . . ." He had lost this battle "because my force was too small. I again repeat that I am not responsible for this & I say it with the earnestness of a General who feels in his heart the loss of every brave man who has been needlessly sacrificed today." He felt "too earnestly tonight — I have seen too many dead & wounded comrades" — a sight only in his mind's eye — "to feel otherwise than that the Govt has not sustained this Army." So there be no misunderstanding this last point, he underlined it: "If I save this Army now I tell you plainly that I owe no thanks to you or any other persons in Washington — you have done your best to sacrifice this Army."

Stunned by this accusation of what amounted to treason, Stanton hurried to the White House to justify himself. "You know — Mr. President that all I have done was by your authority. . . ." Lincoln described the moment for Orville Browning: "McClellan telegraphed to Stanton in very harsh terms, charging him as the author of the disaster." The president could only grit his teeth and tell his distraught general, "Save your Army at all events."

McClellan intended his indictment to reach a larger audience if need be. On June 29 he repeated his particular accounting of Gaines's Mill to General John A. Dix at Fort Monroe: "I for one can never forgive the selfish men who have caused the lives of so many gallant men to be sacrificed." Dix was to consider this confidential, except "if I lose my life make such use of it as you deem best."

Gaines's Mill proved to be the costliest of the Seven Days' battles. Of the Federals' 6,837 casualties, 4,008 were killed and wounded and 2,829 taken prisoner. (The Confederates suffered 7,993 casualties, nearly all of them killed and wounded, almost twice the Federals' count.) Twenty-two Federal guns were captured. The two reinforcing divisions of Slocum and McCall lost between them about 600 more men than the divisions of Morell and Sykes in the original Fifth Corps line, a result of the scattershot manner their troops were pressed into action. Indeed, Slocum's division lost the most men of the four divisions engaged, much to Henry Slocum's embitterment.[34]

Gaines's Mill might easily have become the decisive battle that McClellan envisioned as the centerpiece of his grand campaign — a battle fought defensively, on ground of his choosing, against the Rebels' principal army, with Richmond as the prize. Had he not countermanded the dispatch of Slocum's division at dawn that morning to support the Fifth Corps, Porter would have presented a solidly posted three-division front to the enemy, on choice defensive ground, his flanks secure, his lines stoutly backed by artillery, with a reserve at hand and additional reinforcements on call. "That battle should have been won," said Phil Kearny. "It was lost by imbecility."

But Gaines's Mill as an opportunity never crossed McClellan's mind. He saw instead only the phantom enemy of his imagination, replete now with Stonewall Jackson and P.G.T. Beauregard, menacing him with "vastly superior numbers" on every front.[35]

Saturday, June 28, Day Four of the Seven Days, dawned with the promise of renewed trials for the Federals. "However, the day advanced," wrote the Comte de Paris, "and the enemy did not attack, the hours went by in silence . . ." Gaines's Mill secured the initiative for General Lee, but for the moment he could only watch for McClellan to react. The Yankees might stay and fight for their railroad supply line. They might retreat down the Peninsula, reorganize, and renew their campaign. They might give up both the Chickahominy line and the railroad and retreat southward to the James and their gunboats. Lee was unconcerned that they might lunge straight for Richmond. McClellan had missed his chances on the previous days; surely he would not try it now.

The road network south to the James was limited. The Yankees had to fall back from their lines facing Richmond to Savage's Station on the railroad, turn south, cross White Oak Swamp, and make their way past the hamlet of Glendale to Malvern Hill, overlooking the James. The route covered some 20 miles, but for the Army of the Potomac — nearly 100,000 men, 307 field and heavy-artillery pieces, 3,800 wagons and ambulances, 2,500 beef cattle — navigating that distance, much of it over a single road, proved to be an agonizing and deadly three-day ordeal.

Keyes's Fourth Corps led the way. The engineers rebuilt the White Oak Swamp bridge, earlier destroyed to secure the army's flank. A mile or so upstream, at Brackett's Ford, they built a second bridge. Once across the swamp, Keyes learned of a woods road paralleling the Quaker Road, the main route to the James. This eased his march, but word of his find did not immediately reach those following. The Quaker Road would remain a lumbering mass of men and vehicles and lowing beeves.

Porter's battered Fifth Corps, with the reserve artillery, was next to march. Porter occupied Malvern Hill and Keyes reached Haxall's Landing, on the James, securing the immediate objective of the retreat. The rest of the army had to fight its way free.

On June 28 the fighting was limited to a sharp skirmish on Baldy Smith's front, but the 29th promised a more serious confrontation as Lee determined McClellan's intentions and set out to thwart them. Magruder was to pursue from the Richmond lines toward Savage's Station. Jackson would bridge the Chickahominy and try to catch the Yankees before or at the White Oak Swamp crossing. But again Jackson lagged behind, so initiating any fighting that day was left to Magruder.[36]

The three corps facing Richmond south of the Chickahominy — Sumner's Second, Heintzelman's Third, Franklin's Sixth — pulled back to a new line in front of Savage's Station. McClellan made headquarters south of White Oak Swamp, leaving to his three corps commanders the task of fending off the enemy long enough for the trains to escape, then escape themselves. That day, and thereafter, McClellan stayed to the rear, devoted exclusively to details of the retreat. He named no one to command at Savage's. The three generals acted at their own discretion.

Savage's Station served as the supply railhead for the army, and was crowded with immense stores of provisions, equipment, and ammunition. Here too was a large field hospital filled with wounded. Staff cartographer Robert Sneden described the scene at midday on June 29: "Long trains of wagons were still coming from the woods in front and columns of troops in motion filled the fields in front of Savage's. Amid cracking of whips and braying of mules, all were hurrying to 'the swamp road.' . . . Generals Heintzelman, Sumner, Sedgwick, Franklin, and their staff officers were consulting and giving orders. All were taking the situation coolly. No excitement showed itself on their faces, though all were more or less anxious."

Slocum's bloodied Sixth Corps division was sent on across White Oak Swamp that morning by McClellan, who neglected to mention this to anyone else in the Sixth Corps. At Savage's Franklin was surprised to find only Baldy Smith's division at hand. He was surprised as well to find Sumner's corps nowhere in sight. General Sumner, Heintzelman complained, "had obstinately refused to occupy the position assigned him . . . leaving

Arthur Lumley sketched a munitions train blown up in the evacuation of Savage's Station on June 29. A shell explodes near General Sumner and his staff.

a space of three fourths of a mile unoccupied." Ever since Sumner failed to support Heintzelman at Williamsburg, the two generals had been at swords' points, a situation made worse by Sumner's frequent alarms calling out the men for no cause. Heintzelman likened him to the fabled shepherd boy who cried wolf, and was best ignored. Franklin made complaint to McClellan about Sumner, then he and Smith and Heintzelman determined (as Smith put it) "to try and inveigle" Sumner into taking up the new position by telling him that Smith was in imminent danger of being cut off. "To any appeal for aid he was prompt to respond," Smith said of old Sumner.

Savage's Station now witnessed an orgy of destruction. Anything that could not be carried away was smashed or burned or blown up. There were giant bonfires of hardtack boxes. Stored ammunition was fired, and the result, reported Robert Sneden, "resembled a volcano!" A trainload of artillery shells was set ablaze, the locomotive's throttle tied down and the train sent rushing off toward the demolished rail bridge over the Chickahominy. "Through the roofs and sides of the cars sprang hundreds of live shells, which burst in the woods on either side of the track, screaming like fiends in agony." This carnival of destruction climaxed spectacularly when locomotive and cars spilled off the wrecked bridge into the river.[37]

Heintzelman concluded there was neither space nor need for his corps to remain at Savage's, so he set his men on the march for the rear. He did not inform anyone at Savage's that he was leaving — no doubt deliberately, to avoid debating his decision and command issues with Sumner. Franklin and John Sedgwick discovered his absence when they encountered Confederate troops where Heintzelman's had been. "Why, those men are rebels!" Sedgwick exclaimed. "We then turned back in as dignified a manner as the circumstances would permit," Franklin wrote. Sumner was furious, and on meeting Heintzelman the next day refused to speak to him.

In late afternoon Magruder attacked the Savage's Station line. First to engage was William W. Burns's Philadelphia Brigade, Sedgwick's division. Burns was shot in the face but refused to leave the field, calling on Sumner for help. This only produced confusion, for Sumner seized any regiment that fell under his eye, sending it forward helter-skelter with a shout and a wave of his hat. Franklin, with a clearer grasp of the fighting, ordered up W.T.H. Brooks's Vermont Brigade, and Brooks (despite a leg wound) and Burns soon beat back the attackers. The two sides ended up where they had started, the Federals suffering 919 casualties, the Rebels 444.[38]

Franklin prepared to join the retreat, but Bull Sumner, his fighting blood up, refused to move. "I never leave a victorious field," he insisted. At his wits' end, Franklin showed him McClellan's orders of that morning. "General McClellan did not know the circumstances when he wrote that note," Sumner said with heat. "He did not know that we would fight a battle and gain a victory." Franklin realized if they stayed they would be struck in the morning with redoubled force, and he sent to McClellan to report Sumner's latest obduracy. A headquarters officer soon reached Sumner with unequivocal orders: "Present the accompanying order to Genl E. V. Sumner Comdg 2d Corps. If he fails to comply with the order you will place him in close arrest." The direct order from the general commanding was enough for Edwin Sumner. "Gentlemen," he told his staff, "you hear the orders; we have nothing to do but obey." He and Franklin joined Heintzelman in retreat, and so the Army of the Potomac survived a long day of high command disorder.[39]

Sam Heintzelman's decision to cross the swamp at Brackett's Ford somewhat relieved the congestion at the White Oak Swamp bridge, but still it was a maddeningly slow, tedious, dispiriting night march for everyone. At one point traffic at the bridge came to a dead stop. "Then we heard through the darkness General Richardson swearing like a trooper, and after considerable of that we moved on," wrote one of Israel Richardson's

The field hospital of the 16th New York at Savage's Station on June 28, photographed by James Gibson. Any wounded who could not join the retreat were left to the enemy.

men; "... old 'Dick' with his fusillade of oaths was clearing them out and getting them over...." Phil Kearny hurried his men along, warning that they were "the rear guard of all God's creation."

Nothing wrenched morale more than leaving behind wounded comrades at the Savage's Station field hospital. "Those who could hobble or walk started from the hospital and mixed in with the moving wagon trains," Private Sneden wrote. "Some were taken up by the teamsters, others, carrying their guns, supported a comrade. Some limped on sticks or improvised crutches." Those left to the enemy's care were counted by Lee's medical director as 3,000.[40]

Early on June 30 the rear guard crossed White Oak Swamp bridge and burned the span. The retreat routes through the swamp funneled into the road junction of Glendale two miles to the south. Glendale was as well the target of Jackson's pursuing force and of Lee's columns from Richmond intent on intercepting the Yankees' retreat. Lee determined to make this Day Six of battle decisive. He focused his entire army on the objective of cutting the Potomac army in two. Confederate soldier-historian Porter Alexander would write of Glendale, "Never, before or after, did the fates put such a prize within our reach." Of the Confederacy's few chances for a success so great as to promise independence, Alexander wrote, "this chance of June 30th '62 impresses me as the best of all."

There was full intelligence on the Rebels that morning. From the north, Jackson was known to be advancing on the White Oak Swamp bridge site. From the west, Confederates were detected in force on both the Charles City and Long Bridge roads, close by Glendale. There was no doubt within the Union high command that saving the army's trains — indeed saving the army — would require major fighting at Glendale. The Prince de Joinville, McClellan's trusted adviser, had studied the maps and divined Glendale's critical importance. "My Uncle spoke about this to the General," wrote the Comte de Paris, "who grasped it at once. . . ."

Nevertheless, at this self-evident crisis in his fortunes, what remained of General McClellan's warrior spirit evaporated. He deserted his army, or at least the largest part of it. At noon, following a sketchy inspection of the Glendale lines and a meeting with Sumner, Franklin, and Heintzelman, the commanding general and his entourage "took off at a fast trot" down the Quaker Road and over Malvern Hill to Haxall's Landing on the James. "It is difficult to express the pleasure that everyone felt upon seeing with his own eyes the goal of our efforts, the end of our retreat," Philippe recalled.

Some sixty hours had passed since McClellan determined the collapse of his campaign and committed to retreat. Hour by hour his demoralization intensified. He described himself that day to his wife as "worn out — no sleep for many days. We have been fighting for many days & are still at it. I still hope to save the army." Saving the army meant one thing now: personally seeking out a safe haven on the James River. As to the more immediate crisis at Glendale, however, his loss of the moral courage to command in battle was complete, and he fled the responsibility. Andrew Humphreys of the engineers wrote his wife, "Never did I see a man more cut down than Genl. McClellan was when I visited him on board Com. Rodgers' vessel. . . . He was unable to do anything or say anything."

John Rodgers's gunboat *Galena* was McClellan's haven. At 4:00 p.m. he boarded the *Galena* to confer with Rodgers about the navy guarding the army when it should reach the river. Already at Haxall's McClellan was miles too far from Glendale to exercise any command functions . . . although not too far to escape hearing the rising sounds of battle there. At 4:45, with general and staff aboard, the *Galena* steamed upriver some miles to shell a Rebel column on the riverbank. That evening, wrote the Comte de Paris, "I found the General at table with the naval officers. . . .

When one has led so rude a life for several days, one feels out of place on arriving aboard a ship where everything is proper, whose officers have white linen and where one suddenly finds a good dinner and some good wine."[41]

In common with Savage's Station the day before, McClellan left no one in overall command before he departed Glendale. This decision was surely dictated by Bull Sumner's intransigence at Savage's, but it thrust the Army of the Potomac into one of the worst command tangles it would ever experience. Sam Heintzelman, in congressional testimony, was asked about this peculiar trait of General McClellan's. "Well, sir," he replied, "he was the most extraordinary man I ever saw. I do not see how any man could leave so much to others; and be so confident that everything would go just right." He added, "The corps commanders fought their troops entirely according to their own ideas."

The Federal defenses on June 30 were divided—the rear guard at the White Oak Swamp bridge site facing Jackson's advance from the north, and two to three miles distant, the flank guard at Glendale facing Lee's advance from the west. After leaving his generals at Glendale to sort out matters for themselves, McClellan sent privately to the trusted William Franklin to command the rear guard at the swamp crossing. Franklin's force was a mix of the last to leave Savage's Station the night before—Baldy Smith's Sixth Corps division, Israel Richardson's Second Corps division, Henry M. Naglee's Fourth Corps brigade. When the shooting started, Franklin appealed to ever-generous Sumner, who lent him two brigades from John Sedgwick's Second Corps division.

The command at the Glendale crossroads was if anything even more tangled. The defending infantry was posted in line west of and parallel to the Quaker Road, along which the supply trains were still passing, fronting both the Long Bridge and Charles City roads. On the far right, blocking the Charles City Road, was Henry Slocum's Sixth Corps division. Slocum was separated from his corps commander Franklin and acting independently; as he was short of artillery, Heintzelman loaned him two Third Corps batteries. Phil Kearny's Third Corps division was next in the line. In his contrary way, Kearny took up a position (as Heintzelman put it) "in front of where I was ordered to hold & it was hours before I could move him." Into the resulting gap had appeared George McCall with his laggard Fifth Corps division, inserting himself between Kearny and Hooker's Third Corps division, on the far left. This mix-up left Heintzelman managing a divided command, well separated by McCall's orphaned division; like Slocum, McCall reported to no one. To round out the entanglement,

One of William Franklin's Sixth Corps batteries duels with Stonewall Jackson's artillery at the White Oak Swamp crossing on June 30. Wash drawing by Alfred Waud.

the Second Corps' Bull Sumner went to battle that afternoon in charge of but a single brigade, from Sedgwick's division, posted as a reserve.[42]

General Franklin would encounter no difficulty managing the mix of forces under his command, for Stonewall Jackson's attack proved merely a noisy, prolonged artillery duel, contributing in the end nothing to Lee's battle plan. Franklin was returning to his command from Glendale when Jackson's bombardment opened. "The wood through which I was riding seemed torn to pieces with round shot and exploding shells," he wrote. At the front Baldy Smith was caught bathing, and as shot and shell fell about him he dressed "in what I judged was dignified haste." The shelling caused panic among the supply trains, but inflicted no disruption of Franklin's defenses. There was no follow-up to the shelling, so Franklin and Smith passed quiet hours relieving an abandoned sutler's wagon of its stock of brandy and cigars.[43]

At Glendale the Federal battle line was a ragged, improvised affair. Lacking central direction, each general selected his own position. Slocum on the far right was well separated from Kearny, who held a more advanced posting than anyone else. McCall's line was tied neither to Kearny's on his right nor to Hooker's on his left. Joe Hooker was surprised to discover McCall's division where he expected Kearny's to be, distant 600 yards "and stretching off in an obtuse angle with the direction of my own." McCall was astride the Long Bridge Road, which proved to be the axis of the Confederates' main assault. In Lee's design for June 30, while Jackson attacked the Yankees' rear guard he would strike at Glendale with five divisions, intending to cut McClellan's army in two. Benjamin Huger's division would challenge Slocum on the Charles City Road. James Longstreet's and A. P. Hill's commands, supported by two of Magruder's divisions, took McCall's division as their primary target.

To the Federals' great good fortune, Lee's battle plan fell to pieces just as it had at Mechanicsville four days earlier. Jackson applied only artillery to his task, leaving his powerful infantry force standing idle. Huger fumbled his assignment as well, weakly engaging his artillery and none of his infantry. A confused Magruder marched his divisions first one way and then another, and they too failed to fire a shot. Thus the fighting at Glendale was left to just the twelve brigades of Longstreet and A. P. Hill — a severe enough test for the Yankees, to be sure, and nearly more than they could handle.

McCall's Pennsylvania Reserves, confronting their third fight in five days (after Mechanicsville and Gaines's Mill) were battle-weary and undermanned. John Reynolds had been captured on June 27 and his brigade was under Colonel Seneca G. Simmons. The division had suffered 1,650 casualties at Gaines's Mill, a thousand of those from George Meade's brigade. It was only by chance — a misdirected nighttime march — that the Reserves were not then on Malvern Hill with the rest of the Fifth Corps . . . and only by chance that their posting was at the center of the Glendale defenses.

George McCall's inexperience, or incompetence, was evident in his postings. His flanks were not covered and he positioned his six batteries too far in advance of supporting infantry. Meade regarded the postings as very faulty and told one of his captains he suspected McCall of being either drunk or ailing and under the influence of opium. The opium charge was not new; the Comte de Paris had raised it at Gaines's Mill. Truman Seymour's brigade formed on the left in a large field and well in advance of Joe Hooker's division to his left. Meade's brigade was on the right and not tied to Kearny, while Simmons's lay in reserve. The only other reserve in the Quaker Road sector was one of John Sedgwick's Second Corps brigades.[44]

Longstreet, guiding on the Long Bridge Road, attacked on a three-brigade front. The Rebels stormed out of the thick woods, driving the Yankee skirmishers before them and aiming for McCall's exposed gun line.

On Seymour's front two batteries, from the artillery reserve and unused to such close work, pulled back with unseemly haste. There was bitter fighting around the other four batteries; Seymour's infantry line was breached and his flank turned, and he and most of his men retreated in disorder, leaving a large gap in the battlefront. Joe Hooker was still in a fury about it when he drafted his report: Officers and men of Seymour's brigade "broke through my lines, from one end of them to the other, and actually fired on and killed some of my men as they passed. Conduct more disgraceful was never witnessed on a field of battle."

As Longstreet and Hill tried to widen and deepen the breach, the Federals fought to seal it, striking head-on and from both flanks. Seneca Simmons, only days in command of Reynolds's brigade, led a charge into the gap and was killed. George Meade too rushed into the midst of the fighting. Alanson M. Randol, whose battery was subjected to repeated attacks, remembered seeing Meade pressing his men into the fight, "encouraging & cheering them by word and example." Then Meade was hit, in the right arm and in the chest. He told Randol he was badly wounded and must leave the field. "Fight your guns to the last, but save them if possible." Now, of McCall's three brigade commanders, Simmons was dead, Meade wounded, and Seymour missing in action. A staff man came on a dazed General Seymour behind the lines, on foot, "his hat and clothes pierced by balls. He was alone. I asked him where his Brigade was: he told me it was entirely dispersed." All twenty-six of the guns on McCall's front were captured, abandoned, or withdrawn.

Behind the broken front Sumner and Heintzelman pushed reserves forward as fugitives fled past them. The shrill yip of the Rebel yell marked the enemy's gains, close enough that both Heintzelman and Sumner were grazed by spent bullets. John Sedgwick was nicked twice and his horse killed. Sedgwick's one brigade then present, under William Burns, was thrust into the breach, and Burns met the challenge as he had at Savage's the day before. Sumner called on Franklin to return Sedgwick's other two brigades loaned him, and Franklin did so promptly. Confident now of his own position, Franklin sent along two additional brigades of Richardson's. To the arriving 15th Massachusetts, Sumner called out, "Go in, boys, for the honor of old Massachusetts! I have been hit twice this afternoon, but it is nothing when you get used to it." These 11,700 men proved decisive in stemming the breakthrough.[45]

On the northern shoulder of the broken front Phil Kearny reported Rebels attacking "in such masses as I had never witnessed," a notable appraisal from a soldier of his experience. Guarding his flank was a section of Battery G, 2nd U.S. Artillery, Captain James Thompson, and guarding Thompson was Alexander Hays's 63rd Pennsylvania. Twice Colonel Hays counterattacked to save the guns. Finally Thompson said he was out of ammunition and must withdraw. "I told him to go ahead and I would give him a good chance," wrote Hays in a letter home. "Again it was 'up, 63rd, give them cold steel; charge bayonets, forward, double quick!' In a flash, yelling like incarnate fiends, we were upon them. . . . Such an onset could not last long, and towards dark we retired, having silenced the last shot." This drama was witnessed by Kearny, and Alex Hays was flattered by the attention: "Kearny is somewhat hyperbolical in his expressions, but says it was magnificent, glorious, and the only thing that he saw like the pictures made in the papers. . . ."

Sam Heintzelman, rushing back and forth between his divided command, saw that Hooker now had matters in hand, so he focused on Kearny's needs. He sought out Henry Slocum, whose division on the far right was comparatively idle. Slocum agreed to lend him the New Jersey brigade, Kearny's old command, and with a shout the Jerseymen rushed into the fight at the double-quick. Another reinforcement was Lieutenant Colonel Francis Barlow's 61st New York, loaned from Richardson's division. Barlow wrote, "At a charge bayonets & without firing we went at a rush across the large open field. It was quite dark & very smoky so that we could not distinctly see the enemy in the open ground but they heard us coming & broke & ran. . . ." The 61st ended the day holding its position with the bayonet, its cartridge boxes empty. By then Barlow was leading three regiments as senior officer present.

In the dark woods Kearny was as usual personally (and recklessly) scouting out the fighting. "I got by accident in among the enemy's skirmishers . . . and was mistaken by a rebel Captain for one of his own Generals," he wrote his wife; "he looked stupid enough & said to me, 'What shall I do next, Sir,' to which I replied . . . 'Do, damn you, why do what you have always been told to do,' & off I went." By leading from the front, his men "know that when matters are difficult, I am at their head, between them & danger — at least showing that I *count* on being followed," not exposing them to dangers "I do not share."

As darkness ended the fighting, George McCall concluded a day of general misfortune by losing his way and stumbling into the enemy lines. He was the second Union brigadier general, after John Reynolds, to be taken prisoner in the Seven Days fighting. This left battle-shocked Truman Seymour in command of the Pennsylvania Reserves and colonels in command of its three brigades.[46]

Glendale cost the two armies a roughly equal number of casualties —
3,673 Confederate, 3,797 Federal, plus eighteen guns lost. McCall's and
Kearny's divisions accounted for almost three-fifths of the Federal total.
George Meade's chest wound proved dangerous but not life-threatening.
He recuperated at home in Philadelphia and returned in time for the next
campaign. McCall would be exchanged in August, but ill health and his
unsteady record at Glendale combined to end his military career.

In the absence of the commanding general, the officer corps improvised
very capably at Glendale. Franklin's rear guard had little to do beyond
hunkering down against Jackson's artillery, and Franklin was prompt and
generous in reinforcing McCall. Henry Slocum, not seriously threatened,
reinforced Kearny. Heintzelman added to his solid record of leadership,
managing a divided command even as he fed reinforcements into Mc-
Call's broken front. Edwin Sumner and John Sedgwick and George Meade
were in their element pressing troops into the fighting. Hooker on the left
of the break and Kearny on the right continued to show exceptional skills
at troop leading, although again Kearny did so in the most reckless manner. "He rides about on a white horse, like a perfect lunatic," wrote Richard Auchmuty, adding that a posting on Kearny's staff was decidedly unhealthy. There were some questions about Truman Seymour's indecisive
handling of his brigade, but he would head the Pennsylvania Reserves until the next campaign.[47]

Disaster was averted (narrowly), the army was wounded but intact, and
the Quaker Road remained open. Still lacking any guidance from Mc-
Clellan, his lieutenants continued deciding matters on their own. Convinced that a second day of inaction by Stonewall Jackson was highly unlikely, Franklin sent to Heintzelman to ask how soon his command would
clear the road for the rear guard to withdraw. Heintzelman replied that he
had no orders to move and should not move without them. Slocum, like
Franklin in an exposed position, added his voice for withdrawal, as did
Seymour for McCall's bloodied division. Heintzelman had sent off a staff
officer to find McClellan, report on the day's events, and get his orders. Finally, despairing of hearing from him (the Comte de Paris noted McClellan reading Heintzelman's dispatch aboard the *Galena* and making no reply), Heintzelman and Sumner agreed on retreat. Heintzelman summed
up: "General McClellan had been down the James River & we had to fall
back or be cut off & on our own responsibility."

Slocum pulled back first, followed by Kearny, Seymour, Sedgwick, and
Hooker. Franklin was able to withdraw the rear guard "in parallel" with

the others after one of Baldy Smith's staff rediscovered the woods road General Keyes had found three days earlier. One of Smith's men wrote in disgust, "We pulled up stakes again in the night and skedaddled." They were not pursued. "It was after one a.m. when we took the road," wrote diarist Heintzelman, "& at 2 a.m. were at Gen. Porter's Hd. Qrs. where I met Gen. McClellan who had just heard of what was going on."

A staff man on Malvern Hill recalled McClellan "suddenly coming riding hard up the hill in the dark, about 8.30 p.m. I think, & going at once . . . to read the accumulated dispatches." Earlier, at Haxall's Landing, McClellan implied to Washington that he was in the midst of the battle: "Another day of desperate fighting. We are hard pressed by superior numbers. . . . If none of us escape we shall at least have done honor to the country. I shall do my best to save the Army." He asserted bravely he was sending orders to renew the combat the next day at Glendale, "willing to stake the last chance of battle in that position as any other." But soon enough he found his generals already falling back (without orders, he told the staff disapprovingly). "I have taken steps to adopt a new line. . . ."[48]

At 2:00 a.m. on July 1, McClellan called in topographical engineer Andrew Humphreys and instructed him to lay out lines on Malvern Hill and post the troops coming in from Glendale. "There was a splendid field of battle on the high plateau where the greater part of the troops, artillery, etc. were placed," Humphreys wrote his wife. "It was a magnificent sight." If today was to be the Potomac army's last stand, the place was well chosen.

Malvern Hill was an elevated plateau three-quarters of a mile wide and a mile and a quarter deep that overlooked the James a mile distant. On the west was a sharp drop-off called Malvern Cliffs, and on the east the terrain was wooded and marshy. The Rebels approaching from the north confronted a gradual, open slope leading up to the crest of the hill, where on display was what Alexander Webb called "a terrible array"—the artillery of the Army of the Potomac. Fitz John Porter would be credited with command of the battle fought there that day, but in fact the battle belonged to Henry Hunt, the Potomac army's chief of artillery.

By midday on July 1 Humphreys had the infantry posted and Hunt had the guns positioned to meet what everyone on Malvern Hill recognized was certain to be yet another assault by the relentless enemy. At an early hour General McClellan appeared on the field and rode the lines. The troops' welcome inspirited him: "The dear fellows cheer me as of old as they march to certain death & I feel prouder of them than ever," he told

Deserting the Malvern Hill battlefield for the gunboat *Galena* earned McClellan comments like this when he ran for president in 1864.

Ellen. "I am completely exhausted — no sleep for days — my mind almost worn out — yet I *must* go through it." Going through it would not include taking command of the coming battle, however.[49]

At 10:00 a.m. the *Galena* again weighed anchor with the general aboard. This time his journey was an hour and a half downstream to Harrison's Landing, which Commander Rodgers said was the farthest point on the James that the navy could protect the army's supply line. McClellan spent two hours ashore "to do what I did not wish to trust to anyone else — i.e. examine the final position to which the Army was to fall back." The *Galena*'s log showed him returning to Haxall's Landing at 2:45 that afternoon, and Andrew Humphreys placed him on Malvern Hill at about 4 o'clock, conferring with Porter. McClellan then made a second tour of the lines, after which he remained at the extreme right of the army throughout the period of the heaviest fighting. By the account of his staff officer William Biddle, "We heard artillery firing away off to the left — we were too far to hear the musketry, distinctly. . . ."

Critics would make much of McClellan's *Galena* expedition on July 1, accusing him of abandoning his army on the eve of battle, and he was sensitive to the issue. In testimony before the Committee on the Conduct of the War in March 1863, when asked if he boarded a gunboat "during any part of that day," he replied that he did not remember. During the 1864 presidential campaign cartoonists labeled him "The Gunboat Candidate," lounging aboard the *Galena* as his army fought for its life. In fact, McClellan consulted with Porter during one phase of the Malvern fighting, then deliberately distanced himself from active command. The true, lesser known case of dereliction of duty was absenting himself aboard the *Galena* on June 30 while at Glendale his army did actually fight for its life. At Malvern Hill on July 1, while conforming to the letter of command, George McClellan certainly violated the code of command.[50]

The Fifth Corps' Morell and Sykes and Hunt's reserve artillery were posted on Malvern Hill when McClellan arrived at the James on June 30. He shifted Darius Couch's Fourth Corps division from Haxall's Landing to Malvern. As finally established, the battlefront facing the advancing Rebels was Morell's division on the left and Couch's on the right, a total of 17,800 men. Sykes's and McCall's divisions guarded the western flank. The eastern flank was three army corps strong — Heintzelman's Third, Sumner's Second, Franklin's Sixth. John Peck's Fourth Corps division, with corps commander Keyes, was at the river.

As was now habit, McClellan designated no overall commander when he went off to Harrison's Landing, so Porter, as the general posted on Malvern Hill when the rest of the army reached there, was recognized by all as commander pro tem — by all but old Sumner. Edwin Sumner reflexively assumed the command whenever McClellan was not in sight (which was often enough during the Seven Days), and at one point during the Malvern fighting he ordered Porter to fall back to a new position. Porter ignored him. On the Federal battlefront were eight batteries, 37 guns. Hunt would bring up batteries from his reserve to where they were most needed. Altogether on the plateau there were 171 guns posted for action or in reserve.

General Lee intended to clear the way for his infantry with a massive artillery barrage from a "grand battery." But his guns were poorly handled, while the Yankee batteries were expertly handled, and the barrage scheme collapsed. A series of command misunderstandings then sent the Confederate infantry lunging head-on against Malvern Hill. A single powerful blow might have had at least a chance of breaking the Yankee line, but the assaults were disjointed and beaten back one after another. "It was not war — it was murder," was Confederate general D. H. Hill's verdict.

Henry Hunt ranged back and forth along the gun line, checking post-

In Alfred Waud's drawing of the Malvern Hill fighting on July 1, Federal artilllery fires over Fitz John Porter's infantry line at advancing Confederates in the distance.

ings and battle damage, pulling out batteries that had exhausted their ammunition and replacing them from his reserve. Twice his horse was killed under him, twice he sprang up calling for a new mount. Hunt understood that reserves would be decisive. He described his thinking: "I gathered up some thirty or forty guns . . . brought them up at a gallop, got them into position as rapidly as possible, and finally succeeded in breaking the lines of the enemy." His was a masterful performance.

Captain John C. Tidball's battery was one of those Hunt called up. To his surprise, Tidball found the battery blazing away next to him was commanded by Captain Alanson Randol. He knew Randol had lost his guns at Glendale after a savage struggle. Randol explained that today he was looking for a part to play and came upon this battery of 20-pounder Parrotts whose German gunners had precipitously left the field at Glendale. Their officers apparently absent, Randol appropriated the battery, aided by his lieutenant who spoke a little "Dutch," took it to the front, and administered a lesson in both gunnery and leadership.

Darius Couch had his hands full fending off some of the heaviest Rebel attacks, and he turned to Porter for help. Porter appealed to Sumner, but met reluctance — Sumner, as usual, expected to be attacked any moment, no matter that he was more than a mile from the fighting. Sam Heintzelman was willing: "By God! If Porter asks for help, he wants it, and I'll send him a brigade." He ordered up Sickles's brigade, plus a battery. Thus prodded, Sumner sent forward Meagher's Irish Brigade, and soon the front was stabilized. Couch reported pridefully, "Sumner, Kearny and Sedgwick gave me no little praise for the successes I achieved on this day." Hunt was equally prideful: General McClellan was "in every way and in all respects thoroughly satisfied with me and my work."[51]

Phil Kearny acted his usual ungovernable self. That afternoon, after Heintzelman posted one of the Third Corps batteries, Kearny came along and shifted it elsewhere. Heintzelman returned and demanded to know who had moved the guns. Lieutenant Charles Haydon took up the story: "On being told he rode brim full of wrath for Gen. K. 'You countermand another order of mine & I will have you arrested, Sir' said H. 'Arrest my ass, God damn you,' said Kearny and rode off. . . . Heintzelman looked after him very earnestly for near a minute. A faint smile came over his features & he himself turned around & rode slowly off leaving the battery where he found it."

"The struggle continued until nine o'clock p.m., when the rebels withdrew," wrote artillerist Alexander Webb. "The author, an eye-witness, can assert that never for one instant was the Union line broken or their guns in danger." At 6:10 p.m. Porter had reported to McClellan, "The enemy has renewed the contest vigorously — but I look for success again." By 9:30 he declared victory: "After a hard fight for nearly four hours against immense odds, we have driven the enemy beyond the battle field. . . ." If reinforced, if the men were provisioned and their ammunition replenished, "we will hold our own and advance if you wish." His victorious men "can only regret the necessity which will compel a withdrawal."

The general commanding, however, had already issued orders for the final leg of the retreat, to Harrison's Landing. Porter's report of a complete victory did not move him to reconsider. He explained to Lincoln: "I have not yielded an inch of ground unnecessarily but have retired to prevent the superior force of the Enemy from cutting me off — and to take a different base of operations."[52]

McClellan's lieutenants were dismayed (or worse) by his order to continue the retreat. Darius Couch, who had smothered the assaults on Malvern Hill, recalled his "great surprise" at leaving a victorious field, and his bitterness at abandoning "many gallant men desperately wounded." For staff man William Biddle, "the idea of stealing away in the night from such a position, after such a victory, was simply galling." Israel Richardson observed that "if anything can try the patience and courage of troops," it was fighting all day every day, then falling back every night. Phil Kearny was livid. To fellow officers he declaimed, "I, Philip Kearny, an old soldier, enter my solemn protest against this order to retreat. We ought, instead of retreating, to follow up the enemy and take Richmond. . . . I say to you all, such an order can only be prompted by cowardice or treason!"

In the early hours of July 2 Fitz John Porter and Baldy Smith found time for a conversation as their commands trudged toward Harrison's Landing. Porter described the decisiveness of the victory at Malvern Hill, and said he had spent the night trying to persuade McClellan to change his mind and move against Richmond at daylight. Knowing Porter to be McClellan's closest confidant, and knowing Porter's own native caution, Smith was fully persuaded just how ill judged was McClellan's decision. When he reached Harrison's Landing, he wrote his wife "saying I had arrived safely but that General McClellan was not the man to lead our armies to victory."[53]

Malvern Hill was indeed a decisive victory. Confederate losses on July 1 came to 5,650. The Federal loss was just 3,007, and some 800 of those were stragglers picked up by the enemy during the retreat on July 2. Moreover, in its amphitheater-like setting Malvern was a highly visible victory, for all to witness (all but General McClellan) and a tonic to the fighting men of the battered Army of the Potomac.

A retreat already ugly turned uglier when it began to rain, a downpour that lasted twenty-four hours. "The retreat was a regular stampede, each man going off on his own hook, guns in the road at full gallop, teams on one side in the fields, infantry on the other in the woods," wrote Richard Auchmuty. "At daybreak came rain in torrents, and the ground was ankle deep in mud." To Francis Barlow "it was more like a rout than a 'strategical movement.'" Joe Hooker called it "the retreat of a whipped army. We retreated like a passel of sheep. . . ." John Peck's unbloodied Fourth Corps division acted as rear guard, hurrying along the stragglers and untangling massive tie-ups among the trains. The stunned and wounded Army of Northern Virginia offered no pursuit.[54]

No one excelled George McClellan at inspiriting troops. At Harrison's Landing on July 4, Independence Day, he raised spirits with an address to the army. Like an alchemist he sought to transmute leaden reality into silvery triumph. "Attacked by vastly superior forces, and without hope of reinforcements, you have succeeded in changing your base of operations by a flank movement, always regarded as the most hazardous of military expedients. You have saved all your material, all your trains, and all your guns, except a few lost in battle. . . ." (The Potomac army in the Seven Days lost war matériel beyond counting, wagons by the hundreds, and forty guns in battle.) "Your conduct ranks you among the celebrated armies of history...."

The address played well to the rank and file, which needed assurance that their stout fighting and their costly sacrifices over the past bloody week had not been wasted. What had seemed a retreat was now officially a change of base. "All our banners were flung to wind," Charles Haydon told his journal. "A national salute was fired. The music played most gloriously. Gen. McClellan came around to see us & we all cheered most heartily for country, cause & leader."

If Charles Haydon spoke for a majority of the troops, fellow Third Corps soldier Felix Brannigan represented a vocal and growing minority. The papers speak of the "splendid strategy of McClellan," Brannigan wrote. "I think he was *forced* to it. Anyhow, he gets too much credit for what other people do. McClellan kept at a respectable distance in action, but the real saviours of the army were Heintzelman, Kearny, Hooker, Richardson, and their subordinate generals. They were here, there, and everywhere ... mixing in the thickest of the fray. Heintzelman with his old cloak and battered hat, and the one-armed Kearny, were particularly conspicuous." Henry Ropes, Sedgwick's division, thought "a great deal of faith in McClellan is gone, and I fear will not return."[55]

In the officer corps faith in McClellan was clearly shaken. "You have no idea of the imbecility of management both in action & out of it," Francis Barlow wrote home. "McClellan issues flaming addresses though everyone in the army knows he was outwitted." Everything he saw and heard, said Barlow, "more & more convinces me that McClellan has little military genius & that he is not a proper man to command this Army. I think the Division Genls & about everybody else here have lost confidence in him." Barlow's remark on discontent among the generals of division was perceptive. Of those who expressed opinions, Kearny, Hooker, and Baldy Smith were McClellan's more outspoken critics. Richardson and Couch regarded the final retreat, to Harrison's Landing, as a mistake. Henry Slocum wrote his wife, "I have allowed matters connected with our movements here to worry me until I came near being sick."

The five corps commanders were more discreet. Edwin Sumner's narrow vision focused more on obeying orders than on reasoning why. Still, he favored holding Malvern Hill "if my opinion had been asked about it." Sam Heintzelman, highly critical of McClellan's repeated failures to lead, welcomed his own chances at independent command. Erasmus Keyes was so isolated by McClellan that he scarcely witnessed a shot fired. William Franklin, while a McClellan loyalist, was quietly unhappy with events. "I wept at the mismanagement and waste, and I know other officers who did so too," he told his wife. While Fitz John Porter argued against the final move to Harrison's Landing, he remained a McClellan partisan; he cast all the blame on Washington. Samuel Barlow warned McClellan of "the jealousy of your own Generals, including Sumner, Heintzelman, Kearny & I fear even of Baldy Smith!"[56]

Harrison's Landing was a secure base, with swampy creeks forming its flanks and gunboats as watchdogs. But as an encampment it was a miserable place. Kearny complained that "we are completely boxed up, like *herrings.*" Into some four square miles of lowland were crowded 90,000 men, 25,000 horses and mules, 2,000 beef cattle, almost 3,500 wagons and ambulances, and 289 guns. The water was bad, flies were a constant plague upon man and beast, and it was stiflingly hot and humid. The army's sick list at its peak reached 22 percent.

Malvern Hill was a superior base in every respect — stronger defensively, certainly healthier, and (should it come to that) a proper starting point for a renewed offensive against Richmond. By McClellan's account, the navy was the reason he did not exercise the victor's claim to the Malvern battlefield. Gunboats could guarantee the army's supply line only as far as Harrison's Landing, where the James was wide. Above that it narrowed at Haxall's Landing, and McClellan imagined harassing fire from the south bank.

McClellan might have secured Haxall's himself — and doubled his threat to Richmond — by seizing the south bank of the river with his own or with fresh troops. Ideal for that was Ambrose Burnside's command just then landing at Fort Monroe from North Carolina. But that option did not occur to the Young Napoleon. His only thought now was securing his army from the ravening enemy host.[57]

8. *Summer of Discontent*

IN ONE OF HIS FINAL DISPATCHES from Haxall's Landing, General McClellan told Washington he required 50,000 men to "retrieve our fortunes. More would be well, but that number sent at once, will, I think enable me to assume the offensive." Mr. Lincoln sought to reason with his unreasoning general. Patiently he spelled out the disposition of forces in the Eastern theater and concluded, "Thus, the idea of sending you fifty thousand, or any other considerable force promptly, is simply absurd." McClellan's response was to send Chief of Staff Marcy to Washington with a letter that read, in part, "To accomplish the great task of capturing Richmond & putting an end to this rebellion reinforcements should be sent to me rather much over than much less than 100,000 men."

On July 3, at the War Department, Marcy briefed Secretary Stanton. He said the troops were exhausted from the constant fighting and marching, "but I assured him they were not disheartened or demoralized in the least. . . ." Without the necessary reinforcements, however, Marcy painted a much darker picture. It was possible, in the event "of our being attacked by an overwhelming force, our communications cut off, and a series of battles fought in which we should be defeated, that we might be forced to capitulate."

This "excited Stanton very much," and the president as well. Marcy was called in to face a stern commander-in-chief: "General, I understand you have used the word 'capitulate' — that is a word not to be used in connection with our army." Marcy stammered that he was only speaking of a worst case, and the matter was smoothed over. But Lincoln took no solace from McClellan's next telegram. While boasting that "the movement just completed by this Army is unparalleled in the annals of war," he offered a bleak prospect: "The enemy may attack in vast numbers and if so, our front will be the scene of a desperate battle which if lost will be decisive." At that the president decided he must see the Army of the Potomac for himself.[1]

The presidential party — Lincoln, Stanton, Assistant Secretary of War Peter H. Watson, and Frank Blair, chairman of the House Committee on Military Affairs — reached Harrison's Landing on July 8. Over the past week the encampment was made orderly and the men cleaned up, and Lincoln was pleased with what he saw. Clearly this was not an army on the verge of collapse or capitulation. McClellan told his wife the army did not give Lincoln much of a reception. "I *had to order* the men to cheer & they did it very feebly." But Darius Couch noted that his division greeted the president "with great enthusiasm," and he was seconded by Phil Kearny: "The good President paid us a visit the other day. It seemed a noble thing & was appreciated by the troops." Of "Old Abe's" welcome Felix Brannigan wrote, "Such cheers as greeted him never tickled the ears of Napoleon in his palmiest days."[2]

The president set about interviewing the generals to gauge the Potomac army's strength, condition, and prospects. McClellan estimated his strength at 80,000, and claimed the army's health was the best since the start of the campaign. He said the Rebel army was in full force just four or five miles distant. Lincoln posed a final question: "If you desired, could you remove the army safely?" and recorded McClellan's reply: "It would be a delicate & very difficult matter." Lincoln then separately questioned the five corps commanders. Of each he asked the strength of his corps; his losses in the Seven Days; health conditions in his camps; and an evaluation of the enemy. Finally, two questions: "If it were desired to get the Army away from here could it be safely effected?" and, "Is the Army secure in its present position?"

The five generals' total strength was 81,500, close to McClellan's figure. They estimated casualties at 10,400 (some 5,450 short of the final accounting). Sumner, Heintzelman, and Porter said the health of their men was good, Keyes thought it would get worse, and Franklin reported "not good." (Franklin himself was ill.) None felt immediately threatened by the enemy. "He feels he dare not attack us here," said Porter. As to evacuating Harrison's Landing, there was sharp difference of opinion. Sumner: "I think we could, but I think we give up the cause if we do it." Heintzelman: "Perhaps we could, but think it would be ruinous to the country." Porter: "Impossible — move the Army & ruin the country." Keyes: "I think it could if done quickly." Franklin: "I think we could, and think we better." All five agreed that Harrison's Landing was secure. Lincoln returned to Washington wiser than before, recognizing the alarms of McClellan and Marcy as greatly overblown.[3]

Lincoln also took back with him the remarkable document known as the Harrison's Landing letter — General McClellan's "views concerning the existing state of the rebellion." McClellan originally conceived this paper a week or so previous to the Seven Days, at a time when he felt confident of besieging and conquering Richmond and thereby entitled to propose a potential peace policy. He offered his paper on June 20. Lincoln said he would welcome the general's views, but was concerned about security in transmitting them. McClellan agreed to defer delivery for the present.

The Seven Days changed everything. Now McClellan diagnosed the Potomac army's situation as critical. Confronting the prospect of battlefield martyrdom ("I may be on the brink of eternity"), he reconceived the Harrison's Landing letter to serve, in effect, as his last will and testament on the conduct of the war.[4]

In McClellan's view, a rising tide of abolitionism threatened to radicalize the conduct of the war. (He confronted "rebels on one side, & the abolitionists & other scoundrels on the other," he told his wife.) He was further alarmed by the debate in Congress that spring over a new confiscation bill aimed at Southern civilians. He took as his theme that what had been rebellion was now full-scale war, which "should be conducted upon the highest principles known to Christian Civilization. . . . Neither confiscation of property, political executions of persons, territorial organization of states or forcible abolition of slavery should be contemplated for a moment." The North's military "should not be allowed to interfere with the relations of servitude, either by supporting or impairing the authority of the master" — but slaves seeking military protection as contraband should receive it. "A system of policy thus constitutional and conservative, and pervaded by the influences of Christianity and freedom, would receive the support of almost all truly loyal men, would deeply impress the rebel masses and all foreign nations. . . ." But, he warned, "a declaration of radical views, especially upon slavery, will rapidly disintegrate our present Armies."

McClellan's views were widely held in the Potomac army's officer corps; professed Republicans, professed abolitionists, could be counted on the fingers of one hand. The Sixth Corps' W.T.H. Brooks wrote, "Many I find are restive and impatient with the course of Congress and the authorities, and the radicals who stay at home and foment discord. There can be no peace with confiscation and emancipation staring the whole people in the face." The Fifth Corps' Gouverneur Warren dreaded to see the army

The new general-in-chief, Henry Halleck, gained a reputation as Western theater department head, not as a field commander.

"act out any Abolition programme. It is fighting for the Union, which is unattainable without allowing the Southern people their constitutional rights. . . ."

When he handed his letter to the president, McClellan told Ellen, "He read it in my presence, but made no comments upon it, merely saying, when he had finished it, that he was obliged to me for it. . . . I do not know to what extent he has profited by his visit — not much I fear, for he really seems quite incapable of rising to the height of the merits of the question & the magnitude of the crisis."

Mr. Lincoln, sharing the Harrison's Landing letter with Frank Blair on the return journey to Washington, remarked that the general's advisory reminded him of a story . . . the one about "the man who got on a horse, and the horse stuck his hind foot into a stirrup. The man said, 'If you're going to get on I'll get off.'"[5]

Even before inspecting the Army of the Potomac, Lincoln gave thought to changing the management of the Union's military machine. Old General Scott had urged him to fill the vacant general-in-chief post with his favorite, Henry Halleck, commanding in the Western theater. After visiting Harrison's Landing and sampling the generals' conflicting advice as to the future course of the Potomac army, Lincoln recognized his need for professional military guidance. On July 11 he issued an order naming Major

General Henry Wager Halleck general-in-chief, specifying that "he repair to this Capital so soon as he can. . . ."[6]

Halleck only reached Washington to take up his new duties on July 23, and the interim witnessed much soul-searching regarding the Seven Days. Federal losses came to 15,855, with over 6,000 of those taken prisoner — some two-thirds of whom were the wounded and sick abandoned on the retreat. (The Confederates suffered 20,204 casualties, their toll of dead and wounded nearly double that of the Federals.) Except for his appearance at Oak Grove on Day One of the Seven Days, McClellan absented himself from all the battlefields — conspicuously so at Glendale and Malvern Hill. Gaines's Mill, the one battle where he might have seized the initiative and reshaped the outcome, instead broke his spirit. He surrendered his grand campaign to his delusions about the enemy and retreated to the James River and the gunboats.

In contrast to McClellan, the Potomac army's subordinate commanders did their duty and more during the Seven Days. Fitz John Porter was most prominent, directing the victories at Mechanicsville and Malvern Hill and putting up a staunch fight at Gaines's Mill. Of the other corps commanders, Heintzelman handled a difficult command situation at Glendale with aplomb, and Sumner, despite his bumbling, ended up doing no real harm. Franklin had comparatively little to do during the Seven Days, Keyes even less.

Of division commanders engaged, the strongest leadership was furnished by Hooker, Kearny, Sedgwick, Couch, and Sykes, and the least by McCall. Among the generally capable brigade leaders, John Reynolds showed well before his capture, and William Burns, George Meade, and W.T.H. Brooks were wounded leading their men into the heat of the battle. Henry Hunt demonstrated at Malvern Hill how deadly artillery could be when under unified command.

Just one Union general proved a consistent failure every day of the Seven Days. Unfortunately that was General McClellan. In rationalizing the collapse of his campaign, McClellan discovered it to be God's will. "I think I begin to see his wise purpose in all this. . . . If I had succeeded in taking Richmond now the fanatics of the North might have been too powerful & reunion impossible."[7]

"This war is no longer one of mild measures," Phil Kearny wrote from Harrison's Landing. "When McClellan wrecked us at Richmond, our last chance for a Union party in the South ceased." Moderation had indeed guided George McClellan's war-making rationale — constrict the rebellion to the battlefield, take the measure of the Rebel armies and their misguided leaders, reunite the Union "as it was" without bitterness and societal upset. But McClellan's Peninsula campaign for those goals failed (due primarily to his own failings), discrediting moderation and turning the war in new and uncharted directions. In the North a harder hand of war emerged. The Second Confiscation Act was a step toward seizing the property (particularly slaves) of supporters of the rebellion. John Pope, commanding the new Army of Virginia, issued a set of general orders — with the administration's approval — that freed up soldiers to forage liberally in the rebellious states, acted stringently on allegedly disloyal civilians, and threatened penalties up to summary execution to backers of guerrilla warfare. McClellan questioned if he could serve a government infected with "those radical & inhuman views to which it seems inclined, & which will prolong the struggle. . . ."[8]

Slaves as a major Confederate military resource attracted growing attention from Northern war planners. Phil Kearny offered his views on the topic in a letter published and discussed. "As the blacks are the rural military force of the South," he wrote, they should be seized as contraband of war. "I would use them to spare our whites needed with their colours." In place of the usual regimental pioneer unit, "I would select 50 stalwart Blacks, give them the axe, the pick, & the spade. . . . So too cooks for the companies, Teamsters, even Artillery drivers . . . organize Engineer Regiments of Blacks for the fortifications, Pontoon Regiments of Blacks, Black hospital Corps of nurses. . . . As for the women — employ them in hospitals, and in making cartridges, &c." Such a program would raise combat readiness of the Union army by 50,000 men, just as a beginning. He remarked on the fate of these contraband units. "It eventually would prepare them for freedom — for surely we do not intend to give them up to their rebel masters."[9]

President Lincoln was thinking several steps ahead of General Kearny. He saw the abrupt turn of events on the Peninsula requiring of him a major — indeed a revolutionary — change of policy. On July 13, in conversation with Secretary of State Seward and Secretary of the Navy Welles, he revealed his thoughts on emancipating the slaves by presidential proclamation. He justified it as a matter of military necessity, due to "the reverses before Richmond." Welles quoted the president: He "had about come to the conclusion that we must free the slaves or be ourselves subdued. . . ."

On July 22, to the cabinet, Lincoln read his preliminary Emancipation Proclamation, terming it "a fit and necessary military measure." While his counselors were generally supportive, Secretary Seward argued against is-

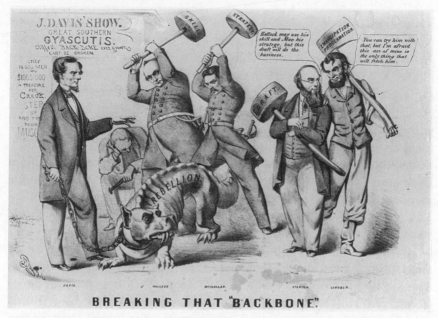

BREAKING THAT "BACKBONE".

Jefferson Davis displays his legendary spiny Gyascutis named "Rebellion," which Halleck attacks with Skill, McClellan with Strategy, and Stanton with the Draft. Lincoln claims his emancipation axe is "the only thing that will fetch him." By Currier & Ives.

suing the proclamation now, with the North still reeling from the collapse on the Peninsula — "It would be considered our last *shriek,* on the retreat." The president admitted the wisdom of that, and set the proclamation aside to await a battlefield victory. He surely appreciated the irony that such a victory might well depend on General McClellan, recent author of the warning that any declaration of Radical views on slavery "will rapidly disintegrate our present Armies."[10]

McClellan just then was trying to recast his grand campaign from the new base on the James. He wrote Lincoln that the Potomac army must be "promptly reinforced & thrown again upon Richmond. If we have little more than half a chance we can take it." His plan for taking it was not revealed. To validate his demand for a massive reinforcement, he claimed that during the Seven Days he had "two hundred thousand enemy to fight — a good deal more than two to one, & they knowing the ground." Lincoln determined to leave it to General Halleck to straighten out this skein of contradictions.

July passed without resolution of these issues, and McClellan complained to a home front supporter of the "inveterate prosecution" that hounded him on the Peninsula, "weakening my command so as to render it inadequate to accomplish the end in view, & then to hold me responsible for the results. I am quite weary of this." Lincoln too was quite weary ... of McClellan's serial complaints. To Senator Browning, he said "if by magic" he reinforced McClellan with 100,000 men today, he would be ecstatic, pledging to "go to Richmond tomorrow." But when tomorrow came, McClellan "would telegraph that he had certain information that the enemy had 400,000 men, and that he could not advance without reinforcements."[11]

Reinforcements was a tender subject for the administration. Stanton's ill-advised closing of recruiting offices in April left the army stretched for manpower, and the reopened offices produced only a trickle of recruits. The reverses on the Peninsula led Lincoln to call on the governors for 300,000 volunteers. However that call fared, it would be summer's end before many new troops became available. Still, the War Department scraped up reinforcements that more than made good the Potomac army's losses — two of McDowell's brigades from Washington, two brigades from David Hunter's Department of the South, three of Ambrose Burnside's brigades brought up from North Carolina. On July 22 Hunter's two brigades and Burnside's three were designated the Ninth Corps, Burnside commanding. The new corps was held at Fort Monroe, waiting on General Halleck for assignment.[12]

McClellan set out to revamp certain commands. When Marcy went to Washington he carried a list of officers that McClellan hoped to be rid of and others he hoped to promote. Marcy advised caution: "There should be as few dissatisfied individuals as possible here till after Congress adjourns" — on July 17 — "for they are ready (your enemies) to pounce upon every shadow of excuse to assail you."

For chief of artillery McClellan wanted the ineffectual William F. Barry out and Henry Hunt in, and he got his wish. Hunt became artillery chief of the Army of the Potomac (and brigadier general), a posting he held throughout the war. The cavalry was overhauled in organization as well as command. Philip St. George Cooke was relieved of the cavalry reserve (a move instigated by Fitz John Porter, who castigated Cooke for the disastrous cavalry charge at Gaines's Mill). To better compete with Jeb Stuart, at least organizationally, a cavalry division was established and headed by George Stoneman, with brigades under William W. Averell and Alfred Pleasonton. Stewart Van Vliet was replaced as the Potomac army's chief quartermaster by Rufus Ingalls, who like Hunt would retain his post until war's end. McClellan rated Ingalls "unequalled as a Chief QM in the field." Another major staff improvement was the appointment of Jonathan Letterman as the army's medical director. Finally, McClellan (again seconded by Porter) classed chief engineer John Barnard difficult to work with, and Barnard left to direct fortifying the capital. His place was taken by James C. Duane.

On his list of command changes McClellan sought was the notation "Keyes relieved for obvious reasons." The Fourth Corps' Erasmus Keyes would not be so easily pushed out. Keyes wrote the president to "ask Your Excellency to maintain me in a command corresponding with my rank." He wrote Republican senator Ira Harris, whom he knew to have Lincoln's ear, in defense of his Peninsula record: "The cloud of envy, jealousy & malice under which this Army has been shrouded can only be removed by listening to & weighing facts." Keyes evaded being relieved, but McClellan saw to it that he did not again hold a command in the Army of the Potomac.[13]

Fitz John Porter, having pressed to get rid of cavalryman Cooke and engineer Barnard, the two he blamed for the Gaines's Mill defeat, sought the head of a third offender, John Martindale. By Porter's reckoning, Martindale abandoned his troops at Gaines's Mill, and he charged him with a like crime at Malvern Hill, where Martindale supposedly counseled "surrender to the enemy while they could obtain terms." A court of inquiry ruled the charges "disproved," but Porter kept Martindale out of the Fifth Corps.

Porter's machinations and his position as McClellan's particular confidant did not sit well with his fellow generals. A particular irritant was his order congratulating the Fifth Corps for valorous conduct in no less than nine Peninsula battles. He condescendingly noted a half-dozen units from the rest of the army "whose assistance has arrived so timely in each of our hours of need." Porter's most-favored status would generate jealousy in any case, but Heintzelman for one thought there was more to it: "There is a good deal said amongst the men & officers about his want of Generalship on the other side of the Chickahominy." It did not help Porter's standing when it became known that he was the only Potomac army general that McClellan personally recommended for promotion.[14]

Secretary Stanton preempted McClellan. On July 5 he initiated a program of promotions to uplift morale in the Potomac army's officer corps. First, the five corps commanders were named major generals of volunteers, with four — Heintzelman, Keyes, Porter, and Franklin — also brevetted brigadier generals in the regular army. Sumner, already a regular-army brigadier, was awarded a major general's brevet in the regulars. These promotions initially caused unrest among such outspoken critics as Hooker and Kearny — "I will not fight their battles for them with the doors to pro-

motion closed on me," said Hooker, and he spoke of resigning — but soon
enough Stanton commenced a second round of promotions to major general, volunteers, for division heads Hooker, Kearny, Couch, Richardson,
Slocum, Peck, Morell, Sedgwick, and Baldy Smith. Kearny grudgingly accepted his promotion "or else would have been passed by the others." Still,
it was "confounding me with the herd & ignoring my achievements." Phil
Kearny was impossible to satisfy.[15]

In these hot weeks at Harrison's Landing illness plagued the officer
corps as well as the enlisted men. William Franklin took sick leave to restore his health. Other generals felled by the unhealthy clime were Darius Couch, Henry Slocum, Dan Butterfield, Sam Heintzelman, and Hiram
Berry. Baldy Smith obtained a leave but with more on his mind than his
health. He quarreled with McClellan and went off to seek duty elsewhere.
McClellan told Ellen, "I don't think he intends returning . . . he had not
even the decency to bid me good bye after all I have done for him! Such is
gratitude." (He meant his defense of Smith against the charge of drunkenness in the Dam No. 1 fight at Yorktown.) On reflection Smith concluded
that loyalty to his division was paramount and he returned. But mutual
trust with McClellan seemed over.

Political general Dan Sickles pulled his War Department strings and
hurried to New York to recruit replacements for his Excelsior Brigade
and to test the waters on running for Congress again. Sickles stayed in the
army, a decision so time-consuming that he missed the Potomac army's
next two campaigns. The equally political Thomas Meagher gained leave
to recruit his Irish Brigade, but Meagher obeyed the order that Sickles ignored, to rejoin his command.

McClellan drew a line in regard to his most trusted lieutenants. Sam
Heintzelman's application for leave was rejected; the general commanding
"feels that he cannot dispense with the presence and aid of a General upon
whose services he would largely count should he be called upon for active
operations." Phil Kearny remained as well, but Kearny's unlimited purse
made his stay something else than a hardship. He had his marquee pitched
in a pleasant grove, he assured his wife, furnished with "my nice French
camp bedstead, my rich furs, braided cloaks, & showy velvet carpet, table
with a gay cover. . . . And then as for comforts — I have a store of Brandy,
& whisky, & Claret, & a basket of Champagne & dozens of ale, & several
boxes of Congress Water, besides lemons, & a nice colored man who can
do anything for me."

A prisoner exchange brought John Reynolds and Orlando Willcox back
to the army. Willcox, captured at Bull Run, was made a brigadier and in

September given a Ninth Corps division. Reynolds took command of the Pennsylvania Reserves, in McCall's place. Otis Howard, who had lost an arm at Fair Oaks, took a Second Corps brigade. George Meade, recovered from his Glendale wounds, returned to his old brigade in the Reserves. He grumbled that with his fighting record he deserved better. Had he "dallied at Washington dancing attendance on the Sec. of War, Genl. Halleck & other official big men I feel pretty sure I could have got a Division." (Wife Margaret took up his cause, writing to Secretary Stanton, enclosing Pennsylvania governor Curtin's recommendation of Meade for major general.)[16]

Critics of every stripe refought the Peninsula campaign. Partisan newspapers excoriated McClellan for retreating from Richmond, or praised him for rescuing the army from disaster. The *New York Leader*: "Direction of the recent campaigns, whether exercised by the President or the Secretary of War, has been a deplorable failure, and only saved from a more fatal result by the masterly genius of McClellan." Treasury Secretary Chase termed McClellan's conduct "shameful, and attributable only to gross neglect & incompetency for which he should at once have been dismissed." Jacobin Zach Chandler took to the Senate floor to damn at length every aspect of McClellan's handling of the campaign.

Fitz John Porter leaped to McClellan's defense. Writing to editor Manton Marble of the Democratic *New York World*, he damned the Republican press for taking the word of "vilifying officers and politicians" and of "radicals and abolitionists" in attacks on McClellan. Marble did Porter's bidding editorially: "The time has come to vindicate General McClellan and his campaign from the misrepresentations of political antagonists and the aspersions of ignorant critics." He named the guilty parties — the "irresponsible" Committee on the Conduct of the War, and "an incompetent civilian," Secretary of War Stanton. (In silent acknowledgment of Porter's leaks, Marble explained that "our position as public journalists has kept us informed of many circumstances in the history of the campaign which are not generally known.")[17]

Henry Halleck, the new general-in-chief, was forty-eight, a paunchy, unmilitary figure of intellectual accomplishment and brusque personality. He graduated third in West Point's class of 1839 and served mostly behind a desk in California during the War with Mexico. As head of the Department of the Mississippi, Halleck had directed the substantial gains in the Western theater from behind a desk in St. Louis. His sole field command was leading the glacier-like advance on Corinth, Mississippi, in May.

When he found his troops referring to him as Old Brains, he remarked to his wife, "A rather coarse title, but I am satisfied with it." The readership of his manual *Elements of Military Art and Science* included Abraham Lincoln. Presidential secretary John Hay wrote of Halleck's "great head" with its "vast stores of learning, which have drifted in from the assiduous reading of a quarter of a century." Quoting "a Western friend" (Lincoln, certainly), Hay declared the general-in-chief "is like a singed cat — better than he looks."

Lincoln had by now quite run out of patience with McClellan. Senator Browning recorded him saying he had sent Halleck to Harrison's Landing to deal with McClellan, and "that he was satisfied McClellan would not fight and that he had told Halleck so, and that he could keep him in command or not as he pleased." This seriously misread the new general-in-chief. Old Brains was a careful, desk-bound army bureaucrat, and exercising command-change authority was alien to his nature. President and cabinet had lost all confidence in McClellan, Halleck told his wife, "& urge me to remove him from command. . . . In other words, they want me to do what they were afraid to attempt!"[18]

General Halleck, with Quartermaster Meigs and General Burnside, reached Harrison's Landing on July 25. Queried about his plans, McClellan proposed crossing to the south bank of the James and capturing Petersburg, through which passed all but one of the railroads reaching Richmond from the south. Sam Heintzelman pressed this scheme on McClellan as a way to break the stalemate, cripple Confederate logistics, and open a new front in the fight for Richmond. Halleck, however, was a devotee of the strategic principle of massing forces, not dispersing them, and he stated "very frankly my views in regard to the danger and impracticability of the plan."

McClellan turned to negotiating reinforcements for an advance directly on Richmond from Harrison's Landing. Scaling back his earlier extravagant demands, he said he needed 30,000 men to give him "a good chance of success." Halleck said the president had only authorized 20,000 reinforcements, including Burnside's Ninth Corps at Fort Monroe. Halleck described the alternative — evacuate the Peninsula and unite the Army of the Potomac with John Pope's Army of Virginia on the Rappahannock, opening a new front. Halleck advised consulting with the officer corps before deciding. McClellan assured Halleck that he faced at Richmond "no less than 200,000."[19]

That evening McClellan met with the six corps commanders plus Brigadier John Newton. He canceled any thought of advancing on Petersburg

After the Army of the Potomac retreated to Harrison's Landing, balloon reconnaisances by aeronaut Thaddeus Lowe were launched from the tender *Curtis* to examine the banks of the James. Pencil and wash drawing by Arthur Lumley.

—Halleck's Western army had failed to cut the Confederacy's east–west rail line, leaving Beauregard free (yet again) to rush east and cut off that portion of the Potomac army out on a limb at Petersburg. Heintzelman was dismayed: "We should have taken Petersburg two weeks ago & cut off supplies & reinforcements from the rebels." Debate turned to withdrawing from the Peninsula. Burnside claimed he, Sumner, and Heintzelman argued for remaining on the Peninsula. Keyes, Franklin, and Newton "were very decidedly in favor of a withdrawal." Porter "did not express any decided opinion." Heintzelman reported the gathering differently. Moving the army to join Pope was voted "both impracticable & otherwise if practicable, not desirable. . . . We were all in favour of an immediate advance" so soon as Burnside's forces arrived.

Heintzelman's contemporary diary seems the more accurate of the two accounts. He would have discounted the opinion of Newton, only a brigade commander, and Burnside was vague about Porter's opinion. Yet Keyes certainly and Franklin probably had not reneged on their earlier statements to the president urging evacuation. Halleck would write (without specifics), "A majority of those whose opinions have been reported to me" favored evacuation. But in fact it appears that four of the six corps commanders — Sumner, Heintzelman, Burnside, and almost certainly Porter — voted for the Army of the Potomac to remain on the Peninsula. This stance by his officer corps must have influenced McClellan, for he told Halleck that with the promised 20,000 reinforcements he would renew his advance on Richmond: He was "willing to try it."

Enemy numbers were discussed. "There is great difference of opinion as to the force in Richmond," Heintzelman wrote; some counted it as a quarter of a million men. "I dont believe it near so many," said skeptic Heintzelman. But Halleck noted the most widely accepted figure (perhaps not surprisingly) was McClellan's 200,000.

During his stay at Harrison's Landing, Montgomery Meigs sought the temperature of the Potomac army. He found it feverish. At a twilight gathering of officers of rank, he wrote, "Mutterings of a march on Washington to 'clear out those fellows' were uttered, when Burnside moved into the circle opposite me and said aloud: 'I don't know what you fellows call this talk, but I call it flat treason, by God!'" At that the circle melted away. Halleck dismissed it as camp talk. For Meigs it represented "a bad spirit in the Army."[20]

Halleck had to be pleased to return to Washington with his mission apparently accomplished — McClellan agreeing to take up the offensive against Richmond from Harrison's Landing, and not requiring unreasonable numbers beyond Burnside's corps already at Fort Monroe. The general-in-chief's satisfaction proved short-lived. In a dispatch dated July 26, the Young Napoleon reverted to his old and maddening ways. He reported troops "pouring into Richmond from the South," which signaled all bets were off. In addition to the Ninth Corps he called for the rest of the men from Burnside's and Hunter's commands in the Carolinas — almost 20,000 — and in addition, 15,000 or 20,000 from Halleck's old command in the West.

McClellan's dispatch, with its arrogant assumptions, its broken agreements, its promise of infinite delay, was the last straw for Abraham Lincoln. He called in Burnside, who had returned to the capital with Halleck, and offered him command of the Army of the Potomac.

The president believed he needed a general from outside the Potomac army, yet not a stranger to its officer corps. Burnside was personable and nonpolitical, "just the same good natured old fellow he always was," as his West Point classmate John Gibbon described him. He had fought at Bull Run and compiled a good record in planting a foothold on the North Carolina coast. Being a friend of McClellan's ought to ease the transition. But Ambrose Burnside was a modest man, with modest ambitions, and the offer flabbergasted him. He did not want the command, said he was not competent to lead a large army; General McClellan could command the Potomac army better than any other general in it. Lincoln had offered, not ordered, so that was the end of the matter for the time being.[21]

Halleck called on McClellan for "that same free interchange of opinions as in former days." McClellan responded in kind, pledging his full and cordial support. But each man mistrusted the other. Halleck told his wife McClellan did not understand strategy "and should never plan a campaign." McClellan's friends have "excited his jealousy" and "he will be disposed to pitch into me . . . in justice to me and to the country he ought now to sustain me. I hope he will, but I doubt it." Already McClellan had assigned Halleck to his enemies list. He knew of the attempt to displace him, for Burnside, with his unhappy propensity to spill out whatever was on his mind, had told his old friend of Lincoln's offer. "I *know* that the rascals will get rid of me as soon as they dare," McClellan told Samuel Barlow. "They are aware that I have seen through their villainous schemes, & that if I succeed my foot will be on their necks." Clearly, the bad spirit Meigs detected in the Potomac army infested its officer corps, starting with the general commanding.[22]

Having raised the reinforcements ante from 20,000 to as many as 60,000, McClellan met stony silence from Washington. He wrote Ellen, "If they leave me here neglected much longer I shall feel like taking my rather large military family to Wasn to seek an explanation of their course." Before that idea took root he had answers. On July 30 Halleck ordered him to send off his sick in preparation for a movement. On August 1 Burnside's Ninth Corps was ordered to Aquia Landing on the Potomac, close by Fredericksburg. And on August 3 Halleck telegraphed, "It is determined to withdraw your army from the Peninsula to Aquia." The telegram put McClellan "into a rage," Heintzelman said.

Joe Hooker brashly persuaded McClellan to challenge the order. Go on the offensive by retaking Malvern Hill, said Hooker; the army could hardly be evacuated while under fire. On August 5 Hooker and John Sedgwick, with 17,000 men of all arms, seized Malvern Hill. Lee was quick to threaten a counterattack. McClellan telegraphed Washington that the Malvern position was "very advantageous" for an advance on Richmond, "and I feel confident that with re-enforcements I could march this army there in five days." Halleck was dismissive: "I have no re-enforcements to send you." McClellan could not nerve himself to run his bluff, and recalled

Hooker's expedition. Once more Robert E. Lee took George McClellan's measure. "I have no idea he will advance on Richmond now," Lee told Stonewall Jackson.[23]

McClellan composed a lengthy protest against the evacuation order. From Harrison's Landing he believed he could advance to within 10 miles of Richmond for the decisive battle — if given the necessary manpower. To that end, all other theaters of war should go on the defensive to free up troops to reinforce him; any resulting "partial reverses" elsewhere would matter little; "it is here on the banks of the James that the fate of the Union should be decided."

"Allow me to allude to a few of the facts in the case," Halleck replied. Using McClellan's own figures he revealed the hollowness of McClellan's argument. "You and your officers at one interview estimated the enemy's forces in and around Richmond at 200,000 men. Since then you and others report they have received and are receiving large re-enforcements from the South. General Pope's army covering Washington is only about 40,000. Your effective force is only about 90,000. You are 30 miles from Richmond, and General Pope 80 or 90, with the enemy directly between you, ready to fall with his superior numbers upon one or the other, as he may elect. Neither can re-enforce the other in case of such an attack."

In light of that stark prospect, said Halleck, he saw no alternative to ordering the evacuation of the Potomac army. He softened the blow, however. "As I told you when at your camp, it is my intention that you should command all the troops in Virginia as soon as we can get them together." With forces concentrated, "I am certain you can take Richmond."

Halleck's decision to evacuate the Peninsula had the certain approval of the president. Clearly Lincoln saw no end to General McClellan's incessant demands for reinforcements, no end to his complaints and his excuses and his delays . . . and, when finally all was said and done, in the end no prospect that he would fight.

From the first moment he did not dare, at Yorktown, to the last moment he would not dare, at Harrison's Landing, McClellan was captive of his delusions about the enemy. His grandest delusion — a count of Richmond's defenders as 200,000 — had induced his command collapse and the flight to the James and finally the humiliating finale at Harrison's. He preached the 200,000 figure to Washington and to his home front supporters and to the newspapers and to his generals. "Since Don Quixote's enumeration of the armies of the Emperor Alifanfaron and King Pentapolin of the Naked Arm," wrote James Russell Lowell, "there has been nothing like our General's vision of the Rebel forces, with their ever-lengthening list of leaders, gathered for the defense of Richmond."

McClellan's grand campaign designed to end the war became itself a delusion. The Peninsula campaign cost the Union some 25,370 casualties and uncounted millions in treasure and ended with nothing whatever to show for it. Confederate losses were the greater (some 30,450), but the Confederacy survived to fight another day and gained credibility in the doing. On August 13 Sam Heintzelman entered a prediction in his diary: "I think the withdrawal of this army of 90,000 men a most suicidal act. As soon as the rebels learn we are retreating they will reinforce Jackson & he can overwhelm Pope before we can aid him." General Lee had exactly that thought.[24]

John Pope came from the West with a chip on his shoulder. His command of the Army of the Mississippi had suited him. His singular accomplishment was capturing the Mississippi River strongholds of Island No. 10 and New Madrid back in April, bagging 5,000 prisoners (he boasted of 7,000), 158 cannon, and many war supplies—all without losing a man. Now he was called East to build a new army out of the three bedraggled armies that during the spring Stonewall Jackson had chased through the Shenandoah Valley. This Army of Virginia promised to be a most troublesome command, and John Pope resented the assignment: "I especially disliked the idea of service in an army of which I knew nothing beyond the personnel of its chief commanders, some of whom I neither admired nor trusted." Still, Pope understood he was there to bring new energy and a new harder tone to the war in Virginia.

Pope was forty, West Point class of 1842, and served capably (two brevets) in the Mexican War. As a Republican in the antebellum army he was a rarity, but with the coming of war his politics helped jump him from captain to brigadier general to major general. A journalist wrote of him, "In person he was dark, martial, and handsome—inclined to obesity ... possessing a fiery black eye, with luxuriant beard and hair. He smoked incessantly, and talked imprudently."

Pope assumed command of the Army of Virginia on June 27 and sorted out his forces. These comprised John C. Frémont's Mountain Department, Nathaniel Banks's Department of the Shenandoah, and Irvin McDowell's Department of the Rappahannock. These departments devolved into corps in the new army. The three corps commanders were senior in rank to Pope, but only Frémont was affronted. There was bad blood there, and

John Pope was brought from the
Western theater to breathe life into
the three ragtag commands making
up the new Army of Virginia.

Frémont asked to be relieved. Washington was happy to oblige him and
the Union army saw no more of the Pathfinder.[25]

Franz Sigel took Frémont's command, designated First Corps. Sigel's
troops included Louis Blenker's German division, whose misadventures
in the Valley gained them infamy as the thieving Dutchmen. Blenker was
gone now, his men scattered among Sigel's division commanders — Robert C. Schenck, the former Ohio congressman quick to retreat at Bull Run;
Adolph von Steinwehr, who served without notice under Blenker; and
Carl Schurz, German revolutionary and like Steinwehr, awaiting the test
of battle. Sigel, a lieutenant under the Grand Duke of Baden and an 1848
insurgent, had compiled a spotty record in the West and held his post due
mostly to his connections in the German American community. He was of
high temper and large gesture — in his long cloak and wide-brimmed hat
he looked, said Alpheus Williams, "as if he might be a descendant of Peter
the Hermit." Whatever Pope thought of Frémont, he thought far worse of
Sigel, calling him "the God damndest coward he ever knew." Sigel, equally
blunt, appraised Pope as "affected with looseness of the brains as others
with looseness of the bowels."

The Second Corps was General Banks's. A Massachusetts governor and
congressman, a Republican stalwart, Banks represented the purest expression of political general. He was derided as Stonewall Jackson's commissary in the Valley, but in fact Banks managed a retreat that saved his men
if not their supplies. His division heads were Alpheus Williams, the former

militia officer whose command promise survived the Valley debacle; and West Pointer Christopher Columbus Augur.

McDowell's Third Corps was the largest, soundest element of the Army of Virginia, with divisions led by Rufus King and James B. Ricketts. West Pointer King was in his first command, and Ricketts, the veteran artillery-man wounded and captured at Bull Run, was leading infantry for the first time. Martinet McDowell still looked to erase the Bull Run stain from his record, and remained as unpopular with the troops as ever. At a review his horse threw him, and from the ranks, sotto voce, came a call for three cheers for the horse.

Pope's brigade commanders were a mixed lot. In McDowell's and Banks's corps such as Abner Doubleday, Marsena R. Patrick, John Gibbon, Samuel S. Carroll, Samuel W. Crawford, George H. Gordon, and George Sears Greene would go on to achieve notice (or better) in the Army of the Potomac; less would be said of those in Sigel's corps.

The variegated elements of the Army of Virginia lacked any shared experience, and what combat record they had was poor. At first glance, said Pope, his new command was "much demoralized and broken down, and unfit for active service. . . . Of some service they can be, but not much just now." Staff man David Strother entered in his diary, "There seems to be a bad feeling among the troops — discouragement and a sense of inferiority which will tell unfavorably if they get into action. . . ." They had not been paid for months, and desertion was endemic; a thousand officers were absent without leave.[26]

Angered at the lack of spirit and the defeatist attitude, Pope issued, on July 14, a blunt address to the Army of Virginia. "I have come to you from the West," he proclaimed, "where we have always seen the backs of our enemies; from an army whose business it has been to seek the adversary and to beat him when he was found. . . ." Warming to his subject, he listed certain phrases he was "sorry to find so much in vogue amongst you. I hear constantly of 'taking strong positions and holding them,' of 'lines of retreat,' and of 'bases and supplies.' Let us discard such ideas." Strong positions should be taken in order to launch attacks, he said. Focus on the enemy's lines of retreat, not your own. "Success and glory are in the advance, disaster and shame lurk in the rear."

Marsena Patrick wrote that Pope's address struck him as "very windy & somewhat insolent." To George H. Gordon it implied "a weak and silly man." Brigadier John P. Hatch said he would "be astonished if with all his bluster anything is done." But in the ranks many recognized Pope's target as the officer corps and many agreed with him. In his diary a cavalryman wrote, "Pleased with Gen'l Pope's address. He seems an energetic — 'go ahead' man — such a one, as this department needs, and has ever needed, and has never had! Our Potomac Generals paid too much attention to reviews and inspections and parades. . . . We have been out-generaled here."[27]

It was well understood that Pope's address skewered General McClellan's way of making war. In Washington, Pope missed no chance to denounce the Young Napoleon. Dining with Treasury Secretary Chase, he claimed McClellan's "incompetency and indisposition to active movements were so great" that should he, Pope, ever need assistance in his operations, "he could not expect it from him." He urged the president to relieve McClellan without delay. He testified to the Committee on the Conduct of the War on McClellan's failings. And he spread his poison among his own generals. George Gordon recalled a talk at headquarters in which Pope described mismanagement on the part of McClellan, "for whom he seemed to entertain a bitter hatred."[28]

Pope's address was followed by notorious general orders that on paper promised to inflict the harshest treatment on Virginia's civilians. Pope would tell General Jacob Cox that the orders were dictated, in substance, by Secretary of War Stanton. But to all and sundry, the orders were General Pope's. The most draconian of them would not be carried out, but nothing lessened their initial impact. General Lee was roused to cold fury. "I want Pope to be suppressed," he told Jackson. "The course indicated in his orders if the newspapers report them correctly cannot be permitted. . . ." He strengthened Jackson "to enable him to drive if not destroy the miscreant Pope."

Pope's General Order No. 5 permitting the army to "subsist upon the country" was interpreted by the rank and file as a license to steal, and Marsena Patrick was outraged. The troops, he told his diary, "believe they have a perfect right to rob, tyrannize, threaten and maltreat any one. . . . This Order of Pope's has demoralized the Army & Satan has been let loose." An officer of Banks's reported, "The lawless acts of many of our soldiers are worthy of worse than death. The villains urge as authority, 'General Pope's order.'"[29]

William Franklin, who knew Pope from the old army, told his wife, "We look with a good deal of interest upon Pope's movements, having a shrewd suspicion that if he does not look out he will be whipped. After his proclamation he deserves it." Fitz John Porter too was acquainted with Pope. To editor Marble of the *New York World* he termed Pope "a vain man (and

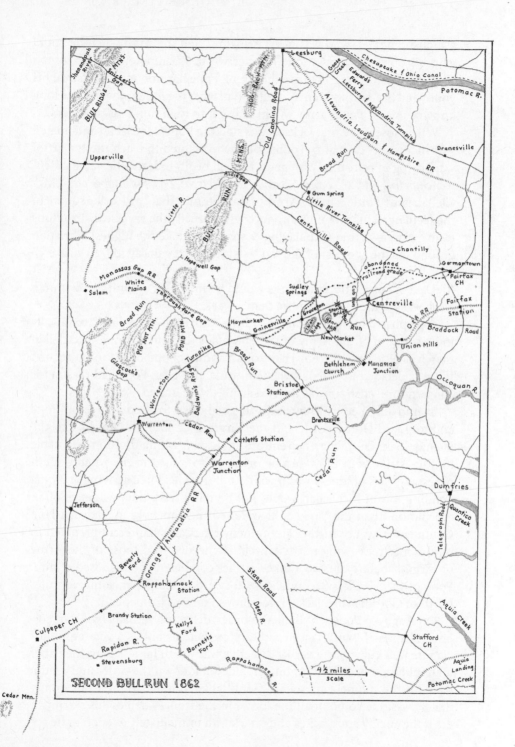

SECOND BULL RUN 1862

4½ miles scale

a foolish one) . . . who was never known to tell the truth when he could gain his object by a falsehood." Porter wrote Washington insider Joseph C. G. Kennedy, "I regret to see that Genl. Pope has not improved since his youth and has now written himself down, what the military world has long known, an ass." Pope's army would only get to Richmond "as prisoners."

When he learned that Jackson was stalking Pope, McClellan anticipated within a week "the paltry young man who wanted to teach me the art of war" being in retreat or whipped. "He will begin to learn the value of '*entrenchments, lines of communication & of retreat, bases of supply etc.*'" McClellan issued orders to the Army of the Potomac that "will strike square in the teeth of all his infamous orders & give directly the reverse instructions to my army — forbid all pillaging & stealing & take the highest Christian ground for the conduct of the war — let the Govt gainsay it if they dare."[30]

McClellan's prediction that Pope would be in retreat or whipped within a week was off the mark by more than a week.

Pope posted his army along the north bank of the Rapidan River awaiting resolution of the Army of the Potomac's dilemma. Should McClellan march on Richmond from Harrison's Landing, Pope ought to be secure. If it was decided to evacuate the Peninsula, however, Pope had reason for concern until such time as the two armies were united.

In mid-July Lee had sent Jackson northward to keep an eye on Pope and to guard Gordonsville and the Virginia Central, the rail link to the Shenandoah. On July 27 he reinforced Jackson with a division, to enable him to "strike your blow and be prepared to return to me when done if necessary." His boldness was rewarded. Burnside's force arriving at Aquia Landing meant McClellan would not be reinforced, then evidence of an evacuation, then the Yankees abandoned their toehold at Malvern Hill. Confident now, Lee further strengthened Jackson's hand and prepared to send Longstreet's wing north as well. He needed to dispose of the Army of Virginia before the two Yankee armies combined and disposed of him. Pope pushed Banks's Second Corps forward to Culpeper, some 20 miles north of Gordonsville. Jackson too moved toward Culpeper.[31]

On August 9 Pope sent Banks an order, delivered verbally by a staff colonel. Nathaniel Banks lacked military credentials but as a veteran politician he well knew that a verbal directive was worth far less than the paper it should have been written on. An aide took down the order and read it back for the colonel's approval: "Genl Banks to move to the front immediately, assume comd of all the forces in the front — deploy his skirmishers if the enemy approaches and attack him immediately as soon as he approaches — and be reinforced from here —" Afterward Pope insisted his order only obliged Banks to take up a defensive position and wait to be reinforced . . . which only confirmed John Pope's reputation as a liar.

Banks's advance took position near Cedar Mountain, some seven miles south of Culpeper. Jackson was known to be close by. Pope intended a general advance that day, with Sigel's First Corps and half of McDowell's Third moving forward in support of Banks's Second. Sigel fumbled his marching orders, McDowell lingered in the rear, and so on August 9 Nathaniel Banks found himself alone with Stonewall Jackson. As the Battle of Cedar Mountain unfolded that day, Jackson would outnumber Banks by 15,000 to 9,000.[32]

Action began at midday with an artillery duel. Then the guns fell silent. It was brutally hot. Division commander Alpheus Williams invited the officers of his old brigade to "a good lunch of coffee, ham, etc." They took their ease under a shade tree, "and everybody seemed as unconcerned and careless as if he was on the lawn of a watering place." Afterward Williams mourned the fact that of all the officers he invited to his luncheon that day, not one survived the next few hours unhurt.

Williams's two brigades, under Samuel Crawford and George H. Gordon, held the right of the line. Crawford had gained notice as the army surgeon who manned the guns at Fort Sumter; this was his first field command. Gordon, a West Pointer and Mexican War veteran, had shared with Williams their Shenandoah Valley travails. Christopher Augur's division held the left. Augur and his three lieutenants — political general John W. Geary and West Pointers Henry Prince and George S. Greene — would see their first serious action this day. Banks accepted that he would be "reinforced from here" to mean the nearby division of James Ricketts. But Pope, at Culpeper, anticipated no fighting and assigned no role to Ricketts.[33]

At about 4:00 p.m. the artillery exchange resumed. Soon enough Banks sighted skirmishers creeping forward to pick off the Union gunners. That, he concluded, was enough of a Confederate approach to satisfy his orders. He signaled his two division commanders to attack. Christopher Augur on the left moved first, with the brigades of Geary and Prince. Geary's advance met a withering blast of artillery and musketry. As he pressed his men forward Geary was hit in the arm and the foot and had to leave the field. His wounding set a deadly trend. Division commander Augur was severely wounded, then Henry Prince of Augur's second brigade was captured. George Greene, the only general officer left, took the division command. The fighting was stalemated.[34]

It was a different story with Banks's other division, under Alpheus Williams. The attack here was launched by Crawford's brigade. Like Christopher Augur, Samuel Crawford was leading his first battle. Nevertheless, his three regiments, 1,500 men, managed to turn Stonewall Jackson's flank, threaten him with disaster, and even put Stonewall himself at grave risk in the bargain.

Crawford's charging line made it across a wheat field, with losses, and reached a woods and struck . . . nothing. Through some oversight Jackson's left flank was uncovered. The triumphant Yankees turned in behind the Rebels. One after another, regiments of a Virginia brigade crumpled and collapsed. A 5th Connecticut veteran described "such a hand to hand conflict with bayonet and gunbutt as was equaled by only a few contests of the war." Geary's and Prince's men firing from the front and Crawford's from the rear left the embattled Confederates seemingly surrounded. One of those surrounded was Stonewall Jackson himself, who had to scramble for safety as he tried to rally reinforcements to mend his broken line.

It was a victory that could not be sealed. Jackson had an entire division at hand, and Banks was woefully slow to bring up his reserves. Ricketts's division of McDowell's corps, the supposed support, never appeared. Crawford's survivors were forced back by counterattacks, then Geary's and Prince's men fell back as well.

It was nearly dark now and for the Union high command one more adventure awaited. Pope had reached the scene, roused by the thunderous gunfire, and was conferring with his generals when Rebel cavalry made a sudden dash into their lines. Chaos erupted. There was a mad dash for horses, and generals and staffs pelted away through the woods in every direction. Alpheus Williams thought the fire "killed some of our horses if nothing else," and "altogether the skedaddle became laughable in spite of its danger."[35]

Cedar Mountain was Nathaniel Banks's battle from start to finish. He believed (properly so) that Pope's verbal order required him to take the offensive. He might have confirmed the order, if just to learn if Ricketts was his support. That he did not was probably deliberate, for he was determined to settle scores with Jackson for his Valley trials, and believed his corps plus Ricketts's division would be enough to do so. Banks had written his wife, "The day we have waited for so long has at last come. I am glad." Yet he neglected to call for Ricketts, and he was too slow to exploit Crawford's breakthrough. "The action was totally unnecessary and about as great a piece of folly as I have ever witnessed on the part of an incompetent general," wrote one of Gordon's officers.

The cost to Banks in officers was severe. Division commander Augur, wounded; brigade commander Geary, wounded; brigade commander Prince, captured. Crawford's brigade that shattered Jackson's flank was itself shattered. Fifty-six of its eighty-eight officers were casualties; the three regiments suffered losses of 49 percent. Federal casualties came to 2,403, against Jackson's 1,418. There was "a good deal of hard feeling between the officers of Genl Banks and Head Quarters — they say that they were needlessly sacrificed." Banks satisfied himself that he had given Stonewall Jackson a check (two days after his victory Jackson pulled behind the Rapidan to regroup). Banks told his wife, "My command fought magnificently," which was true. "It gives me infinite pleasure to have done well," which was self-flattery.[36]

The Army of Virginia's check at Cedar Mountain rudely awakened John Pope to his danger. He telegraphed Halleck, "I am satisfied that one-third of the enemy's whole force is here, and more will be arriving unless McClellan will at least keep them busy and uneasy at Richmond." Halleck sent a sharp dispatch to McClellan: "There must be no further delay in your movements. That which has already occurred was entirely unexpected, and must be satisfactorily explained." Halleck told his wife, "I have felt so uneasy for some days about Genl Pope's army that I could hardly sleep. I can't get Genl McClellan to do what I wish." McClellan told *his* wife he found Halleck's telegram "very harsh & unjust," and in any event, Pope deserved what was coming to him. "I have a strong idea that Pope will be thrashed during the coming week — & very badly whipped he will be & ought to be — such a villain as he is ought to bring defeat upon any cause that employs him." Thus General McClellan's frame of mind as he set about removing the Army of the Potomac from the Peninsula and joining it with Pope's Army of Virginia.

It must be done by the book, McClellan ruled — a careful, calculated disengagement from a powerful, threatening enemy. Halleck's evacuation order was dated August 3. Rather than setting the army on the march for Fort Monroe while removing the sick and the army's baggage by water, McClellan held up the march for ten days. There was no help for this — "Our material can only be saved by using the whole Army to cover it if we are pressed." Porter's Fifth Corps only started from Harrison's Landing on August 14, reached Fort Monroe on August 18, and shipped out for Aquia Landing on August 21. The corps following waited for shipping space. It was August 26 before the last of them began embarking.[37]

On August 13, as McClellan husbanded his forces at Harrison's Landing to fend off attack, Lee ordered the other wing of his army, under Long-

In evacuating Harrison's Landing, the Yankees copied Rebel practice with Quaker guns, these elaborated with carriages and dummy sentries. Drawing by Alfred Waud.

street, to join Jackson on the Rapidan. Lee himself left on the 15th to take command of the evolving campaign. He left two infantry divisions to guard Richmond and a brigade of cavalry to keep an eye on the Army of the Potomac. For more than four months on the Peninsula, George Mc-Clellan had faced a phantom Rebel army of his own devising. Now, as un-knowing as ever, he faced the ghost of a Rebel army.

McClellan felt sure the troops realized he was not responsible for the re-treat. "Strange as it may seem the rascals have not I think lost one particle of confidence in me & love me just as much as ever." But he viewed once-favored lieutenants with less favor. William Franklin and Baldy Smith lacked energy and initiative and "have disappointed me terribly." This rounded out his estrangement from Smith. As to Franklin, he no longer doubted his loyalty — a distrust dating back to Lincoln's ad hoc war coun-cil in January — but "his efficiency is very little." Only Fitz John Porter still earned McClellan's unwavering admiration.

Halleck had promised him command of the two armies so soon as they were united, but McClellan did not hurry north to claim the post. He watched from afar, expecting Pope to come to grief . . . and expecting to be called to pick up the pieces and once again save the Union. On August

21 he was elated to find his plan working. "I believe I have triumphed!!" he wrote Ellen. "Just received a telegram from Halleck stating that Pope & Burnside are hard pressed — urging me to push forward reinforcements, & to *come myself as soon as I possibly can!* . . . Now they are in trouble they seem to want the 'Quaker,' the 'procrastinator,' the 'coward' & the 'traitor'! Bien. . . ."

As the Potomac army haltingly set off on the new campaign, its high command was partially recast. Sumner's Second Corps, Heintzelman's Third, and Franklin's Sixth remained as before, but the Fourth Corps was broken up. To be rid of Erasmus Keyes (Republican, abolitionist), McClellan left him at Yorktown with a one-division corps, part of the Department of Virginia. Keyes's other division, under Darius Couch, was dispatched to the defenses of Washington. Keyes, a victim of his politics, idled at Yorktown for a year, served on the retirement board, and finally resigned in May 1864. He could take pride in his role at Seven Pines, even if only the men of his own corps recognized it.

Burnside's Ninth Corps was first to reach Pope's army, but Burnside himself remained at Falmouth, across the Rappahannock from Fredericksburg, distributing the parts and pieces of the Army of the Potomac as they arrived via Aquia Landing. Jesse L. Reno commanded the Ninth Corps in the field, comprising his own division and that of Isaac I. Stevens. Porter's Fifth Corps followed the Ninth in debarking at Aquia. The divisions of Morell and Sykes remained with Porter, but John Reynolds's Pennsylvania Reserves were stripped from the Fifth Corps and attached to McDowell's corps, Army of Virginia, where they had served in McDowell's Army of the Potomac days. Because of the rapidly shifting campaign, the Second, Third, and Sixth Corps were debarked at Alexandria.[38]

(There now appeared in the capital the somber figure of Brigadier General Charles P. Stone, released after more than six months in military prisons, seeking both justice and a command. No one in the administration had a hand in Stone's release. It was the work of his civilian supporters and Senator James A. McDougall, who posed the question, Who says Stone is a traitor? and answered, "Rumor says it — the great manufacturer of falsehoods." McDougall attached a rider to a military pay bill entitling any serviceman "now under arrest and awaiting trial" to be tried within thirty days. Edwin Stanton had no case — never had a case — against Stone, but still he delayed his release to the last moment. At the White House Lincoln said, by Stone's account, "that if he told me all he knew about the matter he should not tell me much." At Halleck's office Stone found no explanation, no assignment, no orders. McClellan sought Stone for a divisional command, but Stanton turned away the request. There seemed no end to the ordeal of Charles Stone.)[39]

Pope heard nothing regarding command of the joint armies, and assumed Halleck himself would come out from Washington to take the command. Old Brains had no such intention. He — and everyone in the administration — fervently hoped that John Pope, with as much help from the Potomac army as need be, would prevail over the Rebels. A victory by the combined forces under Pope ought to dispose of McClellan without messy political consequences. Heintzelman called it a disgrace. "They want to be rid of McClellan & dont dare to go at it openly. This splendid army has to be broken up to get rid of him. . . ."

Lee fumbled his first advance against Pope's Rapidan line, and Pope hastily pulled back behind the Rappahannock. His move caught General Meade's attention: "It appears that Genl. Pope has been obliged to show *his back* to the enemy & to select a *line of retreat*." Lee probed Pope's new line. On August 22 Jeb Stuart swung around Pope's western flank and raided his headquarters at Catlett's Station on the Orange & Alexandria, the Army of Virginia's supply line. Captured dispatches revealed Pope's situation and the reinforcements he expected, and confirmed Lee's appraisal of the situation — that he had scarcely a moment to spare to strike before Pope became too strong to strike at all.

Lee divided his forces to maneuver around Pope's army and get in his rear — expanding Stuart's raid on the Orange & Alexandria into a full-fledged offensive. On August 25 Jackson's 24,000 men slipped away upstream to cross the Rappahannock at an unguarded ford, and turned north, disappearing behind the Bull Run Mountains. Longstreet's 30,000 stretched their lines to cover Jackson's old postings and continued skirmishing to occupy the Yankees in front of them.[40]

McClellan's lieutenants were uniformly pessimistic as the new campaign unfolded. George Meade told his wife the enemy "are evidently determined to break thro Pope and drive us out of Virginia, when they will follow into Maryland & perhaps Penna. I am sorry to say from the manner in which matters have been mismanaged that their chances of success are quite good." John Reynolds was of like mind: "I am very fearful of the operations. . . . Pope's Army has not seen or met anything like the force we know left Richmond before we did." Phil Kearny wrote bitterly, "*We have no Generals. McClellan is the failure I have proclaimed him. . . . He will only get us in more follies, more waste of blood, fighting by driblets.* He has lost the confidence of all. . . ."

Fitz John Porter was the most public with his complaints. He continued feeding disparaging news and views to editor Marble's *New York World*. Disaster was expected: "Military principles violated in case of Pope & putting Burnside where he is. . . . Pope is a fool. McDowell is a rascal and Halleck has brains but not independent." He echoed McClellan's wishful thought: "Would that this army was in Washington to rid us of incumbents ruining our country."

John Pope, for his part, had no illusions about what to expect from the Army of the Potomac. Influence peddler Joseph C. G. Kennedy had passed around for all to see Porter's July 17 letter with its belittling remarks about Pope. As Pope listened, Phil Kearny denounced the "spirit of McClellanism" infecting officers of the Potomac army and singled out Porter as not to be depended upon. Pope had no illusions about his own army either. He complained that Sigel's troops must march, "because they will not fight unless they are tired and cannot run." He insisted to Halleck that Sigel was "perfectly unreliable" and ought to be replaced. Banks's corps, too, was weak and demoralized and would best be held in the rear. Only McDowell's corps could be counted on.[41]

On August 25, the day Jackson disappeared behind the Bull Run Mountains, Pope's Army of Virginia was arrayed defensively behind the Rappahannock. Sigel's corps held the line to the west and Banks's to the east, with McDowell's corps in support at Warrenton. The pieces of the Army of the Potomac were scattered widely. Jesse Reno's two Ninth Corps divisions had made contact with Banks, but Fitz John Porter's two Fifth Corps divisions were downstream at Kelly's Ford. Porter wanted to know who was issuing orders — was it Halleck, Pope, Burnside? "Does General McClellan approve?" he asked plaintively. Reynolds's Pennsylvania Reserves were attached to McDowell's corps at Warrenton. Of Heintzelman's Third Corps, Kearny's division had reached Warrenton Junction, on the Orange & Alexandria, with Hooker's division following. Sumner's Second Corps and Franklin's Sixth were en route from the Peninsula.

Pope found the command status confusing. He assumed, he told Halleck, "you designed to take command in person." Until then he did not know what forces were his to use. Was he to "command independently" against the enemy? On the subject of command Halleck was silent. McClellan too questioned Halleck. He asked "whether you still intend to place me in the command indicated in your first letter to me, & orally through Genl Burnside. . . . Please define my position & duties." Halleck furnished him no satisfaction. On August 26 McClellan took ship for Alexandria and (as he told Ellen), like Mr. Micawber "am waiting for something to turn up."[42]

When he took command of the Army of Virginia, John Pope found the army's railroad supply network in the hands of Herman Haupt, the railroad construction engineer and superintendent recruited by Secretary Stanton. Haupt had everything in working order and the trains running on time. He noted the evils he had corrected: "Military interference, neglect to unload and return cars, too many heads, and, as a consequence, conflicting orders." The only way to run a railroad, said Herman Haupt, was under a single head, on a fixed schedule. Pope reasoned that since the railroad carried army supplies, he would put army quartermasters in charge and dispense with Haupt. In a matter of days the evils returned: Trains stopped running on time, and often just stopped running. Orders came from the field and from Washington and from everywhere in between. Troops lagged in reaching Pope. Supplies lagged reaching the front. Lack of forage crippled the cavalry. The War Department telegraphed Haupt, "Come back immediately; cannot get along without you; not a wheel moving on any of the roads."

On Haupt's return, Peter Watson of the War Department advised him, "Be patient as possible with the Generals; some of them will trouble you more than they will the enemy." For example, Brigadier General Samuel Sturgis. On August 22 Sturgis brought the Orange & Alexandria to a standstill by commandeering four trains to take his division to the front. Haupt found Sturgis well primed with drink and threatening to arrest *him*, "for disobedience of my orders in failing to transport my command." Haupt had strict orders from Halleck and Pope that he alone ran the railroads, and soon came a telegram from Halleck promising arrest for Sturgis unless he gave up the trains. Believing in his muddled state that the order came from Pope, Sturgis blurted, "I don't care for John Pope a pinch of owl dung!" Savoring his construction, he repeated it several times before staff persuaded him that the order was from the general-in-chief. "He says if you interfere with the railroads he will put you in arrest." "He does, does he?" said Sturgis, drawing himself up. "Well, then, take your damned railroad!"[43]

When Jackson left the Rappahannock on his flank march, he did not escape notice. A Rebel column off to the west, "well closed up and colors flying," was reported to Banks. He forwarded the sighting to Pope: "It seems to be apparent that the enemy is threatening or moving upon the valley of

PERIODICAL SCARE OF THE OLD PARTY AT THE WAR DEPARTMENT.

A Jackson-in-the-box springs another surprise on Secretary of War Stanton, this time in the Shenandoah Valley in August 1862. From the *New York Illustrated News.*

the Shenandoah via Front Royal, with designs on the Potomac, possibly beyond." (Confederate interest in the Valley was well known to Nathaniel Banks.) Pope agreed. For Halleck he gauged the column as 20,000 strong and added, "I am induced to believe that this column is only covering the flank of the main body, which is moving toward Front Royal and Thornton's Gap."

Pope took comfort in this belief. Seeing the Rebels off to the Valley made them, in effect, someone else's problem. There should now be time to properly combine the two armies, and with Halleck in command, meet the new threat. Pope did not set forces on the trail of the enemy column, nor did his cavalry track it.

Before dawn on August 26, near the village of Salem midway between the Blue Ridge and the Bull Run mountains, Jackson roused his column from its bivouac. A turn west (which John Pope anticipated) would lead to Manassas Gap in the Blue Ridge and Front Royal and the Shenandoah. A turn east would lead to Thoroughfare Gap in the Bull Run Mountains and the rear of the Army of Virginia. By noon Jackson's column was passing through Thoroughfare Gap. No Federals barred the way, or sounded the alarm. That afternoon, Lee with Longstreet's troops left the Rappahannock and set out on the same route Jackson had taken.[44]

At 8:00 p.m. on the 26th Colonel Haupt's telegrapher at Manassas Junction reported, "No. 6 train, engine Secretary, was fired into at Bristoe by a party of cavalry — some say 500 strong. . . ." Haupt passed the news to Halleck. Jackson's vanguard, it developed, had cut the Orange & Alexandria at Bristoe Station, then five miles up the line captured Manassas Junction, the Army of Virginia's principal supply depot. By day's end General Pope was aware that his communications were cut, and by more than a party of cavalry. It was belatedly reported to him that a substantial body of Confederate infantry, artillery, and cavalry had traversed Thoroughfare Gap and just then was squarely between his army and Washington.

Once over his surprise, Pope saw opportunity here. McDowell made the case: "If the enemy are playing their game on us and we can keep down the panic which their appearance is likely to create in Washington, it seems to me the advantage of position must all be on our side." This flanking column of Jackson's may have cut communications with the capital, but Pope held the central position in the area of maneuver. If they moved quickly, the Federals might fall on Jackson from two, possibly three directions.

Pope's orders for August 27 had his forces abandon the Rappahannock line and pivot 180 degrees. On the left, McDowell with his own corps, Sigel's corps, and John Reynolds's division would advance from Warrenton northeasterly to Gainesville, on the road Jackson had followed to Manassas Junction. Jesse Reno's two Ninth Corps divisions, with the Third Corps' Phil Kearny, were to march north from the Orange & Alexandria to support McDowell. Banks's corps and Porter's two Fifth Corps divisions would move in support from Warrenton Junction. Joe Hooker's division, Third Corps, was directed up the railroad toward those Rebels who might still be at Bristoe Station. The total force came to some 70,000 men.

These Potomac army units brought a sense of relief to the beleaguered Army of Virginia. David Strother of Pope's staff was curious to meet the Peninsula generals so praised in the papers. "Hooker is a fine-looking man, tall, florid, and beardless," he noted in his diary. "Heintzelman is a knotty, hard-looking old customer with a grizzled beard and shambling one-sided gait. Evidently a man of energy and reliability." Another of Pope's officers, Carl Schurz, described meeting the famous Phil Kearny: "A strikingly fine, soldierly figure, one-armed, thin face, pointed beard, fiery eyes," wearing a jauntily tipped cap that gave him the look of a French legionnaire.

Irvin McDowell saw here the chance to retrieve his fortunes. Washington Roebling of the staff wrote in his journal, "All day long McDowell was in an excited but exhilarated state of mind, very hopeful and confident, but savage as a meat axe, as one poor Wisconsin private can testify, his head being half knocked off because he straggled." Francophile McDowell was heard to mutter that tomorrow would see "une grande bataille, une grande bataille, une grande bataille. . . ."[45]

Pope designed his orders to press Jackson from the west and south with every man then under his control. Advancing on Jackson from the east, by Halleck's order (and Pope's request), was to be Franklin's Sixth Corps of McClellan's army, just then at Alexandria. Colonel Haupt, intent on getting his railroad running, pitched in on his own account. He collected an idle brigade of Franklin's, under George W. Taylor, and two Ohio regiments of Jacob Cox's division, just arrived from western Virginia, and sent them with a work train down the Orange & Alexandria to see how far they could get.

On the map this convergence of Union forces looked most promising. However, these forces were widely scattered to start with, and under a varied lot of generals from a varied range of commands. To further complicate matters, the Potomac army units were arriving from the Peninsula short of cavalry, artillery, transport, ammunition, and provisions. Most columns marched without cavalry in the lead. "Every minute came a new order," Alpheus Williams wrote; "now to march east and now to march west, night and day."[46]

While most Federals spent August 27 marching, three clashes with Stonewall Jackson marked the day. When word reached Washington of the affair at Manassas Junction, the 2nd New York Heavy Artillery was sent out to put things right. At daybreak the "heavies," acting as riflemen in this their first venture outside the capital, stumbled into Jackson's men and met a storm of fire. Colonel Gustav Waagner admitted his men "became a little scattered, but nevertheless the retreat was conducted in tolerably good order." Soon the trains with Colonel Haupt's ad hoc expedition reached the scene. George Taylor's New Jersey brigade (Phil Kearny's ex-command) deployed against the supposed party of raiders and was startled by the same deadly fire that drove off the heavies. Taylor ordered a withdrawal. In the Jerseymen's scramble to get back across the railroad bridge over Bull Run, Taylor fell mortally wounded.

The third clash with Jackson originated on Pope's orders. Sam Heintzelman had his Third Corps at Warrenton Junction, and despite the delays and headaches, he was encouraged. "The rebels have lost the opportunity to defeat Pope," he told his diary. "Our reinforcements are coming in position too rapidly" — just a day or two more. But he was troubled by a command void: "No one appeared to know what to do, or rather to think it necessary to do anything." In Pope's realignment, the Third Corps became the right wing. Phil Kearny and Joe Hooker were two of the best fighting generals in the Potomac army, yet Pope elected to deliver only a half swing. He split the Third Corps, assigning Kearny to the center and Hooker to advance alone up the railroad.

Hooker scouted the Rebel position at Bristoe Station, then swiftly deployed his three brigades to engage Jackson's lieutenant Dick Ewell. Under Cuvier Grover, Joseph B. Carr, and Nelson Taylor (filling in for Dan Sickles, busy politicking in New York), the Yankee brigades fought their way around the Confederates' flank. At sunset Ewell withdrew to Manassas. Limited ammunition prevented any pursuit. Absent Kearny's division, Hooker's fight at Bristoe Station fell short of its promise.[47]

Herman Haupt's estimate of 20,000 Rebels holding Manassas Junction and blocking Pope's supply line came as sobering news for General Halleck — and for General McClellan. From Alexandria he wrote his wife on the morning of the 27th, "Our affairs here now much tangled up & I opine that in a day or two your old husband will be called upon to unsnarl them." Only Franklin's Sixth Corps and Sumner's Second, some 25,000 men, remained under McClellan's command, and Halleck was calling on him to send Franklin's corps to Pope "as soon as possible."[48]

It soon developed that General McClellan doing anything "as soon as possible" was impossible. With Jackson cutting Pope's telegraph link to Washington, reports from the front originated with Fitz John Porter, who retained a roundabout link with Burnside at Falmouth. Announcing battle was imminent, Porter waxed contemptuous: "Would that I were out of this; I don't like the concern." "The strategy is magnificent, and tactics in the inverse proportion." "I find a common feeling of dissatisfaction and distrust in the ability of any one here." "I wish myself away from it, with all our old Army of the Potomac, and so do our companions." Burnside warned Porter about his imprudent language but was obliged to forward these dispatches to headquarters. From reading them McClellan framed his own distinctive view of events.

His first thought was to hold Franklin's corps at Alexandria until it could be massed with Sumner's arriving corps. Halleck said that Franklin "should move out by forced marches." McClellan said the Sixth Corps was not yet fully equipped; Franklin could not "effect any useful purpose in front." The real threat was not to Pope but to Washington itself. "I think our policy now is to make these works perfectly safe, & mobilize a couple of Corps as soon as possible, but not to advance them until they can have their Artillery & Cavalry." He had no time for details, replied the harried general-in-chief. "You will therefore, as ranking general in the field, direct as you deem best." So it happened that no marching orders were issued to the Sixth Corps on August 27 . . . and no marching orders were issued for August 28, either. Franklin told his wife, "We are still in status quo, and I hardly think we will move for a while yet."[49]

David Strother closed his August 27 diary entry with the prediction "To-morrow there will be a grand denouement." That was Pope's prediction as well. His orders for the 28th breathed fire and purpose. He told Phil Kearny, "At the very earliest blush of dawn push forward with your com-mand with all speed to this place . . . and we shall bag the whole crowd." He repeated the image to McDowell, and added, "Be expeditious, and the day is our own." His orders directed all his forces to or toward Manassas Junction.

General Pope's exploits in the Western theater had involved static, for-tified enemy positions — Island No. 10 in the Mississippi, New Madrid in Missouri, Corinth in Mississippi — and that experience perhaps fed his confidence that the next day, August 28, he would find Stonewall Jackson waiting at Manassas to receive his attack. Even the sight during the night of a giant conflagration at his supply base, easily visible to every Yankee soldier within 10 miles, did not persuade him that perhaps his quarry had finished his work there and was moving on.

As was indeed the case. Through the night, the Confederates slipped out of burning Manassas north by west, by various routes, to take up a position on the edge of the battlefield of First Bull Run (as henceforth it would be numbered) just north of the hamlet of Groveton on the Warren-ton Turnpike. Jackson and Lee, in communication by courier, were con-fident now of reuniting the two wings of the Army of Northern Virginia. Their task was to engage Pope in battle before the arrival of any more of McClellan's army made the odds too long.[50]

Thanks to what cavalry was still functioning, McDowell was aware of Longstreet's approach to Thoroughfare Gap. Commanding almost half the combined Federal forces, he initially thought to post four divisions to de-fend the Gap. But none of Pope's orders for August 28 mentioned Long-street or any threat he might pose, and his orders were explicit: McDowell

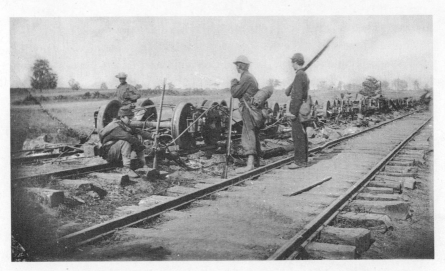

Timothy O'Sullivan photographed a string of Orange & Alexandria rolling stock at Manassas Junction destroyed on August 27 by Stonewall Jackson's raiders.

to "march rapidly on Manassas Junction with your whole force." McDowell decided to not quite obey. He directed James Ricketts's division of his corps to Haymarket, three miles east of Thoroughfare Gap. Ricketts was to keep close watch to the west, and should an enemy force appear, "march to resist it." While less than even a half measure, this seemed to McDowell better than doing nothing.

Then, on August 28, nothing went according to plan. All morning Pope "nipped into delinquents of all grades," wrote Colonel Strother. One delinquent was Fitz John Porter, whose delayed start earned him a black mark in Pope's book. Another was Franz Sigel, whose slow assembly held up those behind him. Sigel then marched off in the wrong direction. This proved merely an irritant, for there was no Stonewall Jackson to fight. Kearny reached Manassas Junction about noon to find Pope's supply base one square mile of ruins. "Long trains of cars lately loaded with stores of all kinds were consumed as they stood on the track, smoking and smoldering, only the iron work remaining entire," Strother wrote. "The whole plain as far as the eye could reach was covered with boxes, barrels, military equipment, cooking utensils, bread, meat, and beans lying in the wildest confusion. The spoilers had evidently had a good time and feasted themselves while they destroyed."[51]

Interrogation of stragglers had Jackson headed to Centreville. Pope ordered McDowell to redirect his pursuit to Centreville. Pope's courier crossed one from McDowell carrying a cavalry report of Longstreet at

Thoroughfare Gap. This caused Pope to think of changing his target to Longstreet. Defeating him or driving him away would isolate Jackson and ensure his defeat as well. New orders, sent at 2:00 p.m., went to McDowell: Halt the march to Centreville and instead assemble at Gainesville, on the Warrenton Pike east of the Gap. Heintzelman's and Reno's corps would also be directed there. That should be force enough to crush Longstreet.

But just then came fresh evidence regarding Jackson, as noted by Heintzelman: The enemy at Centreville "are reported 30,000." By this point John Pope was being swayed by whatever latest word reached him. He abandoned the short-lived movement against Longstreet and reverted to pursuing Jackson — and reverted as well to his conviction that (as he later testified) "we were sufficiently in advance of Longstreet ... to be able to crush Jackson completely before Longstreet by any possibility could have reached the scene of action." At 4:15 p.m. yet another set of orders went to McDowell: "Please march your command directly upon Centreville from where you are." Also redirected to Centreville were Sigel, Kearny, Reno, and Hooker. Figuratively throwing up his hands, McDowell set off to find Pope for a face-to-face meeting.[52]

"A dozen orders were given & countermanded the same day and the troops subjected to a lot of useless marching," complained staff man Washington Roebling. Meanwhile, James Ricketts found himself confronting the vanguard of Longstreet's wing of Lee's army. Ricketts's orders were to "march to resist," so while the rest of McDowell's troops pushed east to seek out Jackson, he pushed west with his division to contest the advance of 30,000 Confederates.

In the forty hours since they learned of Jackson's raid on Manassas, Pope and his confidant McDowell had neither met nor exchanged dispatches to craft joint operations for the swiftly evolving campaign. On August 28, except for his brief flurry of interest in Longstreet, Pope simply ignored that half of the Rebel army and devoted all his energies to cornering Jackson. McDowell had serious concerns about Longstreet's threat, but failed to communicate them to Pope. Had he exercised command discretion and twelve hours earlier attempted to block the narrow defile of Thoroughfare Gap, in the manner of the Spartans at Thermopylae, he might have created a problem for Lee. As it was, Ricketts engaged in a forlorn hope.

Exchanged after his capture at First Bull Run, James Ricketts was in his first infantry command. By the time he approached the Gap it was securely in Longstreet's hands. Veteran gunner Ricketts used his batteries to keep the Rebels at arm's length for a time, held his line until dark, then pulled back to Gainesville. His sole accomplishment that afternoon was to accurately locate Longstreet's half of the Confederate army. Even that, through no fault of his, proved an empty gesture.[53]

McDowell's Corps, Army of Virginia, did the Federals' fighting on August 28. While Ricketts sparred with Longstreet to the west, John Reynolds's and Rufus King's divisions were marching eastward along the Warrenton Pike in search of Jackson. At midday Reynolds had a brief skirmish with Rebel pickets a mile or so short of Groveton. Reynolds's Peninsula veterans chased the intruders away and resumed their march — much to Jackson's disappointment; by the time his troops formed up the Yankees were gone. Jackson recognized that more Yankees ought to be coming his way soon enough, and got ready to bring John Pope to battle.

In late afternoon King's division came in sight — four brigades, led by John P. Hatch, John Gibbon, Abner Doubleday, and Marsena R. Patrick. Just then General King suffered an epileptic seizure, his second in a week. King would be hours recovering, but his lieutenants were not informed that the division was leaderless. None of the four (and only one of their fifteen regiments) had been in battle before, but all four were West Pointers and their men had considerable training and drill.

The Rebels opened on Hatch's lead brigade with artillery, and Hatch replied with his own battery. But Jackson's chief focus fell on the second brigade in the Yankee column, John Gibbon's Westerners — 2nd, 6th, 7th Wisconsin and 19th Indiana. Gibbon was a tough and loyal regular from North Carolina (his three brothers served the Confederacy), a captain of artillery in the old army who had the knack for training volunteers. He had outfitted his men with distinctive black Hardee hats, tall-crowned regulars' headgear that they wore with pride, calling themselves the Black Hat Brigade.

Gibbon sighted horses emerge from the woods north of the turnpike and thought Rebel cavalry, but then the horses turned in unison. "My experience as an artillery officer, told me at once what this meant; guns coming into 'battery'!" Quickly he called up his old command, Battery D, 4th United States, to counter the enemy fire. He spoke with Doubleday, whose brigade was next in line. Since by report Jackson was at Centreville, they decided this must just be horse artillery, and Doubleday suggested storming it. "By heaven, I'll do it!" said Gibbon, and he deployed the 2nd Wisconsin. The 2nd was the division's sole veteran regiment. On July 21, 1861, uniformed then in gray, it had charged Henry Hill and suffered grievously from both enemy and friendly fire. Without warning, battle lines of Confederate infantry came streaming out of the woods to meet the Wisconsin men, and "there burst upon them a flame of musketry."

Gibbon hastily brought up the rest of his brigade and a battle royal erupted. In his memoir, reflecting on three years of combat, Gibbon wrote that at Groveton "for over an hour the most terrific musketry fire I have ever listened to rolled along those two lines of battle. It was a regular stand up fight during which neither side yielded a foot." Gibbon called on General King for support and got no reply. He called on Patrick for support, got no reply, and was blunt in his report: "Patrick's brigade remained immovable and did not fire a shot." (In his journal Patrick noted dismissively that Gibbon "under whose order I know not sailed into the wood" to bring on a fight; lacking orders from King, he stayed out of it.) Doubleday, who had urged on Gibbon, supplied two regiments to brace his line.

The firefight continued until it was too dark to see. Only then did the two sides break apart. John Gibbon wrote his wife of "my desperate fight of Thursday during which my men were literally slaughtered. . . ." The slaughter cost the Black Hat Brigade 725 of the Federals' 1,025 casualties; the 2nd Wisconsin lost nearly two-thirds of its men. Jackson spent 1,250 casualties to reveal his presence to John Pope.[54]

General King, weakened by his seizure, had an unsteady grip on command. (The next morning he turned the division over to John Hatch.) He and his generals debated their predicament. They could not find corps commander McDowell — nor could anyone else. McDowell had ridden off eastward to find Pope, failed to locate him, and as a staff man put it, "could not find our way across the plains of Manassas." They camped in the woods to wait for dawn and enlightenment. King and his lieutenants agreed that their four brigades, one of them crippled, dare not face Jackson alone in the morning. Orders were to head for Centreville, but the enemy blocked that path. Ricketts's division at Gainesville might help . . . if McDowell so ordered. John Reynolds, good soldier that he was, had ridden to the sound of the guns and offered his division for the morning. Would that be in time, or enough help in any case? Without their corps commander to decide such critical matters, a decision was taken and reported to McDowell, wherever he might be found: "Our position is not tenable, and we shall fall back toward Manassas. . . ." Ricketts followed. So it happened that the way was left open on August 29 for Longstreet to unite with Jackson.

Rufus King would afterward be criticized for this decision, in a chorus

Edwin Forbes of *Leslie's Illustrated Newspaper* sketched the rainy retreat of a Yankee column of the Army of Virginia on August 28, falling back to Manassas Junction.

led by John Pope, but with his limited knowledge of larger events it was the only rational choice. The true failure of command was Irvin McDowell's. To absent himself from supervising half the army at a critical moment in the campaign was culpable negligence. He was still missing the next morning, and Pope lost his temper. "God damn McDowell, he is never where he ought to be!"[55]

Notice of the Groveton fight reached Pope in late evening of the 28th. He leaped to the conclusion that Jackson had been intercepted in flight from Centreville. Heintzelman entered in his diary, "From the information we had we supposed the rebels retreating on Gainesville & McDowell on their front & that all we had to do was to follow them rapidly." Pope assured his staff "the game was in our own hands."

John Pope was truly confident he finally had Jackson trapped. He imagined McDowell's corps, the divisions of King and Ricketts, to be west of Jackson on the Warrenton Turnpike. To the south of Jackson was Franz Sigel's corps, three divisions under Robert Schenck, Adolph von Steinwehr, and Carl Schurz. Close by Sigel was Reynolds's division. Pope ordered Sigel to "attack the enemy vigorously" at first light. Certain he had Jackson boxed in from west and south, Pope arranged a strike from the east. To Kearny at Centreville went instructions to march at 1:00 a.m. on August 29: "Advance cautiously and drive in the enemy's pickets to-night, and at early dawn attack him vigorously." Hooker would follow him, said Pope. "Be sure to march not later than 1. . . ."

Phil Kearny, reported one of his colonels, was "in one of his crabbiest moods," his fancy accouterments far to the rear, reduced to coffee and hardtack, his only servant "a damned miscellaneous migratory contraband." In any case he had his fill of John Pope and his repeated orders sending him this way and that way, always with great urgency, never with any result. The least tolerant of men to begin with, Kearny told Pope's messenger, "Tell General Pope to go to Hell. We won't march before morning."[56]

John Gibbon determined to hunt up Pope to brief him on the situation at Groveton, and on the morning of August 29 found him at Centreville in hot temper. Pope had by now learned of King's withdrawal, but knew nothing of McDowell's whereabouts. At Gibbon's urging, he tried to reset the trap for Jackson. Fitz John Porter's corps at Manassas, along with King's (now Hatch's) division, was ordered to march to Gainesville, west of Jackson's position, to cut off his retreat. "I am following the enemy down the Warrenton Turnpike," Pope told Porter. "Be expeditious or we will lose much."

Gibbon volunteered to deliver the orders to Porter at Manassas, where he found as well the missing Irvin McDowell. Without orders himself, McDowell saw his command melting away, but Porter soothed him by pointing out that he was still senior officer. McDowell decided to march toward Gainesville with Porter's Fifth Corps, plus Hatch, with Ricketts to follow. McDowell had yet to see Pope, had yet to deliver Ricketts's report of the 28th that Longstreet was through Thoroughfare Gap and likely to advance in their direction on the 29th.

The orders Gibbon delivered marked Porter's second change of direction that morning. At dawn Colonel Strother had awakened him with Pope's order to march to Centreville for a pending "severe engagement." Porter read the new order and then wrote a dispatch of his own. Porter asked Strother how to spell "chaos." Strother told him, and "at the same time divined what he was thinking about."

Porter was indeed thinking that chaos (he chose not to use the word) described the tangled arrangement of Union forces. His dispatch, to Ambrose Burnside, who forwarded it to Washington, described the Rebels "wandering around loose; but I expect they know what they are doing, which is more than any one here or anywhere knows." He added, "I hope Mac is at work, and we will soon get ordered out of this." Thus Fitz John Porter's state of mind as he went to war on August 29.

By the time he came to issue marching orders to Joe Hooker and Jesse Reno, Pope had calmed down. He directed them to follow Kearny on the Warrenton Pike. Pope now had every man under his command on the move except for Banks's corps, guarding the army's trains. In none of these communications did he mention Longstreet.[57]

On August 28 Sam Heintzelman asked, "I cannot see why troops were not pressed forward from Alex. to attack this force in our front yesterday."

General-in-Chief Halleck had the same thought. That evening he tele-graphed McClellan, "There must be no further delay in moving Franklin's corps toward Manassas. They must go to-morrow morning, ready or not ready." McClellan's reply was apocalyptic: "The enemy with 120,000 men intend advancing on the forts near Arlington and Chain Bridge, with a view of attacking Washington & Baltimore." Morning on August 29 saw Franklin's Sixth Corps march out of Alexandria all of seven miles, to the village of Annandale. There it halted on McClellan's order and spent the day listening to the roar of battle off to the west. In midafternoon, receiv-ing a query from the president, McClellan replied, "I am clear that one of two courses should be adopted — 1st To concentrate all our available force to open communications with Pope — 2nd To leave Pope to get out of his scrape & at once use all our means to make the Capital perfectly safe. No middle course will now answer." In halting Franklin, McClellan had ad-opted course two: to let Pope get out of his scrape as best he might.[58]

Convinced that Jackson was trying to escape, Pope left no room for the possibility that his foe was seeking a battle and held good defensive ground on which to fight it. Jackson's three divisions took advantage of concealing woods and the fills and cuts of the roadbed of an unfinished railroad. First on the scene on the 29th was Franz Sigel's corps. Lacking guidance from anyone who fought at Groveton the day before, Sigel felt his way onto unknown ground.

Sigel's corps was only 9,000 strong, refugees from Pathfinder Frémont's Mountain Department, with an unhappy history against Jackson in the Valley back in the spring. First to engage was Carl Schurz's division. His brigade commanders, Wladimir Krzyzanowski and Alexander Schim-melfennig, were like Schurz émigrés from the revolutionary turmoil in Europe. Only Krzyzanowski had seen action previously, leading the 58th New York at Cross Keys in June.

All was perfectly still, Schurz remembered: "The skirmishers pass the detached groups of timber and enter the forest. The line of battle follows at the proper distance. No sign of the enemy. A quarter of an hour elapses. Perfect stillness all around." He began to wonder if the enemy was there at all. But then Krzyzanowski's advance found A. P. Hill's defenders and opened a bitter, extended firefight in the woods that soon drew in Schim-melfennig's brigade. Schurz's opening gambit was stymied but he managed to hold his own while waiting for support.

To Schurz's left, Robert Milroy rushed his independent brigade into action without benefit of reconnaissance. Milroy was a lawyer and one-time Indiana militia captain with a low opinion of professional soldiers (he called Pope "our miserable humbug-bag of gas"), and he pushed his four little regiments blindly into action. They lost a quarter of their numbers and were knocked back to their starting point.

A pattern of uncoordinated assaults was set. Farther to the left, Robert Schenck's division, supported by John Reynolds's Pennsylvania Reserves, engaged fitfully with infantry and artillery but without unified direction . . . or accomplishment. On the right, however, the arrival of Kearny's division — "Kearny did not start till after daylight & detained us," Heintzelman grumbled — with Hooker and Reno following, seemed to promise a major push by the Army of the Potomac. Schurz was heartened to see orders from Sigel — in field command now that battle was joined — addressed to Kearny, telling him to take action immediately against Jackson's left.[59]

In his report to Sigel, Carl Schurz wrote, "On my right, however, where General Kearny had taken position, all remained quiet, and it became clear to me that he had not followed your request to attack. . . ." Heintzelman recalled, "There was so long delay that I sent to him a second order to move at once." Hooker would complain that despite orders "repeatedly delivered . . . General Kearny's Division did not move until several hours after my division had been driven from the forest. . . ."

Once again, as he had at Seven Pines and Glendale, Phil Kearny marched to his own drum, ignoring orders from a superior he had little respect for — in this case what was worse, from "an officer of a foreign country." (The next day Kearny sent a note to Adolph von Steinwehr, one of Sigel's generals whom Kearny knew from his years abroad, that offered amends. It seemed that Sigel had bristled at a letter critical of German soldiery that Kearny had sent to New Jersey's governor. "I fancied Genl Siegel as extremely arrogant," Kearny admitted, but he asked Steinwehr to apologize for him for the way he reacted to Sigel's messenger . . . and by implication, to the order the man delivered.)

While Kearny's animus toward Sigel was a factor in his slowness to act, there was more to it. This battle presented Kearny with a new command challenge. At Williamsburg, at Seven Pines, at Glendale he had responded to Rebel assaults — the enemy was in plain sight; his task was clear. Here he was ordered to mount an attack of his own devising, against an unseen enemy in an unknown position. He reacted with unaccustomed caution. He sent Orlando Poe's brigade on a turning movement but pulled back when Poe met return fire. In time just three regiments of David Birney's brigade supported Carl Schurz's firefight.

Joe Hooker had particular cause to complain, for his men came close to breaking open the battle. Hooker objected to a frontal assault with just the 1,500 men of Cuvier Grover's brigade, and proposed instead a joint attack with Kearny on the right. General Pope, taking the command, agreed. The Rebels' railroad embankment line was formidable, so Grover sidestepped into the woods a quarter mile to the right. From that cover he launched a sudden charge, "and here occurred" (Grover reported) "a short, sharp, and obstinate hand-to-hand conflict with bayonets and clubbed muskets." The Yankees surged ahead and broke a second line. But they were taking losses and nothing was seen of Kearny on the right, and finally the attack faltered and fell back. Grover returned with two-thirds of the men who started.

Next marked for action, by Pope's disjointed thinking, was Jesse Reno's little Ninth Corps division. James Nagle's brigade spearheaded an assault that like Grover's breached the railroad barricade but soon had its flanks beaten in and collapsed with heavy losses. In each of the day's scattered, mistimed Union offensives, Jackson's lieutenants met the point of attack with superior numbers and prevailed.[60]

At 5:00 p.m. Kearny finally mounted his attack. His advance — John Robinson's and David Birney's brigades — sought to turn Jackson's left. Kearny personally saw his men into the fire. "His simple words, 'Now boys, do your duty!' made our blood thrill and steeled our courage," wrote New Yorker Theodore Dodge. To his wife, Colonel Alex Hays, 63rd Pennsylvania, Robinson's brigade, described an experience entirely typical of the Federal assaults that day. His men answered his order to advance "with a deafening cheer. We drove them before us like sheep until they took shelter behind the railroad." There they met "the most terrible fire I have ever experienced." And there the 63rd stayed, unable to advance, unsupported, running out of ammunition. Hays suffered a bad leg wound, and soon the Rebels counterattacked his undermanned front. After an hour of this punishment they were driven back from the railroad line. Hays, who earned his brigadier's star this day, counted the 63rd's loss as 103 of 357 engaged. Kearny, not attacking in concert with Hooker (or with anyone else), was stymied.[61]

At Pope's headquarters that afternoon, Heintzelman made note, "We are looking for Porter & McDowell." Pope was persuaded that the day-long series of attacks, however limited in results, had fixed Jackson in place so that Porter's and McDowell's corps might turn Jackson's right, and more, cut him off from the rest of Lee's army — which by Pope's calculation would not arrive for another day at least. He staked his expectations on a joint order he had sent Porter and McDowell at 10 o'clock that morning. Whatever he intended by this order, it befuddled both generals. Pope was here repeating his episode with Nathaniel Banks at Cedar Mountain — insisting an order of his had a meaning not at all evident in the order itself.

The joint order told Porter and McDowell to march their two commands toward Gainesville. When they connected with the rest of the army on the line of the Warrenton Pike, "the whole command shall halt. It may be necessary to fall back behind Bull Run at Centreville to-night. I presume it will be so, on account of our supplies." The rest of the enemy force — that is, Longstreet's command — "is moving in this direction at a pace that will bring them here by to-morrow night or the next day." Pope qualified his instructions — "If any considerable advantages are to be gained by departing from this order it will not be strictly carried out" — then qualified *that* by insisting the troops "must occupy a position from which they can reach Bull Run to-night or by morning." Beyond anything else then, the whole army must be prepared promptly to fall back on Centreville. Nothing was said in the joint order of attacking Jackson's right or indeed of attacking anywhere at all.

At midday, pondering Pope's joint order, Porter and McDowell noted strong signs of an enemy force to the north and west, blocking their path to Gainesville. As Porter phrased it, "We had enemies where we expected to find friends." This was, of course, Longstreet's column. Longstreet had made a swift march from Thoroughfare Gap to link up with Jackson's right, then formed his line at a 45-degree angle with Jackson's line. Lee discussed with Longstreet a strike at the flank of Pope's forces just then attacking Jackson, but this Yankee force on the Manassas–Gainesville road on *their* flank caused them to pause. They bided their time to see if the miscreant Pope would walk into their trap.

As he and Porter puzzled over what to do, McDowell was handed a dispatch from cavalryman John Buford, who had been tracking Longstreet. Buford reported seeing, at 8:45 a.m., a large force of infantry, artillery, and cavalry pass through Gainesville. This could only be Longstreet, and meant that he and Jackson were uniting their forces. McDowell had failed to report to Pope James Ricketts's Thoroughfare Gap intelligence of yesterday; now he failed to forward Buford's crucial sighting as well. McDowell told Porter they could not reach Gainesville without a fight. Therefore he was joining the rest of the army, posting his corps to fall back on Centreville, per the joint order. He said, "Porter, you are out too far already; this is no place to fight a battle." Porter had better remain, but if he had to fall back, "do so on my left."[62]

McDowell's corps made contact with the rest of the army at 3:45 p.m. At 4:30, apparently untroubled that his flanking force was now reduced by

Fitz John Porter ran afoul of John
Pope over conflicting orders at
Second Bull Run, the first step in
Porter's eventual downfall.

half, Pope sent to Porter "to push forward into action at once on the enemy's flank, and, if possible, on his rear. . . ." At 5:45 McDowell himself arrived at headquarters. He somehow talked his way clear of the awkward
fact that he had told Porter to remain in harm's way and then marched off
with his own corps to a safer place. He showed Pope John Buford's early-
morning sighting of the enemy arriving in force at Gainesville from Thoroughfare Gap. This, finally, was enough to persuade Pope that Longstreet
was uniting with Jackson, but McDowell either kept silent or forgot the
signs of Rebel troops in numbers on and west of the Manassas–Gainesville
road. Consequently, Pope got it in his head that Longstreet was simply reinforcing Jackson's position north of the Warrenton Pike—not the truth
that Lee with his two lieutenants had formed the wide-open jaws of a trap
for a stubbornly unwary John Pope.

Fitz John Porter and his Fifth Corps were left in limbo. He realized
(through several captures) that he was confronting Longstreet's wing of
the Rebel army; he was saddled with orders that now made even less sense
than before; and he was told by his superior McDowell that he should stay
where he was. He deployed skirmishers and posted his guns, listened to
the cannonading from Pope's front, and hoped for insight. He did not at-

tempt to "feel" the enemy, to estimate, for his own and Pope's benefit, what he was facing. Finally at 4:30 he sent a dispatch reporting the enemy "in strong force on this road" and his decision to fall back. At headquarters at 6 o'clock Heintzelman made note, "Gen. Porter reports the Rebels driving him back & he retiring on Manassas."

Pope's 4:30 courier had crossed Porter's 4:30 courier. That Porter was retreating instead of attacking put Pope in a rage. McDowell calmed him enough that he put aside thoughts of arresting Porter, but just barely. In fact Porter attempted to act on Pope's 4:30 order, which only reached him two hours later, at sunset. But at the front, George Morell argued it would be dark before he could mount an attack with his division; in any case, the idea of attacking here was rooted in what he politely called a misapprehension.

Pope's next order to Porter was threatening: "Immediately upon receipt of this order . . . you will march your command to the field of battle of today and report to me in person for orders. You are to understand that you are to comply strictly with this order, and to be present on the field within three hours after its reception or after daybreak tomorrow morning." This marked the opening gun of John Pope's vendetta against Fitz John Porter.[63]

By day's end on August 29 General Pope was fully delusional about the enemy. His military instincts had proved rudimentary at best. He was unable to fathom the deadly game Lee was playing, unable to grasp that while he bent all his efforts to prevent Jackson from escaping, Jackson was in fact pinning *him* to the ground for a sledgehammer blow by Longstreet. Nothing of Pope's experience in the Western theater prepared him for this, nor was he capable of recognizing the challenge, much less meeting it. His style of command emerged erratic and mistrustful. He split up the Potomac army's Third Corps, dealing directly with Hooker and Kearny and undermining Heintzelman. He also undercut the Ninth Corps' Jesse Reno. He commanded Porter's Fifth Corps through McDowell (when he could be found). He matched his mistrust of Potomac army generals with mistrust of Sigel and Banks of his own army. This hardly inspired confidence among his lieutenants.

To be sure, Pope was handicapped by Irvin McDowell's failings. McDowell never delivered Ricketts's intelligence on Longstreet at Thoroughfare Gap, and was half a day late passing on Buford's sighting of Longstreet's arrival on the field. He avoided command responsibility, and (as Pope complained) was often absent. Porter saw McDowell's motives as self-serving. Porter reported a conversation on August 29 when they received Pope's joint order. "McClellan won't have anything to do with this campaign," McDowell said; "that is decided on." He anticipated victory and expected to claim a major share of it. "I will be at the highest round of the ladder and will take care of such of McClellan's friends as stick to me." Porter said he made no reply.

At 5:00 a.m. on August 30 Pope sent Washington his first report since the fighting began. He spoke of "a terrific battle here yesterday," of driving the enemy from the field "which we now occupy." Prospects seemed bright: "The news just reaches me from the front that the enemy is retreating toward the mountains. I go forward at once to see."

Pope drew this conclusion in part from a clash the evening before along the Warrenton Turnpike. Confederate ambulances were sighted moving westward on the pike, and John Hatch's division was sent in pursuit. The pursuit promptly ran head-on into strong opposition and Hatch sent back for help. McDowell was disbelieving: "Tell him the enemy is in full retreat and to pursue him!" Darkness ended thoughts of pursuit, but not delusions of retreat.

Daylight brought other sketchy reports of an enemy withdrawal. At the front Rebels were overheard talking of pulling back. Enemy troops sighted rearranging their lines were assumed to be heading away. At a council of corps commanders — McDowell, Sigel, Porter, Heintzelman — Pope proposed to strike at Jackson's left, where Kearny had battled, with the corps of Heintzelman, McDowell, and Porter. The high command's conclusions that August 30 morning were summed up in Heintzelman's diary: "McDowell and I went & reconnoitered & were of the impression that the enemy were not in force on their left. We met Sigel as we returned & he holds the center & he was of the impression they had left. When we got to Pope ... he reported the enemy had been moving off towards our left & Thoroughfare Gap all night."[64]

Pope's conviction of an enemy retreating was not shaken by witnesses describing quite the opposite. Porter, in a tense interview, said it had to be Longstreet on and west of the Manassas–Gainesville road. Pope, said Porter, "put no confidence in what I said." Nor did Pope give credence to John Reynolds's claim of Longstreet's presence. Generals James Ricketts, Isaac Stevens, and Marsena Patrick testified to enemy sightings at the front. Patrick said the Rebels were as numerous north of the turnpike as they were the day before. "You are mistaken," Pope told him. "There is nobody in there of any consequence. They are merely stragglers." Such was the confidence at headquarters, Washington Roebling reported, that two of Pope's staff, "who were a little sprung, got up a party to go out on the battle field and count the dead rebs."

Pope's morning idea of striking Jackson's left with three army corps faded away. David Strother watched Pope pacing, "smoking as usual, evidently solving some problem of contradictory evidence in his mind. His preconceived opinions and his wishes decided him. McDowell came in and they spent the morning under a tree waiting for the enemy to retreat."[65]

What agitated Pope's thoughts that morning was what to do about this retreating enemy. Should he promptly pursue, however disorganized or suspect his generals? Should he pause to refit and revictual, mesh the two armies, and make a fresh start? That would be the prudent course. But that would be to admit the Rebels had gotten the best of him, had run rings around him. That, John Pope in his pride would not admit. So at noon on August 30 Pope ordered that his forces "be immediately thrown forward and in pursuit of the enemy, and press him vigorously. . . ." Leading the charge would be Fitz John Porter's Fifth Corps, which in Pope's eyes had so far contributed nothing to the campaign.

The Fifth Corps was shorthanded, for George Morell, along with Charles Griffin's brigade, had gotten lost trying to rejoin the army. Still, Porter's offensive promised to be the largest Federal effort yet—his two Fifth Corps divisions, plus John Hatch's division from McDowell's corps, some 10,000 men. Dan Butterfield replaced the absent Morell. The initial assault wave had three first-time brigade leaders, Colonels Henry Weeks, Charles W. Roberts, and Timothy Sullivan. In support were Sykes's regulars. At 3 o'clock, wrote Major George Hooper, 1st Michigan, "Gen Butterfield rode up to the rear of our line, called for our cheers, and gave the command to charge, and we swept out of the forest like an avalanche."

Pope's instructions called for Porter to pursue along the axis of the Warrenton Turnpike, but Porter recognized the folly in that and struck instead at the Rebels behind the railroad embankment north of the turnpike in the hope of at least starting a retreat. The approach was intimidating—mostly open ground and under the fire of two battalions of artillery at the hinge between Jackson's and Longstreet's lines, posted to deliver deadly enfilade fire. These batteries, wrote Major Hooper, "followed our every movement in this charge, in a way I have never seen equaled before or since . . . and here the slaughter commenced."

Colonel Sullivan's brigade on the right had the best cover and was farthest from the murderous Confederate artillery and got right up to the railroad embankment, but no farther, huddling there and looking for re-inforcement. General Hatch fell wounded. Roberts's brigade, at the cen-ter, and Weeks's, on the left, took fearful losses in the open ground before settling into their own firefight at the embankment. In his inexperience Weeks led his troops into the open in column, easy targets for the enemy guns as they deployed. "From behind this embankment," Marsena Patrick wrote, "a continuous discharge of Musketry was kept up, which it was im-possible to return as the enemy was perfectly protected." Nowhere could they breach the Rebel line. "In this position we remained upward of thirty minutes," Colonel Roberts reported, "our brave boys holding their ground, but falling in scores."

Pope initiated no diversions in support of Porter's assault, and the Union artillery, scattered and lacking central direction, was unsupport-ive. With his lead brigades stymied and with the enemy guns completely dominating the ground over which reinforcements would advance, Por-ter aborted a mission he had considered pointless from the start. The rest of the Fifth Corps and Hatch's brigades stood down, and the advance was recalled. Running the gauntlet of enemy fire, the survivors came back in considerable disorder.

Irvin McDowell, whom Pope had put in charge of the pursuit, now se-riously misread the battlefield. When the Fifth Corps was ordered away to join the rest of the army, John Reynolds's division remained as the only sizable force on the Federal left. Watching Porter's advance falling back in confusion, McDowell ordered Reynolds to support the supposedly weak-ened center. Reynolds had warned McDowell that the Rebels "were not in retreat, and their right was across the pike outflanking us." McDowell "rid-iculed the idea," revealing himself as uncomprehending as Pope, and pres-ently Reynolds marched across the Warrenton Pike, leaving behind open, empty fields and woods in front of James Longstreet's legions.[66]

At 4 o'clock Longstreet unleashed 25,000 men against the Federals' open left flank. Just two Yankee brigades faced the wave of attackers — Gouver-neur Warren's Fifth Corps brigade guarding a battery, and on an eminence called Chinn Ridge, Nathaniel C. McLean's brigade from Sigel's corps. Warren's force totaled a thousand men, and the Rebels stormed over them. As he had at Gaines's Mill, Warren thrust himself into the fighting, man-aging the best retreat he could and saving the battery. A mile or so back where the survivors rallied, "Warren sat immobile on his horse, looking back at the battle as if paralyzed. . . ."

At last the scales fell from McDowell's eyes. He tried to recall Reynolds's

Edwin Forbes labeled this drawing "Infantry Fight on the Left Wing," as Longstreet's
battle force storms a thin line of Yankee defenders at Second Bull Run on August 30.

Pennsylvania Reserves to their blocking position south of the turnpike,
but could only commandeer Reynolds's trailing brigade. The Confederates scattered the Pennsylvanians, capturing a battery. They next targeted Chinn Ridge and the brigade of Colonel McLean, a Cincinnati lawyer whose father, John McLean, had been a long-serving Supreme Court
justice. McLean posted his four Ohio regiments and a battery and determined to at least buy some time.

McLean's 1,200 men beat back the first assaults, and McLean watched
the enemy retire "more rapidly than they had advanced." Division commander Robert Schenck rode up to encourage the defenders, only to be
wounded severely enough to retire him from field command. Presently
masses of troops appeared beyond McLean's left. He ordered a section
of artillery to train on them, but countermanded "upon the assurance of
someone who professed to know the fact that they were our own troops."
As happened to McDowell's batteries at a decisive moment at First Bull
Run, mistaken identity proved fatal this day to holding Chinn Ridge. "Our
own troops" were in fact the enemy, and they turned McLean's flank and
wrecked his brigade. "I do not know that I was ever so angry or mortified
in my life," he remembered.[67]

The fighting was an hour old before McDowell was able to persuade
Pope that this surprise attack was the work of Longstreet, and that it put
the army at grave risk. While McDowell tried to hold the Chinn Ridge

line, Pope turned to the defense of Henry Hill. Should the Confederates seize this high ground overlooking the Warrenton Turnpike, they would outflank the entire Union army.

McDowell collared troops wherever he could find them — the brigades of Zealous B. Tower and John W. Stiles from Ricketts's division, the brigades of John A. Koltes and Wladimir Krzyzanowski from Sigel's corps — to reinforce McLean's collapsing Chinn Ridge defense. It was futile. The Rebels assaulted the ridge from left, right, and center, killing Koltes and wounding Tower, taking a battery, sending the Federals pelting for the rear. Among the dead was Colonel Fletcher Webster, 12th Massachusetts, son of the revered Daniel Webster.

In July 1861 it had been Federals attacking and Confederates defending Henry Hill; today the roles were reversed. Pope gathered the army's odds and ends and spare parts. There were the other two brigades of Reynolds's Pennsylvania Reserves, under Truman Seymour and George Meade, two brigades of Sykes's regulars, under Robert Buchanan and William Chapman, and two small independent brigades, under Robert Milroy and A. Sanders Piatt. At the same time, Pope stood up to the prospect of defeat. He had his right wing begin to disengage for a potential retreat. Orders went to Nathaniel Banks's corps on guard at Bristoe Station to fall back on Centreville. William Franklin, whose Sixth Corps was finally released early that day by McClellan, was told to man the fortifications at Centreville "and hold those positions to the last extremity." The road to Centreville was jammed and "seemed to promise another Bull Run stampede," wrote David Strother.

John Reynolds came with his two Reserves brigades to Henry Hill and took charge. Seizing a regimental flagstaff, Reynolds rode the full length of the battle line and back again, waving the banner and shouting "Forward, Reserves!" and blunting the Rebel advance. George Meade did not exaggerate in writing that when the Reserves "came into action, and held them in check and drove them back . . . we were enabled to save our left flank, which if we had not done the enemy would have destroyed the whole army." Sykes's regulars defended stubbornly, and Jesse Reno aggressively led reinforcements. In contrast, Robert Milroy, who disdained professional soldiers, completely lost his composure and was ordered by Colonel Buchanan of the regulars to "clear out and go away from here." The Henry Hill defenders narrowly held their ground.[68]

The battlefront now became one great confused melee. John Gibbon, whose brigade had been supporting Porter, wrote his wife of his surprise "to find that the enemy was moving in heavy force upon our left, and by his superior numbers & hard fighting was driving us before him. They seemed to advance in every direction. . . . The shot & shell tore thru' the air, and the bullets whistled around our ears in a most astonishing way, but the feeling of personal fear seemed to be almost swallowed up by one of anxiety for the results of the battle. My men behaved splendidly & by their coolness and courage set a good example to some less inclined to be steady." It was due to the coolness and courage of Gibbon and his like that the troops kept to their work.

Pope's orders were now to fall back on all fronts, to re-form on Centreville. In the smoky dusk not everyone got the word. Lines of command and communication became tangled. One of Sigel's batteries took Abner Doubleday's brigade for the enemy and shelled it vigorously. Sam Heintzelman, trying to collect his Third Corps, narrowly escaped being hit on the firing line. "The troops did not fight well," he noted in his diary. "It was evident neither officers or men had any confidence in Pope, nor much in McDowell. . . ." The best of the generals on the firing line — Reynolds, Meade, Kearny, Hooker, Reno, Stevens, Gibbon — managed to break clear of the enemy and withdraw in decent order.

McDowell assigned John Gibbon's Black Hat Brigade to the rear guard. Gibbon was posted on the Warrenton Pike, waiting for the rest of the army to pass, when Phil Kearny rode up to him. "He was a soldierly looking figure as he sat, straight as an arrow, on his horse, his empty sleeve pinned to his breast," Gibbon wrote in his memoir. Kearny cautioned him to wait for his command, on the right, and for Reno, on the left. "He is keeping up the fight and I am doing all I can to help."

In what Gibbon termed a very bitter tone, Kearny said, "I suppose you appreciate the condition of affairs here, sir?" At Gibbon's inquiring look, Kearny repeated, "I suppose you appreciate the condition of affairs? It's another Bull Run, sir, it's another Bull Run!"

"Oh! I hope not quite as bad as that, General," Gibbon said.

"Perhaps not. Reno is keeping up the fight. He is not stampeded. I am not stampeded, you are not stampeded. That is about all, sir, my God that's about all!"[69]

One of Jesse Reno's Ninth Corps officers, Captain Charles F. Walcott, 21st Massachusetts, fresh from the stalwart defense of Henry Hill, had a vivid memory of that night retreat to Centreville. The first troops they met were from Franklin's Sixth Corps, just arrived from Annandale, and he wrote, "Our hearts leaped with joy as we approached the long-hoped-for reënforcements from our Army of the Potomac. But to them we were only a part of Pope's beaten army, and as they lined the road they greeted us with mocking laughter, taunts, and jeers on the advantages of the new route to Richmond; while many of them, in plain English, expressed their joy at the downfall of the braggart rival of the great soldier of the Peninsula." Another witness, Carl Schurz, heard Franklin's generals express "their pleasure at Pope's discomfiture without the slightest concealment. . . ."

The men and officers of the Army of Virginia, along with their poorly grafted detachments from the Army of the Potomac, were tired and footsore and hungry, but rather than being demoralized like their counterparts at First Bull Run, they were angry and disillusioned. General Meade summed up these feelings in a home letter: "In a few words we have been as usual *out-maneuvered* & *out-numbered* and tho not actually *defeated* yet compelled to fall back on Washington for its defense & our own safety." This was an army craving leadership.

From Centreville that evening Pope reported to Washington. "We have had a terrific battle again to-day," he began, and described the enemy's "massing very heavy forces on our left forced back that wing about half a mile." Considering the men and animals were two days without food "and the enemy greatly outnumbering us, I thought it best to draw back to this place at dark. . . . The troops are in good heart, and marched off the field without the least hurry or confusion." He believed the enemy crippled, and he closed, "Be easy; everything will go well."

Come Sunday morning, August 31, however, and John Pope offered General-in-Chief Halleck a darker, chilling vision. While he pledged to give "as desperate a fight as I can force our men to stand up to," he issued a warning: "I should like to know whether you feel secure about Washington should this army be destroyed. I shall fight it as long as a man will stand up to the work. You must judge what is to be done, having in view the safety of the capital."[70]

9. *"Little Mac Is Back!"*

THESE LAST DEADLY DAYS of August 1862 ignited a firestorm of anger and exasperation in Washington. Lieutenant Charles Francis Adams, Jr., 1st Massachusetts Cavalry, caught the temper of the times in a letter to his father, minister to the Court of St. James's in London: "Our rulers seem to me to be crazy. The air of this city seems thick with treachery; our army seems in danger of utter demoralization. . . . Everything is ripe for a terrible panic, the end of which I cannot see or even imagine." Lieutenant Adams, grandson and great-grandson of presidents, was in the capital seeking a posting on Pope's staff, but he soon thought better of it. He told his father, "Do you know that in the opinion of our leading military men Washington is in more danger than it ever yet has been? . . . Do you know that Pope is a humbug and known to be so by those who put him in his present place? Do you know that today he is so completely outgeneraled as to be cut off from Washington?"

On August 29, as the city listened nervously to the distant rumble of gunfire from Bull Run, General-in-Chief Halleck was braced by Secretaries Stanton and Chase, angrily demanding an accounting of what Chase in his journal termed McClellan's "disobedience of orders & subsequent delay of support of Army of Va." Lincoln shared their anger. Indeed, as correspondent Adams Hill reported, "The President was never so wrathful as last night against George." The presidential wrath was directed at McClellan's dispatch proposing "to leave Pope to get out of his scrape" as best he might. John Hay recorded Lincoln's response: "It really seemed to him that McC wanted Pope defeated. . . . The President seemed to think him a little crazy."[1]

On August 30, on receiving Halleck's accounting of McClellan's response to the order to evacuate the Peninsula ("not obeyed with the promptness I expected and the national safety . . . required") and his holding back of Franklin's corps ("should have acted more promptly"), Stanton and Chase resolved to see McClellan relieved of command. They drew up a "remonstrance" to that effect, expecting enough cabinet support to present it to Lincoln as an ultimatum. Either the government or McClellan must go down, they said. That Saturday, as the two secretaries buttonholed their colleagues for signatures on their petition, the rumble of the guns marked a second day of fighting at the Second Bull Run battle.

There was acute distress in the capital. John Sedgwick, on arriving with Sumner's corps, found everything "in the utmost consternation, as much so as after Bull Run. Washington people seem to lose their senses at the most unfounded rumours, but there may be some cause for it now." McClellan told Ellen he was "blue & disgusted. . . . They have taken *all* my troops from me. . . . I have been listening to the distant sound of a great battle in the distance — my men engaged in it & I away! I never felt worse in my life."

Lincoln and Hay went to the War Department for the latest from the front, where Stanton met them and (as Hay put it) "carried us off to dinner." Preparing the ground for his remonstrance, Stanton was severe on McClellan. He said "nothing but foul play could lose us this battle & that it rested with McC. and his friends." Pope's dispatch of that morning claimed the Rebels were in retreat after the fighting on the 29th, and Hay entered in his diary, "Every thing seemed to be going well and hilarious on Saturday & we went to bed expecting glad tidings at sunrise."

A wet, gloomy Sunday brought ill tidings. "Well John we are whipped again, I am afraid," Lincoln told his secretary. "The enemy reinforced on Pope and drove back his left wing and he has retired to Centreville where he says he will be able to hold his men. I don't like that expression. I don't like to hear him admit that his men need holding." He was, Hay noted, "in a singularly defiant tone of mind."[2]

At Centreville that Sunday morning, August 31, Pope called in his generals to decide what to do. When the Sixth Corps finally reached the battle zone on Saturday, William Franklin encountered "an indiscriminate mass of men, horses, guns, and wagons, all going pell-mell to the rear." Today the troops were in better order, formed up in the old Confederate works. But their mood was surly. Sam Heintzelman entered in his diary, "Neither officers or men have the slightest confidence in Pope. They abuse McDowell also." He judged if "we are attacked under Pope we fear another defeat."

Pope's council — Heintzelman, Porter, Reynolds, Franklin, and newly arrived Sumner (elusive McDowell was absent) — all agreed that the army dare not remain at Centreville. They must pull back. Then Pope was handed a dispatch from Halleck, in reply to Pope's of the previous evening saying that after a "terrific battle" the army was falling back on Centreville.

"Don't yield another inch if you can avoid it," Halleck urged. The generals protested, said Porter: "The decision was foolish if not criminal. Each felt that the Government was not truly informed of the condition of affairs — perhaps deceived."

The government was indeed deceived about the dimensions of the defeat — Pope's warning that morning to secure Washington "should this army be destroyed" had not yet reached Halleck — and Fitz John Porter acted to set matters right. His dispatch detailing the army's plight went not to the general-in-chief but to General McClellan. Porter divined who could truly make a difference for this army, and he was not alone. "McClellan would return confidence to officers & men & he would be received with enthusiasm by the whole army," Heintzelman told his diary. Cavalryman George Bayard wrote his father, "We were badly beaten & lost a good deal. I hope to God this will give us McClellan."

Porter told McClellan, "The men are without heart — but will fight when cornered," and without heart "when they know if wounded (as we cannot retain the field against present odds) they are to be left in the care of the enemy." The Rebels would not attack Centreville but try to turn it, he thought. As to that, Porter took particular note that "Lee is here — *Jackson is not now here.*"[3]

Sunday's revelations broke Henry Halleck's spirit. His efforts to rush Franklin's and Sumner's corps to the battlefield had come to nothing. McClellan's recalcitrance and his hectoring left Old Brains in a state of near collapse ("Nerve and pluck all gone," Lincoln remarked). Halleck told his wife, "Few can conceive the terrible anxiety I have had within the last month." Pope's dispatch warning that the army might be destroyed was the final blow. That night Halleck sent McClellan an admission of defeat: "I beg you to assist me in this crisis with your ability and experience. I am utterly tired out." McClellan replied, "You will readily perceive how difficult an undefined position as I now hold must be. At what hour in the morning can I see you?" He closed with an apocalyptic vision: "To speak frankly, & the occasion requires it, there appears to be a total absence of brains & I fear the total destruction of the Army. . . . The question is the salvation of the country."

On reaching the War Department on September 1, McClellan found the president as well as Halleck waiting for him. He described the moment for Ellen: "I received a dispatch from Halleck begging me to help him out of the scrape & take command here — of course I could not refuse, so I came over this morning, mad as a March hare, & had a pretty plain talk with him & Abe." Taking "command here" meant Washington's fortifications.

Belisarius, the general who repeatedly served the emperor Justinian in the days of Rome, is here the model for McClellan, sitting by the wayside "waiting for Justice from the People. Shall I have it?"

THE MODERN BELISARIUS.

He was reluctant, "for things are far gone." He appraised his soldier's duty: "If when the whole army returns here (if it ever does) I am not placed in command of all I will either insist upon a long leave of absence or resign."[4]

That morning at Centreville, John Pope unleashed his pent-up fury and frustration in a dispatch to Halleck. It was his duty "to call your attention to the unsoldierly and dangerous conduct of many brigade and some division commanders of the forces sent here from the Peninsula. Every word and act and intention is discouraging, and calculated to break down the spirits of the men and produce disaster." He detailed the misconduct of one "commander of a corps" (Fitz John Porter) who twice failed to obey marching orders and "worse still, fell back to Manassas without a fight, and in plain hearing . . . of a furious battle, which raged all day." A brigade commander (Charles Griffin) strayed from the battlefield "and made no attempt to join." But the éminence grise behind it all was General McClellan: "You have hardly an idea of the demoralization among officers of high rank in the Potomac Army, arising . . . from personal feeling in relation to changes of commander-in-chief." He urged Halleck to order the army back to Washington "to reorganize and rearrange it. You may avoid great disaster by doing so."

These were the gravest of charges. Halleck took Pope's dispatch to Lincoln, who immediately recalled McClellan. By McClellan's telling, Lincoln said he had reason to believe the Army of the Potomac was not "cheerfully co-operating with and supporting General Pope." He needed McClellan to correct this. The president must be misinformed, said McClellan; his lieutenants, whatever they thought of Pope, would obey his orders and do their duty. Still, the president wanted him to telegraph Fitz John Porter "and try to do away with any feeling that might exist." McClellan said that he cheerfully agreed to do so, and he wrote Porter, "I ask of you for my sake that of the country & of the old Army of the Potomac that you and all my friends will lend the fullest & most cordial cooperation to Genl Pope . . . that for their country's sake they will extend to Genl Pope the same support they ever have to me."

This account of McClellan's, written two years later, makes Lincoln the supplicant: "He thanked me very warmly, assured me that he could never forget my action in the matter, &c. . . ." That cannot have been the tenor of the meeting. John Hay described Lincoln on this day of grim news as defiant morning, noon, and night: "Mr. Hay, we must whip these people now. Pope must fight them, if they are too strong for him he can gradually retire to these fortifications. If this be not so, if we are really whipped and to be whipped we may as well stop fighting." McClellan easily deduced these accusations against his lieutenants came from Pope, and by responding he lent them credence. Surely Lincoln ordered, not asked, him to send this dispatch; surely it was not done cheerfully.[5]

On September 1 Stanton and Chase readied their challenge to Lincoln. When they showed their remonstrance to Attorney General Bates, he told them it was a mistake to catalog McClellan's failings in such a petition — simply declare their lack of confidence in him as army commander. They agreed, and Bates reframed the remonstrance: "The undersigned . . . do but perform a painful duty in declaring to you our deliberate opinion that, at this time, it is not safe to trust to Major General McClellan the command of any of the armies of the United States." Stanton, Chase, Bates, and Interior Secretary Caleb Smith signed. Gideon Welles refused, saying the procedure was disrespectful to the president, but he agreed McClellan should go and would say so if Lincoln asked his view. Secretary of State Seward was out of town and Postmaster General Blair, a McClellan supporter, was not approached. Thus four of the six cabinet members present

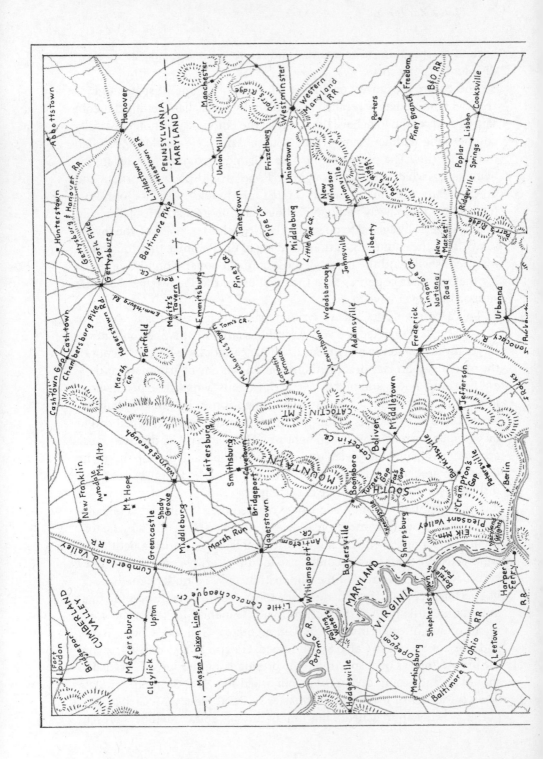

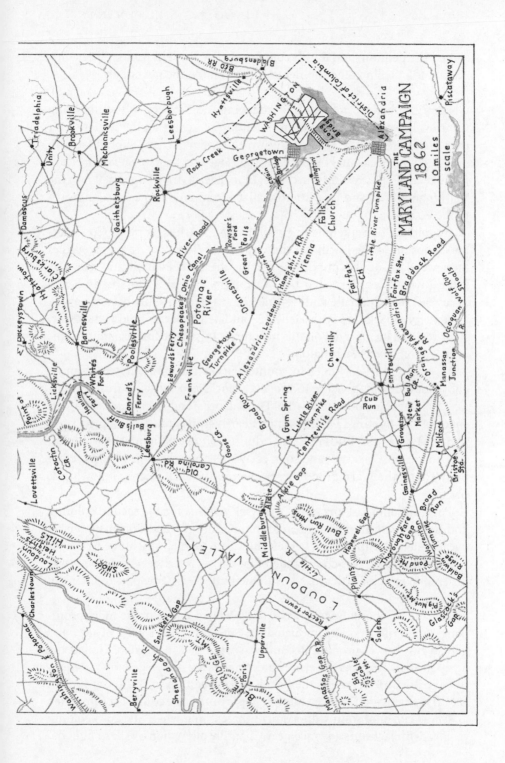

THE
MARYLAND CAMPAIGN
1862

scale
10 miles

signed the petition, and a fifth concurred. They would present their ultimatum to Lincoln at the cabinet meeting at noon the next day.[6]

General Lee had no intention of attacking the Yankees in the imposing
Centreville works. But he had no intention of giving up the initiative either. He elected to use Jackson to turn the enemy's right. Should Jackson
be successful, Lee would follow up with Longstreet's corps. Should Jackson
fail to reach Pope's rear, his threat ought to at least drive Pope back into the
Washington lines and free Lee to realize his ambition to campaign north
of the Potomac.

By midday of September 1 sightings had reached Pope of Confeder-
ate troops off to the north, on the Little River Turnpike. It appeared that
Stonewall Jackson was once more seeking the Yankees' flank and rear. The
Little River Pike intersected the Warrenton Pike at a crossroads, seven
miles east of Centreville and two miles short of the supply base at Fairfax
Court House. Saddled with Halleck's outdated order to hold Centreville,
Pope realized he must act on this new threat or see the final calamity — his
army cut off from Washington.

He organized two forces to counter Jackson. For the first column he
chose Joe Hooker's division to take up a blocking position in front of Fairfax. Heintzelman objected — the Third Corps had done more than its
share of the fighting; Hooker's and Kearny's divisions "are ruined from
their heavy losses." But Pope had admired Hooker's fight at Bristoe Station and against Jackson, and so in early afternoon the Third Corps set off
eastward on the Warrenton Pike, Hooker in the lead, Kearny following as
backup.

Pope did not trust any of his Army of Virginia for the second column,
and he was determined to keep Franklin, Sumner, and Porter under his
eye to defend Centreville. That left the Ninth Corps, which due to the illness of Jesse Reno was commanded that day by Isaac Stevens. Stevens was
ordered to march north cross-lots to the Little River Turnpike to intercept
Jackson.

Brigadier General Isaac I. Stevens was valued as one of the more promising Union officers. He graduated first in West Point's class of 1839 and
gained two brevet promotions and was wounded in Mexico. He left the
army in 1853, and was governor and congressional delegate of Washington Territory. He served in the Port Royal expedition in South Carolina in
1861. This campaign marked his first opportunity as a combat commander.

It was late afternoon with a storm threatening when Stevens's column
tangled with Jackson's advance near Chantilly plantation. A sharp fight de-

Philip Kearny's aggressive reconnoitering was the death of him at the Battle of Chantilly on September 1. Illustration by Rufus Zogbaum.

veloped and Stevens sent back for reinforcements. He sought to press the attack personally, rallying the 79th New York, the regiment he had taken to war. One of the New Yorkers described five color bearers being shot down. Then "Gen Stevens who was passing at the time the last man fell, picked up the colours & was in the act of handing them to some one when he was struck in the head with a rifle ball and instantly killed."[7]

Stevens's death and a maelstrom of lightning and thunder and rain stalled the battle for a time. The aide Stevens had sent for support found Kearny on the Warrenton Turnpike. Told of Stevens's call for help, Kearny turned his command with all speed toward the fighting. Here again, as at Williamsburg, as at Seven Pines, as at Glendale, he was called upon to save the day.

Kearny posted a brigade alongside the embattled Ninth Corps. As the rain stopped the battle heated up, and soon Stevens's troops began to fall back, out of ammunition or with guns fouled by damp powder. Kearny rode up to the 21st Massachusetts in a fury. At Williamsburg he had boasted he could make men follow him to hell, and now he seemed hell-bent on proving it. He cursed the men of the 21st and threatened to turn a battery on them if they did not advance. "Under his sneers, threats, and curses we again moved forward," wrote Captain Charles Walcott. When Kearny refused to believe there were Rebels in their front, Walcott showed him two prisoners they had taken, from the 49th Georgia. "God damn you and your prisoners!" Kearny shouted, and in an uncontrollable rage he spurred his horse ahead. As always (and as senselessly as always), Phil Kearny trusted no one but himself to seek out the enemy.

It was nearly dark now and in the edge of a woods he came on a line of men and called out in his stern officer's voice, "What troops are these?" The answer came back, "49th Georgia." In the Glendale fight back in June the same thing had happened and Kearny bluffed his way out — a Rebel captain mistook him for a Rebel general, he told his wife, "& off I went." These Georgians had sharper eyes. "That's a Yankee officer!" one of them shouted, and Kearny spurred away, crouching low in the saddle. There was a barrage of shots, and a bullet struck him at the base of his spine and coursed through his body and killed him instantly.

Stevens's death and the disappearance of Kearny chilled the Federals' battle ardor and after a final flurry of action in the darkness the two sides parted. The battle at Chantilly ended in a draw, the Federals losing some 700 men, the Confederates some 500.

Kearny had been well known in the old army, and A. P. Hill recognized the body when they brought it in and said with regret, "Poor Kearny! He deserved a better death than this." The next day General Lee sent the body through the lines with a note: "I send it forward under a flag of truce, thinking the possession of his remains may be a consolation to his family." There would be consolation for another family. The flag of the 79th New York that Isaac Stevens was holding when he was killed was presented to his widow.

Phil Kearny had lived for war. "I don't know whether he understood strategy," wrote diarist George Templeton Strong, "but he was a dashing, fearless sabreur who had fought in Mexico, Algeria, and Lombardy, and loved war from his youth up." Kearny proved limited as a commander by inflexible arrogance, and his prospects were stunted by irresponsible reck-lessness, yet the Union army never boasted a more spirited fighting gen-eral. "A stormy end to a stormy life," one of his men mourned. "I have to confess that in spite of pride the news quite unmanned me. The bravest man in the Army of the Potomac has fallen."[8]

John Pope spent September 1 in a slough of despond. He even sought out Fitz John Porter, hoping this confidant of McClellan's might have fresh insight on his dilemma. Porter told him the safety of the army was his responsibility, that on the battlefield he knew more than anyone in Washington. He urged Pope to consult with his generals; it was his right to demand their advice. And so in the midst of the late-afternoon storm Pope met with Porter, William Franklin, Baldy Smith, Henry Slocum, and John Newton. They all advised him to abandon Centreville and fall back on Fairfax Court House. Taking heart, Pope had the orders drawn up. Soon afterward Colonel John C. Kelton, from Halleck's office, joined them. Kelton said he was sent to investigate firsthand, and what he found did not at all match what was believed in Washington. He had come "with power to give orders according to circumstances," and Pope's orders just issued would have been his orders as well.

The bedraggled Union army marched that night for Fairfax Court House and Washington. It left behind its dead and several thousand wounded. It was not pursued. Kelton reported the roads to Washington clogged with stragglers by the thousands.[9]

On Tuesday morning, September 2, Lincoln took the decision he dreaded but now knew he must take. Colonel Kelton described the army's condition in far harsher terms than had Pope. At 7:00 a.m. Lincoln and Halleck walked the few blocks from the War Department to General McClellan's Washington quarters on H Street. "I was surprised this morning when at bkft by a visit from the Presdt & Halleck," McClellan wrote his wife, "— in which the former expressed the opinion that the troubles now impending could be overcome better by me than anyone else. Pope is ordered to fall back upon Washn & as he reenters everything is to come under my command again!" It was God's will, he told her. "A terrible & thankless task. . . . I only consent to take it for my country's sake & with the humble hope that God has called me to it. . . ."

Reinstating McClellan was Lincoln's most wrenching military-command decision of the war. "I must have McClellan to organize the army and bring it out of chaos," he told Gideon Welles (speaking "with much emphasis"), "but there has been a design — a purpose in breaking down Pope, without regard of consequences to the country. It is shocking to see and know this; but there is no remedy at present. McClellan has the army with him."

(Since he had not been relieved of command of the Army of the Potomac, McClellan's reinstatement simply gave him the Army of Virginia as well. But its real meaning was clear: It took the Potomac army out of Pope's hands and returned it to McClellan's.)

"Genl McClellan is now with me & cooperating heartily," Halleck told

The president and his cabinet (meeting on emancipation), engraved by A. H. Ritchie after Francis Carpenter. From left: Edwin M. Stanton, Salmon P. Chase, Lincoln, Gideon Welles, Caleb B. Smith, William H. Seward, Montgomery Blair, and Edward Bates.

his wife. McClellan wired Lincoln that the garrisons in the forts were alerted to receive the troops, commissaries were ready to feed them, cavalry was out to round up stragglers. "If Pope retires promptly & in good order all will yet go well."[10]

At noon that day, in cabinet, the president experienced his counselors' unified hostility to McClellan. Before Lincoln joined the others, their conversation revealed that now even Montgomery Blair objected to McClellan in command. With Seward absent, the four signers of the remonstrance, their unsigned ally Welles, and Blair constituted a cabinet united against the general. But when Stanton entered he announced, in a bitter tone, that McClellan was ordered by the president to command all the forces in defense of Washington. "When Stanton expected by a blow to knock him over, the President put him in power," Welles observed. "There was a more disturbed and desponding feeling than I have ever witnessed in council. . . ."

Lincoln was beset by objections, and Attorney General Bates's notes on the meeting indicate that the remonstrance was shown or read to him. Bates endorsed his copy, "Given to the President Sept. 2d 1862." This accounts for Lincoln's emotional response. By Welles's account, "The President was extremely distressed." In Bates's notes, "The Prest was in deep distress . . . he seemed wrung by the bitterest anguish — said he felt almost ready to hang himself . . . that he was so distressed, precisely because he knew we were earnestly sincere."

When Chase declared that giving McClellan the command "was equivalent to giving Washington to the rebels," the president defended his action. He said McClellan might have the "slows" and be "good for nothing for an onward movement," but he was skilled at organization and defense. These were Halleck's views as well, he said. Bates argued that if Halleck had any doubts about defending the capital "he ought to be instantly broke," that 50,000 men were sufficient to defend it against all the power of the enemy. Only "treachery in our leaders" could lose Washington. The cabinet meeting ended on that note, "leaving the matter as we found it," Chase complained. That evening a still-angry Attorney General Bates wrote a friend, "The thing I complain of is a criminal tardiness, a fatuous apathy, a captious, bickering rivalry, among our commanders who seem so taken up with their quick made dignity, that they overlook the lives of their people & the necessities of their country. They in grotesque egotism, have so much reputation to take care of, that they dare not risk it."[11]

McClellan was well started on taking over Pope's forces, but one all-important step remained — telling the troops, and showing them, who was now in command. At 4 o'clock that Tuesday afternoon he sent a note to Ellen that he was "just about starting out to pick up the Army of the Potomac." With his escort he rode to the city's outer works and the posting of General Jacob Cox. McClellan was in full uniform, with yellow sash and dress sword, and he cheerfully greeted Cox, "Well, General, I am in command again!"

A column of troops from McDowell's corps, headed by John Gibbon's Black Hat Brigade, came into view. Riding out front were Generals Pope and McDowell, and McClellan rode out to meet them. Pope had been told of the command change, and they briefly discussed the bivouacking of the troops, and then they parted. General Gibbon recognized McClellan, and to his wife the next day he wrote, "It did my heart good to hear my brigade cheer when I told them he was in command. They were perfectly wild with delight, hurling their caps in the air and showing the greatest enthusiasm right within hearing too of Genl. Pope. . . ." Jacob Cox wrote in his memoir that he cringed at this "unnecessary affront" to Pope, but Cox had not fought at Second Bull Run and could not conceive of the rage of officers and men. As Gibbon put it, Pope "has turned out a complete failure. I do not know what would have become of us had not McClellan been put in command."

The word was passed to the other returning columns, and well into the night the response was one explosion of celebration after another, whether Army of the Potomac or Army of Virginia troops. Everywhere the cry was "Little Mac is back!" Lieutenant Stephen Weld, Fifth Corps staff, wrote home, "When near Chain Bridge McClellan comes out to meet the weary discouraged soldiers. Such cheers I never heard before, and were never heard in Pope's army. Way off in the distance as he passed the different corps we could hear them cheer him. Everyone felt happy and jolly."

That evening, September 2, 1862, became legend among veterans of the Army of the Potomac. At a stroke, with his unerring skill for self-drama-tization, McClellan transformed the thousands of troops demoralized and embittered from their service under Pope. It was, in retrospect, the Young Napoleon's finest hour. George Meade caught the mood: "Everything tho' new is changed. McClellan's star is again in the ascendant, and Pope's has faded away."[12]

The issue now for the War Department and the White House was what to do with Generals Pope and McDowell. Obviously neither could con-tinue in command roles with this army. On the subject of Pope, Alpheus Williams was merciless: "More insolence, superciliousness, ignorance, and pretentiousness were never combined in one man. It can with truth be said of him that he had not a friend in his command from the smallest drum-mer boy to the highest general officer. All hated him. McDowell was his only companion and McDowell is disliked almost as much, and by his im-mediate command he is entirely distrusted."

Twice defeated on the same battlefield left Irvin McDowell without le-verage. Nor to his credit was his reputation as a martinet. On the retreat from Centreville he attempted to arrest a colonel for some infraction and was met by the leveled rifles of the whole regiment, forcing him to beat a hasty retreat. The papers printed the dying declaration of an officer on the recent battlefield who said he was victim "to McDowell's treachery." Mc-Dowell turned to his patron, Salmon Chase. At Lincoln's nod, Chase sug-gested a solution: request a court of inquiry to clear his name. Lincoln blandly announced he would accept McDowell's request . . . and relieved him of command. "I did not ask to be relieved—I only asked for a court," said McDowell. "I explained as well as I could," said Chase.

The court of inquiry investigated McDowell's conduct from First Bull Run to Second Bull Run and found him blameless. Any untoward actions were "not induced by any unworthy motive"; the dying officer's declara-tion was a "deplorable misapprehension"; the press was wayward, guilty of disseminating "absurd and unjustifiable rumors against general officers. . . ." Yet in the end a certain rough justice was done. Irvin McDowell spent the next eighteen months in Coventry, and ended the war in San Francisco in command of the Department of the Pacific.[13]

John Pope was furious at seeing McClellan in command of the joint armies. He drafted a preliminary report of the recent battle, and on September 4 read it to the president. Gideon Welles, who was present, termed it "not exactly a Bulletin — nor a Report, but a Manifesto — a narrative, tinged with wounded pride and a keen sense of injustice and wrong." Highly critical of the Potomac army, it charged Fitz John Porter with failing to obey Pope's attack order of August 29. Pope added Franklin (arrived too late to do any good) and Charles Griffin (absent from the battlefield) to his list of offenders. In apparent sympathy, Lincoln showed him Porter's August telegrams to Burnside that derided Pope's conduct of the campaign.

Two days earlier, at Fairfax Court House, Porter had confronted Pope with McClellan's telegram calling on Porter and his colleagues to support Pope with the same loyalty they had always shown him. Porter read the telegram as an insult to the Army of the Potomac, and demanded an explanation. Pope, thrown on the defensive, claimed he "knew no cause for the dispatch," that he had made no complaint "and had none to make." To regain his footing, Pope countered with the letter, shown him in Washington, that Porter wrote from Harrison's Landing, harshly critical of Pope's campaign plan and of Pope himself. This was Porter's July 17 letter to Joseph C. G. Kennedy, who thoughtlessly displayed it all over the capital. Porter's charges were unjust, said Pope, for he knew none of the circumstances controlling the campaign. It was a private letter, said Porter, and he regretted that Lincoln and Pope had seen it. Still, what he wrote had turned out to be mostly true; and this or any other concern of Pope's could be explained. Fitz John Porter was an imposing figure, with a well-advertised fighting record, and he could be intimidating. By his account, he and Pope ended their debate with Pope declaring he did not believe Porter "intended to wrong him," that he was "perfectly satisfied with Porter & his command. . . ."

Whatever John Pope found himself saying to Porter on September 2, by September 4 he was fully aggrieved. The Porter-Burnside telegrams "opened my eyes to many matters which I had before been loth to believe. . . ." Pope demanded an investigation. On September 5 Halleck ordered Fitz John Porter, William B. Franklin, and Charles Griffin relieved of duty pending a court of inquiry.[14]

Meantime, as momentous backdrop to these travails, word came that the Rebel army was on the march once more. Lincoln wrote, for Stanton's signature, an order to Halleck to "proceed with all possible dispatch, to organize an army for active operations." Halleck ignored this invitation to take the command; Old Brains was no more inclined to seize the reins now than he had been before Second Bull Run. He redirected the order to McClellan: "There is every probability that the enemy, baffled in his intended capture of Washington, will cross the Potomac, and make a raid into Maryland or Pennsylvania." McClellan must prepare a "movable army" to meet the enemy in the field — only to prepare, not to march. For the next command step, Mr. Lincoln determined to make a change.

Ambrose Burnside had spent the Second Bull Run campaign at Falmouth, shifting the Peninsula forces to Pope's army. Ordered to Washington, he took the night boat from Aquia Landing to reach the capital early on the morning of September 5. At Halleck's office he found Lincoln waiting for him. As Lincoln had told the cabinet, McClellan was indispensable for reorganizing the combined armies and securing the capital, but he had the "slows," was good for nothing in an onward movement. Further, Lincoln had surely been affected by the cabinet's rejection of seeing McClellan in command in any capacity. Consequently, for the second time, he offered Burnside command of the Army of the Potomac. Lincoln later described the setting to Orville Browning: With the Confederates crossing into Maryland, he told Burnside he "must take command of our army, march against the enemy and give him battle."

Burnside had rejected the offer of command when the army was ordered away from the Peninsula, and he rejected it now on the eve of a new campaign — and for the same reason. He said he was not competent to command an army of this size. The responsibility was too great; he was content commanding a corps under McClellan. He told the president that "I did not think there was any one who could do as much with the army as General McClellan could. . . ."

And so, at about 9:00 a.m., September 5, Lincoln and Halleck again walked from the War Department to McClellan's quarters on H Street and met with the general. Halleck testified to the simple proceeding. Lincoln said, "General, you will take command of the forces in the field." Soon after, McClellan wrote Ellen, with obvious emotion, "Again I have been called upon to save the country — the case is desperate, but with God's help I will try unselfishly to do my best & if he wills it accomplish the salvation of the nation."[15]

Lincoln took political cover. Gideon Welles quoted him saying that Halleck awarded field command to McClellan. "I could not have done it, said he, for I can never feel confident that he will do any thing." This was deliberate evasion. In these crisis days Halleck was quite without spine and could not have appointed McClellan on his own. He said he did not know Lincoln's decision beforehand that morning. For the president, George McClellan was as much a political issue as a military problem.[16]

The army machinery lurched into motion with a joint order to Heintzelman, Porter, Franklin — and Pope: Be ready to march with three days' rations. Pope snapped that he had no command. McClellan "has scattered it about in all directions." He demanded clarification. Was it true he was not only superseded but deprived of command entirely? As a matter of justice he wanted his preliminary report published. Halleck soothed him: McClellan had the command "and it is evident that you cannot serve under him willingly." Pope must be at hand to testify in the court of inquiry against Porter, Franklin, and Griffin. Pope's report could not be published now in the interests of unity in a time of crisis. Halleck promised to "never see any injustice done to you. . . ." His note was followed by a one-sentence order: "The Armies of the Potomac and Virginia being consolidated, you will report for orders to the Secretary of War."

John Pope did not go dutifully or quietly or with dignity. He set the tone with a plaint to Stanton that afternoon: "Is it that I am to be deprived of my command because of the treachery of McClellan and his tools?" His preliminary report was leaked to the *New York Times* and published on September 8, creating harsh commentary against the administration. Who leaked it was not determined, but Montgomery Blair had no doubts. General Pope "is the man," Blair told his cabinet colleagues. Pope's father, judge Nathaniel Pope, "was a flatterer, a deceiver, a liar and a trickster. All the Popes are so." Fitz John Porter thought Pope's intent was manifest: "To ruin Gen. McClellan and his friends; his friends, in order to ruin him."

Pope was sent off to head the Department of the Northwest, where the Sioux were rebelling in Minnesota. From there he launched a poison-pen campaign, writing the governor of Illinois, for example, "The Praetorian system is as fully developed and in active operation in Washington as it ever was in Ancient Rome. . . . Already this Potomac Army clique talk openly of Lincoln's weakness and the necessity of replacing him by some stronger man." At the center of this web was General McClellan — "The greatest criminal of all," Pope insisted to Halleck — but McClellan was beyond his reach. So Pope set about plotting against a next-best target, Fitz John Porter.[17]

. . .

McClellan and his personal staff. From left: Herbert von Hammerstein, Edward H.
Wright, Paul von Radowitz, William F. Biddle, Albert B. Colburn, Charles Russell
Lowell, McClellan, Edward M. Hudson, William S. Abert, Arthur M. McClellan.

"It makes my heart bleed to see the poor shattered remnants of my noble Army of the Potomac, poor fellows! and to see how they love me even
now," McClellan wrote Ellen. "I hear them calling out to me as I ride
among them — 'George — don't leave us again!'" His tours of the camps
generated an immense boost in morale among the fighting men. He was
concerned too for the morale of the generals. John Sedgwick, for example,
was resigned: "The enemy have outgeneraled us . . . I look upon a division
as certain; the only question is where the line is to run."

The high command was in shambles and the army was a patchwork.
Losses in the campaign came to 16,800, against some 9,500 for the Rebels. From McClellan's Peninsula command came the Second, Third, Fifth,
and Sixth Corps, in their various current conditions. There was the Ninth
Corps, up from the Carolinas. There were the three corps of the defunct
Army of Virginia, mismatched remnants from Frémont's (Sigel's), Banks's,
and McDowell's commands. There were stray divisions — the Kanawha
Division from western Virginia, and Darius Couch's division from the
old Fourth Corps at Yorktown. And 30,000 new men and new officers
— thirty-six regiments fresh from recruiting stations and training camps.
Half would be assigned to the capital's defenses, half to the field army.

The army was short three corps commanders — McDowell, relieved, and Porter and Franklin, suspended pending their court. Two division commanders, Kearny and Stevens, were dead, and two wounded, Schenck and Hatch. Among brigade commanders, three were dead, four wounded, and one suspended. For McClellan the critical first step was to retrieve his favorites, Porter and Franklin. He also set out to undo several hasty War Department assignments — Hooker heading the Fifth Corps in place of Porter, Reno heading McDowell's corps, and the Franklin-less Sixth Corps attached to Heintzelman's Third Corps.

McClellan went to Stanton with his needs, and to his surprise Stanton "cheerfully" agreed to whatever was necessary. With his remonstrance nulled, with Lincoln taking the decisions on his own, Stanton recognized he must tolerate McClellan at least so long as the emergency lasted. Mc-Clellan asked Lincoln to restore Porter and Franklin to their commands "until I have got through with the present crisis." Lincoln sent him to Halleck, who "must control these questions." With commander-in-chief and secretary of war signed off on the matter, Halleck followed along. Mc-Clellan put his favorites back with the Fifth and Sixth Corps, and Charles Griffin back with his brigade. In derailing the court of inquiry, McClellan turned back Pope's first challenge.[18]

With so many changes required in any case, McClellan undertook a major recasting of the Potomac army. On the Peninsula, to build two new corps for Porter and Franklin, he shrank the corps to two divisions each. This proved to be too little strength for tactical needs, too much slighting of commanders' initiative. He went to three-division corps. For a prospective war of maneuver north of the Potomac, he superimposed a three-wing structure on the army.

Forming the core of this new model army were the two corps — Sumner's Second and Franklin's Sixth — held out of the fighting by McClellan's intransigency. To Sumner's divisions under Richardson and Sedgwick was added a third division, thrown together under the pressure of the moment: one brigade of new recruits, under Dwight Morris; one of untried garrison troops, under Max Weber; and one made up of one new regiment and three old regiments from the Valley fighting, under Nathan Kimball. This new division was headed by William H. French, a regular who formerly led a brigade under Sumner.

In Franklin's Sixth Corps, Couch's stray Fourth Corps division would march alongside the divisions of Slocum and Baldy Smith. The Sixth Corps plus Couch, with Franklin commanding, comprised the left wing in McClellan's new scheme.

However much McClellan despised Irvin McDowell, he recognized his corps was the strongest in the Army of Virginia; what it needed was leadership. Jesse Reno had been assigned in McDowell's place, but McClellan argued for Joe Hooker, who "has more experience with troops." His wish was granted. Hooker moved up to a corps command — renumbered First Corps as it was in the Potomac army in the spring. McClellan had reservations about this corps, but predicted Hooker would "soon bring them out of the kinks, & will make them fight if anyone can." Its First Division had been Rufus King's, then John Hatch's until he was wounded, then King's again before his epilepsy forced him to give way to the recovered Hatch. James Ricketts led the Second Division. John Reynolds's Pennsylvania Reserves, attached to McDowell at Second Bull Run, joined First Corps as its Third Division. But Reynolds would not command in the coming campaign.

Reports of Rebels invading Maryland roused Pennsylvania's Governor Andrew G. Curtin. He mobilized the state's home guard and demanded a high-ranking native son to command it. That could only be, said he, John Reynolds of Lancaster. McClellan protested: Reynolds led one of the army's best divisions and "I cannot see how his services can be spared at the present time." Joe Hooker protested: "A scared Governor ought not to be permitted to destroy the usefulness of an entire division." Anyway, said Hooker, "the rebels have no more intention of going to Harrisburg than they have of going to heaven." But Andrew Curtin was a good Republican and a staunch supporter of the administration, and John Reynolds was soon on his way to Harrisburg.

Reynolds's replacement was George Meade. The promotion was long overdue so far as Meade was concerned. He had grumbled since his return from his Glendale wounding at the injustice of seeing one division after another go to his juniors, including some who had "never heard a ball whistle, in any war." The Pennsylvania Reserves were his, and he told his wife, "I am now ready to meet the enemy, for I feel I am in the position I am entitled to."[19]

Franz Sigel's corps of the Army of Virginia (and Sigel himself) had been held in low regard by Pope, and McClellan had his doubts as well. He designated it Eleventh Corps, Army of the Potomac, but posted it in the Washington defenses for the immediate future.

The third of the Army of Virginia's corps, Nathaniel Banks's, had guarded the army's trains, so it was chosen to campaign in Maryland and designated Twelfth Corps, Army of the Potomac. It had suffered under Stonewall Jackson's lash in the Valley, but division commanders Alpheus Williams and George Sears Greene were capable, and the corps had shown mettle at Cedar Mountain. The Twelfth Corps' problem was its commander. Banks was a political general quite lacking in capacity for field command. Still, he was a Republican of rank and influence, so he was kicked upstairs with a title in the capital's defenses. This left Alpheus Williams, general of volunteers, heading the corps. McClellan wanted a regular in the post and chose John Sedgwick, but Uncle John preferred staying with the division he knew, so the post was scheduled for Joseph K. F. Mansfield, commanding at Suffolk in the Department of Virginia. A white-bearded old regular (West Point 1822), Mansfield had been Winfield Scott's choice to command the Army of Northeastern Virginia, the posting that went instead to McDowell. While waiting for Mansfield, Williams counted five of his eleven regiments as raw recruits, and Greene broke in new commanders for all three of his brigades. The Twelfth, the smallest of the corps, was paired with Sumner's Second Corps, the army's largest corps, to make up the center wing (as it were), with Sumner in command.

While Burnside was at Falmouth, his Ninth Corps engaged two divisions at Second Bull Run, under Jesse Reno and Isaac Stevens. Orlando Willcox, captured at First Bull Run and exchanged in August, replaced the killed Stevens. John G. Parke's division rejoined from Falmouth. The Kanawha Division from western Virginia, Jacob Cox commanding, was added as the Ninth Corps' fourth division.

Jesse Reno was briefly awarded McDowell's corps in this flurry of command changes. When Hooker replaced him, McClellan felt obliged to find Reno an equivalent post. Reno was a West Point classmate of McClellan's and won two brevets in Mexico. He showed well in the North Carolina campaign, made major general, and was marked highly promising. McClellan gave him command of the Ninth Corps, then found a new posting for his old friend Burnside — leading the army's right wing. This comprised Reno's Ninth Corps and Hooker's First Corps, with John Parke as wing chief of staff. Reno's division went to Samuel D. Sturgis and Parke's to Isaac P. Rodman. It was a close-knit group: Burnside, Reno, Parke, Sturgis, and Willcox had all been at West Point at the same time.

McClellan assigned Porter and his Fifth Corps, the divisions of Morell and Sykes, the task of securing Washington while he organized the field army; he treated the Fifth Corps as the army's reserve. A third division was made up for Porter from new Pennsylvania troops — a pair of three-year regiments, and six nine-month militia regiments. The two-brigade division was assigned to engineer Andrew A. Humphreys, who had organized the defenses on Malvern Hill.

Since first organized, the Third Corps had steadily enhanced its battlefield reputation. Joe Hooker and Phil Kearny furnished the Third's cutting edge, and corps commander Sam Heintzelman made sure the troops were ready to fight, directed them to where they needed to be, and saw that reinforcements were at hand and on time. Kearny heaped scorn on Heintzelman (as he heaped scorn on all senior officers), but on the Peninsula no one performed a corps commander's duties better than Heintzelman ... while saving Kearny's skin more than once. McClellan relied on him no less than on his pets Porter and Franklin. But the September crisis left the Third Corps a shadow of what it had been, and separated Heintzelman from the Potomac army.

McClellan was not about to leave Washington to the care of political general Banks and Sigel's suspect corps. He assigned the Third Corps to the city's defenses and Heintzelman to command the critical sector south of the Potomac. Second Bull Run had battered the Third Corps. Its two divisions suffered 2,200 casualties, and with Kearny dead and Hooker transferred, it wanted leadership. The replacements were pale imitations — cavalryman George Stoneman to lead Kearny's division, and Dan Sickles, back finally from recruiting and politicking in New York, to lead Hooker's. These divisions were fated to be passed about from command to command, and by the time the corps was finally reconstituted, Heintzelman was heading the Department of Washington. He would serve out the war in administrative postings. Assigning the Third Corps to defend the capital allowed McClellan to call up Porter's Fifth Corps to the field army in Maryland.

(McClellan sought newly liberated Charles P. Stone to fill one of the command vacancies. Instead of simply appointing Stone, McClellan made obeisance to Secretary Stanton: "I have no doubt as to the loyalty and devotion of General Stone, but am unwilling to use his services unless I know that it meets the approval of the Government." The vindictive Stanton rejected Stone. He remained on the sidelines "while the troops I had commanded were fighting in field after field — always gaining the credit of fully performing their duty — I evidently had not instilled them with treason.")[20]

This shuffling of commanders and reorganizing of commands had its ragged moments, but it was accomplished in a remarkably short time. "McClellan is working like a beaver," said the president. From the first, George McClellan displayed a talent for military administration, and it never showed to better advantage than in these early days of September 1862. With Pope and McDowell vanquished, he could view his high command with satisfaction. Of the six corps commanders, he had personally appointed three (Porter, Franklin, Hooker), Burnside was a trusted friend, and Sumner could be handled if kept on a tight rein. Mansfield was an unknown, but he was a credentialed regular of more promise than Banks. Ten of the seventeen divisional commanders, and twenty-four of forty-nine brigade commanders, had served under McClellan in the Potomac army in one capacity or another.

The start on the Peninsula at reform in the artillery arm — corps artillery detachments — applied now only to Sumner's Second Corps, but two of the new corps, Ninth and Twelfth, had corps batteries. The real reform was the appointment of Henry Hunt as army chief of artillery. There were command changes in the cavalry. When George Stoneman was given Kearny's division, he was replaced as head of the new cavalry division by Alfred Pleasonton. Pleasonton had the undemanding task of leading the cavalry rear guard in the march down the Peninsula in August. His five small cavalry brigades were undermanned, underequipped, and poorly mounted, reflecting the lack of attention to the Potomac army's horse soldiers. McClellan appointed John Buford as chief of cavalry. This was primarily an administrative post — and now a demanding one.

For Alpheus Williams, who had earlier excoriated Pope and McDowell, a bright new day had dawned. "There will be a great battle or a great skedaddle on the part of the Rebels. I have great confidence that we shall smash them terribly if they stand, more confidence than I have ever had at any moment of the war." McClellan was confident as well. On September 7 he announced to Ellen that he was setting out to take command of the army in the field. "I have now the entire confidence of the Govt & the love of the army — my enemies are crushed, silent & disarmed — if I defeat the Rebels I shall be master of the situation."

On that Sunday evening, September 7, Gideon Welles was out for a stroll along Pennsylvania Avenue when McClellan and his entourage passed by. The general recognized the navy secretary and rode over to bid him farewell. Where was he headed, asked Welles, and McClellan replied that he was taking command of the forward movement.

"Well," said Welles, "*onward* is now the word — the country will expect you to go *forward*." That was exactly his intention, McClellan said. "Success to you, then, General with all my heart," said Welles, and general and staff rode off to war.[21]

General Lee had recognized from the first that the South's best hope against the superior resources of the North was a short war, and to accomplish that the best hope was to seize and hold the initiative. He could not breach Washington's defenses and he lacked the munitions to invest them. Withdrawing south or west to refit his army would give up the initiative freshly renewed at Second Bull Run. Maryland was a prospective land of milk and honey. It was also a prospective battleground. On September 4 Lee started his army across the Potomac.

To Jefferson Davis, on September 8, Lee revealed his aggressive intent: "The present posture of affairs, in my opinion, places it in the power of the Government . . . to propose with propriety to that of the United States the recognition of our independence." This derived from "our power to inflict injury upon our adversary. . . ." Lee spoke directly to the matter in a post-war interview. In the interviewer's notes, he "would have had all my troops reconcentrated on Md. side, stragglers up, men rested & I *intended then to attack McClellan,* hoping the best results from state of my troops & those of enemy." He designed to pull the Yankees from their Washington base and bring them to battle on ground of his choosing in western Maryland or southern Pennsylvania. Lee did not yet know that McClellan had re-placed Pope, but the change was of no great moment. He had beaten both generals and was confident of doing so again. In another postwar inter-view, Lee said of McClellan, "He was an able but timid commander."[22]

On September 8, from Rockville, Maryland, McClellan reported the Confederate advance had reached Frederick, but intelligence was "too in-definite to justify definite action. . . . As soon as I find out where to strike I will be after them without an hour's delay." He remained four days at Rockville, completing the army's reorganization. He wrote Ellen, "I have been obliged to do the best I could with the broken & discouraged frag-ments of two armies defeated by no fault of mine . . . under the circum-stances no one else *could* save the country, & I have not shrunk from the terrible task." He felt confident. "I expect to fight a great battle & to do my best at it . . . the men & officers have complete confidence in me & I pray to God that he will justify their trust."[23]

The campaign would be shaped by the particular terrain of western Maryland. A series of natural barriers run in parallel in a roughly north–south direction. East to west, the first is Parr's Ridge, which the Potomac army was approaching by slow marches. Between Parr's Ridge and Ca-toctin Mountain lies the Monocacy River and Frederick, where the Reb-els were concentrating. The next range is imposing South Mountain, and beyond that, Pleasant Valley and Elk Mountain. Farther to the west lies the broad Cumberland Valley of Maryland and southern Pennsylvania. It would not be easy to track the Rebels in this hidden landscape, and intel-ligence reports became McClellan's primary need.

Allan Pinkerton had no agents in Maryland and no capability for scouting. That left most intelligence gathering to the cavalry, and Alfred Pleasonton soon showed himself as inept as Pinkerton. One of his first dispatches had "Lee's corps" combining with Jackson north of the Potomac, "the design being an attack on Washington. This looks probable." At day's end he had Jackson's 60,000 men "going to Baltimore." Such disparate reports raised concerns.

Pleasonton would never gain a direct look at Lee's army, and so his information came from deserters and prisoners, and from civilians who witnessed the Rebels' movements and heard their talk. Extracting information from enemy soldiers required skilled interrogation, for as a Union official in Frederick put it, "Bragging is a favorite game with them, and they do it well." Civilians, with the best intentions, had no concept of troop counting and were easily taken in. Pleasonton, credulously and uncritically, passed all this on to headquarters as gospel.

Pleasonton's count of enemy numbers escalated steadily, and his pronouncements of enemy targets became more assertive. On September 8 "reliable information" put the count of Confederates who had crossed into Maryland at 100,000. "They are to march to *Frederick* thence to *Gettysburg* thence to *York* & thence to *Baltimore*. This can be depended upon up to 11 o'clock today." The next day the count rose to 110,000. "These are the numbers that are given by the rebel officers & men to citizens as they have passed through & which appear to be consistent." McClellan forwarded this latest figure and his latest caution: "I am pretty well prepared for anything except overwhelming numbers."[24]

On September 10 McClellan telegraphed Lincoln that the count of Confederate troops in Maryland ranged from 80,000 to 150,000. Pennsylvania's Governor Curtin forwarded the report of a clergyman in Frederick who counted the Rebels there as "not less than 120,000 men." That evening McClellan defined to Halleck the momentous state of affairs. All the evidence "goes to prove most conclusively that almost the entire Rebel army in Virginia, amounting to not less than 120,000 men, is in the vicinity of Frederick City." They were led by their best generals. "They are probably aware that their forces are numerically superior to ours by at least twenty-five per cent." He assumed his apocalyptic pose. Should stripping Washington of its defenders to reinforce the Potomac army result in the capital's capture by "the gigantic rebel army before us," it would not "bear comparison with the ruin and disasters which would follow a signal defeat of this Army." Once the enemy host was conquered, Washington could easily be recovered. Thus the stakes: Defeat the gigantic Rebel army and "the rebellion is crushed. . . . But if we should be so unfortunate as to meet with defeat, our country is at their mercy."

That the Confederates were 120,000 strong cannot have surprised General McClellan. By his reckoning, they had mobilized 200,000 in defending Richmond. Twelve days earlier they had pressed 120,000 right to the gates of Washington. (If God was once again calling McClellan to save the country, as McClellan believed, surely He would only bless the underdog.) Just then, Lee had about half the men McClellan credited him with; by the time the campaign approached its climax, Lee had one-third that number. This reality was beyond McClellan's imagining. Once again, as he had at Manassas back in the fall and on the Peninsula in the spring and summer and at Washington just days before, George McClellan confronted a phantom Rebel army of his own invention. To meet it he would muster 101,000 men in his own army.[25]

McClellan's alarming reports from Maryland came on the heels of equally alarming reports from the West. A Confederate army under Braxton Bragg had sidestepped Don Carlos Buell and ranged far into Kentucky. In company with Bragg was a second Rebel column under Edmund Kirby Smith. "The morning papers and an extra at mid-day turned us livid and blue," New Yorker George Templeton Strong entered in his diary on September 3. ". . . Stonewall Jackson (our national bugaboo) about to invade Maryland, 40,000 strong . . . Cincinnati in danger. A rebel army within forty miles of the Queen City of the West. Martial law proclaimed in her pork shops." General Halleck, displeased with newspaper critics, had imposed a press blackout, and into the news vacuum rushed speculation and rumor. The *New York Herald* announced the Rebels in Maryland to be "at least 150,000 strong." Philadelphians believed themselves directly in Jackson's sights, reported the *Ledger*: "No such excitement has been seen since the time when the news of the firing upon Fort Sumter was given to the public."

McClellan's enemies were not all "silent & disarmed" as he claimed. Michigan's Jacobin senator Zach Chandler, for one, was in a rage. "Are imbecility *and treason* to be retained and promoted to the end of the chapter." The people of the Northwest had hoped "that traitors in the Army would be punished . . . but the restoration of McLelland Porter & Franklin to command without trial has cast a hopeless gloom over our entire community." If the president has been "bullied by those traitor Generals, how long must it be before he will by them be set aside & a Military Dictator set up."

Chandler's concern was warranted. On the march into Maryland, Colonel Thomas M. Key of McClellan's staff unburdened himself to Nathaniel Paige of the *New-York Tribune*. By Paige's account, "He told me that a plan to countermarch to Washington and intimidate the President had been seriously discussed the night before by the members of McClellan's staff. . . ." Key spoke of "the shaky attitude of Fitz John Porter." These officers had only contempt for the president and wanted the slavery issue sidetracked so there might be a peace negotiated between the armies; they were fighting for a boundary line rather than for the Union. Key stepped in to quell the plot (just as Ambrose Burnside had quelled similar talk at Harrison's Landing). Key believed McClellan knew nothing of the affair. The same or a similar report reached Henry Wilson, chairman of the Senate Committee on Military Affairs. Wilson described for Gideon Welles a conspiracy "among certain Generals for a revolution and the establishment of a provisional government. Has obtained important information from one of McC's staff." No names were mentioned, and Welles wondered if this might be camp talk. Still, should McClellan be victorious in the pending campaign, that might just be revolutionary enough to "overthrow Stanton as well as Lee."[26]

Mr. Lincoln, monitoring the dispatches from Maryland, took note of McClellan's renewed litany of complaints, demands, and excuses. He determined to go himself to McClellan to stiffen his backbone. Halleck and Banks were horrified. Banks warned of roaming Rebel cavalry intersecting "the line of travel proposed by you." Halleck cautioned "against your going beyond the lines of Washington." Lincoln instead stayed close by the War Department telegraph office.[27]

Harper's Ferry triggered a dispute among McClellan, Halleck, and John E. Wool, commanding the Middle Department with headquarters in Baltimore. The 11,500-man garrison there (and the 2,500 men nearby at Martinsburg) guarded the lower Shenandoah and also the Chesapeake & Ohio Canal and the Baltimore & Ohio Railroad, Washington's links with the Midwest. Both posts reported to General Wool. McClellan urged Halleck to evacuate their garrisons and attach them to the Potomac army, for they were prey for capture. Halleck refused, leaving the postings to Wool's care.

Wool telegraphed Dixon S. Miles, in command at Harper's Ferry, "There must be no abandoning of a post, and shoot the first man who thinks of it, whether officer or soldier." Wool felt Colonel Miles required such a bracing order. Nearly cashiered for being drunk at First Bull Run, Miles had been passed off to this hitherto undemanding post. Only on September 12 did Halleck recognize that Wool at Baltimore could order but not act, and he placed Miles under McClellan's orders. His newest headache, said Mc-Clellan, "is to save the garrison at Harper's Ferry."[28]

Beginning on September 10, intelligence reports had the Rebels on the move from Frederick, but where they were bound was a mystery. Pennsylvania's Governor Curtin forwarded multiple sightings of the enemy — Stonewall Jackson at Hagerstown; Stonewall Jackson across the Pennsylvania line near Greencastle; Stonewall Jackson recrossing the Potomac upstream at Williamsport. Other sightings put Rebel forces at Boonsboro, west of South Mountain, and recrossing the Potomac east of Harper's Ferry. To Curtin it appeared certain the enemy was targeting Harrisburg and Philadelphia. Ambrose Burnside echoed general puzzlement: "If they are going into Pennsylvania they would hardly be moving on the Harper's Ferry road, and if they are going to recross, how could they be moving upon Gettysburg?" Halleck warned McClellan that Washington was the enemy's target. "The capture of this place will throw us back six months, if it should not destroy us. Beware of the evils I now point out to you." Pleasonton passed on a report from a "strong Union man" that Joe Johnston with 150,000 men was lurking just south of the Potomac, ready to fall on McClellan's rear. "Whether this be true or not, its consequences would if true be so tremendous that I must call the General's attention to it."[29]

"From all I can gather," McClellan wrote Ellen on September 12, "secesh is skedadelling & I don't think I can catch him unless he is really moving into Penna — in that case I shall catch him before he has made much headway towards the interior. I begin to think that he is making off to get out of the scrape by recrossing the river at Williamsport — in which case my only chance of bagging him will be to cross lower down & cut into his communications near Winchester. He evidently don't want to fight me — for some reason or other."

McClellan kept his own counsel concerning his plans (except when writing his wife). His confidant Fitz John Porter and the Fifth Corps only joined the field army piecemeal. George Sykes's regulars had marched with army headquarters, but Porter with George Morell's division only set out from Washington on September 12. Andrew Humphreys had a miserable time with the corps' third division, the two brigades of new Pennsylvania troops. The Austrian-made muskets of five of the regiments proved defective and were condemned. Only on the 14th did they start for the field. The entire duties of a staff kept him busy, Humphreys told his wife, "for I have had to be Adj. Genl., Qmstr., Comm'y, Ordnance officer &c."

McClellan advanced cautiously, and the marching was easy. "The country is beautiful," William Franklin told his wife, "and Baldy and I are in a

After five days of Confederate occupation, the citizens of Frederick, Maryland, flew their flags and greeted General McClellan enthusiastically. By Edwin Forbes.

tent in the yard of a large brick house the owner of which has not had the decency to ask us in or come near us." He concluded the man was "secesh to the bottom of his heart." John Gibbon too remarked on the Marylanders they passed, teasing his wife, "I am sorry to say that from my observation nearly all the pretty girls are hot rebels, whilst all the old dried up & ugly ones are for the Union!" But he was optimistic: "Thank God we have Pope no longer in command but a man in whom we all have confidence." Israel Richardson's hopes were high as well. "Now is the time to end the war if the North turns out," he told his wife. "The South is risking everything upon their army here." But by George Meade's account, old habits persisted in this army: "The idea of invasion of our territory does not seem to invite any great indignation among the men, who are just as bad plundering & destroying the property of their fellow Union citizens of this state as they were in Virginia."[30]

On the morning of September 13 McClellan and staff followed Jacob Cox's Kanawha Division into Frederick. After five days of Confederate occupation the townsfolk welcomed them eagerly. "When Genl. McClellan came thro' the ladies nearly ate him up, they kissed his clothes, threw their arms around his horse's neck and committed all sorts of extravagances," John Gibbon told his wife. McClellan told Ellen: "I was nearly overwhelmed & pulled to pieces. I enclose with this a little flag that some enthusiastic lady thrust into or upon Dan's bridle. As to flowers!! — they came in crowds!"

Before noon McClellan acknowledged the last of his admirers and was resuming the routine of command when his adjutant Seth Williams interrupted to hand him a packet from Twelfth Corps headquarters. With it was a note from Alpheus Williams, in temporary command of the Twelfth: "General, I enclose a Special Order of Gen. Lee commanding Rebel forces which was found on the field where my corps is encamped. It is a document of interest & is also no doubt genuine." McClellan scanned the enclosure and exclaimed (according to one of the civilians present), "Now I know what to do!"

This "Special Order of Gen. Lee" had been discovered that morning wrapped around three cigars in an envelope lying in a roadside field outside Frederick by Corporal Barton W. Mitchell, 27th Indiana. Corporal Mitchell, realizing the importance of his find, started it up the chain of command to Twelfth Corps headquarters — but not before rewarding himself with one of the cigars (his only reward, as it proved).

Special Orders No. 191, dated September 9, was Lee's plan for seizing the Harper's Ferry and Martinsburg garrisons, which if left in place would block his communications with Virginia. This copy, addressed to General D. H. Hill, was likely lost by a careless courier. S.O. 191 called for three well-separated columns, comprising more than half the Army of Northern Virginia, to maneuver behind the shield of South Mountain so as to scoop up Harper's Ferry and Martinsburg, afterward reassembling at Boonsboro or Hagerstown to resume the campaign.

The Lost Order (as it came to be known) was an intelligence coup unrivaled in all the war. That McClellan fully realized what Fortune had awarded him is evident in the exuberant telegram he sent at noon that day to the president: "I think Lee has made a gross mistake if the plans of the Rebels remain unchanged. . . . I have all the plans of the Rebels and will catch them in their own trap if my men are equal to the emergency." He closed with a pledge: "Will send you trophies."[31]

S.O. 191 resolved the contradictory intelligence of the past few days. The two Rebel columns recrossing the Potomac were not "making off to get out of the scrape" as McClellan thought, but closing in on Harper's Ferry from east and west. (The Martinsburg garrison retreated to Harper's Ferry on September 12.) The third column was to seize Maryland Heights, overlooking Harper's Ferry on the north. Stonewall Jackson led the operation, while James Longstreet's command and D. H. Hill's division marked time at Boonsboro, beyond South Mountain.

At noon on September 13, when he sent his revelatory telegram to Lincoln, McClellan had four army corps — Hooker's First, Sumner's Second, Reno's Ninth, and Williams's Twelfth, plus Sykes's Fifth Corps division, thirteen divisions in all — massed near Frederick, east of the Catoctin range. Reno had the advance that morning, to Middletown in the Catoctins. From Middletown it was six miles to Turner's Gap, where the National Road crossed South Mountain to Boonsboro — where (per the Lost Order) a sizable part of the Confederate army would be found. Franklin's Sixth Corps was six miles to the south at Buckeystown, and Couch's division six miles farther at Licksville. Franklin was a dozen miles from Crampton's Gap in South Mountain. By crossing at Crampton's, he could trap the Rebel column on Maryland Heights.

While he worked out his response to this extraordinary find, McClellan might have been expected to use the afternoon and evening of September 13 to advance forces to or toward the base of South Mountain, ready to storm Turner's and Crampton's Gaps at first light on the 14th. This was a necessary preliminary to whatever response he devised. It involved no risk. It would award him the advantage of surprise. Reports of cannonading at Harper's Ferry confirmed the garrison defending against a still-divided Rebel army.

But General McClellan spent the afternoon entertaining second thoughts. For all it revealed, S.O. 191 held secrets. The march routes it specified did not include places where Rebel troop sightings were already confirmed, at Williamsport on the Potomac and at Hagerstown near the Pennsylvania border. The Rebels must therefore have changed their plans. As with anything that disturbed his initial train of thought, McClellan felt compelled to stop and reconsider. Believing himself (as always) the underdog, caution was his watchword. (S.O. 191 had indeed been modified since its writing. Jackson made a wider swing westward to cross the Potomac at Williamsport, and Lee with Longstreet's two divisions moved on to Hagerstown. That left only D. H. Hill's division and Jeb Stuart's cavalry to guard South Mountain.)

It was 3 p.m. before McClellan took his first step, and it was cautionary. He sent a copy of S.O. 191 to cavalryman Pleasonton with instructions "to ascertain whether this order of march has thus far been followed by the enemy." Pleasonton, with no real knowledge of the matter, replied glibly at 6:15, "As near as I can judge the order of march of the enemy that you sent me has been followed. . . ." McClellan meanwhile began drafting marching orders. They were for the next day, September 14. Eighteen hours passed before a single Federal soldier moved in response to the finding of the Lost Order.[32]

McClellan was at least clear as to purpose: "My general idea is to cut the enemy in two & beat him in detail," he explained to Franklin. While keeping the Lost Order to himself, that evening he offered John Gibbon a hint. "Here is a paper," he gestured, "with which if I cannot whip Bobby Lee, I will be willing to go home." It gave the movements of every division in Lee's army, he said. "Tomorrow we will pitch into his centre and if you people will only do two good, hard days' marching I will put Lee in a position he will find hard to get out of. Castiglione will be nothing to it." Castiglione was Napoleon's classic divide-and-conquer triumph over a scattered Austrian army in 1796.[33]

In a telegram to Halleck at 11:00 p.m. that September 13, to justify his caution, McClellan turned evasive in describing the Lost Order. It only reached him "this evening"; it only disclosed "some of the plans of the enemy." The eight Confederate generals named in the document were evidence of his claim of "120,000 men or more" opposing him. "I have the mass of their troops to contend with & they outnumber me when united." Despite sightings that day placing Longstreet at Hagerstown, McClellan hewed to S.O. 191 and anticipated a major battle at Boonsboro against about half the Rebel host. The outcome was in God's hands. He told Ellen, "I feel as reasonably confident of success as any one well can who trusts in a higher power & does not know what its decision will be."

He employed the army's wing formation to breach South Mountain. Burnside's right wing — Reno's Ninth Corps and Hooker's First — was directed at Turner's Gap. Reno, who advanced to Middletown on the 13th, halted there. Hooker was camped east of Frederick. Had McClellan utilized the afternoon and evening of the 13th to marching Hooker to catch up with Reno, the two corps would have set off in tandem for Turner's Gap on September 14. As it was, Hooker only reached South Mountain that afternoon.

Crampton's Gap was allotted to Franklin's left wing — his Sixth Corps and Couch's division. Franklin was given a busy schedule for September 14, but he too was not awarded a head start on the 13th. He was to seize Crampton's Gap, march south in Pleasant Valley to relieve Harper's Ferry, then countermarch north to reinforce the main army as needed at Boons-

A lithographed view of the Union victory at Fox's Gap on South Mountain on September 14. Wounded future president Rutherford Hayes (23rd Ohio) is at left.

boro. Couch was ordered to join Franklin, but Franklin was not to wait for him.

McClellan did not make his lieutenants privy to the Lost Order, nor did he reveal an overall operational scheme, nor did he impose a timetable. He spent the 14th, a Sunday, at Frederick and Middletown, leaving most matters at the front to wing commanders Burnside and Franklin. Like John Pope, who had expected Stonewall Jackson to wait obligingly at Manassas for the Yankees to trap him, McClellan did not anticipate the Rebels blocking his path to a Castiglione by a defense of South Mountain. Already he had misspent eighteen hours of his unique opportunity. September 14 would add critical hours to the deficit.

Late on the 13th, at Hagerstown, Lee learned from Jeb Stuart that the Yankees were up to something. The Frederick civilian who that morning heard McClellan exclaim, "Now I know what to do!" on reading Corporal Mitchell's find, was a Stuart informant. His report and his sighting of the Federals' advance to Middletown already underway induced Stuart to send his warning to Lee. Lee decided to return with Longstreet to Boonsboro to secure South Mountain while waiting for Jackson to finish matters at Harper's Ferry. It appeared (Lee told Jefferson Davis) that "the enemy was advancing more rapidly than was convenient. . . ." But like McClellan, Lee concluded that September 14 was soon enough to act on the new intelligence.[34]

Pleasonton had pushed the Rebel cavalry screen back from the Catoctins on the 13th, and anticipated doing the same at South Mountain on the 14th. To lend weight to the push he called for infantry. Burnside and Reno sent him Cox's Kanawha Division. The narrow defile where the National Road crossed Turner's Gap looked defensible, so it was decided to flank it. With Eliakim P. Scammon's brigade, Cox advanced up the mountainside toward Fox's Gap, a mile or so south of Turner's. The idea was that so soon as Hooker arrived with the First Corps, he would find Turner's Gap in Reno's hands and follow the Ninth Corps across the mountain. That should pin the Rebels at Boonsboro. In support would then come Sumner's wing — Second and Twelfth Corps — plus Sykes's division.

Jacob Cox was a political general, a lawyer and Ohio state legislator who had quickly adapted to the military life fighting in McClellan's western Virginia campaign in 1861. His Kanawha Division, two brigades of Ohio troops, was called to Washington to man the defenses during the Second Bull Run fighting. Then for the first (and only) time, it was attached to the Army of the Potomac.

As Colonel Scammon's advance approached the crest at Fox's Gap it ran into sharp fire from a Confederate battle line behind a stone wall. This was clearly more than a delaying action by cavalry. Cox reported to Reno that the enemy was in some force on the mountaintop, brought up his second brigade under George Crook, and by 9:00 a.m. there was a full-scale battle for Fox's Gap.

Early that Sunday morning, alerted by General Lee, D. H. Hill rode up to Turner's Gap from Boonsboro to see what the Yankees were about. He was startled to find the vanguard of the Ninth Corps advancing through the valley below, which he recalled as "a grand and glorious spectacle." Hill had five small brigades to defend Turner's Gap, Fox's Gap to the south, and very likely, he decided, his northern flank as well. Until Longstreet arrived from Hagerstown, he would have to fight alone.

Cox's two brigades pressed their advantage in numbers to threaten front and flank of the Fox's Gap defenders. Finally the Yankees stormed the stone wall. "Give 'em hell! Give the sons of bitches hell!" shouted Lieutenant Colonel Rutherford B. Hayes, 23rd Ohio. Hayes went down with a wound in his left arm, but the Rebel line broke and the survivors scattered into the woodland leading to Turner's Gap. (The 23rd Ohio, remarkably, carried a second future president on its rolls, supply sergeant William McKinley.) The Kanawhas had had a hard climb up the mountainside and a hard fight, and at midday Cox determined to wait for support. That support was some time coming, however. Three and a half hours passed in comparative quiet atop South Mountain.[35]

The rest of the Ninth Corps had moved out from Middletown after Cox, Orlando Willcox's division in the lead, the divisions of Samuel Sturgis and Isaac Rodman following. Willcox sent to Cox for directions, and Cox replied that Pleasonton was the man to see. The message was garbled, and Willcox understood he should report to Pleasonton for orders. The cavalryman, unaware of Cox's call for reinforcement, proposed a strike at Turner's Gap from the other flank — completing a textbook double envelopment. Willcox set off on a road that curved up the mountainside to reach Turner's from the north. Burnside caught the mistake, caught Willcox, and countermarched him to support Cox, but it was midafternoon before the fight at Fox's Gap resumed. By then D. H. Hill welcomed the first of Longstreet's troops.

When his division reached the front, Willcox noted the enemy "hidden on the ridge among rocks and trees above us," a contrast to his last fight, in the open on Henry Hill at Bull Run in 1861. Fighting off counterattacks,

Jesse Reno, Ninth Corps commander,
dead of skirmish fire at Fox's Gap.

the Yankees secured Fox's Gap. Sturgis's and Rodman's divisions relieved the thinned and tired ranks of the advance. Cox and Willcox suffered over 700 casualties, evenly divided between them.

Jesse Reno had now committed his entire Ninth Corps to the Fox's Gap operation, and he determined to lead a final push to Turner's Gap. "I must see to this matter in person," he said. It was dusk when he reached the front. Skirmishers stirred up a spurt of counterfire from the woods and a bullet struck Reno squarely in the chest. As he was borne to the rear he saw Sturgis and called out, "Hallo, Sam, I'm dead!" Sturgis replied, "Oh, no, General, not so bad as that, I hope." But Reno knew. "Yes, yes, I'm dead —good by!" and in a few minutes he died. "Poor Reno was shot right through the body and lived only a short time," John Gibbon told his wife. "It is said the bullet went directly thro' his wife's likeness which he had hung around his neck."

In just fourteen days the Army of the Potomac had lost three major generals. Like Phil Kearny and Isaac Stevens, Jesse Reno was a gifted leader of much promise who got too close to the firing line. General Alpheus Williams almost wept when he heard the report of Reno's death. "Of all the major generals," he wrote his family, "he was my *beau* ideal of a soldier."[36]

This Sunday's fight for Turner's Gap was Burnside's to direct as right wing commander, but when McClellan reached the scene in late afternoon he put his own stamp upon it. On a knoll by the National Road, in the spirit of Antoine Gros's depiction of Bonaparte at Eylau, the Young Napoleon sat his big black warhorse Dan Webster and with arm extended pointed his passing troops into the flash and crash and smoke of battle on the mountainside ahead. The men "cheered and cheered again, until they became so hoarse they could cheer no longer," wrote a Massachusetts soldier. ". . . It was like a great scene in a play, with the roar of the guns as an accompaniment."

While approving Burnside's dispositions, McClellan issued battle orders independently of him. When Hooker with the First Corps reached Middletown about 1:00 p.m. he found orders not from Burnside but from McClellan. Reno had urged a diversionary attack mounted against Turner's Gap from the north, and "General McClellan desires you to comply with this request . . . and taking charge of it yourself." That nicely suited Joe Hooker. He had earned a corps command, only to find Burnside suddenly set over him, an outsider who had never before heard a shot fired in the Army of the Potomac. With orders from the army commander himself, Hooker acted on them . . . without reporting to the wing commander. Burnside complained he had to order Hooker "four separate times to move his command into action, and that I had to myself order his leading division (Meade's) to start before he would go." Collaboration was lacking, and the diversionary attack on Turner's Gap that Jesse Reno wanted was not delivered as rapidly as it might have been.[37]

The climb up the mountainside north of Turner's Gap was as testing as the climb to the south at Fox's Gap — difficult enough, said Hooker, "even in advance of a foe in front." George Meade's division on the right and John Hatch's on the left delivered the heavy blows. This was Meade's first action since his promotion to division command, and it roused him to show that he deserved the place. He led his Pennsylvania Reserves with particular aggression this day.

One of Meade's brigade commanders, Truman Seymour, also had something to prove. At Glendale Seymour had been routed and his leadership questioned. Today, on the offensive, he smashed in the Rebel flank with great effect. "Colonel," he shouted, "put your regiment into that corn-field and hurt somebody!" The second of Meade's brigades, under Thomas F. Gallagher, kept up with the pace, but Gallagher himself went down with a wound severe enough to force him out of the service. The third of Meade's brigades, Albert L. Magilton commanding, finished off a notable sweep that evening by the Reserves — a tonic after their unhappy service under Pope. Colonel A. J. Warner, 10th Pennsylvania, noticed his men hanging back, faltering on the attack. "This was the effect of the defeat at Bull Run," he decided. "I did all in my power to push them rapidly forward. . . . In a few minutes confidence took the place of hesitation and all pressed wildly forward driving the enemy."

On the left, Hatch's division advanced in successive brigade lines under Marsena Patrick, Walter Phelps, Jr., and Abner Doubleday. The rough, steep terrain tested the troops almost as much as the Rebels did, and the brigades of Patrick and Phelps became entangled. In trying to straighten them out, Patrick found himself squarely between the skirmish lines. "My orderly gave me warning of 'Gray Coats,'" he entered in his diary, "& I plunged down the Mountain Side followed by a volley from the enemy which passed over my head." John Hatch was not so fortunate, suffering a leg wound serious enough to end his days of field command. But the First Corps seized all the ground north of Turner's, and only darkness kept it from the gap itself.[38]

Hatch's fourth brigade, John Gibbon's, had been pulled aside by Burnside for an advance on Turner's Gap directly up the National Road. The task given the Black Hat Brigade became something of a forlorn hope, a head-on assault against a brigade of well-posted Confederates. Gibbon's troops showed the same mettle in attack as they displayed on defense at Groveton on the Second Bull Run field. Rufus Dawes saw Gibbon "always on the highest ground, where he could see the whole line, giving his orders in a voice so loud and clear as to be heard throughout. Always 'Forward the 7th, Forward the 19th'. . . ." From behind his stone wall a Rebel called out, "Oh you damned black hats, we gave you hell at Bull Run!" and the reply came back, "You thieving scoundrels, no McDowell after you now!" The Black Hats fought their way close to the summit but no farther. Gibbon wrote his wife the next day, "The fight with my brigade continued long after dark, and altho' nearly out of ammunition we held possession of the ground. . . . Every one, from Genl. McClellan down, speaks in the highest terms of my gallant brigade and I of course am proud." Turner's Gap cost the First Corps 923 casualties.

Given the lack of a thought-out, urgent directive from McClellan, Burnside's battle of September 14 was well enough managed by him and his lieutenants. Certainly the victory provided a much-needed boost in morale for the Potomac army. Still, the slow-developing assault on Fox's Gap and the eight-hour delay in the other half of the double envelopment permitted Lee to hold Turner's Gap until morning on the 15th, presenting him with a gift of time to unify his divided army. William Franklin's Sunday fight for Crampton's Gap presented Lee a second gift of time.[39]

Franklin had led a brigade at First Bull Run, but on the Peninsula he saw comparatively light duty while rising to corps command — at Eltham's Landing he had only to defend his bridgehead; during the Seven Days he helped manage the retreat; at Glendale he had only to endure Stonewall Jackson's artillery. At Crampton's Gap, McClellan furnished his old friend instructions detailed but lacking in urgency. Consequently Franklin was his usual deliberate self on September 14.

He set the Sixth Corps on the march at first light, waited (fruitlessly) for Couch's division, and arrived in front of Crampton's Gap about noon. "I think from appearances that we may have a heavy fight to get the pass," Franklin reported. Colonel Joseph J. Bartlett, commanding a brigade in Henry Slocum's division, was summoned to headquarters, where he found Franklin at ease with his old-army comrades — Slocum, Baldy Smith, W.T.H. Brooks, John Newton, Winfield Hancock — "resting upon the ground, in as comfortable positions as each one could assume, after lunch, smoking their cigars." Bartlett was asked where he would attack Crampton's Gap. On the right, he replied. "Well, gentlemen," said Franklin, "that settles it." The gathering, Bartlett was told, had been debating the best approach to the gap, and his vote was the deciding one. Therefore he had the honor of planning and executing the attack. Colonel Bartlett was indignant at the cavalier decision-making of his superiors, all professional soldiers, all more experienced than he.

With that decided, Franklin continued to delay, waiting for Couch's division to join. Darius Couch, however, was elusive. He failed to report, and he could not be found. He only arrived at 10 o'clock that night, having granted his division sixteen hours to march a dozen miles. No explanation was demanded, and none offered.

It was well after 4 o'clock when the brigades of Bartlett and Alfred T. A. Torbert moved against the Confederate battle line sheltered behind a stone wall at the base of the mountain. At 5:20 Franklin notified McClellan, "I have been severely engaged with the enemy for the last hour. . . . The force of the enemy is too great for us to take the pass tonight I am afraid." He promised to renew the attack the next morning.

The officers and men at the front were made of sterner stuff. The enemy's battle line proved paper-thin — some 800 infantry and dismounted cavalry — and collapsed when breached. With the Yankees at their heels, the Rebels retreated up the mountainside and across Crampton's Gap and down the other side. Darkness ended the pursuit. The generals gathered on the mountaintop and (wrote Bartlett) "congratulations were generously and feelingly exchanged all around." In recognition of his role Bartlett was made a brigadier general. He renamed his horse Crampton. In the absence of any urgency from the general commanding, this was victory enough. Casualties at 441 were not excessive. Franklin wrote his wife that Crampton's Gap was "one of the prettiest fights of the war & I arranged the details myself."

"It has been a glorious victory" was McClellan's verdict on the day. He told Halleck, perhaps the enemy would retreat, or perhaps "appear in increased force in the morning. I am hurrying up everything from the rear to be prepared for any eventuality." He boasted to Ellen, "We yesterday gained a glorious & complete victory; every moment adds to its importance."[40]

10. *Wednesday, Bloody Wednesday*

AT HARPER'S FERRY, late in the afternoon of September 13, Colonel Dixon Miles called in Captain Charles H. Russell, 1st Maryland Cavalry, and asked him if he could break out of the tightening Confederate ring and "try to reach somebody that had ever heard of the United States Army, or any general of the United States Army, ... and report the condition of Harper's Ferry." The Rebels held commanding ground on all sides, including towering Maryland Heights to the north, and Miles's message was blunt: He could perhaps hold out for forty-eight hours; then he must surrender.

After an adventurous night evading enemy pickets, Captain Russell found General McClellan at Frederick on the morning of the 14th and delivered Miles's message. Maryland Heights was known to be the key to defending Harper's Ferry, and Russell noticed the general was "very much surprised" at its loss. McClellan hurried a note to Franklin, reminding him of "the necessity of relieving Colonel Miles if possible." Franklin did not alter his deliberate pace against Crampton's Gap.

General-in-Chief Halleck, by insisting on holding Harper's Ferry in the first place, and General Wool, by ordering Miles to defend an indefensible position "at all hazards," doomed the garrison. Miles's blundering defense hastened the inevitable. Stonewall Jackson's gunners opened fire on the afternoon of the 14th and left the garrison nowhere to hide. That night Miles grudgingly allowed his 1,300-man cavalry contingent to attempt a breakout, but he stopped any infantry from following. "I am ordered by General Wool to hold this place," he said, "and God damn my soul to hell if I don't hold it against the enemy."

The troopers crossed the post's pontoon bridge over the Potomac and found an unguarded road on the Maryland shore and made good their escape (capturing a Rebel ordnance train in the bargain). But at first light on September 15 Jackson unleashed a thunderous, crushing bombardment against Miles's lines. At 8:00 a.m., with no sign of rescue, Miles raised the white flag. Just then a last Confederate shell grievously wounded Miles.

Harper's Ferry, photographed by James Gardner in 1865. The Chesapeake & Ohio Canal and the Baltimore & Ohio Railroad curve around the base of Maryland Heights. The rail bridge had been destroyed three times by the Confederates and once by the Federals.

He died the next day. A military commission investigating the Harper's Ferry surrender was unsparing: "Colonel Miles's incapacity, amounting to almost imbecility, led to the shameful surrender of this important post." The commission censured General Wool for assigning Miles to Harper's Ferry, and General McClellan for not effecting a rescue. General Halleck went unnoticed.[1]

The Confederates' windfall at Harper's Ferry included 12,700 prisoners, 73 artillery pieces, 13,000 small arms, 200 wagons, and abundant supplies. Its capture abruptly altered General Lee's thinking. The evening before, acknowledging "the day has gone against us" at South Mountain, he had ordered his army to return to Virginia. But then came word from Jackson that "through God's blessing" Harper's Ferry was in his grasp "and I look to Him for complete success to-morrow." Accepting Jackson's pious certitude, Lee reinstated his campaign. Rather than Boonsboro or Hagerstown per S.O. 191, the army's new assembly point would be the village of Sharpsburg, three miles north of the Potomac.[2]

That Monday, September 15, at his headquarters at Bolivar just east of Turner's Gap, McClellan waited to see if the Rebels would defend South Mountain. Pickets reported them gone from Turner's and Fox's Gaps. "The enemy disappeared during the night," he told Washington. "Our troops are now advancing in pursuit of them." Only then, at 8:00 a.m., did he draft orders for the pursuit.

So as to utilize both mountain crossings, McClellan juggled his high command. He set aside Burnside's right-wing configuration, explaining that Hooker's First Corps, advancing by way of Turner's Gap and "separated from you for the present by force of circumstances," would now take orders from army headquarters. Burnside, with just the Ninth Corps (under Jacob Cox following Jesse Reno's death), would advance by way of Fox's Gap. Joe Hooker was pleased to find Burnside's wing command suspended.

The troops of the First and Ninth Corps had been hard-used on September 14 — a long day of marching, of scrambling up mountainsides, of bloody fighting, of late or no rations, then a long night under arms. Both Hooker and Cox paused on the morning of the 15th to feed and refit their commands and to care for their wounded and bury their dead. Notified of this by Hooker, McClellan reached into Sumner's Second Corps and detached Israel Richardson's division to serve under Hooker and take the lead in the advance from Turner's Gap. The refreshed First Corps would follow, with Sumner's wing bringing up the rear. For McClellan, this kept Hooker, his best fighting general, leading the pursuit, and should checkrein the unpredictable Edwin Sumner.

Burnside left early to join the Ninth Corps at Fox's Gap, but his march orders — be prepared to cooperate with Franklin to the south or Hooker to the north — only reached Fox's at noon. Burnside approved Cox granting the battle-weary Ninth a morning respite (knowing McClellan had approved Hooker doing the same for the First Corps), but notice of this did not reach headquarters. Fitz John Porter, newly arrived from Washington, leading George Sykes's division, was assigned to follow the Ninth Corps through Fox's Gap. Reaching Fox's about noon, Porter found the Ninth taking its ease. He needed only to seek out Burnside or Cox to clarify orders, then move past with Sykes to lead the advance (just as Richardson had taken the advance from the First Corps). Instead, playing the tattletale, Porter halted and complained to McClellan that Burnside "was not moving three hours after the hour designated for him." Back came an order that Porter pass the Ninth Corps and take the lead . . . and to Burnside went a rebuke: "The general also desires to know the reason for your delay in starting this morning."

Porter's snide comment about Burnside delaying the advance reflected his frosty attitude toward the Rhode Islander. Porter had learned that his August dispatches to Burnside, with their disparagement of Pope, were now likely exhibits in the still-pending court of inquiry. That Burnside had warned Porter about his indiscreet remarks, that in any case Burnside was obliged to report without stint from the battlefront, was of little moment to a self-righteous Fitz John Porter.

Ambrose Burnside resented McClellan's rebuke. It implied the Ninth Corps' fighting on the 14th was not deserving of the morning stand-down, and it unjustly implied negligence in carrying out orders. Burnside was already out of sorts, suspecting that Hooker, with whom he squabbled the day before at Turner's Gap, had a hand in removing the First Corps from his control. Whatever the truth of that, Burnside's own position was clouded. Earlier he was relieved as head of the Ninth Corps by Jesse Reno (and now by Jacob Cox); now he was relieved of his wing command. He was, said Cox, "disturbed and grieved at the course things had taken."[3]

At Crampton's Gap on September 15, William Franklin displayed anew his ineptitude for independent command. McClellan's orders directed him to cross into Pleasant Valley and try to rescue the Harper's Ferry garrison. Franklin replied that a Rebel battle line, "a good deal longer than I at first supposed," blocked his way. He took alarm. "If Harper's Ferry has fallen — and the cessation of firing makes me fear that it has — it is my opinion that I should be strongly re-enforced." Bursts of cheering welled up from the Confederate lines. A Billy Yank climbed atop a stone wall and yelled, "What the hell are you fellows cheering for?" A Johnny Reb yelled back, "Because Harper's Ferry has gone up, God damn you!" "I thought that was it," said the disgusted Yank.

Franklin led the two Sixth Corps divisions, Slocum's and Baldy Smith's, plus Couch's late-arriving attached division. He next reported the enemy "outnumber me by two to one. It will, of course, not answer to pursue the enemy under these circumstances." Facing him were hardly 5,000 men, in plain sight; Franklin's advantage was better than three to one. His myopia persisted. He told his wife, "They have been in our front all day making a display of a very large force, too large for us to attack." At 3:00 p.m. he forwarded Smith's report that "the enemy is drawing off in the valley too fast for him." He awaited orders. In reply he was told that General McClellan "will be satisfied if you keep the enemy in your front without anything decisive." Franklin's left wing ended the day in Pleasant Valley about where it began, with nothing tried and nothing gained.[4]

By contrast, the Federals pouring through Turner's Gap that Monday morning had much to report. Joe Hooker put the Rebels rushing for the Potomac "in a perfect panic." Boonsboro citizens "tell me that Lee said publicly last night that they must admit they had been shockingly whipped. Throw forward the cavalry & two or three batteries & we will have the rest of them." George Custer of the staff, in the advance, agreed — "We can capture the entire rebel army" — and added, "Lee reports that he lost fifteen thousand men yesterday."

McClellan proclaimed victory to Washington: "Information this moment rec'd completely confirms the rout & demoralization of the rebel Army." He quoted Hooker's and Custer's boasts without reservation. (Reading these dispatches, Gideon Welles wondered to whom General Lee made such confessions that they should be brought straight to McClellan. "A tale like this from Pope would have been classed as one of his lies.") McClellan wired Winfield Scott news of this "signal victory" over R. E. Lee: "The Rebels routed and retreating in disorder this morning. We are pursuing closely." ("Bravo my Dear General — twice more & its done," Scott replied.) To his wife McClellan was elated: "If I can believe one tenth of what is reported, God has seldom given an army a greater victory than this."

The Rebels' defense of South Mountain on September 14 had denied McClellan his Castiglione — his opportunity, via the Lost Order, to cut Lee's army in half. Now, on September 15, he was content to see the enemy host in flight back to Virginia, its invasion checked. "How glad I am for my country that it is delivered from immediate peril," he told Ellen. That was accomplishment enough, a grant of time to reorganize and refit the Army of the Potomac for a new grand campaign.

Mr. Lincoln, monitoring events at the War Department, proposed to his general a greater ambition: "Your despatches of to-day received. God bless you, and all with you. Destroy the rebel army, if possible."

Soon came notice of an opportunity for McClellan to perhaps do just that — a dispatch marked 12:40 p.m. from Major Albert J. Myer, at a signal station atop South Mountain. "A line of battle," Myer reported, "— or an arrangement of troops which looks very much like it — is formed on the other side of the Antietam creek and this side of Sharpsburg." Twenty minutes later Captain Custer confirmed: "The enemy is drawn up in line of battle on a ridge about two miles beyond Centreville [Keedysville]. They are in full view. Their line is a perfect one about a mile and a half long."[5]

General McClellan was no more inclined to lead the pursuit this day than he had been at Williamsburg back in May. Only a dispatch from Sumner at midafternoon convinced him he should be at the front. Sumner had ridden on ahead of his corps to catch up with Richardson and Hooker in

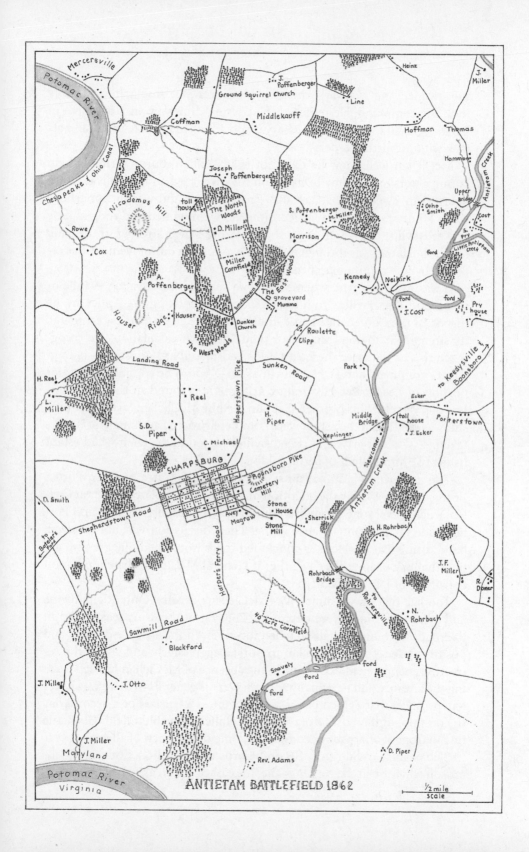

ANTIETAM BATTLEFIELD 1862

½ mile
scale

the advance, and as always whenever McClellan was absent, he arbitrarily took the command. He reported the enemy "drawn up in large force in front. . . . Shall I make the necessary dispositions to attack? And shall I attack without further orders?"

McClellan well knew he dare not (like Williamsburg) permit Edwin Sumner to take the army to battle on his own. He had left Bolivar headquarters to inspect Fox's Gap and Turner's Gap, and was in Boonsboro when Sumner's dispatch reached him. "So we mounted and rode rapidly to Keedysville, halfway to Sharpsburg," wrote David Strother of the staff. "The whole road was through masses of troops and our movement was escorted by one continuous cheering."

It was near 5:00 p.m. when McClellan reached the advance. A mile or so beyond Keedysville, from high ground overlooking the Antietam, he inspected the Confederate battle line beyond the creek. Hooker estimated its strength at 30,000. McClellan made his own calculation. He recognized this as the force the Lost Order had placed at Boonsboro—Longstreet's command and D. H. Hill's division—which he counted as a major portion of Lee's army. His unique arithmetic is found in the headquarters diary kept by his brother, Captain Arthur McClellan: "15th. The pursuit was continued the rebels were completely routed and many prisoners taken. . . . On our arrival at [Keedysville] we found the enemy had established two strong lines of battle 50 000 strong."

The gathering of Yankee brass—McClellan, Sumner, Hooker, Porter, Burnside, Cox—drew the attention of a Confederate battery, and McClellan ordered everyone except his confidant Porter to disperse. He and Porter made their reconnaissance alone. Their discussion was not revealed, but a dismissive Joe Hooker concluded there would be no aggressive action that day or the next day either if General McClellan depended upon the advice of Fitz John Porter.

Too late that day to attack was McClellan's verdict. Only Richardson's and Sykes's divisions were deployed. The rest of the army was halted in the roads in columns that stretched for miles. In the absence of early and positive orders from McClellan to pursue aggressively and attack the retreating enemy relentlessly—or in the absence of McClellan himself leading the advance and personally spurring on his generals—there was never any prospect that September 15 would witness a battle. For a second day the promise of the Lost Order went unfulfilled. Lee's bluff held. His battle line in front of Sharpsburg comprised some 18,000 men of all arms.[6]

The balance of Sumner's Second Corps took position alongside Richardson's division at the center of the line east of the creek, with the Twelfth

Corps of Sumner's wing in reserve. Sykes's division, to the left of Richardson, acted as the nexus for the rest of Porter's Fifth Corps — Morell's division would arrive the next day; Humphreys's division waited at Frederick. The Burnside-Cox Ninth Corps posted to Sykes's left to become the army's left wing. Hooker's First Corps filed into position to Sumner's right, to become the army's right wing. (Hooker initiated this move, putting him well beyond Burnside's reach.) The First and Ninth Corps at opposite ends of the prospective battlefield put period to Ambrose Burnside's wing command. Franklin's Sixth Corps awaited orders in Pleasant Valley.

Captain William J. Palmer, a scout for Pennsylvania's Governor Curtin, visited army headquarters and on September 16 wired Curtin, "The general believes that Harper's Ferry surrendered yesterday morning, and that Jackson re-enforced Lee at Sharpsburg last night. . . . Rebels appear encouraged at arrival of their re-enforcements." This imagined picture of the enemy to be faced on the 16th marked McClellan's final failure to capitalize on the Lost Order.

On September 13–15 McClellan's ingrained, unrelieved caution saved Lee from being divided and conquered. On September 16 McClellan's credulous belief in Rebel capabilities granted Lee yet another twenty-four hours to unite his scattered army. Once more McClellan in his mind's eye confronted a phantom Rebel army. "I have the mass of their troops to contend with & they outnumber me when united," he explained. He wildly miscalculated on both counts. On September 15 not a single man reinforced Lee's 18,000 at Sharpsburg. The cheering supposedly welcoming Jackson was only celebrating the Harper's Ferry surrender. It was midday on September 16 when the first of Jackson's forces began to arrive from Harper's Ferry and they trickled in slowly through the afternoon. Two more divisions reached Sharpsburg at daylight on September 17 after an all-night march. The last of the Army of Northern Virginia's nine divisions, A. P. Hill's, would only arrive late on the 17th. All of these movements went unreported by Union cavalry.

The Confederate army when united, so McClellan claimed, outnumbered him by 25 percent (some 30,000 men), and this conviction ruled his battle planning. Of all the compulsive overcounts of the enemy he had proclaimed since August 1861, this was (so it proved) the most destructive to the Union cause. Not surprisingly, his officer corps fought Antietam in the same mind as he. Captain Charles Russell Lowell of the headquarters staff told a friend, "On Wednesday morning we had their whole army in front of us — about 80,000 on our side and not less than 100,000 on theirs." Alexander S. Webb, chief of staff for the Fifth Corps, gave the

Confederates 100,000 to 130,000 men. The Rebels had "at least 20,000 more men than we had," Alpheus Williams reported. Fitz John Porter assured editor Marble of the *New York World*, "We were much less than the acknowledged strength of the enemy."

McClellan had under command in the Army of the Potomac some 101,200 men. With him on Antietam Creek on September 16 were 75,100. Franklin's 19,500 close at hand in Pleasant Valley raised the total to 94,600 for battle. (Humphreys's Fifth Corps division, 6,600 men, was held at Frederick.) General Lee, when his army was united, would put some 40,000 men on the battlefield.[7]

Dawn on September 16 found the Sharpsburg landscape obscured by fog. At 7:00 a.m. McClellan promised Washington, "Will attack as soon as situation of the enemy is developed." He promised Franklin, "If the enemy is in force here, I shall attack him this morning." In due time the sun burned away the fog and revealed the Rebels still arrayed for battle. McClellan's resolve dissipated with the fog. The headquarters staff, wrote David Strother, "remained nearly all day lying about. . . ." McClellan spent the day "examining the ground, finding fords, clearing the approaches, and hurrying up the ammunition and supply trains. . . ." He did not gather his lieutenants to advise or to explain his intentions.

Generals Sumner and Hooker took their ease near field headquarters at the Philip Pry house, Sumner seated under a tree and Hooker stretched out nearby and dozing as the day warmed. Joseph K. F. Mansfield, newly arrived to take over the Twelfth Corps, spent the day getting acquainted. On a reconnoiter of the left with artillery chief Henry Hunt, McClellan wanted Burnside to close up the Ninth Corps divisions to the Antietam. Their positioning, he said, would be the job of the chief engineer, Captain James C. Duane.

With Burnside's wing command suspended, Jacob Cox urged him to assume command of the Ninth Corps and he would return to his Kanawha Division. Burnside refused. He told Cox he was "unwilling to waive his precedence or to assume that Hooker was detached for anything more than a temporary purpose." Consequently, headquarters' orders went to Burnside, to be handed over to Cox. This blurred responsibilities, and that afternoon neither general took it upon himself to oversee the positioning of the troops or to inspect Antietam crossing sites. At 5:00 p.m. General Hunt stopped again at Burnside's headquarters and saw that most Ninth Corps troops had yet to move. "I dismounted," Hunt recalled, "went in and asked him, why on earth he had not moved." Hunt said McClellan "expected him to be in position by that time." Burnside replied that they were waiting on engineer Duane. Like Porter the day before, Hunt hastened to report the delay to McClellan.

A rebuke, the second in two days, much sharper than the first, was directed at Burnside. General McClellan, wrote adjutant James Hardie, had learned that the Ninth Corps, although ordered to its positions at noon, at sunset "only one division and four batteries had reached the ground intended. . . ." Burnside was reminded of the previous day's delay at Fox's Gap. "I am instructed to call upon you for explanations of these failures on your part to comply with the orders given you." The commanding general "cannot lightly regard such marked departure from the tenor of his instructions." Never had McClellan so strongly chastised a lieutenant. Both incidents grew out of misunderstandings, misreported by Porter and Hunt, easily repairable by McClellan. Instead, he left his old friend Burnside confused and badly rattled.[8]

The challenge McClellan faced was for him unique. Lee was deliberately inviting him to do battle. The two armies were a cannon-shot apart and there was no backing away. In western Virginia in 1861 and at Oak Grove on the first of the Seven Days, McClellan had called for offensives in which his lieutenants managed all the fighting. At South Mountain, too, he was little more than an observer. This time, unlike Glendale and Malvern Hill, he could not take himself to a safer haven, deserting his army and hoping everything would come out right. This time he would have to plan, initiate, and direct a major battle . . . all the while (in his mind) heavily outnumbered.

General Lee, to be sure, assumed substantial risk taking a stand at Sharpsburg. He mined Northern newspapers for intelligence on the Army of the Potomac and had a good idea of the numbers he faced—and a good idea, from the papers, of the inflated numbers the Yankees attributed to the Army of Northern Virginia. At his back was the Potomac, fordable only at Shepherdstown. Yet Lee glimpsed at Sharpsburg an opportunity to once again whip a general he regarded as timid, just as he had whipped him at the gates of Richmond and chased him off the Peninsula and trumped him at Second Bull Run. He posted Longstreet on his right and Jackson on his left, with full confidence in these lieutenants and in the troops they led. As important as anything else, Lee was unwilling to be harried out of Maryland, his ambitions thwarted by his unexpectedly assertive opponent, with nothing more to show than the capture of the Harper's Ferry garrison and all its arms.

Lee chose good defensive ground. His battle line roughly followed a low ridgeline running down the center of the irregular peninsula enclosed by

The Middle Bridge, looking west toward the Confederate battlefront and Sharpsburg, carried the Boonsboro Pike across Antietam Creek. By Alexander Gardner.

the Potomac River and Antietam Creek. "Broken and wooded ground behind the sheltering hills concealed the rebel masses," wrote correspondent George Smalley. Sharpsburg lay behind the ridge, only its church steeples visible to the Federals east of the creek. Between the armies three arched stone bridges spanned the Antietam — the Rohrbach Bridge on the left, on the Ninth Corps front; the Middle Bridge opposite the Union center; and on the right the Upper Bridge on the First Corps front. Only the Upper Bridge was not under the Rebel guns, which dictated that at least the opening of McClellan's offensive would be launched against the Confederates' left or northern flank.

The ground opposite the First Corps appeared more or less level, a checkerboard of fenced crop fields and meadows and woodlots. Southward the terrain became steeper and more broken, most pronounced in the area of the Rohrbach Bridge on the left. For the Federals on the left to engage meant forcing a crossing of the creek, and perhaps for those at the center as well. The Antietam was not very wide nor very deep, but artillery and wagons could only cross at the bridges or at fords. Unless the battle could be won decisively on the northern flank, crossing the creek to support the offensive promised to be a challenge.[9]

At midday on September 16 McClellan finally selected the place and time to open his attack. Joe Hooker had orders to cross the Antietam that afternoon with the First Corps and "attack the enemy on his left flank." The time of attack was to be first light the next morning, Wednesday, September 17. McClellan thereby squandered all the Lost Order's golden opportunities but one — General Lee was brought to battle before he was ready in a place he had not intended.

Hooker's three divisions, under George Meade, James Ricketts, and Abner Doubleday, crossed the Antietam at the Upper Bridge without event. "I could not know whether I was advancing against a mouse or an elephant," Hooker said, but McClellan assured him "I was at liberty to call for re-enforcements if I should need them, and that on their arrival they would be placed under my command. . . ." Meade's advance triggered hot exchanges of fire as it brushed against the enemy outposts, and Hooker sent back to say "the rebels would eat me up" if he was not supported. McClellan crossed the creek to confer, promising him Mansfield's Twelfth Corps. This opening gambit meant no surprise in the September 17 attack.

So far as stiff-necked Edwin Sumner was concerned, his wing command — Second and Twelfth Corps — was intact, and McClellan trod carefully around him. The order sending the Twelfth across the Antietam did not exactly say that Mansfield would come under Hooker's command, only that the Twelfth should take position as "designated for it by General Hooker." Sumner was to have Second Corps ready to march "one hour before daylight to-morrow morning."

McClellan named the Fifth and Sixth Corps as the army's reserve, but his orders to Franklin and to Humphreys reflected indecision. Despite his conviction that Lee had reunited his army on September 15, McClellan delayed until evening of the 16th to order Franklin's Sixth Corps in Pleasant Valley to join the rest of the army — on the 17th. Franklin was also told that McClellan "still desires you to occupy Maryland Heights." This repeated an earlier order to seize the Heights to "secure a tête du pont" to cut off an enemy retreating into Virginia, and Franklin detached Couch's division for that purpose. Thus: Franklin brought just two divisions to the battlefield; they were only available beginning at midday on September 17; and Darius Couch spent the 17th marching uselessly to and fro in Pleasant Valley. As for Andrew Humphreys's Fifth Corps division, marking time at Frederick, it was only ordered at midafternoon on the 17th to join up. McClellan's indecision cost him two divisions for the coming battle.

He showed decision posting his cavalry, but decision of the worst kind. It was "the practice of the centuries" (as trooper George B. Davis put it) to

Gardner photographed the Lutheran church, on Main Street on the eastern outskirts of Sharpsburg, so badly damaged by Federal artillery fire it had to be replaced.

post cavalry to guard an army's flanks in battle. McClellan instead massed Pleasonton's cavalry division behind the center, "ready at a moment's notice, should it be required to make pursuit of the enemy." Not even cavalry vedettes watched the flanks.

Alpheus Williams, back with his division when Mansfield took over the Twelfth Corps, got his troops posted across the Antietam about midnight. He wrote his family he would not "soon forget that night; so dark, so obscure, so mysterious, so uncertain; with the occasional rapid volleys of pickets and outposts, the low, solemn sound of the command as troops came into position, and withal so sleepy that there was a half-dreamy sensation about it all; but with a certain impression that the morrow was to be great with the future fate of our country. So much responsibility, so much intense, future anxiety!"[10]

In not composing a plan of battle for September 17 and in not calling together his high command to consult, McClellan limited counsel from his generals to Fitz John Porter, with whom he spent nearly all the day. Only afterward did he reveal his tactical design, and over time he made revisions to that design, enhanced by fresh hindsight. His first draft in reporting on the battle is perhaps closest to his best hope for the day. It was a simple and reasonably aggressive plan. "The design was to make the main attack upon the enemy's left, and at the same time to create a diversion with the hope of something more, by assailing his right, and as soon as one or both of the flank movements were fully successful, to attack their centre with any reserves that might then be disposable."

This implied coordinated, simultaneous assaults against both Confederate flanks. In the event, however, McClellan backed away from such a commitment. His Antietam battle followed a very cautious, one-step-at-a-time progression. Coordination was absent. Never that day did any two movements of Federal forces begin in tandem. The old warrior Edwin Sumner caught the essence of that bloody Wednesday, complaining afterward of General McClellan "sending those troops into action in driblets, as they were sent."[11]

At daylight on September 17 Joe Hooker made the opening advance. He would testify he had McClellan's assurance there would be attacks "in the centre and on the left" in concert with his attack on the right. Hooker set as the First Corps' target a whitewashed brick building a mile distant on the Hagerstown Turnpike that ran south along the ridgeline and on into Sharpsburg. Soldiers took it for a schoolhouse, but it was in fact a church of the German Baptist Brethren, called Dunkers for their baptism by total immersion. The Dunker church sat on the edge of an open plateau crowded with Confederate artillery. Hooker's line of advance crossed meadows and a 30-acre cornfield, and was flanked by woodlots soon to be known as the East Woods and the West Woods. The ranked batteries were easily seen, but the pastoral landscape concealed the Rebel infantry.

The First Corps was about 9,400 strong. Hooker posted the divisions of James Ricketts on the left and Abner Doubleday on the right, with George Meade's Pennsylvania Reserves in support. All three divisions came out of Pope's Army of Virginia, although the Reserves served under McClellan in the Seven Days. For Ricketts, the artilleryman wounded and captured at First Bull Run, this was his second battle (after Second Bull Run) leading infantry. Doubleday, who fired the first Fort Sumter gun long months before, led a brigade under McDowell and at Turner's Gap under Hooker. He replaced the wounded John Hatch as division commander. Meade was well tested, honed in the Seven Days (where he was wounded), at Second Bull Run, and at Turner's Gap. At Turner's (Meade told his wife) the Reserves "were the admiration of the whole army. . . ."

Joe Hooker believed a basic tenet of "soldiership" was setting an example, especially for volunteer troops. Starting at Williamsburg, he bored right into the heart of the fighting, leading from the front or near the front, showing the way for officers and men. He was not senselessly reckless like Phil Kearny, but still he displayed leadership that was seen and admired. It was noticed by the press, and soon he had a nickname: Fighting Joe. This was a product of chance. A piece of news copy was distributed bearing the typesetter's heading FIGHTING — JOE HOOKER that was taken as the story's headline. Hooker complained that Fighting Joe sounded like a hothead inclined toward "needless dashes at the enemy." Still, it was an accurate-enough label, and well earned.

At the First Corps' first fight, at Turner's Gap, the difficult, concealing terrain forced Hooker to direct the battle impersonally from the rear. In the greater test on the Antietam field, he made it a particular point to show himself to the troops of his new command. On September 17, wrote *New-York Tribune* reporter George Smalley, "Hooker's men were fully up to their work. They saw their General every where in front, never away from the fire, and all the troops believed in their commander, and fought with a will."[12]

Fighting began in the East Woods, where Truman Seymour's brigade, Meade's division, took up last evening's scrap with the Rebel pickets. Forewarned by the Yankees' crossing on the 16th, Jackson had turned his flank into a solidly manned front. Seymour's attempt to push through the East Woods met a hail of fire and was repulsed. This was the sector assigned to Ricketts, and Hooker ordered him to Seymour's rescue. Ricketts led off with Abram Duryée's brigade. A New York merchant long connected with the state militia, Duryée pushed his troops through farmer David R. Miller's cornfield — thereafter known simply as *the* Cornfield — adjacent to the East Woods. As they burst out of the head-high corn, they were surprised by a Rebel battle line that rose up scarcely 200 yards away and delivered a murderous volley. In soldier-historian Ezra Carman's phrase, this opened "a contest of the most deadly character" for the Cornfield. For long minutes the two lines stood and shot each other to pieces before finally taking what cover they could. In half an hour of this Duryée lost a third of his men. Beyond the heavy musketry, a hail of shot and shell fell on the Yankees from the artillery posted in front of the Dunker church. Ricketts's supporting batteries returned the fire, as did Henry Hunt's heavy guns from across the Antietam.

Ricketts intended following Duryée with his other two brigades, but in his inexperience he lost grip on his command. Brigadier George L. Hartsuff rode out ahead to reconnoiter, was badly wounded, and his brigade marked time for thirty minutes until a replacement took over. The conduct of the third brigade commander, William A. Christian, unnerved his men. As the column approached the field, Christian put them through "an unnecessary amount of drilling making a show of us for the benefit of the Rebel artillery." As the shelling intensified, Colonel Christian lost his nerve and hurried to the rear. "He would duck and dodge his head, and go crouching along." (Christian resigned two days later.) Only after considerable delay was the brigade engaged. Furthering the command confusion, Ricketts was injured by his wounded horse falling on him.

The troops of Hartsuff and Christian fought with effect when they finally reached the front under new command. Correspondent Smalley, with Hooker on the battlefield all morning, recorded Hartsuff's advance: "The whole line crowned the hill and stood out darkly against the sky, but lighted and shrouded ever in flame and smoke.... There was no more gallant, determined, heroic fighting in all this desperate day." Yet by mischance and ragged leadership, Ricketts's division fought one brigade at a time, at well-separated intervals, and Jackson met them roughly man for man to stall their progress. It was a pattern repeated all that long day. Duryée's and Hartsuff's men fell back from the carnage to reorganize and replenish ammunition, leaving Christian's brigade, under Colonel Peter Lyle, to hold the line on the south edge of the Cornfield.[13]

To the right, Doubleday's division entered the battle in parallel with Ricketts but somewhat later, after Duryée had triggered the struggle for the Cornfield. Hooker called up Doubleday's Fourth Brigade, John Gibbon's Black Hats, to lead the charge. The brigade was thinned after its baptism of fire at Groveton, then at Second Bull Run and Turner's Gap, but Hooker had it marked as a crack unit — the Iron Brigade.

While Doubleday moved up the brigades of Walter Phelps and Marsena Patrick for support, Gibbon joined Hooker and Meade for instructions. "No enemy was in sight," Gibbon recalled, "but his shells were flying thick over our heads." Much of this fire was coming from Nicodemus Hill off to the right, and Hooker diverted four of his batteries to try to suppress this fire. Gibbon's Iron Brigade advanced astride the Hagerstown Pike. To the left, the 2nd and 6th Wisconsin pushed into the Cornfield where Ricketts's division was still battling, while the 7th Wisconsin and 19th Indiana headed through open fields west of the pike.

Major Rufus Dawes took command of the 6th Wisconsin after his colonel was wounded. As they broke out of the corn, Dawes wrote, "a long line of men in butternut and gray rose up from the ground." The two battle lines opened a tremendous fire. "Men, I can not say fell; they were knocked out of the ranks by dozens. But we jumped over the fence, and pushed on, loading, firing, and shouting as we advanced." With Phelps's New Yorkers adding their weight, the Rebel line wavered. Phelps, a former state militiaman, marveled that he was both unscathed and confident in his leadership. "I do not know how I escaped," he told his wife. ". . . Fortunately I am very cool under fire & the fact of my quietly lighting my pipe when the shot & shell were flying about cutting down my men seemed to enspirit the men and gave them confidence."

West of the pike Gibbon's other two regiments, followed up by Patrick's brigade, pushed the Rebel skirmishers back through farmer Miller's fields and tangled with the enemy front sheltered in the West Woods. "There they were so well protected by the timber and a series of rocky ledges that ran parallel to their line of battle that our troops could not dislodge them," Doubleday wrote. A Confederate counterattack drove the violence to a new pitch and was barely contained. "We were in the hottest of hornet's nests," Gibbon wrote, "and had all we could do to attend to what was in our front whilst the sounds of a severe battle reached our ears from all directions."[14]

With all his brigades but two of Meade's committed, with the fighting in the balance, Hooker sent back for Mansfield's Twelfth Corps. Despite McClellan's assurances of other attacks in concert, the fighting was more than an hour old and headquarters had issued no attack orders elsewhere. On the far left, overlooking the Rohrbach Bridge, Burnside and Cox waited expectantly, listening to the rising roar of battle to the north. On the right flank, Sumner had his Second Corps troops up and ready to march well before dawn. "General Sumner was uneasy and impatient," his son and aide Samuel S. Sumner remembered; "his other Corps, the 12th, had moved during the night, and he wanted to join it and make an attack with the two Corps." Sumner rode to the Pry house to get his orders directly. None were forthcoming. Headquarters functionaries refused to admit him. Sumner and staff sat on the porch steps or paced the yard for more than an hour. An officer who did see McClellan found him in good spirits: "All goes well. Hooker is driving them."[15]

At about 7:00 a.m. the battle picture changed abruptly. Jackson sent in John Bell Hood's division against Hooker's depleted corps. The Rebels, 2,300 strong, came slanting out of the West Woods, formed a line all the way to the East Woods, and charged. The remnants of Ricketts's division were chased back through the East Woods, abandoning a battery. Gibbon's brigade put up a stubborn defense in the Cornfield and along the Hagerstown Pike but had to give ground. "In ten minutes the fortune of the day seemed to have changed," reporter Smalley wrote. Battery B, 4th U.S., Gibbon's old command, unlimbered on the pike and in Mr. Miller's barnyard and blasted the attackers with single then double rounds of canister. Gibbon saw the elevating screw on one piece had run down so that it was firing high and harmlessly. "I jumped from my horse, rapidly ran up the elevating screw until the nozzle pointed almost into the ground in front and then nodded to the gunner to pull his lanyard. The discharge carried away most of the fence in front of it and produced great destruction in the enemy's ranks. . . ."

Meade positioned the First Corps' last reserves, the brigades of Albert Magilton and Robert Anderson, at the fence at the northern edge of the Cornfield, and the Pennsylvanians broke the spearhead of Hood's attack. Meade was in the midst of the fighting; his horse was shot and, he told his wife, "I was hit by a *spent* grape shot, giving me a severe contusion on the right thigh." West of the turnpike, Marsena Patrick described a critical moment. "I ordered the 2 Regts. of Gibbon, as well as my own to throw themselves under the rocky ledge parallel to the road & deliver flank, or crossfire upon the advancing foe." Joe Hooker was everywhere, pressing his officers, filling gaps, rousing the troops. "The tall, soldierly figure of the General, the white horse which he rode, the elevated place where he was, all made him a most dangerously conspicuous mark," Smalley wrote. At last the tide of Hood's assault was spent, and the two sides grudgingly paused in mutual exhaustion. "The cornfield now became neutral ground," said Doubleday, "the fire on both sides being too hot for either party to hold it."[16]

From an observation post on a hill behind the Pry house the progress of the fighting in these early-morning hours could be roughly charted. Shortly after 7 o'clock it became clear that Hooker needed reinforcements, and McClellan took his first tactical decision of the day. At 7:20, at the Pry house, Sumner finally got his orders. "The Comdg. General directs that you move Sedgwick and French across the creek. . . . You will cross in as solid a mass as possible and communicate with Genl. Hooker immediately. Genl. Richardson's Division will not cross till further orders . . . ; halt after you cross until you ascertain if Genl. Hooker wants assistance." Sumner hurried off to start the Second Corps to battle. From his starting point it was two miles to the Dunker church.

McClellan hedged his decision in caution. He waited to commit his strongest corps until Hooker fixed the enemy in place (forestalling any of those surprise flanking moves the Rebels favored). Richardson's division was held back to man the army's defenses until Morell's Fifth Corps divi-

The fighting in Antietam's northern sector left this scene, by Gardner: Confederate dead and an artillery limber in front of the Dunker church and the West Woods.

sion could be marched up to the creek line to replace it. Finally, Sumner was to report to Joe Hooker, the general leading the fighting, thereby coming under Hooker's direction. The last thing wanted was Edwin Sumner in independent command.

The Pry house proved not the best place to follow the shifting battle, and so McClellan and staff mounted and rode south, across the Boonsboro Pike, to Porter's Fifth Corps headquarters east of the Antietam. On high ground near the J. Ecker house, overlooking the center of the battlefield, a redan of fence rails was built for the generals. From here could be seen as far as the East Woods and the ridgeline along which ran the Hagerstown Pike, but not much beyond. Staff man David Strother described the scene. With his telescope resting on the top rail, Porter "studied the field with unremitting attention, scarcely leaving his post during the whole day. His observations he communicated to the commander by nods, signs, or in words so low-toned and brief that the nearest by-standers had but little benefit from them. When not engaged with Porter, McClellan stood in a soldierly attitude intently watching the battle and smoking with the utmost apparent calmness. . . ."[17]

Joseph K. F. Mansfield was in his third day commanding the Twelfth Corps. He was a forty-year regular, served in Mexico (three brevets) and on staff in the years since. Alpheus Williams found General Mansfield "very fussy. He had been an engineer officer and never before had commanded large bodies of troops." The Twelfth Corps (as now numbered) had served under Banks in the Shenandoah and at Cedar Mountain, sat out Second Bull Run, and bore a patched-together look. Williams's brigade commanders, Samuel Crawford and George Gordon, were veterans, but half the infantry were recruits. In George Sears Greene's division the troops were veterans but all three brigade commanders were new. At 7,600 men it was the smallest corps in the army.

The Twelfth was bivouacked a mile to the rear, and when he had it started toward the front Mansfield rode ahead to get his orders. Hooker told him to reinforce the beleaguered First Corps' line that ran in a ragged arc from the East Woods to the West Woods. Williams's division had the lead, and as it came under artillery fire the men were ordered into line of battle. In the new regiments what was known of drill evaporated in the rush of bullets and shells. The generals took them in hand. "I got mine in line pretty well by having a fence to align it on," Williams wrote. The trouble came "in attempting to move them forward or back or to make any maneuver they fell into inextricable confusion and fell to the rear, where they were easily rallied. The men were of an excellent stamp, ready and willing, but neither officers nor men knew anything. . . ."

Mansfield himself posted one of the rookie regiments, then rode to the East Woods where Crawford had found a fight. Mansfield was told there were First Corps men still in the woods, and he shouted to the 10th Maine that they were firing at their own men. The Mainers knew better. As one of them put it, "Those that were firing at us from behind the trees had been firing at us from the first." Mansfield took a closer look and said, "Yes, yes, you are right," and then a bullet took him in the chest. Borne to the rear, he lived through the night but died the next day. Joseph Mansfield had earnestly sought a fighting command for more than a year, and on the Antietam battlefield it had lasted hardly an hour.

Mansfield's wounding put Alpheus Williams back in command of the Twelfth Corps and the work went on. Samuel Crawford took over Williams's First Division, but subsequently no one could find him. A staff man blamed his absence on taking "most of his time to hunt trees that a Minnie ball could not go through." Ezra Carman saw him "ensconced behind a ledge of rocks where nothing could touch him." Williams considered Crawford a skulker who nursed a slight wound into later laurels. Joseph Knipe stepped in for Crawford, and he and George Gordon capably fought the rest of the battle on their own.

Williams sought out Hooker for instructions and found him in a plowed field on the Miller farm. As they talked "amidst a very unpleasant shower of bullets," Williams wrote, up rode a general officer "begging for immediate assistance to protect a battery. He was very earnest and absorbed in the subject . . . when he suddenly stopped, extended his hand, and very calmly said, 'How are you?' It was Gen. Meade. He darted away, and I saw him no more that day." Williams's division had started on the right with Greene's on the left, but soon enough they scattered all across the battlefield.[18]

To brace Doubleday's tenuous position on the far right, Williams detached one of Greene's brigades and its new commander, William B. Goodrich. One of his men watched Goodrich, in peacetime a small-town lawyer and newspaper editor, lead his brigade into combat for the first time: "Our colonel was fifty feet in the rear of the line of battle, his right hand resting on the neck of his little black horse. Calm and brave he was, giving his command, 'Steady! Shoot low!'" Moments later Goodrich was fatally shot through the chest. Greene soon lost the second of his three new brigade commanders, Lieutenant Colonel Hector Tyndale, to a severe head wound. (The Twelfth Corps' casualty list that day included Corporal Barton Mitchell, finder of the Lost Order, and the sergeant he showed it to, John M. Bloss, both wounded, and Captain Peter Kop, who started S.O. 191 up the chain of command, mortally wounded.)

The Twelfth Corps pressed resolutely ahead. It did its duty and more, Williams wrote: "This Corps repulsed the rebels who were exultingly driving Hooker's Corps — drove them back over the open fields, as far as they were at any time." The Confederates were chased from the Cornfield and the East Woods. Greene restrained one of his New York regiments: "Halt, 102nd, you are bully boys but don't go any farther! I will have a battery here to help you." Robert Gould Shaw, 2nd Massachusetts, described the scene: "Beyond the cornfield was a large open field, and such a mass of dead and wounded men, mostly Rebels, as were lying there, I never saw before; it was a terrible sight, and our men had to be very careful to avoid treading on them. . . ." The batteries at the Dunker church withdrew, and the new 125th Pennsylvania reached the church.[19]

Between the Hagerstown Pike and the West Woods, Joe Hooker pressed close behind his advanced line, looking to post artillery. He told John Gibbon he would attend to the annoying Rebel batteries on Nicodemus Hill. On his white horse he was a target, and reporter Smalley noted that "rebel bullets had followed him all day." Finally one found him, tearing through his right foot. Faint from loss of blood, he was carried from the field. Smalley quoted Fighting Joe's last words of command that day: "There is a regiment to the right. Order it forward! Crawford and Gordon are coming up. Tell them to carry those woods and hold them — and it is our fight!"

Hooker sent word to McClellan that George Meade should take the First Corps. James Ricketts had seniority, but McClellan took Hooker's advice.

At 9:00 a.m. Alpheus Williams, now ranking general at the front, reported to headquarters: "Genl Mansfield is dangerously wounded. Genl Hooker wounded severely in foot. Genl Sumner I hear is advancing. We hold the field at present. Please give us all the aid you can. It is reported that the enemy occupy the woods in our advance in strong force." He added, "The head of Genl Sumner's column has just arrived."[20]

Edwin Sumner had wasted not a moment marching to the battleground. The Second Corps crossed the Antietam at a ford west of the Pry house and headed on west, John Sedgwick's division in the lead, William French's to follow. On the march Sumner was handed fresh orders from McClellan. Sent at 8:30 a.m. from the new command post with the Fifth Corps, the dispatch began, "Gen. Hooker appears to be driving the enemy rapidly." Should Hooker not need him, Sumner was to take possession of the East Woods to his right, then "push on towards Sharpsburg and a little to its rear as rapidly as possible." With this dispatch McClellan intended the Second Corps to outflank and complete the destruction of the enemy's left, destruction he thought well started by the First and Twelfth Corps. Sumner had Sedgwick deploy into open fighting order, his three brigades in consecutive lines, facing west.

Headquarters was overoptimistic. Instead of driving the enemy rapidly, Joe Hooker went to the rear in an ambulance; Sumner noted that he "found him wounded." Hooker testified he was semiconscious when Sumner "addressed me, and passed on." Sumner learned nothing from the encounter. He did learn about the battered First Corps in meeting Ricketts and Meade, but this spoke more to the condition of things at the rear than at the front.

Alpheus Williams, commanding the Twelfth Corps, could speak with firsthand authority of happenings at the front, but Sumner made no effort to find him and learn the true conditions on this smoking, blasted battlefield. "I dispatched a staff officer," Williams wrote, "to appraise him of our position and the situation of affairs." The staff man would have repeated to Sumner Williams's warning to headquarters — "It is reported that the enemy occupy the woods in our advance in strong force" — and identified those woods as the West Woods. Sumner brushed him off.

Edwin Sumner had demonstrated that in battle he was not a good listener. He repeatedly ignored his lieutenants in his fumbling direction at

Williamsburg, and on the retreat during the Seven Days he was nearly relieved for going his own contrary way. Williams was astonished that Sedgwick's three brigades "made, without halt or reconnaissance, straight for the woods. . . ." In a private letter he spoke of the hundreds of lives sacrificed by "generals who would come up with their commands and pitch in at the first point without consultation with those who knew the ground or without reconnoitering or looking for the effective points of attacks." He precisely described (and meant) Edwin Sumner.[21]

Sumner determined to carry out McClellan's directive "to push on towards Sharpsburg and a little to its rear" by gaining the West Woods, then turning south. He led with Sedgwick's division only, on a line of march at right angles to the previous lines of attack of Hooker and Williams. The First Corps was at the rear reorganizing. The Twelfth Corps was clinging to the scattered footholds it had gained. French's division lagged behind and Sumner did not wait for it. Richardson's division remained east of the creek by McClellan's order. Sumner sent his son Samuel back to find French and order him to look south for any Rebels he found and (as young Sumner remembered it) "make a vigorous attack in order to aid the advance of the leading division."

The battlefield fell eerily silent. "Not an enemy appeared," wrote Williams. "The woods in front were as quiet as any sylvan shade could be." Reporter Smalley saw Sumner riding with his lead brigade, "his hat off, his gray hair and beard and moustache strangely contrasting with the fire in his eyes and his martial air." Sumner saw that the 1st Minnesota's flag was cased. "In God's name what are your men fighting for?" he bellowed. "Unfurl those colors!"

The West Woods, wrote Smalley, "stretched forward into the broad fields like a promontory into the ocean." Bordering the Hagerstown Turnpike, the woodlot extended a quarter mile north from the Dunker church, was notched back for two roadside grass fields, and continued behind the fields in an irregular line to Miller's farm. Across the pike and into these notch-backs marched the 5,400 men of Sedgwick's division, their three brigade lines 500 yards wide, scarcely 50 yards apart, and without advance skirmishers. It was a formation designed to fight an enemy straight ahead, due west. At 9:10 a.m., alerted by Williams, headquarters sent Sumner a warning: "General McClellan desires you to be very careful how you advance, as he fears our right is suffering." It was delivered too late.[22]

John Sedgwick had in charge veteran troops and lieutenants. Willis A. Gorman, onetime governor of Minnesota Territory, and old regular Napoleon Jackson Tecumseh Dana—presumably slated for West Point from birth — had led their brigades under Uncle John since Yorktown. Oliver Otis Howard, who had led a different Second Corps brigade before his wounding at Seven Pines, joined Sedgwick's division in August. It was close to 9:30 a.m. when a tempest of gunfire from that part of the West Woods to the left overwhelmed the division's flank.

Through the morning General Lee anticipated the Federals' moves rather than reacting to them. Early on he pulled troops from his right to meet the building threat to his left, and now into the West Woods, precisely when needed, came a major reinforcement for Jackson — one of the two divisions that had marched all night from Harper's Ferry. These attackers numbered about 4,400, a thousand fewer than Sedgwick's command, but striking from the flank, combined with surprise, greatly multiplied their force.

First to be hit, and broken, were the rookies of the 125th Pennsylvania, Twelfth Corps, who had earlier gained a lodgment near the Dunker church. "Had I remained in my position two minutes longer," said their colonel, "I would have lost my whole command." He did lose 145 men. In Sedgwick's division the three left-most regiments lost over 600 men in a matter of minutes. The brigade lines were too close together to pivot regiments to face the attack without overlapping, and in any case masses of panicked men fleeing the onslaught broke up the officers' attempts to form. The brigade lines crumpled like rows of dominoes. In the confusion and smoke and din there seemed no way to return fire without hitting a fellow Yankee. One of the first Rebel spearheads struck the trailing brigade of the three, Howard's, and the cry ran through the division that the enemy was behind them.

Sumner could not at first see what was happening, but he soon grasped the danger. Exclaiming "By God, we must get out of this," he rushed toward the broken flank. As he rode through the as-yet-untouched regiments in the second and third lines, shouting and waving his hat, the men thought he was calling for a charge and fixed bayonets. But when he could be heard, it was, "Back boys, for God's sake, move back! You're in a bad fix!" By the account of Henry Ropes, Sumner "ordered us to march off by the right flank. We did so, but the left Regiments gave way in confusion, the enemy poured in upon our rear and now the slaughter was worse than anything I have ever seen before. Sumner walked his horse quietly along waving his hand and keeping all steady near him."

The third line, Howard's brigade, swiftly collapsed after blows from both flank and rear. "With troops that I had commanded longer I could have changed front," was Howard's excuse, "but here, quicker than I can

Alpheus Williams (left), commanding the Twelfth Corps, gained a foothold in the West Woods, but soon afterward John Sedgwick (right), leading his Second Corps division, was blindly directed into the West Woods and there met a deadly flank attack.

write the words, my men faced about and took the back track." Dana suffered a leg wound but refused to go to the rear before he got his men to safety. Sedgwick, rushing all over the field, bore three wounds — leg, wrist, shoulder — but only when near collapse would he leave. To Alpheus Williams, the three brigades "seemed to melt into the earth — so rapidly and mysteriously did they disappear from sight."

Sedgwick's routed, ruined division ended up about where Hooker's early-morning offensive had started. The artillery and a defensive front thrown up by Meade's First Corps survivors and by portions of the Twelfth Corps finally halted the Confederate pursuit. Once again the two sides fell back in mutual depletion and exhaustion. Casualties in Sedgwick's division and in the 125th Pennsylvania came to over 2,300, in hardly thirty minutes of fighting. McClellan's intent to keep Edwin Sumner away from independent command was dashed by circumstances, and the consequence was unrelieved disaster. The First Corps and the Twelfth Corps and one-third of the Second Corps were done for the day, at least on offense.

Shortly after 9:00 a.m., in McClellan's last moments of optimism about the fighting on the right, he sent to Burnside to open a second battlefront by attacking the enemy's other flank. Instead of coordinating the advance of the Ninth Corps with the First Corps, per his supposed design, McClellan waited more than three hours to release Burnside ... and only then because Franklin's Sixth Corps was approaching from Pleasant Valley to replenish the reserve.

That same tender concern for his reserves dictated McClellan's decision to have French's division support Sedgwick rather than Richardson's better-manned, better-led division. The Young Napoleon wanted his most trusted generals — Porter, Franklin, Richardson — to man his defenses in this early-morning engagement with Lee's host.[23]

Neither William French nor his three brigades exactly inspired confidence. French was twenty-five years in the regulars, red-faced and high-tempered and known as a drinker. His one test, at Seven Pines, was hardly the challenge he faced today. His division was patched together from disparate pieces — Max Weber's brigade of garrison troops, Dwight Morris's brigade of new troops, and Nathan Kimball's brigade of Valley veterans to which was attached a regiment of new troops. General French set out with a hazy understanding of what he was supposed to do.

Sumner apparently intended French to follow Sedgwick's division in echelon on the left, protecting the flank and ready in due course to turn southward, in concert with Sedgwick, toward the enemy rear. But French's mismatched regiments were not the marchers that Sedgwick's were, and they fell behind and drifted leftward. Looking left and sighting an enemy force, French dutifully deployed his brigades into battle formation facing south. Supposing it was wanted of him, he pushed ahead to engage . . . and opened a new battlefront.

French struck not the left but the center of Lee's position. Some 600 yards south of the Dunker church, a farm lane ran easterly off the Hagerstown Pike and angled southerly to reach the Boonsboro Pike halfway between Sharpsburg and Antietam Creek. Over the years farmers' wagons and erosion had worn down the roadbed by several feet, creating, for military purposes, a ready-made trench. It would be called the Sunken Road, or more literally, Bloody Lane.

Max Weber's brigade had the lead. His regiments — 4th New York, 1st Delaware, 5th Maryland — had garrison duty but no combat experience. They chased the Rebels out of the William Roulette farmstead toward a skirmish line along a low ridge. As Weber's men approached, this line gave way and as they crested the ridge they were surprised and savaged by a blast of musketry from the Sunken Road beyond. The Yankees were literally mowed down. This first fire took down 450 of Weber's men. Weber fell back to try and regroup.[24]

French gave no thought to turning the Sunken Road position. He ordered Dwight Morris's brigade of recruits to repeat the frontal attack where Weber had failed. The newly mustered-in 130th Pennsylvania left Harrisburg for the war on August 18; the 108th New York left Rochester on August 19; the 14th Connecticut left Hartford on August 25. The latter regiment typified Morris's brigade: no drill, no instruction even in marching, barely able to load its guns: "It was little more than a crowd of earnest Connecticut boys."

The rookies marched up to the ragged line the survivors of Weber's brigade were holding and in their bewilderment the earnest Connecticut boys opened fire too soon, into the 1st Delaware in front of them. The Delawares broke for the rear, crying out that it was a skedaddle. "Some of our men tried to stop them," wrote Samuel Fiske, 14th Connecticut, "and a few of them, it must be confessed, joined in their flight." Still, Fiske believed that for green troops in their first fight, "we behaved well, the men firing with precision and deliberation, though some shut their eyes and fired up in the air." The Pennsylvania and New York boys pushed up alongside, multiplying the confusion. Trying to extract his men from the tangle, Max Weber was wounded and lost a leg. Adding to the din, the six-gun rifled battery of Captain John A. Tompkins sent shells shrieking low over the heads of the infantry and into the Confederate supports behind the Sunken Road. Morris thought his men, "although under fire for the first time, behaved with great gallantry." Yet his brigade, like Weber's, suffered far more casualties than it inflicted.

At about this time, Captain Sam Sumner found French and delivered his father's order to "make a vigorous attack" in aid of Sedgwick's division in the advance. With his decision to attack thus affirmed, French raised his bet and pressed Nathan Kimball's brigade into the frontal assault on the Sunken Road—an assault that had no bearing whatever on Sedgwick's bitter fate in the West Woods. French's failure to keep up on the march, and Sumner's failure to wait for him, left the Second Corps split into two quite separate missions that day.[25]

Nathan Kimball was a citizen-soldier who had led a company at Buena Vista in the Mexican War, experience he put to use in March 1862 when he defeated no less than Stonewall Jackson at Kernstown in the Valley, earning his general's star. He saw his men into the Sunken Road fight with the promise, "Boys, we are going for the Johnnies now, and we'll stay with them all day if necessary!" They charged through the fire, heads down as if in a pelting rainstorm, and met the same bloody reception as the rest of the division. "What we see now looks to us like systematic killing," said

Alfred R. Waud pictured the Samuel Mumma farmhouse and barn, fired early on September 17 by the Rebels to prevent their use by Yankee sharpshooters.

Thomas Galwey, 8th Ohio. Galwey heard General Kimball mutter, "God save my poor boys!" as he tried to secure his wavering line.

Kimball's brigade, along with the survivors of Weber's and Morris's commands, took what cover they found on the reverse slope of the ridgeline and kept up what fire they could, taking cartridges from the dead and wounded. French suffered 1,750 casualties at the Sunken Road, second only to the toll in Sedgwick's division in the West Woods.[26]

In the wake of Sedgwick's calamity, Edwin Sumner pleaded with headquarters, "Re-enforcements are badly wanted. Our troops are giving way." He was missing two divisions, French's and Richardson's — "If you know where they are, send them immediately." This was the first notice of Sedgwick's fate, for the headquarters vantage point did not furnish a view of the distant West Woods fighting. In clearer view was French's contest at the Sunken Road. Morell's Fifth Corps division finally arrived to relieve Richardson, who crossed the Antietam to join battle alongside French. Sumner's cry for help, and Williams's report that Mansfield and Hooker were out of action, painted a grim picture of the northern field. But McClellan waited upon Franklin's Sixth Corps to aid Sumner. For the moment, the struggle at the center engrossed everyone.

Like French before him, Richardson did not think to try and turn the Sunken Road position. The Confederate right was in fact vulnerable to enfilading fire had the Federals' point of attack shifted hardly 200 yards to their left. But Israel Richardson was a straight-ahead, blunt-force sort of general, and he sent in Meagher's Irish Brigade next to French's embattled line. Thomas Francis Meagher's flamboyance rested on a gaudy past. In his days as an Irish revolutionary he was transported to Tasmania, escaped, came to America, and became a leader in New York's Irish community. In 1861 he recruited the Irish Brigade and led it into action under its emerald banners during the Seven Days. Meagher was well known to drink Irish whiskey if he could get it and any other kind if he could not, and so it was on September 17. He ordered his men to fix bayonets, relying "on the impetuosity and recklessness of Irish soldiers in a charge." But a greater-than-ever fire from the Sunken Road knocked the Irishmen back on their heels. As he tried to rally his men Meagher fell off his horse, "and from the shock which I myself sustained, I was obliged to be carried off the field."

But Meagher's reputation had preceded him. At headquarters David Strother told his diary, "Meagher was not killed as reported, but drunk, and fell from his horse." John Gibbon too had the story: "Genl. Meagher was not wounded, but carried off the field dead (*drunk*)." When George Meade saw the papers, he wrote his wife, "If I had only been carried off the field in a stretcher (*dead drunk*) as J. Francis Meagher was I might perhaps be as great a hero. . . ."[27]

Richardson's next brigade was John C. Caldwell's. Citizen-soldier Caldwell had gained his star on the Peninsula, but on this day he roused Richardson's ire. Fighting Dick led from the front and expected the same of his field officers. Thomas Livermore, 5th New Hampshire, saw Richardson rush up to the line on foot, waving his sword, his face "as black as a thunder cloud," and shout, "Where's General Caldwell?" "In the rear," he was told, and some of the men called out, "Behind the haystack!" "God damn the field officers!" Richardson cried, and had the brigade replace Meagher's on the line. "Old Dick Richardson led us in, not merely to fill up a gap, but to make gaps," a captain remembered.

The 5th's Colonel Edward E. Cross was as blunt as General Richardson. He told his veteran Hampshiremen, "You are about to engage in battle. You have never disgraced your state; I hope you won't this time. If any man runs I want the file closers to shoot him; if they don't, I shall myself. That's all I have to say." Meagher's Irishmen welcomed them with a cheer. Thomas Livermore described the scene: "The thundering of artillery, the roaring of bursting shells, the rolling of musketry, and humming of deadly fragments and bullets, and sometimes the yells of the rebels and our own cheers, all seemed to fill the whole horizon and drive Peace away forever."

A mile distant, across the Antietam, McClellan and Porter watched the struggle for the Confederate center. Colonel Strother heard McClellan exclaim, "It is the most beautiful field I ever saw, and the grandest battle! If we whip them today it will wipe out Bull Run forever." But he only watched. He made no move to commit anything of his reserves — Porter's two Fifth Corps divisions under Sykes and Morell — to this grandest battle, even when informed that Franklin's Sixth Corps was at hand from Pleasant Valley.

In General Caldwell's absence, Colonel Francis Barlow, leading in tandem the 61st and 64th New York, was freed to expand his range of command. He went looking for a fight. (Barlow's wife, Arabella, remarked of her husband, "He loves fighting for the sake of fighting, and is really bloodthirsty.") Ranging off to the south from Meagher's position, Barlow found ground to enfilade the right of the Sunken Road position. "They could do us little harm, and we were shooting them like sheep in a pen," wrote one of the New Yorkers. Barlow gathered in 300 prisoners and broke the Rebel line. But before he could further exploit the gain, he was badly wounded. "The Regiment fought splendidly and lost largely," said Barlow, and gained his brigadier general's star.[28]

At nearly the same time, the left of the enemy position was broken as well, by Yankee pressure and a Confederate command failure that caused the evacuation of an entire sector of the line. That triggered a general withdrawal, leaving the Sunken Road empty of all but its dead. The fight surged into the Henry Piper cornfield and farmstead beyond. Israel Richardson sensed the kill, and charged ahead with his triumphant men. They fought off counterattacks from the collapsing Rebel front until finally slowed by a half dozen batteries raking them with shell and canister. Richardson saw he must reinforce to exploit the breakthrough, and he must have artillery to counter the enemy gun line. He pulled back to the ridgeline in front of the Sunken Road and called for support.

Just then, fighting erupted anew at the Dunker church, where George Greene and two Twelfth Corps brigades defended their foothold in the West Woods. Greene's call for help only gained him two small, untested infantry units. Greene had watched Sedgwick's Second Corps division pass out of sight into the West Woods, and therefore felt at least secure about his right flank . . . until one of Sumner's staff found him and told him of

Sedgwick's rout. "Didn't you know it?" Greene's response was "more picturesquely sulphurous than polite." Before he could recast his position, his right was assailed by a sudden Rebel charge, catching his reinforcements unaware and driving them away in panic. Then Greene's left flank was hit a glancing blow by a second enemy column. Soon enough this last Union foothold in the West Woods was streaming back across the Hagerstown Pike to the safety of the East Woods.

The Confederate column that hit Greene's left had been intended to relieve the pressure on the Sunken Road defenders, and it broke off pursuing Greene to strike at French's division. Nathan Kimball's brigade turned to meet the challenge. Kimball defended with two of his veteran regiments from the Valley, supported from John R. Brooke's brigade of Richardson's division, and the charge faltered and fell back.[29]

These various Confederate counterattacks were launched in desperation, for Lee had committed his last reserves at the Sunken Road. Only the line of guns behind the Hagerstown Pike now laced together the center of his position. But taken together with the earlier, devastating counterblows at Hooker's First Corps and at Sedgwick's division, McClellan divined these strikes as clear evidence of the vast hidden strength of his opponent. He redoubled his caution.

When Richardson called for artillery to support a renewal of his attack on the Rebel center, he discovered how badly the Second Corps artillery was managed this day. The Second's objectives were so vague that no corps batteries supported Sedgwick in the advance. Just one corps battery joined the First and Twelfth Corps artillery in driving back the Rebels after Sedgwick's rout. Just one, Captain Tompkins's, was put to use in French's assault on the Sunken Road. (A second corps battery took Tompkins's place when he exhausted his ammunition.) Not one Second Corps battery advanced with Richardson; not one answered his call for artillery support. Instead of the rifled pieces he needed, he was sent Captain William M. Graham's battery of smoothbore Napoleons.

Graham's shots fell short, and Richardson told him to pull back and save his ammunition to accompany the renewed advance. But just then Richardson was caught in the artillery duel and hit by a shell fragment. The one Union general determined to push ahead with the battle was carried to the rear with a wound that six weeks later killed him. "Tell General McClellan," Richardson said, "I have been doing a Colonel's work all day, and I'm now too badly hurt to do a General's."

McClellan was quick to replace Richardson with another general of

Israel Richardson drove his Second Corps division across the Sunken Road, but was mortally wounded trying to exploit his gain.

fighting reputation. He reached into Baldy Smith's newly arrived Sixth Corps division for Winfield Scott Hancock. Hancock made a dashing entrance, galloping with his staff the length of the battle line. But the order he carried, direct from headquarters, belied his appearance. "Now, men, stay here until you are ordered away," he shouted; "this place must be held at all hazards!" The fight for the center was over. General Lee was reprieved.[30]

Israel Richardson's wounding meant that his pause to strengthen his hand before exploiting his breakthrough went unrecognized at headquarters. Despite having the Sunken Road fighting within view, McClellan read Richardson's action not as an opportunity but as a cautionary tale. He explained in his report that Richardson's (now Hancock's) division "was too weak to attack. . . ." In this the Young Napoleon neglected one of the first Napoleon's maxims — reinforce success. The Fifth Corps reserves went unused and Richardson's victory devolved into stalemate. McClellan did allow Alfred Pleasonton to advance four horse batteries across the Middle Bridge but cautioned him, "Do not expose your batteries without necessity." He asked, "Can you do any good by a cavalry charge?" Pleasonton, surely thinking the general commanding had lost his senses, made no reply.[31]

The wounding of Joe Hooker on the northern battlefront cost McClellan the initiative and the direction of the battle. The wounding of Israel

Richardson stunted prospects at the center of the field. Fitz John Porter remarked on the critical role of field generals on this battlefield. Without their individual efforts, he wrote, "no success would have been attained. As soon as they fell fighting ceased. The army rested on its arms. . . . Every officer of standing and worth must expose himself to an unprecedented degree — without he does so, nothing is accomplished."

Whether or not Edwin Sumner would have ceded field-of-battle command to Joe Hooker that morning, he would certainly have accepted Hooker's firsthand knowledge about where and how and when to launch the Second Corps' attack. In the event, Sumner was demoralized by the disaster inflicted on Sedgwick. As usual he assumed control over everyone in sight — his Second Corps (and corps artillery), Williams's Twelfth Corps, Meade's First Corps — and became obsessed with defending against some unseen but massive and impending enemy attack. He reprised his alarmist, doomsday predictions at Williamsburg and after Seven Pines.

Baldy Smith's was the first Sixth Corps division to reach the field, and McClellan sent it to the northern battlefront in response to Sumner's cry for help. Smith found Sumner by the East Woods. "On reporting to him I was told to close my division in mass facing a certain way from which point he expected an attack" — off to the northwest, threatening the army's flank and rear. Smith termed this "inconceivable," and he ignored Sumner's instructions. General Sumner, he decided, "was in no condition to do any more fighting."[32]

With his battle stalled on the right and at the center, McClellan cast anxious eyes to the left and the Burnside-Cox Ninth Corps. Burnside had received two dispatches from headquarters. The first alerted him to prepare for action but await further orders. Burnside read the second dispatch with dismay — the sharp reprimand for his supposed delays on the 15th and 16th. He replied that on the 15th his march orders only reached him at noon. Any delay in posting the Ninth Corps on the 16th was due to conflicting instructions from staff and engineer officers. General Burnside directed him to say, his adjutant wrote, "that he is sorry to have received so severe a rebuke . . . particularly sorry that the general commanding feels that his instructions have not been obeyed."

Between these two friends it had been "Mac" and "Burn" since the 1850s, so the events of the past few days — the suspension of his wing command, the accusation of disobeying orders, the posting of his troops by staff functionaries — left Burnside baffled by his chief's evident loss of confidence in him. His bafflement was warranted. He gave no cause for complaint on the march from Washington or in the South Mountain fighting. His supposed failings on the 15th and 16th were simply miscommunications ... until Porter and Hunt took hold of them. Hunt's critical remarks the previous evening and McClellan's "so severe a rebuke" that morning seem to have withered Burnside's command independence and initiative. Forthwith he acted strictly bound to orders and nothing more. This was evident in his (and Cox's) failure to inspect personally — and thereby to challenge — engineer James Duane's plan for crossing the Antietam.[33]

It was evident (as even McClellan admitted) that Burnside confronted a difficult task forcing a crossing against the well-dug-in Rebels. The valley of the Antietam narrows at the Rohrbach Bridge crossing, with high ground on both sides sloping steeply toward the water. The road from Rohrersville followed the east bank of the creek, turned to cross the bridge, then ran along the west bank before climbing through a ravine to enter Sharpsburg. Storming the bridge — 175 feet long, a dozen feet wide — would require facing point-blank musketry and artillery fire. The position, wrote Jacob Cox, appeared "virtually impregnable to a direct attack over the bridge."

McClellan's 9:10 a.m. order directing the Ninth Corps to open its attack reached Burnside about 10 o'clock. So soon as he had a foothold west of the creek, "you will be supported." This pledge of support dissipated on reports of reverses and checks elsewhere on the battlefield. As the hours passed, Burnside's operation loomed ever larger in McClellan's thinking ... as did his resolution that Burnside must rely on the troops he had started with.[34]

Burnside and Cox devised their own plan of attack. What was asked of them, explained Cox, was "a desperate sort of diversion in favor of the right wing. . . ." A frontal assault on the bridge seemed a forlorn hope, but it would mask the main effort, at a ford two-thirds of a mile downstream that engineer Duane claimed to have found. Isaac P. Rodman's division was assigned to the ford crossing, Samuel D. Sturgis's division to the Rohrbach Bridge, and Orlando B. Willcox's division held in reserve. The Kanawha Division was split up, one brigade assigned to Rodman and the other to Sturgis.

Rodman was a Rhode Island businessman and banker who had led the 4th Rhode Island in the North Carolina operations. The division sat out Second Bull Run at Falmouth, and was in reserve at Fox's Gap. Sam Sturgis was also new to command. A West Pointer and sixteen-year regular, he had transferred from the Western theater in August. His veteran troops served under Jesse Reno in North Carolina and at Second Bull Run and Fox's Gap. Sturgis had commanded the division just three days, since Reno's death.

The Ninth Corps would suffer this day (like Sumner's Second Corps) from a lack of reconnaissance. This was evident in the initial assault on the Rohrbach Bridge. George Crook's Kanawha brigade was assigned the task, and Colonel Crook recalled the moment: "Capt. Christ on Gen. Cox' staff came to see me and said, 'The General wishes you to take the bridge.' I asked what bridge. He said he didn't know. I asked him where the stream was, but he didn't know. I made some remarks not complimentary to such a way of doing business, but he went off, not caring a cent. . . ." Crook advanced over the hills and through the woods more or less by dead reckoning and came out at the creek 350 yards above the bridge. There he remained, skirmishing with the enemy across the water. Meanwhile, the 11th Connecticut, sent to the bridge from another direction to lay down covering fire for Crook, was cut to pieces and its colonel, Henry W. Kingsbury, mortally wounded.

General Rodman no doubt shared Crook's sour view of the way things were managed in the Army of the Potomac. When he reached the spot where engineer Duane reported a usable ford, he found nothing usable about it — steep banks, the eastern bluff sloping right to the water's edge, sharpshooting Confederates lying in wait. Rodman assumed a misunderstanding . . . or Duane had slacked his job. However that might be, no Ninth Corps officer had been ordered or taken it upon himself to confirm Duane's finding or to reconnoiter to the south. Rodman sent out parties to locate a crossing said to be farther down the creek, known as Snavely's Ford, and sat his division down to await their findings. He neglected to report the delay to corps headquarters, and no one there could understand what happened to this critically important element of the battle plan.[35]

Sam Sturgis had charge of the second assault on the bridge. James Nagle's brigade formed on the Rohrersville Road on the east bank of the creek. The rest of the brigade laid down covering fire as two regiments rushed down the road toward the bridge at the double-quick. The Rebels on the western bluff numbered only a few hundred, but they were perfectly posted and the range was hardly a hundred yards. The Yankee column was shredded in minutes.

It was noontime now and McClellan was impatient. "What is Burnside about? Why do we not hear from him?" He sent off an aide with the

Edwin Forbes pictures the 51st New York and 51st Pennsylvania of Ambrose Burnside's Ninth Corps storming across the Rohrbach Bridge, rechristening it Burnside's Bridge.

instruction, "Tell him if it costs him ten thousand men he must go on now." Burnside and Cox gained the prize at a cost of hardly two hundred men. Edward Ferrero's brigade of Sturgis's division got the assignment this time — a 300-yard rush in the open down the hill and across the meadow directly in front of the bridge. Two batteries pounded canister into the hillside across the creek. The fight for the bridge was in its third hour now, and the defenders were thinned by casualties and short of ammunition. Rodman's division found and crossed Snavely's Ford and threatened the Rebels' flank. The 51st New York and 51st Pennsylvania stormed the bridge, their color bearers side by side. As Cox phrased it, "In column with fixed bayonets, and in scarcely more time than it takes to tell it, the bridge was passed. . . ."[36]

At 1:25 that afternoon General McClellan wrote out a telegram for Washington: "We are in the midst of the most terrible battle of the war, perhaps of history — thus far it looks well but I have great odds against me. . . . I have thrown the mass of the Army on their left flank. Burnside is now attacking their right. . . ." The Fifth Corps was "ready to attack the center as soon as the flank movements are developed. It will be either a great defeat or a most glorious victory. I think & hope that God will give us the latter." He thought better of admitting the possibility of "a great defeat" and crossed out the last two sentences, closing with "I hope that God will give us a glorious victory."[37]

From his command post McClellan could now see evidence of fighting on the bluffs west of the Rohrbach Bridge, showing that the Ninth Corps was on the move at last. He had a message from William Franklin, urging a renewed offensive on the right by the Sixth Corps. (It appeared that once General Franklin shed the responsibilities of independent command he shed as well his overarching caution.) Henry Slocum's division had followed Baldy Smith's onto the field, and Franklin proposed to spearhead an assault on the West Woods and the enemy flank. But he found that Sumner had commandeered one of Slocum's brigades for his own purposes. "I sent for it," Franklin testified, "and it finally arrived, and General Sumner with it." There was a heated argument. "But old Sumner came up just then, and countermanded the order because if we failed there the day would be gone." Franklin was insistent. He and Smith "had made up our minds that it was our business to attack" — unless Sumner forbad it. "He assumed the responsibility, and ordered me not to make it." Franklin hurried off an aide to McClellan to argue the decision.

McClellan had sent Lieutenant James H. Wilson to Sumner with instructions "to get up his men and hold his position at all hazards." Sumner said, "Go back, young man, and ask General McClellan if I shall make a simultaneous advance with my whole line at the risk of not being able to rally a man this side of the creek if I am driven back." Perhaps, said Wilson, the general misunderstood the tenor of McClellan's order. But Sumner was fresh from arguing with Franklin. "Go back, young man, and bring an answer to my question," he repeated sternly.

Wilson found McClellan inspired by Franklin's plan for an offensive. Back to Sumner he went with new orders: "Tell the general to crowd every man and gun into ranks, and, if he thinks it practical, he may advance Franklin to carry the woods in front, holding the rest of the line with his own command, assisted by those of Banks [Williams] and Hooker." Edwin Sumner, addicted to obeying orders without question, fought this order. "Go back, young man, and tell General McClellan I have no command. Tell him my command, Banks' command and Hooker's command are all cut up and demoralized. Tell him General Franklin has the only organized command on this part of the field!"

McClellan determined to go himself to the field to settle the matter. He told Henry Hunt he expected to lead the attack in person. His arrival on the northern battlefront marked a potentially Napoleonic moment for the Young Napoleon. Franklin pleaded his case. So did Baldy Smith. Well versed in Sumner's command failings, McClellan surely recognized the demoralization of the old warrior that was evident to all who saw him that afternoon. Nevertheless, his inbred caution pulled him up short of daring. He could not bring himself to overrule Sumner, or to take command himself and personally lead a renewed offensive. McClellan quoted to Fitz John Porter Sumner's declaration: "His command demoralized and scattered — that he could not risk another attack — but if General McClellan was willing to risk a total defeat if he failed, he would advance." Franklin quoted McClellan's declaration: "Things had gone so well on the other parts of the field that he was afraid to risk the day by an attack there on the right at that time."

"Afraid to risk" — an epigraph for the generalship of George McClellan . . . in his own words.[38]

At headquarters Lieutenant Wilson, a brash West Pointer, class of 1860, tried to enlist reporter George Smalley in a plot. Certain of the staff think the battle only half-fought and half-won, said Wilson. "There is still time to finish it. But McClellan will do no more." He wanted Smalley to go to wounded Joe Hooker and see if he could take the command "and drive Lee into the Potomac." Smalley refused to be party to mutiny, but agreed to at least find out the severity of Hooker's wound. That was enough, said Wilson. "All we want you to do is to sound Hooker and let us know what his views are." If he could not ride, let him return in an ambulance, even on a stretcher, "his bugles blowing and his corps flag flying over him." The troops would rally to him.

Smalley found Hooker at the Pry house, in pain but denouncing the stalled battle in "a very copious vocabulary." As Smalley questioned him about whether he might rejoin the fight, Hooker grew suspicious. "What do you mean," he demanded. "Who sent you here?" Smalley spoke of friends who admired his morning's work and were anxious at this critical moment that he "resume his duties." No, no, he could not, said Hooker. "I am perfectly helpless." With that Smalley saw his errand was useless. Bull Sumner's misreading of the northern battlefront would prevail.[39]

Belatedly, orders went out to Andrew Humphreys to lose not a moment bringing up his Fifth Corps division from Frederick. McClellan realized too that assigning Darius Couch's division to Harper's Ferry that day was a fool's errand and issued a recall. But General Couch resumed the elusive ways that had marked his laggardly march to Crampton's Gap on the

14th. He was silent on where and when the recall order reached him; still, he required twelve hours that day to march fewer than 20 miles, nor was he motivated by the thunder of the guns to set a demanding pace. His division, all present and accounted for, reached the battlefield at dark, when the fighting was over.[40]

At about 3 o'clock that afternoon the Antietam battlefield achieved a state of near-suspended animation. On McClellan's order, the northern battlefront stood on the defensive, manned by the bulk of the army's infantry — First Corps, one-third of the Second Corps, Sixth Corps, Twelfth Corps — and the bulk of the army's artillery. The center at the Sunken Road, held by two Second Corps divisions, stood on the defensive. The Fifth Corps stood on the defensive east of the Antietam. If anything decisive was accomplished this day it would have to be by the Ninth Corps. Smalley visited headquarters: "All hazard of the right being again forced back having been dispelled, the movement of Burnside became at once the turning-point of success and the fate of the day depended on him."

It took two hours for Burnside and Cox to secure their foothold across the creek and ready the Ninth Corps to advance. Sturgis's division, having delivered and supported the bridge attacks, needed ammunition replenished; it would act as the reserve. Orlando Willcox's division, with four batteries, was funneled across the narrow bridge, Burnside himself directing traffic. Willcox's brigades under Benjamin C. Christ and Thomas Welsh, plus George Crook's Kanawha brigade, made up the right of the advance. The left was under Isaac Rodman, moving up from Snavely's Ford — the brigades of Harrison S. Fairchild and Edward Harland, with Hugh Ewing's Kanawha brigade. Jacob Cox had field command. Afterward Cox wondered why, of an army of 100,000, it had all come down that day to the Ninth Corps and its 12,000 men.

McClellan's anxiety was acute. He sent Thomas Key of his staff to Burnside to find out the cause of the Ninth Corps' delay. Key reported that Burnside was across the bridge and said he could hold the ground there. McClellan told Key, for delivery to Burnside, "He should be able to do that with five thousand men; if he can do no more I must take the remainder of his troops and use them elsewhere in the field." This was meant as a goad; McClellan harbored no thoughts of an advance elsewhere in the field, much less reinforcing one.[41]

On Willcox's front, on the right, Colonels Christ and Welsh guided on the Rohrbach Bridge road leading into Sharpsburg, with Crook's bri-

The 9th New York, Rush Hawkins's Zouaves, Harrison Fairchild's brigade, has Sharpsburg (right rear) nearly in hand — but finally out of reach. By Edwin Forbes.

gade in reserve. In his memoir Willcox described his battle line advancing "toward Sharpsburg by scarped roads, passing to the higher land above through ravines and woods filled with the infantry and sharpshooters, the turns of the roadway covered by rifle pits and breastworks. . . ." Each colonel employed one of his four regiments as a heavy skirmish line. A battery lent support, one section to duel the Rebel artillery on the heights ahead and one section with the infantry on the road. Willcox progressed slowly but steadily, in short rushes, the Rebels defending every house and haystack and orchard and stone wall, but finally their batteries were driven off commanding Cemetery Hill. Colonel Welsh reported charging the enemy and driving them rapidly in the direction of Sharpsburg, "my troops advancing to the edge of the town." The advance had pushed out ahead of Rodman, however, and began taking enfilading fire from enemy guns. Colonel Christ called for "some demonstration on the left" to neutralize this fire.

Isaac Rodman's command on the left was the least experienced in the Ninth Corps. Antietam was Rodman's first command. His two brigade leaders in the advance (Ewing's Kanawha brigade was in reserve) were civilian soldiers in *their* first command, Colonel Fairchild a banker from New York, Colonel Harland a lawyer from Connecticut.

Fairchild's brigade had a longer march than those on the right, and an artillery array to contend with. Fairchild's New Yorkers met a hail of fire as they stormed the gun line. When finally the guns pulled back, infantry took their place. But these Yankees were resolute and they pushed all the way to the outskirts of Sharpsburg. The cost was heavy — 455 of 940 men who started the charge — and like Willcox's division, they paused to regroup and await support. At army headquarters David Strother watched as "Burnside made his grand effort. His advancing rush was in full view and magnificently done."

On the far left of the line Edward Harland's brigade encountered trouble from the start. It mustered only three regiments — its 11th Connecticut was wrecked in the first attack on the Rohrbach Bridge — and due to a mix-up in orders the 16th Connecticut and the 4th Rhode Island lagged behind while the 8th Connecticut went to battle by itself. The Connecticut boys rushed ahead with the same élan as Fairchild's New Yorkers and overran a Rebel battery. As Rodman turned back to gather up his two trailing regiments, he sighted off to the left a mass of Confederates that seemed to appear out of nowhere.

Here was the final piece of the Army of Northern Virginia: A. P. Hill's division from Harper's Ferry, marched by Hill at a killing pace — 17 miles in eight hours — and just in time to smash squarely into the flank of the Federal advance. By McClellan's negligence no cavalry vedettes were on duty on the army's flank to signal a warning. An angry Jacob Cox wanted to know, too, why Darius Couch's division could not have come up on the left "as well as A. P. Hill's division. Hill came, but Couch did not."

The Rebel spearhead struck the raw new 16th Connecticut and sent it careening to the rear, carrying along with it the 4th Rhode Island. According to a Connecticut diarist, "In a moment we were riddled with shot . . . orders were given which were not understood. Neither the line-officers nor the men had any knowledge of regimental movements." Worse, the command structure collapsed. General Rodman was shot off his horse with a fatal chest wound; like Joseph Mansfield, Isaac Rodman's first combat command role was counted in minutes. Brigade commander Harland had his horse killed under him and struggled to reach the endangered flank on foot. The officer leading the 4th Rhode Island fell wounded.[42]

With the flank broken in, first Fairchild's brigade and then Willcox's two brigades had to fall back from their hard-won gains on the outskirts of Sharpsburg. Sturgis's reserve division was rallied, as were the two Kanawha brigades, and with the exception of the two regiments on the far flank, the withdrawal was generally orderly. Burnside sent to McClellan for the support promised him in the 9:10 a.m. attack order.

Cavalryman Pleasonton attempted to support Burnside from the center, across the Middle Bridge, with his horse batteries, and sought an advance there by Sykes's Fifth Corps infantry. Sykes objected to using his regulars for anything more than supporting the batteries, and at 3:30 Pleasonton was told, "General McClellan directs me to say he has no infantry to spare." When Fitz John Porter affirmed that verdict, the regulars were recalled. In drafting his report, Pleasonton waxed indignant. General Porter, he said, was never at the front and never crossed the Antietam, and "I knew he was ignorant of the state of affairs at that time ... & I further knew that he was the only officer on the field at that moment who was in the situation to take advantage of the embarrassing condition of the enemy. Decisive victory which was then within our grasp was lost to us by this inaction & apathy." (Pleasonton's published report did not include this passage.)

Reporter Smalley was with McClellan at Fifth Corps headquarters and described the denouement to this epic day of battle. McClellan's full attention was focused on the left. "He sees clearly enough that Burnside is pressed — needs no messenger to tell him that. His face grows darker with anxious thought." The general cast a look at the two Fifth Corps divisions nearby — "He turns a half-questioning look on Fitz-John Porter, who stands by his side, gravely scanning the field. They are Porter's troops below, are fresh and only impatient to share in this fight. But Porter slowly shakes his head, and one may believe that the same thought is passing through the minds of both generals. 'They are the only reserves of the army; they cannot be spared.'"

McClellan and Porter and staff mounted and started toward the left, but soon encountered Burnside's messenger. Smalley watched. "His message is: 'I want troops and guns. If you do not send them, I cannot hold my position half an hour.' McClellan's only answer for the moment is to glance at the western sky. Then he turns and speaks very slowly: 'Tell Gen. Burnside this is the battle of the war. He must hold his ground till dark at any cost. I will send him Miller's battery. I can do nothing more. I have no infantry.' Then as the messenger was riding away he called him back. 'Tell him if he *cannot* hold his ground, then the bridge, to the last man! — always the bridge! If the bridge is lost, all is lost.'"[43]

Perhaps inspired by these delivered histrionics, Burnside held his ground and secured the bridge. Without reinforcements, "the command was ordered to fall back to the crests above the bridge," he wrote, "which movement was performed in the most perfect order." He was not overly discouraged by this turn of events; the enemy reinforcements were not forecasted. Visiting the mortally wounded Isaac Rodman that evening, Burnside told him, "It has gone well today, General; tomorrow we will have it out with them again."

It was dark now and gradually the shooting stopped, and the bloodiest single day of the Civil War finally ended. By the account of Robert Gould Shaw, "The crickets chirped, and the frogs croaked, just as if nothing unusual had happened all day long, and presently the stars came out bright, and we lay down among the dead, and slept soundly until daylight." The Pry house had been taken over as a hospital, and so, wrote David Strother, McClellan and staff "rode back to our headquarters camp at Keedysville, where a good supper and a good night's rest closed the day of the great battle."[44]

11. *"An Auger Too Dull to Take Hold"*

CORRESPONDENT GEORGE SMALLEY likely witnessed more of the fighting at Antietam than anyone else on that field, and when he left at 9 o'clock that night to get his story to New York—it would appear in the *Tribune* on Friday, September 19, and be widely picked up by papers across the country and abroad—he appraised the day as "partly a success; not a victory, but an advantage had been gained." There would be more to come, he thought, but he left covering that to his *Tribune* colleagues. "Every thing was favorable for a renewal of the fight in the morning," he wrote. "If the plan of the battle is sound, there is every reason why McClellan should win it."[1]

There was opportunity to win it. First light on September 18 revealed the Confederates manning lines they held at nightfall on the 17th. No significant change in the enemy positions was reported as the day wore on. General Lee, it seemed, was perfectly willing to continue the contest.

Yet only a few in the Army of the Potomac's officer corps favored renewing the battle on September 18. Burnside testified he went to McClellan on the night of the 17th and "told him that if I could have 5,000 fresh troops to pass in advance of my line, I would be willing to commence the attack on the next morning." McClellan said he would think on the matter. Franklin and Baldy Smith, when they could not overcome Sumner's objections to an advance on the 17th, believed they had McClellan's promise to renew the attempt next morning. At 10:00 a.m. on the 18th Franklin sent to McClellan for attack orders, setting Nicodemus Hill as the target. He, like Burnside, received no response.

Franklin and Smith, and to some extent Burnside, were latecomers to Wednesday's savage battle. Those generals immersed in it from dawn to dusk on Wednesday were less than eager to try again on Thursday. At an early hour McClellan rode to the right to consult with Sumner, and the First Corps' Marsena Patrick began his diary entry for September 18, "We were not attacked last night, & this morning Sumner told me that Mc-

Clellan's orders were '*not* to attack'. . . . It seems to be fairly understood, that only Madcaps, of the Hooker stripe, would have pushed our troops into action again without very strong reinforcements." Fitz John Porter affirmed that Sumner was opposed to any advance on Thursday, "and so I believe were other officers." George Meade found the army "a good deal broken and somewhat demoralized." Alexander Webb of the Fifth Corps staff wrote his father a few days later, "Now that all is over you will hear that we ought to have advanced the next day. Well I say that myself but no one thought so at the time. . . . I know of no advocates for a continuance of the battle on the 18th."[2]

At 8:00 a.m. McClellan reported to Washington that after fourteen hours of battle, "We held all we gained except a portion of the extreme left. . . . Our losses very heavy, especially in General officers. The battle will probably be renewed today." He did not explain that any renewed fighting that day would not be initiated by him. Writing his wife at the same hour, he described Wednesday's "terrible battle against the entire rebel army" as a success, "but whether a decided victory depends upon what occurs today. I hope that God has given us a great success. It is all in his hands, where I am content to leave it."[3]

Couch's and Humphreys's late-arriving divisions were quickly posted. Quickly too, McClellan's hopes for 15,000 Pennsylvania militia evaporated. John Reynolds, co-opted by Governor Curtin, pushed and prodded 6,500 militiamen as far as Chambersburg, whereupon two-thirds of them refused to set foot in Maryland; they only enlisted, they said, to defend their home state. Reynolds regarded them as worthless anyway: "They had better have remained at home" was his sour verdict.

In addition to Couch and Humphreys, there were Porter's Fifth Corps and Franklin's Sixth, barely touched by battle on September 17. Porter had suffered 109 casualties in skirmishing beyond the Middle Bridge. Franklin's casualties were 439, mostly in his one brigade in action on the right. The total came to 32,300 fresh troops available that morning.

This figure exceeded Lee's entire army standing defiantly in its lines on September 18 — which fact, however, was quite beyond knowing or imagining by anyone in the Army of the Potomac. Indeed, to an officer corps steeped in McClellan's gross overcounting of enemy numbers, the Rebels' relentlessly aggressive counterstrokes and the terrible fury in the fighting on Wednesday appeared entirely consistent with battling a better-manned enemy — on the right, Hooker's First Corps stopped and beaten back, Mansfield's Twelfth Corps checked, Sedgwick's division of Sumner's Second Corps routed; at the center, the other two-thirds of Sumner's

By accepting a truce to care for the wounded, McClellan signaled that he would not renew the battle on September 18. Alfred Waud sketched the scene at the Dunker church.

corps bloodily stalemated; on the left, Burnside's Ninth Corps flanked and
driven back to the Rohrbach Bridge. Further, Franklin's Sixth Corps manning a last line of defense on the right; Porter's Fifth Corps and Pleasonton's cavalry manning a last line of defense behind the Antietam. "The
multitude of dead Rebels (I saw them) was proof enough how hotly they
contested the ground," wrote Alpheus Williams. ". . . It was thought advisable not to attack further."[4]

The Federals endorsed that decision by accepting a flag of truce to care
for the wounded and bury the dead. A man in the 130th Pennsylvania, one
of the new regiments, was assigned to a burial detail that began the task
of policing the hideous battlefield. He described how half the detail dug a
long pit and the other half moved out in skirmish formation to collect the
dead, "taking the Union men first and placing them in rows on the banks
of the Pit. When the Pit is dug deep enough the Bodies are placed cross-
wise and as many as fourty seven in one Grave. After the Union men were
all gathered up and buried then we commenced gathering up the Rebs. . . .
We seen among the rebels Boys of Sixteen & Fifteen and old Gray headed
men. There was not to the best of my knowledge in all that was buried two
dressed alike."[5]

In his 1864 *Report* McClellan told of his "anxious deliberation" that
Thursday: "One battle lost, and almost all would have been lost. Lee's
army might then have marched as it pleased on Washington, Baltimore,
or New York." Still, he said he intended to renew the contest on the 19th.

Lee relieved him of that decision by pulling out on the night of September 18–19 and crossing back into Virginia at Shepherdstown. Lee's genius and the stellar efforts of his lieutenants and his troops had saved the Army of Northern Virginia from a disastrous defeat, but the cost was too great to grant the Yankees a second chance. McClellan's pursuit was modest. On September 20 Fitz John Porter sent two Fifth Corps brigades across the Potomac at Shepherdstown, where they were promptly attacked by Lee's rear guard and driven pell-mell back across the river.

Confederate casualties at Antietam came to some 10,300, about a quarter of their forces on the field on September 17. Federal casualties were 12,400, about a quarter of the forces McClellan committed to battle. The combined total of 22,700 marked Antietam as the costliest single day of the Civil War. Adding the casualties at South Mountain and Shepherdstown and the prisoners from Harper's Ferry raised the total Federal loss in Maryland to 27,200, against Lee's comparative loss of 14,000. For McClellan, all that counted was that he, the underdog, had evaded defeat and now the enemy was gone. "I have the honor to report that Maryland is entirely freed from the presence of the enemy, who has been driven across the Potomac," he told Washington. "No fears need now be entertained for the safety of Pennsylvania."[6]

Antietam was the only battle George McClellan ever directed (and witnessed) from start to finish, and he was highly pleased with his conduct on September 17. "The spectacle yesterday was the grandest I could conceive of — nothing could be more sublime," he told Ellen. "Those in whose judgment I rely tell me that I fought the battle splendidly & that it was a masterpiece of art."

Except for Fitz John Porter, it is hard to imagine any other of McClellan's generals offering him such praise. Quite the contrary. To correspondent Smalley, Joe Hooker spoke harshly of McClellan, "with whose excessive caution and systematic inertness in the crisis of a great battle he had no patience." Hooker dismissed McClellan as "timid and hesitating when decision is necessary." Edwin Sumner could not understand why McClellan sent in troops "in driblets" — no way to fight a battle. Alpheus Williams saw no art in wasting "our power by impulsive and hasty attacks on wrong points." William Franklin and Baldy Smith were exasperated by McClellan's refusal to use the Sixth Corps offensively on the 17th and by his failure to renew the battle on the 18th. Smith nominated *indecision* as the "nail in McC's coffin as a general." And Ambrose Burnside, stung by

McClellan's unjust rebukes, cannot have thought there was anything masterful about the way his supposed friend managed the battle.[7]

Seeing McClellan characterize his command at Antietam as a splendid masterpiece of art, soldier-historian Ezra Carman observed that "history will not accept this view of a battle in the conduct of which more errors were committed by the Union commander than in any other battle of the war." McClellan's catalog of errors began with putting his army on the field. Despite his conviction that on September 16–17 he was substantially outnumbered, McClellan engaged but eleven of the seventeen divisions in the Army of the Potomac. Of the six unused divisions, two (Couch and Humphreys) he called too late to the battle; two (Smith and Slocum) arrived only at midday and served only as support; and two (Morell and Sykes) remained in reserve. McClellan massed his cavalry uselessly behind his center, leaving the army's flanks unguarded, and a devastating surprise attack was the consequence.

McClellan failed to share any battle plan with his generals. He failed to execute his moves in any coordinated way. Mansfield's Twelfth Corps was not posted for prompt support of Hooker's First Corps. Hooker was repulsed and the Twelfth Corps halted before Sumner's Second Corps reached the battlefield. Holding back Richardson's division seriously weakened Sumner. Richardson was not released until Morell's division took his place on defense. Richardson's breakthrough at the Sunken Road was not exploited. Burnside's Ninth Corps was not committed until Franklin's Sixth Corps reached the field. Franklin was committed for defense only. Porter's Fifth Corps was not committed at all. Not once was success reinforced. Of his 87,400 men actually on the field on Wednesday, McClellan engaged hardly 50,000.

On September 17 McClellan lacked the courage of *any* conviction that he could win this battle; only that he must not lose it. Except for an interval in midafternoon, he consulted no one except the sycophant Porter. When he did go to the field, he was intimidated by a demoralized Sumner — shied away from either overruling Sumner or personally directing an offensive by the Sixth Corps. He shied away from carrying through Richardson's victory at the Sunken Road — "He could not help seeing the chance," wrote an officer, "for it was thundered into his ears, and must have burned his eyes." He broke the shared trust with Burnside, and refused to reinforce the Ninth Corps in either advance or retreat.

George McClellan represents a singular Civil War conundrum. After the Second Bull Run debacle only he could have reorganized and reshaped and revitalized the Army of the Potomac in time to campaign effectively in Maryland. Yet only he could have failed to exploit the remarkable promise of the Lost Order. Only he, by his obsessive overcounting, could have failed to capitalize on the opportunity (unique in all the war) on September 16–17 to wreck the Army of Northern Virginia. Only he could have rested content simply to see the enemy gone. "I have the satisfaction of knowing that God has in his mercy a second time made me the instrument for saving the nation," he told his wife.[8]

Commanding-officer casualties in the Potomac army at Antietam totaled eleven: corps commanders Joseph K. F. Mansfield, mortally wounded, and Joe Hooker, wounded; division commanders Israel B. Richardson and Isaac P. Rodman, mortally wounded, and John Sedgwick, wounded; brigade commanders George L. Hartsuff, N.J.T. Dana, Max Weber, Samuel W. Crawford, Hector Tyndale, all wounded, and William B. Goodrich, killed.

Antietam made Joe Hooker the most celebrated field commander in the Potomac army, thanks to George Smalley's reporting in the *New-York Tribune*. "I see no reason why I should disguise my admiration of Gen. Hooker's bravery and soldierly ability," Smalley wrote. "Remaining nearly all the morning on the right, I could not help seeing the sagacity and promptness of his movements, . . . how keen was his insight into the battle, how every opportunity was seized and every reverse was checked and turned into another success."

That was a fair appraisal. Hooker was slow, however, to utilize the manpower available to him. He had authority over Mansfield's Twelfth Corps, yet the Twelfth was called up too late to meet Hood's counterattack. Still, Hooker's battlefield leadership was widely acknowledged (McClellan saw him appointed brigadier general in the regular army, filling the vacancy created by Mansfield's death), and his wounding marked a turning point in the battle — or so McClellan believed: "Had you not been wounded . . . I believe the result of the battle would have been the entire destruction of the rebel army. . . ."

Hooker's First Corps lieutenants had a mixed record. George Meade performed with his usual competence, especially in turning back Hood's charge; wounded Hooker recognized Meade's worth in signaling McClellan that he should have the corps command. But James Ricketts led his division unsteadily and his brigades engaged in piecemeal fashion. Abner Doubleday and his brigade commanders John Gibbon, Marsena Patrick, and Walter Phelps attacked with spirit and defended stubbornly. The First

Corps lacked a corps artillery reserve, but the divisional batteries were generally well handled on September 17, due in part to the fact that two of the division commanders, Doubleday and Ricketts, were artillerists in the old army.

Mansfield's fatal wounding did not hinder the progress of the Twelfth Corps. Alpheus Williams, far more experienced, resumed his temporary command of the Twelfth — that undermanned, unsung stepchild corps from Pope's army — and directed it to the most battlefield gains of any-one that day. His division regained much of the ground won, then lost, by Hooker, and George Greene's division gained a lodgment in the West Woods, the farthest Federal advance. Greene accomplished this feat with three brigade commanders new to their posts, one of whom was killed (Goodrich) and one wounded (Tyndale). The Twelfth did have a corps ar-tillery reserve, of seven batteries, and they were well handled, notably in aid of the First Corps and Sedgwick's routed division.

By Williams's thinking, the one blot on the Twelfth Corps' record was the absence from the front of Samuel Crawford. It was with outrage, then, that Williams read McClellan's preliminary report on Antietam, which mentioned no name but Crawford's in accounting the Twelfth Corps' part in the battle. Williams wrote McClellan to correct the corps' fighting rec-ord, how it pressed back the enemy "and held those open fields all day, without relinquishing one inch of ground we had taken, except the woods around the Dunkard church." According to brigade commanders Joseph F. Knipe and George H. Gordon, Crawford issued not a single order all day. (In his final report McClellan corrected the record.) Despite his solid fighting history, citizen-soldier Alpheus S. Williams would never hold more than temporary command of the Twelfth Corps.[9]

The Second Corps suffered 5,138 casualties at Antietam, 41 percent of the Federal total and a burden weighing heavily on Edwin Sumner. "Rarely during the war, in my judgment, has an experienced officer so bungled as Sumner did here," wrote Charles A. Whittier, of Sedgwick's staff. Whittier referred primarily to Sumner blindly directing Sedgwick's division into an ambush in the West Woods, but much else was suspect about Sumner's independent commanding. He failed to keep French's division under his control on the march to battle; he failed to keep control of his artillery, which was largely ineffective; and most important, he failed to keep con-trol of himself after Sedgwick's rout. He lost all sense of the battlefield. He predicted doomsday consequences if ordered into further action. Baldy Smith was right: Bull Sumner "was in no condition to do any more fighting." Franklin and Smith could not move him. McClellan would not. The northern battlefront became his personal citadel: six infantry divisions and rank upon rank of artillery.

William French's mismatched Second Corps division was best suited for support — apparently what Sumner had intended — but by mischance it opened a new battlefront at the Sunken Road. French could think of nothing better than launching serial frontal attacks. After being uselessly held back two hours to guard the Antietam Creek line, Israel Richardson's Second Corps division finally joined French. Hampered by one drunken brigadier (Thomas Meagher) and one reluctant one (John Caldwell), but aided by Francis Barlow outflanking the enemy line, Richardson broke through Lee's center. Just then, doing (as he said) a colonel's work in the front lines, Richardson fell wounded. Quite failing to grasp Richardson's accomplishment, McClellan turned defensive at the center, as he had turned defensive on the right.

McClellan began the Maryland campaign with no more loyal lieutenant than Ambrose Burnside, but by September 17 Burnside had to wonder how he had lost the confidence of his longtime friend. Stripped of his wing command; recipient of the severest rebuke McClellan ever issued; suffering headquarters types to move and post his corps — it all added up to a decided distraction that Wednesday. It appears that McClellan listened to only what confidant Fitz John Porter confided.

However that may be, Burnside (and Jacob Cox) confronted a great challenge that day. No other generals dealt with a contested river crossing; none faced terrain as difficult as that west of the Rohrbach Bridge. Had Burnside been more the warrior general, he might have executed his own plan. But he was modest Burnside, who now felt doubly constrained to follow what was laid out for him. Once finally established across the Antietam, the advance on Sharpsburg was well managed . . . except for the inexperienced Rodman on the far left. It was the surprise factor in A. P. Hill's flank attack on Rodman (like the surprise factor in the attack on Sedgwick in the West Woods) that was decisive — and that surprise was due to McClellan's failure to guard his flanks with cavalry.

Artillery chief Henry Hunt had done well gathering the scattered battery commands for the campaign, but on September 17 his tactical control was limited to seven reserve batteries, five of which were heavy guns of position, posted east of the Antietam. For long-range fire they outgunned the Rebels, but artillery support for the infantry was parceled out at the corps and divisional levels — and at Sumner's behest the bulk of the guns guarded the northern battlefront against a supposed attack. To Richardson's call, Hunt confessed, "There were none disposable; all were actively engaged or had been detached to other points. . . ."[10]

In his first flush of triumph on seeing the Rebels gone, McClellan determined to seize the moment and make his self-proclaimed stature as winning general felt at Washington. "An opportunity has presented itself through the Governors of some of the states to enable me to take my stand," he told Ellen on September 20; "— I have insisted that Stanton shall be removed & that Halleck shall give way to me as Comdr in Chief. I will *not* serve under him — for he is an incompetent fool — in no way fit for the important place he holds. . . . Unless these two conditions are fulfilled I will leave the service." He revealed his scheme to Ambrose Burnside, apparently again a kindred spirit. Burnside said they argued until 3 o'clock one morning, he trying to dissuade McClellan "from making any such conditions" for retaining his command, and McClellan being "excessively stubborn" about the matter.

The governors McClellan believed would spearhead his effort to unseat Stanton and Halleck were David Tod of Ohio, known from Department of the Ohio days; Andrew Curtin of Pennsylvania, with whom he dealt during the Maryland campaign; and Maryland's Augustus W. Bradford, whose state was freed from invasion. The occasion was a governors' conference at Altoona, Pennsylvania, on September 24. But McClellan advocates were a decided minority at Altoona. Stanton and Halleck went unmentioned, and Tod, Curtin, and Bradford barely derailed a resolution calling for McClellan's dismissal. McClellan still targeting Stanton and Halleck, only now he thought better of betting his command on the outcome.[11]

Mr. Lincoln, like newspaper readers across the North, got the fullest accounting of Antietam from correspondent Smalley writing in the *New-York Tribune*. McClellan's cryptic telegrams claiming victory on the basis that Maryland was "freed from the presence of the enemy" and Pennsylvania was safe told only that the Rebel army had crossed back into Virginia without challenge by the Army of the Potomac. Antietam, then, was less than the great victory the president had hoped for, yet it was victory enough for his purposes.

On September 22 Lincoln announced to the cabinet members that he was issuing the preliminary Emancipation Proclamation he had discussed with them two months earlier. At that time, in the wake of McClellan's Peninsula defeat, it was decided to wait for a better time, for a victory, to announce the proclamation. That time had come. "The action of the army

David Blythe's lithographed allegory has Lincoln composing his Emancipation Proclamation with his hand on the Bible, resting on a copy of the Constitution. The Army of
the Potomac petitions at right against "guarding the property of traitors."

against the rebels has not been quite what I should have best liked. But
they have been driven out of Maryland, and Pennsylvania is not longer in
danger of invasion." He explained that he "had made a vow — a covenant
— that if God gave us the victory in the approaching battle, he would consider it an indication of Divine will, and that it was his duty to move forward in the cause of emancipation. . . . God had decided this question in
favor of the slave." On January 1, 1863, all persons held as slaves in any state
then in rebellion against the United States "shall be then, thenceforward,
and forever free. . . ."

(At Antietam General McClellan took satisfaction from knowing that
"God has in his mercy a second time made me the instrument of saving
the nation." At Antietam it also appeared that God had made General Mc
Clellan an unwitting, unwilling instrument of abolition.)

The impact of emancipation spread near and far. When news of it
reached London it brought pause to those advocating intervention in
some fashion in the American war. Support for the Confederacy would
now be seen as supporting the slavery regime in the contest. The British
backed away. As Prime Minister Palmerston phrased it, "we must continue merely to be lookers-on till the war shall have taken a more decided
turn."[12]

At home the news created immediate stirrings. L. A. Whitely, Washington correspondent for the *New York Herald,* wrote editor James Gordon Bennett that "a deep and earnest feeling pervades the army" in reference to the proclamation. "The army is dissatisfied and the air is thick with revolution." Unless emancipation was received "more kindly" by the field army in Maryland than those officers he interviewed in the capital, "it will go far towards producing an expression on the part of the Army that will startle the Country and give us a Military Dictator." He wondered if General McClellan might be one to "dictate to the administration. . . ." Whitely's reporting was overheated, yet there was concern as to how the Army of the Potomac (only that army of all the Union's armies) would react to emancipation. Washington tipster T. J. Barnett asked of the proclamation, "Shall it be suffered to retard the war — to demoralize the Army — to mutinize the generals in the field?"

Whitely was right to wonder about the general commanding. McClellan was stunned and appalled by the preliminary Emancipation Proclamation, and by a second proclamation suspending the writ of habeas corpus as it applied to "all persons discouraging volunteer enlistments, resisting militia drafts, or guilty of any disloyal practice. . . ." He wrote Ellen, "The Presdt's late Proclamation, the continuation of Stanton & Halleck in office render it almost impossible for me to retain my commission & self respect at the same time. I cannot make up my mind to fight for such an accursed doctrine as that of servile insurrection — it is too infamous."

With an arrogant confidence in his prerogative as army commander to challenge the civil and political actions of the commander-in-chief, McClellan unburdened himself to a wider audience. He wrote William H. Aspinwall, a New York merchant and conservative Democrat and one of his home front advisers, "I am very anxious to know how you and men like you regard the recent Proclamations of the Presdt inaugurating servile war, emancipating the slaves & at one stroke of the pen changing our free institutions into a despotism — for such I regard as the natural effect of the last Proclamation suspending the Habeas Corpus throughout the land." He added, "If you regard the matter as gravely as I do, would be glad to communicate with you."[13]

Fitz John Porter articulated McClellan's outrage for the *New York World,* the leading antiadministration paper. To editor Manton Marble, Porter derided the "absurd proclamation of a political coward," insisting that it was "ridiculed in the army — caused disgust, discontent, and expressions of disloyalty to the views of the administration, and amounting I have heard, to insubordination." Emancipation, said Porter, would demoralize the army. It would make the South fight all the harder, thereby making the job of the Army of the Potomac (with "much less than the acknowledged strength of the enemy") all the more difficult.

As it happened, except for the cadre devoted to McClellan, the Potomac army's officer corps took the news of emancipation calmly. Charles Wainwright, Hooker's artillery chief, noted in his diary, "I do not hear much said here in the army on the subject, but all think it unadvised at this time." North Carolinian John Gibbon first thought of resigning "if this contest is going to end in an abolition war," but his Union loyalty prevailed. George Meade told his wife, "The day for *compromise,* for a brotherly reconciliation for the old *Union* in reality as well as name, has passed away, and the struggle must be continued till one side or the other is exhausted & willing to give up." Alpheus Williams favored anything to "put an end to this cursed rebellion." He thought fears of slave insurrections were exaggerated; slaves would be freed only as fast as "our troops get possession of Rebel territory, and this was the case before the proclamation. I don't think matters are much changed by that document."[14]

While McClellan waited on Aspinwall, he received a letter from Montgomery Blair, his lone ally (of sorts) in the cabinet. Blair had a cautionary tale to tell. "Whilst the party which elected the President have been wheeled into line against you by the use of the negro question," he began, "you have remained silent with respect to your views of the subject." Blair urged him to declare himself: "Whilst you supposed the object of the war to be the maintenance of the Government yet the natural result would be the extinction of slavery." He had just learned from Lincoln the fate of Major John J. Key of Halleck's staff, brother to Colonel Thomas M. Key of McClellan's staff. Major Key was heard to say that the Rebel army was not destroyed at Sharpsburg due to a plot to make a compromise "which would preserve slavery and the Union at the same time; the president left me saying that he intended his dismissal." Blair urged McClellan to speak out to avoid any association with those who would "effect such a compromise as Major Key has mentioned."

Major John Key was indeed cashiered. On September 27 he with Levi C. Turner, judge advocate's office, appeared before the president. Turner said he had asked Key why "was not the rebel army bagged" after Sharpsburg. "That was not the game," Key replied. Neither army should gain the advantage; both would keep the field until exhausted, "when we will make a compromise and save slavery." To Key's appeal of his dismissal Lincoln replied, "I had been brought to fear that there was a class of officers in the army, not very inconsiderable in numbers, who were playing a game to not beat the enemy when they could, on some peculiar notion as to the proper way of saving the Union. . . . I dismissed you as an example and a warning to that supposed class." The Key case, as Lincoln intended, resonated through the army. It went public in an article (written anonymously by presidential secretary John Hay) that noted of Key, "Striking him down may silence others like him."[15]

McClellan continued stubbornly along his own path. He felt he must declare himself regarding emancipation, and for advice he called in three generals, Ambrose Burnside, Jacob Cox, and John Cochrane, a political general supposedly wise in the ways of Washington. McClellan said he realized the war would probably abolish slavery, but he felt steps to that end should be (by Cox's account) "conservatively careful and not brusquely radical." He said he was urged by certain politicians "and army officers who were near to him" (he named no names) to stand in open opposition to the proclamation. He was assured, he said, that the army was devoted to him and would "as one man enforce any decision he should make."

His guests were as one telling him that taking a public stand against the president's proclamation would be a fatal error and properly regarded as usurpation; those who told him differently were his worst enemies. Cox reminded him that "our volunteer soldiers were citizens as well as soldiers, and were citizens more than soldiers." Not a corporal's guard would stand by him if he challenged the subordination of the military to the civil authority. McClellan appeared to agree that this was probably so. Yet he was not quite done. He called in Baldy Smith, with whom he had apparently mended fences since Harrison's Landing, and showed him the draft of a letter to the president taking, as Smith remembered it, "a pretty strong dissent from the terms of the Proclamation." Smith told him, "General, that letter forwarded would utterly ruin you." The army would not support him, the country would not support him. He "could not imagine a more suicidal thing," said Smith, and he was relieved to see McClellan drop the matter.[16]

William Aspinwall cast the last vote in this tortured debate McClellan had with himself. "Mr. Aspinwall is decidedly of the opinion that it is my duty to submit to the Presdt's proclamation & quietly continue doing my duty as a soldier," McClellan told Ellen. "I presume he is right. . . ." To quell supposed unrest in the Potomac army over the proclamation, McClellan issued a general order reminding the army of the supremacy of the civil over the military: "Discussions by officers and soldiers concerning public measures determined upon and declared by the Government, when carried at all beyond temperate and respectful expressions of opinion," impaired discipline and bred a spirit of political faction. It was a time of mid-term elections, and McClellan pointedly added, "The remedy for political errors, if any are committed, is to be found only in the action of the people at the polls." The overexcited *New-York Tribune* approved, seeing McClellan's general order as a rebuke to the "zanies" and "dangerous ringleaders" in the officer corps who were "threatening the most unutterable vengeance of 'the army' on 'the abolitionists' if they don't stop interfering with Gen. McClellan!"[17]

McClellan's deliberations were interrupted by a visit from the president. After the Seven Days the lack of trustworthy information on the state of the Army of the Potomac drew Lincoln to Harrison's Landing to see matters for himself, and on October 1 he traveled to Sharpsburg for the same purpose. For four days he reviewed troops, visited the wounded, and toured the battle sites. "The President is here," Porter alerted editor Marble. "His visits have been always followed by injury, so look out. Another proclamation or War Order." McClellan told Ellen, "His ostensible purpose is to see the troops & the battle fields. I incline to think that the real purpose of his visit is to push me into a premature advance into Virginia."

President and general spoke at length, and each man came away with different impressions. "The Presdt was very kind personally — told me he was convinced I was the best general in the country etc. etc.," McClellan wrote Ellen. "He was very affable & I really think he does feel very kindly towards me personally." He closed his letter by saying he would think over the whole matter "& do my best to hit upon some plan of campaign that will enable me to drive the rebels entirely away from this part of the country forever."

Affable he may have been, but Lincoln had points to make. He spoke candidly to McClellan of his overcautiousness, what he referred to privately as his "slows." (When photographer Alexander Gardner arrived at Sharpsburg, the president wrote in a note to Mrs. Lincoln, "Gen. McClellan and myself are to be photographed . . . if we can be still long enough. I feel Gen. M. should have no problem. . . .") He believed he made one point forcefully — "that he would be a ruined man if he did not move forward, move rapidly & effectively."

Yet Lincoln had to wonder if what he said — what he ever said or ever wrote — really registered with this general. Indeed, was this the Union's army or the general's? One evening during the visit he stood with his friend Ozias M. Hatch surveying the vast encampment spread before them and asked, "Do you know what this is?" Hatch said it was the Army of the

On Lincoln's visit to the Antietam battlefield, Alexander Gardner seized the occasion to pose the president with McClellan in the flag-draped headquarters tent.

Potomac. "So it is called," said Lincoln, "but that is a mistake; it is only Mc-Clellan's body-guard."[18]

McClellan's hope to be rid of Stanton was fading, but he made a last attempt to be rid of Halleck by assuming his place. He tapped General Cochrane to lobby for him in Washington. A two-term Democratic congressman weaned on New York's Mozart Hall politics, John Cochrane was a War Democrat more skilled finding his way around the capital than around the battlefield. He visited Treasury Secretary Chase, hoping to renew Chase's patronage of the general. In his journal Chase summarized Cochrane's pitch: McClellan would "like to retire from active comd if without disgrace wh. cd. be accomplished & a more active general secured by restoring him to Chief Command." Chase said he would think on it. Cochrane then took his proposal to the White House. Lincoln said that returning McClellan to the post of general-in-chief "had occurred to him," that he "apprehended no serious inconvenience from the loss of Halleck's services." Like Chase, Lincoln said he would give the idea further thought . . . and further thought proved the end of it.

This effort to trade his field command "without disgrace" for the general-in-chief's post marked the climax of McClellan's growing determination that Antietam be his last battle. On September 20 he had told Ellen he believed his military reputation "is safe & that I can retire from the service for sufficient reasons without leaving any stain upon my reputation." Two days later he wrote her, "I feel that the short campaign just terminated will vindicate my professional honor & I have seen enough of public life." If Stanton remained in office, he wrote on the 29th, "I cannot in justice to myself remain in the service. . . ." It seems evident that among his reasons for dragging his feet concerning a new campaign was a reluctance to face Robert E. Lee again.[19]

On October 6, two days after Lincoln returned to Washington, General-in-Chief Halleck telegraphed McClellan, "The President directs that you cross the Potomac and give battle to the enemy or drive him south. Your army must move now while the roads are good." If he advanced directly into the Shenandoah Valley after the Rebels there, McClellan was promised 12,000 to 15,000 reinforcements. If he advanced between the enemy and Washington, covering the capital, he could be reinforced by 30,000 men. "The President advises the interior line, between Washington and the enemy, but does not order it." Halleck told his wife the next day all would be well "if I could only get Genl McClellan to move. He has now lain still *twenty days* since the battle of Antietam, and I cannot persuade him to advance an inch."

McClellan replied, "I see no objective point of strategical value to be gained or sought for by a movement between the Shenandoah & Washn." —Lincoln's interior line. But he saw little strategical value in the Valley line either, except to discourage the Rebels from another dash at Maryland and Pennsylvania. All he offered for the future—certainly not the immediate future—was "to adopt a new & decisive line of operations which shall strike at the heart of the rebellion." To McClellan watchers, that spoke of the Peninsula. "McClellan's heart is not in this movement," correspondent Albert Richardson wrote his editor. "He clings to the Peninsula. As far as I can judge . . . he is in favor of going into winter quarters. If he is kept at the head of the army, it *will* go into winter quarters. . . ."

McClellan's thoughts for this new campaign being pressed on him were different indeed from the president's. Lincoln had in mind seizing the strategic initiative—a major offensive aimed at a showdown battle before winter. Writing his wife, McClellan spoke of a "little campaign," limited by supply issues to just a few days, and if "it is once fought some other line of operations will have to be taken as the one up here leads to no final result." That was the argument he used a year earlier in refusing to challenge Joe Johnston at Manassas. Then, only on the Peninsula might there be a "final result." Now, he would settle for driving the Rebels "entirely away from this part of the country."

Whatever the task, he would once more be outnumbered. That was the intelligence extracted by Darius Couch from an alleged Unionist refugee from Martinsburg, who claimed "that their force in the Valley number 150,000." Soon enough that was the figure circulating in the high command, and in Washington skeptic Sam Heintzelman could only shake his head. He noted in his diary, "The enemy is supposed to have 150,000 men. I dont think so." (General Lee's return for October 20 showed 68,000 men present for duty.)[20]

For three weeks all was quiet on the Potomac as McClellan wrangled with Washington daily, hourly. He could not start south, he insisted, due to shortages of everything, notably clothing and shoes for the men and horses for the cavalry and artillery. He urged the battle-worn regiments be filled out with recruits. He argued for guarding the Potomac line by fortifying Harper's Ferry, building bridges, even constructing a new railroad line. His arguments with the Quartermaster's Department grew heated. There were indeed shortages, but a goodly share of the delay was at the Potomac army end of the supply pipeline. Quartermasters' requisitions were untimely; freight cars sat for days on sidings before being unloaded and returned; rail and wagon transport was mismanaged. Finally the railroad man Herman Haupt was called in again and he issued a barrage of orders "which will remedy the evils complained of."[21]

Had his heart been in this advance, McClellan would surely have stepped in with his unmatched organizational skills to sort out the tangles and get the army's logistics running smoothly. Instead, in a particular display of indifference, on October 9 he and chief of staff (and father-in-law) Randolph Marcy went absent without leave.

In a private car furnished by the president of the Baltimore & Ohio, McClellan and Marcy, in mufti, traveled to Baltimore and then on to Philadelphia where they met Ellen, the McClellans' year-old daughter May, Mrs. Marcy, and a nurse for the baby. The party had traveled from Connecticut to visit the Potomac army. "Genl. McC. wore his citizens dress & managed to slip into the town without attracting much attention," Ellen wrote a friend. They left Philadelphia the next day, October 10, and aboard the B. & O. private car "really enjoyed the trip immensely" to Harper's Ferry. Then by carriage to Pleasant Valley, from where Ellen wrote, "Here

I am in the loveliest valley that you can imagine, in loyal little Maryland at present inhabiting a quaint primitive little farm house and at this present moment as happy as I *can* be, with my husband by my side." Their idyll would last two weeks.[22]

During the forty-eight hours that McClellan and his chief of staff were secretly absent, Jeb Stuart with 1,800 cavalrymen crossed the Potomac upstream from Williamsport, crossed Maryland and the Pennsylvania line, and occupied Chambersburg. A Rebel trooper wrote, "Everything indicated our coming to be unexpected, and not a shadow of opposition appeared." That was not surprising, for just then the Army of the Potomac was leaderless. Only at nightfall on October 10 were McClellan and Marcy back at headquarters. After destroying war supplies in Chambersburg and making off with 1,200 horses from Pennsylvania farmers, Stuart completed his second "ride around McClellan," recrossing the Potomac below Harper's Ferry. The disordered Yankee pursuit never recovered from its late start.

McClellan's secret journey to Philadelphia remained his secret, but he was embarrassed enough as it was by Stuart's exploit. As Colonel Wainwright put it, the raid was "a burning disgrace. . . . I fear our cavalry is an awful botch." McClellan sought to explain to Washington that his cavalry was necessarily widely scattered to watch the many Potomac crossings, and "this severe labor has worked down the horses and rendered many of them unserviceable." In any case, he said, the government had left him short of cavalry to begin with. Halleck replied that the president "directs me to suggest that, if the enemy had more occupation south of the river, his cavalry would not be so likely to make raids north of it."[23]

While the army struggled with logistics, the high command required major sorting out. In the First Corps, John Reynolds returned from his dispiriting interlude with the Pennsylvania militia and, by seniority, displaced George Meade as corps commander while Hooker recuperated. Having in five days risen from leading a brigade to leading a corps, Meade wondered if anything was secure. He told his wife, "Should Hooker get well, he returns, takes command of the Corps, Reynolds comes back to the Division & *I* to a brigade." He hoped his fighting record (and political support from home state Pennsylvania) would reward him with a second star; "then let what may occur I can never have a *less* command than a Division." In November he and Reynolds were named as major generals.

Also in the First Corps, James Ricketts's injuries from his horse falling on him on September 17 would debilitate him for eighteen months. John Gibbon took his division. Among brigade commanders, George Hartsuff's

Antietam wound kept him from further service in the Potomac army, Abram Duryée went on leave and then resigned his commission early in 1863, and Marsena Patrick was named provost marshal for the Potomac army. Their replacements were Nelson Taylor, Adrian R. Root, and William F. Rogers, respectively.

After Antietam Bull Sumner was weary and shaken enough to take a leave of absence. (McClellan tried, and failed, to push him out of the Potomac army into a departmental command somewhere.) Sumner was replaced as Second Corps commander by Darius Couch. Also in the Second Corps, Winfield Hancock, plucked from a Sixth Corps brigade to replace the mortally wounded Israel Richardson, remained in that divisional post. Otis Howard took over the division of the wounded John Sedgwick. Among the brigades, Norman J. Hall replaced the wounded N.J.T. Dana, and John W. Andrews, the wounded Max Weber.

The Ninth Corps' chief of artillery, George W. Getty, took the division of the mortally wounded Isaac Rodman. Jacob Cox's Kanawha Division ended its brief stay with the Army of the Potomac and returned to western Virginia. Additional regiments and a reshuffling of brigades more than made up for the loss of the Kanawhas. With Cox's departure, Orlando Willcox became corps commander. Ambrose Burnside was for the moment put in charge of the three corps posted at Harper's Ferry.

In the Twelfth Corps, Brigadier General Alpheus Williams, U.S. Volunteers, wrote home, "There are so many major generals anxious to command corps that I shall probably have a new commander soon. It is only wonderful that I have held the command so long." He was right. He returned to divisional command and Henry Slocum of the regulars took over the corps. The Twelfth Corps, much reshuffled, was held back to defend Harper's Ferry.

The Fifth Corps, virtually untouched at Antietam, saw only one immediate command change, with plodding George Morell leaving the Potomac army for a post guarding the upper Potomac. Daniel Butterfield assumed his division. In the Sixth Corps, Couch's division of the old Fourth Corps officially became part of the Sixth, and when Couch replaced Sumner in the Second Corps, John Newton took Couch's division. Henry Slocum's departure for the Twelfth Corps raised W.T.H. Brooks to command of Slocum's division. With Winfield Hancock now in the Second Corps, his brigade went to Calvin E. Pratt.[24]

In the weeks following Antietam there was widespread unease and many rumors centered in the Army of the Potomac. "The country groans but nothing is done," Gideon Welles entered in his diary. "We have sinister rumors of peace intrigues and strange management. . . . McClellan is not accused of corruption, but of criminal inaction. His inertness makes the assertions of his opponents prophetic. Many believe him to be acting on the army programme avowed by [Major] Key." Editor William Cullen Bryant, whose *New York Evening Post* supported the administration, linked military stagnation with the forthcoming midterm elections. "These inopportune pauses, this strange sluggishness in military operations seem to us little short of absolute madness," he wrote Lincoln. "Besides their disastrous influence on the final event of the war they will have a most unhappy effect upon the elections. . . ."

The officer corps grew uneasy about the course of the army and about the tenure of the general commanding. McClellan loyalist William Franklin resented Lincoln's visit and his "meddling" in army business. "We hardly know what his object was in coming here, but take it for granted that it bodes no good to us," he told his wife. "Our little Genl is well, but in my opinion loses influence every day." Alpheus Williams, not of the army's old guard like Franklin, met Lincoln on his visit and found him "the most unaffected, simple-minded, honest, and frank man I have ever met." He did wish of the president "a little more firmness, though I suppose the main difficulty with him is to make up his mind as to the best policy amongst the multitude of advisers and advice." Correspondent Albert Richardson wrote his editor, "I am surprised at the number of brigade, division, and regimental commanders who are not only anti-McClellan, but swear that the country is dying of McClellan."

Colonel George D. Ruggles of the headquarters staff felt that "*our* salvation now depends on effecting some changes instanter. . . . McClellan is our Senior Regular Major-General. He has the right by prescription to be General-in-Chief. Let Halleck take half the Republic as his Department — West. Let Hooker take the field here." George Meade was of the same mind, but he saw political forces at work. He told his wife that if McClellan "does not advance soon & do something brilliant, he will be superseded," with Hooker succeeding him. Rumor named McClellan general-in-chief and Halleck returning to the West, "but I can hardly believe this." So long as Stanton "& the ultra Republicans or abolitionists have the influence they are known to have with the Presdt," McClellan could never resume the supreme command. Meade thought Hooker "a capital officer to command an Army Corps, but I should doubt his qualifications to command a large army."[25]

Joe Hooker had no doubts about commanding a large army, and he worked busily toward that goal. His foot wound was just serious enough

GREAT AMERICAN TRAGEDIANS, COMEDIANS,
CLOWNS AND ROPE DANZERS IN
THEIR FAVORITE CHARACTERS

Southerner Adalbert Volck presents Lincoln as jester with a bevy of failed puppets. Simon Cameron is suspended. Gideon Welles (in rowboat) is next to Ben Butler. In front: Frémont, Winfield Scott (in wheelchair), McClellan (on hobbyhorse). Treasury's Chase takes tickets.

to gain him sympathy, and he played the heroic invalid while recuperating in the doctors' quarters at Washington's Insane Asylum. Treasury Secretary Chase and his beautiful daughter Kate came visiting, bearing a gift basket of peaches and grapes. Chase was seeking a new protégé after his disappointments with McDowell and McClellan. Hooker spoke freely of McClellan's missed opportunities on the Peninsula and more recently in Maryland. At Antietam, said Hooker, had he not been wounded, "our victory would have been complete; for I had already gained enough and seen enough to make the rout of the enemy sure." As early as September 24 — in striking contrast to McClellan — Hooker told the press that the Emancipation Proclamation was if anything "issued too late, rather than too early," and was essential to the successful prosecution of the war. Fitz John Porter warned *New York World* editor Marble that Hooker was pursuing the high command and would turn a somersault to get it. "He is ambitious & unscrupulous."

Henry Halleck would welcome being relieved as general-in-chief. Under siege from all sides, he had wilted to near irrelevance. Beyond Pope's debacle and the trials of the Maryland campaign, he confronted a simultaneous Confederate uprising in the Western theater. Braxton Bragg invaded

Kentucky, raised his flag over Frankfort, the state capital, and threatened Cincinnati. But at Perryville, on October 8, a Union army under Don Carlos Buell fended off Bragg's offensive. When Bragg retreated Buell did not pursue. He proved as immobile as McClellan, and Lincoln's patience ran out. On October 24 General Buell was dismissed.

McClellan might have recognized Buell's fate as a cautionary tale. Instead he raised one of his maddening alarms. There was fresh danger from Kentucky, he warned Halleck, in "the fact that a great portion of Bragg's Army is probably now at liberty to unite itself with Lee's command." Halleck replied wearily: "I do not think that we need have any immediate fear of Bragg's army. You are within 20 miles of Lee's, while Bragg is distant about 400 miles." For Henry Halleck it was a last straw. "I am sick, tired, and disgusted with the condition of military affairs here in the East and wish myself back in the Western Army," he told Missouri's Governor Hamilton Gamble. "With all my efforts I can get nothing done. There is an immobility here that exceeds all that any man can conceive of. It requires the lever of Archimedes to move this inert mass. I have tried my best, but without success."[26]

Mr. Lincoln, in a carefully reasoned letter dated October 13, tried *his* best to prod the Young Napoleon into action. "You remember my speaking to you of what I called your over-cautiousness," he began. "Are you not over-cautious when you assume that you can not do what the enemy is constantly doing? Should you not claim to be at least his equal in prowess, and act upon the claim?" As to the route east of the Blue Ridge he had proposed, Lincoln explained that "you are now nearer Richmond than the enemy is by the route that you *can,* and he *must* take. Why can you not reach there before him, unless you admit that he is more than your equal on a march. His route is the arc of a circle, while yours is the chord. The roads are as good on yours as on his." Should Lee again strike north, "he gives up his communications to you absolutely, and you have nothing to do but to follow him, and ruin him." Should Lee move south toward Richmond to hold his communications, "I would press closely to him, fight him if a favorable opportunity should present, and, at least, try to beat him to Richmond on the inside track. I say 'try'; if we never try, we shall never succeed. . . . It is all easy if our troops march as well as the enemy; and it is unmanly to say they can not do it." Lincoln closed by saying, "This letter is in no sense an order." In fact it was an order, if an unstated one. The president had privately set his general a goal. If he did not meet it, he would be dismissed.[27]

. . .

Two more weeks passed without event, marked only by McClellan's assurance that he would "give to your Excellency's letter that full & respectful consideration which it merits. . . ." But he recognized Lincoln's impatience. He showed the letter to Darius Couch, remarking that he might not have the army command much longer. "Lincoln is down on me." Couch said he found no ill feeling in the letter, but McClellan disagreed. "Yes, Couch, I expect to be relieved from the Army of the Potomac, and to have a command in the West."

His litany of complaints continued unabated. One in particular frayed the president's temper — a report McClellan forwarded from a cavalry colonel who said half his horses are "absolutely unable to leave the camp" due to a long list of problems. "I have just read your dispatch about sore-tongued and fatigued horses," Lincoln responded. "Will you pardon me for asking what the horses of your army have done since the battle of Antietam that fatigues anything?" In a lengthy defense of his cavalry, McClellan stressed (perhaps unwisely) all the horse-miles expended chasing after Jeb Stuart in Maryland and Pennsylvania.

Finally supplies arrived and Mrs. McClellan and party went home, and on October 26 — not quite six weeks after Antietam — the Army of the Potomac began crossing into Virginia. McClellan offered no plan or objective. He followed the "inside track" east of the Blue Ridge, between Washington and Lee's army in the Valley, but he ignored Lincoln's prescription for beating the Rebels to Richmond on that inside track. "It is all easy if our troops march as well as the enemy," said the president. McClellan made no pretense of putting his men to that test.

It was nine days before the last of the Potomac army was across the Potomac. After thirteen days of marching, it had advanced 45 miles, averaging less than three and a half miles per day. The five army corps in the advance — First, Second, Fifth, Sixth, and Ninth — were reinforced by the Eleventh Corps and part of the Third. There was frequent cavalry skirmishing but no breakthrough at any of the passes in the Blue Ridge separating the two armies. Lee sent Longstreet's corps south out of the Valley to take a blocking position ahead of the Federals at Culpeper Court House. He held Jackson's corps in the Valley on the Federals' flank.

It was clear that McClellan was setting his usual glacial pace; clear too that glacial was the only pace he knew. When it was known that the Confederates had reached Culpeper, it was obvious that McClellan had no intention of trying to outpace or outmaneuver the Rebels. All that the president's carefully wrought October 13 letter accomplished was to move the army from one side of the Potomac to the other. McClellan's arrogance was in full flower, telling his wife of the "mean & dirty character of the dispatches I receive," full of "wretched innuendo.... But the good of the country requires me to submit to all this from men whom I know to be greatly my inferiors socially, intellectually & morally! There never was a truer epithet applied to a certain individual than that of the 'Gorilla.'"[28]

Lincoln's decision was soon made, but he waited to announce it until the midterm congressional elections were over across the North. He would not award the Democrats so hot an issue as a deposed General McClellan. On November 5, Lincoln wrote out an order to Halleck: "By direction of the President, it is ordered that Major General McClellan be relieved from the command of the Army of the Potomac; and that Major General Burnside take the command of that Army."

Lincoln expounded on his decision to John Hay: "I saw how he could intercept the enemy on the way to Richmond. I determined to make that the test. If he let them get away I would remove him. He did so & I relieved him." John Nicolay explained to his fiancée, "The President's patience is at last completely exhausted with McClellan's inaction and never-ending excuses." His personal regard for the general "led him to indulge him in his whims and complaints and shortcomings as a mother would indulge her baby, but all to no purpose. He is constitutionally *too slow*, and has fitly been dubbed the great American tortoise." Lincoln spoke of the missed opportunities after Antietam to diarist Orville Browning: "The army of the enemy should have been annihilated, but it was permitted to recross the Potomac without the loss of a man, and McClellan would not follow. He coaxed, urged & ordered him, but all would not do." When Francis Preston Blair argued the political risk of relieving McClellan, Lincoln said simply, "He had tried long enough to bore with an auger too dull to take hold."[29]

Secretary Stanton did not discount a coup d'état on McClellan's part, and he planned the change of command with care. He sent his adjutant, Brigadier General Catharinus P. Buckingham, to the army with strict orders. He was to see Burnside first and employ the "strongest arguments" to induce him to accept the command. If he refused it, Buckingham was to return to Washington for new orders ... which then would involve Joe Hooker. On Buckingham's arrival, Burnside spoke, as he had twice before, "of his want of confidence in himself." Buckingham warned of consequences for disobeying an order, but it was the threat of his nemesis Hooker getting the command that brought him around.

With Burnside in tow, Buckingham went to McClellan's tent and handed him Lincoln's order relieving him. "I was much surprised," McClellan told

Alfred Waud sketched McClellan's final review of the Potomac army. "The scenes of to-day repay me for all that I have endured," he wrote to his wife.

Ellen, "—but as I read the order in the presence of Genl Buckingham, I am sure that not a muscle quivered nor was the slightest expression of feeling visible on my face. . . . They shall not have that triumph." To his successor he said with a smile, "Well, Burnside, I turn the command over to you."

Afterward McClellan became introspective in his letter to Ellen. "They have made a great mistake — alas for my country — I know in my inner-most heart she never had a truer servant . . . I do not see any great blun-ders — but no man can judge of himself." In a final analysis he took his usual stance: "Our consolation must be that we have tried to do what was right — if we failed it was not our fault."[30]

McClellan stayed on a few days to help Burnside with the transition. There was a grand review with the firing of artillery salutes and much cheering and displays of emotion. McClellan admonished protesters among his officers to give Burnside the same loyalty they had always given him. "We had a rough time last night," Provost Marshal Patrick told his diary, "as officers & men had been drinking to drown grief & the camp was noisy." George Meade thought "the slightest encouragement from the superior officers would bring on a mutiny in the twinkling of an eye." William Swinton of the *New York Times* did hear a brigade commander (unnamed) predict the army would soon march home, led by its officers. Another brigadier (unnamed but well-read) wanted McClellan to lead the army to Washington "and clear out the Abolition crew, as Cromwell did the Rump Parliament." But with the new day Swinton added, "the efferves-cence will presently die away."

The men in the ranks were content to vent their emotions in letters home. "Well Jim," wrote a man in John Gibbon's division, "I am so mad that I can hardly write, the God-d—— abolitionists of the North have succeeded in their hellish work of removing little Mac. The boys all want to go home." However, a man in the Irish Brigade told his mother, "In spite of my desire for a change, I could not help feeling badly. . . . I regret the necessity of a change but I *do* think that McClellan was awful slow. He seemed to be *afraid* to risk a battle."[31]

What could be the motive "in relieving a successful general in the midst of a campaign," Fitz John Porter asked. "Was there fear Genl. McC. would succeed and the war close or have a tendency to close? Is this a political war alone?" Meade too saw a political motive. As the administration "look on McClellan as the military representative of the Democracy, they have struck a blow at the party thro' him," he told his wife, but this was a great mistake: "It will most certainly result in making a martyr of McClellan, & putting him in the White House." But Meade recognized too McClellan's vice: "He was always waiting to have every thing just as he wanted before he would attack, & before he could get things arranged as he wanted them, the enemy pounced on him. . . . Such a General will never command suc-cess, tho' he may avoid disaster."

Winfield Scott Hancock was notably clearheaded about the Young Na-poleon's dismissal: "I do not sympathize with the movement going on to resist the order. 'It is useless,' I tell the gentlemen around me. 'We are serv-ing no one man: we are serving our country.'"

On November 11 McClellan boarded a special train that would take him out of the war. The color guard tried to stage a protest, but he told them to follow General Burnside loyally and all would be well, and bid them fare-well. The Army of the Potomac would see no more of George McClellan, yet the mark he left on that army proved indelible.[32]

12. *Trial on the Rappahannock*

THAT TWICE BEFORE he pressed the Potomac army command on Burnside (reports of which had leaked out) had tempered Lincoln's choices for a new commanding general. In any case, Burnside had certain qualities that at this critical moment in the army's history commended him to the post. He did well enough on the North Carolina coast and at South Mountain. At Antietam he performed no worse than several other Federal generals. He was an outsider yet not a stranger to the officer corps. He was considered a friend of McClellan's yet did not owe his place to him. Although he fought at First Bull Run and lately in Maryland, he was not so deeply rooted in the Army of the Potomac's culture and politics that his independence was compromised. Just that reason drew Lincoln to Burnside in the first place — he seemed apolitical.

Joe Hooker had the better fighting record, certainly, but Hooker's outspoken faultfinding and unbridled ambition made him, just then, a potentially disruptive leader. Among the other corps commanders, Porter and Franklin were notably McClellan's men, and Sumner was notably unsuited for high command. Lincoln recognized that at this moment — unrest and worse reported in the officer corps, the supposed conspiracy disclosed by Major Key — Ambrose Burnside might be the best antidote for whatever poisons infected the Potomac army's high command. For Henry Halleck, replacing McClellan "became a matter of absolute necessity. In a few weeks more he would have broken down the government." Gideon Welles reflected the administration's wait-and-see attitude: "Burnside will try to do well — is patriotic and amiable, and had he greater power and grasp would make an acceptable if not a great General. . . . We shall see what Burnside can do and how he will be seconded by other generals and the War Department."[1]

McClellan told his wife, "Poor Burn feels dreadfully, almost crazy" about taking the command. In the same vein, he wrote in a note to Mrs. Burnside that her husband "is as sorry to assume command as I am to give it up. Much more so." Burnside's reluctance hardly generated confidence among his lieutenants. George Meade heard from McClellan that at first "B. refused to take the command, said it would ruin the army & the country & he would not be an agent in any such work." In Otis Howard's opinion, "I should feel safer with McClellan to finish what he had planned & was executing so well. . . . I fear we hav'nt a better man." To Alpheus Williams, "Burnside is a most agreeable, companionable gentleman and a good officer, but he is not regarded by officers who know him best as equal to McClellan in any respect." Baldy Smith hoped Burnside would accept advice from those (Smith in particular) who "had his interests at heart." Darius Couch asserted, in the smug comfort of hindsight, "We did not think that he had the military ability to command the Army of the Potomac." But William Franklin saw the need to tamp down a potentially volatile transfer of power. He told his wife, "The feeling of the Army is excessive indignation. Every one likes Burnside, however, and I think that he is the only one who could have been chosen with whom things would have gone on so quietly."[2]

Burnside's approach to high command was a sharp contrast to the imperial trappings of the Young Napoleon. The new commanding general was a large man of thirty-eight years, with luxuriant muttonchop whiskers — the model for sideburns — and an unpretentious manner. Daniel R. Larned of his staff told his sister, "I wish you could see the General commanding the Army of the Potomac footing it into camp without any orderlies — without his shoulder straps, belt or sword." His tent, unlike McClellan's, "is full all the time, & it is as informal as you please." A guard at headquarters wrote his parents, "Old B. came out of his tent at 2 1/2 o'clock this morning in his shirt & warmed his butt at the fire before his quarters, he is a jolly bugger & will joke with a private as quick as an officer." But Burnside took his new responsibilities, however unwelcome, very seriously. "He is working night & day . . . ," Larned wrote. "He has slept but little and is most arduous in his labors and does not spare himself even for the common necessities of health."[3]

Burnside was granted little time for reflection. With the dispatch assigning him the command came one from General Halleck ordering him to "report the position of your troops, and what you purpose doing with them." He was prompt to submit a plan of campaign — a plan in debt to McClellan's thinking on the matter.

In starting across the Potomac on October 26, McClellan had asked Herman Haupt, superintendent of military railroads, for a report on the lines needed to supply an advance into Virginia — the Manassas Gap and the Orange & Alexandria. He asked about the wharves at Aquia Landing, on the lower Potomac, and about the Richmond, Fredericksburg & Potomac from Aquia to Falmouth, across the Rappahannock from Fredericksburg, and about "repairing that road in season to use it for the purposes of this campaign."

Haupt reported the Manassas Gap operable but limited in capacity. The Orange & Alexandria would have to meet the army's immediate needs, he said. Restoring port facilities at Aquia Landing and the R. F. & P. to Falmouth (to Haupt's disgust, both had been unnecessarily left in ruins by Burnside in evacuating the area in September) received a priority go-ahead. Haupt's verdict: to support an advance for any distance beyond Warrenton, the O. & A. would be stretched beyond its capacity to supply an army of 100,000 men; "the Orange & Alexandria Railroad alone will be a very insecure reliance."

Beyond the operational limits of the O. & A., there was the threat of raids on the line by John Singleton Mosby's guerrilla band, and the greater threat by Jeb Stuart, whose most recent "ride around McClellan" was a raw memory in the Potomac army. McClellan's interest in Aquia Landing and the Aquia–Falmouth rail line decided him, on November 6, to order chief engineer James C. Duane to shift the army's bridge train from the Potomac crossing to Washington for potential use in bridging the Rappahannock — indicating that the Young Napoleon was considering a new road to Richmond by way of Fredericksburg. Burnside testified that before the change of command he suggested the Fredericksburg route to McClellan, and McClellan "partially agreed with me." Staff man Daniel Larned remarked that Burnside inherited "a campaign planned & begun by another person & carried on, not as the General would have done perhaps, had he *begun* it."[4]

On November 9 Burnside submitted his plan of campaign. He would open with a feint toward the Rebels at Culpeper, then turn southeast and "make a rapid move of the whole force to Fredericksburg, with a view to a movement upon Richmond from that point." In rejecting an advance astride the Orange & Alexandria, he argued that the enemy would simply fall back along his communications, drawing the Federals farther and farther from their base along a vulnerable, ever-lengthening supply line. But by seizing Fredericksburg the Potomac army would be on the shortest, most direct overland route to Richmond while always staying between the enemy and Washington.

Burnside's plan rested on three assumptions. First, the Federals would gain a march or two on Lee, reach Falmouth and cross the Rappahannock on pontoon bridges laid in timely fashion, and seize lightly guarded Fredericksburg. Second, Herman Haupt's construction crews would re-

pair the Richmond, Fredericksburg & Potomac to Falmouth, rebuild the
rail bridge across the river, then repair the line behind the advancing Potomac army as fast as the Rebels wrecked it. Third, the R. F. & P. would
be supplied from the restored Aquia Landing wharfs and by additional
waterborne stores along the way. Granted these assumptions and these
circumstances, it was a perfectly sound plan. The administration, wrote
Burnside, "will readily comprehend the embarrassments which surround
me in taking command of this army at this place and at this season of the
year." Nevertheless, "I will endeavor, with all my ability, to bring this campaign to a successful issue."[5]

Halleck met with Burnside at Warrenton on November 12, bringing
with him railroad man Haupt and Quartermaster Montgomery Meigs. By
Burnside's account, there was a debate. Halleck was "strongly in favor" of
continuing the march toward Culpeper and beyond, while "my own plan
was as strongly adhered to by me." This was a revived Henry Halleck, shed
at last of insolent McClellan and looking to oversee his successor. The general-in-chief spoke for Lincoln's "inside track" to Richmond, but thanks
to McClellan's modest pace the Rebels had blocked the inside track, ending that race before it began. Haupt supported Burnside's Fredericksburg
plan, stressing the grave difficulties of supporting the Potomac army entirely by means of the Orange & Alexandria. (He hardly needed to remind
his listeners of the O. & A.'s fate just 25 miles from Washington during
Pope's campaign.) Furthermore, supplying and supporting the army by
water and rail from Aquia Landing would greatly simplify Quartermaster
Meigs's task.

An alternative plan—the duplicitous Halleck afterward described it
(falsely) as the plan he and Lincoln approved—was for the army to continue southward, ford the upper reaches of the Rappahannock and Rapidan rivers, and reach Fredericksburg via the south bank of the Rappahannock. While this eliminated the risks of forcing a river crossing at
Fredericksburg, it relied on the unreliable O. & A., and ran its own risks of
being attacked in flank or rear by the Rebels. Burnside rejected this plan
as rife with the unexpected, notably so for a new commanding general in
his first campaign.

Halleck, characteristically, would not make a decision, saying only that
he would take the matter to the president. Before he left, Burnside explained that McClellan's chief engineer James Duane had already, on November 6, ordered the army's bridge train moved from the Potomac crossing at Berlin, Maryland, to Washington for use in the new campaign. He
wanted Halleck to apply his authority to directing the bridge train at Wash-

ington to meet the army on the Rappahannock — once the army marched it would be out of telegraphic communication until it reached Falmouth. On the evening of November 12 Halleck sent a telegram from Warrenton to Brigadier General Daniel P. Woodbury, commanding the engineer brigade at Washington, telling him to order the pontoons and bridge materials to Aquia Creek. He gave Woodbury no details of the purpose of the order nor any timetable nor any priority.

On his return to the capital, Halleck showed Lincoln Burnside's plan and the arguments regarding it, and the president determined to give his new general his head. Halleck telegraphed Burnside on November 14, "The President has just assented to your plan. He thinks it will succeed, if you move very rapidly; otherwise not." The next day Burnside set the Army of the Potomac on the march to Falmouth. "I think the Army has got over the depression caused by McClellan's removal and it is in good heart for anything," wrote Lieutenant Henry Ropes, 20th Massachusetts, "but in case of serious reverse, there would be a great want of confidence."[6]

Burnside reorganized the army for the new campaign. He formalized the three-wing structure McClellan had utilized for the march into Maryland, calling them grand divisions and giving them two corps each. He did this to simplify the exercise of command, but also to settle the matter of what to do with Edwin Sumner. McClellan's attempt to angle Sumner off into a departmental posting had failed, and now he was back from leave, determined not to give away any of his standing. To return Sumner to the Second Corps would bump a string of generals down the command ladder. Giving Sumner the Right Grand Division solved the problem. The Center Grand Division went to Hooker, recovered from his Antietam wound. Fighting Joe was no favorite of Burnside's, but he had seniority and was a newspaper hero for Antietam and could hardly be ignored. William Franklin, with seniority and on good terms with Burnside, was Left Grand Division commander. Being new to the Potomac army, Burnside let seniority be his guide in changes and filling posts.

Sumner's Right Grand Division comprised the Second and Ninth Corps. Couch led the Second, Sumner's old command, with division heads William H. French, Winfield Hancock (replacing the dead Israel Richardson), and Otis Howard (replacing the wounded John Sedgwick). The Ninth Corps, once Burnside's, then Cox's, now Orlando B. Willcox's, had divisions under William W. Burns, Samuel D. Sturgis, and George W. Getty (replacing the dead Isaac Rodman).

Joe Hooker's Center Grand Division contained the Third and Fifth

Burnside with a bevy of his generals, photographed by Alexander Gardner on November 10, 1862. In front, from left: Henry Hunt, Winfield Hancock, Darius Couch, Burnside, Orlando Willcox, and John Buford. At rear, from left: Marsena Patrick, Edward Ferrero, John Parke, a staff man, John Cochrane, and Samuel Sturgis.

Corps. The Third, Sam Heintzelman's since its founding, was posted in Washington during the Maryland campaign and largely revamped. Heintzelman was shifted to departmental command and replaced by George Stoneman, McClellan's onetime chief of cavalry. Phil Kearny's old division went to David Birney and Hooker's old division to political general Dan Sickles. Stoneman's third division was new, two brigades under Amiel W. Whipple, West Point 1841, a topographical engineer. Fitz John Porter's Fifth Corps, untested at Antietam, had a new commander, Daniel Butterfield. Butterfield had started in Robert Patterson's old Army of the Shenandoah and fought his brigade with distinction at Gaines's Mill. His three divisions were led by Charles Griffin, replacing the transferred George Morell; by George Sykes with his regulars; and by Andrew Humphreys with his rookies.

On learning of McClellan's dismissal, Fitz John Porter wrote *New York World* editor Marble, "You may soon expect to hear my head is lopped." He added, "My opinion of it [Pope's campaign] predicting disaster is in their possession and brought up against me as proof of intention to cause disaster." He predicted his fate. The order relieving McClellan also relieved Porter from the Fifth Corps. On November 25 army headquarters announced a general court-martial convened "for the trial of Maj. Gen. Fitz John Porter, U.S. Volunteers." Porter would be charged with disobeying orders and misbehavior before the enemy at Second Bull Run. It seemed that John Pope had his revenge, at least on Porter; Pope's charges against

William Franklin and Charles Griffin were dropped. In his diary David Strother, whose connection with Porter dated back to Patterson's Army of the Shenandoah, blamed Porter for McClellan's downfall: "Fitz John Porter with his elegant address and insinuating plausibility, technical power, and total want of judgment has been the evil genius, has ruined him as he did Patterson." Following McClellan into military exile, Porter awaited trial.

William Franklin's Left Grand Division contained the First and Sixth Corps. The three divisions of John Reynolds's First Corps were commanded by Abner Doubleday, George Meade, and John Gibbon (replacing the injured James Ricketts). The Sixth Corps went to Baldy Smith after Franklin's advancement. Smith's three divisions were newly led: W.T.H. Brooks replaced Henry Slocum, promoted to command the Twelfth Corps; John Newton replaced Darius Couch, promoted to command the Second Corps; and Albion P. Howe, from the old Fourth Corps, took Baldy Smith's division.

Alfred Pleasonton continued to head the army's mounted arm, comprising the brigades of John F. Farnsworth, David M. Gregg, and William W. Averell. Henry Hunt, now brigadier general, remained chief of artillery. Franz Sigel's Eleventh Corps (First Corps in the old Army of Virginia) was designated a general reserve for the Potomac army, and when Burnside set off for Falmouth, Sigel covered Washington. Henry Slocum's Twelfth Corps (Second Corps, Army of Virginia) remained at Harper's Ferry to guard the Potomac line.

Ambrose Burnside's army was in all but its commander's name still George McClellan's army. Halleck granted Burnside full powers to post or remove any officers except corps commanders (the president's prerogative), but his only real change was the grand divisions format — and that copied from McClellan. Most generals were McClellan's generals. In addition to the new grand division commanders, all six corps commanders were new, as were twelve of the eighteen divisional commanders and thirty-five of the fifty-one brigade commanders. Burnside's experience in battle with his lieutenants was minimal — limited at South Mountain to Jesse Reno, who was killed, and to Joe Hooker, who marched to his own drum; limited at Antietam to Jacob Cox, now gone from the army. In the evolving campaign Burnside would have to forge relationships with his generals, and they with him, on the fly. He confided to Franklin that the "awful responsibility" of command weighed on him and left him sleepless. "I pitied Burnside exceedingly," Franklin told his wife.

McClellan left the army short-staffed, taking away with him nearly all the headquarters staff; he needed them, he said, to help prepare the report of his command tenure. (Not missed among the departed was the bumbling Allan Pinkerton.) Burnside had capable John G. Parke as chief of staff, but his administrative grip on the army was not very sure.[7]

The moment the Army of the Potomac crossed the Potomac it began to lay a hard hand on the Virginia countryside. John Pope's general order permitting his army to forage freely in enemy country had migrated into McClellan's army (now Burnside's army) and been widely accepted there. "The people here are all rebels," a Massachusetts soldier told his wife. "We have had a grand time, killing and eating their sheep, cattle and poultry. One farmer here lost nearly three hundred sheep the first night our boys encamped." In the case of a Union man's property a guard would be detailed to protect his goods. Otherwise, "Our officers say nothing if we take a rebel's turkeys, hens, or sheep to eat; they like their share."

Marsena Patrick, the new provost marshal, had witnessed the demoralizing effect of Pope's foraging order on the Army of Virginia and he dreaded its spread to the supposedly better-behaved Army of the Potomac. "I am distressed to death with the plundering & marauding," he told his diary. "I am sending out detachments in all directions & hope to capture some of the villains engaged in these operations." Cavalry was the worst, "stealing, ravaging, burning, robbing. . . ." The conduct of William Averell's cavalry brigade "makes one's blood boil . . . little better than fiends in human shape."[8]

On November 14, the day before the army was to start for Falmouth, General Burnside, "feeling uneasy," had his chief engineer C. B. Comstock telegraph the engineer brigade at Washington to be sure the bridge train sent to the capital from Berlin by Duane's November 6 order was ready to march. Burnside also called for a second bridge train to be "mounted and horsed as soon as possible" to follow the first train.

Daniel Woodbury, head of the engineer brigade, replied the same day that pontoons were only just then starting to arrive from Berlin. He said it would be, at best, two or three days before all the components of a train could be gathered and mounted and ready to march. He added that Duane's November 6 order to send the bridging materials to Washington was only received at Berlin on the afternoon of November 12. He offered no explanation why a telegraphed order had required six days to reach its destination. With that, the first prerequisite of Burnside's campaign — steal a march on the Rebels and bridge the Rappahannock and seize Fredericksburg in one thrust — was endangered before it even began.

Pinning responsibility for the six-day delay proved elusive. As of November 6 McClellan's advance had broken communication with Berlin, and Captain Duane sent the telegraphed order via Washington . . . where the War Department telegraph office, by inscrutable logic, forwarded the order to Berlin by mail, aboard a leisurely packet on the Chesapeake & Ohio Canal. (The Washington–Berlin telegraph line was fully functioning.) This blunder ought to have been caught — except that in the upheaval of McClellan's dismissal Duane failed to follow up when Berlin did not acknowledge his order. Forgetful Duane (or indifferent Duane; it was he at Antietam who misrepresented the ford on Burnside's front) then departed the Potomac army along with McClellan's staff. Burnside trusted Halleck to oversee Woodbury's engineer brigade at the capital, supposing he "fully covered the case." A trust misplaced. "I had advised against the Fredericksburg base from the beginning," Halleck would say, and he lifted not a finger for its support.[9]

Burnside told Woodbury to send the second bridge train by water to Aquia Landing, and went ahead as planned. On November 15 Sumner's Right Grand Division started for Falmouth. Bull Sumner covered the 40 miles at a fast pace and reached Falmouth on the 17th, the rest of the army not far behind, with Burnside himself arriving on the 19th. Where, he asked, was the bridge train?

A bridge train might have forty pontoons, each mounted on a specially adapted wagon that also carried the connecting timbers, or balks; fifteen other adapted wagons for the cross planks, or chesses; and additional wagons with cables, gear, and tools — perhaps sixty wagons all told, with six-horse teams. At Berlin Major Ira Spaulding of the engineers hastily improvised after he finally received his orders on November 12. He took up the Potomac bridges, had the heavy pontoons towed down the C. & O. Canal to Washington, and sent as many of the lightened wagons overland as he had teams to haul them. In the capital Major Spaulding took up his task anew, laboring with Meigs's quartermasters to assemble and mount a train for the overland march. It was a slow process, requiring on short notice 270 fresh horses to be collected, harnessed, and shoed.

General Woodbury would claim that before November 14 "no one informed me that the success of any important movement depended in the slightest degree upon a pontoon train to leave Washington by land." Consequently, surveying the unpromising situation, he went to Halleck and proposed a five-day delay in Burnside's advance. This would put the bridge train back on schedule with the army. Burnside's march could be halted with no harm to the plan. By Woodbury's testimony, Old Brains "replied that he would do nothing to delay for an instant the advance of the army upon Richmond." His proposal, said Woodbury, would not cause delay but prevent it. But Halleck's witless response stood. Burnside was not in-formed or consulted. His march proceeded on the assumption the bridge train would not be unduly delayed.

To act on Burnside's call for a second bridge train, Woodbury had pon-toons "rafted" for towing down the Potomac by steamer. He optimisti-cally expected that the wagons and teams that had delivered the land train would transport these second-train pontoons to Falmouth. The pontoons arrived on November 18, but no wagons and teams were waiting. Delay upon delay had dogged the land train; it did not even leave Washington until the 19th.

To try and make the second train operational, Woodbury extempo-rized, loading the needed pontoon wagons aboard barges for the journey down the Potomac, only to be held up by a winter storm. The land train was bogged down by interminable rain. Stalled at the Occoquan River, un-able to reach either Falmouth or Aquia by road, the desperate engineers rafted the pontoons, disassembled the wagons, and loaded them aboard for towing by a steamer, with the teams going on by road. At last, after vast effort and great difficulties, the two trains were landed, assembled, and reached Falmouth . . . on November 24–25.

Without the initial six-day delay, with initiative and planning in Wash-ington, or with the army's march held up as Woodbury suggested and Hal-leck rejected, one or both bridge trains ought to have arrived at Falmouth in concert with the army. Deceitful Halleck denied everything, even that Woodbury had come to him about delaying the march. As it was, Burnside and the Army of the Potomac hunkered down at Falmouth and watched a full week's worth of opportunity slip away while waiting for the pontoons. Across the Rappahannock, at Fredericksburg, the Army of Northern Vir-ginia assembled in force.[10]

In notable contrast to McClellan, the new commanding general accom-modated advice, proposals, and plans from his officer corps. General Burnside, said Chief of Staff Parke, "would not think of making an im-portant movement of this army without full consultation with his gen-erals." Bull Sumner, finding Fredericksburg empty of Confederates on reaching Falmouth November 17, proposed to Burnside that he cross a force at a nearby ford and seize the town. He was told it was best they first secure their communications. Sumner could appreciate that; he remem-bered only too well the consequences at Seven Pines "of getting astride of a river. . . ."

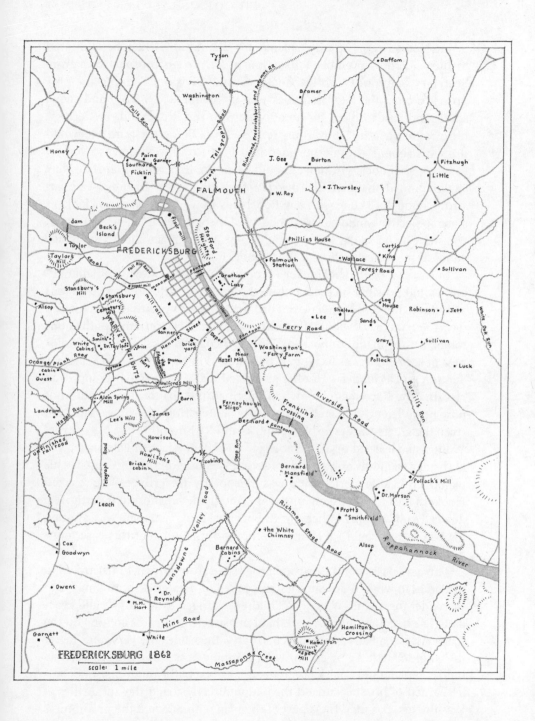

FREDERICKSBURG 1862

scale: 1 mile

Joe Hooker came up with a plan of more ambition, which he submitted to Burnside on November 19 (sending a copy to his prospective patron, Secretary Stanton). With his Center Grand Division, Fighting Joe proposed to cross the Rappahannock well upstream at U.S. Ford and swing south and east to plant his 40,000 men on the Richmond, Fredericksburg & Potomac at Hanover Junction, south of Fredericksburg. He would draw his supplies from a new depot at Port Royal, well downstream on the Rappahannock. His move should catch the Rebels off-guard, for they "have counted on the *McClellan delays* for a long while." In any case he was strong enough to cope with any Rebels his move might stir up. Hooker's stated objective would have warmed Mr. Lincoln's heart: "If Jackson was at Chester Gap on Friday last, we ought to be able to reach Richmond in advance of the concentration of the enemy's forces."

Burnside replied that Hooker's proposal "would be a very brilliant one" and would possibly succeed, but he thought it "a little premature." It was 36 miles to the R. F. & P. via U.S. Ford; with the heavy rains of the past two days there was a question of the ford's viability; the uncertainty of the pontoons' arrival made support for Hooker's column problematical. (Boldness, it seemed, was as lacking in Burnside as in McClellan.) To Secretary Stanton on December 4 Hooker grumbled that if Burnside had approved crossing the Rappahannock when they had the chance, they would not now be suffering "the embarrassments arising from the passage of that river, the greatest obstacle between this and Richmond."[11]

Burnside learned on November 19, the day he reached Falmouth, that his bridge train was only that day leaving Washington, strong evidence his plan to cross at Fredericksburg was in jeopardy. Nevertheless, he rejected Hooker's idea for a crossing upstream, and made no effort to investigate a downstream crossing either. He stubbornly stayed where he was, waiting (as McClellan would say) for something to turn up — in this case, pontoons.

The days passed and Burnside progressed from uneasy to frustrated to baffled as to what to do. Sumner had called on Fredericksburg's mayor to surrender the town: "Women & children, the aged & infirm" should evacuate. The negotiations revealed that Longstreet's corps was coming on the scene. Marsena Patrick noted in his diary, "Burnside feels very blue. Lee & the whole Secesh Army are, or will be, in our front." Burnside made only mild complaint to Halleck about the nonarrival of the pontoons, but Daniel Larned of his staff affixed the blame directly: "Had the authorities at Washington executed their part of the plan with one *half* the promptness and faithfulness that Burnside has done his, our command would have oc-

cupied the City of Fredericksburg three days ago. . . . We are utterly helpless until our pontoon trains arrive."

On November 22 General Sumner dined with Generals Hooker, Meagher, and Pleasonton, wherein "all agree our march to Richmond will be
contested inch by inch." This inspired Sumner to again offer his thoughts
to the general commanding. With the enemy now present in force across
the river, he cautioned that throwing bridges "directly over to the town,
might be attended with great loss" from artillery and from "every house
within musket range. . . ." He proposed instead establishing a "grand battery" of thirty or more heavy guns a mile or so downstream, where the far
shore was an open plain, "which would effectually sweep off every thing
for a long distance." The navy might add gunboats to the barrage. Against
this fire the enemy would be unable to throw up works to prevent the
bridge building. Sumner observed that the Rebels' position on the high
ground behind the town looked very strong. But cross below, form the
whole force in line of battle, "then by a determined march, turn their right
flank, is it not probable that we should force them from the field?" Burnside took note for further consideration.

"We in this Army think this whole campaign is a gross military mistake," force-fed by Radical politicians in Washington, wrote William
Franklin; the true road to Richmond, he told his wife, "is by a more Southern route with less land travel." John Gibbon agreed, and submitted such
a plan to headquarters — hold a bluff at Fredericksburg, where the chance
for a surprise crossing had passed, take a new base at Suffolk, and operate
up the James River to seize the railroad hub of Petersburg. "Once in possession of Petersburg, Richmond will fall." Burnside recognized Gibbon's
plan as too McClellanesque for the occasion.[12]

Mr. Lincoln was monitoring his new general and became concerned
enough that he signaled him they should meet at Aquia Landing for consultation. They met aboard the steamer *Baltimore* on November 27. The
president made a memorandum of the conversation: Burnside said he
could take to battle about 110,000 men, as many as he could handle "to advantage." Their spirits were good. He was committed to crossing the Rappahannock — he offered nothing specific about that — and driving the enemy away, but admitted it would be "somewhat risky."

"I wish the case to stand more favorable than this in two respects," Lincoln wrote. First, he wanted the river crossing "nearly free from risk." Second, he did not want the enemy falling back unimpeded to Richmond's
defenses. He proposed a plan of his own. While Burnside paused where he
was, a 25,000-man force would take post on the south bank of the Rappa-

hannock downstream at Port Royal to divert Fredericksburg's defenders. A second 25,000-man force, escorted by gunboats, would ascend the York and Pamunkey rivers to near Hanover Junction on the R. F. & P. (Hooker's target, reached by the back door) to block the Rebels' escape route. "Then, if Gen. B. succeeds in driving the enemy from Fredericksburg, he the enemy no longer has the road to Richmond."

On November 29 Burnside journeyed to Washington to discuss this new plan with the president and Halleck. Neither general favored it, and Lincoln added a note to his memorandum: "The above plan, proposed by me, was rejected by Gen. Halleck & Gen. Burnside, on the ground that we could not raise and put in position, the Pamunkey force without too much waste of time." Turning aside Lincoln's idea, gaining no counsel from Halleck, Burnside returned to Falmouth no wiser about what he should do.[13]

His thoughts finally turned to a downriver crossing, at a bend called Skinker's Neck a dozen miles from Falmouth. He briefed his generals on December 3 and scheduled the march for the 5th. Irreverent Hooker spoke up that he would like to be on the other shore with 50,000 men and dare anyone to cross. Skinker's Neck was in fact an idea with promise . . . if attempted ten days earlier upon the arrival of the first bridge train. Now Stonewall Jackson's corps was occupying the downstream river line. The march was well started when word came that Skinker's Neck was heavily guarded. The marchers turned back to camp.

Originally Ambrose Burnside had sought, by speed or by maneuver, a new road to Richmond, flushing the enemy into the open. But through miscue and misadventure and mismanagement that opportunity was gone. The Army of Northern Virginia was directly across the river, entrenching as he watched. Afterward Burnside testified to his rationale for fighting at Fredericksburg: "I felt we had better cross here; that we would have a more decisive engagement here, and that if we succeeded in defeating the enemy here, we could break up the whole of their army here, which I think is now the most desirable thing, not even second to the taking of Richmond." Beforehand he assured Baldy Smith he would make the crossing "so promptly that he should surprise Lee, that he knew where Lee's troops were, and that the heart of the movement consisted in the surprise."[14]

At noon on Tuesday, December 9, Burnside called in Sumner, Hooker, and Franklin, his three grand division commanders, and outlined the plan he had settled on. Sumner announced to his staff "the determination to cross the Rappahannock with the Army at daybreak Thursday morning. . . ." Sumner's Right Grand Division would have the advance, crossing on three pontoon bridges to be laid directly opposite Fredericksburg "under at least 150 cannon on our shore." Hooker then to cross as a reserve. Crossing "a mile or two below on 2 bridges" would be Franklin's Left Grand Division. To Washington Burnside staked his claim: "I think now that the enemy will be more surprised by a crossing immediately in our front than in any other part of the river." His three senior commanders, he said, "coincide with me in this opinion."

Sumner, good soldier that he was, may have coincided, but certainly with mixed feelings. Burnside had adopted Sumner's November 23 suggestion for a bridging site a mile or so downstream where the enemy shore was open and vulnerable, but in the same breath he ignored Sumner's very pointed advisory against throwing bridges across right at Fredericksburg's well-defended riverfront. Hooker for the moment held his tongue, his grand division having only a follow-up role in the crossing. Franklin too coincided, recognizing that he had the less risky crossing site of the two.

There was no such unanimity among the Right Grand Division generals that evening when Sumner briefed them. Darius Couch wrote that no words were minced: "The general expression was against the plan of crossing the River." Poor Sumner defended a plan out of loyalty to the commanding general that privately he deplored. Word of the dissenters got back to Burnside, and the next evening he minced no words of his own to the generals gathered at Sumner's headquarters. Otis Howard quoted him, "Your duty is not to throw cold water, but to aid me loyally with advice and hearty service." Couch said Burnside "plainly intimated that his subordinates had no right to express any opinion as to his movements." Burnside took issue with Winfield Hancock's plaints. Hancock replied that while he had meant no personal discourtesy, it was certain to be "pretty difficult" to contend against an entrenched foe at their crossing site. Still, Hancock pledged his loyal support, as did Couch in defending his division commander. Amidst these professions of fealty, bluff William French joined the gathering and asked, "Is this a Methodist camp-meeting?"[15]

At an early hour on December 11 — day 24 since Sumner arrived at Falmouth and found no bridge train waiting — the engineers hauled pontoons and gear to the riverbank and by first light were well started assembling their bridges. Henry Hunt posted 147 guns for support. Initially fog blanketed the river, and the engineers could be heard but not seen as they labored to anchor their pontoons, link them with timber balks, and lay down planking. Downstream the two lower bridges met only sporadic enemy fire, quickly suppressed, and by 11:00 a.m. both were completed. But Franklin was told to hold up his infantry. The middle bridge crossing, at

Alfred Waud sketched the 50th New York Engineers, supported by artillery, assembling a pontoon bridge across the Rappahannock at Fredericksburg on December 11.

the lower end of Fredericksburg, and the upper, two-bridge crossing at the upper end of town, progressed only as long as the fog lasted. The Rappahannock here was hardly 140 yards across, and as one of the engineers put it, "For us to attempt to lay a Ponton Bridge right in their very faces seemed like madness." As the fog lifted the madness turned into "simple murder, that was all."

What Sumner had warned Burnside would happen, happened — sharpshooters filled Fredericksburg's riverfront buildings and their fire riddled the engineer teams and drove them back, leaving the three bridges unfinished about midstream. The artillery Burnside counted on to clear the way pounded the opposite shore, but each time the engineers returned to work the sharpshooters returned to their postings and chased them back. Franklin proposed that he cross the lower bridges and flank the sharpshooters. Burnside rejected that as too risky, insisting on establishing the bridgeheads simultaneously. He demanded the engineers complete the bridges "whatever the cost."[16]

Major Ira Spaulding of the engineers, who had displayed great initiative in getting his bridge train through hell and high water to Falmouth, proposed a solution to the dilemma — row infantry across in pontoon boats to scour the sharpshooters out of their hiding places. The idea got to General Hunt, who with Burnside's approval sought volunteers. In Colonel Norman J. Hall's brigade, Hall volunteered the 7th Michigan, the regiment he had led to war, to cross at the upper bridges. Colonel Harrison S. Fairchild's 89th New York was tapped to cross at the middle bridge. Hunt laid on the heaviest shelling yet, driving the sharpshooters to cover, and the little fleet was poled and paddled with all speed across the river. There were casualties, but the two regiments made landings on the enemy shore. Support followed. Watchers on the Yankee shore went "wild with excitement, cheering and yelling like Comanche Indians."

In house-to-house fighting the Confederates were driven away and the engineers completed the three Fredericksburg bridges, but the hour was late. Otis Howard's Second Corps division crossed and by dark had secured the bridgehead. Charles Devens's brigade, Sixth Corps, secured the lower bridges site. It had been a long and difficult day, especially for the engineers, but Burnside accepted it as a ponderous first step in a deliberate challenge to Lee. "I expect to cross the rest of my command tomorrow," Burnside told Halleck.[17]

Early on December 12 Burnside endorsed a Franklin dispatch, "As soon as he and Sumner are over, attack simultaneously." Nothing came of this spare directive, for it required the entire day to get the army across the river and into position to advance . . . the next day. General Lee watched, detected no Yankee deceptions, and called in Stonewall Jackson from his downriver postings. The entire Army of Northern Virginia was at hand, ready for whatever General Burnside might attempt. These latest of the many delays ended Burnside's last hope for catching the Rebels unwary or out of position. The crossing, John Reynolds contended, "ought to have been a surprise, and we should have advanced at once and carried the heights as was intended."

On the low ridge called Marye's Heights behind Fredericksburg Longstreet had spent three weeks entrenching and posting batteries. At the base of the ridge he had infantry thickly ranked along the Telegraph Road behind a chest-high stone wall — analogous to the Sunken Road at Antietam. Marye's Heights ended at Hazel Run; from there Jackson took post on low wooded hills extending to Hamilton's Crossing on the R. F. & P. Massaponax Creek marked the end of a battle line six miles long.

Burnside's orders set Sumner's objective on the right as "the heights that command the Plank road and the Telegraph road," that is, Marye's Heights. Franklin on the left was to "move down the old Richmond road,

Newspaper artist Arthur Lumley wrote of his drawing of the Federals' sacking of Fredericksburg on December 12 that it was "a fit scene for the French revolution."

in the direction of the railroad," referring to the Richmond Stage Road from Fredericksburg that paralleled the river and the R. F. & P. Hooker's Center Grand Division would stand ready to support either Sumner or Franklin as need be. Nothing was said of timing, of priorities, or in Franklin's case, of objective. Unlike his predecessor, Ambrose Burnside was not haunted by the underdog's role. While he testified to receiving estimates of enemy numbers as high as 200,000, he made his own estimate — less than 100,000. (Lee's actual count was about 78,500.)[18]

Sumner's command — Second and Ninth Corps — had required December 12 to crowd across the three bridges into Fredericksburg. The shelling on the 11th had chased away the last few residents and the town was empty. The troops stood idle, stacking arms and wandering the streets. When Provost Marshal Marsena Patrick reached the scene, "a horrible sight presented itself. All the buildings more or less battered with shells, roofs & walls all full of holes & the churches with their broken windows & shattered walls looking desolate enough." But that was not the worst of it: "The Soldierly were sacking the town! Every house and Store was being gutted!"

Few restraints had marked the Potomac army's passage through Virginia since late October. No restraints marked it now. The sack began with a search for food in the abandoned dwellings, then wine cellars and liquor stocks were raided, fueling a rising tide of plunder and vandalism. Fredericksburg's colonial heritage was ransacked and its artifacts, from carpets to libraries to paintings to spinets, defaced or thrown into the streets. Powerless to restore order, Patrick posted the bridges to at least stop looters from stealing away with their booty. Officers of every rank looked the other way. "Never was a city more thoroughly sacked," wrote a shocked New Hampshire colonel. "The conduct of our men and officers too is atrocious their object seems to be to destroy what they cant steal & to steal all they can." In the annals of the Army of the Potomac it was the ugliest of days; for its officer corps, the most unconscionable of days.[19]

While their troops crossed at the lower bridges — christened Franklin's Crossing — Franklin and John Reynolds (First Corps) and Baldy Smith (Sixth Corps) discussed their next move. Absent fresh orders from headquarters, they agreed, said Smith, that the Left Grand Division should form its 40,000 men "into columns of assault on the right and left of the Richmond road," carry Hamilton's Crossing on the railroad, "and turn Lee's right flank at any cost."

At early evening on the 12th Burnside arrived at Franklin's headquarters to inspect the position and to settle on a plan for the next day. By the accounts of Franklin and Smith, Burnside was attentive and responsive to their proposed plan of attack. Franklin termed it "a long consultation." Smith had Burnside responding, "Yes! Yes!" to their objective — "turn Lee's right flank at any cost." This matched Sumner's November 23 plan that Burnside had already adopted regarding the Franklin's Crossing site — after crossing, "by a determined march, turn their right flank." It seems clear that Sumner's forceful plan was already on Burnside's mind when he heard more or less the same plan from Franklin, Smith, and Reynolds. To be sure, theirs did not include the "whole force" as Sumner's did. Yet Franklin's two full army corps, six divisions, surely counted enough for the task at hand. Burnside promised two of Hooker's divisions to hold the bridges when Franklin's flanking attack commenced — raising Franklin's total to some 60,000 men — and to send written orders for the morrow.

In consequence of those orders, received at 7:30 the next morning, Franklin afterward raised an elaborate construct to defend his conduct when he went to battle on December 13. This construct revealed striking echoes of his last exercise of independent command, at Crampton's Gap on South Mountain in September, where he misjudged his assignment,

William Franklin, leading the
Left Grand Division, misfired in his
assignment to turn the Rebel flank.

shunned both initiative and responsibility, and in his caution quite misread the battlefield.[20]

Ambrose Burnside was strained and wanting sleep, and his orders were poorly framed and hardly a model of clarity. Still, that fails to account for the contrary interpretation Franklin put on them. If at their December 12 council Franklin and his generals came to a firm agreement (as they claimed) with Burnside about a full-blooded assault to turn Lee's right, then Burnside's December 13 orders, however awkward the phrasing, took as a given a fully discussed, already-agreed-upon plan.

"The general commanding," the orders read, "directs that you keep your whole command in position for a rapid movement down the old Richmond road, and you will send out at once a division at least . . . to seize, if possible, the height near Captain Hamilton's" — Prospect Hill, overlooking Hamilton's Crossing — "taking care to keep it well supported. . . ." Seizing Prospect Hill was necessary to open the way for the Left Grand Division to drive between Hamilton's Crossing and the Massaponax and into Lee's rear. Burnside's orders twice spoke of Franklin employing his "whole command" for the operation. Sumner would meanwhile assault the other end of the Confederate line, Marye's Heights, thereby compelling "the enemy to evacuate the whole ridge" . . . or so Burnside hoped.

Before the Committee on the Conduct of the War, Franklin testified to his entirely different reading of the December 13 orders: "It meant that there should be what is termed an armed reconnaissance, or an observation in force made of the enemy's lines, with one division. . . . At that time I had no idea that it was the main attack." This tortured reading, this convenient forgetting what had been discussed and agreed to at the generals' council the previous evening, starkly reveals (once again) William Franklin's incapacity for independent command. He had a telegraphic link with headquarters to clarify his orders if they were "not what we expected." He did not use it. Nor did he take the lead in posting his forces for prompt action on the 13th. Nor did he pay even lip service to gainfully employing his "whole command." He confined the Sixth Corps to keeping open a line of retreat and guarding Franklin's Crossing, even though he had two Third Corps divisions for just that purpose. He assigned the "armed reconnaissance" to John Reynolds.

In the controversy over Franklin's reading of his orders, Burnside made the incisive point: Surely Franklin realized "I did not cross more than 100,000 over the river to make a reconnaissance." Writing his wife, Franklin revealed an untrustworthy state of mind on December 13: "It was not successful and I never thought it would be, but I knew that it had to be made to satisfy the Republicans, and we all went at it as well as though it was all right."[21]

The attack John Reynolds mounted on December 13 bore no resemblance to an armed reconnaissance. He said he read Burnside's orders, shown him by Franklin, to mean an attack on Prospect Hill "with one or two divisions, and to hold that point." Franklin said nothing about holding him to a reconnaissance. Reynolds committed his entire First Corps, George Meade's division in the lead, John Gibbon's division in support on the right, Abner Doubleday's division guarding the left. Meade's division was small and well worn, but Reynolds wanted his most experienced general leading the charge.

Meade led his Pennsylvania Reserves from near the front that day, where he could monitor two new brigade commanders, William Sinclair and C. Feger Jackson. His third brigade was Albert Magilton's. Meade expressed concern they were repeating the Antietam mistake of attacking piecemeal. When he took his objective, where would come the strength to hold it? Franklin said those were Burnside's orders.

In their initial advance, about 10:00 a.m., the Reserves were checked by Rebel artillery off to the left, causing a delay until Doubleday moved up to secure that flank. This left the offense to Meade and Gibbon. At the point of attack Meade deployed the brigades of Jackson and Sinclair, with Magilton's close behind. The Rebel infantry's opening fire checked the Pennsylvanians a second time. Meade ordered a halt while the Yankee guns opened counterbattery fire at the now-revealed targets. Gibbon's division took a supporting position to the right. This was John Gibbon's first battle heading a division, and directing three new brigade leaders.

As his artillery barrage lifted, Meade put his men to the charge. He told his wife, "My men went in *beautifully,* carried every thing before them, and drove the enemy for nearly 1/2 a mile." As it happened, he had struck and exploited a gap in Stonewall Jackson's line — reminiscent of the gap in Jackson's line at Cedar Mountain back in August — threatening a break-through into Lee's rear. But like Banks at Cedar Mountain, Meade received no backing to secure his gains. Doubleday's division was well back and idle, holding the left flank, and Reynolds failed to call on it for Meade's support. Gibbon's division on the right was heavily engaged. Gibbon noted that the troops under two of his new brigade leaders "did not succeed so well." Although he brought up his reserve brigade to steady the line, "the impulsive force of the troops was expended." He was wounded and left the field, and his division stalled.[22]

Meade's foothold was counterattacked, and both his new brigade commanders went down, Feger Jackson killed, William Sinclair wounded. Meade barely escaped death from a bullet that ripped through his hat. An aide he sent back to find support came on David Birney's Third Corps division, brought across to guard the bridges. For Birney it was like the Seven Pines tangle and conflicting orders from Kearny and Heintzelman. He refused Meade's first call, saying he was told to report to General Reynolds and would await his orders. Meade sent back to Birney that he assumed full responsibility for ordering him forward. Again Birney refused. The third time brought Meade himself, in high temper, and he lit into Birney in full voice, enough, said a bystander, to "almost make the stones creep." If nothing else, said Meade, he was a major general and Birney a brigadier general, and that obliged him to obey. Birney finally sent forward two regiments, too late.

Burnside "seemed annoyed" (as an aide put it) on learning that Franklin had made no move to commit any part of Baldy Smith's Sixth Corps to the battle, and he ordered Franklin "to make a vigorous attack with his whole force." In his report Burnside was blunt: "This order was not carried out." Instead, in McClellanesque fashion, Franklin pulled in his horns and assumed a defensive stance, even ordering up two more brigades, from the Ninth Corps, to help guard his bridges. He now had under command twenty-seven of the army's fifty-one infantry brigades.

Meade and Gibbon were forced to give up their fight and fall back. Meade told his wife a great chance was missed — "The slightest straw almost would have *kept* the tide in our favor." As he brought his troops back to their starting point, he encountered Reynolds and burst out, "My God, General Reynolds, did they think my division could whip Lee's whole army?" When Meade reached Franklin's headquarters he made a point of displaying his bullet-riddled hat and said sarcastically, "I found it quite hot enough for me."

Afterward, Meade tended to lay the ultimate blame for the failure of his assault on Prospect Hill on Burnside's inability to communicate. He wrote Franklin, "I have always told Genl. Burnside and told him so the first time I saw him after the battle, that I did not think you were impressed with the importance he attached to the attack ordered on the left." But in the privacy of writing his wife, Meade said of the poorly framed instructions to Franklin, "A *great* captain would have cast them aside & assumed responsibility."[23]

At first, supposing Franklin had launched the intended all-out assault on the enemy's right, Burnside awaited results there before committing Sumner's Right Grand Division. It was reported at 11:00 a.m. that "Meade advanced half a mile, and holds on." Then, "Reynolds has been forced to develop his whole line." Then, the wounding of Francis L. Vinton, one of Baldy Smith's brigadiers, implying that the Sixth Corps was engaged. (Actually the unengaged Vinton was hit by a stray shot.) Cavalry pickets reported enemy troops "moving down the river." That suggested Lee might be stripping his left to support his right. Burnside ordered Sumner to open the assault on Marye's Heights.

During the endless wait "for the means to cross the river," wrote staff man Daniel Larned, the enemy had fortified the Heights until they looked impregnable: "We can count about 20 crests and hills, each mounting from two to five guns, and all can be brought to bear on any given spot." The terrain on the right offered no openings for a turning movement. The left was crimped by a ravine carrying Hazel Run to the Rappahannock. A millrace for runoff from a canal cut through the middle of the field, crossed only at three bridges, one of them damaged. Beyond the millrace lay 500 yards of open ground stretching to the base of Marye's Heights, quite without cover but for some fencing and a handful of houses and outbuildings.

Sumner selected the Second Corps, his old command, now under Darius Couch, to challenge this array. Couch chose his weakest, least experienced division, William French's, to make the first trial. At Antietam French's slapped-together division launched the initial frontal attacks on the Sunken Road, with dismal results. Today promised yet another frontal attack with — plain for all to see — hardly better prospects.

Nathan Kimball, with a brigadier's star earned at Antietam, led his brigade as the first wave. "Boys, we are the attacking brigade," he announced. "Keep steady, aim low, and let every man do his duty. They can't kill all of you but they may hurt some of you." That struck one listener as pretty poor comfort. Kimball's brigade, trailed by French's two other brigades, battled through Longstreet's artillery to within a hundred yards of the stone wall, where Longstreet's infantry then shot them to pieces. This came as a deadly surprise; the Federals knew nothing of Fredericksburg's sunken road in advance. Kimball fell with a wound that ended his days with the Potomac army, and French's division went to ground.

A witness to French's attack, Samuel Fiske, 14th Connecticut, left an account that could as easily apply to any of the seven divisions, one after another, hurled against Marye's Heights that bloody afternoon: "Of whole companies and regiments not a man flinched. The grape and canister tore through their ranks, the fearful volleys of musketry from invisible foes decimated their numbers every few moments; the conflict was hopeless; they could inflict scarcely any damage upon the foe; our artillery couldn't cover them, for they would do more damage to friend than to enemy; yet our gallant fellows pressed on. . . ."[24]

Hancock's division was next up, and Couch ordered him to join French and together storm the heights. To gain a better view, Couch and Otis Howard climbed to the cupola of Fredericksburg's courthouse. They saw a battleground carpeted in blue — the dead and wounded, the living sheltered behind any ripple in the ground from the incessant fire, and French's men slipping back from the front on his orders; William French recognized a losing play when he saw one. That meant Hancock would be replacing French, not supporting him. Couch told Howard to ready his division to support Hancock.

Winfield Hancock had not seen combat since the Peninsula. At Second Bull Run he was in the late-arriving Sixth Corps; at Antietam he replaced the mortally wounded Richardson and stood on the defensive. Today was his first action with the Second Corps. He presented a martial figure on horseback, parading before his waiting men, inspiring them for the ordeal to come. Hancock had spoken out to Burnside that storming Marye's Heights promised to be a "pretty difficult" assignment. Now he dutifully announced that Burnside's orders "must be carried out at all hazards and at all costs."

Like French, Hancock made his advance in brigade front formation — three brigade lines, at intervals of 200 paces, first Samuel K. Zook's brigade, then Thomas F. Meagher's, then John C. Caldwell's. In writing to a friend, Colonel Zook relived what on December 13 became a field officer's nightmare: "I went into the action with no hope of success but with the conviction I was leading my brave battalion to inevitable and useless slaughter." Whatever his premonition, Zook led his men as far forward as anyone that day before his line was shattered by the fire from the stone wall. His horse was killed and he stunned by the fall, but he survived. Meagher's Irish Brigade was similarly driven to ground by the relentless fire. Irish whiskey may have inspired Meagher's flights of oratory bracing his men, but did not render him senseless as it had at Antietam; today he reported "a most painful ulcer in the knee-joint" sent him to the rear. John Caldwell also had an Antietam episode to live down — Israel Richardson damning him for command laxness. He was not lax this day in pressing his men to their limit in front of the stone wall, and it cost him a bullet in the shoulder. Hancock himself came under fire while driving the attack home. A bullet snipped across his overcoat and vest, moving him to remark, "It was lucky I hadn't a full dinner." In hardly 20 minutes Hancock's division was stopped cold. "It was not war, it was madness," wrote a newspaper correspondent.[25]

The Confederate gunners on Marye's Heights quickly sensed the repeating pattern of the Federal attacks and sighted their pieces on the streets leading out of Fredericksburg and on the millrace crossings and created havoc among the attackers well before they came in range of infantry fire. Longstreet would quote his artillerist Porter Alexander as claiming, "A chicken could not live on that field when we open on it." In his own memoir Alexander admitted he might have made such a boast — so well posted were his batteries that "I never thought Burnside would choose that point for attack."

The Federal artillery assigned to Sumner's offensive lacked any central direction and proved nearly useless in supporting the assaulting columns. There was no planning, no thought of establishing grand batteries at the back corners of the battlefield to lay down converging fire support. French's division and most of Hancock's attacked with no artillery support whatever. The big guns of Hunt's artillery reserve, posted on Stafford Heights on the left bank, were at extreme range firing on Marye's Heights and inflicted little damage. Nineteen divisional batteries crowded into Fredericksburg, but just seven saw action, and the Napoleons in four of those seven were too short-ranged to be effective. Couch sent back a plea, "I am losing. Send two rifle batteries." With the army lacking discrete artillery commands, Couch's call was routed to Hunt, who in due course sent across a pair of 3-inch rifle batteries.

Those batteries that did the fighting were thrust into battle piecemeal, to their peril. The gunners on Marye's Heights focused their plunging fire on each one the moment it appeared. Lieutenant George Dickenson's Battery E, 4th U.S., four 10-pounder Parrott rifles, took casualties as it unlimbered, scattering the crews. Dickenson rallied them, but then he was killed and they scattered a second time. Second Lieutenant John Egan took over, recognized that no effective fire could be maintained and that "by remaining longer all my men would be destroyed," and withdrew the battery. In its 30 minutes Battery E lost three men dead, ten wounded, and five horses. In the case of Captain John G. Hazard's Battery B, 1st Rhode Island, General Howard ordered it forward over the protests of the corps' chief of artillery, who insisted, "General, a battery could not live out there." Howard was willing to lose the battery if it would aid the infantry. Hazard pushed his six Napoleons to within 300 yards of the stone wall. He met a blizzard of shot and shell, suffered sixteen casualties, and was no aid whatever to the infantry. One of Howard's brigadiers, Alfred Sully, said the battery was only drawing fire onto his infantry, and he pulled them back. "They might court martial me and be damned, I was not going to murder my men."[26]

Couch pushed the last Second Corps division, Otis Howard's, into the one-sided struggle. These men had served under John Sedgwick at Antietam, and according to Henry Abbott, 20th Massachusetts, were badly scarred by "the recollection of their awful loss & defeat" there. Howard was to widen the battlefront. While Joshua T. Owen and Alfred Sully grounded their brigades among the survivors of the earlier attacks, Howard directed Norman J. Hall's brigade to fresh ground to the right. Captain Abbott appraised Howard as "a most conscientious man, but a very poor general," who "had heard of batteries stormed & rifle pits taken, &c, & without stopping to think whether the rifle pits in question were an analogous case." Worse, Howard attacked not on a brigade front but regiment by regiment, with predictably deadly results. Hall pulled his men back and condemned the operation "as simply ridiculous."

The Second Corps expended, Bull Sumner turned to Orlando Willcox's Ninth Corps. Sam Sturgis's division was told to extend the battlefront to the left, only to meet the same fate as Couch's three divisions — pounded by artillery leaving Fredericksburg and crossing the millrace, slaughtered by rifle fire from the sunken road. Sturgis gained nothing at a cost of over 1,000 of his 4,400 men. He signaled, "for God's sake, send another division," then commanded from behind a brick wall, personally reinforced by a canteen of whiskey.[27]

By now, midafternoon, Ambrose Burnside was trapped in a fog of indecision — the same fog that had engulfed him when the bridge trains did not reach him as scheduled. Word from Franklin's sector was worrying: "Gibbon and Meade driven back from the wood" — Gibbon wounded — "Things do not look so well on Reynolds' front." Burnside's order to Franklin to make a "vigorous attack" with his entire command was ignored. Indeed, Franklin claimed his left was threatened and he needed reinforcements. Burnside meanwhile watched the repeated attacks on Marye's Heights bloodily repulsed. To relieve the (supposed) pressure on Franklin, Burnside could think of nothing better than to throw yet more men against Marye's Heights. For that he called on Hooker's Center Grand Division. Sumner signaled Couch, "Hooker has been ordered to put in everything. You must hold on until he comes in."

Joe Hooker was out of sorts. To begin with, he saw no merit in dividing the army to make two attacks. Then his two favorite divisions — his and Kearny's old commands, now under Sickles and Birney — were sent to serve under Franklin. The remaining Third Corps division, Amiel Whipple's, was posted in Fredericksburg, and just one of its brigades went into battle — under Ninth Corps command. That left Hooker only Dan Butterfield's Fifth Corps. When Burnside ordered it into action, Hooker crossed the river to reconnoiter. He consulted with generals he found there — Couch, French, Hancock, Willcox. "Their opinion, with one exception, was that the attack should not be made at that point." The exception was Couch, who still called for renewed attacks on the sunken road. Displaying an awareness of reality rare in the officer corps that day, Hooker sent a staff man to Burnside to advise against further attacks. The reply came that the attack must be made. Hooker rode back across the river and braced Burnside directly. As Burnside's aide Daniel Larned put it, "Hooker expressed his mind very freely at Hd. Qrs. ungentlemanly & impatient." The two men had clashed before, at South Mountain, and Hooker was not one to employ sweet reason in argument. Burnside stubbornly resisted being challenged in a matter of command. He said the attack would go on as ordered.[28]

Hooker sent orders to the Fifth Corps division of ex-artillery regular Charles Griffin, who had only recently escaped a court for his role at Second Bull Run. Like his predecessors, Griffin dutifully fought his three brigades in succession, and in succession they were riddled by solid shot and shell and case shot and finally by canister as Longstreet's infantry tore them apart. By now there was no attempt to actually storm the sunken road. The newest brigades and regiments simply joined or relieved the earlier survivors to maintain a front in no man's land.

During a lull in the fighting, General Couch heard that one of Han-

By artist Alfred Waud's description, General Andrew Humphreys, Fifth Corps, is shown "charging at the head of the division after sunset on the 13th Dec." His attack on Marye's Heights behind Fredericksburg cost him a quarter of his men dead or wounded.

cock's brigadiers, John Caldwell, reported "the enemy were retreating." This was unlikely intelligence — for one thing, Caldwell had left the field wounded — but it was enough to inspire Darius Couch to take one more swing at the stone wall. With Hooker across the river arguing with Burnside, Couch was ranking general on the field. He turned to Andrew Humphreys's Fifth Corps division and signaled it forward.

Humphreys was fifty-two, West Point class of 1831, trained in the topographical engineers. He had served as an engineer on McClellan's staff and posted the guns on Malvern Hill. Switched to the infantry for the Maryland campaign, his new division of Pennsylvania volunteers and militiamen arrived too late for Antietam. Today Humphreys was itching for action, and he had no problem taking orders from the Second Corps' Couch. In this their first fight, the Pennsylvanians were told to uncap their pieces; they would charge without stopping to fire, relying on the bayonet to carry the sunken road.

To his wife, Humphreys repeated almost precisely what each of the five divisional generals before him had experienced. "Dear Chérie," he wrote. "Yesterday afternoon I led my division into a desperate fight and tried by leading each brigade in succession to take at the point of the bayonet a stone wall behind which a heavy line of the enemy lay." The Rebel musketry "made a continuous sheet of flame. We charged to within 50 yards of it each time but the men could not stand it." Men from earlier attacks hugging the ground over which they charged called out that it was useless, that they would be killed, and pulled at their shoes and pants legs to drag them down and try to save their lives.

Even days later General Humphreys was still caught up in the thrill of the charge. "I felt gloriously," he told his wife, "and as the storm of bullets whistled around me, and as the shells and shrapnel burst close to me in every direction scattering with hissing sound their fragments and bullets, the excitement grew more glorious still. Oh, it was sublime!" His division, as brave as all the others before him, counted just over 1,000 casualties in 4,500 men.

Joe Hooker, back on the field, found two more divisions immediately at hand, George W. Getty's (Ninth Corps) and George Sykes's (Fifth Corps). Getty, on Orlando Willcox's order, made a stumbling, abortive start in the dusk. But someone had finally to stop the madness. It was like attacking "a mountain of rock," Hooker said. "Finding that I had lost as many men as my orders required me to lose, I suspended the attack."[29]

Darkness finally quenched the firing. At army headquarters that evening Burnside's mess included Sumner, Hooker, Chief of Staff Parke, and James Hardie, whom Burnside had sent to monitor Franklin during the day. "We had canned salmon, pears, coffee, &c.," reported Sumner's staff man William Teall. Franklin was sent for, and from 9 o'clock until after midnight Burnside debated next steps with his three grand division chiefs. Telling them to wait up for him, he crossed the river to learn the state of affairs there. Darius Couch assured him, "everything that could be done by troops was done by the Second Corps." It was going on 3:00 a.m. when Burnside returned. "In about 20 minutes they dispersed," wrote Teall, "having determined to storm the crest at 10 a.m. the next morning with the 9th Army Corps, which was to be supported by the 2d Corps." The Ninth was Burnside's old command, and he announced he would lead it personally. By Franklin's account, "the officers were so demoralized that they did their best to keep him out of it." Hooker protested the loudest, but Burnside would not be moved.

On the morning of December 14 generals and staff officers by the dozens milled in and about headquarters, discussing the pending attack. "Nearly all disapproved," noted Colonel Teall. As the high command debated, Teall found an elevated spot and trained his glass across the river. "Our men lay stretched lengthwise on their backs on the ground in straight lines not daring to raise head or hand. If they did they were immediately fired upon by the enemy. What a sight!"

Arthur Lumley sketched Burnside, hat in hand, discussing with Franklin
and staff the evacuation of the army from Fredericksburg.

Loyal, dedicated, dutiful, Bull Sumner took it upon himself to stop this
newest madness. He pulled Burnside aside and diplomatically suggested
a council of war. "Knowing as he did the feeling of the commanding officers generally in reference to the attack he advised it & Genl. B. at once
admitted the propriety of the suggestion," wrote Teall. Burnside himself
would acknowledge his high command was "decidedly against" renewing
the battle; no doubt he secretly welcomed Sumner's intervention. The 10
o'clock attack was set aside, and the council of war debated hour after hour
without a resolution.

Burnside's staff man Daniel Larned reported that "The General was
troubled & anxious all the morning, consulting with officers & much by
himself." It was observed that overnight the Rebels had enhanced their
fortifications on Marye's Heights. Burnside told Sumner he was determined to resign, but Sumner said he must not think of such a thing. After
spending the afternoon looking for answers in Fredericksburg, Burnside
returned to headquarters and ordered the army back across the river —
"poor man, he choked & his tears ran as he gave the order to evacuate."

Daylight on December 16 found the Army of the Potomac safely back
across the Rappahannock. It was the one and only operation of the Fredericksburg campaign that was executed flawlessly.[30]

13. *Joe Hooker in Command*

REPORTER MURAT HALSTEAD summed up Fredericksburg for readers of the *Cincinnati Commercial* in one sentence: "It can hardly be in human nature for men to show more valor, or Generals to manifest less judgment, than were perceptible on our side that day."

Fredericksburg induced severe shock across the North. The *New-York Tribune*'s Henry Villard stated "as strongly as possible that the Army of the Potomac had suffered another, great general defeat; that an inexcusable blunder had been made in attempting to overcome the enemy by direct attack." The *New York Times*'s William Swinton bore similar witness: "The Nation will stand aghast at the terrible price which has been paid for its life when the realities of Fredericksburgh are spread before it . . . and absolutely nothing gained."

That was the nub of it — murderous loss and nothing gained, with demoralizing consequences. The cost for the Union was worse even than Antietam — 12,653, of which 1,284 were dead and 9,600 wounded. The assaults aimed at Marye's Heights accounted for 70 percent of that total. (Confederate losses were 5,309.)

Lincoln had the unsparing news by December 14, from correspondent Villard and railroad man Herman Haupt, both fresh from the battleground. He wanted General-in-Chief Halleck to telegraph Burnside to withdraw the army to safety across the river. Halleck refused. If the president wanted it done he must order it himself. "I hold that a General in command of an army in the field is the best judge of existing conditions," said Halleck. It took Bull Sumner to bring Burnside to his senses and order a withdrawal.[1]

Congressman William Cutler expressed a widespread concern about the management of the Army of the Potomac. "All hopes are placed in the army," Cutler entered in his diary; "— under McClellan nothing was accomplished — now Burnside fails on first trial. McClellans friends chuckle & secretly rejoice over the result." Noting the repeated assaults against Marye's Heights, Elizabeth Blair Lee commented, "Well if I remember the

On January 3, 1863, *Harper's Weekly* recast an Alfred Waud cartoon it had commissioned in 1861 (page 157), replacing Uncle Sam with Columbia who points an accusing finger at Lincoln, Burnside, and Stanton for the bloody debacle at Fredericksburg.

locality none but mad men would attack them there . . . & so it proved to our sorrow." Editors condemned Secretary Stanton and General Halleck for pressing Burnside into a hurried new campaign to justify the dismissal of McClellan. *Harper's Weekly* editorialized that Northerners had borne "imbecility, treachery, failure, privation . . . almost every suffering which can afflict a brave people. But they can not be expected to suffer that such massacres as this at Fredericksburg shall be repeated. Matters are rapidly ripening for a military dictatorship."

Ambrose Burnside determined to set the record straight. "For the failure in the attack I am responsible," he wrote Halleck. The move from Warrenton "onto this line rather against the opinion of the President, Secretary, and yourself, and that you have left the whole management in my hands, without giving me orders, makes me the more responsible." He went up to Washington to deliver his mea culpa personally, and sent a copy to the Associated Press. He backdated it so it would not appear Washington cowed him into writing it. It ran on front pages.[2]

The Committee on the Conduct of the War was sparked to action. Zack Chandler determined to root out the weak in the Army of the Potomac.

"We must have men in command of our armies who are anxious to crush the rebellion or it will never be crushed. . . . The truth is the heart of our Generals is not in the work." The committee journeyed to Falmouth to take testimony from Burnside and grand division chiefs Sumner, Franklin, and Hooker. The testimony went to the press, generating heat in and about the high command.

Burnside's testimony reviewed his appointment to the command (against his wishes) and traced the campaign's misfortunes (his responsibility). He did not point a finger at any of his generals. He named the late arrival of the bridge trains as a primary cause of the defeat: "I understood that General Halleck was to give the necessary orders," indicting Halleck as a party to the defeat. Committeeman John Covode was heard to say, "he was going to raise a howl, & intimated it would not be against Burnside."

Edwin Sumner, as always, dutifully supported his commanding general, even testifying that Burnside's was a wiser course than what McClellan had been pursuing. He said the bridge trains' delay was critical. He did allow that he would have directed the entire army into a single attack (as he had proposed to Burnside) rather than dividing it for two attacks. "But that is a point upon which military men may differ."

William Franklin persuaded himself he bore no responsibility for the failed battle. Blame for the delayed bridges lay in Washington. "I think the whole thing ought to eventuate in the dismissal of Stanton & Halleck," he told his wife, "but whether it will is I am afraid, very doubtful." In his testimony he passed quickly over his own role; he made his attack "according to the order of General Burnside. I put in all the troops that I thought it proper and prudent to put in." He assured his wife, "I ventilated the pontoon business to my heart's content."

Joe Hooker relished this chance to present his views. He touted his proposed crossing upstream at U.S. Ford; his opposition to a downstream crossing; his objection to dividing the army for two attacks; his plea to Burnside to halt the assaults on Marye's Heights. He focused a spotlight on Franklin. It was, he said, his impression that Franklin had enough troops "to have swept everything before him. . . . I have understood that a large portion of Franklin's force was not engaged at all." His testimony impressed Felix Brannigan, 74th New York. "He is *the* General to end the War. . . . It is very disheartening to see able men seniored by ignoramuses. . . ."[3]

High-command casualties were not severe. At division, wounded John Gibbon recovered for the next campaign. At brigade, C. Feger Jackson was dead and Francis L. Vinton badly wounded and discharged; wounded John Caldwell, William Sinclair, and Erastus Taylor would return to duty, and Nathan Kimball to duty in the Western theater. The cavalry suffered a major blow in the death of brigade commander George D. Bayard. "Poor Bayard," Franklin wrote. "He had been sitting under a tree about 20 feet from me" when hit by a shell fragment. "He is a severe loss." Bayard was buried on the day he was to have been married.

Major Rufus Dawes, 6th Wisconsin, expressed a common view in appraising the battle: "This army seems to be overburdened with second rate men in high positions, from General Burnside down . . . our prospects are dark unless we get some stronger minds and clearer heads to lead us." Leadership honors at Fredericksburg were indeed few. On the left, George Meade's breakthrough against Jackson was the sole highlight, and Meade spoke unsparingly of his subsequent lack of support. John Reynolds grasped Burnside's intent (if his superior Franklin did not) and put his First Corps to taking and holding Prospect Hill. In this his initial corps command, Reynolds seemed reluctant to exercise the battlefield initiative that might have steered help to Meade. (Reynolds "knows I think he was in some measure responsible for my not being supported on the 13th," Meade confided to his wife.)

Overriding all else on the left was William Franklin's dismal showing in independent command. He seemed borne down by the responsibility, unable to nerve himself to commit to the offensive. If there was anything to gain at Fredericksburg on December 13, it would be on the left, as Burnside recognized, and he gave Franklin fully half the army for the task — two corps, six divisions, and two additional divisions to guard his bridges. Meade's complaint — "My God, did they think my division could whip Lee's whole army?" — served as epitaph for Franklin's indecisive effort. As much as he liked Franklin personally, said Meade, "from his inertness & fear of responsibility he certainly did not come up to the mark."

The generals on the right had only to carry out orders and find ways to force their men repeatedly against the defenses of Marye's Heights . . . which Sumner's initial attacks demonstrated were impregnable. Burnside did not allow Sumner to cross the river for fear he would try to lead the troops personally, leaving corps commanders Darius Couch and Orlando Willcox on the scene to respond to the slaughter in front of the stone wall. Neither protested nor questioned nor sought to amend Burnside's orders; indeed, to keep up the pace, Couch reached into another corps for Humphreys's division. Only Hooker had the nerve to protest to Burnside and finally to halt the killing.

Three times Ambrose Burnside had proclaimed himself unequal to commanding a great army. Now the merciless trial of battle proved him right. Still, he deserved far more support from superior and subordinate than he received. Choosing Fredericksburg as springboard for a new march on Richmond was sound enough in the circumstances of his taking the command, only to have his plan fatally compromised by Halleck's indifference in the matter of the bridge trains. Their nonarrival first revealed Burnside's inability to think on his feet, to find another way. The bloody repulse on December 13 confirmed that failing. Again it was apathy, by Franklin this time, that destroyed whatever chance there was of breaking Lee's lines. But among the high command there were no subtleties to be taken from December 13. "Very little is said about Burnside," artillerist Charles Wainwright told his diary, "but neither officers nor men have the slightest confidence in him."[4]

Fredericksburg splintered the political as well as the military landscape. Even as the Committee on the Conduct of the War was taking the generals' testimony at Falmouth, Senate Republicans of Radical bent created a governing crisis for the president. In caucus they passed a resolution calling for "a change in and partial reconstruction of the Cabinet." Their target was Secretary of State Seward, whom they took to be the power behind the throne, responsible by manipulation for all that had gone wrong with the war effort. The senators were fed the ugly details in backstairs fashion by Seward's cabinet rival, Treasury Secretary Chase. Presented with Seward's resignation, the president confronted the senatorial cabal with a united cabinet (absent Seward but including an embarrassed Chase) and maneuvered Chase into offering *his* resignation. "I can ride on now," Lincoln exclaimed. "I've got a pumpkin in each end of my bag!" With the two resignations in hand, he accepted neither. The cabal was stymied: To be rid of Seward would cost the favored Chase. By defusing the explosive situation, Lincoln could confront the real crisis — the management of the Army of the Potomac — without additional interference from Congress.[5]

Daniel Larned of Burnside's staff remarked, "*Jealousies* and political intrigue *are* greater enemies than an open foe." Franklin and Baldy Smith furnished proof of Larned's observation. On December 20, the two signed a letter to the president. Because "the plan of campaign which has already been commenced cannot possibly be successful," they proposed the Potomac army return to the Peninsula and base a campaign on the James River — 150,000 men to advance on the north bank of the James, 100,000 on the south bank, carrying three days' rations and 100 rounds, "blankets and shelter tents and a pair of socks and a pair of drawers." This would inevitably produce the destruction of the Rebel army or the investment of the Rebel capital, "and the war will be on a better footing than it now or has any present prospect of being." In reply, Lincoln recalled the fevered debate over McClellan on the Peninsula: "If you go to James River, a large part of the army must remain on or near the Fredericksburg line, to protect Washington. It is the old difficulty." Of course, Smith grumbled, "nothing came of it."

That Baldy Smith would go over Burnside's head, contrary to army regulations, was not unexpected (one of Smith's staff called him "a perfect Ishmaelite to his superior officers, as they found out to their cost"), but Franklin intriguing against his friend was new. Perhaps he hoped to draw attention away from his suspect role on December 13. Perhaps he was putting his name forward in the competition for next army commander. (On that score, he expressed concern that Bull Sumner might get the post — "so by losing Burnside we go from the frying pan into the fire.") Whatever the motives, the joint letter ushered in a generals' revolt against Ambrose Burnside.[6]

It was a revolt rooted in fertile ground. Sam Heintzelman held that Burnside had quite lost the respect of his officers. "I am not surprised when he publishes to the country that he has no confidence in his abilities to command so large an army." The Fifth Corps' Gouverneur Warren proposed the solution many colleagues favored: "We *must* have McClellan back with unlimited and unfettered powers. His name is a tower of strength to everyone here. . . ." Feelings too were strong in the ranks. Henry Abbott, 20th Massachusetts, reported his brigade attending a "sermon & benediction" by General Howard, who closed with a call for three cheers for Burnside. "Several men in a new regiment, the 127th Penn., gave a mockery of 3 cheers. Not a man in the other regiments opened their mouths, except to mutter three cheers for McClellan."[7]

On December 29 Burnside issued orders for a new offensive, this time crossing the Rappahannock downstream. There would be a feint upstream, and a cavalry raid. On December 30 two generals from Baldy Smith's Sixth Corps of William Franklin's Left Grand Division turned up at the president's White House office. The visitors were Brigadier Generals John Newton and John Cochrane, the first, commander of one of Smith's divisions, the second, commander of one of Newton's brigades. Newton was the frontman, a West Pointer who saw just enough action to gain a division. New Yorker Cochrane was the insider, ex–Mozart Hall politico who knew the game well enough that in October McClellan used him to lobby the cabinet and the White House for his return to the general-in-chief's post.

This pairing was there at the behest of (and primed by) Franklin and Smith to undermine Burnside, using the ploy that the troops were too demoralized for a new campaign. When Lincoln suggested they were there to "injure" General Burnside, Newton blanched, but Cochrane slicked things over and testified to the army's sad state of morale. Their point was taken. At 3:30 p.m. that December 30 Lincoln telegraphed Burnside, "I have good reason for saying you must not make a general movement of the army without letting me know."

On the last day of the year Burnside himself called at the White House. Lincoln said that two general officers — whom he would not name — had visited him to warn that the new offensive could not succeed. This put Burnside in a state. He said if he had lost the confidence of his generals he should resign. Lincoln calmed him and told him to return the next day for a fuller discussion. That evening Burnside wrote out his thoughts for the president: "It is my duty to place on paper the remarks I made to you. . . ." He said that Secretary of War Stanton and General-in-Chief Halleck had lost the confidence of the army and of the country. As to his planned offensive, "I am not sustained in this by a single grand division commander," due to "a lack of confidence in me. In this case it is highly necessary that this army should be commanded by some other officer. . . ." He did not couple his proffered resignation with resignations by Stanton and Halleck, but the inference was clear.[8]

January 1, 1863, was irrevocably marked by the signing and issuing of the Emancipation Proclamation, for Abraham Lincoln "the central act of my administration and the great event of the nineteenth century." It was all of that, altering the very thrust of the war. There was concern among proclamation supporters that Fredericksburg and its plunging effect on Union morale might derail emancipation, but Senator Charles Sumner found Lincoln resolute. "The Presdt. says that he could not stop the Proclamation if he would, & would not if he could."

But the "Day of Jubilee" also witnessed Lincoln presented with letters of resignation from the commanding general of the Army of the Potomac and the general-in-chief of all the nation's armies.[9]

On New Year's Day morning Burnside met with the president and Stanton and Halleck at the War Department. Burnside handed his letter to Lincoln, who read it and handed it back without comment. Adopting a confessional manner, Burnside turned to Stanton and Halleck and said he owed it to them to explain that in his letter he had offered his resignation and had expressed his opinion that the two of them lacked the confidence of both the army and the country. After no doubt an awkward moment, he called on them to endorse his new battle plan. Stanton said passing judgment was not a war minister's job. Halleck said the general on the scene must decide the what, where, and when of an advance. "No definite conclusion was come to," wrote an exasperated Burnside. The discussion lagged into the identity of the two generals who went over Burnside's head, and the president dismissed his querulous charges.

That afternoon Lincoln wrote to Halleck reviewing the predicament on the Rappahannock. "If in such a difficulty as this you do not help, you fail me precisely in the point for which I sought your assistance." He wanted Halleck to go to Falmouth, look over the ground, evaluate the temper of the officers, "in a word, gather all the elements for forming a judgment of your own; and then tell Gen. Burnside that you *do* approve, or that you do *not* approve his plan. Your military skill is useless to me, if you will not do this."

Halleck was prompt to reply: "I am led to believe that there is a very important difference of opinion in regard to my relations toward generals commanding armies in the field. . . . I therefore respectfully request that I may be relieved from further duties as General-in-Chief." Lincoln endorsed his letter to Halleck, "Withdrawn, because considered harsh by Gen. Halleck." It was (militarily) a most unpromising start to the year 1863 — one campaign stopped in its tracks, two resignations offered and refused, two discontented generals in the two top commands.[10]

Burnside returned to Falmouth more confounded than ever — his letter of resignation handed back unremarked, his planned advance unendorsed. Then details of his plan leaked out and he had to discard it. He poured out his woes to any lieutenant who would listen. George Meade summed up for his wife: Burnside wrote the president offering his resignation, suggesting Stanton and Halleck be removed as well. "Burnside told me all this himself this morning, & read me the paper, which was right up & down; . . . he could get nothing out of any of them, he came back, & thus matters stand. . . . God only knows what is to become of us & what will be done."

Burnside's confessionals spread dismay through the officer corps and emboldened Franklin and Smith. Hearing him recount his trials with Washington, Franklin wrote his wife, "I am afraid that Burnside is a weak tool in their hands . . . veered around by every wind that comes from Washington." Of opinions, said Smith, Burnside "had none save the reflection from the last person with whom he had talked." Both named the James River as the route to Richmond, scorning further ventures on the Rappahannock. One of Smith's generals, W.T.H. "Bully" Brooks, was so outspo-

ken that Burnside put him in arrest for complaining of government poli-
cies and for "using language tending to demoralize his command." Brooks
protested; his remarks, while perhaps "not in accordance with good man-
ners," were delivered "in a jocular manner."[11]

"There is one great universal condemnation, not of Burnside in particular, but of the whole state of things which has brought us to this pass,"
wrote the 20th Massachusetts's Henry Ropes. Captain Ropes recognized
within this state of things fast-spreading demoralization. He explained, by
way of example, "The men are suffering a great deal for lack of fresh food
and sufficient variety. Diarrhoea and scurvy almost universal," while headquarters dined on canvasback duck and champagne. (This lack of decent
provisions put the army sutlers in peril. A squad of Pennsylvania troopers
charged a train of sutlers' wagons, wrote Felix Brannigan, "hurrahing for
Jeff Davis. Of course the Sutlers took leg-bail, and all the valuables were
left to the mercy of those whom the same Sutlers had, for the last year,
been robbing by extortion prices.")

In these post-Fredericksburg weeks the Army of the Potomac was universally ill fed, ill housed, and ill cared for. "This army is really, the old part
of it, wearied and angered at the neglect we have received, and disgusted,"
wrote Gouverneur Warren, "and the new part of it is very deficient in good
officers, and needs discipline and instruction." The generals, starting with
the general commanding, failed miserably in an officer's fundamental duty
— to take care of his men. In these weeks the Potomac army was the worst
administered it had ever been . . . or ever would be. It was as black a mark
on Burnside's record as Fredericksburg. "Our Potomac army is where it
can do nothing but dissolve, decompose & die," wrote Charles Sumner.
"There must be some speedy extraction, or its present encampment will
be a Golgotha."

In addition to death by neglect — near Aquia Creek, a hospital steward
reported, "is a convalescent camp that is killing the boys off at the rate of
15 or 20 a day" — the most obvious consequence of the Potomac army's
decay was desertion. A New York soldier reported desertions "are of daily
occurrence in almost every Regt. in the field, and sometimes in squads of
fifteen or twenty at a time. . . ." A man in the 24th Michigan wrote his family, "I think that if Uncle Sam don't settle this war pretty quick that it will
play out for the deserters is a going out by great numbers. . . . Company
A has had 7 deserters in one day and Company E has lost about 20 men
by desertion, and other companies is bad but not quite as bad." Payrolls
went unmet, and men supporting families on their army pay took "French
leave" in droves. When there was a payday, it might provide the funds for

deserting. Provost Marshal Patrick reported that in Dan Sickles's division "the Excelsiors are determined to run if they can get a chance, having been paid off today."[12]

Official figures confirm these anecdotal observations. A general order calling on each regiment and battery to list its absentees — absent with leave and absent without leave — produced a confounding statistic: As of January 31, 1863, one in ten men on the Army of the Potomac's rolls was a deserter. The total came to 25,363. The rate of desertion was estimated at 200 a day. Carl Schurz brought the Eleventh Corps to Falmouth, surveyed what he found there — the dismal quarters, the spreading sickness, the "frightful rate" of desertion — and wrote Lincoln, "Connect all this together and you will not be surprised when you see this great army melt away with frightful rapidity."[13]

All the while, dragging at the morale of the officer corps like a dangerous undertow, was the ongoing general court-martial of Fitz John Porter. The Porter court opened in Washington on December 4 and ran on well into the new year. At Falmouth the proceedings were followed closely. General Meade wrote his wife on December 23, "From present appearances the trial of Fitz-John Porter is going rather hard against him." In that event, it was the doing of Edwin Stanton, whose hidden hand guided the verdict from the beginning.

Writing on December 29, Porter told S.L.M. Barlow that he was being tried for something more than his conduct at Second Bull Run. "I have seen sufficient of the court — or of the minds of a few of them, the most of them — to know their conclusion is a foregone one, if not determined by order or the wish of those high in power. . . . I have too many personal enemies & enemies of Genl McClellan on the court." To *New York World* editor Marble he predicted, "Proof strong as holy writ will be required to cause a just verdict to be rendered."[14]

Stanton was determined to take down Porter and through him the last traces of McClellanism in the Potomac army, and he packed the Porter court to do it. Seven of the nine appointed judges were suspect. David Hunter, president of the court-martial, had been shunted aside by McClellan after First Bull Run, and McClellan warned Porter, "Hunter I distrust . . . he is an enemy of mine." After Seven Pines Silas Casey was relieved of his command by McClellan. Ethan Allen Hitchcock served on Stanton's War Board and was easily bullied by the war secretary. N. B. Buford, by the accounts of his wife and his brother, was suborned by Stanton's ally Salmon Chase with promises of promotion for his soldier son.

Judges and figures in the Fitz John Porter court-martial, by Alfred Waud. Clockwise around the table from left: David Hunter, Rufus King, James Ricketts, James Garfield, John Slough, lawyer Reverdy Johnson, Porter, court reporter, prosecutor Joseph Holt, John Pope, N. B. Buford, Silas Casey, Benjamin Prentiss, E. A. Hitchcock.

Porter claimed that James A. Garfield, a Chase protégé, "played the part of Judge Advocate" from the bench. James Ricketts and Rufus King, themselves under investigation for Second Bull Run, should have been recused from Porter's case. When John Tucker of the War Department saw this panel, he told Stanton, "That court will convict General Porter whether guilty or not." Stanton did not deny.[15]

The primary charges against Porter focused on the first day of Second Bull Run, August 29, and his alleged failure to obey lawful commands from Pope — the 10:00 a.m. joint order to Porter and McDowell, and the 4:30 p.m. attack order to Porter. The prosecution made much of Porter's state of mind, as displayed in his August dispatches to Burnside: They "express, on the part of the accused, an intense scorn and contempt for the strategy and movements of the Army of Virginia, a weariness and disgust for his associations with it, added to a bitter fling at his commanding general. . . ."

Pope testified that Porter's July letter to Joseph C. G. Kennedy highly critical of Pope, and the August telegrams of Porter to Burnside, showed that he had been right to suspect Porter's motives from the start. Pope insisted that Longstreet was not yet on the field on the 29th; had Porter obeyed his attack orders "at any time up to 8 o'clock that night, it is my firm conviction that we should have destroyed the army of Jackson."

The prosecution's main witness was Irvin McDowell, and it turned out that General McDowell could remember nothing of his dealings with Porter on August 29 — nothing they discussed about Pope's bizarre joint order, nothing about his ordering Porter's Fifth Corps to remain alone in harm's way, nothing about any enemy blocking forces. Nor could he recall or locate the dispatch Porter sent him confirming that Pope's 4:30 order only reached him at sundown, too late to mount an attack that day. It was perjury by selective amnesia. McDowell, Porter said, "appears to have forgotten almost all that I remember of what took place between us on the 29th of August last. . . ." Porter's defense called witnesses to what did occur that day, a sharp contrast to McDowell's maunderings.

Still, the record showed nothing by Porter about the enemy he had faced — he neither probed its position and strength nor reported it to his superiors. Instead he retreated. The prosecution took this as "the true spirit of the conduct of the accused," a spirit manifest in Porter's expressed contempt for John Pope and all his works.[16]

The judges could hardly ignore the very public turmoil in the Army of the Potomac — the rumors of threatened marches on Washington, the dismissal of Major Key for seditious talk, the high-command bungling at Fredericksburg, the displays of disloyalty to Burnside, the calls for McClellan's return. Fitz John Porter was on trial . . . as was a dysfunctional command he appeared to personify.

The judges rendered their verdict on January 10 and sent it to the president for review. The *New York Times*, pondering the testimony, predicted "the court unanimously acquits Gen. Porter of the charges against him." But Porter suspected more than testimony swayed the judges. He wrote McClellan on January 13, "The court began to smell your return to power and were influenced by it in their decision."

On January 21 President Lincoln, without comment, approved the judges' verdict. Major General Fitz John Porter was found guilty of failure to obey lawful orders and guilty of misbehavior before the enemy. The court sentenced him "to be cashiered, and to be forever disqualified from holding any office of trust or profit under the Government of the United States." "The hounds succeeded at last," Porter wrote McClellan. "This is a terrible blow, but my conscious innocence will sustain me, and my indignation will enable me to fight it out."[17]

(Fitz John Porter fought it out with varying fortune for twenty-three years. With no appeal to a general court-martial finding, he sought a rehearing based on new evidence. The wartime political divide, carried into Reconstruction, immersed the case in partisan squabbles. Finally, in 1878,

President Rutherford B. Hayes appointed a three-man board of army officers to rehear the Porter case. On neutral ground, so to speak, the prosecution case fell apart. Pope's nephew, deliverer of the 4:30 p.m. attack order, confessed he got lost and only reached Porter at sunset, too late to attack. Porter's dispatch to McDowell to that effect turned up among McDowell's papers. General Longstreet testified he was indeed on the field on August 29, blocking Porter's path. The board's report, issued in 1879, overturned the 1863 Porter verdict. It took seven more years — and Democrat Grover Cleveland in the White House — for a "relief bill" to pass, restoring Porter to his colonel's rank in the regular army. Vindicated, he was placed on the retired list.)[18]

The Porter court's decision engrossed the officer corps. "We are all much shocked by it," Franklin told his wife, "considering it unjust and arbitrary in the highest degree." He said that Reynolds, Meade, Hancock, and assorted other generals he spoke to shared his view. It was agreed that politics drove the verdict, and that Porter's close association with the dismissed McClellan had doomed him. "It was necessary for the Administration that . . . some scapegoat had to be found for the shortcomings of their pet, Pope," artillerist Charles Wainwright told his diary, "and in Porter they could hit a friend of McClellan at the same time." Stanton's earlier persecution of Charles Stone was seen as prelude to his pursuit of bigger game in the person of Fitz John Porter.

Yet on closer study General Meade (for one) thought perhaps a kind of rough justice was done. He wrote of Porter, "I do not attribute his failure & shortcomings" at Second Bull Run "to disloyalty & an active desire to have disaster attend to our arms, as I do to his want of judgment & capacity, added to an indifference whether success or disaster followed." Charles Russell Lowell of the headquarters staff wrote, "The evidence leaves little doubt that Porter got 'demoralized,' . . . his frame of mind was un-officer-like and dangerous. This sort of feeling was growing in the army, and the Government and the Country felt that it must be stopped. Porter was made the example." Lowell added, "I accept the lesson." He believed a good many others in the officer corps did too.

Fitz John Porter's cashiering put period to the Army of the Potomac's McClellan era. To be sure, McClellanism as an ultraconservative way of making war was hardly erased from the army's character. McClellan loyalists still populated the officer corps, although keeping their heads down for fear of Edwin Stanton and the Committee on the Conduct of the War. But without McClellan and his acolyte Porter at its head, the Potomac army began to distance itself from opposition politics and to turn more to the business of war making. Talk of colluding with the enemy to preserve slavery and marching on Washington and military coups faded away. Instead of McClellan's army it became the administration's army. It became Mr. Lincoln's army.[19]

This new era was not quite yet, however. First the Army of the Potomac experienced a violent shaking-up. Burnside concluded that the one thing he could not do was do nothing. Quartermaster Montgomery Meigs painted him a melodramatic picture of inaction: "Rest at Falmouth is death to our nation — is defeat, border warfare, hollow truce, barbarism, ruin for ages, chaos!" Burnside determined to cross the Rappahannock upstream at Banks's Ford to strike at Lee from the west. Marching orders were issued for January 20, Hooker's grand division to lead, Franklin's to follow.

These two senior generals, and their staffs, skittered and balked like an unruly team. Hooker "talked very openly about the absurdity of the movement," reported the *New York Times*'s William Swinton, denouncing Burnside as incompetent "and the President and Government at Washington as imbecile and 'played out.'" What was needed, said Hooker, was a military dictator, and the sooner the better. Franklin and Baldy Smith spent the evening of the 19th trying to argue Burnside out of the advance. Diarist Charles Wainwright found Franklin's and Smith's staffs "talking outrageously, only repeating though, no doubt, the words of their generals. . . . Franklin has talked so much and so loudly to this effect ever since the present move was decided on, that he has completely demoralized his whole command." Burnside admitted to George Meade that "some of his Generals had told him he was leading the men to a *slaughter pen.*"

Whatever the merits of the Banks's Ford crossing site, they were washed away when the rains came. Beginning on the evening of January 20 and lasting forty-eight hours, a winter nor'easter struck the Rappahannock front and virtually drowned the Army of the Potomac. "I don't know, of course, how the world's surface looked after the flood in Noah's time," Alpheus Williams wrote, "but I am certain it could not have appeared more saturated than does the present surface of this God-forsaken portion of the Old Dominion." Vehicles sank hub-deep in the mud. The hulking pontoon wagons were rendered immovable — teams doubled and tripled and 150 men on ropes could not budge them. In Potomac army annals it became the Mud March, recalled with a shudder.

Finally Burnside issued recall and the army sloshed back to its Falmouth camps. Deserters were legion. Colonel Wainwright stopped again

Alfred Waud sketched the Mud March, the Army of the Potomac's ill-fated January 1863 offensive that sought to cross the Rappahannock at Banks's Ford amidst a nor'easter. It was claimed "the wagons settled to the hub, and the mules over the fetlock."

at Franklin's headquarters, "where I found him, Smith, and their staffs . . . doing nothing to help things on, but grumbling and talking in a manner to do all the harm possible." Staff rumor had Franklin about to be awarded the army command. Henry Ropes, 20th Massachusetts, wrote his father, "Burnside rode along yesterday and was followed by hooting and yells. The troops are in a dreadful state . . . the Army to the verge of mutiny." John Reynolds was disgusted — Burnside goes off to Washington "to know what to do!! If we do not get some one soon who can command an Army without consulting 'Stanton and Halleck' at Washington I do not know what will become of this Army."[20]

The disaffection among his generals did not escape Burnside's notice, and any gaps in his awareness were filled in by *New York Times* editor Henry J. Raymond, visiting the army and probing the temper of its officer corps. Affable Burnside had a high boiling point but now he boiled over. He drafted General Orders No. 8, with intent to rid his high command of dissidents, malcontents, and the disloyal.

Heading the list was Joe Hooker, guilty of "unjust and unnecessary criticisms of the actions of his superior officers," of "creating distrust in the minds of officers," of "habitually speaking in disparaging terms of other officers." Major General Hooker was dismissed from the military service of the United States. Also dismissed from the service was Bully Brooks, whom Burnside had arrested earlier for demoralizing his command. Burnside had learned the names of the talebearers who had gone over his head to the president, and Generals John Newton and John Cochrane were dismissed. Further, it "being evident" that William B. Franklin, William F. Smith, and Joseph H. Taylor (Sumner's chief of staff) "can be of no further service to this army," they were relieved and ordered to report for assignment.

In one sweep, Burnside purged two of his three grand-division commanders (plus the chief of staff of the third), one corps commander, two division commanders, and one brigade commander. Then he was told that dismissing general officers from the army required the president's approval. Burnside telegraphed Lincoln that he was coming to Washington with "some very important orders, and I want to see you before issuing them." Dining that day with Franklin and Smith, Burnside remarked cryptically, "In a day or two you will hear of something that will surprise you all."[21]

On reaching Washington on January 24, Burnside handed Lincoln General Orders No. 8 and with it his resignation as major general of volunteers. He said he could not effectively lead the army with these dissident officers serving under him. Lincoln must endorse G.O. 8 or accept his resignation. Lincoln said he would consult advisers and see Burnside the next day.

That evening, at a White House reception, *Times* editor Raymond took Lincoln aside and recounted correspondent Swinton's recent interview with Joe Hooker, quoting Hooker's remarks about Burnside's incompetence and his jeremiad against the imbecile and played-out administration and his call for a military dictator. "That is all true — Hooker does talk badly," said Lincoln. "But the trouble is, he is stronger with the country to-day than any other man. Even if the country were told of Hooker's talk they would not believe it."

On Sunday morning, January 25, Lincoln called in Stanton and Halleck and announced, without inviting discussion, his decision to relieve Burnside as commander of the Army of the Potomac and replace him with Hooker. He then called in Burnside and told him his decision. Burnside took it well — perhaps in fact with relief — and said that no one "would be a happier man than I would be" if Hooker gained a victory. Lincoln refused Burnside's resignation. He offered to return him to his previous command in North Carolina, but Burnside said that post was presently in good hands and it was agreed he would take a thirty-day furlough. (On March 17 he was assigned the Department of the Ohio.) It was also agreed that G.O. 8 and Burnside's resignation would not be made public.

Burnside returned to Falmouth to hand over the command. In his farewell to the troops, swallowing his animus, he urged them to give to "the brave and skillful general who has so long been identified with your organization, and who is now to command you, your full and cordial support and co-operation, and you will deserve success." Staff man Daniel Larned made note, "Thus endeth the Drama of 'Burnside and the Army of the Potomac.'" These eighty days of high drama witnessed a disastrous defeat and a near-disastrous internal collapse of the Potomac army. The generals' revolt did not bring on the defeat, but it contributed greatly to the collapse and it triggered the change of command. The cabal succeeded well enough in undermining General Burnside but then failed to steer its hero, General McClellan, back to the command.[22]

Joe Hooker was tall, blue-eyed, clean-shaven, well turned out, an impressive martial figure. Reporter Noah Brooks thought him "by all odds, the handsomest soldier I ever laid my eyes upon. . . . alert and confident, overflowing with animal spirits. . . ." Hooker's fighting record alone was enough to steer him toward the high command, but his ambition for the post was widely seen as tarnished by intrigue.

Along with his command orders came a personal letter of remarkable candor from the president. Lincoln had tried often enough to reason with McClellan by means of personal letters — without apparent success — and in the process brought definition to his role as commander-in-chief. He told Hooker he had good and sufficient reasons to give him the Potomac army, "yet I think it best for you to know that there are some things in regard to which, I am not quite satisfied with you." He said that Hooker was a brave and a skillful soldier, that he had confidence in himself, "which is a valuable, if not an indispensable quality," that he was ambitious, "which, within reasonable bounds, does good rather than harm." But during Burnside's command, "you have taken counsel of your ambition, and thwarted him as much as you could, in which you did a great wrong to the country, and to a most meritorious and honorable brother officer." Further, he said he had heard in such a way as to believe it (i.e., from editor Raymond) "of your recently saying that both the Army and the Government needed a Dictator. Of course it was not *for* this, but in spite of it, that I have given you the command. Only those generals who gain successes, can set up dictators. What I now ask of you is military success, and I will risk the dictatorship. . . . And now, beware of rashness. Beware of rashness, but with energy, and sleepless vigilance, go forward, and give us victories."

John Nicolay said of Lincoln's letter, "It would be difficult to find a severer piece of friendly criticism," but Joe Hooker accepted it with equanimity. He was, after all, where he had long wanted to be. He was heard to say, "That is just such a letter as a father might write to his son," that it ought to be printed "in letters of gold." But he assumed that Burnside was the "author" of the president's criticisms, and when he found a copy of Burnside's unissued G.O. 8, left behind at Potomac army headquarters, he sent it to the *New York Herald*. He said it would make Burnside "more conspicuous than he had ever been before."[23]

Hooker sought Lincoln's assurance that he would not be under the thumb of General-in-Chief Halleck, for whom he nursed a long-standing distrust; neither he nor his army "expected justice" at Halleck's hands. As Hooker told it, in the 1850s in California Halleck partnered in a law firm specializing in land claims, submitting to friends of Hooker's huge bills for essentially doing nothing. Hooker called him out for "his schemes of avarice and plunder." He believed Halleck was behind denying him the army command to succeed McClellan. Halleck, in turn, said he knew sordid things about Hooker's conduct in California; now Hooker "seeks to ward off its effect by making it appear that I am his personal enemy." Lincoln permitted Hooker to bypass Halleck and deal with him, creating an awkward gap in the chain of command.[24]

Hooker bore a second burden from his California years — a reputation for gambling, womanizing, and especially for drinking. The old army was marked by a petty aristocracy of gentlemanly virtues, a mold in which free-spirited Joe Hooker did not exactly fit. Still, twenty months into the Civil War, there had been no reports made, no tales told, of Fighting Joe the worse for drink while leading his troops into battle at Williamsburg and Seven Pines and Oak Grove and Glendale and Second Bull Run and Turner's Gap and Antietam and Fredericksburg. "I am asked on all sides here if he drinks," Charles Wainwright entered in his diary. "Though thrown in very close quarters with him through six months, I never saw him when I thought him the worse for liquor." George Meade said, "Whatever may have been his habits in former times, since I have been associated with him in this Army I can bear testimony of the utter falsehood of the charge of drunkenness."

Joseph Hooker had fought in eight battles for the Potomac army before taking its command, earning his nickname Fighting Joe.

To be sure, it was *said* that Hooker drank, and so Potomac army soldiers revised the tune "Marching Along." Earlier they sang:

> *McClellan's our leader, he's gallant and strong;*
> *For God and our country we are marching along.*

Now they had a new lyric:

> *Joe Hooker's our leader, he takes his whiskey strong;*
> *For God and our country we are marching along.*

Lincoln's secretary John Hay thought he knew how the stories about Hooker and liquor got started. One evening he dined with Hooker and fellow officers. "Hooker drank very little," Hay wrote, "not more than the rest who were all abstemious, yet what little he drank made his cheek hot and red & his eye brighter. I can easily understand how the stories of his drunkenness have grown, if so little affects him as I have seen." Appearances could deceive, and in Joe Hooker's case, they did.

To his diary entry on Hooker's sobriety, Colonel Wainwright added the observation, "I should say that his failing was more in the way of women than whiskey." Bachelor Hooker seems to have made no particular secret of patronizing a Washington brothel on occasion. Indeed, a section of the capital's Second Ward crowded with bawdyhouses was known during the war (and for some years after) as Hooker's Division. Bluenoses in the officer corps were scandalized. Charles Francis Adams, Jr., dismissed Hooker as "a man who . . . in private character is well known to be — I need not say what."

Fighting Joe provoked civilian comment as well. "Injudicious Hooker!" wrote New York diarist George Templeton Strong. "Perhaps he is the fated knight that is to break the spell under which that army has lain enchanted so long," yet the general commanding "should be a man of high moral tone" . . . which did not seem to describe Joe Hooker. In Washington Elizabeth Blair Lee took note, "I regret Genl Hookers appointment still it may do." If only he had the gift of "appreciating clever men & maybe to use them — if so he will get along & well — but I think he lacks every thing but courage. . . ."[25]

Aside from such as Lieutenant Adams, most in the officer corps seemed willing to suspend judgment. Hooker's appointment was hardly a surprise, his fighting record was known and respected, and unlike outsiders Pope and Burnside he was a part of the fabric of the Army of the Potomac. On learning of Hooker's appointment, General Meade spoke of "old regular officers, most of whom are decided in their hostility to him," but as it happened Hooker came to the command just as the core of the old guard departed.

Edwin Sumner was disillusioned and disgusted. There was, he said, "a great deal too much croaking" by his fellow generals. His warrior's spirit had twice been broken — at Antietam, in the deadly rout of Sedgwick's division; then at Fredericksburg, seeing his Second Corps slaughtered at the stone wall — and it was beyond mending. He was sixty-six and tired, and he asked to be relieved of duty with the Army of the Potomac. He was well beyond his time and well above his useful level of command, yet for the Potomac army he had set indelible marks for courage and resolute dedication to duty. Sumner would be assigned to head the Department of the Missouri, but on the journey to his new command he contracted pneumonia and fell mortally ill. His last words were of his beloved Second Corps: ". . . never lost a flag or a cannon! . . . That is true — never lost one."

Participants in the generals' revolt found its consequences personally costly. The army revealed a long memory. The president, with Burnside's G.O. 8 in mind, got rid of William Franklin as neatly as he had gotten rid of McDowell after Second Bull Run. Blandly assuming he "did not wish" to serve under Hooker, Lincoln relieved Franklin of duty with the Army of the Potomac. The press, fed by the Committee on the Conduct of the War, pinned on Franklin the blame for Fredericksburg. He was assigned to the

Department of the Gulf, served there indifferently, and never returned to the Potomac army.

Baldy Smith was next to depart. Hooker was quick to get rid of Smith, for (as he told Stanton) "I recognized in him the evil genius of Franklin, Brooks, and Newton." Smith put on a brave face in his memoir: "Hooker caused me to be promptly relieved from duty with the army, which was progress for I had far less confidence in him than in Burnside." In time Smith would return to the Potomac army, but his role in the generals' revolt put his career largely in eclipse. "The results followed me through the war," he admitted.

Bully Brooks, in June, would start ten months posted at Pittsburgh, had his major general's appointment revoked, and in 1864 resigned. Of the two talebearers, John Cochrane resigned within the month and returned to New York politics; John Newton, in 1864, transferred to the Western theater, had his major general's appointment withdrawn, and ended the war posted in the Florida Keys. Lieutenant Colonel Joseph H. Taylor of the staff ended the war still a lieutenant colonel.[26]

John Gibbon admired Hooker's "gallant bearing" in action, his "coolness and nerve at Antietam," but frowned on the intrigue marking his path to command. Prickly Henry Slocum, troubled by Hooker's reputation, interviewed him and was mollified: "I am willing to follow him. My confidence has greatly increased with him." George Meade, who had known Hooker since West Point, was less concerned how he gained the command than what he would do with it. "I believe Hooker is a good soldier," he told his wife. "The danger he runs, is of subjecting himself to bad influences, such as *Dan Butterfield* & *Dan Sickles* who being intellectually more clever than Hooker . . . will obtain an injurious ascendancy over him. . . . I may however in this be wrong — time will prove." From the Western theater William Sherman remarked, "I know Hooker well, and tremble to think of his handling 100,000 men in the presence of Lee. I dont think Lee will attack Hooker in position . . . but let Hooker once advance or move laterally and I fear the result."

Others questioned if Hooker had the capacity to manage a great army. Mr. Lincoln put the matter succinctly: "Now there's Joe Hooker — he can fight — I think that point is pretty well established — but whether he can 'keep tavern' for a large army is not so sure."[27]

To most everyone's surprise, Joe Hooker proceeded to "keep tavern" brilliantly. As chief of staff for five commands during the War with Mexico, he mastered the fundamentals of army administration, and he managed

MASTER ABRAHAM LINCOLN GETS A NEW TOY.

The *Southern Illus-trated News* takes up the theme of Lincoln as puppeteer, with his latest toy, Fighting Joe. The Emancipation Proclamation serves as backdrop. Disgarded generals fill the shelves.

each of his commands in this new war with high efficiency. An early action as army commander was an application to the War Department: "It will be a great happiness to me to have Brig. Gen. Stone ordered to report as chief of staff." Hooker had known Charles Stone since Mexico and valued his skills. Stone "gladly assented." But Stanton marked the application "not considered for the interests of the service." For Edwin Stanton, loyalty questioned (however falsely) was disloyalty proved.

Hooker turned to Daniel Butterfield for chief of staff. Intensely ambitious Dan Butterfield was an outlander, not West Point, not old army. He had been active in the New York militia, and from the Peninsula on compiled a creditable command record. He wrote a manual, *Camp & Outpost Duty for Infantry,* and turned a disused cavalry call into the haunting lights-out call Taps. He recast Phil Kearny's idea for cap badges (to control straggling) into corps badges worn as symbols of unit pride. Butterfield's claim to chief of staff was his executive experience heading the eastern division of the American Express Company. Provost Marshal Patrick grumbled, "Butterfield now Chief of Staff, delights in papers & Orders." But "papers & Orders" that cracked the whip on the Potomac army was just what was needed.[28]

Hardtack, salt pork, and coffee prevailed in the field, but in Burnside's winter camps it was a debilitating diet. Hooker ordered soft bread issued at least four times a week, fresh potatoes or onions twice a week, desiccated potatoes or mixed vegetables once a week. Corruptors in the Commissary

Department were rooted out; any commissary officer failing to follow this issuing schedule had to produce a certificate from the depot that the provender in question was unavailable. Company cooks were assigned and inspected. Engineer William Folwell wrote home, "Gen. Hooker seems to be gaining the confidence of the army completely. His 'soft bread' order reaches us in a tender spot. . . ."

A system of furloughs was set up for men and officers — keyed to units passing close and frequent inspections. To activate his changes, Hooker added inspectors general and gave them authority. Not a regiment or a battery escaped their notice, and the commanding general made his own inspections. Campsites were regularized and camp sanitation enforced. Hospitals were sanitized. Paydays were reestablished as were clothing issues. Drilling, inspections, and reviews filled the days. Butterfield's paper trails established authority and responsibility, and commanding officers faced sign-off accountability. As Alpheus Williams phrased it, "Everybody must be active, each one above inspecting to see that those below are doing their duty."[29]

Hooker cracked down swiftly on desertion. Provost Marshal Patrick was pressed to pursue and capture, picket lines were tightened, cavalry patrols expanded. At Aquia Landing a patrol captured 400 deserters in the act of building rafts to cross the Potomac into Maryland. Bounties were offered for deserters. So soon as it became evident the army was serious about desertion, the numbers plummeted. Patrick dispensed with court-martial for 344 captured deserters in favor of returning them to their regiments. This approach led the president to proclaim amnesty for deserters returning by April 1. The March 31 return of the Potomac army listed just 1,941 men absent without leave.

Hooker's restoration of army-wide morale following Burnside's debacle was fully as remarkable as the turnaround by McClellan following Pope's debacle. Fighting Joe took charge, striding into the tangles, firing off orders right and left, forcing the military machine to run properly. Darius Couch might deprecate Hooker's character, but granted him due credit: "Hooker by adopting vigorous measures stopped the almost wholesale desertions, and infused new life and discipline in the army." Hooker would confess, "I felt almost dismayed in taking command at the prospect before me," but he added, with pride, "This I regard as the best service I rendered the Country during the war."[30]

He moved as well to reorganize the command structure. Sam Heintzelman, commanding the Washington garrison, decided he could not serve under "a man whose whole reputation was gained under my command."

He proposed that Washington become a separate department. Making the Potomac army responsible for the capital had always weighed down that army's commander, and Hooker was pleased to turn the task over to Heintzelman. He was also pleased to be freed of the defense of Harper's Ferry and the upper Potomac, leaving that to the Middle Department. These changes recast the Army of the Potomac strictly as a field army.

February 6, 1863, would be marked by the cavalry arm as emancipation day. The mounted regiments, companies, and troops scattered from one end of the army to the other, mostly under the tactical direction of infantry officers, were consolidated into a single cavalry corps, under the tactical direction of cavalrymen. To be sure, this hardly brought parity with Jeb Stuart's legions, but it was the key first step. Organizationally, Yankee horse soldiers had caught up with their Rebel counterparts, and they had Joe Hooker to thank.

George Stoneman, McClellan's former cavalry chief, led the new cavalry corps — three divisions, of two brigades each, under Alfred Pleasonton, William W. Averell, and David M. Gregg. A cavalry reserve, mostly regulars, was put under John Buford. Seniority and army politics left Buford, the best general of the four, lowest on the command totem pole. Hooker encouraged mounted aggressions, to "stimulate in the breasts of our men, by successes, however small, a feeling of superiority over our adversaries."

The first aggression took place on March 17, at Kelly's Ford on the upper Rappahannock. William Averell's brigades deliberately went looking for a fight (a first for Potomac army cavalry), found one against Fitzhugh Lee, and had the best of it until Averell withdrew in an excess of caution. "It is good for the first lick," saluted Stanton.

Seeing the cavalry gain headway, Henry Hunt went to Hooker to seek the same thing for the artillery. Hunt's post as chief of artillery was purely administrative, which meant (he testified) "all the duties of a commander, without his power over those I was to command." In Hooker's telling, Hunt "was very anxious to have a Corps made of it, and himself placed in command, to which I demurred." Artillery was assigned to divisions, and "I found that my men had learned to regard their batteries with a feeling of devotion, which I considered contributed greatly to our success." He was unwilling to impose a corps structure on what was for him tried-and-true practice. Henry Hunt had no tolerance for backward thinking, and discussion turned into heated argument. This "ill feeling" left Hunt in the commanding general's doghouse . . . and left the Potomac army's artillery still without any tactical central command.

"We were almost as ignorant of the enemy in our immediate front as if they had been in China," Dan Butterfield testified. Intelligence gathering was in bad odor since the regime of Allan Pinkerton. After Pinkerton's departure the odd spy sufficed for Burnside. Joe Hooker now introduced a genuine innovation by having Provost Marshal Patrick "organize and perfect a system for collecting information as speedily as possible." The consequence was the Bureau of Military Information, which revolutionized the collection and processing of military intelligence. Under the direction of Colonel George H. Sharpe, the B.M.I. broke cleanly with the past. Intelligence was "now collated, compared from many sources, and fully confirmed. The secret service of Gen. Hooker is far superior to anything that has ever been here before."[31]

The army's infantry commands required serious attention. Three of the four grand-division posts were vacated — by Hooker, Sumner, and Franklin — and filling them promised thorny decisions. Hooker chose instead to abolish the grand divisions. The fourth, the Reserve Grand Division, was Franz Sigel's. General Sigel (senior to all the Potomac army's major generals, including Hooker) was unhappy back with the Eleventh Corps. He said he should at least have the army's largest corps. The case went to Lincoln. He said he "has given General Sigel as good a command as he can, and desires him to do the best he can with it." Sigel said, "The reduction of my command . . . makes it exceedingly unpleasant and dispiriting for me,"

Major General Joseph Hooker and his army headquarters staff and chief staff officers. Seated, from left: Henry F. Clark, chief commissary; Henry J. Hunt, chief of artillery; Rufus Ingalls, quartermaster; Hooker; and Daniel Butterfield, chief of staff.

and he resigned. He served out the war (without distinction) apart from the Army of the Potomac.

When George Stoneman exchanged command of the Third Corps for his new cavalry corps posting, it gave Hooker the opportunity to award the vacant Third Corps post to his friend Dan Sickles. Upon learning this, division commander Otis Howard reminded Hooker that his major general's commission predated Sickles's; therefore he should have an equivalent posting. That would be the Eleventh Corps, newly vacated by General Sigel. The Eleventh was the unloved stepchild of the Potomac army. It began as manpower for Pathfinder Frémont's disreputable Mountain Department, suffered through Second Bull Run as a corps in Pope's Army of Virginia, and was grafted onto the Potomac army as Eleventh Corps in McClellan's reorganization. First- and second-generation Germans were heavily represented among its rank and file and its officers, and when Sigel resigned everyone in the corps assumed he would be succeeded by the next-senior general (and fellow German revolutionary), Carl Schurz. But Schurz lacked any military education, and Hooker thought no more of him than he had of Sigel. "I would consider the services of an entire corps as entirely lost to this army were it to fall into the hands of Major General Schurz," he said. General Howard took over the Eleventh Corps.

While Otis Howard was a professional soldier (West Point 1854) and Schurz was not, Howard would prove a poor choice for the roughly half-German Eleventh Corps. Two of three division heads were German; among six brigade commanders were three Germans (and one Pole). They expected to "remain in the hands of one of their own," a disappointed Carl Schurz wrote the president. "They look at me as their natural head and representative." Howard demonstrated courage enough at Fair Oaks, losing an arm leading a charge, but his generalship was lax and uninspired. His true calling was religious orthodoxy. "I think he is the most earnest and devoted Christian that I ever saw, unless I except clergymen," Major Elijah Cavins told his wife. "He is constantly distributing religious tracts or cards with a verse from the Bible printed on them. . . ." This did not sit well with the many freethinkers in the corps, and Howard was soon known contemptuously as Old Prayer Book. His divisions were under Schurz, Adolph von Steinwehr, and Charles Devens. Francis Barlow, recovered from his Antietam wound, led one of the brigades.[32]

The elevation of the unprincipled Dan Sickles to corps command raised hackles in the officer corps. Gouverneur Warren rated him "a defeated democratic politician, tried for murder, morally debased, and of no military experience." But Sickles had been mentored by Hooker and seemed to exert influence over the army commander. His Third Corps divisions were under Amiel W. Whipple and two citizen-soldiers, David B. Birney and Hiram G. Berry. The corps had a demi-brigade, two sharpshooter regiments under Hiram Berdan. Three colonels were promoted from regimental command to brigade command.

The First Corps remained under John Reynolds, but shuffling was required. Abner Doubleday moved over to the Third Division, new Pennsylvania troops replacing the Pennsylvania Reserves, withdrawn for recuperation. James S. Wadsworth took Doubleday's First Division. A wealthy New York landowner and staunch Republican, Wadsworth when military governor in Washington had a disputatious relationship with McClellan. This was his first combat command. With John Gibbon recuperating from his Fredericksburg wound, his Second Division went to John C. Robinson, from the Third Corps. Five of the corps' nine brigades had new commanders.

Darius Couch led the Second Corps, Sumner's old command, as he had at Fredericksburg. Winfield Hancock commanded the First Division and William H. French the Third. On his recovery, John Gibbon took over the Second Division vacated by Howard. (Gibbon confided to his wife, on taking over Howard's headquarters, "I fear we shall not be able to keep up the reputation for sanctity & sobriety which the place held under Howard.") Hancock had a new fourth brigade, John R. Brooke's. French had two new brigade commanders.

George Meade, as a new-made major general, was awarded the Fifth Corps in December. Dan Butterfield, whom he displaced, was quick to pull strings in the capital. Of Senator Zach Chandler he asked, "Have I any friends in Washington?" He wanted it known "that *action* on their part may secure me justice." Hooker soothed him with the chief of staff post. Charles Griffin, George Sykes, and Andrew A. Humphreys headed the Fifth Corps' divisions. Among the four new brigade commanders, Patrick H. O'Rorke replaced Gouverneur Warren, who gave up his brigade to became Hooker's chief topographical engineer.

John Sedgwick, recovered from his Antietam wounds, took the Sixth Corps from the departed Baldy Smith. W.T.H. Brooks, Albion P. Howe, and John Newton led Sedgwick's divisions. A reinforced brigade, called the Light Division, designed for special services, was attached to the Sixth Corps. Four colonels were new brigade commanders.

Henry W. Slocum's Twelfth Corps contained just two divisions, of three brigades each, commanded by Alpheus Williams and John W. Geary; political general Geary bumped old regular George S. Greene back to brigade. In recovering from its Antietam ordeal, the Twelfth Corps had guarded the upper Potomac and then joined the Eleventh Corps in Sigel's Reserve Grand Division.

The Ninth Corps, long associated with Ambrose Burnside, left the Army of the Potomac when Burnside left it. Baldy Smith temporarily commanded the Ninth when it transferred to Fort Monroe. From there the Ninth Corps followed Burnside's fortunes in the Western theater. It (and he) would return to the Potomac army in the spring of 1864.

The army's March 31 return showed 114,243 infantrymen present for duty, a figure not all it appeared. Over a third of them were due for discharge that spring. Early in the war two states, New York and Maine, accepted men for two years instead of the more usual three, to a total of thirty-four regiments. Enlistments would also be up for twenty-six regiments of nine-months' men who had signed on after the collapse of the Peninsula campaign. The fighting morale of such men was sure to lag in advance of their discharge dates. As John Sedgwick put it, "No troops with but a few days to leave are going to risk much in a fight." Commanders began to shift the short-termers to rear-area duties, and General Hooker moved to open his campaign as soon as possible.

The Army of the Potomac went to war in spring 1863 with a new army commander and half its corps commanders new — Sickles, Meade, Howard, and Stoneman. There were four new divisional commanders — Wadsworth, Robinson, Berry, and Devens. One-third of the twenty-four divisional commanders had not attended West Point. Of the sixty-three brigades, just eighteen were under West Pointers. The lower segment of the high command pyramid was increasingly self-taught — citizen-soldier officers for a volunteer army. On this score General Halleck was pessimistic. The great difficulty, he wrote a friend, "is *poor, poorer, worthless* officers. Many of them have neither judgment, sense nor courage." Still, even sour Charles Francis Adams, Jr., had come around: "The army is *decidedly* improving . . . and if Hooker acts as judiciously as indications would warrant us in hoping, we shall, I think, by the first of June be again within sight of Richmond. . . ."[33]

Joe Hooker displayed his own optimism, and early in April he staged an immense review at Falmouth for the president and party. Stoneman's newborn cavalry corps, 10,000 strong, put on a display that Attorney General Bates called "the grandest sight I ever saw." When it came the infantry's turn, four army corps, 75,000 men, went through their paces, and it was generally agreed the show exceeded the best McClellan had put on. "The only cheering thing I have seen this half year is Hooker's army," Bates wrote; ". . . seeing what Hooker has done in the rehabilitation of that army, I do not doubt that he will use it as effectively as he has reformed & inspired it."

Mr. Lincoln never got through to arrogant McClellan (not for lack of trying), and he left most dealings with Burnside to General-in-Chief Halleck. But with Joe Hooker he took an active stance. He prepared a memorandum of understanding. In the present circumstances, he wrote, "there is *no* eligible route for us into Richmond; and consequently a question of preference between the Rappahannock route, and the James River route is a contest about nothing." The prime object must be the enemy's army "in front of us, and is not with, or about, Richmond." There should be no "attacking him in his entrenchments; but we should continually harass and menace him. . . ." He told Hooker, with marked emphasis, "In the next battle be sure to put in all of your men."[34]

General Hooker had led a frontal attack with a division at Williamsburg, with a corps at Antietam, with a grand division at Fredericksburg (where "they could destroy men faster than I could throw them on their works"), and he dismissed it as a bankrupt tactic. Fresh thinking was needed. His initial campaign plan gave the lead role to Stoneman's new cavalry corps. The idea was to pull Lee out of his Fredericksburg lines by severing his railroad supply line. With six brigades, almost 10,000 troopers, Stoneman would cross the Rappahannock well upstream and fall on the Richmond, Fredericksburg & Potomac at Hanover Junction, 35 miles south of Fredericksburg. This should cause Lee to fall back to save his communications. Stoneman "will be able to hold him and check his retreat until I can fall on his rear," Hooker explained.

On April 13 Stoneman started his cavalry columns upstream beyond Kelly's Ford, and by dark on the 14th he had a brigade across the river. But at 2:00 a.m. on the 15th began what diarist Marsena Patrick called "in truth & reality, a terrible rain." It pounded down for twenty-four hours. At nearby Rappahannock Bridge the river rose seven feet. The brigade was fortunate to get back across the torrent. Like Burnside's Mud March, Hooker's first offensive was drowned out.

His second offensive was more fully planned, its prospects resting this time on a coup by the Bureau of Military Information. The B.M.I. had created a highly accurate picture of the size, composition, and location of the Army of Northern Virginia. It also broke the code used by Rebel flag-sig-

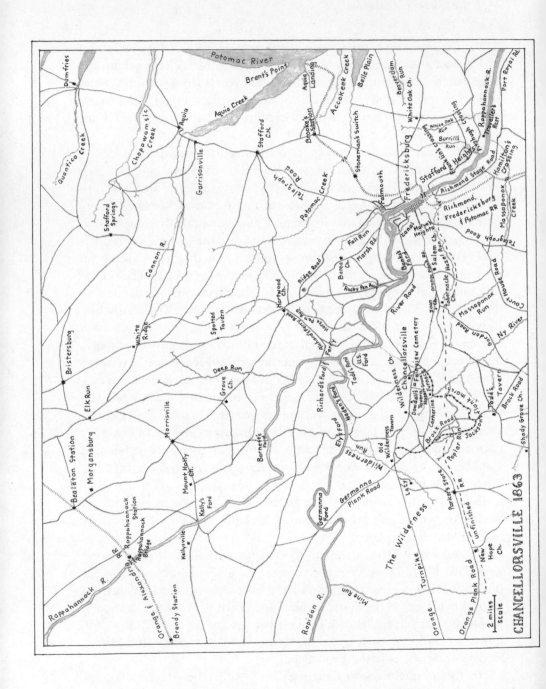

nalmen . . . and learned thereby that the Rebels had broken the Yankee flag code. Chief of Staff Butterfield plotted a ruse.

Stoneman's cavalry did not escape the enemy's notice, and Butterfield had headquarters send a flag message beginning, "Our cavalry is going to give Jones & guerillas in the Shenandoah a smash," with details of the supposed raid. Potomac army signalmen soon decoded an enemy flag-signal reading, "Dispatch received from Yankee signal flag" and quoting Butterfield's ruse message. Lee took the bait. He shifted Jeb Stuart's cavalry westward to counter Stoneman's reported move against Rebels in the Valley. Upstream from Fredericksburg, a 20-mile gap opened between Rebel infantry and Rebel cavalry. Joe Hooker would drive his army into this gap.[35]

Hooker's campaign plan was the most innovative in Potomac army annals to date. A three-corps flanking column, 40,000 men, was to march in secrecy up the Rappahannock past Banks's Ford and U.S. Ford and the junction with the Rapidan River to Kelly's Ford, unguarded now but for a picket post. Met there by a pontoon train, the column would cross the Rappahannock, cross the Rapidan, and march back down the south bank of the Rappahannock to uncover U.S. and Banks's fords for support troops. Reinforced, it would be positioned to turn the Rebels' left flank. Two corps would bridge the river below Fredericksburg, where Franklin crossed in December, to fix the enemy in place and threaten his right flank. The two remaining corps would act where needed. Stoneman's cavalry would cross at Kelly's Ford and restart its Hanover Junction raid. There was more daring here than any Potomac army general had attempted previously. Hooker said later he believed he had eighty chances out of a hundred to make it all work.

Hooker wanted at least a thirty-six-hour jump on the Rebels, wanted his flanking force (his flying column, he called it) across the Rappahannock, and perhaps the Rapidan, before Lee was alerted. That meant employing the three corps camped farthest to the rear — Meade's Fifth, Howard's Eleventh, Slocum's Twelfth — from where they might march unseen to Kelly's Ford. Meade's Fifth Corps was a trusted, veteran force, but in the eyes of the Army of the Potomac the Eleventh and Twelfth Corps were outlanders. The Eleventh, smallest in the army, bore a record of defeat and low morale from its Army of Virginia days, and its new commander Otis Howard was hardly inspiriting. The undermanned Twelfth Corps, another refugee from Pope's army, had fought well at Cedar Mountain and at Antietam under Alpheus Williams and George Greene. Now Williams was pushed back to a division and Greene to a brigade, with less experienced Henry Slocum leading the corps. A quarter of the flying column comprised two-year or nine-month short-termers. This was clearly not the strongest spearhead Hooker could want, but it was the best he could assemble without tipping his hand.

Hooker's left wing — Reynolds's First Corps and Sedgwick's Sixth — was scheduled to cross the Rappahannock below Fredericksburg just as Lee learned of the threat from above Fredericksburg. The Sixth Corps would lay bridges at Franklin's Crossing two miles below the town, where it crossed in December. The First Corps' bridges would be two miles downstream, at Fitzhugh's Crossing. The shore here was swept by the Union artillery, but the hills behind were heavily fortified.

Hooker posted his reserve to reinforce success, wherever gained. Dan Sickles's Third Corps might support Reynolds and Sedgwick if needed. Two of Darius Couch's Second Corps divisions (leaving John Gibbon's division camped in plain sight across from Fredericksburg) would slip away upstream, ready to cross at U.S. or Banks's fords as they were uncovered by the flying column.[36]

At daybreak on Monday, April 27, the three flanking corps set off for Kelly's Ford. Hooker sketched his plan for Lincoln: "The object in crossing high up the river is to come down in rear of the enemy holding strong positions." He was confident. "The only element which gives me apprehension with regard to the success of this plan is the weather." Everything looked as usual at Falmouth. Thaddeus Lowe's balloon rose majestically over the scene, as it did every day in good weather. On the parade ground the Third Corps held a review. But in strict silence the First and Sixth Corps slipped downstream behind Stafford Heights toward their crossing sites.

On April 28, to the west, just thirty minutes behind schedule, the vanguard of the flying column reached Kelly's Ford, paddled across in pontoon boats, and chased off the surprised Rebel picket guard. Unlike November, a pontoon train was there waiting, delivered by the Orange & Alexandria to nearby Bealeton Station. Hooker's orders for the next day directed the advance to the Rapidan crossings and beyond. "The general desires that not a moment be lost until our troops are established at or near Chancellorsville. From that moment all will be ours."

Chancellorsville was not a village nor even a hamlet, but a onetime tavern on the Orange Plank Road 10 miles west of Fredericksburg, ambitiously named by its builder George Chancellor. The Orange Plank Road, running from Orange Court House to Fredericksburg, superseded the older Orange Turnpike. In some places the Plank Road replaced the turnpike, in others they were separate. Chancellorsville stood in a crossroads clearing in the Wilderness, a dark, tangled forest of second-growth timber and brambly undergrowth. Gouverneur Warren remarked of it, "No one can conceive of a more unfavorable field for the movements of a grand army. . . ."

Wednesday, April 29, Day Three of the offensive, proceeded true to Hooker's design. Henry Slocum commanded the flanking wing after it crossed Kelly's Ford. Alpheus Williams's Twelfth Corps led the day's march toward the Rapidan. Williams cast a look at the Potomac army on the march: "Across the river long lines of infantry were winding down toward the river and on the south side brigades were breaking masses and filing up the hills. Batteries of artillery and heavy columns of cavalry were forming large solid squares, which . . . looked like great black blocks on the green surface, massed by some unseen power."

The Twelfth Corps, followed by the Eleventh, approached Germanna Ford on the Rapidan at midday. George Greene reported, "We pressed on, one division of our corps wading, at Germania Ford, water to the armpits and capturing a company of rebel soldiers, who were quietly rebuilding the bridge." The bridge at this rough ford was burned, leaving only the stone piers. The resourceful Yankees, finding stringers and planking the Confederate bridge-builders had stockpiled, put together in two hours a sturdy footbridge anchored against the piers. By night both corps were across the Rapidan.

Meade's Fifth Corps, taking a different road from Kelly's, reached Ely's Ford on the Rapidan in good time. The river was full to its banks and running fast. The plan had been to take up the Kelly's Ford bridge and relay it at Ely's, but Stoneman's cavalry took so long crossing at Kelly's that Meade was only promised the bridge for next morning. Meade's orders — and Meade himself — brooked no tolerance for such delay. He sent his men splashing through the rocky ford, holding rifles and cartridge boxes high. The incautious fetched up against a line of cavalry lifeguards downstream of the ford. The men dried off around bonfires. The schedule was intact. "Everything goes beautifully above," Dan Butterfield reported.

Day Three for the left wing also ended with schedule intact, but after improvisation. By plan, the downstream bridges were to be completed by dawn and bridgeheads emplaced before the Rebels caught on. But bridge building in the dark went badly, especially as directed by the drunken chief engineer, Henry W. Benham. At Franklin's Crossing, Sedgwick's Sixth Corps site, Brigadier David Russell took over, and blessed by an early-morning fog his men paddled unseen across the river in pontoon boats and secured the far bank. By 9:30 a.m. three bridges were in place. Downstream at Fitzhugh's Crossing, Reynolds's First Corps got a later start and took fire from a Rebel picket line guarding the shore. Here Charles Wainwright, corps artillery chief, laid down a barrage behind which the brigade of Westerners once led by John Gibbon, now called the Iron Brigade and now under Solomon Meredith, paddled across. "They landed without very much difficulty and rushed up the bank about the time that we got a good range on the main rifle pit," wrote diarist Wainwright. "Nothing but legs could now save the rebs on the bank. . . ." Two bridges were soon emplaced.

By nightfall on April 29 James Wadsworth's and Bully Brooks's divisions manned the conjoined bridgehead. Should the Rebels mass against him, Butterfield told John Sedgwick, commanding the left wing, that was all to the good. The moves of the flying column "now in progress the general hopes will compel the enemy to fight" on ground he chooses. "He has no desire to make the general engagement where you are, in front of Brooks or Wadsworth." That was useful to know, but it gave Sedgwick no clue as to what Hooker actually expected of him.[37]

Starting midday on April 30 the flying column arrived at Chancellorsville — Meade with the Fifth Corps from Ely's Ford, Slocum with the Eleventh and Twelfth Corps from Germanna Ford — and took up postings in the large clearing there. Alpheus Williams called the site "simply a Virginia 'ville' of one large brick house on the northwest corner of crossroads, built by one Chancellor." Meade's march secured the south bank of U.S. Ford; on the north bank, engineer William Folwell, with a bridge train, was relieved to recognize "our own men on the *rebel shore*." A bridge was laid and Couch's Second Corps divisions under Winfield Hancock and William French crossed and marched for Chancellorsville. Sickles's Third Corps was alerted to cross May 1.

"This is splendid, Slocum," Meade exclaimed; "Hurrah for old Joe! We are on Lee's flank and he does not know it." He thought to continue the march, to seize Banks's Ford, but Slocum had orders: "The general directs that no advance be made from Chancellorsville until the columns are concentrated." Hooker arrived in late afternoon to take the command. He was well satisfied. He was across the Rappahannock in force, with more force to come, and poised on the enemy's flank. The cavalry should be destroying Lee's railroad by now. He intended to give battle on ground of his choosing — to receive attack, not initiate it. No more frontal attacks by this army. In a general order read to the troops, he expressed "heartfelt satisfaction" with events, anticipating "that our enemy must either ingloriously fly, or come out from behind his defenses and give us battle on our own ground, where certain destruction awaits him." General Meade wrote his wife, "We are across the river & out maneuvered the enemy but we are not yet out of the woods."[38]

On the evening of April 29 General Lee had telegraphed Jefferson Davis that the Federals were across the river below Fredericksburg and, by report, across the Rappahannock and the Rapidan above. "Their intention, I presume, is to turn our left, and probably to get into our rear. Our scattered condition favors their operations." So secretive were Hooker's preliminaries that Lee was in a "scattered condition" indeed — two of Longstreet's divisions, a quarter of the army, were engaged at Suffolk below the James River. "The main attack will come from above," Lee told his staff, and he rushed to reinforce his left. Like Sharpsburg, he might have to give up his position, but not before making a fight for it.[39]

On Friday, May 1, believing he had a firm grip on the initiative, Hooker advanced two of the four corps then at Chancellorsville, Meade's Fifth and Slocum's Twelfth. Their objective, halfway to Fredericksburg, was open ground around Tabernacle Church, where the Orange Turnpike and the Orange Plank Road, running separately from Chancellorsville, came together. George Sykes's division set out on the turnpike, and the other two Fifth Corps divisions, under Charles Griffin and Andrew Humphreys, angled to the northeast on the River Road to seize Banks's Ford, to shorten communications between the two wings of the army. Slocum's Twelfth Corps divisions, Alpheus Williams's and John Geary's, took the Plank Road, parallel to and south of Sykes.

Sykes's division on the turnpike, two brigades of regulars and one of volunteers, was first to engage . . . and first to face not the picket posts and cavalry details the flying column had brushed aside these last days but solid ranks of infantry — infantry commanded by Stonewall Jackson. As the fighting accelerated, Sykes found himself quickly outnumbered and both his flanks threatened. Gouverneur Warren, chief topographer, was along as observer, and Sykes sent him for help. Meade, on the River Road to the north, was out of reach. Unless Slocum's Twelfth Corps on the Plank Road to the south promptly joined the battle to even the odds, Sykes doubted he could hold long enough for support to reach him from the rear.

Slocum's column on the Plank Road was nowhere near the fighting and without promise of reaching it. At the first brush with a Rebel picket post, hardly a mile out, Slocum halted, cautiously deployed both his divisions, and crept forward at a snail's pace through the dense Wilderness. Warren reported Sykes's dilemma, staff man Joseph Dickinson reported Slocum's lagging march, and Fighting Joe canceled the operation and ordered the troops back to Chancellorsville.

On the Plank Road Alpheus Williams noted that "the men went back disappointed, not without grumbling." But Hooker based his decision on Sykes's critical situation. "I was completely isolated from the rest of the army," Sykes reported. Meade was too far to the north and Slocum to the south offered no prospect of support. Reinforcements from the rear would be too late. "I soon discovered that I was hazarding too much to continue the movement," Hooker afterward wrote.

Afterward, too, unfriendly lieutenants gave their own versions of events. Laggardly Henry Slocum (who suffered just ten casualties that day) professed shock: "I could not believe that General Hooker wished me to fall back." Darius Couch professed disgust "at the general's vacillation." He had Hooker telling him, "It is all right, Couch, I have got Lee just where I want him; he must fight me on my own ground." From that Couch deduced "my commanding general was a whipped man."

In fact the events of May 1 neither whipped nor discouraged Joe Hooker: "If situated in like manner again I do not hesitate to declare, as my conviction, I should repeat the order." In his scheme for battle he did have Lee where he wanted him — out of the Fredericksburg entrenchments, on a battleground of his own choice, without prospect of frontal attacks of the Burnside kind. Hooker was satisfied to make his fight at Chancellorsville. "The major general commanding trusts that a suspension in the attack to-day will embolden the enemy to attack him," read a circular to his generals.

The singular limitation of choosing to fight defensively was giving up the initiative . . . and Joe Hooker surely was aware of Robert E. Lee's liking for the initiative.[40]

All was quiet in the bridgehead east of Fredericksburg. John Reynolds thought his and Sedgwick's mission indefinite — to "attack when the heights of Fredericksburg are carried or pursue the enemy if he retreats." Hooker had called on Sedgwick for a demonstration in conjunction with the advance from Chancellorsville, but the telegraph between the two wings of the army failed and the message did not get through. Sightings of enemy movements westward, from Lowe's balloon and from ground observers, left little doubt that the First and Sixth Corps crossings had failed to pin many Rebels in their Fredericksburg lines.

Stoneman's raid on Lee's communications produced no results either. Trains on the Richmond, Fredericksburg & Potomac were still arriving at

Potomac army infantry reserves and artillery crowd into the clearing at the Chancellor house (right), Hooker's headquarters, on May 1. Drawing by Alfred Waud.

Fredericksburg. George Stoneman's cavalry service under McClellan had been administrative only, so when Hooker gave him the new cavalry corps it marked Stoneman's first experience of independent field command. He proved the most deliberative of cavalrymen; worse, he seemed incapable of carrying out orders.

Stoneman had the benefit of the B.M.I.'s exacting profile of the Virginia railroads. The Virginia Central running between Richmond and Gordonsville crossed the R. F. & P. at Hanover Junction. Lee's supplies came not only from Richmond but also from the Valley via the Virginia Central, which stockpiled them at Hanover for transshipment north. To sever Lee's rail lifeline, then, meant cutting the R. F. & P. *above* Hanover Junction, best done by burning at least one of three high bridges on the line just north of the junction. Instead, Stoneman confined his (much delayed) efforts to the R. F. & P. *below* Hanover . . . and within forty-eight hours Southern track crews had completed repairs. Much was made of Stoneman coming within a few miles of Richmond, but as a major contributor to Hooker's campaign he was a total failure. Hooker was blunt: "I sent him out to destroy the bridges behind Lee. He rode 150 miles and came back without seeing the bridges he should have destroyed."[41]

Joe Hooker rose early on Saturday, May 2, and rode his lines to be sure everything and everyone was prepared for an attack. Meade's Fifth Corps, the divisions of Humphreys, Griffin, and Sykes, anchored the left on the Rappahannock, guarding the U.S. Ford crossing and extending two miles to the salient covering Chancellorsville. Couch's Second Corps divisions under Hancock and French made up the eastern face of the salient — Gibbon's division remained at Falmouth. The salient's southern face, paralleling the Plank Road, was formed of Slocum's Twelfth Corps divisions under Williams and Geary. Inserted to Slocum's right was Birney's Third Corps division — Sickles's two other Third Corps divisions, Berry's and

Whipple's, formed the reserve. To the right of Birney was Howard's Eleventh Corps, the divisions of von Steinwehr, Schurz, and Devens, extending the line due west a mile and a half and following the Orange Turnpike where it branched off the Plank Road. The count of Chancellorsville's defenders came to 72,300, with 184 guns. The men were everywhere put to entrenching and fortifying.

The Eleventh Corps, the army's smallest, was posted where it arrived from Germanna Ford—at the tail end of the army, well away from any prospective fighting. Howard's line faced south and ended where his manpower ended, "in the air." This troubled Hooker. He told Howard to "refuse" or pull back the end of his line at a right angle to face west, and sent him a supporting Third Corps brigade. Howard said he had no need for a brigade and returned it. He said that to pull his men back from their line would imply to them a retreat . . . which (he might have added) the Eleventh Corps had done enough of. Leaving Howard as he was, Hooker took more direct action to secure his right. In a dispatch marked 1:55 a.m. May 2, he ordering John Reynolds's First Corps, on the far left, to march to U.S. Ford and cross to take a posting behind Howard, facing west—in effect, both refusing and reinforcing his line.

Hooker's order to Reynolds fell victim to a chain of mishaps. The courier taking it to the U.S. Ford telegraph station somehow, on a bright moonlit night, got lost. The order only reached Reynolds after daylight, then garbled communications further delayed the start of his march upriver. By Hooker's calculation, the 16,900 men of the First Corps would be posted to guard the right flank by midday on May 2. As it happened, Reynolds's troops were only starting across the U.S. Ford bridge at 5:30 that afternoon.[42]

On returning from his early-morning inspection that Saturday, Hooker was told of sightings of enemy troop movements to the south at Catharine Furnace, an iron maker's clearing in the Wilderness. At 9:30 a.m. he sent a warning to Howard. The Eleventh Corps, he wrote, was aligned "with a view to a front attack by the enemy. If he should throw himself on your flank . . . determine upon the position you will take in that event," with heavy reserves "well in hand to meet this contingency." He underlined his warning: "We have good reasons to suppose that the enemy is moving to our right." Howard afterward denied receiving this warning, but it is entered in his corps dispatch book, and Carl Schurz reported discussing it in detail with him. As they spoke, a courier brought a second copy, bearing Hooker's additional censure, "The right of your line does not appear to be strong enough." At 10:50 Howard responded, "We can observe a column of infantry moving westward on a road . . . about one and a half miles south of this. I am taking measures to resist an attack from the west." James Biddle of the staff wrote that morning, "Genl. Howard, who is on the right, says he is very strong."

Reassured by Howard's response, Hooker was further reassured by a dispatch from Dan Sickles. Sickles investigated the enemy column sighted at Catharine Furnace. The mission was led by Hiram Berdan's sharpshooters, and as they gained a closer look, it appeared that the Rebels were not moving westward after all. "The enemy column is still moving south," Sickles reported, and he had an inspiration: "I think it is a retreat. Sometimes a regiment then a few wagons — then troops then wagons. . . ."[43]

Early afternoon of May 2, at headquarters at the Chancellor house, was a time for optimism. On the right flank Otis Howard had assured Hooker he was alert and ready to meet an attack from any direction. John Reynolds's First Corps should be reporting for duty on the right at any moment. Indications were that General Lee, recognizing his plight, was pulling out for points south. Alexander Webb, Fifth Corps staff, wrote his wife, "The enemy has started his trains to the rear & is we believe in retreat." Darius Couch noted Hooker telling him "that the enemy were in full retreat in direction of Gordonsville," with Sickles sent to capture their artillery train. Orders went to Sedgwick on the left to pursue — "We know that the enemy is fleeing, trying to save his trains." Howard "did believe, with all the other officers, that he was making for Orange Court House." Such was Howard's optimism that he led his sole brigade in reserve, Francis Barlow's, to join Sickles's push toward Catharine Furnace. Otherwise he paid no heed to Hooker's warnings.[44]

General Lee indeed recognized his plight. Fighting Joe Hooker (Mr. F. J. Hooker, in Lee's dismissive coinage) had stolen a long march on him, crossed the Rappahannock and the Rapidan unopposed, and turned his flank. Yankee cavalry was by report ranging deep in his rear. He was outnumbered, and worse, by poor planning he lacked Longstreet and two of his divisions. Mr. F. J. Hooker parsed his choices about right — he must either come out of his fortifications and fight, or ingloriously fly. Lee and Jackson made a plan of great boldness, born of desperation . . . and, as it happened, blessed by Fortune. They would outflank the flankers.

Hooker's left was too solidly posted to turn, leaving only a long, concealed march to test the Federal right. A local man guided Jackson by hidden ways through the Wilderness to the Orange Turnpike beyond the Federal right. The one sighting, at Catharine Furnace, was misread as a

Edwin Forbes pictured the 1st Ohio Light Battery, Eleventh Corps, offering a lonely defense astride the Orange Turnpike against Stonewall Jackson's surprise flank attack.

retreat. The unprepared Eleventh Corps was taken quite by surprise. One of Schurz's men underlined Otis Howard's negligence: "Everyone who was on the right of that line knows that he did *practically nothing* for 9 hours and would not listen to, or believe the reports sent in, time and time again, about the conditions on our front & flank."

Near 6 o'clock a massive Confederate battle line, guiding on the turnpike, struck the Eleventh Corps "end-on." Howard described the moment for his wife: "On last Saturday Stonewall Jackson attacked my right, with a solid column & with great fury. Col. Von Gilsa's Brigade occupied the point of attack and immediately gave way, broke up & ran upon the other troops with such momentum that they gave way too. Such a mass of fugitives I hav'nt seen since the first Battle of Bull Run."

At the moment of attack Howard was absent, gone with Barlow's brigade toward Catharine Furnace. The general at hand, division commander Charles Devens, overprimed with brandy, waited for someone to tell him what to do. Still waiting, he was wounded in the foot and carried back with his fleeing men. First Devens's division, then Schurz's, finally von Steinwehr's were knocked over like tenpins. As with Sedgwick's division at Antietam, there was no time or chance to redeploy to counter a surprise flank attack. By a reporter's account, "On one hand was a solid column of infantry retreating at double quick from the face of the enemy . . . on the other was a dense mass of beings who had lost their reasoning facilities . . . ;

ambulances, horses, men, cannon, caissons, all jumbled and tumbled together in an apparently inextricable mass. . . ." Beyond von Steinwehr was a large gap in the line, where Sickles had taken his divisions to pursue the sighting at Catharine Furnace. The rout finally fetched up at the Twelfth Corps before Chancellorsville.

Francis Barlow, promoted after Antietam to command an Eleventh Corps brigade, wrote home with candor a few days later: "You know how I have always been down on the 'Dutch' & I do not abate my contempt now, but it is not fair to charge it all on them. Some of the Yankee Regts behaved just as badly & I think that Hooker's failure thus far has been solely from the bad fighting of the men. Howard is full of mortification & disgust & I really pity him."[45]

Hooker acted quickly in the crisis. Reynolds's First Corps was ordered to double-quick from U.S. Ford to patch the northern sector. Sickles was recalled from Catharine Furnace. All batteries faced west. Hooker personally rallied the one division still in reserve, once his and now under Hiram Berry: "'Old Joe' galloped up and called for us his *old division*. Up we went to the front, the boys cheering and swearing." Alpheus Williams saw the headquarters staff rallying fugitives: "Lt. Col. Dickinson of Hooker's staff was riding fiercely about, pistol in hand, and occasionally discharging it at some flying Dutchman. Swords were out and flashing in the setting sun. Such a mixture of Dutch and English and oaths!" One of Schurz's officers took note that the Eleventh Corps once boasted it "fights mit Sigel," but now it "runs mit Howard."

Sickles's rush back from the Furnace in the darkening woods ignited a fresh firestorm. "A tremendous roll of infantry fire, mingled with yellings and shoutings almost diabolical and infernal, opened the conflict on the side of Sickles' division," Williams wrote. Friend could hardly be distinguished from foe, and friendly fire took a toll.

Night finally paused the Confederate attack. Jackson rode ahead on the Plank Road beyond his lines to reconnoiter. There was a blind exchange of gunfire in the darkness. As Jackson and party turned back, North Carolina infantrymen, mistaking them for marauding Yankee cavalry, opened fire. Jackson was hit by three bullets. He was borne back to a field hospital and in the early-morning hours of May 3 his left arm was amputated. Lee ordered Jeb Stuart to command Jackson's corps.[46]

On Sunday, May 3, Hooker took stock. It was certain the Rebels would renew their attack from the west, probably aimed initially at the Third Corps, which had come to rest at Hazel Grove, high, open ground southwest of Chancellorsville. Hooker put engineers Gouverneur Warren and

Cyrus Comstock to laying out a fallback defensive line that would secure the U.S. Ford crossing. At the same time, he recognized opportunity here. Lee had divided his army for the flank attack, and the Yankees were squarely between its two segments. Warren spelled out Hooker's intentions for chief of staff Butterfield at Falmouth: "Lee is massed on our left front, Jackson on our right (so prisoners say) intending to attack at day break. Genl. Hooker made his dispositions accordingly and intends to flank and destroy Jackson. Lee was to be held in check and Sedgwick was to come up and fall on his rear. . . ."

These were difficult days for John Sedgwick. Orders sent him were confusing, or asked more of him than he liked. On the morning of May 2, for example, came an order proposing his Sixth Corps take the offensive against the lone Confederate division the B.M.I. said was defending the entire Fredericksburg position: "It is impossible for the general to determine here whether it is expedient for him to attack or not. It must be left to his discretion." Uncle John had proved a resolute fighting general, but like William Franklin he grew irresolute in independent command. A discretionary order like this puzzled him, and he did nothing. But at 9:00 p.m. came a direct order—to march his corps through Fredericksburg that night to the Plank Road and to the rest of the army. "You will probably fall upon the rear of the forces commanded by General Lee, and, between you and the major general commanding, he expects to use him up."

Certain of renewed fighting on May 3 then, Hooker intended an all-out defense of his Chancellorsville salient; intended his reserve (Meade's and Reynolds's corps) to strike Jackson (Stuart) in the flank; intended Sedgwick's corps to take Lee's forces in the rear and grind them against the eastern face of the salient.[47]

The rout of the Eleventh Corps forced Hooker to realign his defenses. Reynolds's First Corps formed the right, facing west and connected to the Rappahannock. Next in line was Meade's Fifth Corps, brought over from the left to (in effect) take the Eleventh Corps' place. Sickles's Third Corps directly confronted Stuart's forces, supported on the left by Slocum's Twelfth Corps. Couch's Second Corps formed the eastern face of the Chancellorsville salient. Howard's battered Eleventh Corps was tucked away safely on the far left, tying the line to the river and securing the U.S. Ford crossing.

Dan Sickles was at immediate risk. His two divisions had made a disorganized and contested return from their adventuring at Catharine Furnace, and first light on May 3 found them sprawled awkwardly at Hazel Grove. Worse, Hazel Grove formed a salient appended to the larger Chancellorsville salient, vulnerable to attack from two, even three, sides. By Sickles's account, Hooker ordered him "to withdraw from my position on the flank and march my command by the most practicable route" to the Chancellorsville lines.

"The position I abandoned was one that I had held at disadvantage" was all that Joe Hooker would say about this decision. He seems to have reasoned that one salient was enough to defend; he had not time or men to properly defend a second one. However that might be, his reasoning overlooked one critical point — what the enemy might gain by holding Hazel Grove. That gain was quickly evident. Confederate artilleryman Porter Alexander called Hazel Grove "a beautiful position for artillery," within easy range of the Yankee lines and even the Chancellor house. Alexander crowded Hazel Grove with batteries.

It was a scene reminiscent of Malvern Hill on the last of the Seven Days — Confederates deploying a "grand battery" to beat down the Yankee defenses. But McClellan on Day Seven at Malvern Hill had a major advantage over Hooker on Day Seven at Chancellorsville — Henry Hunt. Wielding full command over the Malvern guns, Hunt had shelled the Rebel grand battery to ruin. On this May 3, however, Hooker did not grant tactical artillery command to Hunt, limiting him instead to the reserve artillery north of the Rappahannock.

The Federal batteries guarding the Chancellorsville salient at Fairview Cemetery, bordering the Orange Plank Road, had an advantage in numbers and weight of metal, but were beholden to an array of commanders. General Hunt in command here would certainly have diverted from the infantry battle guns enough to suppress the Rebel grand battery at Hazel Grove. Instead, infantry officers directed the batteries for their own needs. Also missing was Hunt's sure hand at battlefield management — ammunition resupply, and replacement batteries at hand for those on the firing line that exhausted their ammunition. As First Corps artillerist Charles Wainwright saw it that day, "No one appeared to know anything, and there was a good deal of confusion . . . ; all the artillery of the army was running around loose."

John Reynolds sent Wainwright to Hooker to explain the state of affairs: "Every division commander wants his own batteries, and battery commanders will obey no one else's orders." No time for debate, Hooker said. "You take hold and make it right." He ordered Wainwright to "take command of all the artillery and ammunition of this army." This was an important step, to be sure, but not in time to save the Fairview position.[48]

Jeb Stuart, under Lee's order to reunite the army before anything else,

committed every man he had in attacking from the west and southwest. Alpheus Williams's Twelfth Corps division led a stubborn defense of Fairview. Thomas H. Ruger sternly held his brigade to a bloody standoff against an attacking South Carolina brigade. For Ruger it was strikingly like an earlier bloody standoff, in the Cornfield at Antietam. Antietam cost Ruger 646 casualties, Chancellorsville, 614.

The first break in the line came in the Third Corps sector facing west. Williams coordinated his defense with Hiram Berry to his right, "for the maintenance of his line was my safety." Berry was one of those civilian-soldiers who had learned command as he went, in this case under the tutelage of Phil Kearny and Joe Hooker, and he rose from colonel of the 4th Maine to major general of a Third Corps division. In battle it was Berry's habit to deliver his orders personally, so there could be no misunderstandings, and on this day it proved the death of him, felled by a sniper's bullet. He had been a favorite of Hooker's, who knelt by the body and mourned, "My God, Berry, why was this to happen?"

During this brief command hiatus Confederates punched through the line and scooped up a surprised Brigadier General William Hays, whose Second Corps brigade was taking up a supporting position. An incident of a different sort was perpetrated by Joseph W. Revere, one of Dan Sickles's brigadiers. Revere assumed Berry's death put him in command of the division (it did not — Joseph B. Carr was the senior), and without notice he pulled his brigade's six regiments, plus three regiments of the neighboring brigade, out of the battle line and marched them to the rear. They needed ammunition and rations and reorganizing, he said. Hooker met this un-

Dan Sickles, under the Third Corps flag, defends the artillery line at Fairview Cemetery on May 3. By Alfred Waud, on grid paper for the *Harper's Weekly* engravers.

expected crisis by ordering a counterattack by William French's Second Corps men pulled from the eastern face of the salient. Hooker told French to "attack the enemy, and drive him through the woods." French did so.

(Sickles relieved Revere on the spot, and he was court-martialed and cashiered. Lincoln, thinking perhaps of the disgrace to the family name — a grandson of the Revolution's Paul Revere — revoked the sentence and Joseph Revere was allowed to resign.)[49]

The stabilizing effect of French's counterattack was brief. Colonel Wainwright needed more time than he had to unify the artillery command at Fairview, and in any case the Twelfth Corps' infantry support for the guns weakened steadily as regiments were outflanked or fell back with empty cartridge boxes, not to be replaced. "The getting away was worse than the staying," General Williams wrote, for the Rebel artillery had gained almost free rein. It was much the same on the Third Corps front, which Williams had counted on for his safety. Sickles sent urgently to Hooker for reinforcements to hold his crumbling line.

At the Chancellor house Sickles's dispatch was handed to Hooker just at the moment he was knocked senseless by a Confederate solid shot smashing the porch pillar he was standing by. As Hooker told it, the heavy column splintered in two and hit "violently against me . . . which struck me in an erect position from my head to my feet." He lay unconscious for thirty to forty minutes, and came around only with difficulty. His symptoms define severe concussion. William Candler of his staff wrote home, "The blow which the General received seems to have knocked all the sense out of him. For the remainder of the day he was wandering, and was unable to get any ideas into his head." Abner Doubleday made note that Hooker "suffered great pain and was in a comatose condition for most of the time. His mind was not clear, and they had to wake him up to communicate with him."[50]

General Hooker's injury occurred about 9:00 a.m., and for some two hours Potomac army headquarters was rendered mute. In such event, the chief of staff would call the senior general — Darius Couch — to take over, but Butterfield was at Falmouth. Hooker conscious was best described as adrift, rational one moment, befuddled the next. The staff was baffled. With the Confederates momentarily threatening to collapse the salient, Hooker finally saw he must turn the command over to Couch . . . but only conditionally. He ordered him to take the army to the fallback line covering U.S. Ford that the engineers had marked out earlier.

James Biddle of Meade's staff wrote home, "Couch is a regular old granny, and I must say my heart failed me when I saw him in command. Gen. Meade told him what to do, but Couch could not comprehend." Meade went to Hooker to get him to order what was actually needed that moment — a strike with the reserves at the exposed Rebel flank. As aide Alexander Webb phrased it, "Meade begged to go in with our Corps & Reynolds' (5th & 1st) fresh, confident & anxious to fight." Hooker's battle plan for the day had included that very tactic — "to flank and destroy Jackson" — but, wrote Webb, "no, it could *not* be, just at the moment when any cool soldier felt it must be done."

In reporting this turnabout Webb remarked, "Fighting Joe lost himself very suddenly." Indeed, the contrast between the Joe Hooker who two hours earlier demanded French counterattack the enemy, and the Joe Hooker who (said James Biddle) "did not seem to have any energy or to know what to do" and ordered a retreat, can only be explained by the effects of concussion. It appears that the one thought Hooker could keep in his bruised head was to save the army.

Couch hastened to pull Slocum's and Sickles's troops from what remained of the salient and northward through a narrowing corridor to the new defensive line. Directing the retreat personally, Couch was nicked twice by bullets and his horse killed. Winfield Hancock's Second Corps division, in lines facing both east and west a half mile apart, kept the corridor open. Hancock too had his horse killed under him. The posting, wrote the Second Corps' historian, was "subjected to fire at once direct, enfilading, and reverse, receiving shot and shell from every direction except the north." But the lines held where they had to, and by midday the army was compactly arrayed behind a new perimeter, flanks anchored on the Rappahannock, securing the U.S. Ford crossing.[51]

Hooker's prospective battle plan for May 3 also included striking at Lee's rear with the Sixth Corps. He had sent Gouverneur Warren as his proxy to brace Sedgwick and to be sure that officer understood his orders were peremptory: "Any force in front of Gen. Sedgwick must be a small one and must not check his advance." John Sedgwick, already uneasy in independent command, worried the problem of getting over or around Marye's Heights, which blocked his way to the Plank Road. He had some 27,000 men — his three divisions, and John Gibbon's Second Corps division that crossed from Falmouth on a newly laid bridge — but as John Newton observed, "The hard nut was yet to crack; the heights beyond where the rebels were fortified up to their necks. . . ."

Newton's probe in the morning mist closed to within twenty paces of the infamous stone wall when it met a blast of fire. "Every flash of rifle and cannon was distinctly visible," Newton wrote, "and the whole force of the enemy was displayed." Sedgwick sent Albion P. Howe to demonstrate to the left ("he made no visible impression") and Gibbon to demonstrate to the right ("he made no impression"). That only left storming the center, as if it were December again.

"Boys, you see those Heights," Colonel Thomas S. Allen addressed his 5th Wisconsin. "You have got to take them. . . . When the signal 'Forward' is given, you will start at double-quick — you will not fire a gun — and you will not stop until you get the order to halt. You will never get that order." Hiram Burnham announced to his Light Division, "Boys, I have got a government contract. One thousand rebels, potted and salted, and got to have 'em in less than five minutes. Forward! Guide center!" Newton's and Burnham's storming parties were well supported by artillery firing from the flanks. They took heavy casualties — some 1,100 — but pressed on and broke the Rebel line. As they planted their flags atop Marye's Heights the Sixth Corps cheered.[52]

Sedgwick paused to bring up Bully Brooks's fresh division to take the lead before pushing westward on the Plank Road. He assigned Gibbon's division to hold Fredericksburg, but left newly conquered Marye's Heights unoccupied. "We had not the force to hold the heights and *advance too*," wrote a staff man. Hooker's latest order, written just before he was injured and relayed to Sedgwick at 11:30 a.m., was urgent: "You will hurry up your column. The enemy's right flank now rests near the Plank road at Chan-

The desolated Chancellor house, General Hooker's headquarters, set afire by Confederate artillery fire on May 3, served as the epitome of his failed campaign.

cellorsville all exposed. You will attack at once." This proved easier ordered
than carried out. John Sedgwick's natural caution was multiplied by his
feeling of being hemmed in by enemies front and rear.

Bully Brooks, facing an uncertain future for his part in the anti-Burn-
side cabal, felt the need to prove himself that Sunday. He approached
open ground at Salem Church aggressively, on a broad front, two lead brigades in columns ready for quick deployment. General Lee, having driven
Hooker out of his Chancellorsville salient, turned to meet Sedgwick, and
the collision was violent. Initially Brooks pushed the Rebels through a belt
of thick woodland, but in the obscuring clouds of battle smoke his attack
lost cohesion and then momentum, and a counterattack pressed the Yankees back. Sedgwick was not ready with close supports, and soon enough
Brooks found himself where he had started, less 1,500 men. Shaking his
head, he told one of his staff, "Twenty-five years in the army, Mr. Wheeler,
and ruined at last!"

It was evening now and the Rebel counterattack was spent, and Sedgwick formed a defensive perimeter. His advance from Fredericksburg
gained him Banks's Ford, and the engineers laid a bridge there (and a second one the next day), securing his communications. As May 3 ended, the
Federals held three separate bridgeheads — the main army at U.S. Ford, the

Sixth Corps at Banks's Ford, and John Gibbon's two brigades at the Fredericksburg crossing. According to his chief of staff, Sedgwick "scarcely slept that night. . . . He would walk a few paces apart and listen; then returning would lie down again in the damp grass, with his saddle for a pillow, and try to sleep. The night was inexpressibly gloomy."[53]

Gouverneur Warren had left Sedgwick that evening for headquarters, where he found the commanding general often unresponsive. Hooker did say he hoped the enemy would attack him the next day in his new position, but he had no instructions for Sedgwick — "he would have to depend upon himself." Warren felt obliged to send Sedgwick his own interpretation of Hooker's thinking: "He does not desire you to attack them again in force unless he attacks him at the same time." That vague declaration only added to Sedgwick's confusion, but Warren did tell him to look well to the Banks's Ford and Fredericksburg crossings. "You can go to either place if you think it best. To cross at Banks' Ford would bring you in supporting distance of the main body and would be better than falling back to Fredericksburg." Received at 6:30 a.m. on May 4, this was Sedgwick's sole guidance for the day.

For the main army — First, Second, Third, Fifth, Eleventh, and Twelfth Corps — Monday, May 4, passed in comparative quiet. The 5th New York Zouaves, signed up for two years, took advantage of the calm to march for home. There were losses. A sharpshooter mortally wounded Brigadier General Amiel Whipple. Topographical engineer Whipple had gained a division under Burnside, and Chancellorsville was his first serious action. His was the second Third Corps division (after Berry's) to lose its general in two days. The six corps fortified and armed their new salient covering U.S. Ford — Henry Hunt had charge of the guns now — giving up the initiative to General Lee for yet another day. The previous evening Hooker had confided in Colonel Wainwright. "He told me that he should give Lee tomorrow to attack him, and 'then if he does not,' said Hooker, 'let him look out.'"

John Sedgwick's first shock that Monday came not before him but behind him. A staff man watched "the gray-back devils" reoccupy Marye's Heights: "The whole heights swarm with them, — at six o'clock in the morning these works are full again." This severed the Sixth Corps from the Fredericksburg crossing, isolated Gibbon in his bridgehead there, and put Sedgwick on his mettle to defend his own crossing at Banks's Ford. Rumor named the Rebels on Marye's Heights Longstreet's men from distant Suffolk, but in fact they were Jubal Early's who had been driven off the Heights the day before. Sedgwick's chief of staff remarked, "General, it looks as if the Sixth Corps was going to close its career today." "It has somewhat that appearance," Uncle John conceded. "I will tell you a secret: there will be no surrendering."[54]

The attack on Sedgwick did not open until nearly six o'clock that evening, but when it came (said General Albion Howe) it was "delivered with a violence that I had never before encountered." Lieutenant Colonel Thomas Hyde wrote in a memoir, "Oh for the sound of one gun off toward the Wilderness, where three fourths of our army were!" The Sixth Corps defended Banks's Ford on its own.

Howe formed his division on the left and arranged a defense in depth that absorbed the worst of the main Rebel thrust. His line was holding well until the colonel of the 20th New York was wounded. The 20th, a largely German two-year regiment, had already mutinied over its release date. Now, wrote Hyde, without its colonel in control "the 20th New York disgracefully ran," adding to the legend of the Flying Dutchmen of Chancellorsville. Fortunately Colonel Lewis A. Grant's Vermont Brigade, Baldy Smith's old command, "as firm as a rock," blunted the assault and drove it back. Elsewhere on the line artillery was decisive. One of Sedgwick's staff recorded for his wife the effect of a six-gun battery of Napoleons firing canister. "Good God, dear girl, it was awful, the dead seemed piled heaps upon heaps, the shot went right through them, completely smashed the front of the columns." Sedgwick was heard to say, "One more such a repulse as that, my boys," and the day would be theirs. As indeed it was.

General Sedgwick could take satisfaction from his defense of Banks's Ford, yet he saw no future staying where he was — the enemy enclosing him on three sides, believing himself outnumbered, with neither support nor directions from the general commanding. At 9:45 that night he telegraphed Hooker, "The enemy are pressing me. I am taking position to cross the river whenever necessary."[55]

Some thirty-six hours had passed since Joe Hooker's injury, and he was recovered sufficiently to give thought to a possible new direction for his stalled campaign — leave a screening force at the U.S. Ford bridgehead "and with the balance of my force recross the river, march down to Banks's ford and turn the enemy's position in my front in so doing." Before he could tell Sedgwick of this, however, he was taken aback at eleven that night to learn Sedgwick was preparing to cross the river. Hooker's new plan would founder without Banks's Ford.

At midnight, for the first time in his army command, Joe Hooker called on his lieutenants for opinions — not a formal council of war but a consultation. Present were corps commanders Reynolds, Couch, Sickles, Meade, and Howard; Slocum only arrived later. Also present were chief of staff Butterfield, brought over from Falmouth, and engineer Warren. Hooker presented the status of their front and of Sedgwick's front "as clearly as I could." He read them Sedgwick's telegram, but said nothing of his idea for crossing at U.S. Ford, recrossing at Banks's Ford, and striking the enemy's flank; that seemed not an option now. He spoke of the need to protect Washington, of the difficulties of operating in the Wilderness with attacking columns road-bound and presenting only narrow fronts to the enemy. There were two alternatives, he said — an offensive (unspecified) the next day from their present position, or pulling back across the Rappahannock and ending the campaign. He and Butterfield withdrew to "let them confer among themselves."

George Meade was as outspoken as the day before in advocating an offensive, and pointed to the difficulty of evacuating the army in the face of an aggressive enemy. John Reynolds agreed, cast his proxy with Meade, and went to sleep in a corner. Otis Howard also called for an advance. He said his Eleventh Corps had let the army down and needed to make up for it; he would throw his men into battle to clear his tarnished name. (Meade counted four generals as supporting an advance; the fourth must have been late-arriving Slocum). Darius Couch said he knew too little of the situation, so he favored retreat. (In an article years later, Couch wrote that actually he had favored attack, "if I could designate the point of attack." No one at the council recorded him saying that.) Dan Sickles thought it best, for political reasons, to withdraw the army. By Warren's recollection, "in the most abusive language" Sickles turned on Hooker for a campaign going wrong.

When Hooker learned the views of his generals — four to two opposing retreat — he was surprised. But already he had decided the matter himself. He said orders would designate Tuesday, May 5, for the army's withdrawal. When Reynolds was awakened and told the verdict he grumbled, "What was the use of calling us together at this time of night when he intended to retreat anyhow?"[56]

Hooker's faint last hope, recrossing the main army at Banks's Ford, now flickered out. At 1:00 a.m. May 5 a telegram from Sedgwick reported that he was hemmed in by the enemy: "If I had only this army to care for, I would withdraw it to-night. Do your operations require that I should jeopard it by retaining it here? An immediate reply is indispensable, or I may feel obliged to withdraw." That was definite enough, and Hooker's reply was brief: "Withdraw. Cover the river. . . ." Then came a second telegram from Sedgwick, sent before Hooker's withdrawal order reached him:

"I shall hold my position, as ordered, on south of Rappahannock." Sedg-wick's reversal was due to engineer Henry Benham, who warned him not to be responsible for a retreat without a direct order from the general com-manding. His hopes reviving, Hooker countermanded the withdrawal or-der . . . but the telegraph lagged and he was too late. "The bridges at Banks' Ford are swung and in process of being taken up," Sedgwick replied. ". . . The dispatch countermanding my movement over the river was received after the troops had crossed." Joe Hooker could think of nothing better to do. The retreat was on.[57]

Following Sedgwick's lead, John Gibbon retreated from Fredericks-burg, taking up the bridges there. The crossing of the main army at U.S. Ford was delayed by heavy rains and flooding that threatened the bridges — "We all prayed that the bridges might be washed away rather than have that order carried out," wrote the Fifth Corps' Alexander Webb — but the engineers took up one bridge to piece out and re-anchor the other two. The Rebels were taken by surprise, and except for some shells thrown at the Banks's Ford bridges, offered no challenge. By morning on May 6 the Army of the Potomac was safely across the river, marking the end of the Chancellorsville campaign. General Meade wrote his wife, "Poor Hooker himself after he had determined to withdraw said to me in the most de-sponding manner, that he was ready to turn over to me the Army of the Potomac, that he had had enough of it and almost wished he had never been born."[58]

14. *Pennsylvania Showdown*

THE PRESIDENT TRACKED the Chancellorsville campaign at the War Department telegraph office, but reports were sketchy, and so the dispatch he received at 1:25 p.m. on May 6 came as a shock. He was directed, said Chief of Staff Butterfield, "to telegraph you that the army has recrossed the river; that the bridges are up, and that all are under orders to return to camp." A second telegram, from Hooker, elaborated only slightly: "I saw no way of giving the enemy a general battle with the prospect of success which I desire." At 4:00 p.m. president and general-in-chief boarded a steamer for Aquia Landing to take the measure of Fighting Joe and his lieutenants.

Lincoln had anticipated much for this campaign — "He looked upon Hooker as his 'last card,'" said Senator John Sherman — and Butterfield's telegram left him visibly upset and asking, "My God! My God! What will the country say!" On May 7, at Falmouth headquarters, he spoke to the same theme. By General Meade's account, "The Presdt remarked that the result was in his judgment most unfortunate — that he did not blame any one, he believed every one had done all in his power, and that the disaster was one that could not be helped, nevertheless he thought its effect both at home & abroad, would be more serious & injurious, than any previous act of the war."

As it happened, the news of Chancellorsville, instead of bursting on the North with the blunt impact of Fredericksburg, trickled out over a matter of days, limited by censorship and by puzzlement over what had happened. The *what* of Chancellorsville was not easily grasped. (Satirist Robert Henry Newell explained that Hooker arranged his army in a triangle around the Confederates, in successive attacks drove them in retreat across the triangle, displacing the Federals on the far side, until the Confederates held all three sides of the triangle.) Chancellorsville, unlike Fredericksburg, did not trigger an investigation by the Joint Committee on the Conduct of the War. Senators Ben Wade and Zach Chandler did turn up at Falmouth, but said they uncovered nothing worth a hearing. "I have full confidence in Joe Hooker," said Chandler.[1]

Still, for Lincoln the defeat came at a critical moment. Campaigning in Tennessee was in stalemate since the battle at Stone's River at the turn of the year. The navy's trial against the defenses of Charleston Harbor was repelled. For months U. S. Grant's attempts to get at Vicksburg on the Mississippi had been frustrated. Even as Chancellorsville was being fought, Grant was attempting a new and still-uncertain tactic against the Confederate stronghold.

The president might not blame anyone for Chancellorsville, but the Potomac army's officer corps soon enough assigned blame. A fresh generals' revolt sprang up. The ringleaders were corps commanders Henry Slocum and Darius Couch. Couch assured General Halleck of "much dissatisfaction among the higher officers at Hooker's incomprehensible bad management." Slocum promoted a coup—a petition for the signatures of the senior generals to hand to Lincoln, calling for Joe Hooker to be replaced by George Meade.

"Two of my seniors (Slocum & Couch) have told me they were willing to serve under me & preferred me to their present commander," Meade wrote his wife. "I declined to join *Couch* in a representation to the Presdt. when he was down here—and I refused to join Slocum who desired to take action to have Hooker removed. I told both these gentlemen I would not join any movement against Hooker." At that the petitioners backed off. A day or so later a third "senior," John Sedgwick, told Meade he too would be willing to serve under him. (Hooker himself, when asked by Lincoln, named Meade his ablest corps commander.)

George Smalley of the *New-York Tribune* was persuaded by the dissidents to make their case to Meade. At Antietam Smalley undertook a similar mission, that time to Hooker. Now he assured Meade that he was the generals' choice to replace Hooker. Meade "listened with an impassive face. He did not interrupt. He never asked a question . . . a model of military discretion." Smalley knew not what impression he had made, but soon after, Meade wrote his wife, "I think I can truly say that in *the Army* I am over-appreciated. I constantly hear of the most flattering remarks made about me."[2]

Darius Couch judged Hooker unfit to lead. He would publish that Fighting Joe took his courage from a bottle; rather than abstain at Chancellorsville, "it would have been far better for him to have continued in his usual habit in that respect." Couch's notion of duty was to not serve under Hooker. He applied to be relieved of service with the Potomac army. "Gen.

Hooker seemed astounded and returned it," said Couch. He persisted, pressing his suit personally to Lincoln. So it was that Darius Couch exchanged the Second Corps, Army of the Potomac, for leading lowly Pennsylvania militiamen.

Henry Slocum nursed even stronger enmity toward Hooker. He made no secret of "my utter detestation of him as a man." (Lincoln's secretary John Hay portrayed Slocum as "peevish, irritable, fretful. Hooker says he is all that on account of his digestive apparatus being out of repair.") Slocum reported the army's march to Chancellorsville was initially very successful. "Everything after that went wrong, and fighting Joe sunk into a poor driveling cur. The fact is whisky, boasting, and vilification have been his stock and trade." Like Couch, he carried his case against Hooker directly to Lincoln, imploring "for the sake of the Army and the Country, that he should be relieved from the command of that Army." Lincoln sent him back to Falmouth to exist at swords' points with Hooker.[3]

Hooker's generalship spawned other officer corps critics. George Meade: "All I can say is that Hooker disappointed the army & myself in failing to show the nerve & coup d'oeil at the critical moment, which all had given him credit for. . . ." Gouverneur Warren: "We went forward filled with high hopes. . . . But that steady purpose was wanting in the controlling power. We halted, we hesitated, wavered, retired." Winfield Hancock: "I have had the blues ever since I returned from the campaign. Hooker's day is over." John Gibbon: Hooker "committed a great mistake when he backed out from the other side. . . . The *only one* who advised a back out was a man who had no character, private or public, to lose, and him I see the Herald is out in favor of as Genl. Hooker's successor! . . . If Genl. *Sickles* should be appointed to the command of this army we have sunk low." (Alpheus Williams too was outraged by the *New York Herald*'s touting of Sickles: "Matters are not settled by merit but by impudence and brass and well paid reporters. . . . He is a hero without an heroic deed!") Williams was equally harsh on Hooker: "I cannot conceive of greater imbecility and weakness than characterized that campaign. . . ." Otis Howard wrote to his clergyman brother, "Gen. Hooker is said to be impure. . . . Would that you would plead with our Father to convert the soul of Gen. Hooker. It is just what we need."

Among lesser ranks old gossip revived. Thomas Hyde wrote home, "Generals say, 'Nothing better could be expected of a decayed California gambler.' *Such he is.* All clamor for the restoration of McClellan." Accounts of Hooker lying comatose after his injury at the Chancellor house drew George Armstrong Custer to observe (to McClellan) that if anything "prevented him from succeeding, it was a wound he received from a projectile which requires a cork to be drawn before it is serviceable." In Washington Elizabeth Blair Lee heard from a staff officer reporting Hooker drunk all the time "and unfit for duty . . . 'Hooker is stretched on the grass — the Staff standing around & the Army perfectly quiet' . . . draw you your own conclusions from this faithful picture." Colonel Charles Wainwright rejected such gossip. He was with Hooker during the battle and saw no sign of intoxication; "The idea certainly never entered my head."[4]

John Gibbon thought it simply a matter of character. "The great trouble with us is that *principle* is wanting, and a certain set headed by such *Maj. Genls* as *Dan S.* and *Dan B.* is all powerful in its influence. God will not favor a cause where men without character and without principle are placed in the highest positions to the exclusion of high minded and honorable men." For Gibbon, Hooker's "want of *backbone* at the wrong moment" cast him from the same mold as Sickles and Butterfield. For Captain Henry Ropes, McClellan was the answer: "I hear no cries for peace, no desire to give it up, only a cry for a General who can lead us to victory, for the *only* General who can and ought."

These judgments lacked any notice that Hooker's injury on May 3 might be accountable for his erratic behavior that day, might have (as staff man James Biddle put it) "weakened his brain." Gideon Welles told his diary, "The President says if Hooker had been killed by the shot which knocked over the pillar that stunned him, we should have been successful." Concussion was a hidden wound, unrecognized as serious a disablement as a visible wound. Gibbon's view was representative. Hooker, he wrote, "was a good deal stunned whilst leaning against the pillar of a porch when it was shattered by a solid shot, knocking him senseless, but in a couple of hours he was on his horse and among the troops." Instead of suffering a loss of awareness, Hooker was marked down as suffering a loss of nerve.[5]

Hooker's own appraisal of the late battle was ill-advised and further alienated his lieutenants. His strange general order congratulated the army: "If it has not accomplished all that was expected, the reasons are well known to the army" — which reasons were in fact unknown to the army. He next took aim at those he blamed for the defeat — corps commanders George Stoneman, Otis Howard, and John Sedgwick.

On returning from his raid, Stoneman sensed Hooker's displeasure and took medical leave. "His raid was not remarkable for success," noted Gibbon, who guessed (correctly) that Stoneman would not return to the Potomac army. Having picked Stoneman to lead the restructured cavalry, Hooker was pained at his failure. Otis Howard too was a Hooker appoin-

At Chancellorsville, George Stoneman (left) led the Potomac army's cavalry corps with an ineptitude matched by Otis Howard (right) with the Eleventh Corps.

tee, and like Stoneman was guilty in Hooker's eyes of flagrant failure to obey orders: "The 11th corps had been completely surprised and disgracefully routed. . . . I only know that my instructions were utterly and criminally disregarded."

"There will be an effort to throw the blame for the failure on me," John Sedgwick wrote his sister, "but it will not succeed. My friends here will do me justice." In that Uncle John was correct. His Sixth Corps captured Marye's Heights (where Burnside had failed), held its ground at Salem Church, and threw the Rebels back at Banks's Ford. That was the best fighting record of any corps. But to Hooker, Sedgwick fell short of his assignment — to crush Lee between the two wings of the army. The officer corps disagreed with that reading of events. "I think there was some disposition to lay the blame upon Sedgwick," Gibbon wrote, "but the escape from destruction of his corps was so remarkable, and he managed so well, that it could not be done." Hooker confronted Sedgwick about his overcaution (as reported privately to him by Gouverneur Warren), creating "a stormy scene."

George Meade too had run-ins with the general commanding. Pennsylvania's Governor Andrew G. Curtin visited Falmouth to question favorite sons Meade and Reynolds, who were candid in their remarks. Curtin told Lincoln the army's two best corps commanders had lost confidence in General Hooker. Word of this reached Hooker, and he called on Meade for an explanation. Meade said Curtin had no warrant to pass on a private conversation . . . and in any event what he said to the governor was only what he had said to Hooker "at the time the events were occurring." Then the *New York Herald* reported the army retreated due to "the weak councils of its corps commanders." Meade declared that a base calumny. He confronted Hooker to remind him that he was very much a part of the majority that opposed retreat. Alexander Webb of the staff watched as hot-tempered Meade "damned Hooker very freely," and Webb quickly left the tent so he would not be the witness required for court-martial. "God help us all!" was Meade's verdict, and he wrote his wife, "I am sorry to tell you, I am at open war with Hooker."[6]

Joe Hooker would later write of Chancellorsville, "I won greater success on many fields in the war, but nowhere did I deserve it half so much" — a self-serving remark certainly, but it made a fair point. His battle plan opening with such promise was undermined by chance and mischance — the errant courier that kept Reynolds's First Corps from meeting Jackson's surprise attack; communication lapses that diverted the Sixth Corps from an early opportunity to breach the Fredericksburg line; miscommunications that sent Sedgwick prematurely retreating across the Rappahannock; and most notably, Hooker's concussion injury that left him too muddled to command.

To be sure, Hooker's own errors contributed measurably to his downfall — giving up the Hazel Grove position; fumbling direction of the artillery; making no collaborative effort with Sedgwick. Yet these singly or collectively did not assure defeat. Like Ambrose Burnside at Fredericksburg, Joe Hooker at Chancellorsville was badly served by his lieutenants.

"Our great weakness, in my opinion, is in the incompetency of many of our Corps Commanders," Gouverneur Warren wrote of the campaign. "They don't know how to manage and fight troops." Staff officer Alex Webb spoke of brigade and division generals he encountered — "Contemptible blocks with 'stars' on their shoulders in moments of trial have asked *me* what to do! how to do it! & look like sheep when they ought to show character. . . . They all think the enemy wiser & braver & quicker than themselves & such men should not command."

Chancellorsville marked the greatest test yet for the army's corps commanders, and results were inauspicious. Reynolds and Meade, the most experienced at battle, were hardly called upon. On May 1 Henry Slocum's dilatory march with the Twelfth Corps forced Hooker to cancel the day's advance. On May 2 the indifference of the Eleventh Corps' Otis Howard to repeated warnings was plainly dereliction of duty. On May 2 the Third Corps' Dan Sickles poked ineffectually at Jackson's flanking column, misreported the enemy as retreating, and left himself out of position to hold Hazel Grove. The three other corps commanders failed in independent roles. Darius Couch, thrust into the army command on Sunday, shrank from acting with initiative, from making common cause with Reynolds and Meade to rescue the battle. John Sedgwick, like Couch, lacked the initiative and aggressiveness for independent command. He saved his Sixth Corps, certainly, but leading the army's left wing called for more than steady caution. George Stoneman's failure defied understanding. "I had worded my instructions so strongly I thought they would wake up a dead man," said Hooker; "his conduct was criminally insubordinate."[7]

Chancellorsville left the Potomac army's high command in turmoil, yet the army's rank and file was left comparatively stable. Hooker's reforms were well rooted. In May there was no army-wide plunge in morale as in December, no rush to desert. Food, shelter, and medical care continued according to Hooker's standards. Puzzlement was widespread, however. "The men were absolutely astonished at our move," a Wisconsin man told his wife, "for every one felt that we had the best of the Rebs and could hold our position as the saying is till Hell froze over. . . . You cant make any person in this army believe we were whipped." In staff man Stephen Weld's view, "This Army of the Potomac is truly a wonderful army. They have something of the English bull-dog in them. . . . Some day or other we shall have our turn."

The defeat was the Potomac army's costliest yet — 1,694 dead, 9,672 wounded, 5,938 missing, 17,304 in total. The large Sixth Corps suffered the largest loss, 4,611, but the smaller Third and Twelfth Corps, fighting at the Chancellor house, had higher percentage losses, 22 percent for the Third, 21 percent for the Twelfth. Of Otis Howard's casualties, two in five were marked missing, cementing the army's label Flying Dutchmen on the Eleventh Corps.

The Confederates' loss came to 13,460. As evidence of the closeness of the fighting, they lost 30 more dead than the Yankees and just 439 fewer wounded. The singular Confederate loss was Stonewall Jackson, dead of his wounds on May 10. "It is a terrible loss," wrote General Lee. "I do not know how to replace him."

The Federals' heaviest officer casualties fell on the Third Corps at the Chancellor house — division commanders Major General Hiram G. Berry killed and Brigadier General Amiel W. Whipple mortally wounded. One of Berry's brigadiers, Gershom Mott, was wounded. Brigadier Generals William Hays, Second Corps, was captured and Charles Devens, Eleventh Corps, was wounded. Three colonels heading brigades were wounded: Henry W. Brown and William H. Browne, Sixth Corps, and Samuel Ross, Twelfth Corps.[8]

As early as May 7 Mr. Lincoln was asking Hooker, "What next?" A prompt advance would "help to supersede the bad moral effect of the recent one." Should the general lack a plan, "please inform me, so that I, incompetent as I may be, can try and assist in the formation of some plan for the army." The chief executive was now a fully engaged commander-in-chief. Hooker replied that he had a plan; this time all operations would be under his personal supervision. Meade noted, on May 10, "We have been under orders to move & have been for two days in a state of readiness." On May 13 Hooker announced, "I hope to be able to commence my movement to-morrow, but this must not be spoken of to any one." Lincoln immediately ordered him to Washington to consult.

Hooker's new plan — details not revealed — did not survive that evening's White House meeting. Fighting Joe proved not so dedicated to renewing battle after all. Summarizing their meeting, the president noted that the enemy had reoccupied and strengthened its old positions; it was not likely "you can gain any thing by an early renewal of the attempt to cross the Rappahannock." He would not complain "if you do no more, for a time, than to keep the enemy at bay." In closing, Lincoln took up a matter he found deeply disturbing. "I must tell you I have some painful intimations that some of your corps and Division Commanders are not giving you their entire confidence. This would be ruinous, if true. . . ."[9]

Joe Hooker was well aware of the roiling discontent in the officer corps. Instead of chasing down disloyal generals as Burnside had done, he called them into the open. Any aggrieved general seeking a pass to Washington was urged to stop at the White House and complain to the commander-in-chief: "I desired the President himself to . . . learn their views for his own information." (Hooker's patron Treasury Secretary Chase warned him, "I fear it is a mistake to have chiefs of Corps come up here to tell their different stories. . . . We all like to be heroes. . . .") On May 25 John Gibbon made note, "No one whose opinion is worth anything has now any confidence in Genl. H. and the Presdt. has been told so, but whether a change will be made or not, it is difficult to say."

The president, wrote diarist Welles, "has a personal liking for Hooker, and clings to him when others give way." Lincoln appreciated Fighting

Joe's candor, his lack of pretention, certainly his willingness to fight, and initially he resisted calls to replace him. "I tried McClellan twenty times," he told Hooker. "I see no reason why I can't try you at least twice." Nor did he want to appear so inconstant as to change generals after every battle. Still, he was much troubled — as he had been in Burnside's case — by the lack of confidence in Hooker voiced by the officer corps. He began to explore candidates to possibly replace him . . . and discovered a bizarre situation. It seemed just then that no one wanted to command the Army of the Potomac.[10]

When Darius Couch resigned his corps posting, the president brought up the army command, as a courtesy due him for being second in command at Chancellorsville. Couch begged off, citing poor health. Sam Heintzelman, with his seniority, wondered if he might be tapped for the post. "It is an honor not to seek," he decided. Winfield Hancock, who took over the Second Corps from Couch, told his wife he was mentioned for the command: "Give yourself no uneasiness — under no conditions would I accept the command. I do not belong to that class of generals whom the Republicans care to bolster up. I should be sacrificed." John Sedgwick, also approached through an intermediary, wrote his sister, "I think I could have had it if I had said the word, but nothing could induce me to take it."[11]

On May 13 Hooker outlined the state of the army for the president: "My marching force of infantry is cut down to about 80,000, while I have artillery for an army of more than double that number." This reflected not only Chancellorsville's heavy casualties but also the growing number of men, their time up, heading for home. By early July, thirty-four regiments of two-year enlistees, mostly New Yorkers, and twenty-six regiments of Pennsylvania and New Jersey militia called up after the Peninsula defeat — 31,100 men all told — would be gone from the Potomac army. The loss of the two-year men, veterans with veteran officers who had served from the beginning, was especially painful. "I have in my division less than half the men I had in January last," Alpheus Williams wrote. "I cannot believe that the most extravagant self-conceit nor the wildest lunacy could bring anyone to the belief that with our reduced army we can, with the least prospect of success, cross the Rappahannock just now." As Rufus R. Dawes, 6th Wisconsin, put it, "The belligerent Joseph not feeling strong enough to *fight* them here, hopes to keep them by continually shaking his fists at them."

John Sedgwick estimated in mid-May that a thousand men a day were being discharged, and he remarked, "I presume they know in Washington

At Falmouth in May 1863, Edwin Forbes sketched the departure from the Army of the Potomac of a trainload of two-year men, their time up. The loss of two-year men and nine-month militiamen and Chancellorsville casualties totaled some 48,400.

where the reinforcements are to come from." In fact they did not know. In March Congress had cobbled together a conscription bill that was supposed to resolve the growing manpower shortage. In practice, however, by permitting the buying of substitutes and the paying of commutation fees and other inequities, the Enrollment Act produced very few drafted men to fill out the ranks. What it did produce was a growth in volunteering to avoid the draft . . . but volunteers whose motive was the maximum amount of bounty money. Over its course conscription proved one of the more unsavory chapters in the Union war effort. The immediate need, said Hooker, was "partial reorganization."

In John Reynolds's First Corps, the First Division (James S. Wadsworth) lost a brigade of nine-month militiamen and three-quarters of a brigade of two-year men. Wadsworth shrank from four brigades to two. The Second Division (John C. Robinson) went from three brigades to two. The eleven departing regiments of short-termers cost three colonels their brigade posts.

The Second Corps gained fresh, inspirited leadership in the person of Winfield Scott Hancock, advanced from division in place of unenterprising Darius Couch. John C. Caldwell replaced Hancock at division. Gone from the Irish Brigade was Thomas Francis Meagher, with his penchant for Irish whiskey. Refused leave to recruit his thinned ranks in New York,

Meagher resigned. His replacement was proper Irishman Patrick Kelly. Alexander Webb, newly minted a brigadier, came from the Fifth Corps staff to take over the Philadelphia Brigade in John Gibbon's division. Webb, said Gibbon approvingly, "comes down on them with a heavy hand and will no doubt soon make a great improvement." William H. French was shifted to the Middle Department and his division taken by Alexander Hays. The corps lost seven regiments of short-termers.

Chancellorsville cost the Third Corps two division commanders dead, Hiram Berry and Amiel Whipple. (On his deathbed Whipple was brevetted brigadier in the regulars, moving John Gibbon to remark that should he be wounded "& see old Abe browsing round with a parchment in his hand I should take it for granted he has my ticket for the next world.") Casualties and short-termer departures took their toll. Whipple's division was folded into the other two divisions, under David B. Birney and Andrew A. Humphreys, who came over from the Fifth Corps to replace Berry. William W. Brewster took the brigade of Joseph W. Revere, sacked by Sickles for misbehavior in the May 3 fighting.

George Meade's Fifth Corps was scheduled to lose a total of thirteen two-year and nine-month regiments, and like the Third Corps lost a division as a result. Andrew Humphreys's Pennsylvania militia went home and Humphreys moved to the Third Corps. "I am very sorry to lose Humphreys," said Meade. "He is a most valuable officer besides being an associate of the most agreeable character."

In John Sedgwick's Sixth Corps, Hiram Burnham's Light Division took a beating storming Marye's Heights and was afterward broken up and its regiments distributed through the corps, helping to fill gaps left by the eleven departing short-term regiments. Bully Brooks left the Potomac army for the Department of the Monongahela, his division going to Horatio G. Wright. The other two divisions remained under Albion Howe and John Newton.

Otis Howard's Eleventh Corps lost only one short-term regiment. Francis Barlow, promoted to brigade for Antietam, was now promoted to division to replace the wounded Charles Devens. Adolph von Steinwehr and Carl Schurz led the other divisions. The corps, with only six brigades, was seriously undermanned.

Henry Slocum's Twelfth Corps was hard-used in the fight at the Chancellor house. Alpheus Williams wrote of his division, "I have lost half of my field officers, all my adjutant generals, more than *one-third* of all my command, and hence have unusual duties and difficulties to encounter." Losing as well two short-term regiments, his three brigades were combined into two, under newcomer Archibald L. McDougall and veteran Thomas H. Ruger. John W. Geary's Second Division was also short two nine-month regiments but otherwise intact, with brigades under Charles Candy, Thomas L. Kane, and George Sears Greene.[12]

Hooker made it clear that George Stoneman was not wanted in the Potomac army. A desk was found for him at the Cavalry Bureau and Alfred Pleasonton took the cavalry corps. Pleasonton never showed talent for the vital intelligence-gathering part of the job, but his talent for self-promotion boosted him up the command ladder. As trooper Charles Russell Lowell put it, "It is the universal opinion that Pleasonton's own reputation, and Pleasonton's late promotions, are bolstered up by systematic lying." Captain Charles Francis Adams, Jr., called Pleasonton "pure and simple a newspaper humbug." Hooker said afterward he should have put John Buford in the cavalry command. The corps' three cavalry divisions were under Buford, David M. Gregg, and Alfred Duffié.

Henry Hunt was appalled at Hooker's mismanagement of the artillery at Chancellorsville. "I doubt if the history of modern armies," his report read, "can exhibit a parallel instance of such palpable crippling of a great arm of the service in the very presence of a powerful enemy. . . . It is not, therefore, to be wondered at that confusion and mismanagement ensued. . . ." One week after Chancellorsville Joe Hooker quietly reorganized the artillery according to Hunt's specifications. Instead of being assigned to divisions, batteries were formed into brigades, one brigade for each of the seven infantry corps. Two artillery brigades went to the cavalry, and five formed the army's artillery reserve. The corps' artillery brigades were directed by the corps' artillery chiefs, appointed by Hunt on merit. To correct the problems of ammunition resupply so evident at Chancellorsville, each artillery brigade had its own ammunition train under its own command. Hunt termed them brigades in hopes their commanders would gain brigadier rank, but in that he was disappointed. The Potomac army's artillery arm continued notoriously rank-poor, and thereby continued to lose experienced men to higher rank leading infantry. Looking back at Hunt's reformation, veteran artilleryman Tully McCrea remarked, "If what was thus done as a restorative had previously been done as a preventative, the probabilities are that Chancellorsville would have had another and very different ending."[13]

After his hesitant thoughts for a new campaign, Hooker said nothing more on the subject. He reorganized, squabbled with his lieutenants, and watched to see what General Lee might do. He went to Washington to press Stanton and Lincoln for reinforcements. Assurances were given, but actual reinforcing was left to General-in-Chief Halleck, with whom Hooker remained at odds. Hooker called for the 8,600-man "movable force" attached to the Washington garrison. Halleck announced it his duty to retain "the present force in Washington or its vicinity." Returning to Falmouth empty-handed, Hooker warned, "It seems that the enemy will soon be in motion."

That intelligence was the work of Colonel George Sharpe's Bureau of Military Information, which on May 27 detailed the composition and postings of the Army of Northern Virginia. Sharpe concluded that the Rebels were under marching orders — "An order from General Lee was very lately read to the troops, announcing a campaign of long marches and hard fighting, in a part of the country where they would have no railroad transportation." Confirmation of a sort appeared in the *Richmond Examiner* for May 22: "Within the next fortnight the campaign of 1863 will be pretty well decided. The most important movement of the war will probably be made in that time." It seemed clear that again General Lee was heading north.[14]

Chancellorsville persuaded Lee there was no future on the line of the Rappahannock. His victory was dear bought, and like Fredericksburg the Yankees escaped back across the river to fight again. An advance north now seemed his best option. He determined to live off the enemy's country, in the rich farmlands of Maryland and Pennsylvania. And like his ambition in crossing the Potomac the previous September, he went looking for a showdown on Northern soil. He had learned from Northern papers of the departure of two-year men and militia, and believed Hooker's army to be thinned and demoralized. "The General says he wants to meet him as soon as possible and crush him," wrote one of Lee's officers. Gaining Richmond's approval, Lee gathered up his army for the march.[15]

By now Lincoln had heard all the accusations against Hooker, had surveyed candidates to succeed him, had concluded that the Potomac army's officer corps was demoralized and rebellious. He decided to replace Hooker. He called John Reynolds to Washington and on June 2 offered him command of the Army of the Potomac. Reynolds was not so modest as to shy away from the post like Burnside. But he had a proviso. In the messy aftermath of Fredericksburg, Reynolds spoke of the need to get someone who could command "without consulting 'Stanton and Halleck' at Washington. . . . I do not know how it is that the gen'l in command here is obliged to consult Washington every day, and yet there is no one there responsible for failure of operations here. . . ." His condition, then, for taking the command was not to be interfered with from Washington, by the secretary of war or the general-in-chief or apparently by the president either. This was not a condition Lincoln could or would accept. After speaking "very freely" about Hooker and praising Meade for the post, Reynolds returned to the First Corps. He told his staff he had been summoned, was offered and refused the command, and gave his reason as being "unwilling to take Burnside and Hooker's leavings."

But in conversing with Meade, Reynolds recast that story. Meade wrote his wife, "He told me with great naiveté that being informed by a friend in Washington that he was talked of for the command of this Army, he immediately went to the President and told him he did not want the command & would not take it." Labeling Reynolds naive for spinning this tale of a preemptive rejection suggests that Meade saw through his friend's subterfuge — saying he rejected the command before (in effect) it was offered, not mentioning conditions that might tie Meade's hands if (as Reynolds expected) he was next to be called.

Lincoln appears to have found Reynolds's attitude toward the army command suspiciously McClellanesque — "interference" from Washington the paramount problem, to blame for all the Potomac army's woes. These senior generals making bitter complaint against Hooker in command, defining their own duty as *not* to command, stiffened the president's attitude toward the officer corps. He would give Joe Hooker a second chance. As Reynolds reported to Meade, "The Presdt. said he was not disposed to throw away a gun because it missed fire once that he would pick the lock & try it again."[16]

On June 3 the Confederates headed to their step-off point at Culpeper Court House, 30 miles northwest of Fredericksburg. On June 4 Colonel Sharpe's B.M.I. had word of the advance. On June 5 Hooker sent the president his plan for a response. Should this movement be "similar to that of Lee's last year," he expected Lee either to cross the upper Potomac by way of the Shenandoah Valley or to "throw his army between mine and Washington." In either case, "I am of the opinion that it is my duty to pitch into his rear."

Unlike the McClellan era, Mr. Lincoln could now expect the general commanding the Army of the Potomac to give due attention to the commander-in-chief's thinking. Lincoln had sage advice for Fighting Joe. Should Lee move north of the Rappahannock and leave a force at Fredericksburg "tempting you to fall upon it," best ignore the lure. "In one word, I would not take any risk of being entangled upon the river, like an ox jumped half over a fence, and liable to be torn by dogs, front and rear, without a fair chance to gore one way or kick the other. If Lee would come to my side of the river, I would keep on the same side & fight him, or act on the defence." Without the colorful imagery, General Halleck seconded the president.[17]

B.M.I. intelligence included a rumor that Jeb Stuart was planning a major cavalry raid. That suited Joe Hooker's purposes, for he was determined to test his new-formed cavalry command; he gave it as his "great desire to 'bust it up' before it got fairly well under way." That was the flavor of the orders to Pleasonton: "Disperse and destroy the rebel force assembled in the vicinity of Culpeper. . . ."

Pleasonton made a plan: John Buford's cavalry division to cross the Rappahannock at Beverly Ford, David Gregg's and Alfred Duffié's divisions to cross at Kelly's Ford six miles downstream, then join at Brandy Station on the Orange & Alexandria and march six miles to strike Stuart at Culpeper. Pleasonton set his force at 7,900, with two infantry brigades for backup. He set the date as June 9.

The Rebel cavalry was not at Culpeper but scattered about in preparation for leading Lee's march north . . . on June 9. Hardly imagining Hooker so bold, Stuart only lightly picketed the river crossings. By 5:00 a.m. Buford was across the river and scrapping with pickup forces of Rebels in a fight neither side had expected there or then. At Kelly's Ford, Duffié went astray and his and Gregg's division were not across the river until 9:00 a.m. What was to be a battle royal at Culpeper became three battles, separated in time and space, in the general vicinity of Brandy Station.

The initial battle involved Buford's right wing. He was checked when Benjamin F. Davis, commanding the lead brigade, was killed, but soon enough the Yankees pressed on toward Brandy Station. Without threat from Kelly's Ford, Stuart directed everything he could rally to stopping Buford. It was charge and countercharge, to break or turn each other. A Pennsylvania trooper described the melee: "The cutting and slashing, the firing from pistols, carbines, and cannon, the neighing of horses, the yelling of men. . . ."

The drama shifted southward as Gregg's division came onstage, four hours late. Gregg fought for the high ground of Fleetwood Hill, Stuart's headquarters overlooking Brandy Station. David Gregg, at age thirty called Old Reliable, led a charge himself, reported his adjutant: "As they neared the enemy General Gregg showed an enthusiasm that I had never noticed before. He started his horse on a gallop . . . swinging his gauntlets over his head and hurrahing." Judson Kilpatrick directed his brigade with uncoordinated aggression, costing it 156 casualties and affirming his unflattering nickname Kill-cavalry. The third of the Yankee divisions, under Alfred Duffié (in his secret life a deserter from the French cavalry), never joined the central battle. Taking a wide turn to secure the column's flank, Duffié skirmished so cautiously that he failed to answer Gregg's call to support the Fleetwood fighting.

By now, midafternoon, Pleasonton had seen enough. Stuart fought off in turn the Federal attacks and clung to Fleetwood Hill. Pleasonton issued recall, and by evening the Yankees were back across the Rappahannock. Federal casualties were counted as 866, Confederate, 523. Brandy Station was the biggest cavalry battle of the war so far, a distinction it would retain to the end.

For all its fury, Brandy Station did not immediately change anything. Lee's march north was not delayed. Stuart's cavalry raid turned out to be mere rumor. But for Yankee horse soldiers Brandy Station assumed special meaning. As trooper Benjamin Crowninshield put it, that was the day they proved themselves "fully a match for Stuart's cavalry." Admittedly there was more fighting than generalship, but as to the morale of the Potomac army's cavalry corps, June 9, 1863, marked "the turning point of the war."

Stoneman's raid and Brandy Station left the cavalry corps understrength and in disarray. Pleasonton set about reorganizing it. The three divisions were folded into two, under John Buford and David Gregg. In the process, xenophobe Pleasonton displaced or demoted the Frenchman Alfred Duffié, the Englishman Percy Wyndham, and the Italian Luigi di Cesnola. When the cavalry corps gained a third division by transfer from the Washington garrison, Pleasonton replaced its commander, Hungarian Julius Stahel, with Judson Kilpatrick. To fill vacancies at brigade, all-Americans Wesley Merritt, Elon J. Farnsworth, and George Armstrong Custer were each jumped from captain to brigadier general. Custer, said staff man James Biddle, swore he would not cut his hair until he got to Richmond. "It has grown down his back, and he wears a big-brimmed straw hat, presenting a crazy appearance, but he is only so in looks, as he is a good officer & everyone likes him."[18]

Starting on June 10, led by Richard Ewell's corps, the Army of Northern Virginia marched north by west for the Shenandoah Valley. Ewell was followed by James Longstreet's corps, then A. P. Hill's. The Union garrisons in the Valley, the largest at Winchester and Harper's Ferry, were under the purview of Robert Schenck's Middle Department, headquartered at Baltimore. Hooker argued that the present emergency demanded a single head (his) for "all the troops whose operations can have an influence on those of Lee's army." Halleck's response forecast war between general commanding and general-in-chief. Any movement of troops in these commands "you may suggest" will be ordered, said Halleck . . . "if deemed practical." That left the Valley garrisons in a command limbo very like that in the Valley campaign of a year earlier.

Robert H. Milroy commanded the 6,900-man garrison at Winchester. Milroy was "of the extremely nervous, excitable kind" who had raggedly led a brigade at Second Bull Run. On June 11 Halleck at Washington told Schenck at Baltimore that the garrison at Winchester "should be withdrawn." Milroy boasted he could hold his place "against any force the rebels can afford to bring against me." Taking the "should" in Halleck's dispatch as conditional, Schenck told Milroy to be ready to evacuate but await further orders. Lincoln, monitoring this byplay at the War Department telegraph office, asked Hooker if he could aid Milroy — if the head of Lee's army was at Martinsburg and the tail at Fredericksburg, "the animal must be very slim somewhere. Could you not break him?" Hooker replied that just then he could not. On June 14 Lincoln snapped at Schenck, "Get Milroy from Winchester to Harper's Ferry if possible. He will be gobbled up, if he remains, if he is not already past salvation."

Milroy was already past salvation. On June 13 Dick Ewell's swift marchers reached the Winchester post and did indeed gobble it up. Only Milroy and a third of his men escaped, leaving behind 4,000 prisoners and rich stocks of supplies. Coldly determined to rein in Hooker, Halleck was not moved by Milroy's disaster to cede Fighting Joe any independent command authority in the growing campaign.[19]

On June 10 Hooker had proposed a second countermove to Lee's invasion: Leave sufficient force "to check, if not to stop his invasion," and march on Richmond with the rest of the Potomac army. By report Richmond was empty but for a provost guard. "If left to operate from my own judgment . . . I do not hesitate to say that I should adopt this course as being the most speedy and certain mode of giving the rebellion a mortal blow." This was a bold, highly speculative idea, with many moving parts to consider and very little time to do so. But as with Hooker's June 5 scheme to strike at the enemy's rear, the president was unwilling to trust his general to operate entirely from his own judgment. As before (said Lincoln), "I would not go South of the Rappahannock, upon Lee's moving North of it. . . . I think *Lee's* Army, and not *Richmond*, is your true objective point." Follow "on the inside track, shortening your lines, whilst he lengthens his. Fight him when opportunity offers."[20]

One of Joe Hooker's innovations was the Bureau of Military Information, the Army of the Potomac's first successful intelligence-gathering unit. Its chief officers, from left: George H. Sharpe, John C. Babcock, Frederick L. Manning, and John McEntee.

Alfred Pleasonton had delivered scarcely a trace of usable intelligence to McClellan, and he proved equally unhelpful to Hooker, projecting (for example) Pittsburgh as the Rebels' target. But the Bureau of Military Information gained intelligence on enemy movements from a contraband, vouched for by B.M.I. interrogator John McEntee. That was enough for Joe Hooker. On June 13 he set the Potomac army on the march north. Initially his advance comprised two columns, the westernmost Reynolds's First Corps, Sickles's Third, Meade's Fifth, Howard's Eleventh, and Pleasonton's cavalry. In parallel to the east marched Hancock's Second Corps, Sedgwick's Sixth, Slocum's Twelfth, and the reserve artillery. Hooker led the eastern column, John Reynolds the western column.

Earlier Hooker had assured Lincoln that George Meade was his ablest corps commander. Now he apparently thought otherwise. Meade wrote his wife that due to all the talk of his being put forward for the army command, Hooker "has got a spite against me and is determined to show it, and thinks putting me under Reynolds will be the sharpest thing he can do." Whatever his motive, Hooker voiced no regrets naming Reynolds to the wing command: "I never had an officer under me acquit himself so handsomely."[21]

On June 15 in Washington Gideon Welles entered in his diary, "Something of a panic pervades the city this evening. Singular rumors of rebel advances into Maryland. It is said they have reached Hagerstown, and some of them have penetrated as far as Chambersburg." The president called out 100,000 militia for six months' service from Pennsylvania, Maryland, Ohio, and West Virginia. Out of this deepening crisis sprang the name of George Brinton McClellan. Washington tipster T. J. Barnett claimed "McClellan stock was pulsating in the market."

The *New York Herald* took the lead in urging the general be recalled to lead the Army of the Potomac, or at least to lead an army of state militias against the invaders. Such McClellan partisans as artillerist Charles Wainwright seconded the notion: "Nine-tenths of us would look upon McClellan's being placed in command as better than a reinforcement of 25,000 men." Pennsylvania editor Alexander K. McClure thought recalling McClellan "would be the best thing that could be done." Lincoln's reply was dismissive: "Do we gain anything by opening one leak to stop another? Do we gain any thing by quieting one clamor, merely to open another, and probably a larger one?" Little Mac would not again take the field.[22]

"The information sent here by General Pleasonton is very unsatisfactory," Halleck complained. Hooker and Reynolds prodded the cavalry chief for actual, timely sightings of the Rebel forces rather than guesses. Soon enough the Loudoun Valley, east of the Shenandoah, became a cavalry battleground, with Jeb Stuart fending off the attempts of the Yankee troopers to find Lee's army and develop its intentions. There were sharp fights at Aldie (June 17), Middleburg (June 19), and Upperville (June 21), but Stuart's cavalry screen was unbroken and Lee's army unseen.

Hooker followed Lincoln's inside track, covering Washington and Baltimore. He shared no confidences with his generals. "I am as much in the dark as to proposed plans, here on the ground, as you are in Philada," Meade grumbled to his wife. "This is what Joe Hooker thinks profound sagacity, keeping his corps commanders, who are to execute his plans, in total ignorance of them. . . ."

Sam Heintzelman, in command at Washington, told his diary, "The whole North is aroused & Lee's army will not escape if our Generals are worth the parchment their commissions are written on," but he added, "There is very little confidence felt in the Army by the higher officers, or by civilians in Hooker's abilities." John Gibbon was of like mind: "We have, I think, sufficient force to defeat the enemy if it is properly managed. All we want is some competent man to direct matters and I should not be much surprised at any moment to hear of some change." Marsena Patrick thought Hooker adrift. "He acts like a man without a plan and is entirely at a loss what to do. His role now is that of Macawber, 'waiting for something to turn up,' & when something turns up, he plays like a gambler."

In fact Joe Hooker had a plan, as he explained to Chief of Staff Butterfield. General Lee, said Hooker, would duplicate his crossing of 1862. "They are finding great fault with me that I do not attempt to prevent his crossing. Why, I would lay the bridges for him. . . ." On a map of southern Pennsylvania he pointed to the area of Gettysburg, where the battle would be fought, and said, "If Lee escapes with his army the country are entitled to and should have my head for a football." This, to be sure, was Butterfield's after-the-fact recollection, yet it has the inflection of a Joe Hooker boast. There is contemporaneous evidence as well. In a private letter dated June 20, the B.M.I.'s Colonel Sharpe wrote that Lee "must whip us before he goes in force to Md. or Penna. If he don't, we propose to let him go, and when we get behind him we would like to know how many men he will take back." Hooker would not offer battle in the constricting valleys and ranges of western Maryland, but follow Lee across the Potomac, threaten his communications, find a battleground in the open country of southern Pennsylvania . . . and this time manage the fighting under his own eye. "I could choose my position and compel him to attack me," Hooker testified. He understood his open-ended, wait-and-see scheme would not play well to nervous Washington and panicky governors, so he hedged his prospects. This engaged him in rising conflict with Henry Halleck.[23]

Hooker began to duel the general-in-chief over manpower. Citing Pleasonton's estimate of Confederate strength as three corps of 30,000 men each, with 10,000 cavalry (the B.M.I. had yet to estimate Lee's marching strength), setting that against Butterfield's figure for the fighting strength of the Army of the Potomac as 91,400 (with twenty regiments of short-termers still to leave), Hooker felt duty-bound to call for reinforcements. Halleck steadfastly denied him use of the Washington and Valley garrisons. When the Pennsylvania Reserves division returned to the Potomac army, it was one brigade short, held back for the capital's defense. Only on June 25, with the Rebels in Pennsylvania, did Halleck release these troops, and three infantry brigades and a cavalry division. None benefited Joe Hooker.

Hooker glumly watched his special relationship with the president unravel, and his resolution grew strained as the campaign quickened. He could not mistake Washington's lack of trust in him, or the lack of trust by his lieutenants. He knew the army command was offered to John Reynolds, knew that George Meade was the officer corps' choice to succeed him. He had quarreled with Meade and with John Sedgwick. Darius Couch refused to serve under him, Henry Slocum tried his best not to serve under him. Otis Howard he considered incompetent. He barely spoke with anyone other than Dan Sickles and Dan Butterfield and Alfred Pleasonton. Hooker seems to have counted on a display of good generalship on his part being enough to win back his lieutenants. But for the root of his trials he blamed Henry Halleck.

With battle perhaps just around the next corner, George Meade concluded it was too late now to change commanders. In a bout of introspection (writing to his wife, Margaret), Meade appraised his own qualifications apropos the army command, present and past. None could say, he wrote, "I was a *drunkard* or *an unprincipled intriguer,* who had risen by *criticising* & *defaming* my predecessors & superiors. They could not say I was incompetent because I have not been tried, & so far as I have been tried, I have been singularly successful. They could not say I had never been under fire (as by the by is said & truly of McClellan) because it is notorious no General officer, not even Fighting Joe himself has been in more battles, or more exposed." It was, he admitted, fair to ask — did he have the capacity to handle successfully a large army? He did not anticipate that test.[24]

On the morning of June 16 Hooker unburdened himself in a telegram to Lincoln: "You have long been aware, Mr. President, that I have not enjoyed the confidence of the major-general commanding the army, and I can assure you so long as this continues we may look in vain for success, especially as future operations will require our relations to be more dependent upon each other than heretofore."

Lincoln responded with a private letter that sought to reason with this latest discontented commanding general. He downplayed the feud with Halleck. "If you and he would use the same frankness to one another, and to me, that I use to both of you, there would be no difficulty. I need and must have the professional skill of both, and yet these suspicions tend to deprive me of both." Such matters paled before the opportunity awaiting them. "As it looks to me, Lee's now returning toward Harper's Ferry gives you back the chance that I thought McClellan lost last fall. . . . Now, all I ask is that you will be in such mood that we can get into our action the best cordial judgment of yourself and General Halleck. . . ." This was apparently intended to soften the blow that Lincoln delivered at day's end. "To remove all misunderstanding," he telegraphed Hooker, "I now place you in the strict military relation to Gen. Halleck. . . . I shall direct him to give you orders, and you to obey them."[25]

Hooker continued silent as to his plans. Cabinet minister Montgomery Blair reported, "The President said today he got rid of McC because he let Lee get the better of him in the race to Richmond & he seemed to have it in his mind that if Hooker got beat in the present race — he would make short work of him." Gideon Welles thought Lincoln was whistling in the dark. He quoted the president: "How much depends in military matters on one master-mind. Hooker may commit the same fault as McClellan and lose his chance. We shall soon see, but it appears to me he cant help but win."

By June 25 firm intelligence put Ewell's corps well into Pennsylvania and the rest of Lee's army crossing the Potomac to follow. Hooker started the Potomac army across the river. He ordered cavalry to Gettysburg, his point of possible collision, to "see what they can of the movements of the enemy."[26]

On June 27 Harper's Ferry became an issue. Hooker wanted to evacuate the post; he wanted "every available man to use on the field." Halleck replied that much expense had been expended on the works at Harper's Ferry. (He had used the same argument in September 1862 to retain the garrison at Harper's Ferry — for Stonewall Jackson's benefit, as it turned out.) "I cannot approve their abandonment, except in case of absolute necessity." So began a daylong, defining struggle over decision making in the Potomac army.

Hooker inspected Harper's Ferry and shot back, "I find 10,000 men here, in condition to take the field. Here they are of no earthly account . . . a bait for the rebels." He wanted them for a move of his own. Without notice to Halleck, he ordered William French, commanding at Harper's Ferry, to evacuate the post and reinforce the Twelfth Corps to operate against Lee's communications. Hooker's order rested on his claim to manage the army according to his best judgment of the case. (Or as John Reynolds had put it, without at every turn "consulting with 'Stanton and Halleck' at Washington.") Hooker wanted his views validated by Lincoln and Stanton. Halleck was of a different mind.

When French wired the evacuation order to Washington for confirmation, Halleck saw his opening. Rather than Harper's Ferry being bait to the Rebels, he made Harper's Ferry bait to catch Joe Hooker. (There was no mistaking Halleck's conviction in the matter. "Hooker was more than a failure," he would tell U. S. Grant. "Had he remained in command, he would have lost the army and the capital.") In French's account, Hooker's evacuation order was "countermanded in the afternoon." Halleck phrased the countermand deliberately: "Pay no attention to General Hooker's orders."

When French showed this to Hooker, he reacted just as Halleck anticipated he would. He could not submit to the restrictions placed on his command role, Hooker telegraphed, "and earnestly request that I may at once be relieved from the position I occupy." Halleck blandly replied, "Your dispatch has been duly referred for Executive action."

Executive action was swift. The president had not intervened in Halleck's plotting, recognizing that Hooker's resignation was the best way out of a dilemma — no one, it appeared, retained trust in Fighting Joe. No doubt Lincoln accepted the resignation with private regret, yet no doubt with relief at this solution to the glaring problem of Joe Hooker. Lincoln named George Gordon Meade commander of the Army of the Potomac. No other names were considered; the likely candidates had taken themselves out of the running.[27]

Halleck began his instructions to General Meade, "Considering the circumstances, no one ever received a more important command." Except that he cover Washington and Baltimore, no restrictions were placed on him; and specifically, "Harper's Ferry and its garrison are under your direct orders." (That, for Joe Hooker, confirmed Halleck's perfidy.) As a measure of the emergency, "You are authorized to remove from command, and to send from your army, any officer or other person you may deem proper, and to appoint to command as you may deem expedient." This grant had Secretary of War Stanton's imprimatur. Meade could fire and hire without regard to seniority or anything else.

A special train carried James Hardie of the War Department to Fifth Corps headquarters near Frederick in Maryland. At 2:00 a.m. June 28 Meade's aide James Biddle recorded Colonel Hardie arriving "with some mysterious communication for Genl. Meade." As he had when replacing McClellan with Burnside, Secretary Stanton ordered the paperwork go first to the new commanding general, but not for fear of a coup by the deposed general. Hardie was told to make it clear: Meade was not offered the job — he was ordered to it.

Meade wrote Margaret the next day, "Yesterday morning at 3 am I was awakened from my sleep by an officer from Washington entering my tent & after waking me up saying he had come to give me trouble. At first I thought it was either to relieve or to arrest me & promptly replied to him that my conscience was clear. . . ." He read the order assigning him to the

Major General George Gordon Meade, the Army of the Potomac's newest commander, led a brigade in the Seven Days and fought in the army's every campaign since then.

command. "Ah Dearest you know how reluctant we both have been to see me placed in this position, and as it appears to be God's will for some good purpose . . . as a soldier I had nothing to do but accept & exert my utmost abilities to command success. This so help me God I will do. . . ."

At daybreak that Sunday, June 28, Meade and Hardie rode to army headquarters for the change of command. Hooker was aware of Hardie's arrival and anticipated his purpose. Chief of Staff Butterfield was called in and there was discussion about the current state of the army. When Meade emerged from the tent he was met by his son, an aide on his staff. Looking grave, but "with a familiar twinkle of the eye," Meade turned to him and said quietly, "Well, George, I am in command of the Army of the Potomac."[28]

In reporting the command change to a surprised cabinet, Lincoln said that as conflict became imminent, he observed in Hooker "the same failings that were witnessed in McClellan after the battle of Antietam. A want of alacrity to obey, and a greedy call for more troops which could not, and ought not to be taken from other points." When denied the Harper's Ferry garrison, Hooker "had taken umbrage" and resigned. (Treasury Secretary Chase, Gideon Welles noted, "was disturbed more than he cared should appear." It seemed that Chase's protégés — McDowell, McClellan, Pope, now Hooker — had not repaid his patronage.) Lincoln did not refer to the upheaval in the officer corps, but he was sensitive to that issue and it surely shaped his decision. If, as he had been told repeatedly, George Meade was the choice of the Potomac army's generals, this change ought to calm them and align them behind the new commander.

"We reached here last night and I was delighted, on the road, to hear that Genl Meade was in command of the army . . . ," John Gibbon wrote his wife from Frederick. "I now feel my confidence restored & believe we shall whip these fellows." Alpheus Williams "rejoiced at the change of commanders . . . now with a gentleman and a soldier in command I have renewed confidence that we shall at least do enough to preserve our honor and the safety of the Republic." Captain George Meade, the general's son, wrote his mother, "I never saw such universal satisfaction, everyone is delighted. Reynolds, Slocum & Sedgwick have all given in and behaved very well. . . . I think Papa will receive all the assistance the other Corps commanders can give him."

Officer corps morale leaped upward at the command change, but reaction in the ranks was muted. Hooker's reforms in the essentials of a soldier's life — food, shelter, medical care, restored routine — were well established and widely approved. But by now veterans shrugged at this army's command changes. They simply wanted someone to lead them to a victory now and then, and until then they would withhold judgment. It was much the same in Washington. As Lincoln's secretary John Nicolay put it, General Meade "is a good officer so far as he has been tried, but as we have had six different commanders fail in the task he assumes it is idle to say in advance whether or not he will make the seventh."[29]

Joe Hooker bid his chiefs and staff a personal farewell. He explained that he had ordered the troops at Harper's Ferry to reinforce him, and when denied them he could not submit to such treatment and resigned. He said he "had gone into the Army of the Potomac at the beginning, & he had hopes to have gone through with it to the end," but it was not to be. "His farewell to us all was sad and I could not but feel for him," wrote staff man Thomas Hyde, "though I am glad he is going." In his order turning over the command Hooker termed General Meade "a brave and accomplished officer, who has nobly earned the confidence and esteem of this army on many a well-fought field." Charles Wainwright applauded. "His farewell order is excellent, the most modest of all his productions."

When the hurt wore off, Joe Hooker would find pride in his five months commanding the Army of the Potomac. He lifted that army by its bootstraps out of the slough of the Burnside era, and made it (in his eyes at least) "the finest army on the planet." He reformed its intelligence gathering, and reorganized to great advantage both the cavalry and the artillery. He rebuilt it strong enough to survive defeat in May . . . and strong enough in July to meet its greatest test since its founding.

(Hooker always demonstrated a willingness to fight, and after a month —and a campaign— Mr. Lincoln tried to slip him back into the Army of the Potomac. "I have not thrown Gen. Hooker away," he wrote Meade, asking if it would be agreeable for Hooker "to take a corps under you." Meade was to respond "in perfect freedom," but this was the commander-in-chief speaking and Meade had to say, "I shall be very glad to have the benefit" of General Hooker's services. He made his real feelings clear to his wife: "It would be very difficult for Hooker to be quiet under me or any one else, and I sincerely trust . . . it will not be necessary to send him here." Hooker said he would accept the offer if it was still open. When Halleck got wind of this he sent word to Meade to not let it happen. Meade squirmed out from under, saying he would take Hooker if ordered, but he "neither entertained nor expressed any desire upon the subject." Fighting Joe did not rejoin the Potomac army.)[30]

• • •

George Gordon Meade was forty-seven, West Point class of 1835, old army except for a six-year interval (1836–42) in civilian life as a civil engineer. In Mexico he served as an engineer under Zachary Taylor. Correspondent Charles Coffin described him as "tall, thin, a little stooping in the shoulders, quick, comprehending the situation of affairs in an instant, energetic. . . ." Capable, reliable, God-fearing, carrying no baggage as outsider (Pope), as inexperienced (Burnside), as dubious of reputation (Hooker), Meade simply by his appointment brought order to a disordered officer corps. As he noted in his self-appraisal, his battle experience matched or exceeded even Fighting Joe's. Going to war on the Peninsula with the Pennsylvania Reserves, Meade fought his brigade at Gaines's Mill and Glendale, where he was badly wounded, recovered in time for Second Bull Run, then led the Reserves division with distinction at South Mountain, Antietam, and Fredericksburg, and the Fifth Corps at Chancellorsville. But Meade also had a dark side. One of his staff observed "the most singular patches of gunpowder in his disposition, which exploding suddenly, are then gone." George Meade tolerated neither fools nor foibles.

Meade had personal and professional respect for five of his seven corps commanders — Reynolds, Hancock, Sykes (now heading the Fifth Corps), Sedgwick, and Slocum. After Chancellorsville he had doubts about Otis Howard. About Dan Sickles he had grave doubts. He had remarked Sickles's bad influence on Hooker, especially his vote to retreat from Chancellorsville, and he would keep a wary eye on him.

The Pennsylvania campaign Meade found himself leading came at a potentially decisive moment. In Mississippi Grant's bold campaign had left Vicksburg besieged, and on June 24 he reported its capture would "only be a question of time." Complementing a promised major victory in the West with a major victory in the East might well tip the war's balance. Like the previous September, Lincoln saw Lee's crossing the Potomac as a rare opportunity. McClellan had missed that chance. Lincoln hoped Meade would not miss this one.

Meade's officer corps little resembled McClellan's of a year earlier. All McClellan's corps commanders — Sumner, Heintzelman, Keyes, Porter, Franklin — were gone from the Potomac army. Six other corps commanders had come and gone in ensuing campaigns — Sigel, Banks, McDowell, Couch, and Mansfield and Reno killed in battle. Of the eleven divisional commanders in the Seven Days, only Sedgwick, Sykes, and Slocum remained to fight under Meade. Over that year, too, battle killed six divisional infantry commanders — Richardson, Kearny, Stevens, Rodman, Whipple, and Berry — and the cavalry's Bayard. But McClellan's and

Meade's commands were alike in one regard: Each had the overall respect of his officer corps.[31]

Meade set as his first need a chief of staff. Seth Williams, the army's capable adjutant general, said the position was more than he could take on. Gouverneur Warren told his wife, "I was spoken to about being Chief of Staff, but I prefer not to take it." Meade offered the post to Andrew Humphreys, but after discussion Humphreys "declined or deferred it." Incumbent Dan Butterfield was the only one just then who knew where all the pieces of this sprawling army were to be found. Butterfield would in due course betray Meade's trust, but in the next ten critical days he was a dutiful chief of staff.

On June 28, his first day of command, Meade was prompt to issue orders for the next day's march. The Confederate army was said to form a broad arc across southern Pennsylvania, from Chambersburg in the Cumberland Valley and stretching north by east to Harrisburg. Meade picked up the reins where Hooker dropped them. He retained John Reynolds in command of the left wing — Reynolds's First Corps, Sickles's Third, Howard's Eleventh. Hancock's Second Corps and Slocum's Twelfth formed the center. The right wing comprised Sykes's Fifth Corps and Sedgwick's Sixth. The cavalry probe Hooker had directed to the road center of Gettysburg proceeded under John Buford. "Our troops are making tremendous marches some of these days just past," wrote Captain Samuel Fiske, "and, if the enemy is anywhere, we shall be likely to find him and feel of him pretty soon."

The B.M.I. counted Lee's army as of June 27 as 80,000 infantry (cavalry uncounted) and 275 artillery pieces. The count was updated on June 30 (by untutored civilian observers) to 100,000 infantry and cavalry. This overcounted by some 20 percent, but set against his own June 30 return of 104,256 meant that Meade faced battle unburdened by the long-standing Potomac army delusions about enemy numbers. "I am going straight at them, and will settle this thing one way or the other . . . ," Meade told his wife. "We have been reinforced so as to have equal numbers with the enemy. . . ."[32]

By June 30 Meade had formed a plan. On Parr's Ridge, overlooking Pipe Creek just below the Maryland-Pennsylvania line, he would gather his army to receive the enemy. His idea was for Reynolds's left wing to engage the Confederates and then fall back, drawing them onto the Pipe Creek line. But events moved swiftly, and the Pipe Creek plan miscarried. Still, it signaled Meade's thinking. He intended to fight defensively, on ground of his choosing. He believed the Potomac army, especially its officer corps, to be unsettled and uncertain after two consecutive defeats. He believed himself too new in the saddle to attempt the challenges of an offensive. In a circular to his generals, he devoted twenty paragraphs to defense and one sentence to attack.

In late morning on June 30 John Buford led two cavalry brigades into Gettysburg and set about searching out the enemy. General Buford, wrote one of Meade's staff, was "a compactly built man of middle height, with a tawny moustache and a little, triangular gray eye, whose expression is determined, not to say sinister." Buford served Pope as an intelligence gatherer at Second Bull Run, gaining his brigadier's star. Leading a division under Pleasonton, he gained notice as a skilled fighter. John Gibbon, not generous with compliments, called Buford "the best cavalryman I ever saw."

Buford's scouts developed a picture of a menacing enemy, marching on Gettysburg in force from the west, and likely from the north as well. (General Lee, discovering the Federal pursuit, was pulling his scattered army together.) One of Buford's colonels spoke confidently of holding his position for twenty-four hours. "No you won't," Buford told him. "They will attack you in the morning and they will come 'booming' — skirmishers three deep. You will have to fight like the devil to hold your own until supports arrive."[33]

Buford was prescient. By 5:00 a.m. on Wednesday, July 1, A. P. Hill's corps was marching eastward on the Chambersburg Turnpike for Gettysburg. Buford had Meade's orders for the day: Cavalry well out front, "giving timely notice of positions and movements of the enemy." That Buford was already doing. More important to him was Meade's order directing the First Corps to Gettysburg, with the Eleventh Corps in support. Recognizing Gettysburg as a favorable battleground, Buford took a major, and independent, decision. The enemy would get there first unless (as he put it) "arrangements were made for entertaining him until General Reynolds could reach the scene."

Buford's entertainment was a defense in depth on a series of ridgelines west of Gettysburg, Herr's Ridge, McPherson's Ridge, Seminary Ridge closest to the town. At 7:30 a.m. Lieutenant Marcellus E. Jones, 8th Illinois Cavalry, fired the first shot of the Battle of Gettysburg. The Confederates, expecting nothing more than local militia, were surprised to find Buford's 2,950 troopers fighting dismounted as infantry. Buford's tactic bought much-needed time. But at 10:10 he signaled Meade that Hill's

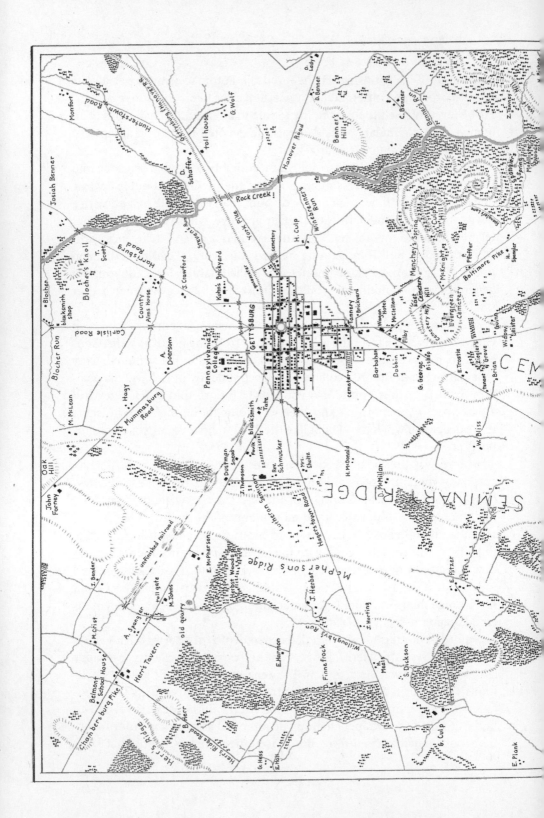

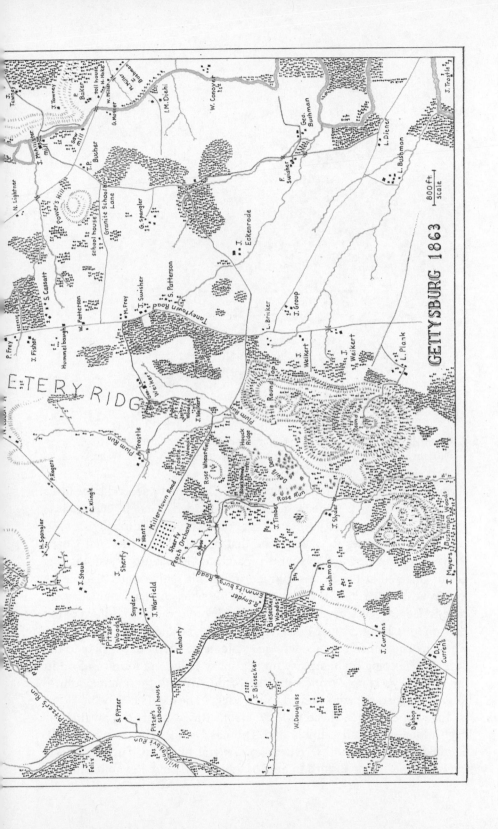

GETTYSBURG 1863

800 ft.
scale

The First Corps' John Reynolds, in command of the Potomac army's left wing, killed on McPherson's Ridge on the first day of Gettysburg. By Alfred Waud.

corps was driving in his forces "very rapidly," and that a second large force was pressing his picket line facing north. He added, "General Reynolds is advancing, and is within 3 miles of this point with his leading division."

Wing commander Reynolds rode that morning with the First Corps with no further instruction than to march to Gettysburg. Reynolds was deeply angered at the Rebels' plundering of his native state. "Hence he was in favor of striking them as soon as possible," Abner Doubleday recalled. "He was really eager to get at them." Word came from Buford of the fight on the Chambersburg Pike. Reynolds spurred ahead into Gettysburg, where he encountered "considerable excitement," then out the pike to the Lutheran Theological Seminary on Seminary Ridge. He found Buford in the seminary's cupola overseeing the battle. "What's the matter, John?" Reynolds called out, and Buford called back, "The devil's to pay!"

Together they rode ahead to McPherson's Ridge, where the cavalry under Colonels William Gamble and Thomas Devin were taking a stand. Gamble called to Reynolds, "Hurry up, General, hurry up! They are breaking our line!" Telling Buford to hold as long as he could, Reynolds hurried back to James Wadsworth's lead division. He ordered Wadsworth to by-pass Gettysburg and march cross-lots toward the fighting. He sent messengers to hasten the march of Otis Howard's Eleventh Corps, and farther to the rear, Dan Sickles's Third Corps. His orders to Howard included posting a "proper reserve" of infantry and artillery on Cemetery Hill, high ground just south of the town.[34]

At Fredericksburg, his initial corps command, John Reynolds hewed to his orders capably enough, but he took no discretionary actions that might have reshaped the stalled attack. On July 1 Reynolds acted, in the absence of orders, decisively and without hesitation. Meade's June 30 instructions read that if the enemy "advance against me, I must concentrate at that point where they show the strongest force." Just now that point was looking like Gettysburg. Reynolds appraised the situation — Buford's cavalry not letting Gettysburg go without a fight; the presence of the First Corps and the pending support of the Eleventh Corps; the high ground immediately south of Gettysburg that looked eminently defensible — and he presented General Meade with a virtual fait accompli.

Reynolds called in his aide Stephen Weld: "He immediately sent me to General Meade, 13 or 14 miles off, to say that the enemy were coming on in strong force, and that he was afraid they would get the heights on the other side of the town; that he would fight them all through the town, however, and keep them back as long as possible." At 11:30 a.m., after a hard ride, Captain Weld delivered Reynolds's message to headquarters at Taneytown in Maryland. General Meade, he wrote, "seemed quite anxious about the matter, and said, 'Good God! if the enemy get Gettysburg, I am lost.'" Weld said Reynolds promised to barricade the streets of Gettysburg to hold back the Rebels, and Meade said, "Good! That is just like Reynolds."

Reynolds had meanwhile directed Wadsworth's division to the McPherson's Ridge battlefront. With a veteran division commander, Reynolds would probably have told him to consult with Buford and then manage his two brigades as the case required. But James Wadsworth was a politician (defeated for governor of New York in 1862) turned general, and today was his first combat command. Perhaps for that reason, wing commander Reynolds chose to manage the fighting himself, from the front, like a brigade commander. He rushed the Iron Brigade's regiments into action, shouting, "Forward men, forward for God's sake and drive those fellows out of the woods! . . . Double quick!" As he turned to urge on the next regiment, wrote his orderly Charles H. Veil, "a Minnie Ball struck him in the back of the neck, and he fell from his horse dead. He never spoke a word, or moved a muscle after he was struck. I have seen many men killed in action, but never saw a ball do its work so *instantly* as did the ball that struck General Reynolds." So perished the general who, had he chosen, would have commanded the Army of the Potomac that day.[35]

Abner Doubleday, leading the First Corps as senior division head, took field command. Wadsworth's two brigades picked up the fight from Buford's weary troopers. The Iron Brigade, John Gibbon's old command, formed the left of the McPherson's Ridge line. It was led by Indiana politician Solomon Meredith, known as Long Sol for his six-foot-seven-inch height. (Mr. Lincoln remarked Meredith as the only Quaker general in the army.) Lysander Cutler's brigade was on the right. Citizen-soldier Cutler was good enough that Gibbon, on being promoted, wanted him for the Iron Brigade, but Meredith had more political pull.

The fight expanded sharply. The Iron Brigade veterans drove back the first Rebel attackers, but on the right Cutler's brigade was nearly flanked. The inexperienced Wadsworth was slow to react, and Cutler complained, "We fight a little and run a little. There are no supports." Quickly Doubleday directed a reinforcement to Cutler that stabilized his front. Losses were heavy.

In the calm before the next storm, the other two First Corps divisions reached the field and Doubleday posted them. The two brigades of Thomas A. Rowley (succeeding Doubleday) reinforced the Iron Brigade on the left, and the two brigades of John C. Robinson went in alongside Cutler on the right. The line there angled to also face north in expectation of meeting a second enemy force. Charles Wainwright posted the batteries of the First Corps' artillery brigade.

At 11:30 a.m. Otis Howard reached the field, in advance of his Eleventh Corps, and found that Reynolds's death thrust him, as ranking general, into Reynolds's place leading the left wing. Howard recalled the press of responsibility: "But, I thought, God helping us, we will stay here till the army comes." John Buford, contemplating Howard in command, contemplating the situation generally, wrote to Meade: "For God's sake, send up Hancock. Everything at odds. Reynolds is killed, and we need a controlling spirit."[36]

Winfield Hancock was soon enough on General Meade's mind. Thanks to the B.M.I. and to Buford, Meade was well informed about the Rebels' approach. But at Taneytown he was 14 miles from the growing fight at Gettysburg. Still with hope for standing defensively at Pipe Creek, he hesitated taking up Reynolds's strong invitation to make the battle at Gettysburg instead. In a noon telegram to Washington he reported on the gathering enemy: "The news proves my advance has answered its purpose. I shall not advance any, but prepare to receive an attack in case Lee makes one." Gripped by indecision, Meade did not order Reynolds reinforced by Sickles's Third Corps, eight miles from Gettysburg, or by Slocum's Twelfth Corps, distant five miles. Then word reached him, about 1:00 p.m., that Reynolds had been killed.

George Meade was only too aware that without Reynolds's guiding hand, command in the army's left wing sank to mediocrity. Abner Doubleday, heading the First Corps, was considered a plodder. Meade had no confidence whatever in politician Dan Sickles, and hardly more confidence in Otis Howard — especially Otis Howard in overall command. He had trusted John Reynolds's judgment implicitly. Now he transferred the trust, and the command, to the Second Corps' Winfield Hancock. In making the change, it was pointed out that Howard was senior to Hancock. He could not help that, Meade said. He knew General Hancock, "but did not know General Howard so well; and that at this crisis he must have a man he knew and could trust." This was Meade's first exercise of the right to hire and fire granted him by Washington. (His second exercise jumped John Gibbon over his senior John Caldwell to command the Second Corps in Hancock's absence.)

By 1:30 Hancock was on his way to Gettysburg to take charge of the battlefield. He carried written orders to "assume command of the corps there assembled, viz, the Eleventh, First, and Third. . . . If you think the ground and position there a better one to fight a battle under existing circumstances, you will so advise the general, and he will order all the troops up."[37]

As the Eleventh Corps, under Carl Schurz now, reached Gettysburg, Howard posted it — the divisions of Alexander Schimmelfennig and Francis Barlow north of the town, confronting what cavalryman Buford warned was Dick Ewell's corps; and in reserve, Adolph von Steinwehr's division on Cemetery Hill south of the town, per Reynolds's earlier order. (Howard would afterward deny receiving Reynolds's order, thereby claiming credit for occupying Cemetery Hill on his own initiative. This is of a piece with Howard at Chancellorsville denying he received Hooker's orders to guard his flank.) The Confederates soon attacked in growing force, from the west against the First Corps, from the north against the Eleventh Corps.[38]

Howard made his headquarters on Cemetery Hill. Reynolds had briefed him the previous evening on Buford's sightings, and from what Buford and Doubleday now told him — and from the fighting unfolding before him—it was obvious the Confederates had a substantial advantage in numbers. Yet only at 1:00 p.m. did Howard send to the nearest support—Slocum's Twelfth Corps and Sickles's Third—and then only a bare-bones report: "Ewell's corps is advancing from York. The left wing . . . is engaging with A. P. Hill's corps." He said nothing of needing support, nothing of Reynolds's death, nothing of holding Gettysburg. Only at 1:30—two hours after reaching Gettysburg—did Howard send again to Slocum and Sickles, this time making it a call for help: "General Reynolds is killed. For God's sake, come up. Howard." Dan Sickles, high command black sheep, responded promptly, marching to the sound of the guns (which he could not yet hear). Henry Slocum, five miles from the fighting, hearing it plainly enough, made no response to Howard's messages.

Unimaginative, wedded to protocol (he was senior to Howard), Slocum recognized only Meade's priority, not Howard's. Howard's brother and aide Charles Howard termed Slocum "too willing to demonstrate the fitness of his name *Slow come*. In fact refused to come up in person saying *he would not assume the responsibility of that day's fighting & of those two corps.*" Another Howard staff man termed Slocum's conduct "anything but honorable, soldierly or patriotic. . . ." Slocum only marched to the battlefield in late afternoon, arriving too late. Dan Sickles arrived too late as well, but not for want of trying. The First and Eleventh Corps fought the battle of July 1 by themselves.[39]

West of Gettysburg, the First Corps had in McPherson's Ridge and Seminary Ridge something on which to anchor a defense. North of the town, however, the Eleventh Corps found militarily featureless terrain, except for a modest elevation called Blocher's Knoll on the far right. July 1 marked Francis Barlow's first battle in divisional command. At Glendale, his initial fight, he led a bayonet charge; at Antietam he searched out and turned the Rebels' Sunken Road position, taking a bad wound in the doing. Fueled today by his usual aggression, Barlow pushed out ahead with Leopold von Gilsa's brigade to seize Blocher's Knoll before the enemy occupied it. Barlow said he acted "as directed" by corps commander Schurz. Schurz said of Barlow's misjudged advance that he was "carried away by the ardor of the conflict." In consequence, Barlow's other brigade, under Adelbert Ames, and the two brigades of Schimmelfennig's division were stretched perilously thin trying to support Barlow and still stay tied to the First Corps.

Colonel von Gilsa's mostly German brigade contained but three regiments, and the Rebels storming Blocher's Knoll was a nightmare repeated—this same brigade had been the initial victim of Stonewall Jackson at

Chancellorsville. The defense of the knoll was brief, despite von Gilsa riding his lines "through a regular storm of lead, meanwhile using the German epithets so common to him." Barlow expected too much of these demoralized men: "We ought to have held the place easily. . . . But the enemies skirmishers had hardly attacked us before my men began to run." He later elaborated: "But these Dutch won't fight. Their officers say so & they say so themselves & they ruin all with whom they come in contact." Barlow fell seriously wounded rallying his faltering command. Confederate General John B. Gordon happened on him on the field and had him carried to the rear for medical care.[40]

Adelbert Ames graduated in West Point's class of 1861 that rushed off to war with the ink on their diplomas hardly dry. He had climbed from second lieutenant to brigadier general, and today was his first brigade command. The collapse of the Blocher's Knoll position left Ames flanked on the right. He tried to counter with an attack of his own, leading it (wisely) on foot, but the fire was now heavy from both front and flank. He fell back on Gettysburg along with the rest of Barlow's division, replacing Barlow in command. Ames summed up: "The whole division was falling back with little or no regularity, regimental organizations having become destroyed." Its flank in turn uncovered, Schimmelfennig's division also fell back in confusion. In hardly an hour of fighting, the Eleventh Corps lost 3,200 men, half its effective force, 1,400 of them as prisoners. The toll was greater, by some 25 percent, than its loss at Chancellorsville.

West of Gettysburg, meanwhile, the First Corps was putting up a strong, sustained fight. Henry Baxter, another first-time brigade commander, held the right of the line where it connected with the Eleventh Corps. Civilian-soldier Baxter had risen from regimental captain to brigadier general, suffering along the way wounds on the Peninsula, at Antietam, and at Fredericksburg. Confronting two brigades in succession, he defeated them both, ambushing the second and driving it in rout. "Up boys, and give them steel!" Baxter called, and they collected prisoners and three Rebel battle flags. Baxter withdrew to replenish ammunition and was replaced by Gabriel Paul's brigade. Paul, thirty years in the old army, was also new to his brigade. As he took up the fight to hold the hinge between the two corps, the retreat of Schimmelfennig's division left his right flank dangerously exposed.[41]

The First Corps' Abner Doubleday performed at his career best trying to hold together a crumbling front plagued by command losses. On the left the Iron Brigade's Long Sol Meredith was struck in the head by a shell fragment and incapacitated. On the right Gabriel Paul was hit in the face and blinded, and three colonels in turn taking over his brigade fell wounded. Brigadier Thomas Rowley, leading Doubleday's division, galloped about in drunken agitation, shouting incoherent orders, posting a brigade directly in front of one of Colonel Wainwright's batteries. Wainwright himself had to work around the unversed James Wadsworth, who would order batteries to the front without infantry support. When Wadsworth was not looking, Wainwright quietly ordered them back.

Otis Howard appeared stunned by the responsibility of battlefield command. Captain Stephen Weld, returned from delivering Reynolds's dispatch to Taneytown, found Howard watching the fighting alongside a battery on Cemetery Hill. Sighting an enemy battle line emerge from a wood, Weld said, "General, those are the rebs, why don't you fire at them?" Howard said they were Federals. "They are not, sir, they are the rebs," said Weld, his sighting soon enough confirmed by hostile fire. Doubleday's adjutant E. P. Halstead had a similar experience. Doubleday sent him to Howard for a reinforcement from von Steinwehr's division in reserve, or otherwise for permission to fall back to better ground. He was refused both. Halstead pointed out a Rebel column threatening Wadsworth's flank, but Howard said, "Those are nothing but rail fences, sir!" A Howard staff man raised his field glasses and reported, "General, those are long lines of the enemy." Perhaps Howard was nearsighted; certainly he was demoralized. In what Halstead described as "a tone of hopeless despair," Howard said to use Buford's cavalry for support.

John Buford's response to that directive was heated: "What in hell and damnation does he think I can do against those long lines of the enemy out there!" Still, he assembled his troopers for a mounted charge, with very doubtful prospects, but fortuitously the enemy advance halted. Buford reported to Pleasonton, "In my opinion, there seems to be no directing person. . . . P.S. — We need help now."[42]

There was no help. The collapse of the Eleventh Corps uncovered Doubleday's postings and threatened to cut them off. Howard finally ordered the First Corps to fall back to Cemetery Hill. General Wadsworth went defiantly: "We are giving the rebels hell with these guns, and I want to give them a few more shots before we leave." The Eleventh's retreat through Gettysburg's narrow streets was disordered, and many prisoners were taken. General Schimmelfennig only escaped by finding a backyard hiding place.

Major General Winfield Scott Hancock arrived on Cemetery Hill at the same time as the survivors of the two corps. He told Howard that he was sent by Meade "to take command of all the forces present." Howard pro-

HANCOCK AT GETTYSBURG—

Alfred Waud's pencil and watercolor study of Second Corps commander Winfield
Scott Hancock symbolizes the general's dominating role at Gettysburg.

tested that he was senior officer. "I am aware of that, General," said Hancock, "but I have written orders in my pocket from General Meade, which
I will show you." Howard could only give way. "I lost no time in conversation," Hancock recalled, "but at once rode away and bent myself to the
pressing task of making such dispositions as would prevent the enemy
from seizing that vital point." One disposition was to occupy Culp's Hill,
key high ground just to the southeast.

"Directing the placing of troops where we turned up was Hancock,
whose imperious and defiant bearing heartened us all," wrote a First
Corps soldier. Winfield Hancock indeed radiated presence — not McClellan parade ground presence, but battlefield presence that turned demoralized fugitives back into soldiers. To Orland Smith, commanding one of
von Steinwehr's brigades on Cemetery Hill, Hancock said, "This position
should be held at all hazards. Now, Colonel, can you hold it?" Smith said
he thought he could. Hancock repeated, forcefully, "Will you hold it?" and
got the answer he wanted — "I will!" Howard, by contrast, told Double-

day that von Steinwehr's men "would probably run off and desert their guns in case the enemy came," and asked him to save the Eleventh Corps' artillery. Fortunately the Confederate generals broke off pursuit, and by nightfall the Federals had the high ground secured and were reinforced by the Third and Twelfth Corps. Hancock reported to Meade, "We can fight here, as the ground appears not unfavorable with good troops." Howard reported to Meade that he led the fighting that day as well as "any of your corps commanders could have done," and being relieved of command "has mortified me and will disgrace me."

In due course, Howard retold events so that Hancock arrived at Gettysburg that afternoon merely to "represent" General Meade, to assist in Howard's labors that saved Cemetery Hill. (Hancock dismissed this reading as "incomprehensible" as to fact.) But Howard's most egregious invention was telling Hancock that evening that during the day's fighting Doubleday's First Corps collapsed first, not Howard's Eleventh Corps. Upon Hancock reporting this to Meade — "Howard says that Doubleday's command gave way" — Abner Doubleday was unjustly relieved of command, and Otis Howard escaped the obloquy he deserved.[43]

General Meade reached Gettysburg in the first moments of Thursday, July 2. Before leaving Taneytown he telegraphed Washington, "I see no other course than to hazard a general battle," and without waiting for Hancock's endorsement of Gettysburg as a battleground he issued marching orders to the rest of the army. On arrival, his generals assured him it was good ground to defend. "I am glad to hear you say so," Meade said, "for it is too late to leave it." With daylight, he told Carl Schurz he expected to have 95,000 men there that day, "enough, I guess, for this business." He added, glancing over the chosen battleground, "Well, we may as well fight it out here just as well as anywhere else." He would fight it out defensively on ground, if not his choice, at least the choice of trusted subordinates John Buford and John Reynolds.

The remnants of the First and Eleventh Corps needed sorting out. The First Corps' battle, managed about as best it could be, was very costly — 62 percent casualties. Reynolds was dead, acting corps commander Doubleday displaced (through Howard's deceit) by John Newton, four of the six brigade commanders wounded, and drunken division commander Thomas Rowley in arrest. Colonel Wainwright's artillery was in hand as was a Vermont brigade just up from Washington, but the rest of the First Corps was held in reserve. The Eleventh Corps survivors, clustered around von Steinwehr's division on Cemetery Hill, were condemned anew as the Flying Dutchmen. Of the Eleventh's other two division commanders, Barlow was wounded and captured, and Schimmelfennig missing and believed captured.

At first light on July 2, accompanied by Howard and Henry Hunt, Meade rode the lines posting infantry and artillery. To the north, Slocum's Twelfth Corps took position on Culp's Hill. Next, on Cemetery Hill, was Howard's thinned-out Eleventh Corps, braced by artillery and backed by the First Corps. From there the line extended southward along Cemetery Ridge, manned by Hancock's Second Corps and Sickles's Third, as far as Little Round Top; beyond was more imposing Round Top. George Sykes's Fifth Corps was in reserve behind the center, with Hunt's artillery reserve. At hand were reinforcements Halleck had denied Joe Hooker — the Pennsylvania Reserves division for the Fifth Corps, and a brigade each for the First, Second, and Twelfth Corps. (John Sedgwick's big Sixth Corps would arrive at day's end, after a forced march of 35 miles in nineteen hours.) At midday Gouverneur Warren wrote his wife, "We are now all in line of battle before the enemy in a position where we cannot be *beaten* but fear being turned."

Meade was indeed concerned that the enemy massed to the north might curl around Culp's Hill and into the Federal rear. He plotted a spoiling attack there by the Twelfth and Fifth Corps, under Slocum. Engineer Gouverneur Warren argued against it due to "the character of the ground." Meade gave up the idea, but Slocum unaccountably still considered himself head of a two-corps right wing, and turned the Twelfth Corps over to Alpheus Williams for the rest of the battle.[44]

Meade and Dan Sickles had earlier struck sparks, with Meade critical of the Third Corps' march discipline. Today, tensely awaiting General Lee's initiative, sparks flew again. Sickles expressed himself unhappy with his assigned position. Ordered to hold Cemetery Ridge to the south of the Second Corps, he found that the ridgeline dropped to level as it reached Little Round Top, seeming not very defensible. Meade repeated to him: Join his right with Hancock's left, and anchor his left on Little Round Top. Sickles asked if there was any flexibility in those instructions. "Certainly," said Meade, "within the limits of the general instructions I have given to you. . . ." Promptly, without notice to anyone, Sickles completely violated those instructions.

Three-quarters of a mile beyond his lines was a peach orchard on a modest elevation. To amateur soldier Sickles this looked like better ground to defend, and he ordered David Birney's and Andrew Humphreys's divisions forward to occupy it. From the Second Corps lines Winfield Han-

Alfred Waud sketched Gouverneur
Warren with a signalman, seeking
defenders for Little Round Top.

cock and John Gibbon watched this movement in astonishment. As a bystander reported, "Gibbon & Hancock both exclaimed, what in hell can
that man Sickles be doing!"

Sickles's blunder created a huge salient in the Federal line, subject to assault from three sides and so thinly manned that neither left nor right was
attached to anything. At 3:00 p.m. Meade was convening a conference of
corps commanders at headquarters when he learned of Sickles's adventuring. When Sickles arrived, and before he could dismount, Meade told him
"in a few sharp words" to return his command to the position he had been
instructed to take. "I never saw General Meade so angry if I may so call it,"
wrote one of the staff. Presently Meade followed after Sickles to inspect his
position.

When historian John C. Ropes interviewed Meade some months
later, Ropes's notes reveal a general still angry. Discovering the major
gap opened between the Second and Third Corps, Meade braced Sickles "and asked him where the devil his troops were. 'Out here, sir,' says
Sickles, and pointed to positions half or three-quarters of a mile in advance. Meade asked what the devil they were out there for. . . ." The new
position was neutral ground between the two sides, said Meade; nei-

ther could hold it. Should he pull back? Sickles asked. He might try, said Meade, but explained, "You cannot hold this position, but the enemy will not let you get away without a fight. . . ." That was hardly spoken when Lee opened his attack . . . on the Third Corps. Should he still withdraw? Sickles asked. "I wish to God you could," said Meade, "but the enemy won't let you!"[45]

Meade had not waited on his inspection of Sickles's bungling before trying to compensate for it. He sent his reserve, Sykes's Fifth Corps, to back up the Third Corps with all speed. Engineer Warren was sent to see if Sickles was anchored on Little Round Top as ordered. Henry Hunt ordered up five batteries from the artillery reserve to support the left. "All was astir on our crest," wrote staff man Frank Haskell. "— Generals and their Staffs were galloping hither and thither. . . ."

Lee's offensive, under Longstreet's command, crashed like successive breakers against the Third Corps sector — against Little Round Top, which overlooked the entire Cemetery Ridge line; against the jumbled terrain in front of Little Round Top manned by David Birney's division; against the Peach Orchard area defended by Andrew Humphreys's division. When Warren reached Little Round Top he was appalled. Except for a flag-signal station, it was empty of Yankees. Sighting an advancing Rebel column hardly a mile away, Warren dispatched a warning to Meade, and sent his aide Ranald S. Mackenzie to tell Sickles to man this key ground as he had been ordered. Sickles "refused to do so, stating that his whole command was necessary to defend his front."

Mackenzie turned to the Fifth Corps, on the march toward the left. Without hesitation, George Sykes ordered his lead brigade, under Colonel Strong Vincent, to Warren. Warren himself rushed to the Fifth Corps. He came on his old brigade, now under Stephen H. Weed, and Colonel Patrick H. O'Rorke's 140th New York. "Paddy!" he shouted, "Give me a regiment!" O'Rorke said he was told to support the Third Corps. "Never mind that," said Warren, "bring your regiment up here and I will take the responsibility." He had the rest of Weed's brigade follow. Little Round Top would be defended.[46]

David Birney's division was staggered by the Rebels' opening assault. Birney bore an inconstant command history. As a citizen-soldier he had learned his trade under Phil Kearny on the Peninsula, but at Seven Pines he became the victim in a dispute over whose orders to obey, Kearny's or Heintzelman's. At Fredericksburg, pledging to Reynolds's orders, he refused Meade's calls to march to the sound of the guns. Today he broke up command unity by repeatedly reaching into one brigade for a regiment or two to patch holes in another brigade. Régis de Trobriand had lost two regiments in this manner when Birney called for a third. Tell General Birney, Colonel de Trobriand replied, that "far from being able to furnish reinforcements to any one, I shall be in need of them myself in less than a quarter of an hour." As was indeed the case.

Birney's men fought stubbornly to hold on to what became battlefield landmarks — Devil's Den, Rose's Woods, the Wheatfield, the Peach Orchard — but were pressed back as if by an avalanche, as de Trobriand described it. He led his brigade in a counterattack to buy time. "I came back covered with dust and glory . . . ," he wrote his daughter, "and after the fight, my men 'cheered' me with three hurrahs, so I need not prove myself as an 'acting Brigade General,' on the field of battle." Hobart Ward's brigade held the far left. Ward had joined the army as a private in 1842, was wounded at Monterrey in 1847, and rejoined in 1861 as colonel, 38th New York. Like Birney, Ward trained under Phil Kearny. He managed a fighting retreat through Devil's Den, escaping with a bullet-riddled hat.

The first supports to arrive were two brigades of James Barnes's Fifth Corps division. (Barnes's third brigade, Strong Vincent's, was directed to Little Round Top.) This was General Barnes's initial battle command — replacing the veteran Charles Griffin, on sick leave — and he misread the field and ordered his reinforcements to pull back. That meant, de Trobriand noted dryly, "Our position was no longer tenable." Barnes fell wounded by a shell fragment, ending his brief field service.

In the Peach Orchard, Charles Graham, a Dan Sickles protégé, got only four of his six regiments to a battle line already stretched too thin and had his flank turned. In the retreat Graham was hit twice and captured. This uncovered the Rhode Island battery of Lieutenant John K. Bucklyn. "I limber up and move slowly to the rear," Bucklyn told his diary. "I have got a case shot through my left shoulder and feel faint. My battery is torn and shattered and my brave boys have gone, never to return. Curse the rebels."[47]

Sickles's misadventure not only left the Third Corps' flanks in the air but its overstretched battle line was absent any reserves. Birney cannibalized one brigade to try and save another, and as the Rebel offensive widened, Sickles cannibalized Andrew Humphreys's division on the right. George Burling's brigade was so picked over that he soon reported not a soldier to his name. This "ruinous habit" was no way to manage a battle, Humphreys told his wife. "They had taken away my reserve brigade to support others, & a large part of my second line I had to bring to my front line & part of it went to others. . . . I remonstrated but uselessly. Finally having driven back the others, the enemy in my front advanced upon me, while those on my left having forced off our troops also gave their attention to me. I have lost very heavily."

Meade's quick action in starting the Fifth Corps to the Third Corps sector before the first shots at least forestalled an immediate collapse of Sickles's line. It was the usual practice for a reinforcing column to come under command of the general on the scene directing the fighting, but Sykes refused "any call from the commander of the Third Corps . . . ; the key of the battle-field was intrusted to my keeping, and I could not and would not jeopardize it by a division of my forces." To be sure, General Sykes released two brigades to Gouverneur Warren for Little Round Top, but nothing to the likes of a Dan Sickles. Sickles was not long in seeking more help. Meade ordered Winfield Hancock to send a Second Corps division to the endangered left — not to report to Sickles but to "General Sykes, commanding Fifth Corps. . . ." Hancock gave the order — "Caldwell, you get your division ready."

John C. Caldwell, the school principal from Maine, was berated at Antietam by Israel Richardson for not being at the front with his men, but at Fredericksburg (where he was wounded) and at Chancellorsville he regained reputation. His was Hancock's old division, four brigades well led by veterans. Caldwell launched a counterattack that was initially successful, regaining Rose's Woods and the Wheatfield. But the cost was heavy, especially among officers. As he did at Fredericksburg, Samuel K. Zook was mounted so that his brigade might see him . . . but so could the enemy, and General Zook went down with a mortal wound. Edward E. Cross chose to go to battle dismounted, but as one of his men wrote, "We were in the open, without a thing better than a wheat straw to catch a Minnie bullet. . . ." Hancock called out, "Colonel Cross, this day will bring you a star," but it was not to be. Cross had been wounded at Seven Pines, Antietam, and Fredericksburg; this time his wound was mortal; he died before the day was out. A third brigade commander, John R. Brooke, seized a regimental flag to lead a charge, then fell wounded and only escaped capture by "a burly fellow under each arm to take me off the field." Of the division's four brigade commanders, only the Irish Brigade's Patrick Kelly was unhurt.[48]

Even as Sykes's Fifth Corps and Caldwell's Second Corps division attempted to salvage Sickles's collapsing salient, a smaller but no less fierce struggle was waged to secure Little Round Top. On Gouverneur Warren's initiative, Strong Vincent's brigade reached the hilltop just in time to blunt the enemy assault. Colonel Vincent was Harvard 1859 and a lawyer, and today marked his first fight as brigade commander. In posting his four regiments, he sent Colonel Joshua L. Chamberlain's 20th Maine to the left. "You understand!" Vincent told Chamberlain, "Hold this ground at all costs!" The 20th Maine was hard-pressed to hold the ground — the left flank of the Army of the Potomac. "The edge of conflict swayed to and fro," Chamberlain would write, "with wild whirlpools and eddies. At times I saw around me more of the enemy than of my own men: gaps opening, swallowing, closing again with sharp convulsive energy." Finally, cartridge boxes empty, Chamberlain ordered bayonets fixed and led a charge, and the Mainers drove their attackers in retreat. Paddy O'Rorke was meanwhile leading his 140th New York in a last-minute charge that secured the right of Vincent's line. Little Round Top was saved. The cost was 27 percent casualties, including the lives of Strong Vincent, Paddy O'Rorke, battery commander Charles Hazlett, and Stephen Weed, leading his reinforcing brigade.[49]

General Caldwell called on Romeyn B. Ayres and his Fifth Corps regulars to help consolidate his gains. As they spoke, Caldwell was surprised to see his front wavering. "Those regiments are being driven back," said the veteran Ayres. "A regiment does not shut up like a jack-knife and hide its colors without it is retreating." A fresh Rebel assault had found another flank to turn; "with dogged silence the men retired slowly and without apparent panic or hurry, for they were perfectly well satisfied of the impossibility of longer holding their ground."

The Federal field command was becoming snarled. Sickles (Third Corps) directed his two division heads, Birney and Humphreys. Sykes (Fifth Corps) had Barnes's and Ayres's divisions in action, with Samuel W. Crawford's Pennsylvania Reserves newly at hand, but Sykes deliberately commanded independently of Sickles. Caldwell's Second Corps division reported not to Sickles but to Sykes. Further, each of these generals rushing to back up the Third Corps had to decipher the battlefield on his own and on the fly. Then, abruptly, there was one less general in the mix. As he pulled back in the face of the latest enemy assault, Dan Sickles was hit by a cannonball that nearly tore off his right leg. At a field hospital the mangled limb was amputated, and he was hurried off to Washington for further care. Meade quickly put the trusted Hancock in charge of the Third Corps as well as the Second — in effect, in charge of the battlefield. The Third Corps went to Birney, the Second to Gibbon. As to Dan Sickles,

Captain Henry Abbott surely spoke for many in the officer corps when he wrote, "The loss of his leg is a great gain to us, whatever it may be to him."[50]

Meade called on Hancock for another brigade for the embattled left, then reached farther afield for reinforcements, to the Twelfth Corps on Culp's Hill. It had been a relatively calm day on Culp's Hill except for a noisy, late-afternoon artillery exchange (which Henry Hunt dismissed — "As soon as I saw it would lead to nothing serious, I returned direct to the Peach Orchard"). Once the Fifth Corps marched off to brace Sickles, right-wing commander (self-appointed) Henry Slocum was left with just the Twelfth Corps, which he had put under Alpheus Williams and to whom he handed Meade's order. "I received the order to detach all I could spare, at least one division, to support our left," Williams reported. He answered the order's "at least one division" with Thomas Ruger's division, plus a new brigade, released by Washington, under Henry Lockwood. The inexperienced Lockwood was senior to Ruger, so Williams contrived to label Lockwood's brigade "unattached," reporting directly to him, and he then led the way to battle.

Williams exchanged parting words with General Slocum. He feared the Rebels "would seize upon our line on the right the moment we left it," and had the Twelfth's other division, under John Geary, extend its line to cover Ruger's absence. Slocum "approved of my suggestions that at least one div. was necessary to hold our entrenchments." But presently Slocum reneged on his approval, and sent Geary with two of his three brigades to follow Williams. That left only George S. Greene's brigade — five New York regiments, some 1,400 men — to hold Culp's Hill. Apparently it was the all-that-could-be-spared phrase in Meade's order that inspired Slocum's ill-conceived second thought. He would later claim Meade ordered the *entire* Twelfth Corps to the left, and took it upon himself to at least retain Greene's brigade. There is no evidence for this claim, however, and it was flatly contradicted by Williams, and indeed contradicted by common sense. Meade would hardly leave Culp's Hill wholly undefended in the face of what was known to be Dick Ewell's army corps. Greene's brigade defending the army's extreme right confronted a challenge fully as testing as Strong Vincent's brigade defending the army's extreme left.[51]

The Third Corps was about done in now, its retreat not always orderly. Fugitives came "like a great billow, rushing with an irresistible force that no troops could check . . . ," wrote a Second Corps man. "They swept over us." But the reinforcements Meade rushed to the left — Sykes's Fifth Corps, Caldwell's Second Corps division, Williams's Twelfth Corps division, even the first arrivals of John Sedgwick's hard-marching Sixth Corps — were

shutting down the Confederate advance and building a new line. In particular need of support was the gun line set up by the reserve artillery's Lieutenant Colonel Freeman McGilvery. McGilvery had once led a battery under him, said General Williams, and just now "was delighted to see me." Williams directed Lockwood's brigade into its first combat, recapturing several lost guns and restoring McGilvery's line. The gun line was further braced by the charge of George L. Willard's brigade, sent into action personally by General Hancock. Back in September, Willard's New Yorkers were victimized at Harper's Ferry by Stonewall Jackson, and today, as they drove the Rebels in retreat, they shouted, "Remember Harper's Ferry!" Their success, however, cost Colonel Willard his life.

"Hancock the Superb" McClellan called him at Williamsburg fourteen months earlier, and today Hancock was once again easily that. Meade, in extremis, finally tapped the First Corps for support, and Captain Henry Abbott watched Hancock personally lead a nine-month Vermont brigade, just up from Washington, to the battlefront. "He led them forward on horseback, with his hat off. They cheered him & as soon as we saw him we sent up a tremendous cheer."

The shift left of Caldwell's division opened a gap in the Second Corps line, soon exploited by the Confederates. Hancock was quickly on the scene—narrowly escaping a volley of musketry—and called out the 1st Minnesota from John Gibbon's division. "Advance, Colonel, and take those colors!" he ordered. "I immediately gave the order 'Forward double-quick,'" said Colonel William Colvill, "and under a galling fire of the enemy, we advanced. . . ." The 1st Minnesota was a truly veteran regiment (it fought at First Bull Run), and it dutifully plugged this fresh hole in the dike . . . at a cost of 68 percent casualties, including Colonel Colvill,

Edwin Forbes pictured the
defenses on Culp's Hill erected
by George S. Greene (right),
enabling him to hold the position
with his single brigade.

wounded. Hancock made note, "I cannot speak too highly of this regiment and its commander in its attack."[52]

General Meade himself constantly appraised the battle, riding close enough that his horse was wounded. Still another gap opened in the line, and Meade and staff found themselves the apparent last line of defense. "He straightens himself in his stirrups," Meade's son wrote, "as do also the aides who now ride closer to him, bracing themselves up to meet the crisis." Then John Newton, commanding the First Corps, rode up with a reinforcing column. Newton offered his flask, the two generals drank a toast, Meade called out, "Come on, gentlemen!" and they posted the troops to fill the gap.

It was dusk now, and after positioning his division, Alpheus Williams came upon General Meade "and a good many other officers on the field and to learn that we had successfully resisted all the Rebel attacks and had punished them severely. There was a pleasant gathering in an open field and gratulation abounded." Someone observed that for a time matters had "seemed pretty desperate." Yes, said Meade, "but it is all right now, it is all right now."[53]

On the far right, however, it was not all right. The Rebels anticipated the failing light shielding an assault on Culp's Hill, but "Pop" Greene was ready for them. George S. Greene, a vigorous sixty-two, was the oldest general officer in the Potomac army. He graduated West Point in 1823 and left the army in 1836 to embark on a distinguished civil engineering career. He fought capably at Cedar Mountain, Antietam, and Chancellorsville; today he fought his brigade more than capably.

The first thing General Greene did on reaching Culp's Hill that morning was to lay out a line of breastworks across the hill, built of logs, cordwood, rocks, and dirt. This became literally a lifesaver when Slocum witlessly sent off the rest of Geary's division. "The enemy made four distinct charges," Greene reported, all of them "effectually resisted" from behind the breastworks. Darkness finally ended it. Except for some Rebel inroads at the base of the hill, the line was intact. A captain in the 60th New York knew what had saved the day: "Without breastworks our line would have been swept away in an instant by the hailstorm of bullets and the flood of men." His battle won, a prideful Pop Greene gestured to his weary troops and told a commissary officer, "Give them the best you have, every man deserves a warm biscuit and a plate of ice-cream."[54]

Otis Howard waited with concern should the Confederates' evening attack expand from Culp's Hill to Cemetery Hill. His Eleventh Corps was depleted and demoralized by the July 1 fighting. Leopold von Gilsa was told by an aide, "You can now command your brigade easily with the voice, my dear Colonel; this is all that is left." The real strength of the position rested with the artillery. Facing west on Cemetery Hill were thirty-three guns. On East Cemetery Hill, the sector between Cemetery Hill and Culp's Hill, facing north and northeast, was a mix of five batteries, twenty-five guns, under First Corps artillery chief Charles Wainwright. Infantry from Adelbert Ames's division was posted behind a stone wall at the base of the hill. No one felt confident about Ames's infantry (including General Ames).

Indeed, when the Confederate attack came in the growing dark, the Eleventh's infantrymen did not stand much longer than they had on July 1. "As soon as the rebels began to fire," Colonel Wainwright told his journal, "the two lines of Deutschmen in front of the batteries began to run, and nearly the whole of them cleared out." As the range shortened Wainwright's gunners went to canister and double charges of canister and case shot without fuzes. A Deutschman who did stand his ground remembered "suddenly, right over my head it seemed, there was a blaze, a crash and a roar as if a volcano had been let loose." A Massachusetts colonel saw this fire "leaving great heaps of dead and wounded just in front of us." Survivors of this blanketing fire got in among the batteries for a time, triggering hand-to-hand combat, the cannoneers wielding rammers, handspikes, and fists. The German gunners, Wainwright admitted, "fought splendidly." Yet it was another Hancock initiative, Samuel S. Carroll's Second Corps brigade, that pushed back the enemy tide. It was full night when the fighting ended.

He pitied General Ames "most heartily," Wainwright wrote. "His men would not stand at all." But the ultimate command failure was Otis Howard's. Howard had led the Eleventh Corps for four months now, during which time he failed to generate any state of trust with officers and men . . . or they with him. Wainwright asked him, "Why don't you have them shot?" to which Howard replied, "I should have to shoot all the way down; they are all alike."[55]

That evening at army headquarters, the little farmhouse of the widow Lydia Leister on the reverse slope of Cemetery Ridge, Meade, with Hancock and Slocum, plotted the next move in a battle certain to be renewed in the morning. Meade told Washington he would hold his position on July 3, not saying if he would attack or defend. He summoned the Bureau of Military Information's George Sharpe for the latest on Lee's army. Colonel Sharpe explained that the B.M.I's interrogation of prisoners identified nearly a hundred Confederate regiments involved in the fighting thus far — none of them from George Pickett's division. "Pickett's division has come up and is now in bivouac," Sharpe said, "and will be ready to go into action fresh tomorrow morning." That marked Pickett as Lee's sole reserve. Meade's reserve was the entire Sixth Corps . . . cause enough for Hancock to raise his fist and exclaim, "General, we have got them nicked!"[56]

Meade called his lieutenants into council. Unlike his predecessors, he wanted a fully informed high command. A dozen generals crowded into the widow Leister's parlor — Meade, Newton (First Corps), Hancock and Gibbon (Second), Birney (Third), Sykes (Fifth), Sedgwick (Sixth), Howard (Eleventh), Slocum and Williams (Twelfth), Chief of Staff Butterfield, engineer Warren. Meade called for the condition and numbers of each command, and Butterfield took notes: "Effective strength" came to 58,000. Birney: "3d Corps used up and not in good condition to fight." Newton: "Thinks it is a bad position" (phrased in John Gibbon's notes, "This was no place to fight a battle in"). Pressed to explain, Newton said, "Correct position of the army but would not retreat."

General Meade posed three questions for comment: (1) "Under existing circumstances is it advisable for this army to remain in its present position or to retire to another nearer its base of supplies"; (2) "It being determined to remain in present position should the army attack or wait the attack of the enemy"; (3) "If we wait attack how long." Meade had already told

Meade's council of generals on the evening of July 2 in the widow Leister's parlor, displaying some artistic license. From left: Alfred Pleasonton (not present), Gouverneur Warren, John Sedgwick, Meade, Daniel Butterfield, David Birney, Otis Howard, Alpheus Williams, Henry Slocum, Winfield Hancock, John Newton, George Sykes, John Gibbon, Carl Schurz (foreground; not present).

Washington he would continue the fight where he was; what he wanted now was consensus.

On the first question his lieutenants were unanimous — "Stay and fight it out" (as Slocum put it). On the second question, to attack or await attack, there was also unanimity — await attack. On the third question, how long to await attack, answers were varied, but the consensus seemed to be, if an attack came it would be the next day. "I recollect there was great good feeling amongst the Corps Commanders at their agreeing so unanimously," Gibbon wrote, "and Genl. Meade announced, in a decided manner, 'Such then is the decision.'" There was no doubt, he added, of Meade "being perfectly in accord with the members of the council."

As the council adjourned, Meade took Gibbon aside and told him, "If Lee attacks tomorrow, it will be *in your front.*" Gibbon asked why he thought so. "Because he has made attacks on both our flanks and failed and if he concludes to try it again, it will be on our centre." Gibbon said he hoped it would be so — "If he did, we would defeat him." Meade felt privately confident. Next morning he wrote a quick note to Margaret, "Dearest love, All well and going on well with the Army. We had a great fight yesterday, the enemy attacking & we completely repulsing them — both armies shattered. To-day at it again what result remains to be seen. Army in fine spirits & every one determined to do or die."[57]

In the small hours of July 3, when the Twelfth Corps' Alpheus Williams returned to Culp's Hill after the war council, he was taken aback to find the breastworks at the base of the hill he had left in John Geary's care now occupied by Rebels. On reporting this to General Slocum, he was told, "Well! drive them out at daylight," an order (Williams thought) more easily made than executed. As regards Slocum sending off two of Geary's brigades the night before — "erroneously I thought then and think now" — Williams did not make an issue of it with his prickly superior.

This would be primarily a Twelfth Corps operation, and Williams assigned Geary's brigades the unenviable task of assaulting their own breastworks. He sought to ease the way with an artillery bombardment, but when the guns ceased fire it was the enemy that seized the moment and attacked. Pop Greene was again ready behind his breastworks, his brigade's fire more deadly than before for being delivered in daylight. As he had the previous evening, Greene rotated his firing lines; as one regiment exhausted its ammunition, another was poised to take its place. He reported "the fire was kept up constantly and efficiently over our whole line, and the men were always comparatively fresh and their arms in good order. . . ." The rest of Geary's division followed Greene's example, and by 11:00 a.m. it was over and Culp's Hill was secure. Pop Greene's men gave three rousing cheers.[58]

Friday morning, July 3, meantime found the Army of the Potomac committing to defense. The Third Corps, with 40 percent casualties on Thursday, was at the rear and out of contention. Sykes's Fifth Corps, battered but resolute, was posted on Cemetery Ridge about where Meade originally intended Sickles to be. Barnes's and Ayers's divisions each had losses of about 25 percent, but Crawford's division was largely intact. To the right of the Fifth Corps, forming the center of the Cemetery Ridge battlefront, was a somewhat tangled array: left to right, Caldwell's Second Corps division, then Doubleday's First Corps division with which Newton had patched the last gap in the line, then the other two Second Corps divisions, under John Gibbon and Alexander Hays. The First and Twelfth Corps manned Cemetery Hill and Culp's Hill, while much of the Eleventh Corps nursed its wounds and its reputation. The army's reserve, John Sedgwick's Sixth Corps, was disbursed far and wide — two brigades guarding the left flank, two supporting the Fifth Corps, two supporting the center, two guarding the right flank. Uncle John grumbled that he might as well go home.

Henry Hunt, Potomac army artillery chief, choreographed his batteries to break the back of Pickett's Charge.

Henry Hunt, master of the army's new artillery scheme, was untiring in organizing, refitting, and posting batteries — "ordered artillery from wherever I could find it, where I thought it could be spared, without any regard to the commands of others. . . ." After his success a year earlier at Malvern Hill massing reserve batteries, Hunt had turned critical of the management of the guns at Antietam, Fredericksburg, and Chancellorsville (where he was banished by Joe Hooker). He determined to make Gettysburg proof of his theory of unified artillery command.

General Meade was up early riding his lines. He sent to Darius Couch and his Pennsylvania militia at Harrisburg to reinforce a victory in the fighting, but in case of a reverse to defend Harrisburg and the Susquehanna line. He told William French at Frederick to harass a retreating enemy, but go to the defense of Washington in the event of a defeat. Following up his alert to John Gibbon to prepare for an attack on the center, he sent the same alert to Sedgwick — prepare to reinforce, for "it is their intention to make the attempt to pierce our center." Correspondent Whitelaw Reid thought Meade "calm, and as it seemed to me, lit up with the glow of the occasion. . . ."

Then, in a turn of high drama, General Lee appeared to confirm Meade's analysis. To the west, along Seminary Ridge, artillery pieces by the dozens, by the scores, were wheeled into battery, forming a great arc extending from the Peach Orchard in the south to the outskirts of Gettysburg in the north. The gun crews faded back to the woods or other cover. Infantry, too, was hidden from view. The guns — 163 of them — stood menacingly in the eerie midday silence. Thomas Hyde of the Sixth Corps staff climbed Little Round Top for a look at this array. "About this time, Generals Meade and Warren came up on the rocks to take a look, and I dodged back to tell the general that it looked like a cannonade pretty soon."

A cannonade pretty soon was also Henry Hunt's conclusion. What he termed the Rebels' "magnificent display" of artillery heralded an infantry attack, almost certainly on the Union center. He rode his own artillery line — 119 pieces, solidly backed by reserves — and issued specific orders to corps artillery chiefs and battery captains. When the enemy bombardment opened, they must not reply for fifteen or twenty minutes, and then with only the most deliberate counterbattery fire. His lesson: They must save their long-range ammunition for the infantry, striking at them the moment they started their advance and continuously until they came within canister range. Hunt did not take the time to pass on his catechism to the commanders of infantry corps and divisions or even to General Meade. He acted as chief of *the* artillery.[59]

The center of the infantry line, Lee's presumed target, was manned by the two Second Corps divisions of John Gibbon and Alexander Hays. Captain John G. Hazard commanded the five batteries of the corps artillery brigade. Hays, on the right, had only the brigades of Thomas A. Smyth and Eliakim Sherrill (replacing George Willard, killed on Thursday). Hays's third brigade, Samuel S. Carroll's, had helped repel the attack on the Eleventh Corps Thursday night, and Otis Howard refused to return it. Howard feared his own men would run without Carroll's bracing. (Carroll's 8th Ohio evaded Howard's clutches and did serve with Hays.) On the left were Gibbon's three brigades, under Alexander S. Webb, Norman J. Hall, and William Harrow. Supporting Gibbon to his left was the First Corps brigade of nine-month Vermonters under George Stannard. Five of these six (excepting Hall) were new to brigade command, but in Gibbon and Hays, and Winfield Hancock, the Army of the Potomac mustered that day the best it had.

In the hot, still noontime everyone waited on General Lee. Gibbon's mess put together a lunch of stewed chicken and potatoes and bread and coffee for him, Hancock, Newton, and Alfred Pleasonton, and Gibbon talked Meade into joining them, saying the commanding general must eat to keep up his strength. Afterward Meade returned to his Leister house headquarters and the generals to their posts, and everyone could only wait. Then, shortly after 1:00 p.m., the quiet was broken by a signal gun. "Almost instantly afterwards," Gibbon recalled, "the whole air above and around us was filled with bursting and screaming projectiles, and the continuous thunder of the guns. . . ." By staff man Frank Haskell's account, "In briefest time the whole Rebel line to the West, was pouring out its thunder and its iron upon our devoted crest."

The Federal line of infantry and guns on that crest offered a target of comparatively little depth, and it was soon evident the Confederate gunners were firing high, many projectiles landing on the reverse slope of Cemetery Ridge. The roiling smoke of their fire and the Yankees' return fire made it hard to see and correct the fall of their shot. Behind the lines was chaos. Shot crashed into and through the Leister house, and General Meade and staff evacuated to the backyard, where it was hardly safer. Meade moved to Slocum's headquarters behind Culp's Hill for a time, but returned to headquarters to stay in touch.

At the front generals sought to spread calm under this unprecedented barrage. Alick Hays rode the lines shouting defiant encouragement to his men. Winfield Hancock rode along at a deliberate pace, his orderly bearing the Second Corps flag, leaving the men cheering. John Gibbon's horse was hit, so he walked the lines. He found the safest place on the field to be the picket line, "the men peering at us curiously from behind the stone wall as we passed along."

When he discovered the artillery obeying Hunt's dictum — initially not returning fire, then doing so with deliberation — Hancock was enraged. (John Geary observed, "Hancock always swore at everybody, above all on the battlefield.") He collared corps artillery chief John Hazard and demanded he give as good as he was getting, to keep up the infantry's morale. Hazard explained Hunt's orders to conserve long-range ammunition for the infantry attack certain to come. Hancock would have none of it. *He* commanded the Second Corps front, including its artillery, and Hazard was under his orders. Hancock turned to Patrick Hart's battery, from the artillery reserve, standing idle. Captain Hart recorded the general's language as "profane and Blasphemous such as a drunken Ruffian would use." The contretemps caught the attention of Hart's boss Freeman McGilvery, brigade commander, reserve artillery. McGilvery, a salty former Maine sea captain, said *he* was under General Hunt's orders, and the time to fire "was not come." It happened that all the Yankee gunners followed Henry Hunt's orders to fire conservatively . . . all except in the Second Corps.[60]

Ammunition supply was a concern of Hunt's — just half the Second Corps' train had reached the field, for example — and on Cemetery Hill he spoke with Generals Howard and Schurz and Eleventh Corps artillery chief Thomas W. Osborn. It was decided the artillery should cease fire, not only to save ammunition but to lure the Rebels into thinking their bombardment had succeeded and to send in the infantry. Learning that General Meade had the same thought — he "expressed the hope that the enemy would attack, and he had no fear of the result" — Hunt ordered all the batteries to cease fire. Soon the guns on both sides fell silent, the battle smoke dissipated, and in the Union lines the cry went up, "Here comes the infantry!" "The enemy in a long grey line was marching towards us over the rolling ground in our front," General Gibbon wrote, "their flags fluttering in the air. . . . Behind the front line another appeared and finally a third and the whole came on like a great wave of men, steadily and stolidly."[61]

History marked it Pickett's Charge — George Pickett's division the B.M.I. said was Lee's only unbloodied force, heavily reinforced from the commands of Johnston Pettigrew and Isaac Trimble, some 13,000 men all told. Hunt's artillery and Hancock's infantry were ready. As the Rebel infantry began its long advance across the open fields, Captain Henry Abbott, Norman Hall's brigade, made note, "The moment I saw them I knew we should give them Fredericksburg. So did every body."

From both ends of the Yankee line Hunt's artillery tore the marching ranks with a deadly crossfire. Benjamin Rittenhouse's Battery D, 5th U.S., posted on Little Round Top, was first to fire. "I watched Pickett's men advance," Rittenhouse reported, "and opened on them with an oblique fire, and ended with a terrible enfilading fire. . . . Many times a single percussion shell would cut out several files, and then explode in their ranks; several times almost a company would disappear, as the shell would rip from the right to the left among them." From Cemetery Hill Major Osborn's thirty-nine pieces shredded the other Confederate front. "They were at once enveloped in a dense cloud of smoke and dust. Arms, heads, blankets, guns and knapsacks were thrown and tossed in to the clear air . . . ," wrote an officer of the 8th Ohio. "A moan went up from the field, distinctly to be heard amid the storm of battle. . . ."

The most devastating artillery fire was delivered by Freeman McGilvery's reserve brigade on the left. McGilvery's forty-one guns were concealed by a rise of ground and untouched by the Rebel bombardment. As Pickett's column came in sight it angled across McGilvery's front, funneling toward the center of Hancock's line. McGilvery was matter-of-fact — the enemy's battle lines "presented an oblique front to the guns under my

command, and by training the whole line of guns obliquely to the right, we had a raking fire through all three of these lines." He added, "The execution of the fire must have been terrible." By the time the Rebel advance was within musketry range, both its flanks were destroyed, leaving but a forlorn hope to contest the Yankee infantry . . . and the artillery's canister. Only Captain Hazard's nineteen guns at the center did not join in this carnival of destruction, having on Hancock's order already expended long-range ammunition. (Henry Hunt always contended but for this "interference," the artillery would have stopped Pickett's Charge in its tracks.)[62]

Now came the infantry's turn. On the far right, the 8th Ohio of Carroll's brigade, freed from Otis Howard's retention, took post along a fence line and sent a Rebel brigade fleeing "in the wildest confusion." Alick Hays shouted to his men, "They are coming boys; we must whip them. . . ." Hays packed his two brigades tightly behind a stone wall so in places the line was three or four ranks deep. Like Pop Greene's tactic, the front rank gave way to a fresh rank to keep up an endless fire. Men in the rear loaded rifles and passed them forward to better marksmen. Hays held back no reserve; he put all his firepower into halting the charge at a distance. On the far left, George Stannard neatly maneuvered his nine-month Vermonters into

July 3, 1863: the climax of Pickett's Charge, painted by Edwin Forbes from his wartime sketches. The copse of trees and the Angle, where the charge peaked, are at the left.

a position to take Pickett's Virginians, pushing toward the Federal center, squarely in the flank.

The fighting narrowed to the center, around a copse of trees and a turn in a stone wall called the Angle. The charge steadily collapsed in on itself, slashed now by musketry and double rounds of canister; now too the Second Corps' guns joined in. Henry Hunt appeared at Andrew Cowan's Sixth Corps battery just called to the front, shouting and firing his pistol. "The display of Secesh Battle flags was splendid and *scary*," Hunt would write his wife. He told her his horse was killed and he was trapped under the animal, but gunners pulled him free. "I have escaped as by a miracle, when it appeared as if there could be no escape."

Winfield Hancock, too, was close to the front, and suffered an ugly wound in the right thigh. A doctor was found and a tourniquet applied. By General Stannard's account, "I reported the condition of the fight to him from time to time while he laid there awaiting an ambulance." John Gibbon, pressing reinforcements toward the center, took a bullet in the shoulder and had to leave the field. Both of Alick Hays's brigade commanders were casualties, Thomas Smyth wounded, Eliakim Sherrill mortally wounded. But there was no consequent slacking of the fire. Men of the 20th Massachusetts took their revenge for the 13th of December, shouting, "Fredericksburg! Fredericksburg!"[63]

Finally all that remained of Pickett's Charge was its narrowing sliver of a spearhead, thrusting into Alex Webb's lines. "When my men fell back," Webb told his wife, "I almost wished to get killed, I was almost disgraced. . . ." But he rallied his Philadelphia Brigade, helped by support from Norman Hall's and William Harrow's brigades. As one of Harrow's colonels put it, "It was impossible to get them in any order. Everyone wanted to be first there and we went up more like a mob than a disciplined force." It became a wild melee, then abruptly it was over, the Rebel spearhead broken, its survivors captured or joining the general retreat to Seminary Ridge. Reaching the battlefront, unneeded now, were the Sixth Corps reinforcements General Meade had positioned behind the center. "Damn the reinforcement, look there," said an exultant Alick Hays, pointing to the disordered enemy withdrawal.

Meade rode up to the front, demanding of Frank Haskell of the staff, "How is it going here?" Haskell replied, "I believe, General, the enemy's attack is repulsed." Was he sure, entirely repulsed? "Yes Sir, we have beaten them," Haskell said. Meade started to reach for his hat "as if to hurrah but checked himself and said, Thank God!" With staff and a party of officers Meade rode the lines, to triumphant cheering for the general commanding.[64]

15. *A Contest of Little Purpose*

SEEING THE CONFEDERATE TIDE crest and recede, wounded Winfield Hancock halted the ambulance carrying him to the rear and dictated a message to General Meade. He had repulsed "a tremendous attack. . . . I have never seen a more formidable attack, and if the Sixth and Fifth Corps have pressed up, the enemy will be destroyed." Sykes's Fifth Corps had not engaged Pickett's attackers, but much damaged from Thursday it was hardly "pressed up" for a counterattack. Nor certainly was Sedgwick's Sixth Corps, scattered in support along the full length of the battlefront. For July 3 Meade had committed his every resource to defense, and it paid off. In the five campaigns since Malvern Hill, a year ago, this was the Army of the Potomac's first clear-cut battlefield victory. He would not jeopardize that. General Lee, said Meade, "was in a strong position, awaiting my attack, which I declined to make, in consequence of the bad example he had set. . . ."[1]

Pickett's Charge ignited sharp cavalry action on both flanks. To the north, Jeb Stuart had just reached Gettysburg after an ill-advised venture to again circumnavigate the Federal army. He took Lee's bombardment as the signal to thrust into the Yankee rear areas. David Gregg's cavalry division blocked the way. Ordered to guard the right, Gregg strengthened his hand by commandeering George Custer's brigade from Judson Kilpatrick's division. Just as Stuart's column came in sight, an order from cavalry headquarters called on Custer to return to Kilpatrick. Gregg ignored it, to Custer's liking. "If you will give me an order to remain," he said, "I will only be too happy to do it."

Gregg's confrontation with Stuart was straight-ahead charge and countercharge, fought by Custer's and John B. McIntosh's brigades. Custer, at twenty-three the youngest general in the Potomac army, was in the action from the start. A bugle sounded the charge of his Michigan troopers: "As the two columns approached each other, the pace of each increased, when suddenly a crash, like the falling of timber. . . . So sudden and violent was the collision that many of the horses were turned end over end and crushed their riders beneath them." In the melee Custer's horse was hit but he seized a riderless mount. The fighting went back and forth for some thirty minutes, the Yankees holding and Stuart finally withdrawing, his charge (like Pickett's) a failure.

In striking contrast, at the other end of the battlefield Judson Kilpatrick demonstrated the aptness of his nickname. Upon Pickett's repulse, Kill-cavalry determined to add his troopers to the day's fight — not against cavalry but against infantry. (A Texan he faced explained that infantry that will stand its ground will defeat cavalry "without any trouble. It was simply a picnic to fight cavalry under such conditions.") When Brigadier Elon Farnsworth got Kilpatrick's order to lead a mounted charge over broken ground in front of Round Top against infantry and artillery, he was aghast. "My God," he told one of his officers, "Kil is going to have a cavalry charge. It is too awful to think of. . . ." It was indeed too awful. Quite unawed by the charging troopers, the Rebel infantrymen shot Farnsworth's brigade to pieces. Farnsworth was among the dead.[2]

That night and into Saturday, July 4 — Independence Day — the Potomac army sorted itself out for what might come next. "Both armies quietly occupied their positions, firing only on the picket lines and with a little artillery," Gouverneur Warren made note. Rations and ammunition were brought up, wounded collected, dead buried. Field hospitals overflowed with Friday's casualties. Rufus Dawes, 6th Wisconsin, wrote his fiancée, "The experiences of the past few days seem more like a fearful, horrible dream than reality. May God save me and my men from any more such trials. Our dearest and best are cold in the ground or suffering on beds of anguish."

Defending against Pickett's Charge cost some 2,300 casualties (about a third of the Confederates' loss). In the Second Corps, Alex Webb's Philadelphia Brigade lost 44 percent, and John Hazard's corps artillery brigade lost a quarter of its gunners. The officer toll that afternoon included corps commander Hancock wounded, division commander Gibbon wounded, brigade commanders Webb and Thomas Smyth wounded and Eliakim Sherrill mortally wounded, and cavalry brigadier Elon Farnsworth killed.

July 4 marked George Meade's seventh day commanding the Army of the Potomac, and for the first time in that week of unending tension he could breathe almost easily. If, as he suspected, the battle at Gettysburg was over, he was the clear winner. He explained to Margaret, "It was a grand battle, and is in my judgment a most decided victory, tho I did not annihilate or *bag* the Confederate Army. . . . At one point things looked a little blue" — no doubt he meant July 2 — "but I managed to get up reinforcements in time to save the day." He then revealed just how intensely the responsibility of command bore on him. He was well, he told her, "tho' at one time I feared I should be laid up with mental excitement."

The 4th saw Gettysburg's citizens celebrate their own day of independence, free of their occupiers. Lee had pulled back to the general line of Seminary Ridge, but it was not apparent what he would do next. In the town a number of First and Eleventh Corps fugitives emerged from hiding, notably General Alexander Schimmelfennig, who had sheltered since July 1 in the Garlach family's backyard. The wounded General Francis Barlow, cared for by Confederate surgeons, was found recuperating in a private home.

On the evening of July 4, as he had on July 2, Meade met with his generals on the state of the army and to collect opinions. Present were John Newton (First Corps, replacing Reynolds), William Hays (Second Corps, replacing Hancock), David Birney (Third Corps, replacing Sickles), George Sykes (Fifth Corps), John Sedgwick (Sixth Corps), Otis Howard (Eleventh Corps), Henry Slocum (Twelfth Corps), Alfred Pleasonton (cavalry), engineer Gouverneur Warren, and Daniel Butterfield, chief of staff. A rough estimate of effective force added up to about 55,000 infantry. Meade posed four questions for discussion.

The first question (as Butterfield recorded it) was, "Shall this army remain here?" No one wanted to abandon a victorious field, yet no one wanted the enemy to get away scot-free. Warren's answer was representative: Stay, "until we see what they are doing." The second question, "If we remain here, shall we assume the offensive?" was answered no, unanimously. The third and fourth questions dealt with pursuing a retreating enemy—pursue in parallel to the east via Emmitsburg, covering Baltimore and Washington; or pursue "on his direct line of retreat." A direct pursuit would be slowed by enemy rear guards and was best done by the cavalry. The flanking route was favored for the infantry, in hopes of intercepting the Rebels at the Potomac. Like the July 2 council, Meade's views were reinforced by his generals. As Warren read the gathering, there was "a tone amongst most of the prominent officers that we had quite saved the country for the time, and that we had done enough; that we might jeopard all that we had won by trying to do too much."[3]

In General Orders No. 68 Meade congratulated his army "for the glorious result of the recent operations." The enemy, baffled and defeated, had withdrawn. "Our task is not yet accomplished, and the commanding general looks to the army for greater efforts to drive from our soil every vestige of the presence of the invader."

Mr. Lincoln told General Halleck he left the telegraph office a good deal dissatisfied. "I did not like the phrase, in Orders, No. 68, I believe, 'Drive the invaders from our soil.'" It seemed a purpose "to get the enemy across the river again without a further collision," not a purpose to prevent his crossing and to destroy him. To the cabinet, while willing to give Meade and the Army of the Potomac all praise for the victory at Gettysburg, the president said he "feared the old idea of driving the rebels out of Pennsylvania & Maryland instead of capturing them was still prevalent among the officers." (Privately to John Hay he termed it "a dreadful reminiscence of McClellan.")

Lincoln's jaundiced view was shaped by two Gettysburg witnesses who furnished him their own peculiar versions of events. On July 5 Lincoln visited Dan Sickles, in the capital recuperating from his amputation. Already he was touted as a (or the) hero of Gettysburg, and a staff man said Sickles "certainly got his side of the story of Gettysburg well into the President's mind and heart that Sunday afternoon" — a story delivered at General Meade's expense. The next day railroad man Herman Haupt reached Washington with his own tale for Lincoln. He said he left Meade at Gettysburg on the 5th "with the impression on my mind that there would be no advance of any considerable portion of the army for some days. . . ."

But the president was buoyed by news from Mississippi that on Independence Day, Vicksburg's 30,000-man garrison surrendered to General Grant. Perhaps, he thought, that might inspire the Army of the Potomac. He had Halleck relay the news, over his signature, to Meade: "Now, if General Meade can complete his work, so gloriously prosecuted thus far, by the literal or substantial destruction of Lee's army, the rebellion will be over." As a further inspiration, Meade was notified he was brigadier general, regular army, "to rank from July 3, the date of your brilliant victory at Gettysburg."[4]

The Northern press, having suffered Fredericksburg and Chancellorsville, was in a celebratory mood. "The tidings from Gettysburg have been arriving in fragmentary instalments, but with a steady crescendo toward complete, overwhelming victory," New Yorker George Templeton Strong told his diary on July 5. The *New York Times* headed its coverage, SPLENDID TRIUMPH OF THE ARMY OF THE POTOMAC. For the *Philadelphia Inquirer* it was VICTORY! WATERLOO ECLIPSED!! The *New York Herald* was carried away: VICTORY! VICTORY! THE DYING STRUGGLES OF THE REBELLION. George Gordon Meade, a week earlier a virtual stranger to the press, was reported a "skilful and courageous leader," praised for his "coolness, decision, and energy." Philadelphia's mayor led a brass band to

Mrs. Meade's doorstep to serenade her in honor of her husband, "the victor of Gettysburg."[5]

On July 5 it became evident that Lee was retreating, and Meade determined to try and seal his victory. "I think we shall have another battle before Lee can cross the river . . . ," he told his wife. "For my part as I have to follow & fight him, I would rather do it at once & in Maryland than to follow into Virginia." Meade gave battle at Gettysburg believing the two armies roughly the same size, and he assumed the two had suffered roughly the same casualties. That meant he faced a still very dangerous foe. Further, having now experienced Robert E. Lee in six campaigns over thirteen months, he knew to stand clear of rashness. Further, heavy rains slowed the army's pace. To urgings from Washington, Meade replied, "I wish in advance to moderate the expectations of those who, in ignorance of the difficulties to be encountered, may expect too much." To do all it could under the circumstances, "I pledge this army to do."

Of major concern to Meade was his badly damaged high command. In the First Corps, replacing trusted John Reynolds with middling John Newton was a decided comedown. A decidedly greater comedown was William Hays taking the Second Corps. Hays was an artilleryman who had gained rank and a brigade in the infantry. At Chancellorsville, his first battle, he was surprised and captured with most of his staff. A prisoner exchange returned him to the Potomac army, and after Hancock's (and then Gibbon's) wounding, the corps command fell into Hays's lap. Wounded Dan Sickles gave up the Third Corps to David Birney, who in turn gave way to his senior, the bibulous William French. George Sykes continued at the Fifth Corps and John Sedgwick at the Sixth. Both Otis Howard, Eleventh Corps, and Henry Slocum, Twelfth Corps, had demonstrated minimal (or less) command skills at Gettysburg. Meade wrote plaintively to Margaret, "I *want corps comdrs.*" He could at least take comfort in a new chief of staff. Dan Butterfield suffered a shrapnel wound on July 2, and as Marsena Patrick phrased it, "to the joy of all, has gone home." Meade gladly replaced him with Andrew Humphreys.[6]

Meade called on ex–Potomac army generals Darius Couch and Baldy Smith for their Department of the Susquehanna militia, but it was a lost cause. The acerbic Smith dismissed these Sunday soldiers as "an incoherent mass . . . quite helpless." Lincoln was of like mind: The militia "will, in my unprofessional opinion, be quite as likely to capture the 'man in the moon' as any part of Lee's army." It rested with the Army of the Potomac to play out the campaign.

The rain-swept pursuit of the Confederate army after Gettysburg, sketched on July 10 by Edwin Forbes. He labeled the fieldpiece a 30-pounder Parrott rifle.

By concealment Lee gained a day's head start, and his direct route to the Potomac crossing at Williamsport was about half the distance of the Yankees' pursuit along the "outside track." Meade moved in three columns, under Sedgwick, Howard, and Slocum. After a false start by Sedgwick against the enemy rear guard, Meade pushed the infantry hard — on July 7, for example, the Twelfth Corps covered 29 miles, the Eleventh, 30 miles. "We are wanderers on the face of the earth, like the Israelites of old," wrote staff man Stephen Weld. "We don't stop 24 hours in the same place, but keep up this eternal marching all the time." Still, spirit in the ranks was high, even to raising a cheer for their staid commanding general — "We are getting quite used to the troops shouting as their Big Injun passes," wrote Meade's son and aide. "The old Pa. reserves did it today."

The cavalry nipped at a wagon train of Confederate wounded, and at a second train filled with booty collected by the invaders. But in a pitched battle of cavalry at Williamsport, Jeb Stuart fought off efforts to damage or delay Lee's main body. A cavalry battle at Hagerstown had a similar outcome. Lee won the race to the Potomac. But providentially for the Yankees, nature intervened.

Lee's army had crossed into Maryland in June at a low-water ford at Williamsport and at a pontoon bridge downstream at Falling Waters. But on July 4 enterprising cavalry from the Middle Department scattered the guard at Falling Waters and broke up the pontoon bridge. Then the rains came. On reaching Williamsport, Lee found the Potomac running 13 feet deep at the ford there. A tiny, rickety cable ferry was his only connection with Virginia. While he waited for the waters to subside and for his engineers to improvise a pontoon bridge, Lee erected an imposing nine-mile line of fieldworks and dug in his army.

On July 11 James Biddle of the staff reported General Meade "in very good spirits & I hope he may be the means of smashing Lee." Meade wrote his wife, "We are now in the immediate vicinity of the enemy and may expect at any hour to be engaged with him. He appears to be getting into a strong position, where he can act on the defensive. I shall be prudent & not act rashly." First Corps artillery chief Charles Wainwright appraised the situation in his diary for July 11: "It would nearly end the rebellion if we could actually bag this army, but on the other hand, a severe repulse of us would give them all the prestige at home and abroad which they lost at Gettysburg, and injure our morale greatly."[7]

Trapped against an impassable river, Lee had no choice but to entrench against attack — in fact (as Colonel Wainwright noted), even to invite attack and perhaps reverse a failed campaign. The Williamsport bridgehead marked something quite new for these two armies. To be sure, over the previous winter Lee enhanced the natural defenses of Fredericksburg in expectation of Hooker's offensive. But never before, in the midst of a campaign of maneuver, had the Army of Northern Virginia entrenched to the hilt and dared the Yankees to attack.

Interviewed afterward by historian John C. Ropes, Meade explained that when he arrived at Williamsport "he had made up his mind to attack Lee without consulting 'any of them,' but on getting there . . . he thought he had better consult his Corps Commanders." His second thought was finding the enemy behind fieldworks.

On the evening of July 12 Meade once again called in his high command. In attendance were James Wadsworth (in place of the ill John Newton), William Hays, William French, George Sykes, John Sedgwick, Otis Howard, and Henry Slocum, plus Alfred Pleasonton, cavalry; Gouverneur Warren, engineers; and Andrew Humphreys, chief of staff. It was not a lineup rich in warrior generals. Meade told his plan to Humphreys beforehand — conduct on the 13th a strong reconnaissance in force, "to be converted into an attack" if a weak spot was found. But, uncertain of his lieutenants' resolve, Meade chose not to order the offensive but to put it to a vote. As he testified, he told his generals he favored "moving forward and attacking the enemy and taking the consequences; but that I left it to their judgment, and would not do it unless it met with their approval."

It did not meet with their approval. "I do not think I ever saw the principal corps commanders so unanimous in favor of not fighting as on that occasion," said Gouverneur Warren. Warren, Pleasonton, and Humphreys supported Meade, but of the seven infantry generals, only Wadsworth and Howard favored an offensive — and their votes were discounted, Wadsworth as a stand-in, Howard because (said Warren) "his troops did not behave well." Sykes and French worried that a defeat would uncover Washington and Baltimore. But the most common view was John Sedgwick's — General Meade had won a great victory, and "he ought not to jeopard all he had gained by another battle at this time."

Meade shaped the vote to his own purpose — simply a day's delay for a full reconnoiter to pinpoint the likeliest place or places to strike. ("General Meade deferred to them so far as to delay until he could examine our own ground and that of the enemy," Humphreys testified.) July 13 was spent in reconnaissance. Meade anticipated "a great battle tomorrow." He ordered a division each from the Second, Fifth, Sixth, and Twelfth Corps to conduct a reconnaissance in force in their respective sectors, starting at 7:00 a.m. on the 14th.

On the morning of the 14th, skirmishers reported the enemy gone. The Potomac had fallen, engineers completed a makeshift pontoon bridge, and overnight Lee took his army back to Virginia. Soldier-correspondent Samuel Fiske told the *Springfield Republican*, "At daybreak we give the word to advance along our whole line. We 'move upon the enemy's works.' Works are ours. Enemy, sitting on the other side of the river, performing various gyrations with his fingers, thumb on his nose."[8]

Upon Meade reporting his lieutenants "unqualifiedly opposed" to attacking the Williamsport bridgehead, Halleck fired back that Meade should act on his own judgment: "It is proverbial that councils of war never fight." Upon Meade reporting that overnight the Rebels had safely crossed the Potomac into Virginia, Lincoln grieved. "We had them within our grasp," he told John Hay. "We had only to stretch forth our hands & they were ours. And nothing I could say or do could make the Army move." As he had the year before with Generals Shields and Frémont in the Shenandoah Valley, the president was making war by map, in one dimension. Gideon Welles entered in his diary on July 14, "On only one or two occasions have I ever seen the President so troubled, so dejected and discouraged." He quoted Lincoln "that there has seemed to him for a full week, a determination that Lee should escape with his force and plunder. . . . There is bad faith somewhere. . . . What does it mean, Mr Welles — Great God what does it mean?"

Lincoln made his displeasure known to Halleck, who telegraphed Meade, "I need hardly say to you that the escape of Lee's army without another battle has created great dissatisfaction in the mind of the President, and it will require an active and energetic pursuit on your part to remove the impression that it has not been sufficiently active heretofore." That was too much for George Meade. Clearly Washington knew nothing (and cared nothing) of the trials he faced getting his limping high command to the Potomac, only to confront a well-dug-in enemy against which any hasty attack was odds-on to fail.

In disgust, Meade asked his quartermaster Rufus Ingalls if he cared to take command of the Army of the Potomac. "No, I thank you," said Ingalls. "It's too big an elephant for me." "Well, it's too big for me, too," said Meade, and he telegraphed Halleck, "The censure of the President conveyed in your dispatch of 1 p.m. this day is, in my judgment, so undeserved that I feel compelled most respectfully to ask to be immediately relieved from the command of this army." Hooker's resignation was accepted promptly; Meade's resignation was rejected promptly. He had not intended his telegram as a censure, said Halleck, "but as a stimulus to an active pursuit. It is not deemed a sufficient cause for your application to be relieved."

"This is exactly what I expected," Meade told his wife; ". . . it is hard after working as I have done & accomplishing as much to be found fault with for not doing impossibilities." He then unburdened himself in replying to a letter of congratulations for Gettysburg from General McClellan. He was, said Meade, "perfectly prepared for a loss of all my rapidly acquired honors the first time the fortune of war fails to smile on me. Already I am beginning to feel the re-action, Lee having crossed the river last night without waiting for me to attack him in one of the strongest positions he has ever occupied."[9]

Meade's observation about the strength of Lee's Williamsport field-works, combined with his complaint to his wife, "I *want corps comdrs*," explains his care and caution following Gettysburg. Lincoln's assertion that there was "bad faith somewhere" in the army's high command was quite unjust. Meade recognized that Lee's going to ground as he did presented new and very difficult problems, and his current crop of lieutenants were hardly problem solvers. Pedestrian John Newton, First Corps, lacked any match to John Reynolds. William Hays, Second Corps, and William

French, Third Corps, were untried and unsteady, respectively. George Sykes, Fifth Corps, and John Sedgwick, Sixth Corps, were steady but exceedingly cautious. Otis Howard with the Eleventh Corps was a command liability. Henry Slocum, Twelfth Corps, had acted the cipher throughout the campaign.

(As it happened, Meade and those of his lieutenants who inspected Lee's abandoned works at Williamsport all expressed relief they had not attempted an attack. "These were by far the strongest I have seen yet; evidently laid out by engineers and built as if they meant to stand a month's siege" was the verdict of artillerist Charles Wainwright. Artillery chief Henry Hunt agreed that an assault "would have been disastrous to us." Meade himself, in a private letter, summed up his dilemma at Williamsport: "I intended to attack Lee, but I would not rush on him blindly & destroy myself & before I had time to feel his weak points he was gone.")

Meade's reputation suffered, then and since, by his putting an offensive at Williamsport to a vote. His two earlier councils, on July 2 and July 4, had simply invited discussion. But on July 12 he made the case for an attack if opportune, but with a lack of fighting generals he wanted a vote of support. He did not get it, and twenty-four hours later the case was nulled. An attack ordered for July 13 would almost certainly have failed . . . but almost certainly would have gained Meade plaudits for trying.

On seeing Meade's request to be relieved of command, the president composed a letter to this latest unhappy general. "I am very — *very* — grateful to you for the magnificent success you gave the cause of the country at Gettysburg," he began, "and I am sorry now to be the author of the slightest pain to you." He explained his deep distress at the evidence (in his mind) that Meade and Couch and Smith "were not seeking a collision with the enemy, but were trying to get him across the river without another battle." He traced the pursuit, the catching of the quarry at the flooded Potomac, "and yet you stood and let the flood run down, bridges be built, and the enemy move away at his leisure, without attacking him. . . .

"Again, my dear general, I do not believe you appreciate the magnitude of the misfortune involved in Lee's escape. He was within your easy grasp, and to have closed upon him would, in connection with our other late successes, have ended the war. As it is, the war will be prolonged indefinitely. . . . Your golden opportunity is gone, and I am distressed immeasureably because of it." He closed by saying, "As you had learned that I was dissatisfied, I have thought it best to kindly tell you why."

Lincoln put the letter in an envelope and endorsed it, "To Gen. Meade, never sent, or signed," and set it aside. His letters to McClellan and to Hooker were meant to persuade; this letter to Meade would only wound. It was not seen in Lincoln's lifetime, nor in Meade's.[10]

The actions of the July 12 war council became fodder for public comment thanks to busybody James Wadsworth. Political general Wadsworth, who on July 1 had led his First Corps division with more verve than skill, resigned and hastened to Washington to spread word of the generals (other than himself) who had voted against fighting. Lee got away, he told John Hay, because "nobody stopped him . . . no idea the enemy intended to get away at once." He told Gideon Welles that Meade hesitated and delayed until too late. "Want of decision and self reliance in an emergency has cost him and the country dear," Welles concluded. Wadsworth was the source for the detailed, negative account of Meade and the July 12 war council in the *New-York Tribune* for July 18, leaked by Wadsworth to his confidant Adams Hill, the *Tribune*'s Washington correspondent.

The *Tribune* article inspired Otis Howard to write to the president to applaud Meade's decisions at Williamsport; otherwise, said Howard, Gettysburg's outcome might "have been turned upon us." Lincoln's reply suggested he had grown less prohibitive and more reflective: "A few days having passed, I am now profoundly grateful for what was done, without criticism for what was not done. Gen. Meade has my confidence as a brave and skillful officer, and a true man." Howard gave the letter to Meade, who sent it, along with an equally supportive private letter from General Halleck, to his wife for safekeeping. "This has all blown over," Meade wrote her, "& I have received very handsome letters both from Halleck & the President doing more than justice to my services."

But in fact, thanks to armchair generals and such talebearers as Wadsworth, undercurrents in Washington eroded Meade's Gettysburg honors, mostly on the grounds that he had "let Lee escape." Typical was the poison pen of Judge Advocate General Joseph Holt. Meade's "conduct in refusing to pursue & press Lee," Holt wrote, "shows that like all the McClellan generals, he is only capable of *defensive* warfare. He could have destroyed Lee's army on the banks of the Potomac as easily as he could have laid his hand on his own swordhilt . . . As it is, it seems to be understood here, that under its present leadership the Army of the Potomac is necessarily without a future, & must sink to the original inglorious rôle assigned to it by McClellan — of being a body guard for Washington."[11]

Meade did not hesitate in resuming the pursuit of the enemy into Virginia. He pushed the Potomac army across the Potomac at Harper's Ferry and Berlin in just two days, in contrast to the nine days McClellan required to cross in *his* pursuit of Lee the previous fall. Meade kept moving, staying east of the Blue Ridge, forcing the pace against Lee in the Shenandoah Valley. In common with McClellan's campaign, Meade was inflicted with supply shortages, but rather than wait and complain he resolved them on the march. "There never was a better army," General Alpheus Williams wrote on July 21, "because from long service and few recruits we are hardened down to the very sublimation of muscle, health, and endurance. The men can march twenty-five to thirty miles a day with sixty pounds — if necessary. They seldom grumble, and come to camp after a hard day's march with jokes and songs."

"The Govt. insists on my pursuing & destroying Lee," Meade told his wife. "The former I can do but the latter will depend on him as much as on me — for if he keeps out of my way, I cant destroy." On July 23 Meade glimpsed an opportunity to destroy. By breaking through Manassas Gap into the Valley, he might cut off Lee's trailing corps, under Dick Ewell. He assigned the operation to William French's Third Corps. General French quickly showed himself incapable of independent command. He crept ahead and lightly skirmished and the day and the opportunity were gone. Meade hurried forward but too late to energize French. Ewell slipped away and Lee moved swiftly out of reach.

On July 31 Meade wrote Margaret, "The Govt. for some reason unknown to me (this is confidential) has directed me to cease the pursuit of the enemy, so I suppose we will have a little quiet for the present. I was in favor of advancing and trying the chances of another battle with Lee." The two armies were back on the Rappahannock line now, about where they had been two months before. "Keep up a threatening attitude," Halleck instructed, "but do not advance." The campaign of Gettysburg was officially ended.[12]

The three days of Gettysburg cost the Union 22,813 casualties, of which 3,149 were dead. There were about 7,300 additional casualties in the march north (mostly captured at Winchester) and in the pursuit south, raising the total campaign loss to some 30,100. (The Confederates' Gettysburg battle loss was remarkably similar, 22,625; and for the campaign as a whole, some 27,125.)

Commanding-officer casualties fell most heavily on the First and Second Corps. The First Corps suffered corps commander John Reynolds killed and six brigade commanders wounded — Solomon Meredith, Gabriel R. Paul, Chapman Biddle, Roy Stone, Langhorne Wister, and George J. Stannard. In the Second Corps, corps commander Winfield Hancock fell wounded, as did division commander John Gibbon. Four of its brigade commanders died — Edward E. Cross, Samuel K. Zook, George L. Willard, and Eliakim Sherrill — and three were wounded — John R. Brooke, Alexander S. Webb, and Thomas A. Smyth. The Third Corps lost corps commander Dan Sickles wounded and brigade commander Charles K. Graham wounded and captured. In the Fifth Corps, division commander James Barnes was wounded, and brigade commanders Strong Vincent and Stephen H. Weed were mortally wounded. In the Eleventh Corps, division commander Francis C. Barlow was wounded. At headquarters, Dan Butterfield and Gouverneur Warren were wounded, and in the cavalry corps, Elon J. Farnsworth was killed. Losses among regimental commanders were heavy — in the Third Corps, for example, seventeen of thirty-seven.[13]

The Potomac army's high command (with exceptions) rose to challenges at Gettysburg as it had not at Chancellorsville, the prime example being the general commanding. Halleck wrote of the new man to Grant, victor of Vicksburg, "Meade has thus far proved an excellent general, the only one, in fact, who has ever fought the Army of the Potomac well. He seems the right man in the right place."

Meade was widely recognized as the right man to rejuvenate a demoralized officer class. Captain Henry L. Abbott, 20th Massachusetts, a close observer of Potomac army generals, explained in a letter to historian John C. Ropes, "Everything we hear of Meade is so honest, so well-conducted, there is such an absence of drunkenness, *whores,* &c. which marked Hooker's Hdqts., there is so much of the old McClellan style & feeling, that we men think we are in the hands of an honest & God-fearing *gentleman.*"

Henry Hunt would examine the management of Gettysburg for a set of articles in *Century* magazine, and he appraised Meade's role for Alex Webb: "Now, Webb, as I have studied this battle, because I have written about it and had to study it, Meade has grown and grown upon me." From the moment he was abruptly placed in command, Hunt wrote, "*all* his acts and intentions, as I can judge of them, were just what they *ought* to have been. . . . He was right in his orders as to Pipe Creek . . . right in pushing up to Gettysburg after the battle commenced, — right in remaining there, — right in making his battle a purely defensive one, — right, therefore, in taking the line he did, — right in not attempting a counter-attack at *any* stage of the battle, — right as to his pursuit of Lee." Rarely, Hunt decided, "has more skill, vigor, or wisdom been shown under such circumstances. . . ."[14]

Hunt's opinions have the merit of experience and assessment. Unlike his predecessors, George Meade excelled at commanding his command-

Edwin Forbes captioned this bit of satire, "The Rebs lament on leaving Pennsylvania. You want us back in the Union, and now we've come you won't let us stay."

ers. On July 1 he entrusted John Reynolds with three of the army's seven infantry corps, and Reynolds rewarded that trust by saving the Gettysburg site (and Cemetery Hill) for a defensive battle. Informed of Reynolds's death and taking the measure of Reynolds's ill-suited successor Otis Howard, Meade sent the charismatic Winfield Hancock to rally the beaten First and Eleventh Corps. Not waiting for Hancock's report, Meade named Gettysburg the battlefield and called up his forces.

On reaching Gettysburg, Meade personally posted defensively for July 2. Acting on the instant to counter Dan Sickles's blundering, he directed the Fifth Corps to back up the Third, posted Sedgwick's arriving Sixth Corps, and had Hancock send a division to meet the crisis on the left. As the battle widened, he drew on the Twelfth Corps and then the First Corps for reinforcement. On July 3 he not only predicted the focus of Lee's attack, positioning substantial reinforcements to meet it, but by silencing his guns drew Lee into advancing his infantry . . . straight at the ranked, deadly Union batteries.

Lacking clairvoyance, Meade did not anticipate Lee's retreat and send ahead to cut it off. Lacking reconnaissance — and warrior generals — he did not dash headlong against the strong Williamsport fieldworks. Meade knew only too well that Robert E. Lee had bested every Yankee general so far sent against him, and that behind his imposing works he would welcome an opportunity to reverse Pickett's Charge. However Mr. Lincoln might wish it, it was not simply a case of stretching forth hands and "they were ours."

The performance of Meade's corps commanders ranged from brilliant to abysmal. Brilliant indeed was the Second Corps' Winfield Hancock, who was everywhere and did everything; on July 2, in particular, he was indispensable to staving off disaster. Before he was killed, John Reynolds ensured that Gettysburg could be the battlefield of Meade's choice. George Sykes handled the Fifth Corps capably in a tangled command situation on July 2, and John Sedgwick rushed the distant Sixth Corps to the battlefield to act as an essential reserve.

Then there was Dan Sickles, whose misstep on July 2 demonstrated why he should never have been entrusted with more than the Excelsior Brigade. Otis Howard showed no better grasp of high command at Gettysburg than he had at Chancellorsville. Henry Slocum veered from overcautious one day to heedless the next.

Sterling individual performances marked the three days. On July 1, John Buford won the time the Union needed to hold and defend the high ground. On July 2, on the left, Gouverneur Warren found Little Round Top undefended and called up the brigades of Strong Vincent and Stephen Weed, both of whom gave their lives holding this sector. On the right flank, Alpheus Williams took the Twelfth Corps from Slocum's palsied hands, and George Greene saved Culp's Hill. On July 3, John Gibbon and Alexander Hays expertly managed the infantry's fight against Pickett's Charge. ("My defences were stone walls," said Hays, "and since Jackson is dead I think I have a claim to his title.") Henry Hunt's inspired direction of the artillery doomed Lee's "grand charge."

At Gettysburg the fighting men of the Potomac army finally got, for the most part, the leadership they had long deserved. "Again I thank God that the Army of the Potomac has at last gained a victory," wrote Elisha Rhodes, 2nd Rhode Island. "I wonder what the South thinks of us Yankees now. I think Gettysburg will cure the Rebels of any desire to invade the North again."[15]

August 1863 was spent rehabilitating the Army of the Potomac and rethinking its mission. Despite his letter (to Otis Howard) expressing confidence in Meade, Lincoln was doubtful about how aggressive a commander he might be. In a conversation at the White House, Gideon Welles asked if Meade was going to have a battle. Lincoln "looked at me earnestly for a moment," Welles told his diary, and said he had no faith that Meade "will attack Lee — nothing looks like it to me. I believe he can never have another as good opportunity as that which he trifled away. . . . No I dont believe he is going to fight."

Secretary Stanton, in one of his impulsive tempers, wanted to bring General Grant east to replace Meade, but Halleck (among others) talked him out of it. Grant too thought it a bad idea — "It would cause me more sadness than satisfaction," he wrote, to be ordered to command the Army of the Potomac. He knew nothing of the Potomac generals, nothing of the Eastern battleground; "dissatisfaction would necessarily be produced by importing a General to command an Army already well supplied with those who have grown up, and been promoted, with it. . . ."

That army was just then in flux. The last two-year men and nine-month militia left for home, and there were other manpower losses. A reinforcing division from the Peninsula was abruptly ordered away to an operation against Charleston. On July 13–16 the first conscription call in New York City had triggered bloody, fiery draft riots that paralyzed the city. "It is a grave business," wrote diarist George Templeton Strong, "a *jacquerie* that must be put down by heroic doses of lead and steel." Grave enough that Halleck had the Potomac army stand down until it was certain that conscription could be effected. "They were afraid to trust this army in another general engagement," Meade told his wife, "for fear that it were crippled or destroyed, *they could not raise another one. . . .*"

A second round of conscription was scheduled for New York, with this time the Army of the Potomac providing security. Four regiments were sent north on July 31. Two weeks later went a reinforcement of some 10,000 men, including the army's two brigades of regulars. This time the draft went smoothly. But the first fruits of conscription, to General Meade, were "miserable creatures. . . . Such worthless material as these men are no addition to this army but only a clog. . . ." If the citizenry did not respond to the draft willingly and heartily, he decided, "the Govt had better make up their minds to letting the South go." To set a stark example for conscripted newcomers, Meade carried out, before the massed Fifth Corps, the firing-squad execution of five substitutes for drafted men who had enlisted for bounty money and were caught deserting. Mr. Lincoln, who often granted clemency in army execution cases, did not intervene in this one.[16]

Meade was called to Washington on August 14 to meet with the president and cabinet. It was his first meeting with Lincoln since taking the command, and his first with any of the cabinet. He described Gettysburg "clearly and fluently," wrote Gideon Welles, who was "better pleased with him than I expected I should be, for I have had some prejudice since

Edwin Forbes's "The Fatal Volley" (August 29, 1863) — the execution of five deserters, seated on their coffins before their open graves, witnessed by the Fifth Corps.

the escape of Lee." The manner in which he was received in Washington, Meade told Margaret, "was certainly most gratifying to me. I really believe I have the confidence of all parties, and will continue to retain it, unless some great disaster should overtake me. . . ."[17]

The makeup of the high command was less gratifying. In a letter to Ambrose Burnside, outspoken John Buford explained that the Army of the Potomac "is in about the same state as when you left it. The same faults exist among corps commanders as has always existed. . . . Too much apathy, too much cold water" thrown on fresh thinking. Staff man James Biddle was more specific for his wife: "Slocum & Howard are slow. French I hear imbibes. Sykes I do not know much about but I do not believe his capacity is more than a Divsn. Newton is nervous & fidgetty. Hays does not amount to anything."

Meade intended at least doing something about mediocre William Hays heading the Second Corps. Hancock's Gettysburg wound was not healing, and Meade told Halleck he was "very anxious" to have a competent commander for the corps. He nominated the army's chief engineer, Gouverneur Warren, a step suggested to him by Hancock himself. This required Warren being made major general, a process caught in red tape that left Warren on tenterhooks. He wrote his wife that he was in his third year of

General Meade was photographed with his principal officers in September 1863. From left: Gouverneur Warren (Second Corps), William French (Third Corps), Meade, Henry Hunt (artillery chief), Andrew Humphreys (chief of staff), George Sykes (Fifth Corps).

unrequited labors on the battlefield. "I feel the necessity for some military reward to sustain me, some mark of appreciation at least." Finally the red tape was cut, Warren was rewarded with the two stars of a major general, and he took the Second Corps. (James Biddle approved: "Warren is active, quick, and a pushing man. . . .")[18]

Another Meade project was doing something about the Eleventh Corps, after Gettysburg more firmly than ever identified within the army as the Flying Dutchmen. "Much feeling exists in this army in regard to the Eleventh Corps," Meade told Halleck. He wanted the corps broken up. He would send Otis Howard with one division to the Second Corps, which, with Warren's promotion just then in abeyance, Major General Howard would command. A second division would go to the Twelfth Corps. A third division, Carl Schurz's, would be guardian of the Potomac army's communications. General Schurz, who saw himself as godfather to the Eleventh, was concerned about morale, and Meade sent him to Halleck to find ways "to be least offensive to the officers and men concerned. . . ."[19]

The scheme was overtaken by events. On September 13 Meade told his wife that Lee "has made a considerable detachment to go somewhere." Two days later he learned the detachment was Longstreet's corps. The

Bureau of Military Information learned the somewhere was Georgia and Braxton Bragg's army. The war in the Western theater was heating up. William Rosecrans's Yankee army pressured Bragg's hold on East Tennessee, and their two armies were now, in mid-September, maneuvering along the Tennessee-Georgia border. With his army reduced by one-third, Lee fell back behind the more defensible Rapidan. Meade moved to press his advantage. "My opinion," Lincoln told Halleck, "is that he should move upon Lee at once in manner of general attack, leaving to developments, whether he will make it a real attack." Before Meade could act on this advice, reports came of Rosecrans's resounding defeat at Chickamauga Creek, in northwestern Georgia, on September 19–20. Rosecrans took refuge in Chattanooga, where he was soon besieged. He cried out for help.[20]

Meade was called to Washington to discuss parting with a portion of his army due to his lack of any active campaigning. He objected with some force, saying that if he was considered too slow or too prudent he should be replaced. "Halleck smiled very significantly," Meade told Margaret, "& said he had no doubt I would be rejoiced to be relieved, but there was no such good luck for me."

Secretary of War Stanton now declared an emergency. On September 23 he convened a midnight war council at the War Department, calling in the president, Secretaries Seward and Chase, General Halleck, Peter Watson and James Hardie of the War Department, and Daniel McCallum, superintendent of military railroads. Rosecrans must be reinforced immediately, Stanton announced. Discussion revealed that forces in the Western theater were too scattered to be certain of getting to Chattanooga in time. Stanton then proposed the reinforcement come from the Army of the Potomac — specifically, the Eleventh and Twelfth Corps, under command of Fighting Joe Hooker.

"This proposition was objected to quite strongly both by Gen Halleck & the President," Chase wrote, on the grounds that Potomac army troops would be too long getting to Rosecrans; in any event, "both were unwilling to withdraw troops from Meade." Stanton argued there was no reason to expect Meade would attack Lee anytime soon. Once the two corps were pulled back to Washington, he said, they could start reaching Rosecrans within five days. Seward and Chase backed Stanton, and McCallum outlined his scheme for taking over the railroads carrying the troop trains. "The scale was now turned," said Chase. At 2:30 a.m. on September 24 Halleck telegraphed Meade and announced the plan.

The plan worked masterfully. The troops had to detrain for two crossings of the Ohio River, and differing rail gauges required three more shufflings. There were trains for troops, trains for artillery, trains for horses and baggage and supplies. A fully equipped army of some 20,000 men traveled the 1,200 miles to Bridgeport, Alabama, 26 miles from Chattanooga, the first of the infantry arriving on the fifth day, the last on the thirteenth day. Hooker wired Stanton, "You may justly claim the merit of having saved Chattanooga for us."

The dispirited Eleventh Corps accepted the transfer West as a fresh start in a new theater of war. That was not the case for the well-traveled Twelfth Corps. It had found a home with the Potomac army. Generals Alpheus Williams, George S. Greene, Thomas H. Ruger, and Joseph Knipe "were quite boiling over," wrote staff man Theodore Lyman; "not only disgusted at leaving the Army of the Potomac, but indignant at being placed under Hooker, whom they despise." Corps commander Henry Slocum boiled over as well, writing Lincoln to tender his resignation rather than serve under Hooker, in whom he professed no confidence. Lincoln mollified him by promising matters would be adjusted once he got West.

Neither corps, nor any of their generals, would return to the Army of the Potomac. Joe Hooker's new posting meant he would no longer be lingering over General Meade's shoulder. Otis Howard and the Eleventh Corps would not be missed. But the Twelfth Corps, which fought well at Antietam, Chancellorsville, and Gettysburg, *would* be missed. Henry Slocum might be a problematical corps commander, but the generals of division and brigade described as boiling over by Colonel Lyman were all first-rate soldiers.[21]

General Meade described for his wife his state of suspense and anxiety at what he termed the "public scene so impatient of what they call the inactivity of the Army of the Potomac." He was even willing to grant General Lee the first move — "He would relieve me very much if he would leave his strong position, and its protections & come out into the open country and give me battle. . . . I have an admirable army for its size and Lee will find it no easy task to overthrow it."

By October 10 it was evident that Lee *was* making the first move. Initially the Yankee cavalry was stymied getting a clear picture of the enemy move, leading waspish Halleck to cite one of Napoleon's maxims for Meade's benefit: "Attack him and you will soon find out." Meade diagnosed the move as an effort to turn his right flank, in seeming imitation of Lee's maneuvers against John Pope the previous fall — or as Provost Marshal Patrick put it, "They are preparing to give us our annual Bull Run Flogging...." Meade backpedaled to stay abreast of the enemy advance. "If Bob Lee will go into those fields there and fight me, man for man," he said, "I will do it this afternoon." On the 13th he missed an opening to cut off a Rebel column due to faulty reconnaissance. "*After it was all over*," he wrote Winfield Hancock, "information was obtained, which, if I had possessed at the time, would have induced me to operate differently." He and Chief of Staff Humphreys firmly agreed that (as Humphreys put it) "any position at or in the near vicinity of the Manassas or Bull Run battle-fields was objectionable because of the former operations there...." Meade would instead take a blocking position in the old lines at Centreville. Skirmishes and cavalry clashes marked the way as the two armies retraced old marches.

On October 14 Gouverneur Warren with the Second Corps did seize an opening, laying an ambush at Bristoe Station on the Orange & Alexandria. Posted at cuts and embankments along the railroad, the divisions of Alex Webb and Alick Hays reprised July 3 at Gettysburg ... against some of the same Rebel troops that had made Pickett's Charge. Generals Warren, Webb, and Hays, it was reported, "gallop up and down the track, encouraging the men with cheers mingled with imprecations." Hays told his wife, "The afternoon affair at Bristoe was one of the prettiest affairs I have ever seen ... we flogged them terribly."

Balked at Centreville, Lee fell back behind the Rappahannock. In the going, he tore up some 20 miles of the Orange & Alexandria. Meade followed, pausing until the tracks could be repaired. He assured Hancock that the Second Corps "has acquired great reputation from the Bristoe affair, and Warren is now our Hero." As for himself, "They are very polite and civil to me at Washington," but once again the enemy had gotten away. He was prepared to be relieved at any moment, he said, "and accordingly keep my sabre packed."[22]

Reports of battle roused Dan Sickles, whose amputation was hardly healed, to take up his crutches and report to the front. He was greeted tumultuously by his old Third Corps. "All the division was lined up on both sides of the road," Régis de Trobriand wrote, "and when the car where our glorious invalid was, arrived, a storm of hurrahs exploded...." "We have great faith here in him," David Birney proclaimed, and envisioned Sickles commanding the Potomac army. But George Meade had had more than enough of Dan Sickles. Gouverneur Warren heard that Sickles would have been court-martialed for his role at Gettysburg had he not been maimed. The Bristoe fighting was over now, and Meade, with fulsome expressions of solicitude, turned Sickles away on the grounds of disability. "I very re-

Two shelved generals, both former commanders of the Third Corps. Sam Heintzelman (right) was pushed from a corps to an administrative posting. Amputee Dan Sickles, when blocked from returning to the Potomac army, became Meade's inveterate enemy.

luctantly yielded assent," said Sickles, and he returned to Washington to initiate a campaign of his own — at Meade's expense — to regain his command.[23]

On October 22–23 Meade was in the capital to consult with Lincoln and Halleck. Lincoln had sent Meade his appraisal of Lee and his army, attaching more than a hint of a direct order — "If Gen. Meade can now attack him on a field no worse than equal for us . . . the honor will be his if he succeeds, and the blame may be mine if he fails." But Halleck was his usual opaque self, urging "something should be done, but what that something was he did not define." Then, on the 24th, came word that deepened Meade's frustration with his Washington masters. A rumor (false) had Lee sending a second corps west, causing Lincoln to "suggest that with all possible expedition the Army of the Potomac get ready to attack Lee. . . ." Meade viewed *this* presidential suggestion as an order, and told his wife, "I am so anxious & worried with the responsibility of my position." He hoped Lee might again take the lead and "relieve me from the solution of a difficult problem which was how to get at him." It was about this time that John Sedgwick made note that "Meade is twenty years older than when he took command."

At least in part to assert himself, Meade took a bold stand and proposed to change the army's base. In a modification of Ambrose Burnside's scheme of the previous December, he would turn Lee's right, "throwing the whole army rapidly and secretly" across the Rappahannock at Banks's Ford and along the river's south bank to the heights behind Fredericksburg. This would shift the army's supply line to Aquia Landing and the Richmond, Fredericksburg & Potomac Railroad for the advance south, as Burnside had intended.

It proved too bold a stand, perhaps rousing too many grim December memories. Halleck transcribed Lincoln's reaction: The proposed change of base seemed unlikely "to produce any favorable result, while its disadvantages are manifest." Halleck concurred: "An entire change of base under existing circumstances, I can neither advise nor approve." Meade wrote Margaret, with some bitterness, "Now I have clearly indicated what I thought feasible & practical and my plan is *disapproved*." He cast a look back at his command role since Gettysburg and "regretted I did not absolutely & firmly decline from the first."[24]

His fresh thinking quashed, Meade dutifully turned to a direct offensive against the Army of Northern Virginia's posting along the south bank of the Rappahannock. At Rappahannock Station, near the wrecked Orange & Alexandria bridge over the river, Lee had a *tête de pont*, a fortified bridgehead, on the north bank as access for counterstriking a Yankee flanking move. Meade divided the army, right wing under Sedgwick to assault the bridgehead, left wing under French to force a crossing downstream at Kelly's Ford. On November 7 the twin assaults went forward.

Régis de Trobriand's Third Corps brigade drew the assignment at Kelly's Ford. Behind artillery and infantry covering fire, the 1st U.S. Sharpshooters was ordered across the waist-deep ford, encouraged by language "not found in military tactics, or the church catechism" from division commander David Birney. Colonel de Trobriand then pushed his regiments across, and the enemy, "who did not expect us there so soon, offered little resistance, and surrendered with a good grace." It was intended to hurry at least a corps across at Kelly's to support the fight at Rappahannock Station, but that proved unnecessary.

Sedgwick assigned Brigadier David A. Russell, that day leading 1st Division, Sixth Corps, to the Rebel bridgehead. When artillery fire failed to drive off the defenders, Russell ordered an infantry assault, with a twist. He sent out a regiment to routinely relieve the skirmish line, but actually to reinforce it for a surprise joint assault. "So quietly and naturally was the whole thing done that the rebels were completely taken in," wrote Charles Wainwright. The assault broke into the enemy works, setting off a hand-to-hand struggle. "The brave old hero, Davy Russell, ordered the charge and rode along close to them," a company captain reported approvingly. A second brigade, under twenty-four-year-old Colonel Emory Upton (West Point class of 1861), was led with such discipline that it carried its section of the works with only the bayonet. In the growing dark the Rebels fled across a pontoon bridge or surrendered. "They were all feeling very jolly at headquarters over this success," said Colonel Wainwright, "and well they may. . . . 'Uncle John,' Russell, and Upton all deserve great credit."

The November 7 assaults inflicted over 2,000 casualties and broke Lee's Rappahannock line beyond repair and sent him hastily retreating behind the Rapidan. With a nighttime head start, the retreat outdistanced the pursuit. General Warren "looked like a man of disappointed hopes," wrote Theodore Lyman, "as he gazed round the country and said, 'There's nobody here — *nobody!*'" Meade told his wife, "*Of course* I am more popular than ever, having been greeted yesterday as I rode through the ranks with great cheering. . . . I am afraid my chances of being relieved are greatly diminished." The president wrote him, "I have seen your dispatches about operations on the Rappahannock on Saturday, and I wish to say, 'Well done.'"[25]

Heartened by success on the Rappahannock, Meade sought a greater success on the Rapidan before winter shut down campaigning. The Orange & Alexandria bridge over the Rappahannock was rebuilt, opening the line as far as Brandy Station, securing the army's supply line. Meade's plan was a mirror image of Joe Hooker's in the spring — Hooker had turned Lee's left to get into his rear at Fredericksburg; Meade would turn Lee's right to get into his rear on the Rapidan.

(This campaign planning prevented Meade from accepting an invitation to attend the ceremonies on November 19 dedicating the military cemetery at Gettysburg. On request, however, he did direct aide Theodore Lyman to prepare a resumé of Meade's Gettysburg report for the benefit of the ceremony's principal speaker, Edward Everett.)

Lee had fortified some 20 miles along the Rapidan's south bank, his line ending downstream at a tributary called Mine Run. It was Meade's thought to shift his five corps eastward rapidly and secretly, cross the river at fords below Mine Run, secure the east–west roadways Orange Turnpike and Orange Plank Road, and drive west to "attack him before he could prepare any defenses." This region was part of the Wilderness of ill fame in the Chancellorsville campaign. The corps commanders — Newton, Warren, French, Sykes, and Sedgwick — were called to a briefing, handed detailed circulars and maps, and treated to a full discussion of timetables and marches. Unlike such predecessors as McClellan and Hooker, George

Meade wanted a fully informed high command. Heavy rains delayed the operation until November 26.

Meade's plan had French's Third Corps, followed by Sedgwick's Sixth, crossing the Rapidan at Jacob's Ford, four miles beyond the Confederate right. Three and a half miles downstream, Warren's Second Corps would cross at Germanna Ford. Four miles farther, Sykes's Fifth Corps and Newton's First would cross at the Culpeper Mine Ford. The crossings were to be simultaneous, and by day's end the army would rendezvous at Robertson's Tavern on the Orange Turnpike, well behind Lee's fieldworks. Per Chief of Staff Humphreys, "The plan promised brilliant success; to insure it required prompt, vigorous action, and intelligent compliance with the programme on the part of corps and other subordinate commanders." Humphreys wrote this retrospectively, to stress the plan's requirements . . . most of which went unmet.[26]

Trouble began straightaway with William French and his Third Corps. French was a burly old regular, red in the face and steeped in alcohol, lacking any trace of enterprise. His experience was smashing a division head-on against unyielding obstacles, at Antietam and at Fredericksburg. During the pursuit into Virginia in July, he had misplayed the chance to cut off the Rebel rear guard at Manassas Gap.

Early on November 26, as the other corps reached their Rapidan crossing sites, the Third Corps was found still asleep. It was three hours getting to the road for Jacob's Ford, then became lost. The lead division was under the inexperienced Henry Prince, whose record comprised being captured at Cedar Mountain in August 1862 and exchanged that December. Eventually Prince approached the ford, but lacking instructions from French, proceeded with great deliberation. After the heavy rains the Rapidan was running high, and when Prince brought up the bridge train it was a pontoon short; the crossing was pieced out with an improvised trestle. Prince's division only started across in late afternoon. Meade had meanwhile held back the other corps for a synchronized crossing. "Meade was very angry (& justly) at this terrible delay & carelessness . . . on the part of the 3' Corps," Provost Marshal Patrick told his diary. The cost, it was feared, was "full notice of our movements to Lee. . . ." At day's end, the lead corps were barely across the Rapidan.

General French managed no better on November 27. Patrick's diary sums up: "The 3' Corps, after fooling away Thursday on the North Side of the River, finally crossed at Jacob's Ferry & again got lost in trying to reach Robertson's Tavern." On Friday, French delayed the "whole Army all day . . . and did not get his position at all that day." In Meade's scheme,

Sykes's Fifth Corps and Newton's First, on the Orange Plank Road, formed the left, and Warren's Second Corps, on the Orange Turnpike, the center. French's lagging Third Corps (trailed by Sedgwick's Sixth) failed to fill out the battlefront on the right, exposing Warren's flank. The hapless Prince again lost his way in the Wilderness. French remained at the rear, by report spending the day living up to his nickname Old Gin Barrel. French reported he was halted, "waiting for General Warren." Meade was furious. "What are you waiting for? No orders have been sent you to wait for General Warren. . . . The commanding general directs that you move forward as rapidly as possible to Robertson's Tavern, where your corps is wanted."

General Lee — awarded a full day's warning — struck the Third Corps before it could connect with the Second. In thick woods with few clearings the fighting was disjointed but sharp. French remained befuddled and Prince's division was roughly handled, but the corps' other divisions, under veterans Joseph Carr and David Birney, finally pushed back the Rebels.[27]

Meade spent November 28 recalculating. The surprise element in his plan was voided by the first-day delays, as were immediate hopes of escaping the entrapping Wilderness for more open ground to the west. Making headquarters at Robertson's Tavern, Meade rearranged his forces. John Sedgwick had become impatient stuck behind the inert French, so Meade pushed his Sixth Corps past the Third to the front, "a very laborious thing, midst mud and soft cross-roads." The battlefront was now (from left) the Second, First, and Sixth Corps, with the Third and Fifth Corps in reserve. Skirmishers found the enemy gone — fallen back behind Mine Run to a line Meade termed formidable: "The western bank of Mine Run . . . on which was the enemy's line of battle, was already crowned with infantry parapets, abatis, and epaulements for batteries. The creek itself was a considerable obstacle. . . ." Staff man James Biddle's impression was "a very strong position, resembling Fredericksburg."

Sunday the 29th was a day of reconnoitering. The weather turned frigid and prospects on the battlefront turned daunting. Robert McAllister, commanding the 11th New Jersey, described the prospective assault for his wife: "Pass over this hill, down into a ravine, over a fence, through a marsh, up another hill, and then over their works. The more we looked at it . . . the more doubtful the result." The best chance seemed, once again, to turn the enemy's right. Gouverneur Warren's Second Corps, reinforced by a Sixth Corps division, was sent southward to see if the Mine Run line could be turned. Warren reported favorably. In a council that evening a "much encouraged" General Meade determined on an assault the next morning by Warren on the left and by Sedgwick on the right. Warren, described by Major Biddle as "full of his position and certain of being able to gain great things," was given priority and reinforced by two of French's divisions (to French's indignation). Warren was heard to say that if he succeeded, "I shall be the greatest man in the army; if I don't, all my sins will be remembered." He was confident enough to think the enemy might be gone by morning.[28]

Orders were that at 8:00 a.m. on November 30, batteries would open and on the left Warren would press his infantry assault. At 9:00 a.m. Sedgwick's Sixth Corps would attack on the right, and the First and Third Corps demonstrate against the center. On Warren's front, men were seen to pin to their clothes slips of paper bearing their name, to ensure their identity for the burial parties.

Artillery opened as scheduled, but nothing was heard from the left. General French, peevish at losing two divisions to Warren, asked Meade, "Where are your young Napoleon's guns; why doesn't he open?" Then, at 8:50, a dispatch from Warren reached headquarters. The enemy's position and strength, he wrote, "seem so formidable in my present front that I advise against making the attack here. The full light of the sun shows me that I cannot succeed." Meade showed this to Humphreys and exclaimed, "My God! Gen. Warren has half my army." Aides rushed off to halt the artillery fire and to cancel Sedgwick's attack. Uncle John, said one of his staff, had expected success on his front. "The General is so savage about it that no one dares to go near him."

Meade hurried to the left to see Warren, "and there they sadly stood, over a fire the orderlies had made for them" (wrote staff man Lyman), declaring the bitter end to the Mine Run operation. Warren explained that overnight the Rebels had reinforced with all the infantry and artillery "that could be put in position." An attack now would be fruitless, and Meade had to agree. Still, it greatly troubled him that his newest corps commander had acted arbitrarily rather than expressing his opinion and referring the decision to the general commanding.

In the fifth day in its extended position, in wintery conditions, the Army of the Potomac was hardly able to either storm or besiege or turn this well-fortified line. On December 1 it fell back to its starting point and went into winter quarters. Provost Marshal Patrick entered in his diary that General Meade "had become so much exasperated at the failure of his plans, or of his Corps Commanders, that he was like a Bear with a sore head & no one was willing to approach him."[29]

· · ·

Mine Run confirmed what Williamsport had implied — it was now a new, very different kind of war. In the field, defenses became paramount. An army might now throw up imposing fieldworks literally overnight, especially where the terrain (in this case, the west bank of Mine Run) was suited to defense to begin with. Nevertheless, while in his report Meade acknowledged failure, "I maintain my plan was a feasible one. Had the columns made the progress I anticipated" on the first day and effected a junction at Robertson's Tavern, he believed the enemy "would have been overwhelmed." Considering that four of his five corps commanders were precisely on schedule that morning of November 26, Meade's claim was not unreasonable.

As to the canceled attack on Warren's front on the 30th, Meade offered no apologies. In the changed circumstances of the moment, hazarding an assault there "would be attended with certain disaster." He wrote with feeling to his wife: "As I have told you before I would rather be ignominiously dismissed, and suffer any thing, than knowingly and willfully have thousands of brave men slaughtered for nothing."

The singular villain of the Mine Run piece was William French, whose conduct on these five days (said Warren succinctly) "was proof of utter incompetency." French ignored Meade's briefing, failed to start the Third Corps as directed, put his worst general in charge, and blundered on from one misjudgment to the next. The initial daylong delay, from which the campaign never recovered, was entirely French's doing. Marsena Patrick, whose ear was close to the ground, told his diary that French "has been tight a good part of the time during this movement."[30]

At least the troops, staff man Lyman decided, had gained new respect for General Meade: "He is not a man who inspires enthusiasm, for he is cold, unbending and not given to granting indulgences, but in time of peril they lean on him, as on a strong wall, and they now feel, more than before, that, when he orders an attack, there is a plan and an object to be gained; and that, without such plan and such object, he will save the men, no matter at what disappointment to himself."

On December 3, soldier-correspondent Samuel Fiske explained to his *Springfield Republican* readers that there had been a game of seesaw here, "in which each side has gone up and gone down, and nobody can say which has kept the longest end of the plank." After a well-conducted retreat "we are safely and perhaps a little ingloriously back again in our old camp." There was disappointment that Meade's army had failed to match the major victory in the Western theater on November 23–25 — George Thomas's Army of the Cumberland, William Sherman's Army of the Tennessee, and Joe Hooker's Eleventh and Twelfth Corps, all under command of U. S. Grant, demolished Braxton Bragg's siege of Chattanooga. Lincoln wondered anew if "this Army of the Potomac was good for anything — if the officers had anything in them. . . ."

The winter encampments of the two armies faced each other across the Rapidan. At his Brandy Station headquarters Meade pondered his future. In the aftermath of Mine Run he wrote the recuperating Winfield Hancock, "I was quite satisfied when I withdrew the army without attacking Lee that it would result in my being relieved." Days and weeks went by and Washington was silent on his fate. But the press was not silent, and General Meade was (unfortunately) a dedicated newspaper reader. He told his wife of a piece in the *Washington Star* headed HESITATING GENERALS that charged him with "running away from Lee" at Williamsport and Mine Run. The *New York Herald,* "inspired by my *friend* Dan Sickles, is constantly harping on the assertion that Gettysburgh was fought by the corps commanders (i.e. D.S.) and the common soldiers & that no generalship was displayed. I suppose after awhile it will be discovered, I was not at Gettysburgh at all."

Hancock enlightened Meade regarding his command status. He had heard rumors that he was being considered as Meade's replacement, said Hancock, but on reporting to General-in-Chief Halleck he was told simply to join his corps when he was ready. Halleck, said Hancock, represented himself as Meade's champion ("No — an officer who gained the battle of Gettysburg is entitled to more consideration"). Meade told Margaret, "The unanimous opinion of all returning officers, together with my report changed the whole aspect of the case. I must say I am gratified some little consideration was extended towards me. . . ."

Meade excelled at military administration, and the army's 1863–64 winter encampment was marked by warm quarters, plentiful food, and generally decent health. A combination of good intentions and high temper, Meade got things done. He had a like-minded collaborator in Chief of Staff Andrew Humphreys. Theodore Lyman described Humphreys as "just as hard as the Commander, for he has a tremendous temper, a great idea of military duty, and is very particular." On becoming wrathy, as Lyman put it, Humphreys "lets go a torrent of adjectives that must rather astonish those not used to little outbursts."[31]

A winter highlight was the "Grand Soiree" staged by the Second Corps celebrating Washington's Birthday. General Meade described it as "quite a gay time." A large ballroom was erected and "beautifully decorated. There were present about 300 ladies many coming from Washington for the oc-

Edwin Forbes portrayed a social highlight of the Army of the Potomac's 1863–64 winter camp, a Washington's Birthday ball staged at Brandy Station by the Second Corps. A special train brought wives and girlfriends and dates from the capital.

casion." Vice President Hannibal Hamlin and senators and congressmen were in attendance, and the noted caterer Gautier furnished "an elegant supper, indeed everything in fine style." Generals treasured their dance cards as souvenirs. The general commanding got to bed at 4:00 a.m.[32]

Winter fighting by the Army of the Potomac was limited to two special operations. By report, prisoners of war housed in Richmond were suffering from overcrowding, disease, and malnutrition, with high mortality rates. Richmond Unionist Elizabeth Van Lew smuggled out the grim statistics to Ben Butler, commanding at Fort Monroe at the tip of the Peninsula. General Butler, of inflated vision and slight military skills, conceived a plan for a cavalry raid on lightly defended Richmond to free the prisoners and perhaps "capture Jeff. Davis" in the bargain. As a diversion, the Second Corps would mount an attack at Morton's Ford on the Rapidan. Nothing of the operation worked. On February 7 Butler's 2,200 troopers were stymied trying to cross the Chickahominy and retreated. On the 6th Alick Hays's division had crossed at Morton's Ford and been sharply repelled at the enemy works, with 261 casualties. After describing this loss, the disgruntled historian of the Second Corps toted up Butler's casualties as six forage caps.[33]

The second special operation was also a raid on Richmond, but more calculated and bearing a secret, ugly stain of mayhem. Brigadier General

Judson Kilpatrick, leading Third Division, Cavalry Corps, intended to succeed where Butler failed. Kill-cavalry's history of command was marked by reckless adventuring, most recently in the destruction of Elon Farnsworth's cavalry brigade at Gettysburg. Staff man Lyman found Kilpatrick "pushing & managing in the extreme . . . an indescribable air between a vulgarian & a crack-brain."

Bypassing the chain of command, Kilpatrick got his idea to Lincoln, delivered by Senator Jacob M. Howard, and Kilpatrick was called to the White House. On February 12 he sketched his plan for the president — a strong force of cavalry to slip around Lee's right, move on Richmond, destroying enemy communications as it went, and liberate the prisoners. Lincoln handed Kilpatrick off to Stanton to develop the plan in its needs and details. When the plan reached Meade it bore the imprimatur of president and secretary of war and he was obliged to approve it — and, to speed its execution, to direct a diversion against Lee's other flank. It was a desperate undertaking, Meade told his wife, but "the anxiety & distress of the public & of the authorities at Washn is so great, that it seems to demand running great risk for the chances of success."

With the expedition approved, Kilpatrick revealed its secret agenda to his partner, Colonel Ulric Dahlgren. Son of Rear Admiral John A. Dahlgren, commanding the South Atlantic Blockading Squadron, the twenty-one-year-old Dahlgren was as reckless an adventurer as Kilpatrick. He had been wounded in a cavalry fight after Gettysburg, requiring amputation of his right leg, but once fitted with a wooden leg he was ready for a new adventure. Hearing rumors of a cavalry raid of some sort ("A secret expedition with us is got up like a picnic," Theodore Lyman complained, "with everybody blabbing and yelping"), Dahlgren volunteered and was accepted as a kindred spirit by Kilpatrick and made second in command. He wrote his father, "A grand raid is to be made and I am to have a very important command . . . it is an undertaking that if I was not in it I should be ashamed to show my face again. . . ."

Notes Dahlgren made of Kilpatrick's instructions for the raid reveal a scheme far more heinous than simply liberating prisoners of war. Once released, the prisoners would be exhorted "to destroy & burn the hateful City & do not allow the Rebel Leader Davis and his traitorous crew to escape . . . prisoners to gut the city . . . Jeff Davis and Cabinet must be killed on the spot." This agenda of arson and assassination would operate at the raiders' direction, but largely carried out by the supposedly enraged prisoners.[34]

Judson Kilpatrick thought up this bloody-minded scheme (with Dahl-

gren his willing collaborator), but even as ruthless and unprincipled a soldier as he would not dare initiate war without quarter and the assassination of Confederate leaders unless he had at least a nod from higher
authority. While Lincoln had approved the potential bonus in Ben Butler's
scheme — capturing President Davis — for this new mission with its secret
objectives the authority Kilpatrick answered to could only be Edwin Stanton. The unscrupulous Stanton was not of a mind to abide by the so-called
rules of war — he had dictated the draconian orders against civilians issued in General Pope's name — and at least by insinuation he planted in
Kilpatrick's mind the mayhem that enraged prisoners of war might inflict
on Richmond and its government when freed.

General Meade launched his diversion early on February 28. The
Sixth Corps marched west as if to turn Lee's left, and 1,500 troopers under George Custer rode south by west with intent to destroy a key railroad bridge near Charlottesville. The bridge proved too well guarded and
Custer withdrew, but he stirred up Rebel defenders sufficiently that the
Kilpatrick-Dahlgren raiders slipped around Lee's right and hurried south
toward Richmond.

The sole success for the 3,600 raiders proved to be their start. Dahlgren
split off with 460 men hoping to find Richmond's southern portal undefended, but he could not cross the James and made a vain effort to reunite
with Kilpatrick. The main body meanwhile approached Richmond from
the north, but when it ran into home-guard defenders Kilpatrick lost his
nerve and after desultory skirmishing took off east for the safety of Ben
Butler's lines on the Peninsula. Dahlgren with some 100 men became separated and on March 2 ran into an ambush and was killed and most of his
men captured. "Kilpatrick's raid was an utter failure," said General Meade.
"Confound the vaporing braggart!" said Theodore Lyman.[35]

Ulric Dahlgren, bold, ambitious, a seeker of fame, was for all that a remarkably foolish young man. Setting off on a secret mission deep behind
enemy lines, he carried with him all his notes and papers spelling out in
detail the raid's hidden agenda of fire and murder. These papers, found
on his body, were soon in Jefferson Davis's hands, and soon after, printed
in full in Richmond's newspapers. The *Dispatch* spoke of the "diabolical
plans" for "booty and butchery, the robbing and marauding." The *Whig* labeled the raiders not soldiers but "assassins, barbarians, thugs," and asked,
"Are they not barbarians redolent with more hellish purposes than were
the Goth, the Hun or the Saracen?"

General Lee was instructed to send photographs of the Dahlgren papers to General Meade by flag of truce, questioning if Dahlgren was act-

ing under orders and "whether the Government of the United States sanctions the sentiments and purposes therein set forth." Meade was appalled at this "pretty ugly piece of business." He demanded a report from Kilpatrick. "All this is false," said Kilpatrick indignantly, and suggested the Rebels had doctored or forged the Dahlgren papers. That too was a theory in the press. Meade replied to Lee that "neither the United States Government, myself, nor General Kilpatrick authorized, sanctioned, or approved the burning of the city of Richmond and the killing of Mr. Davis and cabinet. . . ."

For George Meade, this denial held true for the government and for himself, but he doubted it was true for Kilpatrick. He wrote his wife that Kilpatrick claimed the Dahlgren papers were forgeries, "but I regret to say Kilpatrick's reputation & collateral evidence in my possession rather go against this theory." The collateral evidence was from the Bureau of Military Information. Captain John McEntee accompanied Dahlgren on the mission, and told Marsena Patrick "he thinks the papers are correct that were found upon Dahlgren, as they correspond with what D. told *him*. . . ." B.M.I. agent John Babcock confirmed: The papers "found on Dahlgren's body published in the Richmond papers [are an] Authentic report of contents."

Judson Kilpatrick (left), commanding Third Division, Calvalry Corps, and his second in command Ulric Dahlgren, directed the notorious Richmond Raid in February 1864.

The paper trail to the Kilpatrick-Dahlgren raid's secret agenda ends with Ulric Dahlgren, who posthumously earned not fame but infamy. While Judson Kilpatrick escaped a deserved infamy, General Meade would not have him in his army. In April 1864 Kilpatrick went west to the Army of the Cumberland. To discourage further Yankee raids, Richmond transferred its prisoners to a new prison in Georgia called Andersonville. The *Richmond Inquirer* offered a grim (and prescient) prediction: "We think that these Dahlgren papers will destroy, during the rest of the war, all rosewater chivalry, and that Confederate armies will make war afar and upon the rules selected by the enemy."

Edwin Stanton made a point of shutting off inquiry into the Kilpatrick-Dahlgren affair. At war's end he called on Francis Lieber, keeper of the captured Confederate archives, for the papers found on Dahlgren's body. On December 1, 1865, these papers were delivered to Stanton at the War Department . . . and never seen again.[36]

In December 1863 Congressman Elihu B. Washburne introduced in the new Thirty-eighth Congress a bill to revive the rank of lieutenant general, last held by George Washington (Winfield Scott only held it by brevet). Washburne was the particular champion of U. S. Grant, for whom he intended the rank. As the bill made its way through Congress — Lincoln signed it on February 29 — it generated speculation in the Army of the Potomac. General Meade took note this would make Grant general-in-chief, and he wondered at the fate of Henry Halleck. He also wondered if, "when Grant is responsible for all military operations he may want some one else whom he knows better in command of this Army."

With the Thirty-eighth Congress convened, the Republican caucus, in January 1864, reinstituted the Committee on the Conduct of the War. That too created a stir in the Potomac army. The committee, led by the Jacobin senators Ben Wade and Zach Chandler, deliberately set about recasting the Battle of Gettysburg so as to miniaturize General Meade's role in the victory to the point that he would be replaced — by the Radicals' favorite, Fighting Joe Hooker.

Dan Sickles, incensed at being cast out by Meade, testified to the committee on February 26 and set the agenda. On July 2, said Sickles, he was satisfied that Meade "intended to retreat from Gettysburg." It was only due to his lieutenants (Dan Sickles, notably) that the army stayed to fight. That afternoon, said Sickles, had he not advanced the Third Corps to a new position beyond the lines, "if I had not occupied it in force — would have rendered our position on the left untenable . . . would have turned the fortunes of the day hopelessly against us." Finally, Lee should have been "vigorously attacked before he had an opportunity to recross the river."

Abner Doubleday, wrathful at being displaced in command of the First Corps on July 1 by his junior, John Newton, echoed Sickles's charges and added some of his own: "General Meade is in the habit of violating the organic law of the army to place his personal friends in power. . . . No man who is an anti-slavery man or an anti-McClellan man can expect decent treatment in that army as at present constituted." Albion Howe, yet another displaced general, thought even worse of Meade: under the skin, a lurking Peace Democrat. He testified, "There is a want of heart, of earnestness of purpose in the man who is in command. . . . I do not know as I can express myself better than saying that there is copperheadism at the root of the matter."

On March 3, with these rabid testaments in hand, Wade and Chandler marched to the White House and, "in relation to the incompetency of the general in command of the army," demanded a change. They pressed Hooker as Meade's replacement. But times had changed. The president felt no obligation to Wade and his committee, and in any case he would have Lieutenant General Grant at hand — Grant was called east that day — to look into matters of command.[37]

Lincoln suggested Meade himself should be heard concerning Gettysburg, and on March 5 Meade was called to testify. In Washington, he told his wife, "I was greatly surprised to find the whole town talking of certain grave charges, that had been made against me in the testimony before the Com. on the Conduct of the War of *Genls. Sickles & Doubleday.*" As he explained, "I then occupied 3 hours in giving a succinct narrative of events & you may rest assured I did not spare Genls S or D." He learned, he said, "the ultra-radicals are determined to have me out."

His testimony responded not only to the talk of the town, but to a virulent speech in the Senate on March 2 by Morton Wilkinson of Minnesota, who took his cues from Sickles's testimony. "I believe it can be proven," said Wilkinson, "that before the fight commenced at Gettysburg, the order went forth from the commander . . . to retreat." Exactly the contrary, Meade testified: "No order to retreat was at any time given by me." As to General Sickles on July 2, "I maintain that subsequent events proved that my judgment was correct, and his judgment was wrong." As to Williamsport, he said he refused to dissipate "the fruits of my victory" at Gettysburg by "blindly attacking the enemy without any knowledge of his position." Asked if he had anything more to say, Meade replied, "I would probably have a great deal to say if I knew what other people have said."

The conspiracy grew with the testimony of Alfred Pleasonton and David Birney, and at Sickles's behest, Daniel Butterfield was brought from Tennessee to further invigorate the anti-Meade cabal. Butterfield testified that on the morning of July 2, "General Meade then directed me to prepare an order to withdraw the army from that position." He produced no copy of the order, but to reinforce the point said that at the council of generals that night, "General Meade arose from the table, and remarked that in his opinion, Gettysburg was no place to fight a battle." (In Butterfield's own notes and in John Gibbon's notes, that was said by John Newton.) When Butterfield's testimony about the alleged retreat order became the latest talk of the town, Meade returned to the hearing room and wondered "how it is possible that such an extraordinary idea could have got into his head. . . . I utterly deny, under the full solemnity and sanctity of my oath . . . ever having intended or thought, for one instant, to withdraw that army. . . ." He said what Butterfield claimed was an order to retreat rather than fight was merely a contingency plan any general would draft to assure an orderly retreat in case of defeat; it was not even saved. As he told John Gibbon, this exemplified Butterfield's "hellish ingenuity to rob me of my reputation."[38]

In the committee's printed testimony General Meade clearly bests the conspirators, and he was supported by the testimony of true fighting generals Warren, Hancock, Gibbon, and Hunt. But in playing to the court of public opinion — "to poison the public mind," said Meade — Dan Sickles revealed a hellish ingenuity all his own.

On March 12 a letter signed "Historicus" appeared in the New York Herald offering a "lucid review" of Gettysburg. It was in fact Gettysburg through the skewed lens of Daniel Edgar Sickles, and hardly lucid. It elaborated Sickles's defense of his July 2 actions as earlier presented to the Wade Committee, and represented Sickles as far-seeing, sagacious, and savior of the Union. It presented Meade as anxious to retreat rather than fight, as indifferent to Sickles's warnings of the threat to the army's left, as inept in allowing Lee to escape. A second Historicus letter, on April 4, accelerated the assault on Meade for his "inglorious failure" to profit by the victory — "It will be a singular indifference to public opinion on the part of the government if he is allowed to remain longer in that important post" — and hoped General Grant would speed Meade's departure.

This was the last straw for George Meade. "All this makes me heartsick," he told his wife. Historicus, he told the War Department, had access "not only to official documents but to confidential papers that were never issued to the army, much less made public." He called for a court of inquiry. "I cannot resist the belief that this letter was either written or dictated by Maj. Gen. D. E. Sickles."

Meade was exactly right. Only Dan Sickles could have written these letters, or (much the same thing) dictated them, most probably to Major Henry E. Tremain of his staff, who had a history of writing pseudonymous letters to the press and who could be counted on to attach such adjectives as "sagacious" to Sickles's name. Mr. Lincoln sent a note to Meade sympathizing with his offended sensibilities but rejecting a court of inquiry. "The country knows that, at all events, you have done good service," he said.

Henry Halleck offered more practical advice. No doubt Sickles was behind the Historicus letters, he said, but nothing would suit Sickles better than for Meade to engage him in a personal or newspaper controversy. "He would there be perfectly at home, and, with his facilities for controlling or giving color to the New York press, would have greatly the advantage." Ignore him. "He cannot by these newspaper articles injure your military reputation. . . ." Meade replied, "I am not as philosophical as you are, nor do I consider it good policy to permit such slanders as have been circulated to pass entirely unnoticed." Still, he recognized the folly of getting down in the gutter with the likes of Dan Sickles, and let the matter drop.[39]

Amidst this extended "hullabaloo," as Meade termed it, he undertook a major reorganization of the Army of the Potomac. This was sparked by his urgent need for qualified corps commanders, by his wish for fewer and larger corps in managing a battle . . . and by Stanton's wish to erase any stains of McClellanism from the army.

The First and Third Corps were severely battered at Gettysburg, both losing their commanders, and during the winter, camp rumor had them being broken up. For once camp rumor was right. Gettysburg taught Meade hard lessons about trying to manage seven corps across a sprawling battlefield. The fall campaigning, especially Mine Run, taught him the limitations of some of his (now) five corps commanders. Meade instituted a three-corps army. This meant disbanding the First and Third Corps and a major shuffling of generals. Stanton put in his oar, telling Meade "there were several officers in my army that did not have the confidence of the country and that I was injuring myself by retaining them." Meade told his wife, "I suppose the result will be a pretty general sweeping out."

John Newton was swept out along with the First Corps. He held no claim by merit to the corps command, having been plucked from another corps at Gettysburg to replace the killed John Reynolds. Newton had clouded his career by plotting against Ambrose Burnside a year earlier, and after leading a division (reduced to brigadier) in the Army of the Cumberland, he was exiled to the District of Key West in Florida.

The three First Corps divisions were shoehorned into a four-division Fifth Corps. In the process, only John C. Robinson's First Corps division and Samuel W. Crawford's Fifth Corps division remained relatively intact, while three division commanders—Lysander Cutler, Romeyn B. Ayres, and Joseph J. Bartlett—were back leading brigades. The other two Fifth Corps divisions went to veteran Charles Griffin and politician James Wadsworth, both returning to active duty. The corps' two artillery brigades were combined under Charles Wainwright.

The process cost Fifth Corps commander George Sykes his job. When Winfield Hancock healed enough to return to the Second Corps, he displaced Gouverneur Warren, who (Washington decided) would in turn displace Sykes. Meade tried but failed to keep Sykes as a division commander. George Sykes had served faithfully since First Bull Run. Theodore Lyman called him a stern, Spartan regular, "not brilliant, but like a good clock, always on time." He had roused Stanton's suspicions by taking a role in a proposed testimonial to honor General McClellan—a scheme scotched by Stanton when he learned of it. Sykes was packed off to the Department of Kansas.

The Third Corps was divided between the Second and Sixth Corps. Meade thereby rid himself of the two recent (and inept) Third Corps commanders—Sickles and French—by dissolving their command, ending their wartime service. Of the Third Corps' three divisions, Joseph Carr's moved to the Sixth Corps (James B. Ricketts replacing Carr). David Birney's division moved to the Second Corps (pushing Alexander Hays back to brigade), as did Henry Prince's (Gershom Mott replacing Prince). Two generals recovered from Gettysburg wounds took the other two Second Corps divisions—Francis Barlow replacing (at Hancock's insistence) John C. Caldwell, and John Gibbon replacing Alexander Webb, pushing Webb back to brigade. Albion Howe, who made no friends in testifying to the Wade Committee, was replaced as a Sixth Corps division commander by George W. Getty. The rearranged artillery brigades were under John C. Tidball (Second Corps) and Charles H. Tompkins (Sixth Corps). Alex Webb thought the shakeup still left "some exceedingly slow individuals whom we *know* to be worthy and honest but not exactly suited for commands requiring energy and activity."

Stanton wanted to be rid of cavalry commander Alfred Pleasonton, and

Meade grew receptive to the idea. He explained to his wife that "the opposition I had hitherto made to his removal I no longer should make, since the manner he had talked about me & his testimony to the Comm. on the Conduct of the War." If he did not originate Pleasonton's removal, he certainly helped bring it about.[40]

(The cabal that condemned General Meade before the Wade Committee had reason to regret its intemperance. Sickles, Butterfield, Doubleday, Howe, and Pleasonton were all gone from the Army of the Potomac. David Birney survived — he came to Meade to make peace and to deny "ever having entertained unfriendly feelings towards me, or being a partisan of Sickles. . . .")

Meade went to battle with Stanton over John Sedgwick, commanding the Sixth Corps. To Stanton's thinking, Sedgwick had lagged supporting Butler's scheme to rescue the Richmond prisoners. Worse, Sedgwick organized the aborted testimonial to McClellan. Worse yet, Sedgwick had Arthur McClellan, the general's brother, on his staff. Meade strongly objected to losing Uncle John. Stanton said he would give him command in the Shenandoah Valley, a promotion Meade could hardly object to. Meade chose John Gibbon to replace Sedgwick at the Sixth Corps. But Lincoln intervened. Since leaving the Potomac army in a huff after Fredericksburg, Franz Sigel had paraded his leadership of the German American community. Lincoln listened, and the Valley command went to General Sigel. Sedgwick retained the Sixth Corps, and Gibbon wrote ruefully to his wife, "Genl. Meade tells me I came very near getting one of the corps. . . ."

Meade handled the army reorganization with fair diplomacy. In coping with Stanton's crotchets, he lost one corps commander (Sykes) but retained another (Sedgwick), and did not regret losing Sickles, French, and Pleasonton. He bragged a bit to his wife: "I believe I have gained great credit for the manner in which so dis-agreeable an operation was made acceptable to those concerned." To Chief of Staff Humphreys, "The changes I believe give satisfaction to all except those who lose by it — which I take to be high praise."[41]

Winfield Hancock on a battlefield was a leader beyond compare. He minded his opinions and his politics, and survived unscarred all the high-command upheavals of 1862–63. Hancock was respected by ranks high and low, and was close to Meade. His Gettysburg wound still troubled him, but he said he was ready to campaign. Uncle John Sedgwick was universally admired, and he too was a Meade confidant. Hardly an imaginative general, Sedgwick was solid and reliable, the anvil on which to hammer the enemy. Gouverneur Warren, age thirty-four, was, per reporter

William Swinton, "of a subtle, analytic intellect, endowed with an eminent talent for details, the clearest military *coup d'oeil. . . .*" He was also independent-minded, as he revealed at Mine Run. Warren had not yet earned the full trust Meade had in Hancock and Sedgwick.

Ulysses S. Grant reached Washington on March 8 to be officially commissioned lieutenant general and general-in-chief, and on March 10 he visited General Meade at his headquarters at Brandy Station. Meade was not at all sure what to expect of this meeting. He told his wife he had known Grant slightly during the Mexican War, where he was "considered a clever young officer," but was later compelled to resign "owing to his irregular habits & I have no doubt he is weak on this point." (A widely circulated story had Lincoln asking where Grant got his liquor, so he could send some to his other generals. A good story, Lincoln said when asked about it, but not one of his. "He supposed it was charged to him to give it currency.") Be that as it may, said Meade, "he certainly has been very successful" — Fort Donelson, Vicksburg, Chattanooga — "and that is nowadays the measure of reputation." Neither general stood on ceremony that day (or any day). It was raining, and Meade, in the jacket of a common soldier, opened his tent door, put out his arm, and said, "Good morning, General Grant; pray come in."

The army gossip had Grant replacing Meade as commander of the Potomac army with William F. Smith, a report given credence by the presence of Smith in Grant's party at Brandy Station. Meade had told his wife, of Grant, "It is said he is greatly smitten with Baldy Smith." Smith himself wrote afterward, "The Pres't & Secy had determined on it & thought Grant would certainly do it & relieve them of the responsibility." By the diary of Cyrus B. Comstock of Grant's staff, when he left Chattanooga for Washington Grant did indeed intend to replace Meade with Smith. (Upon Hooker exiling him from the Potomac army, Smith had served Grant as chief engineer in the Tennessee campaign.) Yet it came to pass that George Meade kept his job commanding the Army of the Potomac. In Comstock's diary for March 10, Grant "now says no change & the program is, Halleck here as office man & military adviser. . . ."

Theodore Lyman of Meade's staff described the forty-one-year-old Grant in his journal: "He is rather under middle height, of a spare, strong build; light brown hair, and short light brown beard. His eyes of a clear blue; forehead high; nose aquiline; jaw squarely set. . . . His face has three expressions; deep thought; extreme determination; and great simplicity and calmness." Rufus Dawes, 6th Wisconsin, had a similar impression of

Grant: "He looks like a very common sense sort of a fellow—not puffed up by position nor to be abashed by obstacles."

At their first meeting, Meade told Margaret, he found himself much pleased with Grant, "and most agreeably disappointed in his evidence of mind and character. You may rest assured he is not an ordinary man." Grant was similarly impressed with Meade. Meade spoke "very plainly," offering to step down if Grant had someone else he preferred to lead the Potomac army. "This incident gave me an even more favorable opinion of Meade than did his great victory at Gettysburg," Grant wrote. At whatever point he had made his decision, he assured Meade that he had "no thought of substituting any one for him." He also said he would not command from Washington, but starting that spring, campaign in the field with the Army of the Potomac.[42]

16. "... There Is to Be No Turning Back"

ULYSSES GRANT FOUND that elevation to the top command did not shield him from the grasp of politics, especially politics in a presidential-election year. Indeed, the president wanted assurance about Grant's own ambitions. It was widely remarked that General McClellan might reach for the Democratic nomination, and it was remarked too that a far more successful general like Grant would be a far more viable candidate. A feeler was put out, and a friend of Grant's wrote him about the matter, and Grant replied that such newspaper speculation ended up in his wastebasket. "I already have a pretty big job on my hands," he wrote, "and my only ambition is to see this rebellion suppressed. Nothing could induce me to think of being a presidential candidate. . . ." Shown this letter, Mr. Lincoln then welcomed General Grant warmly.[1]

Beyond army politics, just now national politics intruded on planning for the 1864 spring campaign. An editor complained to Secretary Stanton that "the President has kept that cowardly 'cuss' of a Sigel where he could sacrifice men and position because he was a German," and "placed Hunter — a General who has force of character but brains entirely incommensurate — in the Shenandoah Valley, because he must have a command and is an abolitionist." The editor might have added Ben Butler (because he was a War Democrat) to this rogues' gallery of generals holding high command positions that spring. Butler and Franz Sigel and David Hunter — none Grant's choices, all representing constituencies needed by the president in November — tarnished prospects for the Virginia campaign.

Grant intended to coordinate offensives in the Eastern and Western theaters, pressuring the Confederacy from one end to the other. Until now, he wrote, Federal initiatives had been "without concert, like a balky team, no two ever pulling together." Commanding in the West was William Tecumseh Sherman, "Joe Johnston's army being his objective point and the heart of Georgia his ultimate aim." In the East, Sigel (initially, then Hunter) would operate in the Shenandoah Valley, and Butler's Army of the

Lieutenant General U. S. Grant assumed a casual stance for Mathew Brady's camera, taken in June 1864 amidst the Overland Campaign.

James would operate from Fort Monroe up the James River toward Richmond. As for the Army of the Potomac, Grant told Meade, with striking clarity, "Lee's army will be your objective point. Wherever Lee goes there you will go also."

Grant's thoughts for the Potomac army had evolved. Back in January, answering Halleck's solicitation, he suggested diverting 60,000 men to an invasion of North Carolina, starting from Union-held Suffolk, Virginia, and aiming for Raleigh. This would cut Lee's rail lifeline and "virtually force an evacuation of Virginia. . . ." But on coming east, Grant was made aware that shifting the Army of the Potomac, or any substantial part of it, from in front of the Army of Northern Virginia would mean (Halleck warned) "all the forces which Lee can collect will be moved north. . . ." Lincoln tried out on Grant the same scheme he had tried out on Burnside in November 1862 — send a substantial force up the York and Pamunkey rivers to sever Confederate communications. Grant "listened respectfully" . . . and silently heeded Halleck's warning. Grant and Meade would need to find a way to get directly at or around Lee.

Striking directly at Lee's imposing Rapidan line was not really an option, and in his instructions to Meade, Grant said his only doubt "is whether it will be better to cross the Rapidan above or below him." Logistics infused the matter. To cross above (west of) Lee's line meant depending on the Orange & Alexandria to supply the army, and the farther the advance, the greater the risk of raids by Jeb Stuart and by John Singleton Mosby's guerrilla band. Crossing the Rapidan below (east of) Lee promised in due course a secure supply line based on the Chesapeake and its tributaries. With Meade contributing his Mine Run experience, it was decided to cross the Rapidan below Lee's defenses. Chief of Staff Andrew Humphreys drew up the operational plan.[2]

For this campaign, the Army of the Potomac was not only reorganized, it was reconstituted as well. Just as Hooker had confronted the impending loss of two-year men and nine-month militia in spring 1863, Meade confronted his own manpower crisis in spring 1864 — the expiration of the enlistments of the army's core of old soldiers, the volunteers of '61 who had signed up for three years. Starting in May and June and extending through the summer, the Potomac army, while on campaign, would literally be hollowed out by the loss of its best troops unless ways were found to keep substantial numbers of these veterans, and their veteran officers, in the ranks.

The War Department framed a plan to persuade the veterans to reenlist for three years "or during the war." The plan offered individuals a $400 bounty and a thirty-day furlough to reenlist. Soon the focus shifted to the more practical idea of reenlisting regiment by regiment. If three-quarters of the men in a three-year regiment voted to sign up again, they would get the bounty, the furlough, the designation "veteran volunteers," and retain unit designation, flags, and badges. States and communities added additional bounty money, so the reward for staying the course might reach $700 or more. On March 31 General Meade could tell the War Department that 26,767 veterans had re-signed so far. In time, half the original three-year regiments voted to stay on with the Army of the Potomac. (Most of the rest would muster out during June and July.) Bounty money was important, but thirty days at home was often the deciding factor.[3]

The 6th Wisconsin, of the Iron Brigade, offers a case study. Amidst the fall campaigning after Gettysburg, the 6th's Lieutenant Colonel Rufus Dawes wrote, "Yesterday was one of the hardest days of all our service, and its effect upon the question of veteran enlistment was decidedly unhealthy." Debate intensified in winter quarters, and on December 12 Dawes thought the 6th, "as at present affected, will not re-enlist." He called the regiment together and spelled out as fairly as he could the government's offer and the advantages of a reconstituted regiment of veteran volunteers. The roll of sign-ups grew, but still he was doubtful. The non-combatants — cooks, clerks, hostlers — wanted to go home in July. But in the end, the fighting men "who have stood by the old flag through fair and foul weather, and through many bloody battles" voted to see it through. On January 4, 1864, by 233 of 290, the three-quarter mark was passed and the 6th Wisconsin veteran volunteers entrained for a month's furlough in Milwaukee, where they were welcomed by a brass band and "greeted with salvos of cheers."[4]

To fill the ranks for the spring campaigns, Lincoln called for 500,000 men, then increased by 200,000. As before, few were actually drafted (in this call, only 13,296). Instead, state and community quotas were met by hiring substitutes or by volunteering — some of them patriot volunteers, some of them impoverished patriot volunteers who needed the bounty money, many of them nonpatriots who took the money and ran away at the first opportunity. "The bounty was meant to be an inducement to enlistment; it became, in fact, an inducement to desertion and fraudulent re-enlistment," the army's provost marshal admitted. Alex Webb, commander of a Second Corps brigade, remarked, "We, at the fighting end of the line, are aware of the fact that *here* we do not receive enough men to more than replace the men sent to Genl Hospital."

Soldier-correspondent Samuel Fiske, 14th Connecticut, furnished a taste of the bitter fruit of this corrupt system. A shipment of conscripts, most of them substitutes, arrived in the 14th's camp under guard, already short two killed and several wounded trying to escape. On making his inspection rounds, Captain Fiske was told, "Only ten gone since last roll call." That added up, over just three days, to 60 deserters out of 210 recruits, "and the ratio increasing constantly." Fiske took note, "We can, probably, by letting the enemy go unwatched, and turning our whole attention to these our northern friends, be able to catch some of them as they are deserting." The 14th Connecticut's experience was not universal . . . nor was it unique. Regimental officers learned to shrug off the loss of the worthless bounty-jumpers and turn to making soldiers of those recruits that remained.[5]

The Army of the Potomac's return for April 30, 1864, present for duty, came to 102,869. Attached was Ambrose Burnside's peripatetic Ninth Corps, 19,250 strong. The Ninth had departed the Potomac army after Fredericksburg for the Department of the Ohio, served in Kentucky and in the siege of Vicksburg, and then was itself besieged for a time in Knoxville. As Burnside was senior to Meade, he instead took his orders from General-in-Chief Grant. Special to the Ninth Corps was its Fourth Division, two brigades of U.S. Colored Troops, the first consequence of emancipation in the Army of the Potomac. "As I looked at them, my soul was troubled . . . ," staff man Theodore Lyman told his wife. "Can we not fight our own battles, without calling in these humble hewers of wood & drawers of water, to be bayonetted by the unsparing Southerners?"

Reinforcements of "heavies" received a sardonic greeting from the army's old-timers. These were artillerymen from the heavy batteries in the forts guarding Washington who had enjoyed a good war before Grant's coming. Their ranks were filled, even overfilled, with volunteers who appreciated a good berth — barracks living, three square meals a day, an enemy far distant. Now they were handed rifles and sent off to campaign as infantry. Grant even reached out for heavies from the coastal batteries guarding New York and Boston. Seeing a report of General Edward Canby's sending in artillerymen-cum-infantrymen from New York, Grant told Secretary Stanton, "With men of force like Canby to inspect, troops can be drawn out from all the northern Depts as he has done in N. York." Colonel Lyman made note, "One great good comes of Grant: we get now everything we want, particularly all available men . . ."[6]

The Potomac army's sickly cavalry corps required a command transfusion. The corps had suffered a major blow in the loss of division commander John Buford, dead of typhoid fever in December. Meade then rid

Major General Philip Sheridan, the Army of the Potomac's new commander of the cavalry corps, poses with his chief lieutenants. From left, Henry E. Davies, David M. Gregg, Sheridan, Wesley Merritt, Alfred T. A. Torbert, and James H. Wilson.

himself of distrusted division commander Judson Kilpatrick (Sherman claimed Kill-cavalry. "I know that Kilpatrick is a hell of a damned fool," Sherman said, but just the right sort to invade Georgia), and he abetted the departure of corps commander Alfred Pleasonton. Grant had not interposed in Meade's reorganization of the Potomac army's command, except to furnish a new cavalry corps commander, Philip H. Sheridan. Lyman met Sheridan, "a small broad shouldered, squat man, with black hair & a square head." (To Mr. Lincoln's eye, Sheridan was "a chunky little chap, with a long body, short legs, not enough neck to hang him. . . .") Sheridan had served Grant as a general of infantry in the West. The two vacant division posts were also filled by noncavalrymen — Grant's protégé James H. Wilson, an engineer who had served on the staffs of McClellan and Grant, and Sheridan's West Point classmate Alfred T. A. Torbert, a Sixth Corps brigade commander. The one divisional holdover, David Gregg, was a certified cavalry general.[7]

George Meade had assembled for himself a new model army, its high command slimmed down and pruned of deadwood, political and otherwise. In the Second Corps, Hancock had divisions under Francis Barlow, John Gibbon, David Birney, and Gershom Mott. Warren's Fifth Corps divisions were under Charles Griffin, John Robinson, Samuel Crawford, and James Wadsworth. In Sedgwick's Sixth Corps the divisions were led by

Horatio Wright, George Getty, and James Ricketts. Henry Hunt led the artillery, including a three-brigade artillery reserve. Phil Sheridan was unknown to the cavalry, but it was agreed he had to be an improvement over Pleasonton. Three-quarters of the infantry's brigade commanders were citizen-soldiers who had come up through the ranks; half the brigade commanders were new enough to still be colonels. The Ninth Corps (attached) was a bit problematical, especially corps commander Burnside. Two-thirds of Burnside's command was newly organized. His division commanders were Thomas Stevenson, Robert Potter, Orlando Willcox, and Edward Ferrero, with Ferrero's U.S. Colored Troops of unknown quality.

Meade jotted down, from his intelligence sources, an "Estimate of Lee's Forces April/64." In the Rapidan lines facing him he gave Lee 45,000 veteran infantry, and added 10,000 recruits, 10,000 cavalry, and 3,000 artillery, for a total of 68,000. Under the heading "Accession presumed or probable," he presumed Longstreet's corps, known to have returned from Tennessee, but listed some far-flung not-so-probable reinforcements from Leonidas Polk in Alabama and P.G.T. Beauregard in South Carolina. With allowance for defending Richmond, his total "available in field" for Lee came to 90,000. It is unclear whether Meade took arrivals from Polk and Beauregard as seriously probable; without them the estimate for Lee's field force was 65,000 . . . which by the best estimate is about 1,000 less than the number Lee actually put in the field that spring. In the worst case, then, Lee had about three men to Meade's four; in the best case, he had one to Meade's almost two. It is likely that Meade overestimated Lee's strength to some degree, yet never did he conclude, in McClellanesque fashion, that he was outnumbered. Conventional wisdom called for the offense to outnumber the defense by at least two to one. General Meade was content to hope (as one of his staff put it) "the economical way is to *overwhelm* them."[8]

In the privacy of a letter to his wife, Meade mulled over his rather awkward relationship with Grant. The press, he wrote, was "uniform & consistent in endeavoring to make him out the actual comdr. of this Army," yet in fact Grant "has not given an order, or in the slightest degree interfered with the administration of this Army since he arrived. . . . It is undoubtedly true, he will go with it when it moves, and will in a measure control its movements and should success attend its operations that my share of the credit will be less, than if he were not present. . . .

"Nevertheless, he is so much more active than his predecessor, and agrees so well with me in his views, I cannot but be rejoiced at his arrival. . . . My duty is plain — to continue quietly to discharge my duties, heartily co-operating with him & under him, and leave to truth & justice in time to place me right on the record." It was a hard bargain George Meade set for himself, but true to an unbending inner strength he lived up to it. He and Grant would share a generally strong partnership that withstood many slings and arrows from enemies North as well as South. As for his place in history, in his quiet way, and in time, Meade earned that as well.

As part of a newspaper buildup, Grant was portrayed as a no-nonsense Westerner, a soldier of the simplest needs and tastes. One day Grant invited Meade and staff to dine, and afterward Colonel Lyman wrote his wife, "As you have heard that the Lieut. Gen. never, under any circumstances, eats anything but soldiers' rations, I will state that we had soup, fish, two kinds of meat, three vegetables, pudding, and coffee. . . ."

Grant confessed himself surprised by Meade's army. "The Army of the Potomac is in splendid condition and evidently feels like whipping some body," he wrote a Western colleague. "I feel much better with this command than I did before seeing it." To manage matters at Washington while he traveled with Meade, Grant assigned Henry Halleck the new post of chief of staff of the army. This utilized Halleck's substantial talent for paperwork. Halleck explained to a friend (with an undisguised sigh of relief), "Although I am to perform the same duties as before, the responsibility of *deciding* upon plans of campaign & movements of armies must hereafter rest on the shoulders of others. It will be my business to advise, and *theirs* to decide."[9]

Halleck pointed to the high military stakes in this election year. Should the Federal armies, due to a lack of determination or a failure to recruit, lose headway and allow the Rebels "a few early successes, they expect a reaction at the north against the administration and in favor of a copperhead candidate." Grant took responsibility for that not happening. On the eve of the spring campaign, Lincoln wrote him of his "entire satisfaction with what you have done. . . . The particulars of your plans I neither know, or seek to know. You are vigilant and self-reliant; and, pleased with this, I wish not to obtrude any constraints or restraints upon you."

Grant's reply was one that no other of Mr. Lincoln's generals would have thought to write: "Should my success be less than I desire, and expect, the least I can say is, the fault is not with you."[10]

· · ·

"Everybody begins to feel fidgety & feverish about the move," wrote W. A. Roebling, Fifth Corps staff. "Grant is reticent & glum — Meade is snappish. . . ." Finally April turned to May and the weather cleared and the roads dried, and Grant set dates for the spring offensives. The Army of the Potomac would start on May 4. The same day, Ben Butler's Army of the James assembled aboard a flotilla in Hampton Roads for an advance up the James toward Richmond. On May 2–5 infantry under George Crook and cavalry under William Averell set out from West Virginia to strike at the Virginia & Tennessee Railroad. On May 7 Sherman began his march on Atlanta. On May 9 Franz Sigel started up the Shenandoah Valley.

The Army of the Potomac took center stage. John Gibbon wrote his wife on the evening of May 3, "It is now a little after 9 o'clock and we march at 12. Every thing is ready, we are in fine order and spirits, and as we have good men to direct affairs I have every confidence in our success." At the same time, "there is no disguising the fact that we will have some hard fighting to do, but we are able to do it." To be sure, there was concern in the high command about the inexperience — and the quality — of the army's newest recruits, and resignation at the mustering-out of thirty of the 1861 regiments, due to begin during the second month of campaigning.

But General Meade was confident of his troops. "If hard fighting will do it," he told his wife, "I am sure I can rely on my men. They are in fine condition & in most excellent spirits, and will do all that men can do to accomplish the object." It was remarked by his staff that the general commanding "seemed to be in a particularly good humor today," and that he had even acquired a new hat for the campaign, one "shaped like a puritan witch's, really with his Mephistophelian countenance, he presents quite a sardonic appearance, with it on."[11]

Andrew Humphreys's operational plan of May repeated the premise of the Mine Run operation of November, to turn Lee's right and attack his rear, but on a considerably enlarged scale — a wider, deeper thrust southward that passed the headwaters of Mine Run and its defenses and edged into the open country beyond the Wilderness, that dark and forbidding forest that had ensnared Joe Hooker the previous spring. It called for a secret midnight start, an errorless Rapidan crossing, and a pace fast enough to steal a march on General Lee. The potential drag on this pace was the army's trains. Cutting loose from the Orange & Alexandria for ten days or so, until opening a new supply line via Fredericksburg, meant (said Humphreys) "moving the great trains of the army that distance simultaneously with the troops, so as to keep them under cover of the army." By Quartermaster Rufus Ingalls's count, the "great trains" comprised 3,476 wagons and 590 ambulances, pulled by more than 24,200 horses and mules — numbers considerably exceeding the opening logistics of McClellan's Peninsula campaign in 1862.

The march began in the first moments of Wednesday, May 4. To the surprise of his staff, General Grant was togged out for the occasion in his full-dress lieutenant general's uniform, with sash and sword. Theodore Lyman remarked that several of Grant's staff "were very flippant and regarded Grant as already routing Lee and utterly breaking up the rebellion! — not so the more sober." General Meade did not wear his best, except for his new "witch's hat," and he was all business, pausing on the march to dress down a quartermaster for blocking the road with his trains.

Cavalry led the way, covering the engineers setting the pontoon bridges. The targeted crossings were undefended. Warren's Fifth Corps, trailed by Sedgwick's Sixth, took the Germanna Plank Road and crossed the Rapidan at Germanna Ford and headed into the Wilderness. Hancock's Second Corps crossed farther downstream at Ely's Ford. Most of the trains crossed at Copper Mine Ford, halfway between the two infantry crossings, shielded from the enemy by Warren's and Sedgwick's troops. Humphreys's original thought of pressing the first-day advance straight though the Wilderness to open ground bowed to the reality of moving and guarding the immense trains. Warren's May 4 objective was now Wilderness Tavern, a derelict stage stop at the intersection of the Germanna Plank Road and the Orange Turnpike, squarely in the middle of the Wilderness. Sedgwick halted behind Warren.

Burnside's Ninth Corps brought up the rear. Burnside apparently missed a meeting, for on the evening of May 3 he sought out Chief of Staff Humphreys for help. "He was cramming his pockets with maps, &c.," Humphreys told his wife. "I took some trouble to put him au fait on several matters, and marked out some maps which I got for him ... just the things he wanted to know, yet he had not been informed about them." With Burnside taking his orders from Grant rather than Meade, the Ninth Corps' dealings with the Army of the Potomac were painfully slow and potentially troublesome when fighting began.[12]

Farthest east, the Second Corps was intended as the spear point of the flanking operation. Following the Ely's Ford Road, Hancock took as his objective Chancellorsville, with its relics of Hooker's campaign of a year before, the burned-out Chancellor house and the numerous imperfect

graves. Word of this haunted place made its way to Herman Melville, and
into "The Armies of the Wilderness":

> *In glades they meet skull after skull*
> *   Where pine-cones lay — the rusted gun,*
> *Green shoes full of bones, the mouldering coat*
> *   And cuddled-up skeleton;*
> *And scores of such. Some start as in dreams,*
> *   And comrades lost bemoan:*
> *By the edge of those wilds Stonewall had charged . . .*[13]

   Meade's first essential was to seize control of the road network in the
Wilderness. No column would get very far very fast advancing off-road in
this tangled woodland of scrub pine and oak and underbrush. There were
three principal east–west roadways — the Orange Turnpike, between Orange Court House and Fredericksburg; the Orange Plank Road, in parallel some three miles to the south, joining the Turnpike just west of Chancellorsville; and farther to the south, the Catharpin Road. The primary
north–south roadway was the Brock Road, branching off the Germanna
Plank Road and running south from Wilderness Tavern to Spotsylvania
Court House, thereby intersecting all three east–west roads. There was as
well a spider's web of woods roads and byways sprinkled through the Wilderness. The maps handed to Yankee generals proved faulty. Hooker's 1863

Left: The Second Corps crosses the Rapidan at Ely's Ford on May 4, by Alfred Waud. Right: Waud has Grant composing a telegram to report the crossing to Washington, flanked by Ely Parker (left) and Adam Badeau of his headquarters staff.

campaign, fought in the eastern Wilderness, contributed little knowledge of the western Wilderness, and knowledge from the Mine Run operation was limited. Engineers mapped as the campaign advanced. Certain key locations were misplaced—the intersection of the Brock and Catharpin roads was off by a mile, and the intersection of the Brock and Plank roads was off by a mile and a quarter.

Meade's orders for May 5 called for angling west intending to outflank Mine Run, which he thought Lee might defend; or perhaps Lee might abandon the Rapidan line altogether. Warren's Fifth Corps, moving out the Orange Turnpike, would slant off south by west on a byway to reach the Orange Plank Road at Parker's Store. Sedgwick's Sixth Corps would extend along the Germanna Plank Road to Wilderness Tavern, backing up Warren as the army's right wing. Hancock's Second Corps was to swing south by west from Chancellorsville onto the Catharpin Road, tying in with Warren and becoming the left wing. By day's end, then, Sedgwick should be covering the Orange Turnpike, Warren the Plank Road, Hancock the Catharpin Road, and all three securely connected.

General Meade was not a dedicated supervisor of the cavalry, especially now with the new men Sheridan and Wilson that Grant brought from the West. Rather than putting veteran cavalryman David Gregg to scouting the roadways between the army and the enemy, that assignment went to the new man James Wilson, whose credentials Meade apparently did not check. Wilson's orders were to send out "strong reconnaissances" on the Orange Turnpike and Plank Road and the Catharpin Road "until they feel the enemy"—clear enough in meaning to a cavalryman of experience. But Wilson, not a cavalryman to begin with, not acquainted with cavalry intelligence-gathering, left his scouting job largely undone. Meanwhile, Sheridan, with Gregg's and Alfred Torbert's cavalry divisions, looked east

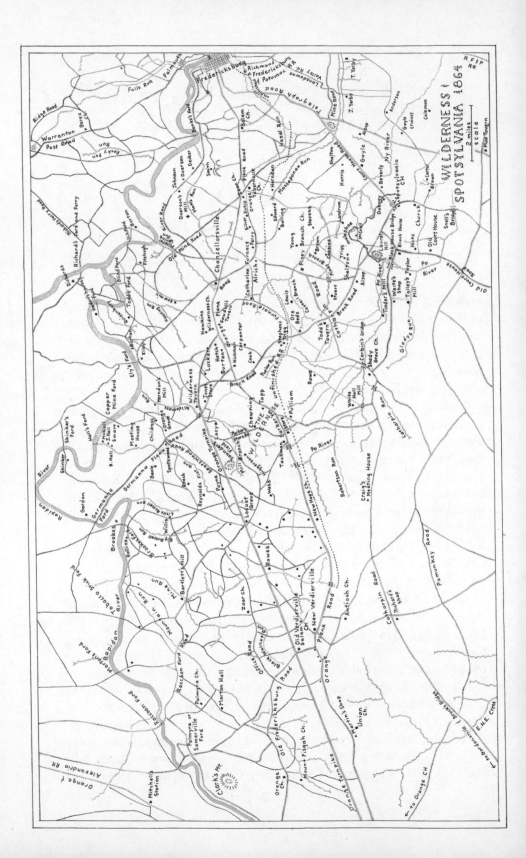

toward Fredericksburg, where Jeb Stuart's cavalry was said to be on the prowl. This proved a wild-goose chase, leaving the Potomac army very poorly served by its new cavalry command on May 4 and 5.[14]

Shortly after 7:00 a.m. on May 5, as Meade's headquarters was setting up at Wilderness Tavern, a dispatch arrived from Gouverneur Warren, Fifth Corps, saying that his pickets sighted Rebel infantry advancing along the Orange Turnpike, hardly two miles from headquarters. Wilson's carelessness had let the infantry be taken by surprise. Warren's command was well scattered. Two divisions, under Samuel Crawford and James Wadsworth, had already started down the track toward Parker's Store on the Plank Road. A third, John Robinson's, was at Wilderness Tavern in reserve. The fourth division, Charles Griffin's, intended as rear guard for the corps, was out on the Turnpike facing the just-discovered Confederate advance. It appeared that General Lee had no intention of taking a stand behind Mine Run, or of abandoning his Rapidan lines either. (When the enemy appears, Dick Ewell was told, "the general's desire is to bring him to battle as soon now as possible.")

Meade did not hesitate accepting the challenge. He met with Warren and told him to attack with his whole corps. "If there is to be any fighting this side of Mine Run, let us do it right off," he said; "what I want is to prevent those fellows from getting back to Mine Run." He sent to Hancock that the enemy was reported on the Turnpike, and he should halt his Second Corps at Todd's Tavern on the Catharpin Road and await further orders. General Meade, it seems, had his fill of congressional complaints and press reports calling him too pacific for a Civil War army commander.

Meade sent a courier to Grant, whose headquarters was still at Germanna Ford where he was shepherding the Ninth Corps, telling him of the enemy force sighted on the Turnpike and describing the actions for battle he had taken. Perhaps, he said, this was only a delaying force rather than an offer of battle, "but of this we shall soon see." Meade's dispatch served as a test case for his relationship with the general-in-chief now that action had begun. He had acted independently, at a moment's notice; would Grant approve, or would he gather decision making into his own hands? Meade was reassured. "If any opportunity presents itself for pitching into a part of Lee's army," Grant replied, "do so without giving time for disposition." The two generals soon established twin headquarters on a knoll near the Lacy house on the Orange Turnpike.[15]

At 7:50 a.m. Warren alerted Charles Griffin, on the Turnpike, to ready his division for attack orders "while the other troops are forming." The other Fifth Corps troops forming were the divisions of Crawford and

Wadsworth, on the Parker's Store Road off to Griffin's left. But actually connecting one or both to Griffin's line meant pressing through a mile or so of the jungle-like Wilderness. To support Griffin's right, Meade assigned Horatio Wright's Sixth Corps division. Wright at least had a track called the Spotswood Road to follow toward the front. Meade told Grant that it appeared Lee was offering battle, and repeated his motto for the day: "If he is disposed to fight this side of Mine Run, he shall be accommodated." Just as he had done during the back-and-forth campaigning the previous fall, Meade welcomed Lee taking the initiative. He need not go find him, or dig him out of his defenses.

A second surprise that morning was also due to cavalryman Wilson's failed reconnaissance — the discovery of Confederate infantry hardly a rifle-shot distant advancing on the Orange Plank Road. (These Rebels were A. P. Hill's men; those on the Turnpike were Dick Ewell's.) Meade endorsed this report with a sharp wake-up call to Wilson, "who, I hope, will himself find out the movement of the enemy." Just then the Plank Road intersection with the Brock Road was not secured by infantry. Until Hancock could bring up his Second Corps from Todd's Tavern, George Getty's division, heading the Sixth Corps advance along the Brock Road, was sent to plug this gaping hole at the center of the Federal position.[16]

John Gibbon described for his wife what it was like fighting in the Wilderness: "The whole country is a dense tangled jungle thro which no line can march & keep in order. In most of it a man cannot see 50 paces & there are but few positions where arty can be placed. Consequently the fight was almost entirely a musketry one." The truth of that analysis was first demonstrated in Charles Griffin's fight on the Orange Turnpike in early afternoon May 5.

"Attack as soon as you can," General Meade ordered Warren and his Fifth Corps at 8:24 a.m., but it took the entire morning and more to amass strength enough to launch an attack. Griffin, in the advance, and Warren fended off headquarters pressure by insisting on flank protection. James Wadsworth's division, recalled from the Parker's Store movement, struggled to advance cross-lots through a mile of boggy, clotted Wilderness to support Griffin's left. Samuel Crawford, a reluctant warrior at Antietam, replayed that role today. Instead of following Wadsworth, Crawford claimed he was needed where he was to guard against an enemy at Parker's Store on the Plank Road. (Crawford's shying away was perhaps linked to the impending discharge of his entire division, two brigades of Pennsylva-

In Alfred Waud's rough sketch, Generals Grant and Meade (pointing) and their staffs watch Gouverneur Warren's distant fight along the Orange Turnpike on May 5.

nia Reserves.) Horatio Wright's Sixth Corps division, ordered to support Griffin's right, was victim to a mix-up. Wright was assigned a reinforcing brigade from Getty's division only at 10:30 a.m., which started out at 11:00, and arrived too late. The Fifth Corps took up the offensive with just Griffin and Wadsworth.

Ex-artilleryman Griffin pushed a two-gun section out the Turnpike to the front while his colonels struggled to form any sort of mobile battle line in the stunted forest. Finally they reached one of the few large openings in the Wilderness, some 60 acres called Saunders' Field. The Rebels fortified the western margin of the field. (Had Wilson's cavalry scouted far enough to reach Saunders' Field, Griffin would have known to bring up more guns to deploy. He had to settle for just the two.) Colonel Lyman took note, "12.50. Reported back at Headq'rs. Just at this moment, heavy musketry from Griffin and apparently from Wright, also from Wadsworth on Griffin's left." It lasted perhaps an hour and a half, "continuous — not by volley, for that is impossible in such woods; but a continuous crackle, now swelling & now abating, and interspersed with occasional cannon." The fight was launched at Meade's insistence and against the judgment of both Warren and Griffin, who feared for their flanks.

They were prophetic. Wadsworth's division, its command disoriented in the thickets, directing by compass, could mount no coherent assault and promptly collapsed in confusion. Even the Iron Brigade was flanked and routed. A staff man reported, "Wadsworth Div. badly handled & fell back." Griffin had a better-organized time of it on Saunders' Field, where Brigadier Joseph Bartlett — the hero of Crampton's Gap back in '62 — stormed his brigade right through the enemy line and down the Turnpike. Soon enough, however, Bartlett was hit from right and left and had to fight for his escape. His horse was killed and he was bloodied. The right flank, lacking Wright's supporting division, was pummeled. The attack failed and fell back, and the two guns were lost. The tinder-dry woods took fire, obscuring the field in billowing smoke.

A furious Charles Griffin came pelting back to headquarters at the Lacy house. "He is stern & angry," Lyman reported. "Says in a loud voice that he drove the enemy, Ewell, 3/4 of a mile, but got no support on the flanks and had to retreat." Griffin's words for the absent Wright were harsh, and he added censure for corps commander Warren before rushing back to the front. General Grant, sitting nearby on a stump, quietly smoking and whittling, heard enough of this tirade that he turned to Meade and snapped, "Who is this Gen. Gregg? You ought to arrest him!" Grant's uniform coat was unbuttoned, Lyman noted, and Meade began to button it up, "as if he were a little boy, saying in a good-natured voice, 'It's Griffin, not Gregg; and it's only his way of talking.'"[17]

As the fire dwindled on the Orange Turnpike it swelled on the Plank Road. The discovery of enemy outriders at Parker's Store had stirred Wilson's cavalry to danger, and there was sharp skirmishing. At midday the threat increased, and the troopers came streaming back "like a flock of wild geese," A. P. Hill's infantry on their heels. This advance toward the Plank Road's intersection with the Brock Road threatened to cut off Hancock's Second Corps from the rest of the army. George Getty's Sixth Corps division was called to the rescue.

The call was delivered, at about 12:30 p.m., by Colonel Lyman. He found Getty out ahead reconnoitering at the crossroads. He hardly needed Meade's dispatch, said Getty, pointing to Rebel skirmishers just 300 yards away on the Plank Road. George Getty was another of those artillerists — he had been Burnside's chief of artillery in the Maryland campaign — who gained rank and a division by shifting to the infantry, and he took to leading foot soldiers. He had sent back to his lead brigade to come at the double-quick, then rallied his little band of staff and orderlies under the headquarters flag to defend this suddenly critical spot. "We must hold this point at any risk," he told them; "our men will soon be up." And so they were, knocking back the enemy skirmishers and holding the crossroads.

Getty had only three brigades with him, his fourth being detached to support Horatio Wright. (Once again, as at Gettysburg, John Sedgwick found his Sixth Corps scattered across the battlefield — Getty on the Plank Road, Wright on the Turnpike, James Ricketts's division holding the Rapidan crossing until Burnside came up.) Hancock marched back from the Catharpin Road to reinforce Getty. Even a driver as forceful as Hancock could not move troops with any speed over the paltry roads and through the woods. "The ground over which I must pass is very bad — a perfect thicket," he explained to headquarters. The lull extended to midafternoon and General Meade grew impatient and sent an order to Getty to advance "at once," with or without Hancock. The latest intelligence showed Longstreet's corps not yet with Lee; now might be the best chance for a victory. General Getty, with misgivings that he was outnumbered, set off into the Wilderness, along the Plank Road as axis.[18]

The Rebels on defense in the woods only revealed their position by an initial, devastating fire, stopping Getty's brigades cold. The Yankees held, however, and it was soon a close-range slugging match, firing at muzzle flashes in the shadows and roiling battle smoke. (Numerous men reported fighting for hours on end in the Wilderness without ever seeing a live Rebel.) The Vermont Brigade's Colonel Lewis A. Grant explained that if his men tried to continue the advance, "the rapid and constant fire of musketry cut them down with such slaughter that it was found impracticable to do more than maintain our then present position." Any advance, another Vermonter agreed, "was simply destruction."

Hancock was there now, feeding his Second Corps brigades into the Plank Road fight. Colonel Lyman watched Hancock in action at the crossroads, "on his fine horse — the *preux chevalier* of this campaign. . . . Now rides up an officer — Maj. Mundy — 'Sir! Gen. Getty is hard pressed and his ammunition nearly out' — 'Tell him to hold on, & Gen. Gibbon will be up to help him!' Another officer, from the left, comes up; 'Sir! Gen. Mott's division has broken, and is coming back!' — 'Tell him to stop them!' roared Hancock, and galloped towards the left and began rallying the retreating troops on the Brock road. 'Maj. Mitchell, go to Gen. Gibbon and tell him to come up on the double-quick!'"

Gershom Mott's little two-brigade division was a shaky refugee from the old Third Corps. Once this was Joe Hooker's division, but mediocre leaders had sapped its resolve. Mott himself was barely two days in command and not a vivid leader in any case, half the regiments were due to be mustered out shortly, and when ambushed in the thickets they would not stand. "Regiment after regiment, like a rolling wave, fell back," admitted brigade commander Robert McAllister. Hancock reinforced with the rest of his troops as they arrived — David Birney's division, John Gibbon's, Francis Barlow's.

Gibbon found it a strange kind of fight: "We are in very strong force but cannot use our artillery & a small force is almost as good as a large one." The front was stabilized at very heavy cost. Samuel Carroll, whose brigade had preserved the right flank at Gettysburg, went to the rescue again, and he was wounded. Alexander Hays, a general decisive in repelling Pickett's Charge, was brought back mortally wounded, shot through the head. At 5:30 p.m. Lyman sent to Meade, "We barely hold our own. . . . General Hancock thinks he can hold the plank and Brock roads, in front of which he is, but he can't advance." He added: "Fresh troops would be most advisable."

The reinforcements were jaded rather than fresh — Wadsworth's Fifth Corps division that had spent the day fighting the Wilderness and the Rebels in equal parts. Wadsworth was "terribly chagrined" at his handling of his troops and wanted a second chance, and it was granted him. Strengthened by a brigade from John Robinson's reserve division, Wadsworth once again struggled through the trackless Wilderness, aiming to tie in with the right of Hancock's forces on the Plank Road. But he was too late, and it grew too dark, to contribute to the fight.[19]

The Army of the Potomac entrenched in place and passed a grim, nerve-racked night under arms. Meade joined Grant at his headquarters that evening to discuss the day and the morrow. May 5 had been General Meade's to command. He initiated a battle plan necessarily improvised on the spot thanks to the cavalry's poor reconnoitering, and while Grant may have advised as the battle expanded, he did not override, issuing orders only to Burnside's Ninth Corps. Once again, as at Mine Run, Meade had concerns about Gouverneur Warren — this time, slow to put his corps into action, slow to press Crawford's and Robinson's divisions to the front. But Warren had a righteous grievance of his own. He believed he should have been allowed to wait for Wright's Sixth Corps division, essential as it was to securing his open right flank . . . and Wright's delay was due to headquarters belatedly attaching an (unneeded) fifth brigade to his division.

The day was a bloody standoff, but Grant was heard to say he felt "pretty well satisfied." He said if Lee had hoped to take the army in the flank he had failed; tomorrow Longstreet would be up, but so would Burnside as a counter. He telegraphed Halleck, "So far there is no decisive result, but I think all things are progressing favorably."

The offensive was ordered resumed at 4:30 a.m. May 6. Warren's Fifth Corps, supported by troops from Sedgwick's Sixth, would engage on the Orange Turnpike, "where you attacked to-day." This should occupy Dick Ewell while Hancock with the reinforced Second Corps made the main push on the Orange Plank Road. Getty's Sixth Corps division was put under Hancock's command (as was, later, Wadsworth's Fifth Corps division), with additional reinforcement expected from Burnside's Ninth Corps. Hancock was admonished to keep "a sharp lookout on your left" for Longstreet.

Meade gathered his commanders to review the plan, and they concluded that 4:30 a.m. was too early to get all the tangled units of Thursday's fighting untangled and ready to fight again. Meade proposed a six o'clock start instead. Grant moved the attack up just half an hour, to five o'clock. Of concern was Lee seizing the initiative, which General Grant "desires especially to avoid."[20]

On Friday, May 6, Lee did seize the initiative. Ewell probed John Sedgwick's front on the Turnpike fifteen minutes before Sedgwick's scheduled 5:00 a.m. advance — Ewell's watch must be fast, said Uncle John — and the two generals traded hard blows to little advantage. Oliver Wendell Holmes, Jr., on General Wright's staff, summed up the stalled advance in his diary: "A simultaneous attack was tried at 5 a.m. advanced some way — not much effected however — a marsh, abattis & battery in our front — Gen. W. managed to keep himself & staff pretty well in range of their shells. . . ."

Warren was also called on for a 5:00 a.m. advance, but with Thursday's fiasco in mind, he delayed until Sedgwick could guard his right flank. He noted too that the Rebel fortifications at Saunders' Field had at least doubled overnight. To Meade's prodding Warren explained, "I think it best not to make the final assault until the preparations are made." Headquarters' response was blunt: "The major-general commanding considers it of the utmost importance that your attack should be pressed with the utmost vigor. Spare ammunition and use the bayonet." But attacking impregnable-looking works was to Gouverneur Warren's thinking suicidal. Instead he made his fight on the Orange Turnpike that day a matter of heavy skirmishing and threatening, holding Ewell's attention from events elsewhere.[21]

Events elsewhere focused on the Orange Plank Road. Winfield Hancock had his four Second Corps divisions, plus a division each from the Fifth (Wadsworth) and the Sixth (Getty). Burnside's Ninth Corps was to support on the right, filling the gap between Hancock and Warren. Already that morning Burnside's peculiar command status had slowed the Ninth Corps' march. Its lead division was blocked by an artillery train, and a staff officer sought Meade's authority to push the artillery aside to make room for the Ninth's infantry. George Meade was a stickler for march discipline, but today he was handcuffed. "No Sir," he said. "I have no command over General Burnside." (Indeed, Meade knew Burnside well enough that had protocol been set aside he surely would have started the Ninth on the road a good deal earlier so as to be on time.)

Staff man Lyman was assigned to the Second Corps to report on the Plank Road offensive. At the intersection of the Plank and Brock roads he found Hancock smiling. "We are driving them, sir; tell General Meade we are driving them most beautifully. Birney has gone in and he is just cleaning them out be-au-ti-fully!" The Confederate line collapsed under this morning assault, driven back in confusion more than a mile. The widow Catherine Tapp witnessed A. P. Hill's men "runnin' up the road." Lyman explained to Hancock that only one division of Burnside's was up and would attack when it could. Hancock's face fell. "I knew it! Just what I expected! If he could attack *now,* we would smash A. P. Hill all to pieces!!"

Two Ninth Corps divisions had started down the road to Parker's Store and got about as far as Crawford had the day before, well short of striking the enemy's rear on the Plank Road in support of Hancock. Confederates on a hillock at the Chewning farm blocked the way. Burnside and his staff chief John G. Parke met with Grant's staff officer Cyrus Comstock and Warren's staff officer W. A. Roebling. A lengthy consultation produced only agreement (said Roebling) that "no one liked the idea of taking the hill by assault. More than an hour was lost doing nothing." Then new orders — the Ninth Corps was needed urgently by Hancock, and Burnside bushwhacked southward through the Wilderness toward the Second Corps.[22]

At 5:40 that morning Colonel Lyman had sent to Meade, "General Hancock went in punctually, and is driving the enemy handsomely." Hancock's own dispatch to headquarters told of forcing the enemy from their position, connecting with Wadsworth's division, and "taking quite a number of prisoners." Hancock had attacked with three divisions — Birney's and Mott's (Second Corps), and Getty's (Sixth Corps), Birney in overall command. Hancock held in reserve on the left his other Second Corps divisions, Gibbon's and Barlow's, Gibbon in command. On the right came Wadsworth's Fifth Corps division, braced with one of John Robinson's brigades.

At 6:20 a.m. Lyman reported, "The left of our assault has struck Longstreet . . . sharp musketry. Longstreet is filing to the south of the plank road — our left; how far not yet developed. . . . Gibbon is just notified of Longstreet's presence by General Hancock." Soon after (per Hancock's report, written nine months later), Gibbon was ordered to attack the Confederate right with Barlow's division. But no such attack was made. Had it been, Hancock wrote, "I believe the overthrow of the enemy would have been assured." Lyman made note, "Hancock complained after, that Gibbon's feeble command of the left wing of his corps changed the face of the day."

John Gibbon, with his unhesitating, no-nonsense manner, was hardly the sort to disobey an order, and on learning of Hancock's complaint, he insisted he never received this attack order. No such order is on record, and Barlow said he knew nothing of it. It appears that either the order was lost in transit, or Hancock misremembered its content ... or in retrospect Hancock was spreading blame for his sharp reverse on the Plank Road.[23]

And a sharp reverse it was. The very success of Hancock's offensive bred confusion, battle lines losing momentum and breaking up to contend with pockets of resistance, lead brigades running short of ammunition, Wadsworth's troops on the right crowding against Birney's and disordering everyone. The lagging Ninth Corp furnished little support. "We kept receiving orders from Generals Hancock, Birney and others, so that 'things were slightly mixed,'" one of Burnside's officers explained. Grant expressed himself "annoyed and surprised" that the Ninth did not attack, and at 11:45 a.m. a complaint was made to Burnside: "Hancock has been expecting you for the last three hours, and has been making his attack and dispositions with a view to your assistance." Only at 5:30 p.m., "from General Meade," was Thomas Stevenson's Ninth Corps division ordered to report to Hancock or Birney for orders.

Longstreet's assault caught the Yankees off balance, striking the gap on the left between Birney's advance and Barlow's division to the rear, waiting expectantly for orders. On Friday, like Thursday, it was nearly impossible to successfully maneuver troops in this crowded, tangled woodland while under attack. To see was to command, but officers could see only fifty paces, if that. The Rebels soon overthrew Hancock's early-morning gains. Gershom Mott's division again failed to stand, carrying some of Hobart Ward's brigade with them. (Ward had a good record at Gettysburg, but now Meade would relieve him for being drunk and leaving his brigade.) John Gibbon sent in Alex Webb's brigade, and Francis Barlow forwarded Paul Frank's, in an effort to slow the Rebels. As he had on Thursday, George Getty blocked the Plank Road with his Sixth Corps division, only this time taking a bullet in the shoulder. The fighting was at close range and exceedingly costly. A beleaguered Ninth Corps officer found "rebs on three sides of us" and was advised, "Get out of there as damned quick as you can!"

A man in the 20th Massachusetts recalled, "Gen. Wadsworth came gal-

Artist Waud sketched James Wadsworth's Fifth Corps division fighting in the Wilderness along the Orange Plank Road on May 6, "near the spot where the General was killed." Republican political general Wadsworth (right) was mourned by Mr. Lincoln.

loping in a very wild and excited manner" and demanded the 20th go forward. Colonel George N. Macy said he was placed there by General Webb "to hold this position at any cost." Wadsworth said excitedly, "I command these troops and order you forward." Macy said, "Very well Sir, but we are the 2nd Corps." Paying no attention, waving his arms, Wadsworth repeated his demand, then rushed off. "Great God," said Macy, "that man is out of his mind." Dutifully the 20th Massachusetts pushed forward and promptly lost a quarter of its men, including Colonel Macy, wounded, and much-admired Major Henry L. Abbott, mortally wounded.

James Wadsworth rode right into the front lines to rally his faltering division — "Nobody could stop him!" said one of his staff — and in due course word came back that he had been shot through the head, falling within the enemy's lines. (Wadsworth died forty-eight hours later.) "A large part of the whole line came back, slowly but mixed up — a hopeless sight!" Colonel Lyman admitted. He drew his sword to try to stop them. "I would get one squad to stop, but, as I turned to another, the first would quietly walk off."[24]

With his mastery for rallying troops either on the advance or on the retreat, Winfield Hancock soon had the works along the Brock Road well

manned. The Confederate counterattack lost its bearings and momentum in the thick woodland, just as Hancock's offensive had earlier, and then came to a halt when Longstreet was seriously wounded in a friendly-fire incident. In the subsequent pause the Yankees strengthened their works and sorted out their tangled ranks. Once staff was attending to these duties, Hancock, still suffering from his Gettysburg wound, "asked me" (Lyman wrote) "to sit down under the trees, as he was very tired indeed. . . . He said that his troops were rallied but very tired and mixed up, and not in a condition to advance."

That was also Hancock's appraisal for Meade. He had just beaten off a last Rebel assault, he said, using Samuel Carroll to do it, despite yesterday's wound. "Carroll, I learn, distinguished himself as usual in a desperate charge," Andrew Humphreys told his wife. Burnside too pitched in to restore the line — "The best thing old Burn did during the day," said Meade. Hancock thought it not advisable "to attack this evening, as the troops I would select are the ones whose ammunition is exhausted. . . ." Meade told him to stand down.

The long day ended with one final, convulsive clash at the opposite end of the battlefield. This was John Sedgwick's sector, quiet now after the earlier blows he traded with Dick Ewell. No cavalry screen guarded the army's right flank — yet another black mark against Sheridan's cavalry corps — and Sedgwick's picketing was lax. A Rebel sortie surprised the Sixth

Corps brigades of Alexander Shaler and Truman Seymour and routed them . . . and captured both Yankee generals. This was the nadir for Truman Seymour. He had experienced rough times at Glendale, at Antietam, and recently at Olustee in Florida, and just the day before he found himself assigned to "Milroy's Weary Boys," the onetime command of Robert Milroy's that ran in the Valley in 1862 and ran at Winchester in 1863, and now in 1864 ran once again.

But Sedgwick quickly moved up infantry supports to blunt the assault. "Halt! For God's sake, boys, rally!" he shouted. "Don't disgrace yourselves and your general in this way!" The sudden racket of musketry inspired outriders of panic — rumor had both Sedgwick and Horatio Wright captured — and an officer rushed up to General Grant to proclaim a crisis. He said he knew Lee's methods well; he would cut off the army from the Rapidan crossings.

Grant turned on the man: "Oh, I am heartily tired of hearing about what Lee is going to do. Some of you seem to think he is suddenly going to turn a double somersault, and land in our rear and on both of our flanks at the same time . . . try to think what we are going to do ourselves, instead of what Lee is going to do."

The day closed on a hideous scene. Fires ignited by musketry and artillery still burned in the forest, and perhaps as many as 200 badly wounded men did not escape the flames. What Theodore Lyman would term the vortex of the fighting along the Orange Plank Road, over two days, "was a sight I could scarcely credit." Not a tree was standing for a distance of some hundreds of yards; "to an unpracticed eye it was just as if a whirlwind had twisted off each trunk and left the top hanging by the torn fibres. But it was the whirlwind of musket balls. . . ."

Melville made note, in "The Armies in the Wilderness,"

> None can narrate that strife in the pines,
>   A seal is on it — Sabæan lore!
> Obscure as the wood, the entangled rhyme
>   But hints at the maze of war —
> Vivid glimpses or livid through peopled gloom,
>   And fires which creep and char —
> A riddle of death, of which the slain
>   Sole solvers are.[25]

It was evident the Confederates now had a contiguous line already (or soon to be) heavily fortified, and any renewed offensive would only renew the whirlwind. "There lay both armies," Lyman wrote, "each behind its

Edwin Forbes portrayed the turning point of the spring 1864 campaign: Grant is cheered
as he leads the Army of the Potomac south from the Wilderness toward Spotsylvania
Court House rather than north to recross the Rapidan in defeat.

breastworks panting and exhausted, and scowling at each other." The moment was General Grant's, and he seized it. At 6:30 a.m. on May 7 he sent
to Meade, "Make all preparations during the day for a night march, to take
position at Spotsylvania Court House" . . . and he added detailed march
directions. The Wilderness battle was declared history.

In reviewing the fighting, Grant remarked to Meade, "Joe Johnston
would have retreated after two such days' punishment," his acknowledgment of a certain difference between the two theaters of war. May 7 marked
a watershed. It did not occur to Grant that day (or to Meade either) to pull
back across the Rapidan, in the manner of Hooker or Burnside (or Mc-
Clellan, changing his base), to lick wounds and regroup and plot some
next campaign. Grant's was a decision not lost on the men of the Army of
the Potomac. That evening the Fifth Corps set off along the Brock Road,
and soon enough, passing by the marching column, came General Grant
and staff — not leading the army north, back across the river, but south,
toward Richmond. "Our men knew what that meant," wrote a man in the
16th Maine. "Somewhere, Grant was seen, and a great burst of cheering
greeted him as he rode swiftly and silently by." Grant sought to quiet the
demonstration — it might alert the enemy, he said — but the cheering continued until he was out of sight.[26]

· · ·

Federal casualties in the two days of the Wilderness came to 17,666 (of which 2,246 were dead), exceeding by some 300 the toll at Chancellorsville the year before. The corps infantry losses were roughly equal: Second Corps, 5,092; Fifth Corps, 5,132; Sixth Corps, about 5,000. The Ninth Corps lost 1,640, reflecting its limited fighting. (Confederate losses are estimated at just over 11,000.)

In the officer corps, Brigadier Generals James Wadsworth (division, Fifth Corps) and Alexander Hays (brigade, Second Corps) were dead. Brigadier George W. Getty (division, Sixth Corps) was wounded, and two Sixth Corps brigadiers, Alexander Shaler and Truman Seymour, were captured. The Fifth Corps lost two brigade commanders wounded, Brigadier Henry Baxter and Colonel Roy Stone, and the Second Corps one, Colonel Samuel S. Carroll. General Grant particularly mourned Alick Hays, a West Point classmate and Mexican War comrade. Wadsworth, whose body was returned under flag of truce, was mourned at the White House, Lincoln telling John Hay, "No man has given himself up to the war with such self sacrificing patriotism as Genl. Wadsworth."[27]

The president waited anxiously for news from the Potomac army. One of the first reports came in the person of *New-York Tribune* reporter Henry Wing, who arrived at the White House on May 7 just from the field. The fighting was still going on, Wing said, but General Grant had given him a message to deliver personally to the president — "Whatever happens, there is to be no turning back." Mr. Lincoln had been waiting three years to hear a general say that, and in his delight he leaned down and gave young Wing a peck on the forehead.[28]

The Army of the Potomac's march south toward Spotsylvania Court House meant not only continuing the effort to turn Lee's right, but the end of the long, frustrating, back-and-forth struggle along the Rappahannock-Rapidan front. Grant was not taking Richmond as his target, as McClellan had. Instead, he took as his target Lee's army, *before* it could reach Richmond's defenses — which goal he could very likely achieve if he reached Spotsylvania first.

The Federals had, in the Brock Road, a more direct path to Spotsylvania than the Confederates, whose roundabout routes included three bridge crossings of the Po River. Lee, as was his wont, was not caught napping, and ordered Longstreet's corps (now under Richard Anderson) to head for Spotsylvania. General Meade's May 7 marching orders for the cavalry "for to-day and to-night" told Sheridan to "have sufficient force on the approaches from the right to keep the corps commanders advised in time of the appearance of the enemy." This was something less than a call to arms for Sheridan to block the Rebels' advance at whatever cost. Still, it called for action "to-day and to-tonight." Neither of these thorny generals communicated further on the matter.

Sheridan responded with a plan to seize all three bridges to block or delay the enemy. But he neither informed Meade nor issued orders to his generals in a timely fashion. Consequently, at one o'clock on the morning of May 8, at Todd's Tavern at the intersection of the Brock and Catharpin roads, Gouverneur Warren's Fifth Corps found two divisions of drowsing cavalrymen and their mounts and their trains blocking the way.

Meade was already in a temper, frustrated over delays in moving thousands of men along a narrow woods road in the dead of night in what he knew was a race. "Never before did I see such slow progress made: certainly not over half a mile an hour," corps artillery chief Charles Wainwright told his diary. At Todd's Tavern, when he learned cavalry generals David Gregg and Wesley Merritt had no orders from Sheridan, Meade brusquely issued them orders so as to break the traffic jam. He enclosed copies in a dispatch to Sheridan, explaining he found the two without orders and "in the way of the infantry and there is no time to refer to you."

When Sheridan came to Meade's headquarters at midday, both men were primed for a blowup. Confederates were now disputing the way and the race to Spotsylvania was being lost, and Meade went at Sheridan "hammer and tongs," as one observer put it, for blocking the infantry and for not blocking the Rebels. Sheridan fired back in language "spiced and conspicuously italicized with expletives" that Meade's orders to Gregg and Merritt conflicted with his own orders (which eventually reached them) and caused all manner of delays. He thought Warren and his Fifth Corps too complaining. Behind this tirade was Sheridan's simplistic argument that cavalry should just fight cavalry, not guard infantry or clear the way or scout or gather intelligence. "I told him," Sheridan wrote in his memoirs, "I could whip Stuart if he (Meade) would only let me."

Meade took the dispute to Grant, who calmly let his general blow off steam until hearing Sheridan's claim he could whip Stuart if let off the leash. "Did Sheridan say that?" Grant asked. "Well, he generally knows what he is talking about. Let him start right out and do it." Meade dutifully issued orders that both deprived him of cavalry and relieved him of a disputatious cavalryman. The next day Phil Sheridan went off with his three cavalry divisions to whip Jeb Stuart, leaving the army with poor maps and no cavalry eyes.[29]

Gouverneur Warren rallies Maryland Brigade troops of his Fifth Corps in the fighting on May 8 at Laurel Hill near Spotsylvania Court House. Drawing by Alfred Waud.

Earlier on May 8, before this expedition was conceived, Wesley Merritt's troopers had tried to clear the Brock Road. First Rebel cavalry delayed them, then Rebel infantry, taking post on a low ridge called Laurel Hill, had Merritt calling for infantry support of his own. Richard Anderson won the race by careful march discipline and plain hard marching. The Yankees lost the race by a serious mishandling of their cavalry and a serious lack of march discipline. Gouverneur Warren, rather than out leading the Fifth Corps and thereby resolving problems, lingered back at the Lacy house for much of the night. With daylight Warren inspected the new battlefront at Laurel Hill, fronting Spotsylvania Court House, and tried to figure out what to do.

He and division commander John Robinson debated. Robinson had only one brigade up and wanted to wait for the others. Warren agonized between attacking now, before the Rebels entrenched, or waiting for reinforcements against a probably dug-in foe. He chose attack now . . . and was repelled by Longstreet's veterans. Warren pressed two more brigades forward. In an attempt to inspire his very tired, very hungry men, he called out, "Never mind cannon! Never mind bullets! Press on and clear this road. It's the only way to get your rations." They too were driven back. General Robinson, "Old Reliable," trying to rally them to use the bayonet, was hit in the left leg, a wound requiring amputation and ending his field command. (Warren complained that Robinson's division "fought with re-luctance," and on May 9 the division was disbanded, its brigades distrib-uted in the Fifth Corps.)[30]

John Sedgwick's Sixth Corps now joined the fight. With it came Gen-eral Meade, in response to Warren's admission that he had "done my best, but with the force I now have I cannot attack again." Meade sought a joint attack by the available troops of the Fifth and Sixth Corps. Warren must attack "with vigor and without delay," said Meade. "I want you to cooper-ate with Sedgwick and see what can be done."

Warren treated cooperation as a last straw, atop an altogether bad day so far, leaving him and Sedgwick exhausted. "Was struck by their worn and troubled aspect," Colonel Lyman noted. Warren spoke bluntly to Meade. He as army commander "can give your orders and I will obey them; or you can put Sedgwick in command and he will give the orders and I will obey them; or you can put me in command and I will give the orders and Sedgwick will obey them; but I'll be God damned if I will *cooperate* with General Sedgwick or anybody else." Already that day Meade had ex-changed highly charged opinions with Sheridan; now a second subordi-nate was venting. But he recognized the strain Warren was experiencing, and calmed his own temper.

This second attack on Laurel Hill, when it finally came, would have benefited by *someone* being in charge. The advance was supposed to strad-dle the Brock Road, but on the right orders went astray and no one moved. On the left it was over quickly, as Lyman reported in his journal: "6:30 p.m. Sharp musketry on our left, for a few moments — the only result of Warren's grand plan of attack — an advance of the Pennsylvania Reserves, who came back in a hurry."[31]

The stress of this day-upon-day combat was unrelenting. John Gibbon explained to his wife, "I am perfectly well but as usual under such excite-ment eat but little & smoke a great deal which does my stomach no good and I feel pretty well worn out. ..." For Rufus Dawes, commanding the 6th Wisconsin in Warren's corps, the definition of "progress" was elusive. "It was not the most encouraging work of my experience," he told his wife, "that first we were defeated, slaughtered, routed almost in every attack we made. By continual, persistent generally unsuccessful assaults, charges, and by skilled maneuvering Gen. Grant worried out the enemy and forced him to fall back to Spots. C.H. ..."

That evening of May 8, "After our late dinner the General let out," Ly-man wrote. Meade confided his frustration with his generals. "Burnside he said was too late, in the Wilderness, to do any good. He wandered down the Parker's Store Road and came in after all the damage was done. Sedgwick was constitutionally slow. The men were now very tired. 'I told Warren today' continued he 'that he had lost his nerve; at which he professed to be very indignant. . . .'"

Gouverneur Warren was not one to let such an accusation pass unremarked. The next morning, May 9, he drafted his own précis of events, marked "confidential," for his friend Chief of Staff Andrew Humphreys. He was blameless — and there was plenty of blame elsewhere. He said if Sedgwick had advanced yesterday according to "the programme of the Genl Orders," he would have been immediately at hand with Warren to defeat the enemy. Whether General Meade "thinks I am capable or not, my want of rank" — seniority, he meant — "makes me incompetent when two corps come together, and I don't think our other two corps commanders are capable." Sedgwick "does nothing of himself." Hancock failed to use all the forces he had in the Wilderness fighting; "I think if he had moved out with his whole command directing near the head in person he could have won." Warren abruptly ended his letter there and put it away, marked "never sent." He had just learned that John Sedgwick was dead.

Captain Oliver Wendell Holmes, Jr., on General Wright's staff, noted in his diary that Wright's Sixth Corps division was taking position that morning when one of Sedgwick's aides rode up "with news that Sedgwick was killed — we had been with him a moment before — he was in an exposed angle between Warren's front & ours & had just been chaffing a man for ducking at the bullets of a sharpshooter; saying 'Why man they couldn't hit an elephant here at this distance' — he was struck on one side of the nose & sunk senseless & soon died." Uncle John's death was deeply personal to every man in the Army of the Potomac who knew him or knew of him. He was widely respected as a mainstay of the high command. A shocked General Grant could hardly believe the report, calling his loss greater than the loss of a division. General Meade had earlier chided Sedgwick about taking more independent command of his corps; "I feel the more grieved at his death because we had not parted entirely in good feeling." Sedgwick had proposed Horatio Wright as his successor if it should come to that, and his wish was honored.[32]

May 9 saw the Second Corps join the coalescing battle line in front of Spotsylvania Court House. So far the Second had done the heaviest fighting and gained the most notice, and Theodore Lyman pictured for his wife the Second's commanders: "As we stood there, under a big cherry tree, a strange figure approached. He looked like a highly independent, mounted

Winfield Scott Hancock, posed with his Second Corps generals of division. From left: Francis C. Barlow, Hancock, David B. Birney, and John Gibbon.

newsboy. He was attired in a flannel checked shirt, a threadbare pair of trousers, and an old blue kepi; from his waist hung a big cavalry sabre; his features wore a familiar sarcastic smile — it was General Barlow, commanding the 1st division of the 2d Corps, a division that for fine fighting cannot be exceeded in the army. There, too, was Gen. Birney, also in checked flannel, but much more tippy than Barlow; and stout Gen. Hancock, who always wears a clean *white* shirt (where he gets them nobody knows); and thither came steel-cold Gen. Gibbon, the most American of Americans, with his sharp nose and up and down habit of telling the truth, no matter whom it hurts."

But for eccentricity, Lyman went on, "you never saw such an old bird as Gen. Humphreys! I do like to see a brave man, but when a man goes out for the express purpose of getting shot at he seems to me in the way of a maniac." The chief of staff, who had reveled in battle-leading his division at Fredericksburg, still responded to gunpowder. "If a few shots are fired on the picket line, he pricks up his ears and cries 'Hey! What's that? I must go and see,' and away he goes at a gallop. . . ." Humphreys told *his* wife, "I don't know what Chiefs of Staff in other armies do, but I go among the troops as much as any Corps Commander, more indeed in some instances."[33]

The Second Corps was directed off to the right, the western end of the position, to explore a possible vulnerability in Lee's line. The Potomac army had Fredericksburg as its new base, and there was concern that Lee might try a turning movement of his own, toward Fredericksburg — perhaps weakening his left to do so. The Confederate line now extended east and west from Laurel Hill, forming a semicircle covering Spotsylvania. The Federal line roughly paralleled it — from west to east, Hancock's Second Corps, Warren's Fifth, Wright's Sixth, and off to the northeast, Burnside's Ninth.

Spotsylvania demonstrated (if further evidence was needed) the Confederates' skill at going to ground. Lyman described the process: "It is a rule that, when the rebels halt, the first day gives them a good rifle-pit; the second, a regular infantry parapet with artillery in position; and the third a parapet with an abattis in front and entrenched batteries behind." He added, "Sometimes they put this three days' work into the first 24 hours." Proof of that was evident when Winfield Hancock attempted to turn Lee's left.

With Grant taking a more directing hand than in the Wilderness, Hancock with three divisions crossed the Po River late on May 9 and prepared to attack on the 10th the enemy's exposed left flank. But morning found the target guarded by an array of fresh entrenchments thrown up overnight. What might have been possible on Monday (with an earlier start) was impossible on Tuesday. Hancock was ordered back across the Po, leaving Francis Barlow's division to maintain a bridgehead as a continuing threat.

Grant changed tack, and a frontal assault was plotted for late afternoon. Hardly had planning begun for that when the Rebels came full-bore after Barlow's bridgehead. Barlow fought them off as best he could, and Hancock hurried to the scene and ordered him back across the river. It was a narrow escape, a bitter ending to any thought of turning the enemy's left.

In the day's attack planning, Hancock, as senior, was to command both his Second Corps and Warren's Fifth Corps, but when Barlow's crisis drew Hancock away, Warren was left in charge. He determined on an independent attack on Laurel Hill, an apparent effort to furbish his reputation under Meade's eye. John Gibbon's division was assigned to the Fifth Corps, and Gibbon did his best to dissuade Warren. The approach was through a woodland full of deadfall. "I told Gen. Warren no line of battle could move through such obstacles to produce any effect," but Meade "seemed to rely wholly upon Warren's judgment in the matter. . . ." Attacking in advance of the day's scheduled offensive, Warren made "a feasible effort" against heavy rifle and artillery fire, "then gave it up."[34]

At age twenty-four, Emory
Upton devised storming tactics
for use against fortifications,
notably the Mule Shoe salient at
Spotsylvania on May 10.

Nothing inventive had thus far surfaced in the Federal command, but now that changed. Meade went to Wright's Sixth Corps to reprise a scheme that had worked in a roughly analogous situation the previous November — the breaking into a fortified Confederate bridgehead on the Rappahannock. The principals would be the same: David A. Russell at division teaming up with Emory Upton (West Point '61) at brigade. The target this time was a bulging salient in the Confederate line that the soldiers called the Mule Shoe. A dozen of the best regiments in the Sixth Corps were put under Upton's command. Engineer Ranald Mackenzie reconnoitered the salient and discovered a covered way that promised surprise.

Colonel Upton's tactical theory relied on a narrow, concentrated thrust by picked troops, delivered rapidly, to break a fortified line, widen the breach, and hold for reinforcements. He divided his force into four lines — the first, with loaded and capped muskets, bayonets fixed, would rush forward without stopping to fire and breach the line. The second line, with muskets loaded but not capped, was to not stop and only fire on reaching the breach, and join in expanding it. The third and fourth lines would advance on targeted objectives, when ordered. Upton coached the officers to continually shout "Forward!" all the way to the target; no one was "to fire a shot, cheer or yell, until we struck their works."

Upton's tactic proved a brilliant success. None stopped to fire, or to help a wounded comrade, but flooded over the parapets and in hand-to-hand fighting broke the Rebel line wide open — paving the way for supports to exploit the victory, just as Upton had predicted. But thanks to command blundering of a high order, there were no supports.

When the Second Corps reached the new battleground, Gershom Mott's poor-performing division had been shunted off to the left to serve as a link between the Sixth and Ninth Corps. When Upton's scheme was adopted, headquarters decided that the Sixth Corps, already furnishing a quarter of its men for Upton's strike force, should not have to furnish the support force too. The Ninth Corps was too far away, so by default the task fell to Mott's division. Mott was put under General Wright's command, but it happened that Wright was not exactly commanding the operation (or did not think he was). He had led the Sixth Corps for hardly a day, and found some orders coming to him and some to Upton and some to Mott. He lacked the boldness to take control of the operation by exercising the discretion assumed of a corps commander. General Meade, with Grant at his shoulder, seemed as indecisive as Wright.

Colonel Lyman thought Gershom Mott "showed a want of force and intelligence." Captain Holmes thought he "seemed somewhat stupid and flurried." Mott was certainly confused, as well he might be. He was not given time to pull his scattered division together, he was not properly positioned to approach the Mule Shoe, and, unbelievably, he was not told the new start time for Upton's attack. At 5:00 p.m., as originally ordered, Mott dutifully advanced on the salient. Upton's attack was only launched at 6:35 — by which time Mott's ragtag column was broken up by artillery and his spiritless men were back where they started. A bewildered Wright appealed to Grant — not Meade — and was told to "pile in the men," but now it was too late for that. With no support and under fierce counterattack, Upton withdrew on David Russell's order — with over 900 prisoners. He estimated his own loss at a thousand men. Captain Holmes, of Wright's staff, was exasperated: "A brilliant magnificent charge made useless except locally by entire failure of promised cooperation . . . nobody did anything to speak of. . . ."[35]

The Second and Fifth Corps now attempted to renew the assault on Laurel Hill, but that too was a fiasco. Warren, in his second try that day (and his fourth try in two days), had no heart for it. "Made an assault towards dark," he wrote. "Not very vigorously made and no result." The attitude in John Gibbon's Second Corps division was much the same. The attack was in the same spot as before, Gibbon wrote, "but with no better success, the only result being the killing and wounding of a certain number of men."

That night, Grant and Meade reviewed a largely lost day, and Lyman monitored the conversation. Wright came in and said "quietly & firmly to Meade; 'General, I don't want Mott's men on my left—they are not a support; I would rather have no troops there!'" Grant was alarmed that Burnside on the far left might now be isolated, especially with no cavalry guard. There was concern that Gouverneur Warren was not measuring up to corps command; "he cannot spread himself over three divisions," Lyman heard it said. "He cannot do it, and the result is partial and ill-concerted and dilatory movements." When Upton's (brief) triumph was mentioned, Meade said, "Well, that is something good at any rate!"

Two brigadier generals, James C. Rice (brigade, Fifth Corps) and Thomas G. Stevenson (division, Ninth Corps), died that day by sharpshooter or stray shot. Already Spotsylvania had claimed three brigade commanders wounded, Andrew W. Denison, William McCandless, and William H. Morris. Francis Barlow relieved brigade commander Paul Frank for drunkenness, the second such charge (after Hobart Ward) stemming from the Wilderness fighting.

In reporting to Washington, General Grant took a positive stance regarding the initial six days of the campaign. "The result to this time is much in our favor," he wrote. Losses were heavy, to be sure, but so were the enemy's. "I am satisfied the enemy are very shaky," only held to the mark by the exertions of their officers and by constant entrenching. Expanding on his earlier pledge to Mr. Lincoln, that there would be no turning back, he said he was resupplying the army "and propose to fight it out on this line if it takes all summer." Secretary Stanton had Grant's declaration included in one of the War Department's daily bulletins, and it received wide play in newspapers across the North.[36]

Grant agreed with Meade in ranking Emory Upton's breakthrough at the Mule Shoe the one "something good" to have come out of May 10. (Grant awarded Upton a field promotion to brigadier general.) He did not doubt that Upton's tactic would have succeeded if launched an hour earlier and "been heartily entered into by Mott's division and the Ninth Corps." Said Grant, "A brigade today—we'll try a corps tomorrow," or so a headquarters orderly remembered it many years later.

May 11 was a day of recuperation. Meade found time for a note to his wife: "We have been fighting continuously for *Six* days, and have gotten I think decidedly the better of the enemy.... I am quite well & in good spirits." But in his diary that day Provost Marshal Patrick found Meade hardly content—"cross as a Bear, at which I do not wonder, with such a man as Grant over him." Grant himself seemed on edge. It was reported that Rebel sharpshooters, in the fashion of guerrillas, had gotten behind the lines and were picking off men. "Grant's under jaw immediately shut, with a snap: 'I want you, Col. Lyman, to tell this to General Meade. Tell him to send a force after them; they have no right there, and let it be understood I want no prisoners taken of any such men.' He has a firm way of speaking, has Ulysses. . . ."

In midafternoon Grant sent the next day's orders to Meade, allowing but thirteen hours for their execution. After dark Hancock's Second Corps, now considered the army's shock troops, was to swing right to left behind the rest of the army and at 4:00 a.m. May 12 strike the Mule Shoe salient. The Fifth and Sixth Corps must move up close for support. Burnside's Ninth Corps, under Grant's rein, was made aware of the "importance of a prompt and vigorous attack."

A salient is inherently difficult to defend because it can be struck from three directions, and its apex is vulnerable because its firepower is diffuse. To follow Upton's example, Francis Barlow's division was chosen to lead a focused strike at the apex, with Burnside immediately supporting the Second Corps, and the Fifth and Sixth Corps standing by to exploit. Meade reviewed the plan with his corps commanders, then Hancock called in division heads Barlow, Birney, and Gibbon for a briefing at the Brown house. There was no time before night for a reconnoiter. Barlow quizzed an officer who had been with Gershom Mott's abortive attack on the 10th, and he sketched on a wall as much of the terrain and the Mule Shoe as he could remember. This, said Barlow, "was the sole basis on which the disposition of my division was made."

Hancock worked out the disposition with Barlow, who was dubious ("No information whatever, so far as I can remember, was given us as to the position and strength of the enemy"), and made the case for a narrow, quick, Upton-like thrust in "two lines of masses" — a two-brigade front, backed by a two-brigade second line; with each regiment doubled on the center, that is, in a column two companies wide, five companies deep. These stacked regiments were to be just five paces apart, the brigades, ten paces apart. To objections that such a massed formation was susceptible to artillery fire, Barlow replied, "I propose to have men enough, when I reach the objective point, to charge through Hell itself and capture all the artillery they can mass in my front." One of his staff thought Barlow depressed, as if leading a forlorn hope.[37]

To widespread surprise (including Barlow's), the opening assault on the Mule Shoe that May 12 succeeded brilliantly. Hancock delayed the 4:00

Alfred Waud captioned his drawing (as engraved in *Harper's Weekly*) "The toughest fight yet — the fight for the salient" at Spotsylvania Court House on May 12.

a.m. start half an hour due to ground fog, but once started, Barlow's men advanced silently and swiftly, not stopping to fire, and overwhelmed the startled defenders. Rebels by the score, by the hundreds, surrendered, flags were seized, batteries taken, even two Confederate generals captured. To the Yankees' good fortune, Lee had been moving artillery out of the salient, anticipating Grant shifting eastward, but even those guns remaining fired hardly a shot; twenty would be captured.

A field telegraph was now operating between corps and headquarters, and at 5:00 a.m. Hancock wired Meade, "Our men have the works, with some hundred prisoners; impossible to say how many; whole line moving up." The operator added, "General Hancock's troops are in second line works." An hour later, Hancock announced, "All of my troops are engaged," and Wright's Sixth Corps should "attack at once." Meade so ordered. But at the breach in the salient all was total confusion. More and more Second Corps troops, then Sixth Corps troops, were rushed in and nobody seemed to know what to do next. Emory Upton's careful May 10 attack briefing had included instructions for *after* the breakthrough. In the hastily formulated May 12 attack plan there was no similar instruction, no coordination among commands.

It was not the enemy's initial counterfire that disordered the attackers, said Barlow. "What did interfere with the restoring of order was the pouring in of fresh troops upon our backs." He rode back in high anger and shouted, "For God's sake, Hancock, do not send any more troops in here." He had to be allowed to re-form "in peace"; the reinforcements should sweep down the enemy lines to secure the breakthrough and the flanks. (Such was Barlow's state of mind that he neglected to address Hancock as "General," which he "never did before or afterwards.") Strong Rebel counterattacks blocked further penetration and induced — now in a driving rainstorm — a great bloody melee inside the apex of the salient.

Hancock telegraphed Burnside, "I am in the inside of second line of enemy's works. Hurry forward, or I may be driven back." While the Second Corps fought at the apex, the Ninth Corps was directed at the eastern face of the salient, to link with the breakthrough. Grant sent Colonel Cyrus Comstock of his staff to keep the Ninth Corps on track. For Ambrose Burnside this was an echo of Antietam, where he had been ordered about by McClellan's officious staff. He announced he "would command his own divisions." Comstock must have turned diplomatic and soothing, for Burnside "apologized most amply & asked my advice again." Or possibly it was Grant's blunt order to attack "as vigorously as possible. . . . See that your orders are executed." In any case, beyond denting the enemy line, Burnside's assaults failed to change much that day. "Rather weak & not fit for a corps commander," was Comstock's verdict.[38]

Throughout the Spotsylvania fighting, Grant was convinced that Lee must be pulling forces from other sectors of his line to defend against the Federal attacks. No results so far demonstrated that to be true. Still, as the May 12 offensive lost momentum, Meade hewed to Grant's theory and ordered Warren's Fifth Corps to attack Laurel Hill as aid to the salient offensive. Warren had already attacked Laurel Hill four times, and he and his officers (and his men) knew perfectly well it was hopeless. As W. A. Roebling put it, "It is not a matter of surprise that they had lost all spirit for that kind of work." In an exchange of telegrams that grew increasingly testy on Meade's part, Warren tried to explain the difficulties of such an attack, how few men it took to hold those entrenchments, and (not in so many words) that it was senseless. Chief of Staff Humphreys took over the exchange, explaining to his old friend that the order was peremptory, and in a "Dear Warren" dispatch signed "Your friend," said Meade would assume "the responsibility and will take the consequences." Meade's temper meanwhile reached boil. He told Grant that Warren "seems reluctant to assault." Grant's response was curt: "If Warren fails to attack promptly, send Humphreys to command his corps, and relieve him."

Warren ordered the attack and pressed it, but it was repulsed, just as the others had been, and at considerable cost. Meade had sent Humphreys to ride herd on Warren, and when Humphreys saw the effort was futile, he called it off. Warren thereby retained his command, but at a cost to his trustworthiness as perceived by Grant and by Meade.

"Thursday May 12th was the date of one of the most fearful combats, which lasted along one limited line and in one spot, more than 14 hours, without cessation. I fancy this war has furnished no parallel to the desperation shown here by both parties." So Theodore Lyman summed up this unique day of battle. On the Federals' part the desperation was to hold open the breach they had made; on the Confederates' part, to hold at the breach long enough for Lee's engineers to construct a new line across the base of the salient. One particular jog in the line — Lyman named it the "Death-angle," others the "Bloody Angle" — acted as a magnet for unrelenting slaughter. "The combat growing hotter & hotter! In some places our men just on one side of the breastwork, and the rebels, 50 feet off, on the other!" In this cauldron much of the fighting was too close-coupled to use artillery, so the guns pounded the rear areas. Commanders took what shelter they could from cannon and sharpshooters. Generals Hancock and Wright were found on liberated chairs on the lee side of a log barn. At the front Brigadier Alex Webb fell with a serious head wound, and newly minted Brigadier Upton had his horse killed under him.[39]

Darkness finally ended the struggle for the salient, and dawn found the Rebels pulled back to their new line, leaving behind a hideous carnage of death, sprawled in rows, heaped in piles; "the place this morning looks like a slaughter pen & is a sight to make any one sick of war," John Gibbon told his wife. Ninth Corps veterans had a standard by which to measure the fighting that day: "Officers and men all agree it was worse than Antietam. . . ." The estimate of Federal losses on May 12 came to about 9,000, for the Confederates, about 8,000, of which 3,000 were prisoners.

General Grant wrote his wife on May 13, "The world has never seen so bloody or so protracted a battle as the one being fought and I hope never will again. The enemy were really whipped yesterday but their situation is desperate. . . . To lose this battle is to lose their cause. As bad as it is they have fought for it with a gallantry worthy of a better."[40]

17. *To James River*

NIGHT AT LAST closed the May 12 fighting, and Theodore Lyman wrote his wife, "This whole death-struggle is almost without a parallel, 8 days, and heavy fighting during seven of them, with night marches and every species of toil! It seems like two giants reeling about each other, bleeding and faint, but unyielding to the last breath."

Next morning Meade wrote a note to Margaret claiming "a decided victory over the enemy, he having abandoned last night the position he so tenaciously held yesterday." He chose "frightful" to describe the casualties on both sides. "Our work is not over but we have the prestige of success which is every thing. . . ." The *New York Times* described Lee's army as "being defeated, demolished, crushed and annihilated by the courage of our soldiers and the masterly generalship of their Commander." Gideon Welles was more reflective. It would not be long, he wrote, "before one or more bloody battles will take place in which not only many dear friends will be slaughtered, but probably the civil war will be decided as to its continuance, or termination. My faith is firm in union success, but I shall be glad when faith is fact." The release of the staggering casualty lists made the newspapers more reflective as well.

Grant was unrelenting. He scheduled another attack for two days hence, May 14, only canceling when torrents of rain turned the battleground to mud. To Halleck he explained, "You can assure the President and Secretary of War that the elements alone have suspended hostilities. . . ."

John Gibbon told his wife on May 14, "The enemy are most persistent in their defense, and I think are now anxious for us to attack him, & consequently I hope we will not gratify them." He thought maneuver the better tactic, "instead of trying to carry their works by assault, the continual fighting for the past 11 days having considerably reduced our effective force." To Gibbon's point, field returns for May 13 gave Hancock 12,115, Warren 14,860, and Wright 11,278, roughly half the number they had started with.

Grant did not share Gibbon's perception. When the rains ended and the roads dried, he set May 18 for yet another trial against the Spotsylvania fortifications. Having run out of ideas, it was decided to attack over "old ground," where Upton and Barlow had earlier broken into the salient. The salient was gone now, of course, which fact offered the rationale for the May 18 attack — it would be unexpected and thereby a surprise. The Second and Sixth Corps were assigned the task.

"But the rebels, surprised once," wrote Lyman, "were not to be surprised a second time." Lee's signalmen spotted the attack forming, the advance was three-quarters of a mile through the tangled detritus of the old salient fortifications and the extensive new fortifications, and it quickly fell victim to the Confederate artillery. Meade grew acerbic: "Even *Grant* thought it useless to knock our heads against a brick wall and directed a suspension of the attack." This dismal operation marked the close to the battle for Spotsylvania Court House.[1]

Spotsylvania cost the Federals 18,399 casualties. In the fifteen days since crossing the Rapidan, the Army of the Potomac, caught up in a wholly new kind of warfare, suffered over 36,000 casualties, including 4,900 dead. (The Confederates lost an estimated 23,700 in this period.) There was as well the continuing drain of three-year men whose time was up — starting in June, thirty more regiments would leave. Replacements thus far came to about 12,000.

Wounded in their many thousands from the Wilderness and Spotsylvania overwhelmed the field hospitals, then faced inexcusable delays for extended care due to malfeasance in Washington. Secretary Stanton had rid himself of independent-minded railroad man Herman Haupt, allowing rebuilding the key rail link between Fredericksburg and Aquia Landing to lag. Stanton then rid himself of the army's crusading surgeon general, William Hammond, whose efforts to reform the hidebound Medical Bureau crossed Stanton once too often. Stanton rigged Hammond's court-martial just as he had rigged Fitz John Porter's. Wounded men literally piled up untreated at Fredericksburg. The reformer Clara Barton enlisted Senator Henry Wilson in her cause, threatening a Senate investigation. Finally Stanton ordered Quartermaster General Montgomery Meigs to take charge at Fredericksburg and clean up the mess. Once the system was working, ambulances lined up night and day at Washington's Sixth Street wharf to meet the steamers loaded with wounded for transfer to the capital's military hospitals.

Seeing early dispatches from the front, Mr. Lincoln remarked to John

Burying the dead from a military hospital at Fredericksburg after the fighting at Spotsylvania Court House, May 1864, photographed by Timothy O'Sullivan.

Hay, "How near we have been to this thing before and failed. I believe if any other General had been at the Head of that army it would have now been on this side of the Rapidan. It is the dogged pertinacity of Grant that wins." Indeed, since crossing the Rapidan Grant had chosen aggression over maneuver against the Army of Northern Virginia. This had secured him the initiative certainly, but created a very costly stalemate. W. A. Roebling, Fifth Corps staff, complained of the deadlock: "Every one knows that if Lee were to come out of his entrenchments we could whip him, but Bob Lee is a little too smart for us; . . . neither of our two commanding Generals seem to be smart enough to do anything beyond mediocrity." As if in response, Grant chose a new course. On May 19 Meade outlined it: "We shall now try to maneuver again so as to draw the enemy out of his stronghold, and hope to have a fight with him before he can dig himself into an impregnable position."[2]

Command changes were needed. Most needed was ending the Ninth Corps' outlander status and making it part of the Army of the Potomac — which meant Ambrose Burnside taking orders from Meade rather than Grant. Had this been the case from the first, Meade would at least have seen that Burnside got to the battles on time. Grant had thought Burnside would object to reporting to a general who once reported to him. In fact, Burnside was pleased. "I am glad to get the order assigning the corps to the Army of the Potomac," he wrote Grant, "because I think good will result from it."

John Robinson's Fifth Corps division had already been broken up and parceled out following Robinson's wounding. Then it was determined that Gershom Mott had failed to breathe life into the moribund Second Corps division he inherited on May 2. Mott's division, Colonel Lyman observed, "that had hitherto behaved so badly, was broken up and put with Birney. A sad record for Hooker's fighting men!" Mott returned to his old brigade. Spotsylvania cost John Gibbon's Second Corps division two of the best brigade commanders in the army. Alex Webb, struck in the head, would recover and return to the Potomac army early in 1865. Samuel Carroll, wounded in the right arm on May 5, was wounded in the left arm on May 13. His surgeon advised amputation, saying it would come to a question between suppuration and constitution. "Well," said Carroll, "I guess old Cons' will carry the day, so we will leave it on!" Carroll's trust was rewarded. He was made brigadier general and returned to the service, although not to the Potomac army.[3]

Picking over Spotsylvania's failings, some on Grant's staff urged him to issue his orders directly to the corps commanders, eliminating delays and chances for misinterpretation by Meade or his staff—in short, take full command of the Army of the Potomac. Staff man Horace Porter had Grant explaining that while he was "fully aware that some embarrassments arise from the present organization," he had too many other responsibilities as general-in-chief to also command this army. And, anyway, coming to the command from the Western theater, he would arouse resentment in the officer corps (he did not refer to John Pope by name).

General Meade, too, was mulling his command status. To visiting senators John Sherman and William Sprague he explained, "At first I had maneuvered the Army, but gradually & from the very nature of things, Grant had taken the control, and that it would be injurious to the Army to have two heads." He admitted to a definition — Grant did the grand strategy, he the grand tactics. He did not lay blame for this situation on Grant. Indeed, "I know he thinks a great deal of me & is most friendly." Still, he felt he was in a false position, but saw no honorable solution to the matter.

Grant and staff also discovered that month of May that George Meade's "irascible temper" bore down hard on perceived folly. Meade's one failing, said Grant, was his temper. "A battle always put him in a fury. He raged from the beginning to the end. His own staff officers would dread to bring him a report of anything wrong." Theodore Lyman acknowledged this failing of his chief — "I can tell you aqua fortis [nitric acid] is mild to the Major General commanding when he gets put out, which is quite not at all infrequently" — but explained that the staff understood Meade's real target was, say, some witless general at the front; they, the messengers, caught the outburst. Alex Webb, who would become Meade's chief of staff, believed "he thought too quick and expected others to think the same — without his source of information." Webb recalled a day that Meade "allowed his tongue to run away with him," and Webb walked off to let his own temper cool. Soon Meade caught up to him, put his arm around his shoulder, and said, "Don't mind, don't think any more about it. It comes to my head and I said it; that is all." Another of Meade's staff, James Biddle, put the matter in perspective: "Genl. Meade's only fault is his irritability, which does not affect him as a general, but only exasperates the unfortunates who are so unlucky as to be the cause of his ire."[4]

Horace Porter's recollection implying that Meade's caution was primarily responsible for the stalemate is misleading. In fact, the army's troubles at Spotsylvania were due primarily to impatience — impatience on General Grant's part.

Meade was more careful and calculating of the odds than Grant . . . and, too, he had the benefit of two years' experience fighting against Robert E. Lee. He took the tactical initiative by translating Emory Upton's feat at the Rappahannock bridgehead back in November to seek a similar success against the Spotsylvania salient, as ordered by Grant for May 10. Upton's planning was timely, but not enough time was allotted to position a proper support force; a day's delay might have awarded a victory to Upton's innovation. It was much the same for the hurried May 12 offensive — there was no time to plan a deliberate exploitation of whatever break might be made in the Confederate lines. This was a very large army with an entrenched high command, and Meade struggled to move it at Grant's arbitrary pace. On May 18 (as John Gibbon pointed out) the enemy was ready, waiting, even anxious for the Yankees to attack, and Grant impatiently ordered this forlorn hope anyway.

Gouverneur Warren, in the Wilderness and again at Spotsylvania, raised his superiors' hackles by questioning and sidestepping orders he believed unworkable, particularly the attack orders against Laurel Hill; Grant ordered him relieved if he did not obey the last of these. Warren credited Meade with saving his corps command that day, but Andrew Humphreys surely had a hand in the saving. In any event, Warren was thereafter on a short leash.

Winfield Hancock continued commanding with driving spirit, making

The newest addition to the Army of the Potomac high command, Horatio Wright, replaced Sixth Corps' John Sedgwick, killed at Spotsylvania.

his Second Corps the army's shock troops in these May battles. He worked well in concert with divisional commanders Francis Barlow, David Birney, and (except for the strayed dispatch on May 6 in the Wilderness) John Gibbon. Hancock said his trouble as corps commander (wrote Theodore Lyman) "is that he can't *see* everything . . . 'Oh! I wish I were a second lieutenant . . . and then I could *see* the men and know what they are doing.'" His indignation at stragglers was tempered by his good nature: "Why men, what *are* you doing here? If this goes on I shall have no command left. Come, come! Go to the front, go to the front!" But Hancock was hampered by his unhealed Gettysburg wound, traveling by ambulance, only mounting when his striking martial presence on horseback was required to rally the troops. It was late June, when bone splinters worked their way out of the wound, that he began a recovery.

After a mostly supporting role at the Wilderness, John Sedgwick was killed before realizing any decisive role at Spotsylvania. Sedgwick thought highly enough of Horatio Wright, a comparative latecomer to the Potomac army, that he was named Uncle John's successor at the Sixth Corps. Wright's approach to corps command proved tentative, especially on May 10 in his weak support of Upton's assault. He might not be able to fill Uncle John's shoes, but he would need to prove he could grow into the job.[5]

As the two armies struggled in the cramped region of the Wilderness and Spotsylvania, related fighting sprawled all across central Virginia. Of most immediate interest to the Army of the Potomac was Phil Sheridan's expedition with the cavalry corps. In consequence of his tendentious argument with Meade on May 8, Sheridan gained Grant's leave to seek out a fight with Jeb Stuart. Sheridan announced to his division commanders, "We are going out to fight Stuart's cavalry in consequence of a suggestion from me . . . and in view of my recent representations to General Meade I shall expect nothing but success." In June 1863 Joe Hooker had ordered his cavalry to find and fight Stuart, resulting in battle at Brandy Station. This time the stimulus originated from the general-in-chief, with Stuart again the deliberate target.

At first light on May 9 Sheridan formed up 12,000 troopers and six horse-artillery batteries in a column stretching some 13 miles and headed south by east for the Telegraph Road linking Fredericksburg and Richmond. His three divisions (seven brigades) were led by Wesley Merritt, David Gregg, and James Wilson. Sheridan made no effort at deception. The pace was at a walk, to ease the horses. The direction was simply toward Richmond, which (Sheridan reasoned) would force Stuart to fight. Stuart pursued with just three of his seven brigades, a decision perhaps dictated by General Lee's need to remain ever informed.

Stuart nipped at the rear guard of the Yankee column, but could not reach the head of it in time to save a major supply depot for Lee's army. George Custer's Michigan brigade led the way across the North Anna River to Beaver Dam Station on the Virginia Central. Warehouses at the station were set ablaze, consuming (by Confederate count) 504,000 rations of bread and 915,000 rations of bacon, as well as a serious loss of medical stores. Sheridan reported two locomotives and 100 cars destroyed as well, along with 10 miles of track (by Confederate count, 26 cars and one mile of track). As a bonus, Custer liberated 378 Federal captives slated for prisoner of war camps.[6]

On May 11 Stuart caught up at the junction of the two roads the two sides were following, where stood an abandoned stage stop called Yellow Tavern. This was just two miles north of Richmond's outer ring of works. Stuart tried to block the way, but was sharply defeated by the powerful Yankee force that fought mostly dismounted. Yellow Tavern was a battle without trenches or parapets, and consequently the full weight of Federal numbers was brought to bear. Beyond numbers, the Federals had in their Spencer seven-shot repeating carbines a major firepower advantage. Jeb Stuart fell mortally wounded in the melee. The South mourned.

To the Potomac army's mounted arm, Yellow Tavern was the first clear-cut, decisive victory in some two years of cavalry battles. Sheridan collected his forces and struck out for Haxall's Landing, on the James behind

Malvern Hill where McClellan had watched (from a distance) his army survive the seventh of the Seven Days. There was a close call when the Yankees had to bridge the Chickahominy, but Richmond could not muster the strength to spring the trap. "Why, what do you suppose we have in front of us?" Sheridan boasted. "A lot of department clerks from Richmond, who have been forced into the ranks. I could capture Richmond, if I wanted, but I can't hold it. . . . It isn't worth the men it would cost."

Sheridan reached Haxall's Landing on May 14 without further event, where guarded by the navy's gunboats he rested and resupplied. Maintaining a leisurely pace, the cavalry corps only rejoined the Potomac army on May 24. The Richmond raid boosted cavalry morale and affirmed Sheridan's posting, and brightened newspaper accounts across the North, yet it had few lasting effects. The Confederates relaid the tracks, replaced the bread and bacon (the medical stores less easily), capable Wade Hampton took Stuart's place, and the Rebel cavalry remained a force to reckon with. Meanwhile, for more than two weeks the Army of the Potomac was left blind, lacking any cavalry-gathered intelligence.[7]

The cavalry accomplished at least its immediate goal of battling Stuart, but the other elements in General Grant's expansive campaign scheme to complement the Potomac army fell apart, piece by piece. In each case it was command failure by generals Grant was saddled with — generals appointed for their politics or their political connections that Lincoln believed he needed in this election year. A prime example was Franz Sigel.

Sigel, the German 1848 insurgent, had come from the Western theater in John Pope's Army of Virginia, muddled through Second Bull Run, ascended to the Grand Reserve Division under Burnside, then sank to heading the little Eleventh Corps under Hooker. That was beneath him, he said, and he resigned. Now, as a means to get out the German American vote in 1864, Lincoln appointed Sigel to head the Department of West Virginia. While grateful for the appointment, Sigel felt cast "into the turbulent sea pond, rather with a frail and leaking bark, to drift along as good as I could."

Aware of Sigel's command history, Grant intended him simply to administer the department while he appointed E.O.C. Ord to command the troops. Ord had left the Potomac army for the Western theater, where he led a corps at Vicksburg. Grant's orders to Ord were to destroy the Virginia & Tennessee Railroad "so that it can be of no further use to the enemy during the rebellion." These dispositions were made, said an offended Sigel, "in such a manner as if I did not exist at all." So Franz Sigel, major general, made his own plans, which left Ord no resources to carry out Grant's mandate. Ord resigned, and a single major thrust at the Rebels' communications was replaced by three minor thrusts, under George Crook, William Averell . . . and Sigel himself.

Crook had led a brigade of the Kanawha Division, Ninth Corps, at Fox's Gap and Antietam. On May 2 he set out with three brigades of infantry, some 6,100 men, to do damage to the Virginia & Tennessee, the Confederates' rail link between Lynchburg, Virginia, and East Tennessee. Crook's march aimed for Dublin Depot, on the railroad in southwestern Virginia. On May 9 he found his way blocked at Cloyd's Mountain by a pickup force under Albert Jenkins.

"The enemy is in force and in a strong position," Crook told one of his colonels. "They may whip, but I guess not." He sent one of his brigades on a wide turning movement, and when that brigade engaged, he attacked in front with his other two brigades, leading the way himself. The Yankees stormed over the skimpy works and routed the defenders, capturing General Jenkins. Future president Rutherford B. Hayes (wounded earlier at Fox's Gap) commanded one of Crook's brigades. He wrote home pridefully of "utterly routing Jenkins's army in the bloody battle of Cloyd's Mountain."

Crook went on to wreck Dublin Depot, tear up track, and burn the rail bridge over the New River. On May 15 he was joined by General Averell, who had a considerably lesser story to tell. At Chancellorsville, Averell had run afoul of Joe Hooker, who considered him faint-hearted in operating against Lee's communications, and Averell was exiled to the Department of West Virginia. Now, with some 2,000 cavalry, he was to attack the important saltworks at Saltville and the lead mines at Wytheville as a corollary to Crook's operation. Both sites turned out to be defended, although not in the numbers Averell imagined, and he was reluctant to commit his troopers to an infantry fight. He backed away and joined with Crook, helping tear up some railroad track — according to Hayes, altogether 18 miles' worth.

General Crook in his report said he saw "dispatches from Richmond" — presumably Richmond newspapers — that claimed Grant was defeated and in retreat. That determined him to declare victory and pull back to West Virginia. He had ordered Averell to continue on to Lynchburg, pulling up rails as he went. Averell, as faint-hearted as ever, said he was short of rations and forage and ammunition, and he too withdrew. Like Sheridan and his Richmond raid, Crook and Averell had adventures in enemy country, won one battle (at Cloyd's Mountain), but together produced no lasting effects. The Confederates had the Virginia & Tennessee back in operation in a month and its defenders were freed up to reinforce General Lee.[8]

In his planning for Franz Sigel's Department of West Virginia, Grant admitted, "I do not calculate on very great results. But it is the only way I can take troops from there. . . . In other words if Sigel cant skin himself he can hold a leg whilst someone else skins." (Grant borrowed this bit of frontier imagery from a conversation he had with Mr. Lincoln.) General Sigel determined to take a role of his own in the campaign, and on May 9, with 9,000 troops, he set off up the Shenandoah Valley.

General Lee regarded any advance in the Valley as a particular threat to both his communications and his commissary, and he made John C. Breckinridge responsible for its defense. Vice president under Buchanan, 1860 presidential candidate, Breckinridge was a political general with martial skills. Starting from Winchester, Sigel marched up the Valley Pike past Strasburg and paused at Woodstock to wait out the rains and calculate what enemy he faced. Dispatches he captured gave the Rebels between 4,000 and 5,000 infantry and marching north toward New Market, 20 miles distant. Sigel's delay at Woodstock gave Breckinridge time to reach and to take his stand at New Market. There, on May 15, the two little armies faced each other.

Taking a leaf from Prince John Magruder's Yorktown book, the Rebels marched and countermarched around and among the trees, confusing Sigel; while he supposed he outnumbered by about two to one, now he was less sure. Putting up a brave front, he said, "We may as well fight them today as any day." He chose a peculiar formation to do so — two lines, one on a low rise and the other a half mile or so in advance — dividing his army in the face of the enemy. Breckinridge massed his forces and took advantage, overrunning the first Yankee line and sending it in a rush back through the second line. Now it was a close-fought struggle, featuring in Confederate annals the legendary tale of a company of teenage cadets from the Virginia Military Institute. Sigel exercised little control of events, frantically rushing about issuing his orders in German to add to the confusion. "In his excitement he seemed to forget his English entirely," wrote his aide D. H. Strother, "and the purely American portion of his staff were totally useless to him." Soon enough the Federal position collapsed in defeat and retreat.

The Federal loss at New Market was 841, the Confederate, some 530. "I came to the conclusion," Strother wrote, "that Sigel is merely a book soldier acquainted with the techniques of the art of war but having no capacity to fight with troops in the field." With the concurrent withdrawal of Crook's and Averell's forces, the Shenandoah Valley and southwestern Virginia were now empty of Yankees. Breckinridge promptly sent 2,500 men to reinforce Lee.⁹

The largest collapse in this catalog of disappointment was the one Grant had the most immediate hopes for — Major General Benjamin F. Butler's James River expedition. Ben Butler, political general, War Democrat with Radical leanings, was described by one of Grant's staff as "sharp, shrewd, able, without conscience or modesty — overbearing. A bad man to have against you." Butler had appeared onstage after Fort Sumter, leading Massachusetts volunteers and proclaiming martial law in Baltimore. He then moved to Fort Monroe on the Peninsula, where he proclaimed runaway slaves as contraband of war. Then he led the army contingent in the capture of New Orleans, proclaiming all manner of things in his controversial administration of the Crescent City. In none of these commands did Butler direct any fighting. Now he was assigned the Army of the James at Fort Monroe, two corps, 36,000 men.

The role of Butler's Army of the James (said Grant) was "to operate on the south side of the James River, Richmond being your objective point." This implied three aims — first, to secure a foothold on the south bank of the James from which, in due course, the united Potomac and James armies might operate against Lee's army and Richmond; second, to secure the James as the army's supply and communications corridor; and third, by its threatening presence, to tie up substantial Rebel forces.

Butler was directed first to City Point, on the south bank where the Appomattox River enters the James. Then a different tack: "Use every exertion to secure footing as far up the south side of the river as you can. . . ." Grant said nothing of any target other than Richmond. Butler saw that taking City Point as a base would require crossing the Appomattox to get at Richmond, so he chose instead to land as far up the south bank as possible.

With the same thinking he applied to Sigel, Grant supplied Butler with two generals for the actual troop-leading — Quincy A. Gillmore, an engineer officer whose specialty was bombardment (Fort Pulaski at Savannah, the defenses of Charleston), and William F. Smith, Grant's engineering officer in the Tennessee campaign. Baldy Smith had spent a rather strange year and a half with the Army of the Potomac. Starting at Yorktown on the Peninsula, he had risen to command the Sixth Corps, yet along the way he did no serious battle-leading — not in the Seven Days, not at Second Bull Run, not at Antietam, not at Fredericksburg; his troops had not reached the field or were in reserve or on the fringes of the action. He spent his spare time undermining his superiors while they assumed he knew how to command a battle. Joe Hooker excised Smith from the Potomac army after Fredericksburg, but in Tennessee he gained enough favor with Grant to make him, for a time, a candidate for the Potomac army command. Smith's new command was the Eighteenth Corps, Gillmore's, the Tenth Corps. Smith and Gillmore would discover that Ben Butler had his own ideas about command.[10]

Their two corps boarded transports at Fort Monroe on May 4, the same day the Army of the Potomac opened its campaign. Passing up the James, the next day they landed a division of U.S. Colored Troops at City Point and the rest of the army beyond at Bermuda Hundred, an irregularly shaped peninsula bounded by the James and the Appomattox. Richmond was 15 miles to the north. The railroad hub of Petersburg was eight miles to the south. Immediately to the west passed the Richmond & Petersburg Railroad, the Confederate capital's lifeline. Butler spent several days fortifying the three-mile neck of land between the two rivers to shelter his army, and lightly probing west toward the railroad.

In addition to the Richmond & Petersburg, four railroads from the rest of the Confederacy entered Petersburg, and for that reason the town had been on the minds of Potomac army generals since the days of McClellan. But not on Grant's mind, or not yet, and Butler's orders came from Grant. The two corps of the Army of the James could have been able to hold Petersburg at least long enough to demolish a good part of its rail connections. And acting from Bermuda Hundred, Generals Smith and Gillmore could surely destroy the Richmond & Petersburg, and keep it destroyed. In that event, Lee would have to fall back to restore his, and Richmond's, communications.

But except for a feeble pass or two at the Richmond & Petersburg, none of this happened. Butler called in Smith and Gillmore and outlined a plan of his own for advancing on Petersburg. The two generals went off and huddled and came up with a different plan for the same purpose, involving bridging the Appomattox. Butler took offense at their "vacillation," said he was "not going to build a bridge for West Point men to retreat over," and in a huff canceled the operation. (Butler's criticism, said Baldy Smith, "was of such a character as to check voluntary advice during the remainder of the campaign.") Instead, Butler announced his "intention of making a subsequent early demonstration" against Richmond.

Richmond somehow kept its collective head despite the multiple threats in these May days — Lee's army defending at Spotsylvania, Yankee cavalry knocking at the city's gates, the Shenandoah Valley and southwestern Virginia invaded — and on May 16 it mustered force enough under P.G.T.

Caricaturist William H. Tevis took U. S. Grant's remark as inspiration for portraying Benjamin F. Butler's entrapment at Bermuda Hundred, on the James near Richmond.

"As if he had been in a bottle strongly corked".

Beauregard to block Butler's advance at Fort Darling, on Drewry's Bluff, the capital's guardian site on the James. The fighting, in a morning fog, was stalemated as the sulking Smith and Gillmore stood on the defensive. Butler tried to get Gillmore to counterattack, to do anything, but without success. As the fog lifted, Smith declared his communications threatened and "immediately ordered a retirement of the whole line." Butler had to fall back to Bermuda Hundred. Smith would lay the blame entirely on Butler, whom he described to Grant "as helpless as a child on the field of battle and as visionary as an opium eater in council. . . ."

Beauregard followed and erected strong works fronting Butler's entrenched line, which both stymied Butler and secured the vital Richmond & Petersburg line. The news was received at Potomac army headquarters: "Butler has just bottled himself up in Bermuda Hundreds and has indeed made a nice mess of it!" Now able to keep Butler quiescent with a modest force, Beauregard sent 7,000 men to reinforce General Lee.

On May 17 General Halleck summed up the day's reports for General Grant. Sheridan's cavalry corps was leaving the James that day to return to the Army of the Potomac — a journey that would take a week. Sigel "is already in full retreat to Strasburg. If you expect anything from him you will be mistaken. He will do nothing but run. He never did anything else." Halleck said David Hunter would replace Sigel. "Butler has fallen back to-day. Do not rely on him."

Remarking on these setbacks, Horace Porter of Grant's staff described the general-in-chief as "not a man to waste any time over occurrences of the past." He has Grant writing out an order "for a general movement by the left flank toward Richmond, to begin the next night, May 19."[11]

Grant renewing the advance by the left flank was predictable, for it shortened his chosen supply line while guarding it. As the Army of the Potomac moved south, so did its water-based logistics, from Belle Plain on the Potomac to Port Royal on the lower Rappahannock. Halleck was told "to stir up the navy" to secure Port Royal. And since the flank movement *was* predictable, Grant decided to set out bait to tempt General Lee. Grant's thinking was similar to Meade's in the fall 1863 campaigning—cede Lee the initiative in the hope he would come out from behind his entrenchments—in this case, by offering him a target of opportunity.

Before the plan could be set in motion, Lee struck first. Upon reaching the current battleground, the Potomac army had initially faced south, toward Spotsylvania, but by now, May 19, it had edged around Spotsylvania and faced west. Holding the army's right (now northern) flank at the Harris house was a division of heavies, the artillerymen who had manned the heavy batteries in the Washington forts, recast as infantry and facing hostile fire for the first time. Robert O. Tyler, known for leading the Potomac army's artillery reserve, had charge of these 7,500 well-drilled but green rookies. In late afternoon Lee sent Dick Ewell on a dash toward the Federals' communications, catching the Yankees by surprise (there being none of Sheridan's cavalry at hand). The Rebels struck two heavy-artillery regiments under Colonel J. Howard Kitching, and soon the rest of the heavies under Tyler were rushed into action.

The heavies' officers knew the drills well enough, but were confused executing them under fire, and formed their lines awkwardly. This being their first fire, "they consequently went in very much jumbled up," wrote Fifth Corps artillery chief Charles Wainwright. "First there was Kitching's brigade firing at the enemy; then Tyler's men fired into his; up came Birney's division and fired into Tyler's; while the artillery fired at the whole damned lot." The heavies bent but did not break . . . and they did not run.

Horace Porter observed the fight, and he complimented Tyler as the

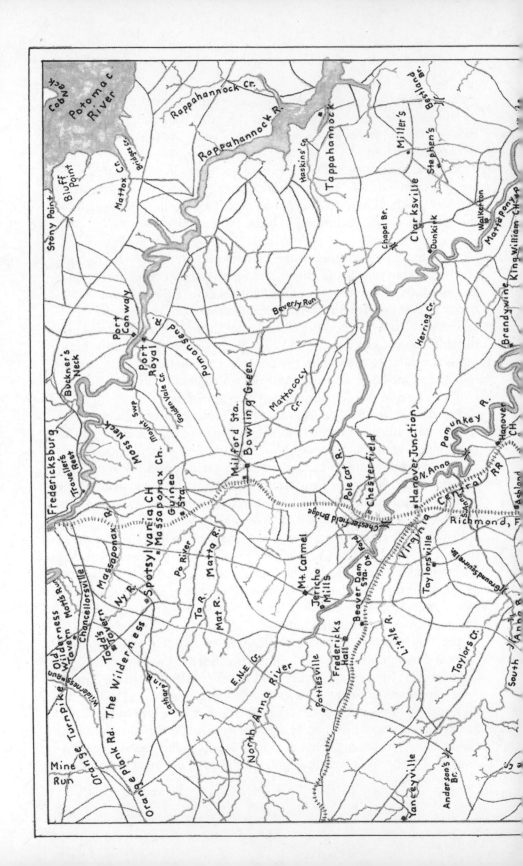

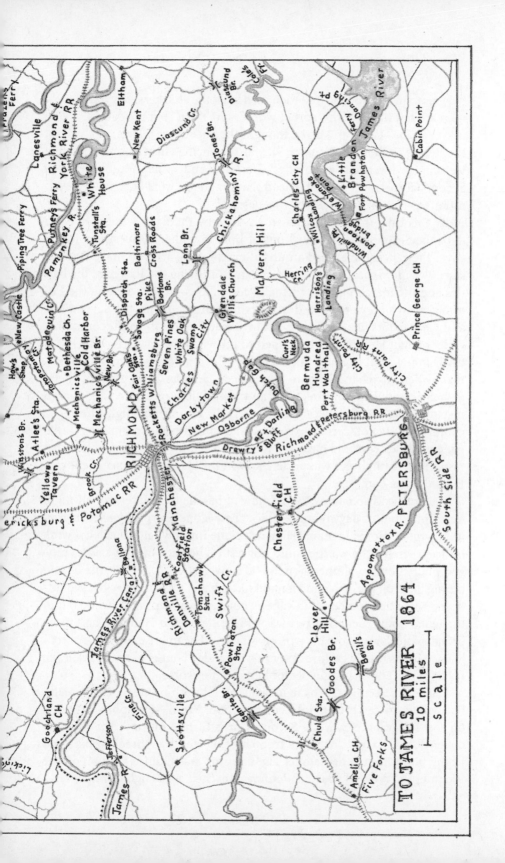

TO JAMES RIVER 1864
10 miles
Scale

heavies managed to hold and then turn back the attackers. "As you see, my men are raw hands at this sort of work," said Tyler, "but they are behaving like veterans." General Warren thought the encounter told as much about the Rebels as about the rookies: "It was the enemy's best troops, and what we supposed were our worst ones." Darkness ended the shooting, and the Second Corps, most trusted to lead the way south, went back to its preparations to march, now postponed a day.[12]

By this time the routine for an advance by the flank was fixed. After dark the Second Corps pulled out of line, the other corps stretching to cover the gap, and marched around the rear of the army to make an early start. For more than two weeks now, since crossing the Rapidan, the battles and the marching were virtually continuous — far exceeding the Potomac army's previous record of sustained engagements, the Seven Days and Chancellorsville — and the strain was telling on the high command. Chief of Staff Humphreys explained to his wife how it was for him — "At times in the front examining the enemy's position & our own operations, then, when any changes are to be made, at Hd. Qrs. arranging for them, giving a multiplicity of directions and instructions and receiving at each instant dispatches that became innumerable, far into the night they keep coming and staff officers keep coming and sometimes all night long. What patience & self control I have had to exercise. I am vastly improved in that respect" — Humphreys was widely known for his range of profane invective — "old as I am."

Generals had somehow to find how to handle this pattern of all-night marching and all-day fighting. Once the Second Corps was set in motion, wrote Colonel Lyman, "Hancock came into my tent to catch a wink of sleep. Tired as he was he could not rest till he had smoked a short pipe and poured out a volume of energetic conversation. . . . After this he laid his big head on his arm and went off like a babe; till waked by his staff officers, when he jumped up (awake as quickly as asleep) and strode out of the tent." Gouverneur Warren was less resilient than Hancock and more problematical. He wrote his wife on May 19, "The intense mental anxiety I have to occasionally endure is very trying indeed but . . . I try to await the result of our efforts resignedly for better or for worse."[13]

Hancock's Second Corps made its march, south by east, not in stealth but willing to catch General Lee's attention. From Massaponax Church on the Telegraph Road, the Second Corps turned off onto the Bowling Green Road. Except for some troopers collected by Alfred Torbert and riding point, it marched alone. The first stop was Guinea Station, on the Richmond, Fredericksburg & Potomac, reached at daylight on May 21. A

Confederate cavalry picket was brushed aside, and the column marched to Bowling Green and nearby Milford Station on the R. F. & P., where a second cavalry picket was dispersed. It was learned that George Pickett's Rebel division had just passed by here, up from North Carolina by way of bottling up Ben Butler at Bermuda Hundred, and on its way to join Lee. Hancock's orders were to get as far south toward Richmond as he could, generally following the line of the railroad. But this report of substantial enemy infantry in the neighborhood gave Hancock pause. He dug in across the Mattapony River by Milford Station to await whatever Lee might throw at him. Hancock reported himself 20 miles in advance of the rest of the army, and mentioned Pickett's division "which had just come up (say last evening) from Plymouth, N.C., and Fort Darling." So that Hancock might not become victim instead of bait, the rest of the army was hastily ordered out after the Second Corps.

Grant and Meade rode together on May 21, accompanying Warren's Fifth Corps in the advance, and at midday they stopped at Massaponax Church. The church pews were carried into the yard under the trees, and the two generals, with staffs in attendance, studied their maps and plotted their course. Photographer Timothy O'Sullivan, who knew a picture opportunity when he glimpsed one, commemorated this unposed example of high command harmony.

The high command paused its march south at Massaponax Church, conferring on pews in the churchyard. Grant is in front of the trees. To his left are Charles Dana, War Department, and John Rawlings, chief of staff. Meade is at the far end of the leftmost pew, studying a map with staffman Theodore Lyman. By Timothy O'Sullivan.

It was a hot, dusty march, Lyman reported, but as they moved south "the country grew more open, with not a few decent houses, and many fields . . . the contrast to the Wilderness tract was most pleasant." Morale brightened for that reason alone — "seeing more & more of the sacred soil, and going south withal, a direction which I pray may continue. The great strife *daily centers more & more on this particular army & that of Lee.*"

Grant was displeased by the intelligence that Pickett's division had left standing guard over Butler at Bermuda Hundred to reinforce Lee, and that Butler could not cut the Richmond & Petersburg rail line. Butler, he complained, could not even keep 10,000 Confederates occupied. ("I know I am employing one-third more of the enemy's force than I have," Butler tried to insist.) Already Grant had demonstrated with the heavies his aversion to idle or wasted manpower. He now had Baldy Smith's Eighteenth Corps shipped off to join the Army of the Potomac. Edward Hincks's black troops remained to garrison City Point on the James.[14]

Lee did not regard Hancock's Second Corps at Milford Station a target of opportunity, as Grant hoped he would, but only as the spearhead of another attempt to turn his right flank . . . which it turned out to be. Lee instead devoted his efforts to swiftly disengaging from Spotsylvania and falling back behind the North Anna River. Flowing southeasterly, the North Anna joins the South Anna at a point some 20 miles north of Richmond to form the Pamunkey. The Pamunkey, in turn, empties into the York River. At the head of navigation on the Pamunkey was White House, once McClellan's logistical base, now to be Meade's logistical base.

Hanover Junction, tucked between the North Anna and the South Anna, was where the Virginia Central from Gordonsville to the west and the R. F. & P. from Fredericksburg to the north intersected and ran in parallel south to Richmond. The northern segment of the R. F. & P. was already lost to Lee, but the Virginia Central carried the Shenandoah Valley's rich produce to Richmond, and to Lee's army. Lee's task was to make of the North Anna a shield to guard Hanover Junction. He wrote Jefferson Davis on May 23 that whatever route Grant's army pursued, "I am in a position to move against him, and shall endeavor to engage him while in motion. . . . I should be very glad to have the aid of General Beauregard in such a blow, and if it is possible to combine, I think it will succeed."

The two armies marched in parallel to the North Anna, and for the first time in almost three weeks, quite out of touch with one another. In this new developing warfare of entrenchments, each hoped to catch the other in motion. But Lee's priority now was getting behind the North Anna before he was flanked. The opportunity was Grant's and Meade's — except due to the cavalry corps' continued absence they were still operating blind. Only on May 24, with the chance gone, did Sheridan rejoin. Beyond killing Jeb Stuart, Phil Sheridan had yet to contribute to the campaign.

Grant's orders to Meade for the army's movements were detailed, spelling out march routes and schedules, implying that Grant was now de facto commander of the Army of the Potomac. This was misleading, however. These orders were in fact products of joint discussion and planning by the two generals — framing orders from which subordinates were then issued their individual orders by Meade. Generals Grant and Meade, wrote staff man James Biddle, "work together very congenially." It was just such a joint planning session that Timothy O'Sullivan photographed at Massaponax Church. Theodore Lyman described a similar session a few days later, at Mt. Carmel Church: "They laid boards across the broad aisle in the mean little church and made a table where sat Grant, Meade, Gen. Williams &c. writing."

(It was also at Mt. Carmel Church that General Meade "got awfully mad" at a perceived insult to his army and to him. Charles A. Dana, assistant secretary of war, was traveling with army headquarters — as Stanton's spy, most believed — and to the gathered generals Dana read aloud a dispatch from General Sherman, in Georgia. Sherman proclaimed, "The army of the West having fought, could now afford to manoeuvre, and that, if his (Grant's) inspiration could make the Army of the Potomac do its share, success would crown our efforts." At that, Lyman reported, Meade's "grey eyes grew like a rattlesnake's" and he said "in a voice like cutting an iron bar with a handsaw: 'Sir! I consider that despatch an insult to the army I command and to me personally. The Army of the Potomac does not require General Grant's inspiration or anybody's else inspiration to make it fight!!'" He did not get over it all day, Lyman said, "and at dinner spoke of the western army as 'an armed rabble.'")[15]

Meade advocated a next step as the Potomac army approached the North Anna. He said there was no reason to force a crossing there (and then at the South Anna). By another swing south by east, clear of the Rebels, they could make an unopposed crossing of the Pamunkey downstream and maintain their flanking threat. Cyrus Comstock of Grant's staff noted in his diary discussing this scheme with Meade. James Biddle of Meade's staff was "pretty certain that Genl. Meade disapproved" of Grant's plan to attack across the North Anna, "and advocated pushing at once for Hanover Town & crossing the Pamunkey there. . . ."

Back in April, writing his wife, Colonel Lyman had added to his initial impression of U. S. Grant the observation that "he habitually wears an expression as if he had determined to drive his head through a brick wall, and was about to do it." General Meade, writing *his* wife, used the Grant-and-brick-wall image at Spotsylvania. Thus Grant rejecting Meade's advice to continue the flanking march was probably not a surprise. Once again Lee's army was in front of him; once again Grant elected to go straight at it.

In part this was because Lee's army *was* his objective; he needed to destroy it before it took refuge in Richmond's defenses. In part this was because a crossing and getting a battle at the North Anna appeared likely. For most of the stretch of river dividing the two armies, the north bank was higher than the south bank. Crossing with artillery dominating the far shore would therefore be easier to force and harder for the Confederates to defend. (It was the opposite at the Rapidan, and the Yankees had elected to flank rather than try to force.)[16]

The Potomac army approached the North Anna on May 23 in three columns. Warren's Fifth Corps, trailed by Wright's Sixth Corps, found an upstream crossing at Jericho Mills. Hancock's Second Corps reached the river five miles downstream at Chesterfield Bridge, where the Telegraph Road crossed. Ox Ford between them was slated for Burnside's last-arriving Ninth Corps.

Gouverneur Warren had concluded that no battlefield could be any worse than Spotsylvania, and he wrote his wife he hoped now for "a battle in an open field without breastworks." His wish was soon granted. The high northern bank at Jericho Mills discouraged the Confederates from even trying to defend the crossing itself. The river here was shallow enough for infantry to wade, and Warren crossed the divisions of Charles Griffin and Samuel Crawford while engineers laid down a pontoon bridge for the artillery and the rest of the corps. Griffin and Crawford started digging in, but Lysander Cutler's division was just reaching the right of the line when A. P. Hill launched a sudden attack.

The Rebels' main thrust struck Cutler's unprepared brigades, which broke under the assault. The Westerners of the Iron Brigade refused their line to try and save their flank but then they too joined the retreat. Rufus Dawes, commanding the 6th Wisconsin, wrote his wife that "General A. P. Hill's corps of the rebel army attacked . . . hoping to make a Ball's Bluff rout of our troops. . . . We came near being driven into the river. . . ." The day was saved by the Fifth Corps artillery under Charles Wainwright. He jammed his guns right into the failing battlefront, firing double-shotted canister. "This was a very ticklish moment," Wainwright told his dairy. "I felt that now was the time to show what artillery could do. . . . I could not help a glow of pleasure and pride as I watched the four little guns moving straight through the fugitive infantry and forming on the very ground a whole brigade had abandoned." His swiftly reinforced gun line held its ground, Griffin and Crawford held their ground, and Griffin sent Joseph Bartlett's brigade to help on the right. The attackers were pressed back, and the ticklish moment passed. Meade sent to Warren, "I congratulate you and your gallant corps for the handsome manner in which you repulsed the enemy's attack." Lee sent to A. P. Hill, "Why did you not do as Jackson would have done—thrown your whole force upon these people and driven them back?" Robert E. Lee found this new kind of warfare not to his liking.

Meanwhile, downstream Hancock's Second Corps confronted a different scene—a Confederate redoubt on the north bank guarding Chesterfield Bridge, which carried the Telegraph Road across the North Anna. Like the similar *tête de pont* on the north bank of the Rappahannock in November, Lee maintained the redoubt to host a potential counterattack north of the river. That purpose expired in the face of the entire Second Corps. John C. Tidball's thirteen corps batteries pounded the redoubt and the Rebel positions along the south bank, and David Birney sent in three brigades to storm the redoubt. Redoubt and bridge were captured. Hancock called a halt at dark and waited for morning to cross the North Anna in force.[17]

By early on May 24 the Second Corps was across the river, and five miles upstream Warren's Fifth Corps completed its crossing, followed by Wright's Sixth Corps. That left, in between at Ox Ford, Burnside's Ninth Corps. Ox Ford was different from Jericho Mills and Chesterfield Bridge in that the south bank there was higher than the north bank and therefore quite defensible.

This was Burnside's final day of taking orders from Grant, and more awkward than usual—the Ninth Corps squarely in the middle of the Potomac army, requiring coordinated decisions, yet not under Potomac army direction. Burnside's dispatch to Grant on the odds for forcing a crossing hardly inspired confidence: "The prospects of success are not at all flattering, but I think the attempt can be made without any very disastrous results, and we may possibly succeed." This was sent at 6:30 a.m., and six hours passed with nothing gained at Ox Ford. An impatient order from Grant—"You must get over and camp to-night on the south side"—earned Burnside's admission that he had been trying all morning without success. Finally he sent a division to cross upstream so as to take the Ox Ford defenders in flank. The first brigade across was James H. Ledlie's, who then recklessly dashed his unsupported command against the Ox Ford fortifications and was routed. That concluded the Ninth Corps' efforts for the day. "General Ledlie made a botch of it. Had too much —— on board, I think," Colonel Stephen Weld discreetly noted in his diary. In fact, Ledlie's staff was as drunk as he was. (Two weeks later, James Ledlie was leading a Ninth Corps division, an indictment of Burnside's management.)

In the well-scattered Federal dispositions, General Lee saw opportunity and seized it. To the west, Warren's Fifth Corps and Wright's Sixth were established across the North Anna. To the east, Hancock's Second Corps was across and established. But in the center, Burnside's Ninth Corps could not dislodge the Confederates anchored on the river. Lee deployed his army in the shape of a wedge between the two wings of the Potomac army — an inverted V with its point at Ox Ford and its flared entrenched legs ever widening the gap separating the Federal forces. The shortest way for either wing to link to or reinforce the other required two river crossings. Hancock reported, "The latest information I have leads me to believe that a large force, if not the whole of Lee's army, is in my front." On the other wing, Warren reported, "I feel satisfied that I should have great difficulty at best in whipping the enemy in my front." The North Anna position was checkmated.[18]

Grant shrugged off his thwarted offensive. On the evening of May 25, in a first since coming east, he convened a gathering of his lieutenants to discuss the next move. Apparently no one argued for butting against this latest brick wall. The choice was to move by either flank. At first Grant leaned to the right flank — passing Lee on the west (and perhaps thereby surprising him), cutting loose from the supply line, aiming at Richmond's northern front. Henry Hunt and Gouverneur Warren spoke out for this approach. Meade, however, repeated what he had earlier championed — rather than forcing a North Anna crossing, march southeast by the left flank, cross the Pamunkey unopposed, then turn west toward Richmond. Cyrus Comstock of Grant's staff noted in his diary on May 26, "I spoke of this to Meade day before yesterday. He thought as I did that it was decidedly the best flank to turn."

"General Grant changed his mind this afternoon, and decided to try again to turn Lee's right," wrote diarist Charles Wainwright. "Can it be that this is the sum of our lieutenant-general's abilities? Has he no other resourse in tactics? Or is it sheer obstinacy?" But Grant was learning — he was heard to admit "this fighting throws in the shade everything he ever saw" — and learning from both the Army of the Potomac and the Army of Northern Virginia. He adopted Meade's plan because moving by the right flank exposed too many imponderables. Leaving the supply line was a risk in itself, and would expose the base at Port Royal to a Confederate raid. On the right, three rivers had to be crossed, likely against opposition. And in any case, it was doubtful that General Lee could be surprised. Grant would move, once again, by the left flank — and without delay.[19]

The move was carefully calculated, leaving no opening for the Confederates to catch the columns on the move. Sheridan's cavalry, returned at last from its adventures, screened the advance. On the other flank, James Wilson's cavalry division made an elaborate feint, skirmishing dismounted in the guise of infantry to suggest a turning move against Lee's left. After nightfall on May 25 the artillery and the trains recrossed the North Anna, and after nightfall the next day the infantry followed. Alfred Torbert's and David Gregg's cavalry divisions, with David Russell's Sixth Corps division, shielded by the Pamunkey, led the way south some 30 miles to a crossing at Hanovertown. Engineers laid down two pontoon bridges, and by noon on May 27 Russell's infantry held a bridgehead west of the Pamunkey. The rest of the army was close behind, the last of it crossing May 29.

These few days of marching peacefully, bands playing, was almost a tonic. "We are all pretty well worn out with our hard work," John Gibbon wrote his wife, "but the last two days we have had some rest & are in good health and spirits ready for the next move. . . . We are engaged in maneuvering now more than in fighting, which *suits me much better*." Cyrus Comstock of Grant's staff took pleasure in reconnoitering, "questioning people a long time about roads &c. if the young ladies were pretty & commiserating with those who had lost chickens, pigs & such. . . ." Charles Dana, in his reporting to Secretary Stanton, brimmed with optimism: "Rebels have lost all confidence, and are already morally defeated. This army has learned to believe that it is sure of victory. Even our officers have ceased to regard Lee as an invincible military genius. . . . Rely upon it the end is near as well as sure." (Dana spent his time listening to Grant's talkative, and mostly idle, staff.)

Before they left the North Anna, the Yankees disposed of what they held of the Virginia Central and R. F. & P. railroads, following Grant's dictum: "I want to leave a gap in the roads north of Richmond so big that to get a single track they will have to import rails from elsewhere." This required more effort than lazy cavalry raiders usually expended (simply

Alfred Waud sketched the cavalry's highly organized railroad destruction — prying up the rails (right) and the ties (left), then piling the ties into a pyre to bend the rails.

pulling up the rails, perhaps tossing them into a stream). Section by section, track was pulled up, the crossties piled and set afire, and the rails laid across the blaze until only a rolling mill could straighten them. Some eight miles of the Virginia Central was thus disabled.

The move to the Pamunkey meant organizational changes. The army's waterborne logistics, which had hopscotched down the coastline to keep pace with the advance, was moved now to White House on the lower Pamunkey. Baldy Smith's Eighteenth Corps voyaged from Bermuda Hundred down the James and up the York and Pamunkey to join the Potomac army. Harking back to his tenuous March command status, Meade wrote Margaret, "Baldy Smith's corps has joined, and he is placed under my command, much to his disgust undoubtedly." That was a fair appraisal. On the eve of the campaign, Smith had written his old crony William Franklin, "Meade is as malignant as he is jealous & as mad as he is either." Burnside was "one of those men who will never get killed in battle." Hancock "is both ambitious and deceitful & now lives by Meade. . . ."

The arrival of the Eighteenth Corps meant awkward scenes with the Ninth Corps and with Ambrose Burnside. In the ugly aftermath of Fredericksburg, Burnside had done his best (but failed) to have Smith relieved of his Potomac army command, and W.T.H. "Bully" Brooks, now one of Smith's division commanders, dismissed from the service. Upon consulting Meade one afternoon, Burnside found both Smith and Brooks present.

As Theodore Lyman phrased it, "Enter Gen. Burnside, whereat great fall in the mercury and Brooks & Smith became military icicles!" "Of course Burnside don't care a fig," said his aide Daniel Larned. But in fact, Larned went on, in the Army of the Potomac "we have been bullyragged round so — & the Corps is spoken of as a superfluity — and no end to the insults & taunts we have received."

(Of Baldy Smith's two other division commanders, in addition to Bully Brooks, John H. Martindale had wriggled out of Fitz John Porter's charge of deserting his men at Gaines's Mill and Malvern Hill, and Charles Devens had been in a drunken stupor facing Stonewall Jackson at Chancellorsville. The Eighteenth Corps' high command was a haven for tarnished generals.)[20]

Meade's spirits rose with the advance to the Pamunkey he had advocated, yet he continued grumbling to his wife about "the false position I am placed in. I think the army realise & appreciate it, but outside the army it appears to be unknown." He complained not of his command relationship with Grant, which was as collegial as ever, but of what the press and the public understood of the campaign. Prideful George Meade commanded a great army in a major campaign . . . or, to the world at large, did he?

Meade was confident Grant "would not intentionally do me injustice . . . & probably is not conscious that in all his dispatches of the operations of this army which he knows has been handled by me he has *only once* . . . mentioned my name & so that the future historians when collecting official documents to compile a truthful view, would absolutely not know, from any evidence Grant's dispatches contain, that I was even present with the army." Meade would learn that Grant did not in fact supply the grist for the War Department's bulletins to the press; still, those bulletins scarcely mentioned Meade's name. As for the reporters with the Potomac army, most were hardly exemplars of journalism. ("I write as often as possible," John Gibbon told his wife, "fearing some of these miserable newspaper reporters will report me dead and write my obituary, as they have done with a number of others. . . ." Gouverneur Warren, reading press accounts of Spotsylvania, remarked that his corps won its victories "in the forenoon, before any of the correspondents got up.") And the acerbic Meade was hardly welcoming to reporters. So, through a combination of circumstances, his pride was bruised. "I see the papers have counted me out entirely," he told Margaret. "I presume therefore, we might as well make up our minds to this state of things. . . ."

Captain Charles Francis Adams, Jr., led a cavalry company attached to

Potomac army headquarters, where he cultivated the staffs of Grant and Meade. In appraising the campaign thus far for his father, Charles Francis Adams, minister to Great Britain, young Adams marveled at the new brand of high command, a major advance over the ragged days of McDowell, McClellan, Pope, Burnside, Hooker. "Grant has this army as firmly as ever he had that of the Southwest . . . ; he has made no parade of his authority, he has given no orders except through Meade, and Meade he treats with the utmost confidence and deference. The result is that even from the most jealously disposed and most indiscreet of Meade's staff, not a word is heard against Grant." (James Biddle did, however, consider Meade the better general of the two.) "The result is of inestimable importance," Adams thought. For the first time, the Army of the Potomac "has a head and confidence in that head. It has leaders and there is no discord among those leaders . . . and all now seem disposed to go in with a will to win." Adams's portrayal is somewhat idyllic, yet he caught the essential bond between Grant and Meade. However much in his home letters Meade chafed at his public anonymity, he worked selflessly and in mutual respect with Grant.[21]

Responding to the Federals' advance, Lee fell back in parallel along the Virginia Central to behind Totopotomoy Creek. To regain contact after their separate movements, both armies sent out cavalry reconnoiters on May 28. They collided head-on near an abandoned manufactory called Haw's Shop, at a crossroads on the fringe of McClellan's 1862 Peninsula campaign. Wade Hampton's troopers fought from behind barricades and the Yankees too fought dismounted — an 1864 new-style cavalry battle. The bitter Haw's Shop struggle only ended when Hampton decided he had enough captures to identify the Federal advance.

From Hanovertown the Potomac army probed ahead on a wide front, trying to further develop Lee's position, running generally behind the Totopotomoy. Beyond lay the Chickahominy, infamous in veterans' Peninsula recollections. The Federals, facing west, had the choice of turning either of Lee's flanks or of driving straight ahead. Lee sought opportunity as well, to strike at a gap, to catch the Yankees on the move. He suspected "a repetition of their former movements." His army was just nine miles from Richmond.

Lee moved first, on June 30, striking from his southern flank to preempt his opponent. Warren's Fifth Corps had crossed the Totopotomoy and was taking position near Bethesda Church. Samuel Crawford's Pennsylvania Reserves division was surprised. The three-year men of the Reserves were in their last two days of service, and careless about entrenching. In five minutes, wrote diarist Charles Wainwright, the lead brigade of

Reserves "were running, and the other two divisions, finding the enemy quite on their flank, were rather indiscriminately hurrying back . . . things looking very squally for a complete turning of our left."

But Warren rallied the Reserves, and Wainwright's corps artillery once again came to the rescue — at canister range — as effectively as it had at Jericho Mills the week before. The Fifth Corps retook its postings, and next day the Pennsylvania Reserves left for home from Bethesda Church . . . just six miles from Beaver Dam Creek, where they had first joined the Army of the Potomac.

General Warren made complaint to headquarters that at Bethesda Church Sheridan's cavalry was supposed to be guarding his flank but had not. Sheridan retorted, "I have had troops on the left of General Warren's corps all day, and connected with him." Warren wondered then why his infantry was taken by surprise by an attack from the left. He decided "the cavalry do not co-operate with us in any reliable way, as far as I can learn." Warren and Sheridan were compiling a mutual record of ill will.[22]

Lee's thrust toward Bethesda Church determined Grant on his next move. He would repeat his advance by the left flank, and attempt the ploy he had tried after Spotsylvania — sending a force past the Confederate flank as bait to draw Lee out of his fortifications. That force would be Baldy Smith's Eighteenth Corps, from Bermuda Hundred, landed at White House on the Pamunkey.

This latest turning movement took focus on a nondescript tavern at a crossroads south of Lee's lines that went by a variety of names. Theodore Lyman listed "Coal Harbor, Cold Harbor, & Cool Arbor, I can't find which is correct, but choose 'Arbor' because it is the prettiest, and because it is so hideously inappropriate." Locals further distinguished between Old Cold Harbor and New Cold Harbor, while disclaiming knowledge of any nearby harbor or arbor. The generals settled on plain Cold Harbor, raising it from obscurity only because it marked an intersection of five roads — roads the Federals needed to (perhaps) finally get between Lee and Richmond.

Grant and Meade might have held their fire for a day or two, keeping Lee guessing while collecting forces and perfecting plans for a sudden surprise strike. But on May 31 Sheridan's cavalry seized the Cold Harbor crossroads to secure the Potomac army's own link with White House, and then dug in and endured a hard fight against infantry to stay there. Time now became critical. Sheridan was ordered by Meade to hold Cold Harbor "at all hazards," but the Eighteenth Corps was not yet at hand to lead (and serve as bait) in the turning movement. A new plan was devised. Horatio Wright's Sixth Corps, at the far right of the line, would make a nighttime march around behind the army to form on the left flank at Cold Harbor, relieve the cavalry, and prepare to attack at daylight, June 1. This movement would create a gap between Wright and Warren's Fifth Corps, and the Eighteenth Corps' new role was to fill the gap and support Wright. As it happened, nothing ventured in this timetable succeeded, creating high temper up and down the Potomac army's chain of command.

Upon the Eighteenth Corps' landing at White House on May 30, Baldy Smith was told to proceed up the Pamunkey to New Castle and await further orders. Smith camped his corps for the night of the 31st three miles short of New Castle. His orders, until he joined the Army of the Potomac, still came from Grant, and they came unaccountably late. Only at daylight on June 1 did Smith receive an order, signed by Grant's staff man Orville Babcock, to "move your command to New Castle and take a position on the right of Maj Gen Wright comd'g 6th A.C. . . . You will place yourself between Genl Wright & Gen Warren. . . ." Dutifully Smith marched to New Castle, where he found no trace of the Fifth or Sixth Corps or anyone else. In time Babcock's blunder was corrected to read "Cold Harbor" for "New Castle," but meanwhile the Eighteenth Corps did not reach Cold Harbor until midafternoon on June 1.

General Wright's Sixth Corps timetable was not achieved either. Meade's order was late reaching him, and Wright had to extract his three divisions from the right flank without notice to the enemy, then make a 15-mile roundabout trek on roads deep in dust in the dark of night. The Sixth Corps only began to relieve Sheridan's troopers at Cold Harbor at 9 o'clock and trailed in until noon. Wright had attack orders, but with an exhausted command he elected to wait for Smith's (also exhausted) command to join him. At 6 o'clock that evening the Sixth and Eighteenth Corps launched an attack originally intended for 6 o'clock that morning.[23]

Over the past month it was vividly demonstrated that in this new mode of warfare, giving the Rebels twelve hours to entrench meant defeat. The June 1 evening assault proved no exception. Two divisions from each corps stormed Lee's lines behind Cold Harbor, and in overall result were thrown back with heavy losses.

Yet a few small gains seemed to hint of promise here. A dent or two was made in the enemy's line, with prisoners taken. Emory Upton's Sixth Corps brigade achieved a real break, only to see it sealed for want of support. "Milroy's Weary Boys, a division always bad," under the leadership of James Ricketts did not this time run away but "suddenly blazed out, and charged with the bayonet." Casualties came to 2,200. The Yankees dug in where they were.

Francis Barlow, one of the best divisional commanders in the army, believed the truth should be heard: "I do not believe that these assaults upon intrenched lines through thick woods, where we do not know the ground, are likely to be successful where the enemy hold their line in force. . . ." Emory Upton was of like mind. He termed June 1 "a murderous engagement. I say *murderous,* because we are recklessly ordered to assault the enemy's intrenchments, knowing neither their strength nor position." Still, Meade's appraisal of the faint June 1 results gained him Grant's agreement to resume the offensive there at first light on June 2.

In his journal for June 1, Colonel Lyman wrote, "General Meade was in one of his irascible fits tonight, which are always founded in good reason though they spread themselves over a good deal of ground that is not always in the limits of the question." Indeed, Meade found fault with the day's operations everywhere he looked. Wright was much too slow. Warren missed a chance to catch a Rebel column in motion, then failed to support the evening attack. Charles Dana summarized for Secretary Stanton: "Grant and Meade are intensely disgusted with these failures of Wright and Warren."

June 1 was indeed a bad day for Gouverneur Warren. His corps artillerist, Charles Wainwright, reported his chief "in one of his pets all yesterday and today, as ugly and cross-grained as he could be. . . . He has pitched into his staff officers most fearfully. . . . One would suppose that a man in his position would be ashamed to show that kind of temper." To Warren's way of thinking, he was again being ordered to do more than he should or could; he was not being listened to. That morning there were sightings of an enemy column moving southward behind their front and Meade expected Warren to strike when the enemy was on the move. Warren explained that the ground was too marshy, that his lines were stretched too thin; "Our skirmish line everywhere comes in sight of entrenchments." Excuses instead of action always grated on George Meade.

That evening, in supporting Wright's and Smith's assault, Warren again appeared to fall short. The Fifth Corps had a new division commander, Henry H. Lockwood. Brigadier General Lockwood had spent most of the war quietly in the Middle Department, gaining rank but no fighting experience — June 1 was his fourth day with the Army of the Potomac. Warren sent him off through the wood without a guide to join the Wright-Smith attack, and Lockwood became hopelessly lost, two miles behind his own lines. Warren, to cover his failings in the episode, labeled Lockwood "too incompetent, and too high rank leaves no subordinate place for him." Poor General Lockwood was relieved the next day.

Late on June 1, amidst this sea of tribulations, there arrived at Meade's headquarters Baldy Smith's engineering officer, who (wrote Lyman) "reports that his superior had arrived, fought &c. &c. but that he had brought little ammunition, no transportation and that 'he considered his position precarious.' 'Then, why in Hell did he come at all for?' roared the exasperated Meade with an oath that was rare with him."[24]

Since crossing the Rapidan, General Grant had followed the same pattern in advancing by the left flank. The move began after nightfall for secrecy. The rightmost corps pulled out, passed behind the rest of the army, and took the lead on the left. This maintained a defensive front and worked well enough if the objective was a march. But as an overnight maneuver for a surprise early-morning attack, it failed every time — again (and most fatefully) on June 1–2.

Winfield Hancock's Second Corps, posted on the right, set out at nightfall on June 1 to transit the rest of the army for an attack at Cold Harbor, in concert with the Sixth and Eighteenth Corps, at 6:00 a.m. June 2. Grant and Meade believed the June 1 advances had edged close enough to the (probably incomplete) enemy entrenchments that one more quick, hard push by the army's best corps would do it — would break open the Rebels' last field defenses.

Whereas General Lockwood had no guide and got lost, General Hancock, with a topographical engineer for a guide, also got lost. Commanders in this campaign consistently overestimated the distances troops could navigate on unknown ground in the dead of night. "Every exertion was made, but the night was dark, the heat and dust oppressive, and the roads unknown," Hancock reported. The Second Corps' vanguard reached Cold Harbor by 6:30 a.m., but the rest of the corps would limp in for hours. Nor was that all. Baldy Smith let it be known he was far from ready to fight that day — his Eighteenth Corps was short of ammunition, his front was too extended. With his talent for irritating superiors, he lectured Meade, "In the present condition of my line an attack by me would be simply preposterous." The attack was rescheduled twice when someone or another was not ready. Grant finally stepped in and told Meade, "In view of the want of preparation for an attack this evening, and the heat and want of energy among the men from moving during the night last night, I think it advisable to postpone assault until early to-morrow morning." He set the hour as 4:30 a.m., June 3.

From the first, Cold Harbor had taken on a life of its own. The cavalry seized it, defended it, and gave way to the infantry. The Rebels must be attacked before they could entrench. The June 1 attack seemed to show promise enough that it must be promptly followed up, on June 2 . . . then delayed to June 3. By June 3 the Potomac army was fully posted facing the Rebels' fortifications — fortifications that Lee's engineers had been seen and heard utilizing a second day to perfect. A week before, confronting a veritable brick wall on the North Anna, Grant had elected to withdraw the army and try another tack. Today the courage to try another tack deserted him, replaced by the determination "to drive his head through a brick wall," as Colonel Lyman had put it. Much blood and effort had already been invested; to pull back would be a confession of defeat.[25]

The Yankee infantrymen had been on the offensive seemingly nonstop for a month now, and during the June 1 fighting they glimpsed these newest imposing enemy works at Cold Harbor, and since then they heard the Johnnies making them stronger. So for this June 3 attack they calculated the odds and adopted a more-or-less code of conduct. In his memoir John Gibbon described how this process worked: "It became a recognized fact amongst the men themselves that when the enemy had occupied a position six or eight hours ahead of us" — in this case, closer to thirty-six hours — "it was useless to attempt to take it. This feeling became so marked that when troops under these circumstances were ordered forward, they went a certain distance and then lay down and opened fire." The saying in the army was, "When the old troops got as far forward as they thought they ought to go 'they sat down and made coffee!'" The more fatalistic men, like those at Mine Run in November, wrote their names on slips of paper which they pinned to their uniforms to identify themselves for the burial parties, and for the home folks.[26]

On June 3 there was no specific plan for breaking the enemy line, as there had been at the Spotsylvania salient on May 12. Nor was there an overall plan, beyond a general advance timed for 4:30 a.m., with corps commanders "making examination of the ground in their fronts, and perfecting their arrangements for the assault." Grant ordered the attack, leaving its execution to Meade. Meade left the details to his corps commanders. The corps were posted, right to left: Burnside's Ninth Corps, Warren's Fifth, Smith's Eighteenth, Wright's Sixth, Hancock's Second. Artillery preparation and support was whatever the corps commanders might make of it.

Colonel Lyman recorded for his journal the progress of the attack as it was reported to headquarters. The Second Corps was first to report: "5.15. Dispatch that Barlow has carried their line in his front, which for the time encouraged us much, but we presently heard he was driven out

Francis Barlow's Second Corps division tries to crack the Rebel line at Cold Harbor on June 3. These are New York heavy artillerymen fighting as infantry. By Alfred Waud.

again. . . ." Hancock soon enough concluded that if Francis Barlow, his most aggressive lieutenant, had been driven back from the crack he found in the enemy line, further efforts would only waste lives. At 6:00 a.m. he wrote Meade, "I shall await your orders, but express the opinion that if the first dash in an assault fails, other attempts are not apt to succeed better." Meade ordered him to renew the attack and "support it well." Hancock explained that John Gibbon had no better luck than Barlow. All efforts were ravaged by Rebel artillery enfilading the attacking columns; "division commanders do not speak encouragingly of the prospect of success since the original attacks failed. Unless success has been gained in other points, I do not advise persistence here."

The other points had less to report. On the Sixth Corps front, "Ricketts carries their first line but is in a very exposed position; Russell cannot succeed on his front." Then, "The 18th Corps also got the first line but were at last obliged to come back." Wright and Baldy Smith declined to renew their failed assaults. Warren and Burnside got barely as far as the enemy's picket line. At 7:00 a.m. Meade tried to end it, signaling Grant, "I should be glad to have your views as to the continuance of these attacks, if unsuccessful." Grant said to suspend any attack certain to fail, but to "pile in troops at the successful point." No successful point was found. Only the Second, Sixth, and Eighteenth Corps seriously engaged that morning — finding, said Lyman, "after some three hours fighting, that all was in vain."

After touring the command posts himself, Grant signaled Meade, at 12:30 p.m., "The opinion of corps commanders not being sanguine of success in case an assault is ordered, you may direct a suspension of further advance for the present."

Veterans, men and officers, saw June 3 as hopeless a venture as December 13 at Fredericksburg, remembered that lesson, and acted accordingly. Finding it as dangerous to retreat as to advance, the troops spent the afternoon digging in where they were. That evening, when the Rebels charged out of their lines in a brief sortie, they were actually welcomed — "Come on! Come on! Bring up some more Johnnies!"

The attack at Cold Harbor on the morning of June 3 cost the Union some 3,500 casualties, a quarter of that number from two regiments of heavies in their first battle. What shocked about Cold Harbor even more than the casualties was that it proved just as senseless as virtually everyone anticipated it would be. Theodore Lyman echoed that common view when he wrote his wife, "I can't say I heard with any great hope, the order, given last night for a general assault at 4.30 the next morning!"[27]

Meade did not at first disclose much of his feelings about Cold Harbor. "The battle ended without any decided result," he told his wife, "we repulsing all attacks of the enemy and they doing the same." In a more forthcoming conversation on June 5, he compared McClellan's approach to Richmond in 1862 ("the true one") to the current so-called Overland Campaign, a running battle against successively erected, ever-more-imposing fieldworks set among woods and swamps. It had become impossible to even plan a battle in these circumstances; "Here, in this country," he explained, "I must fight a battle to reconnoitre a position, as in the assault of day before yesterday."

Other generals remarked Cold Harbor. David Birney: It climaxed a campaign of "bloody and continuous fighting" exceeding all his previous experience. Francis Barlow: "The men feel just at present a great horror and dread of attacking earth-works again." Gouverneur Warren (reported Lyman) "looked haggard; for one trouble he has a tender heart, which cannot grow used to bloodshed. He said: 'For thirty days, now, it has been one funeral procession past me, and it is too much! . . . The men need some rest!'" Warren had a tense encounter with Meade. "The friction increases between them. Meade finds fault with Warren's contradictory spirit which loves to do a thing by a different way from the one ordered."

Meade confirmed the army's entrenching, and Lyman wrote, "Nothing can give a greater idea of deathless tenacity of purpose, than the picture of these two hosts . . . lying down to sleep, with their hands almost on each other's throats!" On June 5 Meade remarked to Margaret that this campaign was affirmation of his decisions not to attack the fortifications at Williamsport and Mine Run. "In every instance that we have attacked the enemy in an entrenched position, we have failed. . . . So likewise whenever the enemy has attacked us in position he has been repulsed. I think Grant has had his eyes opened & is willing to admit now that Virginia & Lee's army is not Tennessee & Bragg's army."[28]

"I have always regretted that the last assault at Cold Harbor was ever made," Grant wrote in his memoir. Indeed, the battle fought there made as much sense as the name of the site, nor was the aftermath enlightening. When it became clear both sides were dug in, on June 5 Grant sent to Lee under flag of truce to propose caring for the wounded and burying the dead lying between the lines. Colonel Lyman was chosen flag-bearer. "My ideas on flags of truce," Lyman admitted, "were chiefly mediæval and were associated with a herald wearing a tabard." Waving a pillowcase tied to a stick, Lyman in due course was able to deliver Grant's letter. For two days Lee fussed over protocol—the wounded were all Federals—before agreeing. The wounded meanwhile died or were shot or were retrieved in nighttime rescues. The truce saved two men.[29]

There were a few days of comparative quiet, and General Meade took advantage of the calm to catch up reading his hometown paper, the *Philadelphia Inquirer*. He found an article extolling his generalship, but with an added anecdote: "History will record, but newspapers cannot that on one eventful night during the present campaign Grant's presence saved the army, and the nation too; not that General Meade was on the point of committing a blunder unwittingly, but his devotion to his country made him loth to risk her last army on what he deemed a chance. Grant assumed the responsibility, and we are still on to Richmond."

The story was picked up by other papers, and enlarged by hearsay and rumor until the "present campaign" was the Wilderness and Meade's counsel was to recross the Rapidan—like his predecessors McClellan and Pope, Burnside and Hooker, General Meade embraced retreat in the heat of battle. Meade was enraged. He explained to his wife the "particular force of this libel which seemed to confirm the charges brought at Williamsport, Centreville & Mine Run, viz, that I was always on the defensive & proposed to run away on the plea of saving the army." It was a reminder too of Dan Sickles's tale of Meade wanting to retreat at Gettysburg. Meade's immediate concern was that the troops' confidence in him would be shaken, and he confronted the *Inquirer* story's author, Edward Cropsey. "I told him it was a base & wicked lie, and that I would make an example of him, which should not only serve to deter others from committing like offenses, but would give publicity to his lie & the truth."

The usual resolution of such cases was for the provost marshal to arrest the errant reporter and send him out of the army, not to return for some period or not to return at all. But the Army of the Potomac's provost marshal was the astringent Marsena Patrick, who nursed a particular dislike for reporters. His thought, acting on Meade's order for removal, was a staged expulsion. Cropsey was mounted backward on a mule, wore placards front and back labeled "Libeler of the Press," and was paraded through the camps to the accompaniment of "The Rogue's March." "It will be a warning to his tribe," said Patrick.

Grant made it known that "Gen. Meade on no occasion advised or counseled falling back toward, much less across, the Rapidan," and any rumors otherwise "are entirely idle and without the shadow of foundation." Edwin Stanton assured Meade "the lying report . . . was not even for one moment believed by the President or myself." But the damage was done and circulated. The incident pushed Meade's temper to new heights. Winfield Hancock and John Gibbon found him one day "laboring under great excitement" about some supposed affront to his command authority. They calmed him and he apologized, Gibbon wrote, saying "he would not have expressed himself quite so freely except to officers of that army whom he regarded as the two best friends he had in it."

As it happened, the inexcusable treatment of Cropsey would haunt Meade to the end of the war. The press corps banded together to exclude his name in their reporting, even to exchanging Grant's name for Meade's in printing official documents. In the ultimate irony, Meade's private complaint of his anonymity in the campaign was now affirmed; he became the Unknown General.

In another headquarters distraction, Brigadier General John G. Barnard, now chief engineer on Grant's staff, put in an appearance. Barnard was not widely welcomed in the Potomac army. He had a checkered past from McClellan days, and Theodore Lyman noted his reputation among the staff: "Thoroughly unreliable . . . a time serving critic . . . a military pedant. . . . Here he is simply in the way. . . ." Meade thought him there "to try and glean a little credit for himself." Barnard would be confined to occasional advice.[30]

Meade's expectation for the Overland Campaign, should they not pry

Lee out of his fortifications for a battle royal, was very like McClellan's expectation in 1862 — a quasi siege of Richmond, a Sevastopol in America. Grant, however, intended to avoid as the next step besieging the Confederate capital. "My idea from the start," he told Halleck on June 5, "has been to beat Lee's army, if possible, north of Richmond, then, after destroying his lines of communication north of the James River, to transfer the army to the south side" and destroy his communications there. Already on May 26 the pontoon train in Washington was ordered to Fort Monroe, "in readiness to proceed up the James River." Only then might he lay siege to Lee in isolated Richmond, "or follow him south if he should retreat." Grant summarized for Congressman Washburne: "All the fight, except defensive and behind breast works, is taken out of Lee's army." Absent a battle royal — Cold Harbor confirmed that — Grant predicted "the balance of the campaign will settle down to a siege." Such an outcome would duplicate his tactics at Vicksburg.

As the Army of the Potomac prepared anew to march, Grant resurrected the peripheral strategies that earlier came to naught or to grief. To carry out his design to cut Lee's communications north of the James, he sent Phil Sheridan and two cavalry divisions to trace the Virginia Central toward Gordonsville, wrecking the line as he went. A grander vision might follow. David Hunter had taken command of the forces of the disgraced Franz Sigel and was starting up the Valley. After his wounding at First Bull Run, Hunter had held a variety of commands in the west and south. He petitioned for a corps command in the Potomac army, and thanks to his stalwart Radical Republicanism he was awarded an independent command in the Valley. Combining Hunter's infantry with Sheridan's cavalry could be imagined doing great damage to Confederate logistics at Gordonsville and Charlottesville, perhaps even at the great supply depot at Lynchburg, in southwestern Virginia. Sheridan set out on June 7, with instructions to cooperate with Hunter. As always when the Valley was threatened, General Lee reacted, starting forces to meet Hunter, and sending Wade Hampton with two cavalry divisions to intercept Sheridan.[31]

Cold Harbor marked the end to the monthlong effort to drive between Lee's army and Richmond. No room remained for maneuver between Lee's right and the city's fortifications, and Grant recognized the futility of laying siege to a city whose communications were intact or nearly so. He therefore set Petersburg, the railroad hub 25 miles south of Richmond, as the Potomac army's new target. Severing Petersburg's rail connections would leave Richmond to wither. Grant plotted a stroke as bold as McClellan's seaborne thrust to the Peninsula two years before. Bold too was

Grant (like McClellan) in leaving Washington uncovered. This time no complaint was heard from the administration.

The direct route to Petersburg lay due south from Cold Harbor, crossing the Chickahominy and then the James. This route would forgo secrecy and pass straight across the face of the Rebel lines, a tactic dangerously vulnerable to attack. Instead the march routes looped east by south through Charles City Court House and well distant from the Rebels, reaching the James at Wilcox Landing and Weyanoke Point, downstream from Harrison's Landing where McClellan had taken refuge after the Seven Days.

To break cleanly and without notice from the Cold Harbor lines and erect an entirely new battlefront, the Union war machine shifted to a higher gear. First, an interior line of entrenchments was erected to shield the withdrawing forces, and a shorter interior line laid out to cover the Chickahominy crossings, with Warren's Fifth Corps slated to man this guardian line — and seemingly threaten a renewed flanking effort. Next, the army would require a new logistical base. In 1862, denied access to the James River by CSS *Virginia*, McClellan depended on the York River and the Richmond & York River Railroad to support his campaign. The James alone served the 1864 campaign, leaving the railroad unneeded. (Grant ordered it dismantled to deny the rails to the Rebels.) Starting on June 9, the White House base was shifted to City Point, on the south bank where the Appomattox enters the James. The Potomac army's own pontoon train was sufficient for the Chickahominy crossings (at low water now and easily bridged, unlike the stormy times of 1862), but to carry the army across the James required a major undertaking — a pontoon bridge of record length, and a flotilla of transports and ferries.

Ben Butler and his Army of the James at Bermuda Hundred was given a major role to play. Butler would supply all the pontoons he could spare for the James River crossing, and rations for the Potomac army vanguard until the City Point base was operating. Most important, Butler would supply the principal initial strike force against Petersburg — Petersburg was eight miles from Bermuda Hundred, 20 miles from the James crossing sites — and for that purpose Baldy Smith's Eighteenth Corps was sent back by water to Bermuda Hundred. This meant coordinating two separate armies in a complex operation against a single target, Petersburg.[32]

The Army of the Potomac set off at nightfall on June 12. Warren's Fifth Corps took the advance to guard the Long Bridge crossing site of the Chickahominy, screened by James Wilson's cavalry. Hancock's Second Corps and Wright's Sixth Corps slipped behind the new interior line, covering the march of Burnside's Ninth Corps and Smith's Eighteenth Corps from the far right. The men were cautioned to disengage as silently as possible, muffling their gear. The march orders were prepared by Andrew Humphreys, who pridefully wrote his wife, "We began our march at dark and drew off without molestation." Meade would direct the Army of the Potomac's march to the James, and Grant would direct Butler's forces, now once more including the Eighteenth Corps.

Baldy Smith marched the Eighteenth eastward to White House on the Pamunkey to embark. Grant's orders left Smith in no doubt of the urgency of the operation — "Send forward your troops . . . as fast as they embark, without waiting for divisions, the object being to get them to Bermuda Hundred at the earliest possible moment." Smith welcomed the reassignment, and onboard a transport on the York he wrote his wife, "I am once more away from the Army of the Potomac, and Meade is, I suppose, as glad as I am."

Once Smith and Burnside were on their way, Hancock and Wright and finally Warren moved out as well. By morning June 13 the tangle of their Cold Harbor lines was empty. Warren's Fifth Corps and Wilson's cavalry division guarded the Chickahominy crossings and maintained the bluff of threatening Richmond. Sheridan's move against the Virginia Central had drawn Hampton's cavalry away, leaving Lee with not enough cavalry to break through Wilson's screen. Lee could only watch and wait to see where the Yankees turned up again.

With the Potomac army on the march, crossings of the James were readied. At Wilcox Landing, and across the river at Windmill Point, wharfs were repaired, and ferries and transports collected. At Weyanoke Point, Godfrey Weitzel, Army of the James chief engineer, prepared the approaches to a monumentally long pontoon bridge to Fort Powhatan on the south bank. At the bridge site the James is an estuary, 1,200 feet wide, 85 feet deep, with strong currents and a tidal rise and fall of some four feet. The approaches — over marshes and tidal flats — required long corduroyed causeways.

Weitzel worked around the clock and everything was ready for the scheduled arrival of the first infantry at midmorning on June 14 . . . everything except the pontoons ordered up from Fort Monroe. An anxious Weitzel had sent a dispatch boat down the James and rousted the captain of the pontoon flotilla, who tied up off Jamestown Island to sleep; "culpable neglect of duty" was Weitzel's verdict. Making up the bridge fell to crews under engineers James C. Duane and George H. Mendell — affixing planking to 101 pontoons stepped out from both shores, braced by three schooners anchored upstream and three downstream to hold against the tides, with a movable section midstream to allow vessels passage, notably the transports carrying the Eighteenth Corps. The bridge was completed by midnight June 14, by General Weitzel's perfectionist accounting a remarkable achievement certainly, but inexcusably late. While the pontoon bridge would carry the bulk of the Potomac army's infantry, artillery, and trains across the James, in the race for Petersburg the Wilcox Landing–Windmill Point crossing was the vital one.[33]

Like Richmond, Petersburg was heavily fortified, the work begun back in 1862 when McClellan threatened. The town, on the south bank of the Appomattox, was enclosed by a well-engineered line 10 miles long river to river, built largely by slave labor. There were massive parapets and deep ditches and redans and abatis and cleared fields of fire for fifty-five artillery emplacements. On May 9 Ben Butler had scorned Baldy Smith's and Quincy Gillmore's plan to launch a surprise attack on Petersburg. On June 9 Butler decided to test Petersburg's defenses after all. His strike force comprised Gillmore's infantry, Edward W. Hincks's U.S. Colored Troops, and August V. Kautz's cavalry division, some 4,500 men in all, Gillmore in command. When Gillmore asked for a battery, Butler was direct: "This is not to be artillery work, but a quick, decisive push."

Only Kautz pushed. His dismounted troopers easily carried a section of works, but under artillery fire and hearing no sounds of battle from Gillmore's main force, he withdrew. Gillmore decided these lines "cannot be carried by the force I have. . . . I am about to withdraw. . . ." Cyrus Comstock of Grant's staff summarized in his diary: "Gillmore makes no serious attack on Petersburg thinking line in his front too strong. Kautz went to Jerusalem road and through enemy's line . . . thinks rebs did not have more than 1500 men in city." Comstock added, "Butler curses & says he will relieve Gillmore. . . ." Butler made his case: "Had the movement been a success, as it easily might have been, Petersburg would have been in our possession. . . ." Grant allowed Gillmore to be relieved at his own request. Twice — May 9 and June 9 — Petersburg escaped the Federals' clutches. Now came a third opportunity.[34]

At 5:30 p.m. on June 13 the advance of the Army of the Potomac, Hancock's Second Corps, reached the James at Wilcox Landing and trailed in through the night. Even this far from the enemy, the men dug in without being told; Yankee infantrymen, Seth Williams observed, had decided that a rifle pit is "a good thing to have in a family where there are small children." Ben Butler reported on the 13th that there were "but about 2,000 men in Petersburg, mostly militia." There was no waiting for the pontoon

William Waud sketched Generals Hancock (seated) and Grant (mounted) watching
the Second Corps board transports and ferries at Wilcox Landing to cross the James to
Windmill Point on June 14. Engineer John Barnard stands between them.

bridge to be completed, yet it required all day on June 14 to cross the Second Corps to Windmill Point aboard the few ferries and transports not being used to return the Eighteenth Corps to Bermuda Hundred. General Hancock was far from his best. The headquarters party came upon him by the roadside, pouring water from a canteen on the Gettysburg wound in his thigh. It had reopened "and troubles him a good deal."

As he did repeatedly during the campaign, General Grant had grown impatient, rushing ahead with his scheme to cross the James without allotting time enough for the logistics of it. Had he delayed a day or two in evacuating Cold Harbor, there would have been an extra day or two to gather the pontoons and have the bridge completed when the army reached the James; time, too, to collect ferries to speed the Wilcox Landing crossing; time, too, to compensate for human error.

At midday on June 14 Grant reported to Halleck, "The enemy show no signs yet of having brought troops to the south side of Richmond. I will have Petersburg secured, if possible, before they get there in much force." Halleck showed Grant's telegram to the president, who telegraphed Grant on June 15, "Have just read your despatch of 1 p.m. yesterday. I begin to see it. God bless you all." This was his first comment to Grant concerning the six-week campaign. Mr. Lincoln had found his general.

Grant boarded a steamer on the 14th to visit Butler and give him orders for "the immediate capture of Petersburg." Baldy Smith's Eighteenth Corps, to be the instrument for the capture, arrived at Bermuda Hundred in early evening. Butler showed Smith a dispatch from Grant that intelligence "looks favorable for the success of your attack on Petersburg to-night," and that Hancock with the Second Corps would start in the morning from Windmill Point for Petersburg. "If the forces going into Petersburg find re-enforcements necessary, by sending back to General Hancock he will push forward." Butler reinforced Smith's two divisions with Edward Hincks's division of black troops and August Kautz's division of cavalry, giving him some 15,500 men. Kautz and Hincks served as guides, and related their experiences of June 9 at the undermanned Rebel works.

Baldy Smith was a general with a thousand excuses, one of the first being that under Butler "no plan was formulated for me to follow." In fact, it was all laid out for him — he could not mistake that for tomorrow he was assigned an independent, high-priority mission to seize Petersburg quickly (calling on Hancock if need be) before the Army of Northern Virginia reached the scene.[35]

General Meade spent June 14 shepherding the James crossings, first at Wilcox Landing, then at the site of the pontoon bridge. At Wilcox Landing he met with Hancock to discuss plans for the next day, and that evening at headquarters Theodore Lyman copied in his journal the movements ordered for June 15: "All the 2d Corps is to cross and to advance tomorrow on Petersburg. The 18th Corps passed up the river in boats, this afternoon, and is to advance on Petersburg tomorrow from Point of Rocks, opposite Butler's left on the Appomattox." At 8:00 a.m. on June 15 Charles A. Dana telegraphed the War Department, "Hancock moves out instantly to Petersburg to support Smith's attack on that place. . . ." On June 15 there was going to be a race and a fight for Petersburg, and contrary to later evasions and excuses, everybody — Smith, Hancock, Meade, Grant — knew to expect it.

Wednesday, June 15, marked the fourth day of Grant's bold maneuver to break free of the trenches and strike deep into the enemy's rear. "Since Sunday," he wrote his wife, "we have been engaged in one of the most perilous movements ever executed by a large army, that of withdrawing from the front of an enemy and moving past his flank crossing two rivers over which the enemy has bridges and rail-roads whilst we have bridges to improvise. So far it has been eminently successful and I hope will prove so to the end." He took a moment that morning to quietly contemplate what he had wrought, standing on a bluff overlooking the James, hands clasped behind him, watching the masses of troops stride across the great pontoon bridge. He lingered only briefly, then set off for the front.[36]

Neither Hancock's troops at Windmill Point nor Smith's at Bermuda Hundred made their intended early starts on June 15. In Hancock's case it was a matter of rations. Grant's order to Butler to have rations waiting for the Second Corps when it crossed the James required interarmy coordination, which at this critical moment fell apart. Hancock found no rations where expected and complained to Meade, who had no say in Butler's doings. Meade finally told Hancock to "move immediately to the position assigned you last evening. . . . It is important that you should move." Rather than at daylight, the Second Corps only marched at 10:30 a.m.

Baldy Smith's delay was a lesser one, only two hours or so, caused by having to fit Hincks's and Kautz's forces into the Eighteenth Corps' order of march. At 9:00 a.m. they encountered a Rebel cavalry outpost some two miles from the Petersburg lines, and Smith sent in a brigade of Hincks's black troops. This was their initial combat, and after the usual first-time confusion they charged the enemy post on the high ground and overran it, capturing a 12-pounder howitzer. Starting at 11 o'clock, the Federals deployed opposite the Confederates' Petersburg line, John Martindale's division on the right, at the Appomattox, then Bully Brooks's and Hincks's divisions. Kautz's cavalry formed on the left.

This would be the Eighteenth Corps' second encounter with a fortified enemy, after Cold Harbor. It would be Baldy Smith's first encounter with independent command, and he wilted under the responsibility of it. Smith had come to command under McClellan, absorbing making war with care and caution and without initiative and risk. For four hours he rode back and forth reconnoitering, by his account suffering from harassing Rebel artillery fire, postbattle stress from Cold Harbor, and the effects of bad water. He concluded, "All the information given to me the night before was erroneous," this despite having with him Hincks and Kautz, who had faced these same enemy works six days before. Baldy Smith could not nerve himself to risk, to recognize that these formidable defenses were, by all accounts, not manned by the Army of Northern Virginia . . . at least not yet. Grant sent to Smith that the Second Corps was on its way, and to call on it. He sent to Gibbon an order "intended for the whole Second Corps" to "push forward as rapidly as possible."

It was 4 o'clock before Smith made up his mind. He would bring up his batteries to soften the defenses and attack in open skirmish formation, to lessen the effectiveness of the enemy's artillery. Then he discovered that his artillery chief, not alerted for action, had taken the battery horses off to water them. While Smith resumed waiting, he learned from Hancock that the Second Corps was nearby and authorized to assist him. Beyond its late start, the Second Corps was hampered by poor maps and advanced to Petersburg in fits and starts. These mundane misfortunes prevented Hancock from reaching the front in time to perhaps inject some spine into General Smith.[37]

At 7:00 p.m., some eight hours after reaching the Petersburg front, Smith took the offensive. His artillery opened, and at the center Bully Brooks's division targeted a salient, crashing through the position with ease, capturing guns and men; the only challenge was scrambling up the steep face of the works. On the left, Hincks's men swarmed around both sides of a battery position and into its rear, celebrating captures. (The black troops "behaved admirably," said Smith. "This is the concurrent testimony of all.") The Rebels, mostly militia and conscripts, fled. Martindale's division on the right completed the conquest. A section of the Petersburg fortifications a mile and a half wide, with sixteen guns, lay in Federal hands. The advance intelligence estimates had proved out — General Beauregard had in fact but 2,200 men to hold the entire Petersburg line. What might have been accomplished at midafternoon was only accomplished at nightfall.

Smith wrote afterward that from the captured lines he could see Petersburg two miles away in the dusk, with no fortifications in sight. He had his own three divisions, only lightly blooded. He knew the Second Corps was close by. General Hincks urged him to continue the advance and capture the town. It was a clear night with a full moon. But it became Smith's excuse that Confederate reinforcements from Richmond "were already pouring into the town," even though as recently as 7:20 p.m. Ben Butler had assured him, "Nothing has passed down the railroad to harm you yet." Without daring to measure risk against reward, Baldy Smith took his stand: "I determined to hold what I had." He termed it the prudent course.

Hancock announced the Second Corps at hand and rode forward to meet Smith and asked what he could do, and got the reply, relieve the Eighteenth Corps in the captured fortifications.

Hancock outranked Smith, but he was new to the battlefield and lacked any real cause to overrule him. If the two debated it was not recorded. Hancock returned to his command hurting, frustrated, and angry. After his last-straw meeting with Smith, his lieutenants found him uncharacteristically abrupt. Theodore Lyman would remark that Hancock's men may have been tired after their day's march, "But, oh! that they had attacked at once. Petersburg would have gone like a rotten branch. In war there is a critical instant — a night — perhaps only a half hour, when everything culminates."

In the Federal ranks there was an immediate reaction to General Smith halting after his victory. A Second Corps artilleryman, talking with his infantry comrades, found wide agreement that the Johnnies would now have at least four or five hours to dig in. "The rage of the intelligent enlisted men was devilish. The most blood-curdling blasphemy I ever listened to I heard that night, uttered by the men who knew they were to be sacrificed on the morrow. The whole corps was furiously excited."[38]

For the Army of the Potomac, June 16 proved not a day marked by any sense of urgency. Baldy Smith, the sole high-command witness to breaking the Petersburg lines on the 15th, might still have exploited his victory at first light on the 16th, but he made no argument for doing so. If anyone else in the officer corps sensed the opportunity missed the night before, he was (just then) quiet about it. Grant was content to turn the battle over to General Meade. At Weyanoke Point, Meade and staff boarded a steamer at 10:30 a.m. and at 2:00 p.m. met Grant at City Point headquarters and assumed the field command. Grant greeted Meade with the observation, "Well, Smith has taken a line of works there, stronger than anything we have seen this campaign! — If it is a possible thing, I want an assault made at 6 o'clock this evening!"

The noteworthy event of the morning was General Beauregard pulling the cork bottling up Ben Butler at Bermuda Hundred. The hard-pressed Beauregard had to choose between Butler and Petersburg, and he chose Petersburg. Butler occupied the Rebel fortifications on his front and pushed forward to tear up the Richmond & Petersburg Railroad. He went no farther, however. For the moment, said Grant, he did not want to open a second front against Petersburg. Butler's troops puttered aimlessly through the afternoon, making no effort to secure their conquest. Evening brought a detachment sent by General Lee that recaptured their lines and regained their battered railroad. Ben Butler ended the day as bottled up as he began it. To this point Lee had reacted in puzzlement to Grant's bold move, but now he was directing his army to the new Petersburg battleground.

Burnside's Ninth Corps, crossing on the pontoon bridge, was marched to Petersburg that day to support the scheduled 6:00 p.m. attack. But it reached there debilitated and was put in reserve. Colonel Lyman came

on the corps as it arrived. "It was pitiable to see the men! — without water, broken by a severe march, scorched by the sun, and covered by a suf-
focating dust." Warren's Fifth Corps was ferried across from Wilcox Landing. Last to cross the James were the army's trains, Wright's Sixth Corps,
and Wilson's cavalry division. The bridge was taken up and shifted to City
Point. The Army of the Potomac was now fully committed to the Petersburg front.

What in moonlight on June 15 was an unobstructed path to Petersburg
was in daylight, by afternoon on June 16, blocked by a fresh line of breastworks. It was deemed (once again) the task of Hancock's Second Corps to
head the offensive. Francis Barlow spoke in favor of turning the enemy's
line on the left, but a reconnaissance by General Barnard of Grant's staff
spoke instead of "the chances in favor" of an advance straight ahead by
Barlow's division. Barlow and Chief of Staff Humphreys made their own
less vague reconnoiter.

It was a carefully planned attack, delivered under General Meade's eye.
Batteries posted by Henry Hunt in the captured works laid down a barrage. At 6 o'clock, with Barlow waving his hat and shouting, "Come on
boys," the assault overran the first line of obstacles and rifle pits but could
not break through the new line of works. The dead included the Irish Brigade's Patrick Kelly. To Barlow's right, Birney's division, with help from
Gibbon, also got the enemy's first line but no farther. The Ninth and Eighteenth Corps contributed demonstrations. All in vain, wrote Lyman: "The
main line was nowhere carried, and our 2d Corps lost 2,500 men."

One of Barlow's men expressed a growing conviction in the ranks: "The
boys dreaded this charge as it seemed a hopeless one. After forming lines
they waited quite awhile before advancing and this led to a calculation
of chances for life and a consequent loss of nerve." That theme was evident to General Hancock as well. Of the day's fighting, he wrote, "I do not
think the men attack with persistence; they appear to be wearied." Another
problem, he added, was leadership — heavy losses among brigade and regimental officers in whom the men had confidence.

Meade sent Lyman back to City Point headquarters to deliver a report
on the day's doings. "Then to Headq'rs and found Gen. Grant just going
to bed. He sat on the edge of his cot, in shirt and drawers and listened to
my report. . . . He smiled, like one who had done a clever thing, and said,
'I think it is pretty well to get across a great river, and come up here and attack Lee in his rear before he is ready for us!'"[39]

June 17 would be the Ninth Corps' day. Burnside joined battle with
three small divisions of two brigades each. (His fourth division, Edward

Ferrero's U.S. Colored Troops, was assigned to guard the army's trains.)
Burnside's opening move, on the army's far left, used a time-honored tactic—a surprise assault before dawn. Robert B. Potter's division slipped
quietly into a ravine leading toward the enemy lines, and at 4:00 a.m. his
men sprang forward and right over the parapets, their surprise complete.
They captured four guns and 600 prisoners and five flags. This success, by
plan, was to be exploited by James H. Ledlie's division. Ledlie was recently
promoted to division despite his besotted conduct on the North Anna.
When he and his division did not appear, he claimed they lost their way
in the same ravine that Potter had no trouble following to the front. Since
Ledlie was found drunk that afternoon, it is safe to assume he had started
early to screw up his courage. Potter dug in facing the Rebels' new second
line.

At 2:00 p.m. Orlando B. Willcox took a turn with his division. Willcox sought artillery to pave his way, but was told there was no time. The
Ninth Corps batteries were not brigaded and under central command like
the rest of the Potomac army, a telling lack today. John F. Hartranft's lead
brigade was somehow misdirected and ran into a murderous enfilading
fire of canister. "Our artillery did nothing at the critical moment," Willcox
noted in his journal. "My troops advanced at a double-quick, unsupported

Edwin Forbes did this panoramic view
of the June 18 attack on the Rebels' final
Petersburg line. The Eighteenth Corps is
engaged, with reinforcements moving up
at left. On the right is the Confederates'
abandoned second defensive line.

in any manner whatever. . . . Hartranft's left struck the enemy's pits, but melted away in a moment." Willcox counted 1,050 survivors of 1,890.

Ledlie's division was picked to lead the day's third offensive, at 6:00 p.m. It was Burnside's ambition to commit his entire Ninth Corps then on the scene, Ledlie's division first, then Potter's, then Willcox's. Leadership went astray, and in the end just two brigades of Ledlie's did the fighting, punching a quarter-mile-wide hole in the second line of works. When called on for support, Ledlie was well to the rear, "hazey-dazey" drunk and unresponsive. His staff officers left in charge were unable to push forward a brigade of heavies; they had seen the fate of heavies in other units. Ledlie's two lead brigades ran out of ammunition and had to give up their gains.[40]

Three days of fighting at Petersburg had accounted no victories except Baldy Smith's initial one, yet produced enough seemingly promising efforts to ensure there would be another fight on June 18, one month to the day since the bungled attack ending the Spotsylvania campaign. The Confederates would make this fight from a new line (their third) encasing Petersburg, more compact and easier to defend . . . and now the defenders included initial arrivals from the Army of Northern Virginia.

Yankee skirmishers sent forth at first light on June 18 discovered the Rebels' second line empty, and glimpsed a new line just a mile from Petersburg. Theodore Lyman reported General Meade stamping about in a "tearing humor" as battle approached. At 5:30 a.m. Meade signaled Grant, "My lines are advancing and will continue to do so until the enemy is found and felt." He ordered forward everything at hand — fourteen divisions — in the belief this was not a "regularly fortified line between the one abandoned and Petersburg. If the time is given them they will make one." That was a logical deduction, and the opening he had been waiting for . . . except that the Rebels had already taken the time. General Beauregard ordered this third line laid out on June 16, as a possible last ditch. On June 18 it was indeed the last ditch, but well near completion, well manned, and well armed with artillery.

The Second Corps led the way again, although not under Hancock this time. His reopened wound left him unable to ride or walk, and he turned over command to David Birney. (Only when the last bone splinter worked its way out of the wound did Hancock begin to heal; he returned to duty in ten days.) The assault was spearheaded by Robert McAllister's brigade, of Gershom Mott's division — Mott replacing Birney, who replaced Hancock. This was a chance for Mott to prove himself, after his troubles at the Wilderness and Spotsylvania. McAllister pushed the enemy skirmishers ahead of him to come up against the new line. He warned that it looked like a deathtrap, but Mott insisted on carrying out orders. "The Rebels poured down upon us lead and iron by musketry and cannon that cut the men down like hail cuts the grain and grass," McAllister told his family. "We had to advance a long distance up a cleared plain. Our ranks melted away, and we could not advance further." John Gibbon sent in three brigades in succession, only to be beaten back with heavy loss.

On the left, Burnside's Ninth Corps and part of Warren's Fifth Corps advanced as far as the shelter of a railroad cut, but every venture beyond was thrown back. In one of them, brigade commander Joshua Chamberlain was seriously wounded. Charles Wainwright noted in his diary, "I cannot say that our men went in well or at all as if they meant to carry the works. In five minutes they were coming back." He tried to rally them but found no officer of rank higher than lieutenant to lead. On the right, John Martindale's Eighteenth Corps division was stopped quickly, gaining hardly 50 yards across the fire-swept open ground fronting the enemy line.

In ordering a general, simultaneous advance, Meade had expected each commander to select the most likely target in his sector, but not all his generals seemed able to meet his expectation or his timetable. "Assault ordered for 12 m. by Gen. Meade," Lyman entered in his journal. "None made then by anybody." Warren and Burnside were particular offenders —

Warren three times canceled his advance. Meade finally snapped at them, "I am greatly astonished at your dispatch of 2 p.m. What additional orders to attack you require I cannot imagine. My orders have been explicit and are now repeated. . . ." Warren's response was that corps commanders must have discretion, "and he would not stand to be thus bullied." It was midafternoon when Meade sent positive orders to Burnside, Warren, and Birney "to attack at all hazards." As he told Birney, "I find it useless to appoint an hour to effect co-operation. . . . You have a large corps, powerful and numerous, and I beg you will at once, as soon as possible, assault in a strong column."

Birney ordered the attack, his second one that day, and it was one attack too many for the Second Corps. Since crossing the Rapidan seven weeks earlier, Grant and Meade had turned the Second into the army's shock troops, finally winnowing down officers and men to the breaking point on this June 18 afternoon. Thomas A. Smyth's brigade of Gibbon's division was ordered to charge over the same ground it had bloodied earlier. "The men did not stir," wrote a company commander. "The more I saw they were going to refuse to go the more urgent I became. . . . The men knew what they could or could not do; they had decided that they could not take this line. . . . The whole Brigade acted the same way; not a man started." When two other of Gibbon's brigades were ordered forward, they did not stir either. Over in Mott's division, Colonel Daniel Chaplin's brigade was told to attack. The only regiment that obeyed was Chaplin's old command, the heavies of the 1st Maine Heavy Artillery. While the rest of the brigade watched, the Mainers were slaughtered — of 900 of them, 632 were casualties.

John Gibbon, as tough and uncompromising a general as any in the Potomac army, was certainly aware of these defections in his division on June 18, yet he offered no comment, took no official action, did not speak of it in his report or even in his memoir. He had already found fault with this storming-the-barricades style of warfare, and he did not begrudge his men the same view.

At 6:30 p.m. Meade could report no successes, only his concern "that Beauregard has been re-enforced by Lee." At 6:50 p.m. Grant ordered a stand-down . . . and quietly announced an end to the Overland Campaign and what it represented. "If this assault does not carry we will try to gain advantages without assaulting fortifications."[41]

18. *Long Road to Appomattox*

NOT ASSAULTING FORTIFICATIONS could only mean in future maneuver and turning flanks and slashing at communications. But first it meant securing the siege itself. Any captured Petersburg lines were utilized where feasible, and engineers laid out extended lines, incorporating favorable terrain. The army's siege train was called for, and the men put down rifles and picked up spades. For this labor the heat was enervating, water was scarce, and the dust was compared to sandstorms in the Sahara. For these two armies gone to ground, forty-seven days passed between rainfalls.

General Meade had judged June 18 his last, best hope for breaking the enemy's new line before it was secured, and in his disappointment he admitted to his staff that evening, "I had hoped all along to have entered Petersburg this day." But Grant reassured him that he was "perfectly satisfied that all has been done that could be done, and that the assaults to-day were called for by all the appearances and information that could be obtained. Now we will rest the men and use the spade for their protection until a new vein can be struck."

In 1862, after the Seven Days, Lincoln had visited the Army of the Potomac to assure himself that it was still a viable fighting force. Now he visited the army to validate its current high command. And having been nominated in convention for a second term on June 8, the president was at City Point as a demonstration of his commander-in-chief credentials. He felt no need to interrogate the generals as he had at Harrison's Landing. He spoke encouragingly to Meade, and he reviewed the troops. Hincks's black troops greeted him with unbridled enthusiasm. "The scene was affecting in the extreme, and no one could have witnessed it unmoved," Horace Porter told his wife. Grant assured the president, "You will never hear of me farther from Richmond than now, till I have taken it. . . . It may take a long summer day, but I will go in." In Washington on June 23 John Hay entered in his diary, "The President arrived today from the field, sun-

Alfred Waud sketched Henry Hunt (left), chief of artillery, and James Duane, chief engineer, laying out postings in the Petersburg siege lines.

burnt and fagged but still refreshed and cheered. He found the army in fine health good position and good spirits."[1]

That the Army of the Potomac was in good spirits was debatable (except for Hincks's black troops, greeting their emancipator). Lieutenant Colonel Stephen Weld, 56th Massachusetts, expressed a more common theme in a June 21 home letter: "The feeling here in the army is that we have been absolutely butchered, that our lives have been periled to no purpose, and wasted." Weld blamed the highest of the high command, that "time and again recklessly and wickedly placed us in slaughter-pens. . . . We can't afford to make many more such bloody attacks as we have been doing. The enemy will outnumber us if we do so." Veteran artillerist Charles Wainwright expressed the blanket judgment, "Never has the Army of the Potomac been so demoralized as at this time." At the high command level, corps commander Gouverneur Warren found himself, after seven weeks of combat, "very much disgusted with our inability so far to force Genl. Lee's lines or get a fight out of him in the open field. We don't seem much nearer beating him than we were when the campaign began."

In addition to failing to capture Petersburg after brilliantly leading the army there, General Grant had to contemplate the failure of his latest peripheral strategy. First to report back was cavalryman Phil Sheridan. With the divisions of David Gregg and Alfred Torbert, Sheridan had ridden off to disable the Virginia Central and to explore joining with David Hunter to make mischief in the Shenandoah Valley. Lee dispatched Wade

Hampton with two divisions to counter Sheridan, which he did to good effect at Trevilian Station, on the railroad half a dozen miles east of Gordonsville. The two-day battle, June 11–12, favored first one side then the other (George Armstrong Custer and his command were very nearly surrounded and wiped out), and ended with Hampton firmly blocking Sheridan's path. The Yankees retreated, having done little damage to the railroad and failing to make contact with Hunter. Sheridan's losses were 1,307, Hampton's 813. Sheridan told Grant, "I regret my inability to carry out your instructions."[2]

Sheridan's expedition might generously be called a setback, but David Hunter's was a disaster. Combining the fractious commands of Franz Sigel, George Crook, and William Averell, Hunter marched up the Valley to carry out Grant's directive: "If Hunter can possibly get to Charlottesville and Lynchburg, he should do so, living on the country." Hunter translated "living on the country" to mean pillage and burning as he went, in Lexington putting the torch to the Virginia Military Institute. Requisitions were laid on the towns they occupied, and David Strother, Hunter's chief of staff, made note, "The soldiers in addition are plundering dreadfully."

On June 5, at Piedmont, Hunter defeated a scratch force of home guards under William E. Jones, killing Jones. But as he neared Lynchburg, he discovered that General Lee had sent the Second Corps, Army of Northern Virginia, Jubal Early commanding, to meet him. Talkative prisoners counted Early's army as 30,000. On June 19, apparently giving some credence to that tale, Hunter turned tail. His retreat continued day and night for 60 miles. "Burning bridges and railroad stations lighted our way," Strother wrote. At Salem, Early's pursuit captured Hunter's artillery and trains. The demoralized Yankees fled into West Virginia. "Starvation being the only enemy we had to contend with, the route to Charleston was taken. . . ." Jubal Early inherited the Shenandoah Valley.[3]

At City Point, meanwhile, harsh accounting was underway. In the month and a half of the Overland Campaign, the Army of the Potomac had suffered some 64,000 men killed, wounded, and missing. At the beginning of May that army had present for duty 122,119 men; at the end of June the number was 86,610. In addition to casualties there was the departure of the three-year men. Replacements fell far short of making good these losses. To be sure, Butler's Army of the James at Bermuda Hundred was next door, so to speak, but the weight of campaigning promised to fall most heavily on the Petersburg front and therefore on the Army of the Potomac. In concert with his earlier scouring of garrisons in the rear areas, Grant called for the Nineteenth Corps from Louisiana. He told Halleck, "We should concentrate our whole energy against the two principal armies of the enemy. In other words, nothing should be attempted, except in Georgia and here. . . ."

Grant did not wring his hands over the missed and lost chances at Petersburg on June 15–18. He shrugged his shoulders instead. "Our work progresses here slowly," he wrote his wife on June 22, "and I feel will progress securely until Richmond finally falls. The task is a big one and has to be performed by some one."

The officer corps was riven by substantial turnover during the campaign. Sixth Corps commander John Sedgwick was dead, as were division commanders James S. Wadsworth and Thomas G. Stevenson, and brigade commanders Alexander Hays and James C. Rice. Division commander George W. Getty was wounded. Thirteen brigade commanders were wounded and two captured and others shifted about. Of the army's forty-one brigades on May 4, just eleven had the same commanders at the close of the campaign. The turnover at the regimental level was even greater. Meade and Hancock both pointed to this loss or change of trusted commanders as crippling to unit morale.

John Gibbon was a careful record-keeper, and in his memoir he recorded the damage inflicted on his Second Corps division in the Overland Campaign. He began the campaign ("in splendid condition and high spirits") with 6,799 officers and men, and in the Wilderness and at Spotsylvania he suffered 47 percent casualties. By the end of June his losses had mounted to 72 percent of the men he originally took into this virtually continuous battle. It was the quality of the loss that made it especially disastrous, Gibbon wrote, "for the very best officers, and the very bravest men were those who fell. These always remained in the ranks and did the fighting and by their example and spirit stimulated the rest." This new-style war of entrenchments spawned a new-style war of attrition.[4]

The officer corps was afflicted with finger-pointing. Winfield Hancock demanded an investigation of a story in the *New York Times* that blamed his Second Corps for not taking Petersburg on June 15. (Grant tried to soothe him, saying Hancock and his corps "cannot be tarnished by newspaper articles or scribblers.") To counter the libel, Hancock claimed he was not told he was expected to join Smith's attack, an evasion of the real but unheroic circumstances (undelivered rations, poor maps) that delayed him.

Complaint was made, then and since, that Meade failed to coordinate his attacks, that he was not up to managing these offensive operations. But Cold Harbor was a stark demonstration that by 1864, whether coordinated or not, no frontal assault on the entrenched Army of Northern Virginia could possibly succeed. And at Cold Harbor Meade recognized that fact before Grant did.

On June 19, the day after his last-chance assault on Petersburg, Meade had a toe-to-toe confrontation with Gouverneur Warren over Warren's repeated delays in carrying out crucial attack orders. Afterward Warren told his wife, "A rupture is probable between me and Genl Meade . . . with whom I had a square understanding today, to the effect that I was no *creature* of his." By Meade's account, "Genl Warren exhibited so much temper and bad feeling forgetting the respect due to me as his superior officer and his senior in years — and ignoring every thing but his own sense of injury. . . ." In earlier disputes with Warren, Meade had shown restraint, but not this time. On June 21 he wrote to Grant to have Warren relieved from duty with the Army of the Potomac.

Meade unburdened himself in the three-page letter with particulars ranging from Mine Run to Spotsylvania to the finale at Petersburg. General Warren's defect, he said, "consists in too great reliance on his own judgment, and in an apparent impossibility on his part to yield his judgment so as to promptly execute orders, where these orders should happen not to receive his sanction or be in accordance with his views. . . . Such a defect strikes at the root of all Military subordination, and it is entirely out of the question that I can command this Army, if each Corps Commander is to exercise a similar independence of action." Meade made note that at Spotsylvania he had resisted Grant's order to relieve Warren; "I no longer feel called to exercise any further patience. . . ."

This time it was Grant who saved Warren's command for him, persuading Meade to withdraw the letter, no doubt using the argument that firing a corps commander would not be good for the army's already-shaken morale. The contretemps got in at least one newspaper, prompting Meade to write candidly to Warren suggesting he best mend his ways — further disharmony and "a separation is inevitable." Warren, his self-righteousness pricked, wrote his wife, "I believe Gen'l Meade is an august and unfeeling man and I dislike his personal character so much now that it is improbable we shall ever have again any friendly social relations. I have also lost all confidence in his ability as a general."[5]

In attempting to fully mobilize what forces he had in order to maintain the initiative and to expand siege operations, General Grant needed to manage perhaps the two most unmanageable generals in the army — Ben Butler and Baldy Smith. At Bermuda Hundred, Butler led the Army of the James and Smith the Eighteenth Corps, and they were as two scorpions in a bottle. Butler, said Cyrus Comstock of Grant's staff, "has the ability to be more dangerous, sharper & more disagreeable than any man I have ever seen." Smith, for his part, dealt in vitriol wherever he went. Diarist Comstock reported, "Some time ago Smith criticised in his ex cathedra way, this campaign as having been a succession of useless slaughters. The general heard of it and told me he did not know which to do, relieve him or talk to him."

Smith made it clear he wanted out from under Butler, and Grant wanted Butler as far away as possible from any battle commanding. This desire was complicated by the fact that onetime War Democrat Butler had gone over to the Radical Republicans. That meant, in this presidential-election year, that Butler needed to be handled with the softest of kid gloves. Grant hoped to resolve the matter by assigning Butler to Fort Monroe, there to administer in peace and quiet his Department of Virginia and North Carolina. Then Grant would insulate Smith and his Eighteenth Corps by putting William Franklin in field command of the Army of the James's two corps, the Eighteenth and the Tenth. General Franklin, after an unhappy exile in the Department of the Gulf, had come to City Point looking for work. But lawyer Butler balked at the plan, remarking that "Department" and "forces in the field" were inseparable; he would stay right where he was. And Franklin, with his record of fealty to McClellan and his intrigues against Burnside, was not welcomed by Washington.

Baldy Smith inserted himself into this imbroglio . . . and in a remarkably short time self-destructed. General Meade wrote his wife on July 7, "I have had a row with Mr. Baldy Smith. We are now avowed antagonists, a much more comfortable position for me than an attempt at friendly relations." Lieutenant Colonel Comstock recorded the saga for his diary: "Smith has constantly been talking against Meade, wishes Franklin to take his place — and a few nights ago . . . insisted on the general's making the change he wished & finally asked the general in the most offensive way, if he expected he was ever going to do any thing with that man (Meade) in command." With Smith saying he would not serve with Butler, Comstock speculated that "as Butler is to stay for the present Smith will probably be shelved." He was exactly right. As more was revealed about Smith's missed opportunity at Petersburg, Grant grew disenchanted with his generalship. Then Smith's blatant intrigue against Meade proved the wrong tactic to use with the general-in-chief. On July 19 Smith was relieved of his command. Grant silenced his protests with the pronouncement, "You talk too much." Smith was ordered to New York to await orders — orders that never came. Theodore Lyman neatly parsed the saga: "Thus did Smith the

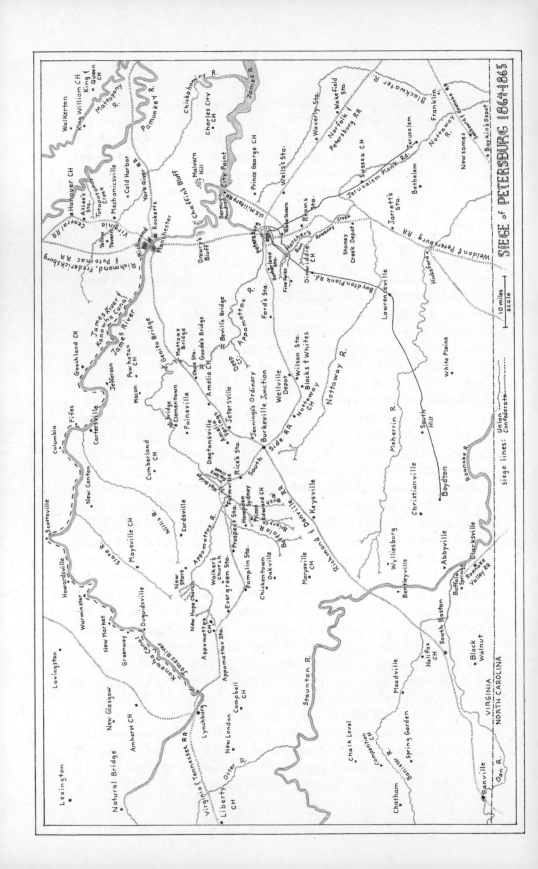

SIEGE of PETERSBURG 1864–1865

siege lines: Union · · · · · · · ·
Confederate · · · · · · · ·

10 miles
scale

VIRGINIA
NORTH CAROLINA

Bald try the Macchiavelli against Butler the cross-eyed, and got floored at the first round!"

Baldy Smith, like John Pope, did not leave quietly. He sent a lengthy screed to Senator Solomon Foot of Vermont to demonstrate to his native state that his relief from command was not "brought about by any misconduct of mine." He seems to have hoped that Foot would take up his case, perhaps with the president. Smith's contrived, convoluted tale involved Grant and liquor, Butler and blackmail: Butler witnessed Grant in his cups, Butler blackmailed him (by threatening to expose his intoxication) into pushing Smith out while keeping him in, ensconced at Bermuda Hundred with full powers over his department and every soldier in it. There is no evidence Foot did anything with the letter, found in his papers after his death, but Smith meanwhile spread his tale of Grant and drink elsewhere. In the postwar years Baldy Smith became a prolific writer, ranging widely through his thousand excuses to recount the course of his Civil War service.[6]

If Petersburg itself was for the time being declared out of reach, at least its railroads could become Potomac army targets. Of its five lines, two had fallen into the Yankees' hands when they crossed the James — a line to City Point, and the Norfolk & Petersburg, to Suffolk and Norfolk. The Richmond & Petersburg had thus far escaped Ben Butler's clutches. Running west from Petersburg was the South Side Railroad, crossing the Richmond & Danville at Burkeville and reaching to Lynchburg, 100 miles from the capital, where it met the Virginia & Tennessee. The Weldon & Petersburg ran south to Weldon, North Carolina, making there a connection with the blockade-running port of Wilmington. Richmond had three railroads of its own for the Yankees to target — the Richmond, Fredericksburg & Potomac, to Hanover Junction; the Virginia Central that touched Gordonsville and Charlottesville to reach Staunton in the Valley; and the Richmond & Danville, reaching to Danville in far southwestern Virginia.

On the Petersburg front, Grant's immediate focus fell on the closest railroad, the Weldon & Petersburg, some three miles beyond the Federals' left marked by the Jerusalem Plank Road. He elected to move quickly, on June 22, advancing as before by the left flank. Horatio Wright's Sixth Corps, little used against Petersburg, was chosen for the operation, in company with the Second Corps. Meade's selection of the Second was thoughtless considering its ordeal on June 18; apparently it drew the assignment because just then it was in reserve. But as the Second Corps' historian remarked, being in reserve had come to mean to the men of the Second being reserved for the heavy fighting. The plan was to get across the Weldon Railroad and dig in there, extending the siege lines. In addition, a cavalry raid was assembled to strike at the South Side and Richmond & Danville railroads to the west. Coordinating the march of the two infantry corps was hurried so as to meet Grant's schedule. This was Wright's first independent command, and the first as well for David Birney, filling in for the recuperating Winfield Hancock.

The landscape south and west of Petersburg was terra incognita to the Federals, made worse by large stretches of scrub forest akin to the Wilderness, and the advance soon went astray. The Second Corps formed the inner half of the wide swing west and the Sixth Corps the outer half, and soon the Sixth fell behind until the two corps were out of touch. Urging on Wright, urging on the attack, Meade told Francis Barlow's Second Corps division, the tie-in to the Sixth Corps, "You will not be dependent on any movement of the Sixth Corps." Until Wright caught up, each corps must look out for itself. Then an inadvertent separation formed within the Second Corps. Barlow's and Gershom Mott's divisions followed supposedly parallel woods roads which in fact diverged until the two commands were out of touch . . . leaving Barlow isolated on both his flanks. Neither Wright nor Birney had their respective corps under close scrutiny or control.

General Lee, as sensitive to threats to Petersburg's railroads as to Richmond's, sent A. P. Hill to counter this latest advance. In midafternoon the Rebels exploited the gaps in the Yankee line. Taken in flank and rear without any warning, Barlow's division collapsed. In turn the flanks of Mott's and then Gibbon's divisions were uncovered, and they too fell back. Two regiments surrendered en masse; a battery was overrun. Gibbon's attempted counterattack to regain the battery floundered.

By Theodore Lyman's account, "General Meade very indignant, ordered an advance along the whole front at 7." Wright's Sixth Corps was only brushed by the enemy attack, but he replied that his men were tired "& could not foresee a good result" from an evening attack. "Ask Gen. Wright, what I am to do tomorrow if I do not advance tonight?" said Meade. When Lyman delivered this message, Wright merely said, "Ah, that I do not know!" The Rebels had no trouble pushing back the Sixth Corps and then withdrew behind their lines. When Wright arrived at headquarters the next day, he found Meade "chafing, with an eye like a rattlesnake and a nose that seemed twice as sharp and long as usual!" An angry commanding general conferred "a long while" with Generals Wright and Birney. The Yankees consolidated their small gains. The Weldon Railroad was now two miles away instead of three.

"I look on June 22d & 23d as the two most discreditable days to this army that I ever saw!" Colonel Lyman told his journal. "There was everywhere, high and low, feebleness, confusion, poor judgment. The only person who kept his plans and judgment clear was Gen. Meade himself." Wright "showed himself totally unfit to command a corps." Grant called it a stampede in reporting to Washington. Cyrus Comstock of Grant's staff took note, "Troops did not fight nearly as well as when we started — best officers & best men gone. . . ."

The 1,700 Second Corps men taken captive was the most shocking statistic. Barlow argued that faulty orders "exposed us to be attacked," yet he added, "It must be admitted that the troops did not meet the attack with vigor and courage and determination." Two of his brigades, he said, were not now to be depended upon, "from loss of commanding and other officers." The Second Corps' command structure was decimated.[7]

Phil Sheridan proved as slow returning from his Trevilian Station raid as from his earlier Richmond raid, leaving the Army of the Potomac with only a single cavalry division, James Wilson's. Meade wanted to postpone Wilson's raid until it could be made with the army's entire cavalry corps, but Grant, with that impatience still marking his planning, overruled him. Wilson was reinforced by August Kautz's small cavalry division from the Army of the James, giving him a force of 4,500 troopers and a dozen guns. On June 22 the Wilson-Kautz raiders set off down the Weldon line to Reams Station, where they burned the station and tore up some track as a preliminary to their target area — the Burkeville junction of the South Side and Richmond & Danville lines, 50 miles west of Petersburg. Burkeville offered rails for tearing up in four directions. It was very hot and the troopers were tired and Rebel cavalry was nipping at their heels, so the destruction was nothing of the order of burned ties and bent and twisted rails. The raiders followed the Richmond & Danville southwest to the rail bridge crossing of the Staunton River, but here they were blocked by home-guard defenders. Wilson calculated that by now he had destroyed some 60 miles of railroad, so he turned for home.

Wilson anticipated the Weldon & Petersburg being in Federal hands by now, but instead he was greeted on his return not only by Hampton's cavalry — Wade Hampton was a far more efficient handler of cavalry than Phil Sheridan — but Rebel infantry as well. At Reams Station, Wilson's and Kautz's men were pursued and slashed at until to escape it was every man for himself. Wilson lost 1,500 men, and all his guns and trains. The Confederates suffered supply shortages after the Wilson-Kautz raid, but not lasting ones. The Richmond & Danville was back in operation in twenty-three days, the South Side a week or so later. On July 16 Theodore Lyman took note, "Those scamps the rebs have repaired the Weldon railroad . . . and have been running trains on it, for three or four days, past our noses." The Yankee cavalry sat out most of July for refitting and remounting.[8]

Engineers set to work extending and elaborating the Petersburg siege lines. It was in no sense a true siege, like Vicksburg. Only by snipping off the Confederates' lines of supply, or by flanking or breaking through their works, could there be a decision. "Our siege is progressing slowly, at a very snail's pace," W. A. Roebling, Fifth Corps staff, wrote on July 12; "no one seems to care about pushing it, we have all lost our energies for the time being, and it requires some great occasion to rouse them again, such as an attack for instance."

John Barnard, Grant's chief engineer, proposed a tactic to break through the enemy works modeled on his intended bombardment against besieged Yorktown in 1862 (six hours of gunnery would do it, he had predicted, but the Rebels retreated). At a sector opposite the Fifth Corps, Barnard would concentrate the fire of 100 cannon. "Two corps massed in successive lines should assault and all the rest be ready to follow up." Charles Dana reported General Meade "totally condemns Barnard's project of assault," saying he had attacked that very spot twelve hours after he got there and failed, and it had since been greatly strengthened. General Barnard was recalled to Washington, to everyone's relief.

If they could not go over the enemy fortifications or turn them, perhaps they could go under them. After the June 18 fighting and the realignment of the siege lines, a sector of the Ninth Corps front was only a hundred yards from an enemy artillery bastion. Lieutenant Colonel Henry Pleasants, commanding the 48th Pennsylvania, promoted the idea of tunneling under the enemy works and blowing them up with a gunpowder mine. Pleasants was by trade a civil engineer, with experience in mining and in railroad tunneling. The 48th, a reenlisted three-year regiment, was raised in coal-mining country, and among the hundred or so remaining original recruits were enough miners to form the core of the tunneling crews. Pleasants took his idea to division commander Robert B. Potter, who approved and sent it to Burnside, who seized on it with enthusiasm. Burnside and his Ninth Corps were not widely accepted in the current campaigning, and this mine project might be the chance for the corps (and for Burnside) to shine. Meade was skeptical but did not object to the project, nor did Grant. The Potomac army's engineering staff offered no support and no matériel. On June 25, in the bank of a creek bed behind the lines, Pleasants started digging his mine gallery.[9]

Grant's thoughts for pressing ahead on the Petersburg front were interrupted by cries of alarm from Washington. Having chased David Hunter's command all the way to the Ohio River, Jubal Early's army corps was free to roam the Shenandoah. On Lee's order, he was to threaten Washington and Baltimore in hopes that Grant "would be compelled either to weaken himself so much for their protection as to afford us an opportunity to attack him, or that he might be induced to attack us." Early reached Harper's Ferry on July 3. Facing him was Franz Sigel and his bedraggled New Market command. Sigel took one look and retreated. Grant's initial response, on July 5, was mild, sending just James Ricketts's division from Horatio Wright's Sixth Corps. But Washington's renewed cries were sufficient that he followed with the rest of the Sixth Corps and then the Nineteenth Corps, up from Louisiana.

The capital's defenders were a ragtag accumulation. Grant had plucked the heavies from the batteries in the forts, Hunter was only now making his slow return from limbo, and in the ranks were 100-day militia, Veteran Reserves, and other casuals. Charles Dana, back at the War Department, waxed sarcastic at the flock of discounted generals inhabiting the capital — Sigel, Lew Wallace, Quincy Gillmore, Darius Couch. "If only the General could spare Butler for the Supreme Command all danger would certainly cease. . . ." In Gideon Welles's view, the administration was hardly better: "The President is enjoined to silence, while Halleck is in a perfect maze — without intelligent decision or self-reliance, and Stanton is wisely ignorant."

On July 9, at the Monocacy River in Maryland, Early attacked a pickup force under Lew Wallace. Braced by Ricketts's newly arrived Sixth Corps division, the Yankees held out for some hours before retreating, badly beaten. For Lincoln this had echoes of 1862, and he telegraphed Grant proposing he leave force enough to hold what he had "and bring the rest with you personally, and make a vigorous effort to destroy the enemie's force in this vicinity. I think there is really a fair chance to do this if the movement is prompt." This was just his thought, he said, not his order.

The Monocacy fight delayed Early for a day, and when he advanced on the Washington lines at Fort Stevens, Wright's other two divisions met him. Mr. Lincoln was there too, and General Wright thoughtlessly invited him to the parapets to observe the skirmishing. John Hay recorded Lincoln's tale: "A soldier roughly ordered him to get down or he would have

THE OLD BULL DOG ON THE RIGHT TRACK.

Bulldog Grant, astride the Weldon Railroad, threatens Jefferson Davis, cowering in his Richmond doghouse guarded by Lee (left) and Beauregard. Presidential hopeful McClellan worries "he'll hurt those other dogs if he catches hold of them," but Lincoln thinks it best "to give the old bull dog full swing to go in and finish them!"

his head knocked off." Another visitor to Fort Stevens, Gideon Welles, "found the President who was sitting in the shade — his back against the parapet toward the enemy." At the White House Hay entered in his diary, "The President is in very good feather this evening. He seems not in the least concerned about the safety of Washington."

In that, the president was right. With no prospects for taking Washington, Early withdrew, but at his own pace, gathering plunder and crossing back into the Valley without hindrance. "They were defiant and insolent," wrote diarist Welles, ". . . but the Bureau Generals were alarmed and ignorant, and have made themselves and the administration appear contemptible." In this presidential-election year, the administration appearing contemptible was a matter of grave concern. The capital might not be in danger, yet to the electorate across the North, Early's exploit was more bad news in a rush of bad news. Grant appeared stymied before Petersburg after an incredible cost in casualties. Sherman appeared stymied before Atlanta. The Rebel army that brazenly threatened the capital even now lurked unchecked in the Valley. In August the Democrats would meet in convention in Chicago, and the betting was on General McClellan as their nominee — that, for the administration, was as bad news as any.[10]

Command against Early was tangled among four departments — Washington, Susquehanna, West Virginia, and the Middle Department. Secretary Stanton warned Grant that his advice and suggestions were not enough; "until you direct positively and explicitly what is to be done, everything will go on in the deplorable and fatal way in which it has gone on for the past week." Grant proposed Henry Halleck take the command, but Halleck slipped away from that role just as he had during the Second Bull Run crisis. Halleck was in a told-you-so temper. He had never favored Grant taking the Army of the Potomac south of the James and thereby leaving Washington uncovered. "I predicted this to Genl Grant before he crossed the James River," he wrote, "and that Lee would play the same game of shuttle-cock between him & Washington that he did with McClellan." Halleck did what he always did in a time of crisis — nothing. Grant turned to Horatio Wright, whose Sixth Corps was the only reliable force at hand, granting him command authority regardless of rank. But Wright was "wanting in audacity" (as Meade put it), and he failed to catch up with Early.[11]

Early's threat to the capital generated all manner of rumors and gossip affecting the Army of the Potomac. With the Petersburg front now more or less quiet, General Meade regularly rode out to inspect his corps commanders' postings. Meade's dealings with Warren were strained, with Wright (before he was sent north) perfunctory, and with Burnside touchy, but with old friend Winfield Hancock dealings were long and cordial. Staff learned that if a day's inspections began with a Hancock "pow-wow," it was going to be a long day.

After one such powwow, on July 12, Meade wrote his wife, "Hancock told me today, he had been confidentially informed, it was intended to remove me from command and that he was to be my successor . . . said he believed it was a political intrigue & intimated a victim was wanted to appease the public & I was to be the man." Hancock said he did not believe this was Grant's doing. "I do not see as I can do any thing to defend myself against unknown enemies on unknown charges . . . ," Meade concluded.

In his reporting to Stanton on July 7, Charles Dana either heard — or started — the same rumor. Dana claimed a change in the army's command "now seems probable." He spoke at length of Meade's notorious temper and said Meade's lieutenants had lost confidence in him. He quoted a "confidential friend" who quoted General Wright saying, "all of Meade's attacks have been made without brains and without generalship." Horatio Wright, it appears, talked out of school after Meade dressed him down for his contribution to the failed attack of June 22–23 on the Weldon Railroad.

The press added this fuel to its fire against Meade. James Biddle of Meade's staff made note, "The trouble is they want to make Meade the scapegoat & are trying to fasten everything that goes wrong in the Army upon him."

Meade went to Grant with Hancock's tale and was assured there was nothing to it; if such a change was ordained, he said, he would know about it. He did say that if more forces than the Sixth and Nineteenth Corps were sent north, he would send Meade with them to take command on the upper Potomac. Meade took such a challenging possibility as a compliment. As for the tale of his relief, he decided that was started by someone "with whom the wish was father to the thought." Cyrus Comstock of Grant's staff, aware of all this gossip, offered a measured critique of George Meade's command status in the Army of the Potomac: "Have talked with very different persons — all snubbed by Meade & think that while they all have private grievances, that he would be first-choice for Comdg. Genl. both among his staff officers & the Maj. Gen's."[12]

Jubal Early's continued presence in the Shenandoah Valley dominated the news, a virtual advertisement for the war-as-a-failure theme the Democrats were sure to trumpet in the upcoming election. Early sent raiding parties into Maryland and Pennsylvania, where as vengeance for David Hunter's depredations in the Valley he burned Chambersburg. A command decision had a higher priority than ever. As Charles Dana told Grant, "There is no head to the whole, and it seems indispensable that you should at once appoint one." Halleck refused to act, and Horatio Wright proved not up to the job. Grant failed to get William Franklin the command of Ben Butler's forces, so he proposed Franklin for this new job. On July 21 Halleck replied, speaking for the president, "General Franklin would not give satisfaction." Over the short compass of three days, the Potomac army careers of William Franklin and Baldy Smith were done, their many missteps unforgiven, although neither man yet suspected his fate. On August 2 a still-hopeful Franklin wrote Smith, "If we had a decent force I would not object to taking the command Grant mentions, and if you will take the Shenandoah Valley in charge I think we could make a good thing of it. . . ."

Grant next wrote directly to the president, on July 25, repeating with more urgency the need to combine the four departments currently in conflict into one "Military Division." He said he would put it under General Meade, and move Hancock to head the Army of the Potomac and Gibbon to head the Second Corps. "Many reasons might be assigned for the changes here suggested," Grant wrote, "some of which I would not care to commit to paper, but would not hesitate to give verbally." It was thereby arranged for president and general-in-chief to meet at Fort Monroe on July 31.

Before his meeting with Lincoln, Grant discussed this new command with Meade, who thought it prudent to express no opinion, just that he would obey any order given him. But he wrote his wife, "So far as having an independent command which the A.P. is not, I would like this change very well." Of course he would have to deal with a new set of generals, and "be managed by the Presdt, Secy & Halleck . . . a pretty trying position that no man in his senses could desire." While claiming indifference to the outcome, Meade appeared receptive to a change.[13]

Neither Lincoln nor Grant left an accounting of their Fort Monroe meeting. A clue to their agenda is Lincoln's jotting on a telegram arranging the meeting: "Meade & Franklin / McClellan / Md. & Penna." Clearly they discussed organization of the forces on the upper Potomac and the command of them. The mention of General McClellan signaled a plot afoot.

The Blair clan had for some time sought to steer McClellan away from the Democratic presidential nomination. In May cabinet member Montgomery Blair felt out McClellan with a quid pro quo: withdraw his name from consideration and "unbosom himself unreservedly & in confidence directly with the President" in return for a military posting in which he "could be most useful. . . ." When Washington fell under threat, Montgomery's influential father Francis Preston Blair stepped in and arranged a meeting with McClellan on July 21 at which he said the same thing, but clothed in the language of patriotism and duty – by McClellan's account, if "I would not permit my name to be used as a candidate for the Presidency in opposition to the present incumbent . . . I would be actively employed by him in a position befitting my rank. . . ." Blair added that Grant had renounced any political ambitions before being named general-in-chief. While Blair said he had not come as an emissary from Lincoln, he afterward reported his conversation with McClellan to the president. The general was noncommittal, he said, but promised to give the matter deep consideration. Lincoln "neither expressed approval nor disapprobation of what I had done. . . ."

When Lincoln and Grant met at Fort Monroe ten days later, no word had come from McClellan. Still, they left the door open. They chose Phil Sheridan to lead the Sixth Corps and a cavalry division on the upper Potomac — not in the top command there but reporting (for the moment) to Hunter. Considering Lincoln's past command politicking with the likes of Nathaniel Banks, Dan Sickles, Ben Butler, or Franz Sigel, to exchange an election for command of a Valley army would be a major coup. But Mc-

Clellan would not bite. In drafting a reply (unsent) to Blair, he said he could not accept such a bargain "for the reason that I do not approve of the policy and measures of the present President."

On Grant's return from Fort Monroe, Meade told his wife he demanded of Grant why he was not chosen for the Valley post. Grant explained that the president, not knowing Meade's wishes on the subject, concluded that to shift him from commanding the Army of the Potomac to what was a lesser posting "might be misunderstood by the public & be construed into a disapprobation of my course. . . ." From this rather convenient explanation it appears that Lincoln deferred to General Grant's wishes here. Grant worked well in partnership with Meade and admired his handling of the Potomac army. What he wanted in the Shenandoah was no-holds-barred aggression of the sort Sheridan offered. Furthermore, Grant was coming to a decision that the Shenandoah Valley must not only be cleared of Confederate soldiers, but that it must no longer provision the Confederate war effort. He likely concluded that George Meade was not a soldier with the stomach for that kind of total, beyond the pale warfare. Phil Sheridan had the stomach for anything.[14]

While high command matters were sorted out, Colonel Pleasants's mine operation pushed ahead steadily. Early on, entirely the work of the poor-relation Ninth Corps, the mine was a novelty, creating (wrote Charles Wainwright) "a good deal of talk and is generally much laughed at." Potomac army engineers scoffed; "neither they, Meade, nor the other corps commanders have any belief in its success."

The work shifts, bossed by a Welsh coal miner named Henry Reese, continued twenty-four hours a day. Timber for the framing was stripped from bridges on the liberated Norfolk & Petersburg, worked up and assembled at a liberated sawmill a half dozen miles away, and installed quietly, without hammering. Springs and quicksand and varied layers of sediments, even marl, were encountered. The gallery was equipped with a ventilating system and lit with candles and lanterns. Burnside sent off to Washington for a theodolite so Pleasants could calculate the exact length (510.8 feet) for his gallery. The only thing not perfected was secrecy, but Confederate counterminers missed their target.

The end of the gallery and two lateral galleries were filled with four tons of carefully placed gunpowder, time fuzes laid, and the chambers tamped with sandbags to direct the blast up and not out. The mine was declared ready on July 28, thirty-four days in the making. And by now the mine had become very important. Prospects elsewhere on the lines proved slim, manpower was draining off to the upper Potomac, and suddenly everyone was interested in Colonel Pleasants's mine.

At Deep Bottom, on the northern loop of the James at Bermuda Hundred, a pontoon bridge and bridgehead were utilized for an offensive by the Second Corps. Hancock would cross and move toward Richmond to see what might be gained, and "break a hole" for two divisions of Sheridan's cavalry to strike at the Virginia Central north of the city. July 27 was Hancock's start date. The mine would be triggered on July 30, in expectation that Lee had pulled men away from Petersburg to contest Hancock.

Hancock crossed at Deep Bottom and tapped the Confederate defenses hard enough to capture four cannon, but Grant's instructions were clear: "I do not want Hancock to attack intrenched lines," just remain and clear the way for the cavalry. Sheridan's dismounted troopers found a stiff fight and held their ground, but their way to the railroad was firmly blocked. At Petersburg the Rebels were seen moving troop trains to the Richmond front, leading Grant to call off Hancock's operation. On July 29 the infantry and cavalry recrossed at Deep Bottom and Hancock hurried back to the Petersburg lines. The operation registered no gain, yet served as a decoy. Lee now had three divisions, half the previous number, holding five miles of Petersburg lines.[15]

General Meade may have been a latecomer to Burnside's mine operation, but now he oversaw thorough planning for it. Colonel Lyman noted, "Very careful & particular directions were given by Gen. Meade for the formation of the assaulting columns and . . . for the easy passage of the troops. . . ." Upon springing the mine, the Ninth Corps' assaulting columns would push rapidly through the breach without pause to seize a lodgment on a ridge called Cemetery Hill, some 500 yards to the rear. A coup de main, Meade called it. Grant stressed the point: "All officers should be fully impressed of the absolute necessity of pushing entirely beyond the enemy's present line if they should succeed in penetrating it. . . ." Ord's Eighteenth Corps would secure the breakthrough on the right and Warren's Fifth Corps on the left. Hancock's Second Corps would act in reserve. To clear the way for a broad attacking front, on the night before, a wide stretch of the Ninth Corps parapets was ordered cut down and trenches filled and abatis removed. "Every preparation to insure success had been made that could have been," General Humphreys told his wife. "Everything that ought to have been looked after, was looked after. The instructions omitted nothing."

Burnside made the attack assignments. Based on the fact they were his freshest men, he chose Edward Ferrero's division of black troops to lead. They were the freshest, said Meade, because they were the rawest, their sole experience being guarding the army's trains during the Overland Campaign, and he overruled the choice. Burnside protested, arguing that the mine operation was his doing and his to lead as he saw fit. Grant upheld Meade. Meade's arguments were two — the inexperience of these troops for such a key assignment; and, in the case of failure, the political repercussions of "shoving those people ahead to get killed because we did not care anything about them." Meade simply wanted the best troops Burnside had to lead the attack . . . and thereby the most promising operation of the campaign went off the rails.

It was said of Ambrose Burnside that he had a laissez-faire attitude toward military management. Command responsibilities could be left to take care of themselves — resulting, for example, in the Potomac army's disastrous collapse of morale following Fredericksburg. "Old B-sides," wrote Lyman, "is one of the 'all-will-come-out-right' sort; a sort of faith pleasant to see even when not backed by strong reasoning." Burnside combined this peculiar faith with the habit of sulking when challenged or questioned or overruled. That had been the case at Antietam when berated by McClellan . . . and now it was the case at Petersburg. In a major lapse of command responsibility, Burnside had the commanders of his other three divisions draw lots for who would lead the mine attack. Division commander James Ledlie drew the lot to lead. Not a poorer general nor a weaker division could be found in the Army of the Potomac.

When called to action, General Ledlie turned to drink, most recently in the June offensive at Petersburg and earlier at the North Anna, where he wrecked his brigade in a solo attack. The division he now led was a poorly run recent inheritance. One of the two brigades was full of heavy-artillerymen and dismounted cavalrymen, none of whom wanted to be there. The other included one three-year regiment shortly due for discharge, and three of the regiments Ledlie had run into the ground at the North Anna, one of which mustered just ninety-eight men and officers. At Burnside's briefing of his generals the evening before the attack, Ledlie was too drunk to grasp what his division was supposed to do in its lead role.

If Burnside did not suspect Ledlie's failings, it only attests to his indifferent notion of command. And on the night of July 29 Burnside was equally indifferent to explicit orders. He neglected to level his works so that the next day's attack could be launched quickly and in line of battle formation. Whatever could go wrong in this battle was already going wrong.[16]

On Saturday, July 30, the mine fuze was lit to explode at 3:30 a.m. A

The Petersburg mine explodes (right rear) on July 30, and supporting batteries (center) open fire. Chief engineer James Duane watches at left. By Alfred Waud.

half hour passed and nothing happened, and Grant went to Meade's head-quarters to ask what was wrong. "Don't know, guess the fuze has gone out," said Meade. Sergeant Henry Reese, who had bossed the tunneling by day and by night, thought the same thing, and resolved to save his handiwork. With Lieutenant Jacob Douty, he went into the gallery and tracked the fuze line until he found it burned out at a defective splice. Reese relit the fuze and they raced for safety. The mine exploded at 4:44 a.m.

"The explosion was the grandest spectacle I ever saw," wrote Colonel Stephen Weld, 56th Massachusetts, waiting to attack. "The first I knew of it, was feeling the earth shaking. I looked up and saw a huge mass of earth and flame rising some 50 or 60 feet in the air, almost slowly and majesti-cally, as if a volcano had just opened, followed by an immense volume of smoke rolling out in every direction." Henry Hunt opened an array of 164 artillery pieces in noisome accompaniment to the explosion.

The rain of debris initially caused Ledlie's attackers to pause, but the far greater delay was simply getting through their own lines. Contrary to Meade's orders, a space only eight or ten feet wide had been cleared, and companies filtered through "by the flank" a few men at a time. Disorga-nized groups advanced into the crater that had been the Rebel artillery bastion — 150 feet by 50 feet and 20 to 30 feet deep. Brigade leaders William F. Bartlett and Elisha Marshall had no orders from Ledlie to do more than hold the captured ground, the ground being the crater. Ledlie himself was in a bombproof far to the rear, furbishing his drunken evening with a drunken morning.

The divisions of Robert Potter and Orlando Willcox struggled through the lines as best they could. These two at least knew the objective was to get *through* the enemy line to the open ground beyond. But when their troops pushed into the crater they piled up against Ledlie's men, who did not know (or did not try) to advance. Attempts to work around the crater became entangled in the enemy works. The effect was very like what had happened on May 12 at Spotsylvania, when far too many men tried to push through a breach with no plan to follow and no guidance. The Petersburg Crater, as it came to be called, witnessed a complete command breakdown — no one in charge and no one trying to take charge.

During the first hour of the assault, there was initially no response from the stunned Confederates, and only light resistance as they began to rally. But in that hour of opportunity the Yankees got no farther than the Crater or the works on each side of it. Meade repeatedly pressed Burnside to push beyond, to seize possession of Cemetery Hill: "Our chance is now; push your men forward at all hazards (white and black), and don't lose time in making formations, but rush for the crest." "There is no object to be gained in occupying the enemy's line. . . . The great point is to secure the crest at once, at all hazards." Their exchanges grew heated, and a befuddled Burnside finally complained that Meade's dispatches were "unofficerlike and ungentlemanly."

Just as the Confederates began to counterattack in force, Burnside's last counter, Edward Ferrero's black division, joined battle. Some of Ferrero's men gained ground on the flanks, others joined the mass of troops crowded into the Crater. General Ferrero was not with his men in this their first battle, however. He huddled with General Ledlie in his bombproof, getting similarly drunk.

It was soon clear that incensed Southerners were giving no quarter to any black man in a Federal uniform. In the face of that terror, and as raw troops frequently did in their first combat, many "ran in all directions except ahead," as Theodore Lyman wrote. "On the other hand I must say that the negroes lost several hundred in killed and wounded, and the place where they had to go up was very hot." Wounded blacks, surrendered blacks, were killed in numbers. A North Carolina soldier recalled, "When I got there they had the ground covered with broken headed negroes and were searching about among the bomb proofs for more, the officers were trying to stop them but they kept on until they finished up." A massacre is evident in the numbers. The Federals listed 410 black soldiers missing in the Battle of the Crater; the Confederates listed 200 black soldiers captured.[17]

To the left of the Crater there was a four-hour back-and-forth discussion with General Warren about aiding Burnside and broadening the attack. Warren could not see an opportunity, or doubted an advance was practical, or argued "our advantages are lost." The Fifth Corps did not engage.

At 9:30 a.m. Meade ordered Burnside to end the action and withdraw. Burnside fought the order, rushing to headquarters and insisting with heat (in another echo of Fredericksburg) that they had not fought long enough; one more "decided effort" would do it. Meade was sharp in rejecting that argument; he remembered Fredericksburg. The retreat was roughly as costly as the advance, for the Confederates now held the high ground — the edges of the Crater — and made deadly use of it. When it was finally over, the Potomac army had lost some 3,800 men. William Bartlett and Elisha Marshall, commanding the two brigades opening the battle, were both captured, Bartlett after his cork leg, replacing the leg he lost at Yorktown, was shot off.

In reporting to Halleck, General Grant composed an epitaph for the "disaster of Saturday last. . . . It was the saddest affair I have witnessed in the war. Such opportunity for carrying fortifications I have never seen and do not expect again to have." General Meade told his wife it was an affair "very badly managed by Burnside, and has produced a great deal of irritation & bad feeling & I have applied to have him relieved. . . . I am afraid our failure will have a most unfavorable influence on the public mind." And on Northern voters, he might have added. That was on Theodore Lyman's mind: "I presume our father Abraham looks on his election prospects as waning, and wants to know of Ulysses the warrior if some *man* or some *plan* can't be got to do some *thing*. The one word he wants to know WHY THE ARMY OF THE POTOMAC DON'T MOVE?"[18]

A grim General Meade set about cleaning up the command debris from the Battle of the Crater. He told his wife, "Having to fight the enemy on one side, with Burnside & others fighting you at the same time, I sometimes wonder how I get along at all." At Meade's insistence, Grant initiated a court of inquiry to investigate who and what went wrong. The court opened on August 8 and a month later issued a finding exclusive to the Ninth Corps — its generals had conceived the project in hopes and wrecked it in blunders. The three principal agents of defeat were General Burnside, for overall mismanagement, and Generals Ledlie and Ferrero, for neglect of duty and "being in a bomb-proof habitually."

Burnside did not stay for the finding. On August 13, seen off by his lieutenants and a brass band, he departed on a thirty-day leave. Watching the scene, Theodore Lyman observed that his leave "will extend itself, I fancy, indefinitely, so far as this army goes." So it did. Burnside's efforts to be recalled went unheeded. ("I don't care where he goes," said Meade, "so as he is not in my army.") In December the Joint Committee on the Conduct of the War took testimony on the Crater battle, and added its favorite scapegoat General Meade to those responsible. By then, February 1865, its report was little noticed.

Ambrose Burnside's record with the Army of the Potomac was an unhappy one almost from first to last, and at the last it seemed all his failings came into play. He said more than once he was not qualified for high command; in fact he was not qualified for much more than brigade command, his posting at First Bull Run.

On August 5 James Ledlie slipped quietly away on leave, allowed to go with only censure. He resigned his commission in January. Edward Ferrero weathered his censure to stay with the Ninth Corps until December, when he transferred to the Army of the James. In like manner, the Ninth Corps' division of U.S. Colored Troops was moved to the Army of the James, ending its unrewarded stay with the Army of the Potomac. In Burnside's absence, his quietly capable chief of staff John Parke took over the Ninth Corps.

The issue with Ben Butler was always the risk that he would actually try to lead a battle. But now that he had dug himself in at Bermuda Hundred and was (grudgingly) accepted there, he seemed content. He took orders well from Grant, and instead of troublemakers under him, he had generals of skill. E.O.C. Ord, one of Grant's favorites, commanded the Eighteenth Corps. When Bully Brooks resigned for health reasons, David Birney came over from the Potomac army to command the Tenth Corps. Theirs was a stable pairing, which lasted until Birney's death from malaria in October.[19]

While Meade and the Army of the Potomac licked wounds and tried to regain order and morale after the mine disaster, Grant turned his attention to the upper Potomac and getting Phil Sheridan firmly in the saddle there. This war theater had now absorbed the Army of the Potomac's Sixth Corps, most of Sheridan's cavalry, and the Nineteenth Corps, up

from Louisiana and originally intended for the Potomac army. All eyes —
including voters' eyes — focused on the Shenandoah. It was essential that
the Lincoln administration regain control of the Valley before November.

In dispatching Sheridan to his new command, Grant outlined his mission in an August 1 telegram to Halleck: "I want Sheridan put in command of all the troops in the field, with instructions to put himself south
of the enemy and follow him to the death. Wherever the enemy goes let
our troops go also." This created a stir at Washington, where Stanton and
Halleck fussed that Sheridan was too young (age thirty-three) and inexperienced; and what was to be done with Hunter? Halleck showed Grant's
telegram to the president.

For the first time since this 1864 campaign began, Mr. Lincoln delivered
sharp, blunt advice to his general-in-chief, based on three years' dealings
with army bureaucracy. In an August 3 telegram he said the instructions
for Sheridan were "exactly right," but then he asked Grant to look over the
dispatches "you may have received from here even since you made that order, and discover, if you can, that there is any idea in the head of any one
here of 'putting our army south of the enemy,' or of 'following him to the
death' in any direction. I repeat to you it will neither be done or attempted,
unless you watch it every day and hour and force it."

With an unspoken "Yes, Mr. President," Grant replied that he would
leave immediately for Washington and meet with the Valley command.
On the scene, in person, in a remarkably short time, Grant slashed through
the thicket of departmental conflicts and War Department obfuscation to
get who and what he wanted for the Shenandoah Valley. He met Hunter
and his variegated command on the Monocacy ("Doing nothing & not
knowing what enemy was doing," Colonel Comstock reported), and issued him orders to drive the Rebels south — and concurrently, "Nothing
should be left to invite the enemy to return. Take all provisions, forage and
stock wanted for the use of your command. Such as cannot be consumed,
destroy." Grant had earlier spelled out this tactic to Halleck in more vivid
terms: In pursuing the enemy south, "eat out Virginia clear and clean as
far as they go, so that crows flying over it for the balance of this season will
have to carry their provender with them."

David Hunter eased matters by resigning, on the grounds that Halleck
distrusted his fitness to command. Grant thought Hunter "showed a patriotism that was none too common in the army." This cleared the way
for Grant to appoint Sheridan commander of the joint forces in the newly
designated Middle Military Division, his orders the same as those issued

to Hunter. Sheridan took direction only from the general-in-chief. As one of Grant's staff put it, "Halleck has no control over troops . . . can give no orders and exercise no discretion. Grant now runs the whole machine independently of the Washington directory." Grant gave Sheridan full rein: "I feel every confidence that you will do the very best, and will leave you as far as possible to act on your own judgment, and will not embarrass you with orders and instructions."[20]

Back at City Point, Grant appraised the hard-earned lessons of trench warfare. Because of the defense's great advantage, he decided the Yankees could hold their own lines with far fewer men, adding manpower to the offense. He thinned the Bermuda Hundred lines to one man per six feet, the Petersburg lines to one man per four feet. When it came to offense, he ordained there be no attacks on fortifications; rather, probes and flankings and reconnaissances in force. With all the cavalry except David Gregg's division in the Valley, offensives would be primarily infantry. Two weeks after the Crater battle, Grant elected to repeat the idea of paired attacks, one from Bermuda Hundred north of the James, the other at Petersburg south of the James, hoping to catch Lee reinforcing one at the expense of the other.

On August 14, seeking surprise, Hancock's Second Corps embarked on transports at City Point for Deep Bottom on the James, to again try Richmond's defenses. The assault would be made alongside David Birney's Tenth Corps, Army of the James, Hancock commanding. There was delay landing Hancock's men, and further delay organizing the attack against the supposedly thinly manned Rebel lines. Surprise was lost and defenses reinforced. Birney found the fortifications in his sector too imposing to offer attack. Francis Barlow, in command of two Second Corps divisions, was not at his best. His assaults were undermanned and unsupported and unsuccessful. Nor was the Second Corps its old self either. Barlow reported, "The troops exhibited such signs of timidity and demoralization that I was convinced it was out of the question to employ them in this work." Hancock concurred: "The troops are not behaving steadily to-day." Hancock stretched out the Deep Bottom operation to a week, skirmishing and probing, to hold the enemy there while its twin offensive proceeded at Petersburg.

On August 17 General Barlow, worn physically and mentally by the Second Corps' constant combat, pushed to the breaking point by the loss of his wife, Arabella, dead of typhus while nursing in army hospitals, turned his division over to Nelson Miles and took medical leave. Cornelia Hancock, nursing at the City Point army hospital, wrote home, "Gen. Barlow is here played out. Why are they not all played out?" Barlow would only return near the war's end.[21]

The twin to Hancock's expedition set off on August 18 — Gouverneur Warren's Fifth Corps, its objective the Weldon Railroad. Meade directed Warren to make a lodgment on the railroad, destroying it as far south as possible. His was a reconnaissance in force, "in which you will take advantage of any weakness of the enemy that you may perceive; but it is not expected you will fight under serious disadvantages or assault fortifications." Warren wrote his wife that for once he had a "very nice set of instructions" and therefore he felt "much softened towards Genl. Meade for making them without my solicitation so much in accordance with my idea of the way things should be."

Warren moved swiftly and seized the railroad close by the Globe Tavern and began digging in. As to General Lee and the Weldon Railroad, said Theodore Lyman, "To touch this has been like touching a tiger's cubs." On the 18th and again on the 19th, Lee lashed out, seeking gaps in the Yankee lines. But Warren pressed counterattacks, Charles Wainwright's batteries came again to the rescue, and the Ninth Corps furnished support. The next day brought a pause, which Warren seized on to rearrange and enlarge his fieldworks. On August 21 Lee struck again in a desperate attempt to recapture his vital railroad. For the Yankees now the tables were turned — they were defending fortifications rather than attacking them. Colonel Wainwright headed his diary entry for August 21, "We have had a love of a fight today." He recorded his artillery wrecking the first line of a Rebel assault. "Their second line managed to advance to within three hundred yards of our line, but could not stand against a direct fire of canister and a cross-fire of case-shot from six and twenty guns." The four-day fight at Globe Tavern was a Federal victory, although close-run at times and costly — 4,300 casualties. Meade visited Warren's headquarters and found him in good spirits, even proposing a counterattack. "Meade thought not," Lyman reported, "as there seemed little to be gained, since we already had the railroad — a great point truly."[22]

To further threaten the Weldon Railroad, Meade called once more on the Second Corps — once too many times, so it proved. He sent two of Hancock's divisions, under Nelson Miles (formerly Barlow's) and John Gibbon, to Reams Station to tear up track as far south as possible. Hancock was warned that an enemy column was sighted passing west of the Fifth Corps "to operate against General Warren or yourself — most probably against your operations," and was cautioned to look out for it. Hancock did not take the threat seriously, concluding that some old fieldworks erected at Reams Station back in June would serve his purposes. As it happened, these works presented problems, among them dilapidation and facing the wrong way when the Rebels attacked on August 25.

John Gibbon's men of four months before, with their experienced officers, would surely have found a way to meet this threat. John Gibbon's men on this day, many of them, ran away or cowered behind the works and surrendered. Most were new, many of them poor excuses for soldiers in the first place, rounded-up draftees and substitutes and bounty jumpers. Gibbon's brigade commanders were all new, colonels or lieutenant colonels; his regiments were led by lieutenants, his companies by sergeants. He described for his wife the attack on his division, "a portion of which behaved very badly, broke without cause. . . . It was a severe and terrible battle and a mortifying one to the 2nd Corps. . . ."

Hancock rallied Miles's forces and held on until dark and then retreated. Reams Station cost the Second Corps 600 killed and wounded and no fewer than 2,000 captured, plus nine guns and twelve regimental flags. His chief of staff found Hancock deeply stirred, "for it was the first time he had felt the bitterness of defeat during the war." He had not called on Meade for reinforcements, he said, because he needed none if his men had fought properly. At least the Petersburg & Weldon was now blocked securely enough that the Confederates were limited to wagoning supplies from a railhead 30 roundabout miles to Petersburg.

Reams Station brewed a contretemps between Hancock and Gibbon. These were two stiff-necked men, with pride uppermost. Gibbon believed the Second Corps (like General Barlow) was burned out, in need of a stand-down for reorganizing and consolidating and retraining. Hancock's response was a "curt private note" suggesting that for the best interests of the service Gibbon "*give up command of my division!*" That left Gibbon "no choice" but to fire back an official application to be relieved of duty with the Second Corps. Before this went further, Hancock initiated a calming discussion. He admitted he was angry when he wrote his note and agreed to withdraw it, and Gibbon agreed to withdraw his application. They parted, Gibbon wrote, "on tolerably good terms, but there was a soreness of feeling remaining. . . ."[23]

For a month the Petersburg besiegers stood down from offensive operations. Recovery and renewal were required. Manpower numbers had fallen steeply. Returns for August 31 showed the three Army of the Potomac corps — Second, Fifth, and Ninth, plus one division of cavalry — to-

This reminds me of a little joke

A *Harper's Weekly* cartoonist adapts one of storyteller Lincoln's favorite lead-in lines to presidential opponent McClellan, who wields a favorite of his own, a besieging spade.

taling only 28,900 for duty. The Army of the James added only 17,000. Parceling out these forces for action would require the most careful planning.

Meanwhile, the siege lines were steadily expanded and logistics took center stage. City Point grew into a bustling port, with a mile of new wharves hosting scores of steamers and barges, and any number of warehouses and barracks and depots. But the marvel was the quickly built 21-mile-long U.S. Military Railroad connecting City Point to the battlefront. It was assembled and operated by railroad men, and by September 26 was running eighteen scheduled trains a day. General Meade and staff rode back and forth to the war by train.

On August 31 the Democrats in convention in Chicago nominated Major General George Brinton McClellan as their candidate for president. Two campaigns, military and presidential, would run in parallel, closely linked, through the fall months. On August 23 the president had had his cabinet members sign, unseen, a memorandum stating, "It seems exceedingly probable that this Administration will not be re-elected. Then it will be my duty to so co-operate with the President elect, as to save the Union between the election and the inauguration; as he will have secured his election on such ground that he can not possibly save it afterwards." As Lincoln predicted, the Democratic platform included a war-is-a-failure plank. McClellan's acceptance letter sought to whitewash that plank with the promise, "The Union is the one condition of peace." That left a war candidate running on a peace platform. The battlefield would likely decide the presidency. The first battlefield went in Lincoln's direction when Sherman announced on September 2 the capture of Atlanta. Grant ordered a 100-gun salute in the Petersburg lines.[24]

No election-winning strategy seemed likely to emerge at Petersburg anytime soon. Instead, embarrassment — on September 16 Wade Hampton's troopers rustled the Potomac army's cattle herd, enriching Rebel diets. But Potomac army troops in the Shenandoah Valley might advance both the war and the politics, and so General Grant again turned his attention to Phil Sheridan. Sheridan's lieutenants were Horatio Wright, Sixth Corps; William H. Emory, Nineteenth Corps; George Crook, heading the mix of Hunter's troops; and two divisions of Potomac army cavalry and one of Hunter's, all under Alfred Torbert.

Sheridan's first move proved tentative — an advance up the Valley only to find Jubal Early too strongly posted for his taste, then a return to his starting point. But he began carrying out Grant's injunction: "Do all the damage to railroads and crops you can. Carry off stock of all descriptions, and negroes, so as to prevent further planting . . . we want the Shenandoah Valley to remain a barren waste." By order, houses were to be spared, but structures related to foodstuffs — barns, corncribs, smokehouses, gristmills — were put to the torch. "The work of destruction seemed cruel," admitted a Pennsylvania cavalryman, "and the distress it occasioned among the people of all ages and sexes was evident on every hand." This draconian policy was a confession of the Federals' failure to either hold the Valley or to sever the Virginia Central Railroad linking the Valley to Richmond.

Recalling Lincoln's advisory that nothing would get done in the Valley unless he watched it every day and every hour, Grant traveled to Sheridan for a face-to-face meeting on taking the offensive. He brought a plan with him, but deferred to Sheridan's plan, slated for September 19, to strike at Early's posting near Winchester. Grant's approval was succinct and clear. As he told his staff, "I ordered Sheridan to move out and whip Early."

At 3:00 a.m. on the 19th, James Wilson's cavalry led the way across Opequon Creek, followed by Wright's Sixth Corps. This was Sheridan's first battle to command, and (typical of first-timers) his plan was too complicated to manage. The way was through a narrow valley, and for some reason Wright brought along all his trains. This blocked the road for the following Nineteenth Corps, creating a massive traffic jam. An attack scheduled for 6:00 a.m. only developed at noon, and then raggedly enough that a gap opened between the two corps that Early exploited. Davy Russell, who had fought so well for John Sedgwick on the Rappahannock, was killed.

Finally Phil Sheridan, like the shade of Phil Kearny, rode right to the front to clear the tangles with shouts and gestures, treating the troops "to a taste of the sweetest swearing that they had ever heard."

George Crook launched a flanking attack and stabilized the line, and at about 5:00 p.m. the entire Yankee army started forward. "Press them, General—they'll run!" Sheridan shouted to the Sixth Corps' George Getty. "Press them, General—I know they'll run!" The assault included a massive cavalry charge—half a mile wide, three ranks deep, a sight to remember, everyone agreed—that overran the collapsing Rebel ranks. Early's army fell back through Winchester in the darkness and kept going. "We just sent them a whirling through Winchester, and we are after them to-morrow," Sheridan's chief of staff reported. "The army behaved splendidly."

Sheridan followed up on September 22, executing a combination flank and frontal attack, by Crook's and Wright's corps, that drove Early off a position at Fisher's Hill, near Strasburg. The Confederates retreated well up the Valley, and Sheridan pursued for a time and then declared victory. Grant ordered a 100-gun salute at Petersburg. Out of concern for his supply line, Sheridan did not take up Grant's suggestion he continue south to break up the Virginia Central. Instead he fell back to Strasburg and a position behind Cedar Creek . . . burning the land as he went. By not finishing off the Virginia Central, Sheridan granted Jubal Early's Valley campaign a certain validity. Having to divide the Potomac army's cavalry corps between Petersburg and the Valley meant in neither place was it strong enough to destroy the railroads there.[25]

To maintain the pressure, Grant scheduled another one-two punch at Petersburg, Butler attacking north of the James, Meade to the south. On September 29 Butler marshaled David Birney's Tenth Corps and E.O.C. Ord's Eighteenth Corps for a direct assault on the Richmond defenses. The plan adopted was Ben Butler's, and perhaps to general surprise it met with some success. Under cover of a morning fog, Ord's men boldly stormed imposing Fort Harrison, which guarded the James River defenses at Chaffin's Bluff. They caught the fort manned by a skeleton force, and Ord's men scaled the parapets and captured the fort and the trench lines right and left. Ord and division commander George J. Stannard were wounded, but their men dug in, turning the works to their purposes. Birney's Tenth Corps made a fierce fight for nearby Fort Gilmer, trying to widen the breach, but could not take it. The attackers included a brigade of black troops whose wounded and captured received no quarter. The next day the Rebels counterattacked at Fort Harrison, only to be thrown back from their own works. It was a small gain against Richmond and a large gain in Yankee morale.

Meade's simultaneous attack on the Petersburg front was large in ambition but small in accomplishment. The design, using Warren's Fifth Corps and Parke's Ninth, was to seize the Boydton Plank Road, by which the wagon trains from the distant railhead of the broken Weldon Railroad reached Petersburg, and then the South Side Railroad, connecting to Lynchburg. Sheridan had most of the cavalry, so this was an infantry affair. It was Parke's first battle command, and he never made firm contact with the Fifth Corps in the advance. In open-field fighting — rare enough in this campaign — the Rebels blocked the advance and held both vital supply lines.

Chief of Staff Humphreys described for his wife the one notable happening on this discouraging day. He and General Meade and Generals Charles Griffin and Joseph Bartlett and assorted staff members were gathered at the front "when a crashing sound, a plunge & a volcanic shower of dirt covered all the officers in front of me. . . . A shell thrown from a battery of the enemy on our flank . . . had passed between Genl. Meade & myself, had taken off a small part of the tail of my horse . . . grazed heavily Genl. Meade's boot close to the knee, passed between Genl. Griffin & Genl. Bartlett, burying itself in the ground five feet behind them & covering them & their staff with dirt. It did not explode." General Meade told *his* wife, "A more wonderful escape I never saw."[26]

In mid-October Sheridan went to Washington to try and get some answers about what to do next with his Valley command. Jubal Early settled the matter for him. In the foggy early dawn of October 19 Early crept up to Cedar Creek and lashed out at the weak link in the Federal position, George Crook's leftovers from David Hunter's old command. Taken in flank and rear, Crook's line broke and fled, forcing back William Emory's Nineteenth Corps and Horatio Wright's Sixth Corps. Wright held command in Sheridan's absence, and despite taking a bullet in the jaw he managed to stem the retreat and start patching together a new line. At that moment Phil Sheridan galloped onto the battlefield like an avenging angel. Sheridan was in Winchester that morning on his return from Washington, and the rising sounds of gunnery drew him south like a magnet. "Sheridan's Ride" would become a legend, and Sheridan a larger-than-life hero in an Army of the Potomac short of heroes — even if "on assignment" on this occasion.

Sheridan did not halt the retreat — Wright had already done that — but

Above: Alfred Waud sketched Phil Sheridan's famous ride to rally his retreating troops and lead them to victory at Cedar Creek in the Shenandoah Valley on October 19. Below: in another Waud sketch, George Armstrong Custer presents Confederate colors captured at Cedar Creek in a ceremony at the War Department in Washington.

he did ride the lines to rally the troops personally and to organize a counterattack, promising they would have their old camps back by nightfall and put Jubal Early to rout in the bargain. He was greeted with cheers — cheers for Little Phil that men in the Sixth Corps, at least, had not delivered since the days of Little Mac. Sheridan was as good as his promise. By 4 o'clock he had everyone lined up and sounded the charge, and the Valley army overwhelmed Early's lines and drove the Rebels south and all but out of the war. "Affairs at times looked badly," Sheridan telegraphed Grant, "but by the gallantry of our brave officers and men disaster has been converted into a splendid victory." At Petersburg there was yet another 100-gun salute. The victory earned Sheridan a major generalship in the regular army.[27]

Grant wanted one more attempt on the Petersburg front before winter — and before the presidential election. That meant the movement would be hedged about with cautions; a victory would be welcome but a defeat would not be tolerated. The objectives were the same as a month earlier: turning the Confederate right to take the Boydton Plank Road and the South Side Railroad. With most of the cavalry in the Valley, there was no opportunity to raid the South Side. Meade planned, and Grant approved, the operation for October 27, utilizing the Second, Fifth, and Ninth Corps.

The plan called for exploring the extent of the enemy line and turning it, always taking note of the order (to John Parke) "If he finds the enemy intrenched and their works well manned, he is not to attack. . . ." In fact the Rebels had enhanced their entrenchments and extended them and manned them well. Hancock got into a sharp fight out on the flank at the Boydton Road and had the better of it, but that was the best result of the day; at least for Hancock it helped fade the August stain of Reams Station. Theodore Lyman summed up for his wife: While the operation was labeled a reconnaissance in force, "it would be more fair to call it an 'attempt,' whose success depended on the enemy not having certain advantages of position. But they were found *to have* those advantages, and so here we are back again, nobody having fought much but Hancock . . . this attempt may be called a *well*-conducted fizzle. . . ."[28]

On November 8, President Lincoln was reelected with 55 percent of the popular vote. As to battlefield victories, the Army of the Potomac, except for Sheridan with the Sixth Corps and the cavalry corps in the Valley, cannot be said to have influenced the outcome. In the soldier voting, however, the men of the Army of the Potomac overwhelmingly rejected their once-revered commander. Of 23,000 voting, seven of ten chose Mr. Lincoln. Of fifty-one Pennsylvania regiments, six registered a majority for McClellan. By all accounts, it was the Democrats' war-as-a-failure platform plank that decided so many soldier voters. They were bound to see the war through to victory to properly honor all those who fell on the way.

According to General Meade, he, Grant, and nearly all the general officers of the Potomac army did not vote in the election. But not all were so neutral in their views. McClellan's candidacy struck Meade as "out of the frying pan into the fire." Henry Hunt and John Gibbon were McClellan men, Gibbon injudiciously so, believing only he, not "this administration and its fanatical principles," could bring the war to a close. Meade took note that Gibbon "was quite calm & seemed to take the result of the election better than I expected." Then there was the case of Lieutenant Colonel Martin T. McMahon, Sixth Corps staff, an outspoken supporter of candidate McClellan. "What is the consequence?" wrote an outraged Colonel Lyman. "He is, without any warning, mustered out of the service!"

McMahon was a victim of the long arm of Secretary of War Edwin Stanton, whose views on disloyalty were expansive indeed. At this time, too, Stanton took final satisfaction in the case of Charles Pomeroy Stone. After his unjust imprisonment, Brigadier General Stone eventually found service in the Department of the Gulf, only to have Stanton abruptly muster him out of the volunteer service, leaving him colonel in the regulars. In the Army of the Potomac Stone wrangled a brigade of regulars in the Fifth Corps and served for a time at Petersburg. But he believed himself under Stanton's surveillance, subject to whispers of disloyalty . . . and it drove him to quit the service. (In a touch of irony, Charles Stone would play a role in the installation of the Statue of Liberty.)[29]

On November 13, General Grant wrote a friend about the consequences of the recent election: "The overwhelming majority received by M. Lincoln, and the quiet with which the election went off, will prove a terrible damper to the rebels. It will be worth more than a victory in the field both in its effect on the rebels and in its influence abroad." Doubts and doubters were banished. The Peace Democrats and the Copperheads were in retreat; the North would not be turning its back on its soldiers. Beyond Virginia the Confederacy was being cleaved apart in these closing months of 1864. Admiral David Farragut had broken into Mobile Bay. From captured Atlanta Sherman's army was marching to the sea. At Nashville the Rebels' Western army was routed. Wilmington, the South's last port for blockade runners, was made a target.

The Army of the Potomac's task in this vast scheme of things was to keep Robert E. Lee caged at Petersburg. Mr. Lincoln caught the essence in a telegram to Grant: "I have seen your despatch expressing your unwillingness to break your hold where you are. Neither am I willing. Hold on with a bull-dog grip, and chew & choke, as much as possible."

The bulldog grip held fast through the muddy Virginia winter. While taking up winter quarters was not officially sanctioned, everyone simply closed up and weatherproofed their quarters — flooring tents, building chimneys for huts, tightening bombproofs. For the Federals at least, it was a well-supplied siege. Grant alerted Meade to be ready to pursue any force Lee might detach to try and halt Sherman's march across the heart of the Confederacy. Supplies and arms were stockpiled, but nothing came of the alarm. Lee's only reinforcement went to Early in the Valley . . . which only lengthened Early's casualty lists.

On December 7, Meade sent Warren's Fifth Corps, reinforced by Gershom Mott's Second Corps division and David Gregg's cavalry division, to put the Petersburg & Weldon permanently out of service. For the first time in this extended railroad war between the two armies, Warren met no opposition. Winter weather caused the most discomfort. Two bridges and some 18 miles of track were destroyed — ties burned and rails twisted — reaching to within 10 miles of the North Carolina border. Warren described the process as "forming a line of battle on the railroad, each division destroying all on its front, and then moving to the left alternately."[30]

Winter saw a shuffling in the Federal high command. The noteworthy change was Winfield Hancock's. The shoddy manpower coming into the army had inspired in the War Department the idea of a Veterans Corps — two- and three-year veteran volunteers who had served their time and might reenlist if the money was right and if they could serve under a general of Hancock's reputation. The money was $400, plus any local bounty, and Hancock was interested. He knew he had twice been spoken of to replace Meade, but now Meade seemed safe in his post, and anyway Meade was a friend. Hancock wrote Francis Barlow, "When Grant told me the other day about the Veterans Corps & that it would in all probability be a separate command I told him that it would suit me . . . I would like a separate command of course."

On November 25 Hancock left his treasured Second Corps for his new post. A count of 20,000 men was projected for the Veterans Corps, but that proved a chimera. Recruiting gained only 4,400. In February 1865 Hancock replaced Sheridan, recalled to the Army of the Potomac, as head of the Middle Military Division, and he was assigned the Nineteenth Corps. But the war ended with his command sitting on the distant sideline, a bittersweet ending for Hancock the Superb.

In command changes made during the winter of 1864–65, General Meade named his chief of staff, Andrew Humphreys (left), to head the Second Corps, and John Gibbon (right) to take over the reconstituted Twenty-fourth Corps.

John Gibbon was the Second Corps' senior division commander, but Meade did not think him right to replace Hancock. "Gibbon has lost ground considerably this campaign," he told his wife. "I think him discontented & in consequence indifferent. He has not shown the energy & fine qualities which so distinguished him up to Gettysburg." Meade nominated Andrew Humphreys for the Second Corps post. Chief of Staff Humphreys was itching for a combat posting. "The Army is terribly dull," he wrote his wife. "So many changes have taken place, so many accustomed faces are absent, wounded; the Army is so strung out in trenches and is so reduced in numbers and altered in composition that it is to the old officers who have witnessed all these transformations, a dull and sad place." Humphreys "made so much matter of it," said Meade, that he was relieved there was this opening for him. Alexander Webb, wounded at Spotsylvania, returned to become Meade's chief of staff.

John Gibbon ended up with an army corps after all. The Army of the James was overhauled, starting at the top. With the election over, Ben Butler's political influence was nothing to worry about. He was sent off to command an expedition against Fort Fisher, guarding Wilmington, the Confederacy's last window on the world. (Butler bungled this assignment and Grant demanded him gone. On January 7, 1865, Butler was replaced as head of the Department of Virginia and North Carolina, and this longtime thorn in the side of the Potomac army was plucked out.) E.O.C. Ord took Butler's place as head of the department and the Army of the James. The James army's two corps, Eighteenth and Tenth, were reconstituted as the new Twenty-fourth Corps (John Gibbon commanding) and the new Twenty-fifth Corps (Godfrey Weitzel). All the white troops in the old corps went to Gibbon and all the black troops to Weitzel. "I am now better satisfied even than if I had gotten the 2d Corps," Gibbon told his wife.[31]

For what most observers in early 1865 could see as the closing act of the rebellion, the Army of the Potomac was led by a cast of generals very different from that of May 1864. Andrew Humphreys, the Second Corps' new commander, had new division commanders Nelson Miles and Thomas Smyth to go with Gershom Mott. The Fifth Corps was the least changed — Gouverneur Warren commanding, division heads Charles Griffin and Samuel Crawford, joined by the new man Romeyn Ayres. The Sixth Corps' command was all new: Horatio Wright at corps, Frank Wheaton, George Getty, and Truman Seymour at division. The Ninth Corps had new commander John Parke and new division commander John Hartranft to go with Orlando Willcox and Robert Potter. Cavalry corps veteran David Gregg resigned, citing personal reasons. Apparently he had burned out, like Francis Barlow. George Crook would take his place.

Somewhat to his surprise, George Meade was still at the helm of the Potomac army. If the ravening press and the vicious Committee on the Conduct of the War were to be believed, General Meade had long deserved cashiering. But in fact, Meade and Grant worked very smoothly together at the operational level, to Grant's full satisfaction. What went wrong at Petersburg — the Crater and Reams Station, for example — were not high-command failures but on-the-scene command lapses, or the unsoldierly manpower now filling up the ranks. To be sure, Meade still marked his home letters with grumblings about the lack of appreciation for his services — and now he had good reason.

As early as May 1864, Grant had proposed Meade for major general in the regular army, but the War Department let the matter lag. Then Sheridan's victory at Cedar Creek aroused the War Department, and a special envoy rushed to the battlefield to present Sheridan with promotion to major general, regular army. Meade acknowledged Sheridan's promotion well deserved, but a coup de théâtre staged by Secretary Stanton and aimed at McClellan — promoted hero takes the rank of onetime hero. Meade had "a very plain conversation" with Grant, who pulled strings in praise of Meade, and his promotion was affirmed — and dated August 18, predating Sheridan's. "Whereat," said Colonel Lyman of his chief, "he was right content." Not for long, however, for Senate confirmation did not follow. Meade imagined all his enemies conspiring against him — Sickles, Butterfield, Baldy Smith, Doubleday, Burnside, the Conduct of the War committee, the newspapers. But on February 1, 1865, the Senate confirmed him . . . by 32 to 5. "I really have more friends than I had any idea of," Meade told his wife.[32]

Just then, at City Point, General Meade found himself conversing alone with three Southern dignitaries who had come through the lines under flag of truce in hopes of meeting President Lincoln to discuss peace. They were Confederate officials of rank: Vice President Alexander Stephens, Assistant Secretary of War John A. Campbell, and Senator R.M.T. Hunter. While their meeting with the president was being negotiated, Meade told his wife that he talked very freely with them. In answer to their query, he said peace could only come with a restoration of the Union and a "final" settlement of the slavery question. To their hopes for a cease-fire to negotiate, Meade thought that out of the question, as was amending the Constitution to "protect the states." When they observed it was a pity matters could not be settled by the generals, Meade "feared there was no chance of that." He urged Margaret to say nothing of this, for he had no authority for

Quarters described as "bombproofs" at Fort Sedgwick, widely known as Fort Hell, in the Petersburg siege lines, photographed in 1865 by Timothy O'Sullivan.

speaking thus. He added that when the three commissioners came within the lines and word got about who they were, soldiers on both sides "cried out lustily, 'Peace! peace!'"

Lincoln met with the commissioners on February 3 at Fort Monroe, and they cannot have gained much hope from their earlier talk with General Meade. The president said he was flexible on how the fighting might be stopped, but this was not two countries negotiating a peace treaty. The only terms were reunion and the abolition of slavery. Stephens, Campbell, and Hunter retired to Richmond empty-handed. On February 5 the war went on.

Once more the Potomac army pushed toward the Boydton Plank Road and the South Side Railroad. The fighting lasted three days, involving primarily the Second Corps, with help from the Sixth and Ninth. As always Lee reacted sharply to threats to these vital supply routes. Constrained by Grant's warning against challenging entrenchments and hampered by sleet and icy temperatures, the offensive gained perhaps four miles to the vicinity of Hatcher's Run, and entrenched. "This brings us no nearer the South Side Railroad," Grant admitted, "but will enable us to secure a good crossing of Hatcher's Run when we do move."

With that the Army of the Potomac stood in place, waiting for the Confederacy's last throes. Generals and staffs went on leave. Generals' wives and children visited the front, including the Grant and Meade families. Visitors of every stripe came to see the war before it was over. They went on tours of the lines, and for the most important the troops were turned out in review. Ladies arrived, said Theodore Lyman, in batches, boodles, posses, parcels. He filled his journal with accounts of officers sent from foreign powers great and small to inspect this latest in siege warfare.

There were more 100-gun salutes as Sherman's conquering army stormed north through the Carolinas. Sheridan finished off his conquest of the Valley, tearing up the Virginia Central (finally) and breaking the James River Canal. He then returned to the Potomac army. On March 2 General Lee wrote to General Grant proposing "a satisfactory adjustment of the present unhappy difficulties by means of a military convention. . . ." Grant was instructed by Lincoln "to have no conference with General Lee, unless it be for the capitulation of General Lee's army. . . ." As to the immediate future, there was the president's second inaugural, on March 4: "With malice toward none; with charity for all; with firmness in the right, as God gives us to see the right, let us strive on to finish the work we are in. . . ."[33]

• • •

Wives and families and visitors were packed off, and on March 24 Grant sent to Generals Meade, Ord, and Sheridan orders for his intended final offensive against the Army of Northern Virginia. It had the double purpose (Grant wrote) "of turning the enemy out of his present position around Petersburg, and to insure the success of the cavalry under General Sheridan . . . in its efforts to reach and destroy the South Side and Danville Railroads." The one new thing here was the force applied — Humphreys's Second, Warren's Fifth, and Wright's Sixth Corps, Army of the Potomac; Gibbon's Twenty-fourth Corps, Army of the James; and the full-strength cavalry corps — to attempt what had been tried repeatedly over the past eight months. Weitzel's Twenty-fifth Corps would hold the Richmond front, Parke's Ninth Corps the Petersburg front. Initiative (not a Potomac army strength) was stressed — any general who saw an opening was to seize it without waiting for orders. Grant told Sherman that he would take personal charge. "I shall start with no distinct view further from holding Lee's forces from following Sheridan. But I shall be along myself and will take advantage of any thing that turns up."

While planning his offensive, Grant invited Lincoln to City Point. "I would like very much to see you, and I think the rest would do you good." It was his quiet way of assuring that the president, who had trusted him with the supreme command, would be in at the kill. Lincoln accepted readily, and on March 24 reached City Point aboard the steamer *River Queen*. The next morning Lincoln telegraphed his arrival to Secretary Stanton, and added, "There was a little rumpus up the line this morning, ending about where it began."

The "little rumpus" was the Army of Northern Virginia's final offensive, General Lee's attempt to disrupt the pending Yankee advance. Before dawn he struck at Fort Stedman, in the Ninth Corps sector where Baldy Smith had missed his golden opportunity to seize Petersburg back in June, and captured it. But John Parke secured the flanks of the breakthrough and counterattacked and drove the Rebels back into their lines. It cost Lee 4,000 men. Clearly General Parke had taken a firm grip on the Ninth Corps. "It was perfectly the Mine turned just the other way!" said Colonel Lyman.

Lyman entered in his journal on March 28, "There were together Grant, Sherman, Meade, and Sheridan, a sight for remembrance!" Sherman had come up by steamer from North Carolina for this highest of high command gatherings to plot strategy. After the generals talked, Grant and Sherman, who faced the two major Confederate forces remaining, Lee's and Joe Johnston's, met with the president to talk of an end to the fighting.

The generals would be in charge of getting to that point; then their duty, said Lincoln, was simply to accept the surrender of the Rebel forces, settling immediate terms for those surrenders. As for guidance, he made it clear he wanted an easy peace. (Or as he put it, in the event, "I'd let 'em up easy, let 'em up easy.") Sherman returned to North Carolina and his army, and the Army of the Potomac set out to finally conquer Robert E. Lee.[34]

Sheridan's 9,000-man cavalry corps marched first, swinging well south by west through Dinwiddie Court House, its eventual target the South Side Railroad but more immediately, a road intersection known as Five Forks, four miles or so west of Lee's fortifications. Sheridan took his orders from Grant rather than Meade. Grant sent him off with the mandate, "I now feel like ending the matter if it is possible to do so. . . ." Ord, commanding the Army of the James, marched with Gibbon's Twenty-fourth Corps. Thus a tripartite high command under Grant: Sheridan, Meade, Ord.

On March 29 Humphreys's Second Corps and Warren's Fifth moved out. The Second Corps started from hard-won Hatcher's Run, with the Fifth Corps farther to the left, the far end of the flanking pivot. First blood was drawn by Charles Griffin's division, Fifth Corps, at the western end of the enemy line. It began to rain late on the 29th and on the 30th it became a downpour, turning the landscape into a quagmire. The storm nearly canceled the operation, but Sheridan pleaded for his deep flanking move to go on. Grant agreed, with infantry support. Sheridan wanted Horatio Wright's Sixth Corps that he had worked with in the Valley. The closest infantry to him was Warren's, but, said Sheridan, "I would not like the Fifth Corps to make such an attempt." He did not get his way — Wright just then was in the Petersburg lines — and Grant gave him the Fifth Corps . . . including command over Gouverneur Warren.

March 31 proved not a good day for General Warren. Still under Meade's orders, he followed his own deliberate habits and his scattered corps was caught by a surprise attack that routed two of his divisions. With Griffin's division he soon enough restored his lines without lasting harm (except for the 1,800 casualties), but Grant was displeased: "I do not understand why Warren permitted his corps to be fought in detail." Why had Warren not followed up with a counterattack before the Rebels could get set? Sheridan's cavalry had a rough day as well. "That night," recorded Theodore Lyman, "Griffin's division was ordered down the Boydton road, to the assistance of Sheridan, by Grant, but, on the advice of Meade, the whole corps was sent — with the happiest fruits, as it proved." Happiest fruits for all but Gouverneur Warren.[35]

Sheridan and Warren had a long history, dating back to their dispute at Spotsylvania, and from the first, on this first day of April, things between them did not go well. When the Fifth Corps reached the cavalry at Dinwiddie Court House, Warren was at the tail of it, pushing rather than leading as Sheridan expected. When Warren did reach the front, he did not report to Sheridan for orders for three hours. Finally, there came a decisive intervention by U. S. Grant. Grant too had a fraught history with Warren, revived by Warren's careless conduct the day before, and when he received a report (false, as it proved) that the Fifth Corps lagged reaching Dinwiddie, Grant sent an aide to Sheridan with a verbal message: "General Grant directs me to say to you, that if in your judgment the Fifth Corps would do better under one of the division commanders, you are authorized to relieve General Warren, and order him to report to General Grant, at headquarters." As a Fifth Corps staff man later put it, "General Grant knew that General Sheridan was not a person who could be intrusted with such a weapon and not use it."

The Rebel defenders — George Pickett's division — had entrenched at Five Forks, and Warren made his battle plan based on a faulty reconnoiter by Sheridan. The first of Warren's flanking divisions, Romeyn Ayres's, barely touched the enemy flank and had to pivot sharply to engage. The second division, under Samuel Crawford, marched harmlessly off into the distance. The third, in reserve, was Charles Griffin's. Griffin alertly saw what was happening, rushed to Ayres's aid, and helped rout Pickett. General Warren, instead of sending an aide after the wandering Crawford and then supervising the attack, went after Crawford himself. His whole corps engaged, but he personally came a bit late to the fight.

That was enough for Phil Sheridan. Without Grant's unsubtle invitation for him to act (or had he rapport with Warren), he surely would have done nothing. Five Forks, after all, was a decisive, overwhelming Federal victory, 5,000 prisoners, very largely the Fifth Corps' doing, and Warren had caused no harm nor delayed the victory. Instead, Sheridan said to Warren's aide announcing the spoils collected, "Tell General Warren that, by God! I say he was not at the front. That is all I have got to say to him." That was followed by Sheridan's written order to Warren, relieving him of his command. Sheridan turned the Fifth Corps over to Charles Griffin. Warren went to Sheridan and asked him if he would reconsider the order. "Reconsider, hell!" Sheridan snapped. "I don't reconsider my decisions. Obey the order!" The war was in the balance, Grant mistrusted Warren to carry it on, and Phil Sheridan served as the ruthless bearer of Grant's bidding.

(Warren sought a court of inquiry, but it was shunted aside in the rush of events. Only in 1879 was a Warren court convened. It dragged on for two years, and in its finding implied, but did not actually say, that Warren was unjustly removed from his corps command. Only after Warren's death, in 1882, was the record of the court of inquiry published. So far as keeping his corps command, Gouverneur Warren was third time unlucky.)[36]

Grant staff man Horace Porter, assigned to Sheridan, rushed back to headquarters with the news of Five Forks, and Grant announced an immediate assault all along the lines. Humphreys should press the Second Corps against the Confederates' right, with Ord lending support. To Meade went the instruction, "Wright and Parke should both be directed to feel for a chance to get through the enemy's line at once, and if they can get through should push on to-night." Wright got the order delayed to 4:00 a.m. April 2, promising he "would make the fur fly!" Everyone should know, said Grant, that everything was being pushed.

Came April 2, the day at long last the Petersburg lines were cracked wide open. Wright's Sixth Corps, making the fur fly, created the first breach after a hard fight, widened and deepened it (killing A. P. Hill), and was joined by Ord with Gibbon's Twenty-fourth Corps. Humphreys linked the Second Corps with (now Griffin's) Fifth Corps at Five Forks. General Meade hurried to the front, and rode the long-fought-over Boydton Plank Road into Petersburg. "As we struck the rear of the column marching onward," Colonel Lyman made note, "the men broke into loud cheers, which were continued all along. It was grand!" Grant too entered Petersburg, and invited Mr. Lincoln to join him. As they sat together on a front porch on Market Street, Lincoln said, "Do you know, general, that I have had a sort of sneaking idea for some days that you intended to do something like this." Grant replied that it was his thought all along that the Army of the Potomac gain the final triumph over Lee's army. "I have always felt confident that our troops here were amply able to handle Lee." And so it was — the Army of the Potomac versus the Army of Northern Virginia — to the very end. The Twenty-fourth Corps (Army of the James) was there to be sure, but it was led by veteran Potomac army general John Gibbon.[37]

Morning on April 3 saw Godfrey Weitzel's Twenty-fifth Corps of black troops enter Richmond as conquerors. The Confederate government had evacuated by rail to Danville, and much of the city was afire. The rest of the Federal forces hurried in pursuit of Lee. "We have had three glorious days," Meade wrote his wife on April 3, "the fighting not so severe as much we have done before, but in the results."

It was supposed that Lee would try to reach Joe Johnston's army in

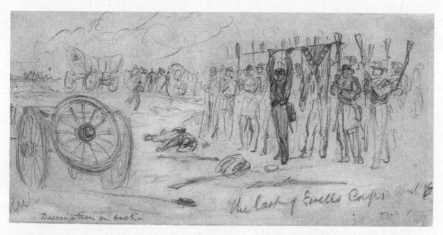

Alfred Waud captioned his sketch "The Last of Ewells Corps April 6." Dick Ewell and the greater part of his army corps were captured at Sailor's Creek.

North Carolina to carry on the fight, and to do so he would have to supply himself from the two railroads left to him, the South Side and the Richmond & Danville. The two lines intersected at Burkeville, 50 miles west of Petersburg, and Burkeville became the target of Sheridan's cavalry, marching with Griffin's Fifth Corps. Behind them came Meade with Wright's Sixth Corps and Humphreys's Second (Francis Barlow was back to command a Second Corps division for the finale). Ord traced the South Side with Gibbon's Twenty-fourth Corps and Parke's Ninth in support.

Lee sought to assemble the pieces of his broken army at Amelia Court House, on the Richmond & Danville some 18 miles northeast of Burkeville, only to find his way blocked midway at Jetersville by Sheridan's cavalry-infantry force. His only recourse now was due west, aiming for Lynchburg, depending on the South Side line. On April 5 Sheridan sent to Grant, "I wish you were here yourself. I feel confident of capturing the Army of Northern Virginia if we exert ourselves. I see no escape for Lee." Grant came up to the front and treated with both Sheridan and Meade. To straighten lines of communication, Meade reclaimed the Fifth Corps to the Potomac army, and Sheridan with the cavalry continued dealing independently with Grant. Sheridan was his usual aggressive self, but Meade, despite suffering from a malarial attack, kept pace, starting his pursuing columns on the road at 1:00 a.m.

Lee's army was exhausted, short of rations and fodder, and leaked men at every mile. Lyman reported, "The way was strewn with ammunition, waggons, tents, camp baggage, muskets. . . ." On April 6 at Sailor's Creek, close by the Appomattox River, the Sixth Corps caught the Rebel rear guard and all but destroyed it, capturing some 6,000 men, including Dick Ewell and most of his generals. Ewell told his captors, "It is murder to continue the contest longer," and said Lee would probably surrender if summoned.

That evening one of Sheridan's staff reached General Meade and read out a dispatch: "I attacked them with two divisions of the Sixth Army Corps and routed them handsomely. . . ." Meade supposed the dispatch was from Wright, Lyman noted, "but, when the name was read, P. H. Sheridan; he exclaimed, 'And so Wright *was not there!*' — 'Oh, yes!' replied the officer. Meade was thoroughly vexed at this combination of fine news and borrowed (yea pilfered) glory." Meade had reason to grumble, for all of Sheridan's engagements were dependent on Potomac army infantry.

Sheridan closed his dispatch, "If the thing is pressed I think Lee will surrender." When shown a copy of this dispatch, Mr. Lincoln sent to Grant, "Gen. Sheridan says, 'If the thing is pressed I think that Lee will surrender.' Let the *thing* be pressed."

At Farmville, on the South Side Railroad, Lee found some rations, and he crossed to the north side of the Appomattox and struck off westward toward Lynchburg. He ordered Lynchburg to have rations and fodder meet him at Appomattox Station. But on April 7 Humphreys with the Second Corps found an Appomattox bridge the Confederates had failed to destroy, and with the Sixth Corps close behind him, stepped up the pursuit. Griffin's Fifth Corps and Gibbon's Twenty-fourth pursued south of the river. Sheridan's troopers set out for Appomattox Station. The April 7 fighting claimed Thomas Smyth, the last Army of the Potomac general to be killed.

Grant recognized his opponent as too proud to open talks. On April 7 he took the initiative with a note sent through the lines addressed to General Lee: "The result of the last week must convince you of the hopelessness of further resistance on the part of the Army of Northern Va. in this struggle. I feel that it is so and regard it as my duty to shift from myself, the responsibility of any further effusion of blood by asking of you the surrender of that portion of the C. S. Army known as the Army of Northern Va."[38]

Lee's response did not concede Grant's view of the situation, but did ask what terms would be offered regarding surrender. "In reply," Grant wrote, "I would say that *peace* being my great desire there is but one condition I insist upon, namely: that the men and officers surrendered shall be disqualified for taking up arms again, against the Government of the United

The county courthouse at Appomattox Court House, April 1865, well picketed by Federal soldiers, photographed after Lee's surrender by Timothy O'Sullivan.

States. . . ." He said he would meet to discuss the particulars of surrender at any place Lee designated. This correspondence continued under flags of truce, and April 8 passed with little gunfire except on Sheridan's front, where he captured Lee's supply trains at Appomattox Station. With Griffin's Fifth Corps and Gibbon's Twenty-fourth he held a blocking position. On Lee's heels were Humphreys's Second Corps and Wright's Sixth. Grant was in good spirits; to Colonel Lyman's amusement he greeted General Meade with a sprightly, "How are you, old fellow." Seeing the truce flags, belligerent Phil Sheridan complained, "Damn them, I wish they had held out an hour longer and I would have whipped hell out of them." He was restrained. It would not be long now.

It ended on April 9, Palm Sunday, at Appomattox Court House, in the parlor of Wilmer McLean, who had moved his family away from the war-torn Bull Run area to these safer precincts. Grant wrote out surrender terms and Lee agreed to them. The critical sentence, ensuring an unhindered transition from war to peace, read, "Each officer and man will be allowed to return to their homes not to be disturbed by United States Authority so long as they observe their parole and the laws in force where they may reside."[39]

General Meade and his Potomac army headquarters were five miles from this history being made in Mr. McLean's parlor, and only at 5:00 p.m. did news reach there of the surrender. Chief of Staff Alex Webb led three cheers for the news and three cheers more for General Meade. Then long-suffering, long-patient George Meade mounted his horse and galloped through the Second and Sixth Corps, waving his hat and spreading the (good) news like a latter-day Paul Revere. A soldier heard him say, "Boys, your work is done. Lee has surrendered. You can go home."

"Such a scene followed as I can never see again," wrote Theodore Lyman. "The soldiers rushed, perfectly crazy, to the road-side, and there crowding in dense masses, shouted, screamed, yelled, threw up their hats and hopped madly up and down! The batteries were run out and began firing, the bands played, the flags waved. The noise of the cheering was such that my very ears rang."

Meade had not been invited to the surrender at the McLean house, but he determined to meet his opposite number before the armies parted. On April 10 he rode through the now-peaceful lines to meet his engineer corps comrade from the old army. "What are you doing with all that gray in your beard?" Lee exclaimed. "That *you* have a great deal to do with!" Meade replied. They talked for some time, Lee admitting that at the surrender he had but 10,000 armed men left for duty. Meade told Margaret of meeting Lee, Longstreet, and many others. They were all affable and cordial, he said, and "uniformly said that, if any conciliatory policy was extended to the South, peace would at once be made."

The war was not yet over. There was still Joe Johnston's army to deal with, and on April 11 Meade led the Second and Sixth Corps back toward Burkeville to attend to that if needed. That left the Fifth Corps and the Twenty-fourth Corps (Army of the James) at Appomattox Court House to mark a ceremonial end to the Army of Northern Virginia. The Federals in that ceremony would of course be from the Army of the Potomac (but with neither Grant nor Meade nor Lee present). On April 12 Charles Griffin chose First Division, Fifth Corps, Joseph Bartlett commanding, to take the formal surrender. Unit by unit the Confederates marched past and stacked arms and returned to their camps and received their paroles. The next day Joshua Chamberlain wrote his sister of the ceremony, of receiving the Confederates "with the honors due to troops, at a shoulder & in silence. They came to a shoulder on passing my flag & preserved perfect order." A half century later Chamberlain relived his emotions of that moment. "On our part not a sound of trumpet more, nor roll of drum; not a cheer, nor word nor whisper of vain-glorying . . . but an awed stillness rather, and breath-holding, as if it were the passing of the dead!"[40]

The Fifth Corps then marched off to join the rest of the Potomac army ... which army, on April 14, suffered its final casualty of the war — the commander-in-chief. The Army of the Potomac had always been Lincoln's army. The president's death shocked and deeply moved General Meade. Meade was never a party to that cohort of generals who derided or patronized the president, and the order to the troops that he prepared announcing the assassination reflected his understanding of just how much the Army of the Potomac owed to Lincoln. "By this army this announcement will be received with profound sorrow, and deep horror and indignation," he wrote. "The President, by the active interest he ever took in the welfare of this army, and by his presence in frequent visits, especially during the recent operations, had particularly endeared himself to both officers and soldiers, all of whom regarded him as a generous friend. An honest man, a noble patriot, and sagacious statesman has fallen! No greater loss, at this particular moment, could have befallen our country."

With Joe Johnston surrendered to Sherman, there was one last thing before the boys could start going home — the Grand Review in Washington. The Army of the Potomac would march first, on May 23, with Sherman's army marching the next day. The review promised to lend the capital a brighter mood, with flags and bunting replacing the mourning and crepe and colors at half-mast for the slain president. May 23 was a fine spring day, blue sky, light breeze. There were reviewing stands along Pennsylvania Avenue, with the main pavilion in front of the White House for distinguished guests. An estimated 75,000 spectators lined the route. Three corps of infantry — Ninth, Fifth, and Second — stepped off at 9 o'clock that morning. (The Sixth Corps and part of Sheridan's cavalry were absent on assignment.) These 80,000 put on a good show. General Meade led the parade to the pavilion, where he dismounted and joined his family in the stands. There were cavalry, engineers, and artillery with the marchers. The Army of the Potomac had been Washington's defender throughout the war years, and it was applauded with enthusiasm.

But the Potomac army that marched down Pennsylvania Avenue in spring 1865 was almost a completely new army, top to bottom, from the Potomac army that went to war on the Virginia Peninsula in spring 1862. Only a handful of officers of position from those first days remained at Appomattox — Meade himself, Henry Hunt, Andrew Humphreys, Charles Griffin, Joseph Bartlett, Truman Seymour (the latter two with the Sixth Corps and not at the Grand Review). Army commanders — McDowell, McClellan, Pope, Burnside, Hooker — had come and gone. Whole army corps had come and gone — First, Third, Fourth, Eleventh, Twelfth.

Grand Review, May 23, 1865: In rank upon rank, the Army of the
Potomac's final march, down Pennsylvania Avenue from the Capitol.

Twenty-one generals were dead and gone serving the Army of the Po-
tomac — Isaac Stevens, Phil Kearny, Jesse Reno, Joseph Mansfield, Israel
Richardson, Isaac Rodman, George Bayard, Hiram Berry, Amiel Whipple,
Samuel Zook, Elon Farnsworth, John Reynolds, John Buford, Alexander
Hays, James Wadsworth, John Sedgwick, Thomas Stevenson, James Rice,
David Birney, David Russell, Thomas Smyth.

Generals left over cause or controversy — Fitz John Porter, Charles
Stone, Dan Sickles, Dan Butterfield, Baldy Smith. Others were pushed out,
for reasons good or ill — Sam Heintzelman, William Franklin, George
Sykes, Gouverneur Warren. The list of ex-Potomac army generals was un-
imaginably long.

For all the turnover at the top — six command postings in two years before General Meade commanded the last nearly two years — the Army of
the Potomac conquered, forcing the surrender of its renowned opponent.
Obscured by the extensive turnover of generals, a vital, solid core of leadership remained, survived, prevailed. It was this lesser-known half of the
high command that held the Potomac army together through one battlefield hellfire after another. Increasingly volunteers as the war dragged on,
they climbed from regiment, brigade, division, and some to corps, furnishing inspiring leadership, trust, and morale.

General Grant, who was said to have wondered, when he became general-in-chief, what was wrong with the Army of the Potomac, had at the end an epiphany. "This army," he said, "has now won a most decisive victory and followed the enemy. That is all it ever wanted to make it as good an army as ever fought a battle." It was for that brave army that Andrew Humphreys spoke on April 9: "One great satisfaction is the fact that the Army of the Potomac has completely destroyed, annihilated the Army of Northern Virginia, its old opponent. This made the most wonderful campaign on record, and will now receive the credit it was entitled to for former deeds."[41]

Epilogue

WHEN GENERAL MEADE galloped through the camps early on the evening of April 9 shouting, "Boys, your work is done" and they could go home, he was a bit premature. Only on June 28 did the books close on the Army of the Potomac. Including its phase being known as the Army of Northeastern Virginia, it had existed four years and one month. Like its men, its generals would scatter to the four winds in the war's aftermath.

General-in-Chief Winfield Scott, who saw the Potomac army through its fledgling beginnings, spent nearly all his few retirement years quartered at West Point. Except for some advice to Mr. Lincoln, his role was done in a matter of a year or so. He died in 1866, age seventy-nine. Scott grieved that McClellan's 1862 Peninsula campaign against Richmond, a replica of his own 1847 campaign against Mexico City, had not similarly ended the war.

Irvin McDowell, commander at First Bull Run of what became the Army of the Potomac, found himself on the shelf and unassigned for long months following Second Bull Run. In 1864 he was ordered to the Department of the Pacific, and spent the years until his retirement in 1882 in various departmental commands, ending finally on the West Coast. Seniority rather than merit earned McDowell a regular-army major generalship in 1872. He left no writings on the war.

George Brinton McClellan, McDowell's successor at the Army of the Potomac and Scott's successor as general-in-chief, chose self-imposed exile to assuage his failed presidential ambitions. He resigned his army commission on Election Day and early in 1865 sailed for Europe. He remained abroad three and a half years where, preceded by his published *Report,* he was widely acclaimed. (Helmuth von Moltke, the Prussian army's chief of staff, said that McClellan would have taken Richmond but for being "shamefully deserted" by the Lincoln government.) McClellan returned to America in 1868, where there was some interest among Democrats in running him again for president . . . only until the Republicans made General

Grant their nominee (the general who took Richmond versus the general who did not).

McClellan made a comfortable living as a railroad executive and engineering consultant, enjoyed lengthy intervals on the Continent, and served three years as governor of New Jersey. He also began a memoir, only rough and half-finished at his untimely death in 1885 at age fifty-eight. This manuscript was taken up by his bumbling literary executor and fleshed out with bits and pieces old and new and home letters that McClellan never intended for publication. The whole was heavily blue-penciled and published under the misleading title *McClellan's Own Story*. General McClellan liked to say that history would do him justice; *Story* only skewed his historical reputation — at least among historians. But in these years he fared well among his contemporaries, and is memorialized by equestrian statues in Washington and Philadelphia.

The next general-in-chief, Henry Halleck, was demoted by General Grant in 1864 to chief War Department clerk, in point of fact his true calling. In 1865 Halleck was ordered to departmental duties in Richmond and after that to the peaceful precincts of the Division of the Pacific. He died in 1872, unmourned for military accomplishment and without literary issue.

Grant, the final wartime general-in-chief, gave up the post for the presidency in 1869. Just as Grant outranked all Civil War generals, his memoir outranked all their such efforts.

John Pope left the Western theater to command the new Army of Virginia, and ended up leading to defeat at Second Bull Run also the forces of McClellan's Army of the Potomac. He was packed off to the Department of the Northwest to contend with the rebelling Sioux. Until his retirement in 1886, Pope remained engaged in Indian pacification matters on the Western plains, where he displayed enlightened policy views rare for the time and place. He wrote on Second Bull Run for the *Battles and Leaders of the Civil War* series.

Pope was hardly enlightened in the matter of the 1878 reopening of the Fitz John Porter court-martial case. He refused to participate in the hearing, and he deplored the overturning of the verdict against Porter for his actions at Second Bull Run. In the years after his cashiering early in 1863, Porter had found employment in mining and engineering projects and service for New York City in such varied positions as fire commissioner, police commissioner, and commissioner of public works. His long battle for vindication was rewarded in 1886 when a Democratic administration — the first since the war — reinstated him as colonel in the regular army and he officially retired. He wrote two articles on the Seven Days for *Battles and Leaders*. Porter lived until 1901, and an equestrian statue honors him in his hometown of Portsmouth, New Hampshire.

In these same years, the Gouverneur Warren case proceeded in parallel notoriety with the Fitz John Porter case. After his abrupt firing from the Fifth Corps by Phil Sheridan on the eve of Appomattox, General Warren applied for a court of inquiry, as was his right. But Grant, as general-in-chief and then as president, squelched any potentially embarrassing review of the case. While he sought to clear Sheridan's stain from his good name, Lieutenant Colonel Warren, Corps of Engineers, supervised projects across the West and Midwest and then on the Atlantic coast. Finally, in 1879, under new president Rutherford B. Hayes, a court of inquiry was convened. Its finding — that Warren's conduct at Five Forks did not justify his being relieved — went to Secretary of War Robert Lincoln, the president's son. Lincoln sat on the finding despite a presidential order that it be published, and Warren never learned of his vindication. On his deathbed, in 1882, his last words were, "I die a disgraced soldier." Three months later the court's finding was released for publication. Today a bronze figure of a resolute General Warren stands on Little Round Top. Warren never knew of that, either. It was erected in 1888.

The third member of the Potomac army's triad of military injustice, Charles Pomeroy Stone, gained neither a hearing nor a court, only a belated recognition. After Secretary Stanton hounded him out of the army in 1864 on the false charge of disloyalty, Stone found a billet abroad, as chief of staff for the army of the khedive of Egypt, whom he served for thirteen years. His last posting before his death in 1887 was New York Harbor, where he supervised the construction of the base for the Statue of Liberty. Stone was buried with full military honors at West Point.

Ambrose Burnside's return with the Ninth Corps to Virginia in 1864 went little better than his stint commanding that army at Fredericksburg, and he waited fruitlessly for assignment after the failed Battle of the Crater at Petersburg. In April 1865 he resigned his commission, officially closing his unhappy connection with the Army of the Potomac. Rhode Island, his native state, bore the goodhearted Burnside no ill will and chose him three times as governor, and as a United States senator as well. He did not attempt to refight old battles. Senator Burnside died in 1881, and an equestrian statue remembers him in Providence.

Massachusetts's Joe Hooker, Burnside's successor to lead the Potomac army, is also remembered with an equestrian statue, at the State House in Boston. Transferred West following Chancellorsville, Hooker showed well as a corps commander at Chattanooga and in the Atlanta campaign. But both Grant and Sherman resented Hooker as being forced on them by the president and in any case as a disruptive presence. When James McPherson, commanding the Army of the Tennessee, was killed at Atlanta, Hooker was the logical (and senior) general to replace him. Instead, Sherman picked for McPherson's place Otis Howard, hardly qualified for army command but cast as deliberate bait to Joe Hooker, who blamed Howard for the Chancellorsville defeat. Hooker rose to the bait; outraged at the insult, he resigned his corps command. He sat out the war and the immediate postwar years in departmental commands, despite strokes suffered in 1865 and 1867 (likely the consequence of his Chancellorsville wounding) that finally forced his retirement. He died in 1879 at age sixty-five. Fighting Joe left no memoir, but he did bombard an early historian of Chancellorsville with fifty-six letters "clarifying" his role in that battle.

George Gordon Meade, the Potomac army's last and longest-serving commander, lived only seven and a half years after the war. His postwar departmental commands were mostly in the East, headquartered (to his pleasure) in his hometown of Philadelphia. He wrote no memoir and suffered in dignified silence the slings and arrows of those, such as Dan Sickles, who would diminish his triumph at Gettysburg. His son and grandson published his wartime letters, carefully selected and edited, in 1913. The soldiers who had truly earned respect at Gettysburg returned respect to their general commanding, symbolized by his imposing equestrian statue on Cemetery Ridge. A second equestrian statue is at Philadelphia, and he is also the feature of a heavily allegorical monument in Washington. Meade suffered postwar bouts of pneumonia as a consequence of his Glendale wounds, the final one taking his life in 1872, age fifty-six.

Meade's nemesis Dan Sickles did not leave a memoir either, but he did leave for posterity the remains of his right leg, amputated at Gettysburg, on display at the National Museum of Health and Medicine in Maryland. Sickles served for a time as military governor in the South, and as ambassador to Spain, a posting he enlivened with an affair with the former queen, Isabella II. He spoke, often in praise of himself, at veterans' gatherings, and in 1893 returned to Congress, where he helped create the Gettysburg National Military Park. Also in benefit of the battlefield, he chaired New York's Monuments Commission, but left it under a cloud of missing funds. Sickles attended the Gettysburg fiftieth reunion in 1913 and died the next year, unrepentant, age ninety-four.

Among the other Potomac army corps commanders, the most distinguished, in both war and peace, was Winfield Scott Hancock. Postwar

Hancock managed commands on the Western plains and in Reconstruction New Orleans before returning East to head the Division of the Atlantic. While he wrote no memoir and refought no battles, he was always solicitous of his Gettysburg reputation, and his equestrian statues mark Gettysburg, Washington, and Philadelphia. In wartime Hancock had kept his politics carefully under wraps, but by the 1870s he revealed presidential ambitions. He was the Democrats' nominee in 1880, and lost to James A. Garfield in the electoral college, 214 to 155, but trailed him by just 7,018 in the popular vote. When he died in 1886 a week short of his sixty-second birthday, his reputation as Hancock the Superb was intact.

In contrast to Hancock, the roster of discarded and failed Potomac army corps commanders was a long one. Sam Heintzelman of the old Third Corps ended the war on courts-martial duty, mustered out of the volunteers, and retired as colonel, 17th Infantry, in 1869. Heintzelman published no memoir, but the diary he kept is a prime inside source for the McClellan era. George Sykes, bumped out of the Fifth Corps in 1864, died in Texas in 1880 as colonel of the 20th Infantry. Erasmus Keyes, of the old Fourth Corps, resigned his commission in 1864 and went on to business success in California. He published a memoir, useful for the 1861–62 Army of the Potomac.

William B. Franklin, pushed out of the Sixth Corps in 1863 and into the Department of the Gulf, resigned from the army at war's end and for two decades ran the Colt Patent Fire-Arms Manufacturing Company in Hartford, Connecticut. He refought his old campaigns in the pages of *Battles and Leaders* and *Annals of the War*. Franklin's compatriot, William F. "Baldy" Smith, once commander of the Second Corps and later the Eighteenth Corps, also left the service and spent his remaining decades in engineering projects. In nine articles Smith exercised his pen to explain (and excuse) his wartime commands.

Otis Howard's hapless Potomac army career took on new life campaigning under Sherman, where there was far less fighting to be responsible for. Postwar Howard made a difficult start with the Freedmen's Bureau, but became a founder of Howard University for freedmen and served as its president. His frontier duty included the campaign against the Nez Perce, and he held a series of departmental commands before his retirement in 1894. Howard wrote an autobiography and contributed articles to *Battles and Leaders*. He is honored (rather generously) with an equestrian statue at Gettysburg.

No such statue honors Henry Hunt, an actual hero of Gettysburg. The artillery's long-standing lack of rank and recognition dogged Hunt even after the war. On retirement as colonel of the 5th Artillery, he was not awarded (as were others) a pension commensurate with his brevet rank of major general. He was governor of the Soldiers' Home in Washington at his death in 1889. Hunt's final contribution to Gettysburg was four articles on the fighting there for *Battles and Leaders*.

Darius Couch and Henry Slocum, corps commanders of only middling skills, both forsook the Army of the Potomac to get away from Joe Hooker, transferring to lesser challenges in the Western theater. Couch left the army in 1865, engaged in business following an unsuccessful run as a Democrat for governor of Massachusetts, and refought his battles in *Battles and Leaders*. Lawyer Slocum also left the army, and he had better success in politics, serving three terms as a congressman from Brooklyn. Horatio Wright, who failed to fill John Sedgwick's shoes at the Sixth Corps, resumed his engineering duties postwar and retired in 1884 as the army's chief engineer.

Phil Sheridan, a newcomer to the Army of the Potomac's cavalry corps in 1864, ended the war as a popular hero for the Shenandoah Valley and Appomattox campaigns. Sheridan afterward directed much of the Western Indian fighting as head of the Military Division of the Missouri, and served as commanding general of the army from 1883 to his death in 1888. His *Personal Memoirs* and an equestrian statue in Sheridan Circle in Washington speak to his memory. Of Sheridan's wartime cavalry officers, the best known was George Armstrong Custer, whose legendary "Custer's Luck" finally expired leading the 7th Cavalry on the Little Bighorn in 1876.

John Gibbon, a major general by brevet, mustered out of the volunteers in 1866 and reverted to colonel in the regulars. He served widely in the Indian wars before his retirement in 1891. His memoir, *Personal Recollections of the Civil War*, is the best such work written by a serving general in the Army of the Potomac.

Like John Gibbon, career soldier Andrew A. Humphreys represented the iron core of the Army of the Potomac that survived and then overcame the years of trials and tribulations. In addition to fighting commands at division and corps, Humphreys served as invaluable chief of staff to General Meade. After the war Humphreys ranked as brigadier general in the regulars and served as the army's chief engineer, retiring in 1879. He wrote two campaign studies, *From Gettysburg to the Rapidan* and *The Virginia Campaign of '64 and '65*.

In Army of the Potomac annals, two citizen-soldiers represented a march to victory that paralleled that of career soldiers Gibbon and Humphreys. Lawyer Francis Channing Barlow enlisted in 1861 as a private, became a battle-worthy brigade and division commander, was twice badly wounded, and left the army a major general. Barlow's postwar public service included New York secretary of state and attorney general, U.S. marshal, and the founding of the American Bar Association. College professor Joshua Lawrence Chamberlain joined in 1861 as a regimental officer and fought through the war, suffering six wounds, resigning as a major general. After the war he was a four-term governor of Maine and president of Bowdoin College. Chamberlain's *The Passing of the Armies,* an account of the twelve days leading to Appomattox, speaks to the final epic of the Army of the Potomac.

Acknowledgments

On the steppingstones leading up to this book trod a number of people of special talents and great generosity. William Marvel once again shared his thoughts and his extensive research regarding any number of Army of the Potomac generals. John J. Hennessy shared insights into what made that army tick. The late Edwin C. Fishel's research into military-intelligence gathering, especially in the McClellan era, is enduring. I am indebted for specialized help to Mark Grimsley, William B. Styple, Thomas G. Clemens, Kelly Nolin, Karen M. Gray, Bob Zeller, Dennis E. Frye, and Eric J. Wittenberg. Donna J. Turner and Douglas Oxenhorn contributed valuable research.

Curatorial staffs, past and present, have lighted my way over the years, and for this volume I add my gratitude to: Michael P. Musick, National Archives; Jeffrey Flannery, Manuscript Division, Library of Congress; Yvonne J. Brooks, Duplication Services, Library of Congress; Mike Buscher, Geography and Map Division, Library of Congress; Olga Tsapina, Huntington Library; John M. Jackson, University Libraries, Virginia Tech; Janie C. Morris, Duke University Library; Kate DuBose, Massachusetts Historical Society; Elisabeth A. Proffen and David Angerhofer, Maryland Historical Society; Laura E. Beardsley, Historical Society of Pennsylvania; Barbara J. Davis, Boston Public Library; Margaret R. Goostray, Boston University Library; Sarah Erwin, Gilcrease Museum; Vivian E. Thiele and David Kuzma, Rutgers University Libraries; Darla Brock, Tennessee State Library and Archives; R. L. Baker, U.S. Army Heritage and Education Center; Mary Linnemann, Hargrett Book & Manuscript Library, University of Georgia; Dennis Northcott, Missouri Historical Society.

Recognition is due David W. Lowe for editing the invaluable Theodore Lyman notebooks, and to the late William E. Gienapp and to Erica L. Gienapp for presenting the diary of Gideon Welles in comprehensible form.

Earl B. McElfresh created the elegant and painstaking maps of battlefields and battle theaters. At Houghton Mifflin Harcourt, Nicole Angeloro, with Laurence Cooper, Chloe Foster, and Melissa Dobson, demonstrated their good nature in expertly putting all the pieces together.

Notes

Works cited by author and short title in the Notes will be found in full citation in the Bibliography. The abbreviation *OR* stands for U.S. War Department, *The War of the Rebellion: A Compilation of the Official Records of the Union and Confederate Armies* (Series I unless otherwise noted). *NOR* stands for U.S. Naval War Records Office, *Official Records of the Union and Confederate Navies in the War of the Rebellion*. *PMHSM* stands for *Papers of the Military Historical Society of Massachusetts*. MOLLUS stands for Military Order of the Loyal Legion of the United States. *CCW* stands for *Report of the Joint Committee on the Conduct of the War*. LC stands for Library of Congress. NA stands for National Archives. HSP stands for Historical Society of Pennsylvania. MHS stands for Massachusetts Historical Society. AP stands for Army of the Potomac.

1. "CIVIL WAR SEEMS INEVITABLE . . ."

1. Stanton to Buchanan, May 16, 1861, George Ticknor Curtis, *The Life of James Buchanan*, 2:548.
2. Timothy D. Johnson, *Winfield Scott: The Quest for Military Glory*, 219. Scott wrote, when Davis became the Confederacy's president, "I am amazed that any man of judgment should hope for the success of any cause in which Jefferson Davis is a leader. There is contamination in his touch": Charles Winslow Elliott, *Winfield Scott: The Soldier and the Man*, 712.
3. Scott's "Views," Oct. 29, 1860, Frank Moore, ed., *The Rebellion Record: A Diary of American Events*, 1:Documents:122–23; Buchanan to Stanton, Apr. 8, 1861, Stanton Papers, LC.
4. Scott to Floyd, Oct. 30, 1860, Moore, *Rebellion Record*, 1:Documents:123; [Jeremiah Black], *Mr. Buchanan's Administration on the Eve of the Rebellion* (New York: D. Appleton, 1866), 104.

5. Emory Upton, *The Military Policy of the United States*, 224; army returns, Dec. 31, 1860, *OR* ser. III, 1:22–26.
6. Scott to Floyd, Oct. 30, 1860, Moore, *Rebellion Record*, 1:Documents:123; Scott to Crittenden, Nov. 12, A.M.B. Coleman, *The Life of John J. Crittenden* (Philadelphia: Lippincott, 1871), 2:219.
7. Porter report, *OR* 1:70–72.
8. Gardner to H. K. Craig, Nov. 5, 1860, Samuel Cooper to Anderson, Nov. 12, *OR* 1:68–69, 72; Elliott, *Winfield Scott*, 678.
9. Anderson to Cooper, Nov. 23, 1860, *OR* 1:75.
10. James D. Richardson, ed., *A Compilation of the Messages and Papers of the Presidents* ([New York]: Bureau of National Literature and Art, 1907), 5:626–39; Seward in *New York Evening Post*, Dec. 6, 1860.
11. Elliott, *Winfield Scott*, 679; Margaret Leech, *Reveille in Washington, 1860–1865*, 1–2, 4–5; E. D. Keyes, *Fifty Years' Observation of Men and Events, Civil and Military*, 65, 318.

12. Washburne to Lincoln, Dec. 17, 1860, Lincoln Papers, LC; Lincoln to Washburne, Dec. 21, Lincoln, *The Collected Works of Abraham Lincoln,* Roy P. Basler, ed., 4:159.

13. Dec. 20, 1860, Edmund Ruffin, *The Diary of Edmund Ruffin,* William Kauffman Scarborough, ed. (Baton Rouge: Louisiana State University Press, 1972), 1:498.

14. Cooper to Anderson, Dec. 1, 1860, Buell to Anderson, Dec. 11, *OR* 1:82–83, 89–90; Samuel W. Crawford, *The Genesis of the Civil War: The Story of Sumter, 1860–1861,* 71–74; Abner Doubleday, *Reminiscences of Forts Sumter and Moultrie in 1860–'61* (New York: Harper, 1876), 60–66; Anderson to Cooper, Dec. 26, *OR* 1:2; Eba Anderson Lawton, *Major Robert Anderson and Fort Sumter, 1861* (New York, 1911), 8; Anderson to G. T. Metcalfe, Dec. 15, Goodyear Collection, Yale University Library. Anderson had disguised his intent by sending schooners loaded with supplies and dependents across the harbor to Fort Johnson, then diverted the supplies to Sumter.

15. Philip G. Auchampaugh, *James Buchanan and His Cabinet on the Eve of Secession* (Lancaster, Pa., 1926), 66–67; George C. Gorham, *Life and Public Services of Edwin M. Stanton* (Boston: Houghton Mifflin, 1899), 1:158–59; John C. Ropes interview with Stanton, 1869, Horatio Woodman Papers, MHS. The account in Gorham is from Joseph Holt.

16. Scott to Floyd, Dec. 28, 1860, to Buchanan, Dec. 30, in Scott memo to Lincoln, Mar. 30, 1861, Lincoln Papers, LC; Curtis, *James Buchanan,* 2:402.

17. Elliott, *Winfield Scott,* 684; Louis T. Wigfall to F. W. Pickens, Jan. 8, 1861, *OR* 1:253; Bruce Catton, *The Coming Fury,* 177–82. Sen. Thomas Bragg entered in his diary on Jan. 8, "This morning we had in the papers a dispatch from N.Y. that the Steam Ship Star of the West had been chartered by the Gov't to take 250 men to Fort Sumpter with supplies also": Bragg diary, Southern Historical Collection, University of North Carolina.

18. Scott (by order) to Slemmer, Jan. 3, 1861, *OR* 1:334; Slemmer report, *OR* 1:333–42; L. Thomas to Israel Vogdes, Jan. 21, Vogdes to Thomas, Feb. 7, *OR* 1:352, 357–58.

19. Scott to Fox, Jan. 30, 1861, Fox to wife, Feb. 7, Fox to Scott, Feb. 8, Gustavus V. Fox, *Confidential Correspondence of Gustavus Vasa Fox,* Robert Means Thompson and Richard Wainwright, eds., 1:3, 6–7, 7–9; Ari Hoogenboom, "Gustavus Fox and the Relief of Fort Sumter," *Civil War History,* 9:4 (Dec. 1963), 383–85.

20. Seward to wife, Dec. 29, 1860, Frederick W. Seward, *William H. Seward* (New York, 1891), 2:488; Sumner to John A. Andrew, Jan. 28, 1861, Andrew Papers, MHS; L. E. Chittenden, *Recollections of President Lincoln and His Administration* (New York: Harper, 1891), 38–39.

21. Charles P. Stone, "Washington on the Eve of the War," *Battles and Leaders of the Civil War,* Robert Underwood Johnson and Clarence Clough Buel, eds., 1:7–11; Stone to Benson J. Lossing, Nov. 5, 1866, Schoff Collection, Clements Library, University of Michigan.

22. Stone, "Washington on Eve of War," *Battles and Leaders,* 1:11–18; army postings, Jan. 1–Apr. 15, 1861, *OR* ser. III, 1:23; E. D. Townsend, *Anecdotes of the Civil War in the United States,* 13–14; Chase to Norman B. Judd, Jan. 20, 1861, to Scott, Dec. 29, 1860, Salmon P. Chase, *The Salmon P. Chase Papers,* John Nevin, ed., 3:51, 43–44; Cameron to Lincoln, Jan. 3, 1861, Scott to Lincoln, Jan. 4, John G. Nicolay and John Hay, *Abraham Lincoln: A History,* 3:250–51; Mather to Yates, Jan. 29, Richard Yates Papers, Lincoln Presidential Library. Mather later claimed he was sent to interview Scott by Lincoln himself, quoting detailed instruc-

tions from the president-elect. In fact Mather was sent by Gov. Yates, and he made no mention of Lincoln in his report to Yates. Don E. Fehrenbacher grades Mather's Lincoln quotation as invented. Fehrenbacher and Virginia Fehrenbacher, eds., *Recollected Words of Abraham Lincoln*, 310–11, 536n308.

23. Elliott, *Winfield Scott*, 692; Keyes, *Fifty Years' Observation*, 350–51; Mrs. Lee to husband, Jan. 1861, Elizabeth Blair Lee, *Wartime Washington: The Civil War Letters of Elizabeth Blair Lee*, Virginia Jeans Laas, ed., 23.

24. Elliott, *Winfield Scott*, 691–92; Leech, *Reveille in Washington*, 31–32.

25. Stone, "Washington on Eve of War," *Battles and Leaders*, 1:24–25; Leech, *Reveille in Washington*, 41–45; Eugene C. Tidball, *"No Disgrace to My Country": The Life of John C. Tidball*, 181–82.

26. Nicolay and Hay, *Lincoln*, 3:333–34, 342; Lincoln to Elihu B. Washburne, to F. P. Blair, Dec. 21, 1860, Lincoln, *Collected Works*, 4:159, 157.

27. Nicolay and Hay, *Lincoln*, 3:376–78; Anderson return, Apr. 4, 1861, Anderson Papers, LC; Anderson to Holt, Feb. 28, in Cameron to Lincoln, Mar. 17, *OR* 1:197; Holt to Lincoln, Mar. 5 (endorsed by Scott), Scott to Lincoln, Mar. 11, Lincoln Papers, LC.

28. Scott to Seward, Mar. 3, 1861, Lincoln Papers, LC. Scott's paper was published in Oct. 1862 (*New York Times*, Oct. 14). In a letter to Scott (Oct. 15, 1862), Chase claimed neither he nor Lincoln had known of the paper. Chase, *Papers*, 3:298–99.

29. Seymour report, *OR* 1:197; Gideon Welles, *The Civil War Diary of Gideon Welles, Lincoln's Secretary of the Navy*, William E. Gienapp and Erica L. Gienapp, eds., 639–41. The opening period of Welles's wartime service — March 1861 to July 1862 — in his *Diary* is a retrospective narrative rather than a contemporaneous account.

30. Lincoln to Scott, Mar. 9, 1861, Lin-
coln, *Collected Works*, 4:279; Scott to Lincoln, to Anderson (draft), Mar. 11, Lincoln Papers, LC; Nicolay and Hay, *Lincoln*, 3:382; Welles, *Diary*, 642–43; Fox to wife, Mar. 19, Fox, *Confidential Correspondence*, 1:9–10. To support his position, Scott gave Lincoln a letter from Ethan Allen Hitchcock, of his Mexican War staff (March 1861, Hitchcock Papers, LC), detailing the case for giving up Sumter: "This alone would secure the border states, and in the end bring back the Seceding States, if any thing will do it."

31. Keyes, *Fifty Years' Observation*, 379; Scott (by order) to Vogdes, Mar. 12, 1861, *OR* 1:360; Catton, *Coming Fury*, 276–77, 282.

32. Lincoln to Cameron et al., Mar. 15, 1861, *OR* 1:196; cabinet members' replies: Lincoln Papers, LC, excerpted in Lincoln, *Collected Works*, 4:285; Cameron reply, Mar. 16, Scott memo to Cameron, c. Mar. 15, *OR* 1:196–98, 200–201; A. Howard Meneely, *The War Department, 1861: A Study in Mobilization and Administration*, 88–91. Scott's memo to Cameron is undated, but clearly it was written on or before Mar. 15, for Cameron's response to Lincoln, dated Mar. 16, makes generous use of Scott's phrasing.

33. Nicolay memo, July 3, 1861, John G. Nicolay, *With Lincoln in the White House: Letters, Memoranda, and Other Writings of John G. Nicolay, 1860–1865*, Michael Burlingame, ed., 46; Scott memo, c. Mar. 15, *OR* 1:200–201; *New York Times*, Apr. 3; Mar. 11, 12, George Templeton Strong, *The Diary of George Templeton Strong: The Civil War, 1860–1865*, Allan Nevins and Milton Halsey Thomas, eds., 109; Stanton to Buchanan, Mar. 16, Curtis, *James Buchanan*, 2:534.

34. Fox to wife, Mar. 27, 1861, Fox, *Confidential Correspondence*, 1:11; Keyes, *Fifty Years' Observation*, 377–78; Montgomery C. Meigs, "The Relations of President Lincoln and Secretary Stan-

ton to the Military Commanders of the Civil War," *American Historical Review,* 26:2 (Jan. 1921), 300. As his memo was addressed to Cameron, Scott would not have shown it to Lincoln, as has been suggested. After his disturbing interview with the president, Scott prepared a 13-page record of his dealings on the Southern forts: Scott to Lincoln, Mar. 30, Lincoln Papers, LC.

35. Nicolay and Hay, *Lincoln,* 3:394–95; Crawford, *Genesis of the Civil War,* 365.

36. Mar. 29, 1861, Edward Bates, *The Diary of Edward Bates: 1859–1866,* Howard K. Beale, ed., 180; Meneely, *War Department, 1861,* 92–93; cabinet members' briefs, Nicolay and Hay, *Lincoln,* 3:430–32; William Ernest Smith, *The Francis Preston Blair Family in Politics* (New York: Macmillan, 1933), 2:9–10; Welles, *Diary,* 645–47.

37. Fox to Lincoln, Mar. 28, 1861, Nicolay and Hay, *Lincoln,* 3:433; Lincoln to Cameron [and Welles], Mar. 29, *OR* 1:226–27; July 3, Orville H. Browning, *The Diary of Orville Hickman Browning,* Theodore Calvin Pease and James G. Randall, eds., 1:476; Lincoln to Robert S. Chew, Apr. 6, Lincoln, *Collected Works,* 4:323.

38. Montgomery Meigs journal, Mar. 29, 31, 1861, Nicolay Papers, LC; Keyes, *Fifty Years' Observation,* 380–84; Nicolay and Hay, *Lincoln,* 3:434–37; Elliott, *Winfield Scott,* 704–6; Scott to Harvey Brown, Apr. 1, *OR* 1:365–66.

39. Oct. 22, 1861, John Hay, *Inside Lincoln's White House: The Complete Civil War Diary of John Hay,* Michael Burlingame and John R. Turner Ettlinger, eds., 28; Michael Burlingame, *Abraham Lincoln: A Life,* 2:119–23.

40. Cameron (Lincoln's draft) to Anderson, Cameron to Fox, Apr. 4, 1861, *OR* 1:235–36; Lincoln to Robert S. Chew, Apr. 6, Lincoln, *Collected Works,* 4:232–33.

41. Hoogenboom, "Gustavus Fox and the Relief of Fort Sumter," *Civil War History,* 9:4 (Dec. 1963), 388–94; Fox to wife, Apr. 6, 1861, to Montgomery Blair, Apr. 17, Fox, *Confidential Correspondence,* 1:26–27, 31–35. Welles recounted Seward's duplicity in the Fort Pickens episode in "Fort Sumter," *The Galaxy,* 10 (Nov. 1870), 613–37.

42. Pickens and Beauregard to L. P. Walker, Apr. 8, 1861, *OR* 1:291; Anderson to L. Thomas, Apr. 8, *OR* 1:294 (seized and enclosed with Pickens to Walker, Apr. 9, *OR* 1:292–93); Samuel W. Crawford, *The History of the Fall of Fort Sumter* (New York, 1898), 421; Pleasant A. Stovall, *Robert Toombs, Statesman, Speaker, Soldier, Sage* (New York, 1892), 226; Walker to Beauregard, Apr. 10, *OR* 1:297. In a further act of deceit, Seward leaked Lincoln's plan for Sumter to a reporter, who telegraphed it to Charleston before the president's message reached Gov. Pickens: [James A. Harvey] to A. G. Magrath, Apr. 6, *OR* 1:287.

43. Catton, *Coming Fury,* 307–11, 314–24; David J. Eicher, *The Longest Night: A Military History of the Civil War,* 36–41.

44. Hoogenboom, "Gustavus Fox and the Relief of Fort Sumter," *Civil War History,* 9:4 (Dec. 1963), 394–97; Fox to Montgomery Blair, Apr. 17, 1861, to wife, May 2, Fox, *Confidential Correspondence,* 1:31–35, 42–43, and original in Fox Papers, New-York Historical Society.

2. AN ARMY FOR BATTLE

1. Scott to Lincoln, Apr. 5, 1861, Nicolay and Hay, *Lincoln,* 4:65–66; John G. Nicolay to Therena Bates, Apr. 14, Nicolay, *With Lincoln in the White House,* 33–34; proclamation, Apr. 15, Lincoln, *Collected Works,* 4:331–32; Russell F. Weigley, *A Great Civil War: A Military and Political History, 1861–1865,* 24; *New York Times,* Apr. 15; Ticknor to Edmund Head, Apr. 21, Anna

Ticknor and George S. Hillard, *Life, Letters, and Journals of George Ticknor* (Boston, 1876), 2:433–34; Apr. 18, Strong, *Diary*, 124; Ellis to Cameron, Apr. 15, Harris to Cameron, Apr. 17, *OR* ser. III, 1:72, 81.

2. Weigley, *A Great Civil War*, 26–27; army postings, Jan. 1–Apr. 15, 1861, *OR* ser. III, 1:23–26; Irvin McDowell to L. Thomas, Apr. 11, 12, *OR* 51.1:322–23, 324; A. K. McClure, *Abraham Lincoln and Men of War-Times* (Philadelphia, 1892), 59–61.

3. Allan Nevins, *The War for the Union*, 1:79; Cameron to Hicks, Apr. 18, 1861, *OR* 2:577; Catton, *Coming Fury*, 341–43.

4. Nicolay memo, Apr. 20, 1861, Nicolay to Therena Bates, Apr. 26, Nicolay, *With Lincoln in the White House*, 34–35, 39; Scott orders, April 21, Butler to Hicks, Apr. 22, 23, *OR* 2:584, 589–90, 593–94; Nicolay and Hay, *Lincoln*, 4:134–36, 153–5; Leech, *Reveille in Washington*, 64–67; Stone to Benson J. Lossing, Nov. 5, 1866, Schoff Collection, Clements Library, University of Michigan; Apr. 24, 1861, Hay, *Inside Lincoln's White House*, 11; Butler report, May 15, Butler proclamation, May 14, Scott to Butler, May 14, 15, 18, *OR* 2:29–30, 30–32, 28, 640–41.

5. Cameron in *New York Herald*, May 8, 1862.

6. Douglas Southall Freeman, *R. E. Lee: A Biography*, 1:350n, 431–32, 436–37; Samuel P. Heintzelman diary, Mar. 5, 1861, Heintzelman Papers, LC; Keyes, *Fifty Years' Observation*, 206; William Allan interview with Lee, Feb. 15, 1868, in Gary W. Gallagher, ed., *Lee the Soldier*, 9–10; Lee to Reverdy Johnson, Feb. 25, 1868, in Alan T. Nolan, *Lee Considered: General Robert E. Lee and Civil War History* (Chapel Hill: University of North Carolina Press, 1991), 178–79; Townsend, *Anecdotes of the Civil War*, 5; Elliott, *Winfield Scott*, 714–15.

7. Frederick W. Seward, *Reminiscences of a War-Time Statesman and Diplomat,*

1830–1915 (New York: Putnam's, 1916), 167–68; Catton, *Coming Fury*, 428, 227–29; army postings, Jan. 1–Apr. 15, 1861, *OR* ser. III, 1:24–25; Elliott, *Winfield Scott*, 718; James L. Morrison, "The Struggle Between Sectionalism and Nationalism at Ante-Bellum West Point, 1830–1861," *Civil War History*, 19:2 (June 1973), 146–47. The regulars surrendered by Twiggs were paroled and in due course reached the East. Twiggs was dismissed from the U.S. Army for treason.

8. Meneely, *War Department, 1861*, 26, 106; Cameron in *New York Herald*, May 8, 1862; Meigs journal, May 10, 1861, Nicolay Papers, LC; Lincoln to Scott, June 5, Lincoln, *Collected Works*, 4:394–95; Leech, *Reveille in Washington*, 67–71; Apr. 30, Hay, *Inside Lincoln's White House*, 14.

9. Meneely, *War Department, 1861*, 137–38; Upton, *Military Policy*, 233–35; proclamation, May 3, 1861, Lincoln, *Collected Works*, 4:353–54; War Dept. G.O. 15, 16, May 4, *OR* ser. III, 1:151–57; Chase to William Dennison, May 16, George B. McClellan Papers, LC. Early in the war New York and Maine accepted men for two years rather than three.

10. Lincoln to Scott, May 24, 1861, Lincoln, *Collected Works*, 4:385; Sandford report, *OR* 2:37–39; Leech, *Reveille in Washington*, 80–82; Frank E. Brownell, "Ellsworth's Career," Peter Cozzens and Robert I. Girardi, eds., *The New Annals of the Civil War*, 17.

11. War Dept. G.O. 26, May 27, 1861, *OR* 2:653; Cameron to governors, Apr. 15, *OR* ser. III, 1:68–69; Chase to W. C. Bryant, Sept. 4, 1862, Chase, *Papers*, 3:259.

12. McDowell testimony, *CCW* 2 (1863), 37; Nicolay and Hay, *Lincoln*, 4:323–24; Heintzelman diary, May 17, 18, 1861, LC.

13. Private diary, July 6, 1861, William Howard Russell, *William Howard Russell's Civil War: Private Diary and Letters, 1861–1862*, Martin Crawford, ed.,

82; Chase to W. C. Bryant, Sept. 4, 1862, Chase, *Papers,* 3:259–60; Tidball, *"No Disgrace to My Country,"* 204.

14. Stephen W. Sears, *George B. McClellan: The Young Napoleon,* 68–71; Chase to McClellan, July 7, 1861, Chase, *Papers,* 3:74; McClellan to Scott, Apr. 27, May 7, George B. McClellan, *The Civil War Papers of George B. McClellan,* Stephen W. Sears, ed., 12–13, 16; Scott to McClellan, May 3, 21, *OR* 51.1:369–70, 386–87.

15. Mark Grimsley, *The Hard Hand of War: Union Military Policy Toward Southern Civilians, 1861–1865,* 28–31; Townsend, *Anecdotes of the Civil War,* 55–56; David W. Miller, *Second Only to Grant: Quartermaster General Montgomery C. Meigs,* 92–93; Montgomery Blair to Lincoln, May 16, 1861, Lincoln Papers, LC.

16. J. B. Elliott, "Scott's Great Snake," 1861, Map Division, LC; May 20, 1861, Strong, *Diary,* 144; *Chicago Tribune,* June 28; *New-York Tribune,* June 26; Sherman to wife, June 12, William T. Sherman, *Sherman's Civil War: Selected Correspondence of William T. Sherman,* Brooks D. Simpson and Jean V. Berlin, eds., 102; Motley to wife, June 20, G.W.C. Motley, ed., *The Correspondence of John Lothrop Motley* (New York: Harper, 1900), 2:143.

17. June 26, 1861, return, *OR* 2:726; John Sherman to Cameron, June 18, McDowell to Townsend, c. June 27, *OR* 2:703, 719–21; [Robert Henry Newell], *The Orpheus C. Kerr Papers: First Series* (New York, 1862), 205; *New-York Tribune,* May 28.

18. Joseph B. Carr, "Operations of 1861 About Fort Monroe," *Battles and Leaders,* 2:148–51; Mitchell Yockelson, "Ambush at Vienna," *North & South,* 2:1 (Nov. 1998), 30–37; Sears, *George B. McClellan,* 80.

19. McDowell to Townsend, c. June 27, 1861, *OR* 2:719–21; McDowell, Sandford testimony, *CCW* 2 (1863), 35–38, 55, 62; Townsend, *Anecdotes of the Civil War,*

56–57; Meigs journal, June 29, Nicolay Papers, LC; Meigs to father, July 18, Meigs Papers, LC. The "You are green" remark is usually attributed to Lincoln, although McDowell in his testimony did not specify who said it.

20. June 26 return, *OR* 2:726; Dept. N.E. Virginia G.O. 13, July 8, 1861, *OR* 51.1:413–14; Elliott, *Winfield Scott,* 718–19; Marvin A. Kreidberg and Merton G. Henry, *History of Military Mobilization in the United States Army, 1775–1945* (Washington: Dept. of Army, 1955), 115–16.

21. Heintzelman diary, July 10, 1861, LC; Willcox to wife, June 30, July 13, Orlando B. Willcox, *Forgotten Valor: The Memoirs, Journals, & Civil War Letters of Orlando B. Willcox,* Robert Garth Scott, ed., 279, 282–83; June 21, Charles B. Haydon, *For Country, Cause & Leader: The Civil War Journal of Charles B. Haydon,* Stephen W. Sears, ed., 30; John Bigelow, *Retrospections of an Active Life* (New York, 1909), 1:360; Sears, *George B. McClellan,* 89–93; McClellan to Townsend, July 14, *OR* 2:204; McClellan proclamation, July 16, McClellan, *Civil War Papers,* 58; *New-York Tribune,* July 16; *New York Herald,* July 15; *Louisville Journal,* July 20.

22. Private diary, July 5, 16, 1861, Russell, *Russell's Civil War,* 81, 86; July 9, 13, 16, William Howard Russell, *My Diary North and South,* 148, 150–51, 158; Vizetelly in *Illustrated London News,* June 15.

23. Patterson to Townsend, June 1, 1861, Scott to Patterson, June 8, *OR* 2:657–58, 670–71; Patterson testimony, *CCW* 2 (1863), 79; Patterson to Townsend, June 16, Scott to Patterson, June 16, *OR* 2:693, 691.

24. McDowell, Patterson testimony, *CCW* 2 (1863), 36, 82; Scott to Patterson, June 16, 25, 1861, *OR* 2:694–95, 725.

25. Townsend to Patterson, July 1, 1861, *OR* 2:157; Patterson, Price, McDowell testimony, *CCW* 2 (1863), 80, 86, 97, 186, 40; Patterson return, June 28, Johnston

return, June 30, *OR* 2:187; Patterson to Townsend, July 4, 6, 9, 13, to Scott, July 6, *OR* 2:158, 160–61, 162–63, 165, 159; D. H. Strother, "Personal Recollections of the War, by a Virginian," *Harper's New Monthly Magazine,* 33 (July 1866), 151–52; Edwin C. Fishel, *The Secret War for the Union: The Untold Story of Military Intelligence in the Civil War,* 44–47. Fishel describes these inflated numbers for Johnston's army as "the first creation of a not very imaginative but often successful Confederate deception effort."

26. Thomas L. Livermore, "Patterson's Shenandoah Campaign," *PMHSM,* 1:22–24, 28–29; Patterson testimony, *CCW* 2 (1863), 85; war council minutes, July 9, 1861, *OR* 2:163–64; Sandford testimony, *CCW* 2 (1863), 55, 59; Scott to Patterson, July 13, *OR* 2:166.

27. Patterson to Townsend, July 13, 1861, *OR* 2:165; Scott, Porter, Sandford, Patterson testimony, *CCW* 2 (1863), 241, 155, 158, 56–57, 106; Livermore, "Patterson's Shenandoah Campaign," *PMHSM,* 1:38, 41n; Scott to Patterson, July 17, 18, Patterson to Townsend, July 18, 20, *OR* 2:167–68, 168, 172; Johnston report, *OR* 2:473; Strother, "Personal Recollections," *Harper's New Monthly Magazine,* 33 (July 1866), 152.

28. July 9, 1861, Russell, *My Diary North and South,* 148; Elliott, *Winfield Scott,* 729; *New York Times,* July 26; Leech, *Reveille in Washington,* 97.

29. McDowell to Townsend, c. June 27, 1861, *OR* 2:719–21; "Strength of the Confederate Army," *Battles and Leaders,* 1:195; July 16–17 return (corrected), *OR* 2:309; Dept. N.E. Virginia G.O. 17, July 16, *OR* 2:303–5; William Marvel, *Burnside,* 19; Sherman to wife, July 15, Sherman, *Sherman's Civil War,* 116. Newspapers on July 16–18 reported McDowell's march, his general order, and his order of battle: Fishel, *Secret War for the Union,* 41–42.

30. D. G. Crotty, *Four Years Campaigning in the Army of the Potomac* (Grand Rapids, Mich., 1874), 20; Dept. N.E. Virginia G.O. 17, July 16, 1861, *OR* 2:304–5; McDowell testimony, *CCW* 2 (1863), 39; Abner R. Small, *The Road to Richmond: The Civil War Memoirs of Major Abner R. Small of the Sixteenth Maine Volunteers,* Harold A. Small, ed., 18.

31. Marvel, *Burnside,* 18–20; William C. Davis, *Battle at Bull Run: A History of the First Major Campaign of the Civil War,* 94–100; Dept. N.E. Virginia G.O. 17, July 16, 1861, G.O. 18, July 18, *OR* 2:304, 743–44; Sherman to wife, July 28, Sherman, *Sherman's Civil War,* 125.

32. Edward G. Longacre, *The Early Morning of War: Bull Run, 1861,* 248–51; Heintzelman to wife, July 18, 1861, Heintzelman Papers, LC; McDowell to Tyler, July 18, *OR* 2:312; Heintzelman diary, July 3, 19, LC; Heintzelman testimony, *CCW* 2 (1863), 29; McDowell to Townsend, July 19, *OR* 2:307; McDowell testimony, *CCW* 1 (1863), 136–37.

33. Tyler, Richardson, Barnard reports, *OR* 2:310–12, 312–14, 328–30; May 24, 30, 1861, Haydon, *Country, Cause & Leader,* 11, 13.

34. Daniel Tyler, *Daniel Tyler, a Memorial Volume, Containing His Autobiography and War Record* (New Haven, Conn., 1883), 51–54; Tyler, Richardson, McDowell testimony, *CCW* 2 (1863), 199–200, 19–21, 39; John G. Barnard, *The C.S.A. and the Battle of Bull Run* (New York: Van Nostrand, 1862), 48–49; Sherman to John Sherman, July 19, 1861, Sherman, *Sherman's Civil War,* 121; Federal casualties: *OR* 2:314; Confederate casualties: Longstreet report, *OR* 2:462; Heintzelman diary, July 19, LC; July 18, Haydon, *Country, Cause & Leader,* 54.

35. Beauregard to Jefferson Davis, Samuel Cooper to Johnston, July 17, 1861, *OR* 2:439–40, 478; Johnston report, *OR* 2:473; T. Harry Williams, *P.G.T. Beauregard: Napoleon in Gray,* 78–80.

36. McDowell, Barnard, Woodbury reports, *OR* 2:318, 329–31, 333; McDowell testimony, *CCW* 2 (1863), 36; McDowell to Townsend, July 20, 1861, *OR* 2:308; Barnard, *The C.S.A. and the Battle of Bull Run* (Van Nostrand, 1862), 49–50.

37. Davis, *Battle at Bull Run*, 153–54; Oliver Otis Howard, *Autobiography*, 1:152; "First Bull Run Notes," Heintzelman Papers, LC; McDowell to Townsend, July 20, 1861, Dept. N.E. Virginia S.O. 37, 39, July 20, *OR* 2:308, 745; Franklin report, *OR* 2:405–6; Longacre, *Early Morning of War*, 282–84; Richardson, McDowell testimony, *CCW* 2 (1863), 22, 40–41.

38. Dept. N.E. Virginia G.O. 22, July 20, 1861, *OR* 2:326–27; Beauregard S.O., July 20, *OR* 2:479–80; Williams, *Beauregard*, 78–80.

39. Scott, Russell testimony, *CCW* 2 (1863), 242, 232; Patterson to Townsend, July 20, 1861, Scott to McDowell, July 21, *OR* 2:172, 746.

40. Private diary, July 17–21, 1861, Russell, *Russell's Civil War*, 88, 90–93; July 21, Russell, *My Diary North and South*, 165.

41. McDowell, Keyes, Tyler testimony, *CCW* 2 (1863), 41–44, 150, 202; Schenck, Wilson, Barnard reports, *OR* 2:357, 362, 331; "First Bull Run Notes," Heintzelman Papers, LC. For Major, not Colonel, Evans, see Longacre, *Early Morning of War*, 522n33.

42. Barnard, Woodbury reports, *OR* 2:329–31, 333; Barnard, McDowell testimony, *CCW* 2 (1863), 160–61, 44; Willcox, *Forgotten Valor*, 289; Williams, *Beauregard*, 81–84.

43. Peter C. Hains, "The First Gun at Bull Run," *Cosmopolitan*, 51 (1911), 391; "First Bull Run Notes," Heintzelman Papers, LC; Porter testimony, *CCW* 2 (1863), 212; Woodbury, McDowell, Richardson, Evans reports, *OR* 2:333, 319, 374, 558–59; E. P. Alexander, *Military Memoirs of a Confederate*, 30–31.

44. McDowell report, *OR* 2:319; Heintzelman diary, Sept. 1, 1861, LC; E. P. Alexander, *Fighting for the Confederacy: The Personal Recollections of General Edward Porter Alexander*, Gary W. Gallagher, ed., 52; Alexander, *Military Memoirs*, 32.

45. McDowell report, *OR* 2:319–20; Ethan S. Rafuse, *A Single Grand Victory: The First Campaign and Battle of Manassas*, 123; Augustus Woodbury, *The Second Rhode Island Regiment: A Narrative of Military Operations* (Providence, 1875), 33; Porter, Burnside reports, *OR* 2:383, 398; McDowell testimony, *CCW* 2 (1863), 40.

46. Marvel, *Burnside*, 24–25; Robert Goldthwaite Carter, *Four Brothers in Blue, or Sunshine and Shadows of the War of the Rebellion* (Austin: University of Texas Press, 1978), 12–13.

47. Heintzelman diary, Sept. 1, 1861, LC; Franklin, Tyler testimony, *CCW* 2 (1863), 33, 201; McDowell report, *OR* 2:319; Sherman to wife, July 28, Sherman, *Sherman's Civil War*, 123; George Wilkes, *The Great Battle, Fought at Manassas* (New York, 1861), 29.

48. "Strength of the Union Army," *Battles and Leaders*, 1:194–95; Heintzelman diary, Sept. 1, 1861, LC.

49. Porter, Tyler, Keyes reports, *OR* 2:383–84, 349–50, 353–55; Averell testimony, *CCW* 2 (1863), 214–15.

50. Ricketts, Griffin, Barry testimony, *CCW* 2 (1863), 242–44, 168–77, 143–47; Heintzelman diary, Sept. 1, 5, 1861, LC.

51. Rafuse, *A Single Grand Victory*, 161; Hazlett, Griffin, Reed testimony, *CCW* 2 (1863), 219, 169, 220–21; Griffin report, *OR* 2:394. Longacre (*Early Morning of War*, 396–98) casts doubt on the Griffin-Barry confrontation, but Horatio B. Reed's testimony in *CCW* 2 (1863), 220, appears to support Griffin's account.

52. Willcox, *Forgotten Valor*, 290–96; Heintzelman diary, Sept. 1, 5, 1861, LC; Jerry Thompson, *Civil War to the Bloody End: The Life & Times of Major General Samuel P. Heintzelman*, 126–30; Franklin to William H. Swift, Aug. 2,

Historical Society of York County, in Mark A. Snell, *From First to Last: The Life of Major General William B. Franklin,* 64; Thomas S. Allen, "The Second Wisconsin at the First Battle of Bull Run," *War Papers,* Wisconsin MOLLUS (1:1891), 46:389–91; Rafuse, *A Single Grand Victory,* 176–77; Federal casualties: *OR* 51.1:17–19.

53. McDowell testimony, *CCW* 2 (1863), 40–41; Sherman to wife, July 28, 1861, Sherman, *Sherman's Civil War,* 124; James B. Fry, "McDowell's Advance to Bull Run," *Battles and Leaders,* 1:191.

54. Schenck, McDowell reports, *OR* 2:360, 320; Townsend, *Anecdotes of the Civil War,* 59; Keyes, *Fifty Years' Observation,* 434–35; Russell to J.C.B. Davis, July 22, 1861, Russell, *Russell's Civil War,* 94; Russell letter, July 22, London *Times,* Aug. 6, in Moore, *Rebellion Record,* 2:Documents:52. Russell's Bull Run letters were printed in American papers starting Aug. 20, and appeared as a pamphlet, *The Battle of Bull Run,* later in 1861.

55. Heintzelman diary, Sept. 5, 1861, LC; McDowell, Richardson reports, *OR* 2:320–22, 376. Richardson preferred charges against Miles for drunkenness.

56. Nicolay to Therena Bates, July 21, 1861, Nicolay, *With Lincoln in the White House,* 51–52; McDowell (by order) to L. Thomas, B. S. Alexander to Thomas, July 21, *OR* 2:747; Townsend, *Anecdotes of the Civil War,* 58–59; Elliott, *Winfield Scott,* 729–30; Scott to McDowell, July 21, *OR* 2:748; Nicolay and Hay, *Lincoln,* 4:358–59; W. A. Richardson in *Congressional Globe* (37th Cong., 1st Sess.), July 24, 246.

57. Mrs. Lee to husband, July 23, 1861, Lee, *Wartime Washington,* 69; Griffin, Kirby, E. P. Alexander reports, *OR* 2:394, 407, 571; Federal casualties: *OR* 51.1:17–19; Confederate casualties: Johnston report, *OR* 2:477.

58. McDowell testimony, *CCW* 2 (1863), 36, 40–41; Scott to Banks, July 22,

1861, *OR* 2:172; Miles Court of Inquiry, *OR* 2:438–39; Richardson report, *OR* 2:375–76; Tidball, *"No Disgrace to My Country,"* 213.

59. Sherman to wife, July 28, 1861, Sherman, *Sherman's Civil War,* 124; Sherman, *Memoirs of General W. T. Sherman* (1875; New York: Library of America, 1990), 208; Franklin to William H. Swift, Aug. 2, Historical Society of York County, in Snell, *From First to Last,* 66; Howard, *Autobiography,* 1:162.

60. McDowell testimony, *CCW* 2 (1863), 40; Townsend to Fitz John Porter, July 23, 1861, Porter Papers, LC.

61. L. Thomas to McClellan, July 22, 1861, *OR* 2:753; Nicolay to Therena Bates, July 23, Nicolay, *With Lincoln in the White House,* 52; enlistment acts, July 22, 25, 1861, *OR* ser. III, 1:380–83; Weigley, *A Great Civil War,* 476n61; John Hay, "The Heroic Age in Washington," Hay, *At Lincoln's Side: John Hay's Civil War Correspondence and Selected Writings,* Michael Burlingame, ed., 126.

3. A NEW ARMY, A NEW ERA

1. Chase to William P. Mellen, July 23, 1861, Chase, *Papers,* 3:79; Feb. 25, 1863, Welles, *Diary,* 142; Scott to Cameron, Oct. 4, 1861, *OR* 51.1:491. Schuyler Hamilton, Scott's military secretary, later said he delivered Scott's advice on McClellan to Lincoln that night at the White House: J. H. Stine, *History of the Army of the Potomac,* 99. Chase may have encouraged the choice of McClellan: Sept. 1, 1862, Welles, *Diary,* 26.

2. Sears, *George B. McClellan,* 28–49, 58–60, 63; McClellan to Fitz John Porter, Apr. 18, 1861, McClellan, *Civil War Papers,* 4–5; Chase to McClellan, July 7, Chase, *Papers,* 3:74.

3. George B. McClellan, *McClellan's Own Story,* William C. Prime, ed., manuscript, McClellan Papers, LC; McClel-

lan to wife, July 27, 1861, McClellan, *Civil War Papers*, 70; Div. of Potomac G.O. 1, July 27, *OR* 51.1:428.

4. Howard to wife, Aug. 1, O. O. Howard Papers, Bowdoin College Library; H.Q. of Army G.O. 15, Aug. 17, AP G.O. 1, Aug. 20, *OR* 5:567, 575; private diary, Sept. 2, Russell, *Russell's Civil War*, 117.

5. McClellan to wife, Aug. 2, 1861, McClellan, "Memorandum for President," Aug. 2, McClellan, *Civil War Papers*, 75, 71–75; draft notes, "Memorandum of Aug. [2], 61," McClellan Papers, LC.

6. McClellan to commanders, Aug. 4, 1861, McClellan Papers, LC; McClellan to McDowell, Aug. 6, *OR* 5:553; McClellan to Scott, Aug. 8, McClellan, *Civil War Papers*, 79–80, endorsed, copy on same day "delivered to the President"; McClellan to wife, Aug. 8, 16, McClellan, *Civil War Papers*, 81, 85–86.

7. Scott to Cameron, Aug. 9, 12, 1861, McClellan to Lincoln, Aug. 10, *OR* 11.3:4–6; McDowell testimony, *CCW* 2 (1863), 40–41.

8. McMurdy to Henry W. Halleck, Sept. 26, 1862, RG 94 (M-619), NA; McClellan to wife, Aug. 19, 1861, to Cameron, Sept. 8, 13, McClellan, *Civil War Papers*, 87, 95–97, 100–101; Confederate return, Oct. 1861, *OR* 5:932.

9. McClellan to Pinkerton, July 30, 1861, McClellan, *Civil War Papers*, 70. There are some two dozen Pinkerton reports, dating from the fall of 1861, in the McClellan Papers, LC. For Pinkerton and his methods, see Fishel, *Secret War for the Union*, especially chs. 4 and 5.

10. Willcox, *Forgotten Valor*, 349; Sherman to wife, Aug. 3, 17, 1861, Sherman, *Sherman's Civil War*, 127, 131; McClellan, *McClellan's Own Story*, 70–71, and manuscript, McClellan Papers, LC; McClellan to Stone, Aug. 18, Stone to Seth Williams, Aug. 28, Sept. 2, *OR* 5:567–68, 582–83. James B. Ricketts, the wounded and captured battery commander at Bull Run, was exchanged in Dec. 1861.

11. Porter to McClellan, Apr. 15, May 10,

Aug. 1, 1861, McClellan Papers, LC; Porter to Cameron, Nov. 1, Fitz John Porter Papers, LC.

12. McClellan to sister, Jan. 1, 1853, McClellan Papers, LC; McClellan to Lincoln, Sept. 6, 1861, to Cameron, Sept. 8, McClellan, *Civil War Papers*, 94, 97; Smith to McClellan, Apr. 15, McClellan Papers; William F. Smith, *Autobiography of Major General William F. Smith, 1861–1864*, Herbert M. Schiller, ed., 29–30; *McClellan's Own Story* manuscript, McClellan Papers.

13. Walter H. Hebert, *Fighting Joe Hooker*, 47–50; Lincoln to Mansfield, June 19, 1861, Lincoln, *Collected Works*, 4:412–13; clipping, Hooker Papers, Huntington Library, cited in Hebert, 49; *McClellan's Own Story* manuscript, McClellan Papers, LC.

14. Sept. 4, 1862, Strong, *Diary*, 252. Kearny's antebellum life can be gleaned from his grandson Thomas Kearny's *General Philip Kearny: Battle Soldier of Five Wars* (New York: Putnam's, 1937); and see Stephen W. Sears, "A One-Armed Jersey Son-of-a-Gun," *The Civil War Monitor*, 4:1 (Spring 2014), 28–39, 74–75.

15. *McClellan's Own Story* manuscript, McClellan Papers, LC; Charles S. Wainwright, *A Diary of Battle: The Personal Journals of Colonel Charles S. Wainwright, 1861–1865*, Allan Nevins, ed., 17.

16. Organization of brigades, Aug. 4, 1861, *OR* 51.1:434–35; organization of divisions, Oct. 15, *OR* 5:15–17; H.Q. of Army S.O. 141, Aug. 24, *OR* 51.1:455; Ralph Kirshner, *The Class of 1861: Custer, Ames, and Their Classmates After West Point* (Carbondale: Southern Illinois University Press, 1999), 4.

17. Almira R. Hancock, *Reminiscences of Winfield Scott Hancock*, 78–80; Edward J. Nichols, *Toward Gettysburg: A Biography of General John F. Reynolds*, 75–76; McClellan to Cameron, Sept. 8, 1861, *OR* 5:589; Cameron to McClellan, Sept. 7, Cameron Papers, LC; Meade

to wife, Aug. 5, Meade Papers, HSP; Freeman Cleaves, *Meade of Gettysburg*, 54; AP S.O. 34, Sept. 5, *OR* 51.1:470–71. Mrs. Meade's given name was Margaretta, but she signed herself Margaret and so her husband and family addressed her.

18. Richard Elliott Winslow III, *General John Sedgwick: The Story of a Union Corps Commander*, 1–4; McClellan, *McClellan's Own Story*, 140; A. M. Gambone, *Major-General Darius Nash Couch: Enigmatic Valor*, 63–66; William E. Doubleday to Chandler, Dec. 6, 1861, Zachariah Chandler Papers, LC; Lincoln to Carl Schurz, Nov. 10, 1862, Lincoln, *Collected Works*, 5:494.

19. R. J. Amundson, "Sanford and Garibaldi," *Civil War History*, 14:1 (Mar. 1968), 40–45; McClellan, *McClellan's Own Story*, 143, and manuscript, McClellan Papers, LC.

20. Enlistment acts, July 22, Aug. 6, 1861, *OR* ser. III, 1:380–83, 401–2; Weigley, *A Great Civil War*, 65–66; T. W. Higginson, "Regular and Volunteer Officers," *Atlantic Monthly*, 4 (Sept. 1864), 355.

21. Meade to wife, Aug. 5, 1861, Meade Papers, HSP; Howard, *Autobiography*, 1:106–7, 113; Smith, *Autobiography*, 30; McClellan to Cameron, Aug. 24, *OR* ser. III, 1:444–45; Aug. 4, Russell, *My Diary North and South*, 180; Régis de Trobriand, *Four Years with the Army of the Potomac*, 89, 417.

22. Upton, *Military Policy*, 260; War Dept. G.O. 47, July 25, 1861, *OR* ser. III, 1:349; AP H.Q. journal, Sept. 20, McClellan Papers, LC; Fred Albert Shannon, *The Organization and Administration of the Union Army, 1861–1865*, 1:186–87; Dec. 25, 1861, Jan. 5, 1862, Wainwright, *Diary of Battle*, 4–5, 7; McClellan, *McClellan's Own Story*, 97; Bragg to wife, Oct. 26, 1861, Edward S. Bragg Papers, Wisconsin Historical Society; May 2, Haydon, *Country, Cause & Leader*, 2–3; Barlow to brother, July 18, Francis C. Barlow, *"Fear Was Not in Him"*:

The Civil War Letters of Major General Francis C. Barlow, U.S.A., Christian G. Samito, ed., 15.

23. L. Van Loan Naisawald, *Grape and Canister: The Story of the Field Artillery in the Army of the Potomac, 1861–1865*, 28–35.

24. Barry report, *OR* 5:67; McClellan to Cameron, Sept. 8, 1861, McClellan, *Civil War Papers*, 95–97; organization of divisions, Oct. 15, *OR* 5:15–17; McClellan, *McClellan's Own Story*, 117.

25. McClellan, *McClellan's Own Story*, 114; Naisawald, *Grape and Canister*, 30–31; AP G.O. 110, Mar. 26, 1862, *OR* 11.3:40–41; Edward G. Longacre, *The Man Behind the Guns: A Biography of General Henry Jackson Hunt, Chief of Artillery, Army of the Potomac*, 98–99; John C. Tidball, "The Artillery Service in the War of the Rebellion, 1861–65," *Journal of the Military Service Institution of the United States*, 12 (1891), 705.

26. McClellan, *McClellan's Own Story*, 118; Moses Harris, "The Union Cavalry," *War Papers*, Wisconsin MOLLUS (1:1891), 46:351; Stephen Z. Starr, *The Union Cavalry in the Civil War*, 1:50, 60, 235. The antebellum regular cavalry was renumbered for wartime service: the 1st and 2nd Dragoons became the 1st and 2nd Cavalry, the Mounted Rifles became the 3rd Cavalry, the old 1st and 2nd Cavalry became the 4th and 5th Cavalry. The 6th Cavalry was new.

27. Benjamin W. Crowninshield, "Cavalry in Virginia During the War of the Rebellion," *PMHSM*, 13:5; organization of divisions, Oct. 15, 1861, *OR* 5:15–17; Harris, "The Union Cavalry," *War Papers*, Wisconsin MOLLUS (1:1891), 46:351; Stephen W. Sears, *To the Gates of Richmond: The Peninsula Campaign*, appendixes I–III; Scott to Lincoln, Sept. 5, Lincoln Papers, LC; McClellan to Lincoln, Sept. 6, McClellan, *Civil War Papers*, 94; AP G.O. 110, Mar. 26, 1862, *OR* 11.3:40–41.

28. AP G.O. 1, Aug. 20, 1861, *OR* 5:575;

George B. McClellan, *Report on the Organization of the Army of the Potomac*, 23; McClellan, *McClellan's Own Story*, 141; F. Stansbury Haydon, *Aeronautics in the Union and Confederate Armies*, 68–71; Edward Hagerman, "The Professionalization of George B. McClellan and Early Civil War Command," *Civil War History*, 21:2 (June 1975), 118; Humphreys to wife, May 1, 1862, Humphreys Papers, HSP.

29. Leech, *Reveille in Washington*, 113; Sears, *George B. McClellan*, 48.

4 · QUIET ALONG THE POTOMAC

1. Williams, *Beauregard*, 99–100; Beauregard to Johnston, Aug. 11, 1861, *OR* 5:778–79; McClellan to Stone, Aug. 18, McClellan, *Civil War Papers*, 86–87.
2. McClellan, *McClellan's Own Story*, 146–47; McClellan to Samuel S. Cox, Feb. 12, 1864, McClellan, *Civil War Papers*, 565. For the arrest of the Maryland legislators, see William Marvel, *Mr. Lincoln Goes to War*, 195–200, and Mark E. Neely, Jr., *The Fate of Liberty: Abraham Lincoln and Civil Liberties*, 14–18.
3. Benjamin Franklin Cooling, *Symbol, Sword, and Shield: Defending Washington During the Civil War*, 76–77; Welles to Cameron, Aug. 20, 1861, McClellan to Welles, Aug. 12, *OR* 5:573, 47; Fox, McClellan testimony, *CCW* 1 (1863), 240–42, 421–22; *Harper's Weekly*, Nov. 2; Hebert, *Fighting Joe Hooker*, 55–61; Hooker to Seth Williams, Oct. 28, Nov. 1, *OR* 5:384–85, 638; Hooker to Seth Williams, Oct. 30, Williams to Hooker, Oct. 31, Barnard to McClellan, Sept. 28, *OR* 5:633–34, 635–36, 606–8.
4. Goldsborough to Welles, Oct. 17, 1861, *NOR* 6:333–34; Pinkerton to McClellan, c. Dec. 16, Barnard to McClellan, Dec. 6, McClellan Papers, LC; Meigs to father, Mar. 9, 1862, Meigs Papers, LC; Barnard to Fox, Feb. 12, Fox, *Confidential Correspondence*, 1:419–22;

Heintzelman diary, Nov. 25, 1861, LC; Welles, *Diary*, 678–79.

5. McClellan to wife, Oct. 10, c. Oct. 11, 1861, McClellan, *Civil War Papers*, 106–7; private diary, Oct. 10, Russell, *Russell's Civil War*, 148.
6. Angus James Johnston II, *Virginia Railroads in the Civil War*, 36–37; Oct. 16, 1861, Russell, *My Diary North and South*, 206; Wade to Chandler, Oct. 8, Chandler to wife, Oct. 12, Zachariah Chandler Papers, LC; Sept. 30, Bates, *Diary*, 194.
7. O'Kane, Wister reports, *OR* 5:218–20; Francis A. Donaldson to brother, Oct. 15, 1861, Donaldson, *Inside the Army of the Potomac: The Civil War Experience of Captain Francis Adams Donaldson*, J. Gregory Acken, ed., 21–26; McClellan to wife, Sept. 29, McClellan, *Civil War Papers*, 104; James Longstreet, *From Manassas to Appomattox: Memoirs of the Civil War in America*, 60; *New-York Tribune*, Oct. 1; private diary, Oct. 3, Russell, *Russell's Civil War*, 141; July 27, Russell, *My Diary North and South*, 179.
8. Private diary, Sept. 2, 1861, Russell, *Russell's Civil War*, 117; Sept. 2, Russell, *My Diary North and South*, 193; Aspinwall to Fox, Sept. 18, Fox, *Confidential Correspondence*, 1:376; Aspinwall to McClellan, Aug. 27, McClellan Papers, LC.
9. McClellan to wife, Aug. 14, 1861, McClellan, *Civil War Papers*, 84; Townsend (in Scott's hand) to McClellan, Sept. 16, Scott to Cameron, Oct. 10, Cameron Papers, LC.
10. Feb. 25, 1863, Welles, *Diary*, 141–42; McClellan to wife, Sept. 27, 1861, McClellan, *Civil War Papers*, 103–4.
11. Scott to Cameron, Oct. 4, 1861, *OR* 51.1:492; John F. Marszalek, *Commander of All Lincoln's Armies: A Life of General Henry W. Halleck*, 104–7; Nicolay and Hay, *Lincoln*, 4:429–30; Oct. 18, Bates, *Diary*, 196–97; McClellan to wife, Oct. 19, McClellan, *Civil War Papers*, 109.

12. Stone to McClellan, Oct. 17, 1861, *OR* 5:621; Stone to McClellan, Oct. 18, McClellan Papers, LC; McCall, Howe testimony, *CCW* 2 (1863), 257, 375–76; Colburn to Stone, Oct. 20, *OR* 5:290; Stone report, *OR* 5:293–94; Stone to McClellan, to Devens, Oct. 20, *OR* 5:290–91, 299–300; McCall testimony, *CCW* 2 (1863), 258–61.

13. Evans, Devens, Stone reports, *OR* 5:349, 405–6, 294–96; Stone to Baker, Oct. 21, 1861, *OR* 5:303.

14. Stone report, *OR* 5:296; Howe, Devens, Lee testimony, *CCW* 2 (1863), 376, 405–11, 476–81; Williams to daughters, June 20, 1863, Alpheus S. Williams, *From the Cannon's Mouth: The Civil War Letters of General Alpheus S. Williams*, Milo M. Quaife, ed., 218; Marvel, *Mr. Lincoln Goes to War*, 211, 236–43; Abbott to father, Oct. 22, 1861, Henry L. Abbott, *Fallen Leaves: The Civil War Letters of Henry Livermore Abbott*, Robert Garth Scott, ed., 60–62; Caspar Crowninshield to mother, Oct. 22, C. P. Putnam Papers, MHS; Roebling to father, [Oct. 24], Roebling Family Papers, Rutgers University Archives.

15. Stone, Gorman reports, *OR* 5:298, 333; Stone to McClellan, Marcy to Stone, Oct. 21, 1861, *OR* 51.1:499; Stone to McClellan, Oct. 21 (two), McClellan, *McClellan's Own Story*, 185; McClellan to Stone, Oct. 21 (two), *OR* 51.1:500, 501; Banks to McClellan, Oct. 22, endorsed by Lincoln, McClellan Papers, LC; Roebling to father, [Oct. 24], Roebling Family Papers, Rutgers University Archives; Federal casualties: *OR* 5:308. The Ball's Bluff prisoners counted in Richmond came to 681 (Marvel, *Mr. Lincoln Goes to War*, 248), while the Federal casualty list listed 714 as missing; the 33 unaccounted for probably drowned, and have been added here to the count of dead.

16. Hay in *St. Louis Missouri Republican*, Oct. 27, Hay, *Inside Lincoln's White House*, 284–85.

17. J. Cutler Andrews, *The North Reports the Civil War*, 677–78n58; Oct. 23, 1861, Strong, *Diary*, 188; *Frank Leslie's Illustrated Newspaper*, Nov. 9; McClellan to division commanders, Oct. 24, McClellan to wife, Oct. 25, McClellan, *Civil War Papers*, 111.

18. Colburn to Stone, Oct. 20, 1861, *OR* 5:290; McCall testimony, *CCW* 2 (1863), 259; Williams to Lewis Allen, Nov. 5, Williams, *From the Cannon's Mouth*, 27; "The Ordeal of General Stone," Stephen W. Sears, *Controversies & Commanders: Dispatches from the Army of the Potomac*, 37.

19. Stone to Colburn, Nov. 1, 1861, McClellan Papers, LC; *New-York Tribune*, Oct. 25, 30; Young report, with Stone endorsement, *OR* 5:327–30; Stone report, *OR* 5:293–99; Stone to Benson J. Lossing, Nov. 5, 1866, Schoff Collection, Clements Library, University of Michigan; Stone supplementary report, *OR* 5:300–302.

20. James A. Hardie to Stone, Jan. 7, 1862, McClellan Papers, LC; Stone G.O. 1, Jan. 2, Moore, *Rebellion Record*, 4:Documents:11; Andrew to Cameron, Nov. 7, 1861, Stone to Seth Williams, Dec. 15, *OR* ser. II, 1:784–85, 786–87; Townsend, *Anecdotes of the Civil War*, 73–74.

21. Sumner speech, *Congressional Globe* (37th Cong., 2nd Sess.), Dec. 18, 1861; Stone to Sumner, Dec. 23, Charles Sumner Papers, Houghton Library, Harvard University.

22. Bruce Tap, *Over Lincoln's Shoulder: The Committee on the Conduct of the War*, 21–24.

23. Henry M. Smith to Charles H. Ray and Joseph Medill, Nov. 4, 1861, Ray Papers, Huntington Library; Chandler to wife, Oct. 27, Chandler Papers, LC; Benjamin F. Wade, *Facts for the People* (Cincinnati, 1864), 2; Oct. 26, 27, Hay, *Inside Lincoln's White House*, 28–29; Trumbull to M. C. Lea, Nov. 5, in Horace White, *The Life of Lyman Trumbull* (Boston: Houghton Mifflin, 1913), 171–72.

24. McClellan to wife, Oct. 30, 31, 1861,

McClellan, *Civil War Papers*, 112–13, 113–14; Scott to Cameron, Oct. 31, *OR* ser. III, 1:611–12; McClellan, *McClellan's Own Story*, 152, and manuscript, McClellan Papers, LC.

25. McClellan to Cameron, Oct. 31, 1861, McClellan, *Civil War Papers*, 114–18. For analysis of McClellan's 150,000 figure for Johnston's army, see Fishel, *Secret War for the Union*, 106–7.

26. Lincoln to McClellan, Nov. 1, 1861, Lincoln, *Collected Works*, 5:9–10; Nov. 1861, Hay, *Inside Lincoln's White House*, 30.

27. McClellan to wife, Nov. 2, 1861, McClellan, *Civil War Papers*, 123; Marszalek, *Henry W. Halleck*, 108–9; Michael Burlingame, ed., *Lincoln's Journalist: John Hay's Anonymous Writings for the Press, 1860–1864* (Carbondale: Southern Illinois University Press, 1998), 136; H.Q. of Army G.O. 97, Nov. 9, *OR* 3:567.

28. John F. Marszalek, *Sherman: A Soldier's Passion for Order* (New York: The Free Press, 1993), 162–63; Sherman to McClellan, Nov. 4, 1861, McClellan Papers, LC; McClellan to Sherman, Nov. 8, McClellan, *Civil War Papers*, 127; McClellan to Lincoln, Sept. 6, to Cameron, Sept. 8, McClellan, *Civil War Papers*, 94, 97; H.Q. of Army G.O. 97, Nov. 9, *OR* 4:349; AP S.O. 136, Nov. 9, *OR* 51.1:503; Keyes to Chase, June 17, 1862, Chase, *Papers*, 3:211–14.

29. Allan Nevins, *Ordeal of the Union: A House Dividing, 1852–1857* (New York: Scribner's, 1947), 2:410; AP S.O. 155, Nov. 25, 1861, *OR* 51.1:507; Sumner testimony, *CCW* 1 (1863), 366; Howard, *Autobiography*, 1:184.

30. Heintzelman diary, Oct. 16, 23, 1861, LC; Meade to wife, Nov. 24, Meade Papers, HSP; Reynolds to sisters, Oct. 14, Reynolds Papers, Franklin and Marshall College, in Nichols, *Toward Gettysburg*, 79; Kearny to Cortlandt Parker, Aug. 29, Dec. 3, Kearny Papers, New Jersey Historical Society.

31. Mary Ellen McClellan to Elizabeth McClellan, c. Dec. 21, 1861, McClellan Papers, LC; Moore, *Rebellion Record*,

3:Diary:85; *Harper's Weekly*, Dec. 7; McClellan to wife, Nov. 20, McClellan, *Civil War Papers*, 137.

32. Bernarr Cresap, *Appomattox Commander: The Story of General E.O.C. Ord*, 64, 69–73; Stuart, Ord, McCall reports, *OR* 5:490–94, 477–80, 474–76; Federal casualties: *OR* 5:489; Confederate casualties: *OR* 5:494; Meade to wife, Dec. 5, 21, 1861, Meade Papers, HSP; *New York Herald*, Dec. 21.

33. Halleck to McClellan, Dec. 6, 1861, *OR* 8:408–10; Buell to McClellan, Nov. 22, *OR* 7:443–44; McClellan to Cameron, Oct. 31, *OR* 5:9.

34. Journal, July 27, 1862, Chase, *Papers*, 1:353–54; Townsend to Jacob D. Cox, Jan. 25, 1887, Cox Papers, Oberlin College Library; McClellan to S.L.M. Barlow, Nov. 8, 1861, McClellan, *Civil War Papers*, 127–28.

35. Nov. 13, 1861, Hay, *Inside Lincoln's White House*, 32; private diary, Oct. 10, Russell, *Russell's Civil War*, 148; McClellan to wife, Nov. 17, McClellan, *Civil War Papers*, 135.

36. Lincoln to McClellan, c. Dec. 1, 1861, Lincoln, *Collected Works*, 5:34–35; Heintzelman diary, July 3, Oct. 20, 1861, Mar. 8, 1862, LC; McClellan to Lincoln, Dec. 10, 1861, McClellan, *Civil War Papers*, 143; Confederate return, *OR* 5:932; Barnard to McClellan, Dec. 5, 6, 1861, and notes, J. G. Barnard, *The Peninsular Campaign and Its Antecedents*, 51–55, 94; Barnard to Sherman, Jan. 6, 1862, John Sherman Papers, LC.

37. Journal, Dec. 12, 1861, July 27, 1862, Chase, *Papers*, 1:317, 353–54; Chase memo, c. Sept. 3, 1862, Jacob S. Schuckers, *The Life and Public Services of Salmon Portland Chase*, 445–46. The sequence of these events requires clarification. Lincoln's interrogatory is undated but was later endorsed by him, "about Dec. 1, 1861." It must have triggered, or energized, McClellan's Urbanna discussions with Barnard, who responded to McClellan (Dec. 5 and 6) before McClellan responded

to Lincoln (Dec. 10). In his Sept. 1862 recollections, Chase said his meeting with McClellan was at "the President's instance," so it follows that Lincoln learned something of the plan from the general before sending him (with the plan) to Chase. Chase placed his meeting with McClellan in Nov., but that is surely an error of recollection. In his journal for Dec. 12, 1861 (*Papers*, 1:317), Chase wrote, "*Genl. McClellan* called at 12 M and remained about an hour and a half," and a few days later Chase met with the New York capitalists.

38. Meade to wife, Dec. 2, 1861, Meade Papers, HSP; Chase memo, c. Sept. 3, 1862, Schuckers, *Chase*, 445; *CCW* 1 (1863), 5; John A. Logan to John A. McClernand, Dec. 27, 1861, McClernand Papers, Lincoln Presidential Library; *New-York Tribune*, Jan. 1, 1862; Meigs, "Relations," *American Historical Review*, 26:2 (Jan. 1921), 292.

5. GRAND ARMY, GRAND CAMPAIGN

1. Dec. 31, 1861, Bates, *Diary*, 220; *New York Express*, Dec. 30; Meade to wife, Jan. 5, 8, 1862, Meade Papers, HSP; Ethan S. Rafuse, "Typhoid and Tumult: Lincoln's Response to General McClellan's Bout with Typhoid . . . ," *Journal of the Abraham Lincoln Association*, 18:2 (Summer 1997), 1–16.

2. Heintzelman diary, Sept. 6, Nov. 25, Dec. 6, 1861, LC; Heintzelman testimony, *CCW* 1 (1863), 119–21.

3. Richardson, McCall testimony, *CCW* 1 (1863), 113–16, 165–66.

4. Franklin, Porter testimony, Wade statement, *CCW* 1 (1863), 122–30, 170–72, 141.

5. McDowell testimony, *CCW* 1 (1863), 131–45.

6. *New-York Tribune*, Dec. 27, 1861; Hans L. Trefousse, *Benjamin Franklin Wade:*

Radical Republican from Ohio (New York: Twayne, 1963), 159; Lincoln to McClellan, Jan. 1, 1862, Lincoln, *Collected Works*, 5:88; journal, Jan. 6, Chase, *Papers*, 1:321–22.

7. Lincoln to Buell, Halleck, Dec. 31, 1861, Buell, Halleck to Lincoln, Jan. 1, 1862, *OR* 7:524, 526; Lincoln endorsement, Jan. 10, 1862, Lincoln, *Collected Works*, 5:95; borrowers' ledgers, LC Archives.

8. Meigs, "Relations," *American Historical Review*, 26:2 (Jan. 1921), 292; McDowell memo, Henry J. Raymond, *Life and Public Services of Abraham Lincoln*, 772–74. In 1864 Raymond showed McDowell's memo to Lincoln, who found nothing to object to except the phrase "the Jacobinism of Congress," which he did not remember using "and which I wish not to be published in any event." (Lincoln to Raymond, Oct. 7, 1864, Lincoln, *Collected Works*, 8:39–40.) In 1865, after Lincoln's death, Raymond published the memo in full.

9. McDowell memo, Raymond, *Life and Public Services of Lincoln*, 774–76; William Franklin, "The First Great Crime of the War," McClure, *Annals of the War*, 77–78; journal, Jan. 11, 1862, Chase, *Papers*, 1:324; McClellan, *McClellan's Own Story*, 157–58. An undated memo by Lincoln (*Collected Works*, 5:119) containing notations on the Occoquan plan probably relates to these January discussions.

10. Meigs, "Relations," *American Historical Review*, 26:2 (Jan. 1921), 292–93; McDowell memo, Raymond, *Life and Public Services of Lincoln*, 776–78; Franklin, "The First Great Crime of the War," McClure, *Annals of the War*, 78–79; Jan. 12, 1862, Browning, *Diary*, 1:523. McClellan's account in his memoir of the Jan. 13 council, describing how he took the measure of those present ("After I had thus disposed of the Secretary of the Treasury . . ."), does not mesh with the accounts of Meigs and McDowell or even his friend

Franklin and is scarcely credible: *Mc-Clellan's Own Story*, 155–59, and manuscript, McClellan Papers, LC.

11. Nov. 13, 1861, Hay, *Inside Lincoln's White House*, 32; Chase memo, c. Sept. 3, 1862, Schuckers, Chase, 446; *McClellan's Own Story* manuscript, McClellan Papers, LC.

12. Stanton to John A. Dix, June 11, 1861, Morgan Dix, ed., *Memoirs of John Adams Dix* (New York: Harper, 1883), 2:19; Nicolay memo, Oct. 2, Nicolay, *With Lincoln in the White House*, 59; Francis Fessenden, *Life and Public Services of William Pitt Fessenden* (Boston: Houghton Mifflin, 1907), 1:231.

13. Alexander M. Reid, quoted in Benjamin P. Thomas and Harold M. Hyman, *Stanton: The Life and Times of Lincoln's Secretary of War*, 131; McClellan, "The Peninsular Campaign," *Battles and Leaders*, 2:163; McClellan to S.L.M. Barlow, Jan. 18, 1862, to Marcy, Jan. 29, McClellan, *Civil War Papers*, 154, 160; Ward to William H. Seward, Jan. 14, Seward Papers, University of Rochester; Stanton to Charles A. Dana, Jan. 24, Dana, *Recollections of the Civil War: With the Leaders at Washington and in the Field in the Sixties*, 5.

14. Ives to Bennett, Jan. 15, 16, 1862, James Gordon Bennett Papers, LC; McClellan to Marcy, Jan. 29, McClellan, *Civil War Papers*, 160; Louis M. Starr, *Bohemian Brigade: Civil War Newsmen in Action* (New York: Knopf, 1954), 77–81.

15. McClellan to Lincoln, Jan. 15, 1862, McClellan, *Civil War Papers*, 154; Tap, *Over Lincoln's Shoulder*, 108–9; [Arthur T. Pierson], *Zachariah Chandler: An Outline Sketch of His Life and Public Services* (Detroit, 1880), 224–26; *New York Herald*, Jan. 19. According to Pierson (224), McClellan "was not formally summoned before the committee then, but simply called in for general consultation." There was no stenographic record.

16. Stone testimony, *CCW* 2 (1863), 265–82; Tompkins testimony, *CCW* 2 (1863), 289–97, and testimony of Downey, De Courcy, Brady, Rea, Berry, Foote, Dimmick, Delany, and Boyle in the same volume; McClellan to Stone, Dec. 5, 1862, McClellan, *Civil War Papers*, 526–27. See "The Ordeal of General Stone," in Sears, *Controversies & Commanders*, 29–50. The 2nd New York militia was redesignated the 82nd New York volunteers.

17. *CCW* journal, 1 (1863), 74, 78, 79; Stanton to McClellan, Jan. 28, 1862, *CCW* 2 (1863), 502; Stone, McClellan testimony, ibid., 426–33, 510; Feb. 3, Bates, *Diary*, 229; McClellan to Marcy, Jan. 29, McClellan, *Civil War Papers*, 160; Pinkerton to McClellan, Feb. 6, McClellan Papers, LC.

18. "Ordeal of General Stone," Sears, *Controversies & Commanders*, 42–48; McClellan to Stone, Dec. 5, 1862, McClellan, *Civil War Papers*, 526–27. Col. Tompkins escaped court-martial when Stone was imprisoned, but his Bull Run misconduct was not forgotten; denied promotion, he left the army in May 1862: McClellan to Stanton, Mar. 24, 1862, Lincoln Papers, LC.

19. *New York Times*, Feb. 11, 1862; Mrs. Lee to husband, Feb. 10, Lee, *Wartime Washington*, 100; Feb. 12, Strong, *Diary*, 206; Feb. 3, Bates, *Diary*, 229.

20. Heintzelman diary, Feb. 10, July 23, 1862, LC; Kearny to Cortlandt Parker, Mar. 4, Kearny Papers, New Jersey Historical Society; Abbott to mother, Feb. 13, Abbott, *Fallen Leaves*, 102–3; Patrick diary, Feb. 28, Patrick Papers, LC; Meade to wife, Feb. 11, Meade Papers, HSP; Burns to Cox, Feb. 3, S. S. Cox Papers, John Hay Library, Brown University.

21. Sedgwick to sister, Feb. 19, 1862, John Sedgwick, *Correspondence of John Sedgwick, Major-General*, 2:38.

22. Heintzelman diary, Dec. 16, 28, 1861, Jan. 1, 10, Feb. 16, 1862, LC; Mar. 6, 1862, Marsena R. Patrick, *Inside Lincoln's*

Army: The Diary of Marsena Rudolf Patrick, David S. Sparks, ed., 48; Smith testimony, *CCW* 1 (1863), 187; McAllister to wife, Jan. 1, Robert McAllister, *The Civil War Letters of General Robert McAllister*, James I. Robertson, Jr., ed., 110–11; Kearny to Cortlandt Parker, Feb. 15, Kearny Papers, New Jersey Historical Society.

23. Brooks to father, Feb. 18, 1862, W.T.H. Brooks Papers, U.S. Army Heritage & Education Center; McClellan to Stanton, Jan. 26, to Thomas A. Scott, Feb. 20, McClellan, *Civil War Papers*, 158, 185; Scott to Stanton, Feb. 2, Stanton to Scott, Feb. 21, Stanton Papers, LC.

24. Feb. 19, 1862, Wainwright, *Diary of Battle*, 18; Feb. 17, Stephen M. Weld, *War Diary and Letters of Stephen Minot Weld, 1861–1865*, 57.

25. Tucker report, Apr. 5, 1862, McClellan Papers, LC.

26. McClellan, *Report*, 42; Lincoln to McClellan, Feb. 3, 1862, Lincoln, *Collected Works*, 5:118–19; McClellan to Stanton, Feb. 3 (draft), McClellan, *Civil War Papers*, 171n. In final editing of this draft, McClellan crossed out "this morning" and replaced it with "in this long letter."

27. President's General War Order No. 1, Jan. 27, 1862, President's Special War Order No. 1, Jan. 31, Lincoln, *Collected Works*, 5:111–12, 115.

28. McClellan, *Report*, 43; McClellan to Stanton, Feb. 3, 1862, McClellan, *Civil War Papers*, 162–71; Lincoln to McClellan, Feb. 3, Lincoln, *Collected Works*, 5:118–19; Confederate return, *OR* 5:1086; Barnard, *The Peninsular Campaign*, 51–55, 94.

29. Tucker to Stanton, Apr. 5, 1862, McClellan Papers, LC.

30. Heintzelman diary, Feb. 21, Jan. 20, 23, 1862, Mar. 18, 1863, and memo, Aug. 10, 1870, Heintzelman Papers, LC.

31. McDowell memo, Raymond, *Life and Public Services of Lincoln*, 773; McDowell, Heintzelman, Meigs, Porter testimony, *CCW* 1 (1863), 144, 118, 159, 176; Wade in ibid., 6–7; Heintzelman diary, Feb. 21, 1862, LC.

32. Journal, *CCW* 1 (1863), 84–85.

33. McClellan, "Peninsular Campaign," *Battles and Leaders*, 2:165; McClellan to Stanton, Feb. 26, 27, 1862, McClellan to wife, Feb. 27, memo to War Dept., [Mar. 1], McClellan, *Civil War Papers*, 191, 192, 191–92, 193–95; Chase memo, c. Sept. 3, 1862, Schuckers, *Chase*, 446.

34. Nicolay memo, Feb. 27, 1862, and recollection, Nicolay, *With Lincoln in the White House*, 72–73, 217n45; White to Joseph Medill and Charles H. Ray, Mar. 3, Ray Papers, Huntington Library; Helen Nicolay, *Lincoln's Secretary: A Biography of John G. Nicolay* (New York: Longmans, Green, 1949), 149; Sumner to John A. Andrew, Mar. 2, Charles Sumner, *The Selected Letters of Charles Sumner*, Beverly Wilson Palmer, ed., 2:103. Nicolay's memo renders Lincoln's remark as, "Why in the —— nation, Gen. Marcy...." In the circumstances, "damnation" best accounts for Nicolay's elision.

35. McClellan memo on Potomac batteries, [Mar. 1, 1862], McClellan to Halleck, Mar. 3, McClellan, *Civil War Papers*, 195–96; Horace White to Charles H. Ray, Mar. 3, Ray Papers, Huntington Library; Mar. 6, 7, Patrick, *Inside Lincoln's Army*, 48–49.

36. Meade to wife, Mar. 9, 1862, Meade Papers, HSP; Ward to Barlow, Mar. 16, S.L.M. Barlow Papers, Huntington Library; James H. Campbell to wife, Mar. 4, Schoff Collection, Clements Library, University of Michigan. Gen. Edwin Sumner was cousin to the abolitionist Sen. Charles Sumner.

37. Heintzelman diary, Mar. 4, 1862, LC; Heintzelman testimony, *CCW* 1 (1863), 121.

38. McClellan, *McClellan's Own Story*, 195–96; McClellan, "Peninsular Campaign," *Battles and Leaders*, 2:165–66. Lincoln scholar Don E. Fehrenbacher

gives this McClellan memoir account a grade of D, suspect: Fehrenbacher, *Recollected Words of Lincoln,* 313.

39. Virginia Woodbury Fox diary, Mar. 7, 1862, Levi Woodbury Papers, LC.

40. Heintzelman diary, Mar. 8, 1862, Barnard to Heintzelman, Oct. 2, 1864, Heintzelman to Barnard, Oct. 14, 1864, Heintzelman Papers, LC; Barnard, *Peninsular Campaign,* 51–52; McDowell in *New York Herald,* Dec. 4, 1864. McClellan gave the date of his interview with Lincoln and the subsequent council of war as March 8, but Heintzelman's diary and Keyes to Stanton (Mar. 14, 1862, Stanton Papers, LC) make it clear that March 7 is the correct date.

41. Heintzelman diary, Mar. 8, 1862, LC; Naglee and Stanton, war council notes, [Mar. 8], Stanton Papers, LC; Naglee to William D. Kelley, Sept. 27, 1864, in *New York World,* Oct. 1, 1864; Barnard to E. D. Townsend, Oct. 3, 1864, Lincoln Papers, LC; President's General War Orders Nos. 2 and 3, Mar. 8, 1862, Lincoln, *Collected Works,* 5:149–50, 151; Mar. 1862, Hay, *Inside Lincoln's White House,* 35; Heintzelman Occoquan memo, Mar. 8, Lincoln Papers.

42. Heintzelman diary, Mar. 8, 1862, LC; McClellan, *McClellan's Own Story,* 222, and manuscript, McClellan Papers, LC; McClellan, army corps memo, c. Jan. 1862, McClellan Papers. This army corps memo is undated, but includes Charles Stone's division in its listing, so it was written before Stone's arrest.

43. President's General War Order No. 3, Mar. 8, 1862, Lincoln, *Collected Works,* 5:151; Heintzelman diary, Mar. 8, LC; W. D. Kelley, *Lincoln and Stanton: A Study of the War Administration of 1861 and 1862* (New York: Putnam's, 1885), 33.

44. Confederate returns, *OR* 5:932, 1086; Johnston to Davis, Feb. 16, 1862, *OR* 5:1074; Bragg diary, Feb. 19, Southern Historical Collection, University of North Carolina; Joseph E. Johnston, *Narrative of Military Operations,* 102–3.

45. Mar. 9, 1862, Nicolay, *With Lincoln in the White House,* 74–75; Welles, *Diary,* 678–82; Montgomery Meigs to father, Mar. 9, Meigs Papers, LC.

46. Fox to Welles, Mar. 9, 1862, *OR* 9:21–22; Hooker to Seth Williams, Mar. 9, Banks to Marcy, Mar. 8, Leavitt Hunt to Heintzelman, Mar. 9, McClellan Papers, LC; McClellan to Lincoln and Stanton, Mar. 9, McClellan, *Civil War Papers,* 200.

47. *New-York Tribune,* Mar. 15, 1862; McClellan to Marcy, Mar. 11, *OR* 51.1:550; Feb. 1862 return, *OR* 5:732; Dawes to sister, Mar. 12, Dawes Papers, Wisconsin Historical Society; McClellan to Stanton, Mar. 11, *OR* 5:742; McClellan to wife, Mar. 11, McClellan, *Civil War Papers,* 202–3; Meade to wife, Apr. 13, Meade Papers, HSP; McClellan, *Report,* 57.

48. *Philadelphia Press,* Mar. 12, 1862; *New-York Tribune,* Mar. 14, 15; M. H. Taylor, *On Two Continents: Memories of Half a Century* (New York, 1905), 116; Hawthorne, "Chiefly About War Matters," *Atlantic Monthly,* July 1862; Mrs. Lee to husband, Mar. 11, Lee, *Wartime Washington,* 109.

49. McClellan to Stanton, Mar. 11, 1862, McClellan, *Civil War Papers,* 201; McClellan, "Peninsular Campaign," *Battles and Leaders,* 2:167; McClellan testimony, *CCW* 1 (1863), 426; McClellan to Stanton, Feb. 3, McClellan, *Civil War Papers,* 168.

50. President's War Order No. 3, Mar. 11, 1862, Lincoln, *Collected Works,* 5:155; Dennison to McClellan, Mar. 14, McClellan Papers, LC; McClellan to Lincoln, Mar. 12, McClellan, *Civil War Papers,* 207.

51. McClellan to Fox, Mar. 12, 1862, McClellan, *Civil War Papers,* 206; Fox to McClellan, Mar. 13, *OR* 9:27; Goldsborough to Fox, Mar. 16, Fox, *Confidential Correspondence,* 1:250.

52. Heintzelman diary, Mar. 11, 13, 1862, LC; *McClellan's Own Story* manuscript, McClellan Papers, LC; Sumner, McDowell testimony, *CCW* 1 (1863), 360, 270; Keyes to Chase, June 17, Chase, *Papers*, 3:212; Keyes, *Fifty Years' Observation*, 438; Smith, *Autobiography*, 32; Barnard to Fox, Mar. 12, *OR* 9:27; McClellan to John Tucker, Mar. 12, *OR* 5:743; McClellan to Stanton, Mar. 13, McClellan, *Civil War Papers*, 207.

53. President's General War Order No. 3, Mar. 8, 1862, Lincoln, *Collected Works*, 5:151; Keyes testimony, *CCW* 1 (1863), 598; war council memo, Mar. 13, *OR* 5:55–56; McClellan to Stanton, Mar. 13, McClellan, *Civil War Papers*, 207; Lincoln to McClellan, Mar. 13, Lincoln, *Collected Works*, 5:157–58 (signed by Stanton but credited to Lincoln).

54. Heintzelman diary, Mar. 13, 1862, LC; address to Army of the Potomac, Mar. 14, McClellan, *Civil War Papers*, 211. McClellan's notes from Napoleon's address (McClellan Papers, LC) read: " . . . you will then return to your firesides, and your fellow citizens will point you out & say 'He belonged to the Army of Italy.'"

55. McClellan to Seth Williams, Mar. 13, 1862, *OR* 5:748; Heintzelman diary, Mar. 14, Seth Williams to Heintzelman, Mar. 14, Heintzelman Papers, LC; Franklin to McClellan, Apr. 7, McClellan Papers, LC; Kearny to wife, Mar. 17, Apr. 24, Kearny Papers, New Jersey Historical Society; McClellan to Stanton, Mar. 14, *OR* 5:754; Howard to wife, Mar. 16, O. O. Howard Papers, Bowdoin College Library.

56. Lincoln to McClellan, Mar. 31, 1862, Lincoln, *Collected Works*, 5:175–76; McClellan to Lincoln, Mar. 31, McClellan, *Civil War Papers*, 219–20. Order of battle: Frank J. Welcher, *The Union Army, 1861–1865*, vol. 1.

57. "Dan Sickles, Political General," Sears, *Controversies & Commanders*, 202–3: Meade to wife, Feb. 23, 1862, Meade Papers, HSP; Brooks to father, Feb. 18, Brooks Papers, U.S. Army Heritage & Education Center.

58. Stanton to McClellan, Mar. 13, 1862, *OR* 5:752; Ethan Allen Hitchcock, *Fifty Years in Camp and Field*, 421–23; Hitchcock diary, Mar. 15, 17, Gilcrease Museum; Hitchcock to Henry Hitchcock, Apr. 25, Missouri Historical Society; Apr. 2, Browning, *Diary*, 1:538–39; Grant to Lincoln, Feb. 9, 1863, Grant, *The Papers of Ulysses S. Grant*, John Y. Simon, ed., 7:301; Thomas and Hyman, *Stanton*, 200–202. Stanton in this period is elucidated in William Marvel, *Lincoln's Autocrat: The Life of Edwin Stanton*, chs. 8 and 9.

59. Stark to Barlow, Mar. 16, 1862, Samuel Ward to Barlow, Mar. 18, McClellan to Barlow, Mar. 16, S.L.M. Barlow Papers, Huntington Library; Edmund C. Stedman to McClellan, Mar. 17, McClellan Papers, LC; Porter to Manton Marble, Mar. 17, Marble Papers, LC.

60. McClellan, *Report*, 72–74, and manuscript, McClellan Papers, LC; McClellan, *McClellan's Own Story*, 254–56; Heintzelman diary, Mar. 17, 1862, LC; Marcy to McDowell, Apr. 1, *OR* 51.1:565; Tucker report, Apr. 5, *OR* 5:46.

61. McClellan to Stanton, Mar. 17, 1862, to Tucker, Mar. 13, *OR* 11.3:10, 5:752; McClellan to Stanton, Mar. 18, to L. Thomas, Mar. 13, McClellan, *Civil War Papers*, 214, 208.

62. Russell to Marcy, Apr. 2, 1862, Russell, *Russell's Civil War*, 236; Barlow to McClellan, Mar. 6, S.L.M. Barlow Papers, Huntington Library; Hay to Nicolay, Apr. 3, Hay, *At Lincoln's Side*, 19.

63. President's War Order No. 3, Mar. 11, 1862, Lincoln, *Collected Works*, 5:151; John W. Garrett to Stanton, Mar. 18, RG 107 (M-473), NA; McClellan to Banks, Mar. 16, Apr. 1, McClellan, *Civil War Papers*, 212, 220–21.

64. Stanton to Lincoln, Mar. 30, 1862, Stanton Papers, LC; McClellan to L. Thomas, to wife, Apr. 1, McClellan,

Civil War Papers, 222–23, 223; Hay to Nicolay, Apr. 1, Hay, *At Lincoln's Side*, 18; Apr. 2, Browning, *Diary*, 1:537–38.

65. McClellan to L. Thomas, to wife, Apr. 1, 1862, McClellan, *Civil War Papers*, 222–23, 223; Wadsworth to Stanton, Apr. 2, Stanton to L. Thomas and Hitchcock, Apr. 2, *OR* 11.3:60–61, 57; Sears, *To the Gates of Richmond*, 32–34; Stanton to Dyer, May 18, *OR* 19.2:726; Hitchcock testimony, *CCW* 1 (1863), 304–5; Sumner to John A. Andrew, May 28, Charles Sumner, *Selected Letters*, 2:115; John C. Ropes, "General McClellan," *PMHSM*, 10:100.

6. TOWARD THE GATES OF RICHMOND

1. Heintzelman diary, Mar. 24–Apr. 1, 1862, and Peninsula notes (Apr. 7, 1863), Heintzelman Papers, LC.

2. McClellan to wife, Apr. 3, 1862, to Stanton, Apr. 3, Mar. 19, McClellan, *Civil War Papers*, 225, 227, 215; Porter to McClellan, Mar. 30, *OR* 51.1:564–65; Fox to Goldsborough, Mar. 24, Goldsborough to Fox, Apr. 21, Fox, *Confidential Correspondence*, 1:251, 261; Goldsborough to McClellan, Apr. 6, *OR* 11.3:80; McClellan to Totten, Mar. 28, to Goldsborough, Apr. 3, McClellan, *Civil War Papers*, 218, 226.

3. Order of march, Apr. 2, 1862, *OR* 11.3:63; Heintzelman diary, Apr. 3, McClellan to Heintzelman, Apr. 4, Heintzelman Papers, LC; Sedgwick to sister, Apr. 3, Sedgwick, *Correspondence*, 2:42; Sears, *To the Gates of Richmond*, 35; McClellan to wife, Apr. 4, McClellan, *Civil War Papers*, 228.

4. Charles H. Howard to Dellie Gilmore, Apr. 10, 1862, C. H. Howard Papers, Bowdoin College Library; McClellan to wife, Apr. 6, to Goldsborough, Apr. 5, McClellan, *Civil War Papers*, 229–30; Porter, Keyes reports, *OR* 11.1:286, 358; Keyes to McClellan, Keyes to Marcy

(two), Apr. 5, *OR* 11.3:69–71; Alexander S. Webb, *The Peninsula: McClellan's Campaign of 1862*, 54; Earl B. McElfresh, *Maps and Mapmakers of the Civil War*, 21 — the map, by Thomas Jefferson Cram, is reproduced on page 84.

5. Magruder report, *OR* 11.1:405–6; Sears, *To the Gates of Richmond*, 37–38; C. Vann Woodward, ed., *Mary Chesnut's Civil War* (New Haven, Conn.: Yale University Press, 1981), 401.

6. McClellan to Totten, Mar. 28, 1862, to Goldsborough, Apr. 5, McClellan, *Civil War Papers*, 218, 229; Seth Williams to Van Vliet, Apr. 5, *OR* 11.1:71–72; Journal of the siege, Apr. 5, *OR* 11.1:320; Arthur McClellan diary, Apr. 5, McClellan Papers, LC.

7. L. Thomas to McClellan, Apr. 4, 1862, *OR* 11.1:10; L. Thomas to McClellan, Apr. 4, Stanton to McClellan, Apr. 6, Lincoln to Stanton, Apr. 3, *OR* 11.3:66, 73, 65–66; McDowell, Hitchcock testimony, *CCW* 1 (1863), 261–62, 305; Hitchcock to Winfield Scott, May 28, E. A. Hitchcock Papers, LC; McClellan to Lincoln, Apr. 5, to wife, Apr. 6, McClellan, *Civil War Papers*, 228, 230; Heintzelman diary, Apr. 5, LC; Franklin to wife, Apr. 9, Historical Society of York County, in Snell, *From First to Last*, 92; Keyes to Ira Harris, Apr. 7, *OR* 11.1:13; Paris journal, Apr. 5, Fondation Saint-Louis.

8. Smith, *Autobiography*, 34–35; Hancock report, *OR* 11.1:309; Heintzelman diary, May 6, 1862, and Peninsula notes (Apr. 7, 1863), Heintzelman Papers, LC; George H. Bangs report, [Apr. 7, 1862], McClellan Papers, LC; McClellan to Stanton, Apr. 7, 1862, McClellan, *Civil War Papers*, 232; Magruder to Lee, Apr. 5, Johnston to Lee, Apr. 22, *OR* 11.3:422, 455–56. In a later diary entry (Aug. 20, 1862), Heintzelman wrote, "I believe the [Yorktown] siege was determined on partly through the influence of Genl. F. J. Porter. I know he was in favor of a siege from the beginning."

9. McClellan to Stanton, Apr. 7, 1862, to wife, Apr. 23, McClellan, *Civil War Papers,* 232, 245; McClellan to wife, Apr. 12, McClellan Papers, LC; McClellan, *Report,* 87.

10. Porter to Marble, Apr. 26, 1862, Manton Marble Papers, LC; Keyes to Harris, Apr. 7, *OR* 11.1:13–14; Key to John Sherman, Apr. 8, McClellan Papers, LC; Key to Chase, Apr. 10, Chase Papers, HSP; Chase to McDowell, May 14, Schuckers, *Chase,* 435.

11. McClellan to Franklin, Apr. 6, 1862, McClellan, *Civil War Papers,* 231; Franklin to McClellan, Apr. 7, McClellan Papers, LC; Franklin to John C. Ropes, Dec. 19, 1893, Ropes Papers, Boston University Library; Sumner to John A. Andrew, Apr. 22, 1862, Andrew Papers, MHS; Lincoln to McClellan, Apr. 6, Lincoln, *Collected Works,* 5:182; McClellan to wife, Apr. 8, to Stanton, Apr. 7, to Lincoln, Apr. 7, 18, McClellan, *Civil War Papers,* 234, 232–33, 233, 241–42.

12. Lincoln to McClellan, Apr. 9, 1862, Lincoln, *Collected Works,* 5:184–85; McClellan to Lincoln, Apr. 14, McClellan, *Civil War Papers,* 239; Stanton to McClellan, Apr. 11, *OR* 11.3:90.

13. McClellan, *Report,* 77; Franklin to wife, Apr. 20, 1862, Historical Society of York County, in Snell, *From First to Last,* 96.

14. Andrews, *The North Reports the Civil War,* 197; Associated Press to Stanton, Apr. 9, 1862, Lincoln Papers, LC; Hay to Nicolay, Apr. 9, Hay, *At Lincoln's Side,* 20; Apr. 9, Bates, *Diary,* 249; Barlow to McClellan, Apr. 14, S.L.M. Barlow Papers, Huntington Library; Montgomery Blair to McClellan, Apr. 9, F. P. Blair to McClellan, Apr. 12, McClellan Papers, LC; McClellan to F. Blair, c. Apr. 17, in Elizabeth Blair Lee, *Wartime Washington,* 129n.

15. Barnard, Barry reports, *OR* 11.1:316–37, 338–49; Stone to L. Thomas, Apr. 13, 1862, *OR,* ser. II, 3:449.

16. McClellan to Smith, Apr. 15, 1862, Mc-Clellan, *McClellan's Own Story,* 284–85; Smith, Brooks reports, *OR* 11.1:364–67, 372–73; McClellan to wife, Apr. 18, Mc-Clellan, *Civil War Papers,* 240; Smith, *Autobiography,* 35; Brooks to father, Apr. 22, Brooks Papers, U.S. Army Heritage & Education Center; *New York Herald,* Apr. 23; McClellan to Lincoln, Apr. 25, Lincoln Papers, LC; Smith to Morrill, Apr. 30, W. F. Smith Papers, Vermont Historical Society; *New-York Tribune,* April 24, May 14.

17. Heintzelman diary, Apr. 29, 1862, LC; Richardson to wife, Apr. 25, Huntington Library; Stanton to Sprague, Mar. 26, *OR* 51.1:559–60; Sprague to Stanton, Apr. 24, May 3, Stanton Papers, LC; Keyes, *Fifty Years' Observation,* 446; McClellan to Smith, Apr. 15, McClellan, *McClellan's Own Story,* 284–85; Stanton to McClellan, Apr. 12, McClellan Papers, LC; McClellan to Stanton, Apr. 13, *OR* 11.3:94.

18. Heintzelman diary, Apr. 30, May 1, 2, 1862, LC; Lincoln to McClellan, May 9, 21, Lincoln, *Collected Works,* 5:208–9, 227; Hamilton petition, May 15, Lincoln Papers, LC; McClellan to Lincoln, May 22, McClellan, *Civil War Papers,* 273; Kearny to wife, May 1, to Cortlandt Parker, May 3, Kearny Papers, New Jersey Historical Society. Hamilton would serve in the Western theater, where intriguing against Grant got him in trouble and in 1863 forced his resignation.

19. Heintzelman diary, May 3, 1862, LC; Pinkerton to McClellan, May 3, *OR* 11.1:268; McClellan to Smith, Apr. 29, McClellan Papers, LC; McClellan to wife, May 3, McClellan, *Civil War Papers,* 252; Sedgwick to sister, Apr. 14, Sedgwick, *Correspondence,* 2:43.

20. Confederate return, c. Apr. 30, 1862, Johnston to Lee, Apr. 29, *OR* 11.3:484, 473; Heintzelman diary, May 4, LC; McClellan to Stanton, May 4, McClellan, *Civil War Papers,* 253.

21. Paris journal, May 12, 1862, Fondation Saint-Louis; Heintzelman diary, May

4, Williamsburg memo (Apr. 18, 1869), Heintzelman Papers, LC.

22. Stoneman, Hooker, Smith reports, *OR* 11.1:423–24, 464, 525–26; Heintzelman diary, May 4, 6, 1862, LC; Keyes to Marcy, May 4, McClellan Papers, LC.

23. McClellan to Stanton, to Scott, to wife, May 4, 1862, McClellan, *Civil War Papers*, 253–55; *New-York Tribune*, May 4; Francis E. Spinner to J. C. Day, May 11, Spinner Papers, Chicago Historical Society; Paris journal, May 12, Fondation Saint-Louis; Hooker to James Nesmith, May 4, Nesmith Papers, Oregon Historical Society; *New York Evening Post*, May 5. Bryant's figure of speech echoed the Roman poet Horace.

24. T. H. Patterson to W. Smith, May 4, 1862, *NOR* 7:311–12; Heintzelman diary, May 3, LC; Franklin report, *OR* 11.1:614–15; Franklin to wife, May 5, Historical Society of York County, in Snell, *From First to Last*, 99; McClellan to Franklin, May 5, *OR* 11.3:143; Franklin to McClellan, Feb. 8, 1884, McClellan, *McClellan's Own Story*, 335–36.

25. McClellan, *McClellan's Own Story*, 323, 327; Rosecrans testimony, *CCW* 3 (1865), 6; McClellan to Stanton, to wife, May 5, 1862, McClellan, *Civil War Papers*, 255–56.

26. May 5, 1862, Wainwright, *Diary of Battle*, 49; Steven H. Newton, *Joseph E. Johnston and the Defense of Richmond* (Lawrence: University Press of Kansas, 1998),133; McClellan to Heintzelman, May 4, Heintzelman Papers, LC; Sumner, Keyes reports, *OR* 11.1:450, 511.

27. Hooker, Smith reports, *OR* 11.1:464, 526; Hooker testimony, *CCW* 1 (1863), 576; Heintzelman diary, May 6, 1862, Williamsburg memo (Apr. 18, 1869), Heintzelman Papers, LC. The Whittaker house is called the Adams house in some accounts.

28. Smith, *Autobiography*, 35–36; Paris journal, May 12, 1862, Fondation Saint-Louis; Heintzelman diary, May 6, LC.

29. Prince de Joinville, *The Army of the Potomac: Its Organization, Its Com-mander, and Its Campaign*, 51; Hooker to James Nesmith, May 5, 1862, Nesmith Papers, Oregon Historical Society; May 5, Wainwright, *Diary of Battle*, 50–51.

30. Hooker, Keyes reports, *OR* 11.1:465–66, 511–12; Sumner to Richardson, May 1, 1862, to Keyes, May 2, *OR* 51.1:589, 592; Heintzelman diary, May 6, LC; Paris journal, May 12, Fondation Saint-Louis. For an excerpt of the count's journal on Williamsburg, edited by Mark Grimsley and translated by Bernatello Glod, see *Civil War Times*, 24:3 (May 1985), 18–26.

31. Heintzelman diary, May 6, 1862, Williamsburg memo (Apr. 18, 1869), Heintzelman Papers, LC; Kearny, Hooker reports, *OR* 11.1:491, 467; Sears, *To the Gates of Richmond*, 74–75; Thomas B. Leaver to brother, May 9, 1862, New Hampshire Historical Society; John W. De Peyster, *Personal and Military History of Philip Kearny, Major-General, United States Volunteers*, 281.

32. Peck report, *OR* 11.1:520; Kearny to Oliver S. Halsted, May 15, 1862, Lincoln Papers, LC; John S. Godfrey to brother, May 8, New Hampshire Historical Society; Kearny to wife, May 7, Kearny Papers, New Jersey Historical Society; Heintzelman to wife, May 6, Heintzelman Papers, LC; Kearny, Berry reports, *OR* 11.1:492, 504; Berry to wife, May 9, Edward K. Gould, *Major-General Hiram G. Berry*, 141; Hooker testimony, *CCW* 1 (1863), 577.

33. James E. Smith, *A Famous Battery and Its Campaigns, 1861–'64* (Washington, 1892), 64; May 7, 1862, Haydon, *Country, Cause & Leader*, 234–35; J. J. Marks, *The Peninsula Campaign in Virginia*, 158; De Peyster, *Personal and Military History of Kearny*, 291; Heintzelman notebook, May 6, Williamsburg memo (Apr. 18, 1869), Heintzelman Papers, LC.

34. Paris journal, May 12, 1862, *Civil War Times*, 24:3 (May 1985), 20; Smith, *Autobiography*, 36–38; Smith, "Memoirs,"

Vermont Historical Society; Smith, Hancock, Brooks, Sumner reports, *OR* 11.1:527–28, 535–37, 556, 451; Thomas W. Hyde, *Following the Greek Cross or, Memories of the Sixth Army Corps,* 51; Hyde, *Civil War Letters of General Thomas W. Hyde,* 15.

35. Paris journal, May 12, 1862, *Civil War Times,* 24:3 (May 1985), 20; McClellan to wife, May 6, McClellan, *Civil War Papers,* 257; McClellan, *Report,* 91; Hooker testimony, *CCW* 1 (1863), 577; Keyes to McClellan, May 5, McClellan, *McClellan's Own Story,* 301; Smith, "Memoirs," Vermont Historical Society; Francis W. Palfrey, "After the Fall of Yorktown," *PMHSM,* 1:156.

36. Smith, *Autobiography,* 38; McClellan to wife, May 6, 1862, to Stanton, May 5, 10, McClellan, *Civil War Papers,* 257, 256, 261; Franklin report, *OR* 11.1:614; McClellan to Stanton, May 9, *OR* 11.3:156–57; McClellan to wife, May 10, McClellan Papers, LC; casualties: *OR* 11.1:618.

37. McClellan to wife, May 6, 1862, McClellan, *Civil War Papers,* 256; McClellan to Stanton, May 7, *OR* 11.3:149; casualties: Sears, *To the Gates of Richmond,* 82; Heintzelman diary, Aug. 19, LC; Darius N. Couch notebook, 1873, Old Colony Historical Society, 112; Smith to John C. Ropes, Feb. 13, 1898, Ropes Papers, Boston University Library; Howard to wife, May 31, O. O. Howard Papers, Bowdoin College Library; Porter to Daniel Butterfield, [May 5, 1862], RG 94 (M-619), NA.

38. McClellan to wife, May 6, 1862, McClellan, *Civil War Papers,* 257; Paris journal, May 12, *Civil War Times,* 24:3 (May 1985), 20–22; Keyes, *Fifty Years' Observation,* 438; Heintzelman diary, May 6, Williamsburg memo (Apr. 18, 1869), Heintzelman Papers, LC.

39. Hooker to James Nesmith, c. May 7, 1862, Nesmith Papers, Oregon Historical Society; Kearny to wife, May 15, Kearny Papers, New Jersey Historical Society; James M. Martin, *History of the Fifty-seventh Regiment, Pennsylvania Veteran Volunteer Infantry* (Meadville, Pa., 1904), 28–29; McClellan to wife, May 6, McClellan, *Civil War Papers,* 256–57; McClellan to J. P. Nicholson, Oct. 21, 1884, Nicholson Papers, Huntington Library.

40. McClellan to Stanton, May 5, 1862, McClellan, *Civil War Papers,* 256; John S. Godfrey to brother, May 12, New Hampshire Historical Society; Hooker to Harris, May 12, Abraham Lincoln Book Shop catalog, Dec. 1988; Hooker to James Nesmith, May 13, Nesmith Papers, Oregon Historical Society; Hooker to "Dr. Welles," May 12, Houghton Library, Harvard University; Hooker to Ten Eyck, May 16, Schoff Collection, Clements Library, University of Michigan; Kearny to Oliver S. Halsted, May 18, *Wilkes' Spirit of the Times,* Nov. 1; Kearny to Halsted, May 15, Lincoln Papers, LC; Heintzelman diary, May 11, LC; McClellan to Stanton, May 11, *OR* 11.3:164–65; *New York Herald,* May 9.

41. McClellan to Stanton, May 8, 1862, McClellan, *Civil War Papers,* 258; Stanton (Lincoln draft) to McClellan, May 9, Lincoln to McClellan, May 9, Lincoln, *Collected Works,* 5:207–8, 208–9; Summary of Events (May 18, 1862), *OR* 11.1:2; Porter G.O. 1, May 17, Franklin G.O. 2, May 23, *OR* 51.1:619, 628; Franklin to Comte de Paris, Sept. 12, 1876, Fitz John Porter Papers, LC; Heintzelman diary, May 6, 7, 19, 1862, LC.

42. Sears, *To the Gates of Richmond,* 89–92; Chase to daughter, May 11, 1862, Chase, *Papers,* 3:193–97.

43. McClellan to Stanton, May 7, 8, 1862, *OR* 11.3:149, 151; McClellan to wife, May 10, McClellan, *Civil War Papers,* 262.

44. McClellan to Stanton, May 10, 1862, McClellan, *Civil War Papers,* 261; James Russell Soley, "The Navy in the Peninsular Campaign," *Battles and Leaders,* 2:269; Goldsborough to Fox, Apr. 24, 28, Fox, *Confidential Corre-*

spondence, 1:263–65; Rogers, Newman reports, *NOR* 7:357–58, 359–60; Sears, *To the Gates of Richmond*, 93–94.

45. McClellan to Lincoln, May 14, 21, 1862, McClellan, *Civil War Papers*, 264–65, 270; R. O. Tyler to Rufus Ingalls, May 17, McClellan Papers, LC.

46. McClellan to wife, May 18, 1862, McClellan, *Civil War Papers*, 268–69.

47. Shields to Stanton, Apr. 20, 1862, Banks to Stanton, Apr. 30, Stanton to McDowell, May 1, *OR* 12.3:94–95, 118–19, 121; McDowell to Stanton, Apr. 18, *OR* 12.1:427–28.

48. Army of Northern Virginia return, May 21, 1862, Army of Potomac return, May 20, *OR* 11.3:530–31, 184; McDowell testimony, *CCW* 1 (1863), 268; McClellan to Lincoln, May 14, McClellan, *Civil War Papers*, 264.

49. Williams to daughter, Apr. 29, 1862, Williams, *From the Cannon's Mouth*, 72; Banks to Stanton, May 12, McDowell to Stanton, May 22, *OR* 12.3:180, 213; Banks to Stanton, May 22, *OR* 12.1:524–25.

50. Lee to Jackson, Apr. 25, 1862, *OR* 12.3:865–66; Banks to Stanton, Stanton to Banks, Apr. 11, *OR* 12.3:66–67; Peter Cozzens, *Shenandoah 1862: Stonewall Jackson's Valley Campaign*, 238–39, 421.

51. McClellan to wife, May 10, 1862, McClellan, *Civil War Papers*, 262–63; P. H. Watson to McClellan, May 17, *OR* 11.3:178.

52. Stanton to McClellan, May 18, 1862, to McDowell, May 17, *OR* 11.1:27, 28; McClellan to Lincoln, May 21, McClellan, *Civil War Papers*, 270–72; Lincoln to McDowell, May 17, to McClellan, May 21, Lincoln, *Collected Works*, 5:219, 226; Webb, *The Peninsula*, 86–87.

53. Heintzelman diary, May 20, 21, 1862, Heintzelman to Henry Wilson, May 21, Heintzelman Papers, LC; Porter to Marble, May 21, Manton Marble Papers, LC.

54. McClellan, "Peninsular Campaign," *Battles and Leaders*, 2:174–75; McClellan to wife, May 22, 1862, McClellan,

Civil War Papers, 274; Richardson to wife, May 26, Huntington Library; Sedgwick to sister, May 27, Sedgwick, *Correspondence*, 2:48; Heintzelman diary, May 20, 25, LC.

55. McDowell testimony, *CCW* 1 (1863), 263; McDowell to Charles A. Heckscher, June 17, 1862, Huntington Library; Lincoln to McClellan, to McDowell, May 24, Lincoln, *Collected Works*, 5:231–32, 232–33; McDowell to Stanton, May 24, *OR* 12.3:220; Sumner to Richard Henry Dana, June 1, Charles Sumner, *Selected Letters*, 2:116.

56. Lincoln to McDowell, May 24, 1862, to Frémont, May 24, to McClellan, May 25, Lincoln, *Collected Works*, 5:230, 234–35, 235–36; McDowell to Lincoln, May 24, *OR* 12.3:220–21; McClellan to Lincoln, May 25, to wife, May 25, 26, McClellan, *Civil War Papers*, 275–76; Gary W. Gallagher, "You Must Either Attack Richmond or Give Up the Job and Come to the Defence of Washington," Gallagher, ed., *The Shenandoah Valley Campaign of 1862*, 8–11.

57. Heintzelman diary, May 27, 1862, LC; McClellan to Lincoln, May 26, to Stanton, May 30, McClellan, *Civil War Papers*, 277, 280; Porter report, *OR* 11.1:681–85; McClellan to wife, May 27, Sumner to Marcy, May 30, McClellan Papers, LC; McClellan to Stanton, May 28, *OR* 11.1:36.

58. Mrs. Lee to husband, June 5, 1862, Lee, *Wartime Washington*, 154; Marcy to Heintzelman, May 27, McClellan Papers, LC; Casey to [Keyes], May 28, *OR* 11.3:197–98; Heintzelman to Keyes, May 29, Keyes to Seth Williams, May 26, Keyes to Heintzelman, May 30, in Keyes testimony, *CCW* 1 (1863), 605–7; Couch notebook, 1873, Old Colony Historical Society, 113; Israel Richardson to wife, May 31, 1862, Huntington Library; Heintzelman diary, May 26, LC; McClellan to Stanton, May 27, McClellan, *Civil War Papers*, 278. Casey's manual was a revision of William J. Hardee's *Light Infantry*

Tactics, undertaken after Hardee went south.

59. May 31, 1862, Wainwright, *Diary of Battle,* 75; Johnston, *Narrative of Military Operations,* 142.

60. Chauncey McKeever to Heintzelman, June 7, 1875, Casey to Heintzelman, June 6, 1862, Heintzelman diary, May 31, Heintzelman Papers, LC; Keyes, *Fifty Years' Observation,* 468–69; Casey report, *OR* 11.1:914–15; Robert Brady, quoted in William J. Miller, "The Disaster of Casey," *Columbiad,* 3:4 (Winter 2000), 33.

61. Heintzelman to Naglee, May 31, 1862, quoted in Thompson, *Civil War to the Bloody End,* 203; May 31, Haydon, *Country, Cause & Leader,* 246; Chauncey McKeever to Heintzelman, Mar. 1, 1863, Heintzelman Papers, LC; Couch report, *OR* 11.1:879–81; Couch notebook, 1873, Old Colony Historical Society, 114.

62. Heintzelman, Keyes reports, *OR* 11.1:813, 873; Heintzelman to Marcy, May 31, 1862 (2), McClellan Papers, LC; Heintzelman diary, May 31, LC.

63. Kearny to Cortlandt Parker, c. June 2, 1862, Kearny Papers, New Jersey Historical Society; Birney to Heintzelman, June 3, Kearny to Heintzelman, June 2, Heintzelman Papers, LC; Birney, Heintzelman reports, *OR* 11.1:852–54, 815; Heintzelman diary, May 31, June 17, 1862, Mar. 10, 1863, LC.

64. Kearny to wife, June 1, 1862, Kearny Papers, New Jersey Historical Society; Walter O. Bartlett to sister, June 21, Bartlett Family Papers, University of Rochester; Heintzelman to "Capt. Adams," Aug. 6, 1865, McClellan to Heintzelman, May 31, 1862, Heintzelman Papers, LC.

65. McClellan to wife, May 26, 1862, McClellan, *Civil War Papers,* 277; Sumner to Marcy, May 30, Heintzelman to Marcy, May 31, McClellan Papers, LC; Sumner, Richardson reports, *OR*

11.1:763, 764; Howard, *Autobiography,* 1:237–38.

66. Couch, Brady, Kirby reports, *OR* 11.1:879–81, 904–5, 795–96; William D. Sedgwick to cousin, June 5, 1862, Sedgwick, *Correspondence,* 2:59–61; Thomas L. Livermore, *Days and Events, 1860–1866,* 67; Ropes to father, June 3, to brother, June 17, Henry Ropes Papers, Boston Public Library.

67. Paris journal, June 13, 1862, Fondation Saint-Louis; Heintzelman diary, June 1, LC; Heintzelman to McClellan (2), May 31, *OR* 51.1:646, 647.

68. Hooker, Richardson, French reports, *OR* 11.1:818–19, 764–66, 783; Heintzelman diary, June 1, 1862, June 2, 1863, LC; Barlow to mother, June 2, Barlow, *"Fear Was Not in Him,"* 71, 74; Howard, *Autobiography,* 1:246–47, 251.

69. McClellan to Stanton, June 1, McClellan, *Civil War Papers,* 285; Freeman, *R. E. Lee,* 2:77.

7. THE SEVEN DAYS

1. Paris journal, June 13, 1862, Fondation Saint-Louis; McClellan to Marcy, May 31, to Army of the Potomac, June 2, to Stanton, June 2, to wife, June 2 (two), McClellan, *Civil War Papers,* 284, 286–87, 285–86, 287–88; Stephen M. Weld to father, June 4, Weld, *War Diary and Letters,* 111.

2. McClellan to wife, June 23, 1862, McClellan, *Civil War Papers,* 306; Seven Pines casualties: Sears, *To the Gates of Richmond,* 146–47.

3. McClellan to Stanton, June 1, 15, 1862, McClellan, *Civil War Papers,* 285, 302; *New-York Tribune,* June 7; Casey to William Sprague, June 7, 1862, Lehigh University Library; McClellan to Stanton, June 5, *OR* 11.1:754; AP S.O. 173, June 7, S.O. 189, June 23, *OR* 11.3:220, 248.

4. May 31, 1862, Wainwright, *Diary of Battle,* 76; Sumner to McClellan, June

4, *OR* 51.1:657; McClellan to Sumner, June 4, *OR* 11.1:750; Sumner to wife, June 4, RG 107 (M-504), NA; Sumner testimony, *CCW* 1 (1863), 362.

5. Paris journal, June 13, 1862, Fondation Saint-Louis; Charles A. Eccleston report, June 6, courtesy Edward S. Belt; Keyes, Civil War Record, RG 94 (M-1098), NA; Keyes to Ira Harris, June 6, Abraham Lincoln Book Shop catalog (Nov. 1989); Keyes to Marcy, June 4, McClellan Papers, LC; Keyes to Chase, June 17, Chase, *Papers*, 3:211–14.

6. Couch notebook, 1873, Old Colony Historical Society, 114; Couch to Marcy, June 1862, Couch Papers, New York Public Library, in Gambone, *Couch*, 266n46; Heintzelman diary, May 31, June 1, 11, LC; Kearny to wife, June 1, Kearny Papers, New Jersey Historical Society; Smith, *Autobiography*, 32.

7. McClellan to Stanton, May 30, June 10, 1862, McClellan, *Civil War Papers*, 281, 295; Halleck to Stanton, June 12, 16, *OR* 16.2:14, 26–27.

8. A. R. Boteler, "Stonewall Jackson in Campaign of 1862," *Southern Historical Society Papers*, 40:165; Meigs to father, May 30, 1862, Meigs Papers, LC; Lincoln to Frémont, May 30, Stanton to Frémont and McDowell, June 2, *OR* 12.3:292, 321; James F. Huntington, "From Winchester to Port Republic," *PMHSM*, 1:322–23; Nicolay to Therena Bates, June 2, Nicolay, *With Lincoln in the White House*, 79–80.

9. Brooks to father, June 22, Brooks Papers, U.S. Army Heritage & Education Center; Gibbon to wife, May 27, Gibbon Papers, HSP; Stanton to McDowell, June 6, L. Thomas to McDowell, June 8, *OR* 12.3:347, 354; Lincoln to McClellan, June 15, 18, 20, to Stanton, June 8, Lincoln, *Collected Works*, 5:272–73, 276, 277–78, *Supplement*, 138; McDowell to McClellan, June 8, *OR* 11.3:220–21; McClellan to Lincoln, June 18, McClellan, *Civil War Papers*, 302–3;

Pinkerton to Andrew Porter, June 15, McClellan Papers, LC; [Pinkerton] to McClellan, June 26, *OR* 11.1:269.

10. McClellan to Stanton, June 14, 1862, McClellan, *Civil War Papers*, 299; Porter to Marble, June 20, Manton Marble Papers, LC; Richardson to wife, May 31, McDowell to Charles A. Heckscher, June 17, Huntington Library; Scott to Lincoln, June 24, Lincoln Papers, LC; Order Constituting Army of Virginia, June 26, Lincoln, *Collected Works*, 5:287.

11. McClellan to Wool, May 23, 1862, McClellan Papers, LC; Lincoln to McClellan, June 1, Lincoln, *Collected Works*, 5:255; War Dept. G.O. 57, June 1, Dix to Stanton, June 9, 26, *OR* 11.3:207, 221, 260–61; Heintzelman diary, June 8, LC.

12. AP S.O. 168, June 2, 1862, *OR* 11.3:210; Heintzelman diary, June 3, 4, 8, 11, LC; Sumner to Marcy, June 1, *OR* 51.1:649; Marcy to Heintzelman, June 2, *OR* 11.3:207; Kearny to O. S. Halsted, Aug. 4, in *Hartford Courant*, Oct. 15.

13. AP S.O. 168, June 2, 1862, *OR* 11.3:210–11; John C. Tidball, "The Artillery Service in the War of the Rebellion, 1861–65," *Journal of the Military Service Institution of the United States*, 12 (1891), 701–2.

14. Barnard report, *OR* 11.1:115; Barlow to brother, June 18, 1862, to mother, June 12, Barlow, *"Fear Was Not in Him,"* 84, 80; Kearny to wife, June 13, Kearny Papers, New Jersey Historical Society; Berry to wife, June 17, Gould, *Hiram G. Berry*, 173–74; McClellan to wife, June 15, to Lincoln, June 18, McClellan, *Civil War Papers*, 301, 303; Lee to Jefferson Davis, June 5, Lee, *The Wartime Papers of R. E. Lee*, Clifford Dowdey and Louis H. Manarin, eds., 184; Sears, *To the Gates of Richmond*, 168–73; Warren to brother, June 16, Warren Papers, New York State Library.

15. Nicolay to Therena Bates, June 5, Nicolay, *With Lincoln in the White*

House, 80; Meigs to father, June 17, Meigs Papers, LC; Meade to wife, June 22, Meade Papers, HSP; McClellan to wife, June 22, McClellan, *Civil War Papers,* 304–5; Porter to Marble, June 20, Manton Marble Papers, LC. Porter wrote historian John C. Ropes in 1881, "We all knew then — we all know now — that there was an influence at work against McC. & you may take it from me … there were two objects to accomplish — McClellan was not to succeed, the war was not to end in a short time": Porter to Ropes, Aug. 8, 1881, John C. Ropes Papers, Boston University Library.

16. McClellan to wife, June 23, 1862, to Heintzelman, June 24, McClellan, *Civil War Papers,* 307, 308.

17. Lincoln to McClellan, Apr. 6, 1862, Lincoln, *Collected Works,* 5:182. Confederate numbers from Leon Walter Tenney, "Seven Days in 1862: Numbers in Union and Confederate Armies Before Richmond" (master's thesis, George Mason University, 1992), with garrison troops subtracted. Union numbers from June 20 return (*OR* 11.3:238), with Fort Monroe garrison subtracted.

18. Hooker, Grover, Sickles reports, *OR* 11.2:108–9, 120–21, 134–36; Heintzelman diary, June 25, 1862, LC; Heintzelman to McClellan, June 25, McClellan report (draft), McClellan Papers, LC; *New York Herald* account, Moore, *Rebellion Record,* 5:Documents, 234; Paris narrative (May 1863), Fondation Saint-Louis. The count's retrospective narrative of the Seven Days was written a year later in England.

19. Oak Grove casualties: *OR* 11.2:37–38; Colburn to Heintzelman, June 25, 1862, Heintzelman Papers, LC; Porter to McClellan, June 25, McClellan Papers, LC; McClellan to Stanton, June 25, McClellan, *Civil War Papers,* 309–10.

20. McClellan to Marcy, June 25, 1862, to Van Vliet, June 25, to Goldsborough, June 26, to Burnside, June 25, to Dix, June 28, McClellan, *Civil War Papers,* 311, 312, 313–14, 310, 324; Clark report, *OR* 11.1:169; [Pinkerton] to McClellan, June 26, *OR* 11.1:269.

21. Porter, "Hanover Court House and Gaines's Mill," *Battles and Leaders,* 2:328; Confederate forces: Tenney, "Seven Days in 1862"; Lee to Davis, June 5, Lee, *Wartime Papers,* 184.

22. Seymour, Amsden reports, *OR* 11.2:399–400, 411; Reynolds report (unpublished), Reynolds Papers, Franklin and Marshall College, in Nichols, *Toward Gettysburg,* 91–92; Sears, *To the Gates of Richmond,* 202–8; casualties: Federal, *OR* 11.2:38–39; Confederate, *OR* 11.2:973–84.

23. McClellan to Stanton, to wife, June 26, 1862, McClellan, *Civil War Papers,* 312–13, 315.

24. McClellan to Stanton, to Marcy, June 26, 1862, McClellan, *Civil War Papers,* 316, 317; Selden Connor to brother, June 27, Connor Papers, John Hay Library, Brown University.

25. Smith, *Autobiography,* 41; Pinkerton report, June 27, 1862, Arthur McClellan diary, June 26, McClellan Papers, LC; Porter report, *OR* 11.2:222; George H. Lyman, "Some Aspects of the Medical Service …," *PMHSM,* 13:200; Paris narrative (May 1863), Fondation Saint-Louis; Porter to John C. Ropes, Feb. 11, 1895, Ropes Papers, Boston University Library; Webb, *The Peninsula,* 187.

26. McClellan, *Report,* 128; Marcy to McClellan, Van Vliet to Ingalls, June 26, 1862, McClellan Papers, LC; Heintzelman to Marcy, June 26, Heintzelman Papers, LC; Barnard report, *OR* 11.1:118–19; William F. Biddle to John C. Ropes, Mar. 27, 1895, Ropes Papers, Boston University Library; McClellan to Stanton, June 27, 1862 (two), McClellan, *Civil War Papers,* 318, 319.

27. Sears, *To the Gates of Richmond,* 213–15; McClellan to Porter, June 27, 1862 (two), McClellan, *Civil War Papers,* 319–20; Porter report, *OR* 11.2:223, 227;

Porter to John C. Ropes, Feb. 11, 1895, Ropes Papers, Boston University Library; Barnard report, *OR* 11.1:118; Porter to Alexander S. Webb, Apr. 3, 1863, Webb Papers, Yale University Library; Marcy to Franklin and Smith, Porter to Marcy, June 27, 1862, McClellan Papers, LC.

28. Union officers' dispatches, June 27, 1862, McClellan Papers, LC; Lowe to Marcy, June 27, *OR* ser. III, 3:290; Josiah Marshall Favill, *The Diary of a Young Officer*, 131.

29. Sears, *To the Gates of Richmond*, 223; Porter to McClellan, [June 27], 1862 (two), McClellan Papers, LC; McClellan to Porter, June 27 (two), McClellan, *Civil War Papers*, 320, 321; Humphreys to wife, July 17, Humphreys Papers, HSP; Auchmuty to mother, July 5, Richard T. Auchmuty, *Letters of Richard Tylden Auchmuty*, 69; Biddle to John C. Ropes, Mar. 27, 1895, Ropes Papers, Boston University Library; Franklin, Sumner to Marcy, June 27, 1862, McClellan Papers, LC. Alexander Webb of the artillery staff, posted with Porter during the fighting, confirmed the "distinct impression then prevailing at the headquarters of the army, that he [Porter] was to hold this large force of the enemy on the left bank of the Chickahominy, in order that General McClellan, with the main army, might break through and take Richmond": Webb, *The Peninsula*, 187.

30. Seymour report, *OR* 11.2:401; Paris narrative (May 1863), Fondation Saint-Louis; Camille Baquet, *History of the First Brigade, New Jersey Volunteers, from 1861 to 1865* (Trenton, 1910), 315; Timothy J. Reese, *Sykes' Regular Infantry Division*, 81, 86–87, 104; Warren to Emily Chase, July 8, 1862, Warren Papers, New York State Library; David M. Jordan, *"Happiness Is Not My Companion": The Life of General G. K. Warren*, 46.

31. Slocum to Stanton, July 19, 1862, Porter to Seth Williams, July 20, Porter

Papers, LC. Slocum's battlefield role at Gaines's Mill was limited by illness: Brian C. Melton, *Sherman's Forgotten General: Henry W. Slocum*, 73–74.

32. Thomas H. Evans, "There Is No Use Trying to Dodge Shot," *Civil War Times Illustrated*, 14:1 (July 1975), 45; Paris narrative (May 1863), Fondation Saint-Louis; Martindale report, *OR* 11.2:290–91; Porter to Seth Williams, Aug. 3, 1862, *OR* 11.3:352; Porter to Stephen M. Weld, Feb. 12, 1878, Porter Papers, MHS; Reynolds to sister, July 3, 1862, Reynolds Papers, Franklin and Marshall College, in Nichols, *Toward Gettysburg*, 96–97; J. W. Ratchford memoir, North Carolina State Archives.

33. Porter, Cooke reports, *OR* 11.2:225–26, 41; Sears, *To the Gates of Richmond*, 245–46; French, Civil War Record, RG 94 (M-1098), NA; James C. Miller, "Serving Under McClellan on the Peninsula in '62," *Civil War Times Illustrated*, 8:3 (June 1969), 26; McClellan to Heintzelman, June 27, 1862, McClellan, *Civil War Papers*, 322.

34. George Alfred Townsend, *Rustics in Rebellion: A Yankee Reporter on the Road to Richmond, 1861–65* (Chapel Hill: University of North Carolina Press, 1950), 141; Heintzelman diary, June 28, 1862, and Peninsula notes (Feb. 25, 1864), Heintzelman Papers, LC; Heintzelman testimony, *CCW* 1 (1863), 355; Paris narrative (May 1863), Fondation Saint-Louis; McClellan to Stanton, June 28, 1862, to Dix, June 29, McClellan, *Civil War Papers*, 322–23, 324–25; July 14, Browning, *Diary*, 1:559; Lincoln to McClellan, June 28, Lincoln, *Collected Works*, 5:289–90; Gaines's Mill casualties: Sears, *To the Gates of Richmond*, 249. The account by David H. Bates, *Lincoln in the Telegraph Office* (1907), 108–10, that the head of the War Department telegraph office deleted the incendiary closing sentence in McClellan's June 28 telegram before showing it to Stanton, is

an invented tale: Marvel, *Lincoln's Autocrat*, 208–9.

35. Kearny to Cortlandt Parker, July 24, 1862, Kearny Papers, New Jersey Historical Society.

36. Paris narrative (May 1863), Fondation Saint-Louis; Sears, *To the Gates of Richmond*, 256; William W. Folwell to fiancée, July 1, 1862, Folwell Papers, Minnesota Historical Society; Keyes, *Fifty Years' Observation*, 480–81. An account by H. L. Thayer, of Gen. Berry's staff (Gould, *Major-General Hiram G. Berry*, 171–72), has a delegation of generals led by Kearny and including Hooker, Heintzelman, and Berry descending on McClellan to protest the decision to retreat, with Kearny's language violent enough to risk arrest. Thayer's account is improbable and lacks any confirmation, particularly in Heintzelman's detailed diary. Possibly it is a garbled recollection of Kearny's outburst after Malvern Hill.

37. McClellan, *Report*, 133; Heintzelman diary, June 29, 1862, Heintzelman to A. H. Gurnsey, Mar. 24, 1866, Heintzelman Papers, LC; Franklin to McClellan, June 29, 1862, McClellan Papers, LC; Robert Knox Sneden, *Eye of the Storm: A Civil War Odyssey*, 73–74; Smith, *Autobiography*, 43.

38. Heintzelman diary, June 29, 30, 1862, LC; Heintzelman to L. Thomas, Apr. 11, 1863, *Battles and Leaders*, 2:181; Franklin, "Rear Guard Fighting During the Change of Base," *Battles and Leaders*, 2:373; Burns in *Battles and Leaders*, 2:374; Sears, *To the Gates of Richmond*, 270–72.

39. Franklin, "Rear-Guard Fighting," *Battles and Leaders*, 2:375; A. V. Colburn to Delos Sacket, June 29, 1862, McClellan Papers, LC; Smith, *Autobiography*, 44–45.

40. Livermore, *Days and Events*, 84; June 29, 1862, Haydon, *Country, Cause & Leader*, 258; Marks, *Peninsula Campaign*, 239, 244; Sneden, *Eye of the Storm*, 72: Guild to Cole, July 3, *OR* ser. II, 4:798.

41. Alexander, *Fighting for the Confederacy*, 109–10; Franklin to McClellan, June 29, 30, 1862, Porter to McClellan, June 29, McClellan Papers, LC; Paris narrative, (May 1863), Fondation Saint-Louis; McClellan to wife, June 30, 1862, McClellan, *Civil War Papers*, 326; Humphreys to wife, July 11, Humphreys Papers, HSP; log of *Galena*, June 30: Lincoln Papers, LC, and Navy Dept. copy, Mar. 31, 1894, John C. Ropes Papers, Boston University Library.

42. Heintzelman testimony, *CCW* 1 (1863), 358–59; Franklin, "Rear-Guard Fighting," *Battles and Leaders*, 2:377; Heintzelman diary, June 30, 1862, LC.

43. Franklin, "Rear-Guard Fighting," *Battles and Leaders*, 2:377–79; Smith, "Memoirs," Vermont Historical Society; Smith, *Autobiography*, 45–46; Sumner report, *OR* 11.2:51; Snell, *From First to Last*, 136–37.

44. Hooker, McCall reports, *OR* 11.2:111, 390; Sears, *To the Gates of Richmond*, 278–79; Alanson M. Randol to Meade, Feb. 2, 1881, Meade Papers, HSP.

45. Hooker draft report, Hooker Papers, Huntington Library; Randol to Meade, Jan. 21, 1881, Meade Papers, HSP; Heintzelman diary, June 30, 1862, Thomas M. Key to Heintzelman, May 26, 1864, Heintzelman Papers, LC; Sedgwick to sister, July 6, 1862, Sedgwick, *Correspondence*, 2:70; Andrew E. Ford, *The Story of the Fifteenth Regiment Massachusetts Volunteer Infantry* (Clinton, Mass., 1898), 176.

46. Kearny report, *OR* 11.2:162; Hays to John B. McFadden, July 7, 1862, John Thornton Fleming, ed., *Life and Letters of Alexander Hays*, 241; William L. Candler to brother, July 7, Candler Papers, Special Collections, Virginia Tech; Heintzelman diary, June 30, LC; Barlow to mother, July 4, Barlow, *"Fear Was Not in Him,"* 92–93; Kearny

to wife, July 5, 10, 15, Kearny Papers, New Jersey Historical Society; W. Roy Mason in *Battles and Leaders*, 2:402n.

47. Glendale casualties: Sears, *To the Gates of Richmond*, 307; Meade to wife, July 1, 1862, R. Biddle Roberts to George Meade II, July 25, 1881, Meade Papers, HSP; Auchmuty to mother, July 22, 1862, Auchmuty, *Letters*, 78.

48. Franklin report, *OR* 11.2:431; Smith, "Memoirs," Vermont Historical Society; Smith, *Autobiography*, 46–47; A. W. Stillwell diary, July 1, 1862, Wisconsin Historical Society; Heintzelman to wife, July 2, diary, June 30, Heintzelman Papers, LC; Paris narrative (May 1863), Fondation Saint-Louis; Franklin to John C. Ropes, Feb. 15, 1895, William F. Biddle to Ropes, Mar. 27, 1895, Ropes Papers, Boston University Library; McClellan to Stanton, to L. Thomas, June 30, 1862, McClellan, *Civil War Papers*, 326, 327; Andrew A. Humphreys to McClellan, Feb. 28, 1864, McClellan Papers, LC.

49. Marcy to Humphreys, July 1, 1862, *OR* 51.1:712; Humphreys to wife, July 5, Humphreys Papers, HSP; Fitz John Porter, "The Battle of Malvern Hill," *Battles and Leaders*, 2:411; Webb, *The Peninsula*, 155; Arthur McClellan diary, July 1, McClellan Papers, LC; McClellan to wife, July 1, McClellan, *Civil War Papers*, 328.

50. Log of *Galena*, July 1, 1862: Lincoln Papers, LC, and Navy Dept. copy, Mar. 31, 1894, John C. Ropes Papers, Boston University Library; McClellan to Reverdy Johnson, Mar. 9, 1864, McClellan, *Civil War Papers*, 568; Humphreys to unknown, Mar. 31, 1863, Alexander S. Webb Papers, Yale University Library; Biddle to Ropes, Mar. 27, 1895, John C. Ropes Papers, Boston University Library; McClellan testimony, *CCW* 1 (1863), 436–37.

51. Hardie to Porter, July 1, 1862, *OR* 51.1:712–13; Sumner, Couch reports, *OR* 11.2:52, 203–4; Porter, "The Battle

of Malvern Hill," D. H. Hill, "McClellan's Change of Base and Malvern Hill," *Battles and Leaders*, 2:415–19, 2:394; Hunt testimony, *CCW* 1 (1863), 574; Tidball, *"No Disgrace to My Country,"* 243–44; Porter memo, Seven Days, Porter Papers, LC; Couch notebook, 1873, Old Colony Historical Society, 118; Hunt letter, July 6, 1862, Henry J. Hunt Papers, LC.

52. July 18, 1862, Haydon, *Country, Cause & Leader*, 265–66; Webb, *The Peninsula*, 167; Porter to McClellan (two), July 1, McClellan Papers, LC; McClellan to Lincoln, July 2, McClellan, *Civil War Papers*, 329.

53. Couch notebook, 1873, Old Colony Historical Society, 118; Biddle to John C. Ropes, Mar. 27, 1895, Ropes Papers, Boston University Library; Jack C. Mason, *Until Antietam: The Life and Letters of Major General Israel B. Richardson*, 164–65; Marks, *Peninsula Campaign*, 294; Smith, "Memoirs," Vermont Historical Society; Smith, *Autobiography*, 47–48. Postwar Alexander Webb said McClellan "sent word to Porter to spike his guns in the hour of victory. Porter went to McClellan on the gunboat and begged him to advance, but he would not": William B. Styple, ed., *Generals in Bronze: Interviewing the Commanders of the Civil War* (Kearny, N.J.: Belle Grove, 2005), 161.

54. Malvern Hill casualties: Sears, *To the Gates of Richmond*, 355; Auchmuty to mother, July 5, 1862, Auchmuty, *Letters*, 72; Barlow to mother, July 4, Barlow, *"Fear Was Not in Him,"* 94; Hooker testimony, *CCW* 1 (1863), 580; Peck report, *OR* 11.2: 217–18.

55. McClellan to Army of Potomac, July 4, 1862, McClellan, *Civil War Papers*, 339; Van Vliet, Meigs reports, *OR* 11.1:158, *OR* ser. III, 2:798; Sears, *To the Gates of Richmond*, 345; July 4, Haydon, *Country, Cause & Leader*, 263; Brannigan to sister, July 16, Felix Brannigan Papers,

LC; Ropes to John C. Ropes, July 11, Henry Ropes Papers, Boston Public Library.

56. Barlow to brother, July 8, 1862, to mother and brother, Aug. 9, Barlow, *"Fear Was Not in Him,"* 96, 105; Slocum to wife, July 10, Charles E. Slocum, *The Life and Services of Major-General Henry Warner Slocum* (Toledo, 1913), 31; Sumner testimony, *CCW* 1 (1863), 366; Franklin to wife, July 4, Historical Society of York County, in Snell, *From First to Last,* 144; S.L.M. Barlow to McClellan, Aug. 9, McClellan Papers, LC.

57. Kearny to wife, July 10, 1862, Kearny Papers, New Jersey Historical Society; Ingalls, Letterman reports, *OR* 11.1:165, 213; Charles Wilkes to Gideon Welles, July 15, McClellan to Goldsborough, July 1, *NOR* 7:574–75, 532–33.

8. SUMMER OF DISCONTENT

1. McClellan to L. Thomas, July 1, 1862, to Stanton, July 3, to Lincoln, July 4, McClellan, *Civil War Papers,* 327, 333, 336–38; Lincoln to McClellan, July 2, Lincoln, *Collected Works,* 5:301; Marcy, undated postwar memo of July 3 meetings, McClellan Papers, LC; July 14, Browning, *Diary,* 1:559.

2. AP circular, July 8, 1862, *OR* 11.3:307; McClellan to wife, July 17, McClellan, *Civil War Papers,* 362; Couch notebook, 1873, Old Colony Historical Society, 119; Kearny to Cortlandt Parker, July 10, 1862, Kearny Papers, New Jersey Historical Society; Brannigan to sister, July 16, Brannigan Papers, LC.

3. Lincoln memo: interviews with officers of Army of Potomac, July 8–9, 1862, Lincoln, *Collected Works,* 5:309–312.

4. McClellan to Lincoln, June 20, July 7, 1862, McClellan, *Civil War Papers,* 304, 344–45; Lincoln to McClellan, June 21, Lincoln, *Collected Works,* 5:279; McClellan to Lincoln, June 22, *OR* 11.1:48.

5. McClellan to wife, Apr. 30, July 9, 1862,

to Lincoln, July 7, McClellan, *Civil War Papers,* 250, 348, 344–45; Brooks to father, June 22, Brooks Papers, U.S. Army Heritage & Education Center; Warren to brother, July 20, Warren Papers, New York State Library; McClellan, *McClellan's Own Story,* 487; Burlingame, *Abraham Lincoln,* 2:329. Col. Thomas M. Key, a Cincinnati jurist who came with McClellan from the Department of Ohio and served as his political adviser, importantly helped draft the Harrison's Landing letter: William B. Styple, *McClellan's Other Story: The Political Intrigue of Colonel Thomas M. Key, Confidential Aide to General George B. McClellan* (Kearny, N.J.: Belle Grove, 2012), 160–62.

6. Lincoln to Halleck, July 2, 1862, *OR* 16.2:88; order making Halleck general-in-chief, July 11, Lincoln, *Collected Works,* 5:312–13.

7. Seven Days casualties: Sears, *To the Gates of Richmond,* 343, 344–45; McClellan to wife, July 10, 1862, McClellan, *Civil War Papers,* 349.

8. Kearny to Cortlandt Parker, Aug. 12, 1862, Kearny Papers, New Jersey Historical Society; Grimsley, *The Hard Hand of War,* 69–70, 75–78; Peter Cozzens, *General John Pope: A Life for the Nation,* 86–88; McClellan to wife, July 17, McClellan, *Civil War Papers,* 362.

9. Kearny to Cortlandt Parker, July 31, 1862 (published in the *Newark Daily Advertiser* and picked up by the *New York World,* among other papers), Kearny to wife, Aug. 12, Kearny Papers, New Jersey Historical Society.

10. July 13, 1862, Welles, *Diary,* 3–4; Burlingame, *Abraham Lincoln,* 2:362–64; McClellan to Lincoln, July 7, McClellan, *Civil War Papers,* 345.

11. McClellan to Lincoln, July 11, 12, 1862, to William H. Aspinwall, July 19, McClellan, *Civil War Papers,* 351–52, 353, 365–66; July 25, Browning, *Diary,* 1:563.

12. Call for 300,000 volunteers, July 1, 1862, Lincoln, *Collected Works,* 5:296–

97; War Dept. G.O. 84, July 22, *OR* 11.3:333.

13. Colburn to Marcy, July 8, 1862, Stanton Papers, LC; Marcy to McClellan, July 13, McClellan Papers, LC; AP S.O. 245, Aug. 27, *OR* 11.3:383; AP S.O. 2, Sept. 5, *OR* 19.2:188; Porter to Seth Williams, July 4, *OR* 11.3:297–98; AP S.O. 194, July 5, *OR* 51.1:715; McClellan, *McClellan's Own Story* manuscript, McClellan Papers, LC; AP G.O. 138, July 10, *OR* 11.3:312–13; War Dept. S.O. 190, Aug. 14, *OR* 12.3:572–73; Keyes to Lincoln, July 10, Aug. 25, *OR* 11.3:313–14, Lincoln Papers, LC; Keyes to Harris, July 5, Schoff Collection, Clements Library, University of Michigan.

14. Porter to Seth Williams, Aug. 3, 1862, *OR* 11.3:352; Porter to Stephen M. Weld, Jr., Feb. 12, 1878, Porter Papers, MHS; Court of Inquiry opinion, Oct. 31, 1862, *OR* 11.3:352; Fifth Corps G.O. 4, July 6, *OR* 11.3:304–5; Heintzelman diary, July 22, LC; McClellan to Stanton, July 7, McClellan, *Civil War Papers,* 341–42. Martindale's revenge was a brevet for Malvern Hill at war's end.

15. Stanton to McClellan, July 5, 1862, to Franklin, July 7, *OR* 11.3:288, 51.1:717; Hooker to James Nesmith, July 11, Nesmith Papers, Oregon Historical Society; Heintzelman diary, Aug. 1, LC; Kearny to wife, Aug. 27, Kearny Papers, New Jersey Historical Society. Division commander George Sykes was only named major general of volunteers in November.

16. Franklin testimony, *CCW* 1 (1863), 622; Stephen R. Taaffe, *Commanding the Army of the Potomac,* 28; Smith, "Memoirs," Vermont Historical Society; McClellan to wife, July 18, 1862, McClellan, *Civil War Papers,* 364; AP S.O. 205, July 16, *OR* 11.3:325; James A. Hessler, *Sickles at Gettysburg: The Controversial Civil War General Who Committed Murder, Abandoned Little Round Top, and Declared Himself the Hero of Gettysburg,* 32; Seth Williams to Heintzelman, Aug. 5, Heintzelman Papers,

LC; Kearny to wife, July 10, 28, Kearny Papers, New Jersey Historical Society; Meade to wife, Aug. 24, Margaretta Meade to Stanton, Aug. 2, Meade Papers, HSP. The Prince de Joinville and his two nephews departed the army for France after the Seven Days.

17. *New York Leader,* July 12, 1862; Chase to Richard C. Parsons, July 20, Chase, *Papers,* 3:229–30; *Congressional Globe* (37th Cong., 2nd Sess.), 3386–92; Porter to Marble, Aug. 5, Marble Papers, LC; *New York World,* Aug. 7.

18. Halleck to wife, May 31, Aug. 9, 1862, Schoff Collection, Clements Library, University of Michigan; Burlingame, ed., *Lincoln's Journalist,* 288; July 25, Browning, *Diary,* 1:563.

19. Heintzelman diary, July 8, 12, 22, 1862, LC; Halleck to Stanton, July 27, *OR* 11.3:337–38; Halleck to McClellan, Aug. 6, *OR* 12.2:9–11.

20. Heintzelman diary, July 26, 31, 1862, LC; Burnside testimony, *CCW* 1 (1863), 638, *OR* 12.2 Supplement, 1005; Halleck to McClellan, Aug. 6, *OR* 11:1:83; Meigs, "Relations," *American Historical Review,* 26:2 (Jan. 1921), 294.

21. McClellan to Halleck, July 26, 1862, McClellan, *Civil War Papers,* 372; July 1862 return, Dept. of North Carolina, *OR* 9:414; July 31 return, Dept. of the South, *OR* 14:367; Burnside testimony, *CCW* 1 (1863), 650; Gibbon to wife, Aug. 9, Gibbon Papers, HSP. Evidence suggests July 27, when McClellan's dispatch reached Washington, as the likeliest date of the command offer to Burnside: Marvel, *Burnside,* 440n6.

22. Halleck to McClellan, July 30, 1862, *OR* 11.3:343; McClellan to Halleck, Aug. 1, to S.L.M. Barlow, July 30, McClellan, *Civil War Papers,* 380–82, 376–77; Halleck to wife, July 28, James Grant Wilson, "General Halleck: A Memoir," *Journal of the Military Service Institution,* 37 (1905), 557.

23. McClellan to wife, July 29, 1862, McClellan, *Civil War Papers,* 375; Halleck to McClellan, July 30, Aug. 3, 6, *OR*

11.1:76–77, 80–81, 78; Halleck to Burnside, Aug. 1, *OR* 12.3:524; Heintzelman diary, Aug. 2, LC; journal, Sept. 23, Chase, *Papers*, 1:396–97; McClellan to Halleck, Aug. 5, *OR* 11.1:77–78; Lee to Jackson, Aug. 7, *OR* 12.3:925–26.

24. McClellan to Halleck, Aug. 4, 1862, McClellan, *Civil War Papers*, 385–86; Halleck to McClellan, Aug. 6, 7, *OR* 11.1:82–84, 11.3:359–60; Sears, *To the Gates of Richmond*, 355; Lowell, "General McClellan's Report," *North American Review*, 203 (Apr. 1864), 558; Heintzelman diary, Aug. 13, LC.

25. Cozzens, *General John Pope*, 63–64; John Pope, *The Military Memoirs of General John Pope*, Peter Cozzens and Robert I. Girardi, eds., 114; George Alfred Townsend, *Rustics in Rebellion: A Yankee Reporter on the Road to Richmond, 1861–1865* (Chapel Hill, University of North Carolina Press, 1950), 192; Lincoln to Banks, Frémont, McDowell, June 26, 1862, Stanton to Frémont, June 27, *OR* 12.3:435, 438.

26. Cozzens, *General John Pope*, 80; Stephen D. Engle, *Yankee Dutchman: The Life of Franz Sigel*, 129; Williams to daughter, Sept. 8, 1862, Williams, *From the Cannon's Mouth*, 107; John J. Hennessy, *Return to Bull Run: The Campaign and Battle of Second Manassas*, 7, 11; Pope to McClellan, July 4, *OR* 11.3:295; June 25, D. H. Strother, *A Virginia Yankee in the Civil War: The Diaries of David Hunter Strother*, ed. Cecil D. Eby, Jr., 62; Speed Butler to father, Aug. 4, William Butler Papers, Chicago Historical Society.

27. Pope to Army of Virginia, July 14, 1862, *OR* 12.3:473–74; July 18, Patrick, *Inside Lincoln's Army*, 108; George H. Gordon, *Brook Farm to Cedar Mountain*, 274; Hatch to father, Aug. 2, 9, John P. Hatch Papers, LC; July 16, Samuel J.B.V. Gilpin diary, LC.

28. Journal, July 21, 22, 1862, Chase, *Papers*, 1:349–50; Pope testimony, *CCW* 1 (1863), 279; Gordon, *Brook Farm to Cedar Mountain*, 275.

29. Army of Virginia G.O. 5, 7, 11: July 18, [10?], 23, 1862, *OR* 12.2:50–52; Jacob D. Cox, *Military Reminiscences of the Civil War*, 1:222; Lee to Jackson, July 27, *OR* 12.3:918–19; Lee to George W. Randolph, July 28, Lee, *Wartime Papers*, 240–41; Patrick diary, July 20, 21, Patrick Papers, LC; James Gillette to mother, July 31, Gillette Papers, LC.

30. Franklin to wife, July 24, 1862, Historical Society of York County, in Snell, *From First to Last*, 155; Porter to Marble, Aug. 5, Marble Papers, LC; Porter to Kennedy, July 17, Porter Papers, LC; McClellan to wife, July 22, Aug. 8, McClellan, *Civil War Papers*, 368, 388; AP G.O. 154, Aug. 9, *OR* 11.3:362–64.

31. Lee S.O. 150, July 13, 1862, Lee to Jackson, July 27, Lee S.O. 181, Aug. 13, *OR* 12.3:915, 918–19, 928–29; Pope to Halleck, Aug. 3, *OR* 12.3:527; Jackson report, *OR* 12.2:182.

32. Lewis Marshall to Banks, Aug. 9, 1862, Nathaniel Banks Papers, LC; Banks, Pope testimony, *CCW* 3 (1865) Misc., 44–46, 47–49; Robert K. Krick, *Stonewall Jackson at Cedar Mountain*, 45.

33. Williams to daughter, Aug. 17, 1862, Williams, *From the Cannon's Mouth*, 100; Williams report, *OR* 12.2:146; Roberts testimony, *OR* 12.1:185–86.

34. Fred Harvey Harrington, *Fighting Politician: Major General N. P. Banks*, 82; Cozzens, *Shenandoah 1862*, 343–44.

35. Williams report, *OR* 12.2:147; Williams to daughter, Aug. 17, 1862, Williams, *From the Cannon's Mouth*, 101; Edwin E. Marvin, *The Fifth Regiment, Connecticut Volunteers* (Hartford, 1889), in Krick, *Jackson at Cedar Mountain*, 159, 180; Beal report, *OR* 51.1:122; Gordon, *Brook Farm to Cedar Mountain*, 321–22.

36. Banks to wife, Aug. 8, Sept. 4, 1862, Banks Papers, LC, in Harrington, *Fighting Politician*, 45, 84; George L. Andrews to wife, Aug. 12, Andrews Papers, U.S. Army Heritage & Education Center; casualties: *OR* 12.2:136–39; Krick, *Jackson at Cedar Mountain*, 372–76; Williams, Crawford reports,

OR 12.2:147, 153; Williams to daughter, Aug. 17, Williams, *From the Cannon's Mouth,* 100; Jesse Reno to Ambrose Burnside, Aug. 16, George Hay Stuart Collections, LC.

37. Pope to Halleck, Aug. 11, 1862, *OR* 12.3:560; Halleck to McClellan, Aug. 10, *OR* 11.1:86; Halleck to wife, Aug. 9, Schoff Collection, Clements Library, University of Michigan; McClellan to wife, Aug. 10, to Halleck, Aug. 12, to Porter, Aug. 17, McClellan, *Civil War Papers,* 389–90, 392, 393; Fifth Corps itinerary, *OR* 12.2:465; Sawtelle to Parke, Aug. 26, *OR* 12.3:681.

38. Lee S.O. 181, Aug. 13, 1862, *OR* 11.3:675; Hennessy, *Return to Bull Run,* 31; McClellan to wife, Aug. 18, 21, 22, McClellan, *Civil War Papers,* 395–96, 397, 399; Halleck to McClellan, Aug. 21, *OR* 11.1:92. Organization and command follows Welcher, *The Union Army,* vol. 1.

39. *Congressional Globe* (37th Cong., 2nd Sess.), Part 2, 1667; "Ordeal of General Stone," Sears, *Controversies & Commanders,* 45–46; Stone testimony, *CCW* 2 (1863), 500.

40. Pope to Halleck, Aug. 25, 1862, *OR* 12.2:66; Heintzelman diary, Aug. 11, LC; Meade to wife, Aug. 21, Meade Papers, HSP.

41. Meade to wife, Aug. 24, 1862, Meade Papers, HSP; Reynolds to sisters, Aug. 18, Reynolds Papers, Franklin and Marshall College, in Nichols, *Toward Gettysburg,* 102; Kearny to Oliver S. Halsted, Aug. 4, in *Hartford Courant,* Oct. 15; Porter to Marble, Aug. 10, Marble Papers, LC; Kennedy to Seward, July 22, Fitz John Porter Papers, LC; Daniel Leasure, "Personal Observations and Experiences in the Pope Campaign in Virginia," *Glimpses of the Nation's Struggle,* Minnesota MOLLUS (1:1887), 26:147–48; Franz Sigel Papers, Western Reserve Historical Society, in Cozzens, *General John Pope,* 98; Pope to Halleck, Aug. 25, *OR* 12.3:653.

42. Porter to Burnside, Aug. 25, 1862, *OR* 12.3:662; Heintzelman diary, Aug. 26, LC; Halleck to Pope, Aug. 24, 26, *OR* 12.3:642, 666; Pope to Halleck, Aug. 25, *OR* 12.2:65–66; McClellan to Halleck, Aug. 24, McClellan to wife, Aug. 27, McClellan, *Civil War Papers,* 405, 406; Halleck to McClellan, Aug. 24, *OR* 11.1:94. McClellan already guessed, "from confidential sources," that he was not slated to command the joint armies: McClellan to Burnside, Aug. 20, McClellan, *Civil War Papers,* 397.

43. Herman Haupt, *Reminiscences of General Herman Haupt,* 70, 73, 80–83, 90; Army of Virginia G.O. 22, Aug. 18, 1862, Stanton to Haupt, Aug. 19, *OR* 12.3:598, 602.

44. Banks to Ruggles, Pope to Halleck (two), Buford to McDowell, Aug. 25, 1862, *OR* 12.3:654–55, 653, 657; Longstreet, "Our March Against Pope," *Battles and Leaders,* 2:516–17.

45. Haupt to Halleck, Aug. 26, 1862, *OR* 12.3:679; McDowell to Pope, Aug. 26, *OR* 12.2:351; Patrick to Third Corps, Aug. 27, *OR* 12.3:686; Army of Virginia G.O., Aug. 27, *OR* 12.2:70–71; William Allan, "Strength of the Forces Under Pope and Lee," Theodore F. Dwight, ed., *The Virginia Campaign of 1862 Under General Pope,* 211; Aug. 27, Strother, *Virginia Yankee in the Civil War,* 89; Carl Schurz, *The Reminiscences of Carl Schurz,* 2:365; Washington Roebling journal, Aug. 27, Fitz John Porter Papers, LC.

46. Halleck to Franklin, Haupt to Halleck, Halleck to Haupt, Aug. 26, 1862, *OR* 12.3:676, 680; Pope to McDowell, Aug. 26, *OR* 12.2:69; Williams to daughter, Aug. 26, Williams, *From the Cannon's Mouth,* 104.

47. Waagner, Brown reports, *OR* 12.2:401–2, 541–43; Haupt, *Reminiscences,* 96–97, 104; Heintzelman diary, Aug. 27, 1862, LC; Aug. 27, Strother, *Virginia Yankee in the Civil War,* 89–90; Grover, Carr reports, *OR* 12.2:438–40, 453–56; Pope, "The Second Battle of Bull Run," *Battles and Leaders,* 2:465.

48. McClellan to wife, Aug. 27, 1862, Mc-Clellan, *Civil War Papers,* 406; Halleck to McClellan, Aug. 27, *OR* 11.1:95.

49. Porter to Burnside, Aug. 27, 1862, *OR* 51.1:763, 12.3:700, McClellan Papers, LC; Burnside testimony, *OR* 12.2 Supplement, 1003; McClellan to Halleck, Aug. 27, McClellan, *Civil War Papers,* 407–9; Halleck to McClellan, Aug. 27, *OR* 11.1:94, 12.3:691; Franklin to wife, Aug. 27, Historical Society of York County, in Snell, *From First to Last,* 161.

50. Aug. 27, 1862, Strother, *Virginia Yankee in the Civil War,* 90; Pope to Kearny, to McDowell, Aug. 27, *OR* 12:2:72; Hennessy, *Return to Bull Run,* 135–36.

51. McDowell to [Sigel], Aug. 27, 1862, *OR* 12.1:175–76; Pope to McDowell, Aug. 27, McDowell G.O. 10, Aug. 28, *OR* 12.2:72, 360; McDowell report, 12.2:335–36; Aug. 28, Strother, *Virginia Yankee in the Civil War,* 90, 91.

52. Hennessy, *Return to Bull Run,* 143–44; Pope to McDowell, Aug. 28, 1862, *OR* 12.3:717; Pope to McDowell, Aug. 28, *OR* 12.2:74 (in reply to McDowell to Pope, Aug. 28, not found); Heintzelman memo book, Aug. 28, Heintzelman Papers, LC; Pope testimony, *OR* 12.1:205; Pope to McDowell, Aug. 28, *OR* 12.2:360–61.

53. Roebling to father, Aug. 29, 1862, Roebling Family Papers, Rutgers University Archives; Leski, Ricketts testimony, *OR* 12.1:168–69, 215–17; Ricketts report, *OR* 12.2:383–84; McDowell G.O. 10, Aug. 28, *OR* 12.2:360.

54. Reynolds report, *OR* 12.2:393; Alan D. Gaff, *Brave Men's Tears: The Iron Brigade at Brawner Farm* (Dayton, Ohio: Morningside House, 1985), 66–67; John Gibbon, *Personal Recollections of the Civil War,* 50–55; Doubleday journal, *OR Supplement,* ser. I, 2:688; Gibbon report, *OR* 12.2:381; Aug. 28, 1862, Patrick, *Inside Lincoln's Army,* 131; Gibbon to wife, Sept. 1, Gibbon Papers, HSP; casualties: Hennessy, *Return to Bull Run,* 187–88, 506n75.

55. Joseph C. Willard diary, Aug. 28, 1862,

Willard Family Papers, LC; King to McDowell, Aug. 28, *OR* 12.3:717–18; Gibbon, *Personal Recollections,* 58.

56. Pope testimony, *OR* 12.1:206; Pope report, *OR* 12.2:37; Heintzelman diary, Aug. 28, 1862, LC; Charles King, "Gainesville, 1862," *War Papers,* Wisconsin MOLLUS (3:1903), 48:281; Sigel, Reynolds reports, *OR* 12.2:266, 393; Pope to Kearny, Aug. 28, *OR* 12.2:74–75; Alexander Hays to wife, Sept. 2, Fleming, ed., *Life and Letters of Alexander Hays,* 266; A. E. Vogelbach to Porter, Aug. 22, 1878, Porter Papers, LC, in Hennessy, *Return to Bull Run,* 195.

57. Gibbon, *Personal Recollections,* 58–60; Pope to Porter, Aug. 29, 1862, *OR* 12.3:729; McDowell testimony, *OR* 12:2 Supplement, 902; Aug. 29, Strother, *Virginia Yankee in the Civil War,* 91–92; Ruggles to Porter, Porter to Burnside, Aug. 29, *OR* 12.3:733; Pope to Heintzelman, to Reno, Aug. 28, *OR* 12.2:75–76.

58. Heintzelman memo book, Aug. 28, 1862, Heintzelman Papers, LC; Halleck to McClellan, Aug. 28, *OR* 12.3:710; McClellan to Halleck, Aug. 28, 29, to Lincoln, Aug. 29, McClellan, *Civil War Papers,* 413–14, 415–16, 416.

59. Schurz, *Reminiscences,* 2:363; Margaret B. Paulus, ed., *Papers of General Robert Huston Milroy,* 1:74, in Hennessy, *Return to Bull Run,* 53; Heintzelman diary, Aug. 29, LC; Schurz report, *OR* 12.2:298.

60. Schurz, Grover, Nagle reports, *OR* 12.2:298, 438–39, 545; Heintzelman to E. D. Townsend, Apr. 19, 1879, Heintzelman Papers, LC; Hooker report, *OR Supplement,* ser. I, 2:742–44; Kearny to Steinwehr, Aug. 30, 1862, Franz Sigel Papers, New-York Historical Society.

61. James Wren diary, Aug. 29, 1862, Antietam National Battlefield, in Hennessy, *Return to Bull Run,* 267; Dodge journal, Aug. 29, Theodore A. Dodge, *On Campaign With the Army of the Potomac: The Civil War Journal of Theodore Ayrault Dodge,* Stephen W. Sears,

ed., 86; Hays to wife, Sept. 2, Fleming, ed., *Life and Letters of Alexander Hays,* 266–67; Kearny report, *OR* 12.2:416.

62. Heintzelman memo book, Aug. 29, 1862, Heintzelman Papers, LC; Pope to Porter and McDowell, Aug. 29, *OR* 12.2:76; Porter to Gouverneur Warren, Apr. 6, 1878, Warren Papers, New York State Library; Hennessy, *Return to Bull Run,* 230; Buford to McDowell, Porter to McDowell, Aug. 29, 1862, Frederick T. Locke testimony, *OR* 12.2 Supplement, 903, 1122, 955–56.

63. Heintzelman memo book, Aug. 29, 1862, Heintzelman Papers, LC; Pope to Porter, Aug. 29, Porter to McDowell, [Aug. 29], *OR* 12.2:525, 524; Hennessy, *Return to Bull Run,* 306; Schofield Board report, *OR* 12.2:519; Morell testimony, *OR* 12.2 Supplement, 968; Pope to Porter, Aug. 29, *OR* 12.2:18.

64. Fitz John Porter, "Campaign in Northern Virginia in 1862," Porter Papers, LC; Stephen M. Weld interview with Porter, Mar. 31, 1877, Porter Papers, MHS; Pope to Halleck, Aug. 30, 1862, *OR* 12.3:741; J. A. Judson to Porter, May 9, 1878, Porter Papers, LC; Hennessy, *Return to Bull Run,* 290–300; Pope report, *OR* 12.2:41; Patrick diary, Aug. 30, 1862, Patrick Papers, LC; Heintzelman diary, Aug. 30, LC.

65. Porter, "Campaign in Northern Virginia in 1862," Roebling journal, Aug. 30, 1862, Porter Papers, LC; Cozzens, *General John Pope,* 164–65; Aug. 30, Strother, *Virginia Yankee in the Civil War,* 95.

66. Pope S.O., Aug. 30, 1862, Pope to Porter, Aug. 30, *OR* 12.2:361; Morell, Griffin testimony, *OR* 12.2 Supplement, 970, 986–87; George C. Hooper, "The Battle of Groveton," *War Papers,* Michigan MOLLUS (1:1893), 50:448; Aug. 30, Patrick, *Inside Lincoln's Army,* 135; Roberts report, *OR* 12.2:471–72; Hennessy, *Return to Bull Run,* 360–61; Reynolds to Porter, Apr. 12, 1863, *OR* 12.3:963–64; Roebling journal, Aug. 30, 1862, Fitz John Porter Papers, LC.

67. Hennessy, *Return to Bull Run,* 367–73; William E. Dougherty in *American History Illustrated* (Dec. 1966), 41; McLean to John C. Ropes, Oct. 6, 1897, Ropes Papers, Boston University Library; McLean report, *OR* 12.2:286.

68. McDowell report, *OR* 12.2:341; Ruggles to Banks, to Franklin, Aug. 30, 1862, *OR* 12.2:78, 77; Aug. 30, Strother, *Virginia Yankee in the Civil War,* 96; Nichols, *Toward Gettysburg,* 115–16; Meade to wife, Sept. 3, Meade Papers, HSP; Hennessy, *Return to Bull Run,* 419.

69. Gibbon to wife, Sept. 1, 1862, Gibbon Papers, HSP; Doubleday journal, *OR* Supplement, ser. I, 2:701; Heintzelman diary, Aug. 30, LC; Gibbon, *Personal Recollections,* 66.

70. Charles F. Walcott, "The Battle of Chantilly," Dwight, ed., *The Virginia Campaign of 1862 Under General Pope,* 143–44; Schurz, *Reminiscences,* 2:382; Meade to wife, Sept. 3, 1862, Meade Papers, HSP; Pope to Halleck, Aug. 30, 31, *OR* 12.2:78–79, 80.

9. "LITTLE MAC IS BACK!"

1. Charles Francis Adams, Jr., to Charles Francis Adams, Aug. 27, 1862, Worthington Chauncy Ford, ed., *A Cycle of Adams Letters, 1861–1865,* 1:176–78; journal, Aug. 29, Chase, *Papers,* 1:366; Hill to Sidney H. Gay, Aug. 31, Gay Papers, Columbia University Library; McClellan to Lincoln, Aug. 29, McClellan, *Civil War Papers,* 416; Sept. 1, Hay, *Inside Lincoln's White House,* 37.

2. Halleck to Stanton, Aug. 30, 1862, *OR* 12.3:739–41; Aug. 31, Welles, *Diary,* 17–18; Sedgwick to sister, Aug. 30, Sedgwick, *Correspondence,* 2:78–79; McClellan to wife, Aug. 30, McClellan, *Civil War Papers,* 419; Sept. 1, Hay, *Inside Lincoln's White House,* 37–38; Pope to Halleck, Aug. 30 (two), 31, *OR* 12.3:741, 12.2:78–79, 80. Hay's diary for Sept. 1, a summary entry, telescopes the content of two Pope dispatches

that reached Washington early morning and midafternoon on Aug. 31.

3. Franklin, "The Sixth Corps at the Second Bull Run," *Battles and Leaders,* 2:540; Heintzelman diary, Aug. 31, 1862, LC; Porter, Second Bull Run memo (1876), Franklin to Porter, July 7, 1876, McClellan Papers, LC; Pope to Halleck, Aug. 30, 31, 1862, Halleck to Pope, Aug. 31, *OR* 12.2:78–79, 80, 12.3:769; Porter to McClellan, Aug. [31], McClellan Papers, LC; Bayard to father, Aug. 31, U.S. Military Academy Library.

4. Apr. 28, 1864, Hay, *Inside Lincoln's White House,* 191–92; Halleck to wife, Sept. 5, 1862, Schoff Collection, Clements Library, University of Michigan; Pope to Halleck, Halleck to McClellan, Aug. 31, *OR* 12.2:80, 11.1:102–3; McClellan to Halleck, Aug. 31 (two), McClellan to wife, Sept. 2, McClellan, *Civil War Papers,* 425, 425–26, 428.

5. Pope to Halleck, Sept. 1, 1862, *OR* 12.2:82–83; McClellan, *Report,* 183; McClellan to Porter, Sept. 1, McClellan, *Civil War Papers,* 427; Sept. 1, Hay, *Inside Lincoln's White House,* 37–38.

6. Journal, Sept. 1, 1862, Chase, *Papers,* 1:367–68; Aug. 31–Sept. 1, Welles, *Diary,* 17–26; Bates, remonstrance and notes, Sept. 2, Lincoln Papers, LC, in Stephen W. Sears, ed., *The Civil War: The Second Year Told by Those Who Lived It* (New York: Library of America, 2012), 428–29.

7. Heintzelman diary, Aug. 31–Sept. 1, 1862, LC; William Todd to parents, Sept. 2, Todd Papers, New-York Historical Society, courtesy Terry A. Johnston, Jr.

8. Charles F. Walcott, "The Battle of Chantilly," Dwight, ed., *The Virginia Campaign of 1862 Under General Pope,* 157–60; Kearny to wife, July 5, 1862, Kearny Papers, New Jersey Historical Society; William B. Styple, ed., *Letters from the Peninsula: The Civil War Letters of General Philip Kearny,* 175; Allen C. Redwood, "Jackson's 'Foot Cavalry'

at the Second Bull Run," *Battles and Leaders,* 2:537–38n; Lee to Pope, Sept. 2, *OR* 12.3:807; Hazard Stevens, *The Life of Isaac Ingalls Stevens* (Boston: Houghton Mifflin, 1900), 2:500; Sept. 4, Strong, *Diary,* 252; Sept. 1, Haydon, *Country, Cause & Leader,* 282.

9. Pope to Halleck, Halleck to Pope, Army of Virginia G.O., Sept. 1, 1862, *OR* 12.2:84, 12.3:785, 12.2:85; Porter, Second Bull Run memo (1876), Franklin to Porter, July 7, 1876, McClellan Papers, LC.

10. McClellan to wife, to Lincoln, Sept. 2, 1862, McClellan, *Civil War Papers,* 428, 428–29; Sept. 7, Welles, *Diary,* 32; War Dept. G.O. 122, Sept. 2, *OR* 12.3:807; Halleck to wife, Sept. 2, Schoff Collection, Clements Library, University of Michigan. The decision to reinstate McClellan was Lincoln's; Halleck issued the order.

11. Sept. 2, 1862, Welles, *Diary,* 26–27; Welles to Montgomery Blair, Nov. 23, 1873, Blair Family Papers, LC; Bates, remonstrance and notes, Sept. 2, 1862, Lincoln Papers, LC, in Sears, ed., *The Civil War: The Second Year Told by Those Who Lived It,* 428–29; Sept. [3], Hay, *Inside Lincoln's White House,* 38; journal, Sept. 2, Chase, *Papers,* 1:368–69; Bates to Francis Lieber, Sept. 2, Lieber Papers, Huntington Library. The Hay diary entry marked Sept. 5 by the editor is in fact, by its content, Sept. 3.

12. McClellan to wife, Sept. 2, 1862, McClellan, *Civil War Papers,* 431; Cox, *Military Reminiscences,* 1:243–44; Halleck to Pope, Sept. 2, *OR* 12.3:797; Gibbon to wife, Sept. 3, Gibbon Papers, HSP; Weld to father, Sept. 4, Weld, *War Diary and Letters,* 136; Meade to wife, Sept. 3, Meade Papers, HSP. In his account of this episode, Cox mistook John Hatch as the general whose men cheered within Pope's hearing.

13. Williams to daughter, Sept. 8, 1862, Williams, *From the Cannon's Mouth,* 111; Cozzens, *General John Pope,* 191;

journal, Sept. 4–6, Chase, *Papers,*
1:370–71; McDowell to Lincoln, Sept.
6, McDowell Court of Inquiry, *OR*
12:1:39–40, 331–32.

14. Journal, Sept. 3, 1862, Chase, *Papers,*
1:369–70; Pope to Halleck, Sept. 3, *OR*
12.2:19–20; Sept. 4, Welles, *Diary,* 30;
Pope testimony, *OR* 12.2 Supplement,
837–40; Porter, memo of Sept. 2, 1862
interview (c. 1876), McClellan Papers,
LC; Porter to L. Thomas, Sept. 10, 1862,
Porter Papers, LC; War Dept. S.O. 223,
Sept. 5, *OR* 19.2:188.

15. Stanton to Halleck, Halleck to McClellan, Sept. 3, 1862, *OR* 19.2:169; Nov. 29,
Browning, *Diary,* 1:589–90; Burnside,
Halleck testimony, *CCW* 1 (1863), 650,
451, 453; McClellan to wife, Sept. 5,
McClellan, *Civil War Papers,* 435. In a
Sept. 4 11:15 p.m. dispatch from Aquia
(*OR* 19.2:175), Burnside stated he would
be in Washington the next morning.
The voyage of the night boat up the
Potomac to Washington was six and
a half to seven hours, bringing Burnside at an early hour to the War Department where he met Lincoln and
rejected the command offer. Lincoln
and Halleck then reached McClellan's
quarters by "about 9 o'clock in the
morning," per Halleck.

16. Sept. 8, 10, 12, 1862, Welles, *Diary,* 34,
39, 40; Halleck to Pope, Oct. 10, *OR*
12.3:820. In an article written after the
deaths of Lincoln and Halleck (*Battles
and Leaders,* 2:552), McClellan fiction-
alized this taking of field command.
Making no mention of Lincoln and
Halleck visiting him at his H Street
quarters, he claimed he took the field
without orders, risking court-martial
and a death sentence had he been defeated. The tale is repeated in *McClellan's Own Story,* 551. Interviewed by
editor Henry J. Raymond in January
1863, Burnside claimed he had great
difficulty persuading McClellan not
to make the dismissal of Stanton and
Halleck a condition of his taking the
field command. Published in *Scribner's*

Monthly for January 1880, the interview was treated scornfully by Mc-
Clellan and Marcy (Marcy to McClellan, Mar. 3, 1880, McClellan Papers,
LC). It appears that Burnside confused
the time when such an argument took
place, for after Antietam McClellan
did seriously consider just that condition for his remaining in command.

17. Halleck to McClellan, Sept. 5, 1862, *OR*
19.2:182; Marcy to Pope, Heintzelman,
Porter, Franklin, Sept. 5, *OR* 51.1:788;
Pope to Halleck (two), Halleck to Pope
(two), Sept. 5, *OR* 12.3:811–13; Pope
to Stanton, Sept. 5, Stanton Papers,
LC; *New York Times,* Sept. 8; Sept. 12,
Welles, *Diary,* 42; Porter to Stephen
M. Weld, Sr., Sept. 12, Porter Papers,
MHS; Pope to Richard Yates, Sept. 21,
Pope to Halleck, Oct. 20, John Pope
Papers, Chicago Historical Society.

18. McClellan to wife, Sept. 5, 1862, to
Halleck, Sept. 6, to Lincoln, Sept. 6,
McClellan, *Civil War Papers,* 435, 436,
436–37; Sedgwick to sister, Sept. 4,
Sedgwick, *Correspondence,* 2:80; War
Dept. S.O. 223, Sept. 5, *OR* 19.2:188; as-
signment of regiments, c. Sept. 6, Mc-
Clellan Papers, LC; Federal casualties:
Darrell Collins, *Army of the Potomac,*
57; Confederate casualties: *Battles and
Leaders,* 2:500.

19. McClellan to Lincoln, Sept. 6, 1862,
to wife, Sept. 12, McClellan, *Civil War
Papers,* 436, 450; Halleck to McClellan,
Sept. 11, McClellan to Halleck, Sept. 11,
McClellan to Curtin, Sept. 11, Hooker
to Seth Williams, Sept. 12, *OR* 19.2:252,
269, 273–74; Meade to wife, Sept. 3, 13,
Meade Papers, HSP.

20. Winslow, *General John Sedgwick,* 42–
43; Heintzelman diary, Sept. 3–22, 1862
passim, LC; Banks memo to Lincoln,
c. Sept. 9, Lincoln Papers, LC; Mc-
Clellan to Stanton, Sept. 7, McClellan,
Civil War Papers, 437; Stone to Benson
J. Lossing, Nov. 5, 1866, Schoff Collection, Clements Library, University of
Michigan.

21. Sept. [3], 1862, Hay, *Inside Lincoln's*

White House, 38; Williams to daughter, Sept. 12, Williams, *From the Cannon's Mouth,* 120–21; McClellan to wife, Sept. 7, McClellan, *Civil War Papers,* 437–38; Sept. 7, Welles, *Diary,* 33.

22. Lee to Davis, Sept. 8, 1862, Lee, *Wartime Papers,* 301; William Allan interview with Lee, Feb. 15, 1868, in Gallagher, ed., *Lee the Soldier,* 8; E. C. Gordon to William Allan, Nov. 18, 1886, Allan Papers, Southern Historical Collection, University of North Carolina.

23. McClellan to Halleck, Sept. 8, 1862, to wife, Sept. 9, McClellan, *Civil War Papers,* 438–39, 439–40.

24. Fishel, *Secret War for the Union,* 214–15; McClellan to wife, Aug. 18, 1862, McClellan, *Civil War Papers,* 396; Pleasonton to Marcy, Sept. 6 (two), *OR* 19.2:192–93, 194–95; *Report of Lewis H. Steiner, M.D., Inspector of the Sanitary Commission* (New York, 1862), 17–18; Pleasonton to Marcy, Sept. 8, 9, McClellan Papers, LC; McClellan to Halleck, Sept. 9, *OR* 19.2:219.

25. McClellan to Lincoln, Sept. 10, 1862, to Halleck, Sept. 10 [misdated Sept. 11 in the *OR*], McClellan, *Civil War Papers,* 443–44, 444–46; Curtin to McClellan, Sept. 10, *OR* 19.2:248.

26. Sept. 3, 1862, Strong, *Diary,* 251–52; *New York Herald,* Sept. 9; *Philadelphia Ledger,* Sept. 2; Chandler to Peter H. Watson, Sept. 10, Stanton Papers, LC; Chandler to Lyman Trumbull, Sept. 10, Trumbull Papers, LC; "Unwritten History of the War," *New-York Tribune,* Mar. 14, 1880; *Washington Capitol,* Mar. 21, 1880, *Dallas Morning News,* Jan. 28, 1886, courtesy William B. Styple; Sept. 10, 12, 1862, Welles, *Diary,* 36, 44.

27. Banks to Lincoln, Halleck to Lincoln, Sept. 12, 1862, Lincoln Papers, LC.

28. McClellan, *Report,* 190; Halleck to Wool, Sept. 5, 1862, *OR* 19.2:189; Halleck to wife, Sept. 9, Schoff Collection, Clements Library, University of Michigan; Wool to Miles, Sept. 5, Halleck to Miles, Sept. 12, *OR* 19.1:523, 758; McClellan to wife, Sept. 12, McClellan, *Civil War Papers,* 450.

29. Curtin to Lincoln and McClellan, Sept. 12, 1862, Miles to Halleck, Sept. 11, *OR* 19.2:267–69, 277, 266; Pleasonton to McClellan, Sept. 12, to Marcy, Sept. 13, McClellan Papers, LC; Burnside to McClellan, Halleck to McClellan, Sept. 12, *OR* 19.2:272–73, 280–81.

30. McClellan to wife, Sept. 12, 1862, McClellan, *Civil War Papers,* 449; Porter, Humphreys reports, *OR* 19.1:338, 370–72; Humphreys to wife, Sept. 12, Humphreys Papers, HSP; Franklin to wife, Sept. 10, Historical Society of York County, in Snell, *From First to Last,* 171; Gibbon to wife, Sept. 13, Gibbon Papers, HSP; Richardson to wife, Sept. 14, in Mason, *Until Antietam,* 172; Meade to wife, Sept. 12, Meade Papers, HSP.

31. Gibbon to wife, Sept. 16, 1862, Gibbon Papers, HSP; McClellan to wife, Sept. 14, McClellan, *Civil War Papers,* 458; S.O. 191 and Williams's note, McClellan Papers, LC; E. C. Gordon interview with Lee, Feb. 15, 1868, in Gallagher, ed., *Lee the Soldier,* 26; McClellan to Lincoln, Sept. 13, 1862, McClellan, *Civil War Papers,* 453. Confirming data on the Lost Order: (1) McClellan time-marked his Sept. 13 telegram to Lincoln "12 M," telegraphic protocol for 12 Meridian, or noon, and it so reads on the War Dept. received file copy (RG 107, M473–50, NA). On the telegrapher's copy made for the president (Lincoln Papers, LC), "12 M" is altered in another hand to read "12 Midnight," i.e., 12 M + idnight. The alteration can only be Lincoln's — the delayed telegram, marked received 2:35 a.m. Sept. 14, misled him into thinking it had been sent at midnight. (2) That Cpl. Mitchell was the sole finder of the Lost Order is confirmed by J. M. Bloss to family, Sept. 25, 1862 (Monocacy National Battlefield, courtesy Thomas G. Clemens). (3) That the Order was

found at midmorning on Sept. 13 and promptly forwarded to McClellan is confirmed in Charles B. Dew, "How Samuel E. Pittman Validated Lee's 'Lost Order' Prior to Antietam: A Historical Note," *Journal of Southern History* 40:4 (Nov. 2004), 865–70. (4) For Cpl. Mitchell (and that he kept one of the cigars), see the papers of Robert W. Menuet, Mitchell's great-great-grandson, in *America's Civil War*, 20:4 (Sept. 2007), 19–22.

32. Julius White report, *OR* 19.1:524; Marcy to Pleasonton, Sept. 13, 1862, *OR* 51.1:829; Pleasonton to Marcy, Sept. 13, McClellan Papers, LC. Troop movements on Sept. 13 were scheduled previous to the Lost Order finding.

33. McClellan to Franklin, Sept. 13, 1862, McClellan, *Civil War Papers*, 454–55; Gibbon, *Personal Recollections*, 73.

34. McClellan to Halleck, Sept. 13, 1862, to wife, Sept. 14, to Franklin, Sept. 13, McClellan, *Civil War Papers*, 456–57, 458, 454–55; Curtin to McClellan, Sept. 13, *OR* 19.2:287; Burnside testimony, *CCW* 1 (1863), 639–40; Marcy to Couch, Sept. 13, McClellan Papers, LC; Lee to Davis, Sept. 16, Lee, *Wartime Papers*, 309–10. Joseph L. Harsh (*Taken at the Flood*, 248–49, and *Sounding the Shallows*, 170–75) contends that before the day of Cpl. Mitchell's find was out, Lee knew McClellan had a copy of S.O. 191. Harsh credits Jeb Stuart with "guessing" this fact, and has Lee maintaining with his lieutenants a cover-up for six years, until Lee revealed all in 1868. In fact, in 1868 Lee's knowledge of the loss and finding of S.O. 191 was derived entirely from hindsight. No evidence supports either Stuart's guesswork or Lee's cover-up. See Stephen W. Sears, "The Curious Case of the Lost Order," *The Civil War Monitor* (Winter 2016).

35. Pleasonton to Marcy, Sept. 14, 1862, McClellan Papers, LC; Jacob D. Cox, "Forcing Fox's Gap and Turner's Gap," D. H. Hill, "The Battle of South Mountain, or Boonsboro,'" *Battles and Lead-*

ers, 2:585–88, 2:560–64; T. Harry Williams, *Hays of the Twenty-Third: The Civil War Volunteer Officer* (New York: Knopf, 1965), 137.

36. Cox, "Forcing Fox's Gap and Turner's Gap," *Battles and Leaders*, 2:587–89; Willcox report, *OR* 19.1:427–29; Willcox, *Forgotten Valor*, 353–55; Fox's Gap casualties: *OR* 19.1:186–87; John David Hoptak, *The Battle of South Mountain*, 82–84; Cox to Ezra A. Carman, Jan. 22, 1897, Huntington Library; D. H. Strother, "Personal Recollections of the War by a Virginian, Antietam," *Harper's New Monthly Magazine*, 36 (Feb. 1868), 277–78; Gibbon to wife, Sept. 16, 1862, Gibbon Papers, HSP; Williams to daughters, Sept. 22, *From the Cannon's Mouth*, 123. In his memoir, Willcox recalled asking the mortally wounded Reno, "General are you badly hurt?" and getting the reply, "Oh yes, Willcox, killed by one of our own men." Confirmation is lacking, but the rumor was current in the army: William B. Jordan, Jr., ed., *The Civil War Journals of John Mead Gould, 1861–1866* (Baltimore: Butternut and Blue, 1997), 191. See also Ezra A. Carman, *The Maryland Campaign of September 1862*, Thomas G. Clemens, ed., 1:343n59.

37. George Kimball in *Battles and Leaders*, 2:551; Ruggles to Hooker, Sept. 14, 1862, *OR* 19.1:50; Burnside report, *OR* 19.1:422–23.

38. Hooker report, *OR* 19.1:214; J. R. Sypher, *History of the Pennsylvania Reserves Corps* (Lancaster, Pa., 1865), 369; James B. Casey, ed., "The Ordeal of Adoniram Judson Warner: His Minutes of South Mountain and Antietam," *Civil War History*, 28:3 (Sept. 1982), 217–18; Burnside report, *OR* 19.1:417; Sept. 14, 1862, Patrick, *Inside Lincoln's Army*, 144.

39. Dawes to mother, Mar. 1, 1863, Dawes Papers, Wisconsin Historical Society; Gibbon to wife, Sept. 15, 1862, Gibbon Papers, HSP; Turner's Gap casualties: *OR* 19.1:186.

40. Hoptak, *Battle of South Mountain*, 180–84; Franklin to McClellan, Sept. 14, 1862 (three), McClellan Papers, LC; Joseph J. Bartlett, "Crampton's Pass," *National Tribune*, Dec. 19, 1889; Timothy J. Reese, *High-Water Mark: The 1862 Maryland Campaign in Strategic Perspective* (Baltimore: Butternut and Blue, 2004), 37; Franklin to wife, Sept. 15, 1862, Historical Society of York County, in Snell, *From First to Last*, 184; McClellan to Halleck, Sept. 14, to wife, Sept. 15, McClellan, *Civil War Papers*, 461, 463.

10. WEDNESDAY, BLOODY WEDNESDAY

1. Russell, Trimble, Powell testimony, Harper's Ferry Military Commission report, *OR* 19.1:720–22, 745, 767; McClellan to Franklin, Sept. 14, 1862, McClellan, *Civil War Papers*, 458–59; Curtin to Stanton, Sept. 15, *OR* 19.2:305; Binney report, *OR* 19.1:539; Military Commission report, *OR* 19.1:799–800.

2. Harper's Ferry captures: *OR* 19.1:549, 951, 955; Chilton to McLaws, Sept. 14, 1862, *OR* 51.2:618–19; Jackson to Chilton, Sept. 14, Jackson to Lee, Sept. 14, Chilton to McLaws, Sept. 15, *OR* 19.1:951, 19.2:608. The Harper's Ferry prisoners were paroled.

3. McClellan to Halleck, Sept. 15, 1862, McClellan, *Civil War Papers*, 461–62; Ruggles to Burnside (two), Marcy to Hooker, Sept. 15, *OR* 51.1:836–37, 837, 834; AP S.O., Sept. 15, *OR* 19.2:297; Porter endorsement on Marcy to Porter, Sept. 15, *OR* 19.2:296; Ruggles to Burnside, Sept. 15, *OR* 51.1:837; Cox, *Reminiscences*. 1:297, 383. Had Burnside received his march orders in good season that morning, he would certainly have started the Ninth Corps forward promptly.

4. Ruggles to Franklin, Sept. 15, 1862, *OR* 19.1:47; Franklin to McClellan, Sept. 15 (two), *OR* 19.1:47, and omitted text in McClellan Papers, LC; W. W. Blackford, *War Years with Jeb Stuart* (New York: Scribner, 1945), 145; Carman, *Maryland Campaign*, 1:431, 437; Franklin to wife, Sept. 15, Historical Society of York County, in Snell, *From First to Last*, 190; Franklin to McClellan, Sept. 15, *OR* 19.2:296, 297; Marcy to Franklin, Sept. 15, *OR* 51.1:836.

5. Hooker to Seth Williams, Custer to Colburn (two), Sept. 15, 1862, McClellan Papers, LC; McClellan to Halleck (two), to Scott, to wife, Sept. 15, McClellan, *Civil War Papers*, 462, 463, 464; Sept. 15, Welles, *Diary*, 45; Scott to McClellan, Sept. 16, Myer, Custer to McClellan, Sept. 15, McClellan Papers, LC; Lincoln to McClellan, Sept. 15, Lincoln, *Collected Works*, 5:426.

6. Sumner to Marcy, Sept. 15, 1862, McClellan Papers, LC; Sept. 15, Strother, *Virginia Yankee in the Civil War*, 108; Carman, *Maryland Campaign*, 1:410, 429 and n107; Hooker report, *OR* 19.1:217; Sept. 15, Arthur McClellan diary, McClellan Papers; McClellan, *Report*, 200.

7. Palmer to Curtin, Sept. 16, 1862, in Curtin to Lincoln, Sept. 16, *OR* 19.2:311; Fishel, *Secret War for the Union*, 224–27; McClellan to Halleck, Sept. 13, McClellan, *Civil War Papers*, 457; Lowell to J. M. Forbes, Sept. 19, Edward W. Emerson, *Life and Letters of Charles Russell Lowell*, 226; Webb to "Mr. Remsen," Sept. 28, Webb Papers, Yale University Library; Williams to Lewis Allen, Nov. 16, Williams, *From the Cannon's Mouth*, 151; Porter to Marble, Sept. 30, Marble Papers, LC; Humphreys report, *OR* 19.1:372; "Strength of the Army of the Potomac at the Battle of Antietam," McClellan Papers, LC. The figures in this latter memo appear in McClellan, *Report*, 214, with Couch's and Humphreys's divisions subtracted for a "Total in action" of 87,164. For the range of estimates of Confederate

numbers, see Carman, *Maryland Campaign*, 2:585–86.

8. McClellan to Halleck, to Franklin, Sept. 16, 1862, McClellan, *Civil War Papers*, 465–66; Sept. 16, Strother, *Virginia Yankee in the Civil War*, 109; Albert D. Richardson, *The Secret Service, the Field, the Dungeon, and the Escape* (Hartford, 1865), 279–80; Williams to daughters, Sept. 22, Williams, *From the Cannon's Mouth*, 123; Cox, "The Battle of Antietam," *Battles and Leaders*, 2:631–32; Hunt to McClellan, Jan. 12, 1876, McClellan Papers, LC; [James A. Hardie] to Burnside, Sept. 16, 1862, *OR* 19.2:308. The rebuke to Burnside was delivered early on Sept. 17: *OR* 19.2:314. Duane was officially appointed chief engineer Oct. 15, retroactive to Sept. 8: *OR* 51.1:885.

9. George W. Smalley in *New-York Tribune*, Sept. 19, 1862; Carman, *Maryland Campaign*, 2:1–13.

10. Hooker, Franklin reports, *OR* 19.1:217, 376; Hooker to Salmon P. Chase, Nov. 3, 1863, Chase, *Papers*, 4:172; Sept. 16, 1862, Strother, *Virginia Yankee in the Civil War*, 109; Ruggles to Sumner, to Franklin, to Pleasonton, Sept. 16, *OR* 51.1:839, 839–40, 840; Ruggles to Franklin, Sept. 15, Humphreys to Marcy, Sept. 17, McClellan Papers, LC; George B. Davis, "The Antietam Campaign," *PMHSM*, 3:55; Williams to daughters, Sept. 22, Williams, *From the Cannon's Mouth*, 125.

11. McClellan, Antietam preliminary report (draft), McClellan Papers, LC; Sumner testimony, *CCW* 1 (1863), 368. In his preliminary report (*OR* 19.1:30), McClellan deleted the phrase "at the same time" from his draft describing the flank attacks.

12. Hooker testimony, *CCW* 1 (1863), 581; Carman, *Maryland Campaign*, 2:570; Meade to wife, Sept. 18, 1862, Meade Papers, HSP; *Harper's Weekly*, Feb. 7, 1863; Smalley in *New-York Tribune*, Sept. 19, 1862.

13. Carman, *Maryland Campaign*, 2:59; John D. Vautier, W. H. Holstead, William P. Gifford letters, Antietam Collection, Dartmouth College Library; Sept. 19, 1862, Samuel W. Moore diary, Antietam National Battlefield; Smalley in *New-York Tribune*, Sept. 19.

14. Gibbon, *Personal Recollections*, 82–83; Rufus R. Dawes, *Service with the Sixth Wisconsin Volunteers*, 90; Phelps to wife, Sept. 18, 1862, quoted in Thomas G. Clemens, "A Brigade Commander's First Fight," *Civil War Regiments* (5:3, 1997), 63; Wood, Doubleday reports, *OR Supplement*, ser. I, 3:541, 535.

15. Cox, *Reminiscences*, 1:334–3; Samuel S. Sumner to George B. Davis, Apr. 4, 1897, John C. Ropes Papers, Boston University Library; Cross journal, quoted in Mike Pride and Mark Travis, *My Brave Boys: To War with Colonel Cross and the Fighting Fifth*, 130.

16. Smalley in *New-York Tribune*, Sept. 19, 1862; Gibbon, *Personal Recollections*, 83; Meade to wife, Sept. 18, Meade Papers, HSP; Sept. 17, Patrick, *Inside Lincoln's Army*, 148; Doubleday report, *OR Supplement*, ser. I, 3:537.

17. Marcy to Sumner, Sept. 17, 1862, RG 393 (entry 45.2), NA, in Marion V. Armstrong, Jr., *Unfurl Those Colors! McClellan, Sumner, and the Second Army Corps in the Antietam Campaign*, 167; D. H. Strother, "Personal Recollections of the War by a Virginian, Antietam," *Harper's New Monthly Magazine*, 36 (Feb. 1868), 281–82.

18. Williams to daughters, Sept. 22, 1862, Sept. 4, 1863, Williams, *From the Cannon's Mouth*, 123, 126, 255; Carman, *Maryland Campaign*, 2:583; John M. Gould, *Joseph K. F. Mansfield: A Narrative of Events Connected with His Mortal Wounding at Antietam* (Portland, Me., 1895), 15–17; E. J. Libby, B. W. Morgan letters, Antietam Collection, Dartmouth College Library; Williams to McClellan, Apr. 18, 1863, McClellan Papers, LC.

19. Williams report, *OR* 19.1:475–76; Donald Brown reminiscences, Colorado Historical Society, in David W. Palmer, *The Forgotten Hero of Gettysburg: A Biography of General George Sears Greene*, 81–82; Tyndale pension records, NA; Stephen W. Sears, *Landscape Turned Red: The Battle of Antietam*, 208; Williams to McClellan, Apr. 18, 1863, McClellan Papers, LC; anon., 102nd New York, Antietam Collection, Dartmouth College Library; Shaw to father, Sept. 21, 1862, Robert Gould Shaw, *Blue-Eyed Child of Fortune: The Civil War Letters of Colonel Robert Gould Shaw*, Russell Duncan, ed., 240.

20. Gibbon, *Personal Recollections*, 86; Smalley in *New-York Tribune*, Sept. 19, 1862; Colburn to Meade, Sept. 17, *OR* 19.2:315; Marcy to Meade, Sept. 17, Meade Papers, HSP; Williams to headquarters, Sept. 17, McClellan Papers, LC.

21. Colburn to Sumner, Sept. 17, 1862, RG 393 (entry 45.2), NA, in Armstrong, *Unfurl Those Colors!*, 171; Sumner, Williams reports, *OR* 19.1:275, 476; Hooker testimony, *CCW* 1 (1863), 581–82; Samuel S. Sumner, "The Antietam Campaign," *PMHSM*, 14:10–11; Samuel S. Sumner to George B. Davis, Apr. 4, 1897, John C. Ropes Papers, Boston University Library; Williams, Civil War Record, RG 94 (M-1098), NA; Williams to Lewis Allen, Sept. 24, 1862, Williams, *From the Cannon's Mouth*, 135. By Ezra Carman's account, Williams did meet with Sumner, but editor Clemens finds no confirmation of this. In any case, whoever met Sumner, he was "not well received.": Carman, *Maryland Campaign*, 2:172, 174n7.

22. Samuel S. Sumner, "The Antietam Campaign," *PMHSM*, 14:11; Williams to daughters, Sept. 22, 1862, Williams, *From the Cannon's Mouth*, 127; Carman, *Maryland Campaign*, 2:9, 193, 575; Smalley in *New-York Tribune*, Sept. 19; Ruggles to Sumner, Sept. 17, *OR* 51.1:842. The warning to Sumner, time-marked 9:10 a.m. in the headquarters order book (McClellan Papers, LC), follows the 9:10 attack order to Burnside. The latter was sent moments before McClellan learned of the reverses on the right.

23. Higgins report, *OR* 19.1:492; George A. Bruce, *The Twentieth Regiment of Massachusetts Volunteer Infantry, 1861–1865* (Boston, 1906), 169; Joseph R. C. Ward, *History of the One Hundred and Sixth Regiment Pennsylvania Volunteers, 1861–1865* (Philadelphia, 1906), 104; Henry Ropes to father, Sept. 20, 1862, Henry Ropes Papers, Boston Public Library; Howard, *Autobiography*, 2:207; Williams, Civil War Record, RG 94 (M-1098), NA; casualties: *OR* 19.1:192–93, 198; Ruggles to Burnside, Sept. 17, *OR* 51.1:844.

24. Carman, *Maryland Campaign*, 2:245–49; French report, *OR* 19.1:323–24. Sumner's initial orders to French are not on record and were apparently verbal: Carman, 2:245.

25. Carman to John C. Ropes, May 23, 1899, Ropes Papers, Boston University Library; W. A. Croffut and John M. Morris, *The Military and Civil History of Connecticut During the War of 1861–65* (New York, 1868), 260; Sept. 18, 1862, Samuel W. Fiske, *Mr. Dunn Browne's Experiences in the Army: The Civil War Letters of Samuel W. Fiske*, Stephen W. Sears, ed., 8–9; Morris report, *OR* 19.1:333; Samuel S. Sumner, "The Antietam Campaign," *PMHSM*, 14:11. Marion V. Armstrong ("Sumner and French at Antietam," *Civil War History* 59:1 Mar. 2013, 67–92) is persuasive that French believed he was acting on orders in attacking the Sunken Road, but less so that Sumner smoothly coordinated the Second Corps' actions that morning.

26. Thomas F. D. Galwey, "At the Battle of Antietam with the Eighth Ohio Infan-

try," *Personal Recollections of the War of the Rebellion,* New York MOLLUS (3:1907), 22:74–78; Galwey, *The Valiant Hours,* W. S. Nye, ed. (Harrisburg, Pa.: Stackpole Books, 1961), 40–42; Sears, *Landscape Turned Red,* 239–40.

27. Sumner to headquarters, Sept. 17, 1862, *OR* 19.1:134 (as received, the flag message read that Sumner was hunting for French's "and Slocum's" divisions; "Slocum" was a transmission error for "Richardson"); Meagher report, *OR* 19.1:294–95; Sept. 18, Strother, *Virginia Yankee in the Civil War,* 113; Gibbon to wife, Sept. 21, Gibbon Papers, HSP; Meade to wife, Sept. 23, Meade Papers, HSP.

28. Livermore, *Days and Events,* 133, 136–38; Cross journal, in Pride and Travis, *My Brave Boys,* 133–34; Robert G. Smith, *A Brief Account of the Services Rendered by the Second Regiment Delaware Volunteers* (Wilmington, 1909), 10–11; Sept. 17, 1862, Strother, *Virginia Yankee in the Civil War,* 110; Maria Lydig Daly, *Diary of a Union Lady, 1861–1865,* Harold Earl Hammond, ed. (New York: Funk & Wagnalls, 1962), 228; Charles A. Fuller, *Personal Recollections of the War of 1861* (Sherburne, N.Y., 1906), 59; Barlow to mother, Sept. 18, 1862, Barlow, *"Fear Was Not in Him,"* 117. Gen. Caldwell would be court-martialed for cowardice but not convicted: Carman, *Maryland Campaign,* 2:288n86.

29. Sears, *Landscape Turned Red,* 246–47, 250; Carman, *Maryland Campaign,* 2:287n83, 2:310–18; Palmer, *Forgotten Hero of Gettysburg,* 93.

30. Carman, *Maryland Campaign,* 2:43–44; Sears, *Landscape Turned Red,* 254, 257; Hancock, Graham reports, *OR* 19.1:279, 343; *New York Times,* Sept. 20, 1862; Benjamin F. Clarkson in *Hagerstown* (Md.) *Weekly Globe,* June 1, 1922, Antietam National Battlefield.

31. McClellan report, *OR* 19.1:60; McClellan to Pleasonton, Sept. 17, 1862, Pleasonton Family Papers.

32. Porter to Manton Marble, Sept. 30, 1862, Marble Papers, LC; Smith, *Autobiography,* 53–55; Smith to George B. Davis, May 9, 1897, W. F. Smith Papers, Vermont Historical Society.

33. Cox report, *OR* 19.1:424; [James A. Hardie] to Burnside, Sept. 16, 1862, Lewis Richmond to Seth Williams, Sept. 17, *OR* 19.2: 308, 314.

34. McClellan preliminary report, *OR* 19.1:31; Cox, "Battle of Antietam," *Battles and Leaders,* 2:650; Burnside report, *OR* 19.1:419; Burnside testimony, *CCW* 1 (1863), 640; Ruggles to Burnside, Sept. 17, 1862, *OR* 51.1:844. In his 1864 *Report* (209), McClellan claimed he sent Burnside the attack order at 8:00 a.m. This was a deliberate falsification, a ploy to make Burnside a scapegoat for Antietam's less-than-decisive outcome. The actual 9:10 a.m. attack order file copy was sequestered (McClellan Papers, LC) and not published until 1897.

35. Cox, "Battle of Antietam," *Battles and Leaders,* 2:650; George Crook, *General George Crook: His Autobiography,* Martin F. Schmitt, ed. (Norman: University of Oklahoma Press, 1946), 97–98; Carman, *Maryland Campaign,* 2:411–12; Marvel, *Burnside,* 137–38. Engineer Duane filed no report detailing his actions at Antietam.

36. Sears, *Landscape Turned Red,* 264–67; D. H. Strother, "Personal Recollections of the War by a Virginian, Antietam," *Harper's New Monthly Magazine,* 36 (Feb. 1868), 283; Alexander Webb to "Mr. Remsen," Sept. 28, 1862, Webb Papers, Yale University Library; Cox, "Battle of Antietam," *Battles and Leaders,* 2:652.

37. McClellan to Halleck, Sept. 17, 1862, McClellan, *Civil War Papers,* 467.

38. Franklin testimony, *CCW* 1 (1863), 626; Franklin to wife, Sept. 19, 1862, Historical Society of York County, in Snell, *From First to Last,* 194; Smith to George B. Davis, May 9, 1897, W. F. Smith

Papers, Vermont Historical Society; James Harrison Wilson, *Under the Old Flag*, 1:114–15; Hunt to McClellan, Jan. 12, 1876, McClellan Papers, LC; Porter to Manton Marble, Sept. 30, 1862, Marble Papers, LC.

39. Wilson, *Under the Old Flag*, 1:116–17; George W. Smalley, "Chapters in Journalism," *Harper's New Monthly Magazine*, 89 (August 1894), 428–29.

40. Williams to Humphreys, Sept. 17, 1862, *OR* 51:1:843; Sixth Corps itinerary, *OR* 19.1:378–79; Couch notebook, 1873, Old Colony Historical Society, 121.

41. Smalley in *New-York Tribune*, Sept. 19, 1862; Cox, *Reminiscences*, 1:350; D. H. Strother, "Personal Recollections of the War by a Virginian, Antietam," *Harper's New Monthly Magazine*, 36 (Feb. 1868), 284. After the 9:10 a.m. dispatch (*OR* 51.1:844), McClellan's orders to Burnside were delivered verbally, and the postwar recollections of their content by staff-officer deliverers are highly suspect, designed to support McClellan's efforts to scapegoat Burnside for the failures at Antietam. See the following examples (all written without knowledge of the 9:10 a.m. attack order, sequestered until 1897 in McClellan's papers): two 1876 Delos B. Sacket letters, McClellan, *McClellan's Own Story*, 609–11; Nelson H. Davis to McClellan, Jan. 31, 1876, McClellan Papers, LC; Edward H. Wright to Fitz John Porter, Mar. 3, 1892, Porter Papers, LC; D. S. Stanley to John C. Ropes, Dec. 1, 1894, and John M. Wilson to Stanley, Nov. 30, 1894, Ropes Papers, Boston University Library; William F. Biddle, "Recollections of McClellan," *United Service Magazine*, 9:5 (May 1894), 468.

42. Willcox, *Forgotten Valor*, 359; Christ, Welsh reports, *OR* 19.1:438, 441; Sears, *Landscape Turned Red*, 282–84; Sept. 17, 1862, Strother, *Virginia Yankee in the Civil War*, 111; Cox, *Reminiscences*, 1:351; Croffut and Morris, *The Military and*

Civil History of Connecticut During the War of 1861–65 (New York, 1868), 271.

43. Marcy to Pleasonton, Sept. 17, 1862, *OR* 51.1:845; Pleasonton draft report, McClellan Papers, LC; Smalley in *New-York Tribune*, Sept. 19. Earlier McClellan ordered two of Morell's brigades to support the right, but then recalled them; in Smalley's account here, the Fifth Corps was intact and in reserve: Morell report, *OR Supplement*, ser. I, 3:466.

44. Burnside report, *OR* 19.1:421; Daniel Ross Ballou, "The Military Services of Maj.-Gen. Ambrose Everett Burnside in the Civil War," *Personal Narratives of Events in the War of the Rebellion*, Rhode Island MOLLUS (10:1905), 41:392; Shaw to father, Sept. 21, Shaw, *Blue-Eyed Child of Fortune*, 241; Sept. 17, Strother, *Virginia Yankee in the Civil War*, 111–12.

11. "AN AUGER TOO DULL TO TAKE HOLD"

1. Smalley in *New-York Tribune*, Sept. 19, 1862.

2. B. F. Fisher to McClellan, Franklin to McClellan, September 18, 1862, McClellan Papers, LC; Burnside testimony, *CCW* 1 (1863), 642; Smith, *Autobiography*, 55; Sept. 18, Strother, *Virginia Yankee in the Civil War*, 112; Sept. 18, Patrick, *Inside Lincoln's Army*, 151; Porter to Manton Marble, Sept. 30, Marble Papers, LC; Meade to wife, Sept. 20, Meade Papers, HSP; Webb to father, Sept. 24, Webb Papers, Yale University Library.

3. McClellan to Halleck, to wife, Sept. 18, 1862, McClellan, *Civil War Papers*, 468, 469.

4. Marcy to Couch, Sept. 17, 1862, Humphreys to McClellan, Apr. 13, 1863, *OR* 51.1:844, 1005–6; William F. Smith, "Notes on Crampton's Gap and Antietam," *Battles and Leaders*, 2:597; Reyn-

olds to sister, Sept. 19, 1862, Reynolds Papers, Franklin and Marshall College, in Nichols, *Toward Gettysburg*, 134; Sears, *Landscape Turned Red*, 301–2; casualties: *OR* 19.1:194–96; Williams to daughters, Sept. 22, Williams, *From the Cannon's Mouth*, 129.

5. John W. Weiser, Oct. 11, 1862, Antietam National Battlefield.

6. McClellan, *Report*, 211–12; casualty totals: Sears, *Landscape Turned Red*, 295–96; casualty details: *OR* 19.1:183–204; McClellan to Halleck, Sept. 19, 1862, McClellan, *Civil War Papers*, 470.

7. McClellan to wife, Sept. 18, 1862, McClellan, *Civil War Papers*, 469; Smalley, "Chapters in Journalism," *Harper's New Monthly Magazine*, 89 (Aug. 1894), 429; journal, Sept. 25, Chase, *Papers*, 1:400; Sumner testimony, *CCW* 1 (1863), 368; Williams to Lewis Allen, Sept. 25, Williams, *From the Cannon's Mouth*, 135; Smith to John C. Ropes, Feb. 11, 1897, Ropes Papers, Boston University Library.

8. Carman, *Maryland Campaign*, 2:499; Benjamin W. Crowninshield, *A History of the First Regiment of Massachusetts Cavalry Volunteers* (Boston: Houghton Mifflin, 1891), 39; McClellan to wife, Sept. 22, 1862, McClellan, *Civil War Papers*, 477.

9. Smalley in *New-York Tribune*, Sept. 19, 1862; McClellan to Lincoln, to Hooker, Sept. 20, McClellan, *Civil War Papers*, 474–75; McClellan preliminary report, *OR* 19.1:30; Williams to McClellan, Apr. 18, 1863, McClellan Papers, LC; McClellan, *Report*, 202.

10. Charles A. Whittier, "Reminiscences of the War, 1861–1865," 1888, Boston Public Library; Smith to George B. Davis, May 9, 1897, W. F. Smith Papers, Vermont Historical Society; Hunt report, *OR* 19.1:206. Demonstrating his animus toward Burnside, Porter demanded an explanation for a rumor that Burnside had preferred charges against Porter for refusing to reinforce him at Antietam. Burnside denied the charge: Burnside to Porter, Oct. 9, 1862, Porter Papers, LC.

11. McClellan to wife, Sept. 20, [21], 1862, McClellan, *Civil War Papers*, 473, 476; M [Randolph Marcy] to Barlow, Oct. 21, S.L.M. Barlow Papers, Huntington Library; Stephen Engle, "'It Is Time for the States to Speak to the Federal Government': The Altoona Conference and Emancipation," *Civil War History*, 58:4 (Dec. 2012) 416–50; Henry W. Raymond, ed., "Excerpts from the Journal of Henry J. Raymond," *Scribner's Monthly*, 19:3 (Jan. 1880), 423. Interviewed by *New York Times* editor Raymond on Jan. 23, 1863, Burnside recalled his argument with McClellan as the time McClellan resumed the Potomac army field command, but in that he was surely mistaken (see Chapter 9, note 16). A post-Antietam date better fits the facts.

12. Smalley in *New-York Tribune*, Sept. 19, 1862; McClellan to Halleck, Sept. 19 (two), McClellan, *Civil War Papers*, 470; journal, Sept. 22, Chase, *Papers*, 1:393–94; Sept. 22, Welles, *Diary*, 54; preliminary Emancipation Proclamation, Sept. 22, Lincoln, *Collected Works*, 5:434; McClellan to wife, Sept. 22, McClellan, *Civil War Papers*, 477; Palmerston to Russell, Oct. 22, G. P. Gooch, ed., *The Later Correspondence of Lord John Russell, 1840–1878* (London, 1925), 328.

13. Whitely to Bennett, Sept. 24, 1862, James Gordon Bennett Papers, LC; Barnett to Barlow, Sept. 25, S.L.M. Barlow Papers, Huntington Library; suspending writ of habeas corpus, Sept. 24, Lincoln, *Collected Works*, 5:436–37; McClellan to wife, Sept. 25, to Aspinwall, Sept. 26, McClellan, *Civil War Papers*, 481–82.

14. Porter to Marble, Sept. 30, 1862, Marble Papers, LC; Sept. 30, Wainwright, *Diary of Battle*, 108–9; Gibbon to wife, Nov. 21, Gibbon Papers, HSP; Meade to

wife, Oct. 1, Meade Papers, HSP; Williams to daughter, Oct. 28, Williams, *From the Cannon's Mouth,* 142.

15. Blair to McClellan, Sept. 27, 1862, Mc-Clellan Papers, LC; Lincoln to John J. Key, Sept. 26, Nov. 24, Lincoln, *Collected Works,* 5:442, 508; [John Hay] in *Missouri Republican,* Oct. 6, Michael Burlingame, *Lincoln's Journalist: John Hay's Anonymous Writings for the Press, 1860–1864* (Carbondale: Southern Illinois University Press, 1998), 317.

16. Cox, *Military Reminiscences,* 1:356, 359–61; Smith, *Autobiography,* 57–58; Smith, "Memoirs," Vermont Historical Society. A report of this McClellan-Smith interview reached the president: Hay, *Inside Lincoln's White House,* 360n247.

17. McClellan to wife, Oct. 5, 1862, McClellan, *Civil War Papers,* 489–90; G.O. 163, Oct. 7, *OR* 19.2:395–96; *New-York Tribune,* Oct. 9.

18. Porter to Marble, Sept. 30, 1862, Marble Papers, LC (Porter completed this letter on Oct. 3); McClellan to wife, Oct. 2, 5, McClellan, *Civil War Papers,* 488, 489–90; Lincoln to Mrs. Lincoln, Oct. 2, collection of Lloyd Ostendorf; David Davis to Leonard Swett, Nov. 26, Lincoln Presidential Library; Nicolay and Hay, *Abraham Lincoln,* 6:175.

19. Journal, Oct. 7, 1862, Chase, *Papers,* 1:416–17; Cochrane, *Memoir of Gen. John Cochrane* (New York, 1879), 30–32; Cochrane to Lincoln, Oct. 26, Lincoln Papers, LC; McClellan to wife, Sept. 20, 22, 29, McClellan, *Civil War Papers,* 476, 477, 486.

20. Halleck to McClellan, Oct. 6, 1862, *OR* 19.1:72; Halleck to wife, Oct. 7, Schoff Collection, Clements Library, University of Michigan; McClellan to Halleck, Oct. 7, McClellan to wife, Oct. 5, 7, McClellan, *Civil War Papers,* 492–93, 489–90, 492; Richardson to Sidney H. Gay, Oct. 31, Gay Papers, Columbia University Library; Couch to Marcy, Oct. 7, McClellan Papers, LC; Oct. 9,

Heintzelman diary, LC; Confederate return for Oct. 20, *OR* 19.2:674.

21. Meade to wife, Oct. 20, 1862, Meade Papers, HSP; Haupt to Stanton, Oct. 20, RG 107 (M-492), NA; Ethan S. Rafuse, *McClellan's War: The Failure of Moderation in the Struggle for the Union,* 357. For a sampling of McClellan's debates with Washington regarding supplies and other issues, see McClellan, *Civil War Papers,* for October 1862.

22. Mary Ellen McClellan to Mary Shipman, Oct. 15, 1862, Shipman Papers, Connecticut Historical Society, courtesy Kelly Nolin; John W. Garrett to McClellan, Oct. 8, McClellan Papers, LC; John C. Gray, Jr., to mother, Oct. 12, John Chipman Gray and John Codman Ropes, *War Letters, 1862–1865,* 1; *Philadelphia Press,* Oct. 15. Apparently McClellan spoke of a visit by his wife when Lincoln was at Sharpsburg —the president suggested they meet in Washington (to McClellan, Oct. 7, Lincoln, *Collected Works,* 5:452) — but the McClellan-Marcy journey to Philadelphia was made without notice to anyone. Among other generals' wives visiting in this period were Mmes. Burnside, Smith, and Franklin.

23. W. W. Blackford, *War Years with Jeb Stuart* (New York: Scribner's, 1945), 168; Oct. 14, 1862, Wainwright, *Diary of Battle,* 115; McClellan to Halleck, Oct. 13, McClellan, *Civil War Papers,* 497–98; Halleck to McClellan, Oct. 14, *OR* 19.2:421.

24. Meade to wife, Sept. 23, Oct. 1, 1862, Meade Papers, HSP; McClellan to Halleck, Oct. 25, *OR* 19.2:483–84; Williams to daughter, Sept. 23, Williams, *From the Cannon's Mouth,* 133. Command changes detailed in Welcher, *The Union Army,* vol. 1.

25. Oct. 18, 1862, Welles, *Diary,* 81; Bryant to Lincoln, Oct. 22, Lincoln Papers, LC; Franklin to wife, Oct. 5, Historical Society of York County, in Snell,

From First to Last, 199–200; Williams to daughter, Oct. 5, Williams, *From the Cannon's Mouth,* 136; Richardson to Sidney H. Gay, Oct. 22, Gay Papers, Columbia University Library; Ruggles to Stewart Van Vliet, Oct. 28, S.L.M. Barlow Papers, Huntington Library; Meade to wife, Oct. 11, 20, Meade Papers, HSP.

26. Journal, Sept. 23, 1862, Chase, *Papers,* 1:396–97; *New-York Tribune,* Sept. 24; Porter to Marble, Sept. 30, Marble Papers, LC; McClellan to Halleck, Oct. 25, McClellan, *Civil War Papers,* 510; Halleck to McClellan, Oct. 26, *OR* 19.1:85; Halleck to Gamble, Oct. 30, *OR* ser. III, 2:703–4.

27. Lincoln to McClellan, Sept. 13, 1862, Lincoln, *Collected Works,* 5:460–61.

28. Darius N. Couch, "Sumner's Right Grand Division," *Battles and Leaders,* 3:105–6; McClellan to Lincoln, Oct. 17, 25, 1862, to wife, c. Oct. 29, McClellan, *Civil War Papers,* 499, 508, 515; McClellan to Halleck, Oct. 22, 25, Lincoln to McClellan, Oct. 25, *OR* 19.2:464, 484–85.

29. Lincoln to Halleck, Nov. 5, 1862, Lincoln, *Collected Works,* 5:485; Sept. 25, 1864, Hay, *Inside Lincoln's White House,* 232; Nicolay to Therena Bates, Nov. 9, 1862, Nicolay, *With Lincoln in the White House,* 90–91; Nov. 29, Browning, *Diary,* 1:590; Francis Preston Blair to Montgomery Blair, Nov. 7, Blair Family Papers, LC. In the midterm elections Democratic gains were substantial but not enough to threaten the Republicans' hold on Congress.

30. Buckingham in *Chicago Tribune,* Sept. 4, 1875, in Comte de Paris, *History of the Civil War in America* (Philadelphia, 1876), 2:555–57; McClellan, *McClellan's Own Story,* 652; Meade to wife, Nov. 9, 1862, Meade Papers, HSP; McClellan to wife, Nov. 7, McClellan, *Civil War Papers,* 519–20.

31. Nov. 11, 1862, Patrick, *Inside Lincoln's Army,* 174; Meade to wife, Nov. 9,

Meade Papers, HSP; Swinton in *New York Times,* Nov. 12; George W. Salter to James M. Wilson, Nov. 9, John Hay Library, Brown University; Robert E. Jameson to mother, Nov. 16, Jameson Papers, LC.

32. Porter to Manton Marble, Nov. 9, 1862, Marble Papers, LC; Meade to wife, Nov. 8, 1862, Jan. 2, 1863, Meade Papers, HSP; Almira R. Hancock, ed., *Reminiscences of Winfield Scott Hancock,* 92. McClellan was ordered to Trenton, New Jersey, but he soon moved to New York City to prepare his final report as commander of the Army of the Potomac.

12. TRIAL ON THE RAPPAHANNOCK

1. Halleck to wife, Nov. 9, 1862, Schoff Collection, Clements Library, University of Michigan; Dec. 3, Welles, *Diary,* 88.

2. McClellan to wife, Nov. 7, 1862, to Mary B. Burnside, Nov. 8, McClellan, *Civil War Papers,* 520, 521; Meade to wife, Nov. 9, Meade Papers, HSP; Howard to brother, Nov. 8, O. O. Howard Papers, Bowdoin College Library; Williams to Lewis Allen, Nov. 16, Williams, *From the Cannon's Mouth,* 151; Smith, *Autobiography,* 59; Couch, "Sumner's 'Right Grand Division,'" *Battles and Leaders,* 3:106; Franklin to wife, Nov. 15, Historical Society of York County, in Snell, *From First to Last,* 203.

3. D. R. Larned to sister, Nov. 27, 1862, to Henry Howe, Nov. 22, Larned Papers, LC; Walter A. Chapman to parents, Oct. 19, Yale University Library.

4. War Dept. G.O. 182, Nov. 5, 1862, Halleck to Burnside, Nov. 5, *OR* 19.2:545, 546; McClellan to Haupt, Oct. 26, 27, to Lincoln, Nov. 7, McClellan, *Civil War Papers,* 511, 513, 519; Haupt to McClellan, Oct. 26, Haupt, *Reminiscences,* 146–47; Ingalls to Meigs, Nov. 6, Haupt

to Burnside, Nov. 9, *OR* 19.2:549, 559–60; Rafuse, *McClellan's War,* 374; Burnside testimony, *CCW* 1 (1863), 649; Larned to Mary B. Burnside, Nov. 9, Larned Papers, LC.

5. Burnside to Collum, Nov. 9, 1862, *OR* 21:99–101.

6. Burnside, Halleck reports, *OR* 21:83–84, 46–48; Burnside, Halleck testimony, *CCW* 1 (1863), 649–50, 673–75; Augustus Woodbury, *General Halleck and General Burnside,* 4–9; Halleck to Daniel Woodbury, Nov. 12, 1862, to Burnside, Nov. 14, *OR* 19.2:572, 579; Ropes to John C. Ropes, Nov. 19, Henry Ropes Papers, Boston Public Library.

7. AP G.O. 184, Nov. 14, 1862, McClellan to Halleck, Oct. 25, *OR* 19.2:583–84, 483–84; William W. Teall to wife, Nov. 13, Tennessee State Library and Archives; War Dept. G.O. 182, Nov. 5, *OR* 19.2:545; Porter to Marble, Nov. 9, Marble Papers, LC; Army HQ S.O. 362, Nov. 25, *OR* 12.2:507; Nov. 14, Strother, *Virginia Yankee in the Civil War,* 129; Halleck to Burnside, Nov. 10, *OR* 19.2:565; Franklin to wife, Nov. 16, Historical Society of York County, in Snell, *From First to Last,* 205; Ruggles S.O., Nov. 7, *OR* 19.2:551. These command changes follow Welcher, *The Union Army,* vol. 1.

8. Edwin O. Wentworth to wife, Nov. 8, 1862, Wentworth Papers, LC; Patrick diary, Nov. 5, 23, Patrick Papers, LC.

9. Burnside testimony, *CCW* 1 (1863), 651; Comstock to Bowers (two), Daniel Woodbury to Comstock, Nov. 14, 1862, *OR* 19.2:580; Augustus Woodbury, *General Halleck and General McClellan,* 8–11; Comstock to Daniel Woodbury, Nov. 15, *OR* 51:1:946; Burnside to Halleck, Nov. 19, *OR* 21:101–3; Halleck to Franklin, May 25, 1863, *OR* 21:1007. Duane's Nov. 6 bridge train dispatch, telegraphed from Rectortown, is missing, but its content is printed in substance in Rufus Ingalls's report, *OR* 21:148.

10. Woodbury to Parke, Nov. 24, 1862, *OR* 21:793–95; Woodbury testimony, *CCW* 1 (1863), 663–65; Ingalls memo, c. Dec. 1862, Magruder to Woodbury, Nov. 25, *OR* 21:148–51, 799–800; Halleck testimony, *CCW* 1 (1863), 675. At Halleck's urging, Burnside put Woodbury in arrest, but relented after his explanation.

11. Sumner, Hooker testimony, *CCW* 1 (1863), 657, 665–66; Hooker to Burnside, Nov. 19, 1862, to Stanton, Dec. 4, Stanton Papers, LC; Parke to Hooker, Nov. 20, *OR* 21:104–5.

12. Burnside report, *OR* 21:85; Slaughter to Sumner, Sumner to Slaughter, Nov. 21, 1862, *OR* 21:784–85; William W. Teall to wife, Nov. 21, Tennessee State Library and Archives; Nov. 25, Patrick, *Inside Lincoln's Army,* 181; Burnside to Halleck, Nov. 22, *OR* 21:103–4; Larned to Henry Howe, Nov. 22, Larned Papers, LC; Sumner to Burnside, Nov. 23, Burnside Papers, RG 94 (entry 159), NA; Franklin to wife, Nov. 25, Historical Society of York County, in Snell, *From First to Last,* 208; Gibbon memo, Nov. 30, *OR* 21:812–13.

13. Lincoln to Burnside, Nov. 25, 1862, to Halleck, Nov. 27, Lincoln, *Collected Works,* 5:511, 514–15; Nov. 29, Browning, *Diary,* 1:590. The Rappahannock flows northwest to southeast at Fredericksburg, but for clarity here the Federals at Falmouth are north of the river, the Confederates at Fredericksburg south of the river.

14. Dec. 3, 1862, Patrick, *Inside Lincoln's Army,* 184; Smith, "Franklin's 'Left Grand Division,'" *Battles and Leaders,* 3:129; Francis Augustín O'Reilly, *The Fredericksburg Campaign: Winter War on the Rappahannock,* 51–52; Burnside testimony, *CCW* 1 (1863), 654; Smith, *Autobiography,* 60.

15. William W. Teall to wife, Dec. 9, 1862, Tennessee State Library and Archives; Burnside to Cullum, Dec. 9, *OR* 21:64; Sumner to Burnside, Nov. 23, Burnside Papers, RG 94 (entry 159), NA; Franklin testimony, *CCW* 1 (1863), 661;

Howard, *Autobiography,* 1:321; Couch notebook, 1873, Old Colony Historical Society, 123; Couch, "Sumner's 'Right Grand Division,'" *Battles and Leaders,* 3:107–8.

16. Hunt report, *OR* 21:181, 183; O'Reilly, *Fredericksburg Campaign,* 54, 61–63, 66, 73–76; Franklin order, Dec. 11, 1862, Franklin Papers, LC; Parke to Franklin, Dec. 11, *OR* 21:107; Wesley Brainerd, *Bridge Building in War Time,* Ed Malles, ed. (Knoxville: University of Tennessee Press, 1997), 158.

17. Hall, Fairchild reports, *OR* 21:282, 346; O'Reilly, *Fredericksburg Campaign,* 78–86; Howard, *Autobiography,* 323–25; Burnside to Halleck, Dec. 11, 1862, *OR* 21:64.

18. Burnside [to Franklin], Dec. 12, 1862, *OR* 21:108; Reynolds to sisters, Dec. 17, Reynolds Papers, Franklin and Marshall College, in Nichols, *Toward Gettysburg,* 155; Burnside to Sumner, Franklin, Hooker, Dec. 10, *OR* 21:106–7; Burnside testimony, *CCW* 1 (1863), 656; Alexander, *Military Memoirs of a Confederate,* 285.

19. Dec. 14, 1862, Patrick, *Inside Lincoln's Army,* 188–89; George C. Rable, *Fredericksburg! Fredericksburg!,* 177–80; John S. Godfrey to brother, Dec. 14, New Hampshire Historical Society.

20. Smith, "Franklin's 'Left Grand Division,'" *Battles and Leaders,* 3:133; Smith, *Autobiography,* 61; Sumner to Burnside, Nov. 23, 1862, Burnside Papers, RG 94 (entry 159), NA; Franklin, "Reply to the report of the Joint Committee on the Conduct of the War," Apr. 6, 1863, *OR* 51:1:1021; Burnside to Franklin, Dec. 13, 1862, *OR* 21:71.

21. Franklin testimony, *CCW* 1 (1863), 707–9; Burnside to Samuel Sturgis, June 7, 1863, Burnside Papers, RG 94 (entry 159), NA; Franklin to wife, Dec. 17, 1862, Historical Society of York County, in Snell, *From First to Last,* 225. Baldy Smith (*Battles and Leaders,* 3:134) offered a flimsy excuse for Franklin's reading of Burnside's Dec.

13 order: The military man, he explained, takes "seize" to mean to occupy an unguarded position, "carry" to attack a defended position. If Burnside had used "carry" instead of "seize" in regard to Prospect Hill, Franklin would have grasped the order's intent. Franklin was also supposedly confused about Burnside's reference to the "old Richmond road." If everyone was agreed on attacking Lee's right, the name of the road leading there was hardly an issue.

22. Reynolds report, *OR* 21:453; Reynolds testimony, *CCW* 1 (1863), 697–98; Dec. 13, 1862, Wainwright, *Diary of Battle,* 143; A. Wilson Greene, "Opportunity to the South: Meade versus Jackson at Fredericksburg," *Civil War History,* 33:4 (Dec. 1987), 303–11; Meade to wife, Dec. 16, 20, Meade Papers, HSP; Gibbon, *Recollections,* 104.

23. O.R.H. Thomson and William H. Rauch, *History of the "Bucktails": Kane's Rifle Regiment of the Pennsylvania Reserve Corps* (Philadelphia, 1906), 235–36; Burnside report, *OR* 21:94–95; Frederick L. Hitchcock, *War from the Inside* (Philadelphia, 1904), 134; Smith, "Franklin's 'Left Grand Division,'" *Battles and Leaders,* 3:136; statements of Cutts, Goddard, *OR* 21:128; Franklin to Meade, Mar. 25, 1863, Meade to Franklin, Mar. 28, Meade to wife, Mar. 30, Meade Papers, HSP.

24. Hardie to Burnside, Dec. 13, 1862, *OR* 21:91; Larned to Henry Howe, Dec. 16, Larned Papers, LC; O'Reilly, *Fredericksburg Campaign,* 255–56; Kimball report, *OR* 21:290; Dec. 15, Fiske, *Mr. Dunn Browne's Experiences in the Army,* 50.

25. Couch, "Sumner's 'Right Grand Division,'" *Battles and Leaders,* 3:108, 113; Zook to E. J. Wade, Dec. 16, 1862, S. K. Zook Papers, U.S. Army Heritage & Education Center; Meagher report, *OR* 21:242; Rable, *Fredericksburg! Fredericksburg!,* 518n51; John W. Forney, *Life and Military Career of Winfield Scott*

Hancock (Philadelphia, 1880), 335; Murat Halstead in *Cincinnati Daily Commercial,* Dec. 18.

26. Longstreet, "The Battle of Fredericksburg," *Battles and Leaders,* 3:79; Alexander, *Fighting for the Confederacy,* 169; Hunt, Egan reports, *OR* 21:183–85, 318–19; Couch to Burnside, Dec. 13, 1862, *OR* 21:117; O'Reilly, *Fredericksburg Campaign,* 397–99.

27. Abbott to father, Dec. 14, 1862, Abbott Family Papers, Houghton Library, Harvard University; Willcox to Sumner, Dec. 13, *OR* 21:162; Oliver C. Bosbyshell, *The Forty-eighth in the War* (Philadelphia, 1895), 97.

28. Hardie to Burnside, Franklin to Burnside, Willcox to Burnside, Sumner to Couch, Dec. 13, 1862, *OR* 21:92, 118–19, 119, 223; Goddard statement, Hooker report, *OR* 21:128, 356; Hooker testimony, *CCW* 1 (1863), 667–68; Larned memo, Dec. 15, Larned Papers, LC.

29. Willcox to Burnside, Dec. 13, 1862, *OR* 21:119; Couch report, 21:223; Couch notebook, 1873, Old Colony Historical Society, 125; Couch, "Sumner's 'Right Grand Division,'" *Battles and Leaders,* 3:114–15; Andrew A. Humphreys to wife, Dec. 14, 17, Henry H. Humphreys letter, Dec. 18, A. A. Humphreys Papers, HSP; Hooker testimony, *CCW* 1 (1863), 668, 669.

30. William W. Teall to wife, Dec. 13, 14, 15, 1862, Tennessee State Library and Archives; Couch, "Sumner's 'Right Grand Division,'" *Battles and Leaders,* 3:117; Franklin to wife, Dec. 17, York County Historical Society, in Snell, *From First to Last,* 224; Burnside testimony, *CCW* 1 (1863), 653; Larned memo, Dec. 15, Larned to Henry Howe, Dec. 16, Larned Papers, LC.

13. JOE HOOKER IN COMMAND

1. *Cincinnati Commercial,* Dec. 18, 1862; Henry Villard, *Memoirs of Henry Villard, Journalist and Financier, 1835–1900* (Boston, 1904), 1:389–90; *New York Times,* Dec. 17; Haupt, *Reminiscences,* 177; casualties: Thomas L. Livermore, *Numbers and Losses in the Civil War in America, 1861–65,* 96.

2. Allan C. Bogue, "William Parker Cutler's Congressional Diary of 1862–63," *Civil War History,* 33:4 (Dec. 1987), 319–20; Mrs. Lee to husband, Dec. 16, 1862, Lee, *Wartime Washington,* 217n1; *Harper's Weekly,* Dec. 27; Burnside to Halleck, Dec. 17, *OR* 21:66–67, and Stanton Papers, LC; *New York Times,* Dec. 23.

3. Chandler to wife, Dec. 18, 1862, Chandler Papers, LC; *Washington Chronicle,* Dec. 24; Burnside, Sumner, Franklin, Hooker testimony, *CCW* 1 (1863), 649–56, 656–60, 661–63, 665–73; Meade to wife, Dec. 20, Meade Papers, HSP; Franklin to wife, Dec. 17, 19, Historical Society of York County, in Snell, *From First to Last,* 228; Brannigan to sister, Dec. 29, Brannigan Papers, LC.

4. Franklin to wife, Dec. 17, 1862, Historical Society of York County, in Snell, *From First to Last,* 227; Elizabeth Blair Lee to husband, Dec. 16, Lee, *Wartime Washington,* 216; Dawes to Mary B. Gates, Dec. 25, 1862, Dawes to sister, Jan. 4, 1863, Dawes Papers, Wisconsin Historical Society; Meade to wife, Dec. 30, 1862, Mar. 17, 1863, Meade Papers, HSP; O.R.H. Thomson and William H. Rauch, *History of the "Bucktails": Kane's Rifle Regiment of the Pennsylvania Reserve Corps* (Philadelphia, 1906), 235–36; Dec. 21, 1862, Wainwright, *Diary of Battle,* 149.

5. Dec. 19, 20, 1862, Welles, *Diary,* 98–106; Francis Fessenden, *Life and Public Services of William Pitt Fessenden* (Boston: Houghton Mifflin, 1907), 1:243–51; Frederick W. Seward, *Seward at Washington, as Senator and Secretary of State . . . 1861–1872* (New York, 1891), 148; Lincoln to Seward and Chase, Dec. 20, 1862, Lincoln, *Collected Works,* 6:12–13.

6. Larned to Henry Howe, Dec. 16, 1862, Larned Papers, LC; Franklin and Smith to Lincoln, Dec. 20, *OR* 21:868–

70; Lincoln to Franklin and Smith, Dec. 22, Lincoln, *Collected Works,* 6:15; Hyde, *Following the Greek Cross,* 117; Smith, *Autobiography,* 63; Snell, *From First to Last,* 236–38; Franklin to Orville E. Babcock, Dec. 24, Babcock Papers, Newberry Library.

7. Heintzelman diary, Jan. 11, 1863, LC; Warren to brother, Dec. 18, 1862, Warren Papers, New York State Library; Henry L. Abbott to George B. Perry, Dec. 17, Abbott, *Fallen Leaves,* 152.

8. Newton, Cochrane, Burnside testimony, *CCW* 1 (1863), 730–40, 740–46, 717–18; Cochrane, *The War for the Union: Memoir of Gen. John Cochrane* (New York, 1875), 48–51; Lincoln to Burnside, Dec. 30, 1862, Burnside to Lincoln, Jan. 1, 1863, *OR* 21:900, 941.

9. Francis B. Carpenter, "Anecdotes and Reminiscences," in Raymond, *Life and Public Services of Lincoln,* 766; Sumner to John Murray Forbes, Dec. 28, 1862, Charles Sumner, *Selected Letters,* 2:135–36.

10. Burnside testimony, *CCW* 1 (1863), 718; Burnside memo, May 24, 1863, Burnside Papers, RG 94 (entry 159), NA; Lincoln to Halleck, Jan. 1, Lincoln, *Collected Works,* 6:31; Halleck to Stanton, Jan. 1, *OR* 21: 940–41. Burnside's various accountings of his Jan. 1 meeting with Lincoln, Stanton, and Halleck led to the fiction that Burnside told Stanton and Halleck to their faces they should resign; see the tangle of correspondence at *OR* 21:1006–12.

11. Meade to wife, Jan. 2, 1863, Meade Papers, HSP; Franklin to wife, Dec. 29, 1862, Jan. 9, 1863, Historical Society of York County, in Snell, *From First to Last,* 235, 243; Smith, *Autobiography,* 59; Burnside G.O. 8 (unissued), Jan. 23, 1863, *OR* 21:998–99; Brooks to Smith, Apr. 27, W. F. Smith Papers, Vermont Historical Society.

12. Ropes to John C. Ropes, Jan. 13, 1863, Ropes to father, Jan. 5, Henry Ropes Papers, Boston Public Library; Brannigan to sister, Jan. 13, Brannigan Papers,

LC; Warren to brother, Jan. 5, Warren Papers, New York State Library; Sumner to Orestes A. Brownson, Jan. 4, Charles Sumner, *Selected Letters,* 2:138; M. Bain Folwell to mother, Jan. 24, Minnesota Historical Society; Sanford N. Truesdell to sister, Jan. 26, University of Chicago Library; John E. Ryder to sister, Jan. 4, to mother, Feb. 1, Michigan Historical Collections, Bentley Historical Library, University of Michigan; Chase to Fessenden, Jan. 7, Chase, *Papers,* 3:357; Patrick diary, Jan. 17, Patrick Papers, LC.

13. Hooker G.O. 3, Jan. 31, 1863, *OR* 25.2:11–12; Jan. 31 return, RG 94 (entry 65), NA; John Bigelow, Jr., *The Campaign of Chancellorsville,* 36; Hooker testimony, *CCW* 1 (1865), 112; Schurz to Lincoln, Jan. 24, Lincoln Papers, LC.

14. Meade to wife, Dec. 23, 1862, Meade Papers, HSP; Porter to S.L.M. Barlow, Dec. 29, Barlow Papers, Huntington Library; Porter to Marble, Dec. 27, Marble Papers, LC.

15. McClellan to Porter, [Dec. 19, 1862], Porter Papers, LC; Henry Gabler, "The Fitz John Porter Case: Politics and Military Justice," Ph.D. diss. (City University of New York, 1979), 309–14; Porter to Stephen M. Weld, Sr., Jan. 23, 1863, Porter Papers, MHS.

16. Pope to McDowell and Porter, Pope to Porter, Aug. 29, 1862, *OR* 12.2:76, 525; Porter to Burnside, Aug. 27, 28, *OR* 12.2 Supplement, 1063–64, 1069–70; judge advocate's review, ibid., 1113–14, 1125; Pope testimony, ibid., 834, 840; McDowell testimony, ibid., 904, 909; Porter defense, ibid., 1107.

17. *New York Times,* Jan. 12, 1863; Porter to McClellan, Jan. 13, 23, McClellan Papers, LC; *OR* 12.2 Supplement, 1050–52.

18. "The Court-Martial of Fitz John Porter," Sears, *Controversies & Commanders,* 67–71.

19. Franklin to wife, Jan. 25, 1863, Historical Society of York County, in Snell, *From First to Last,* 250; Jan. 25, Wainwright, *Diary of Battle,* 161; Meade

to wife, Jan. 26, Meade Papers, HSP; Lowell to H. L. Higginson, Jan. 21, Emerson, *Life and Letters of Charles Russell Lowell*, 231–32.

20. Meigs to Burnside, Dec. 30, 1862, *OR* 21:918; Henry W. Raymond, ed., "Excerpts from the Journal of Henry J. Raymond," *Scribner's Monthly*, 19:3 (Jan. 1880), 420–22; Jan. 19, 20, 21, 1863, Wainwright, *Diary of Battle*, 157–59; Meade to wife, Jan. 23, Meade Papers, HSP; Williams to daughter, Jan. 24, Williams, *From the Cannon's Mouth*, 159; Ropes to father, Jan. 23, Henry Ropes Papers, Boston Public Library; Reynolds to sisters, Jan. 23, Reynolds Papers, Franklin and Marshall College, in Nichols, *Toward Gettysburg*, 158.

21. Henry W. Raymond, ed., "Excerpts from the Journal of Henry J. Raymond," *Scribner's Monthly*, 19:3 (Jan. 1880), 420–22; Burnside G.O. 8 (unissued), Jan. 23, 1863, *OR* 21:998–99; Burnside memo, May 24, Burnside Papers, RG 94 (entry 159), NA; Burnside testimony, *CCW* 1 (1863), 720; Burnside to Lincoln, Jan. 23, *OR* 21:998; Smith, *Autobiography*, 65–66. In G.O. 8 Burnside listed Generals Samuel Sturgis and Edward Ferrero, but later admitted he put them there in error.

22. Burnside testimony, *CCW* 1 (1863), 720–22; Henry W. Raymond, ed., "Excerpts from the Journal of Henry J. Raymond," *Scribner's Monthly*, 19:5 (Mar. 1880), 705; Halleck to Franklin, May 20, 1863, *OR* 21:1008–9; War Dept. G.O. 20, Jan. 25, Burnside G.O., Jan. 26, *OR* 25.2:3, 4–5; Larned to Mary B. Burnside, Jan. 28, Larned Papers, LC. The account of a spirited dispute over the command change in *Battles and Leaders* (3:239–40) is fictional, by an author, Charles F. Benjamin, whose credentials are fictional as well.

23. Noah Brooks, *Washington in Lincoln's Time* (New York, 1895), 52–53, 56; Lincoln to Hooker, Jan. 26, 1863, Lincoln, *Collected Works*, 6:78–79, and *OR* 25.2:4; Nicolay to Robert Lincoln, 1878, in Helen Nicolay, *Lincoln's Secretary: A Biography of John G. Nicolay* (New York: Longmans, Green, 1949), 278; Anson Henry to wife, Apr. 12, 1863, Henry Papers, Lincoln Presidential Library; Hooker to S. P. Bates, [1878], June 29, 1878, Bates Papers, Pennsylvania State Archives; *New York Herald*, Apr. 22, 1863. Hooker sent a copy of Lincoln's Jan. 26 letter to the compilers of the *Official Records*. Reference to a dictator was not in its modern sense of tyrant, but in its more benign Roman sense of a general provisionally taking the command and relinquishing it when the crisis was over.

24. Hooker to S. P. Bates, June 28, 1878, Bates Papers, Pennsylvania State Archives; Hooker testimony, *CCW* 1 (1865), 175, 112; Halleck to William T. Sherman, Sept. 16, 1864, Sherman, *Memoirs* (1875; Library of America, 1990), 590.

25. Jan. 31, 1863, Wainwright, *Diary of Battle*, 162; Meade to wife, Apr. 12, Meade Papers, HSP; Sept. 9, Hay, *Inside Lincoln's White House*, 80; Leech, *Reveille in Washington*, 264; E. N. Gilpin, Apr. 7, 1911, John Bigelow, Jr., Papers, LC; Charles Francis Adams, Jr., to father, Jan. 30, 1863, Ford, ed., *A Cycle of Adams Letters*, 1:249–50; Jan. 26, Strong, *Diary*, 290; Mrs. Lee to husband, Jan. 27, Lee, *Wartime Washington*, 237. The term "hooker" for prostitute long predated the Civil War (*American Heritage Dictionary*, 5th ed., 845), but gossips made the association with the general anyway.

26. Meade to wife, Jan. 26, 1863, Meade Papers, HSP; Sumner testimony, *CCW* 1 (1863), 660; R. I. Holcombe, *History of the First Regiment Minnesota Volunteer Infantry, 1861–1864* (Stillwater, Minn., 1916), 227; Jan. 26, Browning, *Diary*, 1:619; War Dept. G.O. 20, Jan. 25, *OR* 25.2:3; Hooker to Stanton, Feb. 25, 1864,

OR 32.2:468; Smith, *Autobiography*, 66; John H. Eicher and David J. Eicher, *Civil War High Commands*. Franklin defended himself in a pamphlet *A Reply of Maj. Gen. William B. Franklin to the Report of the Joint Committee on the Conduct of the War* (1863). William F. Smith would be reconfirmed a major general in March 1864.

27. Gibbon, *Recollections*, 107; Slocum to Joseph Howland, Feb. 4, 1863, Slocum Papers, New-York Historical Society; Meade to wife, Jan. 26, Meade Papers, HSP; Sherman to wife, Apr. 17, Sherman, *Sherman's Civil War*, 452; John G. Nicolay interview with T. Lyle Dickey, Oct. 20, 1876, Burlingame, *Oral History of Lincoln*, 50.

28. Hooker to L. Thomas, Jan. 26, 1863, *CCW* 1 (1865), 183; Stone to Benjamin J. Lossing, Nov. 5, 1866, Schoff Collection, Clements Library, University of Michigan; Joseph L. Whitney and Stephen W. Sears, "The True Story of Taps," *Blue & Gray*, 10:6 (Aug. 1993), 30–33; badges circular, Mar. 21, 1863, *OR* 25.2:152; Jan. 30, Patrick, *Inside Lincoln's Army*, 209.

29. Hooker G.O. 9, Feb. 7, 1863, *OR* 25.2:57; James A. Huston, "Logistical Support of Federal Armies in the Field," *Civil War History*, 7:1 (Mar. 1961), 40–41; William W. Folwell to fiancée, Feb. 18, Minnesota Historical Society; Hooker G.O. 3, Jan. 30, *OR* 25.2:11–12; Williams to daughter, Mar. 20, *From the Cannon's Mouth*, 169.

30. Hooker to Patrick, Jan. 28, 1863, RG 393 (1:3980), NA; Henry L. Abbott to George B. Perry, Feb. 1, Abbott, *Fallen Leaves*, 168; Shannon, *Organization and Administration of Union Army*, 2:84; Patrick diary, Jan. 31, Patrick Papers, LC; amnesty proclamation, Mar. 10, Lincoln, *Collected Works*, 6:132; Hooker to L. Thomas, Mar. 20, *OR* 25.2:149; Bigelow, *Chancellorsville*, 49; Couch notebook, 1873, Old Colony Historical Society, 128; Hooker to J. W.

De Peyster, Dec. 27, 1875, Hooker Papers, Huntington Library.

31. Heintzelman diary, Jan. 26, 1863, LC; War Dept. G.O. 26, Feb. 2, Hooker G.O. 6, Feb. 6, *OR* 25.2:42, 51; John Bigelow, Jr., "The Battle of Kelly's Ford," *Cavalry Journal*, 21 (1910), 5–28; Stanton to Hooker, Mar. 19, *OR* 25.2:148; Hooker, Hunt, Butterfield testimony, *CCW* 1 (1865), 113, 92–93, 74–75; Hooker to S. P. Bates, Aug. 28, 1876, Bates Papers, Pennsylvania State Archives; Hooker to Patrick, Feb. 4, 1863, RG 393 (1:3980), NA; J. E. Hammond to S.L.M. Barlow, Apr. 22, Barlow Papers, Huntington Library.

32. Hooker G.O. 6, Feb. 5, 1863, *OR* 25.2:51; Sigel to Joseph Dickinson, Feb. 12, endorsed by Hooker Feb. 12, endorsed by Lincoln Feb. 19, *OR* 25.2:70–71; Howard, *Autobiography*, 348–49; Ella Lonn, *Foreigners in the Union Army and Navy* (Baton Rouge: Louisiana State University Press, 1951), 513; Schurz to Lincoln, Apr. 6, Lincoln Papers, LC; Elijah H. C. Cavins to wife, Apr. 1, Indiana Historical Society.

33. Warren to Emily Chase, Apr. 17, 1863, Warren Papers, New York State Library; Gibbon to wife, Apr. 3, Gibbon Papers, HSP; Butterfield to Chandler, Dec. 25, 1862, Zachariah Chandler Papers, LC; Eicher and Eicher, *Civil War High Commands*; Mar. 31, 1863 return, *OR* 25.2:180; short-term men: *OR* 25.2:532, ser. III, 3: 751, 760, 775, *CCW* 1 (1865), 219; Sedgwick to sister, Apr. 30, Sedgwick, *Correspondence*, 2:91; Halleck to Francis Lieber, Apr. 30, Lieber Papers, Huntington Library; Charles Francis Adams, Jr., to Henry Adams, Mar. 22, Ford, ed., *A Cycle of Adams Letters*, 1:265.

34. Bates to James B. Eads, Apr. 1863, Eads Papers, Missouri Historical Society; Lincoln memo, c. Apr. 6–10, Lincoln, *Collected Works*, 6:164–65; Couch notebook, 1873, Old Colony Historical Society, 128.

35. Hooker testimony, *CCW* 1 (1865), 144; Hooker to Lincoln, Apr. 11, 1863, Lincoln, *Collected Works,* 6:169n; Apr. 15, Patrick diary, LC; Stephen W. Sears, *Chancellorsville,* 121–22; intercepted signal, [Apr. 13], RG 111 (entry 27), NA. Butterfield's ruse is detailed by its discoverer, Edwin Fishel, in *Secret War for the Union,* ch. 15.

36. Hooker to S. P. Bates, Apr. 2, 1877, Bates Papers, Pennsylvania State Archives; Sears, *Chancellorsville,* 137–41.

37. Hooker to Lincoln, Apr. 27, 1863, Lincoln, *Collected Works,* 6:190n; Candler to Slocum, Apr. 28, *OR* 25.2:273–74; Warren, Meade reports, *OR* 25.1:196–97, 505–6; Williams to daughter, May 18, Williams, *From the Cannon's Mouth,* 181–83; Palmer, *Forgotten Hero of Gettysburg,* 119; Stephen M. Weld to father, Apr. 29, 30, Weld, *War Diary and Letters,* 187–91; Butterfield to Sedgwick, Apr. 29, Hooker Papers, Huntington Library; Apr. 29, Wainwright, *Diary of Battle,* 185–86; Butterfield to Sedgwick, Apr. 29, *OR* 25.2:292.

38. Williams to daughter, May 18, 1863, Williams, *From the Cannon's Mouth,* 184; Folwell to wife, May 1, Minnesota Historical Society; Richard M. Bache, *Life of General George Gordon Meade* (Philadelphia, 1897), 260; James C. Biddle to wife, May 20, Biddle Papers, HSP; Butterfield to Comstock, Apr. 30, *OR* 25.2:305; AP G.O. 47, Apr. 30, *OR* 25.1:171; Meade to wife, Apr. 30, Meade Papers, HSP.

39. Lee to Davis, Apr. 29, 1863, *OR* 25.2:756–57; Charles Marshall in *Southern Historical Society Papers,* 23 (1895), 210.

40. Hooker circular, May 1, 1863, *OR* 25.2:324; Sykes, Warren reports, *OR* 25.1:525, 198–99; Dickinson in Henry E. Tremain, *Two Days of War: A Gettysburg Narrative and Other Excursions,* 434; Hooker to Sykes, May 1, Francis A. Walker, *History of the Second Army Corps,* 221; Williams to daughter, May 18, Williams, *From the Cannon's Mouth,* 187; Hooker to S. P. Bates, Apr. 2, 1877,

Bates Papers, Pennsylvania State Archives; Slocum in *Brooklyn Eagle,* Feb. 5, 1888, in Melton, *Sherman's Forgotten General,* 102; Couch, "The Chancellorsville Campaign," *Battles and Leaders,* 3:159–61; Hooker circular, May 1, 1863, *OR* 25.2:328.

41. Reynolds to sisters, Apr. 30, 1863, Reynolds Papers, Franklin and Marshall College, in Nichols, *Toward Gettysburg,* 168; Hooker to Butterfield, May 1, *OR* 25.2:338; Stoneman orders, Apr. 12, 28, *OR* 25.1:1065–67; Virginia railroads report, Apr. 1863, Hooker Papers, Huntington Library; Sept. 9, 1863, Hay, *Inside Lincoln's White House,* 79. In Stoneman's orders, Hanover Junction is called Saxton's Junction.

42. Candler to Slocum and Howard, May 1, 1863, *OR* 25.2:334; Graham report, *OR* 25.1:413; Bigelow, *Campaign of Chancellorsville,* 258; Hooker to Butterfield, Butterfield to Hooker, May 2, *OR* 25.2:351; Sears, *Chancellorsville,* 539n6.

43. Van Alen to Howard, May 2, 1863, copy (June 30) by Howard aide H. M. Kellogg, S. P. Bates Papers, Pennsylvania State Archives, also Kellogg copy in John Bigelow Papers, LC; Van Alen circular, May 2, *CCW* 1 (1865), 126; Schurz to Hooker, Apr. 22, 1876, *Battles and Leaders,* 3:219–20, Howard to Hooker, May 2, 1863, ibid. 3:219n; Biddle to wife, May 2, Biddle Papers, HSP; Sickles to Dickinson, May 2, Hooker Papers, Huntington Library.

44. Webb to wife, May 2, 1863, Webb Papers, Yale University Library; Couch notebook, 1873, Old Colony Historical Society, 130; Van Alen to Butterfield, May 2, 1863, *OR* 25.2:363; Howard to J. E. Rankin, Aug. 5, 1869, O. O. Howard Papers, Bowdoin College Library; Howard report, *OR* 25.1:630.

45. H. M. Kellogg to John Bigelow, Jr., Sept. 3, 1907, Bigelow Papers, LC; James H. Peabody, "Battle of Chancellorsville," *G.A.R. War Papers* (Cincinnati, 1891), 53; Howard to wife, May 9, 1863, O. O. Howard Papers, Bowdoin College Li-

brary; John Lee in *Philadelphia Weekly Times,* Feb. 1, 1888; Thomas Cook in *New York Herald,* May 7, 1863; Barlow to family, May 8, Barlow, *"Fear Was Not in Him,"* 130.

46. William C. Wiley letter, May 1863, Patee Library, Pennsylvania State University; Williams to daughter, May 18, Williams, *From the Cannon's Mouth,* 190, 194; George Arrowsmith to brother, May 11, *Reminiscences and Letters of George Arrowsmith* (Red Bank, N.J., 1893), 198.

47. Warren to Butterfield, May 3, 1863, Hooker Papers, Huntington Library; Van Alen to Butterfield, May 2, *OR* 25.2:362; Van Alen to Sedgwick, May 2, *CCW* 1 (1865), 129.

48. Sickles report, *OR* 25.1:390; Hooker testimony, *CCW* 1 (1865), 127; Alexander, *Fighting for the Confederacy,* 204; May 3, 1863, Wainwright, *Diary of Battle,* 193–94.

49. Ruger's losses: *OR* 19.1:198–99, 25.1:184; Williams to daughter, May 18, 1863, Williams, *From the Cannon's Mouth,* 197; Gould, *Major-General Hiram G. Berry,* 267–68; French, Revere reports, *OR* 25.1:363, 460, Revere court-martial, ibid., 460n.

50. Williams to daughter, May 18, 1863, Williams, *From the Cannon's Mouth,* 198; Henry E. Tremain letter, May 7, 1863, Tremain, *Two Days of War,* 328; Hooker memo, May 21, 1877, courtesy Abraham Lincoln Bookshop; Candler letter, May 7, 1863, Bigelow, *Campaign of Chancellorsville,* 363n; Doubleday memo, Doubleday Papers, New-York Historical Society. Gen. Birney testified, "It was some two hours that he [Hooker] was reported to me as being almost insensible": *CCW* 1 (1865), 36.

51. James C. Biddle to wife, May 8, 9, 1863, Biddle Papers, HSP; Alexander S. Webb, "Meade at Chancellorsville," *PMHSM* 3:222–36; Webb to father, May 12, Webb Papers, Yale University Library; Warren to Butterfield, May 3, Hooker Papers, Huntington Library;

Meade to wife, May 8, Meade Papers, HSP; Couch, "Chancellorsville Campaign," *Battles and Leaders,* 3:169–70; Hancock testimony, *CCW* 1 (1865), 67–68; Walker, *History of the Second Army Corps,* 236.

52. Hooker testimony, *CCW* 1 (1865), 129; Van Alen to Butterfield, May 3, 1863, Hooker Papers, Huntington Library; Newton to Henry F. Clarke, May 10, W. F. Smith Papers, Vermont Historical Society; Thomas S. Allen, "Storming of Marye's Heights," ed. George B. Engle, 16, Wisconsin Historical Society; Hyde, *Following the Greek Cross,* 126.

53. Selden Connor to father, May 10, 1863, Connor Papers, John Hay Library, Brown University; Comstock to Sedgwick, May 3, *OR* 25.2:387; Butterfield to Sedgwick, May 3, Hooker Papers, Huntington Library; Camille Baquet, *History of the First Brigade, New Jersey Volunteers* (Trenton, 1910), 250; Martin T. McMahon, "The Sixth Army Corps," *United States Service Magazine,* 5 (1866), 211.

54. Warren testimony, *CCW* 1 (1865), 48; Warren to Sedgwick, May 3, 1863, *OR* 25.2:396; May 3, Wainwright, *Diary of Battle,* 197; Frank A. Haskell to brother, May 4, Haskell, *Haskell of Gettysburg: His Life and Civil War Papers,* eds. Frank L. Byrne and Andrew T. Weaver, 75–76; Martin T. McMahon, *Gen. John Sedgwick: An Address Delivered Before the Vermont Officers' Reunion Society* . . . (Rutland, Vt., 1880), 21–22.

55. Howe testimony, *CCW* 1 (1865), 21; Hyde, *Following the Greek Cross,* 129, 131; Hyde to mother, May 9, 1863, Hyde, *Civil War Letters,* 75; Harry G. Hore to cousin, May 10, Fredericksburg & Spotsylvania National Military Park; Sedgwick to Hooker, May 4, 9:45 p.m., Hooker Papers, Huntington Library [marked in error 9:45 a.m. in the *Official Records*].

56. Hooker, Butterfield testimony, *CCW* 1 (1865), 133–36, 78; Meade to Reynolds,

Sickles, Howard, May 24, 1863, and their replies, OR 25.1:510–511, Warren memo, ibid., 512; Couch, "Chancellorsville Campaign," *Battles and Leaders,* 3:171; Warren to James C. Biddle, May 26, 1877, Warren Papers, New York State Library.

57. Sedgwick to Hooker, May 4, 1863, Hooker to Sedgwick, May 4, Sedgwick to Hooker, May 5 (two), Hooker to Sedgwick, May 5, OR 25.2: 412, 418–19; Abner Doubleday, *Chancellorsville and Gettysburg,* 66–67.

58. Webb to father, May 12, 1863, Webb Papers, Yale University Library; Meade to wife, May 8, Meade Papers, HSP.

14. PENNSYLVANIA SHOWDOWN

1. Butterfield to Lincoln, Hooker to Lincoln, Stanton to Hooker, May 6, 1863, OR 25.2:434–35; John Sherman to William T. Sherman, May 7, W. T. Sherman Papers, LC; Noah Brooks, *Washington in Lincoln's Time* (New York: Century, 1895), 57–58; Meade to wife, May 8, Meade Papers, HSP; [Robert Henry Newell], *The Orpheus C. Kerr Papers: Third Series* (New York, 1865), 139–42; Tap, *Over Lincoln's Shoulder,* 170; Chandler to wife, May 20, Chandler Papers, LC.

2. Couch, Civil War Record, RG 94 (M-1098), NA; Meade to wife, May 8, 10, 20, 1863, Meade Papers, HSP; May 13, Heintzelman diary, LC; Hooker to S. P. Bates, May 30, 1878, Bates Papers, Pennsylvania State Archives; George W. Smalley, *Anglo-American Memories* (New York: Putnam's, 1911), 159–60. In *Battles and Leaders* (3:241), Charles F. Benjamin has Halleck returning to Washington with Hooker's admission that he would be "only too happy" to resign the army command and return to his old division. Like most of this article, this is fiction, as are the author's credentials.

3. Couch, "Chancellorsville Campaign," *Battles and Leaders,* 3:170; Couch notebook, 1873, Old Colony Historical Society; Sept. 27, 1863, Hay, *Inside Lincoln's White House,* 86; Slocum to Joseph Howland, May 29, Howland Papers, New-York Historical Society; Slocum to William H. Seward, Nov. 14, Lincoln Papers, LC.

4. Meade to wife, May 12, 1863, Meade Papers, HSP; Warren to Emily Chase, May 11, Warren Papers, New York State Library; Almira R. Hancock, *Reminiscences of Winfield Scott Hancock,* 94–95; Gibbon to wife, May 6, 12, Gibbon Papers, HSP; Williams to daughter, May 23, June 29, Williams, *From the Cannon's Mouth,* 203, 221; Howard to Rowland Howard, May 16, O. O. Howard Papers, Bowdoin College Library; Hyde to mother, May 9, Hyde, *Civil War Letters,* 77; Custer to McClellan, May 6, McClellan Papers, LC; Mrs. Lee to husband, May 8, Lee, *Wartime Washington,* 266; May 7, Wainwright, *Diary of Battle,* 202.

5. Gibbon to McClellan, May 18, 1863, McClellan Papers, LC; Ropes to John C. Ropes, May 10, Henry Ropes Papers, Boston Public Library; Biddle to wife, May 10, Biddle Papers, HSP; June 20, Welles, *Diary,* 218; Gibbon to wife, May 21, Gibbon Papers, HSP. For the fiction that Hooker publicly confessed a loss of nerve at Chancellorsville (Bigelow, *Campaign of Chancellorsville,* 477–78n), see Sears, *Chancellorsville,* 504–5.

6. AP G.O. 49, May 6, 1863, OR 25.1:171; Gibbon to McClellan, May 18, McClellan Papers, LC; Hooker testimony, CCW 1 (1865), 127, 131; Sedgwick to sister, May 6, Sedgwick, *Correspondence,* 2:92; Gibbon, *Recollections,* 121–22; Meade to wife, May 10, 12, 15, 19, Meade Papers, HSP; Gouverneur Warren to Emily Chase, May 15, Warren Papers, New York State Library; June 12, Wainwright, *Diary of Battle,* 219.

7. Hooker to S. P. Bates, Apr. 2, 1877, Feb.

18, 1879, Bates Papers, Pennsylvania State Archives; Warren to brother, May 8, 1863, Warren Papers, New York State Library; Webb to father, May 12, Webb Papers, Yale University Library; Williams to daughter, May 18, Williams, *From the Cannon's Mouth*, 198.

8. Henry F. Young to wife, May 13, 1863, Wisconsin Historical Society; Weld to mother, June 10, Weld, *War Diary and Letters*, 213; casualties: Sears, *Chancellorsville*, appendix II; Lee to G.W.C. Lee, May 11, Lee, *Wartime Papers*, 482.

9. Lincoln to Hooker, Hooker to Lincoln, May 7, 1863, *OR* 25.2:438; Meade to wife, May 10, Meade Papers, HSP; Hooker to Lincoln, May 13, *OR* 25.2:473; Lincoln to Hooker, May 13, 14, Lincoln, *Collected Works*, 6:215, 217.

10. Hooker testimony, *CCW* 1 (1865), 151; Chase to Hooker, May 23, 1863, Chase, *Papers*, 4:36; Gibbon to wife, May 25, Gibbon Papers, HSP; June 14, *Welles, Diary*, 212–13; Whitelaw Reid, May 25, for *Cincinnati Gazette*, Reid Family Papers, LC.

11. Walker, *History of the Second Army Corps*, 254; May 15, 1863, Heintzelman diary, LC; Almira R. Hancock, *Reminiscences of Winfield Scott Hancock*, 95; Sedgwick to sister, Nov. 16, Sedgwick, *Correspondence*, 2:161–62.

12. Hooker to Lincoln, May 13, 1863, *OR* 25.2:473; short-term men mustered out: *OR* 25.2:532, ser. III, 3:751, 760, 775; *CCW* 1 (1865), 219; Williams to daughters, June 29, May 29, May 23, Williams, *From the Cannon's Mouth*, 221, 204, 203; Dawes to Mary B. Gates, June 7, Dawes Papers, Wisconsin Historical Society; Sedgwick to sister, May 15, Sedgwick, *Correspondence*, 2:128; Gibbon to wife, June 2, 30, Gibbon Papers, HSP; Meade to wife, May 19, Meade Papers, HSP.

13. Lowell to Josephine Shaw, July 12, 1863, Emerson, *Life and Letters of Charles Russell Lowell*, 279; Adams to mother, May 12, Ford, *A Cycle of Adams Letters*, 2:8; Hooker to S. P. Bates, July 12, 1878, Bates Papers, Pennsylvania State Archives; Hunt report, Aug. 1, 1863, *OR* 25.1:252; Army of Potomac S.O. 129, May 12, *OR* 25.2:471–72; Naisawald, *Grape and Canister*, 329–33; McCrea, "Light Artillery: Its Use and Misuse" (1896), in Catherine S. Creary, ed., *Dear Belle: Letters from a Cadet & Officer to his Sweetheart, 1858–1865* (Middletown, Ct.: Wesleyan University Press, 1965), 195.

14. Chase to Hooker, May 23, 1863, Chase, *Papers*, 4:35–36; Hooker to Stanton, May 27, Halleck to Stanton, May 18, *OR* 25.2:527, 504–6; Sharpe report, May 27, *OR* 25.2:528; *Richmond Examiner*, May 22.

15. Stephen W. Sears, *Gettysburg*, 5–7; W. D. Pender to wife, June 23, 1863, Pender, *The General to his Lady: The Civil War Letters of William Dorsey Pender to Fanny Pender*, William W. Hassler, ed. (Chapel Hill: University of North Carolina Press, 1962), 251.

16. Reynolds to sisters, Jan. 23, 1863, Reynolds Papers, Franklin and Marshall College, in Nichols, *Toward Gettysburg*, 158–59; Eleanor Reynolds to J. F. Landis, Aug. 20, 1913, in Nichols, 220–21; June 29, 1863, Wainwright, *Diary of Battle*, 229; Weld, *War Diary and Letters*, 227n; Meade to wife, June 13, Meade Papers, HSP.

17. Sharpe to John McEntee, June 4, 1863, B.M.I., RG 393, NA; Hooker to Lincoln, Halleck to Hooker, June 5, *OR* 27.1:30, 31–32; Lincoln to Hooker, June 5, Lincoln, *Collected Works*, 6:249.

18. Hooker to Lincoln, n.d., B.M.I., RG 393, NA; Butterfield to Pleasonton, June 7, 1863, *OR* 27.3:27; Gary W. Gallagher, "Brandy Station: The Civil War's Bloodiest Arena of Mounted Combat," *Blue & Gray*, 8:1 (1990), 8–22, 44–53; A. E. Bachman memoir, 15–16, U.S. Army Heritage & Education Center; Henry C. Meyer, *Civil War Experiences* (New York, 1911), 28; Buford report, *OR Supplement*, ser. I, 5:229; casualties:

OR 27.1:168–70, 27.2:719; Benjamin W. Crowninshield, *A History of the First Regiment of Massachusetts Cavalry Volunteers* (Boston, 1891), 18; cavalry corps G.O. 18, June 11, S.O. 98, June 28, *OR* 27.3:64, 376; Biddle to wife, July 1, James C. Biddle Papers, HSP.

19. Hooker to Lincoln, Halleck to Hooker, June 5, 1863, *OR* 27.1:30, 31–32; William H. Beach, *The First New York (Lincoln) Cavalry* (New York, 1902), 220; Halleck to Schenck, June 11, Milroy to Schenck, June 11, Schenck to Milroy, June 12, *OR* 27.2:160, 161, 125; Lincoln to Hooker, to Schenck, June 14, Lincoln, *Collected Works*, 6:273, 274; Hooker to Lincoln, June 14, *OR* 27.1:39–40.

20. Hooker to Lincoln, June 10, 1863, Halleck to Hooker, June 11, *OR* 27.1:34–35, 35; Lincoln to Hooker, June 10, Lincoln, *Collected Works*, 6:257.

21. Pleasonton to Seth Williams, June 10, 21, 1863, *OR* 27.3:47–48, 244; McEntee to George H. Sharpe, June 12, B.M.I., RG 393, NA; Hooker to Halleck, June 13, *OR* 27.1:38; Butterfield to Reynolds, June 12, *OR* 27.3:72–73; Meade to wife, June 13, Meade Papers, HSP; Hooker to S. P. Bates, May 30, 1878, Bates Papers, Pennsylvania State Archives.

22. June 15, 1863, Welles, *Diary*, 213; militia proclamation, June 15, Lincoln, *Collected Works*, 6:277–78; Barnett to S.L.M. Barlow, June 22, Barlow Papers, Huntington Library; *New York Herald*, June 18; June 21, Wainwright, *Diary of Battle*, 223; McClure to Lincoln, June 30, *OR* 27.3:436; Lincoln to McClure, June 30, Lincoln, *Collected Works*, 6:311. McClellan did assist Governor Horatio Seymour in mobilizing New York's militia.

23. Halleck to Hooker, June 15, 1863, *OR* 27.1:41–42; Reynolds to Pleasonton, June 13, Hooker circular, June 13, *OR* 27.3:84–85, 88–89; Meade to wife, June 25, Meade Papers, HSP; June 16, 20, Heintzelman diary, LC; Gibbon to wife, June 20, 22, Gibbon, *Recollections*,

125, Gibbon Papers, HSP; June 17, Patrick diary, LC; Julia L. Butterfield, *A Biographical Memorial of General Daniel Butterfield* (New York, 1904). 332n; Sharpe to Jansen Hasbrouck, June 20, George Sharpe Collection, Senate House Museum, Kingston, N.Y., in Fishel, *Secret War for the Union*, 465; Butterfield, Hooker testimony, *CCW* 1 (1865), 80, 177.

24. Pleasonton to Hooker, June 14, 1863, *OR* 27.3:107; Butterfield to Salmon P. Chase, June 11, Chase, *Papers*, 4:61–62; Hooker testimony, *CCW* 1 (1865), 173; Richard T. Auchmuty to mother, June 28, Auchmuty, *Letters*, 92; Meade to wife, June 25, Meade Papers, HSP.

25. Hooker to Lincoln, June 16, 1863, *OR* 27.1:45; Lincoln to Hooker, June 16 (two), Lincoln, *Collected Works*, 6:281–82.

26. Montgomery Blair, cited in Elizabeth Blair Lee to husband, June 23, 1863, Lee, *Wartime Washington*, 276; June 26, Welles, *Diary*, 225; Warren to Hooker, June 24, Hooker to Reynolds, June 25, Hooker to Butterfield, June 27, *OR* 27.3:292, 305–6, 349.

27. Hooker to Halleck, June 26, 1863, Halleck to Hooker, June 27, Hooker to Halleck, June 27, *OR* 27.1:58, 59, 60; Hooker to French, June 25, to Slocum, June 27, *OR* 27.3:317, 354; Halleck to Grant, July 11, *OR* 24.3:498; Stanton interview by John C. Ropes, 1869, Horatio Woodman Papers, MHS; French, Civil War Record, RG 94 (M-1098), NA; Hebert, *Fighting Joe Hooker*, 244–45; Butterfield testimony, *CCW* 1 (1865), 81–82; Halleck to Hooker, June 27, 1863, *OR* 27.1:60; War Dept. G.O. 194, June 27, *OR* 27.3:369. Charles F. Benjamin's account of Hooker's removal (*Battles and Leaders*, 3:239–43) is as fictitious as his account of Hooker's appointment; the author's credentials are fictional as well. The June 27 telegraphic exchange between French and Halleck is not on record, but is inferred from the Stan-

ton interview and from French's report. The content of the countermand is from Hebert. .

28. Halleck to Meade, June 27, 1863, *OR* 27.1:61; Biddle to wife, June 28, James C. Biddle Papers, HSP; Meade to wife, June 29, Meade Papers, HSP; George Meade, *The Life and Letters of George Gordon Meade*, 2:2. Meade understood his power to hire and fire came from Stanton (Gibbon, *Recollections*, 144); Stanton had recently granted similar powers to Grant (Stanton to Charles Dana, May 6, Stanton Papers, LC).

29. June 28, 1863, Welles, *Diary*, 228–29; Chase to Kate Chase, June 29, Chase, *Papers*, 4:72; Gibbon to wife, June 29, Gibbon Papers, HSP; Williams to daughters, June 29, Williams, *From the Cannon's Mouth*, 220–21; George Meade II to Margaret Meade, July 1, Meade Papers, HSP; Nicolay to Therena Bates, June 30, Nicolay, *With Lincoln in the White House*, 117–18.

30. Biddle to wife, June 29, 1863, James C. Biddle Papers, HSP; Hooker G.O. 66, June 28, *OR* 27.3:373–74; Hyde to mother, June 29, *Civil War Letters*, 87; June 28, Wainwright, *Diary of Battle*, 227; Alexander K. McClure, *Recollections of Half a Century* (Salem, Mass., 1902), 347; Lincoln to Meade, July 27, Aug. 11, Lincoln, *Collected Works*, 6:350–51; Meade to Lincoln, July 30, Aug. 11, Lincoln Papers, LC; Meade to wife, Aug. 6, Meade Papers, HSP; Aug. 14, Hay, *Inside Lincoln's White House*, 73–74.

31. Charles C. Coffin, "The May Campaign in Virginia," *Atlantic Monthly*, 14 (July 1864), 127; James C. Biddle to wife, June 29, 1863, Biddle Papers, HSP; Meade to wife, June 25, Meade Papers, HSP; Oct. 13, Theodore Lyman, *Meade's Army: The Private Notebooks of Lt. Col. Theodore Lyman*, David W. Lowe, ed., 49; Grant to Halleck, June 24, *OR* 24.1:37.

32. Meade to G. G. Benedict, Mar. 16,

1870, *Battles and Leaders*, 3:413; Warren to wife, June 28, 1863, Warren Papers, New York State Library (Warren married Emily Chase on June 17); Butterfield to Humphreys, June 28, *OR* 51.1:1064; AP orders, June 28, *OR* 27.3:375–76; Meade to Halleck, June 29, *OR* 27.1:66–67; June 30, Fiske, *Mr. Dunn Browne's Experiences in the Army*, 101; Meade to Halleck, June 28, *OR* 27.1:65; Seth Williams to Reynolds, June 30, July 1, *OR* 27.3:414–15, 460–61; John W. Busey and David G. Martin, *Regimental Strengths and Losses at Gettysburg*, 3rd edition (Hightstown, N.J.: Longstreet House, 1994), 129; June 30 return, *OR* 27.1:151; Meade to wife, June 29, Meade Papers, HSP.

33. Meade circular, July 1, 1863, *OR* 27.3:458–59; Theodore Lyman to wife, Sept. 22, Lyman, *Meade's Headquarters, 1863–1865: Letters of Colonel Theodore Lyman from the Wilderness to the Appomattox*, George R. Agassiz, ed., 21; Buford to Reynolds, to Pleasonton, June 30, *OR* 27.1:923–24; Gibbon, "John Buford Memoir," Gibbon Papers, HSP; A. B. Jerome, "Buford in the Battle of Oak Ridge," in John Watts De Peyster, *The Decisive Conflicts of the Late Civil War* (New York, 1867), 151–52.

34. AP orders, June 30, 1863, *OR* 27.3:416; Buford report, *OR* 27.1:927; John L. Beveridge, "The First Gun at Gettysburg," *Military Essays and Recollections*, Illinois MOLLUS (2:1894), 11:91–92; Buford to Meade, July 1, *OR* 27.1:924; Doubleday to S. P. Bates, Apr. 3, 1874, Bates Papers, Pennsylvania State Archives; Charles H. Veil to David McConaughy, Apr. 7, 1864, McConaughy Collection, Gettysburg College; A. B. Jerome in De Peyster, *Decisive Conflicts of the Late Civil War*, 152–53; Gamble to William L. Church, Mar. 10, 1864, Chicago Historical Society; Abner Doubleday, *Chancellorsville and Gettysburg* (New York: Scribner's, 1882), 126–27; Joseph T. Rosengarten to S. P. Bates,

Jan. 13, 1871, Bates Papers. For Buford, see Eric J. Wittenberg, *"The Devil's to Pay": John Buford at Gettysburg* (El Dorado Hills, Calif.: Savas Beatie, 2014).

35. Meade to Reynolds, June 30, 1863, *OR* 27.1:420; July 1, Weld, *War Diary and Letters*, 229–32; Veil to David McConaughy, Apr. 7, 1864, McConaughy Collection, Gettysburg College. Reynolds's body was carried to Taneytown, then by way of Baltimore and Philadelphia to Lancaster for burial on July 4. Reynolds had been secretly engaged, and eight days after the funeral his intended, Catherine Mary Hewitt, chose to enter a convent of the Sisters of Charity: Mary R. Malony, "General Reynolds and 'Dear Kate,'" *American Heritage*, 15:1 (Dec. 1963), 62–65.

36. Dawes, *Service with the Sixth Wisconsin*, 131–32n; Cutler report, *OR* 27.1:281–82; Howard in *Atlantic Monthly* (July 1876), in Cozzens, ed., *Battles and Leaders of the Civil War*, 5:326; A. B. Jerome in De Peyster, *Decisive Conflicts of the Late Civil War*, 153.

37. Meade to Halleck, July 1, 1863, *OR* 27.1:70–71; George Meade, *The Life and Letters of George Gordon Meade*, 2:36; Charles H. Morgan report, David L. Ladd and Audrey J. Ladd, eds., *The Bachelder Papers: Gettysburg in Their Own Words*, 3:1395; Butterfield to Hancock, July 1, *OR* 27.3:461.

38. Joseph T. Rosengarten to S. P. Bates (Jan. 13, 1871, Bates Papers, Pennsylvania State Archives) affirms Reynolds's order to Howard. Howard's denial is in his *Autobiography* (1:410–12).

39. T. A. Meysenburg to Sickles and Slocum, July 1, 1863, *OR* 27.3:463; Tremain, *Two Days of War*, 19; Charles H. Howard to E. Whittlesey, July 9, C. H. Howard Papers, Daniel Hall to O. O. Howard, Feb. 19, 1877, O. O. Howard Papers, Bowdoin College Library; Charles H. Howard, "First Day at Gettysburg," *Military Essays and Recollections*, Illinois MOLLUS (4:1907), 13:258.

40. Barlow to mother, July 7, 1863, to R. T. Paine, Aug. 12, Barlow, *"Fear Was Not in Him,"* 162, 168; Schurz, *Reminiscences*, 3:10; Schurz, "The Battle of Gettysburg," *McClure's Magazine* (July 1907), 276; William R. Keifer, *History of the One Hundred Fifty Third Regiment Pennsylvania Volunteer Infantry* (Easton, Pa., 1905), 215. Postwar, Gordon's "rescue" of Barlow was a much-heralded incident. See Gregory C. White in *Blue & Gray*, 19:3 (Feb. 2002), 6–7.

41. Ames report, *OR* 27.1:712–13; Sears, *Gettysburg*, 217; Gary G. Lash, "Baxter's Brigade at Gettysburg, July 1," *Gettysburg Magazine*, 10 (1994), 19.

42. July 1, 1863, Wainwright, *Diary of Battle*, 235–37; Weld, *War Diary and Letters*, 233; Doubleday to S. P. Bates, Apr. 3, 1874, Bates Papers, Pennsylvania State Archives; E. P. Halstead, "The First Day of the Battle of Gettysburg," *War Papers*, District of Columbia MOLLUS (1:1887), 42:5–8; Buford to Pleasonton, July 1, 1863, *OR* 27.1:924–25.

43. E. P. Halstead, "The First day of July, 1863," Wadsworth Family Papers, LC; Hancock, "Gettysburg: A Reply to General Howard," Cozzens, *Battles and Leaders*, 5:351, 354; Hancock testimony, *CCW* 1 (1865), 404–5; E. P. Halstead, "The First Day of the Battle of Gettysburg," *War Papers*, District of Columbia MOLLUS (1:1887), 42:6–7; Small, *The Road to Richmond*, 102; Hartwell Osborn, *Trials and Triumphs: The Record of the Fifty-fifth Ohio Volunteer Infantry* (Chicago, 1904), 97; Doubleday to S. P. Bates, Oct. 19, 1875, Bates Papers, Pennsylvania State Archives; Howard, "The Campaign and Battle of Gettysburg," Cozzens, 5:334; Hancock to Meade, Howard to Meade, July 1, 1863, *OR* 27.1:366, 696–97.

44. William H. Paine to George Meade II, May 20, 1886, Meade Papers, HSP; Meade to Halleck, July 1, 1863, *OR* 27.1:71–72; Howard in Cozzens, *Battles*

and Leaders, 5:334; Schurz, *Reminiscences* 3:20–21; Butterfield to Slocum, Slocum to Meade, July 2, 1863, *OR* 27.3:486–87; Warren to wife, July 2, Warren Papers, New York State Library; Warren testimony, *CCW* 1 (1865), 377. Meade confirmed that he ordered a concentration at Gettysburg before receiving Hancock's report: Meade to Reverdy Johnson, Mar. 6, 1864, Stanton Papers, LC. Slocum's misapprehension of his command role is treated in correspondence among Williams, Slocum, and Meade, *OR* 27.1:763–70.

45. Seth Williams to Sickles, June 29, 30, 1863, *OR* 27.3:399, 420; Meade to G. G. Benedict, Mar. 16, 1870, Meade, *Life and Letters,* 2:353–54; Meade testimony, *CCW* 1 (1865), 331–32; Gibbon, *Personal Recollections,* 136; Frank A. Haskell quoted in Henry L. Abbott to John C. Ropes, Aug. 17, 1863, MOLLUS Collection, Houghton Library, Harvard University; William H. Paine, May 22, 1886, and James C. Biddle, Aug. 8, 1880, to George Meade II, Meade Papers, HSP; Ropes to John C. Gray, Jr., Apr. 16. 1864, Gray and Ropes, *War Letters,* 318.

46. Warren to Porter Farley, July 13, 1872, Warren Papers, New York State Library; Haskell, *Haskell of Gettysburg,* 119; Mackenzie to Meade, Mar. 22, 1864, *OR* 27.1:138; Joseph M. Leeper in *National Tribune,* Apr. 30, 1885.

47. De Trobriand, *Four Years with the Army of the Potomac,* 497, 500; De Trobriand to daughter, July 4, 1863, Régis de Trobriand, *Our Noble Blood: The Civil War Letters of Régis de Trobriand,* 116; Bucklyn diary, July 2, Ladd and Ladd, eds., *Bachelder Papers,* 3:72–73.

48. Humphreys to wife, July 4, 1863, Humphreys Papers, HSP; Sykes, Hancock reports, *OR* 27.1:592, 369; John P. Nicholson, ed., *Pennsylvania at Gettysburg* (Harrisburg, 1904), 1:623; Charles A. Fuller, *Recollections of the War of 1861–*

1865 (Sherburne, N.Y., 1906), 93; Pride and Travis, *My Brave Boys,* 235–37; Brooke to Francis A. Walker, Mar. 18, 1886, Ladd and Ladd, eds., *Bachelder Papers,* 2:1234.

49. Maine Gettysburg Commission, *Maine at Gettysburg* (Portland, Me., 1898), 254; Chamberlain, "Through Blood and Fire," *Gettysburg Magazine,* 6 (1992), 51; Sears, *Gettysburg,* 297.

50. William II. Powell, *The Fifth Army Corps (Army of the Potomac),* 535n; Donaldson to aunt, July 21, 1863, Donaldson, *Inside the Army of the Potomac,* 305; Tremain, *Two Days of War,* 89–90; Abbott to John C. Ropes, Aug. 17, MOLLUS Collection, Houghton Library, Harvard University; Hancock report, *OR* 27.1:370.

51. Hancock report, *OR* 27.1:370–71; Hunt, "Second Day at Gettysburg," *Battles and Leaders,* 3:303; Williams to John B. Bachelder, Apr. 21, 1864, Nov. 10, 1865, Ladd and Ladd, eds., *Bachelder Papers,* 1:163, 215; Williams to Slocum, Dec. 1863, Williams, *From the Cannon's Mouth,* 280; Slocum to T. H. Davis, Sept. 8, 1875, S. P. Bates Papers, Pennsylvania State Archives. Meade's order to Slocum for reinforcements for the left is not on record; possibly it was verbal. Williams is the source for its content.

52. Silas Adams, "The Nineteenth Maine at Gettysburg," Maine MOLLUS, *War Papers* (4: 1915), 19:253; Williams to daughters, July 6, 1863, Williams, *From the Cannon's Mouth,* 228; Eric Campbell, "Remember Harper's Ferry . . . ," *Gettysburg Magazine,* 7 (1992), 64–73; Abbott to John C. Ropes, Aug. 1, MOLLUS Collection, Houghton Library, Harvard University; Robert W. Meinhard, "The First Minnesota at Gettysburg," *Gettysburg Magazine,* 5 (1991), 81–83; Hancock report, *OR* 27.1:371.

53. Meade, *Life and Letters,* 2:89; Paul A. Oliver to George Meade II, May 16, 1886, Meade Papers, HSP; Williams to

daughters, July 6, 1863, *From the Cannon's Mouth*, 228.

54. Greene report, *OR* 27.1:855–57; Jesse H. Jones in *Battles and Leaders*, 3:316; Palmer, *Forgotten Hero of Gettysburg*, 165. For Culp's Hill, see A. Wilson Greene, "'A Step All-Important and Essential to Victory': Henry W. Slocum and the Twelfth Corps on July 1–2, 1863," Gary Gallagher, ed., *Three Days at Gettysburg*.

55. John T. Butts, ed., *A Gallant Captain of the Civil War . . . Friederich Otto Baron von Fritsch* (New York, 1902), 80; July 2, 1863, Wainwright, *Diary of Battle*, 242–47; William F. Fox, ed., *New York at Gettysburg* (Albany, 1902), 3:1247; Aldin B. Underwood report, *OR Supplement*, ser. I, 5:218.

56. Meade to Halleck, July 2, 1863, *OR* 27.1:72; Fishel, *Secret War for the Union*, 527–28.

57. "Minutes of Council July 2/63," Meade Papers, HSP; Gibbon, Newton to Seth Williams, Mar. 14, 1864, Meade Papers; Gibbon, *Recollections*, 141–42, 145; Meade to wife, July 3, 1863, Meade Papers. Gibbon seems to be the first to have seen and copied Butterfield's July 2 minutes, in 1881. His *Recollections* were completed in 1885 but not published until 1928.

58. Williams to J. B. Bachelder, Nov. 10, 1865, Ladd and Ladd, eds., *Bachelder Papers*, 1:219; Williams, Greene reports, *OR* 27.1:774–75, 857.

59. R. F. Halsted to Emily Sedgwick, July 17, 1863, Sedgwick, *Correspondence*, 2:134; Hunt testimony, *CCW* 1 (1865), 448; Meade to Couch, to French, July 3, *OR* 27.3:499, 501; Butterfield to Sedgwick, July 3, *OR* 51.1:1078; *Cincinnati Daily Gazette*, July 8; Hyde, *Following the Greek Cross*, 153; Hunt, "The Third Day at Gettysburg," *Battles and Leaders*, 3:371–72.

60. Gibbon, *Recollections*, 146–50; Haskell, *Haskell of Gettysburg*, 145–56; Meade, *Life and Letters*, 2:106; Meade to J. B. Bachelder, Dec. 4, 1869, Ladd and Ladd, eds., *Bachelder Papers*, 1:379, David Shields to Bachelder, Aug. 27, 1884, 2:1067–68; Francis A. Walker, *General Hancock* (New York: Appleton, 1894), 97; Geary to Hunt, July 17, 1879, Hart to Hunt, Aug. 17, 1879, Hunt Papers, LC; Walker in *Battles and Leaders*, 3:385–86.

61. Hunt, "The Third Day at Gettysburg," *Battles and Leaders*, 3:374; Thomas W. Osborn, *The Eleventh Corps Artillery at Gettysburg*, Herb S. Crumb, ed. (Hamilton, N.Y.: Edmonston, 1991), 39; Hunt account, Jan. 20, 1873, Ladd and Ladd, eds., *Bachelder Papers*, 1:430–31; Gibbon, *Recollections*, 150–51.

62. Abbott to father, July 6, 1863, Abbott, *Fallen Leaves*, 188; Rittenhouse, "The Battle of Gettysburg as Seen from Little Round Top," District of Columbia MOLLUS, *War Papers* (1:1897), 42:43; Franklin Sawyer, *A Military History of the 8th Regiment Ohio Vol. Inf'y* (Cleveland, 1881), 131; McGilvery report, *OR* 27.1:884; Hunt; "The Third Day at Gettysburg," *Battles and Leaders*, 3:375. Hunt wrote George Meade II (Sept. 14, 1883), "Had not Hancock interferred with my orders I dont think the enemy assault would have reached our lines.": Meade Papers, HSP.

63. Sawyer report, *OR* 27.1:461–62; Earl J. Hess, *Pickett's Charge—The Last Attack at Gettysburg* (Chapel Hill: University of North Carolina Press, 2001), 198, 237–38; Cowan to J. B. Bachelder, Aug. 26, 1866, Stannard diary, July 3, 1863, Ladd and Ladd, eds., *Bachelder Papers*, 1:282–83, 1:56; Hunt to wife, July 4, 1863, Hunt Papers, LC; Gibbon, *Recollections*, 152–53; Henry L. Abbott report, *OR* 27.1:445.

64. Webb to wife, July 6, 1863, Webb Papers, Yale University; Francis Heath in "The Nineteenth Maine at Gettysburg," Maine MOLLUS, *War Papers* (4: 1915), 19:262; William E. Potter to George Meade II, Dec. 23, 1886, Meade Papers, HSP; Haskell, *Haskell of Gettysburg*, 173–74; Charles H. Morgan re-

port, George Meade II to J. B. Bachelder, May 6, 1882, Ladd and Ladd, eds., *Bachelder Papers,* 3:1364, 2:856.

15. A CONTEST OF LITTLE PURPOSE

1. Hancock to Meade, July 3, 1863, *OR* 27.1:366; Meade to William F. Smith, July 5, *OR* 27.3:539.
2. David M. Gregg, "The Second Cavalry Division ... in the Gettysburg Campaign," Pennsylvania MOLLUS, *Military Essays and Recollections,* (2:1907), 59:124; William E. Miller, "The Cavalry Battle Near Gettysburg," *Battles and Leaders,* 3:404; D. H. Hamilton, *History of Company M, First Texas Volunteer Infantry* (Waco, 1962), 29; Edward G. Longacre, *The Cavalry at Gettysburg: A Tactical Study of Mounted Operations During the Civil War's Pivotal Campaign* (Rutherford, N.J.: Fairleigh Dickinson University Press, 1986), 242.
3. Journal, July 4, 1863, Warren Papers, New York State Library; Dawes to Mary B. Gates, July 6, Dawes Papers, Wisconsin Historical Society; Sears, *Gettysburg,* 468–69; Meade to wife, July 5, Meade Papers, HSP; Butterfield, Warren testimony, *CCW* 1 (1865), 426–27, 378–79. Butterfield testified from his notes of the July 4 council, but the notes themselves are not on record.
4. AP G.O. 68, July 4, 1863, *OR* 27.3:519; Lincoln to Halleck, July 6, Lincoln, *Collected Works,* 6:318; July 7, Welles, *Diary,* 241–42; July 14, Hay, *Inside Lincoln's White House,* 62; Hessler, *Sickles at Gettysburg,* 235–38; James F. Rusling, *Men and Things I Saw in Civil War Days* (New York, 1899), 13; Haupt, *Reminiscences,* 224; Halleck to Meade, July 7, *OR* 27.1:82, 83.
5. July 5, 1863, Strong, *Diary,* 328; July 6: *New York Times, Philadelphia Inquirer, New York Herald.*
6. Meade to wife, July 8, 12, 1863, Meade Papers, HSP; Meade to Halleck, July 8, *OR* 27.1:84; July 9, Patrick, *Inside Lincoln's Army,* 270.
7. Meade to Couch, July 6, 1863, W. F. Smith to Seth Williams, July 8, Lincoln to L. Thomas, July 8, *OR* 27.3:578–79, 611, 612; Edwin B. Coddington, *The Gettysburg Campaign: A Study in Command,* 555; Weld to sister, July 16, Weld, *War Diary and Letters,* 243; George Meade II to mother, July 8, Meade Papers, HSP; Biddle to wife, July 11, Biddle Papers, HSP; Meade to wife, July 12, Meade Papers, HSP; July 11, Wainwright, *Diary of Battle,* 259. See Eric J. Wittenberg, J. David Petruzzi, and Michael F. Nugent, *One Continuous Fight: The Retreat from Gettysburg and the Pursuit of Lee's Army of Northern Virginia, July 4–14, 1863* (New York: Savas Beatie, 2008), and A. Wilson Greene, "From Gettysburg to Falling Waters," in Gary W. Gallagher, ed., *The Third Day at Gettysburg & Beyond* (Chapel Hill: University of North Carolina Press, 1994), 161–94.
8. Ropes to John C. Gray, Jr., Apr. 16, 1864, Gray and Ropes, *War Letters,* 319; Meade, Humphreys, Warren, Wadsworth, Sedgwick testimony, *CCW* 1 (1865), 336–37, 396–97, 381, 415–16, 463; Andrew A. Humphreys, *From Gettysburg to the Rapidan: The Army of the Potomac, July, 1863, to April, 1864,* 5–8; Charles C. Coffin, *The Boys of '61: Four Years of Fighting* (Boston, 1885), 303; Meade circular, July 13, 1863, *OR* 27.3:675; July 14, Fiske, *Mr. Dunn Browne's Experiences in the Army,* 120–21.
9. Meade to Halleck, Halleck to Meade, July 13, 1863, *OR* 27.1:91–92; July 14, Hay, *Inside Lincoln's White House,* 62; July 14, Welles, *Diary,* 247–48; Evelyn Page, ed., "After Gettysburg: Frederick Law Olmsted on the Escape of Lee," *Pennsylvania Magazine of History and Biography,* 75 (Oct. 1951), 440–41; Halleck to Meade (two), Meade to Halleck,

July 14, *OR* 27.1:92–94; Meade to wife, July 14, Meade Papers, HSP; Meade to McClellan, July 14, McClellan Papers, LC.

10. James C. Biddle to wife, Aug. 13, 1863, Biddle Papers, HSP; July 14, Wainwright, *Diary of Battle*, 261; Hunt, "The Third Day at Gettysburg," *Battles and Leaders*, 3:382; Meade to H. A. Walker, Aug. 1, Meade Papers, HSP; Lincoln to Meade (unsent), July 14, Lincoln, *Collected Works*, 6:327–28.

11. Wayne Mahood, *General Wadsworth*, 194–96; July 16, 1863, Hay, *Inside Lincoln's White House*, 63–64; July 17, Welles, *Diary*, 251–52; *New-York Tribune*, July 18; Howard to Lincoln, July 18, Lincoln Papers, LC; Lincoln to Howard, July 21, Lincoln, *Collected Works*, 6:341; Meade to wife, July 31, to H. A. Walker, Aug. 1, Meade Papers, HSP; Halleck to Meade, July 28, *OR* 27.1:104–5; Holt to David Davis, Aug. 18, Davis Papers, Abraham Lincoln Presidential Library.

12. Humphreys, *From Gettysburg to the Rapidan*, 8; Williams to daughters, July 21, 1863, Williams, *From the Cannon's Mouth*, 239; Meade to wife, July 18, 31, Meade Papers, HSP; Meade to Halleck, July 24, Halleck to Meade, July 30, *OR* 27.1:98–99, 108.

13. Union loss: John W. Busey and David G. Martin, *Regimental Strengths and Losses at Gettysburg* (Hightstown, N.J.: Longstreet House, 1994), 239; *OR* 27.1:193; Confederate loss: Busey and Martin, 280; *OR* 27.2:442, 713–16; Sears, *Gettysburg*, 516–32.

14. Halleck to Grant, July 11, 1863, *OR* 24.3:498; Abbott to John C. Ropes, Aug. 17, MOLLUS Collection, Houghton Library, Harvard University; Hunt to Webb, Jan. 19, 1888, *PMHSM*, 3:239. Hunt's three articles are in *Battles and Leaders*, vol. 3.

15. July 14, 1863, Hay, *Inside Lincoln's White House*, 62; Hays to John B. McFadden, July 13, Fleming, ed., *Life and Letters*

of Alexander Hays, 410; July 9, Elisha Hunt Rhodes, *All for the Union: A History of the 2nd Rhode Island Volunteer Infantry*, Robert Hunt Rhodes, ed. (Lincoln, R.I.: Mowbray, 1985), 117.

16. Lincoln to Howard, July 21, 1863, Lincoln, *Collected Works*, 6:341; July 26, Welles, *Diary*, 259; Grant to C. A. Dana, Aug. 5, Grant, *Papers*, 9:146; Halleck to Montgomery Meigs, Aug. 5, *OR* 29.2:8; July 16, Strong, *Diary*, 341; Halleck to Meade, July 29, 30, Meade to Halleck, July 31, *OR* 27.1:105–6, 108; Meade to wife, Aug. 9, Meade Papers, HSP; Lincoln to Meade, Meade to Lincoln, Aug. 27, *OR* 29.2:102. The Jacquerie was a peasant revolt in France in 1358, during the Hundred Years' War.

17. Aug. 14, 1863, Welles, *Diary*, 274; Meade to wife, Aug. 16, Meade Papers, HSP.

18. Buford to Burnside, Aug. 10, 1863, George Hay Stuart Papers, LC; Biddle to wife, Aug. 13, Biddle Papers, HSP; Meade to Halleck, July 19, *OR* 27.1:96–97; Hancock to Warren, Sept. 24, Gilder-Lehrman Papers, New-York Historical Society; Warren to wife, Oct. 14, Warren Papers, New York State Library.

19. Meade to Halleck, July 29, 1863, *OR* 27.1:105, 106.

20. Meade to wife, Sept. 13, 1863, Meade Papers, HSP; Meade to Halleck, Sept. 15, *OR* 29.2:186; Humphreys, *From Gettysburg to the Rapidan*, 11; Lincoln to Halleck, Sept. 15, Lincoln, *Collected Works*, 6:450.

21. Meade to wife, Sept. 24, 1863, Meade Papers, HSP; Sept. 27, Hay, *Inside Lincoln's White House*, 85–86; Sept. 23–24, Chase, *Papers*, 1:450–54; George E. Turner, *Victory Rode the Rails: The Strategic Place of the Railroads in the Civil War* (New York: Bobbs Merrill, 1953), 288–93; Halleck to Meade, Meade to Halleck, Sept. 24, Slocum to Lincoln, Sept. 25, *OR* 29.1:147, 156; Hooker to

Stanton, Oct. 11, *OR* 30.4:291; Sept. 25, Lyman, *Meade's Army*, 42; Lincoln to Rosecrans, Sept. 28, Lincoln, *Collected Works*, 6:486.

22. Meade to wife, Sept. 30, Oct. 4, 12, 1863, Meade Papers, HSP; Halleck to Meade, Oct. 10, *OR* 29.2:278; Oct. 9, Patrick, *Inside Lincoln's Army*, 295; Theodore Lyman to wife, Oct. 12, Lyman Papers, MHS; Meade report, *OR* 29.1:8–10; Meade to Hancock, Nov. 6, Winfield Hancock Papers, Duke University; Humphreys, *Gettysburg to the Rapidan*, 20–26; Walker, *History of the Second Army Corps*, 352; Hays to wife, Oct. 13, Fleming, *Life and Letters of Alexander Hays*, 496.

23. Sickles testimony, *CCW* 1 (1865), 304; de Trobriand to wife, Oct. 13, 1863, de Trobriand, *Our Noble Blood*, 140; Birney to George I. Gross, Oct. 23, David B. Birney Papers, U.S. Army Heritage & Education Center; John C. Gray to John C. Ropes, Nov. 3, Gray and Ropes, *War Letters*, 254.

24. Lincoln to Halleck, Oct. 16, 24, 1863, Lincoln, *Collected Works*, 6:518, 534; Meade to wife, Oct. 23, 27, Nov. 3, 6, Meade Papers, HSP; Sedgwick to sister, Nov. 16, Sedgwick, *Correspondence*, 2:162; Meade to Halleck, Nov. 2, Halleck to Meade, Nov. 3, *OR* 29.2:409–10, 412. Lincoln's Oct. 16 dispatch, proposing an attack at the Rappahannock by Meade ("the honor will be his if he succeeds, and the blame may be mine if he fails"), apparently inspired the tale spun in the 1880s by Robert Todd Lincoln, the president's son, that transmuted the setting back to Williamsport on the Potomac circa July 12 — if Meade's attack fails, Lincoln's order will assume the blame; if Meade wins, he may tear up the order. See Hay, *Inside Lincoln's White House*, 303–4n70.

25. George Lewis, *The History of Battery E, First Regiment Rhode Island Light Artillery . . .* (Providence, 1892), 239; de Trobriand, *Four Years with the Army*

of the Potomac, 549; A. D. Slade, *That Sterling Soldier: The Life of David A. Russell* (Dayton: Morningside House, 1995), 146–51; Nov. 7, 1863, Wainwright, *Diary of Battle*, 299; H. E. Matthews, Mar. 15, 1888, *National Tribune;* Lyman to wife, Nov. 9, 1863, Lyman Papers, MHS; Meade to wife, Nov. 9, Meade Papers, HSP; Lincoln to Meade, Nov. 9, Lincoln, *Collected Works*, 7:7.

26. Oct. 5, 1863, Lyman, *Meade's Army*, 46; AP circular, Nov. 23, *OR* 29.2:480–81; Meade report, *OR* 29.1:13–14; Meade to wife, Dec. 2, Meade Papers, HSP; Humphreys, *Gettysburg to the Rapidan*, 50.

27. Meade, Prince reports, *OR* 29.1:13–14, 760–62; Winslow, *General John Sedgwick*, 126; Nov. 26, 27, 1863, Patrick, *Inside Lincoln's Army*, 313, 314; Martin F. Graham and George F. Skoch, *Mine Run: A Campaign of Lost Opportunities* (Lynchburg, Va.: H. E. Howard, 1987), 50–52; French to Humphreys, Humphreys to French, Nov. 27, *OR* 29.2:498, 500.

28. Meade report, *OR* 29.1:16; Nov. 28, 29, 1863, Lyman, *Meade's Army*, 73–74; Biddle to wife, Dec. 1, Biddle Papers, HSP; McAllister to wife, Dec. 3, McAllister, *Civil War Letters*, 367; Livermore, *Days and Events*, 301; Meade testimony, *CCW* 1 (1865), 345.

29. Meade, Warren reports, *OR* 29.1:16–18, 698; Livermore, *Days and Events*, 302; Nov. 30, 1863, Lyman, *Meade's Army*, 74–75; Warren to Meade, *OR* 29.2:517; Meade to wife, Dec. 2, Meade Papers, HSP; Thomas W. Hyde to mother, Dec. 4, Hyde, *Civil War Letters*, 120; AP circular, Dec. 1, *OR* 29.2:530–32; Dec. 1, Patrick, *Inside Lincoln's Army*, 318. For maps and a narrative of this period, see Bradley M. Gottfried, *The Maps of the Bristoe Station and Mine Run Campaigns* (El Dorado Hills, Calif.: Savas Beatie, 2013).

30. Meade report, *OR* 29.1:17–18; Meade to wife, Dec. 2, 1863, Meade Papers, HSP; Warren to Humphreys, Dec. 3, Warren

Papers, New York State Library; Nov. 30, Patrick, *Inside Lincoln's Army*, 317.

31. Lyman to wife, Dec. 14, 1863, Feb. 22, 1864, Lyman Papers, MHS; Dec. 3, 1863, Fiske, *Mr. Dunn Browne's Experiences in the Army*, 205–6; John Nicolay memo, Dec. 7, Nicolay, *With Lincoln in the White House*, 121; Meade to Hancock, Dec. 11, Hancock Papers, Duke University; Meade to wife, Dec. 7, 28, Meade Papers, HSP.

32. Meade to wife, Feb. 24, 1864, Meade Papers, HSP; Andrew H. Young to wife, Feb. 22, Young Papers, Dartmouth College Library.

33. Virgil Carrington Jones, *Eight Hours Before Richmond* (New York: Henry Holt, 1957), 18–20; I. J. Wistar to S. P. Spear, Feb. 5, 1864, *OR* 33:521–22; Walker, *History of the Second Army Corps*, 396.

34. Feb. 23, 1864, Lyman, *Meade's Army*, 103; Samuel J. Martin, *"Kill-Cavalry": Sherman's Merchant of Terror; The Life of Union General Hugh Judson Kilpatrick* (Madison, N.J.: Fairleigh Dickinson University Press, 1996), 146, 148; Lincoln to Sedgwick, Feb. 11, Lincoln, *Collected Works*, 7:178; Kilpatrick to E. B. Parsons, Feb. 16, *OR* 33:172–73; Meade to wife, Feb. 27, Meade Papers, HSP; Lyman to wife, Mar. 1, Lyman Papers, MHS; Ulric Dahlgren to father, Feb. 26, John A. Dahlgren Papers, LC; Dahlgren papers: entry 721, serial 60, RG 94, NA, and *Richmond Examiner*, Apr. 1.

35. Meade to wife, Mar. 6, 1864, Meade Papers, HSP; Mar. 4, Lyman, *Meade's Army*, 106. For the Kilpatrick-Dahlgren raid, see "Raid on Richmond," Sears, *Controversies & Commanders*, 226–51, and Eric J. Wittenberg, *Like a Meteor Blazing Brightly: The Short but Controversial Life of Colonel Ulric Dahlgren* (Roseville, Minn.: Edinborough Press, 2009).

36. *Richmond Dispatch, Richmond Whig*, Mar. 5, 1864; Lee to Meade, Apr. 1,

Meade to Lee, Apr. 17, *OR* 33:178, 180; Kilpatrick to F. C. Newhall, Mar. 16, to Seth Williams, Apr. 16, *OR* 33:176, 180; Meade to wife, Apr. 18, Meade Papers, HSP; Mar. 12, Patrick, *Inside Lincoln's Army*, 347–48; John C. Babcock statement, Babcock Papers, LC; *Richmond Inquirer*, Mar. 5; James O. Hall, "The Dahlgren Papers: Fact or Fabrication," *Civil War Times Illustrated* (Nov. 1983), 39. See Stephen W. Sears, "The Dahlgren Papers Revisited," *Columbiad*, 3:2 (Summer 1999), 63–87.

37. War Dept. G.O. 98, Mar. 12, 1864, *OR* ser. III, 4:172; Meade to wife, Feb. 29, Meade Papers, HSP; Sickles, Doubleday, Howe testimony, *CCW* 1 (1865), 298, 300, 311, 325, 328, and journal, xix; Halleck to Grant, Mar. 3, *OR* 32.3:13.

38. Meade to wife, Mar. 6, 8, 1864, Meade Papers, HSP; Meade, Butterfield testimony, *CCW* 1 (1865), 329–47, 347–51, 435–39, 417–35; *Congressional Globe*, 38th Cong., 1st sess., 896–900; Meade to Reverdy Johnson, Mar. 6, Stanton Papers, LC; Sickles to Zachariah Chandler, Mar. 30, Chandler Papers, LC; Meade to Gibbon, Mar. 15, Gibbon, *Personal Recollections*, 187.

39. Historicus letters: *New York Herald*, Mar. 12, Apr. 4, 1864, reprinted in Meade, *Life and Letters*, 2:323–31, 337–40; Meade to wife, Mar. 9, 16, Meade Papers, HSP; Meade to E. D. Townsend, Mar. 15, Lincoln to Meade, Mar. 29, Halleck to Meade, Mar. 20, Meade to Halleck, Mar. 22, *OR* 27.1:127–28, 139, 137, 137–38. In *Two Days of War: A Gettysburg Narrative and Other Excursions* (New York, 1905), 373, Tremain admits attacking, as "Eye Witness," Meade's role at Chancellorsville. See Richard A. Sauers, *A Caspian Sea of Ink: The Meade-Sickles Controversy* (Baltimore: Butternut and Blue, 1989), and Edwin B. Coddington, "The Strange Reputation of General Meade: A Lesson in Historiography," *The Historian*, 23:2 (Feb. 1961), 145–66.

40. Meade to wife, Mar. 6, Feb. 14, Mar. 24, 1864, Meade Papers, HSP; Jan. 10, Wainwright, *Diary of Battle,* 314; War Dept. G.O. 115, Mar. 23, *OR* 33:717–18; Mar. 30, Lyman, *Meade's Army,* 116; Webb to father, Mar. 15, Yale University Library. In reference to Lyman's characterization, Sykes earned his nickname Tardy George at West Point, not during the Civil War. The army reorganization here follows Welcher, *The Union Army,* vol. 1.

41. Meade to wife, April 18, 16, 1864, Meade Papers, HSP; Winslow, *General John Sedgwick,* 144–45; Gibbon, *Recollections,* 209; Lincoln to Stanton, Feb. 22, Lincoln, *Collected Works,* 7:199; Gibbon to wife, Apr. 22, Gibbon Papers, HSP; Humphreys to wife, Mar. 27, Humphreys Papers, HSP.

42. Swinton, *Campaigns of the Army of the Potomac,* 412; Meade to wife, Dec. 20, 1863, Mar. 9, 16, 14, 1864, Meade Papers, HSP; Albert B. Chandler, "As Lincoln Appeared in the War Department," *Independent,* 47 (Apr. 4, 1895), 448; Theodore Lyman to wife, Apr. 5, 1864, Lyman Papers, MHS; Smith to William B. Franklin, Apr. 28, Franklin Papers, LC; Mar. 10, Cyrus B. Comstock, *The Diary of Cyrus B. Comstock,* Merlin E. Sumner, ed., 260; Smith, *Autobiography,* 83; Mar. 8, Lyman, *Meade's Army,* 107; Dawes to wife, Mar. 21, Dawes Papers, Wisconsin Historical Society; Ulysses S. Grant, *Memoirs and Selected Letters,* 470.

16. ". . . THERE IS TO BE NO TURNING BACK"

1. Bruce Catton, *Grant Takes Command,* 111–12, 502n10. Grant's letter was addressed to J. Russell Jones.

2. Horatio Woodman to Stanton, May 1864, Woodman Papers, MHS; Grant report, *OR* 36.1:12; Grant to Meade, Apr. 9, Grant to Halleck, Jan. 19, Meade to Grant, Apr. 17, *OR* 33:827–29, 394–95, 889–90; Halleck to Grant, Feb. 17, *OR* 32.2:412; Grant, *Memoirs,* 474. The North Carolina plan was drawn up by Baldy Smith and Cyrus Comstock: Jan. 17, Comstock, *Diary,* 252.

3. War Dept. G.O. 191, June 25, G.O. 376, Nov. 21, 1863, *OR* ser. III, 3:414–16, 1084; Meade to T. M. Vincent, Mar. 31, 1864, *OR* 33:776; Meade to Halleck, Dec. 12, 1863, *OR* 29.2:556 61 with tables, and Frederick H. Dyer, *A Compendium of the War of the Rebellion,* vol. 2.

4. Dawes to fiancée, Oct. 25, Dec. 12, 20, 31, 1863, Jan. 4, 1864, Dawes, *Service with the Sixth Wisconsin,* 217, 231, 232–33, 235–37. Dawes took advantage of his furlough to marry his fiancée.

5. Draft orders, Feb. 1, Mar. 4, 1864, Lincoln, *Collected Works,* 7:164, 245; Provost-Marshal's report, Mar. 17, 1866, *OR* ser. III, 5:636–37, 669; Webb to father, Mar. 15, 1864, Webb Papers, Yale University Library; Aug. 16, 1863, Fiske, *Mr. Dunn Browne's Experiences in the Army,* 150–51.

6. AP return, Ninth Corps return, Apr. 30, 1864, *OR* 36.1:198, 915; Lyman to wife, May 18, Apr. 1, Lyman Papers, MHS; William Marvel, *Tarnished Victory: Finishing Lincoln's War,* 10–11; Grant to Stanton, Apr. 21, Grant, *Papers,* 10:335n. Lyman was prophetic. The division of U.S. Colored Troops guarded the trains, and by the account of a Confederate cavalryman, three black soldiers were captured and "taken out on the road side and shot. . . .": Gordon C. Rhea, *The Battles for Spotsylvania Court House and the Road to Yellow Tavern, May 7–12, 1864,* 351n57.

7. Wilson, *Under the Old Flag,* 1:372; Apr. 13, 1864, Lyman, *Meade's Army,* 122; Philip H. Sheridan, *Personal Memoirs of P. H. Sheridan,* 1:346.

8. Meade, "Estimate of Lee's forces," Apr. 1864, Meade Papers, HSP; Alfred C. Young III, *Lee's Army During the Over-*

land Campaign: A Numerical Study, 229–30; Lyman to wife, Apr. 20, Lyman Papers, MHS. In his memo some of Meade's listings lack clarity; only his totals are used here.

9. Meade to wife, Apr. 13, 1864, Meade Papers, HSP; Lyman to wife, Apr. 24, Lyman Papers, MHS; Grant to John E. Smith, Apr. 26, Grant, *Papers,* 10:357; Halleck to Francis Lieber, Mar. 14, Lieber Papers, Huntington Library.

10. Halleck to Francis Lieber, Jan. 14, 1864, Lieber Papers, Huntington Library; Lincoln to Grant, Apr. 30, Lincoln, *Collected Works,* 7:324; Grant to Lincoln, May 1, Grant, *Papers,* 10:380.

11. Roebling to Emily Warren, Apr. 24, 1864, Roebling Family Papers, Rutgers University Archives; Gibbon to wife, May 3, Gibbon Papers — Meade to wife, May 3, Meade Papers, HSP; *OR* 29.2:556–61; James C. Biddle to wife, May 3, Biddle Papers — Theodore Lyman to wife, May 3, Lyman Papers, MHS.

12. Andrew A. Humphreys, *The Virginia Campaign of '64 and '65, the Army of the Potomac and the Army of the James,* 9–13, and AP orders, May 2, 1864, *OR* 36.2:331–34; Ingalls to Meigs, May 3, *OR* 36.2:355; May 4, Lyman, *Meade's Army,* 131–32; Porter, *Campaigning with Grant,* 41; Humphreys to wife, May 3, Humphreys Papers, HSP. Ingalls's figures do not include the Ninth Corps.

13. Herman Melville, *Battle-Pieces and Aspects of the War,* 1866.

14. Theodore Lyman, "Uselessness of the Maps Furnished to Staff of the Army of the Potomac Previous to the Campaign of May 1864," *PMHSM,* 4:79–80; AP orders, May 2, 5, 1864, *OR* 36.2:332, 371; May 4, 5, Comstock, *Diary,* 263–64; Gordon C. Rhea, "Union Cavalry in the Wilderness: The Education of Philip H. Sheridan and James H. Wilson," Gallagher, ed., *Wilderness Campaign,* 116–17.

15. May 5, 1864, Lyman, *Meade's Army,*

132–33; Gordon C. Rhea, *The Battle of the Wilderness,* May 5–6, 1864, 103; Morris Schaff, *The Battle of the Wilderness* (Boston: Houghton Mifflin, 1910), 128; W. H. Taylor to Ewell, May 4, *OR* 36.2:948; Swinton, *Campaigns of the Army of the Potomac,* 421n; Warren to Humphreys, Humphreys to Hancock, Meade to Grant, Grant to Meade, May 5, *OR* 36.2:413, 406, 403.

16. Locke to Griffin, Meade to Warren, Meade to Grant, Humphreys to Hancock, May 5, 1864, *OR* 36.2:416, 404, 407; Meade endorsement, May 5, *OR* 36.2:418; Getty report, *OR* 36.1:676.

17. Gibbon to wife, May 7, 1864, Gibbon Papers, Maryland Historical Society; Meade to Warren, Locke to Griffin, Crawford to Locke, May 5, *OR* 36.2:404, 416, 418; Mark Grimsley, *And Keep Moving On: The Virginia Campaign, May–June 1864,* 34–39; Upton, Getty reports, *OR* 36.1:665, 676; May 5, Comstock, *Diary,* 264; May 5, Lyman, *Meade's Army,* 133–34; Lyman to wife, May 15, Lyman Papers, MHS; Theodore Lyman, "Addenda . . . on the Battle of the Wilderness," *PMHSM,* 4:167–68. W. A. Roebling claimed, long after the war, that on May 5 Grant threatened to cashier Warren if he did not immediately attack (to Morris Schaff, May 18, 1909, Rutgers University Archives). The aged Roebling's recollections are highly suspect, and there is no supporting evidence.

18. Hazard Stevens, "The Sixth Corps in the Wilderness," *PMHSM,* 4:190–92; May 5, 1864, Lyman, *Meade's Army,* 133–34; Hancock to Humphreys, May 5, *OR* 36.2:409–10; Humphreys, *Virginia Campaign,* 30.

19. L. A. Grant, McAllister reports, *OR* 36.1:697, 488; George C. Benedict, *Vermont in the Civil War* (Burlington, Vt., 1886), 1:424; Lyman to wife, May 15, 1864, Lyman Papers, MHS; May 5, Lyman, *Meade's Army,* 134–35; Gibbon to wife, May 7, Gibbon Papers, Maryland

Historical Society; Lyman to Meade, Humphreys to Warren, May 5, *OR* 36.2:411, 415; Mahood, *General Wadsworth,* 233–34.

20. Warren to C. H. Porter, Nov. 21, 1875, Warren Papers, New York State Library; Horace Porter, *Campaigning with Grant,* 53–54; Grant to Halleck, May 6, 1864, *OR* 36.2:437; Meade to Warren, Meade to Hancock (2), Meade to Grant, W. R. Rowley to Meade, May 5, *OR* 36.2:415, 441, 412, 404–5, 405.

21. Charles A. Page, *Letters of a War Correspondent* (Boston, 1899), 52; diary, May 6, 1864, Oliver Wendell Holmes, Jr., *Touched with Fire: Civil War Letters and Diary of Oliver Wendell Holmes, Jr., 1861–1864,* ed. Mark DeWolfe Howe, 106; Humphreys to Warren (three), Warren to Humphreys, May 6, *OR* 36.2:449, 450, 451–52, 450; Warren report, *OR* 36.1:540.

22. May 6, 1864, Lyman, *Meade's Army,* 136; Lyman to wife, May 16, 1864, Apr. 17, 1866, Lyman Papers, MHS; Roebling report, Warren Papers, New York State Library; Rhea, *Battle of the Wilderness,* 329–30.

23. Lyman to Meade (2), Hancock to Meade, May 6, 1864, *OR* 36.2:439, 440, 439; Hancock report, *OR* 36.1:321; May 6, Lyman, *Meade's Army,* 137–38; Lyman to Meade (10), *OR* 36.2:439–446 passim. See Gibbon, *Recollections,* 387–411, for his dealings with this episode.

24. May 6, 10, 1864, Weld, *War Diary and Letters,* 285–86, 290; Rawlins to Burnside, Humphreys to Lyman, May 6, *OR* 36.2:461, 446; Rhea, *Battle of the Wilderness,* 447–50; C. A. Dana to Stanton, May 9, *OR* 36.1:65; W. T. Mali to E. B. Robins, Oct. 26, 1888, Meade Papers, HSP; Dawes, *Service with the Sixth Wisconsin,* 262; May 6, 8, Lyman, *Meade's Army,* 138, 146; Lyman to wife, May 16, Lyman Papers, MHS.

25. May 6, 1864, Lyman, *Meade's Army,* 138–40; Hancock to Meade, Meade to Hancock, May 6, *OR* 36.2:446, 447;

Humphreys to wife, May 7, Humphreys Papers, HSP; May 6, Comstock, *Diary,* 264; Rhea, *Battle of the Wilderness,* 419; Porter, *Campaigning with Grant,* 69–70; Humpheys, *Virginia Campaign,* 54; Lyman to wife, May 15, 1864, Apr. 17, 1866, Lyman Papers, MHS; Melville, *Battle-Pieces and Aspects of the War,* 1866.

26. Lyman to wife, May 18, 1864, Lyman Papers, MHS; Grant to Meade, May 7, *OR* 36.2:481; May 6, Lyman, *Meade's Army,* 141; Small, *The Road to Richmond,* 134; Porter, *Campaigning with Grant,* 78–79.

27. Casualties: *OR* 36.1:119–36, and Young, *Lee's Army During the Overland Campaign,* 235; Porter, *Campaigning with Grant,* 52; Mahood, *General Wadsworth,* 256; May 14, 1864, Hay, *Inside Lincoln's White House,* 196.

28. Henry E. Wing, *When Lincoln Kissed Me: A Story of the Wilderness Campaign* (New York, 1913), 38.

29. AP orders, May 7, 1864, *OR* 36.2:483–84; May 7, Wainwright, *Diary of Battle,* 355; Forsyth to Gregg, Meade to Gregg, to Merritt, to Sheridan, May 8, *OR* 36.2:553, 552, 551; Porter, *Campaigning with Grant,* 83–84; Sheridan, *Personal Memoirs,* 1:368–69; May 8, Lyman, *Meade's Army,* 144; Starr, *Union Cavalry in the Civil War,* 2:93–96; Humphreys to Sheridan, May 8, *OR* 36.2:552. Burnside's brigade of cavalry remained, but operated largely in the army's rear. Sheridan claimed he did not receive Meade's orders, but his own planning argues otherwise.

30. William D. Matter, *If It Takes All Summer: The Battle of Spotsylvania,* 48; Schaff, *The Battle of the Wilderness,* 91; Warren to Humphreys, May 8, 1864, *OR* 36.2:540.

31. Warren to Humphreys, Meade to Warren, May 8, 1864, *OR* 36.2:540, 541; May 8, Lyman, *Meade's Army,* 145, 146; Wilson, *Under the Old Flag,* 2:395–96. Warren related his outburst to Meade

to Wilson (by Wilson's account) "several years afterwards."

32. Gibbon to wife, May 7, 1864, Gibbon Papers, Maryland Historical Society; Dawes to wife, May 27, Dawes Papers, Wisconsin Historical Society; May 8, 9, Lyman, *Meade's Army*, 146, 148; Warren to Humpheys (unsent), May 9, Warren Papers, New York State Library; diary, May 9, Holmes, *Touched with Fire*, 109–10; Porter, *Campaigning with Grant*, 90.

33. Lyman to wife, May 20, 1864, Lyman Papers, MHS; Humphreys to wife, May 15, Humphreys Papers, HSP.

34. Lyman to wife, May 18, 1864, Lyman Papers, MHS; Hancock to Humphreys, Meade to Hancock, May 10, OR 36.2:599, 600; Gibbon, *Personal Recollections*, 218–19.

35. Upton report, *OR* 36.1:667–68; Rhea, *Battles for Spotsylvania Court House*, 161–75; May 10, 1864, Lyman, *Meade's Army*, 148, 150; May 10, Holmes, *Touched with Fire*, 111, 113.

36. Warren diary, May 10, 1864, New York State Library; Gibbon, *Personal Recollections*, 219; May 10, Lyman, *Meade's Army*, 150–51; Lyman, "Addenda . . . on the Battle of the Wilderness," *PMHSM*, 4:169. Grant to Halleck, May 11, OR 36.2:627–28; Louis M. Starr, *Bohemian Brigade: Civil War Newsmen in Action*, 307.

37. Luman H. Tenney, *War Diary of Luman Harris Tenney, 1861–1865* (Cleveland, 1914), 115; Meade to wife, May 11, 1864, Meade Papers, HSP; diary, May 11, Patrick, *Inside Lincoln's Army*, 372; Lyman to wife, May 22, Lyman Papers, Massachusetts Historical Society; Grant to Meade, May 11, OR 36.2:629; Francis C. Barlow, "Capture of the Salient, May 12, 1864," *PMHSM*, 4:246–59; John D. Black, "Reminiscences of the Bloody Angle," *Glimpses of the Nation's Struggle*, Minnesota MOLLUS (4:1898), 29:422–24.

38. Hancock to Meade (2), Hancock to

Burnside, Grant to Burnside, May 12, 1864, *OR* 36.2:656, 677, 679; Barlow, "Capture of the Salient," *PMHSM*, 4: 254–55; May 12, Comstock, *Diary*, 266.

39. Meade-Warren dispatches, May 12, 1864, *OR* 36.2:661–62; Humphreys-Warren, May 12, ibid., 662–63; Grant-Meade, May 12, ibid., 654; Roebling report, Warren Papers, New York State Library; Jordan, *"Happiness Is Not My Companion,"* 151–52; Lyman to wife, May 22, Lyman Papers, MHS; May 12, Lyman, *Meade's Army*, 155–56.

40. Gibbon to wife, May 13, 1864, Gibbon Papers, Maryland Historical Society; Daniel Larned to sister, May 13, Larned Papers, LC; Rhea, *Battles for Spotsylvania Court House*, 311–12; Grant to wife, May 13, Grant, *Papers*, 10:443–44.

17. TO JAMES RIVER

1. Lyman to wife, May 12, 28, 1864, Lyman Papers, MHS; Meade to wife, May 13, 19, Meade Papers, HSP; *New York Times*, May 14; May 17, Welles, *Diary*, 411; Grant to Halleck, May 16, Meade to Hancock, May 17, OR 36.2:810, 844; Gibbon to wife, May 14, Gibbon Papers, HSP; C. A. Dana to Stanton, May 16, Apr. 30 return, OR 36.1:71, 198; May 17, Lyman, *Meade's Army*, 162.

2. Casualties: OR 36.1:133, 149, and Young, *Lee's Army During the Overland Campaign*, 235, 236; expiring enlistments: OR 29.2:558–61; Humphreys, *Virginia Campaign*, 109–10n; May 9, 1864, Hay, *Inside Lincoln's White House*, 195; Roebling to Emily Warren, May 21, Roebling Family Papers, Rutgers University Archives; Meade to wife, May 19, Meade Papers, HSP. For Stanton's persecution of Hammond, see Marvel, *Lincoln's Autocrat*, 313–17. For the ordeal of the wounded, see Leech, *Reveille in Washington*, 322–25.

3. Army S.O. 25, May 24, 1864, Burnside

to Grant, May 24, *OR* 36.3:169; Second Corps S.O., May 13, *OR* 36.2:711–12; Lyman to wife, May 28, Lyman Papers, MHS; May 15, Lyman, *Meade's Army*, 160.

4. Porter, *Campaigning with Grant*, 114–15; Meade to wife, May 19, 23, June 9, 1864, Meade Papers, HSP; John Russell Young, *Around the World with General Grant* (New York, 1879), 2:299; Lyman to wife, May 27, Lyman Papers, MHS; Alexander Webb interview, 1899, William B. Styple, ed., *Generals in Bronze: Interviewing the Commanders of the Civil War* (Kearny, N.J.: Belle Grove, 2005), 149–50; Biddle to wife, June 4, Biddle Papers, HSP.

5. Warren to Joshua Chamberlain, Nov. 12, 1879, Chamberlain Papers, LC; Lyman to Harland Shaw, June 9, 1864, Lyman Papers, MHS; Meade to wife, June 25, Meade Papers, HSP; Biddle to wife, June 25, Biddle Papers, HSP.

6. Sheridan, *Personal Memoirs*, 1:370; Sheridan to Meade, May 13, 1864, *OR* 36.1:776–77; L. B. Northrup to [J. A. Seddon] May 10, *OR* 51.2:909–10; Johnston, *Virginia Railroads*, 298n17; Robert E. L. Krick, "Stuart's Last Ride: A Confederate View of Sheridan's Raid," Gallagher, ed., *The Spotsylvania Campaign*, 131. Krick speculates that after Gettysburg, Lee wanted "never again to suffer the loss of flexibility brought about by the absence of his cavalry."

7. Rhea, *Battles for Spotsylvania Court House*, 201–12; Theo. F. Rodenbough, "Sheridan's Richmond Raid," *Battles and Leaders*, 4:191. Hampton was only officially appointed head of the Confederate cavalry on Aug. 11.

8. Grant to Ord, Mar. 29, 1864, *OR* 33:758; Sigel Papers, Western Reserve Historical Society, cited in Engle, *Yankee Dutchman*, 175, 177; May 22, Moore, *Rebellion Record*, 11:Documents:14; Crook report, *OR* 37.1:10–12; Hayes to uncle, May 19, Rutherford B. Hayes, *Diary and Letters of Rutherford Birchard Hayes*, Charles Richard Williams, ed. (Columbus: Ohio State Archaeological Society, 1922), 2:463; Johnston, *Virginia Railroads*, 298n27.

9. Grant to Sherman, Apr. 4, 1864, Grant, *Papers*, 10:252–53; Apr. 30, Hay, *Inside Lincoln's White House*, 194; William C. Davis, *Battle of New Market* (New York: Doubleday, 1975), 89, 98, 183; May 15, 16, Strother, *Virginia Yankee in the Civil War*, 226, 229.

10. Apr. 1, 1864, Comstock, *Diary*, 262; Grant to Butler, Apr. 2, 16, 19, *OR* 33:794–95, 885–86, 904–5; William G. Robertson, *Back Door to Richmond: The Bermuda Hundred Campaign* (Newark: University of Delaware Press, 1987), 59.

11. Grimsley, *And Keep Moving On*, 118–29; Smith and Gillmore to Butler, Butler to Smith and Gillmore, May 9, 1864, *OR* 36.2:35; William F. Smith, "Butler's Attack on Drewry's Bluff," *Battles and Leaders*, 4:206–12; Smith to Grant, July 2, *OR* 40.2:595; May 22, Lyman, *Meade's Army*, 170; Halleck to Grant, May 17, Grant to Meade, May 18, *OR* 36.2:840–41, 864–65; Porter, *Campaigning with Grant*, 125. For Butler's operation, see Bruce Catton, *Never Call Retreat*, 343–51.

12. Grant to Halleck, May 19, 1864, to Meade, May 18, *OR* 36.2:906, 864–65; May 19, Wainwright, *Diary of Battle*, 379; Porter, *Campaigning with Grant*, 127; Warren to wife, May 20, Warren Papers, New York State Library.

13. Humphreys to wife, May 15, 1864, Humphreys Papers, HSP; May 18, Lyman, *Meade's Army*, 163; Warren to wife, May 19, Warren Papers, New York State Library.

14. Grant to Meade, May 18, 1864, *OR* 36.2:864–65; Hancock to Seth Williams, Meade to Seth Williams, May 21, *OR* 36.3:49–50, 44; May 21, Lyman, *Meade's Army*, 167; Lyman to wife, May 23, Lyman Papers, MHS; Grant to Halleck, May 22, 25, Butler to Stanton, May 24, *OR* 36.3:77, 183, 176.

15. Lee to Davis, May 23, 1864, Lee, *Wartime Papers*, 747–48; Biddle to wife, May 16, Biddle Papers, HSP; Lyman to wife, June 5, Lyman Papers, MHS; May 24, Lyman, *Meade's Army*, 172–73. The telegram (as paraphrased by Lyman) that infuriated Meade was Sherman to Stanton of May 23, forwarded to Grant: *OR* 38.4:294.

16. May 26, 1864, Comstock, *Diary*, 269; Biddle to wife, June 4, Biddle Papers, HSP; May 26, Patrick, *Inside Lincoln's Army*, 377; Lyman to wife, Apr. 12, Lyman Papers, MHS; Meade to wife, May 19, Meade Papers, HSP.

17. Warren to wife, May 21, 1864, Warren Papers, New York State Library; Dawes to wife, May 24, Dawes, *Service with the Sixth Wisconsin*, 275; May 23, Wainwright, *Diary of Battle*, 385; Meade to Warren, May 23, *OR* 36.3:129; Clement A. Evans, ed., *Confederate Military History* (Atlanta, 1899), 3:460.

18. Burnside to Grant, Rawlins to Burnside, Hancock to Humphreys, May 24, 1864, Warren to Meade, May 25, *OR* 36.3:166, 167, 155, 192; Gordon C. Rhea, *To the North Anna River: Grant and Lee, May 13–15, 1864*, 336–42; May 24, Weld, *War Diary and Letters*, 296–97. There is no evidence that Lee intended an offensive from his wedge formation: Grimsley, *And Keep Moving On*, 145–46.

19. May 26, 1864, Comstock, *Diary*, 269; May 26, Wainwright, *Diary of Battle*, 388; Lyman to wife, May 24, Lyman Papers, MHS; Grant to Meade, May 25, to Halleck, May 26, *OR* 36.3:183, 206–7.

20. Grant to Halleck, May 26, 1864, *OR* 36.3:206–7; Gibbon to wife, May 26, 31, Gibbon Papers, HSP; May 28, Comstock, *Diary*, 270; Dana to Stanton, May 26, *OR* 36.1:79; Grimsley, *And Keep Moving On*, 148; Meade to wife, June 4, Meade Papers, HSP; Smith to Franklin, Apr. 28, Franklin Papers, LC; June 4, Lyman, *Meade's Army*, 191; Larned to sister, June 5, Larned Papers, LC.

21. Meade to wife, June 5, 9, 12, May 16, 1864, Meade Papers, HSP; Gibbon to wife, May 15, Gibbon Papers, HSP; Warren to brother, May 20, Warren Papers, New York State Library; Charles Francis Adams, Jr., to father, [May] 29, Ford, ed., *A Cycle of Adams Letters*, 2:134; Biddle to wife, June 5, Biddle Papers, HSP.

22. Gordon C. Rhea, "The Battle of Haw's Shop, May 28, 1864," *North & South*, 4:4 (Apr. 2001), 42–57; Lee to Anderson, May 30, 1864, *OR* 36.3:851; May 30, Wainwright, *Diary of Battle*, 392–94; Warren to Humphreys, Sheridan to Humphreys, Warren to Crawford, May 30, *OR* 36.3:336, 361, 351. 1,759 Pennsylvania Reserves reenlisted as the 190th and 191st Pennsylvania, Army of the Potomac: J. R. Sypher, *History of the Pennsylvania Reserve Corps* (Lancaster, Pa., 1865), 547.

23. Grant to Meade, May 30, 1864, *OR* 36.3:323; Lyman to wife, June 11, Lyman Papers, MHS; Sheridan report, *OR* 36.1:794; Meade to Wright, May 31, Grant to Smith, May 30, *OR* 36.3:404, 371; Babcock to Smith, June 1, Grant, *Papers*, 10:499.

24. Humphreys, *Virginia Campaign*, 175–76; Lyman to wife, June 2, 1864, Lyman Papers, MHS; Barlow to Meade, Meade to Grant, Comstock to Meade, June 1, *OR* 36.3:437, 432–33, 433; Upton to sister, June 5, Peter S. Michie, *The Life and Letters of Emory Upton*, 109; June 1, Lyman, *Meade's Army*, 185; Dana to Stanton, June 1, *OR* 36.1:85; June 1, Wainwright, *Diary of Battle*, 396; Ricketts to Warren, Warren to Meade (2), Meade to Warren, June 1, *OR*, 36.3:447, 447–48, 449, 451–52; Fifth Corps S.O. 131, June 2, *OR* 36.3:495.

25. Meade to Hancock, June 1, 1864, Grant to Meade, Smith to Meade, June 2, *OR* 36.3:432–33, 478, 505; Hancock report, *OR* 36.1:344; Lyman to wife, Apr. 12, Lyman Papers, MHS.

26. Gibbon, *Personal Recollections*, 229; Porter, *Campaigning with Grant*, 174–

75. Porter's account of names pinned on uniforms has been called apocryphal because it was not reported elsewhere, a dubious objection.

27. AP circular, June 2, 1864, *OR* 36.3:479; June 3, Lyman, *Meade's Army*, 188–90; Meade-Hancock, June 3, *OR* 36.3:525–31 passim; Porter, *Campaigning with Grant*, 177; Grant-Meade, June 3, *OR* 36.3:525–27 passim; Grant, *Memoirs*, 585; Lyman to wife, June 9, 14, Lyman Papers, MHS; Gordon C. Rhea, *Cold Harbor: Grant and Lee, May 26–June 3, 1864*, 362. See Rhea's discussion of Cold Harbor casualties at 358–62.

28. Meade to wife, June 4, 5, 1864, Meade Papers, HSP; June 3, 5, Lyman, *Meade's Army*, 189–90, 192; Barlow to F. A. Walker, June 6, *OR* 36.3:646–47.

29. Grant, *Memoirs*, 586–88; Lyman to wife, June 20, 1864, Lyman Papers, MHS.

30. *Philadelphia Inquirer*, June 2, 1864; Meade to wife, June 9, 17, Meade Papers, HSP; June 8, Lyman, *Meade's Army*, 195–96; June 8, Patrick, *Inside Lincoln's Army*, 381; Grant to Isaac P. Clark, June 22 (published in *New York Times*, July 10), Stanton to C. A. Dana, June 10, Meade Papers, HSP; Gibbon, *Personal Recollections*, 239–40; I. S. Pennypacker, *General Meade* (New York, 1901), 318. The *Inquirer* reporter's surname is sometimes given as Crapsey, but Cropsey is his editor's and his byline spelling: George Harding to Margaret Meade, Aug. 13, Meade Papers, HSP. Chief of Staff Humphreys advised against Cropsey's expulsion and Meade suspended the order, but Patrick had already carried it out: Humphreys to wife, Aug. 9, Humphreys Papers, HSP; Grant to Isaac N. Morris, July 12, Grant, *Papers*, 11:227.

31. Grant to Halleck, to Meade, June 5, 1864, *OR* 36.3:598–99, 599; Seth Williams to H. W. Benham, May 26, *OR* 36.3:232; Grant to Washburne, June 9, Grant, *Papers*, 11:32; Hunter to Charles Halpine, Mar. 10, Halpine Papers, Huntington Library; Grant to Hunter, June 6, *OR* 37.1:598.

32. Earl J. Hess, *In the Trenches at Petersburg: Field Fortifications & Confederate Defeat*, 16–17; Grant to J. J. Abercrombie, June 7, 1864, to Butler, June 11, to Herman Biggs, June 12, *OR* 36.3:690, 754–55, 769.

33. June 12, 1864, Lyman, *Meade's Army*, 201; Humphreys to wife, June 14, Humphreys Papers, HSP; Grant to Meade, June 11, *OR* 36.3:745–46; Rawlings to Smith, June 13, *OR* 40.2:17; Smith to wife, June 13, William F. Smith, "The Movement Against Peterburg, June, 1864," *PMHSM*, 5:108; Mendell, Weitzel reports, *OR* 40.1:300–301, 676–77; Humphreys, *Virginia Campaign*, 202–3. For the movement to the James, see Gordon C. Rhea, "Grant's Disengagement from Cold Harbor," in Gary W. Gallagher and Caroline E. Janney, eds., *Cold Harbor to the Crater: The End of the Overland Campaign*, 176–209.

34. Hess, *In the Trenches at Petersburg*, 10–12; Butler to Gillmore, June 8, 1864, Gillmore to Butler, June 9, *OR* 36.3:705, 719; June 9, Comstock, *Diary*, 272; Butler to Grant, June 14, Grant to Butler, June 17, *OR* 36.2:282, 286.

35. June 26, 1864, Lyman to wife, Lyman Papers, MHS; Butler to Grant, Grant to Halleck, June 13, Grant to Meade, to Butler, June 14, Grant to Butler and Smith, to Gibbon, June 15, *OR* 40.2:12, 18–19, 19, 36, 73, 63; June 13, Lyman, *Meade's Army*, 201; Lincoln to Grant, June 15, Lincoln, *Collected Works*, 7:393; Grant report, *OR* 36:1:25; Smith, "Movement Against Peterburg," *PMHSM*, 5:80.

36. June 14, 1864, Lyman, *Meade's Army*, 204; Dana to Stanton, June 15, *OR* 40.1:19; Grant to wife, June 15, Grant, *Papers*, 11:55; Porter, *Campaigning with Grant*, 199.

37. Meade to Hancock, June 15, 1864, *OR* 40.2:57; David M. Jordan, *Winfield Scott Hancock: A Soldier's Life*,

142–43; Samuel A. Duncan report, *OR* 51.1:265–66; Smith, *Autobiography,* 99, 102–4; Smith, "Movement Against Petersburg," *PMHSM,* 5:89.

38. Hess, *In the Trenches at Petersburg,* 18–19; Thomas L. Livermore, "The Failure to Take Petersburg, June 15, 1864," *PMHSM,* 5:68; Smith, *Autobiography,* 104–5; Butler to Smith, June 15, 1864, Butler to Grant, June 16, *OR* 40.2:83, 98; Lyman to wife, June 28, Lyman Papers, MHS; Gibbon, *Personal Recollections,* 243; Frank Wilkeson, *Recollections of a Private Soldier in the Army of the Potomac* (New York: Putnam's, 1887), 162. In 1897 a signalman's diary surfaced which seemed to show that Smith halted on the night of June 15 on an order from Butler. No such order has been found, however, and Smith admitted he did not recall receiving it, nor did he mention receiving it in his wartime report. Furthermore, Butler's on-the-record dispatches to Smith that evening urged him on after he had already halted. The diary and documentation, all three decades after the fact, supported yet another Smith excuse.

39. Grant to Meade, to Butler, Barlow to Meade, Barnard to Meade, Hancock to Meade, June 16, 1864, *OR* 40.2:86, 98, 92–93, 87, 91; June 16, Lyman, *Meade's Army,* 206–8; Richard F. Welch, *The Boy General: The Life and Careers of Francis Channing Barlow,* 150–52; June 18, Comstock, *Diary,* 274.

40. Hess, *In the Trenches at Petersburg,* 25–29; Marvel, *Burnside,* 385–87; Willcox, *Forgotten Valor,* 542–44; Weld, *War Diary and Letters,* 312.

41. June 18, 1864, Lyman, *Meade's Army,* 211, 213; Hess, *In the Trenches at Petersburg,* 29–37; Meade to Grant, to Birney, to Warren and Burnside, June 18, *OR* 40.2:156, 165, 179; McAllister to family, June 19, McAllister, *Civil War Letters,* 445; June 18, Wainwright, *Diary of Battle,* 424–25; Meade to Birney, to Grant, Grant to Meade, June 18, *OR* 40.2:167, 156.

18. LONG ROAD TO APPOMATTOX

1. June 18, 1864, Lyman, *Meade's Army,* 214–15; Grant to Meade, June 18, *OR* 40.2:157; Porter to wife, June 24, Horace Porter Papers, LC; June 26, Browning, *Diary,* 1:673; June 23, Hay, *Inside Lincoln's White House,* 210.

2. Weld to father, June 21, 1864, Weld, *War Diary and Letters,* 318; June 19, Wainwright, *Diary of Battle,* 426; Warren to brother, June 21, Warren Papers, New York State Library; Eric J. Wittenberg, *Little Phil: A Reassessment of the Civil War Leadership of Gen. Philip H. Sheridan,* 37–41; Sheridan report, *OR* 36.1:785.

3. Grant to Halleck, May 25, 1864, *OR* 36.3:183; Strother, *Virginia Yankee in the Civil War,* 241, 266–68, 273.

4. Catton, *Grant Takes Command,* 303; Apr. 30, 1864 returns: *OR* 36.1:198, 915; June 30 return: *OR* 40.2:542; Grant to Halleck, June 23, *OR* 40.2:330–31; Grant to wife, June 22, Grant, *Papers,* 11:110; Gibbon, *Personal Recollections,* 227–28. Gibbon included in his calculations a reinforcement of a fourth brigade during the campaign.

5. Hancock report, Hancock to S. Williams, June 26, 1864, Grant to Meade, June 28, *OR* 40.1:304, 313–15; Warren to wife, June [19], July 24, Warren Papers, New York State Library; Meade to Rawlins, June 21 (withdrawn), Meade Papers, HSP; Meade to Warren, July 22, *OR* 40.3:393–94.

6. June 27, July 17, 1864, Comstock, *Diary,* 277, 282; Smith to Rawlins, June 21, Smith to Grant, July 2, *OR* 40.2:301, 595; Grant to Halleck, July 6, *OR* 40.3:31; July 20, Lyman, *Meade's Army,* 236; Meade to wife, July 7, Meade Papers, HSP; Smith, *Autobiography,* 116; Lyman to wife, July 24, Lyman Papers, MHS; Smith to Foot, July 30, Grant, *Papers,* 11:207–9n; Aug. 19, Patrick, *Inside Lincoln's Army,* 415.

7. Walker, *History of the Second Corps,*

543; Humphreys, *Virginia Campaign,* 226–29; Meade to Grant, June 20, 1864, Grant to Halleck, June 24, *OR* 40.2:231, 372–73; Meade to Barlow, June 22, Barlow report, *OR* 40.1:326, 328; June 22–23, Lyman, *Meade's Army,* 219–25; June 22, Comstock, *Diary,* 276; Barlow report, *OR* 40.1:329.

8. Meade to wife, June 30, 1864, Meade Papers, HSP; Edward E. Longacre, *Lincoln's Cavalrymen: A History of the Mounted Forces of the Army of the Potomac, 1861–1865,* 287–93; Wittenberg, *Little Phil,* 42, 46–47; Johnston, *Virginia Railroads,* 213–15; Lyman to wife, July 22, Lyman Papers, MHS.

9. Roebling to Emily Warren, July 12, 1864, Roebling Family Papers, Rutgers University Archives; Barnard memo, July 2, Townsend to Grant, July 4, *OR* 40.2:584–85, 619; Dana to Stanton, July 4, 5, 1864, *OR* 40.1:33, 34; Hess, *In the Trenches at Petersburg,* 45.

10. Lee to Seddon, July 19, 1864, Lee, *Wartime Papers,* 822; Dana to Rawlings, July 11, Grant, *Papers,* 11:210–11; July 8, 12, 13, Welles, *Diary,* 442, 446, 448; Lincoln to Grant, July 10, Lincoln, *Collected Works,* 7:437; July 11, Hay, *Inside Lincoln's White House,* 221. Justice Oliver Wendell Holmes, formerly on Wright's staff, liked to tell the story that at Fort Stevens he yelled at the president, "Get down, you damn fool!" Holmes likely embroidered the tale; if that was indeed his phrasing, Lincoln would surely have quoted it to Hay.

11. Dana to Grant, July 12, 1864, *OR* 37.2:223; Halleck to Francis Lieber, July 6, Lieber Papers, Huntington Library; Meade to wife, July 15, Meade Papers, HSP.

12. Lyman to wife, July 12, 1864, Lyman Papers, MHS; Meade to wife, July 12, 15, Meade Papers, HSP; Dana to Stanton, July 7, *OR* 40.1:35–36; Biddle to wife, July 18, Biddle Papers, HSP; July 7, Comstock, *Diary,* 279.

13. Halleck to Grant, July 21, 1864, Grant to Lincoln, July 25, *OR* 40.3:360, 436;

Franklin to Smith, Aug. 2, Smith Papers, Vermont Historical Society; Dana to Grant, July 12, *OR* 37.2:223; Meade to wife, July 29, Meade Papers, HSP.

14. Grant to Lincoln, July 30, 1864, Lincoln, *Collected Works,* 7:470n; Montgomery Blair to S.L.M. Barlow, May 1, Barlow Papers, Huntington Library; F. P. Blair in *National Intelligencer,* Oct. 8; McClellan to F. P. Blair (unsent), July 22, McClellan, *Civil War Papers,* 583–85; Grant to Halleck, Aug. 1, *OR* 37.2:558; Meade to wife, Aug. 3, Meade Papers, HSP.

15. July 21, 1864, Wainwright, *Diary of Battle,* 439; Hess, *In the Trenches at Petersburg,* 45–49, 79–85; July 27, Lyman, *Meade's Army,* 238; Grant to Meade, July 27, 28, *OR* 40.3:505, 553.

16. Lyman to wife, Aug. 3, 1864, Lyman Papers, MHS; AP Orders, July 29, Grant to Meade, July 24, *OR* 40.1:134–35, 129; Humphreys to wife, July 31, Humphreys Papers, HSP; Burnside, Meade, Grant testimony, *CCW* 1 (1865), Petersburg, 17–18, 127–28, 111; Marvel, *Burnside,* 396, 399–400.

17. July 30, 1864, Lyman, *Meade's Army,* 240–43; July 30, Weld, *War Diary and Letters,* 353; Humphreys to wife, July 31, Humphreys Papers, HSP; Hess, *In the Trenches at Petersburg,* 90–104; Meade to Burnside, Burnside to Meade, July 30, *OR* 40.1:141, 141–42, 143; Lyman to wife, July 31, Lyman Papers, MHS; Bryce A. Suderow, "The Battle of the Crater: The Civil War's Worst Massacre," *Civil War History,* 43:3 (Sept. 1997), 222–24.

18. Warren-Humphreys, July 30, 1864, *OR* 40.1:148–52 passim; Burnside testimony, Court of Inquiry, *OR* 40.1:65; Grant to Halleck, Aug. 1, *OR* 40.1:17; Meade to wife, July 31, Meade Papers, HSP; Aug. 5, Lyman to wife, Lyman Papers, MHS.

19. Meade to wife, July 31, Aug. 13, 1864, Meade Papers, HSP; Court of Inquiry, *OR* 40.1:125–29; Grant to Meade, Aug.

13, *OR* 42.2:142; Lyman to wife, Aug. 17, Lyman Papers, MHS; *CCW* 1 (1865), Petersburg, 1–12.

20. Grant to Halleck, Aug. 1, 1864, Lincoln to Grant, Aug. 3, Grant to Halleck, July 14, *OR* 37.2:558, 582, 300–301; Grant to Lincoln, Aug. 4, *OR* 42.2:38; Aug. 5, Comstock, *Diary*, 285; Grant to Hunter, Aug. 5, *OR* 36.1:29–30; Grant, *Memoirs*, 616; T. S. Bowers to Rawlins, Aug. 10, James H. Wilson, *The Life of John A. Rawlins* (New York, 1916), 257; Grant to Sheridan, Aug. 7, *OR* 43.1:719.

21. Grant to Butler, Aug. 12, 1864, Grant to Meade, Aug. 14, Hancock to Grant, Aug. 14, *OR* 42.2:136, 169, 173; Walker, *History of the Second Army Corps*, 569–79; Barlow report, *OR* 42.1:248; Cornelia Hancock, *South After Gettysburg: Letters of Cornelia Hancock, 1863–1868*, Henrietta Stratton Jaquette, ed. (New York: Crowell, 1956), 145.

22. Humphreys to Warren, Aug. 17, 1864, *OR* 42.2:251; Warren to wife, Aug. 17, Warren Papers, New York State Library; Aug. 21, Lyman, *Meade's Army*, 254; Aug. 21, Wainwright, *Diary of Battle*, 453–55.

23. Meade to Grant, Aug. 22, 1864, Humphreys to Hancock, Aug. 24, *OR* 42.2:391–92, 449; Hess, *In the Trenches at Petersburg*, 135–40; Gibbon, *Personal Recollections*, 259–62; Gibbon to wife, Aug. 27, Gibbon Papers, HSP; Walker, *History of the Second Army Corps*, 598; Aug. 25, Lyman, *Meade's Army*, 257.

24. AP return, Aug. 31, 1864, *OR* 42.1:39; Lincoln memorandum, Aug. 23, Lincoln, *Collected Works*, 7:514; McClellan to Democratic Nomination Committee, Sept. 8, McClellan, *Civil War Papers*, 595–96.

25. Grant to Sheridan, Aug. 26, 1864, *OR* 43.1:916–17; Henry P. Moyer, *History of the Seventeenth Regiment Pennsylvania Volunteer Cavalry* (Lebanon, 1911), 211; Porter, *Campaigning with Grant*, 298; Wittenberg, *Little Phil*, 63; George T. Stevens, *Three Years in the Sixth Corps* (Albany, 1866), 391; J. W. Forsyth to J. D. Stevenson, Sept. 19, *OR* 43.2:124; Grant to Sheridan, Sept. 26, *OR* 43.2:177.

26. Hess, *In the Trenches at Petersburg*, 160–66; Humphreys to wife, Oct. 2, 1864, Humphreys Papers, HSP; Meade to wife, Oct. 3, Meade Papers, HSP.

27. Catton, *A Stillness at Appomattox*, 307–17; Roy Morris, Jr., *Sheridan: The Life and Wars of General Phil Sheridan*, 211–19; Sheridan to Grant, Oct. 19, 1864, *OR* 43.2:410.

28. Grant to Meade, Oct. 24, 1864, *OR* 42.3:317–18; Lyman to wife, Oct. 28, Lyman Papers, MHS.

29. Sears, *George B. McClellan*, 385–86; Meade to wife, Nov. 22, 1864, Aug. 30, Nov. 13, Meade Papers, HSP; Gibbon to wife, Aug. 30, Gibbon Papers, HSP; Lyman to wife, Oct. 17, Lyman Papers, MHS; "The Ordeal of General Stone," Sears, *Controversies & Commanders*, 46–47.

30. Grant to J. Russell Jones, Nov. 13, 1864, Grant, *Papers*, 12:415–16; Lincoln to Grant, Aug. 17, Lincoln, *Collected Works*, 7:499; Grant to Meade, Nov. 15, *OR* 42.3:620; Dec. 7–11, Lyman, *Meade's Army*, 304–7; Warren report, *OR* 42.1:444.

31. Jordan, *Winfield Scott Hancock*, 169–75; Hancock to Barlow, Nov. 3, 1864, Barlow Papers, MHS; Meade to wife, Dec. 13, Meade Papers, HSP; Humphreys to wife, Nov. 9, Humphreys Papers, HSP; Gibbon to wife, Jan. 14, 1865, Gibbon Papers, HSP.

32. Longacre, *Lincoln's Cavalrymen*, 322–23; Meade to wife, Nov. 20, 24, Dec. 23, 1864, Feb. 3, 4, 1865, to Henry A. Cram, Jan. 21, Meade Papers, HSP; Dana, *Recollections of the Civil War*, 248–49; Dec. 4, Lyman to wife, Lyman Papers, MHS.

33. Meade to wife, Feb. 1, 1865, Meade Papers, HSP; Hess, *In the Trenches at Petersburg*, 229–33; Grant to Meade, Feb. 6, to Sheridan, Feb. 8, *OR* 46.2:417, 495;

Lee to Grant, Mar. 2, Stanton [Lincoln] to Grant, Mar. 3, *OR* 46.2:824, 802; Second Inaugural Address, Lincoln, *Collected Works*, 8:332–33.

34. Grant to Meade, Ord, Sheridan, Mar. 24, 1865, *OR* 36.1:52–53; Grant to Sherman, Mar. 22, *OR* 47.2:948–49; Grant to Lincoln, Mar. 20, Lincoln to Grant, Mar. 20, Lincoln to Stanton, Mar. 25, *OR* 46.3:50, 109; Mar. 25, 28, Lyman, *Meade's Army*, 349, 351; Catton, *Grant Takes Command*, 437–38; Thomas Thatcher Graves in *Battles and Leaders*, 4:728.

35. Grant to Sheridan, Mar. 29, 30, 1865, Sheridan to Grant, Mar. 31, Grant to Meade, Mar. 31, *OR* 46.3:266, 325, 380, 337; Mar. 31, Lyman, *Meade's Army*, 354.

36. Orville Babcock, Frederick T. Locke testimony, Warren Court of Inquiry, *OR Supplement* 9:901, 366; William W. Swan, "The Five Forks Campaign," *PMHSM*, 6:408; "Gouverneur Kemble Warren and Little Phil," Sears, *Controversies & Commanders*, 255, 279–84.

37. Porter, *Campaigning with Grant*, 442–43, 451; Grant to Meade, Apr. 1, 1865, *OR* 46.3:397; Apr. 1, 2, Lyman, *Meade's Army*, 356–58; Grant, *Memoirs*, 711.

38. Meade to wife, Apr. 3, 1865, Meade Papers, HSP; Sheridan to Grant, Apr. 5, 6, *OR* 46.3:582, 610; Apr. 6, 8, Lyman, *Meade's Army*, 364, 367; Gibbon to wife, Apr. 7, Gibbon Papers, HSP; Lincoln to Grant, Apr. 7, Lincoln, *Collected Works*, 8:392; Grant to Lee, Apr. 7, Grant, *Papers*, 14:361.

39. Lee to Grant, Apr. 7, 1865, Grant to Lee, Apr. 8, Lee to Grant, Apr. 8, Grant to Lee, Apr. 9, Lee to Grant, Apr. 9, Grant to Lee, Apr. 9, Grant, *Papers*, 14:361n, 367, 267n, 371, 371n, 373–74; Apr. 8, Lyman, *Meade's Army*, 367; Catton, *Grant Takes Command*, 462.

40. April 9, 10, 1865, Lyman, *Meade's Army*, 369, 371; William Marvel, *A Place Called Appomattox*, 242, 258–64; Lyman to wife, Apr. 9, Lyman Papers, MHS; Meade to wife, Apr. 10, Meade Papers, HSP; Chamberlain to sister, Apr. 13, Chamberlain Papers, Bowdoin College; Joshua L. Chamberlain, *The Passing of the Armies: An Account of the Final Campaign of the Army of the Potomac*, 261.

41. G.O. 15, Apr. 15, 1865, *OR* 46.3:789; Leech, *Reveille in Washington*, 414–16; Grant to Sherman, Apr. 3, *OR* 46.3:510; Humphreys to wife, Apr. 9, Humphreys Papers, HSP. Grateful acknowledgment is made to John J. Hennessy for access to his study of the subordinate command of the Army of the Potomac.

Bibliography

MANUSCRIPTS

Andrew, John A. Massachusetts Historical Society.
Antietam Collection. Dartmouth College Library.
Banks, Nathaniel P. Manuscript Division, Library of Congress.
Barlow, Samuel L. M. Huntington Library.
Bennett, James Gordon. Manuscript Division, Library of Congress.
Biddle, James C. Historical Society of Pennsylvania.
Birney, David B. U.S. Army Heritage & Education Center.
Blair Family Papers. Manuscript Division, Library of Congress.
Bragg, Edward S. Wisconsin Historical Society.
Brannigan, Felix. Manuscript Division, Library of Congress.
Brooks, W.T.H. U.S. Army Heritage & Education Center.
Burnside, Ambrose. RG 94, Entry 159, National Archives.
Cameron, Simon. Manuscript Division, Library of Congress.
Candler, William L. Special Collections, Virginia Tech.
Carman, Ezra A. Manuscript Division, Library of Congress; New York Public Library.
Chandler, Zachariah. Manuscript Division, Library of Congress.
Chase, Salmon P. Historical Society of Pennsylvania.
Connor, Selden. John Hay Library, Brown University.
Couch, Darius N. Old Colony Historical Society, Taunton, Mass.
Cox, Jacob D. Oberlin College Archives.
Dawes, Rufus R. Wisconsin Historical Society.
Franklin, William B. Historical Society of York County, Pa.
Gay, Sidney H. Columbia University Library.
Generals' Reports of Civil War Service. RG 94 (M-1098), National Archives.
Gibbon, John. Historical Society of Pennsylvania; Maryland Historical Society.
Gilder-Lehrman Papers. New-York Historical Society.
Godfrey, John S. New Hampshire Historical Society.
Hatch, John P. Manuscript Division, Library of Congress.
Heintzelman, Samuel P. Manuscript Division, Library of Congress.
Hitchcock, Ethan Allen. Gilcrease Museum; Manuscript Division, Library of Congress.
Hooker, Joseph. Huntington Library; Samuel P. Bates Papers, Pennsylvania State Archives;
    Nesmith Papers, Oregon Historical Society.
Howard, Charles H. Bowdoin College Library.
Howard, Oliver Otis. Bowdoin College Library.
Humphreys, Andrew A. Historical Society of Pennsylvania.
Kearny, Philip. New Jersey Historical Society.
Larned, Daniel Reed. Manuscript Division, Library of Congress.

Lieber, Francis. Huntington Library.

Lincoln, Abraham. Manuscript Division, Library of Congress.

Lyman, Theodore. Massachusetts Historical Society.

Marble, Manton. Manuscript Division, Library of Congress.

McClellan, George B. Manuscript Division, Library of Congress.

McDowell, Irvin. Huntington Library.

Meade, George Gordon. Historical Society of Pennsylvania.

Meigs, Montgomery C. Manuscript Division (Nicolay Papers), Library of Congress.

MOLLUS Collection. Houghton Library, Harvard University.

Nicolay, John G. Manuscript Division, Library of Congress.

Paris, Comte de, Phillipe d'Orléans. "Voyage En Amerique, 1861–1862." Fondation Saint-Louis, Amboise, France.

Patrick, Marsena R. Manuscript Division, Library of Congress.

Pinkerton, Allan. Manuscript Division (McClellan Papers), Library of Congress.

Pope, John. Chicago Historical Society.

Porter, Fitz John. Manuscript Division, Library of Congress; Massachusetts Historical Society.

Ray, Charles H. Huntington Library.

Reynolds, John F. Franklin and Marshall College.

Richardson, Israel B. Huntington Library.

Roebling, Washington A. Roebling Family Papers, Rutgers University Archives.

Ropes, Henry. Boston Public Library.

Ropes, John C. Boston University Library.

Schoff Collection, William L. Clements Library, University of Michigan.

Seward, William H. University of Rochester.

Sigel, Franz. New-York Historical Society; Western Reserve Historical Society.

Slocum, Henry W. New-York Historical Society.

Smith, William F. Vermont Historical Society.

Stanton, Edwin M. Manuscript Division, Library of Congress.

Stone, Charles P. Schoff Collection, William L. Clements Library, University of Michigan.

Sumner, Charles. Houghton Library, Harvard University.

Teall, William W. Tennessee State Library and Archives.

Warren, Gouverneur K. New York State Library.

Webb, Alexander S. Yale University Library.

Zook, Samuel K. U.S. Army Heritage & Education Center.

BOOKS AND ARTICLES

Abbott, Henry L. *Fallen Leaves: The Civil War Letters of Major Henry Livermore Abbott.* Robert Garth Scott, ed. Kent, Ohio: Kent State University Press, 1991.

Adams, Michael C. C. *Our Masters the Rebels: A Speculation on Union Military Failures in the East, 1861–1865.* Cambridge, Mass.: Harvard University Press, 1978.

Alexander, E. P. *Fighting for the Confederacy: The Personal Recollections of General Edward Porter Alexander.* Gary W. Gallagher, ed. Chapel Hill: University of North Carolina Press, 1989.

———. *Military Memoirs of a Confederate.* New York: Scribner's, 1907.

Andrews, J. Cutler. *The North Reports the Civil War.* Pittsburgh: University of Pittsburgh Press, 1955.

Armstrong, Marion V., Jr. *Unfurl Those Colors! McClellan, Sumner, and the Second Army Corps in the Antietam Campaign.* Tuscaloosa: University of Alabama Press, 2008.

Auchmuty, Richard T. *Letters of Richard Tylden Auchmuty, Fifth Corps, Army of the Potomac.* Ellen Schermerhorn Auchmuty, ed. Privately printed, 1895.

Barlow, Francis C. *"Fear Was Not in Him": The Civil War Letters of Major General Francis C. Barlow, U.S.A.* Christian G. Samito, ed. New York: Fordham University Press, 2004.

Barnard, J. G. *The Peninsular Campaign and Its Antecedents.* New York: D. Van Nostrand, 1864.

Bates, Edward. *The Diary of Edward Bates: 1859–1866.* Howard K. Beale, ed. Washington, D.C.: Government Printing Office, 1933.

Battles and Leaders of the Civil War. Robert Underwood Johnson and Clarence Clough Buel, eds. 4 vols. New York: Century, 1887–88.

Beatie, Russel H. *Army of the Potomac.* I: *Birth of Command: November 1860–September 1861* (2002) and II: *McClellan Takes Command: September 1861–February 1862* (2004). Cambridge, Mass.: Da Capo Press. III: *McClellan's First Campaign: March 1862–May 1862* (2007). New York: Savas Beatie.

Bigelow, John, Jr. *The Campaign of Chancellorsville.* New Haven: Yale University Press, 1910.

Browning, Orville H. *The Diary of Orville Hickman Browning.* Theodore Calvin Pease and James G. Randall, eds. 2 vols. Springfield: Illinois State Historical Library, 1925, 1933.

Burlingame, Michael. *Abraham Lincoln: A Life.* 2 vols. Baltimore: Johns Hopkins University Press, 2008.

Carman, Ezra A. *The Maryland Campaign of September 1862.* I: *South Mountain* (2010). II: *Antietam* (2012). Thomas G. Clemens, ed. New York: Savas Beatie.

Catton, Bruce. Army of the Potomac. I: *Mr. Lincoln's Army* (1951). II: *Glory Road* (1952). III: *A Stillness at Appomattox* (1953). Garden City, N.Y.: Doubleday.

————. *The Centennial History of the Civil War.* I: *The Coming Fury* (1961). II: *Terrible Swift Sword* (1963). III: *Never Call Retreat* (1965). Garden City, N.Y.: Doubleday.

————. *Grant Moves South* (vol. 1). *Grant Takes Command* (vol. 2). Boston: Little, Brown, 1960, 1968.

Chamberlain, Joshua Lawrence. *The Passing of the Armies: An Account of the Final Campaign of the Army of the Potomac.* New York: Putnam's, 1915.

Chase, Salmon P. *The Salmon P. Chase Papers.* John Niven, ed. Vols. 1–4. Kent, Ohio: Kent State University Press, 1993–97.

Civil War, The. I: *The First Year Told By Those Who Lived It* (2011). Brooks D. Simpson, Stephen W. Sears, Aaron Sheehan-Dean, eds. II: *The Second Year . . .* (2012). Stephen W. Sears, ed. III: *The Third Year . . .* (2013). Brooks D. Simpson, ed. IV: *The Fourth Year . . .* (2014). Aaron Sheehan-Dean, ed. New York: Library of America.

Cleaves, Freeman. *Meade of Gettysburg.* Norman: University of Oklahoma Press, 1960.

Coddington, Edwin B. *The Gettysburg Campaign: A Study in Command.* Rev. ed. Dayton, Ohio: Morningside House, 1979.

Collins, Darrell L. *The Army of the Potomac: Order of Battle, 1861–1865, with Commanders, Strengths, Losses and More.* Jefferson, N.C.: McFarland, 2013.

Commager, Henry Steele, ed. *The Blue and the Gray: The Story of the Civil War Told by Participants.* Indianapolis: Bobbs-Merrill, 1950.

Comstock, Cyrus B. *The Diary of Cyrus B. Comstock.* Merlin E. Sumner, ed. Dayton, Ohio: Morningside House, 1987.

Cooling, Benjamin Franklin. *Counter-Thrust: From the Peninsula to the Antietam.* Lincoln: University of Nebraska Press, 2007.

————. *Symbol, Sword, and Shield: Defending Washington During the Civil War.* Hamden, Conn.: Archon Books, 1975.

Cox, Jacob D. *Military Reminiscences of the Civil War.* 2 vols. New York: Scribner's, 1900.

Cozzens, Peter. *General John Pope: A Life for the Nation.* Urbana: University of Illinois Press, 2000.

————. *Shenandoah 1862: Stonewall Jackson's Valley Campaign.* Chapel Hill: University of North Carolina Press, 2008.

————, ed. *Battles and Leaders of the Civil War,* vols. 5 and 6. Urbana: University of Illinois Press, 2002, 2004.

Cozzens, Peter, and Robert I. Girardi, eds. *The New Annals of the Civil War.* Mechanicsburg, Pa.: Stackpole Books, 2004.

Crawford, Samuel W. *The Genesis of the Civil War: The Story of Sumter, 1860–1861.* New York: Webster, 1887.

Cresap, Bernarr. *Appomattox Commander: The Story of General E.O.C. Ord.* San Diego: A. S. Barnes, 1981.

Cullum, George W. *Biographical Register of the Officers and Graduates of the U.S. Military Academy.* 2 vols. New York: D. Van Nostrand, 1868.

Curtis, George Ticknor. *The Life of James Buchanan.* 2 vols. New York: Harper, 1883.

Dana, Charles A. *Recollections of the Civil War: With the Leaders at Washington and in the Field in the Sixties.* New York: D. Appleton, 1902.

Davis, William C. *Battle at Bull Run: A History of the First Major Campaign of the Civil War.* Garden City, N.Y.: Doubleday, 1977.

Dawes, Rufus R. *Service with the Sixth Wisconsin Volunteers.* Marietta, Ohio, 1890.

De Peyster, John W. *Personal and Military History of Philip Kearny, Major-General, United States Volunteers.* New York: Rice and Gage, 1869.

De Trobriand, Régis. *Four Years with the Army of the Potomac.* Boston: Ticknor and Co., 1889.

————. *Our Noble Blood: The Civil War Letters of Régis de Trobriand, Major-General U.S.V.* William B. Styple, ed. Nathalie Chartrain, trans. Kearny, N.J.: Belle Grove Publishing, 1997.

Detzer, David. *Donnybrook: The Battle of Bull Run, 1861.* Boston: Houghton Mifflin, 2004.

Dodge, Theodore A. *On Campaign with the Army of the Potomac: The Civil War Journal of Theodore Ayrault Dodge.* Stephen W. Sears, ed. New York: Cooper Square Press, 2001.

Donaldson, Francis Adams. *Inside the Army of the Potomac: The Civil War Experience of Francis Adams Donaldson.* J. Gregory Acken, ed. Mechanicsburg, Pa.: Stackpole Books, 1998.

Doubleday, Abner. *Chancellorsville and Gettysburg.* New York: Scribner's, 1882.

Dubbs, Carol Kettenburg. *Defend This Old Town: Williamsburg During the Civil War.* Baton Rouge: Louisiana State University Press, 2002.

Dwight, Theodore F., ed. *The Virginia Campaign of 1862 Under General Pope.* Boston: Military Historical Society of Massachusetts, 1895.

Dyer, Frederick H. *A Compendium of the War of the Rebellion.* 2 vols. Des Moines, Iowa, 1908.

Eicher, David J. *The Longest Night: A Military History of the Civil War.* New York: Simon & Schuster, 2001.

Eicher, John H., and David J. Eicher. *Civil War High Commands.* Stanford, Calif.: Stanford University Press, 2001.

Elliott, Charles Winslow. *Winfield Scott: The Soldier and the Man.* New York: Macmillan, 1937.

Emerson, Edward W. *Life and Letters of Charles Russell Lowell.* Boston: Houghton Mifflin, 1907.

Engle, Stephen D. *Yankee Dutchman: The Life of Franz Sigel*. Fayetteville: University of Arkansas Press, 1993.

Favill, Josiah Marshall. *The Diary of a Young Officer*. Chicago: R. R. Donnelley, 1909.

Fehrenbacher, Don E., and Virginia Fehrenbacher, eds. *Recollected Words of Abraham Lincoln*. Stanford, Calif.: Stanford University Press, 1996.

Fishel, Edwin C. *The Secret War for the Union: The Untold Story of Military Intelligence in the Civil War*. Boston: Houghton Mifflin, 1996.

Fiske, Samuel W. *Mr. Dunn Browne's Experiences in the Army: The Civil War Letters of Samuel W. Fiske*. Stephen W. Sears, ed. New York: Fordham University Press, 1998.

Fleming, George Thornton, ed. *Life and Letters of Alexander Hays*. Pittsburgh, 1919.

Ford, Worthington Chauncy, ed. *A Cycle of Adams Letters, 1861–1865*. 2 vols. Boston: Houghton Mifflin, 1920.

Fox, Gustavus V. *Confidential Correspondence of Gustavus Vasa Fox*. Robert Means Thompson and Richard Wainwright, eds. 2 vols. New York: Naval History Society, 1920.

Freehling, William W. *The Road to Disunion*. II: *Secessionists Triumphant, 1854–1861*. New York: Oxford University Press, 2007.

Freeman, Douglas Southall. *Lee's Lieutenants: A Study in Command*. 3 vols. New York: Scribner's, 1942–44. Abridged in 1 vol. by Stephen W. Sears, New York: Scribner's, 1998.

———. *R. E. Lee: A Biography*. 4 vols. New York: Scribner's, 1934–35.

Gallagher, Gary W., ed. *Lee the Soldier*. Lincoln: University of Nebraska Press, 1996.

———, ed. Military Campaigns of the Civil War. *The Third Day at Gettysburg & Beyond* (1994); *The Fredericksburg Campaign: Decision on the Rappahannock* (1995); *Chancellorsville: The Battle and Its Aftermath* (1996); *The Wilderness Campaign* (1997); *The Antietam Campaign* (1999); *The Richmond Campaign of 1862: The Peninsula and the Seven Days* (2000); *The Shenandoah Valley Campaign of 1862* (2003); *The Shenandoah Valley Campaign of 1864* (2006); *The Spotsylvania Campaign* (2010); with Caroline E. Janney, *Cold Harbor to the Crater: The End of the Overland Campaign* (2015). Chapel Hill: University of North Carolina Press.

———, ed. *Three Days at Gettysburg: Essays on Confederate and Union Leadership*. Kent, Ohio: Kent State University Press, 1999.

Gambone, A. M. *Major-General Darius Nash Couch: Enigmatic Valor*. Baltimore: Butternut & Blue, 2000.

Gibbon, John. *Personal Recollections of the Civil War*. New York: Putnam's, 1928.

Glatthaar, Joseph T. *Partners in Command: The Relationships Between Leaders in the Civil War*. New York: Free Press, 1994.

Gordon, George H. *Brook Farm to Cedar Mountain in the War of the Great Rebellion*. Boston: James R. Osgood, 1883.

Goss, Thomas J. *The War Within the Union High Command: Politics and Generalship During the Civil War*. Lawrence: University Press of Kansas, 2003.

Gould, Edward K. *Major-General Hiram G. Berry*. Rockland, Maine, 1899.

Grant, Ulysses S. *Memoirs and Selected Letters*. New York: Library of America, 1990.

———. *The Papers of Ulysses S. Grant*. John Y. Simon, ed. 31 vols. Carbondale: Southern Illinois University Press, 1967–2009.

Gray, John Chipman, and John Codman Ropes. *War Letters, 1861–1865*. Boston: Houghton Mifflin, 1927.

Greene, A. Wilson. *Breaking the Backbone of the Rebellion: The Final Battles of the Petersburg Campaign*. Mason City, Iowa: Savas Publishing, 2000.

Grimsley, Mark. *And Keep Moving On: The Virginia Campaign, May–June 1864*. Lincoln: University of Nebraska Press, 2002.

———. *The Hard Hand of War: Union Military Policy Toward Southern Civilians, 1861–1865.* Cambridge: Cambridge University Press, 1995.

Hancock, Almira R. *Reminiscences of Winfield Scott Hancock.* New York: Webster, 1887.

Harrington, Fred Harvey. *Fighting Politician: Major General N. P. Banks.* Philadelphia: University of Pennsylvania Press, 1948.

Harsh, Joseph L. *Sounding the Shallows: A Confederate Companion for the Maryland Campaign of 1862.* Kent, Ohio: Kent State University Press, 2000.

———. *Taken at the Flood: Robert E. Lee and Confederate Strategy in the Maryland Campaign of 1862.* Kent, Ohio: Kent State University Press, 1999.

Hartwig, D. Scott. *To Antietam Creek: The Maryland Campaign of September 1862.* Baltimore: Johns Hopkins University Press, 2012.

Haskell, Frank A. *Haskell of Gettysburg: His Life and Civil War Papers.* Frank L. Byrne and Andrew T. Weaver, eds. Kent, Ohio: Kent State University Press, 1989.

Hassler, Warren W., Jr. *Commanders of the Army of the Potomac.* Baton Rouge: Louisiana State University Press, 1962.

Haupt, Herman. *Reminiscences of General Herman Haupt.* Milwaukee: Wright and Joys, 1901.

Hay, John. *At Lincoln's Side: John Hay's Civil War Correspondence and Selected Writings.* Michael Burlingame, ed. Carbondale: Southern Illinois University Press, 2000.

———. *Inside Lincoln's White House: The Complete Civil War Diary of John Hay.* Michael Burlingame and John R. Turner Ettlinger, eds. Carbondale: Southern Illinois University Press, 1997.

Haydon, Charles B. *For Country, Cause & Leader: The Civil War Journal of Charles B. Haydon.* Stephen W. Sears, ed. New York: Ticknor & Fields, 1993.

Haydon, F. Stansbury. *Aeronautics in the Union and Confederate Armies: With a Survey of Military Aeronautics Prior to 1861.* Baltimore: Johns Hopkins Press, 1941.

Hebert, Walter H. *Fighting Joe Hooker.* Indianapolis: Bobbs-Merrill, 1944.

Heitman, Francis B. *Historical Register and Dictionary of the United States Army.* 2 vols. Washington, D.C.: Government Printing Office, 1903.

Hennessy, John J. *The First Battle of Manassas: An End to Innocence, July 18–21, 1861.* Revised Edition. Mechanicsburg, Pa.: Stackpole, 2015.

———. *Return to Bull Run: The Campaign and Battle of Second Manassas.* New York: Simon & Schuster, 1993.

Hess, Earl J. *Field Armies & Fortifications in the Civil War: The Eastern Campaigns, 1861–1864* (2005); *Trench Warfare Under Grant & Lee: Field Fortifications in the Overland Campaign* (2007); *In the Trenches at Petersburg: Field Fortifications & Confederate Defeat* (2009). Chapel Hill: University of North Carolina Press.

Hessler, James A. *Sickles at Gettysburg: The Controversial Civil War General Who Committed Murder, Abandoned Little Round Top, and Declared Himself the Hero of Gettysburg.* New York: Savas Beatie, 2009.

Hitchcock, Ethan Allen. *Fifty Years in Camp and Field: Diary of Major-General Ethan Allen Hitchcock, U.S.A.* W. A. Croffut, ed. New York: Putnam's, 1909.

Holmes, Oliver Wendell, Jr. *Touched with Fire: Civil War Letters and Diary of Oliver Wendell Holmes, Jr., 1861–1864.* Mark DeWolfe Howe, ed. Cambridge, Mass.: Harvard University Press, 1946.

Hoptak, John David. *The Battle of South Mountain.* Charleston, S.C.: History Press, 2011.

Howard, Oliver Otis. *Autobiography of Oliver Otis Howard, Major General, United States Army.* 2 vols. New York: Baker & Taylor, 1907.

Howe, Thomas J. *Wasted Valor: The Petersburg Campaign, June 15–18, 1864.* Lynchburg, Va.: H. E. Howard, 1988.

Hubbell, John T., and James W. Geary, eds. *Biographical Dictionary of the Union: Northern Leaders of the Civil War.* Westport, Conn.: Greenwood Press, 1995.

Humphreys, Andrew A. *From Gettysburg to the Rapidan: The Army of the Potomac, July, 1863, to April, 1864.* New York: Scribner's, 1883.

———. *The Virginia Campaign of '64 and '65, the Army of the Potomac and the Army of the James.* New York: Scribner's, 1883.

Humphreys, Henry H. *Andrew Atkinson Humphreys: A Biography.* Philadelphia: John C. Winston, 1924.

Hyde, Thomas W. *Civil War Letters by General Thomas W. Hyde.* Privately printed, 1933.

———. *Following the Greek Cross, or Memories of the Sixth Army Corps.* Boston: Houghton Mifflin, 1895.

Johnson, Timothy D. *Winfield Scott: The Quest for Military Glory.* Lawrence: University Press of Kansas, 1998.

Johnston, Angus James, II. *Virginia Railroads in the Civil War.* Chapel Hill: University of North Carolina Press, 1961.

Johnston, Joseph E. *Narrative of Military Operations.* New York: D. Appleton, 1874.

Joinville, Prince de. *The Army of the Potomac: Its Organization, Its Commander, and Its Campaign.* New York: Anson D. F. Randolph, 1862.

Jones, Archer. *Civil War Command and Strategy: The Process of Victory and Defeat.* New York: Free Press, 1992.

Jones, R. Steven. *The Right Hand of Command: Use and Disuse of Personal Staffs in the American Civil War.* Mechanicsburg, Pa.: Stackpole Books, 2000.

Jordan, Brian M. *Unholy Sabbath: The Battle of South Mountain in History and Memory, September 14, 1862.* New York: Savas Beatie, 2012.

Jordan, David M. *"Happiness Is Not My Companion": The Life of General G. K. Warren.* Bloomington: Indiana University Press, 2001.

———. *Winfield Scott Hancock: A Soldier's Life.* Bloomington: Indiana University Press, 1988.

Keyes, E. D. *Fifty Years' Observation of Men and Events, Civil and Military.* New York: Scribner's, 1885.

Kreiser, Lawrence A., Jr. *Defeating Lee: A History of the Second Corps, Army of the Potomac.* Bloomington: Indiana University Press, 2011.

Krick, Robert K. *Stonewall Jackson at Cedar Mountain.* Chapel Hill: University of North Carolina Press, 1990.

Ladd, David L., and Audrey J. Ladd, eds. *The Bachelder Papers: Gettysburg in Their Own Words.* 3 vols. Dayton, Ohio: Morningside House, 1994.

Lee, Elizabeth Blair. *Wartime Washington: The Civil War Letters of Elizabeth Blair Lee.* Virginia Jeans Laas, ed. Urbana: University of Illinois Press, 1991.

Lee, Robert E. *The Wartime Papers of R. E. Lee.* Clifford Dowdey and Louis H. Manarin, eds. New York: Bramhall House, 1861.

Leech, Margaret. *Reveille in Washington, 1860–1865.* New York: Harper, 1941.

Lincoln, Abraham. *The Collected Works of Abraham Lincoln.* Roy P. Basler, ed. 9 vols. New Brunswick, N.J.: Rutgers University Press, 1953–55. *Supplement,* Westport, Conn.: Greenwood Press, 1974.

Livermore, Thomas L. *Days and Events, 1860–1866.* Boston: Houghton Mifflin, 1920.

———. *Numbers and Losses in the Civil War in America, 1861–65.* Boston: Houghton Mifflin, 1901.

———. "Patterson's Shenandoah Campaign." *Papers of the Military Historical Society of Massachusetts* (1895). 1:1–58.

Long, E. B., with Barbara Long. *The Civil War Day by Day: An Almanac, 1861–1865.* New York: Doubleday, 1971.

Longacre, Edward G. *The Early Morning of War: Bull Run, 1861.* Norman: University of Oklahoma Press, 2014.

———. *Lincoln's Cavalrymen: A History of the Mounted Forces of the Army of the Potomac, 1861–1865.* Mechanicsburg, Pa.: Stackpole Books, 2000.

———. *The Man Behind the Guns: A Biography of Henry Jackson Hunt, Chief of Artillery, Army of the Potomac.* New York: A. S. Barnes, 1977.

Longstreet, James. *From Manassas to Appomattox: Memoirs of the Civil War in America.* Philadelphia: Lippincott, 1896.

Lyman, Theodore. *Meade's Army: The Private Notebooks of Lt. Col. Theodore Lyman.* David W. Lowe, ed. Kent, Ohio: Kent State University Press, 2007.

———. *Meade's Headquarters, 1863–1865: Letters of Colonel Theodore Lyman from the Wilderness to the Appomattox.* George R. Agassiz, ed. Boston: Atlantic Monthly Press, 1922.

Mahood, Wayne. *General Wadsworth: The Life and Times of Brevet Major General James S. Wadsworth.* Cambridge, Mass.: Da Capo Press, 2003.

Marks, J. J. *The Peninsula Campaign in Virginia.* Philadelphia: Lippincott, 1864.

Marszalek, John F. *Commander of All Lincoln's Armies: A Life of General Henry W. Halleck.* Cambridge, Mass.: Harvard University Press, 2004.

Marvel, William. *Burnside.* Chapel Hill: University of North Carolina Press, 1991.

———. *Lincoln's Autocrat: The Life of Edwin Stanton.* Chapel Hill: University of North Carolina Press, 2015.

———. *Lincoln's War.* I: *Mr. Lincoln Goes to War* (2006). II: *Lincoln's Darkest Year: The War in 1862* (2008). III: *The Great Task Remaining: The Third Year of Lincoln's War* (2010). IV: *Tarnished Victory: Finishing Lincoln's War* (2011). Boston: Houghton Mifflin Harcourt.

———. *A Place Called Appomattox.* Chapel Hill: University of North Carolina Press, 2000.

Mason, Jack C. *Until Antietam: The Life and Letters of Major General Israel B. Richardson, U.S. Army.* Carbondale: Southern Illinois University Press, 2009.

Matter, William D. *If It Takes All Summer: The Battle of Spotsylvania.* Chapel Hill: University of North Carolina Press, 1988.

McAllister, Robert. *The Civil War Letters of General Robert McAllister.* James I. Robertson, Jr., ed. New Brunswick, N.J.: Rutgers University Press, 1965.

McClellan, George B. *The Civil War Papers of George B. McClellan: Selected Correspondence 1860–1865.* Stephen W. Sears, ed. New York: Ticknor & Fields, 1989.

———. *McClellan's Own Story.* William C. Prime, ed. New York: Charles L. Webster, 1887.

———. *Report on the Organization of the Army of the Potomac, and of Its Campaigns in Virginia and Maryland.* Washington, D.C.: Government Printing Office, 1864.

McClintock, Russell. *Lincoln and the Decision for War: The Northern Response to Secession.* Chapel Hill: University of North Carolina Press, 2008.

McClure, A. K., ed. *The Annals of the War: Written by Leading Participants, North and South.* Philadelphia: Times Publishing, 1879.

McElfresh, Earl B. *Maps and Mapmakers of the Civil War.* New York: Harry N. Abrams, 1999. "A Civil War Watercolor Map Series." Olean, N.Y.: McElfresh Map Co.

McPherson, James M. *Battle Cry of Freedom: The Civil War Era.* New York: Oxford University Press, 1988.

————. *Tried by War: Abraham Lincoln as Commander in Chief.* New York: Penguin Press, 2008.

Meade, George. *The Life and Letters of George Gordon Meade.* 2 vols. New York: Scribner's, 1913.

Meigs, Montgomery C. "The Relations of President Lincoln and Secretary Stanton to the Military Commanders in the Civil War." *American Historical Review,* 26:2 (Jan. 1921), 285–303.

Melton, Brian C. *Sherman's Forgotten General: Henry W. Slocum.* Columbia: University of Missouri Press, 2007.

Meneely, A. Howard. *The War Department, 1861: A Study in Mobilization and Administration.* New York: Columbia University Press, 1928.

Michie, Peter S. *The Life and Letters of Emory Upton.* New York: D. Appleton, 1885.

Military Order of the Loyal Legion of the United States (MOLLUS). *Papers,* 1887–1915. Reprint: 62 vols. numbered serially, index. Wilmington, N.C.: Broadfoot Publishing, 1991–97.

Miller, David W. *Second Only to Grant: Quartermaster General Montgomery C. Meigs.* Shippensburg, Pa.: White Mane Books, 2000.

Miller, William J., ed. *The Peninsula Campaign of 1862: Yorktown to the Seven Days.* 3 vols. Campbell, Calif.: Savas Publishing, 1993–97.

Moore, Frank, ed. *The Rebellion Record: A Diary of American Events.* 11 vols. and supplement. New York: Putnam's, 1861–63; Van Nostrand, 1864–68. Reprint: New York: Arno Press, 1977.

Morgan, James A., III. *A Little Short of Boats: The Fights at Ball's Bluff and Edwards Ferry, October 21–22, 1861.* Ft. Mitchell, Ky.: Ironclad Publishing, 2004.

Morris, Roy, Jr. *Sheridan: The Life and Wars of General Phil Sheridan.* New York: Crown, 1992.

Naisawald, L. Van Loan. *Grape and Canister: The Story of the Field Artillery of the Army of the Potomac, 1861–1865.* New York: Oxford University Press, 1960.

Neely, Mark E., Jr. *The Fate of Liberty: Abraham Lincoln and Civil Liberties.* New York: Oxford University Press, 1991.

Nevins, Allan. *The War for the Union.* 4 vols. New York: Scribner's, 1959–71.

Nichols, Edward J. *Toward Gettysburg: A Biography of General John F. Reynolds.* State College: Pennsylvania State University Press, 1958.

Nicolay, John G. *With Lincoln in the White House: Letters, Memoranda, and Other Writings of John G. Nicolay, 1860–1865.* Michael Burlingame, ed. Carbondale: Southern Illinois University Press, 2000.

————. *An Oral History of Abraham Lincoln: John G. Nicolay's Interviews and Essays.* Michael Burlingame, ed. Carbondale: Southern Illinois University Press, 1996.

Nicolay, John G., and John Hay. *Abraham Lincoln: A History.* 10 vols. New York: Century, 1890.

O'Reilly, Francis Augustín. *The Fredericksburg Campaign: Winter War on the Rappahannock.* Baton Rouge: Louisiana State University Press, 2003.

Palmer, David W. *The Forgotten Hero of Gettysburg: A Biography of General George Sears Greene.* Trenton, N.J.: Xlibris, 2004.

Papers of the Military Historical Society of Massachusetts. 15 vols. Boston, 1895–1918. Reprint: Wilmington, N.C.: Broadfoot Publishing, 1989–1990.

Patchan, Scott C. *Shenandoah Summer: The 1864 Valley Campaign.* Lincoln: University of Nebraska Press, 2007.

Patrick, Marsena R. *Inside Lincoln's Army: The Diary of Marsena Randolph Patrick, Provost*

Marshal General, Army of the Potomac. David S. Sparks, ed. New York: Thomas Yosel-off, 1964.

Patterson, Robert. *A Narrative of the Campaign in the Valley of the Shenandoah in 1861.* Philadelphia: John Campbell, 1865.

Pope, John. *The Military Memoirs of General John Pope.* Peter Cozzens and Robert I. Girardi, eds. Chapel Hill: University of North Carolina Press, 1998.

Porter, Horace. *Campaigning with Grant.* New York: Century, 1897.

Powell, William H. *The Fifth Army Corps (Army of the Potomac).* New York: Putnam's, 1896.

Pride, Mike, and Mark Travis. *My Brave Boys: To War with Colonel Cross and the Fighting Fifth.* Hanover, N.H.: University Press of New England, 2001.

Rable, George C. *Fredericksburg! Fredericksburg!* Chapel Hill: University of North Carolina Press, 2002.

Rafuse, Ethan S. *McClellan's War: The Failure of Moderation in the Struggle for the Union.* Bloomington: Indiana University Press, 2005.

———, *A Single Grand Victory: The First Campaign and Battle of Manassas.* Wilmington, Del.: Scholarly Resources, 2002.

———, ed. *Corps Commanders in Blue: Union Major Generals in the Civil War.* Baton Rouge: Louisiana State University Press, 2014.

Raymond, Henry J. *The Life and Public Services of Abraham Lincoln.* New York: Darby and Miller, 1865.

Reardon, Carol. *With a Sword in One Hand & Jomini in the Other: The Problem of Military Thought in the Civil War North.* Chapel Hill: University of North Carolina Press, 2012.

Reese, Timothy J. *Sykes' Regular Infantry Division, 1861–1864: A History of Regular United States Infantry Operations in the Civil War's Eastern Theater.* Jefferson, N.C.: McFarland, 1990.

Report of the Joint Committee on the Conduct of the War. Vols. 1–2 (1863 series). Vol. 1 (1865 series). Washington, D.C.: Government Printing Office. Reprint: Wilmington, N.C.: Broadfoot Publishing, 1998–99.

Rhea, Gordon C. *Overland Campaign I: The Battle of the Wilderness, May 5–6, 1864* (1994). II: *The Battles for Spotsylvania Court House and the Road to Yellow Tavern, May 7–12, 1864* (1997). III: *To the North Anna River: Grant and Lee, May 13–15, 1864* (2000). IV: *Cold Harbor: Grant and Lee, May 26–June 3, 1864* (2002). Baton Rouge: Louisiana State University Press.

Russell, William Howard. *My Diary North and South.* New York: Harper & Brothers, 1863.

———. *William Howard Russell's Civil War: Private Diary and Letters, 1861–1862.* Martin Crawford, ed. Athens: University of Georgia Press, 1992.

Ryan, Thomas J. *Spies, Scouts, and Secrets in the Gettysburg Campaign.* El Dorado Hills, Calif.: Savas Beatie, 2015.

Schaff, Morris. *The Battle of the Wilderness.* Boston: Houghton Mifflin, 1910.

Schuckers, Jacob S. *The Life and Public Services of Salmon Portland Chase.* New York: D. Appleton, 1874.

Schurz, Carl. *The Reminiscences of Carl Schurz.* 2 vols. New York: McClure, 1907.

Sears, Stephen W. *Chancellorsville.* Boston: Houghton Mifflin, 1996.

———. *Controversies & Commanders: Dispatches from the Army of the Potomac.* Boston: Houghton Mifflin, 1999.

———. *George B. McClellan: The Young Napoleon.* New York: Ticknor & Fields, 1988.

———. *Gettysburg.* Boston: Houghton Mifflin, 2003.

———. *Landscape Turned Red: The Battle of Antietam.* New York: Ticknor & Fields, 1983.

———. *To the Gates of Richmond: The Peninsula Campaign.* New York: Ticknor & Fields, 1992.

Sedgwick, John. *Correspondence of John Sedgwick, Major-General.* 2 vols. New York: De Vinne Press, 1902–3. Reprint (1 vol): Baltimore: Butternut and Blue, 1999.

Shannon, Fred Albert. *The Organization and Administration of the Union Army, 1861–1865.* 2 vols. Cleveland: Arthur H. Clark Co., 1928.

Shaw, Robert Gould. *Blue-Eyed Child of Fortune: The Civil War Letters of Colonel Robert Gould Shaw.* Russell Duncan, ed. Athens: University of Georgia Press, 1992.

Sheridan, Philip H. *Personal Memoirs of P. H. Sheridan.* 2 vols. New York: Charles L. Webster, 1888.

Sherman, William T. *Sherman's Civil War: Selected Correspondence of William T. Sherman, 1860–1865.* Brooks D. Simpson and Jean V. Berlin, eds. Chapel Hill: University of North Carolina Press, 1999.

Sifakis, Stewart. *Who Was Who in the Civil War.* New York: Facts on File, 1988.

Simpson, Brooks D. *Ulysses S. Grant: Triumph over Adversity, 1822–1865.* Boston: Houghton Mifflin, 2000.

Small, Abner R. *The Road to Richmond: The Civil War Memoirs of Major Abner R. Small of the Sixteenth Maine Volunteers.* Harold A. Small, ed. Berkeley: University of California Press, 1939.

Smith, William F. *Autobiography of Major General William F. Smith, 1861–1864.* Herbert M. Schiller, ed. Dayton, Ohio: Morningside House, 1990.

Sneden, Robert Knox. *Eye of the Storm: A Civil War Odyssey.* Charles F. Bryan, Jr., and Nelson D. Lankford, eds. New York: Free Press, 2000.

Snell, Mark A. *From First to Last: The Life of Major General William B. Franklin.* New York: Fordham University Press, 2002.

Sommers, Richard J. *Richmond Redeemed: The Siege of Petersburg.* Rev. ed. El Dorado Hills, Calif.: Savas Beatie, 2014.

Stampp, Kenneth M. *And the War Came: The North and the Secession Crisis, 1860–1861.* Baton Rouge: Louisiana State University Press, 1950.

Starr, Louis M. *Bohemian Brigade: Civil War Newsmen in Action.* New York: Knopf, 1954.

Starr, Stephen Z. *The Union Cavalry in the Civil War.* Vols. 1–2. Baton Rouge: Louisiana State University Press, 1979, 1981.

Stewart, A. M. *Camp, March and Battle-Field, or Three Years and a Half with the Army of the Potomac.* Philadelphia: J. B. Rogers, 1865.

Stine, J. H. *History of the Army of the Potomac.* Washington, D.C., 1893.

Strong, George Templeton. *The Diary of George Templeton Strong: The Civil War, 1860–1865.* Allan Nevins and Milton Halsey Thomas, eds. New York: Macmillan, 1952.

Strother, David Hunter. "Personal Recollections of the War by a Virginian." *Harper's New Monthly Magazine,* 33–36 (1866–68).

———. *A Virginia Yankee in the Civil War: The Diaries of David Hunter Strother.* Cecil D. Eby, Jr., ed. Chapel Hill: University of North Carolina Press, 1961.

Styple, William B., ed. *Letters from the Peninsula: The Civil War Letters of General Philip Kearny.* Kearny, N.J.: Belle Grove Publishing, 1988.

Sumner, Charles. *The Selected Letters of Charles Sumner.* Beverly Wilson Palmer, ed. Vol. 2. Boston: Northeastern University Press, 1990.

Swinton, William. *Campaigns of the Army of the Potomac.* New York: Charles B. Richardson, 1866.

Taaffe, Stephen R. *Commanding the Army of the Potomac.* Lawrence: University Press of Kansas, 2006.

Tanner, Robert G. *Stonewall in the Valley: Thomas J. "Stonewall" Jackson's Shenandoah Valley Campaign, Spring 1862.* Mechanicsburg, Pa.: Stackpole Books, 1996.

Tap, Bruce. *Over Lincoln's Shoulder: The Committee on the Conduct of the War.* Lawrence: University of Kansas Press, 1998.

Tate, Thomas K. *General Edwin Vose Sumner, USA: A Civil War Biography.* Jefferson, N.C.: McFarland, 2013.

Tenney, Leon Walter. "Seven Days in 1862: Numbers in Union and Confederate Armies Before Richmond." Master's thesis, George Mason University, 1992.

Thomas, Benjamin P., and Harold M. Hyman. *Stanton: The Life and Times of Lincoln's Secretary of War.* New York: Knopf, 1962.

Thompson, Jerry. *Civil War to the Bloody End: The Life & Times of Major General Samuel P. Heintzelman.* College Station: Texas A & M University Press, 2006.

Tidball, Eugene C. *"No Disgrace to My Country": The Life of John C. Tidball.* Kent, Ohio: Kent State University Press, 2002.

Townsend, E. D. *Anecdotes of the Civil War in the United States.* New York: Appleton, 1884.

Tremain, Henry E. *Two Days of War: A Gettysburg Narrative and Other Excursions.* New York: Bonnell, Silver and Bowers, 1905.

Trudeau, Noah Andre. *Bloody Roads South: The Wilderness to Cold Harbor, May–June 1864.* Boston: Little, Brown, 1989.

——. *The Last Citadel: Petersburg, Virginia, June 1864–April 1865.* Boston: Little, Brown, 1991.

Union Army, The. 8 vols. Madison, Wis.: Federal Publishing Co., 1908.

Upton, Emory. *The Military Policy of the United States.* Washington, D.C.: Government Printing Office, 1917.

U.S. Naval War Records Office. *Official Records of the Union and Confederate Navies in the War of the Rebellion.* 30 vols. Washington, D.C.: Government Printing Office, 1894–1922.

U.S. War Department. *The War of the Rebellion: A Compilation of the Official Records of the Union and Confederate Armies.* 128 parts in 70 vols. and atlas. Washington, D.C.: Government Printing Office, 1880–1901. *Supplement,* 100 vols. Wilmington, N.C.: Broadfoot Publishing, 1994–2000.

Venter, Bruce M. *Kill Jeff Davis: The Union Raid on Richmond, 1864.* Norman: University of Oklahoma Press, 2016.

Wainwright, Charles S. *A Diary of Battle: The Personal Journals of Colonel Charles S. Wainwright, 1861–1865.* Allan Nevins, ed. New York: Harcourt, Brace & World, 1962.

Walker, Francis A. *History of the Second Army Corps, in the Army of the Potomac.* New York: Scribner's, 1887.

Warner, Ezra J. *Generals in Blue: Lives of the Union Commanders.* Baton Rouge: Louisiana State University Press, 1964.

Webb, Alexander S. *The Peninsula: McClellan's Campaign of 1862.* New York: Scribner's, 1881.

Weigley, Russell F. *A Great Civil War: A Military and Political History, 1861–1865.* Bloomington: Indiana University Press, 2000.

——. *Quartermaster General of the Union Army: A Biography of M. C. Meigs.* New York: Columbia University Press, 1959.

Welch, Richard F. *The Boy General: The Life and Careers of Francis Channing Barlow.* Madison, N.J.: Fairleigh Dickinson University Press, 2003.

Welcher, Frank J. *The Union Army, 1861–1865: Organization and Operations.* Vol. 1: *The Eastern Theater.* Bloomington: Indiana University Press, 1989.

Weld, Stephen M. *War Diary and Letters of Stephen Minot Weld, 1861–1865.* 2nd ed. Boston: Massachusetts Historical Society, 1979.

Welles, Gideon. *The Civil War Diary of Gideon Welles, Lincoln's Secretary of the Navy.* William E. Gienapp and Erica L. Gienapp, eds. Knox College Lincoln Studies Center. Urbana: University of Illinois Press, 2014.

Wert, Jeffry D. *From Winchester to Cedar Creek: The Shenandoah Campaign of 1864.* Carlisle, Pa.: South Mountain Press, 1987.

———. *The Sword of Lincoln: The Army of the Potomac.* New York: Simon & Schuster, 2005.

Willcox, Orlando B. *Forgotten Valor: The Memoirs, Journals, & Civil War Letters of Orlando B. Willcox.* Robert Garth Scott, ed. Kent, Ohio: Kent State University Press, 1999.

Williams, Alpheus S. *From the Cannon's Mouth: The Civil War Letters of General Alpheus S. Williams.* Milo M. Quaife, ed. Detroit: Wayne State University Press, 1959.

Williams, Kenneth P. *Lincoln Finds a General: A Military Study of the Civil War.* 5 vols. New York: Macmillan, 1949–59.

Williams, T. Harry. *Lincoln and His Generals.* New York: Knopf, 1952.

———. *McClellan, Sherman and Grant.* New Brunswick, N.J.: Rutgers University Press, 1962.

———. *P.G.T. Beauregard: Napoleon in Gray.* Baton Rouge: Louisiana State University Press, 1955.

Wilson, James Harrison. *Under the Old Flag.* 2 vols. New York: D. Appleton, 1912.

Winslow, Richard Elliott, III. *General John Sedgwick: The Story of a Union Corps Commander.* Novato, Calif.: Presidio Press, 1982.

Wittenberg, Eric J. *Little Phil: A Reassessment of the Civil War Leadership of Gen. Philip H. Sheridan.* Washington, D.C.: Brassey's, 2002.

Woodbury, Augustus. *General Halleck and General Burnside.* Boston: John Wilson, 1864.

Woodward, C. Vann, ed., *Mary Chesnut's Civil War.* New Haven, Conn.: Yale University Press, 1981.

Young, Alfred C., III. *Lee's Army During the Overland Campaign: A Numerical Study.* Baton Rouge: Louisiana State University Press, 2013.

Illustration Credits

Chapter 1. National Archives, 2; *Battles and Leaders of the Civil War*, 4; Century Collection, 11, 28–29; Library of Congress, 13, 19.

Chapter 2. M. and M. Karolik Collection, Museum of Fine Arts, Boston, 31; Library of Congress, 33, 41, 47, 51, 74; Becker Collection, Boston, 39; Geography and Map Division, Library of Congress, 44; *New York Illustrated News*, Sept. 2, 1861, 64.

Chapter 3. National Archives, 80, 88 (2); Library of Congress, 87, 89, 95, 97; Musée de la Marine, Paris, 102.

Chapter 4. National Archives, 107, 124–25; Library of Congress, 110, 122, 130; Miriam and Ira D. Wallach Print Collection, New York Public Library, 115.

Chapter 5. Library of Congress, 135, 140, 153, 157, 163; National Archives, 143; John Hay Library, Brown University, *Harper's Weekly*, Jan. 25, 1862, 147; M. and M. Karolik Collection, Museum of Fine Arts, Boston, 161; Brian C. Pohanka Collection, 173.

Chapter 6. Musée de la Marine, Paris, 178; M. and M. Karolik Collection, Museum of Fine Arts, Boston, 184; Graphic Arts Collection, Princeton University Library, 191; Library of Congress, 198, 201, 204, 223; U.S. Naval Historical Center, 211; James S. Schoff Collection, William L. Clements Library, University of Michigan, 215; Century Collection, 225.

Chapter 7. Boston Athenaeum, 233; Miriam and Ira D. Wallach Print Collection, New York Public Library, 241; Anne S.K. Brown Military Collection, Brown University Library, 250–51, 268; Library of Congress, 257, 259, 262, 270.

Chapter 8. Library of Congress, 281, 292, 300, 310, 314, 325; Miriam and Ira D. Wallach Print Collection, New York Public Library, 287; *New York Illustrated News*, Aug. 9, 1862, 305; National Archives, 278, 320.

Chapter 9. Louis A. Warren Lincoln Library and Museum, 332; *Battles and Leaders of the Civil War*, 337; Library of Congress, 340, 346, 357, 361, 363.

Chapter 10. Library of Congress, 369, 378, 380, 386, 392 (left), 395, 399, 403, 407; National Archives 392 (right).

Chapter 11. Library of Congress, 413, 420, 425, 435; Louis A. Warren Lincoln Library and Museum, 431.

Chapter 12. Library of Congress, 442, 452, 454, 456, 464, 466.

Chapter 13. *Harper's Weekly*, Jan. 3, 1863, 468; Library of Congress, 477, 481, 503, 510–11, 514; National Archives, 485; Hargrett Book and Manuscript Library, University of Georgia, 488; U.S. Army Heritage and Education Center, 491; Century Collection, 506.

Chapter 14. Library of Congress, 523 (2), 528, 536, 550, 557, 560, 566, 572, 576–77; National Archives, 542, 567; U.S. Army Heritage and Education Center, 570.

Chapter 15. Library of Congress, 584, 592, 595, 596, 608; National Archives, 600, 611 (2).

Chapter 16. Library of Congress, 621, 630, 631, 635, 642, 643, 645, 648, 653, 657; National Archives, 625, 651.

Chapter 17. National Archives, 662; Library of Congress, 665, 672, 677, 684, 692, 700, 706–7.

Chapter 18. Library of Congress, 711, 722, 729, 741 (2), 745 (2), 747, 753, 755, 758; *Harper's Weekly*, September 17, 1864, 737.

Index